HANDBOOK
of
PSYCHOLOGY

HANDBOOK
of
PSYCHOLOGY

VOLUME 12
INDUSTRIAL AND ORGANIZATIONAL PSYCHOLOGY

Walter C. Borman

Daniel R. Ilgen

Richard J. Klimoski

Volume Editors

Irving B. Weiner

Editor-in-Chief

John Wiley & Sons, Inc.

Library of Congress Cataloging-in-Publication Data:

Handbook of psychology / Irving B. Weiner, editor-in-chief.
     p. cm.
    Includes bibliographical references and indexes.
    Contents: v. 1. History of psychology / edited by Donald K. Freedheim — v. 2. Research methods in psychology / edited by John A. Schinka, Wayne F. Velicer — v. 3. Biological psychology / edited by Michela Gallagher, Randy J. Nelson — v. 4. Experimental psychology / edited by Alice F. Healy, Robert W. Proctor — v. 5. Personality and social psychology / edited by Theodore Millon, Melvin J. Lerner — v. 6. Developmental psychology / edited by Richard M. Lerner, M. Ann Easterbrooks, Jayanthi Mistry — v. 7. Educational psychology / edited by William M. Reynolds, Gloria E. Miller — v. 8. Clinical psychology / edited by George Stricker, Thomas A. Widiger — v. 9. Health psychology / edited by Arthur M. Nezu, Christine Maguth Nezu, Pamela A. Geller — v. 10. Assessment psychology / edited by John R. Graham, Jack A. Naglieri — v. 11. Forensic psychology / edited by Alan M. Goldstein — v. 12. Industrial and organizational psychology / edited by Walter C. Borman, Daniel R. Ilgen, Richard J. Klimoski.
    ISBN 0-471-17669-9 (set) — ISBN 0-471-38320-1 (cloth : alk. paper : v. 1)
— ISBN 0-471-38513-1 (cloth : alk. paper : v. 2) — ISBN 0-471-38403-8 (cloth : alk. paper : v. 3)
— ISBN 0-471-39262-6 (cloth : alk. paper : v. 4) — ISBN 0-471-38404-6 (cloth : alk. paper : v. 5)
— ISBN 0-471-38405-4 (cloth : alk. paper : v. 6) — ISBN 0-471-38406-2 (cloth : alk. paper : v. 7)
— ISBN 0-471-39263-4 (cloth : alk. paper : v. 8) — ISBN 0-471-38514-X (cloth : alk. paper : v. 9)
— ISBN 0-471-38407-0 (cloth : alk. paper : v. 10) — ISBN 0-471-38321-X (cloth : alk. paper : v. 11)
— ISBN 0-471-38408-9 (cloth : alk. paper : v. 12)
    1. Psychology. I. Weiner, Irving B.

BF121.H1955 2003
150—dc21

2002066380

Printed in the United States of America.

10 9 8 7 6 5 4 3 2 1

Editorial Board

To the Society for Industrial and Organizational Psychology

Handbook of Psychology **Preface**

Psychology at the beginning of the twenty-first century has become a highly diverse field of scientific study and applied technology. Psychologists commonly regard their discipline as the science of behavior, and the American Psychological Association has formally designated 2000 to 2010 as the "Decade of Behavior." The pursuits of behavioral scientists range from the natural sciences to the social sciences and embrace a wide variety of objects of investigation. Some psychologists have more in common with biologists than with most other psychologists, and some have more in common with sociologists than with most of their psychological colleagues. Some psychologists are interested primarily in the behavior of animals, some in the behavior of people, and others in the behavior of organizations. These and other dimensions of difference among psychological scientists are matched by equal if not greater heterogeneity among psychological practitioners, who currently apply a vast array of methods in many different settings to achieve highly varied purposes.

Psychology has been rich in comprehensive encyclopedias and in handbooks devoted to specific topics in the field. However, there has not previously been any single handbook designed to cover the broad scope of psychological science and practice. The present 12-volume *Handbook of Psychology* was conceived to occupy this place in the literature. Leading national and international scholars and practitioners have collaborated to produce 297 authoritative and detailed chapters covering all fundamental facets of the discipline, and the *Handbook* has been organized to capture the breadth and diversity of psychology and to encompass interests and concerns shared by psychologists in all branches of the field.

Two unifying threads run through the science of behavior. The first is a common history rooted in conceptual and empirical approaches to understanding the nature of behavior. The specific histories of all specialty areas in psychology trace their origins to the formulations of the classical philosophers and the methodology of the early experimentalists, and appreciation for the historical evolution of psychology in all of its variations transcends individual identities as being one kind of psychologist or another. Accordingly, Volume 1 in the *Handbook* is devoted to the history of psychology as it emerged in many areas of scientific study and applied technology.

A second unifying thread in psychology is a commitment to the development and utilization of research methods suitable for collecting and analyzing behavioral data. With attention both to specific procedures and their application in particular settings, Volume 2 addresses research methods in psychology.

Volumes 3 through 7 of the *Handbook* present the substantive content of psychological knowledge in five broad areas of study: biological psychology (Volume 3), experimental psychology (Volume 4), personality and social psychology (Volume 5), developmental psychology (Volume 6), and educational psychology (Volume 7). Volumes 8 through 12 address the application of psychological knowledge in five broad areas of professional practice: clinical psychology (Volume 8), health psychology (Volume 9), assessment psychology (Volume 10), forensic psychology (Volume 11), and industrial and organizational psychology (Volume 12). Each of these volumes reviews what is currently known in these areas of study and application and identifies pertinent sources of information in the literature. Each discusses unresolved issues and unanswered questions and proposes future directions in conceptualization, research, and practice. Each of the volumes also reflects the investment of scientific psychologists in practical applications of their findings and the attention of applied psychologists to the scientific basis of their methods.

The *Handbook of Psychology* was prepared for the purpose of educating and informing readers about the present state of psychological knowledge and about anticipated advances in behavioral science research and practice. With this purpose in mind, the individual *Handbook* volumes address the needs and interests of three groups. First, for graduate students in behavioral science, the volumes provide advanced instruction in the basic concepts and methods that define the fields they cover, together with a review of current knowledge, core literature, and likely future developments. Second, in addition to serving as graduate textbooks, the volumes offer professional psychologists an opportunity to read and contemplate the views of distinguished colleagues concerning the central thrusts of research and leading edges of practice in their respective fields. Third, for psychologists seeking to become conversant with fields outside their own specialty and for persons outside of psychology seeking information about psychological matters, the *Handbook* volumes serve as a reference source for expanding their knowledge and directing them to additional sources in the literature.

The preparation of this *Handbook* was made possible by the diligence and scholarly sophistication of the 25 volume editors and co-editors who constituted the Editorial Board. As Editor-in-Chief, I want to thank each of them for the pleasure of their collaboration in this project. I compliment them for having recruited an outstanding cast of contributors to their volumes and then working closely with these authors to achieve chapters that will stand each in their own right as

valuable contributions to the literature. I would like finally to express my appreciation to the editorial staff of John Wiley and Sons for the opportunity to share in the development of this project and its pursuit to fruition, most particularly to Jennifer Simon, Senior Editor, and her two assistants, Mary Porterfield and Isabel Pratt. Without Jennifer's vision of the *Handbook* and her keen judgment and unflagging support in producing it, the occasion to write this preface would not have arrived.

IRVING B. WEINER
Tampa, Florida

Contents

PART THREE
THE WORK ENVIRONMENT

Contributors

Clayton P. Alderfer, PhD
Graduate School of Professional Psychology
Rutgers University
Piscataway, New Jersey

John R. Austin, PhD
Pennsylvania State University
Pittsburgh, Pennsylvania

Bruce J. Avolio, PhD
School of Management
Center for Leadership Studies
Binghamton University
Binghamton, New York

Jean M. Bartunek, PhD
Department of Organization Studies
Boston College
Chestnut Hill, Massachusetts

Bradford S. Bell
School of Industrial and Labor Relations
Cornell University

Yair Berson, PhD
Polytechnic University
New York, New York

Walter C. Borman
University of South Florida
Tampa, Florida

John W. Boudreau, PhD
ILR Human Resource Studies
Cornell University
Ithaca, New York

Daniel M. Cable, PhD
Kenan-Flagler Business School
University of North Carolina at Chapel Hill
Chapel Hill, North Carolina

Michael A. Campion, PhD
Krannert Graduate School of Management
Purdue University
West Lafayette, Indiana

Wayne F. Cascio, PhD
Department of Management
University of Colorado
Denver, Colorado

Terry Connolly, PhD
Department of Management and Policy
University of Arizona
Tucson, Arizona

Jose M. Cortina, PhD
Department of Psychology
George Mason University
Fairfax, Virginia

Denise Daniels, PhD
Business and Economics Department
Seattle Pacific University
Seattle, Washington

Fritz Drasgow, PhD
Department of Psychology
University of Illinois at
    Urbana-Champaign
Champaign, Illinois

Michael Frese, PhD
Department of Psychology
University of Giessen
Giessen, Germany

Adrian Furnham, PhD
Department of Psychology
University College London
London, England

Jeffrey H. Greenhaus, PhD
Department of Management
Drexel University
Philadelphia, Pennsylvania

Leaetta M. Hough, PhD
The Dunnette Group, Ltd.
St. Paul, Minnesota

William C. Howell, PhD
Department of Psychology
Arizona State and Rice Universities
Gold Canyon, Arizona

Charles L. Hulin, PhD
Department of Psychology
University of Illinois at Urbana-Champaign
Champaign, Illinois

Daniel R. Ilgen
Michigan State University
East Lansing, Michigan

Michael J. Ingerick
Department of Psychology
George Mason University
Fairfax, Virginia

Timothy A. Judge, PhD
Department of Business
University of Iowa
Iowa City, Iowa

Dong I. Jung, PhD
Department of Management
San Diego State University
San Diego, California

Angelo J. Kinicki, PhD
Arizona State University
Phoenix, Arizona

Richard J. Klimoski
George Mason University
Fairfax, Virginia

Steve W. J. Kozlowski, PhD
Department of Psychology
Michigan State University
East Lansing, Michigan

Kurt Kraiger, PhD
Department of Psychology
University of Colorado
Denver, Colorado

Roxanne M. Laczo
Department of Psychology
University of Minnesota
Minneapolis, Minnesota

Terence R. Mitchell, PhD
School of Business
University of Washington
Seattle, Washington

Frederick P. Morgeson, PhD
Department of Management
Texas A&M University
College Station, Texas

Stephan J. Motowidlo, PhD
Department of Psychology
University of Minnesota
Minneapolis, Minnesota

Lisa Ordóñez, PhD
Department of Management and Policy
University of Arizona
Tucson, Arizona

Cheri Ostroff, PhD
Teachers College
Columbia University
New York, New York

Robert E. Ployhart, PhD
Department of Psychology
George Mason University
Fairfax, Virginia

Peter M. Ramstad
Personnel Decisions International
Minneapolis, Minnesota

Ann Marie Ryan, PhD
Department of Psychology
Michigan State University
East Lansing, Michigan

Sara L. Rynes, PhD
Department of Management
   and Organizations
Tippie College of Business
University of Iowa
Iowa City, Iowa

Paul R. Sackett, PhD
Department of Psychology
University of Minnesota
Minneapolis, Minnesota

Neal Schmitt, PhD
Department of Psychology
Michigan State University
East Lansing, Michigan

Adrienne D. Sims
Graduate School of Professional Psychology
Rutgers University
Piscataway, New Jersey

Sabine Sonnentag, PhD
Department of Psychology
University of Konstanz
Konstanz, Germany

John J. Sosik, PhD
Department of Management
Penn State Great Valley
Malvern, Pennsylvania

Melinda M. Tamkins
Teachers College
Columbia University
New York, New York

Darin Wiechmann
Department of Psychology
Michigan State University
East Lansing, Michigan

CHAPTER 1

Stability and Change in Industrial and Organizational Psychology

WALTER C. BORMAN, RICHARD J. KLIMOSKI, AND DANIEL R. ILGEN

Handbooks Past and Present

In the mid-1970s Marvin D. Dunnette edited the first handbook of industrial and organizational psychology (Dunnette, 1976). This prodigious work brought together the writings of the leading scholars in the field under one cover and acted as a foundation and guide for the field for the next 15 years. In the early 1990s Dunnette did it again. The second edition, edited by Dunnette and Leaetta M. Hough, maintained the same high quality of the first but expanded significantly from one to four volumes, each approximately 800 pages (Dunnette & Hough, 1990, 1991, 1992, 1994, vols. 1–4, respectively). The definitive reviews and even visionary statements targeted virtually all areas of industrial and organizational psychology and again set the standards for the field.

Knowing the standard to which we would be inevitably compared, we undertook the task of editing the present volume with great trepidation. Ours was a more modest and somewhat different objective. As a single volume nested within a handbook for all of psychology, our purpose was to provide the depth and breadth that would capture the domain of industrial and organizational psychology in a way valuable for scholars and students in that field domain; however, we also strove to create a volume to which those outside the field could turn in order to gain an appreciation of the latest thinking in this area of interest. To accomplish these purposes, we have again assembled a collection of leading scholars in the field. We asked them to describe the work in their area, but to do so in a way that would speak to both those inside and outside the field; we

believe they did this very well—and did it in such a way that this volume can serve as a sequel to the handbook of the 1990s, informing and guiding industrial and organizational psychology in the early part of the twenty-first century.

What follows begins by addressing the field of industrial and organizational psychology as a whole and describing some of the major accomplishments and new directions that have occurred since the publishing of the Dunnette and Hough handbook. After some discussion of our discipline and advancements in this field, we turn to a preview of individual chapters.

Industrial and Organizational Psychology: Overarching Models

Industrial and organizational psychology is the study of human behavior in organizations; the behaviors of interest contribute to either the effectiveness of organizational functioning, the satisfaction and well-being of those who populate the organizations, or both. These behaviors and the people who exhibit them exist in a dynamic open system (Katz & Kahn, 1978). Behaviors observed in the present are influenced by past behaviors and conditions, as well as by the anticipation of future ones. Individuals are systems nested within other systems—such as teams and work groups—that are nested under larger organizational systems. All of these systems are open to the outside through connections to family members, customers, and multiple other potential sources of influence on organizational members' behavior.

Open Systems

Although open systems models capture the complexities of a psychology bound by the context in which the behaviors occur, the field of industrial and organizational psychology has—for the most part—constrained its domain to that of the interface between individuals and their environments, where that environment is physical (tasks, jobs, working conditions, organizational structures) or social (superiors, subordinates, peers). Furthermore, the beliefs, feelings, and behaviors of interest within that domain are limited to those for which there is some reason to believe that understanding them will enhance our ability to influence organizational effectiveness or individual well-being.

Fit

Underlying the psychological focus on individuals in organizational settings is the implicit assumption that both the organization and the individual are best served when there is a good fit between the goals, expectations, and conditions of organizations (e.g., jobs) with the characteristics of the people in them. From a prescriptive viewpoint, there are many ways to obtain a good fit. One is to consider organizations and people as relatively fixed entities. From this position, characteristics of each entity are assessed and the match is accomplished through selection—selection of people by organizations or organizations by people. The second option to obtain fit is to modify either or both of the two domains. In the case of changing people, training and development are primary mechanisms. Job design, organizational development, organizational design, or policies and practices related to goals, work rules, and other factors are relevant for changing organizations. For any particular case, multiple factors influence the fit, and the fit is a dynamic interaction between people and the organization, with each influencing the other over time. In addition, of course, while efforts at producing good fit are underway, both the individual and the organization are subject to evolutionary forces outside of the control of either the leaders of an organization or those whom they trust as advisors.

For much of industrial and organizational psychological research, the person-organization (P-O) fit has been implicit. In the last decade, considerably more effort has been devoted to developing it explicitly. The P-O model posits that a fit between applicants' personal characteristics and attributes of the organization contributes in important ways to individual performance and retention, as well as to organizational effectiveness. One way to demonstrate support for the P-O model is to find interactions between applicants' personal characteristics and organizational attributes. For example, Cable and Judge (1994) showed that a fit between applicants' personality and pay system characteristics enhanced the prediction of pay preferences and job attractiveness over and above the main effects of pay system characteristics themselves. Gustafson and Mumford (1995) found that individuals' personality predicted job satisfaction and performance better when the type of job situation was taken into account, supporting a P-O fit interpretation.

An important issue with P-O fit is how to conceptualize and measure it. Kristof (1996) pointed out that there has been considerable confusion on this issue. For example, P-O fit may be conceived of as person-environment congruence that confounds P-O fit with person-vocation and person-job fit. Also, fit has been measured *directly* by obtaining a single judgment of congruence between applicant and organizational characteristics and *indirectly* by getting independent judgments of person and organization characteristics and then assessing the similarities and differences. Finally, for the indirect approach, various indexes of fit are of course possible. Edwards (1994) provided a useful discussion of fit indexes and recommended a polynomial regression approach to overcome certain measurement problems. However, subsequent analysis (Kristof, 1996; Schneider, Goldstein, & Smith, 1995) has shown that this method poses some limitations as well.

The most compelling theoretical approach to modeling P-O fit is the attraction-selection-attrition (ASA) model (Schneider, 1987). Those who advocate this approach argue that individuals are attracted to organizations whose members are similar to them in relation to personality, values, and other attributes. Organizations in turn find attractive and are more likely to select those who possess knowledge, skills, and abilities similar to the ones that their organizational members possess. After they have been offered a job, those more similar are more likely to accept the job and are also more likely to be successfully socialized into the organization. Over time, those who do not fit well are more likely to leave—either on their own accord or because of problems on the job. Thus, the continuous process of attraction, assimilation, and attrition over time creates a force toward a fit between the people employed in the organization at any one time and the needs and expectations of that organization. The process is a less-than-perfect one in the sense that it does not create a perfect fit between all employees, their work, and those with whom they work, but it does create a force toward fit.

An important component of ASA theory is the *gravitational hypothesis;* this hypothesis posits that over time, people will gravitate to organizations that have values, attitudes, and so on that are similar to theirs. Empirical tests of this hypothesis have shown some support. For example, Wilk, Desmarais, and Sackett (1995) found that general cognitive ability is a good predictor of movement to jobs of higher or lower complexity 5 years later.

Schneider et al. (1995) provided an update on ASA research and thinking. Regarding personnel selection in the ASA context, these authors point out that if P-O fit is to be considered important, organizational diagnosis should be included in the job analysis strategy *and* that personality is likely to be a useful predictor of turnover and job performance because of the positive individual and organizational outcomes associated with homogeneity. Schneider et al. (1995) also argued that organizational homogeneity in personality, attitudes, and values is usually good early in the life of an organization because of its positive effect on cooperation and communication; however, such homogeneity over time may lead to an inability for the organization to adapt to changing external environments.

On balance, as organizational flexibility in effectively using employees is increasingly required (e.g., more movement of organization members from job to job or task force to task force), the P-O fit model may be more relevant compared to the person-job match strategy (e.g., Kristof, 1996) of the past. We think that both models will continue to have merit.

Aptitude-Treatment Interaction

Using Gough's (1957) terminology, in which *aptitude* represents individual difference characteristics of people and *treatment* is broadly defined as situations encountered by people (job characteristics, working conditions, supervisors, performance goals, etc.), John Campbell (1999) cogently argued that *all* industrial and organizational psychology is captured by aptitudes, treatment, and their interaction. In almost all cases, the dependent variables important to the field can be captured by individual, work group, or team performance; withdrawal behaviors such as absenteeism, turnover, or lack of attention to work; self-evaluation of the job or facets of the work setting (e.g., job satisfaction); or self-evaluation of fair treatment at work. Constructs that fall into either the aptitude domain, the treatment domain, or both are always invoked, and the task becomes that of measuring these constructs validly and explaining observed relationships by attempting to account for or control variability in constructs other than the ones of interest that would provide alternative explanations for observed covariation.

Almost all past and present work in industrial and organizational psychology falls squarely within the aptitude-treatment interaction model. It has served industrial and organizational psychology well in the past and will (in our opinion) continue to do so—with one caveat. How it does so is relatively clear when conditions and personal characteristics are relatively sta-

ble; however, the more we attempt to incorporate dynamic open systems properties into our work, the less clear is the guidance of the model. In many cases, we have remained within the model and simply treated our research and practice using its principles and acting *as if* people and situations were stable. In other cases, we treat continuous dynamic conditions as discrete events and use these events as means of dealing with time in a dynamic sense—sometimes without a very clear idea about scaling properties of the links between the discrete events over time.

INDUSTRIAL AND ORGANIZATIONAL PSYCHOLOGY IN THE 1990s

The chapters contained in this book represent the central content areas of industrial and organizational psychology. A comparison of the domain of issues addressed with earlier handbooks in the field shows a great deal of overlap; work continues in most of the same areas as before. Yet such a comparison underestimates change and progress. It does so because the events of change are more specific and idiosyncratic than the broad domains that come to represent most subdisciplines of the field. Furthermore, some of the more innovative work often does not fit neatly into one content domain; rather, it spans several. Therefore, before describing the content of this volume, we introduce some of the works of the 1990s that we believe have been particularly important for advancing the field of industrial and organizational psychology, but was not an explicit topic for any single chapter. In doing this, we have clustered this work into research that falls squarely within the aptitude-treatment model (advances by elaboration) and research that has wrestled with the open systems characteristics of human behavior in organizations, in turn placing some strains on working within the aptitude-treatment framework (advances through extension).

Advances by Elaboration

Models of Job Performance

A central behavior of concern in industrial and organizational psychology is that of individuals' performance on their jobs. Job performance is often the criterion that industrial and organizational psychologists attempt to predict from knowledge of characteristics of the performer and of the conditions under which the job is performed. Although it is appealing to think of performance as a unidimensional construct that varies along a single dimension from good to bad, the construct is rarely (if ever) that simple. Rather, job performance is a complex, multidimensional criterion, and addressing the criterion problem is a highly important endeavor.

In the 1990s Campbell observed that although job performance plays a central role in much of industrial and organizational psychology, little had been done to develop a comprehensive theory of what is meant by job performance. He and his colleagues addressed this issue by explicating the latent variables that best characterize the performance requirements of (ideally) all jobs associated with work. They (Campbell, Gasser, & Oswald, 1996; Campbell, McCloy, Oppler, & Sager, 1993) identified eight dimensions (e.g., Core Technical Proficiency; Oral and Written Communication; Supervision and Leadership) that they felt captured all important performance factors across the domain of jobs. Five of the eight latent performance constructs emerged consistently in the Project A research (a large-scale selection and classification study conducted in the U.S. Army to be described in the next section; Campbell & Knapp, 2001) across a large number of jobs studied in this research program.

This type of criterion model is important because it makes possible the scientific study of predictor-construct/job-performance-construct links. For personnel selection especially, but more broadly for other areas of industrial and organizational psychology (e.g., training, job design interventions, etc.), a taxonomy of performance helps organize accumulating research findings according to the effects of independent variables on individual criterion performance constructs. Findings from Pulakos, Borman, and Hough (1988) and McCloy, Campbell, and Cudeck (1994) confirm the usefulness of this research direction. Pulakos et al. found very different patterns of personality predictor-criterion relations across three different performance constructs, and McCloy et al. found that cognitive ability predicted a declarative knowledge criterion construct, whereas certain personality predictors were linked to a motivation-related criterion.

During the 1990s, other work continued by extending the typical model of searching for predictors of standard performance criteria—typically ratings of job performance. Work begun by Hunter (1983) using meta-analyses of relationships between cognitive ability, job knowledge, task proficiency, and overall performance ratings continued to show that cognitive ability had a direct effect on the acquisition of job knowledge. In his path model, performance ratings were a function of both knowledge and proficiency. Schmidt, Hunter, and Outerbridge (1986) added job experience to this model, and Borman and his colleagues (Borman, White, & Dorsey, 1995; Borman, White, Pulakos, & Oppler, 1991) added personality factors, behavioral indicators (e.g., number of disciplinary actions), and rater-ratee relationship factors to the mix. Each of these factors significantly increased the variance accounted for in performance ratings. These studies, along with others, have helped identify the factors and cues that supervisors use when making summary overall performance judgments, and such research helps us to understand better the job performance construct and certain critical antecedents of performance.

Project A: The U.S. Army Selection and Classification Research

From 1982 through 1994, the U.S. Army Research Institute and a consortium of private research firms conducted perhaps the largest-scale personnel research project ever attempted (Campbell & Knapp, 2001). The acknowledgment section of the final technical report listed 366 persons who worked on the project at one stage or another. The majority were industrial and organizational psychologists.

Project A (1982–1989) and the follow-up, the Career Forces Project (1990–1994), involved two major validation samples—one concurrent and one predictive. The Project A concurrent sample allowed for the evaluation of the validities of a wide range of predictor measures against the job performance of military personnel during their first tour of duty. A second longitudinal sample provided validation results for these same predictors against performance in training programs, first-tour job performance, and second-tour performance as a noncommissioned officer (NCO) supervisor. To provide an idea of the magnitude of these validation efforts, approximately 9,500 soldiers participated in the first-tour concurrent validation study; roughly 45,000 recruits were tested at the beginning of the longitudinal validation research. Criterion data were collected on about 30,000 at the end of training, 10,000 during this cohort's first tour, and 1,500 during their second tour.

The experimental predictor test battery included measures of an incredibly wide variety of individual differences. Development of the tests was driven by job analyses of a representative sample of 21 enlisted jobs (most of which had civilian counterparts). The predictor battery included measures of general and specific cognitive abilities, perceptual and psychomotor abilities, personality, vocational interest, and biographical information.

Criterion measures were extensive as well. For first-tour performance, researchers administered end-of-training measures, work sample and job knowledge tests, peer and supervisor ratings on Army-wide and job-specific dimensions, and administrative measures such as disciplinary actions and awards or commendations. For second tour, all of these measures were administered along with peer and supervisor ratings on special leadership dimensions, a situational judgment test, and supervisory role-play exercises. A more extended description of these contributions can be found in the recently released book on Project A and the Career Forces Project (Campbell & Knapp, 2001).

The preceding provides a feel for the magnitude of the data collections and the effort put forth on the predictor and criterion development as well as validation of the measures; all of this was critical for the project to meet its objectives. More important for the science of personnel selection and classification were the substantive contributions derived from the project's analyses and results.

First, for both the individual differences predictor and the job performance criterion domains, the emphasis on latent variables and latent structure rather than methods (e.g., ratings) or particular measures (e.g., a biodata survey) was highly important for generalizing results. The strategy was extremely successful in specifying job performance as reflecting a consistent five-factor structure (core technical proficiency, general soldiering proficiency, effort and leadership, personal discipline, and physical fitness/military bearing). Each of the factors was represented by multiple methods. For example, effort and leadership had as components number of administrative awards and certificates, the Army-wide rating factor, technical skill and effort, and the job-specific rating overall composite. This performance model was confirmed for multiple jobs in the first-tour sample, and a similar model was derived and confirmed for the second-tour NCO sample. Also, on the predictor side exploratory and subsequent confirmatory factor analyses identified latent variables in each of the domains represented (e.g., perceptual abilities, personality).

Especially important for the science of personnel selection, the different performance latent variables were related to different combinations of and individual predictor latent variables in theoretically meaningful ways. General cognitive ability was the primary predictor of the two technical proficiency performance factors, whereas some of the personality constructs were more predictive of the personal discipline and physical fitness/military bearing constructs. These empirical results support Campbell's taxonomy of performance, with constructs widely relevant to the population of jobs. As mentioned in a previous section, this specification of performance constructs should encourage accumulation of research findings according to the effects of individual differences and other organizationally relevant variables on individual performance constructs (e.g., Campbell et al., 1993).

Second, if anyone still believed that job performance could be captured by a single dimension, sometimes termed the ultimate criterion, that notion was laid to rest in Project A. Different criteria and different criterion measures were necessary to adequately capture the performance space. For example, work sample and job knowledge tests measured maximum performance on elements of job performance that were primarily a function of human abilities, whereas ratings tapped components that were more motivationally driven. None of these measures was more ultimate than any other; each was important and appropriate for measuring a particular aspect of job performance.

Third, Project A research confirmed the results that general cognitive ability is a robust predictor of job performance across jobs (Schmidt & Hunter, 1998). However, the results also showed that—with a wide range of predictor and criterion variables selected to capture the heterogeneity in both domains across jobs—differential prediction across jobs was relatively strong. This finding provides another example of how research can increase our understanding of individual-differences/job-performance linkages by identifying specific criterion constructs rather than working with the overall job performance construct.

Thus, the Project A research program provided industrial and organizational psychologists with an unprecedented opportunity to study relationships between a broad array of individual differences and job performance constructs. Perhaps most noteworthy was the specification of job performance, resulting in a replicable multidimensional model of performance. This depiction of performance coupled with a combination concurrent and predictive validity design allowed researchers to learn a considerable amount about specific linkages between the individual differences and each one of these performance constructs.

Development of the Occupational Information Network (O*NET)

A major contribution of industrial organizational psychology to human behavior at work has been in the form of taxonomies and structures for describing the world of work. However, as the world's economy has matured and shifts in the kind of work being performed have occurred (in developed countries in particular), it became increasingly clear that there was a need for new systems for characterizing work and the demands it places on people and organizations. The system that best described jobs in place was that of the Dictionary of Occupational Titles. In it, jobs were located in a three-dimensional space defined by the human characteristics needed to perform the job, the way in which data were handled in the job, and the physical characteristics of the job (i.e., People x Data x Things). A coding system based on the descriptive taxonomy located thousands of jobs within the space and was extremely useful for estimating what was needed to perform particular jobs (skills, abilities, educational requirements, etc.), and how those jobs fit into families of similar jobs.

In the early 1990s, the U.S. Department of Labor convened a panel of industrial and organizational psychologists to plan the development of a database that would eventually replace the Dictionary of Occupational Titles as the primary information source for jobs in the U.S. economy. This panel designed a plan for a content model that could describe jobs according to both person and job requirements (Advisory Panel for the Dictionary of Occupational Titles, 1993; Campion, Gowing, Lancaster, & Pearlman, 1994).

The content model is depicted in Figure 2.1. The idea was to build taxonomies of descriptors in each of these areas and then to score each target occupation on each of the descriptors. As an example, in the abilities domain, the plan was to develop a comprehensive model of all abilities relevant to work and then to get ratings for an occupation on each of the abilities regarding how much each ability was required to accomplish work in that occupation. After the ratings were obtained for every descriptor in the content model—the occupation's ability, skill, generalized work activity, and so forth—requirements would be numerically defined, making possible a variety of practical applications. In fact, the ultimate goal was to obtain content model ratings on all occupations in the U.S. economy to make the O*NET maximally useful. Anticipated applications included (a) supporting educational policy and skill standards, (b) informing school-to-work transitions, (c) helping dislocated workers find jobs, (d) helping employers select employees, (e) identifying job families, (f) linking job requirements to disability or medical standards, (g) identifying training needs for target occupations, (h) developing wage and salary systems, and (i) serving as input dimensions for performance appraisal systems.

The content model descriptors have been developed (Peterson, Mumford, Borman, Jeanneret, & Fleishman, 1999; Peterson et al., 2001). The taxonomies in most of the domains build upon earlier model development efforts. For example, the abilities model is based on Fleishman's research on the Functional Job Analysis System (F-JAS; Fleishman & Mumford, 1988). The skills taxonomy borrows from the work done on the Secretary of Labor's Commission on Achieving Necessary Skills (SCANS; Peterson, 1992) project and from the National Skill Standards Board. The generalized work activities model took as a starting point job components emerging from work on the Position Analysis Questionnaire (McCormick, Jeanneret, & Mecham, 1969), and supervisory dimensions represented in several models of supervisory behavior, including those of Hemphill (1960), Mitchell (1978), and Borman and Brush (1993). Finally, the work styles dimensions were derived from a view of personality that collapse the dimensions of personality into five primary ones, referred to as the "Big Five" (Goldberg, 1990), and from work Guion and colleagues (e.g., Raymark, Schmit, & Guion, 1997) did to develop a personality-related job analysis survey.

Two additional features of the O*NET content model and database reinforce its flexibility and overall usefulness. The first is that with so many different types of descriptors (i.e., skills, abilities, work activities, etc.), multiple windows to the world of work are available to the user. Different applications are likely to require different sets of descriptors, and this condition can be met with O*NET. Second, the content model is organized hierarchically so that users can enter the database at the level appropriate for their applications. At the most specific levels the user can obtain fine-grained occupational information. If more general information about occupations is required, users can enter the database at a more generic, aggregated level. Additionally, O*NET provides a common nomenclature for describing different jobs. The cross-job descriptors essentially place all jobs on the same metric, thus avoiding the necessity to develop a new descriptive system for each job.

Work is continuing to refine the descriptors and obtain job incumbent ratings on as large a population of occupations as possible. The hope is that the O*NET database will become sufficiently populated such that all of the applications described previously can be realized.

Advances Through Extension

Project A and O*NET both represent large-scale developments in industrial and organizational psychology that were incremental advances in thinking or practice. In some sense they were new solutions to traditional problems historically addressed by the field. In this section we highlight breakthroughs that might be characterized as extending into new directions for the field. We shall begin with what is often referred to as the *levels issue*.

Levels of Analysis

The historical focus of theory and practice in our field has been the individual. Indeed, many early industrial psychologists thought of themselves as differential psychologists whose attention was focused primarily on individual differences in knowledge, skills, abilities, and other attributes that were then related to critical behavior in organizational settings.

As industrial and organizational psychology attempted to deal with the broader organizational environment in which individuals are imbedded to include work teams and larger units, it became necessary to recognize that important behavioral constructs occur at different levels in the organization. The multilevel nature of the relevant behavioral phenomena raised many conceptual and measurement issues. Some constructs are meaningful at multiple levels, and the nature of the meaning must be carefully specified.

Consider the case of cognitive ability. At the individual level, cognitive ability is a construct that represents a person's ability to accomplish some specified domain of behaviors. However, if cognitive ability is considered at the team or group level, it also may be meaningful, such as the case in which there might be interest in the level of cognitive ability of members of a classroom or a team in a team-based organization. Yet at the team level, each individual possesses some level of cognitive ability and the members are likely to differ in it. Assuming they do differ, what best represents team ability? Is it the average of all members, the ability level of the highest member, the lowest? The answer to this question is not clear. What is clear, however, is that variance among team members which had no analogue at the individual level exists at the team level and cannot be ignored. The best representation of team cognitive ability will depend on the theory in which its use is imbedded. Thus, if team ability is something that is to be related to performance on a task in which all members can put forth their own ideas, work relatively autonomously, and pool their work, then the average of all members may be appropriate. If, however, the task is one in which a good idea from one team member can carry the team, then the cognitive ability of the brightest member may be more appropriate.

The previous example was one in which the construct could have meaning at both the team and the aggregate level. In other cases, constructs are only meaningful at one level even though multiple levels are involved. Returning to teams, individuals comprise teams and have individual-level characteristics, but some constructs only occur at the team level. Cooperation is one of these constructs. Individuals can create conditions of cooperation that vary from low to high, but cooperation is a between-person phenomenon. Thus, as levels are introduced, how behavior is observed, measured, and studied when considered as activity embedded in multiple levels requires a perspective different from that taken by industrial and organizational psychology in its early development.

Increasingly—by chance or by design—people work in groups or teams. This level of analysis enjoys great status in the field today. Although the literature on social collectives—like that on groups—is well developed and has been evident for some time (e.g., Forsythe, 1999; McGrath, 1984), the research on work groups and teams represents a distinct breakthrough because it has integrated group dynamics with task work, work flow, and work procedures. This literature is well

represented in this volume and details the distinction between what might be called *individual-in-team* behavior (i.e., as a result of the social forces operating on an individual in a social context) from truly team-level phenomena (Klimoski & Zukin, 1999; see chapter by Kozlowski & Bell in this volume).

Although they are less common in today's scholarship, still other levels of description have found favor. At a macrolevel, a number of investigators have found it important and useful to acknowledge and measure societal-level phenomena. Arguably, these phenomena represent both the context that the worker (or applicant) experiences and the environment in which the organization must operate. Similarly, macroforces stemming from developments in popular culture (including the entertainment media) and the educational system are known to affect parameters of interest to those doing research on personnel selection, recruiting, training, or work motivation. Indeed, even specific trends in industry sectors (e.g., consumer products, transportation) can represent a contextual (boundary condition) or might be transformed into a variable of interest.

This trend to use alternative levels of analysis has several implications; two are noted here. The first is the need for specificity. As never before, researchers are required to be clear about the levels in which they are interested and the ones to which they wish to generalize. A version of this point is the possibility that we may get the best models or the best prediction if we presume that more than one level is operative to produce an outcome of interest. Thus, Hofmann and Stetzer (1996), in attempting to understand workplace safety, found—as tradition would have it—that individual differences were important in the prediction of unsafe behaviors. But it was also true that the safety behavior of the supervisor (e.g., wearing safety gear) and the risk-taking norms of the work group were involved. Because these different aspects of the problem are usually intertwined, one must think not only of the effects of multiple but also those of interpenetrating levels. Similarly, Zaccaro and Klimoski (2001) chose to focus on senior organizational leadership as a way of capturing the effects of individual and executive team factors on the organizational level of functioning, but they also recognized that phenomena at that level would have first- (e.g., structural design) and second-order (e.g., communications-information flow) effects.

A second implication is the need for the clear articulation of explanatory mechanisms—that is, we must specify the processes that we believe are operating. Clearly, when characterizing individuals, we can and often do invoke subcognitive (e.g., habitual), cognitive, and affective processes. It is also likely that these processes will be relevant at most higher levels of analysis. For example, the behavior of organizations is largely the result of sets of individuals for whom such processes are controlling. The challenge, however, lies in deciding when to move up the level of analysis to attend to other processes. Alternative processes include interpersonal (dyad and team), social (group and team), informational (team and organization), and political (team, organization, or interorganization) ones.

A Renewed Interest in Viewing Workers as Individuals

Earlier in this chapter, we characterized the field of industrial and organizational psychology as one that is concerned with the satisfaction and well-being of those who populate work organizations; yet some people might argue the point. This is because many in the field historically have adopted the perspective of an organization's management in their approach to the framing of research questions or to practice (see historical treatments by Katzell & Austin 1992; Schmitt & Klimoski, 1991). However, during the 1990s there was a great deal of interest in issues and questions that are or could be framed in terms of the needs and expectations of the individual as an applicant or as an employee.

To illustrate, several investigators have attempted to model the forces affecting the organizational entry process whereby an individual becomes an applicant and then as an applicant decides to accept an offer made by the organization (e.g., Rynes, Bretz, & Gerhart, 1991). Others have focused on the dynamics of the first few days, weeks, or months on the job as they are experienced by the new employee. Guided by the seminal ideas of Louis (1980), researchers have concentrated on the way individuals make sense of the new environment by both passive and active means (e.g., Ashforth, Saks, & Lee, 1998; Morrison, 1993). At times the issue has been framed relative to learning (Ostroff & Kozlowski, 1992) or alternatively, one of understanding how a new hire comes to adopt an organizational identity (Albert, Ashforth, & Dutton, 2000). These notions are evidenced in the chapters in this volume on recruitment, culture and climate, and motivation.

We have seen that as part of this focus on the individual, scholars have placed a special emphasis on issues of fairness and social justice in the workplace—often associated with what has come to be called the psychological contract (Morrison & Robinson, 1997; Robinson, 1996; Rousseau, 1995). Indeed, perceived fairness is often linked to the development of trust in the workplace. It is not surprising that modeling trust, its antecedents, and its consequences has become a major theme in the literature. Investigators have sought out parsimonious and powerful explanatory mechanisms for understanding how individuals self-regulate in the workplace (Kramer & Tyler, 1996). Finally, those studying leadership processes also have contributed to this literature on the development of trust—especially in the context of the socialization

of newcomers (Liden, Wayne, & Stilwell, 1993). Fairness and trust are covered in some detail in this volume in chapters addressing such issues as motivation, stress, job attitudes, and organizational development.

The theme of the individual's point of view has also been woven into recent treatments of the effects of various personnel practices. These include applicant testing (e.g., Gilliland, 1993; Ployhart & Ryan, 1998), training (Colquitt, LePine, & Noe, 2000), performance standards (Bobko & Colella, 1994), affirmative action programs (Kravitz & Klineberg, 2000) and layoff policies (Wanberg, Bunce, & Gavin, 1999). In these and in other papers like them, it is the worker's view that is being made salient and is the focus of attention. Such issues discussed in this volume's chapters on personnel selection, diversity, and job performance.

Finally, it would be appropriate to include in our characterization of this trend to viewing the worker's needs and interests as important by pointing out what appears to be renewed attention to work associated with empirically derived models of career patterns and career management (e.g., Hall & Mirvis, 1995; London, 1995), research on the interface between work and family (e.g., Zedeck, 1992), or research on workers' daily lives (Hage, 1995). In this volume, these topics are addressed in chapters on training, culture and climate, careers, and organizational development and change.

Methods, Models, and Theories

The 1990s began with continued frequent use of studies employing meta-analytic techniques for summarizing multiple data sets in which covariation between the same variables was employed. In 1992, Schmidt went so far as to argue that meta-analysis was likely to provide all of the knowledge needed about relationships between variables in industrial and organizational psychology (Schmidt, 1992). The only reason for conducting original studies (according to this view) would be to supply meta-analysts with the data needed to establish *the* scientific findings regarding the variables. Meta-analytic work is certainly valuable for summarizing research findings, but the importance of individual studies in their own right is not diminished and continues to be demonstrated.

To provide a brief summary of the role of meta-analysis in industrial and organizational research, we did a search of the literature in the leading journals of the field and found 119 meta-analytic studies conducted since 1992. These studies are summarized in Table 1.1. As can be seen, the largest number of studies involved the job performance construct. Examples of findings include point estimates for links between job performance and role ambiguity and conflict, supervisory expectations, job experience, feedback interventions, homogeneity of

TABLE 1.1   Summary of Meta-Analysis Content in Industrial and Organizational Psychology, 1992–2001

Content Category	Number of Meta-Analyses
Job performance	62
Leadership	8
Turnover	9
Goal theory and motivation	13
Ethnic group and gender	11
Job satisfaction and organizational commitment	22
Selection predictors	35
Training	4
Miscellaneous	17

work teams, and the purpose of the job performance ratings. A count of studies linking job performance and each of the other seven categories in Table 1.1 shows three with leadership constructs, one with turnover, seven with goal theory or other motivation-related variables, three with ethnic group or gender, four with job satisfaction or organizational commitment, and 27 with various selection predictors such as the interview, biodata, and personality constructs. We counted 18 meta-analyses summarizing relations between personality predictors and job performance constructs.

The next largest number of studies involve relations between selection predictors and—in the vast majority of cases—job performance. As mentioned previously, personality-performance linkages received by far the most attention. The third largest number of studies summarize relations between job satisfaction or organizational commitment and constructs such as flexible work schedules, vocational interest congruence, and job level. Regarding other categories, two are with leadership constructs, three are with turnover, three are with goal theory and motivational constructs (e.g., participation in decision making), two are with selection predictors, and two link job satisfaction with gender.

Correlations between goal theory or other motivation-related constructs and several other constructs have also been summarized using meta-analysis. The vast majority of these relations have been between motivation constructs (e.g., participation in decision making, task involvement, or expectancy variables) and job performance or job satisfaction.

Meta-analyses involving ethnic group and gender are the fifth most numerous. In this category, relationships have been studied with such variables as cognitive ability, job performance and satisfaction, leadership effectiveness, and negotiation outcomes.

As shown in Table 1.1, nine meta-analyses involving turnover have appeared in the literature from 1992 to 2001. Four of these meta-analyses examined relations between turnover and job satisfaction or organizational commitment. Leadership constructs were included in eight additional

meta-analyses. Overall leadership effectiveness, as well as specific constructs such as initiating structure, consideration, and leader-member exchange have been linked primarily to job performance and job satisfaction. Finally, four studies involving training (e.g., managerial training and cross-cultural training) have related training to performance outcomes.

The purpose of this exercise was to demonstrate the breadth of meta-analytic activity in industrial and organizational psychology. Clearly, the method has been useful for better informing us about covariation among primary variables of interest in the field. As with any method, however, there is need for caution—particularly as it relates to the need to recognize that a number of subjective calls must be made when using the method. Of particular importance is the need to be aware of overcorrection for unreliability in circumstances under which reliability may be underestimated (Murphy & DeShon, 2000).

As important as meta-analysis may be for cumulating data across multiple samples, perhaps its major contribution in the long run is the use of the method for model testing and also its role in a shift away from a singular reliance on statistical significance testing (Schmidt, 1996). For example, Hom, Caranikas-Walker, Prussia, and Griffeth (1992) combined meta-analyses with structural equation modeling to validate a model of turnover presented earlier by Mobley, Griffeth, Hand, and Meglino (1979) and to compare it to two other models. Similarly, Colquitt et al. (2000) employed meta-analytical techniques to test hypotheses about cognitive and motivational predictors of training outcomes in ways that combined the power of meta-analysis for estimating population relationships from multiple studies along with the ability to develop theoretically informed models that could then be evaluated. Thus, meta-analysis and other major methodological advances such as hierarchical linear modeling (HLM), structural equation modeling (SEM), and confirmatory factor analysis (CFA) are having a positive effect on the field at the interface between theory and data. When used appropriately, the methods require that the investigators carefully specify the theory underlying their empirical work and then construct models that fit the theory. The data are then compared to the models and judgments are made about the degree of fit between the data and the theoretical models.

All of the previously mentioned methods of model testing involve data gathered from observations of human behavior. Other modeling techniques exist that use computer models to test assumptions from theories that have been informed by observations of behaviors at work. These models, called computational models, are frequently used in the cognitive sciences and in the organizational sciences but rarely appear in the industrial and organizational psychology literature

(Hulin & Ilgen, 2000). One model (WORKER) developed for addressing withdrawal behaviors at work is grounded in the extensive literature on absenteeism, turnover, tardiness, and other withdrawal behaviors and is extremely valuable for informing us about interactions among key variables over time that neither theory nor empirical observations are likely to uncover on their own (Hanisch, Hulin, & Seitz, 1986). A recently published book, edited by Ilgen and Hulin (2000), offers a number of illustrations of ways in which computational modeling can and should be added to the growing trend toward model testing in our field. With this and other statistical model testing methods that are now available, there is a strong trend toward better integrating theory with data in industrial and organizational psychology.

Strategic Human Resource Management

Another major shift in thinking in the field of industrial and organizational psychology relates to the recognition that much of what we do as a field relative to scholarship and practice must be framed in terms of the business case; although this has always been true to some extent (for practitioners at least), it is increasingly recognized that our theories and models need to add value in the view of society for us to have the luxury of pursuing our scholarship. Moreover, because numerous other fields of endeavor are competing for such respect (and for the resources that follow), our contributions must do well in the marketplace for useful ideas.

As a term, *strategic HRM* (human resource management) has been around for a relatively short period of time (Devanna, Fombrum, & Tichy, 1981; Lengnick-Hall & Lengnick-Hall, 1988; Wright, 1998). However, several of the concepts underlying it have a bit of a history. For example, notions of *utility* in personnel selection (Brogden, 1949) were created more than 50 years ago to show how and when a selection device would demonstrate value in improving the quality of the workforce over what was currently the case. Similarly, the logic of utility and cost/benefit analysis have become the basis for assessing the value of any intervention affecting the organization's so-called human capital (see chapter by Boudreau & Ramstad in this volume). What is somewhat different, however, is that the unit of analysis is not just the pool of applicants or a personnel initiative (e.g., a new training program), but rather that of the organization. In short, the problematic of HRM is one of ensuring that the organization as a whole is well served as it attempts to succeed in the larger marketplace, including the global arena.

More specifically, Wright and McMahan (1992) define strategic HRM as "the pattern of planned human resource deployments and activities intended to enable the firm to achieve its goals" (p. 298). In this regard, several contemporary writers are interested in modeling how the management of human resources can contribute to such things as matching personnel activities to business strategies, forecasting manpower needs (given certain strategic objectives), or finding ways to align personnel practices to strategy and structure (e.g., Boxall, 1998; Lepak & Snell, 1998, Taylor, Beechler, & Napier, 1996). Still others attempt to deal with the implications of restructuring, downsizing, and mergers or acquisitions (e.g., Gratten, Hailey, Stiles, & Truss, 1999). Finally, writers in this area are attempting to address the issue of metrics and measurement systems that will reveal the HR contributions to company performance (e.g., Rogers & Wright, 1998). It is also worth noting that this trend has promoted the need for and the use of the multilevel and dynamic modeling approaches described briefly in an earlier section as the firm, its policies and practices, and employees' reactions to these policies and practices are involved (e.g., Shaw, Delery, Jenkins, & Gupta, 1999).

Taking a strategic perspective has allowed practitioners in our field to relate in meaningful ways what they do professionally to the most senior organizational leaders. Not only are they able to better empathize with their clients, but they are also capable of making a business case for what they do. When they accomplish this goal, there is a greater likelihood that the research and findings of industrial and organizational psychologists will be given the same credibility and weight as is given to the work of consultants with backgrounds in other fields such as engineering and economics.

In fact, the field of industrial and organizational psychology is often referred to as an applied science. Its members are often described as scientist-practitioners. In this regard, we feel that professional practice should be based on good theories, models, and data. At the same time, however, all good theories must be grounded in organizational realities. Thus, unlike many other social sciences (e.g., economics), we hold ourselves accountable for (and take some pride in) being able to make valid predictions (rather than merely descriptions or postdictions) relative to the impact of our interventions or recommendations. Moreover, we seek to modify our models in light of prediction errors.

Chapters Comprising This Handbook

The remainder of this volume contains 22 chapters on specific topics in industrial and organizational psychology. The first eight chapters address the nature of work and behavior at work that typically is described as personnel psychology.

They are followed by six chapters that address organizational psychological issues of motivation, attitudes, teams, and customer relations. From these discussions, we turn to issues of the organizational, work, and social environment that influence behavior in the present environment and over a career.

In the chapter on job analysis, Sackett and Laczo (this volume) point out that many choices must be made before conducting this critical first step in the vast majority of our industrial and organizational interventions. Such choices as whether the job analysis should be general or more fine-grained, focused on job activities or worker attributes, and so forth must of course align with the purpose of the job analysis. These authors also provide excellent sections on some contemporary hot topics—most notably, competency modeling, cognitive task analysis, and strategic job analysis.

Motowidlo (this volume) provides a carefully crafted definition of the job performance construct—"the total expected value to the organization of the discrete behavioral episodes that an individual carries out over a standard period of time." This definition implies that performance is behavior, not results—a distinction also made several years ago by Campbell (Campbell, Dunnette, Lawler, & Weick, 1970). The author reviews in detail Campbell's recent theory of job performance (briefly noted earlier in this chapter) and other attempts to define elements of the performance space (e.g., contextual performance and organizational citizenship behavior). It is important to note that Motowidlo describes a model in which knowledge, skill, motivation, and habits are the direct determinants of job performance. These variables are in turn determined primarily by individual differences and by training and development opportunities. This model provides a rich theoretical framework for our field's most important independent variables and job performance.

To illustrate how much the area of recruitment has grown in the last 25 years, Rynes and Cable (this volume) point out that in the first *Handbook of Industrial and Organizational Psychology* (Dunnette, 1976), less than one page was devoted to recruiting (Guion, 1976). Coverage in the 1991 Handbook increased to a full chapter (Rynes, 1991), and the last 10 years have seen still more research activity. In this highly informative review, Rynes and Cable make a strong case for the increasing importance of recruitment as a corporate strategy; attracting and retaining people—especially for key positions—is critical for gaining competitive advantage in our global economy. Also covered in this chapter is research on recruitment sources (e.g., Web sites), affirmative action, applicant reactions to selection procedures, vacancy characteristics (e.g., pay and benefits), and social processes related to recruitment. Finally, these authors also look to the future by calling for recruiting research to move beyond the individual level of analysis and instead to aggregate results to the organizational level and study cross-organizational differences in recruiting practices.

Schmitt, Cortina, Ingerick, and Wiechmann (this volume) present a comprehensive model of personnel selection that has as components individual differences (e.g., ability, personality), mediators (e.g., job knowledge, motivation), performance, and individual and organizational distal outcomes (e.g., customer satisfaction, withdrawal behavior, social responsibility). It is becoming evident (and very well documented in this chapter) that declarative knowledge, procedural knowledge and skill, and motivation mediate relationships between individual differences and job performance. But the authors go beyond this general observation to discuss specific links. For example, cognitive ability is the primary predictor of declarative knowledge; perceptual speed and psychomotor ability are the primary predictors of procedural knowledge and skill; and personality is the primary predictor of elements of motivation. Schmitt et al. also differentiate between components of job performance, separating task and contextual performance (Borman & Motowidlo, 1997), but also introducing the construct of adaptive performance (Pulakos, Arad, Donovan, & Plamondon, 2000) to the mix. These distinctions are likely to be quite important for providing differential predictions for the individual-differences/mediator-variables/job-performance relations. Finally, the authors provide a concise, focused review of our predictor domains, including physical abilities, job experience, personality, biodata, and the interview.

Fritz Drasgow (this volume) provides an illuminating review of research on human abilities—especially in relation to job performance. He first discusses the major approaches to studying intelligence: factor-analytic research, information-processing approaches, and neuropsychological research. The author then draws on his own work with situational judgment tests (SJTs, tests that present difficult real-world situations and ask test takers to select the most effective response in a multiple-choice form) to suggest that constructs such as social intelligence or tacit knowledge as measured by SJTs might be employed to provide incremental validity beyond general cognitive ability in predicting job performance. These constructs and related personality variables appear to predict the contextual performance (e.g., supporting and helping other individuals in the organization or the organization itself, volunteering for assignments and putting forth extra effort) component of job performance—a component shown to be important beyond task performance for contributing to overall performance (e.g., Motowidlo & Van Scotter, 1994).

Hough and Furnham (this volume) review the burgeoning literature on personality and the prediction of job performance. These authors make a good case for increasing the scientific understanding of personality-performance links by evaluating relations between relatively specific performance constructs and individual components of job performance. They also discuss alternative methods for measuring personality, including the use of biodata, others' reports or descriptions, computerized assessment, and genetic testing. Their position on the slanting of responses or faking in a personnel selection context is that response distortion is not likely to affect validity substantially, although there is considerable disagreement on this topic (e.g., Rosse, Stecher, Miller, & Levin, 1998).

The approach to training offered by Kraiger (this volume) reflects the major ways in which this area has been treated in both theory and practice. Thus, training does involve both instruction and learning. However, it also is embedded in attempts to change the organization. In addition to detailing these distinctions, the chapter goes on to highlight key issues in measurement that must be resolved if we are going to make great strides in this area.

In their excellent chapter on utility, Boudreau and Ramstad (this volume) go well beyond a review of cost-benefit analysis and thinking. These authors argue that industrial and organizational psychology must become more strategic to influence human resource decisions before such decisions are made rather than justify interventions after the fact. They observe that there often exist in organizations key jobs that can create uniqueness and competitive advantage; and that these jobs are not necessarily the highest paid (e.g., trash sweepers at Disney World and repair technicians at Xerox). An implication of this chapter is that utility analysis should broaden from a rather esoteric technical topic to include an examination of all links between investments in industrial and organizational and in human resources (HR) programs and individual and organizational effectiveness.

Extensive literatures on work motivation and job satisfaction are reviewed and organized in models that provide excellent frameworks for identifying major themes and pointing out gaps in our current knowledge. A chapter is devoted to each topic. Terence R. Mitchell and Denise Daniels (this volume) identify eight theoretical motivational positions (expectancy theory, self-efficacy, goal setting, moods and affect, need theories, dispositions, reinforcement theory, and justice). For each position, they review the progress to date and suggest new directions. All these positions are introduced within an overarching model that provides an excellent means for seeing the relationships among them. Hulin and Judge (this volume), in their treatment of job satisfaction, also provide models that depict the nature of various positions on job satisfaction. They use these models to show what has been found in the past, to discuss what we now know, and to discuss some of the controversies that have been raised regarding the nature of job satisfaction and its covariation with important behaviors at work.

Avolio, Sosik, Jung, and Berson (this volume) do an excellent job of summarizing the many crosscurrents in the field of organizational leadership. To their credit, they are also able to provide a synthesis around what they term a full-range theory of leadership. Although it remains to be seen if their approach will satisfy all of our needs, it does offer a very useful way to consider leadership as simultaneously an input, process and output phenomenon—one that has been conceptualized as operating at several levels of analysis (e.g., dyad, team, unit, firm, and even nation-state). It also is interesting to note that the piece reflects the efforts of four generations of scholars who were able to find some common ground in producing this chapter in spite of the extensive and complex literature that exists.

Although the interplay between theory and practice can be found in several chapters, it is a major theme for Austin and Bartunek (this volume) on organizational development. The authors effectively show how theories of organizations and theories of change combine to affect practice and the likelihood of favorable outcomes. They also go on to show how important it is to integrate knowledge from the field if we are going to have truly grounded theories of organizational dynamics and planned change.

A topic that has enjoyed rapid development in the last decade or so is that of work teams and groups. Perhaps this phenomenon was due to a high level of funding for basic and applied research in the United States by the military that has a great need to know about creating and managing effective command and control or action teams. It may have also been a result of a shift toward teams as a design solution for creating effective and adaptable work organizations. In any event, we in the field of industrial and organizational psychology are now able to understand more than ever before just how and why work teams and groups function and can be made more effective. It is also fortunate that we have such a good summary of these developments in the chapter by Kozlowski and Bell (this volume). This chapter offers a unique multilevel perspective on how individuals, dyads, and teams function as nested systems. A signature feature of this chapter is the authors' treatment of applied problematics (like staffing and training of teams) within a conceptual framework that has been extensively informed by research.

Ryan and Ployhart (this volume), in their chapter about customer service behavior (CSB), use an innovative contingency approach to understanding, predicting, and influencing CSB.

Their argument is that the specific customer service situation will often influence the effectiveness of different types of CSB. The authors define the CSB situation along a number of dimensions, including intangibility (e.g., giving a haircut is low, providing financial advice is high) and standard versus customized service required. In fact, Ryan and Ployhart provide tables that present research questions for each of several industrial and organizational areas (e.g., job performance, selection, climate and attitudes, etc.) under different situational CSB conditions. Thus, for selection, for example, a research question is *Will cognitive ability and job knowledge be better predictors of customer service performance in customized service situations than in standard service situations?* The authors also review research on the selection of customer service employees; service climate in organizations; mood, emotions, and CSB; the training and socialization of CSB; and the design of customer service jobs.

Wayne F. Cascio (this volume) turns attention to a number of factors that a global economy and its effect on the rapid pace of change are likely to have on research topics in industrial and organizational psychology as well as on its practice. Relying heavily on case studies and best practices reported in the organizational literature, Cascio provides a number of examples of how corporations have adjusted staffing, training, and motivational practices to respond to rapid change, globalization, a multicultural workforce, and other factors that play a major role in work at the beginning of the twenty-first century.

In the chapters about performance and job analysis, the authors deal with the measurement and description of jobs and work. In these cases, the work setting is—for the most part—taken as a given. In the chapter on work design, Frederick P. Morgeson and Michael A. Campion (this volume) return again to the nature of work but do so from the standpoint of designing work—particularly as it influences work motivation. They present a number of different perspectives on the design of work and examine the impact of social and structural factors on work. They also pay particular attention to the distinction between the physical nature of work and the perceptions of that work from the standpoint of the person who occupies the work role. Issues of measurement as well as those of the content of work are discussed.

The issue of work place stress has never been more salient than it is currently. Because of the terrorist attacks on September 11, 2001; the anthrax scares; and the widespread economic recession, more individuals in the United States and elsewhere are under more work-related stress than they have been in recent memory. Thus, it is important that we are able to offer in this volume such a fine chapter by Sonnentag and Frese (this volume) on stress in organizations. This chapter

reports on many large-scale studies from a variety of nations, thus ensuring that the conclusions offered are reliable and generalizable.

Although many of the chapters deal with behaviors that are anchored in particular organizational processes such as selection or training, Connelly and Ordóñez (this volume) examine the process of decision making, a process that deals with multiple content areas and applies across the board in almost every organizational setting. They present basic theoretical views of how inferences are made and then turn to predictions of behavioral choices. There is high agreement that such choices are guided by judgments about preferences held by the decision maker, yet a number of different theories have been proposed to explain how these preferences are derived and how they affect judgments. The authors review work on these different theories and discuss their impact for understanding decision making in organizations.

Greenhaus (this volume) provides the only chapter that takes employees' perspectives on work over the entire life span of work. He begins by focusing on the meaning of career success and then examines the nature of success for women and for men as they perform multiple roles both on and off the job. Attention is directed at changes within the person over time and at organizational interventions, such as training, career transitions, and providing mentors, to enhance the likelihood of career success. He provides an extensive review of a large and diverse literature.

William Howell (this volume) first provides a highly interesting history of HF/E (human factors and ergonomics). He also covers a variety of professional issues in HF/E, including graduate school training, research and practice issues, and job settings for HF/E types. In addition, Howell summarizes the content of the HF/E field, reviewing topics such as mental workload, situational awareness, and computer-supported cooperative work. Finally, he closes the chapter with a description of a new movement in HF/E that is challenging the traditional strongly cognitive perspective. The ecological approach emphasizes field observations and understanding systems in vivo; according to Howell, this approach is likely to help bring HF/E and industrial and organizational psychology closer together.

The issue of levels is made a major theme in the chapter by Ostroff, Kinicki, and Tamkins (this volume). The authors rightly point out that culture has been treated at the organizational level, whereas climate has been viewed as both an individual- and organizational-level construct. As they argue, however, it is the individuals as members of a work organization that create and define both culture and climate. The authors offer a unique and valuable way to show how the field indeed must simultaneously treat these constructs at more than one level, yet link them through the notion of emergent properties.

Diversity in the workforce is even more critical than it was in the past for effective organizational functioning, as we begin the twenty-first century. It is a condition in which many industrial and organizational psychologists have been involved for some time—both in building theories of behavior related to diversity issues and in developing employment practices that foster diversity. In their chapter on diversity, Alderfer and Sims (this volume) accept the position that understanding diversity effects is critical to effective organizations, but they argue that much of the research that has been conducted in the past fails to consider the complexities of understanding diversity—largely because researchers fail to consider the impact of their own race, ethnicity, gender, and so on as they relate to the study of diversity. Alderfer and Sims consider the notion that we all bring our own theories of diversity to any setting; moreover, when we study behavior in the workplace, those we study are reacting to our race, ethnicity, gender, etc., in ways that influence what we observe. Rarely are these factors taken into account. Alderfer and Sims address such issues in detail as they critique diversity research in the field and suggest ways to approach diversity in the future.

In sum, the chapters of this volume are meant to provide exposure to the domain of industrial and organizational psychology and to describe the material in a way that is useful for first-time readers and for those whose own work is more focused on our own field. It is expected that some will read the whole volume, whereas others will turn only to particular chapters that address their concerns. The authors have written the chapters so that each chapter can stand alone. We trust that the volume will serve readers across the spectrum of knowledge about industrial and organizational psychology.

REFERENCES

Advisory Panel for the Dictionary of Occupational Titles. (1993). *The new DOT: A database of occupational titles for the twenty-first century.* Washington, DC: U.S. Department of Labor, Employment and Training Administration.

Albert, S., Ashforth, B. E., & Dutton, J. E. (2000). Special topic forum on organizational identity and identification. *Academy of Management Review, 25,* 113–121.

Ashforth, B. E., Saks, A. M., & Lee, R. T. (1998). Socialization and newcomer adjustment: The role of organizational context. *Human Relations, 51,* 897–926.

Bobko, P., & Colella, A. (1994). Employee reactions to performance standards. *Personnel Psychology, 47*(1), 1–30.

Borman, W. C., & Brush, D. H. (1993). Toward a taxonomy of managerial performance requirements. *Human Performance, 6,* 1–21.

Borman, W. C., & Motowidlo, S. J. (1997). Task performance and contextual performance: The meaning for personnel selection research. *Human Performance, 10,* 99–109.

Borman, W. C., White, L. A., & Dorsey, D. W. (1995). Effects of ratee task performance and interpersonal factors on supervisor and peer performance ratings. *Journal of Applied Psychology, 80,* 168–177.

Borman, W. C., White, L. A., Pulakos, E. D., & Oppler, S. H. (1991). Models of supervisory job performance ratings. *Journal of Applied Psychology, 76,* 863–872.

Boxall, P. (1998). Achieving competitive advantage through human resource strategy: Toward a theory of industry dynamics. *Human Resoruce Management Review, 8*(3), 265–288.

Brogden, H. E. (1949). When testing pays off. *Personnel Psychology, 2,* 171–183.

Cable, D. M., & Judge, T. A. (1994). Pay preferences and job search decisions: A person-organization fit perspective. *Personnel Psychology, 47,* 317–348.

Campbell, J. P. (1999). The definition and measurement of performance in the new age. In D. R. Ilgen & E. D. Pulakos (Eds.), *The changing nature of performance* (pp. 399–430). San Francisco: Jossey-Bass.

Campbell, J. P., Dunnette, M. D., Lawler, E. E., & Weick, K. E. (1970). *Managerial behavior, performance, and effectiveness.* New York: McGraw-Hill.

Campbell, J. P., Gasser, M. B., & Oswald, F. L. (1996). The substantive nature of performance variability. In K. R. Murphy (Ed.), *Individual differences and behavior in organizations* (pp. 258–299). San Francisco: Jossey-Bass.

Campbell, J. P., & Knapp, D. J. (Eds.). (2001). *Exploring the limits in personnel selection and classification.* Mahwah, NJ: Erlbaum.

Campbell, J. P., McCloy, R. A., Oppler, S. H., & Sager, C. E. (1993). A theory of performance. In N. Schmitt & W. C. Borman (Eds.), *Personnel selection in organizations* (pp. 35–70). San Francisco: Jossey-Bass.

Campion, M., Gowing, M., Lancaster, A., & Pearlman, K. (1994). *United States Department of Labor Database of Occupational Titles reinvention project: DOT transition team final report.* Washington, DC: U.S. Office of Personnel Management.

Colquitt, J. A., LePine, J. A., & Noe, R. A. (2000). Toward an integrative theory of training motivation: A meta-analytic path analysis of 29 years of research. *Journal of Applied Psychology, 85,* 678–707.

Devanna, M., Fombrum, N., & Tichy, N. (1981). Human resources management: A strategic perspective. *Organizational Dynamics, 10*(Winter), 51–67.

Dunnette, M. D. (1976). *Handbook of industrial and organizational psychology* (1st ed.). Chicago: Rand McNally.

Dunnette, M. D., & Hough, L. M. (Eds.). (1990). *Handbook of industrial and organizational psychology* (2nd ed., Vol. 1). Palo Alto, CA: Consulting Psychologists Press.

Dunnette, M. D., & Hough, L. M. (Eds.). (1991). *Handbook of industrial and organizational psychology* (2nd ed., Vol. 2). Palo Alto, CA: Consulting Psychologists Press.

Dunnette, M. D., & Hough, L. M. (Eds.). (1992). *Handbook of industrial and organizational psychology* (2nd ed., Vol. 3). Palo Alto, CA: Consulting Psychologists Press.

Dunnette, M. D., & Hough, L. M. (Eds.). (1994). *Handbook of industrial and organizational psychology* (2nd ed., Vol. 4). Palo Alto, CA: Consulting Psychologists Press.

Edwards, J. R. (1994). The study of congruence in organizational behavior research: Critique and a proposed alternative. *Organizational Behavior & Human Decision Processes, 58,* 51–100.

Fleishman, E. A., & Mumford, M. D. (1988). The ability rating scales. In S. Gael (Ed.), *Handbook of job analysis for business, industry, and government* (pp. 917–935). New York: Wiley.

Forsythe, D. R. (1999). *Group dynamics* (3rd ed). Belmont, CA: Wadsworth.

Gilliland, S. W. (1993). The perceived fairness of selection systems: An organizational justice perspective. *Academy of Management Review, 18,* 694–734.

Goldberg, L. R. (1990). An alternative "Description of personality": The Big-Five factor structure. *Journal of Personality and Social Psychology, 59,* 1216–1229.

Gough, H. G. (1957). *The California psychological inventory manual.* Palo Alto, CA: Consulting Psychologists Press.

Gratton, L., Hailey, H., Stiles, P., & Truss, C. (Eds.). (1999). *Strategic human resource management.* New York: Oxford University Press.

Guion, R. (1976). Recruiting, selection, and job placement. In M. D. Dunnette (Ed.), *Handbook of industrial and organizational psychology* (pp. 777–828). Chicago: Rand McNally.

Gustafson, S. B., & Mumford, M. D. (1995). Personal style and person-environment fit: A pattern approach. *Journal of Vocational Behavior, 46,* 163–188.

Hage, J. (1995). Post industrial lives: New demands, new prescriptions. In A. Howard (Ed.), *The changing nature of work* (pp. 485–512). San Francisco: Jossey-Bass.

Hall, D. T., & Mirvis, P. H. (1995). Careers as lifelong learning. In A. Howard (Ed.), *The changing nature of work* (pp. 323–361). San Francisco: Jossey-Bass.

Hanisch, K. A., Hulin, C. L., & Seitz, S. T. (1996). Mathematical/computational modeling of organizational withdrawal processes: Benefits, methods, and results. In G. Ferris (Ed.), *Research in personnel and human resources management* (Vol. 14, pp. 91–142). Greenwich, CT: JAI Press.

Hemphill, J. K. (1960). *Dimensions of executive positions.* Columbus: Ohio State University, Bureau of Business Research.

Hofmann, D. A., & Stetzer, A. (1996). A cross level investigation of factors influencing unsafe behaviors and accidents. *Personnel Psychology, 49,* 307–340.

Hom, P. W., Caranikas-Walker, F., Prussia, G. E., & Griffeth, R. W. (1992) A meta-analytical structural equations analysis of a model of employee turnover. *Journal of Applied Psychology, 77,* 890–909.

Hulin, C. L., & Ilgen, D. R. (2000). Introduction to computational modeling: The good that modeling does. In D. R. Ilgen & C. L. Hulin (Eds.), *Computational modeling of behavior in organizations* (pp. 3–18). Washington, DC: American Psychological Association Press.

Hunter, J. E. (1983). A causal analysis of cognitive ability, job knowledge, job performance and supervisor ratings. In F. Landy, S. Zedeck, & J. Cleveland (Eds.), *Performance measurement and theory* (pp. 257–266). Hillsdale, NJ: Erlbaum.

Ilgen, D. R., & Hulin, C. L. (Eds.). (2000). *Computational modeling of behavior in organizations.* Washington, DC: American Psychological Association Press.

Katz, D., & Kahn, R. L. (1978). *The social psychology of organizing* (2nd ed.). New York: Wiley.

Katzell, R. A., & Austin, J. T. (1992). From then to now: The development of industrial and organiztional psychology in the U.S.A. *Journal of Applied Psychology, 77,* 803–835.

Klimoski, R., & Zukin, L. (1999). Selection and staffing for team effectiveness. In E. Sundstrom (Ed.), *Supporting work team effectiveness* (pp. 63–94). San Francisco: Jossey-Bass.

Kramer, R. M., & Tyler, T. R. (1996). *Trust in organizations.* Thousand Oaks, CA: Sage

Kravitz, D., & Klineberg, S. (2000). Reactions to two versions of Affirmative Action among whites, blacks, and hispanics. *Journal of Applied Psychology, 85,* 597–611.

Kristof, A. L. (1996). Person-organization fit: An integrative review of its conceptualizations, measurement, and implications. *Personnel Psychology, 49,* 1–50.

Lengnick-Hall, C. A., & Lengnick-Hall, M. (1988). Strategic human resource management: A review of the literature and a proposed typology. *Academy of Management Review, 13*(3), 454–470.

Lepak, D. P., & Snell, S. A. (1998). Virtual HR: Strategic human resource management in the 21st century. *Human Resource Management Review, 8*(3), 215–234.

Liden, R., Wayne, S., & Stilwell, D. (1993). A longitudinal study on the early development of leader-member exchanges. *Journal of Applied Psychology, 78*(4), 662–674.

London, M. (Ed.). (1995). *Employees, careers and job creation.* San Francisco: Jossey-Bass.

Louis, M. R. (1980). Surprise and sensemaking: What newcomers experience in entering unfamiliar organizational settings. *Administrative Science Quarterly, 25,* 226–251.

McCloy, R. A., Campbell, J. P., & Cudeck R. (1994). A confirmatory test of a model of performance determinants. *Journal of Applied Psychology, 79,* 493–505.

McCormick, E. J., Jeanneret, P. R., & Mecham, R. C. (1969). *The development and background of the Position Analysis Questionnaire (PAQ)* (Tech. Rep. No. 5). West Lafayette, IN: Purdue University, Occupational Research Center.

McGrath, J. (1984). *Groups: Interaction and performance.* Englewood Cliffs, NJ: Prentice Hall.

Mitchell, J. L. (1978). *Structured job analysis of professional and managerial positions.* Unpublished doctoral dissertation, Purdue University, West Lafayette, IN.

Mobley, W. H., Griffeth, R. W., Hand, H. H., & Meglino, B. M. (1979). Review and conceptual analysis of the employee turnover process. *Psychological Bulletin, 86,* 493–522.

Morrison, E. W. (1993). Longitudinal study of the effects of information seeking on newcomer socialization. *Journal of Applied Psychology, 35,* 1036–1056.

Morrison, E. W., & Robinson, S. L. (1997). When employees feel betrayed: A model of how psychological contract violation develops. *Academy of Management Journal, 22,* 226–256.

Motowidlo, S. J., & Van Scotter, J. R. (1994). Evidence that task performance should be distinguished from contextual performance. *Journal of Applied Psychology, 79,* 475–480.

Murphy, K. R., & DeShon, R. (2000). Inter-rater correlations do not estimate the reliability of job performance ratings. *Personnel Psychology, 53,* 873–900.

Ostroff, C., & Kozlowski, S. W. J. (1992). Organizational socialization as a learning process: The role of information acquisition. *Personnel Psychology, 45*(4), 849–874.

Peterson, N. G. (1992). *Methodology for identifying SCANS competencies and foundation skills.* Washington, DC: American Institutes for Research.

Peterson, N. G., Mumford, M. D., Borman, W. C., Jeanneret, P. R., & Fleishman, E. A. (Eds.). (1999). *The occupation information network (O*NET).* Washington, DC: American Psychological Association.

Peterson, N. G., Mumford, M. D., Borman, W. C., Jeanneret, P. R., Fleishman, E. A., Levin, K. Y., Campion, M. A., Mayfield, M. S., Morgeson, F. P., Pearlman, K., Gowing, M. K., Lancaster, A. R., Silver, M. B., & Dye, D. M. (2001). Understanding work using the Occupational Information Network (O*NET): Implications for practice and research. *Personnel Psychology, 54,* 451–492.

Ployhart, R. E., & Ryan, A. M. (1998). Applicants reactions to the fairness of selection procedures: The effects of positive rule violations and time of measurement. *Journal of Applied Psychology, 83,* 3–16.

Pulakos, E. D., Arad, S., Donovan, M., & Plamondon, K. (2000). Adaptability in the workplace: Development of a taxonomy of adaptive performance. *Journal of Applied Psychology, 85,* 612–624.

Pulakos, E. D., Borman, W. C., & Hough, L. M. (1988). Test validation for scientific understanding: Two demonstrations of an approach to studying predictor-criterion linkages. *Personnel Psychology, 41,* 703–716.

Raymark, P. H., Schmit, M. J., & Guion, R. M. (1997). Identifying potentially useful personality constructs for employee selection. *Personnel Psychology, 50,* 723–736.

Robinson, S. L. (1996). Trust and breach of the psychological contract. *Administrative Science Quarterly, 41,* 574–599.

Rogers, E. W., & Wright, P. M. (1998). Measuring organizational performance in strategic human resource management research: Problems, prospects, and performance information markets. *Human Resource Management Review, 8*(3), 311–331.

Rosse, J. G., Stecher, M. E., Miller, J. L., & Levin, R. A. (1998). The impact of response distortion on preemployment personality testing and hiring decisions. *Journal of Applied Psychology, 83*(4), 634–644.

Rousseau, D. (1995). *Promises in action: Psychological contracts in organizations.* Newbury Park, CA: Sage.

Rynes, S. L. (1991). Recruitment, job choice, and post-hire consequences: A call for new research directions. In M. D. Dunnette & L. M. Hough (Eds.), *Handbook of industrial and organizational psychology* (2nd ed., Vol. 2, pp. 399–444). Palo Alto, CA: Consulting Psychologists Press.

Rynes, S. L., Bretz, R. D., & Gerhart, B. (1991). The importance of recruitment in job choice: A different way of looking. *Personnel Psychology, 44,* 487–521.

Schmidt, F. L. (1992). What do data really mean? Research findings, meta-analysis, and cumulative knowledge in psychology. *American Psychologist, 47,* 1173–1181.

Schmidt, F. L. (1996). Statistical significance testing and cumulative knowledge in psychology: Implications for training researchers. *Psychological Methods, 1,* 115–129.

Schmidt, F. L., & Hunter, J. E. (1998). The validity and utility of selection methods in personnel psychology: Practical and theoretical implications of 85 years of research findings. *Psychological Bulletin, 134*(2), 262–274.

Schmidt, F. L., Hunter, J. G., & Outerbridge, A. N. (1986). Impact of job experience and ability on job knowledge, work sample performance, and supervisory ratings of job performance. *Journal of Applied Psychology, 71,* 431–439.

Schmitt, N., & Klimoski, R. (1991). *Research methods in human resources management.* Cincinnati, OH: South-Western.

Schneider, B. (1987). The people make the place. *Personnel Psychology, 40,* 437–453.

Schneider, B., Goldstein, H. W., & Smith, D. B. (1995). The attraction, selection and attrition framework: An update. *Personnel Psychology, 48,* 747–773.

Shaw, J. D., Delery, J. E., Jenkins, G. D., & Gupta, N. (1999). An organizational level analysis of voluntary and involuntary turnover. *Academy of Management Journal, 41*(5), 511–525.

Taylor, S., Beechler, S., & Napier, N. (1996). Toward an integrative model of strategic international human resource management. *Academy of Management Review, 21*(4), 959–985.

Wanberg, C. R., Bunce, L. W., & Gavin, M. B. (1999). Perceived fairness in layoffs among individuals who have been laid off: A longitudinal study. *Personnel Psychology, 52*(4), 59–84.

Wilk, S. L., Desmarais, L. B., & Sackett, P. R. (1995). Gravitation to jobs commensurate with ability: Longitudinal and cross-sectional tests. *Journal of Applied Psychology, 80,* 79–85.

Wright, P. M. (1998). Introduction: Strategic human resource management research in the 21st century. *Human Resource Management Review, 8*(3), 187–191.

Wright, P. M., & McMahan, C. C. (1992). Theoretical perspectives for strategic human resource management. *Journal of Management, 18,* 295–320.

Zaccaro, S., & Klimoski, R. J. (Eds.). (2001). *The nature of organizational leadership.* San Francisco: Jossey-Bass.

Zedeck, S. (1992). *Work, families, and organizations.* San Francisco: Jossey-Bass.

PART ONE
PERSONNEL PSYCHOLOGY

CHAPTER 2

Job and Work Analysis

PAUL R. SACKETT AND ROXANNE M. LACZO

Job analysis is a broad term commonly used to describe a wide variety of systematic procedures for examining, documenting, and drawing inferences about work activities, worker attributes, and work context. In light of recent workplace changes that de-emphasize traditional conceptions of rigidly defined jobs, the broader term *work analysis* is sometimes advocated (Sanchez & Levine, 1999). We see the tools and techniques developed under the job analysis label as applicable to changing work structures, and the use of the term *job analysis* is not meant to convey a narrow focus on rigidly prescribed jobs.

There has been criticism in recent years of job analysis as an outdated concept; our sense is that that criticism is based on one narrow purpose of job analysis—namely, the formalization of job duties through a written job description, resulting in a rigid prescription of job duties. Job analysis is generally viewed within Industrial and Organizational (I/O) psychology as a foundational activity carried out to support some organizational activity requiring job information (e.g., developing a selection system, designing a training program). That jobs are becoming more flexible and less prescribed does not negate or even reduce the need for the work of I/O psychologists in these domains, and we see no reduction in the need for or importance of job analysis in the work of I/O psychologists.

In this chapter we open with a conceptual overview of the range of choices facing the individual conducting a job analysis. We do not attempt to detail the extensive array of available job analytic techniques; Gael's (1988) two-volume handbook remains the most detailed available source of information; Harvey (1991) and Sanchez and Levine (2001) are other handbook chapters on the topic. We then discuss a set of topics that reflect important changes and challenges to job analysis that have emerged over the last decade. This discussion is of necessity selective; we cannot review all job analysis research in the space available here. The first topic is the development of the Occupational Information Network (O*NET; Peterson, Mumford, Borman, Jeanneret, & Fleishman, 1999), a comprehensive job analysis system designed to replace the Dictionary of Occupational Titles (DOT; U.S. Department of Labor, 1991). It represents a major effort to develop a comprehensive and flexible set of job descriptors. Second, we discuss the growing trend toward the incorporation of personality variables in job analysis, paralleling the growth of interest in personality within the field of I/O psychology overall. Third, we examine the growth of competency modeling, which is often presented as an alternative to or replacement for job analysis. Fourth, we review developments in the field of cognitive task analysis, which involves efforts to understand unobservable cognitive processes. Fifth, we examine the growth of strategic job analysis, which focuses on analysis for changing job situations and projections about work in the future. Sixth (and finally), we discuss recent developments focusing on the topic of sources of inaccuracy in job analysis.

OVERVIEW: JOB ANALYSIS REQUIRES MANY CHOICES

When one encounters job analysis for the first time, one often confronts a seemingly bewildering array of methods and techniques. They vary on a number of dimensions that we briefly outline here to set the stage for a discussion of why and how choices are made among these techniques.

Activity Versus Attribute

Perhaps the most fundamental distinction in job analysis is that between a focus on the activities performed by the worker and a focus on the attributes contributing to successful performance of these activities. A focus on activities is sometimes labeled *work-oriented* and involves an examination of the tasks or behaviors performed on the job. A focus on attributes is sometimes labeled *worker-oriented* and involves an examination into characteristics (e.g., knowledges, skills, abilities) that contribute to successful job performance. Some techniques focus solely on activities (e.g., task inventory approaches), whereas others focus solely on attributes (e.g., Fleishman's Ability Requirements Scale; Fleishman, Quaintance, & Broedling, 1984). Other approaches incorporate separate analyses of both activities and attributes, followed by some process for linking activities and attributes (i.e., determining which attributes contribute to the performance of which activities). Thus, the choice can be made to focus solely on activities, to focus solely on attributes, or to incorporate both in the analysis.

General Versus Specific

In either activity- or attribute-oriented job analysis, decisions have to be made as to level of detail and specificity needed. For example, job activities of a child welfare caseworker can be described in highly specific terms (e.g., interviews child to determine whether the child is being physically or sexually abused), in moderate specific terms (e.g., conducts interviews), or in very general terms (e.g., gathers information verbally). All three of these activities do indeed describe the job: It is not that one is more correct than another is. The degree of detail needed may vary from one application to

another, and thus a critical decision to be made in any job analysis application is the determination of the position on the specificity-generality continuum that is most appropriate.

Qualitative Versus Quantitative

A job can be described qualitatively, as in the case of a narrative description of job duties, or quantitatively, as in methods that involve numeric evaluations on a fixed set of scales. For example, one standardized job analysis questionnaire, the Position Analysis Questionnaire (PAQ; McCormick & Jeanneret, 1988), involves rating the degree to which 187 statements are descriptive of the job in question. Thus, the same job can be described qualitatively via a narrative or a listing of job activities, attributes, or both, or it can be described quantitatively as a profile of rating on the 187 PAQ items (or a smaller set of dimensions derived from these 187 items).

Taxonomy-Based Versus Blank Slate

Quantitative approaches to job analysis, as introduced in the previous section, can make use of preestablished taxonomies of job characteristics; alternatively, they may be developed without the use of such taxonomies. As noted previously, the PAQ is one example of a taxonomy-based approach, working at the level of relatively general work activities applicable across a broad range of jobs. An example at the level of job attributes is the Fleishman Ability Requirements Scales; with these scales, jobs can be rated regarding how much each of 52 abilities is needed for job performance. In contrast are approaches that use observers or informants (e.g., incumbents or supervisors) to generate lists of job activities or attributes; after they are developed, such lists may be rated on time spent, criticality, or other dimensions as a means of narrowing the list to the most critical activities or attributes. Because these *blank slate* approaches develop activity-attribute lists for specific jobs or job families, they have the potential for a higher degree of detail and specificity than do taxonomy-based approaches.

Observer-Based Versus Informant-Based

Information about work activities and attributes is sometimes obtained via direct observations of the work by a trained job analyst, who then distills these observations into qualitative descriptions or quantitative evaluations of work activities or attributes. In other circumstances, information comes directly from informants—most commonly job incumbents or their direct supervisors—who may be asked to list job activities and attributes or to evaluate activities and attributes on a variety of scales (e.g., the frequency with which an activity is performed or the criticality of an attribute to effective job performance). The use of multiple informants (at times hundreds or thousands of incumbents) permits the examination of consistency in responding and the identification of clusters of respondents with differing patterns of work activities.

KSA Versus KSAO

There is a long tradition of focusing on knowledges, skills, and abilities (KSAs) in conducting attribute-oriented job analysis. This perspective is seen by some as limiting in that it does not include other personal characteristics linked to job performance or valued by the organization, such as personality traits, attitudes, and values. Adding *other personal characteristics* to the KSA acronym allows a broader range of attributes to be included in the picture of the job that emerges from the analysis. Broadening job analysis to incorporate the full range of these other characteristics is one hallmark of techniques labeled *competency modeling,* which have gained in popularity recently and are viewed by some as supplanting traditional job analysis; we treat competency modeling in detail later in this chapter.

Single Job Versus Job Comparison

In some applications, the focus is on a single job, as in the case of an assignment to develop a selection system for an entry-level firefighter. In other cases, the focus is on documenting similarities and differences between jobs or positions. Examples include comparing jobs within an organization to determine whether multiple jobs can be treated as the same for some given purpose (e.g., can the same selection system be used for multiple job titles?), documenting job similarity across firms for purposes of transporting some HR system (e.g., can a selection system developed in one firm be used in another?), and examining commonalities and interrelationships among jobs in a firm for internal staffing purposes (e.g., promotions, career ladders).

Descriptive Versus Prescriptive

There is a long tradition of viewing job analysis as a set of methods for describing a job as currently constituted. Also worthy of recognition, however, are a variety of situations in which the goal is to be prescriptive rather than descriptive. Examples include scenarios in which the work of one or more expert performers is studied with the goal of prescribing procedures to be followed by others or prescriptions about activities or attributes for an about-to-be-created job that does not

currently exist. Strategic job analysis (discussed later in this chapter) is also an example of a job analysis technique used for the purpose of forecasting future job requirements.

JOB ANALYSIS METHODS MUST ALIGN WITH PURPOSE: ONE SIZE DOES NOT FIT ALL

Any given job analysis application can be classified in terms of the previously outlined categories. Note that these choices are not orthogonal. In some cases, a decision about one variable constrains choices on others. The KSA versus KSAO distinction, for example, comes into play only if one has chosen to conduct an attribute-oriented job analysis rather than solely an activity-oriented analysis. As another example, the qualitative versus quantitative distinction may be a choice when one's objective is the analysis of a single job; when comparing multiple jobs, however, a quantitative approach is a virtual necessity. If, for instance, each of 50 jobs is described in terms of a profile of ratings of attribute requirements using a common set of attribute requirement scales, the comparison of various jobs is manageable, which it would not be if 50 separate qualitative analyses had been conducted.

One set of key points we wish to emphasize early in this chapter is that job analysis is not a mechanical, off-the-shelf, routine activity. Neither is it a one-size-fits-all activity, in which a single type of job analysis data, after data are obtained, can be used to support virtually any human resource activity. Clearly inappropriate is the position that one can identify a preferred job analysis method and apply it to any situation. We believe that these points are not well appreciated, and we develop in the following discussion a series of examples to illustrate the complexities of job analysis and the need for careful professional judgment in the choice of a job analysis method for a particular application.

The first example, dealing with the theme of generality versus specificity in the choice of the job descriptor, involves a job analysis of the job *psychologist* as described by Sackett (1991). A dispute had arisen as to whether different specialties within psychology—clinical, counseling, I/O, and school—were similar enough that a common licensing exam was appropriate for these four specialties. The Educational Testing Service (ETS) was commissioned to conduct a comparative job analysis of these four areas (Rosenfeld, Shimberg, & Thornton, 1983). An inventory of 59 responsibilities and 111 techniques and knowledge areas was designed and mailed to a carefully selected sample of licensed psychologists. The study found a common core of responsibilities among all four specialties and chided various practice areas for emphasizing the uniqueness of their own group.

We assert that a survey instrument could have been designed that would have produced different results. The more general the data collected, the more likely it is that jobs will appear similar; conversely, the more specific the inventory items, the greater the apparent differences among jobs. The art of job analysis lies in determining a level of specificity that meets the purposes of the particular job analysis application. Consider some of the statements comprising the ETS inventory. Responsibility 1 is *Conduct interviews with client-patient, family members, or others to gain an understanding of an individual's perceived problem.* This item is endorsed by a high proportion of respondents from all specialties, yet it can mean dramatically different things—from interviewing a corporate executive to gain insight into an organization's incentive pay plan to interviewing a 7-year-old suspected victim of child abuse. More examples include *Observe the behavior of individuals who are the focus of concern* and *Formulate a working hypothesis or diagnosis regarding problems or dysfunctions to be addressed.* Again, these items can refer to dramatically different activities. More to the point, given that the purpose of the job analysis was to support the creation of one or more licensing exams, these areas can require different skills, abilities, training, and experience. By being more specific and rephrasing Responsibility 1 as multiple tasks (*interview business clients, interview adult patients, interview children*), the chances of concluding that the jobs are different increase. By getting even more general (*gather information verbally*), the chances of concluding that the jobs are similar increase. Each of these levels of specificity present information that is true. However, the question of which level of specificity is appropriate depends on the purpose for which the information is being collected.

A second example, also from Sackett (1991), illustrates that one may reach different conclusions if different categories of job descriptors are chosen (e.g., focusing on job activities vs. focusing on abilities required for job performance). In a multiorganization study of bank teller and customer service jobs (Richardson, Bellows, Henry, & Co., 1983), a 66-item activity questionnaire (e.g., *cashes savings bonds, verifies signatures, types entries onto standardized forms*) and a 32-item ability requirement questionnaire (e.g., *ability to sort and classify forms, ability to compute using decimals, ability to pay attention to detail*) were administered. Although the vast majority of incumbents held the title *paying and receiving teller,* 20 other job titles were found (e.g., new accounts representative, customer service representative, drive-in teller, safe deposit custodian). The issue was whether these 20 jobs were sufficiently similar to the job of paying and receiving teller that a selection test battery developed for the paying and receiving tellers could also be used for the other

jobs. A correlation between each job and the paying and receiving teller was computed, first based on the activity ratings and then based on the ability ratings. In a number of cases, dramatically different findings emerged. The new accounts representative, customer service representative, and safe deposit custodian correlated .21, .14, and .09, respectively, with the paying and receiving teller when the jobs were compared based on similarity of rated activities. These same three jobs correlated .90, .92, and .88 with the paying and receiving teller when comparing the jobs based on similarity of rated ability requirements. Thus, the use of different job descriptors leads to different conclusions about job similarity. Conceptually, one could argue that for purposes of developing an ability test battery, the ability requirements data seem better suited. If data on these same jobs were being collected to determine whether a common training program for new hires was feasible, one might argue that the activity data seem better suited. The question *Which jobs are sufficiently similar that they can be treated the same?* cannot be answered without information as to the purpose for which the jobs are being compared.

As a third example, consider one additional aspect of the choice of the job descriptor—namely, the nature of the data to be collected about the descriptor chosen. It is common to ask job experts to rate the importance of each job component. However, importance can be conceptualized in a number of ways, three of which are discussed here. Using abilities as an example, one approach to importance is in terms of time: What proportion of total time on the job is spent using the ability in question? A second approach examines contribution to variance in job performance: To what extent does the ability in question contribute to differentiating the more successful employees from the less successful ones? A third approach is in terms of level: What degree of a given ability is needed for successful job performance? Conceptually, it is clear that these three can be completely independent. The abilities that are used most frequently may be possessed by virtually all incumbents and thus not contribute to variance in job performance. A given ability may contribute equally to variance in job performance in two jobs, yet the level of ability needed may differ dramatically across the jobs. Thus, even if it were agreed that abilities required is the appropriate job descriptor for a particular application, operationalizing ability as importance, frequency of use, contribution to variance in performance, or level required can lead to different conclusions.

The use of one operationalization of importance when another seems better suited is found in Arvey and Begalla's (1975) examination of the job of homemaker. They compared the PAQ profile for the position of homemaker with each of the large number of profiles in the PAQ database. These comparisons were made to determine which jobs were amenable to entry by homemakers. Jobs most similar in PAQ profiles were patrolman, home economist, airport maintenance chief, and kitchen helper; a number of supervisory positions followed closely (electrician foreman, gas plant maintenance foreman, fire captain) in the list of the 20 most similar positions. Arvey and Begalla note that a major theme running through many of the occupations listed was a troubleshooting emergency-handling orientation.

Based on this list of most similar occupations, it is not clear that the goal of identifying jobs amenable to entry by homemakers was met. Arvey and Begalla note this potential problem and interpret their findings with appropriate caution. The rating scales used in the PAQ typically reflect time spent. We would hypothesize that different patterns of similarity would be found if level required rather than time spent were used to rate items. Conceptually, level required seems better suited to the tasks of identifying jobs amenable to entry by homemakers. Jobs very similar in the amount of time spent on the PAQ dimension *processing information* may be very different in the level of information processing involved.

In sum, careful alignment of the needs of a specific job analysis application with the various choices made in conducting job analysis is at the heart of successful job analysis. We turn now to a discussion of a variety of recent developments in job analysis.

FROM THE DICTIONARY OF OCCUPATIONAL TITLES TO THE O*NET

For decades the DOT was the most comprehensive source of occupational information available, containing information on over 12,000 jobs. However, as Dunnette (1999) noted, a number of features limited its usefulness, including (a) a focus on occupation-specific narrative information, thus limiting the opportunities for cross-job comparison; (b) a focus on tasks rather than on worker attributes; and (c) difficulties in keeping the information current due to the time and expense involved in updating job information. In the early 1990s an advisory panel was constituted to review the DOT.

In 1993 the Advisory Panel for the Dictionary of Occupational Titles (APDOT) released its final report, offering a detailed blueprint for a replacement for the existing DOT (APDOT, 1993). They offered a number of recommendations, including (but not limited to) recommendations that the DOT should cover all occupations in the U.S. economy, that a single occupational classification system should be used, that structured job analysis questionnaires be the primary strategy for data collection, and that a flexible, automated, readily accessible database be created.

Two additional recommendations will be singled out here as of exceptional importance. The first is that the information to be obtained about each occupation should be based on what APDOT called its *Content Model*. The content model calls for collecting broad information about each occupation, falling into four categories: (a) worker attributes, including aptitudes, occupation-specific knowledge and skill, and personal qualities; (b) work context, including information about the organizational context (such as organizational culture) and the work context (such as physical working conditions); (c) labor market context, including future employment prospects for the occupation; and (d) work content and outcomes, including tasks performed, services rendered, and products produced.

Within this Content Model, the worker attributes category is of particular importance because it reflects APDOT's recommendations as to the basis for content-oriented occupational clustering. Of particular interest is a set of five descriptors that APDOT offered as an approximate hierarchy from generality to specificity:

1. Aptitudes and abilities, including cognitive, spatial-perceptual, psychomotor, sensory, and physical abilities.
2. Workplace basic skills, defined as developed abilities required to some degree in virtually all jobs, including reading, writing, and arithmetic. APDOT acknowledged the close relationship of these to the aforementioned aptitude-ability category.
3. Cross-functional skills, defined as developed generic skills required across broad ranges of jobs. Examples include information gathering, negotiating, and organizing and planning.
4. Occupation-specific skills, defined as ability to perform activities that are relatively job specific, such as reading blueprints, repairing electrical appliances, and operating a milling machine.
5. Occupation-specific knowledge, defined as understanding of facts, principles, processes, and methods specific to a particular subject area. Examples include knowledge of patent law, knowledge of financial planning, and knowledge of spreadsheet software.

Pearlman (1993), a member of APDOT, argues persuasively for the adoption of the APDOT content model in addressing questions about skill requirements. He notes that the term *skills* is used by different people to refer to virtually every category within the worker attributes section of the content model. Pearlman labels the skills literature a veritable Tower of Babel, with the term *skills* used to refer to everything from basic abilities to workforce basic skills to cross-functional generic skills to occupation-specific skills.

In many cases, the term is extended to what the content model calls personal qualities, such as responsibility, sociability, and honesty. Thus, the adoption of the terminology of the content model would permit progress to be made by ensuring that there is a common understanding when talking about *closing the skills gap* or *setting skill standards.*

It is significant that rather than choosing among these different levels of attribute requirements, APDOT called for obtaining information about attribute requirements at each of these levels; this leads to the second APDOT recommendation's being singled out as of particular importance—namely, that the information about occupations be detailed and the database be sufficiently flexible to permit differentiation and clustering of occupations based on user needs. Thus, APDOT recognized the key point that purpose must drive occupational clustering and that if the DOT is to meet multiple purposes, then information about attribute requirements must be available at multiple levels and user-specific clustering must be available.

Ideally, an occupational database could be developed that would permit infinite flexibility in occupational clustering. A user could identify the set of descriptors that meet the purpose at hand and generate occupational clusters based specifically on the chosen set of descriptors. A counselor working with an individual job seeker could choose a set of descriptors that reflect the skills, experience, education, and interests of the job seeker and identify the occupations with requirements that closely match the job seeker. An educational institution providing training in particular skills could identify occupations

requiring those skills. An employer considering eliminating a particular job could identify jobs with similar requirements to determine whether redeployment is a viable alternative to downsizing. The ongoing development of the O*NET reflects continuing efforts to bring this ideal to reality.

An extensive program of research that refined the APDOT Content Model and developed and evaluated an extensive series of job analysis questionnaires to tap each component of the model is described in a book summarizing the O*NET research, edited by Peterson et al. (1999). Figure 2.1 presents the O*NET Content Model that served as the organizing blueprint for the program of research.

The O*NET research illustrates many of what we view as the crucial issues in job analysis highlighted in the opening section of this chapter. The O*NET researchers developed nine separate questionnaires to assess abilities, skills, knowledges, training and education requirements, generalized work activities, work context, organizational context, occupational values, and work styles. They recognized the central premise that the purpose of job analysis drives the information needed; thus, in order to serve multiples purposes a wide range of types of information was needed. They also recognized the importance of the differing scales on which job activities and attributes could be rated; thus, they gave careful attention to the choice of the rating scales used for each questionnaire. For example, skills were evaluated on three scales: level needed, importance, and need for the skill at point of job entry. This approach thus permitted the user to determine which descriptor best fits the needs of a particular application.

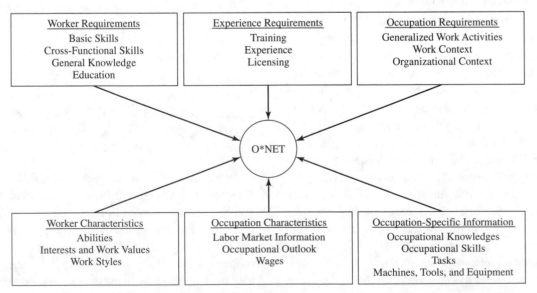

Figure 2.1   O*NET content model. From Peterson et al. (1999), p. 25. Copyright © 1999 by the American Psychological Association. Reprinted with permission.

For each of the nine questionnaires listed previously, data from multiple incumbents in each of roughly 30 occupations were obtained. For each questionnaire, interrater agreement was examined, as was the factor structure of the questionnaire items. Agreement between incumbents and job analysts was examined for some of the questionnaires. Across the nine questionnaires, over 300 pieces of job information were collected; the separate factor analyses of each questionnaire produced a total of 38 factors. These 38 were used as to basis for cross-domain comparison; a second-order factor analysis of these 38 factors produced four factors: management-achievement, manual-physical, office work, and technical versus interpersonal. Thus, an occupation can be characterized at varying levels of detail: 300 individual ratings, 38 first-order factor scores, or 4 broad second-order factor scores.

All of this information is contained in a relational database that is accessible to the general public at http://www.online.onetcenter.org. The system has considerable flexibility. One can start with a skill or ability profile and find occupations matching the profile; alternately, one can start with an occupation and find occupations with similar characteristics.

Several comments about O*NET are in order. First, because of the overarching interest in comparing occupations, the O*NET focuses on job information that is applicable across occupations rather than on occupationally specific information (e.g., detailed task information). In addition, it uses an occupational classification system that results in 1,122 occupations, as opposed to the roughly 12,000 occupational groupings in the DOT; thus, the information is relatively general. It is certainly possible that work within a given occupation varies in important ways in any single organization from the occupational profile for the occupation contained in the O*NET, and individual organizations or individuals using O*NET might for a variety of purposes wish to examine similarities and differences between O*NET ratings and firm-specific ratings. Some of the individual items reflect features that surely vary across organizations (e.g., the work values item *workers on this job have coworkers who are easy to get along with*).

Second, the O*NET remains a work in progress. As described previously, only a small number of occupations have been thoroughly examined. Although the current O*NET data base does contain ratings of 1,122 occupations on several content domains, only about 30 have been thoroughly examined. The ratings of the bulk of the occupations were rated by job analysts based on written job information. We are concerned that analysts may have relied in part on job stereotypes in the absence of sufficient job detail, and thus that the ratings reflect raters' implicit theories about the structure of work. These caveats aside, the O*NET does represent a major achievement in its design of a comprehensive framework for conceptualizing occupational information.

JOB ANALYSIS FOR IDENTIFYING PERSONALITY DIMENSIONS RELEVANT TO JOB PERFORMANCE

The well-documented revival of interest in personality as a determinant of job performance within I/O psychology has also had an impact on job analysis. At least one commentator (Jackson, 1990) has posited that the failure to incorporate personality in the scope of job-analytic efforts was an important contributor to the long period of dormancy in the use of personality measures. We discuss here a variety of ways in which personality variables have recently been incorporated into job-analytic work.

The first is the use of a job-analytic tool to directly evaluate the job relevance of each dimension within a multidimensional instrument. As an example, the well-known Neuroticism, Extraversion, Openness Personality Inventory (NEO-PI) has an instrument labeled the NEO Job Profiler (Costa, McCrae, & Kay, 1995). The NEO-PI has six subdimensions for each of the Big Five personality dimensions, resulting in a total of 30 subdimensions. The NEO Job Profiler lists and defines each subdimension, and each is rated separately on a dichotomous job relevance scale; the relevant dimensions are then rated on a desirability-undesirability continuum. This approach thus represents direct ratings of the relevance of personality dimensions for the job in question.

The second approach is also linked to a specific personality instrument but involves rating whether job behaviors that have been linked to the personality dimensions of interest are part of the job in question. An example of this approach is the use of a behavioral rating form linked to the Personnel Decisions International Employment Inventory (EI; Paajanen, Hansen, & McClellan, 1993). The EI measures factors in the domain of dependability, responsibility, and conscientiousness. An extensive list of work behaviors reflecting manifestations of these factors was developed, and ratings of the relevance of those behaviors for the job in question help determine the applicability of the EI to the situation at hand. This behavioral rating form is also used for criterion development purposes: The subset of behaviors rated by managers as relevant to the target job become the basis for a criterion instrument with which supervisors rate employees on each of the behaviors. Thus, for criterion-related validation purposes the EI is correlated with rating on a job-specific set of behaviors initially rated as relevant to the situation. In sum, the first approach involves direct rating of the relevance of personality dimensions; the second approach outlined here involves ratings by managers of the relevance of job behaviors that have been linked by researchers to the personality dimensions measured by the EI.

A third example is the work of Raymark, Schmit, and Guion (1997) on development of the Personality-Related Position Requirements Form (PPRF), which also involves the rating of specific job behaviors that are then linked to personality dimensions. The distinction we make here is that this work is not designed to support a specific personality measure; rather, it is a general approach to identifying the personality characteristics relevant to a job. Raymark et al. describe a multistage research process resulting in a set of 12 personality dimensions, hierarchically structured under the Big Five. A large sample of psychologists made ratings linking a large set of behaviors to these dimensions. The result is a 107-item behavioral rating form from which the relevance of each of the 12 personality factors can be inferred. Raymark et al. document that this form does reliably differentiate between various occupations. They acknowledge that the question yet unanswered is whether those personality dimensions identified as relevant are indeed more predictive of job performance than are the less relevant dimensions. Another example of this approach—namely, the use of behavior ratings, which are then linked to personality dimensions—is the O*NET work under the rubric of *work styles* (Borman, Kubisiak, & Schneider, 1999).

The examples used here all involve what we termed in the initial section of this chapter *taxonomic* as opposed to blank slate approaches to job analysis. As noted there, blank slate approaches are job specific and involve using various mechanisms to produce lists of important job activities, job attributes, or both. Many applications such as personnel selection work involve obtaining both and then using subject matter expert (SME) judgments to link activities and attributes. It is common for such a linkage process to also be used to infer the importance of various job attributes, where attribute importance is a function of the number and importance of the activities to which attributes are linked. To the extent that a traditional KSA framework is adopted, such a process will not include personality characteristics among the relevant job attributes. If a broader KSAO framework is adopted, carefully defined personality characteristics can become part of the set of job attributes under consideration; much applied work now does so. We offer as a cautionary note the observation that it is critical to describe all activities at the same level of detail and specificity if one wishes to infer relative attribute importance from linkages to activities. The tradition of detailed KSA analysis means that it is likely that cognitively loaded work activities are described in considerable detail. In some settings we see softer, less cognitively loaded aspects of work described at a higher level of generality. If,

using a simplified example, the activity *adds, subtracts, multiplies, and divides whole numbers* is written as four separate task statements, but the activity *responds to inquiries from coworkers, customers, and media representatives* is written as a single summary statement, a conclusion about the relative importance of cognitively loaded versus less cognitively loaded attributes is likely to be drawn that is different from the one that would be drawn if the same level of detail is used for both domains.

In sum, a variety of approaches have emerged that incorporate personality factors into job analysis. The relative merits of direct judgments of personality dimension importance versus approaches that involve judgments about job behaviors, from which inferences about relevant personality dimensions are drawn, remains an interesting issue not resolved at present.

COMPETENCY MODELING

Easily the most visible change in the analysis of work in the last decade is the rise of a variety of approaches under the rubric *competency modeling*. The origins of the competency modeling approach to job analysis can be traced back to an article that first proposed the use of competencies in organizational settings (McClelland, 1973). Titled "Testing for Competence, Not Intelligence," the paper posited that intelligence was not related to job performance and that a wide range of characteristics—labeled *competencies*—could be identified that differentiated between superior and average performers. Barrett and Depinet (1991) document the wide range of errors in McClelland's paper, including mischaracterizing the research linking cognitive ability to job performance and failing to acknowledge the wide array of measures of constructs other than cognitive ability used in employment settings. Despite its serious shortcomings, the paper was quite influential; McClelland and a variety of coworkers continued to develop the notion of competencies (Boyatzis, 1982; Spencer & Spencer, 1993).

More recently, the assertion that task-based approaches are unable to capture the changing nature of work has strengthened the call for competency-based systems in organizations (Lawler, 1994). Although the practice of competency modeling has become widespread—often as a replacement for job analysis—the field of I/O psychology has certainly not led the charge (Schippmann et al., 2000). Until the results of a recent Society for Industrial and Organizational Psychology (SIOP) task force project comparing competency modeling and job analysis were published (The Job Analysis and Competency Modeling Task Force; Schippmann et al., 2000), attempts to meaningfully distinguish between the two general methods of analyzing jobs were few. In addition, despite the current popularity of competency modeling in organizations, consistent definitions of the term *competency* do not exist, and even authorities in the field are unable to arrive at a clear meaning of the term (Schippmann et al., 2000).

In general, competency modeling refers to the practice of identifying the characteristics or attributes that are needed for effective performance on the job—specifically, those characteristics held by exceptional performers (DuBois, 1999). Although these characteristics or competencies typically consist of the well-known KSAs, other authors also include such variables as motives, traits, or attitudes (e.g., Spencer & Spencer, 1993). Elsewhere, competencies are defined as the actual behaviors that distinguish superior performers from poor performers (Dalton, 1997). A competency model ideally consists of a set of competencies that have been identified as necessary for successful performance, with behavioral indicators associated with high performance on each competency specified to illustrate successful performance on that competency.

A number of issues are associated with the competency modeling approach to analyzing jobs. First is the notion that competency modeling is a replacement for traditional forms of job analysis. The problem with this line of thought is the misguided assumption that job analysis methodologies purport to identify *only* the tasks and activities associated with a job and fail to assess the personal characteristics and attributes associated with success on the job (e.g., Spencer & Spencer, 1993). This assertion is simply incorrect; examples of worker-oriented job analysis focusing on worker attributes abound, as has been illustrated throughout this chapter.

A second problem is the lack of clarification of what the term *competency* actually refers to. For example, in a recent book detailing the practice of competency modeling, Lucia and Lepsinger (1999) offer examples of the competencies required for various positions. For a sales consultant, competencies included communication skills, product knowledge, computer literacy, sociability, self-confidence, mental agility, and analytical skills, to name a few. Although some of these competencies refer to personality characteristics (e.g., sociability), it is difficult to differentiate many from the KSAs studied in a typical job analysis (e.g., product knowledge, computer literacy). In addition, competencies reflecting personality characteristics such as sociability are certainly included in KSAO approaches to job analysis. Finally, many competencies that appear throughout the literature and in competency models are ill-defined concepts with no clear meaning (e.g., the meaning of a competency such as visioning; Pearlman & Barney, 2000). Pearlman and Barney (2000) also add that any deficiencies in the meaning of a competency

will translate into deficiencies in selection tools (or otherwise) that make use of those constructs. Thus, the meaning and definition of individual competencies require further clarification before they can be accurately measured and put into use in organizations.

Finally, until recently there has been a general failure to meaningfully distinguish between competency modeling and job analysis. Lucia and Lepsinger (1999) identify two major goals of competency modeling: the identification of the skills, knowledge, and characteristics required to do the job and the identification of behaviors related to success on the job. It is unclear how these particular goals differ from those of a typical job analysis. Lucia and Lepsinger also identify a number of business needs that competency models can address—for example, clarifying expectations, hiring the best people, and maximizing productivity. Again, it is difficult to imagine that these particular needs cannot be addressed via job-analytic procedures. Lastly, Lucia and Lepsinger outline the benefits of using competency-based HR systems. For example, they propose that in selection systems, competency models can help provide a complete picture of the job requirements; for succession planning, competency models clarify the skills, knowledge, and characteristics required for the job. These benefits parallel the benefits of using job analysis to enhance HR systems. Thus, despite the increasing reliance on competency modeling in organizations, it is doubtful that the process represents something unique from what most people currently think of as job analysis.

Basing their conclusions on a review of the literature and interviews with experts in the field, Schippmann et al. (2000) attempted to clarify the distinction between the two approaches. Their report identified 17 variables on which competency modeling and job analysis could be compared, and they rated each variable according to the level of rigor at which they were practiced. These variables are summarized in Table 2.1. The first 10 variables represent evaluative, front-end activities that can be expected to influence the quality of the inferences to be drawn from the resulting analysis. Job analysis was seen as demonstrating more rigor on every evaluative criterion, with the exception of establishing a link to business goals and strategies. The final seven variables are meant to be nonevaluative and focus on the uses of the resulting information and the type of characteristics investigated. In this case, job analysis was generally rated as less rigorous than was competency modeling, except for the focus on technical skills and the development of selection and decision applications.

Although they provide a useful comparison of the two methodologies, the variables listed in Table 2.1 can be distilled into a smaller number of dimensions that represent the

TABLE 2.1   Level of Rigor Comparison: Competency Modeling Versus
Job Analysis

Variable
Evaluative criteria
1. Method of investigation and data collection.[b]
2. Type of descriptor content collected.[b]
3. Procedures for developing descriptor content.[b]
4. Level of detail of descriptor content.[b]
5. Linking research results to business goals.[a]
6. Extent of descriptor content review.[b]
7. Ranking or prioritizing of descriptor content.[b]
8. Assessment of reliability of results.[b]
9. Retention criteria for items and categories.[b]
10. Documentation of research process.[b]
Nonevaluative criteria
1. Focus on core competencies.[a]
2. Focus on technical skills.[b]
3. Organizational fit versus job match.[a]
4. Focus on values and personality orientation.[a]
5. Face validity of content.[a]
6. Training and development applications.[a]
7. Selection and decision applications.[b]

Note.   Taken from Schippmann et al. (2000).
[a]Rated more rigorous for competency modeling.
[b]Rated more rigorous for job analysis.

most fundamental differences between competency model-ing and job analysis. These dimensions are breadth of analy-sis, unit of analysis, type of characteristic studied, general use of data, and methodological rigor. Each dimension is dis-cussed in the following paragraphs.

The first major dimension on which competency modeling and job analysis differ concerns the completeness of the re-sulting picture of a job. As mentioned previously, the primary purpose of competency modeling is to identify those charac-teristics that differentiate superior from average performers (Spencer & Spencer, 1993); thus, it focuses on attributes rather than activities, whereas job analysis may focus on either or both. More crucially, when job analysis focuses on attributes, the goal is commonly to present a complete picture of job requirements.

Second, competency modeling generally focuses on any at-tribute that is related to performance, and as such it includes the full range of KSAOs; thus, it is indistinguishable in its domain coverage from worker-oriented job analysis with a KSAO focus. Job analysis—depending on the methodology—can be work-oriented, focusing on the tasks and activities involved in a job; it can be worker-oriented, focusing on the KSAs neces-sary to perform the job (and therefore is broader than competency modeling); or it may incorporate elements of both approaches.

Third, the unit of analysis for a competency model can vary from a single job to an entire organization. When the focus is on a single job or job family, the differences between

competency modeling and traditional job analysis are much smaller. However, the notion of an organization-wide compe-tency model is something conceptually very different. Any set of characteristics relevant across an entire organization is of necessity quite broad. Specifying a set of attributes valued across the organization is typically an attempt to specify what the organization will value and reward. Note the future tense: The specification of what the organization will value and re-ward is often part of an attempt at organizational change. The set of attributes specified in the competency model may not come from an analysis of the attributes of current employees, but rather may reflect top managers' vision as to what will be valued and rewarded in the future.

For example, one large organization offered an organization-wide competency model including the following 10 compe-tencies: business awareness, communication, teamwork, resilience, influencing others, critical thinking, managing con-flict and change, results orientation, innovation, and functional excellence. We do not identify the organization in order to make a point about the generic nature of such models: We challenge the reader to make any inferences as to what kind of organiza-tion this is. Note what a model of this sort does. The intent is that all subsequent human resource activities be designed with this model in mind; thus, these characteristics would be incor-porated in performance appraisal systems and selection sys-tems. A characteristic such as teamwork can be given greater emphasis in the evaluation of current employees or in the selec-tion of future employees than was the case in the past. Note that what is commonly viewed as *doing one's job* is relegated to a catchall competency—namely, functional excellence; thus, the organization is emphasizing that a set of features broader than simply excellence in the performance of prescribed job tasks is to be valued and rewarded. In short, when the term *competency modeling* is used to refer to an organization-wide model rather than to a job-specific model, the differences from traditional job analysis are much more than semantic.

Fourth, and following from the previous point, compe-tency modeling is more prescriptive or future-oriented than is job analysis, often emerging from espoused firm values or from the beliefs of senior managers and based on inferences about future work requirements (Dalton, 1997; McLagan, 1997). Job analysis is commonly (but not necessarily) de-scriptive in nature, providing a picture of the job as it is con-stituted at a particular point in time. This distinction is encapsulated by the greater focus in competency modeling on linking research results to business strategy as outlined in Table 2.1. More specifically, competency modeling has a greater focus than does job analysis on the integration of the desired qualities of individuals with organizational strategies and goals—and in using this information to inform human resources (HR) systems (DuBois, 1999; Lucia & Lepsinger, 1999; McLagan, 1997).

Finally, competency modeling and job analysis can differ greatly on the level of methodological rigor and validation that each entails. There is no intrinsic reason that the two must differ, but in practice the differences are often substantial. Traditional job analysis commonly involves multiple methods, careful selection of SMEs, documentation of the degree of agreement among multiple informants, and links between attributes and activities to support hypothesized attribute requirement. Although some descriptions of competency modeling procedures reflect similar rigor (e.g., Spencer & Spencer, 1993), in other instances the focus is on the speed with which a set of competencies can be identified, such as asking managers to check what they believe to be relevant attributes from a preset list (e.g., Mansfield, 1996).

So what is competency modeling? Despite all of the hype surrounding the practice of competency modeling in organizations, it appears to be a form of worker-oriented job analysis that focuses on broader characteristics of individuals and on using these characteristics to inform HR practices. As such, it is inappropriate to proclaim that competency modeling is a replacement for job analysis because each approach has a different focus, and the appropriateness of either methodology should depend on the purpose of the analysis (Cronshaw, 1998). This point leads to the question of what value competency modeling has for organizations. To some extent, the second set of nonevaluative variables in Table 2.1 addresses this question. First, competency modeling attempts to identify variables related to overall organizational fit and to identify personality characteristics consistent with the organization's vision (Schippmann et al., 2000). Second, competency modeling has a high degree of face validity to the organization and can be written in terms that managers in the organization understand. Taken together, these two factors may explain why managers are more excited today about competency modeling than they are about job analysis.

Ideally, an integration of the rigor of traditional job analysis with the broad focus of competency modeling can be achieved. Although we have emphasized in various places in this chapter the broadening of job analysis from a KSA focus to a KSAO focus, the data presented by Schippmann et al. show that the typical job analysis effort today remains focused more heavily on technical skills than on personality characteristics and values. Competency modeling's broader KSAO focus is certainly consistent with the movement in I/O psychology over the last decade to incorporate noncognitive variables more heavily in our research and practice. I/O psychologists also should be more attentive to the need for offering timely solutions to organizations. Competency modeling

practice makes clear the need for less time-consuming job analysis procedures. As other commentators have noted (Guion, 1998), in some settings—particularly job analysis for personnel selection—job analysis is done largely for purposes of legal defensibility: Rigor and detail become ends in themselves. That extraordinary detail is needed to meet legal requirements in such instances should not spill over into the notion that all job analysis is a 6-month process. As always, the purpose of job analysis should remain in the forefront.

COGNITIVE TASK ANALYSIS

The term *cognitive task analysis* (CTA), sometimes referred to as *cognitive job analysis,* has been defined in various ways and is associated with numerous methodologies. Generally, CTA refers to a collection of approaches that purport to identify and model the cognitive processes underlying task performance (Chipman, Schraagen, & Shalin, 2000; Shute, Sugrue, & Willis, 1997), with a particular focus on the determinants of expert versus novice performance for a given task (Gordon & Gill, 1997; Means, 1993). Although the term *CTA* first emerged in the late 1970s, the field has grown substantially in the last decade, and some authors seem to have forgotten that most methodologies are adapted from the domain of cognition and expertise (see Olson & Biolsi, 1991, for a review of knowledge representation techniques in expertise). Instead, CTA is sometimes treated as if it evolved entirely on its own (Annett, 2000). The value added for CTA is not that it represents a collection of new activities for analyzing performance, but that it represents the application of cognitive techniques to the determination of expert versus novice performance in the workplace, facilitating high levels of knowledge and skill (Lesgold, 2000).

CTA is often contrasted with behavioral task analysis. Whereas the former seeks to capture the unobservable knowledge and thought processes that guide behavior (i.e., *how* people do their jobs), the latter seeks to capture observable behavior in terms of the actual task activities performed on the job (i.e., *what* people do on their jobs). Proponents of CTA claim that due to the increasing use of technology in the workplace, jobs are becoming increasingly complex and mentally challenging, necessitating a more cognitive approach to the analysis of job tasks (e.g., Gordon & Gill, 1997; Ryder & Redding, 1993; Seamster, Redding, & Kaempf, 2000); thus, it is believed that task analysis methodologies may be inadequate procedures for capturing how people perform in jobs that require cognitive skill. However, separating the unobservable cognitive functions of a job from the observable behavioral functions of jobs may limit the usefulness of the overall analysis, and both types of information are often necessary for a complete understanding of the tasks involved (Chipman et al., 2000; Gordon & Gill, 1997; Shute et al., 1997). Therefore, rather than be considered a replacement for task analysis approaches, CTA should be considered a supplement because neither method alone may be able to provide all of the information necessary for analyzing how an individual performs his or her job (Ryder & Redding, 1993).

At the same time, situations probably exist in which CTA is not necessary for fully understanding task performance. Because approaches to CTA are generally time-consuming, labor-intensive, and expensive endeavors (Potter, Roth, Woods, & Elm, 2000; Seamster et al., 2000), it would be wise to first consider the nature and purpose of the analysis before choosing a CTA methodology over a different job analysis methodology. Although most examples of CTA have been conducted for highly complex jobs (e.g., air traffic controllers, air force technicians; Means, 1993), some investigations have been conducted for more commonplace jobs outside of the military domain (e.g., Mislevy, Steinberg, Breyer, Almond, & Johnson, 1999, for dental hygienists; O'Hare, Wiggins, Williams, & Wong, 1998, for white-water rafting guides; Hoffman, Shadbolt, Burton, & Klein, 1995, for livestock judges). It is easy to imagine the application of CTA techniques to any job that requires some degree of decision-making or cognitive skills; again, however, such analysis may not be necessary in order to gain an understanding of what constitutes effective performance.

As with traditional types of job analysis, CTA methodologies abound, and although they share the common goal of understanding the cognitive processes that underlie performance, there is little comparative information available as to which methods are appropriate under different circumstances and for different job settings (Chipman et al., 2000). (Seamster et al., 2000, do provide suggestions for which methods are appropriate for different skill domains.) In addition, there appears to be no evidence that any single approach is useful across all domains (Schraagen, Chipman, & Shute, 2000), or that different methods will result in the same data (Gordon & Gill, 1997); thus, the use of multiple approaches with multiple experts would likely yield the most meaningful information (Potter et al., 2000). Chipman et al. (2000) suggest that the following issues should be taken into consideration when choosing a CTA methodology: the purpose of the analysis, the nature of the task and knowledge being analyzed, and the resources available for conducting the analysis, including relevant personnel.

Some of the more common CTA techniques include PARI (prediction, action, results, interpretation), DNA (decompose, network, and assess), GOMS (goals, operators, methods, and selection), and COGNET (cognition as a network of tasks). Examples of techniques borrowed from the domain of expertise include interviews and protocol analysis. Information on these and other procedures is available in Hoffman et al. (1995); Jonassen, Tessmer, and Hannum (1999); Olson and Biolsi (1991); and Zachary, Ryder, and Hicinbothom (1998).

Because the use of CTA as a job-analytic technique is relatively recent, a number of issues have yet to be resolved. First, for someone new to the field of CTA, there is little documented information available concerning how to actually perform the different techniques, making replication difficult (Shute et al., 1997). In addition, the procedures are somewhat complex and difficult (Gordon & Gill, 1997), are not refined to the extent that standardized methods exist (Shute et al., 1997), and require that the analyst become familiar with the technical details of the particular domain being studied (Means, 1993). Thus, the amount of time and effort required by each individual involved in the analysis and the lack of information on how to conduct a CTA potentially limits the usefulness of the procedures in operational settings. This limitation is evidenced by the limited number of CTAs that are being performed by a relatively limited number of persons who are generally experienced in the domain of cognitive science (Seamster et al., 2000).

Second, there is little information available on how to use the data collected during a CTA—specifically, on how to go from the data to a solution, such as the design of training programs or other systems within organizations (Chipman et al., 2000; Gordon & Gill, 1997). The large quantity of data generated by a CTA makes development of a design solution even more difficult (Potter et al., 2000).

Third, there is a lack of information on the quality of the data gleaned from CTA techniques. Thus, researchers need to assess the relative strengths and weaknesses of the different techniques to determine the conditions under which the use of each technique is optimal—and finally, to assess the reliability and validity of the different techniques. Reliability could be assessed by comparing the results of different analysts using the same procedures, and validity assessment would involve comparing the results of multiple experts using multiple procedures (Shute et al., 1997). The lack of this kind of information is probably a result of the intensive nature of the data collection process.

To conclude, CTA represents an intriguing way of analyzing jobs. However, the lack of information available concerning the relative merits of different methodologies for conducting CTA limits applicability at present. An interesting area that is gaining in study is the application of CTA methodologies to team tasks and decision making to determine the knowledge shared by team members and how it is used to elicit effective performance (e.g., Blickensderfer, Cannon-Bowers, Salas, & Baker, 2000; Klein, 2000).

STRATEGIC JOB ANALYSIS

Traditional forms of job analysis generally assume that the job is a static entity, and SMEs are generally chosen based on the assumption that they have experience with or knowledge of the job in question. However, due to changing jobs and organizations, some would argue that the notion of a static, unchanging job may no longer be appropriate. In addition, new jobs are being created all the time—partially a result of downsizing, globalization, and the increased use of computer technology (Schneider & Konz, 1989). Thus, the use of SMEs with prior knowledge and experience may not be possible (Sanchez & Levine, 1999), and new methods of determining the tasks and abilities required on future jobs become necessary. The goal of strategic job analysis is to determine the tasks that will be performed and the abilities required for effective performance in jobs (that may or may not currently exist) as they are expected to exist in the future (Schneider & Konz, 1989). Strategic job analysis therefore represents a shift from descriptive job analysis (what is currently done on the job) to predictive job analysis (what will be done on the job in the future; Cronshaw, 1998).

Few empirical examples of strategic job analysis currently exist (e.g., Arvey, Salas, & Gialluca, 1992; Bruskiewicz & Bosshardt, 1996), and most working examples in the literature are based upon personal business experience or suggestions about what might constitute effective forecasting techniques (Pearlman & Barney, 2000; Sanchez, 1994; Sanchez & Levine, 1999; Schneider & Konz, 1989). Arvey et al. (1992) suggested that existing relationships between task- and ability-based job-analytic information could be used to predict the skill requirements of future jobs, assuming a stable covariance structure of task-ability matrices that adequately captured the domain of skills and abilities to be forecasted. They found that if only a limited number of tasks were known, future skill requirements could be forecasted based on current knowledge about which tasks predicted which abilities. However, as Arvey et al. point out, the ability to forecast future job requirements does not assure that those skills or abilities will actually be essential to that job.

Using a very different methodology, Bruskiewicz and Bosshardt (1996) compared job-analytic ratings made by a group of SMEs involved in creating a new position (immediately prior to when the position was filled) to ratings made by a group of incumbents who had been working in the new position for 9 months. High levels of agreement between SMEs

and incumbents were found, and SMEs with more direct experience in the job design process provided ratings most similar to those of incumbents. However, because those SMEs were directly involved in the redesign process, it is likely that they were completely familiar with what the job would entail and thus were not providing a true predictive forecast. A more informative study would have involved SMEs completing two concurrent job analysis questionnaires prior to being informed that they would be involved in the redesign process—one for the job as it existed prior to redesign and one for the job as they would forecast it to exist in the future. After the redesign process, incumbent ratings of the job as it currently existed could be gathered and compared to the previous SME forecasts to assess the accuracy of their predictions.

Although empirical analyses of strategic job analysis are few in number, prescriptive information is provided in the literature. Group discussion techniques are the most commonly recommended methodology for conducting a strategic job analysis (Pearlman & Barney, 2000; Sanchez, 1994; Sanchez & Levine, 1999; Schneider & Konz, 1989). These techniques generally involve bringing together a group of SMEs (e.g., incumbents, managers, strategy analysts) and brainstorming about the expected task and ability requirements of future jobs. SMEs may be asked to identify possible organizational or environmental conditions that could affect future jobs (e.g., changing labor markets, technology, demographics, political or economic trends; Sanchez & Levine, 1999; Schneider & Konz, 1989), to think about what aspects of jobs are the most likely to change and what skills or attributes are important to those aspects (Pearlman & Barney, 2000), or to visualize how future tasks might be performed—particularly in consideration of likely technological change (Sanchez & Levine, 1999).

Although a seemingly useful tool for the development of business strategy and the prediction of future human resource functions, strategic job analysis represents a relatively new field of study and many issues have yet to be resolved. Although the group discussion techniques listed previously are reportedly in use by the authors, no evidence exists as to their utility as forecasting tools; thus, a primary concern lies in assessing the validity of strategic job analytic information—namely, how to accurately examine and describe existing jobs in the future or jobs that do not currently exist (Cronshaw, 1998; Schneider & Konz, 1989). Because the world of work has undergone so many changes in recent years (e.g., see Howard, 1995), the possibility of even more change in the future is likely, making it a difficult task to accurately predict variables that may affect how work and jobs will be conceived of or the skills and abilities that will be required for future jobs. If future predictions can be shown to be valid predictors of actual requirements and activities, it would be possible to defend the development of (for example) selection systems based on this kind of information (Schneider & Konz, 1989). However, until more empirical evidence for the validity of strategic job analytic information is obtained, the usefulness of the method cannot be determined.

A second point to be made is that some of the activities described under strategic job analysis are activities that any competent job analyst could be expected to perform. For example, it is reasonable to expect that a job analyst would inquire about the future of a target job—particularly if that job had recently changed or could be expected to change in a predicable way. A third potential concern lies in determining who the most accurate judges of future skills and abilities are. As with traditional forms of job analysis, the best practice would likely be to gather information from as many sources as possible (e.g., Schneider & Konz, 1989). Finally, it is also possible that techniques other than group discussion may be useful ways to gather information for the future. For example, CTA techniques may be useful for forecasting jobs that involve complex tasks or technical skills. Clearly, the emphasis on changing work structures and processes means that strategic job analysis will continue to be a significant activity.

ACCURACY IN JOB ANALYSIS

Morgeson and Campion (1997) presented an important challenge to the field with a provocative article that drew on a wide variety of literatures in setting forth a framework that identified 16 potential social and cognitive sources of inaccuracy in job analysis. The word *potential* is critical; in many cases the authors were making a conceptual argument that a potential source of inaccuracy is feasible rather than offering documentation of actual effects. Morgeson and Campion suggested that researchers have largely ignored issues of accuracy; given the central role of job analysis as a foundational activity for much of the work of I/O psychologists, they believe that this inattention is a serious problem. We provide an overview of Morgeson and Campion's sources of inaccuracy and offer a variety of comments.

We do not develop here all 16 of the themes in the Morgeson and Campion work. The 16 are grouped into four broader categories; we offer exemplars from each category. The first is social influence processes, which largely apply in settings in which job analysis judgments are made in groups rather than by individuals. If group consensus is required, pressures for conformity may be a source of bias; if a group product is required, the lack of individual identifiability may diminish motivation to devote attentional resources to the task. The second

is self-presentation processes, involving impression management, social desirability, and demand effects. Concerns about incumbents' inflating the importance of their jobs are a long-standing concern and result in the common practice of using multiple sources of job analysis information. The third is limitation in the information-processing systems of respondents. Demands for large numbers of ratings or for fine differentiations among job characteristics may result in information overload, which may be resolved by some heuristic process to simplify the rating task. The final source is bias in information-processing systems, with examples including extraneous effects of features such as respondent job satisfaction or dissatisfaction.

We offer a number of comments on these issues. At the forefront is the fundamental issue of the criterion for job analysis accuracy: How would we know whether an analysis is accurate or inaccurate? One argument is that one draws conclusions about job analysis accuracy from the outcomes of the HR system or program developed on the basis on the job analysis (Sanchez & Levine, 1999). If the job analysis is used to select predictors and the predictors prove to exhibit criterion related validity, then one uses these consequences to infer that the job analysis was accurate. This is not fully satisfactory—for example, one would never know whether an important predictor was excluded from the validation study due to an omission in the job analysis. Note also that in a number of instances there is not an external criterion of HR system effectiveness on which to draw. In some applications—as in the reliance on content-oriented evidence of selection system validity—the job analysis information itself is the evidence on which one's conclusion about the selection system rides.

Harvey and Wilson (2000) address the problem of job analysis accuracy by arguing that the term *job analysis* should be restricted to documenting observable work activities. The verification of incumbent information about work activities by job analysts permits conclusions to be drawn about job analysis accuracy. They propose *job specification* as the term for the process of making inferences about job attributes. We agree that the documentation of work activities is more straightforward and amenable to independent verification than is the process of making inferences about required job attributes. We note, however, that job analysis is broadly used as an umbrella term for a wide range of activities involving the systematic study of work, including both activities and attributes, and we do not view restriction of the use of the term as viable.

We see considerable value in the perspective taken by Guion (1998). Guion posits that job analysis is not science: It is an information-gathering tool to aid researchers in deciding what to do next. It always reflects subjective judgment. With careful choices in decisions about what information to collect and how to collect it, one will obtain reliable and useful information. Careful attention to the types of issues raised by Morgeson and Campion can increase the likelihood that useful information will result from job analysis. But we do not see an available standard for proving the accuracy of a job analysis. The documentation of one's choices and the use of sound professional judgment in job analysis decisions is the best that can be expected.

CONCLUSION

Job analysis has long been an important foundational tool for I/O psychologists. The last decade has seen more significant new developments than has been the case for several decades. The content model underlying the O*NET reflects a major effort toward a comprehensive model of job and worker characteristics, and it represents a highly visible manifestation of the notion that multiple purposes require multiple types of job information. I/O psychology's rediscovery of personality has led to the development of a variety of dedicated tools for identifying the personality requirements of jobs and has led to a broadening of the traditional KSA framework to include personality characteristics under the KSAO rubric. The business world's embracing of competency modeling reflects a change in the way organizations view job information; the challenge is to meld the breadth and strategic focus of competency modeling with the rigor of traditional job analysis methods. Cognitive task analysis is the subject of considerable research, with the jury still out as to feasibility and value of widespread I/O applications. Strategic job analysis may become a more important tool as organizations look increasingly towards the future. As work and organizations continue to change, we look forward to continuing developments in job and work analysis.

REFERENCES

Advisory Panel for the Dictionary of Occupational Titles (APDOT). (1993). *The new DOT: A database of occupational titles for the 21st century.* Washington, DC: U.S. Employment Service, U.S. Department of Labor Employment and Training Administration.

Annett, A. (2000). Theoretical and pragmatic influences on task analysis methods. In J. M. Schraagen, S. F. Chipman, & V. L. Shalin (Eds.), *Cognitive task analysis* (pp. 3–23). Mahwah, NJ: Erlbaum.

Arvey, R. D., & Begalla (1975). Analyzing the homemaker job using the Position Analysis Questionnaire. *Journal of Applied Psychology, 60,* 513–517.

Arvey, R. D., Salas, E., & Gialluca, K. A. (1992). Using task inventories to forecast skills and abilities. *Human Performance, 5,* 171–190.

Barrett, G., & Depinet, R. (1991). Reconsideration of testing for competence rather than intelligence. *American Psychologist, 46,* 1012–1024.

Blickensderfer, E., Cannon-Bowers, J. A., Salas, E., & Baker, D. P. (2000). Analyzing knowledge requirements in team tasks. In J. M. Schraagen, S. F. Chipman, & V. L. Shalin (Eds.), *Cognitive task analysis* (pp. 431–447). Mahwah, NJ: Erlbaum.

Borman, W. C., Kubisiak, U. C., & Schneider, R. J. (1999). Work styles. In N. G. Peterson, M. D. Mumford, W. C. Borman, P. R. Jeanneret, & E. A. Fleishman (Eds.), *An occupational information system for the 21st century: The development of O*NET* (pp. 213–226). Washington, DC: American Psychological Association.

Boyatzis, R. E. (1982). *The competent manager: A model for effective performance.* New York: Wiley.

Bruskiewicz, K. T., & Bosshardt, M. J. (1996, April). *An evaluation of a strategic job analysis.* Paper presented at the 11th Annual Conference of the Society for Industrial and Organizational Psychology, San Diego, CA.

Chipman, S. F., Schraagen, J. M., & Shalin, V. L. (2000). Introduction to cognitive task analysis. In J. M. Schraagen, S. F. Chipman, & V. L. Shalin (Eds.), *Cognitive task analysis* (pp. 3–23). Mahwah, NJ: Erlbaum.

Costa, P. T., Jr., McCrae, R. R., & Kay, G. G. (1995). Persons, places, and personality: Career assessment using the Revised NEO Personality Inventory. *Journal of Career Assessment, 3,* 123–139.

Cronshaw, S. F. (1998). Job analysis: Changing nature of work. *Canadian Psychology, 39,* 5–13.

Dalton, M. (1997). Are competency models a waste? *Training and Development, 51,* 46–49.

DuBois, D. D. (1999). Competency modeling. In D. G. Langdon, K. S. Whiteside, & M. M. McKenna (Eds.), *Intervention resource guide: 50 performance improvement tools* (pp. 106–111). San Francisco: Jossey-Bass/Pfeiffer.

Dunnette, M. D. (1999). Introduction. In N. G. Peterson, M. D. Mumford, W. C. Borman, & E. A. Fleishman (Eds.), *An occupational information system for the 21st century: The development of O*NET* (pp. 3–7). Washington, DC: American Psychological Association.

Fleishman, E. A., Quaintance, M. K., & Broedling, L. A. (1984). *Taxonomies of human performance: The description of human tasks.* San Diego, CA: Academic Press.

Gael, S. A. (1988). *The job analysis handbook for business, industry, and government* (Vols. 1 and 2). New York: Wiley.

Gordon, S. E., & Gill, R. T. (1997). Cognitive task analysis. In C. E. Zsambok & G. Klein (Eds.), *Naturalistic decision making* (pp. 131–141). Mahwah, NJ: Erlbaum.

Guion, R. M. (1998). *Assessment, measurement, and prediction for personnel decisions.* Mahwah, NJ: Erlbaum.

Harvey, R. J. (1991). Job analysis. In M. D. Dunnette & L. M. Hough (Eds.), *Handbook of industrial and organizational psychology* (Vol. 2, pp. 71–63). Palo Alto, CA: Consulting Psychologists Press.

Harvey, R. J., & Wilson. M. A. (2000). Yes, Virginia, there is an objective reality in job analysis. *Journal of Organizational Behavior, 21,* 829–854.

Hoffman, R. R., Shadbolt, N. R., Burton, A. M., & Klein, G. (1995). Eliciting knowledge from experts: A methodological analysis. *Organizational Behavior and Human Decision Processes, 62,* 129–158.

Howard, A. (1995). *The changing nature of work.* San Francisco: Jossey-Bass.

Jackson, D. N. (1990). *Quantitative perspectives on the personality-job performance relationship.* APA Division 5 Presidential Address, Boston.

Jonassen, D. H., Tessmer, M., & Hannum, W. H. (1999). *Task analysis methods for instructional design.* Mahwah, NJ: Erlbaum.

Klein, G. (2000). Cognitive task analysis of teams. In J. M. Schraagen, S. F. Chipman, & V. L. Shalin (Eds.), *Cognitive task analysis* (pp. 417–429). Mahwah, NJ: Erlbaum.

Lawler, E. E. (1994). From job-based to competency-based organizations. *Journal of Organizational Behavior, 15,* 3–15.

Lesgold, A. (2000). On the future of cognitive task analysis. In J. M. Schraagen, S. F. Chipman, & V. L. Shalin (Eds.), *Cognitive task analysis* (pp. 451–465). Mahwah, NJ: Erlbaum.

Lucia, A. D., & Lepsinger, R. (1999). *The art and science of competency models: Pinpointing critical success factors in organizations.* San Francisco: Jossey-Bass/Pfeiffer.

Mansfield, R. S. (1996). Building competency models: Approaches for HR professionals. *Human Resource Management, 35,* 7–18.

McClelland, D. (1973). Testing for competence rather than for "intelligence." *American Psychologist, 28,* 1–14.

McCormick, E. J., & Jeanneret, P. R. (1988). Position analysis questionnaire (PAQ). In S. A. Gael (Ed.), *The job analysis handbook for business, industry, and government* (Vol. 2, pp. 825–842). New York: Wiley.

McLagan, P. (1997). Competencies: The next generation. *Training & Development, 51,* 40–47.

Means, B. (1993). Cognitive task analysis as a basis for instructional design. In M. Rabonowitz (Ed.), *Cognitive science foundations of instruction* (pp. 97–118). Hillsdale, NJ: Erlbaum.

Mislevy, R. J., Steinberg, L. S., Breyer, F. J., Almond, R. G., & Johnson, L. (1999). A cognitive task analysis with implications for designing simulation-based performance assessment. *Computers in Human Behavior, 15,* 335–374.

Morgeson, F. P., & Campion, M. A. (1997). Social and cognitive sources of potential inaccuracy in job analysis. *Journal of Applied Psychology, 82,* 627–655.

O'Hare, D., Wiggins, M., Williams, A., & Wong, W. (1998). Cognitive task analysis for decision centered design and training. *Ergonomics, 41,* 1698–1718.

Olson, J. R., & Biolsi, K. J. (1991). Techniques for representing expert knowledge. In K. Anders Ericsson & J. Smith (Eds.), *Toward a general theory of expertise* (pp. 240–285). Cambridge, England: Cambridge University Press.

Paajanen, G. E., Hansen, T. L., & McClellan, R. A. (1993). *PDI Employment Inventory and PDI Customer Service Inventory manual.* Minneapolis, MN: Personnel Decisions.

Pearlman, K. (1993). *The skill standards project and the redesign of the nation's occupational classification system.* Washington, DC: U.S. Department of Labor.

Pearlman, K., & Barney, M. F. (2000). Selection for a changing workplace. In J. F. Kehoe (Ed.), *Managing selection in changing organizations: Human resource strategies* (pp. 3–72). San Francisco: Jossey-Bass.

Peterson, N. G., Mumford, M. D., Borman, W. C., Jeanneret, P. R, & Fleishman, E. A. (Eds.). (1999). *An occupational information system for the 21st century: The development of O*NET.* Washington, DC: American Psychological Association.

Potter, S. S., Roth, E. M., Woods, D. D., & Elm, W. C. (2000). Bootstrapping multiple converging cognitive task analysis techniques for system design. In J. M. Schraagen, S. F. Chipman, & V. L. Shalin (Eds.), *Cognitive task analysis* (pp. 317–340). Mahwah, NJ: Erlbaum.

Raymark, P. H., Schmit, M. J., & Guion, R. M. (1997). Identifying potentially useful personality constructs for employee selection. *Personnel Psychology, 50,* 723–736.

Richardson, Bellows, Henry, & Co. (1983). *The candidate profile record.* Washington, DC.

Rosenfeld, M., Shimberg, B., & Thornton, R. F. (1983). *Job analysis of licensed psychologists in the United States and Canada.* Princeton, NJ: Educational Testing Service.

Ryder, J. M., & Redding, R. E. (1993). Integrating cognitive task analysis into instructional systems development. *Educational Technology Research and Development, 41,* 75–96.

Sackett, P. R. (1991). Exploring strategies for clustering military occupations. In A. K. Wigdor & B. F. Green (Eds.), *Performance assessment for the workplace* (pp. 305–330). Washington, DC: National Academy Press.

Sanchez, J. I. (1994). From documentation to innovation: Reshaping job analysis to meet emerging business needs. *Human Resource Management Review, 4,* 51–74.

Sanchez, J. I., & Levine, E. L. (1999). Is job analysis dead, misunderstood, or both? New forms of work analysis and design. In A. I. Kraut & A. K. Korman (Eds.), *Evolving practices in human resource management* (pp. 43–68). San Francisco: Jossey-Bass.

Sanchez, J. I., & Levine, E. L. (2001). The analysis of work in the 20th and 21st centuries. In N. Anderson, D. S. Ones, H. K Sinangil, & C. Viswesvaran (Eds.), *Handbook of industrial, work, and organizational psychology* (pp. 70–90). London: Sage.

Schippmann, J. S., Ash, R. A., Battista, M., Carr, L., Eyde, L. D., Hesketh, B., Kehoe, J., Pearlman, K., Prien, E. P., & Sanchez,

J. I. (2000). The practice of competency modeling. *Personnel Psychology, 53,* 703–740.

Schneider, B., & Konz, A. M. (1989). Strategic job analysis. *Human Resource Management, 28,* 51–63.

Schraagen, J. M., Chipman, S. F., & Shute, V. J. (2000). State of the art review of cognitive task analysis techniques. In J. M. Schraagen, S. F. Chipman, & V. L. Shalin (Eds.), *Cognitive task analysis* (pp. 467–487). Mahwah, NJ: Erlbaum.

Seamster, T. L., Redding, R. E., & Kaempf, G. L. (2000). A skill-based cognitive task analysis framework. In J. M. Schraagen, S. F. Chipman, & V. L. Shalin (Eds.), *Cognitive task analysis* (pp. 135–146). Mahwah, NJ: Erlbaum.

Shute, V., Sugrue, B., & Willis, R. E. (1997, March). *Automating cognitive task analysis.* Paper presented at the annual meeting of the American Educational Research Association, Chicago.

Spencer, L. M., & Spencer, S. M. (1993). *Competence at work: Models for superior performance.* New York: Wiley.

U.S. Department of Labor. (1991). *Dictionary of Occupational Titles* (4th ed., rev.). Washington, DC: U.S. Government Printing Office.

Zachary, W. W., Ryder, J. M., & Hicinbothom, J. H. (1998). Cognitive task analysis and modeling of decision making in complex environments. In J. A. Cannon-Bowers & E. Salas (Eds.), *Making decisions under stress: Implications for individuals and team training* (pp. 315–344). Washington, DC: American Psychological Association.

CHAPTER 3

Job Performance

STEPHAN J. MOTOWIDLO

Studies of personnel practices and programs designed to improve human work performance have used a wide variety of criterion measures, including supervisory ratings, productivity indexes, absenteeism, turnover, salary, and promotion. Although all of these measures might be presumed to reflect performance—at least to some degree—there has been very little discussion about the conceptual status of the underlying performance construct itself. Over the last 20 years, however, researchers have been paying more and more attention to conceptual issues at the root of the so-called criterion problem (see Austin & Villanova, 1992, for a detailed analysis of historical trends). The past decade in particular saw an increasingly energetic literature on the behavioral content of job performance and its causal antecedents (e.g., Borman & Motowidlo, 1993; Campbell, 1990; Campbell, Gasser, & Oswald, 1996; Organ, 1997; Sackett, 2002; Schmidt & Hunter, 1992; Van Dyne, Cummings, & Parks, 1995; Viswesvaran & Ones, 2000).

This chapter builds upon ideas developed over the past 20 years or so to present a formal definition of job performance that incorporates explicit and fully articulated assumptions about the conceptual meaning of variation in the performance construct. Then it reviews some current efforts to define the behavioral content and antecedents of job performance.

WHAT IS JOB PERFORMANCE?

A Definition

A definition of job performance should be useful for the full range of strategies and interventions that the field of

industrial and organizational (I/O) psychology might utilize to improve human performance in work organizations. Many of these strategies involve recruitment and selection, training and development, or motivation. In addition, other strategies that might involve removing constraints that prevent individuals from contributing to organizational objectives and providing individuals with enhanced opportunities for organizational contributions could also affect performance directly. Thus, a definition of performance should allow for variation attributable to differences in (a) traits measured in selection programs, (b) participation in training and development programs, (c) exposure to motivational interventions and practices, and (d) situational constraints and opportunities.

Job performance is defined as the total expected value to the organization of the discrete behavioral episodes that an individual carries out over a standard period of time. This definition is a slightly revised version of the definition of performance we presented in a previous publication in connection with a theory of individual differences in task and contextual performance (Motowidlo, Borman, & Schmit, 1997). One important idea in this definition is that performance is a property of *behavior*. In particular, it is an aggregated property of multiple, discrete behaviors that occur over some span of time. A second important idea is that the property of behavior to which performance refers is its *expected value* to the organization. Thus, the performance construct by this definition is a variable that distinguishes between sets of behaviors carried out by different individuals and between sets of behaviors carried out by the same individual at different times. The distinction is based on how much the sets of behaviors (in the aggregate) are likely to contribute to or detract from organizational effectiveness. In a word, variance in performance is variance in the expected organizational value of behavior.

Performance Refers To Behavior

Behavior, performance, and results are not the same. Behavior is what people do. Performance is the expected organizational value of what people do. Results are states or conditions of people or things that are changed by what they do in ways that contribute to or detract from organizational effectiveness. Therefore, results are the route through which an individual's behavior helps or hinders an organization in reaching its objectives, which is what makes it appealing to focus on results when considering individual performance.

There are two conceptual and practical advantages, however, to tying the performance construct to an individual's behavior rather than to the results of that behavior. First, states or conditions of things or people that are changed by an individual's behavior are also often affected by other factors not under the performer's control. This argument presumes a distinction between two types of situational constraints and opportunities. One type affects the probability that people will carry out behaviors that are expected to help or hurt the organization. This type is a determinant to job performance as defined earlier. Situational factors of this type make it either easier or more difficult for people to carry out actions that have the potential to contribute to or detract from organizational effectiveness by directly interfering with or facilitating behavioral responses. For example, availability of appropriate tools or raw materials will affect the probability that people perform behaviors that involve using those tools to operate on the raw materials in order to produce organizational goods and services; however, a second type of situational constraints and opportunities affects valued organizational results without necessarily affecting individuals' performance behaviors. For instance, economic factors and market conditions can have direct effects on sales volume and profitability without necessarily constraining or facilitating individual performance behaviors involved in the production of goods and services. Thus, although situational opportunities and constraints that affect an individual's behavior are viewed as determinants of job performance, situational opportunities and constraints that affect only the results of an individual's behavior are not viewed as determinants of job performance.

Second, if psychology is a science of behavior, and if psychologists want to understand and manage job performance, we are probably best off to construe performance as a behavioral phenomenon. Defining performance according to properties of behavior instead of results of behavior allows us to develop an understanding of the psychological processes that govern selection, training, motivation, and facilitating or debilitating situational processes; it also allows us to apply most fruitfully psychological principles to the management of these processes.

From one perspective, work behavior is a continuous stream that flows on seamlessly as people spend time at work. During the course of an 8-hour workday, however, people do many things that neither help nor hinder the accomplishment of organization goals. Such behaviors have no effect on their performance. Thus, streams of work behavior are punctuated by occasions when people do something that does make a difference in relation to organizational goals; these are the behavioral episodes that make up the domain of job performance.

This raises the question of how the beginnings and endings of behavioral episodes in the performance domain might be identified so that performance episodes can be distinguished from the rest of the behavioral stream that is not relevant for organizational goals. Studies by Newtson and his colleagues (Newtson, 1973; Newtson, Engquist, & Bois, 1977) support the idea that when people observe an individual's behavior, they naturally segment it into discrete units to process social information. Newtson et al. (1977) argued that people perceive behavior as a series of coherent action units separated by break points that define their beginnings and endings. Furthermore, perceivers can generally agree where the break points are, although there is some flexibility about their location in the behavioral stream—depending in part on perceivers' purposes and situational factors.

In the realm of personnel research more directly, coherent units of action can be isolated from continuous streams of work behavior through the application of some methods of job analysis. For example, the task inventory procedure identifies specific tasks that make up a job and estimates the extent to which incumbents are involved in executing them. Task statements included in such inventories describe activities that are discrete units of work with identifiable beginnings and endings (McCormick, 1979). For instance, an inventory of tasks for a metal machinist's job might include statements such as the following: interpret engineering drawings, drill center holes, adjust cutting tools and machine attachments, grind tools and drills to specifications, and calibrate mechanical or electronic devices (McCormick, 1979, p. 136).

The critical incident technique is another job analysis method that can be used to identify coherent action units in the stream of work behavior. Critical incidents are examples of particularly effective or ineffective behavior in a circumscribed sphere of activity (Flanagan, 1954; McCormick, 1979), which—for our purposes—is work activity. Three examples of critical incidents drawn from an analysis of police officer jobs (Dunnette & Motowidlo, 1976, p. 92) are shown below:

> After an officer became aware that a dangerous intersection had no traffic control devices and that a high hedge was obstructing the view, he took it upon himself to contact the traffic engineers to have signs posted and the owner of the hedge to have it cut (effective).

> The officer took a gun away from a woman in a domestic dispute but gave it back to her before her husband had left, so that she had it reloaded as her husband was leaving (ineffective).

> At a propane gas tank leak, the officer requested cars to block specific intersections. He then shut down two nearby companies and began evacuating the area, all without receiving orders from his supervisor (effective).

Performance Is the Expected Organizational Value of Behavior

Performance refers only to behaviors that can make a difference to organizational goal accomplishment. The performance domain embraces behaviors that might have positive effects and behaviors that might have negative effects on organizational goal accomplishment. Thus, behavioral episodes in the performance domain for any given individual might have varying expected values for the organization that range from slightly to extremely positive for behaviors that can help organizational goal accomplishment and from slightly to extremely negative for behaviors that can hinder organizational goal accomplishment.

Because performance behaviors have varying positive or negative consequences for the organization, behaviors like those described in critical incidents are better candidates for the performance domain than are behaviors like those described in task activity statements. Activity statements in task inventories can be extremely useful for analyzing a job according to the degree to which incumbents are involved with various tasks and for providing detailed reports of precisely what incumbents have to do in order to satisfy the demands of their jobs. What they do not typically provide, however, is specific information about how incumbents might do these tasks in ways that contribute to or detract from the accomplishment of organizational goals. A machinist who has a sophisticated understanding of engineering symbols and takes the time to understand important details of engineering drawings probably contributes more to organizational goal accomplishment than does a machinist who has only a cursory understanding of engineering symbols and impatiently scans them only superficially. Both can be said to be executing the task, which is to interpret engineering drawings, but one executes it in a way that

is more organizationally valuable because it is more likely to yield correct interpretations of the drawings.

Conversely, critical incidents describe work behaviors that are particularly effective or ineffective. As seen in the examples of police officer performance, they do capture essential behavioral features that differentiate degrees of contribution to organizational goal accomplishment. Thus, they are close analogues to the behavioral episodes that comprise the domain of job performance.

The notion of a behavioral performance domain that includes behavioral episodes of varying organizational value, all performed by the same individual over some period of time, echoes Kane's (1986) concept of a *performance distribution*. His approach to performance distribution assessment acknowledges that situational changes can affect an individual's motivation or opportunity to perform with the result that the individual works at varying levels of effectiveness at different times during the course of the performance period. Borman (1991) illustrated how the shape of the distribution of these performance episodes over time can yield useful information beyond just an individual's typical performance level. Two performers may have exactly the same modal performance level, but if one performs close to his or her minimum level most of the time and the other performs close to his or her maximum level most of the time, these differences may imply diagnostically useful differences in ability and motivation.

Sackett, Zedeck, and Fogli (1988) raised some similar issues in a study of relations between measures of typical and maximum performance in a sample of supermarket cashiers. They measured typical cashier accuracy by unobtrusively measuring number of errors (cashier slip voids) per shift over a 4-week period. They also unobtrusively measured typical cashier speed over the same period as mean number of items processed per minute. To measure maximum speed and maximum accuracy, they developed a work sample simulation consisting of shopping carts with a standard set of grocery items to be checked out. Cashiers were asked to do their best in checking out the standard grocery carts and asked to place an equal emphasis on speed and accuracy. Sackett et al. found that speed on the job correlated .14 with speed in the job simulation in a sample of new hires and .32 in a sample of current employees. They also found that accuracy on the job correlated .17 with accuracy in the job simulation in a sample of new hires and .11 in a sample of current employees. They concluded that measures of maximum performance are not necessarily highly related to measures of typical performance and that it is inappropriate to treat them as interchangeable.

It should be noted, however, that maximum performance in a job simulation like the one used by Sackett et al. (1988)

is not the same thing as maximum performance on the job during any particular performance period, as described in Kane's (1986) model of performance distribution assessment. Maximum performance in a job simulation may represent an upper limit on actual job performance, but maximum performance on the job could well be substantially below that upper limit, depending on situational job factors that constrain motivation and opportunity. Correlations between performance in a job simulation and typical performance on the job reported by Sackett et al. (1988) were not strong enough to argue that maximum performance measured on a simulation is a good substitute for typical performance measured on the job. The strength of the relation between maximum performance on the job and typical performance on the job, however, remains an open question.

The definition of performance as expected behavioral value over a standard period of time is fully consistent with assumptions argued by others that an individual's performance can vary over time with changes in motivational factors and situational constraints. Nothing in the definition denies that it might be interesting and important—both conceptually and practically—to study differences in individual distributions of performance episodes (Kane, 1986) and typical versus maximum performance levels of individuals over time (Sackett et al., 1988). However, the expected behavioral value definition of performance does not take distributional differences into account when scaling the total expected value of behaviors carried out over the course of the performance period.

Moreover, this definition of performance does not conflict with arguments on either side of the debate about dynamic criteria (Austin, Humphreys, & Hulin, 1989; Barrett, Caldwell, & Alexander, 1985). The total expected value of an individual's behavior could change idiosyncratically and systematically from one performance period to another (Hofmann, Jacobs, & Gerras, 1992; Ployhart & Hakel, 1998), but the extent to which this happens is an empirical issue, not a definitional one.

As has been mentioned, a behavior's effects on organizational effectiveness are carried through the changes it brings about in the states or conditions of things or people that represent favorable or unfavorable organizational consequences. Thus, the value of a behavior is determined by its favorable or unfavorable organizational consequences. However, the same behavior can be successful in yielding a favorable organizational outcome on some occasions but not on others, depending on situational factors that share causal influence on the outcome and that are independent of an individual's behavior.

The value of a behavior to the organization does not depend on the actual outcome of that behavior when carried out on any one occasion by any one individual. It does depend on the expected outcomes of that behavior if it were to be repeated over many occasions by many individuals. This point is similar to one of Organ's (1997) definitional requirements for organizational citizenship behavior (OCB):

> Finally, it was required that OCB contain only those behaviors that, in the aggregate, across time and across persons, contribute to organizational effectiveness. In other words, not every single discrete instance of OCB would make a difference in organizational outcomes; for example, I might offer help to a coworker that actually turns out to be dysfunctional for that person's performance, but summated across the categories of relevant behaviors, the effect would be positive. Or, if you will, lots of people who frequently offer help to coworkers will contribute to the effectiveness of the organization (p. 87).

The expected organizational value of a behavioral episode can be defined more formally in language borrowed from expectancy theory (Vroom, 1964) in terms of (a) its instrumentality for organizational outcomes and (b) the degree to which these outcomes have positive or negative valence for the organization. Thus, expected organizational value of a behavior is like the concept of valence in expectancy theory. It is the product of the instrumentality of a behavior for a relevant organizational outcome times the valence of that outcome for the organization, with these products summed over all such relevant organizational outcomes of the behavior.

Defining a behavior's value according to its expected results instead of according to its actual results makes it possible to assess individual performance by observing an individual's behavior without requiring information about the consequences of that behavior. This approach is convenient because behavioral consequences might not become known for days, weeks, or even years after the behavior is carried out. After organizationally valuable behaviors are identified, it also becomes sensible to develop selection systems, training programs, motivational interventions, and adjustments for situational constraints to encourage people to carry such behaviors out more frequently, even though the behaviors encouraged by these means will not yield organizationally valuable outcomes with perfect consistency. The same kinds of personnel practices can also aim to discourage people from carrying out behaviors that have negative organizational value because they are expected to yield unfavorable organizational consequences. This argument assumes, of course, that such positively and negatively valued behaviors can be identified with the level of specificity necessary to guide the development and implementation of effective personnel programs and practices.

BEHAVIORAL DIMENSIONS OF JOB PERFORMANCE

Definitions of categories or dimensions of behavior that make up the performance domain must begin with some notion of behaviors that are organizationally valued either positively or negatively. Consequently, the problem of identifying behaviors that have positive or negative expected value for the organization is closely tied to the problem of developing a taxonomic structure of the performance domain. Viswesvaran and Ones (2000) reviewed several taxonomic models of performance and discussed some of the similarities and differences between them. Different taxonomies are probably most useful for different purposes and no one way to slice up the behavioral domain is likely to be most useful overall (Coleman & Borman, 2000). The definition of performance offered in this chapter does not necessarily favor any one taxonomy over another as long as they can identify categories or dimensions that consist of behaviors believed to have positive or negative expected valued for the organization. To illustrate how different kinds of behavioral dimensions or clusters can be extracted from the performance domain, the paragraphs that follow describe a few of the taxonomic models that are currently being discussed in this literature.

Campbell's Multifactor Model

Campbell (1990) defined eight behavioral dimensions of performance that he claimed "are sufficient to describe the top of the latent hierarchy in all jobs in the *Dictionary of Occupational Titles*. However, the eight factors are not of the same form. They have different patterns of subgeneral factors, and their content varies differentially across jobs. Further, any particular job might not incorporate all eight components" (Campbell, 1990, p. 708). The eight factors appear in the following list:

1. Job-specific task proficiency: How well someone can do tasks that make up the core technical requirements of a job and that differentiate one job from another.
2. Non-job-specific task proficiency: How well someone can perform tasks that are not unique to the job but that are required by most or all jobs in an organization.
3. Written and oral communications: How well someone can write or speak to an audience of any size.
4. Demonstrating effort: How much someone commits to job tasks and how persistently and intensely someone works at job tasks.
5. Maintaining personal discipline: How much someone avoids negative behavior such as alcohol abuse, rule breaking, and absenteeism.
6. Facilitating team and peer performance: How well someone supports, helps, and develops peers and helps the group function as an effective unit.
7. Supervision: How well someone influences subordinates through face-to-face interaction.
8. Management and administration: How well someone performs other, nonsupervisory functions of management such as setting organizational goals, organizing people and resources, monitoring progress, controlling expenses, and finding additional resources.

Campbell did not specifically mention examples of behavioral episodes with varying levels of expected organizational value. It is not difficult, however, to imagine what they might be from the definitions he provided for the behavioral categories. For example, in the first dimension (job-specific proficiency), behaviors that represent quick, error-free task execution would carry positive expected value, and—at the other end—behaviors that represent very slow or incomplete task execution would carry negative expected value. Similarly, in the sixth dimension (facilitating peer and team performance) behaviors that represent generous help and support for coworkers in need would carry positive expected value and behaviors that represent indifference toward coworkers in need, or hostile and hurtful acts toward coworkers would carry negative expected value. Thus, performance in each of the behavioral areas described in Campbell's model can be defined according to the expected values of all the behaviors that fall under the same behavioral category. For example, performance on the factor job-specific task proficiency can be defined as the sum of the expected values of all behaviors related to job-specific task proficiency that an individual carries out over some standard period of time.

Task Versus Contextual Performance

Borman and Motowidlo (1993) distinguished between task performance and contextual performance out of concern that research and practice in the area of employee selection tended to focus only on a part of the performance domain and tended to exclude or downplay another part that is also important for organizational effectiveness. To explain how these two parts of the performance domain differ, we suggested that the part that tended to be most frequently recognized and targeted by selection research and practice refers to activities like those that usually appear on formal job descriptions. We called it *task performance* and suggested that it might take either of two forms. One involves activities that directly transform raw materials into the goods and services that are the organization's products. Such activities include selling merchandise in a retail store, operating a production machine in a manufacturing plant, teaching in a school, performing surgery in a hospital, and cashing checks in a bank.

The second form of task performance involves activities that service and maintain the technical core by replenishing its supply of raw materials, distributing its finished products, or providing important planning, coordination, supervising, or staff functions that enable it to function effectively and efficiently. When these task activities are performed effectively, they are behavioral episodes with positive expected organizational value because they facilitate the production of organizational goods and services. When performed ineffectively, however, they can have negative expected value because they might hinder the production of organizational goods and services. Thus, the domain of task performance includes behavioral episodes that represent task activities that are performed well and behavioral episodes that represent task activities that are performed poorly, with corresponding variability in their expected organizational value.

We argued that the part of the performance domain that was relatively ignored in selection research is also organizationally valuable, but for reasons different from those that explain the organizational value of task performance. We called it *contextual performance* because we defined it in terms of behavior that contributes to organizational effectiveness through its effects on the psychological, social, and organizational context of work. Individuals can contribute through the context of work in several different ways.

One way is by affecting other individuals in the organization so that they become more likely to carry out organizationally valuable behaviors themselves. For instance, to the extent an individual's actions promote positive affect in others, defuse hostilities and conflict, and encourage interpersonal trust, such actions will have positive expected organizational value because their effects on the social context of work improve interpersonal communication and cooperation and make it easier to coordinate individuals' efforts on interdependent tasks. To the extent actions that show unusual dedication to the task or organization are modeled by others who become inspired to behave similarly themselves, such actions will have positive expected organizational value because their effects on the psychological context of work motivate others to exert greater effort in the service of organizational objectives. Effects like these on patterns of interpersonal interaction and task motivation spread from the individual level to the group level as they affect group characteristics such as cohesiveness, teamwork, and morale that govern individual behavior within groups and consequently affect group members' performance. They can also spread more generally to the organizational level through effects on organization-wide norms, culture, and climate that in turn can affect individuals' performance broadly throughout the organization.

Another way to contribute through the context of work is by increasing the individual's own readiness to perform organizationally valuable behaviors. Things people do to develop their own knowledge and skill, for example, have positive expected organizational value because enhancements in knowledge and skill should improve their performance in areas related to the enhanced knowledge and skill. Similarly, actions such as consuming alcohol or drugs at work have negative expected value because they diminish an individual's readiness to perform effectively. Other actions such as actively resisting the debilitating effects of stressful work situations, adapting flexibly to changing work demands, and taking the initiative to carry out organizationally valuable actions instead of just responding passively to situational demands also fall under the category of behaviors that have positive expected value because of their effects on an individual's readiness to contribute to organizational objectives.

A third way to contribute through the context of work is through actions that affect the organization's tangible resources. For instance, actions such as cleaning up the conference room after a meeting, using personal resources such as the family automobile or computer for organizational business, and conserving electricity by shutting off lights when leaving an office all have positive expected value because of their effects on tangible aspects of the organizational context. At the other end, actions such as theft, sabotage, and waste or destruction of organizational resources or facilities have negative expected value also because of their effects on tangible aspects of the organizational context.

These three broad forms of contextual performance emphasize different features of the psychological, social, and organizational context of work. The first one focuses on contextual elements in the form of psychological states of other individuals and related characteristics of groups and the organization as a whole. Behaviors that affect these psychological states and corresponding group or organizational characteristics have positive or negative expected value because they affect the likelihood that other individuals will carry out actions that contribute to organizational effectiveness. The second one focuses on contextual elements in the form of an individual's own readiness to contribute. Behaviors that affect an individual's own readiness have positive or negative expected value depending on whether they increase or decrease the likelihood that the individual will carry out subsequent actions that contribute to organizational effectiveness. The third one focuses on contextual elements in the form of tangible organizational resources. Behaviors that affect these elements have positive or negative expected value depending on whether they preserve or squander organizational resources.

Borman and Motowidlo (1993) described five types of contextual activities: volunteering to carry out task activities that are not formally a part of the job; persisting with extra enthusiasm or effort when necessary to complete own task activities successfully; helping and cooperating with others; following organizational rules and procedures even when personally inconvenient; and endorsing, supporting, and defending organizational objectives (Borman & Motowidlo, 1993). Although these behavioral descriptions mention only behaviors likely to have positive organizational value, we intended that they would also include behaviors that have negative organizational value. This idea was made explicit where Borman and Motowidlo (1993) wrote

> On the other hand, it is clear that organizational behavior at the low end of these (contextual) dimensions can be very troublesome for organizations. Employees who ignore standard procedures when personally inconvenient, rebel against reasonable organizational rules, consistently question supervisors' judgment, or deride the organization to fellow employees and persons outside the organization definitely contribute to problems and can seriously undermine organizational effectiveness. (p. 94)

Coleman and Borman (2000) empirically refined our original five-factor taxonomy of contextual performance. They reviewed behavioral patterns that were mentioned in our original taxonomy, in discussions of organizational behavior (Organ, 1988) and prosocial organizational behavior (Brief & Motowidlo, 1986), and in our model of soldier effectiveness (Borman, Motowidlo, & Hanser, 1983) and decomposed the patterns into 27 different behavioral concepts. They had expert judges categorize the 27 concepts according to their behavioral content and through factor analysis, multidimensional scaling analysis, and cluster analysis of their judgments identified underlying dimensions that they labeled *interpersonal support, organizational support,* and *job-task conscientiousness.*

Borman, Buck, et al. (2001) reported further refinements to the three-dimensional model developed by Coleman and Borman (2000). They started with 5,000 examples of job performance that were collected over the years in 22 studies by researchers at Personnel Decisions Research Institutes. They culled out about 2,300 examples of contextual performance and sorted them into the three dimensions developed by Coleman and Borman. Then they redefined the three categories (and relabeled one) based on the types of examples

that ended up in each category. The revised category definitions follow:

- Personal support: Helping others by offering suggestions, teaching them useful knowledge or skills, directly performing some of their tasks, and providing emotional support for their personal problems; cooperating with others by accepting suggestions, informing them of events they should know about, and putting team objectives ahead of personal interests; showing consideration, courtesy, and tact in relations with others as well as motivating and showing confidence in them.
- Organizational support: Representing the organization favorably by defending and promoting it; expressing satisfaction and showing loyalty by staying with the organization despite temporary hardships; supporting the organization's mission and objectives, complying with organizational rules and procedures, and suggesting improvements.
- Conscientious initiative: Persisting with extra effort despite difficult conditions; taking the initiative to do all that is necessary to accomplish objectives even if not normally parts of own duties and finding additional productive work to perform when own duties are completed; developing own knowledge and skills by taking advantage of opportunities within and outside the organization using own time and resources.

Again, although these definitions mention only effective behaviors, the categories are meant to include ineffective behaviors as well. In fact, the computerized adaptive rating scales developed by Borman, Buck, et al. (2001) to measure these dimensions of contextual performance specifically include behaviors intended to represent four levels of effectiveness: very effective, effective, somewhat ineffective, and very ineffective.

The defining difference between task and contextual performance lies in the reason behaviors in each domain have some level of positive or negative expected value for the organization. The reason is either a contribution to organizational goods and services or a contribution to the psychological, social, and organizational context of work. Some behaviors, however, can have expected value for both reasons, which complicates efforts to assign behaviors to one category or the other. Some behaviors can directly help or hurt the production of goods and services, thereby contributing to task performance; the same behaviors can simultaneously help or hurt the social, organizational, or psychological context of work, thereby contributing also to contextual performance.

Behaviors listed in the definitions of contextual performance dimensions are meant to be prototypical of the kinds of behaviors that would have expected value for maintaining or enhancing the psychological, social, and organizational context of work. Their implications for task performance are also sometimes readily apparent, however, especially in the conscientious initiative dimension. Behaviors such as persisting with extra effort despite difficult conditions and taking the initiative to do all that is necessary to accomplish objectives contribute to an individual's contextual performance partly because—when observed by others in the organization—they can serve as models that inspire others to behave similarly. They can also help to establish and reinforce norms that support and encourage such behaviors. At the same time, of course, the same acts can enhance the performer's own production of organizational goods and services, thereby contributing to his or her task performance. Then task performance can be defined as the total expected value of an individual's behaviors over a standard period of time for the production of organizational goods and services. Contextual performance can be defined as the total expected value of an individual's behaviors over a standard period of time for maintaining and enhancing the psychological, social, and organizational context of work. These definitions acknowledge that some behaviors might have consequences both for producing goods and services and for maintaining and enhancing the psychological, social, and organizational context of work.

If there are no other reasons a behavior might have positive or negative organizational value besides those behind the distinction between task and contextual performance, behaviors covered by these two dimensions combined exhaust the domain of job performance. If Campbell's (1990) multifactor model can describe the latent structure of all jobs, by implication it too covers the entire domain of job performance. This means that the two taxonomic frameworks refer to the same domain of performance behaviors. The difference between them is in how the behavioral domain is partitioned. Campbell's model seems to divide behaviors primarily according to their content. The distinction between task performance and contextual performance divides behaviors according to their organizational consequences, recognizing that some behaviors might have implications for both kinds of consequences.

Organizational Citizenship Behavior

According to Organ (1997), ideas about organizational citizenship behavior developed from his conviction that job satisfaction affected "people's willingness to help colleagues and work associates and their disposition to cooperate in varied and mundane forms to maintain organized structures that govern work" (Organ, 1997, p. 92). His student, Smith (Smith, Organ, & Near, 1983), tried to define specific behaviors that reflected this willingness and disposition by asking managers to describe things they would like their subordinates to do but that they could not require subordinates to do by force, offers of rewards, or threats of punishment. By asking what managers would like their subordinates to do, Smith et al. seemed to be focusing on behaviors that would have positive expected value for the organization. These interviews produced 16 behavioral items. Another sample of managers rated a subordinate by indicating the degree to which each item characterized the subordinate. Factor analysis produced one factor that was interpreted as altruism (highest factor loadings for the items *Helps others who have been absent, Volunteers for things that are not required,* and *Helps others who have heavy workloads*) and another that was interpreted as generalized compliance (highest factor loadings for the items *Does not take extra breaks, Does not take unnecessary time off work,* and *Punctuality*).

Organ (1988) defined organizational citizenship behavior as "individual behavior that is discretionary, not directly or explicitly recognized by the formal reward system, and that in the aggregate promotes the effective functioning of the organization" (Organ, 1988, p. 4). He proposed another set of dimensions of such behaviors that included altruism, conscientiousness, sportsmanship, courtesy, and civic virtue. Podsakoff, MacKenzie, Moorman, and Fetter (1990) developed an instrument that came to be widely used to measure these five dimensions. It includes items such as *Helps others who have been absent* and *Helps others who have heavy work loads* for altruism; *Attendance at work is above the norm* and *Does not take extra breaks* for conscientiousness; *Consumes a lot of time complaining about trivial matters* (reversed) and *Always focuses on what's wrong, rather than the positive side* (reversed) for sportsmanship; *Takes steps to try to prevent problems with other workers* and *Is mindful of how his or her behavior affects other people's jobs* for courtesy; and *Attends meetings that are not mandatory but are considered important* and *Attends functions that are not required, but help the company image* for civic virtue.

More recently, Organ (1997) acknowledged conceptual difficulties associated with definitional requirements that organizational citizenship behaviors are discretionary and not formally rewarded. He redefined organizational citizenship behavior according to the definition that Borman and Motowidlo (1993) suggested for contextual performance: "contributions to the maintenance and enhancement of the social and psychological context that supports task performance" (Organ, 1997, p. 91). However, this revised definition has been largely ignored by researchers in this area who persist in using Organ's (1988) original definition of organizational citizenship behavior and instruments developed to measure the construct according to its original definition.

LePine, Erez, and Johnson (2002) conducted a meta-analysis to determine whether the five dimensions of organizational citizenship behavior were empirically distinct. They concluded that relations between these dimensions at the population level are generally about as high as their reliability estimates. This finding calls into question the common practice of drawing conclusions about different aspects of organizational citizenship behavior. It also suggests that organizational citizenship behavior might best be viewed as a multidimensional latent variable (Law, Wong, & Mobley, 1998)—perhaps interpretable as either a trait or state reflecting "willingness to help colleagues and work associates and their disposition to cooperate" (Organ, 1997, p. 92). LePine et al. note, however, that an alternative explanation for their meta-analytic findings might be that the common variance in different dimensions of organizational citizenship is halo error. This possibility would suggest that although dimensions of organizational citizenship might not be distinguishable by currently available measures, they might still be conceptually distinguishable and perhaps empirically distinguishable too if effects attributable to halo can be controlled.

The literature on organizational citizenship behavior is rich and extensive enough to have stirred up some intriguing conceptual questions because different researchers defined, interpreted, and measured the concept in different ways at different times. These questions pose several interesting definitional challenges. First, does organizational citizenship behavior refer only to behaviors that have positive expected value for the organization, as implied in its early definition (Smith et al., 1983) and in discussions that distinguish it from behaviors with negative expected value such as anticitizenship behaviors (Podsakoff & MacKenzie, 1997) and counterproductive behaviors (Sackett, 2002)? Or does it also include behaviors with negative expected value, as implied by the inclusion of behavioral items that are scored in reverse for organizational citizenship behavior in instruments such as the one developed by Smith et al. (1983; *Takes undeserved breaks* and *Great deal of time spent with personal phone conversations*) and the one developed by Podsakoff et al. (1990; e.g., *Tends to make mountains out of molehills* and *Is the classic squeaky wheel that always needs greasing*)? Second, is organizational citizenship behavior best viewed as a multidimensional latent variable that is represented by the common variance shared by its various dimensions and that reflects either (a) something like agreeableness and the dependability components of conscientiousness or (b) a motivational state elicited by organizational conditions that affect feelings of satisfaction or equity? Or is it the aggregated sum of those dimensions? Or is it just a useful classification label for conceptually distinct dimensions of behavior such as altruism, conscientiousness, and so on? Third, is it best defined as discretionary and not formally rewardable? Or is it best defined as equivalent to contextual performance in these respects?

Many of the behaviors subsumed under the label *organizational citizenship behavior* resemble behaviors embraced by our definition of contextual performance. If the concept of organizational citizenship behavior is identical to the concept of contextual performance, the expected behavioral value definition of contextual performance should apply equally well to organizational citizenship behavior. The unsettled questions raised in this literature, however, make it doubtful that all researchers who work in this area would agree that organizational citizenship behavior is the total expected value of an individual's behaviors (including behaviors with both positive and negative expected values) over a standard period of time for maintaining and enhancing the psychological, social, and organizational context of work.

Organizational citizenship behaviors are also represented in Campbell's (1990) multifactor model. If they include only behaviors with positive expected value, such behaviors would be included at the top ends of Campbell's dimensions, demonstrating effort, maintaining personal discipline, and maintaining team and peer performance, which appear especially likely to include behaviors motivated by willingness to help and cooperate.

Counterproductive Behavior

Organizational citizenship behavior poses an especially interesting contrast to organizationally dysfunctional forms of behavior such as antisocial behavior (Robinson & O'Leary-Kelly, 1998), incivility (Andersson & Pearson, 1999), withholding effort (Kidwell & Bennett, 1993), deviant workplace behaviors (Robinson & Bennett, 1995), and counterproductive behavior (Sackett, 2002). The contrast is between behaviors that are carried out to help and cooperate (and have positive expected organizational value) and behaviors that are carried out to hurt and hinder (and have negative expected organizational value). Some efforts to define or identify the content of such dysfunctional organizational behaviors are reviewed briefly in the following discussion.

Robinson and O'Leary-Kelly (1998) studied correlates of antisocial behavior at work with an instrument that asked people to rate the extent to which—over the past year—they "damaged property belonging to (their) employer, said or did something to purposely hurt someone at work, did work badly, incorrectly, or slowly on purpose, griped with cowork-ers, deliberately bent or broke a rule(s), criticized people at work, did something that harmed (their) employer or boss, started an argument with someone at work, and said rude things about (their) supervisor or organization" (p. 662).

Andersson and Pearson (1999) distinguished incivility from other forms of interpersonal mistreatment such as anti-social behavior, deviant behavior, violence, and aggression by defining it as "low-intensity deviant behavior with am-biguous intent to harm the target, in violation of workplace norms for mutual respect. Uncivil behaviors are characteris-tically rude and discourteous, displaying a lack of regard for others" (p. 457). Some examples of incivility are sending a nasty or demeaning note, treating someone like a child, un-dermining someone's credibility in front of others, neglecting to greet someone, interrupting someone who is speaking, leaving trash around for someone else to clean, and not thanking someone who exerted special effort (Pearson, Andersson, & Porath, 2000).

Kidwell and Bennett (1993) argued that the common ele-ment underlying behavioral patterns characterized as shirking, social loafing, and free riding is propensity to withhold effort. They distinguished this propensity from providing extra effort, which is part of the concept of organizational citizenship be-havior, by suggesting that although providing extra effort might not be enforceable through formal contracts or obliga-tions, withholding effort generally is sanctioned by such formal contracts. Thus, providing extra effort might be seen as an ex-ample of extrarole behavior, but withholding effort would be an example of negatively valued in-role behavior.

Robinson and Bennett (1995) defined employee deviance as "voluntary behavior that violates significant organizational norms and in so doing threatens the well-being of an organiza-tion, its members, or both" (p. 556). They collected critical incidents describing things people did that were thought to be deviant or wrong from a sample of 70 research participants. Another sample of research participants rated the similarity of incidents to a target behavior. Multidimensional scaling yielded a two-dimensional solution that finally produced a ty-pology with four categories of workplace deviance: production deviance (e.g., leaving early, taking excessive breaks, inten-tionally working slow, wasting resources), property deviance (e.g., sabotaging equipment, accepting kickbacks, lying about hours worked, stealing from company), political deviance (e.g., showing favoritism, gossiping about coworkers, blaming coworkers, competing nonbeneficially), and personal aggres-sion (e.g., sexual harassment, verbal abuse, stealing from coworkers, endangering coworkers).

Perhaps the most general and inclusive term to describe organizationally dysfunctional behaviors such as these is *counterproductive behavior,* which—according to Sackett (2002)—"refers to any intentional behavior on the part of the organizational member viewed by the organization as con-trary to its legitimate interests." Based on results of Gruys' (1999) dissertation, Sackett enumerated 11 categories of counterproductive behaviors: theft, destruction of property, misuse of information, misuse of time and resources, unsafe behavior, poor attendance, poor quality work, alcohol use, drug use, inappropriate verbal actions, and inappropriate physical actions. Sackett argued that empirical evidence from several sources converges on the possibility of a general factor of counterproductive behavior and accordingly suggested that a hierarchical factor model might well represent patterns of covariation in the occurrence of counterproductive behaviors. This hierarchical model would have a general factor, group factors below it, and specific factors such as theft, absence, and safety below them.

As mentioned, Sackett's (2002) definition of counterpro-ductive behaviors includes the requirement that such behav-iors are intentional. If this stipulation means including only behaviors that people carry out deliberately to hurt other indi-viduals or the organization at large, it rules out behaviors that have negative effects that were not intended, such as acciden-tal behaviors and behaviors that have negative effects because well-intentioned performers lacked the knowledge or skill necessary to carry them out effectively. Defining counterpro-ductive behaviors as necessarily intentional pits the concept squarely against the motivational basis for organizational citi-zenship behavior in willingness to help and disposition to co-operate. Although the motivational antecedents of the two performance domains might seem to be opposites of each other, however, some organizational citizenship behaviors such as helping others who have been absent and helping others who have heavy work loads are not obviously the oppo-site of some counterproductive behaviors such as theft and ab-senteeism. This makes it important and interesting to ask whether it makes better sense to define organizational citizen-ship behavior and counterproductive behavior as opposite ends of the same dimension or as entirely separate dimensions.

Counterproductive behaviors are represented at the bottom ends of both task performance and contextual performance. They are distinguished from other (dysfunctional) behaviors at the bottom ends of these dimensions by the requirement that counterproductive behaviors are intentional. Task and contex-tual performance also refer to mindless or accidental behav-iors that have negative expected value as well as behaviors carried out with the intention of having a positive effect on productivity or the work context but that end up having negative expected value because the individual is deficient in the task-specific or contextual knowledge or skill necessary for executing an effective behavior. Similarly, counterproductive behaviors are probably represented at the bottom of all eight of Campbell's (1990) performance dimensions, although the dimension *maintaining personal discipline* is likely to be especially well saturated with counterproductive behavior (Sackett, 2002).

Accepting the twin requirements in Sackett's (2002) definition that counterproductive behaviors are both intentional and contrary to the organization's interests, counterproductive performance could be defined as the total expected value to the organization of behaviors that are carried out over a standard period of time with the intention of hurting other individuals or the organization as a whole and that have negative expected organizational value.

The General Performance Factor

Reporting results of a meta-analytic study of correlations between performance ratings, Viswesvaran, Schmidt, and Ones (1996) concluded that there is a general factor in supervisory performance ratings that is independent of halo; they suggest that this factor explains 49% of the total variance in the ratings. One explanation they offer for the general factor is that all dimensions of job performance are probably determined in part by general mental ability and conscientiousness. Then the common variance across performance dimensions that is the general factor would represent that portion of the total variance in performance that is attributable to general mental ability and conscientiousness.

Although the primary focus in the study reported by Viswesvaran et al. (1996) was on testing for a general factor, Viswesvaran and Ones (2000) noted that arguing for a general factor of job performance does not preclude specific factors of job performance in addition. In fact, they proposed a hierarchical model with a general factor at the top, group factors below it, and more specific factors below them. If the general factor reflects primarily the joint operation of conscientiousness and cognitive ability, each of the group and specific factors would represent other sets of common antecedents—perhaps reflecting the operation of different traits, participation in training and development opportunities, exposure to motivational interventions, situational opportunities and constraints, or any combination of these.

Structuring the performance domain according to covariance between performance dimensions essentially identifies performance factors according to commonalities in their antecedents. This strategy for slicing up the behavioral content of the performance domain is different from a strategy like Campbell's (1990) that appears to be based only on similarity of behavioral content within dimensions and from a strategy

like that followed by Borman and Motowidlo (1993) that distinguishes between task and contextual performance on the basis of their consequences or reasons for their positive or negative expected organizational value.

ANTECEDENTS OF JOB PERFORMANCE

Several theoretical and empirical reports published over the past 20 years presented causal models of performance that explain relations between basic traits such as cognitive ability and personality and job performance in terms of intervening variables such as knowledge, skill, and sometimes other variables that are also presumed to mediate effects of basic traits on performance. Hunter (1983) reported one of the first accounts of this sort. It was a meta-analysis based on a total sample of 3,264 cases that examined relations between cognitive ability, job knowledge, work sample performance, and supervisory ratings of job performance. Average correlations across the studies in his meta-analysis supported a model that has direct causal paths from ability to both job knowledge and work sample performance, a direct path from job knowledge to work sample performance, and direct paths from both job knowledge and work sample performance to supervisory ratings of performance. It is important to note that the effect of ability on knowledge was substantially stronger than was its effect on work sample performance, and it had no effect on supervisory ratings except through its effects on job knowledge and work sample performance. If work sample performance can be construed to be a measure of job skill (Campbell et al., 1996), and if supervisory ratings measure performance on the job, Hunter's results show that ability directly affects job knowledge and skill and that it affects job performance only through its effects on knowledge and skill.

Schmidt, Hunter, and Outerbridge (1986) added job experience to the variables tested by Hunter (1983). Using data from four of the studies that were included in Hunter's meta-analysis, they showed that besides ability, experience also has a direct affect on job knowledge and a smaller direct effect on job sample performance. There were no direct effects of experience on supervisory ratings. Thus, both experience and ability have a substantial direct effect on knowledge and smaller direct effects on skill as measured through work sample performance, and neither variable affects job performance as measured by supervisory ratings except through their effects on job knowledge and skill.

Borman, White, Pulakos, and Oppler (1991) added two personality variables, dependability and achievement orientation, and two related outcome variables, number of awards and number of disciplinary actions, to the set of variables that

Hunter (1983) analyzed. Correlations between these variables in nine military jobs supported a causal model in which ability affected knowledge, knowledge affected skill, and skill affected job performance. Neither ability nor knowledge had direct or other indirect effects on job performance. In addition, dependability had direct effects on knowledge, number of disciplinary actions, and job performance. Achievement orientation had direct effects on number of awards and job performance.

Campbell (1990) and his associates (Campbell et al., 1996; Campbell, McCloy, Oppler, & Sager, 1993) presented a theory of performance that formalized relations found by Hunter (1983) and Borman et al. (1991) between ability, job knowledge, skill, and job performance. They argued that there are three direct determinants of job performance: declarative knowledge, procedural knowledge and skill, and motivation. Declarative knowledge is knowledge of facts, principles, and procedures—knowledge that might be measured by paper-and-pencil tests, for example. Procedural knowledge and skill is skill in actually doing what should be done; it is the combination of knowing what to do and actually being able to do it. It includes skills such as cognitive skill, psychomotor skill, physical skill, self-management skill, and interpersonal skill and might be measured by simulations and job sample tests.

Motivation is the combination of choice to exert effort, choice of how much effort to exert, and choice of how long to continue to exert effort. Individual differences in personality, ability, and interests are presumed to combine and interact with education, training, and experience to shape declarative knowledge, procedural knowledge and skill, and motivation. Thus, individual differences in cognitive ability and personality should have only indirect effects on performance mediated by knowledge, skill, and motivation.

Motowidlo et al. (1997) presented a theory of individual differences in job performance that also incorporates this idea. The theory divides job performance into task performance and contextual performance (Borman & Motowidlo, 1993) and predicts that cognitive ability is a better predictor of task performance, whereas personality variables such as extraversion, agreeableness, and conscientiousness are better predictors of contextual performance. Knowledge, skills, and work habits are intervening variables in the theory and are learned through experience as basic tendencies in ability and personality interact with external influences in the environment. One set of knowledge, skills, and habits is presumed to directly affect task performance, and a different set of knowledge, skills, and habits is presumed to directly affect contextual performance. Thus, the theory predicts that cognitive ability is associated more with technical knowledge and skill and that personality characteristics are associated more with contextual knowledge and skill, which include some forms of interpersonal knowledge and skill. Borman, Penner, Allen, and Motowidlo (2001) reviewed evidence showing that the personality constructs of conscientiousness and dependability correlate more highly with contextual performance than with task performance.

These empirical and theoretical statements argue that cognitive ability, experience, and conscientiousness affect job performance primarily through their effects on knowledge and skill—especially knowledge. Schmidt and Hunter (1998) summarized research in this area by concluding that ability is related to job performance because more intelligent people learn job knowledge more quickly and more thoroughly, experience is related to job performance because more experienced people have had more opportunity to learn job-relevant knowledge and skill, and conscientiousness is related to job performance because more conscientious people "exert greater efforts and spend more time 'on task'" (p. 272). Thus, if cognitive ability, experience, and conscientiousness are all determinants of job knowledge and skill, three different causal mechanisms seem to be involved. Capacity for learning is the causal mechanism for effects of ability, opportunity to learn is the causal mechanism for effects of experience, and motivation to learn is the casual mechanism for effects of conscientiousness.

Causal mechanisms associated with ability, experience, and conscientiousness are implicated in the acquisition and retention of all kinds of knowledge and skill. However, another causal mechanism that involves interpersonally oriented personality factors may be associated only with knowledge and skill that reflect patterns of behavior consistent with the personality factors. This causal mechanism involves a match between knowledge content and interpersonally oriented personality factors. When the most effective response to a situation is one that represents high levels of a particular personality trait, people high on that trait are more likely to know how to deal with the situation. For instance, highly aggressive people will tend more than will less aggressive people to believe that aggressive responses are often appropriate and effective ways of handling various social situations. Thus, for social situations in which aggressive responses actually are most appropriate or best by some criterion of effectiveness, aggressive people will know better how to handle such situations effectively.

Thus, the fourth mechanism suggested here is knowledge is gained through dispositional fit. It involves three components. First, people harbor beliefs about the best way to handle difficult social situations, and these beliefs tend to be consistent with their basic traits. Second, work situations differ in the degree to which they demand responses that reflect some level of a given trait. Third, when a person's belief about the best response to a situation agrees with the type of response actually required in that situation for maximum effectiveness, the person essentially has more knowledge about how that situation should be handled because his or her beliefs are correct.

This fourth causal mechanism implies that different domains of knowledge and skill (and therefore different behavioral dimensions of job performance) are influenced by different personality characteristics. Thus, to test effects of these personality characteristics on knowledge, skill, and performance, it is necessary to isolate a behaviorally homogeneous dimension of job performance and specific domains of knowledge and skill that are related to it.

Schmit, Motowidlo, DeGroot, Cross, and Kiker (1996) accomplished this task in a study of relations between customer service knowledge, customer service performance, and extraversion in a sample of 160 sales associates in a chain of retail stores. Customer service knowledge was measured through a situational interview that asked sales associates how they would handle various difficult situations with customers, and customer service performance was measured through supervisory ratings. They found that extraversion correlated .32 ($p < .05$) with knowledge and .24 ($p < .05$) with performance. Knowledge correlated .32 ($p < .05$) with performance. Hierarchical regressions testing the incremental validity of extraversion and knowledge showed that knowledge explained 6.6% of the incremental variance in performance after extraversion, but extraversion explained only 1.8% of the incremental variance in performance after knowledge. These results provide preliminary evidence that extraversion is related to customer service knowledge and that much of its effect on customer service performance is mediated by knowledge.

Motowidlo, Brownlee, and Schmit (1998) extended the study by Schmit et al. (1996) by testing a wider array of personality variables and by including measures of ability, experience, and customer service skill in addition to customer service knowledge and performance in another sample of retail store associates. They collected measures of agreeableness, extraversion, conscientiousness, and neuroticism with the NEO. Five Factor Inventory and cognitive ability with the Wonderlic. They measured customer service knowledge through six situational interview questions that asked how the store associates would handle difficult customer situations. Moreover, they measured customer service skill through role-play simulations that required store associates to deal with a difficult customer (role-played by a researcher) in three of the situations described in the interview questions. Finally, they collected ratings of customer service performance from supervisors.

Correlations between relevant variables were submitted to a path analysis in which the order of causal precedence was presumed to be the following: first, personality, ability, and experience as the exogenous variables; second, knowledge; third, skill; and fourth, performance. Results showed significant paths (a) from extraversion, ability, and experience to knowledge; (b) from ability, experience, neuroticism, and knowledge to skill; and (c) from skill to performance. These results confirm findings reported by Schmit et al. (1996) and provide further support for the prediction that extraversion affects job performance (i.e., customer service performance) through its effects on job knowledge.

SUMMARY

Job performance was defined in this chapter as the total expected value to the organization of the discrete behavioral episodes that an individual carries out over a standard period of time. This definition makes allowance for sources of variance that stem from individual differences in stable traits, participation in training and development programs, and exposure to motivational interventions; it also allows for situational factors that directly facilitate or constrain actions that might have positive or negative value for the organization. It does not, however, make allowance for effects of other types of situational factors that affect only organizationally relevant outcomes without affecting performance behaviors that are also partial causes of such outcomes. Thus, this definition offers a single construct of performance that should be useful for psychological research and practice in the areas of employee selection, training, motivation, and the management of situational opportunities and constraints.

Besides allowing the performance construct to be broken down into different sources of variance corresponding to different strategies for organizational intervention, the definition also allows the performance domain to be divided into different behaviorally homogeneous categories or dimensions. The performance literature includes examples of very different bases for identifying interesting and important behavioral dimensions of performance, such as manifest behavioral content (Campbell, 1990), organizationally relevant consequences (Borman & Motowidlo, 1993), motivational antecedents (Organ, 1988; Sackett, 2002), or other antecedents such as ability and personality traits (Viswesvaran et al., 1996). No single taxonomic structure is likely to prove best for all purposes, and the performance definition presented here does not favor any one over others—provided they can identify differences between behavioral episodes in the performance domain.

Empirical and theoretical reports in the performance literature are converging on an overall model of performance that identifies variables such as knowledge, skill, motivation, and habits as direct determinants of the expected value of an individual's behaviors over time. Knowledge, skill, and habits are presumably jointly determined by individual differences in stable traits and by training and development opportunities. Motivation is presumably jointly influenced by stable traits, by situational factors, and perhaps by training and development opportunities as well.

If ability, experience, and conscientiousness affect job performance through their effects on job knowledge, the mechanisms through which this happens might involve capacity, opportunity, and motivation to learn. A fourth mechanism—knowledge through dispositional fit—might explain how some interpersonally oriented personality characteristics such as extraversion affect relevant behavioral dimensions of job performance through their effects on relevant types of job knowledge. This idea implies that effects of at least some stable traits on job performance can only become fully understood when specific types of knowledge and specific relevant behavioral dimensions of job performance are identified.

More generally, identifying behaviorally homogeneous dimensions of job performance makes it possible to identify traits that might be differentially correlated with different parts of the overall performance domain (e.g., Borman et al., 2001; Campbell, 1990; Viswesvaran & Ones, 2000). But it also makes it possible to study potentially important differences in motivation and learning processes that might govern different parts of the performance domain and to study different kinds of situational opportunities and constraints that affect performance behavior as well. In sum, defining job performance according to the expected value of behavior and identifying behaviorally homogeneous dimensions of performance lets I/O psychologists explore the possibility that many of the antecedents of performance might vary across different behavioral dimensions and that psychological processes that involve stable individual differences, learning, motivation, and situational constraints might be different for different behavioral dimensions of performance.

REFERENCES

Andersson, L. M., & Pearson, C. M. (1999). Tit for tat? The spiraling effect of incivility in the workplace. *Academy of Management Review, 24,* 452–471.

Austin, J. T., Humphreys, L. G., & Hulin, C. L. (1989). Another view of dynamic criteria: A critical reanalysis of Barrett, Caldwell, and Alexander. *Personnel Psychology, 42,* 583–596.

Austin, J. T., & Villanova, P. (1992). The criterion problem: 1917–1992. *Journal of Applied Psychology, 77,* 836–874.

Barrett, G. V., Caldwell, M. S., & Alexander, R. A. (1985). The concept of dynamic criteria: A critical reanalysis. *Personnel Psychology, 38,* 41–56.

Borman, W. C. (1991). Job behavior, performance, and effectiveness. In M. D. Dunnette & L. M. Hough (Eds.), *Handbook of industrial and organizational psychology* (2nd ed., Vol. 2, pp. 271–326). Palo Alto, CA: Consulting Psychologists Press.

Borman, W. C., Buck, D. E., Hanson, M. A., Motowidlo, S. J., Stark, S., & Drasgow, F. (2001). An examination of the comparative reliability, validity, and accuracy of performance ratings made using computerized adaptive rating scales. *Journal of Applied Psychology, 86,* 965–973.

Borman, W. C., & Motowidlo, S. J. (1993). Expanding the criterion domain to include elements of contextual performance. In N. Schmitt & W. C. Borman (Eds.), *Personnel selection in organizations* (pp. 71–98). San Francisco: Jossey-Bass.

Borman, W. C., Motowidlo, S. J., & Hanser, L. M. (1983). *A model of individual performance effectiveness: Thoughts about expanding the criterion space.* Symposium presented at the meeting of the American Psychological Association, Anaheim, CA.

Borman, W. C., Penner, L. A., Allen, T. D., & Motowidlo, S. J. (2001). Personality predictors of citizenship performance. *International Journal of Selection and Assessment, 9,* 52–69.

Borman, W. C., White, L. A., Pulakos, E. D., & Oppler, S. H. (1991). Models of supervisory job performance ratings. *Journal of Applied Psychology, 76,* 863–872.

Brief, A. P., & Motowidlo, S. J. (1986). Prosocial organizational behaviors. *Academy of Management Review, 11,* 710–725.

Campbell, J. P. (1990). Modeling the performance prediction problem in industrial and organizational psychology. In M. D. Dunnette & L. M. Hough (Eds.), *Handbook of industrial and organizational psychology* (2nd ed., Vol. 1, pp. 687–732). Palo Alto, CA: Consulting Psychologists Press.

Campbell, J. P., Gasser, M. B., & Oswald, F. L. (1996). The substantive nature of job performance variability. In K. R. Murphy (Ed.), *Individual differences and behavior in organizations* (pp. 258–299). San Francisco: Jossey-Bass.

Campbell, J. P., McCloy, R. A., Oppler, S. H., & Sager, C. E. (1993). A theory of performance. In N. Schmitt & W. C. Borman (Eds.), *Personnel in organizations* (pp. 35–70). San Francisco: Jossey-Bass.

Coleman, V. I., & Borman, W. C. (2000). Investigating the underlying structure of the citizenship performance domain. *Human Resource Management Review, 10,* 25–44.

Dunnette, M. D., & Motowidlo, S. J. (1976). *Police selection and career assessment.* Washington, DC: U.S. Government Printing Office.

Flanagan, J. C. (1954). The critical incident technique. *Psychological Bulletin, 51,* 327–358.

Gruys, M. L. (1999). *The dimensionality of deviant employee performance in the workplace.* Unpublished doctoral dissertation, Minneapolis, MN: University of Minnesota.

Hofmann, D. A., Jacobs, R., & Gerras, S. J. (1992). Mapping individual performance over time. *Journal of Applied Psychology, 77,* 185–195.

Hunter, J. E. (1983). A causal analysis of cognitive ability, job knowledge, job performance, and supervisory ratings. In F. Landy, S. Zedeck, & J. Cleveland (Eds.), *Performance measurement and theory* (pp. 257–266). Hillsdale, NJ: Erlbaum.

Kane, J. S. (1986). Performance distribution assessment. In R. A. Berk (Ed.), *Performance assessment: Methods and applications* (pp. 237–273). Baltimore: Johns Hopkins University Press.

Kidwell, R. E., & Bennett, N. B. (1993). Employee propensity to withhold effort: A conceptual model to intersect three avenues of research. *Academy of Management Review, 18,* 429–456.

Law, K. S., Wong, C. S., & Mobley, W. H. (1998). Toward a taxonomy of multidimensional constructs. *Academy of Management Review, 23,* 741–755.

LePine, J. A., Erez, A., & Johnson, D. E. (2002). The nature and dimensionality of organizational citizenship behavior: A critical review and meta-analysis. *Journal of Applied Psychology, 87,* 52–65.

McCormick, E. J. (1979). *Job analysis.* New York: AMACOM.

Motowidlo, S. J., Borman, W. C., & Schmit, M. J. (1997). A theory of individual differences in task and contextual performance. *Human Performance, 10,* 71–83.

Motowidlo, S. J., Brownlee, A. L., & Schmit, M. J. (1998, April). *Relations between individual differences in personality, ability, and experience and knowledge, skill, and performance in servicing retail customers.* Paper presented at the meeting of the Society for Industrial and Organizational Psychology, Dallas, TX.

Newtson, D. (1973). Attribution and the unit of perception of ongoing behavior. *Journal of Personality and Social Psychology, 28,* 28–38.

Newtson, D., Engquist, G., & Bois, J. (1977). The objective basis of behavior units. *Journal of Personality and Social Psychology, 35,* 847–862.

Organ, D. W. (1988). *Organizational citizenship behavior: The good soldier syndrome.* Lexington, MA: Lexington Books.

Organ, D. W. (1997). Organizational citizenship behavior: It's construct clean-up time. *Human Performance, 10,* 85–97.

Pearson, C. M., Andersson, L. M., & Porath, C. L. (2000). Assessing and attacking workplace civility. *Organizational Dynamics, 29,* 123–137.

Ployhart, R. E., & Hakel, M. D. (1998). The substantive nature of performance variability: Predicting interindividual differences in intraindividual performance. *Personnel Psychology, 51,* 859–901.

Podsakoff, P. M., & MacKenzie, S. B. (1997). The impact of organizational citizenship behavior on organizational performance: A review and suggestions for further research. *Human Performance, 10,* 133–151.

Podsakoff, P. M., MacKenzie, S. B., Moorman, R. H., & Fetter, R. (1990). Transformational leader behaviors and their effects on followers' trust in leader, satisfaction, and organizational citizenship behaviors. *Leadership Quarterly, 1,* 107–142.

Robinson, S. L., & Bennett, R. J. (1995). A typology of deviant workplace behaviors: A multidimensional scaling study. *Academy of Management Journal, 38,* 555–572.

Robinson, S. L., & O'Leary-Kelly, A. M. (1998). Monkey see, monkey do: The influence of work groups on the antisocial behavior of employees. *Academy of Management Journal, 41,* 658–672.

Sackett, P. R. (2002). The structure of counterproductive work behaviors: Dimensionality and relationships with facets of job performance. *International Journal of Selection and Assessment, 10,* 5–11.

Sackett, P. R., Zedeck, S., & Fogli, L. (1988). Relations between measures of typical and maximum job performance. *Journal of Applied Psychology, 73,* 482–486.

Schmidt, F. L., & Hunter, J. E. (1992). Development of a causal model of processes determining job performance. *Current Directions in Psychological Science, 1,* 84–92.

Schmidt, F. L., & Hunter, J. E. (1998). The validity and utility of selection methods in personnel psychology: Practical and theoretical implications of 85 years of research findings. *Psychological Bulletin, 124,* 262–274.

Schmidt, F. L., Hunter, J. E., & Outerbridge, A. N. (1986). Impact of job experience and ability on job knowledge, work sample performance, and supervisory ratings of job performance. *Journal of Applied Psychology, 71,* 432–439.

Schmit, M. C., Motowidlo, S. J., DeGroot, T., Cross, T., & Kiker, D. S. (1996, April). *Explaining the relationship between personality and job performance.* Paper presented at the meeting of the Society for Industrial and Organizational Psychology, San Diego, CA.

Smith, C. A., Organ, D. W., & Near, J. P. (1983). Organizational citizenship behavior: Its nature and antecedents. *Journal of Applied Psychology, 68,* 653–663.

Van Dyne, L., Cummings, L. L., & Parks, J. M. (1995). Extra-role behaviors: In pursuit of construct and definitional clarity (a bridge over muddied waters). *Research in Organizational Behavior, 17,* 215–285.

Viswesvaran, C., & Ones, D. S. (2000). Perspectives on models of job performance. *International Journal of Selection and Assessment, 8,* 216–226.

Viswesvaran, C., Schmidt, F., & Ones, D. S. (1996, April). *Modeling job performance: Is there a general factor?* Poster presented at the eleventh annual meeting of the Society for Industrial and Organizational Psychology, San Diego, CA.

Vroom, V. H. (1964). *Work and motivation.* New York: Wiley.

CHAPTER 4

Recruitment Research in the Twenty-First Century

SARA L. RYNES AND DANIEL M. CABLE

The study of recruitment as an academic pursuit has increased dramatically over the past 25 years. In the first edition of the *Handbook of Industrial & Organizational Psychology,* the topic of recruitment filled less than a page (Guion, 1976). By the second edition, it had expanded to 45 pages (Rynes, 1991).

Despite all the research activity between 1976 and 1991, the substantive findings produced by these efforts were rather modest. For example, research consistently showed that certain recruiter characteristics were reliably associated with applicant impressions of recruiter effectiveness. However, these impressions did not seem to matter to applicants' actual job choices (Taylor & Bergmann, 1987)—particularly after vacancy characteristics (e.g., pay) were taken into account (Rynes & Miller, 1983). Similarly, research on recruitment sources suggested that modest improvements in employee retention might be obtained by recruiting primarily through informal sources, particularly employee referrals. However, research on other posthire outcomes (e.g., performance) showed no consistent patterns, and almost no research examined the effect of sources on prehire outcomes such as quality of the applicant pool or job acceptance rates.

In addition to these modest empirical findings, pre-1990s recruitment research was also restricted by a narrow range of research questions and an almost exclusive concentration on the individual level of analysis. In combination, these features left many of the most important questions about recruitment unanswered—such as whether recruitment effectiveness can be improved through recruiter selection or training, how to attract applicant populations other than graduating college students, and whether recruitment practices that work for high-paying, high-status firms also work for firms with the opposite characteristics.

The purpose of this chapter is to assess the progress that has been made since publication of the last handbook and to make recommendations for the next decade of recruitment research. We organize our review around the model for future recruitment research suggested by Rynes in the 1991 *Handbook* (reproduced here in Figure 4.1). Generally speaking, this model suggested that future researchers place increased emphasis on the broader context in which recruitment occurs, the interdependencies between different phases of the recruitment process, and the potential trade-offs between quantity and quality in recruitment outcomes.

RECRUITMENT CONTEXT

Prior to the 1990s, the vast majority of recruitment research had been conducted at the individual level of analysis, either in campus placement offices or within the confines of a single

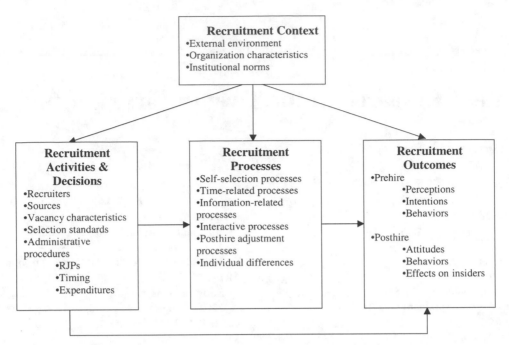

Figure 4.1 Model for future recruitment research. From Rynes (1991, p. 430).

organization. As a result, considerable leaps of faith were required in order to translate research findings into recommendations for organizational recruitment. Although research at individual or dyadic levels can provide clues about possible higher-level processes and outcomes, it cannot be assumed that phenomena at the microlevel translate directly into similar effects at the organizational level (Klein, Dansereau, & Hall, 1994; Rousseau, 1985). Thus, moving to higher levels of analysis is necessary in order to provide relevant answers to many important recruitment and staffing questions (Rynes & Barber, 1990; Schneider, Smith, & Sipe, 2000; Taylor & Collins, 2000).

For these reasons, Rynes (1991) recommended that future research focus more on the *context* in which recruitment occurs. Although Figure 4.1 includes three contextual features presumed to be relevant to recruitment, only one—organizational characteristics—has received sustained attention over the past decade.

Organizational characteristics are important to the study of recruitment for several reasons. First, many applicants are at least as concerned about picking the right *organization* as about choosing the right *job*. For example, previous research has shown that organizational characteristics such as location, size, or industry are sometimes used as prescreens before specific vacancy characteristics are ever considered (e.g., Barber & Roehling, 1993; Turban, Campion, & Eyring, 1995). Second, the human resource (HR) strategy literature has shown that organizations tend to evolve relatively unique

bundles of HR practices that can have important influences on the overall climate of an organization as well as on the way specific job attributes (such as pay) are administered and interpreted (e.g., Delery & Doty, 1996; Schuler & Jackson, 1987). Third, it is not at all clear that recruitment practices that are effective for some types of organizations (e.g., the use of informal recruitment sources and stock options by high-growth companies) will be equally effective when used by organizations with different characteristics.

Fortunately, psychologists' knowledge of recruitment practices at the organizational level has improved somewhat over the past decade. Three different types of studies have contributed to our knowledge. First, a limited number of studies have demonstrated that differences in organizational characteristics are reliably associated with differences in recruitment practices. Second, studies from the strategic HR literature have suggested that differences in HR practices (including recruitment) are associated with reliable differences in organizational performance. Third, some research has examined how a number of organization-level characteristics are associated with applicant reactions and intentions.

Turning to the first issue, Barber, Wesson, Roberson, and Taylor (1999) found that larger organizations were more likely than were smaller ones to use dedicated HR staff for recruitment, provide training for recruiters, initiate recruitment further in advance of hiring, allow applicants more time to accept positions, use campus placement offices, and use more screening devices (particularly drug tests). In addition,

Rynes, Orlitzky, and Bretz (1997) found differences in the extent to which organizations recruit new college graduates versus experienced workers. Specifically, organizations recruited larger proportions of experienced workers (rather than new graduates) to the extent that they were growing rapidly and had short-term staffing strategies, older workforces, and less dynamic business environments.

Of course, simply knowing that different types of organizations pursue different kinds of recruitment practices does not indicate whether certain practices are generally more effective than others or (alternatively) whether effectiveness depends on fit with other features of the environment. A number of studies have examined this question with respect to HR practices in general, but none has focused closely on organizational recruitment.

For example, Huselid (1995) showed that two factors representing high-performance HR practices were associated with organizational profitability 1 year later. However, the only recruitment-related variable in this study was the organizational selection ratio, which may not be a recruitment practice at all, but rather a proxy for (or outcome of) company visibility or reputation. Moreover, the Huselid study did not investigate the independent effects of the selection ratio, but rather combined it with three other items into an employee motivation factor. In contrast, Delaney and Huselid (1996) did examine the separate effects of a number of HR practices (including selection ratios) on managerial perceptions of organizational performance. However, they found no effects for selection ratio. Finally, Terpstra and Rozell (1993) found a correlation between organizational profits and evaluation of recruitment source effectiveness, although causal interpretation is ambiguous. Thus, although the literature on linkages between general HR practices and organizational performance has grown rapidly in recent years, it is fair to say that recruitment practices have not figured prominently in this body of work.

The third contribution to organization-level research comes from studies that have examined the relationships between organization-level characteristics (particularly image or reputation) and applicant attraction. Two early studies (Gatewood, Gowan, & Lautenschlager, 1993, and Turban & Greening, 1996) showed that corporate image was associated with student perceptions of organizational attractiveness and propensity to apply for jobs. However, these findings still left three important questions: (a) What are the components of organizational image, (b) to what extent can this image be modified in the eyes of job seekers, and (c) *why* does image matter to job seekers?

Turning to the first question, Gatewood and colleagues (1993) examined two kinds of image: overall corporate image (i.e., reactions to company name alone) and recruitment image (reactions to corporate employment advertisements). These two measures were found to correlate moderately with one another ($r = .45$), as well as heavily with company familiarity to applicants ($r = .95$ for overall image and $r = .51$ for recruitment image). In addition, Gatewood et al. applied multidimensional scaling to students' reactions to actual job advertisements. This analysis suggested that there were three dimensions to corporate recruiting image: total information in the advertisement, emphasis on telecommunications and technology, and general information about the company. Only the first of these dimensions was found to correlate significantly ($r = .96$) with overall recruitment image, suggesting that recruitment image may be bolstered by the provision of more information in advertisements.

Turban and Greening (1996) also found that student assessments of corporate reputation were rather closely associated with familiarity. Specifically, they reported that measures of organizational familiarity obtained from one sample of college students correlated .52 with reputation and .49 with organizational attractiveness in other student samples. In addition, they assessed the extent to which corporate social performance (CSP) was associated with college seniors' ratings of company reputation and attractiveness. Correlations ranging from .15 to .25 were found between student assessments of company reputation and the CSP dimensions (e.g., community and employee relations). Both reputation and attractiveness as an employer were also correlated with organizational profitability ($r = .25$ and .23, respectively). After controlling for company assets and profitability, CSP explained an additional 7% of the variance in student assessments of company attractiveness.

Cable and Graham (2000) used three different methodologies to assess the predictors of corporate reputation among job seekers. First, using verbal protocol analysis of student reactions to job descriptions, they found four topics that stimulated the most discussion about reputation: industry, opportunities for growth, organizational culture, and company familiarity. Second, policy capturing confirmed the effect of these variables on reputation, but also showed that profitability ($\beta = .26$) and pay level ($\beta = .16$) affected reputation judgments. Finally, they conducted a two-stage field survey, separated by 3 weeks. In the first phase, subjects evaluated six organizations with respect to their familiarity, perceived career opportunities, industry, organizational culture, profitability, and pay level. Three weeks later, subjects gave overall reputational assessments for the six companies. Simple correlations and regressions of reputation measures on earlier dimensional assessments produced the following results: profitability ($r = .73$, $\beta = .49$), industry

($r = .55$, $\beta = .16$), and familiarity ($r = .49$, $\beta = .11$). Two other variables that had large simple correlations—opportunities for growth ($r = .55$) and organizational culture ($r = .59$)—had almost no association with reputation ($\beta = .08$ and .04, respectively) after profitability, industry, and familiarity were taken into account.

The second unanswered question—whether firms can change their recruitment images—has not been directly assessed via field experiments. However, the preceding studies seem to suggest that the most feasible route for improving corporate recruitment image may be to increase applicant familiarity by providing more information. For example, Gatewood et al. (1993) found that recruitment image was strongly related ($r = .96$) to the total amount of information provided in employment advertisements, and that recruitment image explained more variance in students' self-reported propensities to apply than did overall corporate reputation. Similarly, Turban and Greening (1996) found that student familiarity was higher for companies that recruited on campus, provided materials to the campus placement office, or both. Finally, Cable, Aiman-Smith, Mulvey, and Edwards (2000) showed that companies' recruitment images can be affected not only by recruitment advertisements, but also by product or service advertisements. For example, students who were most influenced by product advertising tended to overestimate the amount of risk-taking in the corporate culture and to underestimate the degree of rules orientation.

Thus, previous results suggest that application behaviors may be positively influenced by mere provision of greater information. However, there are at least three important caveats to this tentative conclusion. First, none of the studies has examined actual application behaviors, but rather perceptions of organizations or self-reported propensities to apply for jobs. Second, there have been no field experiments to demonstrate the effects of modified advertisements on quantity or quality of applications to specific, real organizations. Third, most of the research on organizational image has restricted itself to organizations that are already familiar to most people. This may be an important boundary condition because it is not clear that unknown organizations will reap the same benefits from advertising as do firms that are already familiar to applicants (Barber, 1998). Indeed, a recent study by Cable and Turban (in press) showed that the amount of information that individuals retained from recruitment advertisements was moderately correlated ($r = .22$) with their familiarity with the organization to begin with.

Finally, few studies have sought to determine *why* organizational image or reputation might influence application decisions. However, several reasons for expecting such a linkage have been advanced. First, social identity theory

(Ashforth & Mael, 1989) suggests that people seek to associate themselves with organizations that enhance their self-esteem. Thus, job seekers may pursue high-reputation companies to bask in such organizations' reflected glory or to avoid the negative outcomes (e.g., lowered self esteem) incurred from working for employers with a poor image (Ashforth & Kreiner, 1999; Dutton, Dukerich, & Harquail, 1994). Second, a positive reputation may signal that an organization is likely to provide other desirable job attributes, such as high pay and strong opportunities for career growth and development (Rynes, 1991). Finally, a positive reputation may make applicants more receptive to whatever information an organization provides (Barber, 1998).

In the most direct examination of these hypotheses to date, Cable and Turban (in press) observed the reactions of 368 subjects to job postings that manipulated company reputation, pay level, and human resource philosophy. Company reputation was manipulated by producing advertisements for one high- and one low-reputation firm (as assessed by *Fortune* rankings and an independent student sample) in each of four industries. Results suggested that company reputation influenced subjects' perceptions of specific job characteristics (thus supporting signaling theory), as well as their expected pride from becoming an organizational member (supporting social identity theory). In addition, the impact of reputation on application likelihood was partially mediated by perceptions of job characteristics and completely mediated by expected pride from membership. Finally, subjects were willing to pay a premium (in the form of lower salaries) to join companies with positive reputations. This relationship, too, was mediated by the pride that individuals expected to attain through membership.

In summary, the past decade has begun to shed light on the relationships between organizational characteristics, recruitment practices, and applicant attraction. The most important conclusions from this body of research involve the importance of industry, organizational familiarity, and financial profitability to organizational image and also involve the importance of organizational image to applicant attraction. On the other hand, considerable work remains to be done. For example, few definitive recommendations for organizational practice can be offered, although a tentative suggestion to increase information provision, general marketing, and familiarity as ways of improving image can be provided. In addition, almost no research exists to indicate whether certain practices work better in some types of organizations than they do in others. For many of these questions, different types of methodologies (such as field experiments or cross-level surveys) will be required. Because similar methodological issues apply to several of the sections that follow, they are discussed in greater detail later in the chapter.

RECRUITMENT ACTIVITIES AND PRACTICES

Prior to 1990, three aspects of recruitment had received considerable research attention: recruiters, recruitment sources, and realistic job previews (RJPs). However, it was suggested that other recruitment practices were also likely to have an effect on recruitment processes and outcomes—particularly the attractiveness of vacancy characteristics, the stringency of selection standards, and administrative procedures other than RJPs (e.g., recruitment timing and expenditures). Post-1990 research in each of these areas is reviewed in the following sections.

Recruiters

Pre-1991 research on recruiters had clearly established links between applicants' perceptions of recruiter traits (especially positive affect and enthusiasm) and their perceptions of the organization itself (e.g., job attractiveness, treatment of employees). However, nearly all such findings were generated immediately after initial campus interviews, using a single questionnaire to ask about recruiter characteristics, job attractiveness, expectancies of receiving an offer, and intentions of further job pursuit. As such, nearly all findings were subject to concerns about demand characteristics and common method variance.

In addition, there were reasons to doubt the strength and duration of the observed effects. For example, in the only longitudinal recruitment study prior to 1991, Taylor and Bergmann (1987) found that recruiter effects on applicant evaluations vanished after the campus interview stage. Similarly, Rynes and Miller (1983) and Powell (1984) found that recruiter effects faded to insignificance after vacancy characteristics were taken into account. These findings caused Rynes (1991) to conclude that "recruiters probably do not have a large impact on actual job choices" (p. 413).

Much of the recruiter research conducted since 1991 has validated earlier findings. For example, several studies have reconfirmed that there are moderate correlations between applicants' perceptions of recruiter characteristics following initial campus interviews and broader assessments of organizational characteristics (e.g., Goltz & Giannantonio, 1995; Turban & Dougherty, 1992). Similarly, additional research on recruiter demographic characteristics has continued to find weak, conflicting, or nonexistent effects of gender or race on overall applicant impressions (Maurer, Howe, & Lee, 1992; Turban & Dougherty, 1992).

However, a few studies have changed researchers' interpretation of earlier findings or added depth with respect to knowledge of interviewer behaviors and their effects on applicants. For example, a study by Rynes, Bretz, and Gerhart (1991) suggested a role for recruiters in applicants' job search and choice decisions that was somewhat larger than that suggested by the pessimistic conclusion drawn in the earlier *Handbook* chapter. Rynes et al. used structured, longitudinal interviews to discover how job seekers determine whether an organization provides a good fit to their wants and needs. Content analysis of interview responses suggested that although perceived job and organizational attributes were the major determinants of perceived fit, recruiters and other organizational representatives were the second-most important. In addition, recruiters were also associated with *changes* in many job seekers' assessments of fit over time—16 of 41 individuals mentioned recruiters or other corporate representatives as reasons for deciding that an initially favored company was no longer a good fit, whereas an identical number mentioned recruiters as a reason for changing an initial impression of poor fit into a positive one.

Another question that has received attention since the last review is whether—or how—recruiter training affects recruiter behaviors and applicant reactions. Prior to 1991, the only study to include recruiter training as an independent variable found no relationship between training and applicant impressions (Taylor & Bergmann, 1987). Since then, two studies (Connerley, 1997; Stevens, 1998) have addressed the issue in greater detail.

Based on content analysis of 39 tape-recorded campus interviews, Stevens (1998) found distinct differences in the interview behaviors of trained versus untrained recruiters. Specifically, relative to untrained recruiters, trained recruiters were more likely to begin the interview with a preamble, spend less time discussing non-task-related topics, stick more closely to a standard script sequence (establishing rapport, asking questions, taking questions from applicants, disengagement), and asked more screening-oriented questions. In addition, trained recruiters were perceived by applicants to be better prepared and more professional than were untrained recruiters. However, there were no effects on applicants' intentions to accept job offers after preinterview impressions were taken into account (although the small sample size needs to be kept in mind). Connerley (1997) also found that trained recruiters were perceived by applicants to have significantly higher interpersonal effectiveness ($r = .11$) and overall effectiveness ($r = .14$), although she did not test the effects of training on intentions to accept an offer.

Stevens' (1998) finding that trained interviewers tend to ask more screening-oriented questions is interesting in light of previous speculation that applicants may be differentially affected by recruitment- versus selection-oriented interviews (Rynes, 1989). At least two studies have directly addressed this question. In a field study of post-campus-interview reactions, Turban and Dougherty (1992) found that recruiters who focused mostly on recruitment (as opposed to selection) created more positive impressions among applicants and were less likely than were selection-oriented recruiters to be perceived as intimidating. In addition, Barber, Hollenbeck, Tower, and Phillips (1994) and Stevens (1998) found that applicants received and absorbed more information from recruitment-oriented recruiters than from selection- or dual-oriented ones.

Despite these positive effects of recruitment focus on applicant's feelings about recruiters, Turban and Dougherty (1992) found that the *jobs* associated with recruitment-focused interviews tended to be viewed as *less* attractive than they did when recruiters were focused more evenly on recruitment and selection. Similarly, Barber, et al. (1994) found that applicants were less likely to drop out of the applicant pool when recruiters used a combined recruitment-plus-selection approach rather than a recruitment-only approach. Thus, at least two studies (although not Stevens, 1998) suggest that recruiters who do not balance recruitment selling with applicant screening may have the unintended effect of devaluing their vacancies in applicants' eyes.

Finally, Connerley and Rynes (1997) conducted a field survey to determine whether various types of organizational support for recruitment (e.g., preinterview training, recruitment feedback, and rewards) were associated with recruiters' self-perceptions of recruiting effectiveness and applicants' perceptions of recruiter effectiveness. Regression analyses suggested that none of the forms of organizational support influenced recruiters' ($n = 252$) perceptions of their effectiveness. Rather, recruiter self-perceptions of effectiveness were associated most closely with their self-perceptions of interpersonal skills ($\beta = .52$), amount of prior recruitment experience ($\beta = .28$), and self-perceived toughness in screening candidates ($\beta = .13$).

On the applicant side ($n = 1,571$), two organizational support activities were weakly associated with applicants' perceptions of recruiter effectiveness: preinterview support activities ($\beta = .10$) and hours of training ($\beta = .05$). In addition, applicants found recruiters who provided more information to be less effective ($\beta = -.10$), suggesting again that too much of a selling focus may be detrimental to applicant perceptions.

Recruitment Sources

Prior to the last *Handbook,* research on recruitment sources had focused almost exclusively on relationships between sources and posthire outcomes, particularly performance and turnover. The most widely reported finding at that time was that employees recruited through informal sources—particularly referrals—appeared to have higher rates of job survival. In contrast, findings with respect to performance and other dependent variables were highly variable across studies.

Since the last *Handbook,* one study (Kirnan, Farley, & Geisinger, 1989) has supported the finding of higher job survival rates for employees recruited through informal sources. However, two other studies (Werbel & Landau, 1996; Williams, Labig, & Stone, 1993) found no differences between recruitment source and turnover.

With respect to job performance, recent studies have been just as mixed as earlier research. For example, Kirnan et al. (1989) found no relationship between recruitment source and insurance sales performance, and Williams et al. (1993) found no relationships between source and nursing performance. On the other hand, Blau (1990) reported higher performance among bank tellers hired through direct application, whereas Werbel and Landau (1996) found that insurance agents recruited through college placement were higher performers than were those hired through newspaper ads.

Also unresolved at the time of the last *Handbook* were the underlying mechanisms behind source-outcome relationships (where observed). Two potential explanations had been offered: (a) the *realistic information* hypothesis, which proposes that some sources provide more or better information to applicants, and (b) the *prescreening* or *individual differences* hypothesis, which suggests that different sources attract applicants with differing qualifications and other outcome-related attributes.

Some recent source research has been devoted primarily to testing these two hypotheses. In general, this research suggests that different sources indeed produce applicants with different individual characteristics, job-related information, or both. For example, Kirnan et al. (1989) found that referrals produced applicants with higher scores on an empirically validated application blank. They also found that women and minorities were disproportionately attracted through formal sources, whereas White males had disproportionate access to referrals. Both Williams et al. (1993) and Griffeth, Hom, Fink, and Cohen (1997) found that different recruitment sources produced nursing applicants with both differing qualifications and different degrees of knowledge about the job. Blau (1990) found that walk-in bank tellers had ability scores higher than those of applicants from other sources and that referrals had more realistic information about the job. Werbel and Landau (1996) found that insurance agents hired through college placement offices were younger and better educated than were those from other sources and that referrals had less realistic expectations than did walk-ins or agency hires.

Finally, Vecchio (1995) reported that different sources systematically produce applicants with different racial, gender, educational, and income characteristics.

Although most studies have found at least some source-related differences in applicant characteristics, information, or both, the specific nature of those relationships tends to vary widely across studies. In addition, although such differences are consistent with hypotheses that realism or individual differences mediate observed relationships between sources and posthire outcomes, their mere existence is not sufficient to establish intermediary processes. Rather, direct tests of mediation are necessary.

Recent tests of mediation have not been strongly supportive of either the individual differences or the realistic information hypothesis. For example, neither Werbel and Landau (1996) nor Williams et al. (1993) found any support for mediating effects of qualifications and prehire knowledge on posthire outcomes. Moreover, although Vecchio (1995) did not directly test for mediator effects, he did find that source-related differences in affective outcomes remained even after he controlled for individual differences. Griffeth et al. (1997) did find a mediating effect of realism on posthire affective outcomes but did not assess job performance.

Finally, at least two studies have found that source-related individual differences tend to be larger within applicant pools than they are among new hires (Kirnan et al., 1989; Williams et al., 1993). This finding suggests that observed source effects are likely to be attenuated posthire, presumably because the best individuals are hired from within each source. As a result, both Kirnan et al. (1989) and Williams et al. (1993) caution against placing too much emphasis on source per se as a predictor of posthire outcomes.

Overall, the relatively weak and inconsistent findings for source-outcome processes and relationships have led researchers to recommend that future source research focus more on prehire outcomes (Barber, 1998; Rynes, 1991; Werbel & Landau, 1996; Williams et al., 1993). An example of such research is provided by Kirnan et al. (1989), who found that informal sources produced higher job offer and acceptance rates than did formal sources.

The recent discovery of complexities in source usage suggests that source research may have to become more sophisticated if reliable effects are to be detected. For example, many applicants appear to use multiple sources to identify their future employers (Vecchio, 1995), and results can vary widely depending on how multiple-source cases are coded or classified (Williams et al., 1993). In addition, the same source can be used in very different ways. For example, companies can passively wait for individuals to apply via their Web sites, or they can actively solicit applications by raiding internal company directories or responding immediately to hits from applicants at targeted universities or competing employers.

These considerations suggest that prior operationalizations of source (usually *1* for the primary source and *0* for all others) have probably been seriously deficient. What may be more important than the source per se is how much support and information accompanies source usage or the extent to which a source embeds prescreening on desired applicant characteristics. Overall, the weak and inconsistent prior results combined with the considerable variance in how different firms use the same source, suggest that little progress will be made by conducting research as usual.

Administrative Procedures

As with recruiters, administrative practices are believed to be capable of affecting job applicants in one of two ways: Either they signal something about the company's broader characteristics (e.g., efficiency, profitability), or they influence applicants' expectations of receiving job offers (Rynes, Heneman, & Schwab, 1980). At the time of the last *Handbook,* the study of administrative practices had been overwhelmingly dominated by studies of RJPs. Since that time, there has been a marked drop-off in RJP studies and a considerable increase in studies of applicant reactions to affirmative action policies and employer selection procedures.

Realistic Job Previews

Most early RJP research assessed the effects of RJPs on posthire outcomes. This approach was seriously deficient from a recruitment perspective, given the possibility of adverse applicant self-selection in the face of more (and usually more negative) information. Thus, Rynes (1991) recommended that subsequent RJP research focus more explicitly on applicant attraction. In addition, it was suggested that future research pinpoint the *types* of applicants most strongly affected by RJPs because it seemed plausible that the applicants most likely to withdraw on the basis of negative information would be those with the most options (e.g., Rynes et al., 1991).

As far as we know, only one study (Bretz & Judge, 1998) has attempted to investigate this question, using both experimental and field methodologies. However, in the experimental portion, examination of the experimental stimuli suggests that the authors actually manipulated the *attractiveness* of job attributes (e.g., "expectations are high but will be recognized when these expectations are met" vs. "expectations are high, and you can expect to be criticized for poor performance but seldom praised for good performance," p. 332) rather than the realism of information provided about a given attribute. A slightly different type of confound applies to the field portion of this research, in that applicants were simply asked to report how much negative information they had received about each company early in the recruitment process. *Negative information received* would be expected to be a function of at least two properties: actual job and organizational attractiveness and degree of honesty or accuracy in portraying those attributes. As such, the study does not appear to be a true test of the relationships between realism, applicant attraction, and applicant characteristics.

A recent meta-analysis by Phillips (1998) found an average correlation of $-.03$ between RJPs and applicant withdrawal. Although this relationship was statistically significant due to the large number of subjects involved ($N = 6,450$), it is clearly not a large effect. Nevertheless, these results do suggest that there are not likely to be large withdrawals from recruitment pools as a consequence of more realistic information. With respect to other outcomes, Phillips reported that RJPs correlated $-.06$ with voluntary turnover, $-.05$ with all types of turnover, $-.01$ with job satisfaction, $.01$ with organizational commitment, and $.05$ with job performance. Given these modest findings, we do not see RJPs as a major priority for future recruitment research.

Affirmative Action

A number of general patterns have begun to emerge from recent research on applicant reactions to various types of affirmative action (AA) policies (for a more complete review, see Kravitz et al., 1997). Perhaps the most consistent (though hardly surprising) finding from this research is that applicant reactions to AA tend to depend on one's demographic status. Specifically, African Americans tend to have the most favorable views toward AA, followed by women and to a lesser extent, Hispanics (e.g., Barber & Roehling, 1993; Highhouse, Stierwalt, Bachiochi, Elder, & Fisher, 1999; Kravitz & Klineberg, 2000; Truxillo & Bauer, 1999). In short, AA is most popular with likely beneficiaries and least popular with White males. It should be noted, however, that although reactions to AA tend to vary by gender and ethnicity, reactions to discriminatory questions (e.g., about age, marital status, gender, or ethnicity) appear to be consistently negative (Saks, Leck, & Saunders, 1995).

Ethnic differences in reactions to AA have been explained in terms of both self-interest and justice theories, with perceived unfairness mediating many of the observed relationships between ethnicity and applicant reactions (Heilman, McCullough, & Gilbert, 1996; Kravitz & Klineberg, 2000).

Other individual-level mediators of reactions to AA include perceptions of workplace discrimination, personal experiences with discrimination, and political orientation—especially among Whites (Kravitz & Klineberg, 2000).

Minimizing negative reactions to AA policies is very important because such reactions have been associated with negative outcomes for both beneficiaries and nonbeneficiaries alike (at least in experimental research). For example, experimental beneficiaries of AA have been found to suffer from lower self-esteem (Heilman, Lucas, & Kaplow, 1990) and reduced perceptions of competence by others (Heilman, Block, & Lucas, 1992), while nonbeneficiaries have reported reduced enthusiasm for work, diminished organizational attractiveness, and a reduction in prosocial behaviors (e.g., Heilman et al., 1996; Truxillo & Bauer, 1999).

Because of these potentially negative outcomes, it is useful to know whether reactions to AA depend on the specific types of plans utilized as well as the rationalizations for employing them. On this issue, Whites have been found to react less negatively to tie-breaker plans than to preferential-treatment AA plans, whereas Blacks and Hispanics react in the opposite fashion (Kravitz & Klineberg, 2000). AA also appears to raise fewer concerns when merit is emphasized as central to the decision-making process (Heilman, Battle, Keller, & Lee, 1998) and when various rationales are provided for AA adoption (e.g., the need to make up for past discrimination or to account for test score unreliability; Heilman et al., 1996; Truxillo & Bauer, 1999).

Another finding is that in the absence of explicit information about a company's selection procedures, nonbeneficiaries of AA (i.e., White males) tend to make unfavorable assumptions about the fairness of selection procedures (e.g., to assume that they are more qualified than are beneficiaries or that merit was not considered in the decision; Heilman et al., 1996; Heilman et al., 1998). Thus, researchers recommend that employers think carefully about the messages they wish to transmit concerning their AA programs and that they not leave interpretation to applicant imaginations (Kravitz & Klineberg, 2000; Truxillo & Bauer, 1999).

Selection Procedures

Since publication of the last *Handbook,* there has been a dramatic increase in research examining applicant reactions to a wide variety of selection procedures (e.g., Campion, Palmer, & Campion, 1997; Murphy, Thornton, & Prue, 1991; Sackett & Wanek, 1996). However, by far the most research has been conducted on reactions to cognitive ability tests—often with a secondary purpose of determining whether there are racial differences in such reactions (e.g., Chan & Schmitt, 1997). A recent review of this literature located at least 40 such studies conducted between 1985 and 1999 (Ryan & Ployhart, 2000).

The most common theoretical framework for analyzing applicant reactions has been justice theory (e.g., Gilliland, 1993). Studies conducted in this tradition have (not surprisingly) found substantial correlations between perceived fairness of selection procedures, overall perceptions of the selection process, and perceived organizational attractiveness. However, most of these studies have employed cross-sectional research designs and used questionnaires with strong demand characteristics (e.g., self-report items concerning perceived justice of selection procedures followed by items concerning organizational attractiveness). Moreover, available evidence suggests that these differences have little impact on applicant behaviors such as withdrawal from the selection process or rejection of job offers (e.g., Ryan, Sacco, McFarland, & Kriska, 2000).

In combination, previous findings and the characteristics of previous research raise serious questions about how much additional effort to invest in this area. Although Ryan and Ployhart (2000) make a number of well-reasoned suggestions for future research, they argue (and we agree) that the top priority must be to show that any of these differences in perceived justice are important enough to affect any applicant behaviors of practical interest. Without such evidence, little is likely to be gained from further examinations of correlations between race, perceived justice, and organizational attractiveness.

Vacancy Characteristics

Because vacancy characteristics such as pay and benefits are important to applicants and potentially manipulable by employers, Rynes (1991) argued that they should be studied more directly as part of recruitment research. Several studies responded to this call. For example, Barber and Roehling (1993) used verbal protocol analysis to examine which of 10 attributes were attended to most heavily in hypothetical decisions to apply to companies. Results showed that participants paid the most attention to location, salary, benefits, and attributes that were extreme or unusual in some way.

Cable and Judge (1994) used policy capturing to examine students' reactions to multiple pay and benefits preferences. In general, they found that participants preferred high pay levels to low ones, individually based pay to team-based pay, fixed pay to variable pay, and flexible benefits to fixed. However, they also found that these preferences were stronger for some types of individuals than for others. For example, materialistic applicants placed greater emphasis on pay level than did low materialists, and individuals with high self-efficacy placed greater value on individualistic pay than did those with low self-efficacy.

Trank, Rynes, and Bretz (2002) used attribute importance ratings to determine whether college students with different levels of academic achievement (test scores and grade point average or GPA) and social achievement (leadership and extracurricular activities) place differential importance on various job and organizational characteristics. Results suggest that in general, students with high ability and achievement place relatively greater importance on interesting and challenging work than do other students. However, on many other attributes, students with high *academic* achievement appeared to have different preference patterns from those with high *social* achievement. For example, students with high social achievement placed *more* importance on high pay level than did low achievers, whereas those with high academic achievement placed *less* importance on this factor. More generally, high social achievers placed more importance on extrinsic rewards, expected to spend less time with their first employer, and expressed stronger tendencies toward self-employment than did high academic achievers. Finally, high achievers of both types were less attracted to job rotation and cross-functional career paths than were low achievers.

Konrad and colleagues (Konrad, Corrigall, Lieb, & Ritchie, 2000; Konrad, Ritchie, Lieb, & Corrigall, 2000) conducted two meta-analyses of gender differences in job attribute preferences. One meta-analysis included 31 studies of managers and business students, whereas the other examined 242 samples from a broad range of ages and settings. Although some gender differences in attribute preferences were observed, the authors concluded that these differences were not large enough to be important determinants of women's lower employment and earnings status.

In the only field study of vacancy characteristics and applicant attraction over the past decade, Williams and Dreher (1992) examined a variety of relationships between the compensation systems of 352 banks and their relative success in applicant attraction. As would be expected, pay levels were positively related to job acceptance rates. However, contrary to expectations, high pay levels were *positively* associated with the time required to fill vacancies and not at all associated with applicant pool size. Further investigation of these surprising results suggested that the banks tended to use pay in reactive fashion, such that higher pay or benefit levels often reflected *prior* difficulties in attracting workers. Thus, rather than treating pay and benefit levels as strategic decisions that persist over time, the organizations in that study treated them as attributes to be tinkered with in response to ad hoc changes in labor supply.

Although many details remain to be discovered, it seems quite safe to conclude that pay level is at least moderately important in most applicants' job choices. In addition, other forms of pay (e.g., contingent pay increases, benefits) are also important—perhaps increasingly so as they become more variable across employers (Heneman, Ledford, & Gresham, 2000) and more volatile over time (e.g., the value of stock options). Further advances await more explicit examination and more sophisticated methodologies.

Selection Standards and Applicant Quality

Early research showed that one of the main sources of flexibility in applicant attraction involves the raising or lowering of selection standards as workers become more—or less—available (e.g., Malm, 1955; Thurow, 1975). By broadening applicant pools and loosening selection standards as labor markets tighten, most employers are generally able to fill most of their vacancies. However, because changes in recruitment pools and hiring standards may have implications for subsequent productivity as well as immediate attraction (Dreher & Sackett, 1983), it is crucial to assess the *quality* of individuals attracted under various recruitment and selection procedures.

The 1990s produced the tightest U.S. labor market in decades, a change that undoubtedly led to broadened applicant pools and reduced selection standards in many organizations. Yet despite calls for updated research on this topic (Rynes, 1991), none has been forthcoming. In part, we suspect that this paucity of research is due to the legal sensitivities of conducting research in this area (see Boehm, 1982). In addition, research at the organizational level is hampered by the fact that most organizations use different selection criteria and thus cannot be compared on anything other than subjective assessments of screening rigor or selection ratios (which are probably confounded with organizational visibility and image). Thus, the most promising sites for such research may be multibranch organizations with similar types of work but with selection criteria that perhaps vary in stringency across locations (e.g., consulting firms or the military).

RECRUITMENT PROCESSES

A case can be made that the recruitment literature has more than enough studies demonstrating that recruiters, sources, or realistic previews are sometimes related to both pre- and post-hire outcomes. What is missing is a clear understanding of why, and under what conditions, such relationships are likely to emerge. Thus, the time has come to pay closer attention to the design and measurement issues necessary to isolate recruitment processes. (Rynes, 1991, p. 437)

As shown in Figure 4.1, the previous *Handbook* suggested six processes in need of additional research: applicant self-selection, time-related processes, information-related processes, interactive processes, individual differences, and posthire adjustment. Not surprisingly, progress across these areas has been uneven, with the greatest amount of attention paid to individual differences (in the form of person-organization fit). We now review recent findings with respect to the first five (i.e., prehire) processes, plus a short section on social processes. Posthire processes are not reviewed due to space limitations and extensive coverage in previous reviews.

Applicant Self-Selection

At the time of the last *Handbook,* one major unresolved issue was whether the modest posthire benefits of RJPs might be nullified by increases in the numbers of those self-selecting out, thereby raising the costs of generating sufficiently large applicant pools and job acceptances. As indicated earlier, a recent meta-analysis suggests that this is not the case (Phillips, 1998). However, an equally if not more important question concerns the *quality* of those who self-select out in the face of more accurate (and usually more negative) RJP information. If higher quality applicants—who presumably have more market alternatives—are disproportionately dissuaded by the provision of negative information, then the modest posthire benefits of higher retention might be gained at the expense of losing more qualified new hires.

Direct evidence on this question is lacking in the RJP literature. However, indirect evidence suggests that negative recruitment features in general (e.g., unattractive job attributes, unfriendly recruiters, recruitment delays) are evaluated more critically by higher quality applicants. For example, Bretz and Judge (1998) found that higher quality job seekers (as measured by quantity and quality of work experience, academic achievement, and extracurricular activities) attached greater weight to negative information communicated early in the recruiting process than did less qualified applicants. Rynes et al. (1991) found that students with higher grades were more likely to withdraw from the recruitment process after organizational delays and also were more likely to make negative attributions about the organization (rather than about themselves) in explaining the delay. Similarly, after controlling for a variety of other applicant characteristics, Connerley and Rynes (1997) found that students with higher grades generally perceived recruiters to be less effective. On the other hand, some evidence suggests that negative judgments are tempered for those with greater previous work experience (Bretz & Judge, 1998; Rynes et al., 1991).

As with research on vacancy characteristics and selection standards, ascertaining the effects of RJPs on the quantity (and especially the quality) of applicants generated is likely to be most convincingly pursued via field experiments or in cross-sectional research in organizations with multiple sites and relatively standardized recruitment and selection procedures. Without standardized procedures, assessment of applicant quality (and quality-related self-selection) is nearly impossible.

Time-Related Processes

Both organizational recruitment and individual job search are processes that occur over time; this raises the possibility that variables such as early-versus-late search start and timeliness of follow-through will influence both the quantity and quality of applicants attracted at various stages. Thus, the previous *Handbook* recommended that recruitment researchers examine timing effects in markets with clearly defined recruitment cycles (e.g., college recruitment), as well as possible order effects (e.g., recency, contrast) on applicant evaluations of vacancies (e.g., see Soelberg, 1967).

Although recent research has not examined these precise questions, several studies have examined time-related recruitment processes. For example, in their study of how applicants determine their fit with various organizations, Rynes et al. (1991) inadvertently discovered that delays between recruiting phases were a fairly important cause of applicants' dropping companies from further consideration. Specifically, 50% of the students in their sample turned down at least one site visit due to late timing. However, in contrast to earlier findings (e.g., Arvey, Gordon, Massengill, & Mussio, 1975; Sheppard & Belitsky, 1966), applicants who were most likely to lose interest in specific companies due to delays were those who tended to have the *most* employment alternatives. This difference is almost certainly due to the fact that Arvey et al. (1975) and Sheppard and Belitsky (1966) studied noncollege populations who typically do not have the luxury of choosing among multiple organizations but rather have to find their own alternatives in sequential fashion. With respect to college recruitment, however, the message seems clear: Not only do delays between recruitment phases lose applicants, but they are likely to cost the most sought-after applicants.

Another focus of recent research is whether and how applicants' information-seeking processes change over time. Blau (1994) found support for two stages of search among a sample of diverse job seekers: a preparatory phase during which job seekers generated possible alternatives and an active phase during which they actually applied for vacancies and sought more detailed information. Similarly, a longitudinal study of college and vocational school students by Barber, Daly, Giannantonio, and Phillips (1994) showed that job seekers narrowed the field of considered options over time, investigated more deeply into the characteristics of those options, and switched their emphasis from formal to informal sources of information. Both these studies support earlier work by Rees (1966), Soelberg (1967), and Osborn (1990), all of whom suggested that periods of expansive, general search (called *extensive search* by Rees) tend to be followed by narrower, more detail-oriented intensive search.

Finally, Powell and Goulet (1996) found that applicants' postinterview intentions were relatively good predictors of their subsequent behaviors (e.g., acceptance of second interviews and job offers), even after controlling for number of other offers and number of previous turndowns. This finding somewhat reduces concerns about the common practice of assessing applicants' behavioral intentions at early phases of the recruiting process without following them through to ultimate decisions.

Social Processes

Barber, Daly, et al.'s (1994) finding that informal sources (e.g., friends and relatives) play a large role in the active phase of job search draws attention to the highly social nature of the job choice process. Social processes in job search and choice have been discussed in considerable detail by Granovetter (1974) and more recently by Kilduff (1990). Specifically, Kilduff found that master's of business administration (MBA) students were disproportionately likely to interview with the same companies as were those students they perceived to be similar to themselves or who were viewed as personal friends, even after controlling for similarities in job preferences and academic concentration. Additionally, several authors have shown that social referral processes are often correlated with demographic characteristics such as gender or race and that these differences have consequences for subsequent search and choice outcomes (e.g., Kirnan et al., 1989; Leicht & Marx, 1997).

The relatively heavy emphasis on social relationships that emerges from field research suggests a number of recruiting tactics for organizations. For example, in campus recruiting, the importance of social ties suggests the likely effectiveness of strategies that build an ongoing campus presence and that provide high-quality internship experiences that cause interns to spread the word about the company upon their return to campus. Indeed, recent surveys of practice suggest that organizations have in fact been placing more emphasis on these tactics in recent years (e.g., Thornburg, 1997).

Information-Related Processes

Two issues have received the bulk of attention with respect to the way applicants process information: how applicants make judgments about unknown attributes on the basis of known characteristics (signaling) and the effects of initial applicant beliefs on subsequent actions, beliefs, and decisions. Turning to the first question, earlier research had clearly established that applicants tend to use *recruiter* characteristics as signals of broader organizational characteristics (Harris & Fink, 1987) as well as expectations of receiving an offer (Rynes & Miller, 1983). However, little work had been done to determine how *known* job and organizational attributes influence applicants' beliefs about attributes that are more difficult to discover.

To address this deficiency, Barber and Roehling (1993) used verbal protocol analyses (VPA) to examine how applicants made inferences about a variety of job characteristics. In the unprompted condition in which subjects simply talked through their reactions to various job descriptions, industry and firm size were the most common sources of inferences about more specific job characteristics. In the prompted condition (in which subjects were asked directly to estimate job challenge, responsibility, etc.), job title and industry were used most often to make inferences about job challenge and responsibility, salary was used to make inferences about work hours, and firm size and benefits were used to make inferences about job security.

Rynes et al. (1991) used interviews with actual job seekers to determine how they made inferences from various recruitment experiences. They found that delays in recruitment processes were common sources of inferences about organizational (in)efficiency and influenced job seekers' expectations of receiving a job offer. They also found that some candidates interpret the number of women and minorities met during site visits as indicative of organizational attitudes toward diversity. Finally, they found considerable individual differences in the extent to which job seekers viewed recruitment practices as reflective of broader organizational characteristics. Specifically, recruitment practices were more likely to be viewed as representative of the company when job seekers had less previous experience, when recruiters were not from the HR department, and when the practices were experienced on the site visit rather than during the campus interview.

Other information-processing studies have examined how early impressions or beliefs of job applicants affect their job search behaviors and subsequent impressions or choices. Although this issue has been rather widely studied on the recruiter side of the process (under the rubric of self-fulfilling prophecies; e.g., Dipboye, 1982), it has rarely been investigated with respect to applicants. However, Stevens (1997) recently conducted such an investigation, using information from 106 pre- and postinterview surveys and 24 audiotaped campus interviews. Similar to findings from the recruiter side (e.g., Dougherty, Turban, & Callender, 1994; Phillips & Dipboye, 1989), she found that applicants with more positive prior beliefs about an organization were more likely to use positive impression management techniques and to ask positive-leaning questions designed to produce favorable information about the organization.

Stevens also found that applicants' impressions of recruiters were positively correlated with their impressions of the organization and that perceptions of recruiters partially mediated relationships between preinterview and postinterview job beliefs. It is interesting to note that applicants who expected to receive job offers evaluated recruiters more positively even though objective coding of the interviews did not reveal more positive recruiter behaviors. Based on the overall pattern of results, Stevens (1997) speculated that one of the reasons for the relatively modest impact of recruiters on job choice is that for many applicants, the likelihood of job acceptance may be substantially determined before formal recruitment activities begin.

Interactive Processes

A second aspect of self-fulfilling prophecies concerns *interactive* effects, or the impact that preinterview impressions of one party to the interview (e.g., recruiters) can have on the other party (e.g., applicants). To investigate this possibility, Liden, Martin, and Parsons (1993) had college students play the role of interviewee in interviews in which the recruiter was either warm or cold, as manipulated via eye contact and smiling. Independent judges then rated applicants' verbal and nonverbal behaviors. As predicted, overall results showed that applicants interviewed by warm recruiters displayed more effective verbal and nonverbal behaviors in return (see also Dougherty et al., 1994). However, Liden et al. (1993) also found that high self-esteem applicants were barely affected by recruiter behaviors, whereas low-self-esteem individuals were significantly affected on both verbal and nonverbal behaviors.

In an interesting twist on the more common attempt to examine how recruiter behaviors influence applicants, Stevens (1997) evaluated whether applicants' behaviors had any discernible impact on recruiters. In an analysis of 24 audiotaped campus interviews, she found that applicants' use of positive confirmatory questioning about the company did not cause recruiters to answer questions in more positive ways.

In fact, when applicants asked more positive questions and had more positive prior beliefs about the job and company, interviewers were rated as both less personable and less informative by outside observers. The author attributed this result, which generally differs from findings with respect to recruiter influences on applicants (Dougherty et al., 1994; Phillips & Dipboye, 1989), to applicants' lesser degree of control over the course and direction of the employment interview.

Individual Differences and Person-Organization Fit

Although research on the role of vacancy characteristics has lagged over the past decade, research on the topic of person-organization (P-O) fit has flourished. The P-O fit literature differs from the vacancy characteristics literature at least three ways. First, the vacancy characteristics literature primarily focuses on the main effects of various job attributes in applicant decisions (e.g., whether fixed pay is generally preferred to variable pay). In contrast, the concept of fit implies an interactive process whereby certain attributes are assumed to be attractive to some applicants but unattractive or less attractive to others. Second, the vacancy characteristics literature tends to focus primarily on *job* attributes (pay, coworkers, career path, type of work), whereas the P-O fit literature tends to focus on *organizational* attributes (e.g., size, location, or culture). Third, the fit literature has tended to focus relatively more on subjectively construed attributes, such as values and beliefs (e.g., Chatman, 1991; Meglino, Ravlin, & Adkins, 1989).

The increase in P-O fit research makes sense in light of a number of trends in the broader environment. For example, diversity in HR systems—particularly compensation systems and work schedules—has increased noticeably over the past decade (Heneman et al., 2000; Levering & Moskowitz, 2001) and thus made fit a more salient issue. Additionally, research on P-O fit among current employees (as opposed to job seekers) has shown that a wide variety of positive outcomes (e.g., employee satisfaction, retention, and performance) correspond with higher levels of congruency or fit (Chatman, 1991).

Early fit research was mostly experimental (e.g., Bretz, Ash, & Dreher, 1989), with researchers maintaining tight control over extraneous factors while trying to determine whether P-O fit played any role in individuals' job choice decisions. For example, using a policy capturing design, Judge and Bretz (1992) showed that most individuals prefer organizations that display fairness, concern for others, high achievement, and honesty (i.e., main effects). However, they also found that individuals' primary value orientations interacted with organizational characteristics such that individuals were relatively more interested in firms with values similar to their own.

Turban and Keon (1993) examined how self-esteem and need for achievement moderated the effects of organizational characteristics on attraction to hypothetical organizations. They found that in general, most applicants preferred decentralized organizations and performance-based pay to centralized organizations and seniority-based pay. However, they also found that preferences for performance-based pay and organizational size varied with differences in subjects' need for achievement.

As noted earlier, Cable and Judge (1994) built on these results in a policy-capturing study that examined how personality traits are related to multiple pay and benefits preferences. They found that subjects generally preferred certain types of pay systems (e.g., high pay levels, individual-based pay), but also that certain types of applicants placed greater emphasis on particular pay attributes (e.g., individuals with high self-efficacy placed greater value on individualistic pay).

Although experimental studies provide advantages of tight control and clear causality in studying fit, they also present limitations (Schwab, Rynes, & Aldag, 1987). Such limitations include the use of hypothetical jobs and choices, demand characteristics (e.g., researchers choose which job attributes are manipulated and which individual differences are measured), and lack of contextual fidelity in relation to real labor markets (e.g., subjects sometimes evaluate dozens of scenarios in one sitting).

Fortunately, there have also been a number of field studies of fit over the past decade. For example, Rynes et al. (1991) employed structured interviews with real job seekers to find out how they assessed their fit with various companies at two points during the job search. The most commonly mentioned determinants of fit included general company reputation, attitude toward the product or industry, perceived status of the job seeker's functional area in the company, training and career opportunities, geographic location, and popular press reports. A comparison with the earlier section on organizational image in this review reveals a general similarity between elements associated with fit and those associated with image. In addition, about a third of the job seekers in Rynes et al. also mentioned the behaviors of recruiters and other company representatives as indicators of good or poor fit.

Cable and Judge (1996) conducted another field study that examined job seekers' subjective P-O fit perceptions and the sources of those perceptions. Results revealed that P-O fit perceptions were predicted by perceived values congruence and that job seekers placed substantial weight on P-O fit relative to other job and organizational attributes (e.g., pay, location) when choosing jobs. Results from this longitudinal study also extended previous research on the P-O fit construct by demonstrating that job seekers' subjective fit perceptions mediated the effect of perceived values congruence on job choice intentions and subsequent work attitudes.

Judge and Cable (1997) examined the dispositional basis of job seekers' organizational culture preferences and also investigated how these preferences interact with organizational cultures to affect applicant attraction. Results suggested that the Big Five personality traits (conscientiousness, extraversion, emotional stability, agreeableness, and openness to experience; Barrick & Mount, 1991) were generally related to hypothesized dimensions of culture preferences. Analyses also indicated that both objective P-O fit (congruence between applicant preferences and the recruiting organization's reputed culture) and subjective fit (applicants' direct assessments of fit) were related to organization attraction.

Saks and Ashforth (1997) examined job seekers' subjective perceptions of P-O fit, focusing on the role of information sources and self-esteem. This longitudinal study showed that P-O fit was not related to self-esteem but was related to the number of formal information sources used (e.g., newspaper advertisements, campus recruiters). This study also suggested that although subjective P-O fit and subjective person-*job* fit are correlated ($r = .56$), they are distinct constructs (see Kristof-Brown, 2000, for similar evidence from the recruiter side).

In evaluating the recent research on P-O fit in recruitment, it is clear that several advances have been made since the previous *Handbook*. For example, researchers have demonstrated that many different organizational attributes can be associated with applicants' impressions of fit, including size, geographic dispersion, values, culture, and pay systems. However, one potential problem with fit research to date is that almost all psychological characteristics of applicants (e.g., personality characteristics, values) have been found to be associated with preferences for like-measured organizational attributes. The fact that nearly all investigated characteristics have yielded evidence of fit raises questions about the truly critical dimensions of fit that actually drive job choices.

Although published studies have all found at least some evidence of interactions or fit in applicant impressions, it is important to remember that most have found even larger main effects for such variables as pay level, performance-based pay, individual- rather than team-based pay, flexible benefits, fair treatment, concern for others, and achievement orientation. Thus, on many attributes, organizations may be well-advised to think at least as much in terms of best practices as of fit. On the other hand, there are clearly some

organizational characteristics that are evaluated significantly differently by different types of applicants (e.g., organizational size; Barber et al., 1999).

Recent research has also provided information about results to be expected using different measures of fit (Kristof, 1996). For example, subjective holistic measures of fit generally do a better job of predicting outcomes than do direct measures of fit, which are typically calculated as difference or distance scores between organizational and applicant characteristics on multiple dimensions. This finding is not all that surprising, given that subjective perceptions of fit (a) are measured from a single source; (b) do not suffer from the same degree of unreliability as difference scores; and (c) are global estimates of total organizational fit and thus are broader than any one set of organizational factors that researchers might measure.

Still, the fact that objective measures of fit are not as predictive as subjective ones appears to place limits on organizations' ability to predict or influence fit on the basis of objective practices and characteristics. Moreover, from a research perspective, current measures of subjective fit often tread dangerously close to other, better-established constructs such as attractiveness, expected utility, or job satisfaction (when applied to current employees). Thus, to the extent that future fit research relies on subjective perceptions, fit researchers should be required to demonstrate the discriminant validity of the various fit constructs (e.g., P-O and P-J).

Finally, investigations of fit have moved from experimental studies to studies of actual job seekers making real choices. Thus, research in this area has moved beyond demonstrating that P-O fit *can* affect job seekers' reactions to paper organizations, to showing how actual job seekers acquire and utilize fit perceptions during the job search process. However, to continue this trend toward generalizability, it is important for future P-O fit research to move beyond college students, who comprise the vast majority of subjects in this area to date. In addition, it will be important to minimize the demand characteristics associated with most fit research so that the dimensionality of fit—as well as the critical incidents that trigger fit perceptions—arise more directly from job seekers' own language and experiences than from researchers' assumptions (for examples from the recruiter side, see Bretz, Rynes, & Gerhart, 1993, and Kristof-Brown, 2000).

To summarize, over the past decade, research on recruitment and applicant attraction has made progress in a number of areas (Table 4.1). Because some of the conclusions in Table 4.1 are more tentative than others are, the reader is encouraged to return to earlier sections of the chapter for information about the nature of the evidence underlying each conclusion.

TABLE 4.1   Tentative Conclusions from the Past Decade of Recruitment Research

Organizational Characteristics
Location, size, and organizational image are important factors in job seekers' application decisions.

Organizational reputation or image is highly correlated with organizational familiarity and moderately correlated with profitability and industry.

Organizational image appears to be important to applicant decisions both because it sends signals about more specific job attributes and because it influences expected pride from membership (social identity).

The most likely routes to improving organizational image are to improve familiarity and to increase the amount of information available to applicants.

Recruiters and Other Organizational Representatives
Recruiters can make a difference to applicants' job choices, particularly at the extremes of recruiter effectiveness. However, recruiter effects are typically overshadowed by job and organizational attributes.

Line recruiters and representatives met on site visits are more influential (in either direction) than staff recruiters and representatives met on campus.

Applicants regard trained recruiters as somewhat more effective than untrained ones, although the effects on job choices are probably not large.

Trained recruiters are more likely to follow a standardized protocol in interviews and to ask more screening-related questions. Thus, they are probably likely to produce more valid selection decisions.

Although applicants *like* recruiters who spend more time recruiting than selecting, attraction to the job itself may suffer if recruitment is overemphasized relative to selection.

Recruitment Sources
Results are very inconsistent across studies. Even the strongest conclusion from pre-1991 research—that informal sources are superior to formal ones in terms of posthire outcomes—appears to be open to question.

Sources differ in terms of the types of applicants they produce and the amount of information they appear to provide. However, the precise *nature* of these differences varies across studies.

Individuals often use more than one source in locating and applying for jobs. The typical practice of coding only one source is problematic and can have a substantial effect on study results.

The same source (e.g., the Internet) can be used in very different ways by different employers. Thus, the types of applicants attracted and the amount of information associated with the same source can also vary dramatically across employers.

White males still have better access than other groups to informal sources of referral.

Realistic Job Previews (RJPs)
RJPs are associated with consistent, but very small, increases in employee retention.

RJPs do not appear to cause greater applicant self-selection out of the application process. The issue of whether different *types* of employees self-select as a result of RJPs remains unexamined.

Affirmative Action Policies
In general, AA policies are perceived positively by those who might benefit from them, and negatively by White males.

Negative reactions to AA can be minimized by placing a strong emphasis on merit (e.g., AA as tie-breaker policies) and explaining the reasons behind the policy.

Selection Procedures
Applicant reactions to selection procedures can be explained largely in terms of perceived fairness or justice.

In general, applicants appear to accept the use of cognitive ability tests in selection.

Although there are sometimes differences in perceived test fairness across demographic groups, there is little evidence that the use of testing causes job seekers to drop out of applicant pools.

Vacancy Characteristics
Pay and benefits are of at least moderate importance in job choice. However,

importance varies across individual and market characteristics.

In general, college students prefer high pay levels, pay raises based on individual rather than team performance, fixed rather than variable pay, and flexible rather than fixed benefits.

Job challenge and interesting work appear to be particularly important to students who have exhibited high academic and social achievement.

High pay levels, strong promotion opportunities, and performance-based pay are relatively more important to students with high levels of social achievement (e.g., extracurriculars and offices).

High academic achievers (high GPA and test scores) are more attracted by commitment-based employment philosophies than are high social achievers.

Organizations appear to modify vacancy characteristics in reactive rather than strategic fashion, thus limiting potential recruitment effectiveness.

Applicant Quality & Self-Selection
High-quality applicants (as assessed via grades and number of job offers) generally appear to be more critical of recruiting practices (e.g., recruiters and recruiting delays). However, those with greater work experience may be slightly more forgiving.

Time-Related Processes
In campus recruiting contexts, delays between recruitment phases can cause significant dropout from applicant pools. Dropout will probably be most severe among applicants with the most opportunities.

In other types of labor markets, dropout may be heaviest among those who need immediate employment.

Applicants appear to go through two phases of job search: (a) a broad, exploratory phase in which general information is sought mostly through formal sources, and (b) a more focused stage in which informal sources are increasingly used to gain detailed information about a small subset of identified alternatives.

Social Processes
Social referrals are still unequal by race and gender, and they have effects for employment outcomes.

Job seekers' social networks explain variance in job choices over and above general preferences and specific academic preparation.

Information-Related Processes
Recruiter characteristics are often used to make inferences about organizational and job characteristics and likelihood of receiving an offer.

Organization-level characteristics, particularly size and industry, are used to make inferences about more specific vacancy characteristics.

Applicants' preinterview beliefs about organizations affect their interview performance and impressions. Applicants with positive pre-interview beliefs exhibit more positive impression management behaviors, ask more positive confirmatory questions, and perceive recruiter behaviors more positively.

Interactive Processes & Self-Fulfilling Prophecies
Recruiter behaviors (particularly warmth) have a clear effect on applicant interview performance. Applicant behaviors have much less effect on recruiter behaviors, suggesting that recruiters have much more control over interview processes and outcomes than do applicants.

Individual Differences and Person-Organization (P-O) Fit
Although there are some organizational characteristics that are widely favored by most job seekers (e.g., fairness, high pay), the strength—and sometimes direction—of preferences varies according to individual differences in values, personality, or beliefs.

Recruiters and other organizational representatives are often mentioned as sources of applicant beliefs about P-O fit.

Some of the main determinants of perceived P-O *fit* are the same as factors influencing perceived organizational *image*.

Subjective holistic measures of fit produce better predictions than objective, multiattribute estimates of fit.

P-O fit and person-job fit are moderately to highly related, yet conceptually distinct, constructs.

MOVING TOWARD THE FUTURE

In Table 4.2, we make suggestions for future research in a number of specific areas. However, we use this last section of the text to address some of the more general substantive and methodological needs in recruitment.

Substantive Issues

One important factor that has received little attention to this point is that there have been many dramatic changes in the *practice* of recruitment over the past decade (Taylor & Collins, 2000). Technological advances and the tightest labor market in decades have combined to dramatically alter the range of tactics organizations use to attract new talent and that individuals use to seek new employers. These developments remain almost completely uninvestigated by researchers.

Many of the shifts in recruitment practices have resulted from rounds of corporate downsizing and the subsequent weakening of internal labor markets (Cappelli, 1999). In traditional internal labor markets, employees are brought into

organizations through a small number of entry-level jobs and then are promoted up through a hierarchy of increasingly responsible (and lucrative) positions. In recent years, however, high-level jobs have not been restricted to internal candidates, and new employees have been hired from the outside at virtually all levels. Although downsizing and the weakening of internal promotion channels initially put employees at a distinct disadvantage relative to employers, these same practices also weakened employee loyalty and trust in management. Consequently, as labor markets began to tighten, employers suddenly found themselves in an unenviable position.

The loosening of ties between employers and employees has created new forms of labor exchange that behave much more like financial markets than like conventional labor markets (Cappelli, 1999; Useem, 1999). Consider this recent description of labor markets by Pink (1998, p. 87):

As more and more people declare free agency, a genuine market—with brokers, exchanges, and an evolving set of rules—is emerging for their talent . . . If you think of yourself as talent and you're looking for an agent, you need to meet the people at

TABLE 4.2 Areas for Future Recruitment Research

Organizational Characteristics
Examination of best practice versus contingency models of relationships between recruiting practices and organization-level outcomes (e.g., do the same types of practices work for organizations with negative versus positive images? for unknown versus well-known organizations?).

Cross-level research on the impact of recruitment practices on employee characteristics and organizational outcomes.

Field experiments on the effectiveness of attempts to improve organizational recruitment image (or to establish an image where none currently exists).

Examination of recruitment strategies and philosophies (e.g., how are decisions about recruitment practices made? To what extent are recruitment decisions strategic versus reactive? Are strategic approaches to recruitment more successful than reactive ones?).

Recruitment Sources
Effectiveness of new or growing sources of recruits, including company Web sites, temporary employment agencies, talent auctions, "raids" of competitors, and rerecruiting of former employees.

Effects of rewarding current employees with cash or prizes for successful applicant referrals.

Process examinations of results from different ways of using the same source (e.g., the huge variations in Internet recruiting practices).

Applicant Reactions to Selection Procedures
Examine new or emerging selection procedures such as Web quizzes, personality inventories, and lotteries as (sometimes disguised) prescreening. and recruitment techniques.

Examine "distance recruiting" via technologies such as videoconferencing.

Shift emphasis from perceived fairness of procedures to *impressiveness* of procedures (e.g., can creative selection devices be used to *attract,* as well as screen, high-quality employees?).

Vacancy Characteristics
Examine effects of short-term monetary incentives (e.g., "exploding" offers, signing bonuses) on posthire outcomes.

Effects of salary compression and inversion caused by increased external hiring.

Effects of increasing individualization of recruiting packages (e.g., flexible benefits, alternative work schedules).

Field experiments and organization-level examinations of changes or variations in vacancy characteristics.

Updated research on preferences for variably pay, especially stock ownership and options.

Time-Related Processes
Effects of recent timing trends in recruitment, such as: earlier college recruiting cycles, exploding offers, reduced cycle time for extending offers, extending offers years in advance of college graduation, and so on.

Examine relationships between recruitment timing and applicant pool size and quality.

Social Processes
Explore effects of recruiting entire teams of employees (e.g., entire graduating classes from key programs) or using corporate acquisitions as recruitment devices.

Explore ways to make referrals a more effective source for women and minorities.

Individual Differences and Person-Organization Fit
Conduct more process-oriented fit research with fewer demand characteristics to examine the most critical dimensions of fit.

Examine fit issues with respect to cognitive ability (in addition to more traditional fit research on personality and values).

MacTemps Inc.—they can help you manage your career. If you think of yourself as a stock and you're looking for a broker, you need to meet the people at M-Squared—they can help you get a good price. And if you think of yourself as an investor and you're looking to put some money into the human-capital market, you need to meet the people at IMCOR—they can help you devise an investment strategy.

In comparison with earlier practices, these new forms of labor exchange are characterized by shorter-term relationships between employers and employees, more explicit fixed-duration contracts, and better market information—particularly for job seekers (Useem, 1999). The amount of salary information available to job seekers has exploded in recent years—not only in general but also in very specific terms (e.g., Korn Ferry will put an explicit valuation on potential clients' skills and experience).

As a result of these changes, the recruitment of new employees has increasingly involved monetary incentives—both to prospective hires and to those who identify and recruit them. Current employees are often paid large finders' fees for successful referrals, and the amount of money spent on executive recruiters more than doubled in the mid-1990s (Useem, 1999). New hires are offered large signing bonuses, stock options, and salaries that sometimes far exceed those of current employees with many years of experience. Individuals post their resumes in so-called human talent auctions on Monster.com, selling their services to the highest bidder.

These trends raise important questions about the types of employees likely to be attracted through such practices. For example, in 1971, Lawler wrote the following summary of research on individual differences in pay importance: "The employee who is likely to value pay highly is a male, young (probably in his twenties); he has low self-assurance and high neuroticism; he belongs to few clubs and social groups; he owns his own home or aspires to own one and probably is a Republican and a Protestant." More recently, Cable and Judge (1994) found that high importance of pay level was associated with materialism and risk-seeking, and Trank and colleagues (2002) found a correlation between the importance of high pay and the tendency to be less committed to particular employers. Clearly, additional research examining individual differences in the attractiveness of different forms of pay would be useful. For the moment, however, available evidence suggests caution in placing too much emphasis on up-front, noncontingent high pay *levels* in attracting and retaining employees.

Another change in the practice of recruitment is that there has been a dramatic relaxation of historical (but tacit) no-raid agreements. Corporate recruiters are increasingly acting like external search firms, hacking into the internal directories of competitors and raiding their employees (Kuczynski, 1999; Useem, 1999). These practices—combined with increased Internet surfing by currently employed individuals—are moving labor markets toward a world in which "employees keep their credentials in play more or less constantly. . . . (becoming) active yet passive lookers, perhaps content with their station in life but always on the watch for that dream job" (Useem, 1999, 74).

The long-term impact of all these changes has yet to be examined, but clearly should be. For example, studies of Internet recruiting should be incorporated into increasingly complex studies of recruitment sources that take into account multiple source usage by applicants, as well as the multiplicity of ways that different employers use the Internet for recruiting. Similarly, studies of emerging compensation issues associated with recruitment (e.g., exploding offers, signing bonuses, salary compression) are some of the most important questions to be studied in the area of vacancy characteristics.

In addition to the numerous developments in recruitment practice, the other major understudied area involves recruitment decision making in organizations. With only a few exceptions (e.g., journalistic case studies such as Nakache, 1997, or organization-level surveys such as Barber et al., 1999; Rynes & Boudreau, 1986; Rynes et al., 1997), we know very little about how or why particular recruitment decisions are made in organizations. We therefore do not know the extent to which organizational decision makers actually pursue the steps necessary to develop a recruitment strategy (e.g., Breaugh, 1992) or—if they do—the extent to which such plans are derailed by the frenetic pace of change in external labor markets.

In order to conduct research that is meaningful to practice, it seems essential to know how such decisions are being made and whether differences in decision strategies are associated with differences in recruiting success (see also Breaugh & Starke, 2000, and Taylor & Collins, 2000). Although the prescriptive literature suggests that proactive strategies are likely to be associated with greater recruiting success, it also appears that a high degree of adaptiveness is required because of the increasing turbulence in external labor markets. Thus, future studies of the effectiveness of different combinations of fixed strategy and flexible responsiveness would be useful.

Methodological Issues

For the past decade, nearly all reviewers of the recruitment literature have concluded that recruitment researchers need to augment their traditional focus on individual reactions with research at higher levels of analysis (e.g., Barber, 1998;

Breaugh & Starke, 2000; Rynes & Barber, 1990). In fact, Taylor and Collins (2000) suggest that shifting to a much higher proportion of organization-level research (roughly 70% organizational, 30% individual) is the single most important step for increasing the relevance of recruitment research to practice: "Such a shift would allow researchers to examine recruitment practices across a population of organizations, permitting the assessment of context as a determinant of the kinds of practices implemented, and providing opportunities to assess the practice effects on organization level outcomes" (pp. 324–325).

However, as earlier organization-level research has shown, attributing causality, accurately apportioning variance across predictors, and determining the actual processes by which organizational practices such as recruitment are associated with organization outcomes is a difficult business (e.g., March & Sutton, 1997). Therefore, in addition to increasing the number of cross-sectional, organization-level surveys, the implementation of more complex designs is also highly desirable.

One important step for increasing our understanding of organization-level processes would be to use cross-level (not just organization-level) research. Schneider and colleagues (2000) suggest that one particularly fruitful cross-level design would be to examine the links between organizational differences in staffing practices and aggregate individual performance because "most managers of organizations are uninterested in which of the people on the shop floor are superior (the traditional individual differences focus); rather, the concern is for the aggregate of the shop floor workers" (pp. 110–111).

Such studies can best be done through experimental or quasi-experimental research in which organizational or subunit differences in recruitment practices are subsequently related to differences in aggregated individual performance. Such designs make most sense and are most likely to be interpretable when the organizations and types of work involved are at least reasonably similar, as in different locations of the armed forces or large consulting firms. Although a full discussion of cross-level issues is beyond the scope of this chapter, we refer readers to the excellent discussion of cross-level issues in a highly related area (selection; Schneider et al., 2000) as well as more general discussions of cross-level issues (e.g., Klein & Kozlowski, 2000; Rousseau, 1985).

In addition to cross-level research, supplementing cross-sectional organizational research with longitudinal data could help ameliorate problems of questionable causality (e.g., see Huselid, 1995). Another valuable supplement to organization-level research would be to get participants' reactions to puzzling findings after results have been obtained. A good example of this approach can be found in Williams and Dreher (1992), who did follow-up surveys to evaluate alternative explanations and to clarify the most likely direction of causality.

Another important methodological need in several areas of recruitment research—particularly organizational image and P-O fit research—is to reduce the demand characteristics present in most research. For example, it has become increasingly common for researchers to measure subjects on some well-known personality or values instrument (such as the Neuroticism, Extraversion, Openness Personality Inventory or the Organizational Culture Profile; O'Reilly, Chatman, & Caldwell, 1991) and then correlate individual difference scores with subjects' perceptions of the desirability of various organizational characteristics (e.g., openness, participative management, or achievement orientation). Although such studies almost always confirm at least some of the hypothesized relationships, the demand characteristics associated with this approach beg the question of whether personality is in fact one of the most important individual differences for predicting or explaining fit.

Therefore, we strongly recommend an increase in basic descriptive research and inductive theory building as opposed to the present near-monopoly of deductive testing of individual difference models generated in other subfields of I/O psychology (particularly selection). In calling for more inductive and process-oriented research, we echo Cooper and Locke's (2000) arguments that the failure to closely study phenomena in field settings *before* moving to deductive hypothesis testing is a major cause of perceived research irrelevance:

> You cannot build a sensible theory without facts. Theory building should be an inductive process. You should start by gathering facts pertinent to the issue you want to study from observation of reality.... It is no wonder that practitioners almost never read the academic literature. Aside from the jargon and mind-numbing statistics, the theories developed may have very little to do with the real world or, if they do, may deal with such minute segments of it that it is not worth the manager's time to study them. (pp. 340–341)

CONCLUDING REMARKS

Recent advances in technology and the growing intensity of market competition have elevated recruitment to a preeminent role in organizational struggles for competitive advantage. After many years of taking a backseat to other areas of I-O and HR, applicant attraction now has central billing in many companies' strategic portfolios. In fact, in a recent survey of worldwide executives by Andersen Consulting (now Accenture), 80% said that attracting and retaining people will be the number one force in business strategy by the end of the decade (Byrne, 1999). Even if labor shortages ease in the future, increasing recognition of the economic value of hiring the best possible people will continue to keep recruitment at the forefront of corporate strategy—particularly for key positions.

It is interesting, however, that the same forces that have led to an increased emphasis on recruitment are likely—in the longer run—to place even more pressure on employee *retention*. Economic theory suggests that in a world of perfect competition, perfect information, perfect information processing, and perfect mobility, the ability of recruitment to influence applicants' judgments would be severely limited (Rynes et al., 1980). Rather, choices to join and leave organizations would be made almost exclusively on true characteristics of the jobs and organizations themselves.

As technological advances, changing recruitment norms, and flexible work arrangements increasingly chip away at past market imperfections, the opportunities to influence applicants through such practices as advertising, signaling, and timing are reduced. In addition, the decline of internal labor markets, the reduction of employment loyalties, the growing feasibility of telecommuting, and the increasing frequency with which workers switch jobs all suggest that if the expectations of newly attracted workers are not met, they will soon be lost to competitors.

Thus, the attraction of new workers—but even more so, their retention—is increasingly likely to rest on the true characteristics of jobs and organizations rather than on recruitment hype or the relatively strong job-seeking inertia formerly generated by protected internal labor markets. In such a world, recruitment is probably best thought of as merely the price of admission to play in a much bigger and more difficult quest for competitive advantage through people. Still, although recruitment is only the first phase of the new talent game, failure to win at it is increasingly likely to result in elimination from the entire tournament.

REFERENCES

Arvey, R. D., Gordon, M., Massengill, D., & Mussio, S. (1975). Differential dropout rates of minority and majority job candidates due to "time lags" between selection procedures. *Personnel Psychology, 38,* 175–180.

Ashforth, E., & Kreiner, G. (1999). "How can you do it?" Dirty work and the challenge of constructing a positive identity. *Academy of Management Review, 24,* 413–434.

Ashforth, E., & Mael, F. (1989). Social identity theory and the organization. *Academy of Management Review, 14,* 20–39.

Barber, A. E. (1998). *Recruiting employees: Individual and organizational perspectives.* Thousand Oaks, CA: Sage.

Barber, A. E., Daly, C. L., Giannantonio, C. M., & Phillips, J. M. (1994). Job search activities: An examination of changes over time. *Personnel Psychology, 47,* 739–765.

Barber, A. E., Hollenbeck, J. R., Tower, S. L., & Phillips, J. M. (1994). The effects of interview focus on recruitment effectiveness: A field experiment. *Journal of Applied Psychology, 79,* 886–896.

Barber, A. E., & Roehling, M. V. (1993). Job postings and the decision to interview: A verbal protocol analysis. *Journal of Applied Psychology, 78,* 845–856.

Barber, A. E., Wesson, M. J., Roberson, Q. M., & Taylor, M. S. (1999). A tale of two job markets: Organizational size and its effects on hiring practices and job search behavior. *Personnel Psychology, 52,* 841–867.

Barrick, M. R., & Mount, M. K. (1991). The big five personality dimensions and job performance: A meta-analysis. *Personnel Psychology, 44,* 1–26.

Blau, G. (1990). Exploring the mediating mechanisms affecting the relationship of recruitment source to employee performance. *Journal of Vocational Behavior, 37,* 303–320.

Blau, G. (1994). Testing a two-dimensional measure of job search behavior. *Organizational Behavior and Human Decision Processes, 59,* 288–312.

Boehm, V. R. (1982). Are we validating more but publishing less? (The impact of governmental regulation on published validation research: An exploratory investigation). *Personnel Psychology, 35,* 175–187.

Breaugh, J. A. (1992). *Recruitment: Science and practice.* Boston: PWS-Kent.

Breaugh, J. A., & Starke, M. (2000). Research on employee recruitment: So many studies, so many remaining questions. *Journal of Management, 26,* 405–434.

Bretz, R. D., Ash, R. A., & Dreher, G. F. (1989). Do people make the place? An examination of the attraction-selection-attrition hypothesis. *Personnel Psychology, 42,* 561–581.

Bretz, R. D., & Judge, T. A. (1998). Realistic job previews: A test of the adverse self-selection hypothesis. *Journal of Applied Psychology, 83,* 330–337.

Bretz, R. D., Rynes, S. L., & Gerhart, B. (1993). Recruiter perceptions of applicant fit: Implications for individual career preparation and job search behavior. *Journal of Vocational Behavior, 43,* 310–327.

Byrne, J. (1999, October 4). The search for the young and gifted. *Business Week, 3649,* 108–112.

Cable, D. M., Aiman-Smith, L., Mulvey, P. W., & Edwards, J. R. (2000). The sources and accuracy of job applicants' beliefs about organizational culture. *Academy of Management Journal, 43,* 1076–1085.

Cable, D. M., & Graham, M. E. (2000). The determinants of organizational reputation: A job search perspective. *Journal of Organizational Behavior, 21,* 929–947.

Cable, D. M., & Judge, T. A. (1994). Pay preferences and job search decisions: A person-organization fit perspective. *Personnel Psychology, 47,* 317–348.

Cable, D. M., & Judge, T. A. (1996). Person-organization fit, job choice decisions, and organizational entry. *Organizational Behavior and Human Decision Processes, 67,* 294–311.

Cable, D. M., & Turban, D. B. (in press). The value of reputation in a recruitment context. *Journal of Applied Social Psychology.*

Campion, M. A., Palmer, D. K., & Campion, J. E. (1997). A review of structure in the selection interview. *Personnel Psychology, 50,* 655–702.

Cappelli, P. (1999). *The new deal at work: Managing the market-driven workforce.* Boston: Harvard Business School Press.

Chan, D., & Schmitt, N. (1997). Video-based versus paper-and-pencil method of assessment in situational judgement tests: Subgroup differences in test performance and face validity perceptions. *Journal of Applied Psyhology, 82,* 143–159.

Chatman, J. A. (1991). Matching people and organizations: Selection and socialization in public accounting firms. *Administrative Science Quarterly, 36,* 459–484.

Connerley, M. L. (1997). The influence of training on perceptions of recruiters' interpersonal skills and effectiveness. *Journal of Occupational and Organizational Psychology, 70,* 259–272.

Connerley, M. L., & Rynes, S. L. (1997). The influence of recruiter characteristics and organizational recruitment support on perceived recruiter effectiveness: Views from applicants and recruiters. *Human Relations, 50,* 1563–1586.

Cooper, C. L., & Locke, E. A. (Eds.). (2000). *Industrial and organizational psychology: Linking theory with practice.* Oxford, England: Blackwell.

Delaney, J. T., & Huselid, M. A. (1996). The impact of human resource management practices on perceptions of organizational performance. *Academy of Management Journal, 39,* 949–969.

Delery, J. E., & Doty, D. H. (1996). Modes of theorizing in strategic human resource management: Tests of universalistic, contingency, and configurational performance predictions. *Academy of Management Journal, 39,* 802–835.

Dipboye, R. L. (1982). Self-fulfilling prophecies in the employment interview. *Academy of Management Review, 7,* 579–586.

Dougherty, T. W., Turban, D. B., & Callender, J. C. (1994). Confirming first impressions in the employment interview: A field study of interviewer behavior. *Journal of Applied Psychology, 79,* 659–665.

Dreher, G. F., & Sackett, P. R. (1983). *Perspectives on employee staffing and selection.* Homewood, IL: Irwin.

Dutton, J. E., Dukerich, J. M., & Harquail, C. V. (1994). Organizational images and member identification. *Administrative Science Quarterly, 39,* 239–263.

Gatewood, R. D., Gowan, M. A., & Lautenschlager, G. J. (1993). Corporate image, recruitment image, and initial job choices. *Academy of Management Journal, 36,* 414–427.

Gilliland, S. W. (1993). The perceived fairness of selection systems: An organizational justice perspective. *Academy of Management Review, 18,* 694–734.

Goltz, S. M., & Giannantonio, C. M. (1995). Recruiter friendliness and attraction to the job: The mediating role of inferences about the organization. *Journal of Vocational Behavior, 46,* 109–118.

Granovetter, M. S. (1974). *Getting a job: A study of contacts and careers.* Cambridge, MA: Harvard University Press.

Griffeth, R. W., Hom, P. W., Fink, L. S., & Cohen, D. J. (1997). Comparative tests of multivariate models of recruiting source effects. *Journal of Management, 23,* 19–36.

Guion, R. M. (1976). Recruiting, selection, and job placement. In M. D. Dunnette (Ed.), *Handbook of industrial and organizational psychology* (pp. 777–828). Chicago: Rand-McNally.

Harris, M. M., & Fink, L. S. (1987). A field study of applicant reactions to employment opportunities: Does the recruiter make a difference? *Personnel Psychology, 40,* 765–783.

Heilman, M. E., Battle, W. S., Keller, C. E., & Lee, R. A. (1998). Type of affirmative action policy: A determinant of reactions to sex-based preferential selection? *Journal of Applied Psychology, 83,* 190–205.

Heilman, M. E., Block, C., & Lucas, J. A. (1992). Presumed incompetent? Stigmatization and affirmative action efforts. *Journal of Applied Psychology, 77,* 536–544.

Heilman, M. E., Lucas, J. A., & Kaplow, S. R. (1990). Self-derogating role consequences of preferential selection: The moderating role of initial self-confidence. *Organizational Behavior and Human Decision Processes, 46,* 202–216.

Heilman, M. E., McCullough, W. F., & Gilbert, D. (1996). The other side of affirmative action: Reactions of nonbeneficiaries to sex-based preferential selection. *Journal of Applied Psychology, 81,* 346–357.

Heneman, R. L., Ledford, G. E., Jr., & Gresham, M. T. (2000). The changing nature of work and its effects on compensation design and delivery. In S. L. Rynes & B. Gerhart (Eds.), *Compensation in organizations: Current research and practice* (pp. 195–240). San Francisco: Jossey-Bass.

Highhouse, S., Stierwalt, S. L., Bachiochi, P., Elder, A. E., & Fisher, G. (1999). Effects of advertised human resource management practices on attraction of African American applicants. *Personnel Psychology, 52,* 425–442.

Huselid, M. A. (1995). The impact of human resource management practices on turnover, productivity, and corporate financial performance. *Academy of Management Journal, 38,* 635–672.

Judge, T. A., & Bretz, R. D. (1992). Effects of work values on job choice decisions. *Journal of Applied Psychology, 77,* 261–271.

Judge, T. A., & Cable, D. M. (1997). Applicant personality, organizational culture, and organization attraction. *Personnel Psychology, 50,* 359–394.

Kilduff, M. (1990). The interpersonal structure of decision making: A social comparison approach to organizational choice. *Organizational Behavior and Human Decision Processes, 47,* 270–288.

Kirnan, J. P., Farley, J. A., & Geisinger, K. F. (1989). The relationship between recruiting source, applicant quality, and hire performance: An analysis by sex, ethnicity, and age. *Personnel Psychology, 42,* 293–308.

Klein, K. J., Dansereau, F., & Hall, R. J. (1994). Levels issues in theory development, data collection, and analysis. *Academy of Management Review, 19,* 195–229.

Klein, K. J., & Kozlowski, S. W. J. (2000). *Multilevel theory, research, and methods in organizations.* San Francisco: Jossey-Bass.

Konrad, A. M., Corrigall, E., Lieb, P., & Ritchie, J. E., Jr. (2000). Sex differences in job attribute preferences among managers and business students. *Group and Organizational Management, 25*(2), 108–131.

Konrad, A. M., Ritchie, J. E., Jr., Lieb, P., & Corrigall, E. (2000). Sex differences and similarities in job attribute preferences: A meta-analysis. *Psychological Bulletin, 126,* 593–625.

Kravitz, D. A., Harrison, D. A., Turner, M. E., Levine, E. L., Chaves, W., Brannick, M. T., Denning, D. L., Russell, C. J., & Conard, M. A. (1997). *Affirmative Action: A review of psychological and behavioral research.* Bowling Green, OH: The Society for Industrial & Organizational Psychology.

Kravitz, D. A., & Klineberg, S. L. (2000). Reactions to two versions of affirmative action among Whites, blacks, and Hispanics. *Journal of Applied Psychology, 85,* 597–611.

Kristof, A. L. (1996). Person-organization fit: An integrative review of its conceptualizations, measurement, and implications. *Personnel Psychology, 49,* 1–50.

Kristof-Brown, A. L. (2000). Perceived applicant fit: Distinguishing between recruiters' perceptions of person-job and person-organization fit. *Personnel Psychology, 53,* 643–672.

Kuczynski, S. (1999, March). You've got job offers! *HR Magazine, 44*(3), 50–58.

Lawler, E. E., III. (1971). *Pay and organizational effectiveness: A psychological view.* New York: McGraw-Hill.

Leicht, K. T., & Marx, J. (1997). The consequences of informal job finding for men and women. *Academy of Management Journal, 40,* 967–987.

Levering, R., & Moskowitz, M. (2001, January 8). The 100 best companies to work for. *Fortune, 143*(1), 148–168.

Liden, R. C., Martin, C. L., & Parsons, C. K. (1993). Interviewer and applicant behaviors in employment interviews. *Academy of Management Journal, 36,* 372–386.

Malm, F. T. (1955). Hiring procedures and selection standards in the San Francisco Bay area. *Industrial and Labor Relations Review, 8,* 231–252.

March, J. G., & Sutton, R. I. (1997). Organizational performance as a dependent variable. *Organization Science, 8,* 698–706.

Maurer, S. D., Howe, V., & Lee, T. W. (1992). Organizational recruiting as marketing management: An interdisciplinary study of engineering graduates. *Personnel Psychology, 45,* 807–833.

Meglino, B. M., Ravlin, E. C., & Adkins, C. L. (1989). A work values approach to corporate culture: A field test of the value congruence process and its relationship to individual outcomes. *Journal of Applied Psychology, 74,* 424–432.

Murphy, K. R., Thornton, G. C., III, & Prue, K. (1991). Influence of job characteristics on the acceptability of employee drug testing. *Journal of Applied Psychology, 76,* 447–453.

Nakache, P. (1997, September 29). Cisco's recruiting edge. *Fortune, 136*(6), 275–276.

O'Reilly, C. A., Chatman, J., & Caldwell, D. F. (1991). People and organizational culture: A profile comparison approach to assessing person-organization fit. *Academy of Management Journal, 34,* 487–516.

Osborn, D. P. (1990). A reexamination of the organizational choice process. *Journal of Vocational Behavior, 36,* 45–60.

Phillips, A. P., & Dipboye, R. L. (1989). Correlational tests of predictions from a process model of the interview. *Journal of Applied Psychology, 74,* 41–52.

Phillips, J. M. (1998). Effects of realistic job previews on multiple organizational outcomes: A meta-analysis. *Academy of Management Journal, 41,* 673–690.

Pink, D. H. (1998, August). The talent market. *Fast Company, 16,* 87–116.

Powell, G. N. (1984). Effects of job attributes and recruiting practices on applicant decisions: A comparison. *Personnel Psychology, 70,* 706–719.

Powell, G. N., & Goulet, L. R. (1996). Recruiters' and applicants' reactions to campus interviews and employment decisions. *Academy of Management Journal, 39,* 1619–1640.

Rees, A. (1966). Labor economics: Effects of more knowledge-information networks in labor markets. *American Economic Review, 56,* 559–566.

Rousseau, D. M. (1985). Issues of level in organizational research: Multi-level and cross-level perspectives. *Research in Organizational Behavior, 7,* 1–37.

Ryan, A. M., & Ployhart, R. E. (2000). Applicants' perceptions of selection procedures and decisions: A critical review and agenda for the future. *Journal of Management, 26,* 565–606.

Ryan, A. M., Sacco, J. M., McFarland, L. A., & Kriska, S. D. (2000). Applicant self-selection: Correlates of withdrawal from a multiple hurdle process. *Journal of Applied Psychology, 85,* 163–179.

Rynes, S. L. (1989). The employment interview as a recruitment device. In R. W. Eder & G. R. Ferris (Eds.), *The employment interview: research and practice* (pp. 127–141). Beverly Hills: Sage.

Rynes, S. L. (1991). Recruitment, job choice, and post-hire consequences: A call for new research directions. In M. D. Dunnette & L. M. Hough (Eds.), *Handbook of industrial and organizational psychology* (2nd ed., Vol. 2, pp. 399–444). Palo Alto, CA: Consulting Psychologists Press.

Rynes, S. L., & Barber, A. E. (1990). Applicant attraction strategies: An organizational perspective. *Academy of Management Review, 15,* 286–310.

Rynes, S.L., & Boudreau, J. W. (1986). College recruiting in large organizations: Practice, evaluation and research implications. *Personnel Psychology, 39,* 729–757.

Rynes, S.L., Bretz, R. D., Jr., & Gerhart, B. (1991). The importance of recruitment in job choice: A different way of looking. *Personnel Psychology, 44,* 487–521.

Rynes, S.L., Heneman, H. G., III, & Schwab, D. P. (1980). Individual reactions to organizational recruiting: A review. *Personnel Psychology, 33,* 529–542.

Rynes, S. L., & Miller, H. E. (1983). Recruiter and job influences on candidates for employment. *Journal of Applied Psychology, 68,* 146–154.

Rynes, S. L., Orlitzky, M. O., & Bretz, R. D. (1997). Experienced hiring versus college recruiting: Practices and emerging trends. *Personnel Psychology, 50,* 309–339.

Sackett, P. R., & Wanek, J. E. (1996). New developments in the use of measures of honesty, integrity, conscientiousness, dependability, trustworthiness, and reliability for personnel selection. *Personnel Psychology, 49,* 787–829.

Saks, A. M., & Ashforth, B. E. (1997). A longitudinal investigation of the relationships between job information sources, applicant perceptions of fit, and work outcomes. *Personnel Psychology, 50,* 395–426.

Saks, A. M., Leck, J. D., & Saunders, D. M. (1995). Effects of application blanks and employment equity on applicant reactions and job pursuit intentions. *Journal of Organizational Behavior, 16,* 415–430.

Schneider, B., Smith, D. B., & Sipe, W. P. (2000). Personnel selection psychology: Multilevel considerations. In K. J. Klein & S. W. J. Kozlowski (Eds.), *Multilevel theory, research, and methods in organizations* (pp. 91–120). San Francisco: Jossey-Bass.

Schuler, R. S., & Jackson, S. E. (1987). Linking competitive strategies with human resource management practices. *Academy of Management Executive, 1,* 209–213.

Schwab, D. P., Rynes, S. L., & Aldag, R. J. (1987). Theories and research on job search and choice. In K. M. Rowland & G. R. Ferris (Eds.), *Research in personnel and human resources management* (Vol. 5, pp. 129–166). Greenwich, CT: JAI Press.

Sheppard, H., & Belitsky, A. H. (1966). *The job hunt.* Baltimore: Johns Hopkins Press.

Soelberg, P. O. (1967). Unprogrammed decision making. *Industrial Management Review, 8,* 19–29.

Stevens, C. K. (1997). Effects of preinterview beliefs on applicants' reactions to campus interviews. *Academy of Management Journal, 40,* 947–966.

Stevens, C. K. (1998). Antecedents of interview interactions, interviewers' ratings, and applicants' reactions. *Personnel Psychology, 51,* 55–85.

Taylor, M. S., & Bergmann, T. J. (1987). Organizational recruitment activities and applicants' reactions at different stages of the recruitment process. *Personnel Psychology, 40,* 261–285.

Taylor, M. S., & Collins, C. J. (2000). Organizational recruitment: Enhancing the intersection of research and practice. In C. L. Cooper & E. A. Locke (eds.), *Industrial and organizational psychology: Linking theory with practice* (pp. 304–334). Oxford, England: Blackwell.

Terpstra, D. E., & Rozell, E. J. (1993). The relationship of staffing practices to organizational level measures of performance. *Personnel Psychology, 46,* 27–48.

Thornburg, L. (1997). Employers and graduates size each other up. *HR Magazine, 42*(5), 76–79.

Thurow, L. (1975). *Generating inequality.* New York: Basic Books.

Trank, C. Q., Rynes, S. L., & Bretz, R. D., Jr. (2002). Attracting applicants in the war for talent: Individual differences in work preferences by ability and achievement levels. *Journal of Business and Psychology, 16,* 331–345.

Truxillo, D. M., & Bauer, T. N. (1999). Applicant reactions to test score banding in entry-level and promotional contexts. *Journal of Applied Psychology, 84,* 322–339.

Turban, D. B., Campion, J. E., & Eyring, A. R. (1995). Factors related to job acceptance decisions of college recruits. *Journal of Vocational Behavior, 47,* 193–213.

Turban, D. B., & Dougherty, T. W. (1992). Influence of campus recruiting on applicant attraction to firms. *Academy of Management Journal, 35,* 739–765.

Turban, D. B., & Greening, D. W. (1996). Corporate social performance and organizational attractiveness to prospective employees. *Academy of Management Journal, 40,* 658–672.

Turban, D. B., & Keon, T. L. (1993). Organizational attractiveness: An interactionist perspective. *Journal of Applied Psychology, 78,* 184–193.

Useem, J. (1999, July 5). For sale online: You. *Fortune, 140*(1), 66–78.

Vecchio, R. P. (1995). The impact of referral sources on employee attitudes: Evidence from a national sample. *Journal of Management, 21,* 953–965.

Werbel, J. D., & Landau, J. (1996). The effectiveness of different recruitment sources: A mediating variable analysis. *Journal of Applied Social Psychology, 26,* 1337–1350.

Williams, C. R., Labig, C. E., & Stone, T. H. (1993). Recruitment sources and posthire outcomes for job applicants and new hires: A test of two hypotheses. *Journal of Applied Psychology, 42,* 163–172.

Williams, M. L., & Dreher, G. F. (1992). Compensation system attributes and applicant pool characteristics. *Academy of Management Journal, 35,* 571–595.

CHAPTER 5

Personnel Selection and Employee Performance

NEAL SCHMITT, JOSE M. CORTINA, MICHAEL J. INGERICK, AND DARIN WIECHMANN

PERFORMANCE MODEL

Our model begins with the notion that there are two major individual difference determinants of performance: *can-do* and *will-do* factors. This notion underlies most of the history of industrial/organizational (I/O) psychology, if not of psychology in general. In the performance domain itself, this distinction is often referred to as the difference between *maximal* (can-do) and *typical* (will-do) performance. The can-do factors include what has been referred to as *g* (general cognitive capacity), and lower order abilities (e.g., spatial perception, math and verbal abilities, reasoning, etc.). The relative importance of *g* and the existence and number of lower order ability factors has been debated for most of the past century (Carroll, 1993; Murphy, 1996; Spearman, 1927). Also included in the can-do category are physical abilities (e.g., manual dexterity, strength, coordination, stamina).

Fleishman's taxonomy of physical ability and his measures (Fleishman & Reilly, 1992) have dominated this area of research within the personnel-selection arena (J. C. Hogan, 1991). Another can-do characteristic is the experience an individual brings to a job. While not an ability in the traditional sense, the experience that an individual brings to a job situation certainly contributes to his or her competent handling of that situation. Job experience has played a central role in various theories of job performance (Borman, White, Pulakos, & Oppler, 1991; Campbell et al., 1993; Schmidt, Hunter, & Outerbridge, 1986). Recent attempts to clarify the meaning and importance of job experience (Quinones, Ford, & Teachout, 1995) should help to enhance our understanding of the manner in which experience affects performance either directly or through mediators, as is suggested by our model.

The will-do factor in our model is represented by personality and integrity. In the last decade, the interest in personality determinants of performance is obvious to anyone reading the journals that publish personnel-selection research. This renewed interest began with the meta-analysis published by Barrick and Mount (1991) establishing *conscientiousness* as a valid predictor of performance across job situations and establishing other of the Big Five dimensions as valid predictors in some circumstances. Many I/O researchers (e.g., Hogan & Roberts, 1996; Hough, 1998a) believe that the Big Five do not represent an all-inclusive taxonomy of personality. Often, constructs such as the *need for achievement* are found to be particularly predictive of performance. In many jobs, a sense of *integrity* has been found to be relevant to our understanding of counterproductive behavior (Ones, Viswesvaran, & Schmidt, 1993). In any case, conscientiousness, need for achievement, and integrity are all motivational in nature and therefore belong among the will-do factors.

Finally, it is important to note that can-do and will-do factors are often thought to interact to determine performance. That is, one must be both able and motivated to perform well, and if either of these characteristics is low or absent, performance will be inadequate. For a variety of reasons discussed later in this chapter, such interactive hypotheses are often not supported. In any event, we have ample evidence of the importance of both factors in the determination of performance.

The can-do and will-do variables are thought to lead to *declarative knowledge* (knowledge about facts and things), *procedural knowledge* or skill (knowing how to do something as well as what to do), and *motivation* (a combination of three choices: what to do, how much energy to expend on the activity, and how long to continue expending energy). Viewing these three variables as mediators of the individual difference-performance relationship is consistent with the Campbell et al. (1993) theory.

Performance is behavior that is a direct function of declarative and procedural knowledge and motivation. Our notions about performance include the major performance dimensions specified by Campbell et al. (1993), but we have grouped them into task proficiency, contextual behavior, and adaptive performance. The distinction between task proficiency and contextual behavior is consistent with work that indicates that these two major dimensions of work behavior are conceptually and empirically distinct (Borman & Motowidlo, 1993, 1997; Motowidlo, Borman, & Schmit, 1997). *Task proficiency* involves those behaviors that contribute to the technical core of the organization. Additionally, they tend to be role-prescribed and built into the formal reward structure. *Contextual work behavior* supports the environment in which the technical core must function, rather the technical core itself. Interest in several of the aspects of contextual behavior that are

listed in Figure 5.1 have generated significant bodies of literature (e.g., team effectiveness, Hackman, 1991; organizational citizenship behavior, Podsakoff & MacKenzie, 1997; customer service, Schneider & Bowen, 1995). *Adaptive performance* can be defined as the proficiency with which employees self-manage novel work experiences (London & Mone, 1999). Adaptive performance is considered separately because it appears to be an important part of job performance that does not fit neatly into either the task performance or the contextual performance categories (Pulakos, Arad, Donovan, & Plamondon, 2000).

Individual job performance and performance aggregated over individuals has a variety of outcomes, both individual and organizational. The introduction of the notion that performance can be aggregated and that outcomes include organizational level variables as well as individual variables means that our research must consider levels of analysis issues (Klein & Kozlowski, 2000). A significant body of such literature has been generated in the last decade (see Schneider, Smith, & Sipe, 2000, for a review). Some of the variables in the last column of Figure 5.1 can be both individual and organizational. Such is the case for productivity measures. Customer satisfaction is almost always an aggregated or organizational-level variable, although there might be cases in which organizational members serve a single client and an individual level of analysis without aggregation is appropriate. Withdrawal and counterproductive behaviors could be treated as individual or organizational. Litigation and social-responsibility measures are likely to be organizational.

Figure 5.1 represents some familiar ideas and variables. For example, the individual difference constructs mentioned have been studied by psychologists for most of the last century, as has the construct of job performance (Austin & Villanova, 1992). Distinctions among knowledge components, performance dimensions, and organizational-level indices of performance are notions that are relatively new to the personnel-selection literature and did not appear in literature reviews similar to this one even a decade ago (Guion, 1991). More recent reviews (Hough & Oswald, 2000) reflect these trends. This figure and our preceding discussion of it represent an outline of the issues we address in this chapter.

Theories of Job Performance and Job Analysis

Figure 5.1 is presented as a general model of job performance. Models of job performance in specific work situations may involve only portions of Figure 5.1 and will almost always include more detail about the nature of the can-do and will-do of the job (often referred to as *knowledge, skill, ability, and other requirements,* or *KSAOs*) and the performance

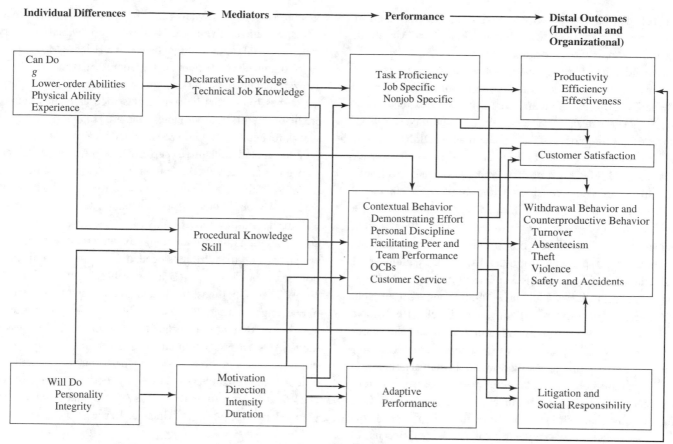

Figure 5.1 Model relating individual differences, mediators, performance, and distal outcomes.

domains relevant to the job under consideration. These models of job performance are constructed based on reviews of the literature, the experience of the I/O psychologist, and a formal job analysis. A *job analysis* involves the specification of the work behaviors required of job incumbents and hypotheses about the KSAOs required to perform those work behaviors. The work involved in a thorough job analysis is time consuming and expensive. This work is described well in a variety of sources (Goldstein, Zedeck, & Schneider, 1993; Schmitt & Chan, 1998). A detailed job analysis may be necessary when litigation is a possibility (Varca & Pattison, 1993) or when one is trying to document that selection procedures constitute a representative sample of the domain of work behavior (i.e., they are content valid). However, aspects of these detailed analyses may be unnecessary if the researcher can abstract from previous such analyses the basic structure of work and its attendant KSAO requirements. This abstraction is one of the basic components of science—*parsimony*. The most significant recent development in job analysis is the development of such an abstraction by the U.S. Department of Labor in the form of the Occupational Information Network, or O*NET.

O*NET represents an extremely rich source of accumulated information about a broad range of jobs. It provides lists of job tasks and related KSAOs (categorized as broad occupational requirements, worker requirements, and worker characteristics) as well as the level and importance of the KSAOs required for most major jobs in our economy. In addition, experience, educational, and licensing and certification requirements as well as occupational characteristics are specified for most jobs. Much of the work involved in forming a basic model of performance on these jobs can be done by consulting this computerized database. The need for extensive new job analyses in specific situations should be minimal. Long-term and consistent updating of this database is essential, particularly given reports that some jobs as traditionally structured no longer exist (e.g., see Bridges, 1994). Traditional employment arrangements have been changed as a function of outsourcing, the use of temporary employees, and the creation of individual career paths (Hall, 1996). One important research effort might involve the documentation of such changes and the implications for various aspects of the content model underlying the O*NET. The O*NET database is the result of many different streams of accumulated research data and represents a significant integrative effort that should prove widely useful (Peterson, Mumford, Borman, Jeanneret, & Fleishman, 1999).

To study the changing nature of work, researchers need measures of work that are valid, comprehensive, and applicable across different contexts. We have measures focused on specific task activities (Fleishman & Quaintance, 1984), motivational properties of jobs (Hackman & Oldham, 1980) and the ergonomic and biological requirements of work (Grandjean, 1980). Each of these approaches risks overlooking aspects of work considered important from other perspectives. Campion and Thayer (1985) presented the *Multimethod Job Design Questionnaire,* which integrated four more-specific approaches (motivational, mechanistic, biological, and perceptual-motor) to the measurement of work. This instrument has proven useful in a variety of contexts (Campion & McClelland, 1993; Wong & Campion, 1991). Recently, Edwards, Scully, and Brtek (1999) have evaluated the psychometric and factorial nature of the instrument. Tests of the a priori 4-factor structure were not encouraging, but a 10-factor structure was interpretable and subscales based on this factor solution were reasonably reliable in all but two cases. Further, each of the 10 scales included items that belonged to one of the four major factors (with the exception of a single item on one scale). Because of its multidisciplinary nature, this instrument may provide a relatively efficient means to track changes in jobs. A similar effort to develop generalized work activities is reported by Jeanneret, Borman, Kubisiak, and Hanson (1999).

THE NATURE OF PERFORMANCE

Until 10 or 15 years ago, I/O psychology had a tendency to focus on predictors of performance to the exclusion of performance itself, in spite of numerous pleas to attend better to the so-called criterion problem (Campbell, 1990; Dunnette, 1963; Wallace, 1965). Appreciation of the need to better understand the performance side of the equation *prior* to consideration of the predictor side has increased, thanks in part to some influential sources (Austin & Villanova, 1992; Binning & Barrett, 1989; Campbell, 1990). Consistent with this concern regarding the nature of performance and much recent research, we discuss the differences between task and conceptual performance. We also discuss the possibility of a third major performance dimension: adaptive performance.

Why focus on the task–contextual performance distinction? One reason for this choice was the attention paid to contextual performance versus task performance in recent years (Conway, 1999; Motowidlo & Van Scotter, 1994; Van Scotter & Motowidlo, 1996). Many recently discussed aspects of performance fall relatively neatly into the contextual category (e.g., prosocial organizational behaviors, Brief & Motowidlo, 1986; organizational spontaneity, George & Brief, 1992; organizational citizenship behaviors, Organ, 1988). Finally, research has found that behaviors classified as contextual are predicted by different variables than are behaviors classified as task related (Motowidlo & Van Scotter, 1994).

Why include adaptive performance? Adaptive performance has also received attention in the last couple of years (Pulakos et al., 2000; Ilgen & Pulakos, 1999), and with good reason. Although the task-contextual distinction describes well the day-to-day activities in most job settings, there exists an overarching concern about the dynamic nature of today's workplace and the attributes needed to negotiate the fluctuations associated with it (Bridges, 1994; Ilgen & Pulakos, 1999). That is, both task-related and contextual requirements may change on a regular basis, and the successful employee may be the one who identifies these changes and possesses the KSAOs necessary to modify behavior accordingly. Without some consideration of adaptive performance, some theoreticians and researchers believe, any model of performance becomes too static to represent the vagaries and exigencies of the modern workplace (Pearlman & Barney, 1999).

Task Performance

Every definition of job performance includes the notion of task performance or proficiency. For Katz and Kahn (1978), these are role-prescribed behaviors. For Campbell (1990), these are core tasks. For Borman & Motowidlo (1993), these are the tasks that involve or maintain the technical core. We focus on the approach suggested by Borman and Motowidlo (1993). Task-related behaviors contribute to the technical core of the organization. Additionally, although they tend to be role-prescribed (as in Campbell's notion of job-specific task proficiency) and built into the formal reward structure, they are not necessarily so.

The term *technical core* is used here a bit loosely. The technical core, as defined by Borman and Motowidlo (1993), involves the transformation of raw materials (machine parts, stitches, unenlightened students) into organizational products (machines, closed wounds, less unenlightened students). As can be seen from these examples, the term *raw materials* is not restricted to pig iron and rolls of fabric. Raw materials are those that are to be manipulated in some fashion to become whatever it is that the organization in question produces, and any behaviors that contribute, either directly or indirectly, to the manipulation process are labeled *task related.* As another example, the technical core of managerial jobs may involve the need to transform people through conflict resolution or efforts to motivate.

Task-related behaviors are typically predicted well by ability and experience-related individual differences (Hunter & Hunter, 1984; Schmidt, Hunter, Outerbridge, & Goff, 1988), and less well by dispositional sorts of variables (Cortina, Goldstein, Payne, Davison, & Gilliland, 2000). Task-related behaviors have also been shown to relate to scores from structured interviews (McDaniel, Whetzel, Schmidt, & Maurer, 1994), biodata forms (Rothstein, Schmidt, Erwin, Owens, & Sparks, 1990), and a variety of other types of predictors. In the latter cases, the predictability would likely result from the fact that these predictors index ability or experience.

It is task-related performance on which we have traditionally focused our attention. The reason for this is unclear, although it may be a result of the fact that traditional job analyses based on task statements are less likely to uncover contextual behaviors (Borman & Motowidlo, 1993). Regardless of the cause of this omission, both the changing nature of work and, perhaps relatedly, a realization that most jobs are composed of more than task-related behaviors have forced us to consider contextual aspects of performance.

Contextual Performance

Borman and Motowidlo (1993) explain that contextual behaviors support the environment in which the technical core must function, rather than the technical core itself. Contextual behaviors also differ from task-related behaviors in that contextual behaviors are likely to be constant across jobs, whereas task-related behaviors vary. Examples of contextual behaviors are persisting with enthusiasm and extra effort, volunteering to carry out activities that are not part of one's formal job, and following organizational rules and procedures even when they are personally inconvenient. Such behaviors are less likely to be role-prescribed and less likely to be built into a formal reward structure than are task-related behaviors. Nevertheless, they are crucial to organizational functioning.

Van Scotter and Motowidlo (1996) further distinguished between two aspects of contextual performance: job dedication and interpersonal facilitation. *Job dedication* behaviors are those that include "self-disciplined, motivated acts," whereas *interpersonal facilitation* includes "cooperative, considerate, and helpful acts" (p. 525). These authors found that although many of the variables that predict task performance also predict job dedication, the same could not be said of interpersonal facilitation. Conway (1999) also found evidence that job dedication and interpersonal facilitation were distinct, although he also found that the nature of this

distinction may vary across jobs and across information source (e.g., supervisors vs. peers).

Kiker and Motowidlo (1999) found that task and contextual performance combined both additively and multiplicatively to influence reward decisions such that, although both were helpful, interpersonal effectiveness paid off more for technically effective people than for technically ineffective people. This study indicates the differential use of information on these two aspects of performance by organizational decision makers. Overall, the available evidence suggests that the nature and determinants of task-related and contextual performance differ, and that each may be an important determinant of a variety of organizational outcomes.

Adaptive Performance

Many (perhaps most) of today's jobs require versatility and tolerance for ambiguity in addition to whatever individual tasks they involve. In the most comprehensive treatment of adaptive performance to date, Pulakos et al. (2000) developed an eight-factor taxonomy of adaptive performance. The eight factors were (a) handling emergencies or crisis situations, (b) handling work stress, (c) solving problems creatively, (d) dealing with uncertain and unpredictable work situations, (e) learning work tasks, technologies, and procedures, (f) demonstrating interpersonal adaptability, (g) demonstrating cultural adaptability, and (h) demonstrating physically oriented adaptability. It should be noted that these dimensions are not suggestive of the technical core for most jobs; nor do they appear to be redundant with either the job-dedication or interpersonal-facilitation aspects of contextual performance (although there is sure to be some overlap). Thus, the suggestion that such behaviors be added to any conceptualization of job performance is not unfounded.

Although the concept of adaptive performance is too new to have generated a great deal of research, it is possible to speculate as to the nomological net in which it is likely to exist. First, cognitive ability might predict some (e.g., learning new tasks) but not other (e.g., cultural adaptability) dimensions of adaptive performance (Pulakos et al., 2000). Second, dispositional variables might play an important role in the prediction of adaptive performance (LePine, Colquitt, & Erez, 2000). Among the leading candidates would be variables such as behavioral flexibility, emotional stability, and situational awareness. Third, studies similar to Conway (1999) and Kiker and Motowidlo (1999) might show that dimensions of adaptive performance contribute to the prediction of overall ratings of performance and to reward decisions over and above task-related and contextual performance. Adaptive performance may also be particularly modifiable by training or situational differences (Chan, 1997). Adaptive performance might be shown to predict long-term organizational effectiveness in ways that contextual and task-related performance do not. All these statements represent hypotheses at this point; we do not believe there exists convincing evidence that adaptive performance and its correlates are distinguishable from task and contextual performance.

Summary

We have discussed three aspects of job performance: task-related performance, contextual performance, and adaptive performance. Each should provide a unique contribution to the prediction of organizational effectiveness. For example, the employees in a given organization may be exceptional with regard to the technical core of the organization, but if they fail to cooperate with one another, or if they are unwilling to expend extra effort at crucial times, organizational effectiveness will suffer. Likewise, high levels of task-related performance without adaptive performance may result in stagnation over time, or in an inability to cope with changing circumstances, thus leading to deterioration of organizational effectiveness in the long term. It seems reasonable to posit that only when all three aspects of performance are emphasized is effectiveness optimized. Finally, and most important for selection research, is the possibility that these different performance dimensions have different individual difference determinants.

PROXIMAL ANTECEDENTS OF PERFORMANCE: DECLARATIVE KNOWLEDGE, PROCEDURAL KNOWLEDGE AND SKILLS, AND MOTIVATION

Campbell and colleagues (Campbell, 1990, 1999; Campbell et al., 1993) identified three proximal determinants of job performance: (a) declarative knowledge, (b) procedural knowledge and skills, and (c) motivation. Consistent with the model formulated by Campbell and colleagues, we propose that these variables mediate the effects of more distal can-do (i.e., abilities) and will-do (i.e., dispositional traits) individual differences on performance. In this section, we (a) define declarative knowledge, procedural knowledge and skills, and motivation; (b) discuss how these variables may influence different dimensions of performance (task, contextual, and adaptive performance); and (c) review the measurement of these variables, including new approaches to their assessment.

Definitions of the Variables

Declarative knowledge is knowledge about facts and things (Campbell, 1990). As noted by Campbell, examples of declarative knowledge include knowledge of facts, principles,

goals, and self. In the context of Campbell and colleagues' model of performance, declarative knowledge consists of knowledge of performance-relevant tasks and behaviors. Similar to cognitive ability, declarative knowledge can be conceived as a hierarchical arrangement of knowledges at differing levels of specificity. For example, declarative knowledge can be decomposed by occupation or job, by performance dimension (i.e., Motowidlo et al., 1997), by task, and so on, as is typically done in a job analysis. Additionally, the amount of declarative knowledge one possesses is different from the manner in which that knowledge is organized in memory (i.e., mental models–knowledge structures; Dorsey, Campbell, Foster, & Miles, 1999). Declarative knowledge is therefore best viewed as a multifaceted construct reflecting both the amount and structure of one's knowledge.

Procedural knowledge and skills consist of the knowledge and skills necessary to perform various activities (Campbell, 1990). Procedural knowledge and skills are differentiated from declarative knowledge in that the former pertain to the *processes* underlying relevant performance behaviors (i.e., how to do things). Procedural knowledge and skills are not limited to cognitive processes and can include psychomotor, physical, self-management, and interpersonal processes as well (Campbell, 1990). In short, procedural knowledge and skills will reflect the task domain from which they are acquired and (subsequently) applied.

As defined by Sternberg and colleagues (Sternberg, Wagner, Williams, & Horvath, 1995) *tacit knowledge,* a component of practical intelligence (Sternberg et al., 2000), is similar to Campbell's conceptualization of procedural knowledge and skills. However, tacit knowledge differs from Campbell's definition in that it is closely tied to a given work context and is acquired through an individual's personal experiences (i.e., self-learning), rather than through formal training or education. Hence, tacit knowledge reflects an individual's aptitude more so than it does his or her level of achievement (Borman, Hanson, & Hedge, 1997).

As defined by Campbell (1990), *motivation* represents the combined effect of three choice behaviors, which are (a) the choice to expend effort, (b) the choice of level of effort to expend, and (c) the choice to persist in the expenditure of that level of effort. Campbell's definition is consistent with the emphasis of much of the motivational theory and research conducted during the 1960s and 1970s on choice processes (i.e., volition). However, despite its central importance to many work-related behaviors, there is currently no single, commonly agreed upon conceptualization of motivation (Kanfer & Heggestad, 1997). The proliferation of motivational theories and the absence of integrative frameworks relating distal traits to motivational variables have been fundamental roadblocks to furthering our understanding of motivation and its influence on workplace behaviors (Kanfer, 1990; Locke & Latham, 1990).

Nevertheless, recent advances in understanding motivation have been made, particularly from an individual-difference perspective, and can be summarized as follows. First, motivation encompasses both distal (goal-setting) and proximal (self-regulation; Kanfer, 1990; Kanfer & Ackerman, 1989) processes. These processes operate sequentially, varying in their proximity to outcome variables such as performance and satisfaction. Second, motivation represents a constellation of traits and skills, such as the taxonomy proposed by Kanfer and Heggestad (1997, 1999). In their framework, Kanfer and Heggestad posit that motivation consists of stable, trait-based individual differences such as achievement, motivation, and anxiety, which in turn (combined with task and environmental conditions) influence more proximal self-regulatory skills such as motivational and emotional control. The constructs comprising this constellation will differ in terms of both their content (goal orientation, self-efficacy) and their stability (trait vs. state). For example, as suggested by Kanfer and Heggestad, motivational skills will tend to be domain specific and malleable (to some degree). Hence, motivational skills exhibit the same properties as self-efficacy, in that they are context dependent and amenable to learning and environmental contingencies. Kanfer and Heggestad's (1997) taxonomy has received initial empirical support (Kanfer & Ackerman, 2000).

Antecedents and Outcomes

Within Campbell and colleagues' model (Campbell, 1990, 1999; Campbell et al., 1993), the components (or dimensions) of performance are a joint function of individual differences in declarative knowledge, procedural knowledge and skills, and motivation. This section briefly reviews support for these hypothesized linkages.

Declarative knowledge and procedural knowledge are determined by different ability constructs (Ackerman, 1987). These ability constructs can be classified into three categories: (a) *general intelligence* (i.e., cognitive ability), (b) *perceptual speed,* and (c) *psychomotor abilities* (Kanfer & Ackerman, 1989). To these constructs some researchers might add *practical intelligence,* if it is not reflected in traditional measures of general intelligence. Practical intelligence may contribute to the acquisition of knowledge and skills (i.e., tacit knowledge) independent of general intelligence in a variety of performance contexts (see Sternberg et al., 2000), although this point is sharply disputed by others (Schmidt & Hunter, 1993). More data should be provided on the nature of practical intelligence and how it relates to both performance and measures of more traditional constructs.

In brief, research demonstrates that declarative knowledge is better predicted by cognitive ability, while procedural knowledge and skills more strongly reflect perceptual speed and psychomotor abilities (Kanfer & Ackerman, 1989; McCloy, Campbell, & Cudeck, 1994). However, much of this research has been conducted within the context of skill acquisition involving very technical, cognitively demanding tasks, and the results may not generalize to other performance domains. Hence, there is a need to consider the type of knowledge and skill (i.e., technical, interpersonal, etc.), because the knowledge and skill in question will be differentially predicted by certain kinds of traits (Motowidlo et al., 1997). For example, dispositional traits will be more highly predictive of knowledge and skills involving interpersonal relationships or interacting with others (i.e., social skills), whereas cognitive ability might better predict technical knowledge and skills related to the tasks performed.

Motivation is related to stable, dispositional traits, such as conscientiousness (McCloy et al., 1994), achievement motivation (Kanfer & Heggestad, 1997; McCloy et al., 1994), emotional stability (Kanfer & Heggestad, 1997), and goal orientation (Ford, Smith, Weissbein, Gully, & Salas, 1998). Furthermore, motivation encompasses more state-like or proximal motivational process variables, such as task-specific self-efficacy and goal-setting, which mediate the influence of distal dispositional traits on performance (Gellatly, 1996; Phillips & Gully, 1997). Predictors of self-efficacy are not limited to dispositional variables, because cognitive ability appears to be positively related to self-efficacy (Phillips & Gully, 1997). However, this relationship may not be causal, but due to overlapping variance that cognitive ability shares with some of the stable, dispositional traits (i.e., achievement motivation, locus of control) that contribute to efficacy perceptions. The latter argument is consistent with the work of Ackerman (Ackerman & Heggestad, 1997) demonstrating that cognitive, dispositional, and interest traits can be clustered into trait complexes consisting of a mixture of both cognitive and noncognitive traits.

Additionally, declarative knowledge, procedural knowledge and skills, and motivation can influence each other. For example, in the context of skill acquisition, declarative knowledge is considered a precursor to procedural knowledge and skills (Kanfer & Ackerman, 1989). However, experts' inability to verbalize the procedures behind successful task completion (i.e., Langer & Imber, 1979) would seem to contradict this point. Further, motivational processes can impact the acquisition (and hence the quality) of declarative knowledge and procedural knowledge and skills, by shifting limited cognitive resources away from skill acquisition and towards self-regulatory activities (Kanfer & Ackerman, 1989). There is evidence (i.e., DeShon, Brown, & Greenis, 1996), however, that self-regulatory activities may not demand major cognitive resources, and may thereby be detrimental to skill acquisition. A possible explanation for this finding is that individual differences in motivational control skills ameliorate the deleterious effects of self-regulatory activities, such that individuals high on these skills are able to successfully minimize the negative influence of self-regulatory activities on performance, whereas individuals low on such skills cannot.

In terms of their influence on job performance, declarative knowledge, procedural knowledge and skills, and motivation have been demonstrated by research to be direct determinants of performance, and to mediate the effects of distal traits such as cognitive ability and dispositions (Borman et al., 1991; McCloy et al., 1994; Schmidt et al., 1986). However, these models (with the exception of McCloy et al.) employed measures of overall performance. If the different performance dimensions described previously are differentially predicted by different sets of variables (Campbell et al., 1993; Motowidlo et al., 1997), it is important to consider the varying effects certain combinations of these determinants will have on different dimensions of performance. In short, it seems conceptually reasonable that declarative knowledge, procedural knowledge and skills, and motivation seem to combine in different ways to influence a given dimension of performance, but more research on various aspects of performance and their ability, knowledge, and motivational components is needed.

As described above, the types of knowledge and skills (and motivation) that are most predictive of a certain dimension of performance will largely depend on the nature of the performance domain (Motowidlo et al., 1997). For example, an individual's social skills (i.e., procedural knowledge and skills related to interpersonal relationships and social interactions) will be more predictive of contextual performance whereas an individual's technical knowledge and skills will better predict his or her task performance. Similarly, self-knowledge and emotional-control skills might be more highly predictive of adaptive performance behaviors. Currently, evidence for these suppositions is indirect or theoretical (Borman & Motowidlo, 1993; Motowidlo & Van Scotter, 1994). Future research modeling these effects will greatly contribute to our understanding of the components of performance and their immediate determinants. Examples of such research as it relates to the modeling of the effects of distal dispositional traits on performance include Gellatly (1996) and Barrick and Mount (1993).

Additionally, the effects of these determinants on performance may not always be direct. For example, motivation has traditionally been viewed as a moderator of the influence of ability determinants of performance. However, research tends not to find significant evidence for such an interaction (Sackett, Gruys, & Ellingson, 1998). This could be due to the

general confusion regarding the conceptualization of motivation. Furthermore, it could reflect the fact that many of these studies have used distal dispositional variables (i.e., conscientiousness), rather than more proximal motivational constructs such as self-efficacy, goal-setting, or motivational skills, as indicators of motivation.

Measurement

Traditional measurement strategies for assessing declarative knowledge, procedural knowledge and skills, and (to a lesser extent) motivation include job-sample tests and simulations, situational judgment inventories, job-knowledge tests, and structured interviews. Within the past decade, research involving these approaches has continued to yield information on their predictive relationship with performance (i.e., McDaniel, Bruhn Finnegan, Morgeson, Campion, & Braverman, 2001; McDaniel et al., 1994), subgroup differences compared to traditional cognitive ability tests (Clevenger, Pereira, Wiechmann, Schmitt, & Schmidt Harvey, 2001), and the nature and consequences of applicant reactions (Chan & Schmitt, 1997; Rynes & Connerly, 1993).

Although largely post hoc, more and more attention is being paid to the construct validity of these approaches, particularly that of structured interviews and situational judgment tests (Cortina et al., 2000; Huffcutt, Roth, & McDaniel, 1996; Ployhart & Ryan, in press). In general, job-sample tests and job-knowledge tests are more indicative of maximal than typical performance (Schmitt & Chan, 1998). Hence, test scores are not likely to reflect an individual's motivation (Sackett, Zedeck, & Fogli, 1988). Conversely, interviews appear to reflect both can-do and will-do determinants of performance (Huffcutt et al., 1996). Ployhart and Ryan recently validated a construct-oriented approach to the development of situational judgment tests that may serve as a model for future research in the assessment of the construct validity of structured interviews.

Mental models–knowledge structures and cognitive task–verbal protocol analysis represent two nontraditional approaches to measuring declarative knowledge and procedural knowledge and skills. Mental models–knowledge structures represent an organized set of domain-level knowledge that can be activated to describe, predict, and explain behavior (Marshall, 1993). Within I/O, mental models–knowledge structures have been applied to the study of teams and training outcomes. For recent treatments of mental models and teams, see Kraiger and Wenzel (1997) or Langan-Fox, Code, and Langfield-Smith (2000).

Mental models–knowledge structures have also been used as measures of training effectiveness (Kraiger, Ford, & Salas, 1993). Of interest to the Campbell et al. (1993) model, there is evidence that training interventions lead to changes in trainees' knowledge structures, and that more highly developed knowledge structures are positively related to posttraining task performance (Dorsey et al., 1999; Kraiger & Wenzel, 1997). Furthermore, knowledge-structure assessments have low to moderate correlation with traditional declarative-knowledge tests (Dorsey et al.). These findings suggest that, rather than being an alternative measure of declarative knowledge, knowledge-structure assessments actually measure aspects of an individual's knowledge, such as organization, differently than do traditional declarative-knowledge tests (Kraiger & Wenzel, 1995). This unique variance might reflect higher levels of knowledge acquisition, such as expertise (Kraiger et al., 1993), and could add incremental validity to the prediction of task performance. As evidenced by the lack of convergent validity among different approaches to measuring knowledge structures (Dorsey et al., 1999), more research is needed in differentiating between the method and content of knowledge-structure assessments (Kraiger et al., 1993).

An extension of traditional task-analysis techniques, *cognitive task analysis (CTA)* yields information about the knowledge, thought processes, and goal structures that underlie observable performance (Chipman, Schraagen, & Shalin, 2000). Cognitive task analysis emphasizes the multidimensional nature of job performance and job expertise by making explicit the knowledge and cognitive requirements of effective performance (Dubois & Shalin, 2000). As such, CTA holds promise for advancing theoretical understanding of job expertise and knowledge, as well as (more practically) the development of job knowledge and job-sample tests (Dubois & Shalin, 1995, 2000). For a recent treatment of cognitive task analysis and its application to work contexts, including team-based environments, see Schraagen, Chipman, and Shalin (2000).

Verbal protocol analysis (VPA) methods are based on the proposition that verbal protocols are observable behaviors of cognitive processes (Ericsson & Simon, 1993). Verbal protocol analysis methods are a set of techniques, in addition to structured interviews and critical incidents, for assessing cognitive processes employed during decision making and task performance. Within I/O, VPA has been applied to the investigation of cognitive processes in performance appraisals (Martin & Klimoski, 1990), problem solving and strategy formation (Ball, Langholtz, Auble, & Sopchak, 1998), questionnaire responding (Barber & Wesson, 1998), and applicant job-search decisions (Barber & Roehling, 1993). For an overview of VPA methods and their validity, see Ericsson and Simon (1993).

These nontraditional measurement strategies have yet to be widely applied in personnel-selection research. However,

they reflect a shift away from the behavioral emphasis on which traditional predictor- and criterion-measurement approaches (and not coincidentally, the theories and models they support) have been almost exclusively based. As such, these approaches hold promise for furthering our understanding of the nature of job performance and its determinants (Campbell et al., 1993; Campbell, Gasser, & Oswald, 1996; Schmitt & Chan, 1998).

Summary

The purpose of this section was to discuss and review research related to the three proximal determinants (declarative knowledge, procedural knowledge and skills, and motivation) of job performance proposed by Campbell and colleagues (Campbell, 1990, 1999; Campbell et al., 1993). Future research addressing these determinants is needed, particularly with respect to fully delineating the nature and set of constructs associated with motivation. The fact that performance is a function of the joint influences of declarative knowledge, procedural knowledge and skills, and motivation has important implications for prediction and measurement. *How* individual differences on these determinants combine to influence the different dimensions of performance has not been explicitly specified, even within Campbell and colleagues' model. The way in which these determinants combine (i.e., additive, compensatory, etc.) to predict performance, and the weights associated with each of the determinants (e.g., Murphy & Shiarella, 1997) raise both theoretical and practical considerations, not the least of which is the validity of selection decisions.

INDIVIDUAL DIFFERENCE CORRELATES OF KNOWLEDGE, MOTIVATION, AND PERFORMANCE

Not much validation work has considered knowledge and motivation explicitly as mediators of KSAO-performance relationships. Most such research has simply assessed the KSAO-performance relationship directly or ignored the distinction between individual differences and mediators. The results of these more traditional studies of KSAO-performance relationships are summarized in this section.

Cognitive Ability

Another recent meta-analysis (Schmidt & Hunter, 1998) has reconfirmed the finding that cognitive ability measures are among the most valid predictors of job performance across all job situations. Nevertheless, the use of these measures remains controversial (Neisser et al., 1996) mostly because of their sizable subgroup differences. Partly in response to these differences and to new research findings, and partly because of a belief that cognitive ability or intelligence has been too narrowly defined, new theories of intelligence have been formulated and investigated.

Hierarchical models of intelligence (Spearman, 1927) posit the existence of a single general factor *g,* collectively defined by different specific ability factors. A contemporary hierarchical model is described by Carroll (1993). Citing the results of a large number of factor-analytic studies, Carroll describes three levels of specificity. At the most general level is *g.* The second level consists of seven broad abilities: fluid intelligence, crystallized intelligence, auditory perception, memory ability, retrieval ability, visual perception, and cognitive speediness, and each of these broad abilities can be further subdivided into more specific abilities. Murphy (1996) has argued that hierarchical models suggest that general versus specific ability constructs can be used for different purposes. The single general factor may be all that is needed if we want only a parsimonious prediction of performance. Ree, Earles, and Teachout (1994) have demonstrated that specific abilities that are relatively independent of *g* provide no incremental predictive contribution when related to job-relevant criteria. However, if the researcher wants to understand and explain performance, then the ability to link specific abilities at the lower levels of a theory of intelligence to performance helps describe the nature and content of the tasks performed by the individual.

Three other theories of intelligence have received attention in the broader psychological literature. Naglieri and Das (1997) have presented a neuropsychological theory of intelligence that posits three major functional areas of intelligence: *planning, attention,* and *simultaneous or successive information processing.* Given the interest in information processing in some areas of I/O psychology, it is somewhat surprising that this theory and the authors' operationalizations of these concepts have gained no attention in the personnel-selection area. Gardner (1999) posits a number of intelligences, including the traditional linguistic, spatial, and mathematical dimensions in addition to *interpersonal* and *intrapersonal dimensions,* claiming that different dimensions have been important to different cultures at different times. Gardner's interpersonal and intrapersonal dimensions also seem similar to some aspects of *emotional intelligence* (Mayer, Salovey, & Caruso, 2000), another concept that has been discussed by those who seek to broaden the concept of intelligence beyond the traditional verbal and mathematical components. Gardner's dimensions of intelligence include more than what we usually identify as intelligence, but not many personnel-selection researchers would deny the importance of many of his dimensions (e.g., interpersonal) in job performance. Sternberg (2000) divides intelligence into three major areas. The *componential* part of intelligence is composed of problem-solving abilities; the *contextual* component involves an understanding of how to modify or adapt to a situation or select a new environment; and the *experiential* component relates to the manner in which individuals can use their past experience in problem solving. Perhaps Sternberg's greatest influence on personnel selection is his notion of *practical intelligence* (Wagner, 2000), which appears central to most situational judgment measures that have become popular and useful selection tools (Clevenger et al., 2001). The constructs measured by situational judgment measures are not clear. Some (Schmit, Motowidlo, DeGroot, Cross, & Kiker, 1996) have argued that they are measures of job knowledge related to the way interpersonal or administrative situations are handled in a given organizational context. With the exception of the situational judgment test, these alternate views of intelligence have had minimal impact on personnel selection.

In sum, general cognitive ability measures are valid predictors of supervisory ratings (usually overall performance or a summed composite of dimensional ratings). Whether additional cognitive factors provide incremental validity is, in part, a function of how broadly or narrowly one defines cognitive ability and job performance. Efforts continue, with minimal success (Bobko, Roth, & Potosky, 1999; Sackett, Schmitt, Ellingson, & Kabin, 2001), to minimize subgroup differences in personnel-selection measures. These differences are mostly a function of the use of measures of cognitive ability or of constructs closely related to cognitive ability, such as paper-and-pencil measures of job knowledge. In an interesting departure from the usual individual-level analysis of predictor-criterion relationships, Neuman and Wright (1999) showed that aggregated measures of team cognitive ability were related much better to team job performance than were individuals' cognitive ability and job performance.

Physical Ability

Most of what we know about physical ability derives from the work of Fleishman and his associates (Fleishman & Reilly, 1992) and J. C. Hogan (1991). Hogan provides data indicating that measures of physical ability are valid in a wide variety of contexts, but that there are large mean differences in physical-ability measures across gender groups and that validities within gender groups are often near zero. These results, along with concerns regarding requirements of the Americans with Disabilities Act (ADA), have dampened enthusiasm for the use of physical-ability measures. The procedure described by Good, Maisel, and Kriska (1998) to set the cutoff score for the use of a visual acuity test might be helpful in providing defensible means of using physical-ability tests. Psychomotor ability, which implies the use of a combination of cognitive, sensory, and muscular activity, has not been widely studied in the selection context usually because of the difficulty of developing appropriate instrumentation. Ackerman and Cianciolo (1999) provide an innovative computerized touch panel to measure psychomotor abilities. They provide initial evidence of the construct- and criterion-related validity of these measures and discuss the challenge associated with the development of dynamic versus static versions of this test.

Experience

Experience in a job like the one for which an applicant is being considered should be a reasonable proxy for both the can-do and will-do factors believed to be important for job success, and Rynes, Orlitzky, and Bretz (1997) present evidence that employers evaluate experienced hires versus inexperienced college graduates more favorably on a wide variety of dimensions. Most previous studies have operationalized experience as years on a job, position, or organization (see McDaniel, Schmidt, & Hunter, 1988, for a meta-analysis of the validity data). Quinones et al. (1995) have maintained that research has found mediocre results for the validity of job-experience variables because experience is often measured inappropriately. In the framework they provide, experience is measured at three different levels of specificity (task, job, and organization) and in three different modes (type, amount, and time). Job tenure is only one of the resulting nine types; we have very little data on the other eight types. In a performance model, it is important to specify the nature of the work experience and how it relates to some potential aspect of the job-performance domain. Tesluk and Jacobs (1998) provide an elaboration of this idea about experience that should generate additional research on experience-performance relationships that will enhance the utility of job-experience measures.

Motivational and Noncognitive Traits

The 1990s gave rise to a new interest in the use of personality and motivational characteristics in personnel selection, beginning with the meta-analysis by Barrick and Mount (1991) indicating that personality, especially measures of conscientiousness, was a valid predictor of job success. A second major factor stimulating further work on personality has been the contention of personality theorists that the myriad of available personality measures and constructs can be reduced to the *Big Five:* Conscientiousness, Neuroticism, Extraversion, Agreeableness, and Openness to Experience (Digman, 1990). Subsequent reviews of the personality literature in personnel selection (Hogan & Roberts, 1996; Hough, 1998b) have indicated that the Big Five may be too broad; that is, that significant increments in understanding can be achieved by considering additional narrower personality characteristics. Some empirical research supports this contention. Frei and McDaniel (1998) and Mabon (1998) provide support for a customer service orientation measure, as does the research by Hogan and colleagues (Hogan & Hogan, 1995). Siebert, Crant, and Kraimer (1999) provide evidence of the importance of a proactive personality in predicting career success, and Judge, Erez, and Bono (1998) point to the importance of a positive self-concept in predicting job performance. Hogan and Shelton (1998) present evidence for the importance of self presentation and social skills in job success and argue for seven personality dimensions. One factor that seems to be common to several of these studies was similar to achievement motivation, which Conway (2000) also found to be an important factor in managerial success.

Several other studies of the use of personality measures should be noted. Tett, Jackson, Rothstein, and Reddon (1999) present evidence that attention to the hypothesized direction of the relationship between personality and performance criteria provides significantly larger estimates of the validity of personality. Sackett et al. (1998) did not find evidence for an interaction between personality and ability in the prediction of performance. This notion has a long history and is reflected in our model of performance (see Figure 5.1). Barrick, Stewart, Neubert, and Mount (1998) found that aggregated team-member personality constructs were related to team performance. Finally, increased concern and attention to the measurement of contextual performance as described previously will likely increase the predictive utility of personality measures (Hogan, Rybicki, Motowidlo, & Borman, 1998).

Concern about the ability to fake personality measures continues. There is certainly evidence that job applicants can and do fake (Jackson, Wroblewski, & Ashton, 2000; Rosse, Stecher, Miller, & Levin, 1998). There is evidence suggesting that faking has little impact on criterion-related validity (Hough, 1998a). However, if there are individual differences in faking, different people will be selected if the best scores on personality measures are used to make decisions and attempts to correct for faking or social desirability are successful (Ellingson, Sackett, & Hough, 1999; Viswesvaran & Ones, 1999). James's conditional reasoning (James, 1998) represents an innovative approach to personality measurement that may help to remove the effects of social desirability as well as provide valid measures of job performance. James constructed reasoning problems in which respondents were asked to indicate their justification for an argument. These justifications were such that they indicated either a need for achievement or fear of failure, and were scored accordingly. James reports that the respondents accepted the statement that they are doing a judgment task and that they had no suspicion that the measure was an index of personality. He also reported impressive validities in the prediction of student grades among a group of student respondents. As James indicated, the conditional-reasoning approach to personality measurement should generate an interesting set of research questions and the potential for substantial improvements in the measurement of personality if original results replicate and generalize to other groups, outcomes, and situations.

Biodata, or scored versions of background experiences, hobbies, or preferences, probably represent alternate sources of information about motivation and personality. Early versions of these measures were scored application blanks; current versions of many biodata instruments are indistinguishable in format, and sometimes content, from many personality instruments (Mumford & Stokes, 1992). Two recent studies (McManus & Kelly, 1999; Mount, Witt, & Barrick, 2000), however, indicate that biodata measures have incremental validity over that afforded by measures of the Big Five personality constructs. Another issue central to the study and use of biodata has been the organizational specificity of biodata scoring keys. Given the variability in content, scoring key development, and uses of biodata, it is perhaps not surprising that this research has failed to produce much that is generalizable other than the fact that biodata appear to be valid predictors of a variety of performance criteria (Schmidt & Hunter, 1998). On the other hand, Rothstein et al. (1990) showed that developing a scoring key with the use of experts and responses from individuals in multiple organizations resulted in a scoring key whose validity generalized to multiple organizations. Also, Carlson, Scullen, Schmidt, Rothstein, and Erwin (1999) demonstrated the generalizability of the validity of a key developed in one organization to 24 other organizations. They attributed their success to the development of a common and valid criterion across organizations, large sample sizes, and the use of theory in developing items. The latter focus (on the development of rational scoring keys or constructs) has continued to receive a great deal of research attention (Stokes, 1999).

One concern that some (e.g., Pace & Schoenfeldt, 1977) have expressed about biodata is the potential for differences in racial or ethnic groups who approach various life and work experiences from a different cultural perspective. Schmitt and Pulakos (1998) reported differential response patterns across racial groups, especially for items related to the manner in which members of different subgroups reported interacting with other people.

Measures of Fit

Kristof (1996) has redirected the attention of personnel-selection researchers to the importance of a fit between individual differences and organizational environments. Werbel and Gilliland (1999) have extended these ideas with hypotheses about three different types of fit and their relationships to different potential work outcomes. *Person-job fit* should be based on ability, personality, and experience measures and should be most highly related to job proficiency measures and work innovations. *Person-workgroup fit* should be based on interpersonal attributes and ability and should be related to measures of workgroup effectiveness, unit cooperation, and interpersonal communication. *Person-organization fit* should be based on an analysis of values and needs and should result in job attitudes and organizational citizenship behaviors. Some support for these notions has been provided in studies by Van Vianen (2000) and Chan (1996), but research on fit-performance relationships of any type is relatively rare. Given that the objective of finding the right person for a job is at least the implicit goal of most selection systems, it is somewhat surprising that these fit hypotheses have not received more attention and support (although there may be significant methodological shortcomings in the research that has been conducted; Edwards, 2002).

METHODS OF MEASUREMENT

Aside from developments in the constructs measured, the last several years have seen significant changes in the methods used to measure those constructs. These changes have resulted from technology and from increased concern about the reactions of examinees as well as for concerns related to measurement and validity.

Technological Changes

The single most significant change in the method of measurement has been brought about by technology changes. For the past two decades, various paper-and-pencil tests have been administered and scored by computer. These simple page-turners provide a very cost effective and efficient way to collect test data and, for power tests at least, computerized tests seem to be equivalent to their paper-and-pencil counterparts (Mead & Drasgow, 1993). More recently, the use of *computer adaptive tests* (McBride, 1998) has also become widespread. Using items whose psychometric characteristics have been calibrated using item response theory, the computer matches the test item to the best estimate of the examinee's ability and discontinues testing when the accuracy of ability estimation does not improve in a useful manner with the addition of more items. Today, various Web-based assessments are becoming common, and CD-ROM and full-motion video and sound technology allow the simulation of complex jobs (e.g., Hanson, Borman, Mogilka, Manning, & Hedge, 1999).

Some of the advantages of computer-based testing are obvious—for example, standardization, ease of administration and scoring, and opportunity for increased realism in the development of test stimuli. However, we have probably not used this technology to assess constructs that are novel or not easily assessed in other ways as often as we should if we are to take full advantage of the technology. Two good examples of this type of work are the studies by Ackerman and Cianciolo (1999), who developed a computerized measure of psychomotor ability that was not possible in paper-and-pencil form; and Drasgow, Olson, Keenan, Moberg, and Mead (1993), who developed a computer simulation of conflict-resolution skills. Some other, similar examples of the innovative use of computer technology are described in Drasgow and Olson-Buchanan (1999). The liabilities of computerized assessments have also been described (Drasgow & Olson-Buchanan, 1999; McBride, 1998). Foremost among these liabilities are the cost and complexities of development, and in the case of Web-based testing, the security of the test materials and the examinees' responses. There remain many important research issues: reliability and validity of these tests, the incremental utility of these relatively expensive processes over more traditional test forms, the relative impact on subgroups who may not have the same experience with technology (Hoffman & Novak, 1998), the possibility of scoring open-ended computer responses (e.g., Bejar, 1991), and how to maximize the feedback provided to examinees (Schmitt, Gilliland, Landis, & Devine, 1993).

Interviews

Perhaps because the employment interview is so routinely used in employee selection at all levels in most organizations, and because it represents a context for the study of a wide variety of social and cognitive psychological theories (Eder & Harris, 1999), the interview has received a great deal of research attention for most of the past century (Wagner, 1949). Recent meta-analyses of interview validity (McDaniel

et al., 1994) have indicated some significant improvement in the validity and reliability of the employment interview. Most of these improvements are attributed to the increased use of structured interviews. Improvements in the interview include the following. First, consideration of content is important; that is, questions that are based on the findings of a job analysis and are demonstrably job related are superior to unplanned conversational interviews. Second, the same questions (in-depth, if necessary) should be asked of all candidates to provide a standardized instrument. Third, the use of rating scales that define good and bad answers to each question are helpful. Fourth, interviewer training that specifies how the interview is to be conducted, provides practice and feedback with respect to the conduct of the interview, and details the type of rater errors that can serve to diminish interview reliability and validity can serve to improve the psychometric quality of interview judgments. Campion, Palmer, and Campion (1997) have detailed the nature of these and other improvements in the selection interview and have examined the research literature on the impact of each. Most importantly for practice, these authors suggest that any combination of the 15 factors they examined would enhance the utility of the interview. Also important for employee-selection practice in this context is the finding that aspects of interview structure are related to positive outcomes in litigation (Williamson, Campion, Malos, Roehling, & Campion, 1997).

There is continued research (e.g., Burnett & Motowidlo, 1998; Huffcutt & Roth, 1998) on how interview decisions are made and what information is being used to make decisions. There is new interest in the types of constructs measured in the interview and how that relates to interview validity (Cortina et al., 2000) and the incremental validity of the interview when it is used along with other measures (Pulakos & Schmitt, 1996). It would seem that research directed to the question of what KSAOs are being measured reliably and validly in the interview (rather than whether the interview per se is reliable and valid) would provide greater understanding and progress in the long term.

Cross-Cultural Research

With the increased globalization of our economy, two research and practice issues have attracted the attention of those interested in personnel selection. The first issue involves the selection and success of individuals assigned to company facilities located in other countries. There is little empirical literature on *expatriate selection* (see Black, Mendenhall, & Oddou, 1991; Ronen, 1989), but that literature points to three skills: self-skills that relate to the individual's own capacity to maintain his or her mental health and well-being; relationship skills referring to the person's ability to develop successful interactions with persons in the host country; and perception skills that relate to the expatriate's ability to perceive and evaluate the behavior of people in the host country. The technical competence of the individual to perform his or her assigned duties may also play some role. Other variables such as previous experience with other cultures may be a factor, but the person's nonwork life and family adjustment are probably much more important. The importance of the latter concerns was reaffirmed in a recent study of expatriate withdrawal by Shaffer and Harrison (1998).

The second cross-cultural issue that has received some attention is the appropriateness of *translations of assessment devices* for use with people who do not speak or write English (e.g., Budgell, Raju, & Quartetti, 1995). Most of the research on the adequacy of translations has involved the use of measures of job attitudes (Ryan, Horvath, Ployhart, Schmitt, & Slade, 2000). This relatively small body of literature indicates that some ideas or test items are very difficult, if not impossible, to translate with the same psychological meaning even when very thorough back-translation techniques are used. Even when these instruments can be translated reasonably well, it is important to consider the host country's own practices with respect to selection (Levy-Leboyer, 1994). Clearly, there is a great need for more understanding of the applicability of our personnel-selection practices to other cultures. Efforts such as those represented by the work of Schmit, Kihm, and Robie (2000), in which the researchers set out to develop an instrument that could be used globally, should become more frequent and will provide useful models for research and practice in international selection.

Reactions to Selection Procedures

In the last decade, personnel-selection researchers have given increased attention to the reactions of job applicants both to the tests they are required to take and to the employment process. This research usually indicates that examinees react more favorably to procedures they view as job related (e.g., Elkins & Phillips, 2000); that they are more concerned about the outcomes of the selection process than they are about the process itself (e.g., Bauer, Maertz, Dolen, & Campion, 1998; Gilliland, 1994); that explanations for the processes employed result in better reactions than do no explanations (Horvath, Ryan, & Stierwalt, 2000); and that perceptions of affirmative action procedures are variable (Heilman, Battle, Keller, & Lee, 1998). There is a much smaller body of research relating these reactions to various personal or organi-

zational outcomes, and most of this research employs an intention to take a job or recommend the organization to one's friends (e.g., Schmitt & Chan, 1999).

The primary source of theoretical hypotheses regarding the impact of selection procedures on applicant reactions has been *organizational justice theory* (Gilliland, 1993). Although empirical research does confirm the importance of various aspects of procedural justice, it is usually true (as stated previously) that the outcomes of a selection decision for the applicant involved often play a much more significant role in employee perceptions.

Ryan and Ployhart (2000) have provided a very useful and critical review of the literature on applicant reactions to employee-selection procedures. They call for improvements in the measurement of test-taking attitudes and reactions measures, greater attention to outcomes other than organization perceptions or intentions measures, more focus on individual-difference (including demographic measures) antecedents of test reactions, greater attention to the role of social information in the selection context, and more theoretical emphasis in areas other than justice theory. On a practical level, Schmitt and Chan (1999) provide a series of suggestions they believe are supported by this research literature. Both the actual and perceived job-relatedness of selection procedures should be maximized. The use, development, and validation of the procedures should be explained to the applicants. All staff that deal with applicants should be trained to treat applicants with respect and courtesy. Applicants should be provided with feedback that is as timely as possible and feedback that is detailed, providing suggestions for remedial action if possible, and feedback that is designed to support the applicant's self-efficacy. Organizational personnel should take the time to make sure applicants understand the selection process and when they will be informed with respect to potential actions and outcomes. Finally, the entire process should be conducted as applicants are told it will be, and should be conducted consistently across applicants.

METHODOLOGICAL ISSUES AND POTENTIAL MODERATED RELATIONSHIPS

Some of the issues related to methods and moderators have been covered in other sections of the chapter (e.g., job analysis). Other such issues remain, and it is these on which this section of the chapter focuses. Specifically, this section includes a discussion of validation, prediction over time, other moderators, and performance modeling.

Validation

Although the term *validity* is used in many different ways, it is defined here as the degree to which evidence and theory support the interpretation of test scores for various proposed uses of the test (AERA, APA, NCME, 1999). Validation is, therefore, the compilation of evidence of inferential appropriateness. It is important to note that validity is not an attribute of a test, but is instead an attribute of the uses to which scores from a test are put. For example, cranial circumference scores from a good measuring tape may be perfectly appropriate (i.e., valid) for inferences about age in preadolescents, but they are likely inappropriate (i.e., not valid) for inferences about one's capability to deal with complex problem-solving situations.

The situation in a selection context is often quite complicated because validation involves establishing the connection between a selection tool and the outcome of interest. This outcome may be some of the performance constructs discussed earlier or some of the distal outcomes in Figure 5.1 that will be discussed shortly. This process can involve the validation of measures of predictor constructs, measures of criterion constructs, or measures of criterion constructs that may serve as predictors of some other outcome. Nevertheless, the inferences of primary interest in a selection context are those having to do with criteria, and validation involves the investigation of the appropriateness of those inferences regardless of whether they are based on direct measures (e.g., work samples) or indirect measures (e.g., cognitive ability).

Although we still speak of content, construct, and criterion-related validation (Binning & Barrett, 1989), it is now recognized that there are no different types of validity, only different strategies for justifying inferences (SIOP, 1987) and different inferences that might be justified (e.g., statistical conclusions vs. construct-related conclusions; Cook & Campbell, 1979). Validation involves theory development and testing, and any information about the test or job in question can contribute to a basis for conclusions regarding test scores (Binning & Barrett, 1989).

With these realizations has come an increased appreciation of the need to take a more complex view of job performance, as described previously (Campbell, 1990). This has, in turn, led to increased efforts to match particular predictors to particular aspects of performance. Examples of research showing differential relationships between different performance dimensions and different predictor constructs were provided earlier in this chapter (e.g., Motowidlo & Van Scotter, 1994). Additional evidence suggesting a more complex view of validation comes in the form of studies focusing not on bivariate predictor-criterion relationships but on incre-

mental validity. This is useful from a practical standpoint in that it allows an examination of contribution over and above existing selection procedures. Pulakos and Schmitt (1995) demonstrated the incremental validity of an experience-based interview over and above cognitive ability in predicting composite performance ratings. McManus and Kelly (1999) showed that four of the Big Five personality factors predicted contextual performance over and above a biodata instrument and that extraversion alone contributed to the prediction of task-related performance over and above the biodata instrument. Mount et al. (2000) found similarly encouraging results for the contribution of biodata scores beyond both personality and cognitive ability.

Consideration of incremental validity can also be useful from a theoretical perspective. Cortina et al. (2000) showed that structured interviews contributed to the prediction of performance over and above both cognitive ability and conscientiousness. In addition to the practical implications, these results refute suggestions that interviews merely are poor measures of cognitive ability or indirect measures of conscientiousness. Goffin, Rothstein, and Johnston (1996) showed similar results for assessment centers and personality. The incremental validity evidence from these studies informs not only practice, but also our understanding of commonly used selection tools.

Finally, although *banding* is discussed later in the chapter, it is worth mentioning here that the trend toward taking a more complex view has also spread to procedures for constructing equivalence bands around selection scores. Aguinis, Cortina, and Goldberg (1998) developed a banding procedure that takes into account not only predictor reliability, but also criterion reliability and criterion-related validity. Banding test scores usually involves consideration of the unintended consequences of testing (Messick, 1998) or the explicit consideration that more than performance outcomes must be considered in test use. Taken as whole, the evidence suggests that our field has taken a much-needed step in the direction of more complex characterizations of work behavior and models for predicting it.

Prediction Over Time

The importance of time in models of performance prediction has been recognized for several years (Henry & Hulin, 1987). Perhaps the most ubiquitous finding in longitudinal studies of performance prediction has been the *superdiagonal* or *simplex* pattern of correlations in which predictor-criterion relationships are highest at Time 1 and decrease steadily as the separation in time between the predictor and the criterion increases (Humphreys, 1960). Among the implications of such a pattern is that the rank order of job applicants would change over time such that the person most likely to perform well tomorrow may not be the person most likely to perform well next year.

Ackerman (1987) has suggested that deterioration is not uniform, but varies with the type of predictor and the consistency of the task on which performance is measured. For inconsistent tasks, higher order cognitive abilities continue to predict performance over time. For consistent tasks, the predictiveness of higher order cognitive abilities deteriorates substantially over time, whereas the importance of lower order abilities such as perceptual speed and psychomotor ability wax in importance.

Keil and Cortina (2001) showed that although deterioration occurred regardless of task consistency and type of ability, the deterioration was curvilinear, conforming to a cusp catastrophe model such as those found in the work of S. Guastello (Guastello & Guastello, 1998). Ployhart and Hakel (1998) showed that there were individual differences in performance changes over time, and that the latent growth parameters representing these changes were predicted by biodata scores.

Although this area has a long history, research has been sporadic. The fact that the inferences involved in personnel selection are always longitudinal (i.e., using scores today to predict performance in the future), it is critical that the role time might play in selection models be examined in much more detail than it has been in the past.

Moderators

There are, of course, many different potential moderators of the relationships among individual difference variables, including those identified in our model as mediators such as declarative knowledge and motivation, and, on the other hand, performance and outcomes. We are also cognizant of the research that indicates that most predictors used by personnel-selection specialists are valid in most contexts in which they are used (Schmidt & Hunter, 1998). However, validities do vary in practically significant ways. Our purpose here is merely to highlight a few factors that have accounted for such variability in recent research.

Beginning with the individual difference–mediator relationships, *job type* seems important to consider as a moderator. Certainly, different individual difference variables should predict knowledge for different jobs (Campbell et al., 1993). Similarly, motivation to perform in a job might be predicted to a different degree by a given individual difference variable than it is for a different job (e.g., extraversion predicting motivation to perform in a job with a large social component,

but not predicting motivation in a job with a more typical social component).

The same might be true for *task complexity* such that cognitive ability may relate to knowledge and motivation for complex jobs to a greater degree than it would for simple jobs, particularly over longer periods of time (Ackerman, 1987). Complexity, of course, has long been recognized as an important moderator of the cognitive ability–performance rating relationship (Hunter & Hunter, 1984). Other similarly functioning moderator candidates might be *climate for updating* (Tracey, Tannenbaum, & Kavanagh, 1995) and *psychological contract violation* (Robinson & Morrison, 1995).

The mediator-performance relationship might also be moderated by a variety of factors. We might infer from Barrick and Mount (1993) that autonomy would moderate the relationship between knowledge-motivation and performance, and this might be particularly true for the more discretionary aspects of performance. Other candidates that might be perceived are organizational support (Grover & Crooker, 1995), role conflict and extracurricular demands (Galinsky & Stein, 1990), dynamaticity (Hesketh & Neal, 1999), psychological contract violation (Robinson & Morrison, 1995), and perceived reasons for contract violation (Turnley & Feldman, 1999).

Finally, there is also likely to be a variety of factors that influence the relationship between performance and more distal outcome variables. One obvious example is market conditions, such that low performance is less likely to lead to negative consequences in a tight labor market than in a looser market. Likewise, high performers might be more likely to leave an organization when there are fewer alternatives available. Also, becoming more important is personal *skill development* (London & Mone, 1999). Those who have taken time to develop their skills continuously will find it easier to obtain subsequent employment.

Performance Models

Beginning with the work of Hunter (1986), personnel-selection researchers have also proposed and tested a variety of increasingly complex performance models. These models include cognitive and noncognitive measures, mediators, and both contextual- and task-proficiency measures (e.g., Borman et al., 1991; Pulakos, Schmitt, & Chan, 1996). These models are similar to that depicted in Figure 5.1 and we suspect that there will be many more future attempts to test theories of job performance that include a broader array of individual difference and contextual variables. Testing these models usually requires the use of structural equation modeling and other multivariate techniques rather than correlation and regression analyses, which have usually been the primary data-analytic tools in selection research.

Summary

In this section, we discussed topics relevant for validity and validation, prediction over time, and moderators of the relationships between the classes of variables included in our model. Obviously, this discussion was selective; there is a much larger body of such research. We are encouraged by the increased appreciation of the complexity of relationships among variables relevant for selection reflected in the consideration of multiple predictors, multiple and specific criteria, and the boundary conditions within which the relationships among them operate.

DISTAL OUTCOMES OF THE SELECTION PROCESS AND EMPLOYEE PERFORMANCE

In this section, we consider relatively distal outcomes associated with the can-do and will-do variables studied in personnel selection. In most cases, these outcomes are the result of an employee's behavior rather than the behavior itself, although we realize that, in some cases (e.g., withdrawal and counterproductive behavior), this distinction does not apply. Prediction of these distal outcomes using can-do and will-do measures has often proceeded without consideration of potential mediators.

Aspects of Productivity

Although the term *productivity* is used often, its definition has been far from consistent (Pritchard, 1992). Adding to the confusion is the fact that productivity can be considered at a variety of levels of analysis. For example, Pritchard (1992) defines *organizational productivity* as how well an organization uses its resources to achieve its goals. Payne (2000) modified this definition in an attempt to define *individual productivity* as how well an individual uses available resources to contribute to organizational goals. Payne (2000) goes on to explain that productivity is a combination of *efficiency* (ratio of inputs to outputs) and *effectiveness* (amount and quality of output relative to some standard or expectation).

I/O psychologists tend to focus on effectiveness, although it is usually referred to as *job performance* (Pritchard, 1992) or perhaps as *productivity*. This confusion stems in large part from a lack of clear delineation among the concepts of productivity, performance, efficiency, and effectiveness.

Campbell, Dunnette, Lawler, and Weick (1970) provided a useful distinction between performance and effectiveness, but that distinction has been largely ignored. Payne (2000) provided a similar delineation at the individual level of analysis. First, effectiveness is distinguished from performance through consideration of the value associated with a given behavior. Specifically, effectiveness is a function of performance dimensions (i.e., value-free markers of behavior), value weights for those dimensions determined by the organization and its goals, and situational factors. Second, efficiency is the sum of input to (value-free) performance ratios plus situational factors. Third, productivity is efficiency plus effectiveness plus any additional situational factors that might be influential. Finally, organizational productivity is a function of the productivity of its individuals plus higher level situational factors.

Thus, in considering productivity as an outcome in a model of personnel selection, we must consider both efficiency and effectiveness. Clearly, those employees or components of an organization that produce more of the behaviors that are strongly tied to the goals of the organization will be more productive. Also, those employees or components that can produce those behaviors with less input (e.g., time, money, materials) will be more productive. Those individual, group, or organizational attributes that increase these behaviors or decrease the amount of input required to generate them will contribute to productivity.

Clearly, higher task-related, contextual, and adaptive performance will lead to higher effectiveness (all else equal), and therefore, higher productivity. This ignores, however, the weights attached to the different aspects of performance and the efficiency with which those aspects of performance are produced. With respect to efficiency, Payne (2000) examined a new construct called *efficiency orientation (EO)*, which is defined as "the tendency to approach a task with the goal of obtaining the most out of the resources used" (p. 23). Those who tend to approach a task with the intention of maximizing output given a fixed amount of input, or of reducing input given a high level of output, are more likely to minimize input to output ratios, thus making them more efficient. This, in turn, results in higher individual productivity.

Withdrawal Behavior

In some jobs, the most important aspect of performance is the presence of the employee. In production jobs that are controlled by an assembly line, in which completion of a task (not its quality) is of central interest, the most important performance variable is whether the worker comes to work and remains at work. In these jobs, tardiness, absenteeism, and turnover are often used as the primary outcome or performance index. Even for jobs in which the employee has flexibility with respect to where and when he or she does the required tasks, turnover, absenteeism, and tardiness, broadly defined, are important. Using these as performance indices produces a variety of well-known definitional and measurement problems (Johns, 1994). Hulin (1991) has argued that these variables and others should be considered in the aggregate as measures of a *withdrawal construct*. Hanisch (1995) has presented a model that includes organizational, job, and work withdrawal constructs. Each of these aggregate variables has multiple, and more specific, behavioral manifestations. For example, work withdrawal might be indicated by tardiness, leaving work early, absenteeism, taking long and unauthorized work breaks, and increased drug abuse. A worker who cannot withdraw in this manner may strike out at the organization in other ways such as stealing supplies, filing grievances, or in extreme cases, in a violent manner. On the positive side, an engaged worker might display organizational citizenship behaviors such as organizing parties, cleaning the workplace, or volunteering for special projects. Attitudinal correlates of these behaviors include work and organizational commitment. In the Hanisch (1995) model, individual differences (values, personality, work attitudes) play a role in moderating the relationship between cognitive and attitudinal antecedents (e.g., stress, pay inequity, satisfaction) and withdrawal. Hanisch, Hulin, and Roznowski (1998) reviewed a series of studies in which this general model was used to predict withdrawal constructs as a function of sexual harassment, job attitudes, and organizational commitment. As expected, these aggregate withdrawal measures are more highly correlated with various predictors than is usually found with single indicator measures of withdrawal.

This *theory of adaptive behavior* suggests that researchers will achieve a greater understanding of such behaviors by studying them as aggregates rather than as isolated measures of performance. The theory also suggests that different isolated withdrawal behaviors are a function of the same psychological processes, that they should be correlated, and that they have a common set of antecedents including individual difference variables. Although this theory provides a promising new approach to a set of variables that have proved difficult to understand and predict, there is not, to our knowledge, any research that has focused on the use of these variables as criteria in selection research.

Harrison and Martocchio (1998), in their excellent review of the literature on absenteeism, argue similarly with respect to the time period over which absenteeism is aggregated in research studies. These authors provide a discussion of absenteeism theory and empirical research suggesting that personality and demographic variables are distal long-term determinants of absenteeism that might determine attitudes toward attendance at work, organizational commitment, job satisfaction, job involvement, and social context, which in turn determine the short-term daily decision to attend work. They provide a fairly short and simple list of precursors of absenteeism that should be helpful in subsequent selection research in which the major outcome of interest is attendance.

Counterproductive Behavior

There is a great deal of research in personnel selection on integrity testing (Ones et al., 1993; Sackett & Wanek, 1996). *Integrity tests* are usually paper-and-pencil tests that purport to identify individuals likely to lie or steal from an organization or to present security risks. Sackett and Wanek (1996) reported that validity studies in which theft criteria were used reported relatively low predictive validity (.09–corrected to .13). When broader job-performance criteria are used, validities are substantially better (.27–corrected to .39). The latter finding is consistent with the notion that some integrity tests are tapping into a broader conscientiousness factor that is usually a valid predictor of job performance (Murphy & Lee, 1994).

More recently, discussions of lying or stealing have often considered these behaviors or negative aspects of performance as part of a constellation of counterproductive behaviors that includes arson, bribery, blackmail, discrimination, fraud, violence, sabotage, harassment of coworkers, and even some forms of whistle-blowing (Giacalone & Greenberg, 1997; Murphy, 1993). Like the withdrawal behaviors discussed previously, these counterproductive behaviors may be the result of similar psychological processes. Spector (1997) argues that these acts may be the result of reactions to frustration. If this is the case, then, from a personnel-selection perspective, it would be most important to identify those individuals who are most susceptible to frustration and who are likely to act in an antisocial fashion to that frustration. Measurement of counterproductive behavior, like measurement of withdrawal behavior, is difficult. Many of these variables occur rarely; hence we have the usual base-rate problems in predictive studies (Martin & Terris, 1991). In addition, for obvious reasons, it is often difficult to identify the persons who engage in counterproductive behavior (Murphy, 1993).

Even with these problems, there are some promising studies of several of these behaviors. The work of Fitzgerald and colleagues (Fitzgerald, Drasgow, Hulin, Gelfand, & Magley, 1997; Magley, Hulin, Fitzgerald, & DeNardo, 1999) has contributed greatly to our understanding of the nature of sexual harassment as well its antecedents and outcomes. The use of background checks has been suggested as a means of detecting violence-prone individuals (Mantell, 1994), although very little research on their effectiveness exists (Slora, Joy, Jones, & Terris, 1991). Mantell (1994) suggests a check of driving records and of military, criminal, and credit history as well as a series of situational interview questions as means of identifying violence-prone individuals. Giacalone, Riordan, and Rosenfeld (1997) provide an analysis of the nature of sabotage as well as various possible explanations for this behavior. Miceli and Near (1992, 1997) have done much to further our understanding of positive and negative whistleblowing, although there are no data of which we are aware that provide empirical evidence of the relationship between individual differences and subsequent acts of whistleblowing.

Our understanding of this broad range of counterproductive behavior is only beginning to develop. Given the huge potential individual, social, and financial costs of some of these acts, research on this area of work performance is certainly overdue. Beyond the direct costs of these behaviors, there are often also unanticipated but significant legal implications (Ryan & Lasek, 1991).

Accidents and Health and Safety Outcomes

Accidents are indicators of performance, rather than performance itself. In addition, most types of accidents occur rarely; hence we have the same base-rate problem in research on accidents we did for some of the counterproductive and withdrawal behaviors noted in the previous section. Moreover, accidents likely have causes (work conditions, machine malfunction, etc.) other than individual differences. As a consequence, researchers usually focus on predicting and understanding unsafe behavior rather than accidents per se. Studies of accidents have often taken the form of post hoc analysis of case studies (Kaempf, Klein, Thordsen, & Wolf, 1996), the analysis of near-miss accidents (Hofmann & Stetzer, 1998), and the development of checklist measures and observational techniques to measure a person's safe behavior (Hofmann & Stetzer, 1996). All these methods focus on human performance in the accident situation as opposed to the occurrence of the accident itself. However, very few of these research efforts have focused on individual characteristics as determiners of accident behavior as did early efforts (Whitlock, Clouse, & Spencer, 1963). The focus has been on the design of the workplace or the safety climate in the organization or the workgroup (Hofmann & Stetzer, 1996).

The concept of *accident-proneness,* defined as a quality of persons with individual difference characteristics that make them more likely than others to have accidents in any situation, has received limited support (McCormick & Ilgen, 1985; Whitlock et al., 1963) and little attention in recent years. A sequential model of the occurrence of accidents presented by McCormick and Ilgen suggests that individual differences should be involved in the perception of an unsafe situation, our cognitive evaluation of the situation, our decisions to avoid a situation, and our ability to avoid that situation. With greater understanding and better measurement of the criterion space (i.e., unsafe behavior), it seems personnel-selection researchers should rediscover this area of research.

Litigation and Social Responsibility

Over the past three or four decades, personnel selection and its impact on members of diverse groups have been the subject of legislation (Civil Rights Acts of 1964 and 1991; ADA), professional guidelines (AERA, APA, & NCME, 1999; SIOP, 1987), executive orders (e.g., President Johnson's executive order 11246 establishing the Office of Federal Contract Compliance), governmental guidelines (Uniform Guidelines on Employee Selection Procedures, 1978) and extensive litigation and case law development (for a review see Sharf & Jones, 1999). These external events have challenged personnel-selection researchers to reexamine not only the usual validity and reliability issues addressed in much of this chapter, but also the impact that these measures have on the opportunities afforded members of diverse groups in our society. The latter has stimulated a new term, *consequential validity* (Messick, 1998), which refers to the broad set of outcomes that result from use of a selection procedure in addition to the prediction of some organizationally relevant criterion.

The research that this external attention generated has clarified some points. First, tests have not been found to be psychometrically biased in that predicted outcomes for various protected groups do not seem to be lower than actual outcomes. Second, there are large minority-majority subgroup differences on some tests, especially cognitive ability tests. Various attempts to remove these subgroup differences in measured cognitive ability may serve to diminish subgroup differences, but large differences in subgroup performance remain and often produce legally defined levels of adverse impact on minority groups (Sackett et al., 2001). There is no general agreement as to how to prevent discrimination or its past effects. Affirmative-action programs seem to have negative consequences for perceptions of employees who are thought to be hired based on group membership rather than merit (Heilman et al., 1998), although most of this research has been conducted in the laboratory and does not consider similar impact over a long period of time. Affirmative-action programs do seem to result in employment improvement for minority groups and women (Kravitz et al., 1997), although reverse discrimination cases now indicate that race or irrelevant class membership criteria cannot be used in selection decisions.

The results regarding the lack of predictive bias in ability tests and large subgroup differences in test scores suggest that overall utility of a selection procedure will be diminished when tests are not utilized in an optimal manner (Boudreau, 1991). However, studies conducted at the organizational level (Leonard, 1990; Steel & Lovrich, 1987) do not indicate a relationship between the proportion of minorities or women in organizations and organizational efficiency measures. In an analysis of 3,200 employers in four large metropolitan areas, Holzer and Neumark (1996) showed little evidence of substantially weaker job performance among most groups of minority and female affirmative-action hires. Consideration of the outcomes related to various human resource interventions including selection at the organizational level has become increasingly common in human resources research (e.g., Schneider et al., 2000). This research, an increased sense of the importance of corporate social responsibility (see the October 1999 issue of the *Academy of Management Journal*), and the recognition on the part of many large corporations (Doyle, 2000) that a well-educated, highly diverse workforce composed of people who have learned to work productively and creatively with individuals from many races, religious, and cultural histories are all important to maintaining organizational global competitiveness. These trends suggest that personnel-selection researchers need to broaden the criteria by which they judge individual and organizational effectiveness. Such broadening may change the KSAOs we judge to be important for success and may change the research questions we ask when considering the KSAO-performance relationships across various subgroups in our society.

Customer Satisfaction and Loyalty

Considerable attention has been focused in the professional literature and in the popular media on the need for organizations to be more sensitive to quality issues and customer satisfaction. In addition, the number and proportion of the workforce that is directly involved in service to customers has continued to rise over the past two decades. This increased emphasis on service quality and customer satisfaction has generated some interest in the relationship between employee behavior and attitudes and customer satisfaction. In most studies of customer service, the performance

measure is a survey measure administered to customers (e.g., Johnson, 1996; Schneider, White, & Paul, 1998). Factor analyses of these dimensions (Johnson; Schneider et al.) generally reveal factors related to courtesy or interpersonal treatment, competence, convenience or efficiency, and ability to resolve problems. Rogg, Schmidt, Shull, and Schmitt (2001) found that these customer satisfaction indices were also highly related (>.70) to what they described as an objective measure of service quality, the number of times a customer needed to return to have his or her car repaired by auto dealerships. The latter index might be preferred by some researchers, but it should be pointed out that sometimes the employee may not be in complete control of the service rendered; that is, the company's product is defective in ways that the employee cannot correct.

Hogan, Hogan, and Busch (1984) report on the development and validation of the Service Orientation Index as part of the Hogan Personality Inventory. A recent meta-analysis (Frei & McDaniel, 1998) of attempts to measure service orientation as an individual difference predictor of supervisory ratings included a very large number of studies using this index. Vinchur, Schippman, Switzer, and Roth (1998) also provide evidence for the successful prediction of sales performance using a wide variety of biodata and personality measures. Results indicated that the average corrected validity of these measures was .50 and that service orientation was positively correlated with conscientiousness, extraversion, and agreeableness and unrelated to cognitive ability. The work on effectiveness in sales occupations (Schmitt, Gooding, Noe, & Kirsch, 1984) is also relevant and usually indicates the importance of personality or motivation variables (Ghiselli, 1973). Selection research in the area of customer service should be conducted using behavioral measures derived from customers but also attending to various organizational constraints and aids (Schneider, Wheeler, & Cox, 1992).

SOCIETAL AND ORGANIZATIONAL ISSUES

There are a number of larger issues that are affecting selection practices in organizations, or at least the manner in which they are examined. On most of these issues, there are few empirical studies, but we believe that research addressing these concerns is needed and will be conducted in the next several years. The first three of these issues demand that we attend to levels-of-analysis issues in our research on selection (Klein & Kozlowski, 2000; Schneider et al., 2000). Both theory and data analyses must be oriented appropriately to a consideration of variables at individual, group, or organizational levels.

First, there seems to be an increasing interest in examining the effect of human resource efforts including selection at the organizational level. Terpstra and Rozell (1993) represent the only systematic study of the relationship between specific selection practices and organizational-level measures of performance. They reported correlational data supporting the conclusion that organizations employing relatively greater numbers of selection practices (e.g., structured interviews, cognitive ability tests, biodata, and evaluations of recruiting sources) had higher annual profit, profit growth, and overall performance. Studies assessing a wider variety of human resource criteria and their relationship to organizational outcomes have become more common (e.g., Huselid, Jackson, & Schuler, 1997; Shaw, Delery, Jenkins, & Gupta, 1998). Typically, these studies report statistically significant, but low (<.10) correlations between these organizational-level variables. The measures of human resource efforts used in these studies are often simple, single-item measures and the studies themselves are usually cross-sectional surveys. Much more conceptual and empirical work is needed in assessing the impact of selection on organizational performance.

Second, Johns (1993) has argued that selection researchers must view their efforts as organizational interventions subject to the same mechanisms and processes described in the innovation-diffusion and implementation literatures rather than as technical improvements that any rational manager would adopt if he or she understood validity data. Johns (1993) presents a number of propositions, the central thesis being that variance in the adoption of psychology-based interventions is a function of the decision-making frame of managers, the nature of the I/O theory and research presented to them, and critical events and actors in the external environment of the adopting organization. Most practitioners will be able to cite technically meritorious practices that are not adopted or are modified in inappropriate ways for a variety of social and organizational reasons. Validation work that includes assessment and evaluation of the roles of these factors may prove useful in discerning individual difference-performance relationships.

Third, there is a trend among organizational scholars to think of selection as a means to further organizational strategic objectives. Traditionally, the focus in selection research has been on the match between a person and a job. A common notion among strategic planners (Snow & Snell, 1993) is to view selection as a method of staffing an organization with persons whose KSAOs help effectively implement organizational strategy. This idea is similar to the job-match focus, but some believe that selection should or can drive organizational strategy. If organizations hire a great many innovative personnel, over a period of time its research and development efforts may become more important than its production capabilities. If selection is to propel strategy, we may need to focus on broader KSAOs that indicate an individual's capacity to adapt to and change her or his environment (Chan, 1997; Pulakos et al., 2000).

Today, many organizations have facilities or markets in countries throughout the world. This globalization requires communication among people from different cultures and frequently the relocation of personnel from one country or culture to another. Because of the enormous expense associated with these moves, the selection, training, adaptation, and repatriation of these international assignees has begun to receive research attention (Black et al., 1991). The empirical literature available suggests that previous experience, interpersonal skills and self-efficacy in dealing with people of diverse cultures, nonwork life concerns, and the nature of the host country's culture have been found to be critical in expatriate adjustment. Certainly, adjustment to other cultures requires a set of nontechnical interpersonal skills that are not normally evaluated by organizations.

Fifth, many organizations have outsourced parts of their human resource function including selection in efforts to downsize. When this happens, the function is often provided by consultants. When this is the case, it is critical that organizational personnel value the service provided and understand the manner in which it is to be used. Without adequate implementation plans and sufficiently committed and trained personnel, even the best developed assessment center or structured interview will not be used appropriately and will undoubtedly fail to contribute what it otherwise might to the identification of human talent. The impact of outsourcing on the effectiveness of selection procedures and even the type and quality of the procedures that are developed has not been examined.

There are undoubtedly other external societal issues that influence the capability of personnel-selection researchers in their attempts to understand and predict employee performance. These represent some we believe should or will be important in the short term.

CONCLUSION

Personnel-selection research has clearly expanded from its early interest in documenting predictor-criterion relationships. There has been great progress in considering a broader range of predictors and outcomes and in their measurement. Sophisticated performance models are being proposed and tested. The broader social significance of personnel selection and the reactions of examinees to our procedures are receiving greater attention. We believe these are positive trends and hope that the many questions we posed throughout this chapter will be addressed in the near future.

REFERENCES

Ackerman, P. L. (1987). Individual differences in skill learning: An integration of psychometric and information processing perspectives. *Psychological Bulletin, 102,* 3–27.

Ackerman, P. L., & Cianciolo, A. T. (1999). Psychomotor abilities via touch-panel testing: Measurement innovations, construct, and criterion validity. *Human Performance, 12,* 231–273.

Ackerman, P. L., & Heggestad, E. D. (1997). Intelligence, personality, and interests: Evidence for overlapping traits. *Psychological Bulletin, 121,* 219–245.

Aguinis, H., Cortina, J. M., & Goldberg, E. (1998). A new procedure for computing equivalence bands in personnel selection. *Human Performance, 11,* 351–365.

American Educational Research Association, American Psychological Association, & National Council on Measurement in Education. (1999). *Standards for educational and psychological testing.* Washington, DC: American Psychological Association.

Austin, J. T., & Villanova, P. (1992). The criterion problem: 1917–1992. *Journal of Applied Psychology, 77,* 803–835.

Ball, C. T., Langholtz, H. J., Auble, J., & Sopchak, B. (1998). Resource-allocation strategies: A verbal protocol analysis. *Organizational Behavior & Human Decision Processes, 76,* 70–88.

Barber, A. E., & Roehling, M. V. (1993). Job postings and the decision to interview: A verbal protocol analysis. *Journal of Applied Psychology, 78,* 845–856.

Barber, A. E., & Wesson, M. J. (1998). Using verbal protocol analysis to assess the construct validity of an empirical measure: An examination of the OCP. In J. A. Wagner (Ed.), *Advances in qualitative organization research* (Vol. 1, pp. 67–104). Greenwich, CT: JAI Press.

Barrick, M. R., & Mount, M. K. (1991). The Big-Five personality dimensions in job performance: A meta-analysis. *Personnel Psychology, 44,* 1–26.

Barrick, M. R., & Mount, M. K. (1993). Autonomy as a moderator of the relationships between the Big Five personality dimensions and job performance. *Journal of Applied Psychology, 78,* 111–118.

Barrick, M. R., Stewart, G. L., Neubert, M. J., & Mount, M. K. (1998). Relating member ability and personality to work-team processes and team effectiveness. *Journal of Applied Psychology, 83,* 377–391.

Bauer, T. N., Maertz, C. P., Jr., Dolen, M. R., & Campion, M. A. (1998). Longitudinal assessment of applicant reactions to employment testing and test outcome feedback. *Journal of Applied Psychology, 83,* 892–903.

Bejar, I. I. (1991). A methodology for scoring open-ended architectural design problems. *Journal of Applied Psychology, 76,* 522–532.

Binning, J. F., & Barrett, G. V. (1989). Validity of personnel decisions: A conceptual analysis of the inferential and evidentiary bases. *Journal of Applied Psychology, 74,* 478–494.

Black, J. S., Mendenhall, M., & Oddou, G. (1991). Toward a comprehensive model of international adjustment: An integration of multiple theoretical perspectives. *Academy of Management Review, 16,* 291–317.

Bobko, P., Roth, P. L., & Potosky, D. (1999). Derivation and implications of a meta-analytic matrix incorporating cognitive ability, alternative predictors, and job performance. *Personnel Psychology, 52,* 561–589.

Borman, W. C., Hanson, M. A., & Hedge, J. W. (1997). Personnel selection. *Annual Review of Psychology, 48,* 299–337.

Borman, W. C., & Motowidlo, S. J. (1993). Expanding the criterion domain to include elements of contextual performance. In N. Schmitt & W. C. Borman (Eds.), *Personnel selection in organizations* (pp. 71–98). San Francisco: Jossey-Bass.

Borman, W. C., & Motowidlo, S. J. (1997). Task performance and contextual performance: The meaning for personnel selection research. *Human Performance, 10,* 99–110.

Borman, W. C., White, L. A., Pulakos, E. D., & Oppler, S. H. (1991). Models of supervisory job performance ratings. *Journal of Applied Psychology, 76,* 863–872.

Boudreau, J. W. (1991). Utility analysis for decisions in human resource management. In M. D. Dunnette & L. M. Hough (Eds.), *Handbook of industrial and organizational psychology* (pp. 621–746). Palo Alto, CA: Consulting Psychologists Press.

Bridges, W. (1994, September 19). The end of the job. *Fortune, 130,* 62–74.

Brief, A. P., & Motowidlo, S. J. (1986). Prosocial organizational behaviors. *Academy of Management Review, 11,* 710–725.

Budgell, G. R., Raju, N. S., & Quartetti, D. A. (1995). Analysis of differential item functioning in translated assessment instruments. *Applied Psychological Measurement, 19,* 309–321.

Burnett, J. R., & Motowidlo, S. J. (1998). Relations between different sources of information in the structured selection interview. *Personnel Psychology, 51,* 963–982.

Campbell, J. P. (1990). Modeling the performance prediction problem in industrial and organizational psychology. In M. D. Dunnette & L. M. Hough (Eds.), *Handbook of industrial and organizational psychology* (Vol. 1, 2nd ed., pp. 687–732). Palo Alto, CA: Consulting Psychologists Press.

Campbell, J. P. (1999). The definition and measurement of performance in the new age. In D. R. Ilgen & E. D. Pulakos (Eds.), *The changing nature of performance* (pp. 399–429). San Francisco: Jossey-Bass.

Campbell, J. P., Dunnette, M. D., Lawler, E. E., III, & Weick, K. E., Jr. (1970). *Managerial behavior, performance, and effectiveness.* New York: McGraw-Hill.

Campbell, J. P., Gasser, M. B., & Oswald, F. L. (1996). The substantive nature of job performance variability. In K. R. Murphy (Ed.), *Individual differences and behavior in organizations* (pp. 258–299). San Francisco: Jossey-Bass.

Campbell, J. P., McCloy, R. A., Oppler, S. H., & Sager, C. E. (1993). A theory of performance. In N. Schmitt & W. C. Borman (Eds.), *Personnel selection in organizations* (pp. 35–70). San Francisco: Jossey-Bass.

Campion, M. A., & McClelland, C. L. (1993). Follow-up and extension of the interdisciplinary costs and benefits of enlarged jobs. *Journal of Applied Psychology, 78,* 339–351.

Campion, M. A., Palmer, D. K., & Campion, J. E. (1997). A review of structure in the selection interview. *Personnel Psychology, 50,* 655–702.

Campion, M. A., & Thayer, P. W. (1985). Development and field evaluation of an interdisciplinary measure of job design. *Journal of Applied Psychology, 70,* 29–43.

Carlson, K. D., Scullen, S. E., Schmidt, F. L., Rothstein, H. R., & Erwin, F. (1999). Generalizable biographical data validity can be achieved without multi-organizational development and keying. *Personnel Psychology, 52,* 731–755.

Carroll, J. B. (1993). *Human cognitive abilities: A survey of factor-analytic studies.* Cambridge, England: Cambridge University Press.

Chan, D. (1996). Cognitive misfit of problem-solving style at work: A facet of person-organization fit. *Organizational Behavior and Human Decision Processes, 68,* 167–181.

Chan, D. (1997). *Individual differences and learning perspectives on the construct of adaptability: An integrative person-situation approach.* Paper presented at the annual meeting of the Academy of Management, Boston.

Chan, D., & Schmitt, N. (1997). Video-based versus paper-and-pencil method of assessment in situational judgment tests: Subgroup differences in test performance and face validity perceptions. *Journal of Applied Psychology, 82,* 143–159.

Chipman, S. F., Schraagen, J. M., & Shalin, V. L. (2000). Introduction to cognitive task analysis. In J. M. Schraagen, S. F. Chipman, & V. L. Shalin (Eds.), *Cognitive task analysis* (pp. 3–24). Mahwah, NJ: Erlbaum.

Clevenger, J., Pereira, G. M., Wiechmann, D., Schmitt, N., & Schmidt Harvey, V. (2001). Incremental validity of the situational judgment inventory relative to cognitive ability, conscientiousness, experience, and job knowledge. *Journal of Applied Psychology, 86,* 410–417.

Conway, J. M. (1999). Distinguishing contextual performance form task performance for managerial jobs. *Journal of Applied Psychology, 84,* 3–13.

Conway, J. M. (2000). Managerial performance development constructs and personality correlates. *Human Performance, 13,* 23–46.

Cook, T. D., & Campbell, D. T. (1979). *Quasi-experimentation: Design and analysis issues for field settings.* Chicago: Rand-McNally.

Cortina, J. M., Goldstein, N. B., Payne, S. C., Davison, H. K., & Gilliland, S. W. (2000). The incremental validity of interview scores over and above cognitive ability and conscientiousness scores. *Personnel Psychology, 53,* 325–352.

DeShon, R. P., Brown, K. G., & Greenis, J. L. (1996). Does self-regulation require cognitive resources? Evaluation of resource allocation models of goal setting. *Journal of Applied Psychology, 81,* 595–608.

Digman, J. M. (1990). Personality structure: Emergence of the five factor model. *Annual Review of Psychology, 41,* 417–440.

Dorsey, D. W., Campbell, G. E., Foster, L. L., & Miles, D. E. (1999). Assessing knowledge structures: Relations with experience and posttraining performance. *Human Performance, 12,* 31–57.

Doyle, R. A. (2000, August 14). GM supports University's stand on affirmative action. *The University Record* (Vol. 55, No. 37). Ann Arbor: University of Michigan.

Drasgow, F., & Olson-Buchanan, J. B. (1999). *Innovations in computerized assessment.* Mahwah, NJ: Erlbaum.

Drasgow, F., Olson, J. B., Keenan, P. A., Moberg, P., & Mead, A. D. (1993). Computerized assessment. *Personnel and Human Resources Management, 11,* 163–206.

DuBois, D., & Shalin, V. L. (1995). Adapting cognitive methods to real-world objectives: An application to job knowledge testing. In P. D. Nichols, S. F. Chipman, & R. L. Brennan (Eds.), *Cognitively diagnostic assessment* (pp. 189–220). Hillsdale, NJ: Erlbaum.

DuBois, D., & Shalin, V. L. (2000). Describing job expertise using cognitively oriented task analyses (COTA). In J. M. Schraagen, S. F. Chipman, & V. L. Shalin (Eds.), *Cognitive task analysis* (pp. 41–56). Mahwah, NJ: Erlbaum.

Dunnette, M. D. (1963). A note on the criterion. *Journal of Applied Psychology, 47,* 251–254.

Eder, R. W., & Harris, M. M. (Eds.). (1999). *The employment interview handbook.* Thousand Oaks, CA: Sage.

Edwards, J. R. (2002). Alternatives to difference scores: Polynomial regression analysis and response surface methodology. In F. Drasgow & N. Schmitt (Eds.), *Advances in measurement and data analysis* (pp. 350–400). San Francisco, CA: Jossey-Bass.

Edwards, J. R., Scully, J. A., & Brtek, M. D. (1999). The measurement of work: Hierarchical representation of the multimethod job design questionnaire. *Personnel Psychology, 52,* 305–334.

Elkins, T. J., & Phillips, J. S. (2000). Job context, selection decision outcome, and the perceived fairness of selection tests: Biodata as an illustrative case. *Journal of Applied Psychology, 85,* 479–484.

Ellingson, J. E., Sackett, P. R., & Hough, L. M. (1999). Social desirability corrections in personality measurement: Issues of applicant comparison and construct validity. *Journal of Applied Psychology, 84,* 155–166.

Ericsson, K. A., & Simon, H. A. (1993). *Protocol analysis: Verbal reports as data.* Cambridge, MA: MIT Press.

Fitzgerald, L. F., Drasgow, F., Hulin, C. L., Gelfand, M. J., & Magley, V. J. (1997). The antecedents and consequences of sexual harassment: A test of an integrated model. *Journal of Applied Psychology, 82,* 578–589.

Fleishman, E. A., & Quaintance, M. K. (1984). *Taxonomies of human performance: The description of human tasks.* New York: Academic Press.

Fleishman, E. A., & Reilly, M. E. (1992). *Handbook of human abilities.* Palo Alto, CA: Consulting Psychologists Press.

Ford, J. K., Smith, E. M., Weissbein, D. A., Gully, S. M., & Salas, E. (1998). Relationships of goal orientation, metacognitive activity, and practice strategies with learning outcomes and transfer. *Journal of Applied Psychology, 83,* 218–233.

Frei, R. L., & McDaniel, M. A. (1998). Validity of customer service measures in personnel selection: A review of criterion and construct evidence. *Human Performance, 11,* 1–27.

Galinsky, E., & Stein, P. J. (1990). The impact of human resource policies on employees: Balancing work-family life. *Journal of Family Issues, 11,* 368–383.

Gardner, H. (1999). *Intelligence reframed.* New York: Basic Books.

Gellatly, I. R. (1996). Conscientiousness and task performance: Tests of cognitive process model. *Journal of Applied Psychology, 81,* 474–482.

George, J. M., & Brief, A. P. (1992). Feeling good-doing good: A conceptual analysis of the mood at work-organizational spontaneity relationship. *Psychological Bulletin, 112,* 310–329.

Ghiselli, E. E. (1973). The validity of aptitude tests in personnel selection. *Personnel Psychology, 26,* 461–478.

Giacalone, R. A., & Greenberg, J. (1997). (Eds.). *Antisocial behavior in organizations.* Thousand Oaks, CA: Sage.

Giacalone, R. A., Riordan, C. A., & Rosenfeld, P. (1997). Employee sabotage: Toward a practitioner-scholar understanding. In R. A. Giacalone & J. Greenberg (Eds.), *Antisocial behavior in organizations* (pp. 231–257). Thousand Oaks, CA: Sage.

Gilliland, S. W. (1993). The perceived fairness of selection systems: An organizational justice perspective. *Academy of Management Review, 18,* 694–734.

Gilliland, S. W. (1994). Effects of procedural and distributive justice in reactions to a selection system. *Journal of Applied Psychology, 79,* 691–701.

Goffin, R. D., Rothstein, M. G., & Johnston, M. G. (1996). Personality testing and the assessment center: Incremental validity for managerial selection. *Journal of Applied Psychology, 81,* 746–756.

Goldstein, I. L., Zedeck, S., & Schneider, B. (1993). An exploration of the job analysis-content validity process. In N. Schmitt & W. C. Borman (Eds.), *Personnel selection in organizations* (pp. 3–32). San Francisco: Jossey-Bass.

Good, G. W., Maisel, S. C., & Kriska, S. D. (1998). Setting an uncorrected visual acuity standard for police officer applicants. *Journal of Applied Psychology, 83,* 817–824.

Grandjean, E. (1980). *Fitting the task to the man: An ergonomic approach.* London: Taylor & Francis.

Grover, S. L., & Crooker, K. J. (1995). Who appreciates family-responsive human resource policies: The impact of family-friendly policies on the organizational attachment of parents and non-parents. *Personnel Psychology, 48,* 271–288.

Guastello, S. J., & Gaustello, D. D. (1998). Origins of coordination and team effectiveness: A perspective from game theory and nonlinear dynamics. *Journal of Applied Psychology, 83,* 423–437.

Guion, R. M. (1991). Personnel assessment, selection, and placement. Physical abilities. In M. D. Dunnette & L. M. Hough (Eds.), *Handbook of industrial and organizational psychology* (Vol. 2, pp. 327–398). Palo Alto, CA: Consulting Psychologists Press.

Hackman, J. R. (Ed.). (1991). *Groups that work (and those that don't).* San Francisco: Jossey-Bass.

Hackman, J. R., & Oldham, G. R. (1980). *Work redesign.* Reading, MA: Addison-Wesley.

Hall, D. T. (1996). Protean careers of the 21st century. *Academy of Management Executive, 10,* 9–16.

Hanisch, K. A. (1995). Behavioral families and multiple causes: Matching the complexity of responses to the complexity of antecedents. *Current Directions in Psychological Science, 4,* 156–162.

Hanisch, K. A., Hulin, C. L., & Roznowski, M. (1998). The importance of individuals' repertoires of behaviors: The scientific appropriateness of studying multiple behaviors and general attitudes. *Journal of Organizational Behavior, 19,* 463–480.

Hanson, M. A., Borman, W. C., Mogilka, H. J., Manning, C., & Hedge, J. W. (1999). Computerized assessment of skill for a highly technical job. In F. Drasgow & J. B. Buchanan (Eds.), *Innovations in computerized assessment* (pp. 197–220). Mahwah, NJ: Erlbaum.

Harrison, D. A., & Martocchio, J. J. (1998). Time for absenteeism: A 20–year review of origins, offshoots, and outcomes. *Journal of Management, 24,* 305–350.

Heilman, M. E., Battle, W. S., Keller, C. E., & Lee, R. A. (1998). Type of affirmative action policy: A determinant of reactions to sex-based preferential selection. *Journal of Applied Psychology, 83,* 190–205.

Henry, R. A., & Hulin, C. L. (1987). Stability of skilled performance across time: Some generalizations and limitations on utilities. *Journal of Applied Psychology, 72,* 457–462.

Hesketh, B., & Neal, A. (1999). Technology and team performance. In D. R. Ilgen & E. D. Pulakos (Eds.), *The changing nature of performance* (pp. 21–55). San Francisco: Jossey-Bass.

Hoffman, D. L., & Novak, T. P. (1998). Bridging the racial divide on the Internet. *Science, 280,* 390–391.

Hofmann, D., & Stetzer, A. (1996). A cross-level investigation of factors influencing unsafe behavior and accidents. *Personnel Psychology, 49,* 307–340.

Hofmann, D., & Stetzer, A. (1998). The role of safety climate and communication in accident interpretation: Implications for learning from negative events. *Academy of Management Journal, 41,* 644–657.

Hogan, J. C. (1991). Physical abilities. In M. D. Dunnette & L. M. Hough (Eds.), *Handbook of industrial and organizational psychology* (Vol. 2, pp. 753–831). Palo Alto, CA: Consulting Psychologists Press.

Hogan, J. C., Hogan, R., & Busch, C. M. (1984). How to measure service orientation. *Journal of Applied Psychology, 69,* 167–173.

Hogan, J. C., & Roberts, B. W. (1996). Issues and non-issues in the fidelity/bandwidth tradeoff. *Journal of Organizational Behavior, 17,* 627–638.

Hogan, J. C., Rybicki, S. L., Motowidlo, S. J., & Borman, W. C. (1998). Relations between contextual performance, personality and occupational advancement. *Human Performance, 11,* 189–208.

Hogan, R. T. (1991). Personality and personality measurement. In M. D. Dunnette & L. M. Hough (Eds.), *Handbook of industrial and organizational psychology* (Vol. 2, pp. 873–919). Palo Alto, CA: Consulting Psychologists Press.

Hogan, R. T., & Hogan, J. C. (1995). *Hogan Personality Inventory Manual* (2nd ed.). Tulsa, OK: Hogan Assessment Systems.

Hogan, R. T., & Shelton, S. (1998). A socioanalytic perspective on job performance. *Human Performance, 11,* 129–144.

Holzer, H., & Neumark, D. (1996). *Are affirmative action hires less qualified: Evidence from employer-employee data on new hires.* Cambridge, MA: National Bureau of Economic Research.

Horvath, M., Ryan, A. M., & Stierwalt, S. L. (2000). The influence of explanations for selection test use, outcome favorability, and self-efficacy on test-taker perceptions. *Organizational Behavior and Human Decision Processes, 83,* 310–330.

Hough, L. M. (1998a). Effects of intentional distortion in personality measurement and evaluation of suggested palliatives. *Human Performance, 11,* 209–244.

Hough, L. M. (1998b). Personality at work: Issues and evidence. In M. D. Hakel (Ed.), *Beyond multiple choice: Evaluating alternatives to traditional testing for selection* (pp. 131–166). Mahwah, NJ: Erlbaum.

Hough, L. M., & Oswald, F. L. (2000). Personnel selection. *Annual Review of Psychology, 51,* 631–664.

Huffcutt, A. I., & Roth, P. L. (1998). Racial group differences in employment interview evaluations. *Journal of Applied Psychology, 83,* 179–189.

Huffcutt, A. I., Roth, P. L., & McDaniel, M. A. (1996). A meta-analytic investigation of cognitive ability in employment interview evaluations: Moderating characteristics and implications for incremental validity. *Journal of Applied Psychology, 81,* 459–473.

Hulin, C. L. (1991). Adaptation, persistence, and commitment in organizations. In M. D. Dunnette & L. M. Hough (Eds.), *Handbook of industrial and organizational psychology* (pp. 445–505). Palo Alto, CA: Consulting Psychologists Press.

Humphreys, L. G. (1960). Investigation of the simplex. *Psychometrika, 25,* 313–323.

Hunter, J. E. (1986). Cognitive ability, cognitive aptitudes, job knowledge, and job performance. *Journal of Vocational Behavior, 29,* 340–362.

Hunter, J. E., & Hunter, R. F. (1984). Validity and utility of alternate predictors of performance. *Psychological Bulletin, 96,* 72–98.

Huselid, M. A., Jackson, S. E., & Schuler, R. S. (1997). Technical and strategic human resource management effectiveness as determinants of firm performance. *Academy of Management Journal, 40,* 171–188.

Ilgen, D. R., & Pulakos, E. D. (1999). Employee performance in today's organizations. In D. R. Ilgen & E. D. Pulakos (Eds.), *The changing nature of performance: Implications for staffing, motivation, and development* (pp. 1–20). San Francisco: Jossey-Bass.

Jackson, D. N., Wroblewski, V. R., & Ashton, M. C. (2000). The impact of faking on employment tests: Does forced choice offer a solution. *Human Performance, 13,* 371–388.

James, L. R. (1998). Measurement of personality via conditional reasoning. *Organizational Research Methods, 1,* 131–163.

Jeanneret, P. R., Borman, W. C., Kubisiak, U. C., & Hanson, M. A. (1999). Generalized work activities. In N. G. Peterson, M. D. Mumford, W. C. Borman, P. R. Jeanneret, & E. A. Fleishmann (Eds.), *An occupational information structure for the 21st century: The development of O*Net* (pp. 101–121). Washington, DC: American Psychological Association.

Johns, G. (1993). Constraints on the adoption of psychology-based personnel practices: Lessons from organizational innovation. *Personnel Psychology, 46,* 569–592.

Johns, G. (1994). How often were you absent? A review of the use of self-reported absence data. *Journal of Applied Psychology, 79,* 574–591.

Johnson, J. W. (1996). Linking employee perceptions of service climate to customer satisfaction. *Personnel Psychology, 49,* 831–852.

Judge, T. A., Erez, A., & Bono, J. E. (1998). The power of being positive: The relation between positive self-concept and job performance. *Human Performance, 11,* 167–188.

Kaempf, G., Klein, G., Thordsen, M., & Wolf, S. (1996). Decision making in complex command and control environments. *Human Factors, 38,* 220–231.

Kanfer, R. (1990). Motivation theory and industrial and organizational psychology. In M. D. Dunnette & L. M. Hough (Eds.), *Handbook of industrial and organizational psychology* (Vol. 1, pp. 75–170). Palo Alto, CA: Consulting Psychologists Press.

Kanfer, R., & Ackerman, P. L. (1989). Motivation and cognitive abilities: An integrative aptitude-treatment interaction approach to skill acquisition. *Journal of Applied Psychology, 74,* 657–690.

Kanfer, R., & Ackerman, P. L. (2000). Individual differences in work motivation: Further explorations of a trait framework. *Applied Psychology: An International Review, 49,* 470–482.

Kanfer, R., & Heggestad, E. D. (1997). Motivational traits and skills: A person-centered approach to work motivation. *Research in Organizational Behavior, 19,* 1–56.

Kanfer, R., & Heggestad, E. D. (1999). Individual differences in motivation: Traits and self-regulatory skills. In P. L. Ackerman & P. C. Kyllonen (Eds.), *Learning and individual differences: Process, trait, and content determinants* (pp. 293–313). Washington, DC: American Psychological Association.

Katz, D., & Kahn, R. L. (1978). *The social psychology of organizations.* New York: Wiley.

Keil, C. T., & Cortina, J. M. (2001). Degradation of validity over time: A test and extension of Ackerman's model. *Psychological Bulletin, 127,* 673–691.

Kiker, D. S., & Motowidlo, S. J. (1999). Main and interaction effects of task and contextual performance on supervisory reward decisions. *Journal of Applied Psychology, 84,* 602–609.

Klein, K. J., & Kozlowski, S. W. J. (Eds.). (2000). *Multilevel theory, research, and methods in organizations.* San Francisco: Jossey-Bass.

Kraiger, K., Ford, J. K., & Salas, E. (1993). Application of cognitive, skill-based, and affective theories of learning outcomes to new methods of training evaluation. *Journal of Applied Psychology, 78,* 311–328.

Kraiger, K., & Wenzel, L. H. (1997). Conceptual development and empirical evaluation of measures of shared mental models as indicators of team effectiveness. In M. T. Brannick & E. Salas (Eds.), *Team performance assessment and measurement: Theory, methods, and applications* (pp. 63–84). Mahwah, NJ: Erlbaum.

Kravitz, D. A., Harrison, D. A., Turner, M. E., Levine, E. L., Chaves, W., Brannick, M. T., Denning, D. L., Russell, C. J., & Conard, M. A. (1997). *Affirmative action: A review of psychological and behavioral research.* Bowling Green, OH: Society for Industrial and Organizational Psychology.

Kristof, A. L. (1996). Person-organization fit: An integrative review of its conceptualization, measurement, and implications. *Personnel Psychology, 49,* 1–48.

Langan-Fox, J., Code, S., & Langfield-Smith, K. (2000). Team mental models: Techniques, methods, and analytic approaches. *Human Factors, 42,* 242–271.

Langer, E. J., & Imber, L. G. (1979). When practice makes imperfect: Debilitating effects of overlearning. *Journal of Personality and Social Psychology, 37,* 2014–2024.

Leonard, J. S. (1990). The impact of affirmative action regulation and equal employment law on Black employment. *Journal of Economic Perspectives, 4,* 47–63.

LePine, J. A., Colquitt, J. A., & Erez, A. (2000). Adaptability to changing task contexts: Effects of general cognitive ability, conscientiousness, and openness to experience. *Personnel Psychology, 53,* 563–593.

Levy-Leboyer, C. (1994). Selection and assessment in Europe. In H. C. Triandis, M. D. Dunnette, & L. M. Hough (Eds.), *Handbook of industrial and organizational psychology* (pp. 173–190). Palo Alto, CA: Consulting Psychologists Press.

Locke, E. A., & Latham, G. P. (1990). *A theory of goal setting and task performance.* Upper Saddle River, NJ: Prentice-Hall.

London, M., & Mone, E. M. (1999). Customer driven employee performance. In D. R. Ilgen & E. D. Pulakos (Eds.), *The changing nature of performance* (pp. 119–153). San Francisco: Jossey-Bass.

Mabon, H. (1998). Utility aspects of personality and performance. *Human Performance, 11,* 289–304.

Magley, V. J., Hulin, C. L., Fitzgerald, L. F., & DeNardo, M. (1999). Outcomes of self-labeling sexual harassment. *Journal of Applied Psychology, 84,* 390–402.

Mantell, M. (1994). *Ticking bombs: Defusing violence in the workplace.* Burr Ridge, IL: Irwin.

Marshall, S. P. (1993). Assessing schema knowledge. In N. Frederiksen, R. J. Mislevy, & I. I. Bejar (Eds.), *Test theory for a new generation of tests* (pp. 155–179). Hillsdale, NJ: Erlbaum.

Martin, S. L., & Klimoski, R. J. (1990). Use of verbal protocols to trace cognitions associated with self- and supervisor evaluations of performance. *Organizational Behavior & Human Decision Processes, 46,* 135–154.

Martin, S. L., & Terris, W. (1991). Predicting infrequent behavior: Clarifying the impact on false-positive rates. *Journal of Applied Psychology, 76,* 484–487.

Mayer, J. D., Salovey, P., & Caruso, D. (2000). Models of emotional intelligence. In R. J. Sternberg (Ed.), *Handbook of intelligence* (pp. 396–422). Cambridge, England: Cambridge University Press.

McBride, J. R. (1998). Innovations in computer-based ability testing. In M. D. Hakel (Ed.), *Beyond multiple choice: Evaluating alternatives to traditional testing for selection* (pp. 23–40). Mahwah, NJ: Erlbaum.

McCloy, R. A., Campbell, J. P., & Cudeck, R. (1994). A confirmatory test of a model of performance determinants. *Journal of Applied Psychology, 79,* 493–505.

McCormick, E. J., & Ilgen, D. R. (1985). *Industrial and organizational psychology.* Englewood Cliffs, NJ: Prentice Hall.

McDaniel, M. A., Bruhn Finnegan, E. B., Morgeson, F. P., Campion, M. A., & Braverman, E. P. (2001). Predicting job performance using situational judgment tests: A clarification of the literature. *Journal of Applied Psychology, 86,* 730–740.

McDaniel, M. A., Schmidt, F. L., & Hunter, J. E. (1988). A meta-analysis of the validity of methods for rating training and experience in personnel selection. *Personnel Psychology, 41,* 283–314.

McDaniel, M. A., Whetzel, D. L., Schmidt, F. L., & Maurer, S. D. (1994). The validity of the employment interview: A comprehensive review and meta-analysis. *Journal of Applied Psychology, 79,* 599–616.

McManus, M. A., & Kelly, M. L. (1999). Personality measures and biodata: Evidence regarding their incremental predictive value in the life insurance industry. *Personnel Psychology, 52,* 137–148.

Mead, A. D., & Drasgow, F. (1993). Equivalence of computerized and paper-and-pencil cognitive ability tests: A meta-analysis. *Psychological Bulletin, 114,* 449–458.

Messick, S. (1998). Test validity: A matter of consequence. *Social Indicators Research, 45,* 35–44.

Miceli, M. P., & Near, J. P. (1992). *Blowing the whistle: The organizational and legal implications for companies and employees.* Lexington, MA: Lexington.

Miceli, M. P., & Near, J. P. (1997). Whistle-blowing as antisocial behavior. In R. A. Giacalone & J. Greenberg (Eds.), *Antisocial behavior in organizations* (pp. 130–149). Thousand Oaks, CA: Sage.

Motowidlo, S. J., Borman, W. C., & Schmit, M. J. (1997). A theory of individual differences in task and contextual performance. *Human Performance, 10,* 71–84.

Motowidlo, S. J., & Van Scotter, J. R. (1994). Evidence that task performance should be distinguished from contextual performance. *Journal of Applied Psychology, 79,* 475–480.

Mount, M. K., Witt, L. A., & Barrick, M. R. (2000). Incremental validity of empirically keyed biodata scales over GMA and the five factor personality constructs. *Personnel Psychology, 53,* 299–323.

Mumford, M. D., & Stokes, G. S. (1992). Developmental determinants of individual action: Theory and practice in applying background measures. In M. D. Dunnette & L. M. Hough (Eds.), *Handbook of industrial and organizational psychology* (Vol. 3, pp. 61–138). Palo Alto, CA: Consulting Psychologists Press.

Murphy, K. R. (1993). *Honesty in the workplace.* Pacific Grove, CA: Brooks/Cole.

Murphy, K. R. (1996). Individual differences and behavior in organizations: Much more than g. In K. R. Murphy (Ed.), *Individual differences and behavior in organizations* (pp. 3–30). San Francisco: Jossey-Bass.

Murphy, K. R., & Lee, S. L. (1994). Personality variables related to integrity test scores: The role of conscientiousness. *Journal of Business and Psychology, 8,* 413–424.

Murphy, K. R., & Shiarella, A. H. (1997). Implications of the multidimensional nature of job performance for the validity of selection tests: Multivariate frameworks for studying test validity. *Personnel Psychology, 50,* 823–854.

Naglieri, J. A., & Das, J. P. (1997). Intelligence revised: The planning, attention, simultaneous, successive (PASS) Cognitive Processing Theory. In R. F. Dillon (Ed.), *Handbook on testing* (pp. 136–163). Westport, CT: Greenwood Press.

Neisser, U., Boodoo, G., Bouchard, T. J., Jr., Boykin, A. W., Brody, N., Ceci, S. J., Halpern, D., Loehlin, J. C., Perloff, R., Sternberg, R. J., & Urbina, S. (1996). Intelligence: Known and unknowns. *American Psychologist, 51,* 77–101.

Neuman, G. A., & Wright, J. (1999). Team effectiveness: Beyond skills and cognitive ability. *Journal of Applied Psychology, 84,* 376–389.

Ones, D. S., Viswesvaran, C., & Schmidt, F. L. (1993). Comprehensive meta-analysis of integrity test validities: Findings and implications for personnel selection and theories of job performance. *Journal of Applied Psychology, 78,* 679–703.

Organ, D. W. (1988). *Organizational Citizenship Behavior: The good soldier syndrome.* Lexington, MA: Lexington Press.

Pace, L. A., & Schoenfeldt, L. F. (1977). Legal concerns in the use of weighted applications. *Personnel Psychology, 30,* 159–166.

Payne, S. C. (2000). *Efficiency orientation: Establishing measurement and predictive properties.* Unpublished doctoral dissertation, George Mason University, Fairfax, VA.

Pearlman, K., & Barney, M. F. (1999). Selection in a changing workplace. In J. Kehoe (Ed.), *Managing selection in changing organizations: Human resource strategies.* San Francisco: Jossey-Bass.

Peterson, N. G., Mumford, M. D., Borman, W. C., Jeanneret, P. R., & Fleishman, E. A. (1999). *An occupational information system for the 21st century. The development of O*NET.* Washington, DC: American Psychological Association.

Phillips, J. M., & Gully, S. M. (1997). Role of goal orientation, ability, need for achievement, and locus of control in the self-efficacy and goal-setting process. *Journal of Applied Psychology, 82,* 792–802.

Ployhart, R. E., & Hakel, M. D. (1998). The substantive nature of performance variability: Predicting interindividual differences in intraindividual performance. *Personnel Psychology, 51,* 859–901.

Ployhart, R. E., & Ryan, A. M. (in press). A construct-oriented approach for developing situational judgment tests in a service context. *Personnel Psychology.*

Podsakoff, P. M., & MacKenzie, S. B. (1997). Impact of organizational citizenship behavior on organizational performance: A review and suggestions for future research. *Human Performance, 10,* 133–152.

Pritchard, R. D. (1992). Organizational productivity. In M. D. Dunnette & L. M. Hough (Eds.), *Handbook of industrial and organizational psychology* (Vol. 3, 2nd ed., pp. 442–472). Palo Alto, CA: Consulting Psychologists Press.

Pulakos, E. D., Arad, S., Donovan, M. A., & Plamondon, K. E. (2000). Adaptability in the workplace: Development of a taxonomy of adaptive performance. *Journal of Applied Psychology, 85,* 612–624.

Pulakos, E. D., & Schmitt, N. (1995). Experience based and situational interview questions: Studies of validity. *Personnel Psychology, 48,* 289–307.

Pulakos, E. D., & Schmitt, N. (1996). An evaluation of two strategies for reducing adverse impact and their effects on criterion-related validity. *Human Performance, 9,* 241–258.

Pulakos, E. D., Schmitt, N., & Chan, D. (1996). Models of job performance ratings: An examination of ratee race, ratee gender, and rater level effects. *Human Performance, 9,* 103–120.

Quinones, M. A., Ford, J. K., & Teachout, M. S. (1995). The relationship between work experience and job performance: A conceptual and meta-analytic review. *Personnel Psychology, 48,* 887–910.

Ree, M. J., Earles, J. A., & Teachout, M. S. (1994). Predicting job performance: Not much more than g. *Journal of Applied Psychology, 79,* 518–524.

Robinson, S. L., & Morrison, E. W. (1995). Psychological contracts and OCB: The effect of unfulfilled obligations on civic virtue behavior. *Journal of Organizational Behavior, 16,* 289–298.

Rogg, K. L., Schmidt, D. B., Shull, C., & Schmitt, N. (2001). Human resource practices, organizational climate, and customer satisfaction. *Journal of Management, 4,* 431–449.

Ronen, S. (1989). Training the international assignee. In I. L. Goldstein (Ed.), *Training and development in organizations* (pp. 417–454). San Francisco: Jossey-Bass.

Rosse, J. G., Stecher, M. D., Miller, J. L., & Levin, R. A. (1998). The impact of response distortion on preemployment personality testing and hiring decisions. *Journal of Applied Psychology, 83,* 634–644.

Rothstein, H. R., Schmidt, F. L., Erwin, F. W., Owens, W. A., & Sparks, P. P. (1990). Biographical data in employment selection: Can validities be made generalizable? *Journal of Applied Psychology, 75,* 175–184.

Ryan, A. M., Horvath, M., Ployhart, R. E., Schmitt, N., & Slade, L. A. (2000). Hypothesizing differential functioning in global employee opinion surveys. *Personnel Psychology, 53,* 531–562.

Ryan, A. M., & Lasek, M. (1991). Negligent hiring and defamation: Areas of liability related to pre-employment inquiries. *Personnel Psychology, 44,* 293–319.

Ryan, A. M., & Ployhart, R. E. (2000). Applicants' perceptions of selection procedures and decisions: A critical review and agenda for the future. *Journal of Management, 26,* 565–606.

Rynes, S. L., & Connerly, M. L. (1993). Applicant reactions to alternative selection procedures. *Journal of Business & Psychology, 7,* 261–277.

Rynes, S. L., Orlitzky, M. O., & Bretz, R. D., Jr. (1997). Experienced hiring versus college recruiting: Practices and emerging trends. *Personnel Psychology, 50,* 309–340.

Sackett, P. R., Gruys, M. L., & Ellingson, J. E. (1998). Ability-personality interactions when predicting job performance. *Journal of Applied Psychology, 83,* 545–556.

Sackett, P. R., Schmitt, N., Ellingson, J. E., & Kabin, M. B. (2001). High-stakes testing in employment, credentialing, and higher education: Prospects in a post-affirmative action world. *American Psychologist, 56,* 302–318.

Sackett, P. R., & Wanek, J. E. (1996). New developments in the use of measures of honesty, integrity, conscientiousness, dependability, trustworthiness, and reliability for personnel selection. *Personnel Psychology, 49,* 787–830.

Sackett, P. R., Zedeck, S., & Fogli, L. (1988). Relations between measures of typical and maximum job performance. *Journal of Applied Psychology, 73,* 482–486.

Schmidt, F. L., & Hunter, J. E. (1993). Tacit knowledge, practical intelligence, general ability, and job knowledge. *Current directions in psychological science, 2,* 7–8.

Schmidt, F. L., & Hunter, J. E. (1998). The validity and utility of selection methods in personnel psychology: Practical and theoretical implications of 85 years of research findings. *Psychological Bulletin, 124,* 262–274.

Schmidt, F. L., Hunter, J. E., & Outerbridge, A. N. (1986). Impact of job experience and ability on job knowledge, work sample performance, and supervisory ratings of job performance. *Journal of Applied Psychology, 71,* 432–439.

Schmidt, F. L., Hunter, J. E., Outerbridge, A. N., & Goff, S. (1988). Joint relation of experience and ability with job performance: Test of three hypotheses. *Journal of Applied Psychology, 73,* 46–57.

Schmit, M. J., Kihm, J. A., & Robie, C. (2000). Development of a global measure of personality. *Personnel Psychology, 53,* 153–193.

Schmit, M. J., Motowidlo, S. J., DeGroot, T. G., Cross, S. S., & Kiker, S. S. (1996). *Explaining the relationship between personality and job performance.* Paper presented at the 11th Annual Conference of the Society for Industrial and Organizational Psychology, Orlando, FL.

Schmitt, N., & Chan, D. (1998). *Personnel selection: A theoretical approach.* Thousand Oaks, CA: Sage.

Schmitt, N., & Chan, D. (1999). The status of research on applicant reactions to selection tests. *International Journal of Management Reviews, 1,* 45–62.

Schmitt, N., Gilliland, S. W., Landis, R. S., & Devine, D. (1993). Computer-based testing applied to selection of secretarial applicants. *Personnel Psychology, 46,* 149–163.

Schmitt, N., Gooding, R. Z., Noe, R. A., & Kirsch, M. P. (1984). Meta-analyses of validity studies published between 1964 and 1982 and the investigation of study characteristics. *Personnel Psychology, 37,* 407–422.

Schmitt, N., & Pulakos, E. D. (1998). Biodata and differential prediction: Some reservations. In M. D. Hakel (Ed.), *Beyond multiple choice: Evaluating alternatives to traditional testing for selection* (pp. 167–182). Mahwah, NJ: Erlbaum.

Schneider, B. J., & Bowen, D. E. (1995). *Winning the service game.* Boston: Harvard Business School Press.

Schneider, B. J., Smith, D. B., & Sipe, W. P. (2000). Personnel selection psychology: Multilevel considerations. In K. J. Klein & S. W. J. Kozlowski (Eds.), *Multilevel theory, research, and methods in organizations* (pp. 91–120). San Francisco: Jossey-Bass.

Schneider, B. J., Wheeler, J. K., & Cox, J. F. (1992). A passion for service: Using content analysis to explicate service climate themes. *Journal of Applied Psychology, 77,* 705–716.

Schneider, B. J., White, S. S., & Paul, M. C. (1998). Linking service climate and customer perceptions of service quality: Test of a causal model. *Journal of Applied Psychology, 83,* 150–163.

Schraagen, J. M., Chipman, S. F., & Shalin, V. L. (Eds.). (2000). *Cognitive task analysis.* Mahwah, NJ: Erlbaum.

Shaffer, M. A., & Harrison, D. A. (1998). Expatriates' psychological withdrawal from international assignments: Work, nonwork, and family influences. *Personnel Psychology, 51,* 87–118.

Sharf, J. C., & Jones, D. P. (1999). Employment risk management. In J. F. Kehoe (Ed.), *Managing selection strategies in changing organizations* (pp. 271–318). San Francisco: Jossey-Bass.

Shaw, J. D., Delery, J. E., Jenkins, G. D., Jr., & Gupta, N. (1998). An organization-level analysis of voluntary and involuntary turnover. *Academy of Management Journal, 41,* 511–525.

Siebert, S. E., Crant, J. M., & Kraimer, M. L. (1999). Proactive personality and career success. *Journal of Applied Psychology, 84,* 416–427,

Slora, K. B., Joy, D. S., Jones, J. W., & Terris, W. (1991). The prediction of on-the-job violence. In J. W. Jones (Ed.), *Preemployment honesty testing: Current research and future directions* (pp. 171–183). Westport, CT: Quorum Books.

Snow, C. C., & Snell, S. A. (1993). Staffing as strategy. In N. Schmitt & W. C. Borman (Eds.), *Personnel selection in organizations* (pp. 448–480). San Francisco: Jossey-Bass.

Society for Industrial and Organizational Psychology. (1987). *Principles for the validation and use of personnel selection procedures.* College Park, MD: Author.

Spearman, C. (1927). *The abilities of man.* New York: MacMillan.

Spector, P. (1997). The role of frustration in antisocial behavior. In R. A. Giacalone & J. Greenberg (Eds.), *Antisocial behavior in organizations* (pp. 1–17). Thousand Oaks, CA: Sage.

Steel, B. S., & Lovrich, N. P. (1987). Equality and efficiency trade-offs in affirmative—real or imagined? The case of women in policing. *Social Science Journal, 24,* 53–70.

Sternberg, R. J. (2000). Intelligence and creativity. In R. J. Sternberg (Ed.), *Handbook of intelligence* (pp. 611–630). Cambridge, MA: Cambridge University Press.

Sternberg, R. J., Forsythe, G. B., Hedlund, J. R., Horvath, J. A., Wagner, R. K., Williams, W. M., Snook, S. A., & Grigorenko, E. L. (2000). *Practical intelligence in everyday life.* New York: Cambridge University Press.

Sternberg, R. J., Wagner, R. K., Williams, W. M., & Horvath, J. A. (1995). Testing common sense. *American Psychologist, 50,* 912–927.

Stokes, G. S. (Ed.). (1999). The next one hundred years of biodata. (Special Issue). *Human Resource Management Review, 9,* 111–242.

Terpstra, D. E., & Rozell, E. J. (1993). The relationship of staffing practices to organizational level measures of performance. *Personnel Psychology, 46,* 27–48.

Tesluk, P. E., & Jacobs, R. R. (1998). Toward an integrated model of work experience. *Personnel Psychology, 51,* 321–355.

Tett, R. P., Jackson, D. N., Rothstein, M., & Reddon, J. R. (1999). Meta-analysis of bi-directional relations in personality-job performance research. *Human Performance, 12,* 1–30.

Tracy, J. B., Tannenbaum, S. I., & Kavanagh, M. J. (1995). Applying trained skills on the job: The importance of the work environment. *Journal of Applied Psychology, 80,* 239–252.

Turnley, W. H., & Feldman, D. C. (1999). The impact of psychological contract violations on exit, voice, loyalty, and neglect. *Human Relations, 52,* 895–922.

Uniform Guidelines on Employee Selection Procedures. (1978). *Federal Register, 43,* 38290–38315.

Van Scotter, J. R., & Motowidlo, S. J. (1996). Interpersonal facilitation and job dedication as separate facets of contextual performance. *Journal of Applied Psychology, 81,* 525–531.

Van Vienen, A. E. M. (2000). Person-organization fit: The match between newcomers' and recruiters' preferences for organizational cultures. *Personnel Psychology, 53,* 113–149.

Varca, P. E., & Pattison, P. (1993). Evidentiary standards in employment discrimination: A view toward the future. *Personnel Psychology, 46,* 239–258.

Vinchur, A. J., Schippman, J. S., Switzer, F. S., III, & Roth, P. L. (1998). A meta-analytic review of predictors of job performance for salespeople. *Journal of Applied Psychology, 83,* 586–597.

Viswesvaran, C., & Ones, D. S. (1999). Meta-analysis of fakability measures: Implications for personality measurement. *Educational and Psychological Measurement, 59,* 197–210.

Wagner, R. (1949). The employment interview: A critical summary. *Personnel Psychology, 2,* 279–294.

Wagner, R. K. (2000). Practical intelligence. In R. J. Sternberg (Ed.), *Handbook of intelligence* (pp. 380–395). Cambridge, England: Cambridge University Press.

Wallace, S. R. (1965). Criteria for what? *American Psychologist, 20,* 411–417.

Werbel, J. D., & Gilliland, S. W. (1999). Person-environment fit in the selection process. In G. R. Ferris (Ed.), *Research in personnel and human resources management* (pp. 209–244). Stamford, CT: JAI Press.

Whitlock, G. H., Clouse, R. J., & Spencer, W. F. (1963). Predicting accident proneness. *Personnel Psychology, 16,* 35–44.

Williamson, L. G., Campion, J. E., Malos, S. B., Roehling, M. V., & Campion, M. A. (1997). Employment interview on trial: Linking interview structure with litigation outcomes. *Journal of Applied Psychology, 82,* 900–913.

Wong, C., & Campion, M. A. (1991). Development and test of a task level model of motivational job design. *Journal of Applied Psychology, 76,* 825–837.

CHAPTER 6

Intelligence and the Workplace

FRITZ DRASGOW

Research on intelligence, dating back to Spearman's 1904 article "'General Intelligence,' Objectively Determined and Measured," has been an area of keen interest to psychologists and the general public. Books such as Herrnstein and Murray's (1994) *The Bell Curve* have created controversy, consternation, and commitment among different constituencies. Few areas of psychology—indeed few areas of scientific inquiry—have created such intense debate.

This chapter summarizes several areas of research on intelligence. The first, and probably foremost, area consists of factor analytic studies investigating the latent structure of cognitive ability. This line of research dates back to Spearman and is called the psychometric approach to the study of intelligence. Some of the most eminent and controversial psychologists of the twentieth century have worked in this area, including Thurstone, Burt, Guilford, Thompson, Vernon, and Cattell. In a work of remarkable scholarship, John Carroll (1993) reanalyzed 461 correlation matrices from this literature using a single methodology to provide

a coherent and compelling account of the factor analytic findings.

Information processing approaches to intelligence constitute the second line of research summarized here. This work is characterized by carefully controlled experimental investigations of how people solve problems. In the psychometric literature, item responses are often aggregated up to subtest or total test scores prior to analysis; in contrast, information processing research often decomposes item responding into more basic elemental components and processes to understand intelligence.

Neuropsychological approaches to intelligence form the third area of research summarized in this chapter. Neuropsychology attempts to link the brain and behavior and thereby provide a deeper understanding of intelligence. Until recently, many of the most important findings in this area resulted from case studies of individuals with tragic brain damage. Advances in methods for imaging brain activity, such as functional magnetic resonance imaging (fMRI) and positron-emission tomography (PET), allow investigations of site-specific activation when individuals solve problems of a particular type. This research is exciting because it has the potential for connecting what is known about the latent structure of cognitive ability from psychometric research with the underlying hardware of the brain.

The author is grateful to Walter C. Borman, Lloyd G. Humphreys, and David Lubinski for their valuable feedback on an earlier draft of this chapter.

Factor Fractionation

When considering research on the nature and structure of intelligence, it is important to keep in mind a point made by Truman Kelley in 1939 and repeatedly made by Lloyd Humphreys. Kelley stated that "evidence of existence of a factor [should] be not cited as evidence that it is important" in his famous "Mental Factors of No Importance" paper (1939, p. 141). Humphreys (1962) wrote that "test behavior can almost endlessly be made more specific, . . . factors [of intelligence] can almost endlessly be fractionated or splintered" (p. 475). With the advent of confirmatory factor analysis (CFA; Jöreskog, 1966) and convenient software implementations such as the LISREL computer program (Jöreskog & Sörbom, 1996), this problem has been exacerbated. In samples exceeding a few hundred, CFA can be likened to an electron microscope in that it can reliably determine the number of factors that are required to reproduce a correlation matrix, a number often substantially exceeding that expected on the basis of substantive theory.

How can researchers avoid extracting and interpreting "factors of no importance"? In factor analytic studies of test batteries of the sort pioneered by Thurstone (1938), there does not appear to be any way to differentiate substantively important factors from inappropriately splintered factors. Thus, research of a different kind is needed in which the pattern of relations with important criterion variables is examined. When a factor is fractionated, this research asks whether the newly split factors (a) correlate meaningfully with other important variables such as job performance, (b) exhibit a pattern of differential relations with such variables, and (c) increase our ability to understand and explain these variables. Vernon (1950) emphasized that "only those group factors shown to have significant practical value in daily life are worth incorporating in the picture" (p. 25). McNemar (1964), Lubinski and Dawis (1992, pp. 13–20), and Lubinski (2000) further elaborated on the pitfalls of factor fractionation and the importance of examining the scientific significance of factors.

For example, suppose a large sample completes an algebra test. It is likely that CFA could be used to demonstrate that a word-problem factor can be differentiated from a calculation factor (i.e., a factor determined from items that ask examinees to solve quadratic equations, solve two equations in two unknowns, etc.). Although statistically separable and likely to be correlated with performance on tasks requiring mathematical skill, the word-problem factor and the calculation factor would be highly correlated (probably in excess of .95), would have very similar correlations with other variables, and would not have a multiple correlation with any important criterion variable higher than the simple correlation of the original algebra test. Thus, there is no reason to fractionate the original algebra factor.

Intelligence and Performance

In industrial and organizational (I/O) psychology, two of the most important and often-studied variables are training proficiency and job performance. A large and compelling literature shows that intelligence predicts these two important classes of criterion variables (Humphreys, 1979, 1984; Hunter, 1980).

During the past decade, Borman and Motowidlo (1993, 1997; see also Motowidlo & Van Scotter, 1994) have argued for differentiating between *task* and *contextual* performance. Essentially, task performance consists of an employee's performance on the tasks listed on the job description of his or her job and is related to general cognitive ability (Hunter, 1986). Contextual performance (or, as it is sometimes called, organizational citizenship behavior; Organ, 1988) has been defined variously; a recent account (Coleman & Borman, 2000) lists organizational support, interpersonal support, and conscientious initiative as its main components.

Although it has been argued that there is "not much more than g" (Ree & Earles, 1991; Ree, Earles, & Teachout, 1994; see also Herrnstein & Murray, 1994) that is useful when predicting training proficiency and job performance, enlarging the criterion space to include contextual job performance seems likely to increase the range of individual differences required to predict and understand behavior in the workplace. Personality, for example, has been found to be an important predictor of contextual job performance (McHenry, Hough, Toquam, Hanson, & Ashworth, 1990). What has been variously labeled as social intelligence, situational judgment, and tacit knowledge appears to be related to contextual job performance. Therefore, social intelligence is included here as an element of intelligence, and research relevant both to the measurement of social intelligence and to the use of social intelligence to predict job performance is reviewed.

In sum, this chapter reviews psychometric approaches, information processing models, and neuropsychological findings concerning intelligence. To avoid spurious proliferation of intelligence factors, desiderata involving relations with other important variables are utilized. In this consideration of relations with other variables, contextual performance is examined (to the extent that research is available) in addition to the usual training and task performance variables. To enhance prediction of this enlarged criterion space, social intelligence is examined.

GENERAL MENTAL ABILITY

Psychometric Approaches to Intelligence

During the past century, the psychometric approach to intelligence has been the focus of a tremendous amount of research. Obviously, it is impossible to provide a comprehensive review of a century's research in this chapter. More detail can be found in Carroll (1993), who provides a fascinating review, summarizing substantive findings, methodological advances, and the personal perspectives of key figures. In this chapter, the contributions of Spearman, Thurstone, Vernon, Guilford, Cattell, and Carroll are described.

Spearman

Although Galton, Wundt, and others had studied intelligence previously, it is probably fair to say that contemporary theories of intelligence and corresponding methodologies for research originated with Charles Spearman. Spearman was an Englishman who studied experimental psychology with Wundt. After completing his doctorate, Spearman returned to England and made many important contributions until his death in 1945.

Substantively, Spearman is best known for his two-factor theory of intelligence. Actually, this theory postulated two *types* of factors, not two factors. The first type is the general factor, which Spearman labeled *g*, and the second type consists of specific factors. Spearman used the general factor as the explanation of why students' grades in the classics were correlated with grades in other courses such as math and music. Indeed, much of Spearman's research was directed to documenting the pervasive influence of the general factor. Specific factors were used to explain why performance in different domains had less than perfect correlations; performance in a given domain was influenced by general ability as well as domain-specific ability.

Spearman believed that general intelligence involved three fundamental processes, which he called the *apprehension of experience,* the *eduction of relations,* and the *eduction of correlates.* To educe means "to draw out; elicit" or "to infer from data; deduce" (*Webster's New World College Dictionary,* 1997, p. 432). The legacy of Spearman can be seen in the inductive and deductive reasoning factors found in Carroll's (1993) reanalysis of cognitive ability correlation matrices.

Spearman also made important methodological contributions to the study of intelligence. In his 1904 paper he examined the "hierarchy of the intelligences" (pp. 274–277) and provided a means for determining the "intellective saturation" of a variable, which was defined as the "extent to which the considered faculty is functionally identical with General Intelligence" (p. 276). These saturations are essentially factor loadings; later (Hart & Spearman, 1912) Spearman introduced a method for computing the loadings on a single general factor.

The law of tetrad differences (Carroll, 1993, attributes this term to a paper by Spearman & Holzinger, 1925) was introduced to test the two-factor model. Let r_{ij} denote the correlation between tests i and j. Suppose the general factor is the sole reason that a set of variables have nonzero correlations and the loading of test i on the general factor is denoted λ_i. Then the correlation r_{ij} should equal the product of λ_i and λ_j (plus sampling error). Consequently, for any four variables the tetrad difference,

$$\text{Tetrad Difference} = r_{13}r_{24} - r_{23}r_{14}$$
$$= (\lambda_1\lambda_3)(\lambda_2\lambda_4) - (\lambda_2\lambda_3)(\lambda_1\lambda_4)$$

should differ from zero only due to sampling error. Investigating tetrad differences, to which Spearman devoted great effort, is akin to the modern analysis of residuals. Computer programs such as LISREL (Jöreskog & Sörbom, 1996) provide a matrix of residuals, which are obtained by subtracting the matrix of correlations reproduced on the basis of the parameters estimated for a hypothesized model from the original correlation matrix.

As described later, subsequent researchers have developed models of intelligence that incorporate additional factors. In fact, Spearman's focus on a single ability may seem odd because there are measures of so many different abilities currently available. To provide a perspective for Spearman's interest in a single dominant ability (and to illustrate later theories of intelligence), it is instructive to consider the correlations among a set of cognitive ability tests. Table 6.1 presents the correlations of the 10 subtests that constitute the Armed Services Vocational Aptitude Battery (ASVAB) along with their internal consistency reliabilities. These correlations, provided by Ree, Mullins, Mathews, and Massey (1982), were obtained from a large sample (2,620 men) and have been corrected to estimate the correlations that would have been obtained from a nationally representative sample.

The ASVAB subtests assess a rather wide range of abilities. Arithmetic Reasoning and Math Knowledge measure quantitative reasoning; Word Knowledge and Paragraph Comprehension assess verbal ability; General Science is largely a measure of science vocabulary; Auto-Shop Information, Mechanical Comprehension, and Electronics Information assess technical knowledge required for increasingly sophisticated military occupational specialties; and Numerical Operations and Coding Speed assess very simple skills (e.g., 7 + 9 = ?) albeit

TABLE 6.1   Correlation Matrix of ASVAB Form 8A Subtests

Subtest	AR	MK	WK	PC	GS	AS	MC	EI	NO	CS
Arithmetic Reasoning (AR)	(.90)									
Math Knowledge (MK)	.79	(.87)								
Word Knowledge (WK)	.70	.62	(.92)							
Paragraph Comprehension (PC)	.70	.60	.82	(.80)						
General Science (GS)	.71	.65	.83	.74	(.84)					
Auto-Shop Information (AS)	.60	.52	.68	.63	.70	(.88)				
Mechanical Comprehension (MC)	.69	.64	.67	.64	.71	.75	(.87)			
Electronics Information (EI)	.68	.61	.76	.69	.78	.79	.75	(.83)		
Numerical Operations (NO)	.59	.58	.52	.55	.48	.40	.45	.46	na	
Coding Speed (CS)	.52	.51	.48	.49	.43	.42	.45	.46	.64	na

Note. Internal consistency reliabilities (KR–20) appear in the diagonal within parentheses; internal consistency reliabilities were not computed for speeded tests.

in a highly speeded context. Although it is not surprising that the quantitative reasoning tests correlate highly ($r = .79$) and the verbal tests correlate highly ($r = .82$), the magnitude of the quantitative-verbal correlations is surprisingly large (rs between .60 and .70). Indeed, the quantitative-verbal correlations are only about .10 to .20 smaller than are the within-trait correlations. Moreover, the technical tests have remarkably high correlations with the verbal and quantitative skills (e.g., Word Knowledge correlates .67 with Mechanical Comprehension), and even the speeded tests have sizable correlations with the power tests (all correlations greater than .40).

Table 6.2 contains the factor loadings obtained when a single common factor (i.e., Spearman's two-factor model) is fit to the ASVAB correlation matrix using maximum likelihood estimation as implemented in LISREL (Jöreskog & Sörbom, 1996). Table 6.2 also contains the residuals. Residuals are obtained by using the estimated factor loadings to compute the fitted correlation matrix (i.e., the correlations expected from the estimated factor loadings). The fitted correlations are then subtracted from the observed correlations to produce the residuals. For example, Table 6.2 shows that the factor loadings of Arithmetic Reasoning and Math Knowledge were

estimated to be .83 and .75. For this single common factor model, the expected correlation is therefore $.83 \times .75 = .62$. The fitted correlation is then subtracted from the actual correlation, $.79 - .62$, to obtain a residual of .17, which is shown in Table 6.2.

As reported in Table 6.2, all of the tests have large loadings; the two speeded subtests have loadings of about .6, whereas the eight power tests have loadings of about .8. Note the large positive residuals between Arithmetic Reasoning and Math Knowledge and between Numerical Operations and Coding Speed and the more moderate positive residuals among the three technical tests. The correlations among the three verbal tests have been reasonably well modeled (residuals of .08, .05, and .00) by estimating their loadings as quite large (.89, .84, and .88). Thus, the general factor in this solution appears strongly related to verbal ability, with mathematical and technical abilities also highly related.

Fit statistics for the solution shown in Table 6.2 indicate substantial problems. The root mean squared error of approximation (RMSEA; Steiger, 1990) is .19; the adjusted goodness of fit statistic is .67; and the nonnormed fit index is .83. All three of these indices, as well as the matrix of residuals, indicate that Spearman's two-factor model is unable to

TABLE 6.2   Factor Loadings and Residuals for Spearman's Two-Factor Model Fitted to the ASVAB

Subtest	Factor Loadings	Residuals									
		AR	MK	WK	PC	GS	AS	MC	EI	NO	CS
AR	.83	—									
MK	.75	.17	—								
WK	.89	−.03	−.05	—							
PC	.84	.01	−.03	.08	—						
GS	.88	−.02	−.02	.05	.00	—					
AS	.79	−.06	−.08	−.02	−.04	.00	—				
MC	.82	.01	.02	−.05	−.05	−.01	.10	—			
EI	.87	−.04	−.04	−.01	−.04	.01	.10	.04	—		
NO	.61	.09	.12	−.02	.04	−.06	−.08	−.05	−.06	—	
CS	.57	.05	.08	−.02	.01	−.07	−.03	−.01	−.03	.30	—

TABLE 6.3   Factor Loadings and Residuals for Four Correlated Factors Fitted to the ASVAB

Subtest	Factor Loadings				Residuals									
	Q	V	T	S	AR	MK	WK	PC	GS	AS	MC	EI	NO	CS
AR	.93				—									
MK	.85				.00	—								
WK		.92			−.02	−.04	—							
PC		.86			.03	−.01	.02	—						
GS		.90			.02	.01	.00	−.03	—					
AS			.86		−.04	−.07	−.03	−.03	.01	—				
MC			.85		.06	.06	−.03	−.01	.03	.02	—			
EI			.91		−.00	−.01	.01	−.01	.05	−.01	−.02	—		
NO				.85	−.01	.03	−.01	.05	−.04	−.05	.01	−.02	—	
CS				.75	−.01	.02	.01	.05	−.03	.02	.06	.04	.00	—

Note. Q = quantitative; V = verbal; T = technical; S = speed. Omitted factor loadings were fixed at zero.

account for the correlations among the ASVAB subtests. Instead, a consideration of the content of the subtests suggests that four factors are required to describe adequately the correlations in Table 6.1 (i.e., factors representing quantitative, verbal, technical, and speed abilities).

Nonetheless, it is clear that a single general factor explains much of the association seen in Table 6.1. In fact, Spearman's response to the residuals in Table 6.2 may well have been "swollen specifics." That is, Spearman might have argued that including two measures of a single skill (e.g., Arithmetic Reasoning and Math Knowledge) in a test battery causes the quantitative specific factor falsely to appear to be a general factor.

Thurstone

Louis Leon Thurstone's (1938) *Primary Mental Abilities* monograph stands as a landmark in the study of intelligence. A total of 218 college students completed 56 tests during five 3-hour sessions. The tests were carefully selected, and detailed descriptions of the items were provided in the monograph. A dozen factors were extracted and rotated, and seven primary factors were clearly interpretable: spatial, perceptual, numerical, verbal relations, word fluency, memory, and inductive reasoning.

In his study of cognitive abilities, Thurstone made many methodological innovations that contributed to the development of factor analysis. These innovations, developed over a period of years, were summarized in his *Multiple Factor Analysis* (1947) text, which a half-century later continues to provide a remarkably lucid account of factor analysis. Central to his approach was the use of multiple factors, interpretable due to the "simple structure" of factor loadings, to explain the correlations among a set of tests. To obtain these interpretable factors in an era when calculations were performed by hand, Thurstone devised a computationally simple

method for extracting factors. He clearly articulated the distinctions between common variance, specific variance, and error variance and provided means to estimate a variable's communality (i.e., its common variance). When factors are extracted according to algebraic criteria (e.g., Thurstone's centroid method or principal axes), Thurstone maintained that the resulting factor loading matrix is not necessarily psychologically meaningful. Consequently, he developed orthogonal and oblique rotation methods to facilitate interpretation. Simple structure, which Thurstone used to guide rotation, is now used as the principal model for the relation of latent (the factors) and manifest (i.e., the tests) variables.

For a battery of psychological tests, it is ordinarily impossible to obtain simple structure when the latent variables are required to be uncorrelated. For this reason, Thurstone introduced the idea of correlated factors and used such factors when rotating to simple structure. In LISREL terminology, Thurstone treated his tests as manifest variables (Xs) and used exogenous latent factors (ξs) to explain the correlations among the manifest variables. The results of this analysis are a factor loading matrix (Λ_x in LISREL notation) and a matrix (Φ) of factor correlations. Table 6.3 provides the factor loading matrix and residuals obtained by using LISREL to fit four correlated factors to Table 6.1; the factor correlations are given in Table 6.4.

Fitting four correlated factors to the ASVAB correlations shown in Table 6.1 is much more satisfactory. The RMSEA is

TABLE 6.4   Correlations of Four Factors Fitted to the ASVAB

Factor	Factor			
	Q	V	T	S
Quantitative (Q)	—			
Verbal (V)	.83	—		
Technical (T)	.80	.90	—	
Speed (S)	.76	.68	.62	—

.093; the adjusted goodness of fit is .90; and the nonnormed fit index is .95.

In this formulation of factor analysis, a general factor is not needed to describe the pervasive relations between manifest variables (and will not emerge in a factor analysis if Λ_x is specified to show simple structure) because the factor correlations in Φ explicitly model the associations of the latent variables. Note that the factor correlations shown in Table 6.4 are all large and positive. Interestingly, Carroll (1993) noted that "an acrimonious controversy between Spearman and his 'British' school, on the one hand, and Thurstone and his 'American' school, on the other" (p. 56) arose about the existence of a general factor. Carroll feels "fairly certain that if Spearman had lived beyond 1945, it would have been possible for him and Thurstone to reach a rapprochement" (p. 56).

It was not until 1957 that Schmid and Leiman showed the algebraic equivalence of correlated primary factors and a representation with a second-order general factor and orthogonal first-order factors. When viewed from the perspective of structural equation modeling, it is easy to see that the debate between advocates of a general factor and advocates of correlated primary factors was pointless. When Φ contains many large positive correlations between factors, the question is not whether a general factor exists but rather *whether a single general factor can account for the factor correlations.* To examine this question within the LISREL framework, the tests can be taken as endogenous manifest variables (Ys); primary factors are taken as endogenous latent variables (ηs); and the issue is whether paths (in the Γ matrix) from a single exogenous latent factor (ξ, i.e., the general factor) to each η can account for the correlations between tests loading on different factors. With a large battery of the sort analyzed by Thurstone (1938), more than a single general factor may be required to model adequately the observed correlation matrix.

Fitting this model to the ASVAB data yields estimates of paths from the second-order general factor ξ to the endogenous Quantitative, Verbal, Technical, and Speed factors of .88, .96, .92, and .73. The factor loading matrix Λ_y is virtually identical to the factor loading matrix (Λ_x) shown in Table 6.3. The residuals are also similar, except that rather large residuals remain between the Quantitative subtests and Speed subtests. For example, the residual between Math Knowledge and Numerical Operations was .13. Consequently, the fit statistics dropped slightly: the RMSEA is .11; the adjusted goodness of fit is .88; and the nonnormed fit index is .94. These results clearly show that the issue is not whether a general factor exists, but instead whether a model with a *single* general factor can account for the correlations among Thurstonian primary factors. The models described

by Vernon (1950) and Carroll (1993) suggest that for large batteries of tests that sample diverse abilities the answer will ordinarily be negative.

Vernon

Philip E. Vernon, a junior colleague of Spearman, developed a model that addressed the main weakness of his senior mentor. Specifically, the law of tetrad differences fails for the correlation matrix presented in Table 6.1 and for almost any test battery unless the tests have been very carefully selected so that their tetrad differences vanish. A theory of intelligence that satisfactorily describes only some (very carefully selected) sets of tests is not satisfactory, and Spearman was criticized for this problem.

Vernon (1950) acknowledged that "almost any specific factor (in Spearman's sense) can be turned into a primary factor, given sufficient ingenuity in test construction" (p. 133) and warned against "highly specialized factors, which have no appreciable significance for everyday life [and] are not worth isolating" (p. 133). Such factors are sometimes called *eye twitch factors* (Charles L. Hulin, personal communication, August 21, 1977). Instead, Vernon argued that "factorists should aim not merely to reduce large numbers of variables to a few components that account for their intercorrelations, but also to reduce them to the fewest components which will cover most variance" (p. 133).

To this end, Vernon (1950) developed the *hierarchical group-factor theory* of intelligence illustrated in Figure 6.1. At the apex is general intelligence, *g*, which Vernon suggested would account for about 40% of the variance in the scores of a test battery. Vernon used *v:ed* and *k:m* to denote two "major group factors," which collectively might explain approximately 10% of the variance in test scores. The construct *v:ed* refers to a verbal-educational higher order factor, which explains the relations among reading comprehension, logical reasoning, and arithmetic reasoning after partialling out *g*, and *k:m* refers to a major group factor defined by spatial and mechanical abilities. Vernon believed the minor

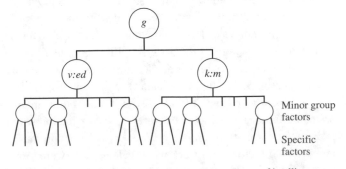

Figure 6.1   Vernon's hierarchical group-factor theory of intelligence.

TABLE 6.5   Carroll's Factor Loadings for a Correlation Matrix Published by Schutz (1958) After Schmid-Leiman Transformation

Test	g	Gc	Gf	Verbal	Numerical	Space	Reasoning
Word meaning	**.56**	**.43**	−.01	**.53**	−.02	.01	−.01
Odd words	**.62**	**.44**	.02	**.50**	.03	.00	.01
Remainders	**.53**	**.22**	.18	−.01	**.64**	.04	−.01
Mixed arithmetic	**.56**	**.25**	.16	.02	**.62**	−.03	.01
Hatchets	**.50**	.01	**.35**	.01	.01	**.58**	.00
Boots	**.49**	.00	**.36**	.00	.00	**.58**	.00
Figure changes	**.60**	.18	**.27**	−.02	−.06	.03	**.27**
Mixed series	**.65**	.21	**.26**	−.02	.07	.00	**.25**
Teams	**.53**	.21	**.18**	.05	.00	−.04	**.21**

Note. Salient loadings are bolded. g = general intelligence; Gc = crystalized intelligence; Gf = fluid intelligence.
Source: Adapted from Carroll (1993, p. 95).

group factors (reading comprehension, logical reasoning, spatial ability, etc.) explained about 10% of the variance in test scores, and he attributed the remaining 40% to specific factors and error of measurement.

Vernon's model in LISREL notation appears very different from Thurstone's simple structure. As shown in Table 6.3, each test loads on just one factor in an ideal simple structure. In Vernon's model, each test would load on the general factor g (denoted as ξ_1 in LISREL notation); v:ed and k:m would be latent variables (ξ_2 and ξ_3); the m minor group factors would be latent variables denoted ξ_4 to ξ_{m+3}; and all latent variables would be uncorrelated. A test hypothesized to assess the first minor group factor within the v:ed domain would have loadings estimated on three factors: ξ_1, ξ_2, and ξ_4 (assuming that the first minor group factor was denoted as the fourth factor). Although the factors in Table 6.5 are labeled according to Carroll's (1993) conceptualization, they illustrate the pattern of large (in bold) and small (not bold) loadings expected in Vernon's model. Note that all tests are expected to load on g; about half of the tests are expected to load on one of the two major group factors (Gc); the other tests are expected to load on the other major group factor (Gf); and the factors labeled Verbal, Numerical, Space, and Reasoning play the role of minor group factors.

An interesting effect is that if the loadings expected to be small in Table 6.5 are fixed at zero and the bolded loadings are treated as parameters to be estimated, a program such as LISREL is unable to obtain a maximum likelihood solution. Without further constraints, such a pattern of fixed and free loadings is underidentified (McDonald, personal communication, December 1, 2000). McDonald (1999, pp. 188–191) describes the constraints that must be implemented for factor loadings to be estimable. LISREL 8.30 does not allow such constraints; instead, CALIS (SAS Institute, 1990) can be used.

The prepotence of g in Vernon's model nicely explains the large correlations among all variables seen in Table 6.1. The quantitative, verbal, technical, and speed factors apparent in Table 6.1 would correspond to minor group factors in Vernon's model and, as expected, clearly explain much less variance. The v:ed and k:m major group factors are not obvious in Table 6.1, presumably because the ASVAB battery of tests is too limited in scope.

Guilford

Factor fractionation was taken to an extreme in J. P. Guilford's (1967, 1985) structure of intellect (SOI) model. Guilford factorially crossed *contents* (i.e., the type of information processed) with *operations* (i.e., the mental activity or process applied to the content) and *products* (i.e., the output of the operation) to arrive at SOI abilities. Contents included visual, auditory, symbolic, semantic, and behavior categories; operations included evaluation, convergent production, divergent production, memory, and cognition; and products included units, classes, relations, systems, transformations, and implications (Guilford, 1967, 1985). This three-way classification can be represented as a cube with 5 rows, 6 columns, and 5 slabs, for a total of 150 primary abilities.

Guilford spent much of his career developing multiple measures of the various abilities defined by the SOI cube. Great energy and effort was devoted to this program of research. Carroll (1993) noted that "Guilford must be given much credit for conducting a series of major factorial studies in which hypotheses were to be confirmed or disconfirmed by successive studies in which new tests were continually designed to permit such testing of hypotheses" (p. 58).

On the other hand, there is much to criticize. For example, Guilford wrote that "any genuine zero correlations between pairs of intellectual tests is sufficient to disprove the existence of a universal factor like g" (1967, p. 56) and that of "some 48,000 correlations between pairs of tests, about 18% were below .10, many of them being below zero" (1985, p. 238). The problem with Guilford's argument is that eye twitch factors are unlikely to correlate with other eye twitch factors, so zero correlations between measures of obscure abilities are neither surprising nor particularly meaningful. Moreover, as noted previously, an important desideratum in evaluating psychometric factors is their practical significance. Research with broad abilities such as the ASVAB's verbal, quantitative, and technical abilities has found that they add little incremental validity to that provided by g when predicting training performance (Ree & Earles, 1991) and job performance (Ree et al., 1994); it appears unlikely that the factors identified by Guilford would meet with more success.

A more fundamental criticism of the SOI model lies in its factorial combination of content, operation, and product to characterize human abilities. There is no a priori reason why the mind should be well described by factorially crossing these three factors. Indeed, new statistical methodologies such as hierarchical regression trees (Breiman, Friedman, Olshen, & Stone, 1984) and neural networks (Freeman & Skapura, 1992) suggest the need for nonlinear approaches to understanding complex phenomena.

Cattell

Raymond B. Cattell was a student of Spearman in the 1930s (Carroll, 1993) and spent most of his career at the University of Illinois at Urbana-Champaign. In addition to his academic appointment, Cattell also founded the Institute for Personality and Ability Testing (IPAT) and made numerous contributions to the study of personality.

Cattell (1971) described a variety of influences that led to his (1941, 1943) notions of fluid and crystalized intelligence, often denoted Gf and Gc. Among these were his consideration of the correlations of Thurstone's (1938) primary factors, which he felt revealed more than one general factor, as well as the different kinds of abilities assessed by culture-fair tests (i.e., perceptual) and traditional intelligence tests (e.g., verbal comprehension).

Cattell (1971) wrote that "fluid intelligence shows itself in successfully educing complex relations among simple fundaments whose properties are known to everyone" and that Gf "appears to operate whenever the sheer perception of complex relations is involved" (p. 98). Thus, Gf reflects basic abilities in reasoning and related higher mental processes (e.g., inductive reasoning). On the other hand, crystalized intelligence reflects the extent of an individual's base of knowledge (vocabulary, general information). Cattell wrote that this crystalized intelligence operates "in areas where the judgments have been taught systematically or experienced before" (p. 98).

Cattell (1971) described an interesting mechanism that explains why cognitive ability tests have large positive correlations. Cattell suggested that individuals are born with "a single, general, relation-perceiving ability connected with the total, associational, neuron development of the cortex" (p. 117). This ability is what Cattell viewed as fluid intelligence. Through experience, individuals learn facts, relationships, and techniques for solving problems. This pool of acquired knowledge, which depends on opportunity to learn, motivation, frequency of reward, and so forth, is what Cattell viewed as crystalized knowledge. Cattell's *investment theory* hypothesizes that "as a result of the fluid ability being *invested* in all kinds of complex learning situations, correlations among these acquired, crystallized abilities will also be large and positive, and tend to yield a general factor" (p. 118). However, correlations of measures of fluid and crystallized intelligence will not be perfect because of the various other factors affecting crystallized intelligence.

Carroll

John B. Carroll (1993) conducted a massive review and re-analysis of the factor analytic literature. He first compiled a bibliography of more than 10,000 references and identified approximately 1,500 "as pertaining to the correlational or factor analysis of cognitive abilities" (p. 78). Ultimately, 461 data sets were selected on the basis of being well suited to factor analysis (e.g., at least three tests were included as measures of each factor that was hypothesized; a reasonable representation of factors was included; the sample of individuals was broad).

One of the problems in comparing factor analytic results from different researchers lies in their use of different statistical methods. The seriousness of this problem can be seen in the acrimonious debate between the British and American researchers. To allow valid comparisons across studies, Carroll (1993) used a single, consistent methodology, which he carefully described in his book (pp. 80–101). Exploratory factor analysis (EFA) provided the fundamental basis for Carroll's analysis.

Carroll decided to use EFA to "let the data speak for themselves" (p. 82). Because EFA results are often unstable and sampling variability can play an unacceptably large role in samples of moderate size (i.e., a few hundred; Idaszak, Bottom, & Drasgow, 1988), CFA has largely replaced EFA. However, CFA requires the researcher to specify, prior to beginning the analysis, the pattern of fixed (at zero) and free (to be estimated) factor loadings as well as any higher order structure. Thus, to use CFA to reanalyze, say, Thurstone's (1938) correlation matrix, the researcher would need to specify the pattern of fixed and free loadings for tests such as Block-counting, Lozenges, and Flags. The contents of such tests are not apparent from their names, and the traits they assess are not obvious. Of course, careful consideration of the contents of each test would allow tentative hypotheses to be made, but application of CFA to all of Carroll's 461 sets of tests would have been incredibly difficult and impossibly time consuming. Consequently, EFA was the only viable option for this massive reanalysis.

Carroll's analysis included some of the most reliable and trustworthy procedures developed in the long history of EFA. For example, the number of factors was determined in part by Montanelli and Humphreys's (1976) parallel analysis, which compares the eigenvalues of a correlation matrix (with squared multiple correlations on the diagonal) to the eigenvalues of a correlation matrix for random data simulating the same number of people and variables. The parallel analysis criterion suggests extracting a factor only when the eigenvalue of the real data exceeds the corresponding eigenvalue of the random data.

Varimax (Kaiser, 1958) was used for orthogonal rotation, and Tucker and Finkbeiner's (1981) direct artificial personal probability function rotation (DAPPFR) was used for oblique rotation; in my experience, these rotation methods are the best available. When DAPPFR produced correlated first-order factors (which Carroll reports was usually the case), the resulting factor correlation matrix was factor analyzed to produce second-order factors. When the second-order factors were also correlated, a third-order factor analysis was performed; no higher order analysis was needed (Carroll, 1993, p. 89).

When second-order or third-order factors were obtained, Carroll performed a Schmid-Leiman (1957) transformation.

Carroll (1993) noted that the "Schmid-Leiman transformation can be thought of as one that redistributes variances from correlated factors to orthogonal factors" (p. 90) and demonstrates the equivalence of Thurstonian correlated factors with Vernon's hierarchical representation. When a test battery allowed a third-order analysis, each test obtained a loading on the third-order factor, loadings on each second-order factor, and loadings on each first-order factor. Table 6.5, adapted from Carroll's (1993, p. 95) Table 3.2, illustrates the end result of a reanalysis. Note that all nine tests have sizable loadings on the general factor g; four tests have moderate-sized loadings on crystalized intelligence Gc; five tests have moderate loadings on fluid intelligence Gf; and each test has a loading on its first-order common factor.

Reminiscent of Vernon's (1950) hierarchical model shown in Figure 6.1, Carroll's (1993) *three stratum model* is shown in Figure 6.2. At the apex is general cognitive ability. Whereas Vernon had two broad factors (*v:ed* and *k:m*) at the second level, Carroll obtained many more; eight of the most important are shown in Figure 6.2, and several others appear in Carroll's Table 15.14 (pp. 620–622). Following Carroll (see p. 625), the distance between g and each second-order factor (e.g., *Gf*) in Figure 6.2 reflects the approximate strength of relationship, with shorter distances indicating stronger association. Table 6.6 lists some of the first-order factors that define the second-order factors.

The second-order factor most strongly related to g is fluid intelligence, *Gf*. It is defined by the first-order factors of induction, deduction, and quantitative reasoning. Carroll (1993) stated that it is "concerned with the basic processes of reasoning and other mental activities that depend only minimally on learning and acculturation" (p. 624).

Also closely related to g is crystalized intelligence, *Gc*. Carroll (1993) found many first-order factors related to *Gc*, including verbal ability, reading comprehension, and lexical knowledge. From the first-order factors that Carroll found to

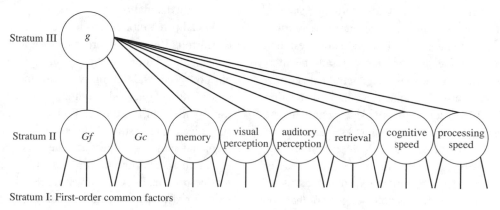

Figure 6.2   Carroll's three-stratum theory of intelligence. Adapted from Carroll (1993, p. 626).

TABLE 6.6 Some First-Order Factors Identified by Carroll (1995)

Second-Order Factor	First-Order Factors		
	Power Factor	Speed Factor	Misc. Factor
Gf	Deduction (.41) Induction (.57) Quantitative (.51)		
Gc	Verbal ability (.49) Reading comprehension Lexical knowledge (.37)		Reading speed
Memory	Memory span (.36)	Associative memory (.43) Free recall memory Meaningful memory	
Visual perception	Visualization (.57)	Spatial relations (.40) Closure speed (.42) Flexibility of closure (.45) Perceptual speed (.37)	Length estimation
Auditory perception	Hearing threshold Speech sound discrimination Musical discrimination		
Retrieval	Originality (.40)	Ideational fluency (.38) Naming facility Word fluency (.43)	
Cognitive speed			Perceptual speed (.37) Rate of test taking Numerical facility (.45)
Processing speed			Simple reaction time (.08) Choice reaction time Semantic processing speed

Note. Median loadings of tests on the third-order *g* are provide in parentheses when available.

be related to *Gc*, this factor could have been labeled Verbal Ability. Cattell's (1971) investment theory would predict a much wider array of first-order factors lying beneath *Gc*, including perhaps science knowledge, mechanical knowledge, and knowledge of other subjects taught in high school. A general-knowledge first-order factor did occasionally appear under *Gc*.

Actually, the empirical distinction between *Gf* and *Gc* was not sharp and clear in several data sets. Carroll (1993) obtained a second-order factor in some cases that was a combination of the first-order factors that usually define *Gf* and *Gc*, such as verbal ability, deduction, and quantitative reasoning. This combination may be the result of inadequately designed test batteries and the vagaries of sampling. It would be interesting to use CFA methods on these data sets to determine whether a latent structure that makes a sharp distinction between *Gf* and *Gc* first-order factors fits significantly worse than does the combination structure obtained by Carroll.

Carroll (1993) also identified a second-order memory factor. First-order factors lying beneath this second-order factor include memory span, associative memory, free recall memory, and meaningful memory. Carroll suggested that the latent structure of memory has been understudied, noting that

"our database does not include enough information to clarify the true structure of memory and learning abilities at higher strata" (p. 605). In their paper "Reasoning Ability Is (Little More Than) Working-Memory Capacity?!" Kyllonen and Christal (1990) certainly argued for the importance of memory, but Carroll found the median loading of memory span factors on *g* to be a less promising .36. The distinction between short term memory and working memory (Engle, Tuholski, Laughlin, & Conway, 1999)—working memory involves Baddeley's (1986) central executive—appears to be the critical distinction.

Visual perception is another second-order factor obtained by Carroll (1993). First-order factors defining visual perception include, among others, visualization, spatial relations, closure speed, and flexibility of closure. Some of these first-order tests had relatively high median loadings on *g* (e.g., .57 for visualization, .45 for flexibility of closure, and .42 for closure speed), suggesting that some of these item types should be included in a broad test of general cognitive ability.

A rather small number of studies have investigated auditory perception, but Carroll was nonetheless able to identify a second-order factor for this domain. Prior to the widespread availability of multimedia computers, research investigating auditory perception had been more difficult than factorial studies of abilities that can be assessed via paper-and-pencil tests. Multimedia computerized tests of musical aptitude (Vispoel, 1999) and other auditory abilities can now be easily developed and administered, so research in this area is warranted.

Carroll (1993) found a second-order retrieval factor, which he described as the "capacity to readily call up concepts, ideas, and names from long-term memory" (p. 612). The first-order factor found most often beneath retrieval was ideational fluency. Tests used to assess this construct require examinees rapidly to list exemplars of some category. For example, examinees might be given three minutes to write as much as they can about a given theme, identify objects that are round, or enumerate things that might happen on an airplane trip. Another first-order factor in this domain is word fluency, which can be assessed by tests that give examinees a few minutes to list words that begin with the letter R, make as many anagrams as possible from a given word, unscramble words (e.g., "rabvle" is "verbal"), and so forth. Carroll found both ideational fluency and word fluency factors to have fairly large median loadings (.38 and .43, respectively) on *g*.

The final two second-order factors shown in Figure 6.2 are cognitive speed and processing speed. First-order factors underlying cognitive speed include perceptual speed (which also sometimes appears under the second-order visual perception factor), numerical facility (e.g., the ASVAB Numerical Operations test), and the rate of test taking. The second-order processing speed factor includes first-order factors such as simple reaction time, choice reaction time, and semantic processing speed. The distance of these second-order factors from *g* in Figure 6.2 indicates their relatively weak association with general cognitive ability.

Summary of the Psychometric Approach

Humphreys (1984, p. 243) defined intelligence as an individual's "entire repertoire of acquired skills, knowledge, learning sets, and generalization tendencies considered intellectual in nature that [is] available at any one period of time." Factor analytic research has carefully analyzed the latent structure of this repertoire of knowledge, skills, and problem-answering strategies; the most important finding lies in the tremendously important general ability *g*. A handful of second-order factors are also necessary to model correlation matrices that show patterns of first-order factors more highly associated than expected on the basis of a single general factor. Thus, *Gf*, *Gc*, memory, visual perception, auditory perception, retrieval, and cognitive speed factors are required for adequately describing the broad structure of the repertoire. Countless first-order

factors can be obtained, but they seem unlikely to explain additional variance in important workplace behaviors. Instead, their main use lies in helping to define and understand the higher order factors.

Cattell (1941) proposed investment theory to explain how crystalized skills and abilities develop over the life span. He envisioned *Gf* as one's fundamental reasoning capability and believed that *Gc* grew as a function of one's fluid intelligence and investment of time and energy.

Of relevance to this conceptualization is Tuddenham's (1948) comparison of White enlisted men's intelligence in World Wars I and II. Using the Army Alpha test of intelligence, Tuddenham reported a gain of about one standard deviation in test scores over this period. Such an increase in scores is difficult to explain if the Army Alpha test is thought to assess fundamental reasoning capacity. The World War II men averaged about two years more education than the earlier sample (Tuddenham, 1948), so the increase can be explained if Humphreys's definition of intelligence as a repetoire is used.

Flynn's (1984, 1987) research is also relevant. The *Flynn effect* refers to large gains in intelligence test scores over time. Flynn compiled longitudinal results from 14 nations for tests with "culturally reduced content" that assess "decontextualized problem solving" (i.e., tests that generally fit better into the *Gf* category) and tests with greater verbal content (i.e., fitting better into the *Gc* category). Flynn (1987, p. 185) found "strong data for massive gains on culturally reduced tests," and, for nations where such comparisons were possible, "gains on culturally reduced tests at twice the size of verbal gains."

Thus, the view of *Gf* as one's inherent reasoning ability is inconsistent with Flynn's data (if we are willing to assume that there has not been a major change in the gene pool in the past half-century). Instead, Flynn's findings appear to be more consistent with Humphreys's (1984) definition of intelligence as an individual's repertoire of knowledge, skills, and problem-solving strategies.

In addition to education, test scores can be affected by coaching. It is important to note that item types vary in their susceptibility to coaching. For example, it is difficult to develop effective coaching strategies for some item types (Messick & Jungeblut, 1981). On tests of verbal ability that use a synonyms or antonyms format, students must substantially increase their vocabulary to raise test scores, which is a very difficult task. Messick and Jungeblut reported that SAT–Verbal scores increase linearly with the logarithm of time spent studying; based on a variety of regression equations, they predicted a 7-point gain for 10 hours of SAT-V preparation, a 20- to 25-point gain for 100 hours of study, and a 30- to 35-point gain for 300 hours. Flynn's (1984, 1987) results, on the other hand, suggest that tests with culturally reduced content are more coachable. Specifically, the simplest explanation for Flynn's findings is that one can learn problem-solving strategies that substantially increase scores on culturally reduced tests. Indeed, test developers should conduct coachability studies of new item types to ensure that they are resistant to easily learned strategies for answering items.

Flynn (1987) concluded that "psychologists should stop saying that IQ tests measure intelligence" (p. 188). If we accept Humphreys's definition, then Flynn's results provide compelling evidence that intelligence tests do measure intelligence, but some test formats are more coachable than others (i.e., scores are more affected by problem-answering strategies).

Flynn defined intelligence as "real-world problem-solving ability" (p. 188), a definition quite different from Humphreys's and not within the psychometric mainstream. What would a test of real-world problem solving look like? Test development for such an assessment instrument could begin with interviews of a fairly large number of people who would be asked to describe situations where they had to solve important problems; this is essentially Flanagan's (1954) method of critical incidents. Test development could then follow the approach described by Motowidlo, Dunnette, and Carter (1990) and used by Olson-Buchanan et al. (1998). The resulting test would likely be viewed as a situational judgment test and look much more like the assessments described later in the section on social intelligence; the test would not appear similar to the tests that usually define first-order factors beneath *Gf*, *Gc*, or memory.

Information Processing Approaches to Intelligence

Whereas the psychometric approach to the study of intelligence examines covariation among total test scores, the information processing approach decomposes responses to individual items into more elemental parts. Performance on these elemental parts can then be related to traditional measures of intelligence to identify the specific process or processes that constitute intelligence.

One of the most influential information processing conceptualizations is Sternberg's (1977) componential model of intelligence. This approach begins with the *component,* which is defined as "an elementary information process that operates upon internal representations of objects or symbols" (p. 65). Sternberg noted that a "component may translate a sensory input into a conceptual representation, transform one conceptual representation into another, or translate a conceptual representation into a motor output" (p. 65).

Componential theories consist of two parts. First, the researcher must identify the elemental components required to perform a task; examples are given later. The researcher must also identify the processes by which the components are combined; this is often most easily described by a flowchart. The goal of the componential theory is to decompose response time (RT) to an item into its constituent parts; these parts include the time required to execute each component as influenced by the combination rules. For example, an item response might require *a* ms for encoding, *d* ms for responding, and the lesser of two processing times, *b* and *c*. Thus, response time would be decomposed into $RT = a + \min(b, c) + d$.

Sternberg (1977) used a within-subject design to estimate the durations of the components for each respondent. These estimates are called the component scores. To evaluate a particular componential model, Sternberg examined the proportion of variance in response times accounted for by the model for each respondent. In one study, the best-fitting model accounted for 85% of the variance in response times for the most predictable respondent and 69% of the variance for the least predictable (the R^2 values were apparently not corrected for capitalization on chance).

To illustrate a componential model, consider an analogy A is to B as C is to D′, which Sternberg (1977) denoted (A:B::C:D′). Sternberg's model begins with encoding whereby an individual "identifies attributes and values of each term of the problem" (p. 135). Then, in successive steps, it is necessary to discover the rule relating A to B, discover the rule relating A to C, and then form a hypothesis about D′. Next, the match between a true-false alternative D and the hypothesized D′ is evaluated, and finally the response is made. According to this model, the total time needed to solve the problem should equal the sum of the times needed to perform each step. Information processing models have been developed for a variety of tasks, including inductive reasoning (Pellegrino, 1985), deductive reasoning (Johnson-Laird, 1985), and verbal reasoning (Hunt, 1985).

Although important from the perspective of basic psychology, attempts to find a specific component that is strongly associated with intelligence (and that can therefore be interpreted as the essence of intelligence) have not been successful. Kyllonen and Christal (1990) wrote,

> One of the hopes for this research was that complex cognitive abilities, such as reasoning ability, would be reducible to more elementary components, such as the inference component. Despite some successes (see Pellegrino, 1985, for a review), in one important sense this research can be looked upon as a modest failure. No one component was shown over different studies to be the essence of reasoning ability. (p. 427)

Thus, it appears that trying to derive the meaning of intelligence from a componential analysis of item responses can be likened to trying to learn about beauty by examining the Mona Lisa with a microscope.

This line of research does provide a detailed answer to the snide question of "Exactly what does an intelligence test measure?" Information processing models show that intelligence test items assess a variety of interrelated processes and mechanisms. However, componential models provide little insight for understanding workplace behavior because they view intelligence from a distance that is too close.

Kyllonen and his colleagues have retained an information processing perspective but view intelligence from a distance better suited for understanding. The cognitive abilities measurement (CAM) project described by Kyllonen (1994) is grounded on his "consensus information-processing model" (p. 310) depicted in Figure 6.3. This model utilizes two long-term memories, one for procedural knowledge and one for declarative knowledge. The cognitive processing system retrieves information from these systems into working memory, where it is manipulated and a response is ultimately generated through the motor processing system. Clearly, Kyllonen takes a more molar view of intelligence than do the componential researchers.

Kyllonen and Christal (1989, 1990) suggested that performance on cognitive tasks is primarily a function of four of the components shown in Figure 6.3: procedural knowledge, declarative knowledge, cognitive processing speed, and working memory capacity. Certainly, greater amounts of declarative and procedural knowledge and faster cognitive processing should be related to superior performance. Kyllonen and Christal (1990) speculated that "the central factor is

working-memory capacity. Working memory is the locus of both declarative and procedural learning . . . , and limitations in working memory are responsible for the difficulties of learning new facts (Daneman & Green, 1986) and procedures (Anderson & Jeffries, 1985)" (p. 392).

Baddeley's (1986) definition of working memory capacity as the degree to which an individual can simultaneously store and manipulate information is central to Kyllonen and Christal's (1990) research. This definition was used to develop several tests. For example, in the Alphabet Recoding test, examinees are given three letters (e.g., GVN is presented on a first computer-administered screen) and instructed to move forward or backward a certain number of letters (e.g., +2 on the second screen), and then type the answer (IXP). Interestingly, Kyllonen and Christal (1990) found strong relationships between their measures of reasoning ability and working memory capacity, with correlations estimated to be between .80 and .88 across four studies.

The work of Kyllonen and his colleagues has clear connections with the psychometric approach and Carroll's (1993) three-stratum model. Kyllonen's measures of reasoning ability might form a first-stratum factor lying beneath fluid intelligence, and his measures of working memory capacity appear to be related to the second-order memory factor. However, Baddeley's (1986) conceptualization of working memory capacity is different from the digit span and free recall tests ordinarily used to define memory factors in psychometric studies in that he describes a central executive process responsible for controlled attention. Clearly, manipulating information held in short term memory is cognitively challenging, and if tests of this sort are used to define a memory factor, it would be expected to be closer to g than a memory factor defined by tests such as digit span. It would be interesting to include several working memory capacity tests in a battery that used inductive, deductive, and quantitative first-order factors to identify second-order fluid intelligence as well as more standard first-order memory factors to define second-order memory; Kyllonen and Christal's (1990) working memory capacity appears to be a combination of Gf and memory.

Summary of the Information Processing Approach

This line of research has very carefully examined how people solve various types of questions. In effect, it identified the molecules of intelligence. Moreover, as illustrated by Sternberg's (1977) large proportions of variance explained, information processing models provide a substantially complete description of how examinees solve problems.

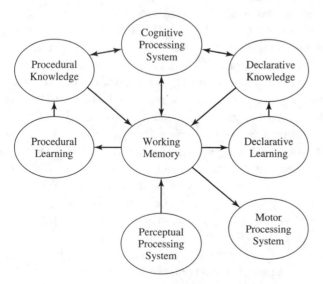

Figure 6.3 Kyllonen's (1994) consensus information processing model.

No single element of the componential models has been found to be preeminent. Consequently, more recent research in this area has taken a more molar view. Kyllonen's model shown in Figure 6.3, for example, focuses on higher order constructs such as procedural knowledge, declarative knowledge, and working memory. It provides important insights and should guide the development of a variety of new tests.

Neuropsychological Approaches

Psychometric researchers view the brain as a black box whose functioning can be empirically investigated by examining the covariation in performance across diverse tasks. In contrast, neuropsychologists explicitly study the brain, functions of various parts of the brain, and interrelations of various functions. Although a detailed review of neuropsychological approaches to the study of intelligence is beyond the scope of this chapter, it is interesting and important to summarize some of the basic findings about the underlying hardware of the brain.

Parts of the brain are specialized for particular functions. In overview, the left side performs verbal information processing, and the right side processes visuospatial information and emotion. As an example of the specialization of the brain, different areas underlie the production and comprehension of speech. Paul Broca was a French neurologist who, in the 1860s, noticed that some patients could not produce speech but were able to understand speech (Banich, 1997). Broca performed autopsies on deceased patients and found damage to the left anterior hemisphere. Other patients with damage in the analogous location of the right hemisphere did not suffer a loss of fluent speech production (Banich, 1997). This inability to produce speech is called Broca's aphasia.

Wernicke's aphasia, in contrast, consists of loss of speech comprehension but fluent production of grammatically correct (but nonsensical) speech. It is caused by damage to the posterior left hemisphere (Banich, 1997). Again, damage to the mirror-image side of the right hemisphere does not cause this deficit.

Based on these anatomical findings, it seems plausible to hypothesize that the abilities to comprehend speech and produce speech are distinct and would be separable in carefully designed psychometric studies. To date, there has been little formal development of psychometric assessments of either speech production or comprehension. With the advent of multimedia computers, assessments of speech comprehension could be developed in a relatively straightforward manner. Examinees equipped with headphones could be presented with audio clips; after listening to the clip, multiple-choice questions could be presented either as audio clips or as text on the computer's monitor.

Speech production is of course critically important in many occupations; its assessment is typically via unstructured interviews (or the *job talk* in academic circles). Computerized assessment of speech production is likely to become a reality within a few years; speech recognition software that converts speech to text (e.g., Dragon Dictate) could be linked with software used to grade essays (e.g., Page & Peterson, 1995) to produce virtually instantaneous scores.

Neuropsychological research provides important insights into our understanding of memory. Cohen (1997) pointed out that

> Memory is not a unitary process. Rather, it must be thought of as a collection of memory systems that operate cooperatively, each system making different functional contributions and supported by different brain systems. Normal memory performance requires many of the brain's various systems, which ordinarily operate together so seamlessly that intuitively appreciating the separate systems and the distinct contributions of each is difficult. (p. 317)

For example, working memory is not a unitary system. Cohen (1997) noted that auditory-verbal working memory can be severely compromised in some patients while their working memory for spatial relations and arithmetic remains perfectly intact. This has implications for developing assessments of working memory capacity; a richer assessment can be constructed by including items that tap into the different types of working memory. Although working memory has several distinct components, they all appear to be situated in the same part of the brain: the dorsolateral prefrontal cortex (Cohen, 1997).

Neuropsychological research clearly demonstrates the distinction between procedural memory and declarative memory that is part of Kyllonen's (1994) information processing model. Originally proposed by Cohen and Squire (Cohen, 1981, 1984; Squire & Cohen, 1984) and further elaborated by Cohen and Eichenbaum (1993), declarative memory accumulates facts and events and provides the means to learn arbitrary associations (e.g., people's names, phone numbers); it is mediated by the hippocampal system, which includes the hippocampus, the amygdala, and the adjoining cortex. In contrast, skill acquisition and performance (e.g., riding a bicycle) are effected by procedural memory. Amnesia is caused by damage to the hippocampal system and affects declarative but not procedural memory. Thus, it is possible to teach patients with amnesia new skills; they do not have a conscious awareness of their recently acquired skills, but they can perform them (Cohen, 1997).

The executive functions, which "include the ability to plan actions toward a goal, to use information flexibly, to realize the ramifications of behavior, and to make reasonable inferences based on limited information" (Banich, 1997, p. 369), are also studied by neuropsychologists. Banich noted that these activities are multifaceted and include the ability "to create a plan and follow through with it, to adapt flexibly, to sequence and prioritize, to make cognitive estimations, and to interact in a socially astute manner" (p. 370). Lezak (1995, pp. 43–44) provided a vivid description of a once-successful surgeon who suffered hypoxia as he was having minor facial surgery. His reasoning ability was spared (he continued to score high average to very superior on intelligence tests), but he was utterly unable to plan. He ultimately worked as a truck driver for his brother; after each individual delivery, it was necessary for him to call his brother for instructions about his next destination. The executive functions are typically compromised by damage to the prefrontal cortex.

In the past, conducting neuropsychological research was very difficult because it had been limited to observing patients with brain damage. In many cases, it was not possible to understand fully the nature and extent of brain damage until an autopsy was performed following a patient's death. Recently developed brain imaging methods have been embraced by neuropsychologists because they allow direct, immediate observations of brain functioning. By tracking blood flow, researchers can see the parts of the brain that are active when specific activities are performed. PET examines brain activity via a radioactive agent, and fMRI examines changes in neuronal activity by using a contrast agent to track blood flow.

An example of this research is provided by Duncan et al. (2000), who used PET to examine brain activity while research participants performed tasks with high factor loadings on g (called high g tasks) and tasks with matching content but low factor loadings on g (low g tasks). The high g tasks were associated with increased activity of a specific area, namely, the lateral frontal cortex. For tasks with verbal content, the high g task was associated with increased activity in the left lateral frontal cortex relative to a matching low g task. In contrast, there was increased activity in both hemispheres' lateral frontal cortex for tasks involving spatial content. Duncan et al.'s (2000) study is important because it found that the brain performed intellectual activities in relatively specific sites, rather than in multiple diffuse areas.

Summary of the Neuropsychological Approach

Until recently, conducting research linking psychometric theories of intelligence with the brain has been difficult if not impossible. Now PET and fMRI provide methods for imaging that make such research possible. As these methods become more available to researchers, it is likely that many important studies will be conducted.

Connections with neuropsychology deepen and enrich our understanding of intelligence. For example, inclusion of procedural and declarative memories in Kyllonen's (1994) model has been shown to have an anatomical justification. Duncan et al.'s (2000) research has identified specific sites for reasoning and demonstrates that reasoning about verbal and spatial material involves different parts of the brain.

The executive functions identified in neuropsychological research suggest important directions for research by test developers. Situational judgment tests (discussed later) seem to provide a means for assessing executive functions, but to date they have not been developed with this in mind. Methods for assessing the executive functions are needed, as is research examining the relation of executive functions and job performance.

INTELLIGENCE AND PERFORMANCE

Two streams of research are important for understanding the relation of intelligence and performance. First, the topic of learning and skill acquisition has been of interest to psychologists since the beginning of psychology as a discipline. This research has ordinarily utilized laboratory studies of "subjects" learning relatively narrow tasks. In the other stream of research, job and training performance have been related to various measures of intelligence and aptitude in field studies. Across the entire gamut of predictors of job performance, Schmidt and Hunter (1998) noted that there have been "thousands of research studies performed over eight decades and involving millions of employees" (p. 271).

Laboratory Studies of Skill Acquisition

Ackerman's 1987 literature review and series of experiments reported in a 1988 article provide a definitive picture of skill acquisition. Ackerman (1988, pp. 289–290) noted that skill acquisition is usually described as consisting of three phases (although different researchers use various terms for the phases). In the first phase, sometimes termed the *declarative stage,* heavy cognitive demands are made on the learner as he or she begins to understand and perform the task; responses are slow, and many errors occur. The next phase is sometimes called the *knowledge compilation stage.* Here strategies for performance are developed, and responses become faster and with fewer errors. Finally, in the *procedural stage* fast and accurate responses become highly automatic responses.

Schneider and Shiffrin (1977) defined *automatic processing* as "activation of a learned sequence of elements in long-term memory that is initiated by appropriate inputs and then proceeds automatically—without subject control, without stressing the capacity limitations of the system, and without necessarily demanding attention" (p. 1) and contrasted it with *controlled processing,* which "requires attention, is capacity-limited (usually serial in nature), and is controlled by the subject" (p. 1). The declarative stage of skill acquisition requires controlled processing, whereas automatic processing is used in the procedural stage.

Schneider and Schffrin (1977) and Ackerman (1987, 1988) identified an important characteristic of the task that affects skill acquisition. *Consistent tasks* are characterized by "invariant rules for information processing, invariant components of processing, or invariant sequences of information processing components that may be used by a subject to attain successful task performance" (Ackerman, 1987, p. 4). *Inconsistent tasks* are tasks where invariant rules or components do not exist. The key point is that skill acquisition for consistent tasks goes through the three stages just described and that the final stage is characterized by automatic processing; inconsistent tasks interrupt this process and always require controlled processing.

In a series of eight experiments, Ackerman (1988) showed that human ability requirements differ across the stages of skill acquisition and across the two types of tasks. Controlled processing is resource intensive; intelligence, as a measure of cognitive resources, is strongly correlated with performance in the declarative stage of skill acquisition. For consistent tasks, intelligence becomes less important as performance becomes automated. Perceptual speed, which is relatively unimportant for controlled processing, becomes more strongly related to performance during the compilation stage but ultimately diminishes in importance. When performance becomes highly automated, it is primarily influenced by an individual's psychomotor ability; psychomotor ability is much less important for performance in earlier stages that demand controlled processing. This pattern of relationships suggests that performance in assembly-line jobs would initially be related to workers' cognitive ability, but *g* would quickly diminish in importance, and psychomotor abilities would ultimately determine performance.

In contrast, inconsistent tasks always require controlled processing, and cognitive ability consequently remains highly correlated with performance regardless of practice. In many managerial and technical jobs, individuals face continuously changing problems and issues. Here, Ackerman's findings imply that general cognitive ability is always an important determinant of performance.

Intelligence and Performance: Training and Job Criteria

The relation of intelligence and performance on the job and in training has been studied extensively for much of the past century. This literature was so vast and the effects of sampling variability so pernicious that the findings were essentially incomprehensible until statistical methods for aggregation across studies were introduced by Frank Schmidt and John Hunter in 1977. Their meta-analytic procedure, which they termed *validity generalization,* provides a means for combining results across studies to estimate a population mean correlation between intelligence (or some other type of predictor) and a measure of job or training performance. In addition to minimizing the effects of sampling (because results of many studies can be combined), validity generalization allows corrections for range restriction and unreliability in job performance ratings. The method also allows researchers to estimate the population standard deviation of the validity coefficient; that is, after correcting for the effects of sampling, range restriction, and criterion unreliability, to what extent does the intelligence–job performance correlation vary across settings? A population standard deviation of zero implies that the relation of intelligence and job performance is invariant across settings and organizations.

In one of the most comprehensive studies, Hunter (1980) analyzed the results of validation studies of the General Aptitude Test Battery (GATB) across 512 jobs. Because of the rich sample, Hunter was able to partition the jobs into five levels of complexity and perform analyses separately for job performance criteria and training performance criteria. Hunter found that job complexity moderated the relation between intelligence and performance; as expected, the relationship was stronger for more complex jobs. Of note, a substantial association was found for all but the least complex job category (feeding and off bearing). Moreover, the relation of intelligence and performance was very similar across both types of criterion measures.

Based on Hunter's (1980) research, Schmidt and Hunter (1998) suggested that the best estimate of the correlation of intelligence and job performance is .51 and that the best estimate of the correlation of intelligence and training performance is .56. Note that these estimates assume that the criterion is measured without error. Moreover, the estimates assume that there is no prior selection of job applicants; that is, the correlation estimated is that which would be expected if a simple random sample of job applicants entered a training program or was hired for a job of medium complexity.

Schmidt and Hunter's methodology and substantive findings have been controversial. For example, many individual studies do not report information about range restriction and criterion unreliability, so the validity generalization procedure does not directly correct correlations from individual studies. Instead, assumed distributions of range restriction and criterion unreliability are utilized; these distributions represent best guesses based on the evidence available. Imprecision in the assumed distributions may cause the second digit in the estimates just given to be inaccurate, but the best available evidence indicates that the correlation of intelligence and performance in jobs of at least moderate complexity is approximately .5 for a random sample of job applicants.

It is important to note that empirical studies using intelligence to predict job performance will not obtain correlations of approximately .5 even when large samples are obtained; instead, it is much more likely that a correlation of .25 will be observed. This will occur because job performance is always measured with error, which will reduce the correlation. Moreover, there is at least indirect selection on intelligence due to direct selection on other preemployment procedures (e.g., interviews) used in the hiring process. R. L. Thorndike's (1949) report of a study of World War II pilots remains a landmark in demonstrating the consequences of selection; because of the war, an entire applicant pool of 1,036 candidates entered a pilot training program (only 136 would have qualified under prewar requirements for admission). An overall validity of .64 for the selection composite was observed for this large sample, whereas the validity computed using only the sample of 136 qualified candidates was only .18. Unless an organization is willing to hire a simple random sample of unscreened applicants, validities much less than R. L. Thorndike's .64 or Schmidt and Hunter's (1998) .51 will be observed.

Intelligence and Performance: More Than *g*?

Ree and Earles (1991) and Ree et al. (1994) examined the extent to which specific abilities assessed by the ASVAB provided validity incremental to that of general cognitive ability for predicting job and training performance. These researchers used the first principal component from the ASVAB as their measure of g; they reported that other plausible methods for estimating g from the ASVAB tests correlated in excess of .996 with the first principal component. The remaining principal components served as the measures of specific abilities. This partitioning of variance is useful because the measures of specific variance are orthogonal to the measure of g and, moreover, because all of the specific variance is utilized.

Ree and his colleagues first computed the simple correlation between their measure of g and the job or training school criterion measure and corrected for restriction of range. Next, the validity of the total test battery was estimated via multiple regression (with a multivariate correction of restriction of range), and then the multiple correlation was adjusted for capitalization on chance. Finally, the difference between the adjusted multiple correlation and the simple correlation was computed; it represents the incremental validity provided by

the specific knowledge, skills, and abilities assessed by the ASVAB.

As a summary of their basic findings, Ree et al. (1994) reported that the simple correlation of g (corrected for range restriction and averaging across occupations) with various measures of job performance was about .42. After a multivariate correction for range restriction and correction for capitalization on chance, the multiple correlation of the ASVAB battery with job performance averaged about .44. Thus, the incremental validity of the specific abilities assessed by the ASVAB was .02, which led to the remarkable conclusion that predicting job performance is "not much more than g," to quote the article's title.

There are at least three limitations regarding Ree et al.'s (1994) conclusion. First, the ASVAB does not provide reliable assessments of the various second-stratum factors of Carroll's (1993) model depicted in Figure 6.2. Reliable and valid measures of these factors, as well as important first-order factors, need to be included in the type of study conducted by Ree et al. Second, Ree et al. considered only measures of cognitive ability; Schmidt and Hunter (1998) provided estimates of incremental validity for predicting job and training performance from other types of measures such as work samples, integrity tests, and measures of conscientiousness. Incremental validities large enough to have practical importance were found for several of the measures. Third, the criterion measures used by Ree et al. might best be described as assessments of task performance; measures of Borman and Motowidlo's (1993) contextual job performance were not included.

It appears premature to conclude unequivocally that there is "not much more than g." Nonetheless, the work of Ree and his colleagues as well as numerous other practitioners who have used test batteries assessing cognitive abilities to predict task performance demonstrate that a search for incremental validity in this context is unlikely to be successful. Instead, to obtain incremental validity, it is probably necessary to use individual differences outside the cognitive domain to predict some measure of job behavior other than task performance.

SOCIAL INTELLIGENCE

Lezak's (1995) report of a surgeon who became a truck driver needing special assistance despite intact reasoning abilities demonstrates that more than g is required for successful job performance. The executive functions summarized by Banich (1997) suggest several types of assessments that might be related to job performance. This section addresses the usefulness of interpersonal skills or social intelligence as predictors of performance in the workplace.

To understand the relation of social intelligence and job performance, it is important to think carefully about the aspects of job performance for which incremental validity might be obtained. In this regard, Borman and Motowidlo's (1993) distinction between task and contextual performance is important. Borman and Motowidlo (1997) argued that

> contextual activities are important because they contribute to organizational effectiveness in ways that shape the organizational, social, and psychological context that serves as the catalyst for task activities and processes. Contextual activities include volunteering to carry out task activities that are not formally part of the job and helping and cooperating with others in the organization to get tasks accomplished. (p. 100)

Thus, a major part of contextual performance appears to be intrinsically social in nature.

Is contextual performance important in the workplace? Motowidlo and Van Scotter (1994) conducted a study to address this question. Using a sample of 421 U.S. Air Force mechanics (which is not a job where one would expect contextual performance to be especially salient), Motowidlo and Van Scotter obtained job performance ratings from three different supervisors. One rated overall job performance; one rated task performance; and one rated contextual performance. Contextual performance was assessed by a 16-item scale; these items asked supervisors how likely it was that the mechanic would perform various contextual behaviors, including "cooperate with others in the team," "persist in overcoming obstacles to complete a task," "defend the supervisor's decisions," and "voluntarily do more than the job requires to help others or contribute to unit effectiveness" (p. 477). The ratings of task performance correlated .43 with overall performance; remarkably, the contextual performance measure correlated .41 with overall performance. Thus, in a prototypical blue-collar job, contextual performance and task performance appear to be equally important components of overall job performance. Similar results have been reported by Borman, White, and Dorsey (1995); Dunn, Mount, Barrick, and Ones (1995); Ferris, Judge, Rowland, and Fitzgibbons (1994); and Werner (1994).

Collectively, these findings show that cooperating with others and helping coworkers are important in virtually every job. The extent to which an employee actually enacts such behaviors appears likely to be a function of both willingness to help and the capability (a) to recognize situations where one should help others or defend the organization and (b) to know what steps to take. These capabilities appear to have a knowledge component; consequently, social intelligence may be related to the performance of appropriate behaviors.

Measurement of Social Intelligence

Two distinct conceptual approaches to the measurement of social intelligence have been taken, although both seem to have originated with E. L. Thorndike's (1920) definition of social intelligence as "the ability to understand and manage men and women, boys and girls—to act wisely in human relations" (p. 228). In the first line of research, instruments explicitly intended as measures of social intelligence were developed. One of the earliest measures was the George Washington University Social Intelligence Test developed by Moss, Hunt, Omwake, and Ronning (1927). The other line of research consisted of situational judgment tests (SJTs) that are intended primarily to predict job performance. Early examples include the How Supervise? test (File, 1945; File & Remmers, 1948) and the Supervisory Judgment Test (Greenberg, 1963).

In additional to the conceptual approaches, two technological approaches have been taken. Until recently, social intelligence tests and SJTs have utilized a paper-and-pencil format. In contrast, video assessments have used either a videotape (Stricker, 1982; Weekley & Jones, 1997) or multimedia computer (Olson-Buchanan et al., 1998) format.

Explicit Measures of Social Intelligence

Walker and Foley (1973) provided a review of research on social intelligence during the 50 years following E. L. Thorndike's 1920 paper. They noted that the two key elements of E. L. Thorndike's definition were "the ability to (a) understand others and (b) act or behave wisely in relating to others" (p. 842). They further noted that O'Sullivan, Guilford, and deMille (1965) viewed social intelligence as the ability to understand other people's feelings, thoughts, and intentions. Walker and Foley also cited Flavell, Botkin, and Fry (1968) as providing "the single most extensive analysis and investigation of the development of various aspects of social-cognitive functioning" (p. 844). Flavell et al. argued that effective social interacting requires five steps. First, an individual must recognize the *existence* of other people's perspectives (i.e., an individual needs to realize that others may perceive a particular situation very differently than he or she does). Second, the individual must understand the *need* to consider other people's perspectives. Third, the individual must have the ability to *predict* how others will perceive a situation. Fourth is the need for *maintenance* of perceptions of others' perspectives when they conflict with one's own views. The last step is the *application* of this understanding of others' views to determine one's behavior in a particular situation.

It is important for social intelligence to exhibit discriminant validity from other constructs. Unfortunately, Riggio (1986) noted that "difficulties in assessing social intelligence, particularly the inability to discriminate social intelligence from general intelligence, led to the demise of this line of research" (p. 649). Riggio's (1986) Social Skills Inventory represents a more recent attempt to develop a measure of social intelligence. It utilizes a "typical performance" format rather than a "maximal performance" format. For example, an item is "At parties I enjoy speaking to a great number of different people" (p. 652). Thus, distinguishing the Social Skills Inventory from cognitive ability is unlikely to be a problem; however, establishing discriminant validity vis-à-vis personality is clearly important.

Riggio (1986) viewed social intelligence as "not a single entity but, rather, a constellation of many more basic skills" (p. 650). The Social Skills Inventory includes six of these more basic skills: emotional expressivity, the ability to communicate one's affect and attitudes; emotional sensitivity, the ability to "decode others' emotions, beliefs, or attitudes, and cues of status-dominance" (p. 650); social expressivity, the ability to express oneself verbally and initiate conversations; social sensitivity, the ability to understand others' verbal statements and recognize social rules and norms; emotional control, "the ability to regulate emotional communications and nonverbal displays" (p. 650); and social control, an individual's social self-presentation skill. Riggio reported high internal consistency and test-retest reliabilities for his instrument and generally satisfactory results in an exploratory factor analysis. However, some of the subscales of the Social Skills Inventory had large correlations with scales of the 16 Personality Factor (16 PF) instrument (Cattell, Eber, & Tatsuoka, 1970). For example, the Social Control scale correlated .69 with the 16 PF Shy-Venturesome scale and −.78 with the Social Anxiety scale.

Descriptions of emotional intelligence (Goleman, 1996) sometimes seem similar to social intelligence. Emotional intelligence has been hypothesized to encompass

> a set of conceptually related psychological processes involving the processing of affective information. These processes include (a) the verbal and nonverbal appraisal and expression of emotion in oneself and others, (b) the regulation of emotion in oneself and others, and (c) the use of emotion to facilitate thought. (Davies, Stankov, & Roberts, 1998, p. 990)

In a series of three studies, Davies et al. examined a variety of measures that have been suggested as measures of emotional intelligence. These measures either had low reliability or, when reliable, correlated highly with well-known personality scales. Davies et al. concluded, "The three studies reported here converge on a conclusion that, as presently postulated, little remains of emotional intelligence that is unique and psychometrically sound" (p. 1013).

Situational Judgment Tests

SJTs present descriptions of workplace situations and ask the respondent how he or she would respond. They are often developed by interviewing job incumbents and asking about critical incidents (Flanagan, 1954). Information gleaned from these interviews is then transformed into the items constituting an SJT. As a result of this process, the items on SJTs are viewed as interesting and face valid by job applicants and employees (Richman-Hirsch, Olson-Buchanan, & Drasgow, 2000; Smither, Reilly, Millsap, Pearlman, & Stoffey, 1993). McDaniel and Nguyen (2001) provided a summary of the constructs assessed in SJTs as well as test development procedures.

McDaniel, Morgeson, Finnegan, Campion, and Braverman (2001) described the history of SJTs. These authors noted a flurry of activity in the 1940s but less emphasis during the ensuing decades. Motowidlo et al.'s (1990) "low fidelity simulation" appears to have reenergized work in this area. Numerous papers were presented at academic conferences in the 1990s, although fewer have been published in journals. Particularly noteworthy is the research by Weekley and Jones (1997); they reported the development of two SJTs, one for hourly employees of a discount retailer and the other for employees of a nursing home organization.

Relation of Situational Judgment Tests to Job Performance

There has been much research examining the relation of SJTs to measures of job performance. For example, cross-validation samples demonstrated that Weekley and Jones's (1997) video-based SJTs were substantially related to job performance. In preparation for their meta-analysis, McDaniel et al. (2001) identified 102 validity coefficients for 39 different SJTs based on data from 10,640 research participants. They then conducted a meta-analysis, correcting for range restriction and unreliability in measures of job performance. After these corrections, McDaniel et al. estimated the population mean correlation of SJTs with job performance to be .34.

Due to the large number of correlations McDaniel et al. (2001) identified, they were able to examine the moderating effect of g on the SJT-job performance relationship. High-g tests were defined as SJTs with mean correlations with g in excess of .50; medium-g SJTs had correlations with g

between .35 and .50; and low-g SJTs had correlations below .35. McDaniel et al. estimated the mean population validity of high-, medium-, and low-g SJTs to be .41, .18, and .34. Although confidence intervals for these point estimates were not provided, it is unlikely that the high g and low g validities differ significantly from one another.

The implication of McDaniel et al.'s meta-analysis is that researchers can build predictive SJTs that are more or less related to general cognitive ability. Of course, the incremental validity of an SJT will be greater when it has a smaller correlation with g. In some cases it may be very useful, however, to construct an SJT with a very large correlation with g. For example, in a tight labor market, applicant reactions to selection procedures can be very important. It is unlikely that applicants for senior executive positions would enjoy taking a test like the Wonderlic, and consequently they might drop out of the recruitment process. However, a senior executive might be intrigued (and hence remain a job candidate) by an SJT that is fundamentally a cognitive ability test in disguise. Consistent with McDaniel et al.'s (2001) meta-analysis, Weekley and Jones (1999) concluded that "SJTs represent a method and not a construct" (p. 695).

Linking Situational Judgment Tests and Social Intelligence

Chan and Schmitt (1997) conducted a study that examined how administration medium affected an SJT's correlation with g (and the resulting Black-White score difference). Two forms of SJTs were developed; the forms had identical content, but one was administered via paper and pencil, and the other used a video-based administration. The paper-and-pencil version was found to correlate .45 with a measure of reading comprehension, but the correlation for the video version was just .05. Particularly noteworthy were the effect sizes for Black-White differences: $-.95$ for paper-and-pencil administration versus $-.21$ for video presentation. Thus, the paper-and-pencil form is moderately confounded with g; the video version is independent of g and may well represent a pure measure of social intelligence.

Olson-Buchanan et al.'s (1998) video-based SJT had near-zero correlations with measures of cognitive ability but predicted overall job performance and managers' skills at resolving conflict in the workplace. Their measures of cognitive ability also predicted overall job performance but did not significantly predict conflict resolution performance.

A hypothesis that explains the pattern of results obtained by McDaniel et al. (2001) and Olson-Buchanan et al. (1998) is that high-g SJTs predict job performance, and especially task performance, because of the strong g-job performance relationship. On the other hand, low-g SJTs may measure mainly social intelligence uncontaminated by g; they may have stronger relations with measures of contextual performance because of its fundamental social nature. Clearly, further research is needed to understand why both high- and low-g SJTs have similar validities.

CONCLUSIONS

Psychometric, cognitive, and neuropsychological approaches to investigating intelligence provide complementary perspectives to this important area of human functioning. Convergent evidence across disciplinary lines greatly strengthens the confidence of our conclusions.

Carroll's (1993) three-stratum model depicted in Figure 6.2 represents a landmark accomplishment in the psychometric study of intelligence. It is a comprehensive elaboration of Vernon's (1950) hierarchical model that summarizes and integrates literally hundreds of factor analytic studies.

Comparing Carroll's (1993) model to Spearman's original theory presented in 1904, it is interesting to see how far research has progressed. Spearman's theory could adequately describe a correlation matrix if one test beneath each of the eight stratum II factors were included; if more than one test beneath a stratum II (or stratum I) factor were included, Spearman's theory is not supported. Nonetheless, for understanding performance in the workplace, and especially task performance and training performance, g is key. As demonstrated by Ree and his colleagues (Ree & Earles, 1991; Ree et al., 1994), g accounts for an overwhelming proportion of the explained variance when predicting training and job performance.

The information processing models for cognitive ability test items of Sternberg (1977), Hunt (1985), and others provided important information about what intelligence tests measure. Specifically, no one element of these componential models emerged as the fundamental process of intelligence, thus suggesting that intelligence should be viewed as a mosaic of microprocesses. For understanding and predicting job behavior, a more macro-level perspective better serves researchers. Kyllonen's (1994) consensus information processing model provides a useful framework for understanding performance on cognitive ability tests. His demonstration of the importance of working memory should influence psychometric researchers. Moreover, computerized assessment greatly facilitates measurement of time-related phenomena such as working memory and should allow measures of working memory to be routinely included in test batteries. Baddeley's (1986) research on the structure of working memory provides a solid conceptual foundation for developing test specifications for assessments in this area.

To date, there has been little interaction between researchers with psychometric and neuropsychological perspectives. In part, this has been due to the difficulty in measuring brain activity while performing psychometric tasks. The recent paper by Duncan et al. (2000) demonstrates the value of such collaborations.

Research on social and emotional intelligence has had a dismal history. Measures of these abilities have been found to be either unreliable or confounded with cognitive ability. Nonetheless, neuropsychologists (e.g., Wendy Heller, personal communication, December 3, 2000) can describe individuals who are unable to keep jobs, who are unable to remain married, or who are unable to interact appropriately with others following head injuries despite intact cognitive abilities. Clearly, important abilities have been compromised in such individuals, but standard measures of cognitive skills are insensitive to the consequences of the injuries. Measures of social intelligence unconfounded with g are needed.

Video-based SJTs may provide the type of assessment that is needed. It would be fascinating to use PET or fMRI to examine the locus of brain activity for individuals responding to the two versions of Chan and Schmitt's (1997) SJT. One might hypothesize left lateral frontal cortex activity for the paper-and-pencil SJT because verbal reasoning is used to process the items. In contrast, the brain may be more active in the right hemisphere for the video SJT because this is where emotions are processed. Such results would explain why video-based SJTs have been found to be unrelated to cognitive ability by Chan and Schmitt (1997) and Olson-Buchanan et al. (1998).

In conclusion, despite a century of research on intelligence, much work remains. Is working memory as important as Kyllonen and Christal (1990) believe? How should assessments of working memory be constructed, and will they add incremental validity to predictions of important job behaviors? Will measures obtained from other tasks in the cognitive domain add incremental validity? Will video-based assessments finally provide a means for assessing social intelligence? What will brain imaging studies find when they examine individuals answering video-based assessments? Will video-based SJTs predict contextual job performance better than g? Clearly, intelligence research represents an area with many important and exciting issues as yet unresolved.

REFERENCES

Ackerman, P. L. (1987). Individual differences in skill learning: An integration of psychometric and information processing perspectives. *Psychological Bulletin, 102,* 3–27.

Ackerman, P. L. (1988). Determinants of individual differences during skill acquisition: Cognitive abilities and information processing. *Journal of Experimental Psychology: General, 117,* 288–318.

Anderson, J. R., & Jeffries, R. (1985). Novice LISP errors: Undetected losses of information from working memory. *Human-Computer Interaction, 1,* 107–131.

Baddeley, A. D. (1986). *Working memory.* Oxford, England: Oxford University Press.

Banich, M. T. (1997). *Neuropsychology: The neural bases of mental function.* Boston: Houghton Mifflin.

Borman, W. C., & Motowidlo, S. J. (1993). Expanding the criterion domain to include elements of contextual performance. In N. Schmitt & W. C. Borman (Eds.), *Personnel selection* (pp. 71–98). San Francisco: Jossey-Bass.

Borman, W. C., & Motowidlo, S. J. (1997). Task performance and contextual performance: The meaning for personnel selection research. *Human Performance, 10,* 99–109.

Borman, W. C., White, L. A., & Dorsey, D. W. (1995). Effects of ratee task performance and interpersonal factors on supervisor and peer performance ratings. *Journal of Applied Psychology, 80,* 168–177.

Breiman, L., Friedman, J. H., Olshen, R. A., & Stone, C. J. (1984). *Classification and regression trees.* Belmont, CA: Wadsworth.

Carroll, J. B. (1993). *Human cognitive abilities: A survey of factor-analytic studies.* New York: Cambridge University Press.

Cattell, R. B. (1941). Some theoretical issues in adult intelligence testing. *Psychological Bulletin, 38,* 592.

Cattell, R. B. (1943). The measurement of adult intelligence. *Psychological Bulletin, 40,* 153–193.

Cattell, R. B. (1971). *Abilities: Their structure, growth, and action.* Boston: Houghton Mifflin.

Cattell, R. B., Eber, H. W., & Tatsuoka, M. M. (1970). *Handbook for the 16 PF* (4th ed.). Champaign, IL: Institute for Personality and Ability Testing.

Chan, D., & Schmitt, N. (1997). Video-based versus paper-and-pencil method of assessment in situational judgement tests: Subgroup differences in test performance and face validity perceptions. *Journal of Applied Psychology, 82,* 143–159.

Cohen, N. J. (1981). *Neuropsychological evidence for a distinction between procedural and declarative knowledge in human memory and amnesia.* Unpublished doctoral dissertation, University of California, San Diego.

Cohen, N. J. (1984). Preserved learning capacity in amnesia: Evidence for multiple memory systems. In L. R. Squire & N. Butters (Eds.), *Neuropsychology of memory* (pp. 83–103). New York: Guilford Press.

Cohen, N. J. (1997). Memory. In M. T. Banich (Ed.), *Neuropsychology: The neural bases of mental function* (pp. 314–367). Boston: Houghton Mifflin.

Cohen, N. J., & Eichenbaum, H. E. (1993). *Memory, amnesia, and the hippocampal system.* Cambridge, MA: MIT Press.

Coleman, V. I., & Borman, W. C. (2000). Investigating the underlying structure of the citizenship performance domain. *Human Resources Management Review, 10,* 25–44.

Daneman, M., & Green, I. (1986). Individual differences in comprehending and producing words in context. *Journal of Memory and Language, 25,* 1–18.

Davies, M., Stankov, L., & Roberts, R. D. (1998). Emotional intelligence: In search of an elusive construct. *Journal of Personality and Social Psychology, 75,* 989–1015.

Duncan, J., Seitz, R. J., Kolodny, J., Bor, D., Herzog, H., Ahmed, A., Newell, F. N., & Emslie, H. (2000). A neural basis for general intelligence. *Science, 289,* 457–460.

Dunn, W. S., Mount, M. K., Barrick, M. R., & Ones, D. S. (1995). Relative importance of personality and general mental ability in managers' judgments of applicant qualifications. *Journal of Applied Psychology, 80,* 500–509.

Engle, R. W., Tuholski, S. W., Laughlin, J. E., & Conway, A. R. A. (1999). Working memory, short-term memory, and general fluid intelligence: A latent variable approach. *Journal of Experimental Psychology: General, 128,* 309–331.

Ferris, G. R., Judge, T. A., Rowland, K. M., & Fitzgibbons, D. E. (1994). Subordinate influence and the performance evaluation process: Test of a model. *Organizational Behavior and Human Decision Processes, 58,* 101–135.

File, Q. W. (1945). The measurement of supervisory quality in industry. *Journal of Applied Psychology, 30,* 323–337.

File, Q. W., & Remmers, H. H. (1948). *How Supervise? manual 1948 revision.* New York: Psychological Corporation.

Flanagan, J. C. (1954). The critical incident technique. *Psychological Bulletin, 51,* 327–358.

Flavell, J. H., Botkin, P. J., & Fry, C. L. (1968). *The development of role-taking and communication skills in children.* New York: Wiley.

Flynn, J. R. (1984). The mean IQ of Americans: Massive gains 1932 to 1978. *Psychological Bulletin, 95,* 29–51.

Flynn, J. R. (1987). Massive IQ gains in 14 nations: What IQ tests really measure. *Psychological Bulletin, 101,* 171–191.

Freeman, J. A., & Skapura, D. M. (1992). *Neural networks: Algorithms, applications, and programming techniques.* Reading, MA: Addison-Wesley.

Goleman, D. (1996). *Emotional intelligence.* New York: Bantam Books.

Greenberg, S. H. (1963). *Supervisory Judgment Test manual.* Washington, DC: U.S. Civil Service Commission.

Guilford, J. P. (1967). *The nature of human intelligence.* New York: McGraw-Hill.

Guilford, J. P. (1985). The structure-of-intellect model. In B. B. Wolman (Ed.), *Handbook of intelligence: Theories, measurements, and applications* (pp. 225–266). New York: Wiley.

Hart, B., & Spearman, C. (1912). General ability, its existence and nature. *British Journal of Psychology, 5,* 51–84.

Herrnstein, R. J., & Murray, C. (1994). *The bell curve.* New York: Free Press.

Humphreys, L. G. (1962). The organization of human abilities. *American Psychologist, 17,* 475–483.

Humphreys, L. G. (1979). The construct of intelligence. *Intelligence, 3,* 105–120.

Humphreys, L. G. (1984). General intelligence. In C. R. Reynolds & R. T. Brown (Eds.), *Perspectives on bias in mental testing* (pp. 221–247). New York: Plenum.

Hunt, E. (1985). Verbal ability. In R. J. Sternberg (Ed.), *Human abilities: An information processing approach* (pp. 31–58). New York: Freeman.

Hunter, J. E. (1980). *Validity generalization for 12,000 jobs: An application of synthetic validity and validity generalization to the General Aptitude Test Battery (GATB).* Washington, DC: U.S. Department of Labor, Employment Service.

Hunter, J. E. (1986). Cognitive ability, cognitive aptitudes, job knowledge, and job performance. *Journal of Vocational Behavior, 29,* 340–362.

Idaszak, J. R., Bottom, W. P., & Drasgow, F. (1988). A test of the measurement equivalence of the Revised Job Diagnostic Survey: Past problems and current solutions. *Journal of Applied Psychology, 73,* 647–656.

Johnson-Laird, P. N. (1985). Deductive reasoning ability. In R. J. Sternberg (Ed.), *Human abilities: An information processing approach* (pp. 173–194). New York: Freeman.

Jöreskog, K. G. (1966). Testing a simple structure hypothesis in factor analysis. *Psychometrika, 31,* 165–178.

Jöreskog, K. G., & Sörbom, D. (1996). *LISREL 8: User's reference guide.* Chicago: Scientific Software International.

Kaiser, H. F. (1958). The varimax criterion for analytic rotation in factor analysis. *Psychometrika, 23,* 187–200.

Kelley, T. L. (1939). Mental factors of no importance. *Journal of Educational Psychology, 30,* 139–143.

Kyllonen, P. C. (1994). CAM: A theoretical framework for cognitive abilities measurement. In D. K. Detterman (Ed.), *Current topics in human intelligence: Vol. 4. Theories of intelligence* (pp. 307–359). Norwood, NJ: Ablex.

Kyllonen, P. C., & Christal, R. E. (1989). Cognitive modeling of learning abilities: A status report of LAMP. In R. Dillon & J. W. Pellegrino (Eds.), *Testing: Theoretical and applied issues* (pp. 66–87). New York: Freeman.

Kyllonen, P. C., & Christal, R. E. (1990). Reasoning ability is (little more than) working-memory capacity?! *Intelligence, 14,* 389–433.

Lezak, M. D. (1995). *Neuropsychological assessment* (3rd ed.). New York: Oxford University Press.

Lubinski, D. (2000). Scientific and social significance of assessing individual differences: "Sinking shafts at a few critical points." *Annual Review of Psychology, 51,* 405–444.

Lubinski, D., & Dawis, R. V. (1992). Aptitudes, skills, and proficiencies. In M. D. Dunnette & L. M. Hough (Eds.), *Handbook of industrial and organizational psychology* (Vol. 3, 2nd ed., pp. 1–59). Palo Alto, CA: Consulting Psychology Press.

McDaniel, M. A., Morgeson, F. P., Finnegan, E. B., Campion, M. A., & Braverman, E. P. (2001). Use of situational judgment tests to predict job performance: A clarification of the literature. *Journal of Applied Psychology, 86,* 730–740.

McDaniel, M. A., & Nguyen, N. T. (2001). Situational judgment tests: A review of practice and constructs assessed. *International Journal of Selection and Assessment, 9,* 103–113.

McDonald, R. P. (1999). *Test theory: A unified treatment.* Mahwah, NJ: Erlbaum.

McHenry, J. J., Hough, L. M., Toquam, J. L., Hanson, M. A., & Ashworth, S. (1990). Project A validity results: The relationship between predictor and criterion domains. *Personnel Psychology, 43,* 335–354.

McNemar, Q. (1964). Lost: Our intelligence? Why? *American Psychologist, 19,* 871–882.

Messick, S., & Jungeblut (1981). Time and method in coaching for the SAT. *Psychological Bulletin, 89,* 191–216.

Montanelli, R. G., Jr., & Humphreys, L. G. (1976). Latent roots of random data correlation matrices with squared multiple correlations on the diagonal: A Monte Carlo study. *Psychometrika, 41,* 341–348.

Moss, F. A., Hunt, T., Omwake, K. T., & Ronning, M. M. (1927). *Social Intelligence Test.* Washington, DC: Center for Psychological Service.

Motowidlo, S. J., Dunnette, M. D., & Carter, G. W. (1990). An alternative selection procedure: The low-fidelity simulation. *Journal of Applied Psychology, 75,* 640–647.

Motowidlo, S. J., & Van Scotter, J. R. (1994). Evidence that task performance should be distinguished from contextual performance. *Journal of Applied Psychology, 79,* 475–480.

Olson-Buchanan, J. B., Drasgow, F., Moberg, P. J., Mead, A. D., Keenan, P. A., & Donovan, M. (1998). Conflict resolution skills assessment: A model-based, multi-media approach. *Personnel Psychology, 51,* 1–24.

Organ, D. W. (1988). *Organizational citizenship behavior: The good soldier syndrome.* Lexington, MA: Lexington Books.

O'Sullivan, M., Guilford, J. P., & deMille, R. (1965). *The measurement of social intelligence* (Psychological Laboratory Report No. 34). Los Angeles: University of Southern California.

Page, E. B., & Peterson, N. S. (1995). The computer moves in essay grading: Updating the ancient test. *Phi Delta Kappan*, March, 561–565.

Pellegrino, J. W. (1985). Inductive reasoning ability. In R. J. Sternberg (Ed.), *Human abilities: An information processing approach* (pp. 195–225). New York: Freeman.

Ree, M. J., & Earles, J. A. (1991). Predicting training success: Not much more than *g. Personnel Psychology, 44,* 321–332.

Ree, M. J., Earles, J. A., & Teachout, M. S. (1994). Predicting job performance: Not much more than *g. Journal of Applied Psychology, 79,* 518–524.

Ree, M. J., Mullins, C. J., Mathews, J. J., & Massey, R. H. (1982). *Armed Services Vocational Aptitude Battery: Item and factor analyses of Forms 8, 9, and 10* (Air Force Human Resources Laboratory Technical Report No. 81-55). Brooks Air Force Base, TX: Air Force Human Resources Laboratory.

Richman-Hirsch, W. L., Olson-Buchanan, J. B., & Drasgow, F. (2000). Examining the impact of administration medium on examinee perceptions and attitudes. *Journal of Applied Psychology, 85,* 880–887.

Riggio, R. E. (1986). Assessment of basic social skills. *Journal of Personality and Social Psychology, 51,* 649–660.

SAS Institute Inc. (1990). *SAS/STAT user's guide, version 6* (4th ed., Vol. 1). Cary, NC: Author.

Schmid, J., & Leiman, J. M. (1957). The development of hierarchical factor solutions. *Psychometrika, 22,* 53–61.

Schmidt, F. L., & Hunter, J. E. (1977). Development of a general solution to the problem of validity generalization. *Journal of Applied Psychology, 62,* 529–540.

Schmidt, F. L., & Hunter, J. E. (1998). The validity and utility of selection methods in personnel psychology: Practical and theoretical implications of 85 years of research findings. *Psychological Bulletin, 124,* 262–274.

Schneider, W., & Shiffrin, R. M. (1977). Controlled and automatic human information processing: I. Detection, search and attention. *Psychological Review, 84,* 1–66.

Schutz, R. E. (1958). Factorial validity of the Holzinger-Crowder Uni-Factor tests. *Educational & Psychological Measurement, 18,* 873–875.

Smither, J. W., Reilly, R. R., Millsap, R. E., Pearlman, K., & Stoffey, R. W. (1993). Applicant reactions to selection procedures. *Personnel Psychology, 46,* 49–76.

Spearman, C. (1904). "General intelligence," objectively determined and measured. *American Journal of Psychology, 15,* 201–293.

Spearman, C., & Holzinger, K. J. (1925). Note on the sampling error of tetrad differences. *British Journal of Psychology, 16,* 86–88.

Squire, L. R., & Cohen, N. J. (1984). Human memory and amnesia. In G. Lynch, J. L. McGaugh, & N. M. Weinberger (Eds.), *Neurobiology of learning and memory* (pp. 3–64). New York: Guilford Press.

Steiger, J. H. (1990). Structural model evaluation and modification: An interval estimation approach. *Multivariate Behavioral Research, 25,* 173–180.

Sternberg, R. J. (1977). *Intelligence, information processing, and analogical reasoning: The componential analysis of human abilities.* Hillsdale, NJ: Erlbaum.

Stricker, L. J. (1982). Interpersonal competence instrument: Development and preliminary findings. *Applied Psychological Measurement, 6,* 69–81.

Thorndike, E. L. (1920). Intelligence and its use. *Harper's Magazine, 140,* 227–235.

Thorndike, R. L. (1949). *Personnel selection.* New York: Wiley.

Thurstone, L. L. (1938). Primary mental abilities. *Psychometric Monographs,* No. 1. Chicago: University of Chicago Press.

Thurstone, L. L. (1947). *Multiple factor analysis.* Chicago: University of Chicago Press.

Tucker, L. R., & Finkbeiner, C. T. (1981). *Transformation of factors by artificial personal probability functions* (Research Report No. RR-81-58). Princeton, NJ: Educational Testing Service.

Tuddenham, R. D. (1948). Soldier intelligence in World Wars I and II. *American Psychologist, 3,* 54–56.

Vernon, P. E. (1950). *The structure of human abilities.* London: Methuen.

Vispoel, W. (1999). Creating computerized adaptive tests of music aptitude: Problems, solutions, and future directions. In F. Drasgow & J. B. Olson-Buchanan (Eds.), *Innovations in computerized assessment* (pp. 151–176). Hillsdale, NJ: Erlbaum.

Walker, R. E., & Foley, J. M. (1973). Social intelligence: Its history and measurement. *Psychological Reports, 33,* 839–864.

Webster's New World College Dictionary (3rd ed.). (Ed.), Victoria Neufeldt. New York: Macmillan.

Weekley, J. A., & Jones, C. (1997). Video-based situational testing. *Personnel Psychology, 50,* 25–49.

Weekley, J. A., & Jones, C. (1999). Further studies of situational tests. *Personnel Psychology, 52,* 679–700.

Werner, J. M. (1994). Dimensions that make a difference: Examining the impact of in-role and extra-role behaviors on supervisory ratings. *Journal of Applied Psychology, 79,* 98–107.

CHAPTER 7

Use of Personality Variables in Work Settings

LEAETTA M. HOUGH AND ADRIAN FURNHAM

Personality theories and the constructs and measures that stem from them have significantly influenced the science and practice of industrial and organizational (I/O) psychology. Our understanding of the role of personality variables and their effect on work performance is dramatically greater than it was even a decade ago. There has been a recent renaissance in the field of I/O psychology that traces its roots to a greater understanding and use of personality variables (Hough, 2001).

This chapter describes the history of personality theory, taxonomies, and constructs and their role in I/O psychology. We also summarize meta-analytic evidence of the criterion-related validity of personality variables according to predictor and criterion construct, highlighting the usefulness of personality variables. We describe the evidence related to variables thought to moderate criterion-related validity, such as intentional distortion and item frame-of-reference, and we present methods for incrementing validity. We then turn to methods and issues of personality measurement, discussing them according to self-report and self-evaluation, others' reports and descriptions, objective measures, interviews, modes of assessment, and cultural and language issues in-

volved in personality assessment. Last, we describe legal issues and relevant evidence related to the use of personality inventories in the workplace in the United States.

BRIEF HISTORY OF THE ROLE OF PERSONALITY THEORY AND VARIABLES IN I/O PSYCHOLOGY

Relevance to Theories of Work Performance

The importance of personality variables to the psychology of work is demonstrated by their prominent role in current theories of work performance. Although researchers have long theorized that motivation is a determinant of performance (e.g., performance is a function of ability $\times$ motivation; see Campbell & Pritchard, 1976), few theorists conceptualized motivation as a personality variable. Theories of work performance now explicitly incorporate personality variables as determinants of performance. Earlier models of the determinants of work performance (as measured by supervisory ratings) included cognitive ability, job knowledge, and task proficiency (e.g., Hunter, 1983). F. L. Schmidt, Hunter, and

Outerbridge (1986) added job experience and demonstrated its importance. Borman, White, Pulakos, and Oppler (1991) expanded upon these models by adding awards, disciplinary actions, and two personality variables, dependability and achievement orientation, which are facets of the broad Conscientiousness construct in the five-factor model of personality (Costa & McCrae, 1995a). The Borman et al. (1991) model accounted for more than twice the variance in job-performance ratings than the Hunter (1983) model. Summarizing research on the determinants of work performance, F. L. Schmidt and Hunter (1992) described a causal model in which general mental ability, job experience, and conscientiousness determine job performance. They concluded that general mental ability has a major causal impact on the acquisition of job knowledge but that its impact on job performance is indirect, whereas conscientiousness has both a direct effect on job performance and an indirect effect on performance through its influence on the acquisition of job knowledge. According to Motowidlo, Brownlee, and Schmit (1998), capacity, opportunity, and motivation to learn are the causal mechanisms for cognitive ability, experience, and conscientiousness, respectively. They speculate that a fourth causal mechanism involves a match between knowledge content and interpersonally oriented personality variables. We certainly agree that such a fourth mechanism is involved in determining performance.

The early 1990s produced general theories of work performance in which a personality variable, conscientiousness, played a central role in determining performance. In the years ahead, we are likely to see more personality variables included in general models in the form of congruence between work-content variables and personality (including vocational-interest) variables as well as in models of performance involving specific job-performance constructs. Such trends can already be seen in Motowidlo, Borman, and Schmit's (1997) theorizing and research on the determinants of contextual versus task performance, Motowidlo et al.'s (1998) work on the determinants of customer service (which involve more personality variables than conscientiousness), Barrick, Stewart, and Piotrowski's (2002) work on the role of extraversion and conscientiousness variables in the performance of sales representatives, and Hurtz and Donovan's (2000) meta-analyses of personality predictors of job performance and contextual performance.

Relevance to Theories of Work Adjustment

The importance of personality variables to the psychology of work is also seen in their role in theories of work adjustment (e.g., job satisfaction, stability). Holland (1973, 1985), in his theory of vocational choice that has dominated career and vocational counseling (Furnham, 2001), described interest variables as personality variables, suggesting a hexagonal model of six interest categories, each of which represented a distinct personality type: Realistic, Investigative, Artistic, Social, Enterprising, or Conventional (i.e., RIASEC theory). His theory assumes there are six corresponding kinds of job environments. He hypothesized that vocational and job satisfaction, stability, morale, productivity, and achievement depend on the fit between one's personality and one's work environment (Holland, 1973).

Similarly, Dawis and Lofquist (1984) incorporated personality characteristics into their set of needs for various job rewards (or reinforcers) in their theory of work adjustment. Their set of 20 needs includes 12 personality characteristics: Achievement, Activity, Advancement, Authority, Independence, Moral Values, Recognition, Responsibility, Security, Social Service, Social Status, and Variety, all of which readily fit into the five-factor model of personality (e.g., Extraversion, Emotional Stability, Conscientiousness, Agreeableness, and Openness to Experience). Dawis and Lofquist argue that both individuals and jobs can be characterized according to skills and needs or reinforcers and that work adjustment (performance and satisfaction) is the degree of correspondence or fit between the individual's skills and needs and the job's skill requirements and reinforcers.

Much of the appeal of Holland's theory lies in its simple schema for separately classifying personality and jobs into six types, as well as its approach to measuring the congruence between people and jobs in a two-dimensional Euclidean space (Furnham & Schaffer, 1984). Holland's six personality types provide a simple structure of the world of work that yields manageable information amenable to career planning and guidance. Equally important is the contribution that personality variables in both the hexagonal (RIASEC) and work-adjustment models have made to the prediction of occupational membership, job involvement and satisfaction, training performance, and job proficiency (Hough, Barge, & Kamp, 2001).

Relevance of Different Personality Variables to Different Theories

Comparison of the two research orientations indicates that researchers investigating the usefulness of the Big Five factors and the RIASEC personality types theorize and focus on different criteria: work performance versus work adjustment. In an integration and comparison of these two research orientations, De Fruyt and Mervielde (1997) found that although there is considerable overlap between the two personality models, the realistic and investigative types are not well represented in the Big Five. In later research, they found that Holland's RIASEC personality types and the Big Five personality factors independently contribute to the prediction of two work-related outcomes—employment status and nature of employment. RIASEC types were superior in explaining the nature of employment (jobs that are Realistic, Investigative, Artistic, Social, Enterprising, or Conventional) whereas two Big Five variables (Extraversion and Conscientiousness) were superior in predicting employment status such as employed or unemployed (De Fruyt & Mervielde, 1999).

Interestingly, in vocational psychology, a hexagon model of six personality types (i.e., RIASEC) has dominated interest-assessment and research (Rounds, 1995) whereas in personality psychology, and now in theories of individual work performance in I/O, the five-factor model reigns as king (see Goldberg, 1995; Mount & Barrick, 1995; Wiggins & Trapnell, 1997). In spite of the favored status of the Big Five in examining the relationships between personality variables and *individual* work performance, Holland's RIASEC types are emerging as important constructs in theories of *team* performance (Muchinsky, 1999).

The Hogans (R. T. Hogan, Hogan, & Roberts, 1996) use variables from both these interest-based and personality-based models to predict individual work performance. They first classify jobs into homogeneous categories using Holland's RIASEC and then examine the criterion-related validity coefficients of the Big Five variables. This approach assumes that job type moderates the validity of Big Five variables for predicting individual job performance. The use of job type as a moderator variable is probably a useful approach to examining the validity of personality constructs in the absence of good definition and measurement of the criterion space. Much of the older research on the validity of personality variables used *overall* job performance as the criterion, regardless of job type. Thus, when summarizing validity coefficients of personality constructs from such studies, classifying jobs according to similar interest patterns and then analyzing validities within those groups is likely to lead to greater understanding of the circumstances in which a relationship exists. Grouping jobs according to similar interest patterns and examining relationships of personality variables with overall job performance is, however, a surrogate for examining the relationships between personality variables and performance constructs directly.

Future Directions

In today's world of work in which the concept of *job* has lost much of the meaning it once had, understanding relationships between personality variables and well-defined work performance and adjustment constructs is crucial. It is those relationships that will endure, even in cases in which particular job titles or job classifications do not. We need to build theories explaining such relationships. When meta-analyses are conducted, correlation coefficients should be summarized according to well-defined, specific, work-related constructs rather than overall job performance. Given the dynamic rather than static nature of many jobs in an information and service economy and in a more team-oriented workforce, building our science and our theories on relationships based only on overall job performance is akin to building a sand castle out of—and on top of—quicksand.

PERSONALITY THEORIES AND TAXONOMIES AND THEIR IMPORTANCE TO I/O PSYCHOLOGY

Personality psychology has a rich history, and I/O psychologists have benefited significantly from its theories and research. Currently, many personality psychologists adhere to a dynamic view of the person $\times$ situation interaction. Nonetheless, our thinking about personality-trait variables focuses on a more static view. For example, our general theories of performance (e.g., that performance is determined by general cognitive ability, job experience, and *conscientiousness*) are almost exclusively influenced by personality-trait theory, and in contrast with a dynamic point of view, traits reflect a consistency in behavior over time. In this performance model, although job experience obviously changes with time, conscientiousness is assumed to exert the same influence over the course of time. Similarly, practitioners involved in organizational development, especially team-building activities, focus on traits. For example, regardless of its Jungian heritage (and Jung's theory of collective unconscious), the Myers-Briggs Type Indicator (MBTI) is typically administered to participants involved in team building, with the results interpreted according to trait theory.

This almost exclusive focus of I/O psychology on trait theory as well as a static view of the influence of traits is likely to change. Indeed, it *is* changing (e.g., G. L. Stewart, 1999). Our research and theories will undoubtedly become more sophisticated as we incorporate research on dynamic criteria and investigate longitudinally the relative contributions of the knowledge and motivational determinants of work performance (Hough & Oswald, 2000). For now, however, trait psychology and its concern with taxonomic structure dominate much of our thinking and research about personality.

Taxonomies of Personality Variables

Taxonomic structures are important. The description of scientific phenomena afforded by taxonomies usually precedes (and facilitates) their explanation. In I/O psychology, the taxonomic structure of personality variables affects the magnitude of their relationships with criteria of interest (Hough, 1992; Hough & Ones, 2001; Hough & Schneider, 1996).

Indeed, conclusions about the usefulness of personality variables and the nature of the personality-performance relationship depend upon the taxonomic structure used.

Trait psychologists view personality as consisting of a variety of dimensions on which people differ. There is a seemingly infinite number of ways that individuals can differ, with more personality theories, variables, and measures emerging every year. Thus, one of the main research questions trait psychologists must address is *What is an adequate taxonomy of trait variables and more particularly, what is an adequate taxonomy of trait variables for I/O psychology?* Many personality psychologists (e.g., Digman, 1990; Goldberg, 1995; McCrae & Costa, 1997; Wiggins & Trapnell, 1997) believe the quest should end—that the five-factor model is the answer.

Five-Factor Model

The five-factor model has its roots in the so-called *lexical hypothesis* of Galton (1884), that personality traits are captured in the words that people use to describe one another and are thus encoded in dictionaries. Allport and Odbert (1936) expanded Galton's already lengthy list, and throughout much of the last half of the twentieth century one of the great research tasks of personality psychology has been to reduce their list to a scientifically acceptable number of underlying factors.

Fiske (1949) was the first to identify five factors from self and others' ratings of target persons. Tupes and Christal (1961/1992), however, were the first to identify a variant of what we now often call the *Big Five*. They labeled their five factors Surgency, Emotional Stability, Agreeableness, Dependability, and Culture. Norman (1963) confirmed their findings, concluding that the pattern matrices appeared to be reasonably good approximations of simple structure (although intercorrelations among unit-weighted factor composites show that the five factors are clearly not orthogonal—the intercorrelations typically exceed .30). Today, the Big Five labels are *Extraversion, Conscientiousness, Agreeableness, Neuroticism* (also known as *Emotional Stability* or *Adjustment*), and *Openness to Experience*. Goldberg's (1990, 1992) list of adjectives for each factor is now considered to constitute the standard definitions of the Big Five. Costa and McCrae developed the Neuroticism, Extraversion, Openness Personality Inventory (NEO-PI; Costa & McCrae, 1992), a personality inventory that has become widely used to measure the Big Five. Although they also identified six facets for each factor (Costa & McCrae, 1995a), there is considerably less agreement about the structure of personality at the facet level (Goldberg, 1997). Others have developed measures of the Big Five as well. (See Block, 1995; Digman, 1990; John, 1990a, 1990b; Schneider & Hough, 1995; and Wiggins &

Trapnell, 1997, for detailed descriptions of the history of the five-factor model.)

During the last 20 years of the twentieth century, a host of studies correlated established personality measures with the NEO-PI (the best known of the Big Five personality inventories) in an effort to demonstrate the overlap between the inventories and the NEO-PI and thus the comprehensiveness of the five-factor model. That is, comprehensiveness of the Big Five can be examined by regressing the NEO-PI onto scales of other personality inventories. If, across a large number of other personality inventories, the variance accounted for by the NEO-PI is high, the Big Five can be argued to be comprehensive. Examples of the other inventories that have been compared to the NEO-PI include Gough's California Psychological Inventory (McCrae, Costa, & Piedmont, 1993); the California Q-Set (McCrae, Costa, & Busch, 1986), Cattell's Sixteen Personality Factor (16PF; Gerbing & Tuley, 1991), the Comrey Personality Scales (Hahn & Comrey, 1994), Edwards Personal Preference Schedule (EPPS; Piedmont, McCrae, & Costa, 1992), the Eysenck Personality Inventory (Costa & McCrae, 1995b), the Fundamental Interpersonal Relations Orientation–Behavior (FIRO-B; Furnham, 1996b), Holland's Vocational Preference Inventory (Costa, McCrae, & Holland, 1984), Holland's Self-Directed Search (De Fruyt & Mervielde, 1997), the Learning Styles Questionnaire (Furnham, 1996b), Jackson's Personality Research Form (Costa & McCrae, 1988), the Minnesota Multiphasic Personality Inventory (MMPI; Costa, Zonderman, Williams, & McCrae, 1985), Tellegen's Multidimensional Personality Questionnaire (Church & Burke, 1994), the MBTI (Furnham, 1996a), and Wiggins' Interpersonal Adjective Scales (McCrae & Costa, 1989). Despite different theoretical origins, labels, and formats, these studies show considerable overlap between the different personality inventories and the Big Five as measured by the NEO-PI.

A summary of this research and many other studies demonstrates that the five-factor model is robust across different cultures, languages, types of assessment, rating sources, genders, and factor extraction and rotation methods, and that (a) Extraversion and Neuroticism are the most robust—they were replicated reliably in almost all studies; (b) Conscientiousness is next most reliably replicated; (c) there is less evidence for Agreeableness; and (d) Openness to Experience is the least replicable, and its construct validity is the most controversial (Hough & Ones, 2001). In our rapidly changing world of work, Openness to Experience may become one of the more important personality variables in emerging theories of the determinants of specific performance constructs. Much work is needed to refine this construct. One clear bifurcation in Openness to Experience is that of the artistic component and the intellectual component. We urge researchers to consider methods other than factor analytic methods.

Criticisms of the Five-Factor Model. The five-factor model is not without its critics. Highly respected personality psychologists such as Block (1995), Eysenck (1991, 1992), Loevinger (1994), McAdams (1992), Pervin (1994), Tellegen (1993), Waller and Ben-Porath (1987), and Zuckerman (1992) have criticized it severely. In our field, Hough and her colleagues (Hough, 1997; Hough & Schneider, 1996) and Paunonen and Jackson (2000) criticize the five-factor model as not comprehensive. Indeed, a close examination of the articles cited previously (as well as others in which a Big Five inventory was compared to various well-known personality inventories) reveals that the following variables are not well represented in the Big Five: (a) masculinity-femininity, or what Hough (1992) refers to as *rugged individualism* (see Costa et al., 1985; Goldberg, 1990; Paunonen & Jackson, 2000; Saucier & Goldberg, 1998); (b) consideration (see Tokar, Fischer, Snell, & Harik-Williams, 1999; (c) aggression and hostility (see Zuckerman, Kuhlman, & Camac, 1988; Zuckerman, Kuhlman, Joireman, Teta, & Kraft, 1993); (d) impulsivity, sensation seeking, risk taking, and harm avoidance (see Ashton, Jackson, Helmes, & Paunonen, 1998; Zuckerman et al., 1988; Zuckerman et al., 1993); (e) social adroitness and social insight (see Ashton et al., 1998; Detwiler & Ramanaiah, 1996; Schneider, Ackerman, & Kanfer, 1996); (f) religiosity, devoutness, and reverence (see Goldberg, 1990; Paunonen & Jackson, 2000; Saucier & Goldberg, 1998); (g) morality, honesty, ethical versus unethical beliefs, and false friendliness (see Ashton, Lee & Son, 2000; De Raad & Hoskens, 1990; Paunonen & Jackson, 2000); (h) villainy, monstrousness, and brute personality (De Raad & Hoskens, 1990); (i) cunning, sly, deceptive, and manipulative personality (see Paunonen & Jackson, 2000; Saucier & Goldberg, 1998); (j) conservatism, orthodoxy, and traditional, down-to-earth personality (see Ashton et al., 1998; John, 1990a; Paunonen & Jackson, 2000); (k) prejudice (see Saucier & Goldberg, 1998); (l) egotism, conceit, and snobbery (see Block, 1995; McCrae et al., 1986; Paunonen & Jackson, 2000); (m) sensuality, seductiveness, eroticism, and sexiness (see Paunonen & Jackson, 2000; Saucier & Goldberg, 1998); (n) frugality, miserliness, and thriftiness versus materialism (see De Raad & Hoskens, 1990; Paunonen & Jackson, 2000; Saucier & Goldberg, 1998); (o) wittiness, humorousness, and amusing personality (see De Raad & Hoskens, 1990; Goldberg, 1990; Paunonen & Jackson, 2000); (p) folksiness (see Saucier & Goldberg, 1998); (q) autonomy granted to others (see Pincus, Gurtman, & Ruiz, 1998); (r) imaginative and aesthetic sensitivity (see Digman & Inouye, 1986); (s) absorption (see Church & Burke,

1994); (t) positive valence (emotionality), a characteristic particularly relevant to personality disorders (see Almagor, Tellegen, & Waller, 1995; Benet & Waller, 1995; Waller & Zavala, 1993); and (u) negative valence (emotionality), another characteristic particularly relevant to personality disorders (see Almagor et al., 1995; Benet & Waller, 1995; Saucier, 1997; Waller & Zavala, 1993).

In addition to criticizing the Big Five as not being comprehensive, Hough, Paunonen, and their colleagues argue that the Big Five confound constructs, merging variables that are too heterogeneous and thereby obscuring relationships between personality variables and criteria of interest (e.g., Ashton, Jackson, Paunonen, Helmes, & Rothstein, 1995; Hough, 1989, 1992, 1997; Hough, Eaton, Dunnette, Kamp, & McCloy, 1990; Hough & Schneider, 1996; Jackson, Paunonen, Fraboni, & Goffin, 1996; Paunonen, 1998; Paunonen, Jackson, Trzebinski, & Forsterling, 1992; Paunonen & Nicol, 2001; Paunonen, Rothstein, & Jackson, 1999; Schneider & Hough, 1995). They argue that understanding the relationships between personality variables and work-related criteria and our ability to build meaningful theories are significantly reduced when variables are collapsed into the Big Five. Hough especially criticizes the Big Five factor Conscientiousness because it confounds dependability with achievement, as well as the Big Five factor Extraversion because it confounds sociability with dominance (surgency). In the European literature, Robertson and Callinan (1998) also argue that more emphasis needs to be given to the facet level of the Big Five and the relationship of facets to different performance criteria.

In spite of the serious criticisms of the five-factor model, it has provided an important taxonomic structure for organizing and summarizing relationships between personality variables and criteria in I/O psychology, advancing our theories and practice (Hough, 2001). An examination of the meta-analyses in our journals that involve personality variables reveals the five-factor model is our personality taxonomy of choice, and we know more about the determinants of work performance as a result. For example, Barrick, Mount, and Judge (2001) reviewed 15 meta-analyses that had summarized criterion-related validities according to the Big Five. They concluded that Conscientiousness is a valid predictor regardless of the criterion measure or occupation, and that Emotional Stability predicts overall work performance, although it is less consistently related to specific performance criteria and occupations. In spite of the importance and contribution of the five-factor model to our understanding of the determinants of job performance, there are other personality models and other methods (besides factor analysis) for developing personality taxonomies. For instance, circumplex models of personality have been developed (Plutchik & Conte, 1997). These and other approaches, such as the nomological-web clustering approach described in the next section, have potential for advancing our understanding of the determinants of work performance beyond that of the five-factor model.

A Construct Validity Approach to Taxonomic Structure

Most personality taxonomies, including the five-factor model, are based on factor analysis of intercorrelations between *personality* variables. Hough argues for a nomological-web clustering approach in developing a taxonomy of personality variables (see Hough & Ones, 2001). She proposes a bootstrapping, clustering strategy in which personality variables within a taxon demonstrate the same pattern of relationships with other variables, including work-related criterion variables (not just other personality variables). That is, validity of the taxon is empirically demonstrated through cluster analysis of the profiles of relationships that target variables have with other variables. It is a flexible taxonomy that is expected to change as empirical evidence and theory suggest refinements to the structure and the taxons.

The origins of the approach lie in Hough and her colleagues' efforts to group personality scales into the Big Five factors. They found that, although the components or facets may correlate most highly with their respective Big Five factor, many facets within a Big Five factor correlate differently with criteria of interest to I/O psychologists (Hough, 1989, 1992, 1997; Hough et al., 1990; Hough, Ones, & Viswesvaran, 1998). For example, the Big Five factor Conscientiousness is diverse; two of its facets, achievement orientation and dependability, show different patterns of correlations with other variables and thus should not be combined into one taxon. Similarly, affiliation, a facet of the Extraversion factor, should not be combined with the other facets of Extraversion. When its profile of relationships with other variables (nomological web) is compared to the profile of other facets of Extraversion, affiliation belongs in a separate taxon.

Using this strategy, Hough and Ones (2001) developed an initial set of working taxons of personality variables. After reviewing an extensive amount of literature, they independently classified existing personality scales into an initial set of taxons, resolving differences through additional review of literature. They present a working taxonomic structure of personality variables and invite others to refine it through theory and empirical evidence. They argue that a refined set of taxons will enable researchers and practitioners to understand better the relationships between personality variables and work-related criteria, to build better theories of work performance, and to predict more quickly and accurately job performance that involves new configurations of work and work circumstances.

Bandwidth Issues

Conflicting Viewpoints

A point-counterpoint exchange in the mid-1990s debated the merits of broad versus narrow personality traits. Ones and Viswesvaran (1996a) argued strongly for broader personality variables, such as Conscientiousness, rather than narrow, more specific variables, such as Order. They described a trade-off between the *fidelity* (measurement precision) and *bandwidth* (heterogeneity-homogeneity) of broad versus narrow measures. They argued that broad measures typically result in higher internal-consistency estimates than narrow measures, and that the more reliable broad measures have greater criterion-related validity than narrow measures. J. Hogan and Roberts (1996) argued that the real issue is whether the bandwidth of the predictor and the criterion match. Schneider, Hough, and Dunnette (1996) agree that predictors should match criteria in terms of specificity, arguing that the best criterion-related validities are attained when researchers use a construct-oriented approach to match predictors to criteria. The underlying cause for the three sets of researchers' different orientations toward broad versus narrow predictors is their different focus on broad versus narrow *criteria*. Ones and Viswesvaran prefer broad, overall criteria such as overall job performance and thus almost always prefer broad predictors; whereas J. Hogan, Roberts, Schneider, Hough, and Dunnette regard both narrow and broad criteria as important, preferring to focus on the construct relevance of the predictor (and its components) for the criterion.

The real issue is how test development and test use should proceed. Although this issue is not directly addressed in the bandwidth debate, Hogan and Hough prefer to develop narrow measures and then combine relevant measures to form broader predictor composites for particular prediction situations (J. Hogan, personal communication, July 12, 2001; Hough, 2001; see also R. T. Hogan et al., 1996). Goldberg (1997) and Paunonen and his colleagues (Paunonen et al., 1999; Paunonen & Nicol, 2001) agree. Ones and Viswesvaran (2001), on the other hand, prefer development and use of broad measures, arguing that criteria of interest are broad. They describe broad measures of this type, which they label *criterion-focused occupational personality scales (COPS)*. Examples of some COPS are integrity tests, service-orientation scales, and managerial potential scales.

Reality and Solution

Off-the-shelf measures of both narrow and broad variables are needed. Many applied situations exist in which there are many incumbents in essentially the same, relatively stable job and for which there are typically many applicants. In this situation, an off-the-shelf broad COPS-type measure may be practical and all that is needed.

There are also now many employment situations (and will be more in the future) in which jobs and assignments are one of a kind. The world of work is changing; the concept of *job* is changing. For these situations, practitioners need off-the-shelf, narrow measures that can be combined to form broad predictor composites—composites that are tailored for the prediction situation. Practitioners need to be able to build predictor equations for jobs that have unique configurations of performance constructs; they need to synthesize validities.

For effective prediction in these situations, we need to have accumulated knowledge about the relationship between predictors and criteria at a more narrow rather than a broad construct level. Practitioners need look-up tables (generated through meta-analyses) showing the relationships between narrow predictor measures and specific performance constructs. We need theories of determinants of performance constructs that are more specific than overall job performance, and that incorporate notions of dynamic criteria and predictors whose usefulness change over time.

Research of this type is already in the literature. G. L. Stewart (1999), for example, examined the differential usefulness of broad versus narrow traits at different stages of job performance, finding that two facets of Conscientiousness, order and achievement, correlated differently with performance at different stages of job performance. Not only did the two facets provide incremental validity beyond Conscientiousness, achievement correlated more strongly with performance in the maintenance stage (once the work is learned and routinized), and order correlated more strongly with performance in the transition stage (when work changes and new tasks must be learned and accomplished). We also need more meta-analyses, like that of Hurtz and Donovan (2000), that examine the relationship between personality variables and contextual performance constructs. We recommend, however, that facet-level validities, similar to some of the analyses Borman, Penner, Allen, and Motowidlo (2001) conducted, also be reported. As Paunonen and Nicol (2001) point out, "it might be only one facet of the Big Five that is entirely responsible for the criterion prediction or that the Big Five facets are differentially aligned with the various facets of a multidimensional criterion" (p. 166).

Two more examples of current research demonstrate the usefulness of this approach. In a meta-analysis of the predictors of job performance for salespeople, Vinchur, Schippmann, Switzer, and Roth (1998) found more useful levels of validity at the facet level of Conscientiousness—that is, achievement orientation was a better predictor than Conscientiousness. W. H. Stewart and Roth (2001) meta-analyzed the relationship between a narrow measure (risk propensity) and

specific criteria (growth versus income goals) for entrepreneurs as well as the usefulness of the narrow measure for differentiating entrepreneurs and managers. The narrow measure not only differentiated between entrepreneurs and managers, it also differentiated between entrepreneurs who were growth oriented versus those who were income oriented. Such research helps build better theories and helps practitioners build better prediction equations. We need more of this type of research.

VALIDITY EVIDENCE FOR PERSONALITY VARIABLES

Much of this chapter has focused on evidence and issues of construct validity of personality variables. Our argument has been that greater construct validity of our taxonomic structure of personality variables enhances our understanding and prediction of work-related criteria. We have argued that reporting relationships at a narrow or facet level will advance our theories and models and our use of them. We have also argued that broad or compound variables can and do increment criterion-related validity when the compound variable consists of criterion construct-relevant facets.

An important piece of evidence for construct validity is criterion-related validity. In this section we describe criterion-related evidence of personality variables for predicting several work performance and work adjustment criteria. We also describe evidence of incremental validity when personality variables are used in combination with other individual difference variables, as well as variables (such as measurement method, time of measurement, criterion construct, and intentional distortion) that moderate, or are often thought to moderate, validity.

Criterion-Related Validity of Personality Variables

Criterion-related validity studies and meta-analyses of relationships between personality variables and work-related criteria have grown exponentially in the last decade, and such research continues unabated. A review of the titles of articles published during the last few years in the major journals in our field indicates that the number of studies examining the relationship of personality variables with criteria is greater than any other domain of individual difference variables. The change in focus over the years is striking.

Validities From Meta-Analytic Studies

We summarize meta-analytically-derived validities of several personality variables (Big Five factors, several Big Five facets, compound variables, and other personality variables including social desirability scales) for predicting work-related criteria. Results are shown in Tables 7.1–7.3. Table 7.1

TABLE 7.1 Personality Variables and Their Meta-Analyzed Validities for Predicting *Broad* Work Performance Criteria

Overall Job Performance

Personality Variable	Source	$\bar{r}$	ρ_s	ρ_p	ρ_c	ρ_{pc}	ρ_{cr}	ρ_t	ρ_a
Emotional Stability	$N = 11,635$; $k = 87$; Barrick & Mount, 1991	.04						.07	
	$N = 28,587$; $k = 186$; Hough, 1992	.11							
	$N = 5,027$; $k = 35$; Hurtz & Donovan, 2000	.09						.14	.15
	$N = 2,799$; $k = 22$; Salgado, 1997 *European settings*	.08						.12	.18
	$N = 1,800$; $k = 14$; Anderson & Viswesvaran, 1998	.10			.13	.15			
	$N = 4,106$; $k = 20$; Judge & Bono, 2001a	.16				.19			
	$N = 900$; $k = 10$; Tett et al., 1991 (cf. Tett et al., 1994) *confirmatory studies*	.15			.19	.22		.27	
	$N = 69,889$; $k = 202$; Hough et al., 1998 *managerial jobs*	.04						.08	
	$N = 3,134$; $k = 24$; Vinchur et al., 1998 *sales jobs*	.05					.10		
	$N = 678$; $k = 4$; Mount et al., 1998 *team settings*	.16			.23				
	$N = 908$; $k = 7$; Mount et al., 1998 *dyadic service jobs*	.08			.11			.12	
overall weighted ave.		.06			.09	.09	.13	.13	.13
Self-esteem	$N = 5,145$; $k = 40$; Judge & Bono, 2001b	.18				.26			
Agreeableness	$N = 11,526$; $k = 80$; Barrick & Mount, 1991	.04						.06	
	$N = 12,722$; $k = 69$; Hough, 1992	.04							
	$N = 5,803$; $k = 38$; Hurtz & Donovan, 2000	.07						.10	.12
	$N = 2,574$; $k = 19$; Salgado, 1997 *European settings*	.00						-.01	-.02

Overall Training Success

Personality Variable	Source	$\bar{r}$	ρ_s	ρ_p	ρ_c	ρ_{pc}	ρ_{cr}	ρ_t	ρ_a
Emotional Stability	$N = 3,283$; $k = 19$; Barrick & Mount, 1991	.04						.07	
	$N = 8,685$; $k = 69$; Hough, 1992	.12							
	$N = 644$; $k = 2$; Hurtz & Donovan, 2000	.06						.08	.09
	$N = 470$; $k = 6$; Salgado, 1997 *European settings*	.11						.18	.27
	$N = 4,520$; $k = 15$; Salgado, 2000	.11						.16	
overall weighted ave.		.10						.15	.19
Agreeableness	$N = 3,685$; $k = 19$; Barrick & Mount, 1991	.06						.10	
	$N = 988$; $k = 7$; Hough, 1992	.08							
	$N = 644$; $k = 2$; Hurtz & Donovan, 2000	.12						.18	.21
	$N = 415$; $k = 5$; Salgado, 1997 *European settings*	.12						.19	.31

Overall Educational Success

Personality Variable	Source	$\bar{r}$	ρ_s	ρ_p	ρ_c	ρ_{pc}	ρ_{cr}	ρ_t	ρ_a
Emotional Stability	$N = 3,784$; $k = 14$; Salgado, 2000	-.01						-.04	-.02
	$N = 70,588$; $k = 162$; Hough, 1992	.20							
overall weighted ave.		.19						.38	
Self-esteem	$N = 1,654$; $k = 11$; Salgado, 2000	-.03						-.04	
	$N = 7,330$; $k = 15$; Hough, 1992	.01							

138

Meta-analytic results (continued). Column headings: $\bar{r}$, ρ_s, ρ_p, ρ_c, ρ_{pc}, ρ_{cr}, ρ_t, ρ_a.

[Trait continued from previous page] — left panel

	$\bar{r}$	ρ_s	ρ_p	ρ_c	ρ_{pc}	ρ_{cr}	ρ_t	ρ_a	Source
	.07						.09	.11	N = 1,841; k = 16; Anderson & Visweswaran, 1998
	.22			.27	.28		.33		N = 280; k = 4; Tett et al., 1991 (cf. Tett et al., 1994) — confirmatory studies
	.03			.05	.06	.08	.05	.04	N = 42,218; k = 99; Hough et al., 1998 — managerial jobs
	.03				.06				N = 2,342; k = 23; Vinchur et al., 1998 — sales jobs
	.20			.27			.33		N = 678; k = 4; Mount et al., 1998 — team settings
	.09			.12			.13		N = 908; k = 7; Mount et al., 1998 — dyadic service jobs
overall weighted ave.	.04			.05	.06	.08	.05	.07	

[Trait continued from previous page] — right panel

	$\bar{r}$	ρ_s	ρ_p	ρ_c	ρ_{pc}	ρ_{cr}	ρ_t	ρ_a	Source
	.07							.11	N = 3,289; k = 13; Salgado, 2000
overall weighted ave.	.07						.00	.10	

Extraversion — left panel

	$\bar{r}$	ρ_s	ρ_p	ρ_c	ρ_{pc}	ρ_{cr}	ρ_t	ρ_a	Source
Extraversion	.06								
	.06						.10		N = 12,396; k = 89; Barrick & Mount, 1991
	.06						.09	.09	N = 5,809; k = 37; Hurtz & Donovan, 2000
	.06						.09	.14	N = 2,799; k = 22; Salgado, 1997 — European settings
	.05			.07	.07		.05	.07	N = 2,186; k = 17; Anderson & Visweswaran, 1998
	.10			.13	.16				N = 2,302; k = 15; Tett et al., 1991 (cf. Tett et al., 1994) — confirmatory studies
	.05						.09		N = 108,607; k = 379; Hough et al., 1998 — managerial jobs
	.09					.18			N = 3,112; k = 27; Vinchur et al., 1998 — sales jobs
	.14			.19			.22		N = 678; k = 4; Mount et al., 1998 — team settings
	.05			.06			.07		N = 829; k = 6; Mount et al., 1998 — dyadic service jobs
overall weighted ave.	.05			.07	.08	.11	.09	.10	

Extraversion — right panel

	$\bar{r}$	ρ_s	ρ_p	ρ_c	ρ_{pc}	ρ_{cr}	ρ_t	ρ_a	Source
	.15						.26	.15	N = 3,101; k = 17; Barrick & Mount, 1991
	.07							.10	N = 3,585; k = 12; Salgado, 2000
	.12						.17	.19	N = 644; k = 2; Hurtz & Donovan, 2000
	.01						.02	.03	N = 383; k = 4; Salgado, 1997 — European settings
	.12						.17		N = 3,468; k = 14; Salgado, 2000
overall weighted ave.	.13						.20	.26	

(Continued)

TABLE 7.1 (Continued)

Overall Job Performance

	$\bar{r}$	ρ_s	ρ_p	ρ_c	ρ_{pc}	ρ_{cr}	ρ_t	ρ_a
Dominance-potency	.09						.27	
	N = 30,642; *k* = 248; Hough, 1992							
	.16					.28		
	N = 11,823; *k* = 125; Hough et al., 1998 *managerial jobs*							
	.15						.19	
	N = 2,907; *k* = 25; Vinchur et al., 1998 *sales jobs*							
overall weighted ave.	.11					.21	.19	
Sociability-affiliation	.02						−.01	
	N = 3,782; *k* = 31; Hough, 1992							
	−.01					.12		
	N = 19,454; *k* = 102; Hough et al., 1998 *managerial jobs*							
	.06							
	N = 2,389; *k* = 18; Vinchur et al., 1998 *sales jobs*							
overall weighted ave.	.00					.00	.00	
Energy level	.12					.20		
	N = 8,937; *k* = 22; Hough et al., 1998							
Openness to Experience	−.02						−.03	
	N = 9,454; *k* = 55; Barrick & Mount, 1991							
	.01							
	N = 10,888; *k* = 36; Hough, 1992							
	.03						.05	.06
	N = 4,881; *k* = 33; Hurtz & Donovan, 2000							
	.00						.01	.02
	N = 1,629; *k* = 11; Salgado, 1997 *European settings*							
	.05			.07	.08			
	N = 1,656; *k* = 14; Anderson & Viswesvaran, 1998							
	.18			.24	.27			
	N = 1,304; *k* = 10; Tett et al., 1991 (cf. Tett et al., 1994) *confirmatory studies*							
	.05					.08		
	N = 46,614; *k* = 110; Hough et al., 1998 *managerial jobs*							

Overall Training Success

	$\bar{r}$	ρ_s	ρ_p	ρ_c	ρ_{pc}	ρ_{cr}	ρ_t	ρ_a
Dominance-potency	.07							
	N = 8,389; *k* = 70; Hough, 1992							
Sociability-affiliation	.01							
	N = 2,953; *k* = 9; Hough, 1992							
Openness to Experience	.14						.25	
	N = 2,700; *k* = 14; Barrick & Mount, 1991							
	.02							
	N = 8,744; *k* = 35; Hough, 1992							
	.08						.13	.14
	N = 644; *k* = 2; Hurtz & Donovan, 2000							
	.11						.17	.26
	N = 477; *k* = 4; Salgado, 1997 *European settings*							
	.13						.18	
	N = 2,071; *k* = 12; Salgado, 2000							

Overall Educational Success

	$\bar{r}$	ρ_s	ρ_p	ρ_c	ρ_{pc}	ρ_{cr}	ρ_t	ρ_a
Dominance-potency	.12							
	N = 63,057; *k* = 128; Hough, 1992							
Sociability-affiliation	.01							
	N = 2,953; *k* = 9; Hough, 1992							
Openness to Experience	.00						.00	
	N = 1,654; *k* = 11; Salgado, 2000							
	.13							
	N = 3,628; *k* = 8; Hough, 1992							

	$\bar{r}$	ρ_s	ρ_p	ρ_c	ρ_{pc}	ρ_{cr}	ρ_t	ρ_a	$\bar{r}$	ρ_s	ρ_p	ρ_c	ρ_{pc}	ρ_{cr}	ρ_t	ρ_a	$\bar{r}$	ρ_s	ρ_p	ρ_c	ρ_{pc}	ρ_{cr}	ρ_t	ρ_a
	.06					**.11**																		
	N = 804; k = 8; Vinchur et al., 1998 ***sales jobs***																							
	.10			**.14**			**.16**																	
	N = 678; k = 4; Mount et al., 1998 ***team settings***																							
	.11			**.15**			**.17**																	
	N = 829; k = 6; Mount et al., 1998 ***dyadic service jobs***																							
overall	$\bar{r}$	ρ_s	ρ_p	ρ_c	ρ_{pc}	ρ_{cr}	ρ_t	ρ_a	$\bar{r}$	ρ_s	ρ_p	ρ_c	ρ_{pc}	ρ_{cr}	ρ_t	ρ_a	$\bar{r}$	ρ_s	ρ_p	ρ_c	ρ_{pc}	ρ_{cr}	ρ_t	ρ_a
weighted ave.	**.04**			**.05**	**.06**	**.07**	**.06**	**.07**	**.06**						**.10**	**.13**	**.09**							
Conscien-tiousness	**.13**						**.23**		**.13**						**.23**		**.21**						**.28**	
	N =12,893; k = 92; Barrick & Mount, 1991								N = 3,585; k = 17; Barrick & Mount, 1991								N = 2,214; k = 15; Salgado, 2000							
	.15						**.22**	**.24**	**.02**						**.03**	**.03**								
	N = 7,342; k = 42; Hurtz & Donovan, 2000								N = 741; k = 3; Hurtz & Donovan. 2000															
	.10						**.16**	**.26**	**.15**						**.24**	**.39**								
	N = 2,241; k = 18; Salgado, 1997 ***European settings***								N = 324; k = 3; Salgado, 1997 ***European settings***															
	.13			**.18**	**.20**				**.12**						**.17**									
	N = 2,449; k = 19; Anderson & Viswesvaran, 1998								N = 4,617; k = 16; Salgado, 2000															
	.12			**.16**	**.18**																			
	N = 450; k = 7; Tett et al., 1991 (cf. Tett et al., 1994) ***confirmatory studies***																							
	.07						**.11**																	
	N = 50,367; k = 186; Hough et al., 1998 ***managerial jobs***																							
	.11					**.21**																		
	N = 2,186; k = 19; Vinchur et al., 1998 ***sales jobs***																							
	.13			**.18**			**.21**																	
	N = 678; k = 4; Mount et al., 1998 ***team settings***																							
	.20			**.26**			**.29**																	
	N = 908; k = 7; Mount et al., 1998 ***dyadic service jobs***																							
overall	$\bar{r}$	ρ_s	ρ_p	ρ_c	ρ_{pc}	ρ_{cr}	ρ_t	ρ_a	$\bar{r}$	ρ_s	ρ_p	ρ_c	ρ_{pc}	ρ_{cr}	ρ_t	ρ_a								
weighted ave.	**.09**			**.13**	**.14**	**.18**	**.15**	**.17**	**.12**						**.18**	**.22**								
Achievement	**.19**								**.21**								**.29**							
	N = 3,182; k = 31; Hough, 1992								N = 1,160; k = 9; Hough, 1992								N = 12,639; k = 31; Hough, 1992							
	.09						**.17**																	
	N = 11,926; k = 78; Hough et al., 1998 ***managerial jobs***																							

(Continued)

TABLE 7.1 (Continued)

	Overall Job Performance								Overall Training Success								Overall Educational Success							
	$\bar{r}$	ρ_s	ρ_p	ρ_c	ρ_{pc}	ρ_{cr}	ρ_t	ρ_a	$\bar{r}$	ρ_s	ρ_p	ρ_c	ρ_{pc}	ρ_{cr}	ρ_t	ρ_a	$\bar{r}$	ρ_s	ρ_p	ρ_c	ρ_{pc}	ρ_{cr}	ρ_t	ρ_a
sales jobs — $N=1{,}319$; $k=8$; Vinchur et al., 1998	.14					.25																		
overall weighted ave.	.11					.20	.21																	
Dependability — $N=21{,}029$; $k=114$; Hough, 1992	.07						.03		.11								.12							
managerial jobs — $N=5{,}078$; $k=62$; Hough et al., 1998	.02					.18																		
sales jobs — $N=1{,}702$; $k=15$; Vinchur et al., 1998	.10																							
overall weighted ave.	.06					.11	.09																	
Compound Variables																								
Integrity tests (socialization) — $N=7{,}550$; $k=23$; Ones et al., 1993 *applicants and predictive validity*	.25						.41																	
personality based — $N=37{,}683$; $k=138$; Ones et al., 1993	.22						.35							.38										
overall weighted ave.	.23						.36																	
Violence scales — $N=4{,}003$; $k=14$; Ones et al., 1994						.41																		
Drug and alcohol scales — $N=1{,}436$; $k=7$; Ones & Viswesvaran, 2001	.14			.19																				
Managerial potential scales — $N=11{,}009$; $k=87$; Ones et al., 1998	.26						.42																	
Service orientation scales — $N=6{,}945$; $k=41$; Frei & McDaniel, 1998	.24					.50																		
$N=6{,}944$; $k=33$; Ones & Viswesvaran, 2001	.27			.39																				
overall weighted ave.	.25			.37		.53																		

Note — Overall Training Success: Dependability row $N=4{,}710$; $k=34$; Hough, 1992. Integrity tests row $N=2{,}364$; $k=8$; Ones & Viswesvaran, 1998c.

Note — Overall Educational Success: Dependability row $N=18{,}661$; $k=42$; Hough, 1992.

142

	r̄	ρ$_s$	ρ$_p$	ρ$_c$	ρ$_{pc}$	ρ$_{cr}$	ρ$_t$	ρ$_a$	N; k; source
Stress tolerance scales	.34							.41	N = 1,010; k = 13; Ones & Viswesvaran, 2001
Internal locus of control scales	.19				.28				N = 2,517; k = 11; Hough, 1992 (N = 225; k = 2; Hough, 1992)
	.14				.22				N = 4,310; k = 35; Judge & Bono, 2001a
	.09			.12	.13				N = 719; k = 7; Tett et al., 1991 (cf. Tett et al., 1994) *confirmatory studies*
overall weighted ave.	.15			.20	.24				
Type A personality	−.11			−.14	−.16				N = 164; k = 2; Tett et al., 1991 (cf. Tett et al., 1994) *confirmatory studies*
Rugged individualism	.05				.03		−.02		N = 3,410; k = 32; Hough, 1992 (N = 1,614; k = 11; Hough, 1992) (N = 12,358; k = 27; Hough, 1992)
	.11				.20				N = 811; k = 5; Vinchur et al., 1998 *sales jobs*
overall weighted ave.	.06				.11				
Generalized self-efficacy	.19				.23				N = 1,122; k = 10; Judge & Bono, 2001a
Specific self-efficacy	.19				.22				N = 182; k = 2; Colquitt et al., 2000
Social desirability	.01	.01			.22	.19	−.09	−.11	N = 9,966; k = 14; Ones et al., 1996 (N = 4,547; k = 7; Ones et al., 1996) (N = 3,125; k = 16; Ones et al., 1996)

Note. r̄ = sample-size weighted mean observed validities; ρ$_s$ = validities corrected for sampling error only; ρ$_p$ = validities corrected for predictor unreliability; ρ$_c$ = validities corrected for criterion unreliability; ρ$_{pc}$ = validities corrected for unreliability in both predictor and criterion; ρ$_{cr}$ = corrected for range restriction and unreliability in the criterion; ρ$_t$ = corrected for range restriction and unreliability in both predictor and criterion; ρ$_a$ = corrected for range restriction, unreliability in both predictor and criterion, and imperfect predictor construct measurement.

TABLE 7.2 Personality Variables and Their Meta-Analyzed Validities for Predicting *Specific* Work Performance Constructs

Personality Variable	Task/Tech	Contextual	Counterprod	Cust Svc	Sales	Creativity	Leadership	Combat
Emotional Stability	$\bar{r}=.09$, $\rho_t=.13$, $\rho_a=.14$; N = 1,243; k = 8; Hurtz & Donovan, 2000	$\bar{r}=.14$; N = 1,151; k = 6; Borman et al., 2001; **citizenship**	$\bar{r}=-.15$		$\bar{r}=-.07$, $\rho_{cr}=-.12$; N = 2,157; k = 14; Vinchur et al., 1998; **objective sales criteria**	$\bar{r}=-.05$; N = 442; k = 8; Hough, 1992	$\bar{r}=.17$; $\rho_{pc}=.24$; N = 8,025; k = 48; Judge, Bono et al., 2001; **all settings**	$\bar{r}=.19$; N = 3,880; k = 13; Hough, 1992
	$\bar{r}=.05$; N = 9,364; k = 23; Hough, 1992	$\bar{r}=.16$; N = 9,562; k = 15; Hough, 1992; **effort**	$\bar{r}=-.41$; N = 21,431; k = 9; Hough, 1992; **irresponsible behavior**		$\bar{r}=.18$; N = 778; k = 3; Hough, 1992	$\bar{r}=.02$[1]; k = 66; Feist, 1998; **creative scientists**	$\rho_{pc}=.15$; k = 9; Judge, Bono et al., 2001; **business settings [subset of 'all settings' above]**	
		$\bar{r}=.09$, $\rho_t=.13$, $\rho_a=.14$; N = 2,581; k = 15; Hurtz & Donovan, 2000; **job dedication**	N = 36,210; k = 15; Hough, 1992; **unlawful behavior**		$\bar{r}=.10$, $\rho_t=.15$; N = 356; k = 3; Salgado, 2000	$\bar{r}=-.07$[1]; k = 128; Feist, 1998; **artists vs. non-artists**		
		$\bar{r}=.10$, $\rho_{pc}=.12$; N = 847; k = 5; Organ & Ryan, 1995; **generalized compliance**	$\bar{r}=-.04$, $\rho_t=-.06$; N = 3,107; k = 15; Salgado, 2000; **counterproductivity**					
		$\bar{r}=.10$, $\rho_t=.16$, $\rho_a=.17$; N = 3,685; k = 21; Hurtz & Donovan, 2000; **interpersonal facilitation**	$\bar{r}=.03$, $\rho_t=.04$; N = 2,491; k = 12; Salgado, 2000; **absenteeism**					
		$\bar{r}=.12$, $\rho_c=.16$; $\rho_t=.19$; N = 1,491; k = 10; Mount et al., 1998; **interactions with others**	$\bar{r}=-.04$, $\rho_t=-.08$; N = 2,121; k = 5; Salgado, 2000; **accidents**					
		$\bar{r}=.13$; N = 2,067; k = 31; Hough, 1992; **teamwork**	$\rho_s=-.02$; N = 3,106; k = 13; Arthur et al., 1991; **accidents**					
		$\bar{r}=.05$, $\rho_{pc}=.06$; N = 1,201; k = 6; Organ & Ryan, 1995; **altruism**	$\bar{r}=-.12$; N = 3,288; k = 23; Clarke & Robertson, 1999; **accidents**					

(Continued)

overall wtd. ave.	$\bar{r} = .05$	$\bar{r} = .13$	$\bar{r} = -.27$	$\bar{r} = .01$	
		$\rho_c = .17$		$\rho_{cr} = .01$	
		$\rho_{pc} = .15$			
	$\rho_t = .08$	$\rho_t = .20$	$\rho_t = -.43$	$\rho_t = .01$	
	$\rho_a = .09$	$\rho_a = .21$			
Low anxiety	$\bar{r} = .13$; $\rho_{pc} = .15$ $N = 368$; $k = 4$; Colquitt et al., 2000; **skill acquisition**				
Agreeableness	$\bar{r} = .05$, $\rho_t = .07$, $\rho_a = .08$ $N = 1,754$; $k = 9$; Hurtz & Donovan, 2000	$\bar{r} = .13$ $N = 1,554$; $k = 7$; Borman et al., 2001; **citizenship**	$\bar{r} = -.08$ $N = 24,259$; $k = 4$; Hough, 1992; **irresponsible behavior**	$\bar{r} = -.02$, $\rho_{cr} = -.03$ $N = 918$. $k = 12$; Vinchur et al., 1998; **objective sales criteria**	$\bar{r} = -.29$ $N = 174$; $k = 3$; Hough, 1992	$\bar{r} = .06$; $\rho_{cr} = .08$ $N = 9,081$; $k = 42$; Judge, Bono et al., 2001; **all settings**
	$\bar{r} = .02$	$\bar{r} = .06$, $\rho_t = .08$, $\rho_a = .10$ $N = 3,197$; $k = 17$; Hurtz & Donovan, 2000; **job dedication**	$\bar{r} = -.13$, $\rho_t = -.20$ $N = 1,299$; $k = 9$; Salgado, 2000; **counterproductivity**	$\bar{r} = -.10$, $\rho_t = -.13$ $N = 311$: $k = 3$; Salgado, 2000	$\bar{r} = -.03^l$ $k = 64$; Feist, 1998; **creative scientists**	$\rho_{pc} = -.04$ $k = 10$; Judge, Bono et al., 2001; **business settings [subset of 'all settings' above]**
	$N = 7,837$; $k = 4$; Hough, 1992	$\bar{r} = .17$ $N = 329$; $k = 7$; Hough, 1992; **teamwork**	$\bar{r} = .03$, $\rho_t = .04$ $N = 1,339$; $k = 8$; Salgado, 2000; **absenteeism**		$\bar{r} = -.10^l$ $k = 63$; Feist, 1998; **artists vs. non-artists**	
		$\bar{r} = .11$, $\rho_t = .17$, $\rho_a = .20$ $N = 4,301$; $k = 23$; Hurtz & Donovan, 2000; **interpersonal facilitation**	$\bar{r} = .00$, $\rho_t = -.01$ $N = 1,540$; $k = 4$; Salgado, 2000; **accidents**			
		$\bar{r} = .17$, $\rho_c = .23$, $\rho_t = .27$ $N = 1,491$; $k = 10$; Mount et al., 1998; **interactions with others**	$\bar{r} = -.17$ $N = 5,090$; $k = 15$; Clarke & Robertson, 1999; **accidents**			
		$\bar{r} = .10$, $\rho_{pc} = .13$ $N = 916$; $k = 6$; Organ & Ryan, 1995; **altruism**				

TABLE 7.2 (Continued)

	Task/Tech	Contextual	Counterprod	Cust Svc	Sales	Creativity	Leadership	Combat
(continued)		$\bar{r} = .08$, $\rho_{pc} = .11$; N = 916; k = 6; Organ & Ryan, 1995; **generalized compliance**						
overall wtd. ave.	$\bar{r} = .03$; $\rho_t = .05$, $\rho_a = .06$	$\bar{r} = .11$, $\rho_c = .14$, $\rho_{pc} = .14$; $\rho_t = .16$, $\rho_a = .19$	$\bar{r} = -.09$; $\rho_t = -.13$	$\bar{r} = -.04$	$\rho_{cr} = -.06$, $\rho_t = -.05$		$\bar{r} = .22$; $\rho_{pc} = .31$	
Extraversion	$\bar{r} = .04$, $\rho_t = .06$, $\rho_a = .07$; N = 1,839; k = 9; Hurtz & Donovan, 2000	$\bar{r} = .08$; N = 1,832; k = 8; Borman et al., 2001; **citizenship** $\bar{r} = .03$, $\rho_t = .05$, $\rho_a = .05$; N = 3,130; k = 16; Hurtz & Donovan, 2000; **job dedication** $\bar{r} = .06$, $\rho_t = .10$, $\rho_a = .11$; N = 4,155; k = 21; Hurtz & Donovan, 2000; **interpersonal facilitation** $\bar{r} = .09$, $\rho_c = .12$, $\rho_t = .14$; N = 1,412; k = 9; Mount et al., 1998; **interactions with others** $\bar{r} = .08$, $\rho_{pc} = .08$; N = 869; k = 5; Organ & Ryan, 1995; **altruism**	$\bar{r} = .01$, $\rho_t = .01$; N = 2,383; k = 12; Salgado, 2000; **counterproductivity** $\bar{r} = .05$, $\rho_t = .08$; N = 1,799; k = 10; Salgado, 2000; **absenteeism** $\bar{r} = -.02$, $\rho_t = -.04$; N = 2,341; k = 7; Salgado, 2000; **accidents** $\bar{r} = .09$; N = 6,141; k = 32; Clarke & Robertson, 1999; **accidents**		$\bar{r} = .12$, $\rho_{cr} = .22$; N = 2,629; k = 18; Vinchur et al., 1998; **objective sales criteria** $\bar{r} = .10$, $\rho_t = .13$; N = 403; k = 3; Salgado, 2000	$\bar{r} = .14$[1]; k = 135; Feist, 1998; **creative scientists** $\bar{r} = .08$[1]; k = 148; Feist, 1998; **artists vs. non-artists**	$\bar{r} = .22$; $\rho_{pc} = .31$; N = 11,705; k = 60; Judge, Bono et al., 2001; **all settings** $\rho_{pc} = .25$; k = 13; Judge, Bono et al., 2001; **business settings** [subset of 'all settings' above]	

146

	$\bar{r} = .06$, $\rho_{pc} = .07$; $N = 934$; $k = 6$; Organ & Ryan, 1995; **generalized compliance**		$\bar{r} = .05$		$\bar{r} = .12$	
	$\bar{r} = .06$ $\rho_c = .08$ $\rho_{pc} = .07$ $\rho_t = .10$ $\rho_a = .11$		$\rho_t = .07$		$\rho_{cr} = .22$ $\rho_t = .15$	
overall wtd. ave.						
Dominance-potency	$\bar{r} = .02$; $N = 17,001$; $k = 23$; Hough, 1992	$\bar{r} = .17$ $N = 17,156$; $k = 16$; Hough, 1992; **effort**	$\bar{r} = -.06$ $N = 38,578$; $k = 14$; Hough, 1992; **irresponsible behavior**	$\bar{r} = .15$, $\rho_{cr} = .26$ $N = 2,278$; $k = 14$; Vinchur et al., 1998; **objective sales criteria**	$\bar{r} = .21$ $N = 550$; $k = 11$; Hough, 1992	$\bar{r} = .24$; $\rho_{pc} = .37$ $N = 7,692$; $k = 31$; Judge, Bono et al., 2001; **all settings**
		$\bar{r} = .08$ $N = 2,307$; $k = 39$; Hough, 1992; **teamwork**	$\bar{r} = -.29$ $N = 29,590$; $k = 10$; Hough, 1992; **unlawful behavior**	$\bar{r} = .25$ $N = 1,1.1$; $k = 7$; Hough, .992	$\bar{r} = .19^1$ $k = 42$; Feist, 1998; **creative scientists**	$\bar{r} = .08$ $N = 2,695$; $k = 9$; Hough, 1992
					$\bar{r} = .08^1$ $k = 42$; Feist, 1998; **artists vs. non-artists**	
overall wtd. ave.	$\bar{r} = .16$		$\bar{r} = -.16$	$\bar{r} = .18$ $\rho_{cr} = .32$		
Sociability-affiliation	$\bar{r} = .06$; $N = 736$; $k = 2$; Hough, 1992			$\bar{r} = .08$, $\rho_{cr} = .15$ $N = 279$; $k = 4$; Vinchur et al., 1998; **objective sales criteria**	$\bar{r} = .07^1$ $k = 23$; Feist, 1998; **creative scientists**	$\bar{r} = .24$; $\rho_{pc} = .37$ $N = 5,827$; $k = 19$; Judge, Bono et al., 2001; **all settings**
				$\bar{r} = .19$ $N = 667$; $k = 1$; Hough, 1992	$\bar{r} = .01^1$ $k = 35$; Feist, 1998; **artists vs. non-artists**	$\bar{r} = -.02$ $N = 600$; $k = 2$; Hough, 1992
overall wtd. ave.				$\bar{r} = .16$ $\rho_{cr} = .30$		

(Continued)

147

TABLE 7.2 (Continued)

	Task/Tech	Contextual	Counterprod	Cust Svc	Sales	Creativity	Leadership	Combat
Openness to Experience	$\bar{r}=-.01$, $\rho_t=-.01$, $\rho_a=-.01$ $N=1,176$; $k=7$; Hurtz & Donovan, 2000 $\bar{r}=.16$ $N=700$; $k=2$; Hough, 1992	$\bar{r}=.01$, $\rho_t=.01$, $\rho_a=.01$ $N=2,514$; $k=14$; Hurtz & Donovan, 2000; **job dedication** $\bar{r}=.03$, $\rho_t=.05$, $\rho_a=.05$ $N=3,539$; $k=19$; Hurtz & Donovan, 2000; **interpersonal facilitation** $\bar{r}=.06$, $\rho_c=.09$, $\rho_t=.10$ $N=1,412$; $k=9$; Mount et al., 1998; **interactions with others**	$\bar{r}=.10$, $\rho_t=.14$ $N=1,421$; $k=8$; Salgado, 2000; **counterproductivity** $\bar{r}=-.15$ $N=1,414$; $k=2$; Hough, 1992; **irresponsible behavior** $\bar{r}=.00$, $\rho_t=.00$ $N=1,339$; $k=8$; Salgado, 2000; **absenteeism** $\bar{r}=.05$, $\rho_t=.09$ $N=1,660$; $k=5$; Salgado, 2000; **accidents** $\bar{r}=.20$ $N=1,147$; $k=10$; Clarke & Robertson, 1999; **accidents**		$\bar{r}=.03$, $\rho_{cr}=.06$ $N=951$; $k=6$; Vinchur et al. 1998; **objective sales criteria** $\bar{r}=-.03$, $\rho_t=-.04$ $N=251$; $k=2$; Salgado, 2000	$\bar{r}=.18$ $k=52$; Feist, 1998; **creative scientists** $\bar{r}=.21$[1] $k=93$; Feist, 1998; **artists vs. non-artists**	$\bar{r}=.16$; $\rho_{pc}=.24$ $N=7,221$; $k=37$; Judge, Bono et al., 2001; **all settings** $\rho_{pc}=.23$ $k=9$; Judge, Bono et al., 2001; **business settings [subset of 'all settings' above]**	
overall wtd. ave.	$\bar{r}=.05$ $\rho_t=.05$ $\rho_a=.05$	$\bar{r}=.03$ $\rho_c=.04$ $\rho_t=.05$ $\rho_a=.04$	$\bar{r}=.03$ $\rho_t=.05$		$\bar{r}=.02$ $\rho_{cr}=.03$ $\rho_t=.02$			
Conscientiousness	$\bar{r}=.10$, $\rho_t=.15$, $\rho_a=.16$ $N=2,197$; $k=12$; Hurtz & Donovan, 2000 $\bar{r}=-.04$, $\rho_{pc}=-.05$ $N=839$; $k=6$; Colquitt et al., 2000; **skill acquisition**	$\bar{r}=.24$ $N=2,378$; $k=12$; Borman et al., 2001; **citizenship** $\bar{r}=.12$, $\rho_t=.18$, $\rho_a=.20$ $N=3,197$; $k=17$; Hurtz & Donovan, 2000; **job dedication**	$\bar{r}=-.18$, $\rho_t=-.26$ $N=1,737$; $k=10$; Salgado, 2000; **counterproductivity** $\bar{r}=-.04$, $\rho_t=-.06$ $N=2,155$; $k=10$; Salgado, 2000; **absenteeism**		$\bar{r}=.17$, $\rho_{cr}=.31$ $N=1,774$; $k=15$; Vinchur et al., 1998; **objective sales criteria** $\bar{r}=.16$, $\rho_t=.22$ $N=987$; $k=9$; Salgado, 2000	$\bar{r}=.07$[1] $k=48$; Feist, 1998; **creative scientists** $\bar{r}=-.29$[1] $k=52$; Feist, 1998; **artists vs. non-artists**	$\bar{r}=.20$; $\rho_{pc}=.28$ $N=7,510$; $k=35$; Judge, Bono et al., 2001; **all settings** $\rho_{pc}=.05$ $k=8$; Judge, Bono et al., 2001; **business settings [subset of 'all settings' above]**	

	$\bar{r} = .11, \rho_t = .16,$ $\rho_a = .18$ $N = 4,301; k = 23;$ Hurtz & Donovan, 2000; **interpersonal facilitation**	$\bar{r} = -.03, \rho_t = -.06$ $N = 2,094; k = 6;$ Salgado, 2000; **accidents**			
	$\bar{r} = .13, \rho_c = .18,$ $\rho_t = .20$ $N = 1,491; k = 10;$ Mount et al., 1998; **interactions with others**	$\bar{r} = -.16$ $N = 5,156; k = 22;$ Clarke & Robertson, 1999; **accidents**			
	$\bar{r} = .04,$ $\rho_{pc} = .04$ $N = 1,231; k = 7;$ Organ & Ryan, 1995; **altruism**				
	$\bar{r} = .17,$ $\rho_{pc} = .23$ $N = 1,231; k = 7;$ Organ & Ryan, 1995; **generalized compliance**				
overall wtd. ave.	$\bar{r} = .06$ $\rho_{pc} = .08$ $\rho_t = .09$ $\rho_a = .10$	$\bar{r} = .14$ $\rho_c = .19$ $\rho_{pc} = .16$ $\rho_t = .20$ $\rho_a = .22$	$\bar{r} = -.12$	$\bar{r} = .17$ $\rho_{cr} = .30$ $\rho_t = .23$	$\rho_t = -.12$
Achievement	$\bar{r} = .02$	$\bar{r} = .21$ $N = 15,554; k = 6;$ Hough, 1992	$\bar{r} = -.19$ $N = 19,476; k = 4;$ Hough, 1992; **irresponsible behavior**	$\bar{r} = .23, \rho_{cr} = .41$ $N = 1,259; k = 10;$ Vinchur et al., 1998; **objective sales criteria**	$\bar{r} = .14$ $N = 116; k = 2;$ Hough, 1992	$\bar{r} = .23; \rho_{pc} = .35$ $N = 4,625; k = 16;$ Judge, Bono et al., 2001; **all settings**
		$N = 15,530; k = 4;$ Hough, 1992; **effort**			
	$\bar{r} = .13, \rho_{pc} = .17$ $N = 356; k = 2;$ Colquitt et al., 2000; **skill acquisition**	$\bar{r} = .14$ $N = 233; k = 3;$ Hough, 1992; **teamwork**	$\bar{r} = -.42$ $N = 5,918; k = 2;$ Hough, 1992; **unlawful behavior**	$\bar{r} = .27$ $N = 162; k = 2;$ Hough, 1992	
overall wtd. ave.	$\bar{r} = .02$ $\rho_{pc} = .03$	$\bar{r} = .21$	$\bar{r} = -.24$	$\bar{r} = .23$ $\rho_{cr} = .42$	

149

(Continued)

TABLE 7.2 (Continued)

	Task/Tech	Contextual	Counterprod	Cust Svc	Sales	Creativity	Leadership	Combat
Depend-ability	$\bar{r} = .05$	$\bar{r} = .14$	$\bar{r} = -.24$		$\bar{r} = .10, \rho_{cr} = .18$	$\bar{r} = -.07$	$\bar{r} = .18; \rho_{pc} = .30$	$\bar{r} = .08$
	$N = 25,237; k = 13$; Hough, 1992	$N = 25,408; k = 11$; Hough, 1992; **effort**	$N = 98,676; k = 69$; Hough, 1992; **irresponsible behavior**		$N = 359; k = 5$; Vinchur et al., 1998; **objective sales criteria**	$N = 268; k = 5$; Hough, 1992	$N = 5,020; k = 16$; Judge, Bono et al., 2001; **all settings**	$N = 1,490; k = 5$; Hough, 1992
		$\bar{r} = .17$	$\bar{r} = -.58$		$\bar{r} = .06$			
		$N = 1,340; k = 25$; Hough, 1992; **teamwork**	$N = 25,867; k = 22$; Hough, 1992; **unlawful behavior**		$N = 2,236; k = 5$; Hough, 1992			
			$\rho_s = -.16$					
			$N = 3,242; k = 28$; Arthur et al., 1991; **accidents**					
overall wtd. ave.		$\bar{r} = .14$	$\bar{r} = -.31$		$\bar{r} = .07$ $\rho_{cr} = .12$			

Compound Variables

Integrity tests (socialization)

- $\bar{r} = .20, \rho_t = .29$; $N = 93,092; k = 62$; Ones et al., 1993; **personality-based scales, applicants, predictive validity, counterproductivity**
- $\rho_{cr} = .52$; $N = 759; k = 5$; Ones & Viswesvaran, 1998c; **accidents**
- $\rho_{cr} = .69$; $N = 1,970; k = 14$; Ones & Viswesvaran, 1998c; **property damage**
- $\bar{r} = .18, \rho_{cr} = .26$; $N = 11,079; k = 17$; Ones et al., 1994; **violence on the job**
- $\bar{r} = .20, \rho_{cr} = .26$; $N = 25,594; k = 50$; Schmidt et al., 1997; **substance abuse**

overall wtd. ave.

- $\bar{r} = .20$
- $\rho_{cr} = .27$
- $\rho_t = .29$

Violence scales	$\rho_{cr} = .46$ $N = 533; k = 4$; Ones et al., 1994; **counterproductivity**	$\bar{r} = .34, \rho_{cr} = .48$ $N = 1,265; k = 11$; Ones et al., 1994; **violence on the job**		
overall wtd. ave.	$\bar{r} = .34$ $\rho_{cr} = .47$			
Managerial potential	$\bar{r} = .15, \rho_t = .24$ $N = 5,123; k = 20$; Ones et al., 1998; **managerial jobs**	$\bar{r} = .16, \rho_t = .26$ $N = 2,270; k = 16$; Ones et al., 1998; **managerial jobs, organizational citizenship**	$\bar{r} = .19, \rho_t = .30$ $N = 2,948; k = 20$; Ones et al., 1998; **managerial jobs, counterproductivity**	
Service orientation	$\bar{r} = .30, \rho_c = .42$ $N = 740; k = 5$; Ones & Viswesvaran, 2001; **counterproductivity**	$\bar{r} = .23, \rho_c = .34$ $N = 4,401; k = 15$; Ones & Viswesvaran, 2001; see also Table 7.1		
Stress tolerance	$\bar{r} = .30, \rho_c = .42$ $N = 594; k = 5$; Ones & Viswesvaran, 2001; **counterproductivity**			
Internal locus of control	$\bar{r} = .06$ $N = 8,333; k = 2$; Hough, 1992	$\bar{r} = .16$ $N = 599; k = 3$; Borman et al., 2001; **citizenship**	$\bar{r} = -.12$ $N = 8,333; k = 2$; Hough, 1992; **irresponsible behavior**	$\bar{r} = .08; \rho_{pc} = .13$ $N = 2,347; k = 15$; Judge, Bono et al., 2001; **all settings**
	$\bar{r} = .03, \rho_{pc} = .04$ $N = 386; k = 7$; Colquitt et al., 2000; **skill acquisition**	$\rho_{cr} = -.20$ $N = 1,909; k = 13$; Arthur et al., 1991; **accidents**	$\bar{r} = .13$ $N = 9,039; k = 6$; Hough, 1992; **effort**	$\bar{r} = -.09$ $N = 1,616; k = 10$; Clarke & Robertson, 1999; **accidents**
overall wtd. ave.	$\bar{r} = .06$ $\rho_{pc} = .08$	$\bar{r} = .13$	$\bar{r} = -.12$	

(Continued)

TABLE 7.2 (Continued)

	Task/Tech	Contextual	Counterprod	Cust Svc	Sales	Creativity	Leadership	Combat
Rugged individualism	$\bar{r}$ = **.01**	$\bar{r}$ = **−.03**	$\bar{r}$ = **.02**					$\bar{r}$ = **.25**
	N = 153; k = 3; Hough, 1992	N = 198; k = 2; Hough, 1992; **effort**	N = 6,152; k = 3; Hough, 1992; unlawful **behavior**					N = 595; k = 2; Hough, 1992
		$\bar{r}$ = **.06**						
		N = 306; k = 4; Hough, 1992; **teamwork**					
overall wtd. ave.		$\bar{r}$ = **.02**						
Specific self-efficacy	ρ_{pc} = **.34**							
	N = 21,616; k = 157; Stajkovic & Luthans, 1998							
	ρ_{pc} = **.48**							
	N = 526; k = 7; Stajkovic & Luthans, 1998; **low-complexity task, field setting**							
	ρ_{pc} = **.32**							
	N = 3,411; k = 22; Stajkovic & Luthans, 1998; **medium-complexity task, field setting**							

152

$\rho_{pc} = .20$

$N = 4{,}236; k = 26;$
Stajkovic & Luthans, 1998; **high-complexity task, field setting**

$\bar{r} = .36, \rho_p = .40$

$N = 1{,}658; k = 16;$
Sadri & Robertson, 1993

$\bar{r} = .26, \rho_{pc} = .32$

$N = 2{,}745; k = 20;$
Colquitt et al., 2000

overall wtd. ave. $\bar{r} = .30$
$\rho_p = .33$
$\rho_{pc} = .33$

Social desirability $\bar{r} = .00, \rho_p = .00$ $\bar{r} = -.03, \rho_p = -.03$

$N = 3{,}230; k = 6;$ $N = 1{,}479; k = 6;$
Ones et al., 1996   Ones et al., 1996;
counterproductivity

Note. $\bar{r}$ = sample-size weighted mean observed validities; ρ_s = validities corrected for sampling error only; ρ_p = validities corrected for predictor unreliability; ρ_c = validities corrected for criterion unreliability; ρ_{pc} = validities corrected for unreliability in both predictor and criterion; ρ_{cr} = corrected for range restriction and unreliability in the criterion; ρ_t = corrected for range restriction and unreliability in both predictor and criterion; ρ_a = corrected for range restriction, unreliability in both predictor and criterion, and imperfect predictor construct measurement.
[1]We converted the reported $\bar{d}$ to $\bar{r}$; calculation of d did not include sample-size weighting.

153

TABLE 7.3   Personality Variables and Their Meta-Analyzed Validities for Predicting Work Adjustment Criteria

	Job Satisfaction	Tenure
Big Five		
Emotional Stability	$\bar{r} = .20$; $\rho_{pc} = .24$ $N = 7,658$; $k = 21$; Judge & Bono, 2001a	$\bar{r} = .01$; $\rho_t = .02$ $N = 1,495$; $k = 13$; Barrick & Mount, 1991
	$\bar{r} = .24$; $\rho_{pc} = .29$ $N = 24,527$; $k = 92$; Judge, Heller, & Mount, 2002	$\bar{r} = .02$; $\rho_t = .03$ $N = 5,775$; $k = 12$; Salgado, 2000
overall wtd. ave.	$\bar{r} = .23$; $\rho_{pc} = .28$	$\bar{r} = .02$; $\rho_t = .03$
Self-esteem	$\bar{r} = .20$; $\rho_{pc} = .26$ $N = 20,819$; $k = 56$; Judge & Bono, 2001a	
Agreeableness	$\bar{r} = .13$; $\rho_{pc} = .17$ $N = 11,856$; $k = 38$; Judge, Heller, & Mount, 2002	$\bar{r} = .06$; $\rho_t = .09$ $N = 1,838$; $k = 15$; Barrick & Mount, 1991
		$\bar{r} = -.02$; $\rho_t = -.03$ $N = 5,024$; $k = 9$; Salgado, 2000
overall wtd. ave.		$\bar{r} = .00$; $\rho_t = .00$
Extraversion	$\bar{r} = .19$; $\rho_{pc} = .25$ $N = 20,184$; $k = 75$; Judge, Heller, & Mount, 2002	$\bar{r} = -.03$; $\rho_t = -.03$ $N = 1,437$; $k = 13$; Barrick & Mount, 1991
		$\bar{r} = -.06$; $\rho_t = -.09$ $N = 6,038$; $k = 13$; Salgado, 2000
overall wtd. ave.		$\bar{r} = -.05$; $\rho_t = -.08$
Openness to Experience	$\bar{r} = .01$; $\rho_{pc} = .02$ $N = 15,196$; $k = 50$; Judge, Heller, & Mount, 2002	$\bar{r} = -.08$; $\rho_t = -.11$ $N = 1,628$; $k = 12$; Barrick & Mount, 1991
		$\bar{r} = .02$; $\rho_t = .02$ $N = 4,853$; $k = 8$; Salgado, 2000
overall wtd. ave.		$\bar{r} = -.01$; $\rho_t = -.01$
Conscientiousness	$\bar{r} = .20$; $\rho_{pc} = .26$ $N = 21,719$; $k = 79$; Judge, Heller, & Mount, 2002	$\bar{r} = .09$; $\rho_t = .12$ $N = 2,759$; $k = 19$; Barrick & Mount, 1991
		$\bar{r} = .06$; $\rho_t = .08$ $N = 6,083$; $k = 13$; Salgado, 2000
overall wtd. ave.		$\bar{r} = .07$; $\rho_t = .09$
Compound Variables		
Internal locus of control	$\bar{r} = .24$; $\rho_{pc} = .32$ $N = 18,491$; $k = 80$; Judge & Bono, 2001a	
Generalized self-efficacy	$\bar{r} = .38$; $\rho_{pc} = .45$ $N = 12,903$; $k = 12$; Judge & Bono, 2001a	

Note. $\bar{r}$ = sample-size weighted mean observed validities; ρ_s = validities corrected for sampling error only; ρ_p = validities corrected for predictor unreliability; ρ_c = validities corrected for criterion unreliability; ρ_{pc} = validities corrected for unreliability in both predictor and criterion; ρ_{cr} = corrected for range restriction and unreliability in the criterion; ρ_t = corrected for range restriction and unreliability in both predictor and criterion; ρ_a = corrected for range restriction, unreliability in both predictor and criterion, and imperfect construct measurement.

shows meta-analyzed validities of personality variables for predicting broad work-related criteria: overall job performance, overall training success, and overall educational success. Table 7.2 shows meta-analyzed validities for predicting specific work performance criteria: technical proficiency, contextual performance (e.g., effort, teamwork, interpersonal facilitation, organizational citizenship, generalized compliance, altruism), counterproductive and dysfunctional behavior (e.g., absenteeism, irresponsible behavior, unlawful behavior, violence on the job, accidents), customer service, sales effec-

tiveness, creativity, leadership, and combat effectiveness. Table 7.3 shows validities for predicting work adjustment criteria: job satisfaction and tenure. When possible, we used Hough and Ones' (2001) personality taxons to organize the entries in the tables.

We have several observations about the tables. First, validities vary within cells, some of which is due to methodological differences in the studies. For example, some of the variation within cells is due to the number and types of corrections made to observed validities. We therefore report the meta-analyzed validities according to type of correction. We also report the observed validities (sample-size-weighted mean observed validities) to show the differences in observed and theoretical values. For each meta-analytic entry we also report other information that may contribute to variation in the magnitude of the validities in a cell (e.g., sample size, number of studies, type of job examined, setting, and specific criterion construct).

Second, and perhaps more important, the validities of personality variables vary according to criterion construct. Although few meta-analyses are conducted at the facet level, a comparison of the validities of facets reveals interesting differences at that level as well—some facets from the same Big Five factor show different patterns of correlations with criterion constructs. Unfortunately, few meta-analyses have included facet-level validity analyses, perhaps because researchers more often report validities at a broader variable level. More researchers should report validities at the facet level, thus enabling meta-analysis of relationships at that level.

Third, compared to other Big Five variables, Conscientiousness correlates most highly with overall job performance, a conclusion similar to that of Barrick et al. (2001). However, depending upon the job, conscientiousness facets—achievement and dependability—are differentially important. For example, dependability correlates .18 with overall job performance in sales jobs and .03 with overall job performance in managerial jobs. A comparison of the levels of validity for achievement and dependability for managerial jobs alone reveals that achievement correlates .17 with overall job performance, whereas dependability correlates .03 with overall job performance.

Fourth, although Conscientiousness correlates most highly with overall job performance for many jobs, the validities of other personality variables are often higher for specific performance constructs. For example, Conscientiousness correlates .05 with leadership in business settings whereas Extraversion, Openness to Experience, and Emotional Stability correlate .25, .23, and .15, respectively, with leadership in business settings. Creativity is another criterion construct for which variables other than Conscientiousness are better predictors. For example, Conscientiousness correlates 2.11 with creativity, whereas Openness to Experience correlates .20 with creativity. These findings highlight the importance of understanding the criterion or performance constructs to be predicted.

Fifth, compound variables often show the highest levels of validity when the criterion is complex. As Hough and Ones (2001) point out, "when compound variables are formed by appropriately weighting and combining homogeneous vari-

ables that each correlate with an aspect of the criterion of interest, validity of the compound variable will be higher than any of the individual, homogeneous variables" (p. 247). Ones and Viswesvaran (1998c) summarized Ones's previous meta-analyses, showing that true score correlations between integrity tests and Big Five factors are .42 for Conscientiousness, .40 for Agreeableness, .33 for Emotional Stability, .12 for Openness to Experience, and −.08 for Extraversion. Ones and Viswesvaran (1996b) found that true score correlations between customer service scales and Big Five factors are .70 for Agreeableness, .58 for Emotional Stability, and .43 for Conscientiousness. Similarly, Frei and McDaniel (1998) found that the customer service scales correlate strongly with Agreeableness, Emotional Stability, and Conscientiousness. Inspection of the validities of these personality factors provided in Tables 7.1 and 7.2 indicates that individual Big Five variables correlate with relevant criteria at a lower level than the compound variables, and that test developers made wise choices regarding which variables to include and emphasize when developing these compound measures.

We also summarized validities within several of the cells in Tables 7.1–7.3, but urge caution in interpreting the results for several reasons. (Dr. Frederick Oswald computed the overall weighted averages shown in Tables 7.1–7.3.) First, few of the studies within a cell are independent. That is, some studies are included in multiple meta-analyses in a cell; other studies are included in only one. The summary values also confound job types and criterion constructs. For example, within the Contextual Performance criterion, criteria as diverse as altruism and job dedication were included. Within the Counterproductive and Dysfunctional Behavior criterion, criteria as diverse as accidents and unlawful behavior were included. As shown by the range in validities within each cell, these variables (and likely others as well) appear to moderate validity, making an overall summary less useful.

Validities of Other Personality Variables

Meta-analysis has been applied to the validities of many personality variables, but obviously not to all, and certainly not to emerging personality constructs. Meta-analyses existed for several non–Big Five variables (i.e., violence scales, drug and alcohol scales, stress tolerance scales, locus-of-control scales, Type A personality scales, rugged individualism scales, generalized self-efficacy scales, specific self-efficacy scales, and social desirability scales), and we reported the results in Tables 7.1–7.3. Several of the variables show useful correlations with criteria.

Promising *compound* variables for which no meta-analyses exist include core self-evaluation (Judge & Bono,

2001a, 2001b), proactive personality (Bateman & Crant, 1993; Crant & Bateman, 2000), sociopolitical intelligence (J. Hogan & Hogan, 1999), and emotional intelligence and social competence (Goleman, 1998; Mayer, Salovey, & Caruso, 2000; Schneider, Ackerman, & Kanfer, 1996). We will see much more of these variables.

Incremental Validity of Personality Variables When Used in Combination With Other Variables

As the foregoing discussion of compound personality variables indicates, personality variables can be used in combination with each other as well as with variables from other individual difference domains to increase overall predictive accuracy. Just as theories of performance suggest, the evidence is clear that personality variables improve the overall validity of prediction (e.g., Borman et al., 1991; F. L. Schmidt & Hunter, 1998). This is not a surprising finding given that personality variables do correlate with performance criteria but are essentially uncorrelated with cognitive ability variables (Ackerman & Heggestad, 1997; Hough, Kamp, & Ashworth, 1993).

Possible Moderator Variables

We have commented on several variables that moderate validity of personality variables—taxonomic structure, match between complexity of predictor and complexity of criterion (assuming construct relevance), stage in work experience or job tenure (maintenance vs. transition), type of job, and criterion construct relevance (a theoretical link between predictor and criterion). Two possible moderators not yet discussed are intentional distortion and item frame-of-reference.

Intentional Distortion

The most frequently expressed concern about factors moderating the validity of self-report personality measures is intentional distortion. The literature is very clear: When instructed to do so, people can distort their responses to self-report personality measures in either a positive or negative (especially a negative) direction, depending upon the instructions. However, in applied, real-life settings (i.e., nonlaboratory conditions), the majority of the evidence indicates that intentional distortion exists but is not as serious a problem as suggested in laboratory settings. As a result, construct- and criterion-related validity are not affected or are less affected in real-life, applied settings than in simulated, laboratory settings, where construct and criterion-related validity are seriously

affected. Meta-analyses of directed-faking studies using within-subjects designs indicates that compared to their responses in the honest condition, people change their substantive (e.g., Emotional Stability, Extraversion) personality scale scores an average of 0.72 standard deviations in the positive direction when instructed to fake good (Viswesvaran & Ones, 1999). For between-subjects designs, compared to scores in the honest condition, scores were 0.60 standard deviations higher when instructed to fake good. When instructed to fake bad, meta-analyses of directed-faking studies using within-subjects designs indicates that compared to their responses in the honest condition, people change their substantive personality scale scores an average of 1.47 standard deviations in the negative direction, although in the one study ($N = 23$) that included a measure of Extraversion, scores on that scale actually increased (Viswesvaran & Ones, 1999). For between-subjects designs, scores were 1.67 standard deviations lower in the fake-bad conditions. The Viswesvaran and Ones (1999) meta-analysis also indicates that social desirability scales detect such distortion. In fake-good studies with a within-subjects design, scores on the social desirability scales were 2.26 standard deviations higher in the fake-good conditions. In fake-bad studies with a within-subjects design, scores on the social desirability scales were 3.66 standard deviations lower in the fake-bad conditions.

In real-life applicant settings, distortion is not as severe, especially when warnings about detection of and consequences for distortion are included in the administration directions to applicants. Hough and Ones (2001) examined the effect sizes of differences between applicant and incumbent personality scale scores, concluding that distortion in actual applicant settings is not as great as that produced in directed-faking studies. In one of the largest studies (using 40,500 applicants and 1,700 incumbents), Hough (1998a) found some, but not serious, distortion. Directions to applicants in her studies had included warnings about detection and consequences for distortion. A meta-analysis of the amount of distortion with and without warnings indicates that warnings reduce distortion about 0.23 standard deviations (Dwight & Donovan, 1998).

A comparison of the effects of intentional distortion on validity shows that setting (i.e., laboratory settings vs. real-life, applied settings) moderates the effect of intentional distortion on validity. Hough (1998a) examined criterion-related validities of personality scales separately for studies conducted in laboratory settings versus real-life, applied settings. She found little, if any, change in criterion-related validity in real-life, applied settings but dramatic change (lower criterion-related validity) in laboratory settings. She concluded that setting moderates criterion-related validity, and that criterion-related validity remains intact in real-life applicant settings. A similar conclusion is appropriate for the effects of intentional distortion on construct validity of personality scales. Construct validity is negatively affected in directed-faking studies (e.g., Ellingson, Sackett, & Hough, 1999), but not nearly as seriously in real-life applicant settings (e.g., Collins & Gleaves, 1998; Ellingson, Smith, & Sackett, 2001; Ones & Viswesvaran, 1998a).

These data, plus evidence from meta-analyses of the predictive criterion-related validities from studies involving applicants versus incumbents, indicate that (a) validities are comparable for the two groups (e.g., Ones, Viswesvaran, & Schmidt, 1993) and (b) intentional distortion is a mythical moderator variable in real-life business settings. In addition, although social desirability is related to emotional stability and conscientiousness (Furnham, 1986; Ones, Viswesvaran, & Reiss, 1996), meta-analysis establishes that social desirability does not function as a predictor, practically useful suppressor, or mediator of criterion-related validity of personality scales (Ones et al., 1996).

Nonetheless, concern persists. Some (e.g., Holden & Hibbs, 1995; Snell, Sydell, & Lueke, 1999; Zickar, 2001; Zickar & Drasgow, 1996) argue that traditional measures of intentional distortion are inadequate or inappropriate, and some (e.g., Rosse, Stecher, Levin, & Miller, 1998; Zickar, Rosse, Levin, & Hulin, 1996) argue that the validity coefficient is an inappropriate index for examining the effects of distortion on hiring decisions. For a thorough review of these views, we refer interested readers to Hough and Ones (2001).

Research about the effects of coaching on personality scale scores and their validity is likely to advance our understanding of this area. Alliger, Lilienfeld, and Mitchell (1996) are among the few who have examined this for personality variables. They have found that *obvious items* (items for which the personality characteristic being measured is obvious) can be distorted without detection by traditional measures of social desirability; *subtle items,* however, are resistant to coaching and distortion.

Some researchers are developing new strategies to reduce intentional distortion. Bernal, Snell, Svyantek, and Haworth (1999), for example, developed a hybrid scaling technique that uses a *decoy construct* to mislead test takers into thinking it is the construct of interest to the test administrators, thereby making it more difficult for people to distort their responses in the desired way. James (1998) has also developed a new approach, called *conditional reasoning,* to measure personality constructs that produces scales that are resistant to intentional distortion. These approaches are in their infancy and will undoubtedly receive further research attention.

Frame of Reference Provided in the Item

Items in personality inventories differ in their *frames of reference,* or amount of context that is provided. Some measures consist simply of adjectives, whereas others consist of items that are complete sentences. Items that are complete sentences can be contextualized such that respondents describe themselves in a work setting, whereas other items may ask respondents to describe themselves in general. Schmit, Ryan, Stierwalt, and Powell (1995) compared the criterion-related validities obtained using general personality items with validities obtained using items asking about the person in contextualized work-related settings. The more general items produced lower validity coefficients than the contextualized items. Similarly, an adjective form of the Big Five resulted in lower criterion-related validities than were obtained with a form consisting of complete sentences (Cellar, Miller, Doverspike, & Klawsky, 1996). Additional research suggests that error variances are slightly lower for contextualized (at-work) items compared to general or noncontextualized items (Robie, Schmit, Ryan, & Zickar, 2000). Taken together, these different lines of evidence suggest that the frame of reference or the context provided in items may increase the criterion-related validities of personality variables for work-related criteria.

MEASUREMENT METHODS AND ISSUES

Although stage theories such as Kohlberg's (1969) theory of moral development are not out of fashion, we focus on measurement issues involved in operationalizing *trait* concepts. We discuss them in terms of self-report and self-description or self-evaluation, others' reports or descriptions of the target person, objective measures, and interviews. We also describe and evaluate different assessment modes and discuss cross-cultural factors and their effects on the quality of personality measurement.

Self-Report, Self-Description, and Self-Evaluation Measures

Most personality measures that I/O psychologists use are a combination of self-report and self-description or self-evaluation—for example, the CPI (Gough, 1996), the Hogan Personality Inventory (HPI; R. T. Hogan & Hogan, 1992), and the NEO-PI-R (Costa & McCrae, 1992). This type of measure is criticized as being susceptible to intentional distortion. However, one form of self-report, *biodata,* is at least potentially verifiable.

Biodata Measures

Biographical information, or biodata, has a long and illustrious history in psychology. (Readers who want an in-depth discussion of biodata are referred to Mumford & Stokes, 1992; Stokes, Mumford, & Owens, 1994.) It is a method of measuring a variety of constructs including cognitive ability, physical ability, and personality. It is regarded as one of the best predictors of behavior (F. L. Schmidt & Hunter, 1998). Only recently, however, has research with biodata been construct oriented. Mumford and Stokes (1992) developed item-generation procedures that enable test developers to target personality or other constructs for measurement using biographical information. Evaluations of biodata scales generated using Mumford and Stokes's approach indicate such scales have construct validity (Mumford, Costanza, Connelly, & Johnson, 1996), although items that ask the respondent to recall events that deal with personal relationships, trauma, race, or religion have the potential to be viewed as invasive (Mael, Connerly, & Morath, 1996).

Others' Reports, Descriptions, and Observations

Hogan (1991) argues that one of the purposes of self-report personality measures is to obtain a description of the individual's *reputation*—how the individual is perceived and evaluated by others. Similarly, Gough (1987) suggests that an important function of self-report personality inventories is to characterize people according to how others characterize them. Others' descriptions of the target person are thus important, and they have been investigated both as a way of validating self-assessment (Funder & West, 1993) and for the purpose of understanding lay theories and lay language when describing personality (Mervielde, Buyst, & de Fruyt, 1995).

Over the past 20 years a number of replicated findings have appeared. Correlations between self and others' ratings typically range between .30 and .60, with the correlation increasing with acquaintanceship. Funder, Kolar, and Blackman (1995) tested three hypotheses to explain these findings, concluding that interjudge agreement stems mainly from mutual accuracy. Some studies have examined how well participants can estimate their own scores on a test. In one of a long series of studies, Furnham (1997) demonstrated that participants can predict reasonably well ($r = .50$) their Extraversion, Neuroticism, and Conscientiousness scores but that correlations drop with dimensions such as Openness and Agreeableness. When individuals' self-description personality test scores are compared with assessment-center judges' ratings of the target individual, scores are consistently and logically correlated with assessment-center ratings of variables used by business

people (e.g., drive to achieve, intuition, resilience, and interpersonal sensitivity; Furnham, Crump, & Whelan, 1997). Studies of others' ratings and descriptions also suggest that the Big Five dimensions of personality are important dimensions that people use to structure their perceptions of others (Digman & Shmelyou, 1996; Mervielde & de Fruyt, 2000). Other studies have examined the difference in criterion-related validity of self-ratings versus others' ratings for predicting job performance, finding that others' ratings tend to have higher validity (Mount, Barrick, & Strauss, 1994; Nilsen, 1995).

Objective Measures

Cattell (1957) defined an *objective personality test* as any test that showed reasonable variability, could be objectively scored, and whose purpose is indecipherable to the subject. An objective personality measure does not rely on self-report (either by interview or questionnaire). Instead, it uses some objective behavior (such as reaction time) to measure personality.

Cattell and Warburton (1967) compiled an impressive compendium of more than 800 objective personality and motivation tests for use in experimental research. Although most of the interest in objective personality tests has been in the applied, clinical literature (e.g., Cimbolic, Wise, Rossetti, & Safer, 1999; L. Schmidt & Schwenkmezger, 1994), we expect greater I/O interest in the future primarily because of concern about the effects of intentional distortion. Elliot, Lawty-Jones, and Jackson (1996), for example, demonstrated that an objective measure (time taken to trace a circle) of a personality construct was less susceptible to intentional distortion than a self-report measure of the same construct.

Conditional Reasoning Measures

Similarly, intentional distortion is not a problem in conditional reasoning measures. *Conditional reasoning measures* are tests in which the individual responds to cognitive ability–like questions for which there are no correct answers, although, depending upon one's standing on the characteristic being measured, there *appear* to be correct answers (cf. James, 1998; James & Mazerolle, in press). The primary assumptions are that people rely on reasoning processes, which are supposedly logical, to justify their behavior and choices and that people who are high on a personality construct tend to use different justifications for their behavior than people who are low on the construct. Scale development requires identifying the main justifications that people high and low on the construct use to justify their behavior. The test appears to be a reading comprehension test with right and wrong answers. People who are high on the construct choose the supposed right answer—the answer that justifies their preferred behavior. People who are low on the construct choose a different right answer—the one that justifies *their* preferred behavior. These measures are still in their infancy, and considerable work needs to be done to demonstrate construct validity of the measures. They do, however, appear promising.

Genetic Testing

With the mounting evidence of the genetic and biological bases of personality (e.g., Bouchard, 1997; Plomin & Crabbe, 2000; Saudino, 1997; Zuckerman, 1995), we expect greater interest in and use of genetic testing in the future. As Matthews and Deary (1998) note: "The architecture of the inheritance of personality and biochemical mediators of behavioural consistency will be revealed, not by traditional behaviour genetics, but by the leads given by molecular genetic studies of personality" (p. 121). Mouth swabs (DNA testing) may very well replace self-report personality questionnaires in the next decade, at least in countries where it is not prohibited by legislation.

Interview

The interview is the most frequently used method of assessing applicants for jobs. Meta-analyses of the criterion-related validity of interviews indicate they do correlate with job performance, with validities equal to .29 for *psychological interviews* (interviews conducted by psychologists who are assessing personal traits such as Conscientiousness), .39 for *job-related interviews* (interviews that assess past behavior and job-related information but that are not primarily behavioral or situational interviews), and .50 for *situational interviews* (interviews that ask the interviewees to describe what they would do in a hypothetical situation) (McDaniel, Whetzel, Schmidt, & Maurer, 1994). Depending upon the amount of structure in the questions asked of the interviewees and the structure or guidelines provided to interviewers on how to evaluate the information obtained, meta-analysis indicates that mean validities range from .20 for the least degree of structure to .57 for the greatest degree of structure (Huffcutt & Arthur, 1994). Although these meta-analyses provide useful information about the validity of interviews, they provide no information about the constructs measured or about their construct validity (Hough, 2001). Research aimed at understanding the validity of the interview for measuring personality variables suggests the interview is not a good measure of the Big Five factors (Barrick, Patton, & Haugland,

2000). For the two Big Five factors that correlate with overall job performance for most jobs, Conscientiousness and Emotional Stability, interviewer ratings correlated only .16 (not significant) and .17 (n.s.), respectively, with self-ratings of the same variables. Type of interview—job-relevant, situational, and behavioral—did not moderate the correlations. Thus, although the interview is often thought to measure personality characteristics, the limited evidence that exists suggests otherwise.

Mode of Assessment

There are many ways in which personality traits can be assessed. By far the most popular method is still the paper-and-pencil test, on which participants read questions (often statements about behavior) and respond by marking an answer. Technological developments have enabled test publishers to offer computer-administered versions of their established tests, and computer-administered tests are now quite common.

Measurement Equivalence

Much research has been undertaken on the structure of variables measured and the psychometric properties of variables administered via paper and pencil versus computer. Most research, including meta-analyses, has found highly equivalent results in structure, means, standard deviations, and correlations as well as near-perfect rank orderings for the two modes of administration (Bartram & Baylis, 1984; Finger & Ones, 1999; King & Miles, 1995; Richman, Kiesler, Weisband, & Drasgow, 1999). Moderator-variables analyses indicate that when paper-and-pencil tests are converted to computerized tests, administration should allow respondents to backtrack and change their answers to ensure greater equivalence of measurement (Richman et al., 1999). Anonymity also appears to moderate the equivalence of test scores between the two modes of testing, with greater distortion occurring in the computerized version when anonymity is lacking (Richman et al., 1999). Finally, supervision appears to be an important component in administering a computerized test. Structural models of personality fit the data from supervised computerized personality tests much better than they fit the data from the same test when unsupervised (Oswald, Carr, & Schmidt, 2001).

Response Latency

Only a limited number of studies have examined the relationship between response latency and personality variables.

However, extensive research based on the arousal hypothesis shows that extraverts trade speed for accuracy (Eysenck, 1967). In addition, the obsessive component of neurosis is associated with taking longer to respond to most items, especially those concerned with abnormal behavior. Furnham, Forde, and Cotter (1998) recorded the time taken by job applicants to complete the Eysenck Personality Profiler (EPP). They found that (a) a primary factor from Neuroticism correlated with time taken—the more obsessive took more time; (b) two primary factors from Extraversion were correlated with time taken—inhibited and submissive people took longer; (c) five of the seven primary factors from Psychoticism correlated negatively with time taken—careful, controlled, responsible, practical, and unadventurous subjects took longer to complete the questionnaire; and (d) neurotic individuals who were more obsessive and anxious tended to ponder questions longer before answering. Using the 60-item Eysenck Personality Questionnaire–Revised (EPQ-R), Merten and Ruch (1996) and Merten and Siebert (1997) found a slight trend for high P(sychoticism), high E(xtraverion), and low L(ie) scorers to respond more quickly to personality items, although in general the two studies did not replicate very well, perhaps because, as they point out, the sample sizes were small.

These results suggest that response latency may be one useful unobtrusive measure of personality; item-by-item analysis (as carried out by Merten & Siebert, 1997) may yield even more insights into the types of questions that trouble some personality types. The increasing use of computer-administered tests, during which response latencies can be recorded, means that research into unobtrusive measures of response style will no doubt increase.

Measures of response latency have also been developed and touted as potentially superior to traditional measures of intentional distortion (e.g., Holden & Hibbs, 1995). However, as Hough and Ones (2001) point out, when only cross-validated results are examined, measures of response latency and traditional social desirability scales both correctly identify approximately the same number of respondents in honest and fake conditions. Nevertheless, a combination of response latency and traditional measures of distortion has yielded more accurate classification than either type used alone (Dwight & Alliger, 1997). We urge caution in using measures of response latency to measure intentional distortion because (a) response time is correlated with familiarity with the job applied for (Vasilpoulos, Reilly, & Leaman, 2000); (b) as discussed previously, response latency is correlated with substantive personality variables such as extraversion, neuroticism, and psychoticism; and (c) speed of response to

personality items may change with coaching and practice (Hough & Ones, 2001).

Virtual Reality

In addition to being able to measure response variables, computers are more capable of simulating reality than are other technologies. An important advantage of virtual-reality technology is the ability to simulate both hazardous and rare environments and tasks. According to Aguinis, Henle, and Beatty (2001), virtual-reality technology provides other advantages as well. For example, it allows for higher levels of standardization and structure and thus greater measurement precision and greater predictive validity than do other simulation-based techniques, such as role-playing.

Cross-Cultural Issues

Three distinct lines of research characterize the study of cross-cultural differences in personality. One line of research examines the taxonomic structure of personality within and across cultures and languages. A second line of research focuses on the behavioral correlates of personality variables in different cultures. A third line of research focuses on the development of cross-cultural, construct-equivalent measures of personality variables. Although cross-cultural psychologists have a special interest in demonstrating cross-cultural variability in behavior, personality psychologists seem eager to demonstrate structural and functional *in*variance across cultures.

The first group of studies—those that examine taxonomic structures across cultures and languages—can be further divided into two streams of research. One uses responses to adjectives (or dictionaries of words) to examine personality structure in different cultures and languages. The other uses responses to statements on questionnaires. The two strategies yield different results.

Eysenck and Eysenck (1985) summarized research that used questionnaires consisting of statements to investigate the taxonomic structure of personality in different cultures. They reviewed studies of adults in 24 countries and children in 10, and concluded that "essentially the same dimensions of personality emerge from factor analytic studies of identical questionnaires in a large number of different countries, embracing not only European cultural groups but also many quite different types of nations. This of course was to be expected in view of the strong genetic components underlying those major dimensions of personality" (p. 108). More recently, McCrae, Costa, del Pilar, Rolland, and Parker (1998) used factor analytic evidence for Filipino and French translations of the Big Five NEO-PI to conclude that the five-factor model is a biologically based human universal, noting other studies that have replicated the structure of the NEO-PI-R as translated into Spanish, Portuguese, Italian, Dutch, German, Croatian, Russian, Hebrew, Japanese, Korean, and Chinese. Such conclusions have not been unchallenged. Bijnen, van der Net, and Poortinga (1986), for example, argued that statistical tests used to judge the similarity of factor structures are unreliable; even with a randomly generated data set, they found high levels of similarity between factor structures. Moreover, although structure may be universal, there may be small but consistent cross-cultural differences in the *level* of traits (i.e., such that individuals in one country are more extraverted than those in another) or in *how* people complete personality questionnaires (Kallasmao, Allik, Realo, & McCrae, 2000).

The stream of research that uses adjectives (the *lexical* or *natural-language approach*) was stimulated by the work of Digman and Takemoto-Chock (1981). This approach has often found poor cross-cultural replications (e.g., Di Blas & Forzi, 1999; De Raad, Perugini & Szirmak, 1997). For example, Neuroticism did not emerge in Italian; Openness did not emerge in Hebrew (although the other four dimensions did); and in Spain, a seven-dimensional solution seemed necessary to describe personality parsimoniously. Although these researchers have used somewhat different methods, De Raad (1998) concluded:

> A study of the various studies participating in the crusade for cross-lingual personality-descriptive universals makes it clear that researchers are unlikely to find one and only one canonical, cross-culturally valid trait structure.... Even under relatively optimal conditions, with congruencies computed after target rotation, confirmation of Factor V [Openness] is not found in several languages. (p. 122)

A second approach to studying cross-cultural differences in personality focuses on the behavioral correlates of personality variables in different cultures and languages. Furnham and Stringfield (1993), for example, compared personality (MBTI) and management practice scores in two cultural groups, finding interesting and predictable differences. Whereas Extraversion-Introversion was an important correlate of managerial appraisal in a Chinese sample, Thinking-Feeling (from the MBTI) was more relevant in a European sample. Cross-cultural replications nearly always yield both similarities and differences, but it remains unclear whether the latter are due primarily to unique substantive variance

or to errors in measurement (e.g., small samples, poor translation, cultural differences in response set) because the two are often confounded.

A third approach involves development of measures that are cross-culturally equivalent. Schmit, Kihm, and Robie (2000), for example, involved psychologists from many different cultures in all phases of development and validation of the Global Personality Inventory (GPI). They utilized psychologists from different cultures to help define the constructs and write items, thereby enhancing the probability of construct equivalence after translation.

Several issues arise when transporting personality measures across languages and cultures. However, the globalization of so many features of life, increasing educational levels, and the Internet may reduce cultural and linguistic variance, making the use of personality questionnaires derived in the West increasingly more applicable in other countries of the world.

LEGAL ISSUES IN THE UNITED STATES

The Civil Rights Acts (CRA) of 1964 and 1991, the Americans With Disabilities Act (ADA) of 1990, and the Age Discrimination in Employment Act (ADEA) of 1967 (amended 1978) have had significant effect on the use of tests in industry in the United States. Nonetheless, as Sharf and Jones (2000) point out, "risks from tort liability far exceed the risks posed by federal statutory civil rights violations in almost every case" (p. 274).

Age and Civil Rights Acts

The U.S. CRAs of 1964 and 1991 make it illegal to discriminate against people on the basis of their race, religion, sex, or national origin, and the ADEA makes it illegal to discriminate against people on the basis of their age. In personnel selection, discrimination against these protected groups is examined in terms of adverse impact. *Adverse impact* is calculated as the percentage of applicants of one group—for example, Blacks—who are hired compared to the percentage of White applicants who are hired. Mean score differences between the two groups is thus an important determinant of adverse impact.

Just as the concept of the Big Five has provided an organizing strategy for summarizing validities of personality measures, it also provides a strategy for summarizing mean score differences between protected groups. Hough, Oswald, and Ployhart (2001) summarized mean score differences of Blacks and Whites, Hispanics and Whites, East Asians and Whites, American Indians and Whites, women and men, and older and younger adults on a variety of individual difference variables, including personality constructs. They found minimal differences between age groups and ethnic or cultural groups at the Big Five factor level but larger differences between men and women on Agreeableness and at the facet level of Conscientiousness, and very large differences between men and women on Rugged Individualism (masculinity and femininity). Given the small differences in personality scores between ethnic or cultural groups and age groups and the personality factors that constitute integrity tests (i.e., Conscientiousness, Emotional Stability, and Agreeableness), not surprisingly, Ones and Viswesvaran (1998b) found minimal differences between age and ethnic or cultural groups on integrity tests, and small differences between men and women, with women scoring somewhat (e.g., 0.16 standard deviations) higher than men. Hough, Oswald, and Ployhart (2001) also compared groups on social desirability scores, finding that Hispanics, on average, score somewhat over half a standard deviation higher than Whites. Incorporating appropriate personality measures in personnel prediction equations can reduce adverse impact and, as described earlier, increase validity.

Americans With Disabilities Act

The ADA prohibits disability-related inquiries of applicants, and it prohibits a medical examination before a conditional job offer. The Equal Employment Opportunity Commission (EEOC) issued its enforcement guidelines for ADA in 1995. Their guidelines that are applicable to personality testing in the workplace appear in Hough (1998b). An important conclusion is that, although some personality inventories (such as the MMPI) are considered medical exams because they were designed to determine an applicant's mental health, most personality inventories that are used in the workplace are not, and thus can be used prior to a conditional job offer. Nonetheless, employers should examine the personality inventories they use to ensure that the way they are using them is not prohibited under ADA. Moreover, current legislative discussions about genetic testing with its potential for identifying diseases and abnormalities may result in legislation that limits the ability of U.S. employers to use genetic testing to measure personality characteristics.

SUMMARY AND CONCLUSIONS

Personality variables enhance our theories and understanding of workplace behavior and performance. Indeed, studies suggest that when personality variables are included, they can more than double the variance accounted for in supervisory ratings of overall job performance. Taxonomies of personality variables have been critically important in enabling researchers to summarize and examine the importance of personality variables for predicting behavior. Our summary of the meta-analyses of criterion-related validities of personality variables indicate that personality variables are useful for predicting overall job performance; and, for example, when customer service, interpersonal effectiveness, and integrity are important to the job, personality variables become even more useful for predicting behavior and performance. We also know that predictive accuracy of personality variables increases when the predictor and criterion are matched in terms of their complexity and theoretical relevance. For self-report personality inventories, intentional distortion does not appear to moderate criterion-related validity in real-life applicant settings. Intentional distortion does, however, moderate validity, decreasing it dramatically in experimental, laboratory, or simulated applicant settings. Other moderator variables include taxonomic structure of the personality variables, type of job, other- versus self-report, and item frame-of-reference (more work context appears better). Mode of measurement (i.e., paper-and-pencil versus computerized) does not appear to moderate validity, but more research is needed as computer administration increases in its user-friendliness and in its possibilities for innovative measurement.

Globalization of the world's economies and of the workplace increases our interest in and concern about cross-cultural testing. Nonetheless, globalization also reduces the differences among cultures, increasing the transportability of many of our personality measures. Indeed, developing countries may be as eager to import Western ideas and measures of personality as we are to export them.

In the years ahead, personality testing in work settings will be even more prevalent than today. It is likely to be more objective and more tailored to the situation. These are exciting times for applied personality researchers.

REFERENCES

Ackerman, P. L., & Heggestad, E. D. (1997). Intelligence, personality, and interests: Evidence for overlapping traits. *Psychological Bulletin, 121,* 219–245.

Aguinis, H., Henle, C. A., & Beaty, J. C., Jr. (2001). Virtual reality technology: A new tool for personnel selection. *International Journal of Selection and Assessment, 9,* 70–83.

Alliger, G. M., Lilienfeld, S. O., & Mitchell, K. E. (1996). The susceptibility of overt and covert integrity tests to coaching and faking. *Psychological Science, 7,* 32–39.

Allport, G. W., & Odbert, H. S. (1936). Trait-names: A psycho-lexical study. *Psychological Monographs, 47*(No. 211).

Almagor, M., Tellegen, A., & Waller, N. G. (1995). The Big Seven model: A cross-cultural replication and further exploration of the basic dimensions of natural language trait descriptors. *Journal of Personality and Social Psychology, 69,* 300–307.

Anderson, G., & Viswesvaran, C. (1998). *An update of the validity of personality scales in personnel selection: A meta-analysis of studies published between 1992–1997.* Paper presented at the 13th Annual Conference of the Society for Industrial and Organizational Psychology, Dallas, TX.

Arthur, J., Jr., Barrett, G. V., & Alexander, R. A. (1991). Prediction of vehicular accident involvement: A meta-analysis. *Human Performance, 4,* 89–105.

Ashton, M. C., Jackson, D. N., Helmes, E., & Paunonen, S. V. (1998). Joint factor analysis of the Personality Research Form and the Jackson Personality Inventory: Comparisons with the Big Bive. *Journal of Research in Personality, 32,* 243–250.

Ashton, M. C., Jackson, D. N., Paunonen, S. V., Helmes, E., & Rothstein, M. G. (1995). The criterion validity of broad factor scales versus specific trait scales. *Journal of Research in Personality, 29,* 432–442.

Ashton, M. C., Lee, K., & Son, C. (2000). Honesty as the sixth factor of personality: Correlations with Machiavellianism, primary psychopathy, and social adroitness. *European Journal of Personality, 14,* 359–368.

Barrick, M. R., & Mount, M. K. (1991). The Big Five personality dimensions and job performance: A meta-analysis. *Personnel Psychology, 44,* 1–26.

Barrick, M. R., Mount, M. K., & Judge, T. A. (2001). Personality and performance at the beginning of the new millennium: What do we know and where do we go next? *International Journal of Selection and Assessment, 9,* 9–30.

Barrick, M. R., Patton, G. K., & Haugland, S. N. (2000). Accuracy of interviewer judgments of job applicant personality traits. *Personnel Psychology, 53,* 925–951.

Barrick, M. R., Stewart, G. L., & Piotrowski, M. (2002). Personality and job performance: Test of the mediating effects of motivation among sales representatives. *Journal of Applied Psychology, 87,* 43–51.

Bartram, D., & Baylis, R. (1984). Automated testing: Past, present and future. *Journal of Occupational Psychology, 57,* 221–237.

Bateman, T. S., & Crant, J. M. (1993). The proactive component of organizational behavior: A measure and correlates. *Journal of Organizational Behavior, 14,* 103–118.

Benet, V., & Waller, N. G. (1995). The Big Seven factor model of personality description: Evidence for its cross-cultural generality in a Spanish sample. *Journal of Personality and Social Psychology, 69,* 701–718.

Bernal, D. S., Snell, A. F., Svyantek, D. J., & Haworth, C. L. (1999, April). *The hybrid scaling technique: Faking out the fakers with a new method of scale construction.* Symposium conducted at the 14th Annual Conference of the Society for Industrial and Organizational Psychology, Atlanta, GA.

Bijnen, E. J., van der Net, T. Z., & Poortinga, Y. H. (1986). On cross-cultural comparative studies with the Eysenck Personality Questionnaire. *Journal of Cross-Cultural Psychology, 17,* 3–16.

Block, J. (1995). A contrarian view of the five-factor approach to personality description. *Psychological Bulletin, 117,* 187–215.

Borman, W. C., Penner, L. A., Allen, T. D., & Motowidlo, S. J. (2001). Personality predictors of citizenship performance. *International Journal of Selection and Assessment, 9,* 52–69.

Borman, W. C., White, L. A., Pulakos, E. D., & Oppler, S. H. (1991). Models of supervisory job performance ratings. *Journal of Applied Psychology, 76,* 863–872.

Bouchard, T. J., Jr. (1997). Genetic influence on mental abilities, personality, vocational interests and work attitudes. In C. L. Cooper & I. T. Robertson (Eds.), *International review of industrial and organizational psychology* (pp. 373–394). Chichester, England: Wiley.

Campbell, J. P., & Pritchard, R. D. (1976). Motivation theory in industrial and organizational psychology. In M. D. Dunnette (Ed.), *Handbook of industrial and organizational psychology* (1st ed., pp. 63–130). Chicago: Rand McNally.

Cattell, R. (1957). *Personality, motivation, structure and measurement.* Yonkers, NY: World Book Company.

Cattell, R., & Warburton, F. (1967). *Objective personality and motivation tests.* Champaign: University of Illinois Press.

Cellar, D. F., Miller, M. L., Doverspike, D. D., & Klawsky, J. D. (1996). Comparison of factor structures and criterion-related validity coefficients for two measures of personality based on the five factor model. *Journal of Applied Psychology, 81,* 694–704.

Church, A. T., & Burke, P. J. (1994). Exploratory and confirmatory tests of the Big Five and Tellegen's three- and four-dimensional models of personality structure. *Journal of Personality and Social Psychology, 66,* 93–114.

Cimbolic, P., Wise, R., Rossetti, S., & Safer, M. (1999). Development of a combined objective ephebophila scale. *Sexual Addiction and Compulsivity, 6,* 253–266.

Clarke, S., & Robertson, I. (1999). *Selecting for safety: Personality and accident involvement.* Unpublished manuscript, Manchester School of Management, UMIST, Manchester, UK.

Collins, J. M., & Gleaves, D. H. (1998). Race, job applicants, and the five-factor model of personality: Implications for black psychology, industrial/organizational psychology, and the five-factor theory. *Journal of Applied Psychology, 83,* 531–544.

Colquitt, J. A., LePine, J. A., & Noe, R. A. (2000). Toward an integrative theory of training motivation: A meta-analytic path analysis of 20 years of research. *Journal of Applied Psychology, 85,* 678–707.

Costa, P. T., Jr., & McCrae, R. R. (1988). From catalogue to classification: Murray's needs and the Five-Factor Model. *Journal of Personality and Social Psychology, 55,* 258–265.

Costa, P. T., Jr., & McCrae, R. R. (1992). *Revised NEO Personality Inventory (NEO-PI-R) and NEO Five-Factor Inventory (NEO-FFI) professional manual*. Odessa, FL: Psychological Assessment Resources.

Costa, P. T., Jr., & McCrae, R. R. (1995a). Domains and facets: Hierarchical personality assessment using the Revised NEO Personality Inventory. *Journal of Personality Assessment, 64,* 21–50.

Costa, P. T., Jr., & McCrae, R. R. (1995b). Primary traits of Eysenck's P-E-N-system: Three-and five-factor solutions. *Journal of Personality and Social Psychology, 69,* 308–317.

Costa, P., McCrae, R., & Holland, J. (1984). Personality and vocational interests in an adult sample. *Journal of Applied Psychology, 60,* 390–400.

Costa, P. T., Jr., Zonderman, A. B., Williams, R. B., & McCrae, R. R. (1985). Content and comprehensiveness in the MMPI: An item factor analysis in a normal adult sample. *Journal of Personality and Social Psychology, 48,* 925–933.

Crant, J. M., & Bateman, T. S. (2000). Charismatic leadership viewed from above: The impact of proactive personality. *Journal of Organizational Behavior, 21,* 63–75.

Dawis, R. V., & Lofquist, L. H. (1984). *A psychological theory of work adjustment: An individual difference model and its applications*. Minneapolis: University of Minnesota.

De Fruyt, F., & Mervielde, I. (1997). The five-factor model of personality and Holland's RIASEC interest types. *Personality and Individual Differences, 23,* 87–103.

De Fruyt, F., & Mervielde, I. (1999). RIASEC types and Big Five traits as predictors of employment status and nature of employment. *Personnel Psychology, 52,* 701–727.

De Raad, B. (1998). Five big, big five issues: Rationale, content, structure, status and cross-cultural assessment. *European Psychologist, 3,* 113–124.

De Raad, B., & Hoskens, M. (1990). Personality-descriptive nouns. *European Journal of Personality, 4,* 131–146.

De Raad, B., Perugini, M., & Szirmak, Z. (1997). In pursuit of a cross-lingual reference structure of personality traits: Comparisons among five languages. *European Journal of Personality, 11,* 167–185.

Detwiler, F. R. J., & Ramanaiah, N. V. (1996). Structure of the Jackson Personality Inventory from the perspective of the five-factor model. *Psychological Reports, 65,* 947–950.

Di Blas, L., & Forzi, M. (1999). Refining a descriptive structure of personality attributes in the Italian language. *Journal of Personality and Social Psychology, 76,* 451–481.

Digman, J. M. (1990). Personality structure: Emergence of the five-factor model. In M. R. Rosenzweig & L. W. Porter (Eds.), *Annual review of psychology* (Vol. 41, pp. 417–440). Palo Alto, CA: Annual Reviews.

Digman, J. M., & Inouye, J. (1986). Further specification of the five robust factors of personality. *Journal of Personality and Social Psychology, 50,* 116–123.

Digman, J., & Shmelyou, A. (1996). The structure of temperament and personality in Russian children. *Journal of Personality and Social Psychology, 50,* 116–123.

Digman, J. M., & Takemoto-Chock, M. K. (1981). Factors in the natural language of personality: Re-analysis and comparison of six major studies. *Multivariate Behavioral Research, 16,* 149–170.

Dwight, S. A., & Alliger, G. M. (1997). *Using response latencies to identify overt integrity test dissimulators*. Paper presented at the 12th Annual Meeting of the Society for Industrial and Organizational Psychology, St. Louis, MO.

Dwight, S. A., & Donovan, J. J. (1998). *Warning: Proceed with caution when warning applicants not to dissimulate (revised)*. Paper presented at the 13th Annual Meeting of the Society for Industrial and Organizational Psychology, Dallas, TX.

Ellingson, J. E., Sackett, P. R., & Hough, L. M. (1999). Social desirability correction in personality measurement: Issues of applicant comparison and construct validity. *Journal of Applied Psychology, 84,* 155–166.

Ellingson, J. E., Smith, D. B., & Sackett, P. R. (2001). Investigating the influence of social desirability on personality factor structure. *Journal of Applied Psychology, 86,* 122–133.

Elliot, S., Lawty-Jones, M., & Jackson, C. (1996). Effect of dissimulation on self-report and objective measures of personality. *Personality and Individual Differences, 21,* 335–343.

Eysenck, H. (1967). *The biological bases of personality*. Springfield, IL: Thomas.

Eysenck, H. J. (1991). Dimensions of personality: 16, 5, or 3? Criteria for a taxonomic paradigm. *Personality and Individual Differences, 12,* 773–790.

Eysenck, H. J. (1992). Four ways five factors are *not* basic. *Personality and Individual Differences, 13,* 667–673.

Eysenck, H., & Eysenck, M. (1985). *Personality and individual differences*. New York: Plenum.

Feist, G. J. (1998). A meta-analysis of personality in scientific and artistic creativity. *Personality and Social Psychology Review, 2,* 290–309.

Finger, M. S., & Ones, D. S. (1999). Psychometric equivalence of the computer and booklet forms of the MMPI: A meta-analysis. *Psychological Assessment, 11,* 58–66.

Fiske, D. W. (1949). Consistency of the factorial structures of personality ratings from different sources. *Journal of Abnormal and Social Psychology, 44,* 329–344.

Frei, R. L., & McDaniel, M. A. (1998). Validity of customer service measures in personnel selection: A review of criterion and construct evidence. *Human Performance, 11,* 1–27.

Funder, D., Kolar, D., & Blackman, M. (1995). Agreement among judges of personality: Interpersonal relations, similarity, and acquaintanceship. *Journal of Personality Assessment, 69,* 229–243.

Funder, D., & West, S. (1993). Consensus, self-other agreement and accuracy in personality judgment: An introduction. *Journal of Personality, 61,* 457–496.

Furnham, A. (1986). Response bias, social desirability and dissimu- lation. *Personality and Individual Differences, 7,* 385–400.

Furnham, A. (1996a). The big five vs. the big four: The relationship between the *Myers-Briggs Type Indicator* (MBTI) and the *NEO-PI* five factor model of personality. *Personality and Individual Differences, 21,* 303–307.

Furnham, A. (1996b). The FIRO-B, the Learning Style Question- naire and the five factor model. *Journal of Social Behaviour and Personality, 11,* 285–299.

Furnham, A. (1997). *The psychology of behaviour at work.* Sussex, England: Psychologist Press.

Furnham, A. (2001). Vocational preference and P-O fit: Reflections on Holland's theory of vocational choice. *Applied Psychology, 50,* 5–29.

Furnham, A., Crump, J., & Whelan, J. (1997). Validating the NEO personality inventory using assessor's ratings. *Personality and Individual Differences, 22,* 669–675.

Furnham, A., Forde, L., & Cotter, T. (1998). Personality and test taking style. *Personality and Individual Differences, 24,* 19–23.

Furnham, A., & Schaffer, R. (1984). Person-environment fit, job satisfaction and mental health. *Journal of Occupational Psychol- ogy, 57,* 295–307.

Furnham, A., & Stringfield, P. (1993). Personality and occupational behaviour: Myers-Briggs Type Indicator correlates of manager- ial practices in two cultures. *Human Relations, 46,* 827–848.

Galton, F. (1884). Measurement of character. *Fortnightly Review, 36,* 179–185.

Gerbing, D., & Tuley, M. (1991). The 16PF related to the five-factor model of personality. *Multivariate Behavioural Research, 26,* 271–289.

Goldberg, L. R. (1990). An alternative "description of personality": The big five factor structure. *Journal of Personality and Social Psychology, 59,* 1216–1229.

Goldberg, L. R. (1992). The development of markers of the Big- Five factor structure. *Psychological Assessment, 4,* 26–42.

Goldberg, L. R. (1995). What the hell took so long? Donald W. Fiske and the Big-Five factor structure. In P. E. Shrout & S. T. Fiske (Eds.), *Personality research, methods and theory: A festschrift honoring Donald W. Fiske* (pp. 29–43). Hillsdale, NJ: Erlbaum.

Goldberg, L. R. (1997). A broad-bandwidth, public-domain, person- ality inventory measuring the lower-level facets of several five- factor models. In I. Mervielde, I. Deary, F. De Fruyt, & F. Ostendorf (Eds.), *Personality psychology in Europe* (Vol. 7, pp. 7–28). Tilburg, The Netherlands: Tilburg University Press.

Goleman, D. (1998). *Working with emotional intelligence.* New York: Bantam Books.

Gough, H. (1987). *California Personality Inventory administrator's guide.* Palo Alto, CA: Consulting Psychologist Press.

Gough, H. G. (1996). *CPI manual* (3rd ed.). Palo Alto, CA: Consulting Psychologists Press.

Hahn, R., & Comrey, A. L. (1994). Factor analysis of the NEO-PI and the Comrey Personality Scales. *Psychological Reports, 75,* 355–365.

Hogan, J., & Hogan, R. (1999, April). *Leadership and socio- political intelligence.* Paper presented at the Kravis-de Roulet Leadership Conference, Claremont McKenna College, CA.

Hogan, J., & Roberts, B. W. (1996). Issues and non-issues in the fidelity-bandwidth trade-off. *Journal of Organizational Behav- ior, 17,* 627–637.

Hogan, R. T. (1991). Personality and personality measurement. In M. D. Dunnette & L. M. Hough (Eds.), *Handbook of industrial and organizational psychology* (2nd ed., Vol. 2, pp. 873–919). Palo Alto, CA: Consulting Psychologists Press.

Hogan, R. T., & Hogan, J. (1992). *Hogan Personality Inventory manual.* Tulsa, OK: Hogan Assessment Systems.

Hogan, R. T., Hogan, J., & Roberts, B. W. (1996). Personality mea- surement and employment decisions. *American Psychologist, 51,* 469–477.

Holden, R. R., & Hibbs, N. (1995). Incremental validity of response latencies for detecting fakers on a personality test. *Journal of Research in Personality, 29,* 362–372.

Holland, J. (1973). *Making vocational choices: A theory of careers.* Englewood Cliffs, NJ: Prentice Hall.

Holland, J. (1985). *Making vocational choices: A theory of voca- tional personalities and work environments.* Englewood Cliffs, NJ: Prentice Hall.

Hough, L. M. (1989). Development of personality measures to sup- plement selection decisions. In B. J. Fallon, H. P. Pfister, & J. Brebner (Eds.), *Advances in industrial organizational psychology* (pp. 365–375). Amsterdam, The Netherlands: Elsevier Science.

Hough, L. M. (1992). The "Big Five" personality variables— construct confusion: Description versus prediction. *Human Per- formance, 5,* 139–155.

Hough, L. M. (1997). The millennium for personality psychology: New horizons or good old daze. *Applied Psychology: An Inter- national Review, 47,* 233–261.

Hough, L. M. (1998a). Effects of intentional distortion in personal- ity measurement and evaluation of suggested palliatives. *Human Performance, 11,* 209–244.

Hough, L. M. (1998b). Personality at work: Issues and evidence. In M. Hakel (Ed.), *Beyond multiple choice: Evaluating alternatives to traditional testing for selection* (pp. 131–166). Hillsdale, NJ: Erlbaum.

Hough, L. M. (2001). I/O*wes* its advances to personality. In B. Roberts & R. T. Hogan (Eds.), *Personality psychology in the workplace* (pp. 19–44). Washington, DC: American Psychologi- cal Association.

Hough, L. M., Barge, B., & Kamp, J. (2001). Assessment of person- ality, temperament, vocational interests, and work outcome preferences. In J. P. Campbell & D. J. Knapp (Eds.), *Exploring *the limits of personnel selection and classification* (pp. 111–154). Mahwah, NJ: Erlbaum.

Hough, L. M., Eaton, N. L., Dunnette, M. D., Kamp, J. D., & McCloy, R. A. (1990). Criterion-related validities of personality constructs and the effect of response distortion on those validities [Monograph]. *Journal of Applied Psychology, 75,* 581–595.

Hough, L. M., Kamp, J., & Ashworth, S. D. (1993). *Development of Project A Temperament Inventory: Assessment of Background and Life Experiences (ABLE)* (Institute Report No. 259). Minneapolis, MN: Personnel Decisions Research Institutes.

Hough, L. M., & Ones, D. S. (2001). The structure, measurement, validity, and use of personality variables in industrial, work, and organizational psychology. In N. Anderson, D. S. Ones, H. K. Sinangil, & C. Viswesvaran (Eds.), *Handbook of industrial work and organizational psychology,* Vol. 1 (pp. 233–377). London: Sage.

Hough, L. M., Ones, D. S., & Viswesvaran, C. (1998). *Personality correlates of managerial performance constructs.* Symposium conducted at the 13th Annual Convention of the Society for Industrial and Organizational Psychology, Dallas, TX.

Hough, L. M., & Oswald, F. L. (2000). Personnel selection: Looking toward the future–remembering the past. *Annual Review of Psychology, 51,* 631–664.

Hough, L. M., Oswald, F. L., & Ployhart, R. E. (2001). Determinants, detection, and amelioration of adverse impact in personnel selection procedures: Issues, evidence, and lessons learned. *International Journal of Selection and Assessment, 9,* 152–194.

Hough, L. M., & Schneider, R. J. (1996). Personality traits, taxonomies, and applications in organizations. In K. Murphy (Ed.), *Individual differences and behavior in organizations* (pp. 31–88). San Francisco: Jossey-Bass.

Huffcutt, A. I., & Arthur, W., Jr. (1994). Hunter and Hunter (1984) revisited: Interview validity for entry-level jobs. *Journal of Applied Psychology, 79,* 184–190.

Hunter, J. E. (1983). A causal analysis of cognitive ability, job knowledge, job performance, and supervisor ratings. In F. Landy, S. Zedeck, & J. Cleveland (Eds.), *Performance measurement and theory* (pp. 257–266). Hillsdale, NJ: Erlbaum.

Hurtz, G. M., & Donovan, J. J. (2000). Personality and job performance: The Big Five revisited. *Journal of Applied Psychology, 85,* 869–879.

Jackson, D. N., Paunonen, S. V., Fraboni, M., & Goffin, R. D. (1996). A five-factor versus six-factor model of personality structure. *Personality and Individual Differences, 20,* 33–45.

James, L. R. (1998). Measurement of personality via conditional reasoning. *Organizational Research Methods, 1,* 131–163.

James, L. R., & Mazerolle, M. D. (in press). *Personality at work.* Thousand Oaks, CA: Sage.

John, O. P. (1990a). The "Big Five" factor taxonomy: Dimensions of personality in the natural language and in questionnaires. In L. A. Pervin (Ed.), *Handbook of personality: Theory and research* (pp. 66–100). New York: Guilford Press.

John, O. P. (1990b). The search for basic dimensions of personality. In P. McReynods, J. C. Rosen, & G. J. Chelune (Eds.), *Advances in psychological assessment* (pp. 1–37). New York: Plenum Press.

Judge, T. A., & Bono, J. E. (2001a). Relationship of core self-evaluations traits—self-esteem, generalized self-efficacy, locus of control, and emotional stability—with job satisfaction and job performance: A meta-analysis. *Journal of Applied Psychology, 86,* 80–92.

Judge, T. A., & Bono, J. E. (2001b). A rose by any other name: Are self-esteem, generalized self-efficacy, neuroticism, and locus of control indicators of a common construct? In B. Roberts & R. T. Hogan (Eds.), *Personality psychology in the workplace* (pp. 93–118). Washington, DC: American Psychological Association.

Judge, T. A., Bono, J. E., Ilies, R., & Werner, M. (2001). *Personality and leadership: A qualitative and quantitative review.* Manuscript submitted for publication.

Judge, T. A., Heller, D., & Mount, M. K. (2002). Five-factor model of personality and job satisfaction. *Journal of Applied Psychology, 87,* 530–541.

Kallasmao, T., Allik, J., Realo, A., & McCrae, R. (2000). The estonian version of the NEO-PI-R: An examination of universal and culture-specific aspects of the five-factor model. *European Journal of Personality, 14,* 265–278.

Karp, S. L. (Ed.). (1999). *Studies of objective/projective personality tests.* Brooklandville, MD: Objective/Projective Tests.

King, W. C., Jr., & Miles, E. W. (1995). A quasi-experimental assessment of the effect of computerizing noncognitive paper-and-pencil measurements: A test of measurement equivalence. *Journal of Applied Psychology, 80,* 643–651.

Kohlberg, L. (1969). Stage and sequence: The cognitive-developmental approach of socialization. In D. A. Goslin (Ed.), *Handbook of socialization theory and research.* Chicago: Rand McNally.

Loevinger, J. (1994). In search of grand theory. *Psychological Inquiry, 5,* 142–144.

Mael, F. A., Connerly, M., & Morath, R. A. (1996). None of your business: Parameters of biodata invasiveness. *Personnel Psychology, 49,* 613–650.

Matthews, G., & Deary, I. (1998). *Personality traits.* Cambridge, England: Cambridge University Press.

Mayer, J. D., Salovey, P., & Caruso, D. (2000). Models of emotional intelligence. In R. J. Sternberg (Ed.), *Handbook of intelligence* (pp. 396–420). New York: Cambridge University Press.

McAdams, D. P. (1992). The five-factor model *in* personality: A critical appraisal. *Journal of Personality, 60,* 329–361.

McCrae, R. R., & Costa, P. T. (1989). The structure of interpersonal traits: Wiggins' circumplex and the five-factor model. *Journal of Personality and Social Psychology, 56,* 586–595.

McCrae, R. R., & Costa, P. T., Jr. (1997). Personality trait structure as a human universal. *American Psychologist, 52,* 509–516.

McCrae, R. R., Costa, P. T., Jr., & Busch, C. M. (1986). Evaluating comprehensiveness in personality systems: The California Q-Set and the five-factor model. *Journal of Personality, 54,* 430–446.

McCrae, R., Costa, P., del Pilar, G., Rolland, J. P., & Parker, W. (1998). Cross-cultural assessment of the five-factor model: The revised NEO Personality Inventory. *Journal of Cross-Cultural Psychology, 29,* 171–188.

McCrae, R. R., Costa, P. T., Jr., & Piedmont, R. L. (1993). Folk concepts, natural language, and psychological constructs: The California Psychological Inventory and the five-factor model. *Journal of Personality, 61,* 1–26.

McDaniel, M. A., Whetzel, D. L., Schmidt, F. L., & Maurer, S. D. (1994). The validity of employment interviews: A comprehensive review and meta-analysis. *Journal of Applied Psychology, 79,* 599–616.

Merten, T., & Ruch, W. (1996). A comparison of computerized and conventional administration of the German version of the Eysenck Personality Questionnaire and the Carnell Rating Scale for Depression. *Personality and Individual Differences, 20,* 281–291.

Merten, T., & Siebert, K. (1997). A comparison of computerized and conventional administration of the EPQ-R and the CRS. *Personality and Individual Differences, 20,* 283–286.

Mervielde, I., Buyst, V., & de Fruyt, F. (1995). The validity of the big five as a model for teacher's ratings of individual differences in children aged 4 to 12. *Personality and Individual Differences, 18,* 525–534.

Mervielde, I., & de Fruyt, F. (2000). The big five personality factors as a model for the structure of children's peer nominations. *European Journal of Personality, 14,* 91–106.

Motowidlo, S. J., Borman, W. C., & Schmit, M. J. (1997). A theory of individual differences in task and contextual performance. *Human Performance, 10,* 71–83.

Motowidlo, S. J., Brownlee, A. L., & Schmit, M. J. (1998). *Effects of personality characteristics on knowledge, skill, and performance in servicing retail customers.* Unpublished manuscript.

Mount, M. K., & Barrick, M. R. (1995). The Big Five personality dimensions: Implications for research and practice in human resources management. *Research in Personnel and Human Resource Management, 13,* 153–200.

Mount, M. K., Barrick, M. R., & Stewart, G. L. (1998). Five-factor model of personality and performance in jobs involving interpersonal interactions. *Human Performance, 11,* 145–165.

Mount, M. K., Barrick, M. R., & Strauss, P. P. (1994). Validity of observer ratings of the Big Five personality factors. *Journal of Applied Psychology, 79,* 272–280.

Muchinsky, P. M. (1999). Applications of Holland's theory in industrial and organizational settings. *Journal of Vocational Behavior, 55,* 127–135.

Mumford, M. D., Costanza, D. P., Connelly, M. S., & Johnson, J. F. (1996). Item generation procedures and background data scales: Implications for construct and criterion-related validity. *Personnel Psychology, 49,* 361–398.

Mumford, M. D., & Stokes, G. S. (1992). Developmental determinants of individual action: Theory and practice in applying background measures. In M. D. Dunnette & L. M. Hough (Eds.), *Handbook of industrial and organizational psychology* (2nd ed., Vol. 2, pp. 61–138). Palo Alto, CA: Consulting Psychologists Press.

Nilsen, D. (1995). *Investigation of the relationship between personality and leadership performance.* Unpublished doctoral dissertation, University of Minnesota, Minneapolis.

Norman, W. T. (1963). Toward an adequate taxonomy of personality attributes: Replicated factor structure in peer nomination personality ratings. *Journal of Abnormal and Social Psychology, 66,* 574–583.

Ones, D. S., Hough, L. M., & Viswesvaran, C. (1998, April). *Validity and adverse impact of personality-based managerial potential scales.* Symposium conducted at the 13th Annual Convention of the Society for Industrial and Organizational Psychology, Dallas, TX.

Ones, D. S., & Viswesvaran, C. (1996a). Bandwidth-fidelity dilemma in personality measurement for personnel selection. *Journal of Organizational Behavior, 17,* 609–626.

Ones, D. S., & Viswesvaran, C. (1996b). *What do pre-employment customer service scales measure? Explorations in construct validity and implications for personnel selection.* Paper presented at the 11th Annual Conference of the Society for Industrial and Organizational Psychology, San Diego, CA.

Ones, D. S., & Viswesvaran, C. (1998a). The effects of social desirability and faking on personality and integrity assessment for personnel selection. *Human Performance, 11,* 245–269.

Ones, D. S., & Viswesvaran, C. (1998b). Gender, age, and race differences on overt integrity tests: Results across four large-scale job applicant data sets. *Journal of Applied Psychology, 83,* 35–42.

Ones, D. S., & Viswesvaran, C. (1998c). Integrity testing in organizations. In R. W. Griffin, A. O'Leary-Kelly, & J. M. Collins (Eds.), *Dysfunctional behavior in organizations: Vol. 2. Nonviolent behaviors in organizations* (pp. 243–276). Greenwich, CT: JAI.

Ones, D. S., & Viswesvaran, C. (2001). Personality at work: Criterion-focused occupational personality scales (COPS) used in personnel selection. In B. W. Roberts & R. T. Hogan (Eds.), *Applied personality psychology: The intersection of personality and I/O psychology* (pp. 63–92). Washington, DC: American Psychological Association.

Ones, D. S., Viswesvaran, C., & Reiss, A. D. (1996). Role of social desirability in personality testing for personnel selection: The red herring. *Journal of Applied Psychology, 81,* 660–679.

Ones, D. S., Viswesvaran, C., & Schmidt, F. L. (1993). Comprehensive meta-analysis of integrity test validities: Finding and implications for personnel selection and theories of job performance [Monograph]. *Journal of Applied Psychology, 78,* 679–703.

Ones, D. S., Viswesvaran, C., Schmidt, F. L., & Reiss, A. D. (1994). *The validity of honesty and violence scales of integrity tests in predicting violence at work.* Paper presented at the Annual Meeting of the Academy of Management, Dallas, TX.

Organ, D. W., & Ryan, K. (1995). A meta-analaytic review of attitudinal and dispositional predictors of organizational citizenship behavior. *Personnel Psychology, 48,* 775–802.

Oswald, F. L., Carr, J. Z., & Schmidt, A. M. (2001). *The medium and the message: Dual effects of supervision and web-based testing on measurement equivalence for ability and personality measures.* Symposium presented at the 16th Annual Conference of the Society for Industrial and Organizational Psychology, San Diego, CA.

Paunonen, S. V. (1998). Hierarchical organization of personality and prediction of behavior. *Journal of Personality and Social Psychology, 74,* 538–556.

Paunonen, S. V., & Jackson, D. N. (2000). What is beyond the Big Five? Plenty! *Journal of Personality, 68,* 821–835.

Paunonen, S. V., Jackson, D. N., Trzebinski, J., & Forsterling, F. (1992). Personality structure across cultures: A multimethod evaluation. *Journal of Personality and Social Psychology, 62,* 447–456.

Paunonen, S. V., & Nicol, A. A. A. M. (2001). The personality hierarchy and the prediction of work behaviors. In B. W. Roberts & R. T. Hogan (Eds.), *Personality psychology in the workplace* (pp. 161–191). Washington, DC: American Psychological Association.

Paunonen, S. V., Rothstein, M. G., & Jackson, D. N. (1999). Narrow reasoning about the use of broad personality measures in personnel selection. *Journal of Organizational Behavior, 20,* 389–405.

Peabody, D., & Goldberg, L. R. (1989). Some determinants of factor structures from personality-trait descriptors. *Journal of Personality and Social Psychology, 57,* 552–567.

Pervin, L. A. (1994). A critical analysis of current trait theory. *Psychological Inquiry, 5,* 103–113.

Piedmont, R., McCrae, R., & Costa, P. (1992). An assessment of the Edwards Personal Preference Schedule from the perspective of the five-factor model. *Journal of Personality Assessment, 58,* 67–78.

Pincus, A. L., Gurtman, M. B., & Ruiz, M. A. (1998). Structural analysis of social behavior (SASB): Circumplex analyses and structural relations with the interpersonal circle and the five-factor model of personality. *Journal of Personality and Social Psychology, 74,* 1629–1645.

Plomin, R., & Crabbe, J. (2000). DNA. *Psychological Bulletin, 126,* 806–828.

Plutchik, R., & Conte, H. R. (1997). *Circumplex models of personality and emotions* (1st ed.). Washington, DC: American Psychological Association.

Richman, W. L., Kiesler, S., Weisband, S., & Drasgow, F. (1999). A meta-analytic study of social desirability distortion in computer-administered questionnaires, traditional questionnaires, and interviews. *Journal of Applied Psychology, 84,* 754–775.

Robertson, I., & Callinan, M. (1998). Personality and work behaviour. *European Journal of Work and Organizational Psychology, 7,* 321–340.

Robie, C., Schmit, M. J., Ryan, A. M., & Zickar, M. J. (2000). Effects of item context specificity on the measurement equivalence of a personality inventory. *Organizational Research Methods, 3,* 348–365.

Rosse, J. G., Stecher, M. D., Levin, R. A., & Miller, J. L. (1998). The impact of response distortion on preemployment personality testing and hiring decisions. *Journal of Applied Psychology, 83,* 634–644.

Rounds, J. B. (1995). Vocational interests: Evaluating structural hypotheses. In D. Lubinski & R. V. Dawis (Eds.), *Assessing individual differences in human behavior* (pp. 177–232). Palo Alto, CA: Davies-Black.

Sadri, G., & Robertson, I. T. (1993). Self-efficacy and work-related behaviour: A review and meta-analysis. *Applied Psychology: An International Review, 42,* 139–152.

Salgado, J. F. (1997). The five factor model of personality and job performance in the European community. *Journal of Applied Psychology, 82,* 30–43.

Salgado, J. F. (2000). *The Big Five personality dimensions as predictors of alternative job performance criteria.* Paper presented at the 15th Annual convention of the Society for Industrial and Organizational Psychology, New Orleans, LA.

Saucier, G. (1997). Effects of variable selection on the factor structure of person descriptors. *Journal of Personality and Social Psychology, 73,* 1296–1312.

Saucier, G., & Goldberg, L. R. (1998). What is beyond the Big Five? *Journal of Personality, 66,* 495–524.

Saudino, K. J. (1997). Moving beyond the heritability question: New directions in behavioral genetic studies of personality. *Current Directions in Psychological Science, 6,* 86–90.

Schmidt, F. L., & Hunter. J. E. (1992). Development of a causal model of processes determining job performance. *Current Directions in Psychological Science, 1,* 89–92.

Schmidt, F. L., & Hunter, J. E. (1998). The validity and utility of selection methods in personnel psychology: Practical and theoretical implications of 85 years of research findings. *Psychological Bulletin, 124,* 262–274.

Schmidt, F. L., Hunter, J. E., & Outerbridge, A. N. (1986). Impact of job experience and ability on job knowledge, work sample performance, and supervisory ratings of job performance. *Journal of Applied Psychology, 71,* 432–439.

Schmidt, F. L., Viswesvaran, C., & Ones, D. S. (1997). Validity of integrity tests for predicting drug and alcohol abuse: A meta-analysis. In W. J. Bukoski (Ed.), *Meta-analysis of drug abuse prevention programs* (pp. 69–95). Rockville, MD: NIDA Press.

Schmidt, L., & Schwenkmezger, P. (1994). Differential diagnosis of psychiatric disorders using personality tests and questionnaires. *Diagnostica, 40,* 27–41.

Schmit, M. J., Kilm, J. A., & Robie, C. (2000). Development of a global measure of personality. *Personnel Psychology, 53,* 153–193.

Schmit, M. J., Ryan, A. M., Stierwalt, S. L., & Powell, A. B. (1995). Frame-of-reference effects on personality scale scores and criterion-related validity. *Journal of Applied Psychology, 80,* 607–620.

Schneider, R. J., Ackerman, P. L., & Kanfer, R. (1996). To "act wisely in human relations": Exploring the dimensions of social competence. *Personality and Individual Differences, 21,* 469–481.

Schneider, R. J., & Hough, L. M. (1995). Personality and industrial/organizational psychology. In C. L. Cooper & I. T. Robertson (Eds.), *International review of industrial and organizational psychology* (pp. 75–129). Chichester, England: Wiley.

Schneider, R. J., Hough, L. M., & Dunnette, M. D. (1996). Broadsided by broad traits: How to sink science in five dimensions or less. *Journal of Organizational Behavior, 17,* 639–655.

Sharf, J. C., & Jones, D. P. (2000). Employment risk management. In J. F. Kehoe (Ed.). *Managing selection in changing organizations* (pp. 271–318). San Francisco: Jossey-Bass.

Snell, A. F., Sydell, E. J., & Lueke, S. B. (1999), Towards a theory of applicant faking: Integrating studies of deception. *Human Resources Management Review, 9,* 219–242.

Stajkovic, A. D., & Luthans, F. (1998). Self-efficacy and work-related performance: A meta-analysis. *Psychological Bulletin, 124,* 240–261.

Stewart, G. L. (1999). Trait bandwidth and stages of job performance: Assessing differential effects for conscientiousness and its subtraits. *Journal of Applied Psychology, 84,* 959–968.

Stewart, W. H., Jr., & Roth, P. L. (2001). Risk propensity differences between entrepreneurs and managers: A meta-analytic review. *Journal of Applied Psychology, 86,* 145–153.

Stokes, G. S., Mumford, M. D., & Owens, W. A. (Eds.). (1994). *Biodata handbook: Theory, research, and use of biographical information in selection and performance prediction.* Palo Alto, CA: Consulting Psychologist Press.

Tellegen, A. (1993). Folk concepts and psychological concepts of personality and personality disorder. *Psychological Inquiry, 4,* 122–130.

Tellegen, A., & Waller, N. G. (n.d.). *Exploring personality through test construction: Development of the Multidimensional Personality Questionnaire.* Unpublished manuscript.

Tett, R. P., Jackson, D. N., & Rothstein, M. (1991). Personality measures as predictors of job performance: A meta-analytic review. *Personnel Psychology, 44,* 703–742.

Tett, R. P., Jackson, D. N., Rothstein, M., & Reddon, J. R. (1994). Meta-analysis of personality–job performance relations: A reply to Ones, Mount, Barrick, and Hunter (1994). *Personnel Psychology, 47,* 157–172.

Tokar, D. M., Fischer, A. R., Snell, A. F., & Harik-Williams, N. (1999). Efficient assessment of the Five-Factor Model of personality: Structural validity analyses of the NEO Five-Factor

Inventory (Form S). *Measurement and Evaluation in Counseling and Development, 32,* 14–30.

Tupes, E. C., & Christal, R. E. (1992). Recurrent personality factors based on trait ratings. *Journal of Personality, 60,* 225–251. (Original work published 1961)

Vasilopoulos, N. L., Reilly, R. R., & Leaman, J. A. (2000). The influence of job familiarity and impression management on self-report measure scale scores and response latencies. *Journal of Applied Psychology, 85,* 50–64.

Vinchur, A. J., Schippmann, J. S., Switzer, F. S., & Roth, P. L. (1998). A meta-analytic review of predictors of job performance for salespeople. *Journal of Applied Psychology, 83,* 586–597.

Viswesvaran, C., & Ones, D. S., (1999). Meta-analyses of fakability estimates: Implications for personality measurement. *Educational and Psychological Measurement, 59,* 197–210.

Waller, N. G., & Ben-Porath, Y. S. (1987). Is it time for clinical psychology to embrace the Five-Factor Model of personality? *American Psychologist, 42,* 887–889.

Waller, N. G., & Zavala, J. D. (1993). Evaluating the Big Five. *Psychological Inquiry, 4,* 131–134.

Wiggins, J. S., & Trapnell, P. D. (1997). Personality structure: The return of the Big Five. In R. Hogan, J. Johnson, & S. Briggs (Eds.), *Handbook of personality psychology* (pp. 737–765). San Diego, CA: Academic.

Zickar, M. J. (2001). Conquering the next frontier: Modeling personality data with item response theory. In B. Roberts & R. T. Hogan (Eds.), *Personality psychology in the workplace* (pp. 141–160). Washington, DC: American Psychological Association.

Zickar, M. J., & Drasgow, F. (1996). Detecting faking on a personality instrument using appropriateness measurement. *Applied Psychological Measurement, 20,* 71–87.

Zickar, M. J., Rosse, J. G., Levin, R. A., & Hulin, C. L. (1996). *Modeling the effects of faking on personality tests.* Unpublished manuscript.

Zuckerman, M. (1992). What is a basic factor and which factors are basic? Turtles all the way down. *Personality and Individual Differences, 13,* 675–682.

Zuckerman, M. (1995). Good and bad humors: Biochemical bases of personality and its disorders. *Psychological Science, 6,* 325–332.

Zuckerman, M., Kuhlman, D. M., & Camac, C. (1988). What lies beyond E and N?: An analysis of scales believed to measure basic dimensions of personality. *Journal of Personality and Social Psychology, 54,* 96–107.

Zuckerman, M., Kuhlman, D. M., Joireman, J., Teta, P., & Kraft, M. (1993). A comparison of three structural models for personality: The Big Three, the Big Five, and the Alternative Five. *Journal of Personality and Social Psychology, 65,* 757–768.

CHAPTER 8

Perspectives on Training and Development

KURT KRAIGER

This chapter covers theory and practice in the area of training and development. *Training* and *development* refer to systematic processes initiated by (or at the direction of) the organization resulting in the relatively permanent changes in the knowledge, skills, or attitudes of organizational members. Generally, the term *training* is reserved for activities directed at the acquisition of knowledge, skills, and attitudes for which there is an immediate or near-term application (e.g., an upcoming promotion), whereas *development* is reserved for the acquisition of attributes or competencies for which there may be no immediate use (Noe, 2002).

There has been a tremendous surge in training research over the past 15 years, resulting in exciting new theories and applications. During the same time, the role and look of training in applied settings are changing (Bassi, Benson, & Cheney, 1998). Human resource (HR) advocates see training as one of several alternatives for ensuring that workers possess the knowledge and skills to perform their jobs successfully, while HR skeptics (often, non-HR stakeholders in organizations) see training as either as a catchall to solve all performance problems or a cost center to be controlled or downsized during lean times.

The role of training and the perceived value of employee learning are changing. Evidence from benchmarking studies by the American Society for Training and Development (ASTD) suggests that organizations are investing more heavily in employee training and development (Van Buren, 2001). The medium for training continues to shift from traditional hands-on or instructor-led modes to computer-based forms of delivery, resulting both in enthusiasm about the possibility for cost-effective delivery of core knowledge to all employees and in the onset of highly leveraged partnerships between traditional training companies and new-economy software businesses. Finally, the notion of ensuring and leveraging employees' competencies has infiltrated newer theories of organizational change such as learning organizations or knowledge management systems (London & Moore, 1999; Pfeffer & Sutton, 2000; Tannenbaum & Alliger, 2000).

The interaction of research and practical developments makes this a pivotal time in the training and development field. The dynamics of change and growth call for a solid conceptual foundation so that theoretical and empirical advancements continue to have an impact on practice. The objective for this chapter is to provide a broad overview of theory and practice in training, with respect to emerging methods and technologies for ensuring training success. In so doing, the chapter considers training and development from three perspectives: training and development as instruction, as learning, and as organizational change. Finally, specific attention is given to the role of measurement in training and development.

TRAINING AS INSTRUCTION

Background

In its most literal sense, *training* is synonymous with *instruction;* training is the method by which job-related information is conveyed to learners. Thus, it is natural that over the years researchers and practitioners have been concerned with identifying optimal instructional strategies, a term that refers to a set of tools (e.g., job aids or overheads), methods (e.g., demonstrations or practice), and content (e.g., critical tasks or job-relevant competencies) that, when combined, create a purposeful instructional approach (Salas & Cannon-Bowers, 1997). Generally, researchers interested in training as instruction have focused either on general principles of learning (across instructional approaches) or on specific instructional approaches or methods.

Early research in the 1950s and early 1960s focused on general learning principles. Given the predominance of Skinnerian behavioral learning theories of that era, it is not surprising that learning principles had a similar stimulus-response flavor. Much of the research of this era was sponsored by the military, set in the laboratory, and focused on the learning of psychomotor tasks. Many of these learning principles were summarized in a classic article by Gagne (1962). Gagne described a number of learning principles appropriate for improving the efficiency of military training, including overlearning tasks to improve retention or transfer, and ensuring an identical match between elements of training and conditions of practice in the transfer setting. Notably, Gagne argued that application of these learning principles was a necessary but not sufficient condition for learning; he called for more attention to be paid to needs assessment and training design issues to properly sequence learning events and improve skill acquisition and retention.

The period from the mid-1960s to the mid-1980s saw not only a considerable decline in training research, but a change in emphasis from the study of general learning principles to the validation of specific instructional approaches. Very often, these instructional methods were rooted in behaviorally based learning paradigms (e.g., Decker & Nathan, 1985; Goldstein & Sorcher, 1974). Authors in the *Annual Review of Psychology* regularly decried this research as atheoretical, uninspiring, or virtually nonexistent (e.g., Campbell, 1971; Goldstein, 1980; Latham, 1988; Wexley, 1984). Campbell noted that the sparse empirical work tended to compare new and old training methods, rather than attempting to advance our knowledge of needs analysis, instructional processes, or evaluation. Latham capped this era by noting that it had almost become a tradition for *Annual Review* authors to lament the lack of attention to theory and research influencing practice, and by calling for a return to research on the psychological and structural variables needed to maintain what is learned in training on the job.

In contrast, the last 10 to 15 years have seen not only a resurgence of training research, but also a renewed interest

in the general study of conditions for effective instruction. In the most recent *Annual Review* chapter, Salas and Cannon-Bowers (2001) labeled this period a "decade of progress," one that has seen an "explosion" of training research. The focus of study continutes to be specific training methods, such as dyadic protocols (Arthur, Day, Bennett, McNelly, & Jordan, 1997; Shebilske, Regian, Arthur, & Jordan, 1992), training simulators (e.g., Gopher, Weil, & Bareket, 1994; Jentsch & Bowers, 1998), or computer-based instruction (e.g., Brown, 2001). However, characteristics of effective training or instruction have reemerged as an area of inquiry (see Colquitt, LePine, & Noe, 2000; Noe & Colquitt, 2002, for reviews). Emerging training methods will be discussed shortly. The next section reviews research on training effectiveness because this research has led to guidelines on designing and implementing effective instructional strategies regardless of the specific research methods.

Training Effectiveness

The rebirth of interest in training research can be traced principally to three influential papers appearing between 1985 and 1990 (Baldwin & Ford, 1988; Howell & Cooke, 1989; Noe, 1986). The first of these was by Noe, who proposed and later tested (Noe & Schmitt, 1986) a model of training effectiveness. Noe's fundamental thesis was that training success was determined not only by the quality of training (or the effectiveness of a specific method), but by interpersonal, social, and structural characteristics reflecting the relationship of the trainee and the training program to the broader organizational context. Variables such as organizational support or an individual's readiness for training could augment or negate the direct impact of the training itself. Noe's original model has been refined several times, both by other authors (Cannon-Bowers, Salas, Tannenbaum, & Mathieu, 1995) and by Noe and his colleagues (Colquitt et al., 2000); an updated training effectiveness model is reproduced in Figure 8.1.

As shown in Figure 8.1, learning during training is influenced by factors both prior to and during the training itself. As noted previously, specification of these pretraining influences was one of Noe's (1986) primary contributions. Generally, pretraining influences may be categorized as organizational-level, social- or team-level, or individual-level influences. Examples of organizational-level pretraining influences include perceived organizational support for training and whether training is mandatory or optional. Trainees may be more motivated to attend training when they see it as consistent with organizational goals, supported by top management, and required of all members.

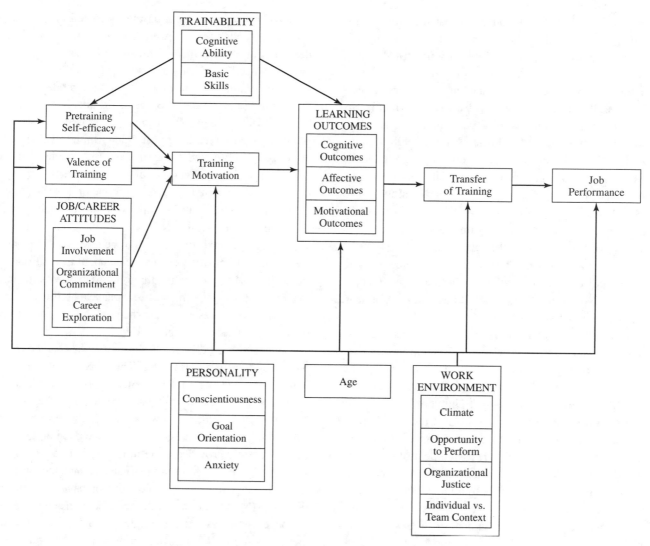

Figure 8.1 Noe and Colquitt's revised training effectiveness model.

An important social influence is the supervisor, who can positively or negatively influence trainees' motivation for training or their perceptions of the utility of training. Supervisors can positively influence training outcomes by referring positively to the training process, by clarifying probable learning outcomes or how those outcomes will be advantageous to job performance or future development, and by providing interpersonal or technical support to trainees prior to and during training. For example, supervisors can provide backup while workers attend training. Peers or coworkers can exert a similar social impact on trainees. Often this influence can be negative, as when peers make derogatory comments about the training content or the trainer.

Individual-level variables refer to trainees' readiness for training as well as their course-specific motivation to learn. *Readiness for training* is a general state of preparedness for

training: Trainees should have sufficient cognitive ability to learn the material; they should have sufficient understanding of their jobs to see how the tasks, knowledge, and skills covered in training are relevant to that job; and they should be relatively free from anxieties and fears about the learning environment (Noe & Colquitt, 2002). *Motivation to learn* is evident when trainees believe that training is relevant and are willing to exert effort in the learning environment. Motivation to learn may result from prior successful experiences with similar training programs or training in general, from generally high self-efficacy, or from positive influences from organizational-level and social- or team-level influences. Motivation influences training effectiveness in three ways: by affecting whether the employees decide to attend training, by influencing the amount of effort trainees exert to learn, and by influencing whether trainees choose to apply skills on the job (Quiñones, 1997).

Training effectiveness models posit that individual characteristics (including trainability, personality, age, and attitudes) influence training motivation; and, in turn, learning during training; and later, the transfer of training and job performance. For example, an individual with a mastery orientation is generally more motivated to learn, and in fact learns more, than an individual with a performance orientation (Colquitt & Simmering, 1998; Fisher & Ford, 1998; Phillips & Gully, 1997). *Mastery orientation* refers to an individual's desire to master or learn the material, the willingness to make mistakes, and the lack of concern about performing well to impress others. Other attitudes such as self-efficacy, valence, job involvement, organizational commitment, and career exploration have been shown to be related to training motivation as well (Colquitt et al., 2000; Facteau, Dobbins, Russell, Ladd, & Kudisch, 1995; Mathieu, Martineau, & Tannenbaum, 1993; Noe & Schmitt, 1986; Tannenbaum, Matthieu, Salas, & Cannon-Bowers, 1991).

Work-environment characteristics may influence pretraining states as well. These characteristics include organizational climate, managerial support, and organizational justice. For example, trainees who perceive the work climate to be supportive are more likely to attend training programs and to exhibit high levels of motivation to learn (Maurer & Tarulli, 1994; Noe & Wilk, 1993). Perceptions of organizational justice are related to issues around the assignment of trainees to training situations. According to the research, trainees hold more favorable attitudes toward training when they have input into training design or when they choose to attend training as opposed to be being assigned to do so (Baldwin, Magjuka, & Loher, 1991; Hicks & Klimoski, 1987). Additionally, performance in remedial training is more positive if trainees perceive the assignment to training as fair or just (Quiñones, 1995).

In summary, the training effectiveness literature has identified a number of individual and organizational-level factors that affect trainees' motivation and capacity to do well in training. Researchers in this area have made considerable progress over the past 15 years and are now able to offer practical insights and guidelines on the planning and maintenance of effective training programs (Noe & Colquitt, 2002).

Effective Training Design

Principles of effective training design have been widely known for more than 40 years. Early research on the acquisition of motor skills led to the delineation of a number of learning principles to guide effective design (e.g., Gagne, 1962; McGehee & Thayer, 1961). A number of these principles are listed in the later section on transfer of training. Since

the advent of modern learning theory rooted in information processing models (e.g., Newell & Simon, 1972), instructional designers and industrial/organizational (I/O) psychologists have expanded their lists of features of an effective instructional environment to account for multiple modern learning paradigms (e.g., Cannon-Bowers, Rhodenizer, Salas, & Bowers, 1998; Gagne & Medsker, 1996). What situations promote effective learning in training? Initially, adult learners must be motivated to learn. This may come from perceived utility or applications of the material, internally or externally determined goal orientation, or a sense of surprise—the training material falls well outside their expectations (see Dweck, 1986; Noe & Colquitt, 2002; Schank & Joseph, 1998). Next, for training to be effective, it must create or maintain positive expectancies about the utility of the training, present information that is consistent with the information-processing and memory-storage capabilities of learners, and provide cues that aid in the retrieval or application of the learned material (Gagne & Medsker, 1996).

Generally, most effective training methods can be characterized by four basic principles: They present relevant information or concepts to be learned; they demonstrate the knowledge, skills, and abilities to be learned; they provide opportunities to practice new skills; and they provide feedback to trainees during and after practice. Noe and Colquitt (2002) recently provided a useful list of a number of characteristics of effective training: (a) Trainees understand the objectives, purpose, and intended outcomes of the training program; (b) the training content is meaningful and relevant to job experiences (i.e., examples, exercises, assignments, etc. are based on job-relevant information); (c) trainees are provided with learning aids to help them learn, organize, and recall training content (i.e., diagrams, models, and advanced organizers); (d) trainees have the opportunity to practice in a relatively safe environment; (e) trainees receive feedback on their learning from trainers, observers, peers, or the task itself; (f) trainees have the opportunity to observe and interact with other trainees; and (g) the training program is efficiently coordinated and arranged.

Despite the advances in the development of principles of instructional effectiveness and the ongoing introduction of new innovative instructional methods (e.g., Arthur et al., 1997), organizations remain dependent on traditional forms of instruction (e.g., classroom lecture, videos, and case studies) for the majority of their training (Industry Report, 1997; Van Buren, 2001). Nonetheless, in contrast to the applied research of 30 to 40 years ago that tended to compare method to method without much consideration to the underlying learning paradigms (Campbell, 1971), modern research in training and instructional psychology is positioned to build and test new instructional methods rooted in sound learning principles and tailored to specific combinations of content, audience, and training media.

Emerging Training Methods

This section selectively reviews developments in training methods, including computer-based training, team training, cross-cultural training, and alternative corporate models of training delivery. Note that the most popular or prototypical training methods—lecture and experiential learning—are not explicitly addressed. The intent is not to review the most common training methods but those that may shape our understanding of the processes of instruction and learning over the next decade. Two excellent examples of ongoing research and development in training methods are team training and computer-based training. The tracking of training trends by ASTD suggests that in the coming years, organizations intend to deliver more and more training via learning technologies. Although the anticipated growth of team training in particular has not been similarly documented, team training should be in greater demand given the increasing popularity of self-managed work teams and the centrality of work teams to methods of managed change in organizations (Guzzo & Dickson, 1996). Cross-cultural training and alternative models for corporate training have received less attention by training researchers, but may be equally important to organizations competing in the new digital, global economies.

Computer-Based Training (CBT)

Recent survey evidence suggests a shift away from instructor-led, classroom training toward learner-centered, technology-mediated training. For example, Bassi and Van Buren (1999) predicted that companies would reduce classroom training by nearly 20% between 1997 and 2000, replacing most of the traditional forms of training with various forms of computer-based training (CBT). *Computer-based training* is the presentation of text, graphics, video, audio, or animation via computer for the purpose of building job-relevant knowledge and skill. Among the most common forms of CBT (and the focus of this section) are computer-based instruction, computer-aided instruction, multimedia learning environments (delivered via CD-ROM or desktop systems), intranet- and Internet-based instruction, Web-based instruction, and more recently, e-learning. One recent analysis predicted that U.S. corporations' spending on Web-based training or e-learning will grow from $2.2 billion in 2000 to $14.5 billion in 2004 (Brennan & Anderson, 2001).

Additional forms of CBT include intelligent tutoring systems (e.g., Burns & Parlett, 1991), full-scale simulations (Salas, Bowers, & Rhodenizer, 1998), and virtual-reality training (e.g., Steele-Johnson & Hyde, 1997). Common to the first of these forms are two important characteristics: The training content and methods of presentation may be customized to the needs and preferences of the individual trainee; and the learner can exert influence or control over the content, pace, or style of training. As Brown and Ford (2002) noted, customization and learner control are in some senses opposite sides of the same coin. *Customization* refers to designers' efforts to build training programs that can be adapted based on important learner characteristics. *Learner control* represents efforts by learners themselves to modify the learning environment to their own purposes. Thus, CBT is designed to be adaptive to individual learners.

This section focuses on these learner-centered technologies primarily because of their greater popularity and flexibility in business settings. Organizations are moving toward greater adoption of learner-centered CBT for several reasons. The first is greater flexibility; trainees do not have to attend prescheduled training programs, but can learn when they want, often just in time as job requirements change. The second reason is that organizations anticipate that implementing CBT can reduce training costs. Although it may be more expensive to create a CBT program, the expectation is that higher developmental costs can be recouped through reduced trainer costs and reduced travel costs associated with sending employees to training. Interestingly, few studies have documented sustained cost savings (e.g., Hall, 1997; Whalen & Wright, 2000), and it is possible that ongoing system maintenance, technical support, and software and hardware upgrades may offset potential savings in many large-scale CBT applications.

Regardless of whether, in the long run, the implementation of CBT results in the anticipated gains in flexibility, availability, and cost savings, it is easy to imagine that the use of CBT will become increasingly widespread during the next decade. Accordingly, two practical questions are (a) how effective is CBT? and (b) how can the effectiveness of CBT be maximized?

Perhaps surprisingly, the first question is difficult to answer. Despite literally hundreds of studies comparing computer-based and instructor-led training (e.g., Simon & Werner, 1996; Williams & Zahed, 1996), there are few firm conclusions regarding the relative advantages and disadvantages of CBT. There is some evidence that it reduces training times for learners (Kulik & Kulik, 1991). Regarding impact on learning, the most comprehensive review of the literature was conducted by Russell (1999), who reviewed several hundred studies and reported that there was no evidence that online learning had a negative impact on either student learning or student satisfaction with courses. Some evidence suggested that online courses resulted in greater learning. However, the report and its conclusions have been widely criticized primarily due to the quality of the courses reviewed; very few of the studies he reviewed presented a fair test of the two instructional methods.

Consider a prototypical study in which a traditional instructor-led training course is being adapted for Web-based training. Prior to putting the course on the Internet, the course designers must conduct a quick needs assessment to verify the relevancy of critical knowledges and skills, or collect realistic examples to be simulated in the course. The course materials may be updated during the process, and some thought is put into optimal ways of presenting information on the Web. The course is then offered on a trial basis to trainees who self-select into the pilot test. Should the pilot reveal the new CBT course to be more effective, is there any reason to doubt that, had the same process been applied to convert a CBT course to classroom instruction, a similar advantage for the traditional method would have been found? Consider also issues of individual differences for learning environments and the suitability of different skills to CBT (e.g., calculating interest on a mortgage vs. providing performance feedback); it easy to imagine that there may never be a definitive conclusion reached regarding the superiority of one method over the other.

Consequently, it is not surprising that most scholars agree that the most powerful influence on learning from instructional technologies is not the technology itself, but what is delivered with that technology (Clark, 1994). That is, poorly designed training will not stimulate and support learning regardless of the extent to which appealing or expensive technology is used to deliver it (Brown & Ford, 2002). This leads to the second question: How can CBT be designed to maximize the effectiveness of training?

Traditionally, this question has been addressed through research on choices of training media (e.g., text vs. graphics) or on user interfaces (e.g., Krendl, Ware, Reid, & Warren, 1996; Mayer, Moreno, Boire, & Vagge, 1998). However, a recent chapter by Brown and Ford (2002) offers an interesting alternative perspective on increasing CBT effectiveness. Brown and Ford noted that in all forms of CBT, the learner is an important intermediary between training features and training outcomes. That is, regardless of the instructional feature embedded in the program, it will work only through deliberate cognitive processing by the learner. Accordingly, they propose that CBT be designed in such a way that it promotes active learning by trainees. Trainees demonstrating active learning are motivated, mastery-oriented, and mindful.

According to Brown and Ford, learners who are motivated hold two expectancies: that effort exerted during training will result in learning, and that learning during training will be useful for achieving valued outcomes back on the job. After Dweck (1986), a *mastery orientation* consists of a belief structure that holds that ability is malleable and mistakes are attributable to effort. Learners with a mastery orientation will persist during training, persevering through challenges. In contrast, a *performance orientation* consists of beliefs that abilities are fixed and mistakes are attributable to ability. In a training context, subjects with a performance orientation are less concerned with mastering material and more concerned with achieving high scores or appearing competent. *Mindfulness* involves the deliberate, systematic expending of cognitive effort to evaluate information and integrate it with previous knowledge. Mindful processing suggests that learners actively engage material during the learning process—for example, reading training materials carefully and expending effort thinking about the job-related implications of a newly learned principle.

Brown and Ford (2002) argued that for learner-centered instructional technologies to be maximally effective, they must be designed to encourage active learning in participants. Brown and Ford offered a set of principles and guidelines for designing CBT rooted in four key thematic areas: (a) designing information structure and presentation to reflect both meaningful organization (or chunking) of material (e.g., Yang & Moore, 1995) and ease of use (e.g., Krendl et al., 1996); (b) balancing the need for learner control with guidance to help learners make better choices about content and process (e.g., Tennyson & Elmore, 1997); (c) providing opportunities for practice and constructive feedback (e.g., Azevedo & Bernard, 1995); and (d) facilitating metacognitive monitoring and control to get learners to be mindful of their cognitive processing and in control of their learning processes (e.g., Ford, Smith, Gully, Weissbein, & Salas, 1998; Georghiades, 2000).

In summary, although it appears that CBT will become increasingly popular, there is yet little evidence that suggests it is either more effective or cost efficient than traditional forms of training. However, by attending to design principles and capitalizing on customization and learner control, CBT designers can encourage active learning and more effective computer-based training.

Team Training

As organizations become more enamored with the use of self-managed work teams, there has been considerable research by I/O psychologists on both the characteristics of effective teams and methods for designing effective team training (Cannon-Bowers & Salas, 1998; Sundstrom, McIntyre, Halfhill, & Richards, 2000). The increased popularity of teams in organizations and the special demands of teams in training suggest the importance of understanding effective principles for team training.

As in individual-based training, team-training advocates recommend starting with a needs assessment (or, more specifically, a team-based training needs assessment; e.g., Salas & Cannon-Bowers, 2000; Schraagen, Chipman, & Shalin, 2000). Salas and Cannon-Bowers recommended the following steps for conducting a team-training analysis. Step one is to conduct a skills inventory to identify job-level tasks, as well as the team competencies (knowledge, skills, and attitudes) associated with particular tasks (Cannon-Bowers, Tannenbaum, Salas, & Volpe, 1995). There are two primary differences between team-training needs assessment and traditional forms. The first is the recognized importance in team-training needs analysis of determining interdependencies among team members and ascertaining what skills are required to master the coordination requirements present within team tasks. The second is the focus on identifying the cognitive skills and knowledge needed to interact as a team (e.g., knowledge of team-member roles and responsibilities or interpositional knowledge); this is often accomplished through a team-based cognitive task analysis (see Schraagen et al.).

Step two is to develop training objectives based on the results of step one; training objectives should address both task-work and teamwork skills (after Morgan, Glickman, Woodard, Blaiwes, & Salas, 1986). *Task-work skills* are those needed by team members to perform individual job tasks, whereas *teamwork skills* are behavioral, cognitive, and attitudinal skills needed to communicate, interact, and coordinate tasks effectively with other team members. Examples of teamwork skills and knowledge include a shared understanding of teammate characteristics and preferences, as well as common *cue-strategy associations* (meaning that team members can execute similar strategic responses to on-the-job cues or stimuli). In general, training should be sequenced so that task-work skills are mastered before teamwork skills are taught (Salas, Burke, & Cannon-Bowers, 2002).

Step three is to design exercises and training events based on the objectives from step two. Important to the success of team training is the opportunity for guided practice during training (Salas et al., 2002). Guided practice sessions provide both opportunities to practice new skills and opportunities for timely constructive feedback. Additionally, there are several recently developed, team-based strategies that have been empirically supported (see Cannon-Bowers & Salas, 1998; Swezey & Salas, 1992). The most popular of these techniques is *team coordination training,* sometimes referred to as *crew resource management training.* Depending on the underlying paradigm for team effectiveness, team coordination training focuses either on specific attitudes promoting cooperation and team-based activities or on teamwork skills that facilitate information exchange, cooperation, and coordination of job-related behaviors (Swezey & Salas; Weiner, Kanki, & Helmreich, 1993).

Another team-training strategy is *cross-training.* Based on shared mental model theory, cross-training attempts to provide exposure to and practice with other teammates' tasks, roles, and responsibilities in an effort to increase shared understanding and knowledge among team members (e.g., Cannon-Bowers, Salas, Blickensderfer, & Bowers, 1998; Volpe, Cannon-Bowers, Salas, & Spector, 1996). As team members learn the requirements for successful performance for other positions, they are better able to provide resources or support to assist other team members do their jobs. Yet another strategy, *guided team self-correction,* involves providing guidance to team members in reviewing team events; identifying errors and exchanging feedback; making statements of expectations; and, based on revelations during this self-correction event, developing plans for the future (Smith-Jentsch, Zeisig, Acton, & McPherson, 1998).

The fourth and final step is to design measures of team effectiveness based on the objectives set at step two, evaluate training effectiveness, and use this information to guide future team training. Although a review of methods for measuring team effectiveness and team processes is beyond the scope of this chapter, suffice it to say that evaluation measures should be related to team objectives and should assess outcome-oriented constructs such as collective efficacy (e.g., Marks, 1999), shared knowledge structures (e.g., Kraiger, Salas, & Cannon-Bowers, 1995), team situational awareness (e.g., Stout, Cannon-Bowers, & Salas, 1996/1997), and shared mental models (e.g., Rasker, Post, & Schraagen, 2000).

Cross-Cultural Training

Of interest to organizations that must send employees to other countries to conduct business is the topic of international training. *Cross-cultural training* refers to formal programs designed to prepare persons of one culture to interact effectively in another culture or to interact more effectively with persons from different cultures (see Bhawuk & Brislin, 2000, for a major review). Cross-cultural training usually includes components of awareness or orientation—helping trainees to be aware of their own cultural values, frameworks, and mores. Successful cross-cultural training programs often contain behavioral components as well, providing opportunities for trainees to learn and practice culturally appropriate behaviors (Brislin & Bhawuk, 1999; Landis & Bhagat, 1996; Triandis, 1995).

Early forms of cross-cultural training used either lectures or experiential learning (e.g., Harrison & Hopkins, 1967). In contrast, more modern techniques make use of demonstrations or written scenarios that focus on trainees' understanding of social cues, cultural differences in values, or strategies for learning within or assimilating different cultures. These techniques include cultural assimilators (Harrison, 1992), the contrast-American technique (Stewart, 1966), the cultural analysis system (Lee, 1966), and cultural self-awareness training (Kraemer, 1973). The *culture assimilator method* has emerged as one of the most valid cross-cultural tools. Trainees review critical incidents that focus on cultural differences, select one of several alternative behavioral options, and receive feedback on the cultural implications of both their preferred choices and the desired responses. Initial programs were specific to unique nations (e.g., the Honduras; O'Brien, Fiedler, & Hewett, 1970), cultures, or subcultures (e.g., the hard-core unemployed within the United States; Weldon, Carlston, Rissman, Slobodin, & Triandis, 1975). A recent exciting advancement is the development of the *culture-general assimilator* (Brislin, Cushner, Cherrie, & Yong, 1986; Cushner & Brislin, 1996), which contains more than 100 critical incidents based on a general model of competencies valuable for multiculture navigation. Although the method is new, preliminary research supports the efficacy of the training (see Landis & Bhagat, 1996, for a review).

More generally, several reviews in the early 1990s suggested that across training methods, cross-cultural training is effective. In a qualitative review of 29 studies, Black and Mendenhall (1990) found that participants in cross-cultural training reported improved interpersonal relationships, a reduction in their experience of culture shock, and improvement in their performance on the job. A subsequent meta-analysis of 21 studies found a positive effect of cross-cultural training on trainees' self-development, relationships with host nationals, adjustment during sojourn, and job performance (Deshpande & Viswesvaran, 1992).

Alternative Methods for Corporate Training

An increasingly popular strategy for training employees, particularly managers and technical specialists, is the *corporate university*. A corporate university training model extends the customer base for training beyond current employees and managers to include stakeholders outside the company, often vendors, clients, or professional students at a local university.

In addition to presenting a curriculum that emphasizes core competencies and professional development skills, the corporate university may be responsible for conveying a sense of corporate culture, teaching cross-functional skills, and forming partnerships with educational institutions (Meister, 1998). Although the corporate university label connotes off-site training, the integrated curriculum may be delivered through a combination of on-site, off-site, and virtual locations. An early and still prototypical corporate university was Motorola University; other examples of organizations offering university training curricula are Cisco Systems, Disney, Chase Manhattan, and the U.S. Air Force. In a recent survey of Fortune 500 companies, 84% of 140 responding organizations indicated that they had implemented or planned to implement a corporate university. Although the costs of initiating and maintaining such training models may be high, sponsoring organizations cite a number of practical benefits, including operating training as a line of business, linking training to business goals, coordinating all training under one roof (so to speak), and cutting down cycle time for new business development.

The linking of corporate training with mainstream universities is also a trend in executive education. In order to stay competitive, organizations are investing continually in the development and training of their top managers and executives. Since these same individuals are kept very busy with the running of their companies, methods must be developed for providing easy-access, streamlined, or just-in-time training opportunities. One response has been a greater reliance on Web-based training or distance learning (e.g., Byrne, 1995). A second strategy is for organizations and universities to partner together to design short courses customized to the needs of the company's executive force (Reingold, 1999). Popular topics in both models include leadership, entrepreneurship, global management, and e-business. Perhaps more importantly, individuals attending these customized courses have the opportunity to focus for a short time on business-related problems while they network with their peers from other geographical locations or divisions within the company.

Trends such as corporate universities, distance learning, and specialized executive courses suggest that organizational training units are continuing to rethink their roles in managing the education and development opportunities for their constituents. Accordingly, training professionals are making an increasing commitment to outsourcing training services (Noe, 2002). *Outsourcing* refers to a reliance on an external supplier to provide traditional in-house services such as training. The case for outsourcing is that external vendors may be able to provide a wider array of training courses more efficiently and less expensively than an in-house training department. For example, it may be less practical for a small to midsize organization to develop a technical support training program for a few incumbents than it would be to send those individuals to a course developed, maintained, and delivered by an outside vendor. From the external vendor's perspective, building a large client base enables the vendor to offer more cost-effective services and encourages the development of more innovative partnerships and platforms for offering its curricula. The increasing popularity of outsourcing may create concerns about the long-term viability of traditional training operations. In the short term, it is clear that their growing influence requires that training professionals must expand their skill sets to include competencies such as analyzing the utility of conducting operations internally or externally, identifying and selecting vendors, negotiating contracts, project management, vendor management, and database management (Noe).

TRAINING AS LEARNING

A second influential paper sparking the resurgence of interest in training research was a chapter by Howell and Cooke (1989) entitled "Training the Information Processor: A Review of Cognitive Models." The chapter introduced training research to the field of cognitive psychology. Since training is about facilitating learning, and a significant strand of cognitive psychology research involves how humans learn, it is somewhat curious that it took training scholars as long as it did to connect to this discipline. Howell and Cooke presented an overview of a generic information-processing/cognitively based learning model, but did not explicitly address many implications for training. A subsequent chapter by Lord and Maher (1991) on cognition in the revised I/O handbook attempted to make more direct linkages between cognitive psychology research and I/O theories, including training. However, a monograph on learning outcomes by Kraiger, Ford, and Salas (1993) and a later chapter by Ford and Kraiger (1995) were what most directly implicated cognitively based theories of learning for training. Couched as a training evaluation model, Kraiger et al.'s monograph presented a typology of learning outcomes, arguing that training impacts learners in the form of cognitive, behavioral, or affective change.

The effect of this series of papers has been to transform our perspective on training and development away from the process by which work-related knowledge, skills, rules, concepts, or attitudes are communicated or emphasized, and toward an understanding of how learners (i.e., trainees) acquire, organize, master, and generalize this content. As noted by Ford and Kraiger (1995), this change in perspective holds several important consequences for planning and facilitating the learning process. First, the acquisition of knowledge and skills in training are important but imperfect indicators of true learning (Schmidt & Bjork, 1992). Acquisition during training may reflect temporary rather than permanent changes in knowledge, skills, and behaviors, and trainees may demonstrate attitudes, knowledge, or on-the-job skills that were not evident in training. Schmidt and Bjork summarized a number of studies that demonstrate how conditions of practice may be manipulated to facilitate or hinder later transfer. Specifically, by introducing difficulties for the learner during practice (e.g., lessening feedback or providing variation in task stimuli), initial acquisition rates may be decreased, but retention and generalization to new tasks may be increased due to the additional, deeper processing necessary during practice (Ghodsian, Bjork, & Benjamin, 1997; Schmidt & Bjork). While this research is directly relevant to issues of transfer of training discussed later, it also underscores the value to training design of understanding how individuals learn.

Second, learning is multidimensional and may be evident in cognitive, affective, or behavioral changes (Kraiger et al., 1993). A taxonomy of learning outcomes in training was proposed by Kraiger et al., then later refined and expanded by Jonassen and Tessmer (1996/1997) and Kraiger (2002). The taxonomies categorize broad classes of outcomes—affective, behavioral, and cognitive—along with specific categories and outcomes under each class. For example, Kraiger (2002) identified seven categories of cognitive outcomes: declarative knowledge, structural knowledge, formation of concepts and procedures, situated problem-solving, ampliative skills, self-knowledge, and executive control. Examples of specific outcomes within situated problem-solving include identifying and defining problems and evaluating solutions.

These modern taxonomies attempt to be more realistic, explicit, and comprehensive than previous efforts describing how persons actually learn. Recall your first efforts to master a word-processing program. You did more than simply learn word-processing or progress toward a behavioral objective of typing and formatting a certain number of words within a prescribed time period or level of accuracy. You may have needed to be convinced that word processing offered advantages over typing on a typewriter; you may have experienced a reduction in computer anxiety; you acquired a new vocabulary (e.g., *font size* and *cut and paste*); and you memorized, practiced, and eventually became fluid in executing key strokes and mouse-click sequences to copy data, format text, and load and save files. Each of these experiences represents a different affective, cognitive, or behavioral outcome.

The implication of understanding training as learning has not yet been fully explored by training researchers. As will be noted shortly, researchers are just now beginning to include multiple measures of learning outcomes in their evaluation designs. The application of learning outcomes to needs assessment and training design (Ford & Kraiger, 1995) may be equally important but, to date, has been less explored by researchers and practitioners. By understanding the multidimensional nature of learning, better decisions can be made during the planning and designing of training. For example, if a preliminary needs assessment identifies problem solving as an important job skill, subsequent cognitive task analyses can specify the types of problems most commonly encountered and whether it is more important that trainees be able to identify problems, generate solution options, or evaluate potential solutions. As instructional designers become more comfortable with cognitive and affective outcomes, new methods for affecting the motivation, organization, self-monitoring, and advanced cognitive skills of learners will be proposed and tested.

A note of warning is also in order. Previously, I have argued for caution in applying research findings from cognitive psychology to the training domain (Kraiger, 1995). Consider the construct of transfer of training. In the I/O literature, *transfer of training* refers to "the degree to which trainees effectively apply the knowledge, skills, and attitudes gained in a training context to the job" (Baldwin & Ford, 1988, p. 63). However, to cognitive psychologists, transfer involves "change in the performance of a task as a result of the prior performance of a different task" (Gick & Holyoak, 1987, p. 10). Thus, learning tasks and transfer tasks are differentiated only in terms of similarity or time. There are other key differences as well: The transfer criterion in I/O is usually job performance, while it is often speed of learning (similar tasks) in the cognitive domain; the learning and transfer domains are very different in the typical training situation, while they may be very similar in a cognitive psychology study. Finally, transfer tasks are often performed relatively soon after initial learning tasks in cognitive studies (rarely more than a week later), while trainees sometimes wait months or more to apply training to their jobs. Accordingly, if studies from cognitive science suggest that withholding feedback from learners facilitates later transfer (e.g., Schmidt & Bjork, 1992), then applied research is necessary to show that the same phenomenon holds in a training application before advocating this as a general principle of (real-

world) transfer (Ghodsian et al., 1997). Nonetheless, it is clear that studies of learning and transfer hold tremendous potential value for training researchers and that better training will result from more attention to how and what trainees really learn.

TRAINING AS ORGANIZATIONAL CHANGE

Transfer of Training

A third influential paper sparking the resurgence of interest in training research was a 1988 review on transfer of training by Baldwin and Ford. They positioned transfer of training as an extension of learning during training and speculated that transfer failure was a function not only of bad training, but, like Noe (1986), a function of individual and organizational factors. Their review was timely because training writers of the era were suggesting that only 10 to 20% of what is learned in training is applied to the job (Newstrom, 1986). Then and now, for training to have impact, training practitioners must plan for transfer.

Formally, transfer of training occurs where there is "effective and continuing application, by trainees to their jobs, of the knowledge and skills gained in training—both on and off the job" (Broad & Newstrom, 1992, p. 6). Inspired by the theoretical work of Baldwin and Ford (1988), there have been any number of transfer of training models including those by Broad and Newstrom, Foxon (1993, 1994), Thayer and Teachout (1995), Kozlowski and Salas (1997), and Machin (2002). Foxon's model emphasizes intentions to transfer, while Kozlowski and Salas's distinguishes horizontal and vertical transfer (with the latter referring to generalization and application of learned skills to more complex tasks). Thayer and Teachout's model emphasizes the role of transfer climate, while Broad and Newstrom's and Machin's models emphasize transfer interventions at pretraining, training, and post-training time periods.

Pretraining influences on transfer greatly resemble the pretraining influences on learning in training effectiveness models discussed previously. For example, high self-efficacy and learner motivation prior to training is likely to enhance later transfer (e.g., Thayer & Teachout, 1995). In the interest of space, the focus of this section will be on training and posttraining interventions.

Training Interventions to Improve Transfer

Baldwin and Ford (1988), citing the work of McGehee and Thayer (1961), argued that specific instructional techniques will increase initial learning and enhance later transfer. These techniques (or learning principles) include (a) using identical elements (e.g., ensuring the fidelity of the training setting relative to the work setting; see also Holding, 1991), (b) teaching general principles (e.g., describing how a principle can be applied across multiple situations; see also Detterman, 1993), (c) providing stimulus variability (e.g., varying examples or practice conditions), and (d) varying conditions of practice (e.g., how often trainees practice the tasks; see also Schmidt & Bjork, 1992).

Consistent with Kozlowski and Salas (1997), transfer may also be enhanced when trainees develop adaptive expertise through training (Hesketh, 1997a, 1997b; Smith, Ford, & Kozlowski, 1997). The probability of transfer increases because trainees become more adept at recognizing and responding to novel stimuli across a range of complex tasks and settings. Ford and Weissbein (1997) suggested three training design features to build adaptive expertise and improve the transfer of training: discovery learning, use of error-based learning, and developing of trainees' metacognitive skills.

Finally, transfer intentions (Foxon, 1993, 1994) may be enhanced through the use of in-training, transfer-enhancing activities including goal setting (Hesketh, 1997a; Stevens & Gist, 1997), encouraging the development of specific implementation plans for achieving transfer goals (Gollwitzer, 1999), and relapse prevention, which is a strategy for preparing trainees to deal with the problematic situations they may face after training (Marx, 1982).

Posttraining Interventions to Improve Transfer

Baldwin and Ford (1988) proposed that after training, work environment characteristics may affect transfer outcomes. One characteristic is the presence of *situational constraints* (Hesketh, 1997b). Peters, O'Connor, and Eulberg (1985) identified potential work constraints as support from one's supervisor and peers, opportunity to use one's knowledge and skills on the job, and scheduling of activities. Similarly, Ford and his colleagues identified trainees' opportunity to perform trained tasks on the job as a potential deterrent to transfer (Ford, Quiñones, Sego, & Sorra, 1992; Quiñones, Sego, Ford, & Smith, 1995/1996). These researchers suggested that factors such as supervisor attitudes and workgroup support, and individual characteristics such as trainee self-efficacy and career motivation may result in trainees' having differential opportunities to apply trained skills on the job.

Finally, research by Rouiller and Goldstein (1993) and Tracey, Tannenbaum, and Kavanagh (1995) suggested that the organizational support and transfer climate can affect transfer effectiveness. *Organizational support* was defined by Rouiller and Goldstein (1993) as situations or conse-

quences that inhibit or help trainees apply trained skills back on the job. These include situational cues (prompting application at appropriate times) and linking consequences (including feedback) to performance. *Transfer climate* is defined in terms of trainee perceptions of supervisor and peer support for newly learned behaviors. Organizations hoping to facilitate transfer can ensure that trainees have the opportunity to perform newly learned skills, that supervisors understand training goals and encourage transfer attempts, and that peers and supervisors offer positive feedback and support for transfer. Research on transfer climate suggests that climate matters at least in part because of its effects on trainee characteristics: Facilitating climates increase trainee focus, motivation, and intentions to transfer (Rouiller & Goldstein, 1993; Tracey et al., 1995).

Learning Organizations

An extreme level of organizational support, learning, and transfer is the transformation to a true learning organization. A *learning organization* is one that has an enhanced capacity to learn, adapt, and grow or change (Gephart, Marsick, Van Buren, & Spiro, 1996). As detailed by Jeppesen (2002), there are a number of drivers for organizations to develop the capacity for rapid learning and internal dissemination of knowledge, including the change from a capital-intensive to a knowledge-intensive economy; rapid technological innovation; and greater global competition. Perhaps even more critical in an era of tight labor markets, organizations that provide better learning and growth opportunities have an advantage when competing for talented employees (Buckingham & Coffman, 1999). Note that learning and growth opportunities are not necessarily synonymous with the provision of formal training programs. Some companies may offer considerable training opportunities but are not perceived as positive learning environments, while other companies that offer less formal training may be perceived as ones with tremendous opportunities for personal growth (Tannenbaum, 1997).

Gephart et al. (1996) described some of the key features of learning organizations: a continuous learning environment (in which employees share knowledge and create or apply new knowledge through doing their jobs); systems for creating, capturing, and sharing knowledge; encouraging flexibility and experimentation on the job; and maintaining a learning culture (in which learning is rewarded and supported by management and through organizational decision making). Methods for creating and sharing knowledge include using technology and software to store and share information; publishing directories or yellow pages (so to speak) of employee expertise; hiring a chief information officer to facilitate the exchange of information within the company; allowing employees to take sabbaticals to acquire new expertise; and maintaining on-line resources such as journals or training manuals (Gephart et al., 1996; Noe, 2002). Methods for building and maintaining learning cultures include instituting performance-measurement systems that emphasize progress and improvement rather than control and accountability; establishing organizational infrastructure that reinforces knowledge and learning through multiple media choices; scanning inside and outside the organization for new knowledge and practices; and the use of work teams that emphasize collaboration and job sharing (Jeppesen, 2002).

Tannenbaum (2002) suggests that to promote individual learning, organizations (including true learning organizations) must diversify their learning portfolios by augmenting formal training with a commitment to better on-the-job training (OJT) and more N-of-1 or personalized learning opportunities. Although OJT is often unstructured, unmonitored, and unsupported by modern organizations, it remains one of the primary means by which employees learn their jobs. In several recent cross-organizational studies, employees reported that only 10 to 30% of their job-relevant knowledge and skills were acquired through formal job training (Pfeffer & Sutton, 2000; Tannenbaum, 1997). There are many potential benefits for OJT, including the use of job experts as instructors, and fewer expenditures for planning and design and actual training costs. Yet, the potential impact of OJT may be negated if organizations fail to provide even minimal support in terms of such standard operating procedures as identifying needs, setting objectives, training trainers, and holding OJT trainers and learners accountable for results. Accordingly, authors such as Noe (2002) and Rothwell and Kazanas (1990) have provided prescriptions centered on formalizing and providing minimal structure to previously ill-structured, informal OJT.

Regarding personalized learning, organizations are increasingly asking their members to take greater responsibility for planning and accomplishing personalized instruction. So-called *self-directed learning* works best when job demands are constantly changing and when members have access to electronic performance support systems and computer-based training, receive detailed performance feedback (often through 360-degree systems), and believe the organization supports and reinforces continual learning.

MEASUREMENT ISSUES IN TRAINING

The roles of needs assessment and training evaluation are specified in the fundamental *instructional systems design (ISD) model* (e.g., Goldstein & Ford, 2001), one that has remained virtually unchanged for more than 30 years. Yet data

suggest that these processes frequently are *not* routinely followed in organizations, and there has been limited theoretical or empirical work on either topic over the past four decades. The next two sections address issues regarding needs assessment and training evaluation.

Needs Assessment

The Need for Needs Assessment

With respect to needs assessment, several points are worth making. Across multiple disciplines, the needs-assessment process is perceived as an essential starting point in virtually all instructional design models (e.g., Dick & Carey, 1996; Goldstein & Ford, 2001; Noe, 2002; Robinson & Robinson, 1995). The second point is that despite the assumed importance of needs assessment, in practice, many training programs are initiated without it. While research on needs-assessment practices is not as widespread as research on training evaluation, available evidence suggests that instructional designers do *not* always make use of formal needs-assessment processes when planning training programs (Loughner & Moeller, 1998; Saari, Johnson, McLaughlin, & Zimmerle, 1988; Wedman & Tessmer, 1993). For example, survey research by Loughner and Moeller indicated that professional instructional developers spend, on average, less than 25% of their time on formal task analysis. Furthermore, there are no research-based guides for selecting the most appropriate needs-assessment methods given foreknowledge of the performance problem or anticipated learning outcomes. The third point is that in contrast to other areas of training, there is very little ongoing research or theory development with respect to needs assessment (Salas & Cannon-Bowers, 2001; Tannenbaum & Yukl, 1992).

That said, what should be the role of needs assessment and what are the future research questions with respect to needs assessment? Despite an apparent lack of interest in needs assessment by both practitioners and researchers, the process remains a fundamental, critical first step in planning training. In fact, research evidence on training effectiveness and transfer of training underscores its importance. As noted earlier, pretraining motivation for learning in trainees is an important determinant of training success (e.g., Baldwin & Magjuka, 1997; Colquitt et al., 2000). The adult-learning literature suggests that learner motivation increases as adults perceive the training as relevant for daily activities (e.g., Bowden & Merritt, 1995; Knowles, 1990), so that a thorough needs assessment should be able to both diagnose motivational deficiencies and ensure the relevance of training activities or clarify trainee expectancies prior to attending training.

Additionally, research on transfer of training has shown that organizational climate can either facilitate or hinder posttraining transfer (Rouillier & Goldstein, 1993; Tracey et al., 1995). Accordingly, in planning for both training and later transfer, it would be beneficial to assess initial states of trainee motivation and organizational support for transfer. Not only can such an assessment diagnose potential trouble spots, but also data on frequently performed tasks and obstacles to transfer can be useful for designing interventions for enhancing trainee motivation and ability to transfer by enabling the construction of higher fidelity training simulations. The critical role of needs assessment was underscored by Hesketh (1997b), who recommended that traditional training needs analysis be replaced with a *transfer of training* needs analysis, the goal of which is to identify organizational constraints to the transfer of training.

Yet another potential but underutilized benefit from a more extensive needs assessment is the diagnosis of individual learning styles. The importance of aptitude by treatment interactions was discussed years ago by educational psychologists (e.g., Cronbach & Snow, 1977), but has fallen out of favor with psychologists in general (Sternberg & Grigorenko, 1997) and has been historically ignored by training researchers (Warr & Allen, 1998). However, training effectiveness research has renewed interest in individual aptitude, attitudes, and personality characteristics as determinants of training outcomes (e.g., Baldwin & Magjuka, 1997; Colquitt & Simmering, 1998; Martocchio & Judge, 1997; Ree & Earles, 1991). If trainee attitudes and personal characteristics are predictive of main effects in training, it seems logical to explore the interactions of these states and traits with specific instructional methods.

Of some interest to instructional psychologists has been the relationship between individual learning styles and learning success. *Learning style* refers to an individual preference for how information is presented or acted upon for purposes of mastering learning content. Intuitively, matching learner preferences with instructional styles should result inboth more positive attitudes toward training and greater learner achievement. In practice, there have been several impediments to measuring and matching based on preferred learning styles. First, research evidence generally has not demonstrated the value of matching styles and instructional methods (Sternberg & Grigorenko, 1997). Sternberg and Grigorenko have suggested that the absence of reliable, valid learning-style instruments may account for much of the lack of positive research support. Second, in typical large-scale corporate training environments, instructional designers may not have the opportunity or resources to design separate training interventions for each subset of learners. Note, however, that the growing popularity of various forms of technology-mediated learning offers the opportunity to tailor learning environments to individuals (Brown & Ford, 2002). There is some evidence in the CBT literature that accounting for individual differences is efficacious. A recent review of technology-based instruction suggests that trainees differ in preferred levels of learner control, and that matching desired to actual control may increase trainee motivation in computer-based learning environments (Brown, Milner, Ford, & Golden, in press). Accordingly, the growing popularity of CBT suggests the need to more accurately assess individual learning styles and offer guidance to learners for choosing appropriate learning interactions. Regarding Sternberg and Grigorenko's concerns about the psychometric quality of state-of-the-art learning-style instruments, recent renewed interest in learning styles coupled with more rigorous instrument development has resulted in several reliable, valid assessment tools (Dalton, 1999; Towler & Dipboye, 2001).

Competency Modeling

One emerging trend among training and development practitioners is the use of competency models to drive training curricula. A *competency* is a cluster of interrelated knowledge, skills, values, attitudes, or personal characteristics that are presumed to be important for successful performance on the job (Noe, 2002). In contrast to traditional job analysis, competency-modeling approaches tend to be more worker focused than task focused, more closely linked with business objectives, and more likely to generalize within an organization but not across job families (Shippman et al., 2000). Determining the competencies for a particular cluster of jobs may include a formal job analysis, but should also include an examination of emerging business strategies and a quantitative comparison of the characteristics of highly successful and less successful job incumbents (Kochanski, 1997). Once validated, an organization-specific competency model may be used to design training programs or personal development plans, 360-degree style performance appraisals, long-term staffing plans, or screening and selection tools (Noe, 2002).

Given the recent popularity of competency modeling, it is worth asking whether this approach adds value to the training operation beyond traditional needs assessment models. Since it appears that thorough needs assessments are done infrequently at best, and since I have suggested that some up-front needs assessment is preferable to no needs assessment, the growing use of competency analyses reflects positively on training practice. Whether the use of a competency approach provides better design input than a traditional needs assessment is an empirical question that has yet to be addressed. Competency-model advocates prescribe analysis at the organizational, job, and person (performance) levels, but then, so did proponents of traditional needs assessment. Competency models are unique in that they cluster knowledge, skills, attitudes, and values, whereas the product of a job analysis would indicate the relative importance of discrete knowledge, skill, ability, and other requirements (KSAOs), but not necessarily group them together. However, at the training-development stage, the competent designer would make decisions (perhaps with input from incumbents or analysts) about the grouping of KSAOs for pedagogical reasons. Thus, given the current state of the competency-modeling literature, the approach is welcome for renewing interest in pretraining assessment, but has yet to successfully counter concerns that it is nothing more than old wine in new bottles.

Future Research Needs

As noted before, there has been both a lack of research on needs assessment and a lack of empirically supported guidelines to influence needs-assessment choices. Thus, the general area of needs assessment represents open territory for future training researchers. Some interesting, practical research questions are outlined in the following paragraphs.

Traditional approaches to needs assessment (e.g., Goldstein & Ford, 2001) specify the requirement to conduct organizational, job, or task analyses, and person analyses. Within this framework, some unanswered questions include the following: Are all three levels of analysis necessary, and under what conditions is a subset of these analyses acceptable? In what order should these be carried out? Traditionally, organizational analyses are recommended prior to job and task analyses, but could organizational decision makers make better decisions about commitment to training if they understand what tasks are to be trained or exactly what the performance deficiencies are? How much convergence is there among different constituents (e.g., decision makers, managers, and employees) with respect to problem identification, and what methods are optimal for resolving differences in discrepancies among sources?

Regarding organizational analysis, should the same processes and sources used to identify training resources be used to assess climate for transfer? What are useful ways for assessing and building commitment to training through organizational analysis? How do prior experiences with training affect perceptions of the utility of training solutions identified during training?

Regarding job and task analysis, there are a number of interesting questions pertaining to methods of data collection and translating information on tasks and individual competencies into training content. For example, what are the implications for training design of basing the analysis on current tasks or KSAOs, as opposed to framing the question in terms of forecasted future KSAOs (e.g., Arvey, Salas, & Gialluca, 1992; Wilson & Zalewski, 1994). What qualifies someone as a subject-matter expert? Can the characteristic of automaticity often found in true experts inhibit their ability to explain basic tasks to job analysts (Ford & Kraiger, 1985)? What are the best ways of combining traditional forms of job and task analysis, with their focus on observable behaviors, with new methods of cognitive task analysis (Ryder & Redding, 1991)? Here, *cognitive task analysis* refers to procedures for understanding the mental processing and requirements for job performance—for example, the roles of decision making and memory aids (see Dubois, 2002; Schraagen et al., 2000).

Regarding person analysis, topics of interest include identifying optimal ways of assessing trainee readiness, motivation to learn, preferred learning styles, mastery orientation, and performance deficits, and of determining to what extent these attributes overlap. Recent research has only now begun to show the links between these individual attributes and training outcomes, so it is not surprising that less emphasis has been placed on the development of psychometrically sound measures or providing evidence of the convergent and discriminant validity of existing measures. Other research questions pertain to the validity of individual reports of training needs or trainee readiness. Given that novice learners often "don't know what they don't know" (e.g., Nelson & Leonesio, 1988; Weaver & Kelemen, 1997), what are the best ways of soliciting employees' opinions on needed training while at the same time enhancing their interest in upcoming training?

As additional research on needs assessment is conducted, I/O psychologists will be able to make more practical suggestions enabling organizations planning on training to make efficient uses of their resources.

Training Evaluation

Historical Patterns

A second major area of training measurement concerns training evaluation. Since the early 1960s, training programs have been evaluated in terms of Kirkpatrick's (1994) four levels of evaluation. The four levels were originally suggested by Kirkpatrick in the late 1950s in response to requests from practitioners for useful techniques for evaluating training programs. Thus, while the four levels soon assumed model-like status (see Holton, 1996), they were originally offered as practical guidelines drawn from Kirkpatrick's personal experience. Specifically, Kirkpatrick recommended assessing, in sequence, the following four outcomes: trainees' reactions (how well trainees liked the training), learning (what principles, facts, or skills were learned), behavior (what were the resulting changes in job behavior), and results (what were the tangible results from training). Kirkpatrick's four levels have been characterized as hierarchical, indicating both that higher levels should not be assessed unless satisfactory results are achieved at prior levels and that changes at higher levels are more beneficial to the organization than changes at lower levels.

Kirkpatrick's (1976, 1994) four-level hierarchy remains the standard for evaluation practice. Accordingly, recent surveys of organizations' evaluation practices have been organized around the four levels (Twitchell, Holton, & Trott, 2001; Van Buren, 2001). These surveys found that although most organizations assess the first level, or reactions to training, fewer than half measure learning during training, and, depending on the survey source, only 10–30% measured changes in on-the-job behavior or performance results. The consistency of these findings with those of prior surveys (e.g., Catalanello & Kirkpatrick, 1968) led Twitchell et al. to conclude that "it would appear that evaluation practices today are not much more widespread than thirty years ago, except at Level 2" (p. 96).

Emerging Trends in Evaluation

It is easy to look pessimistically at modern evaluation practices and believe that, unlike in other areas of training and development, nothing much is changing: Training researchers and practitioners continue to use an atheoretical model proposed 40 years ago, and the prevalence of behaviorally based or performance-based evaluation measures remain unchanged from 30 years ago. However, it can also be argued that seeds for change in evaluation practices have been sown, such that we may continue to see growth toward better, more construct-based evaluation practices in the next decade.

First, the last decade has seen several thoughtful critiques of the Kirkpatrick approach (Alliger & Janak, 1989; Alliger, Tannenbaum, Bennett, Traver, & Shortland, 1997; Holton, 1996; Kraiger, 2002; Kraiger et al., 1993), and the limitations of this approach are gradually being recognized by both researchers and practitioners. In brief, criticisms of the approach are as follows: (a) The approach is largely atheoretical, and to whatever extent that it may be theory based, it is based on a 1950s behavioral perspective that ignores modern, cognitively based theories of learning. (b) It is overly simplistic in that it treats constructs such as trainee reactions and learning as unidimensional. (c) The approach makes assumptions about positive relationships between training outcomes that are not supported by research (see Alliger et al., 1997) or do not make sense intuitively. For example, Kirkpatrick argued that trainees cannot learn if they do not like the train-

ing. Although meta-analytic research suggests that trainee reactions and learning are in fact correlated (Alliger et al.) the relationship is not that strong. (d) The approach does not account for the purpose for evaluation; it is not always necessary to move from a level-2 to a level-3 evaluation simply because that is the next step, but it is important that data collection be conducted with a mind toward how the data may be useful to the training function. As discussed by Kraiger (2002), there are generally three purposes for training evaluation: decision making (e.g., deciding whether to keep a course), feedback (e.g., identifying strengths and weaknesses of trainers or trainees), and marketing (e.g., using results of the evaluation to sell the training to other organizations or future trainees). A more practical approach to evaluation would recognize that what is to be measured should be guided by the intended uses of the data, not by what was measured last.

Second, researchers have begun to appreciate the multidimensional nature of common evaluation targets. For example, Warr and Bunce (1995) argued that participant reactions are not a unitary construct, but a multidimensional one composed of feelings of affect or satisfaction toward training, perceived utility, and perceived difficulty. Alliger et al. (1997) concurred in principle, but suggested that reactions typically comprise two dimensions—affect and utility. Finally, Morgan and Casper (2001) administered 32 common-reaction questions to more than 9,000 trainees and factor-analyzed respondents' answers. Their analyses suggested that there were six factors underlying participant reactions to training: satisfaction with the instructor, satisfaction with the training and administration process, satisfaction with the testing and evaluation process, utility of training, satisfaction with materials, and course structure. A useful practitioner-focused article that captures the dimensionality of trainee reactions was recently published by Lee and Pershing (1999), who defined and provided sample questions for 10 dimensions of participant reactions, including content and program materials, delivery methods, instructor, instructional activities, program time or length, the training environment, and logistics and administration.

As discussed previously, the multidimensional nature of participant learning was recognized by Kraiger et al. (1993). Their typology is not only more consistent with modern learning theory, but provides greater precision in determining how trainee learning should be assessed. To date, there have been relatively few published applications of Kraiger et al.'s taxonomy, particularly in the applied domain. The use of new measures proposed in the taxonomy tend to be restricted to academically focused tests of training methods geared toward learning outcomes in the taxonomy, such as knowledge organization (Kraiger, Salas, & Cannon-Bowers, 1995) or metacognition (Schmidt & Ford, 2001; Toney & Ford, 2001).

Building on an expanded outcomes framework suggested by Jonassen and Tessmer (1996/1997), Kraiger (2002) has recently proposed an updated taxonomy that is linked explicitly to training purpose and provides sample measures for each outcome. For example, under the general learning construct of "forming concepts and principles," Kraiger provides five possible outcomes including "forming concepts" (e.g., identifying examples of statistical problems that can be solved using analysis of covariance) and "applying rules" (e.g., calculating the sample size necessary to ensure adequate statistical power in a simple training design). If one of the strengths of the Kirkpatrick (1994) approach is its simplicity, then the logical pathways from training purpose to suggested learning measures in Kraiger may be at the same time equally straightforward yet more comprehensive.

A third reason for optimism with respect to training evaluation is the growing understanding that less rigorous research designs may still be useful for decision-making purposes. One of the popular reasons provided by training professionals that more extensive evaluations (e.g., measuring changes in on-the-job behavior) are not performed is that strong experimental designs (i.e., those with pretesting and control groups) are not possible due to lack of resources, poor timing, or ethical considerations of withholding treatment from control group subjects (Twitchell et al., 2001). However, depending on the use of evaluation information, high quality, rigorous evaluation designs may not be necessary (Sackett & Mullen, 1993; Tannenbaum & Woods, 1992). As Sackett and Mullen noted, evaluation is very often made merely to determine whether a target performance level has been achieved (e.g., whether a paramedic is street ready). In these circumstances, formal evaluation designs may not be necessary at all, particularly if the researcher has confidence in the validity of the performance measure. When evaluation is done for decision-making purposes, true experimental designs may have less power to detect training effects than weaker preexperimental designs under some conditions (Sackett & Mullen, 1993). When true experimental designs are impractical, there are useful alternatives, including Haccoun and Hamtiaux's (1994) internal referencing strategy, and the use of reasoned logic based on knowledge of the measures and the intended impact of training (McLinden, 1995, Sackett & Mullen, 1993). As training practitioners learn more about how to build the case for training without having cleanly and absolutely isolated the training, then perhaps more extensive evaluations will be attempted.

In summary, in many ways the practice of training evaluation looks no different than it did 40 years ago. However, a growing appreciation of the limitations of old methods, the emergence of expanded taxonomies of potential measures, and a new understanding for the value of less rigorous research designs may spark more widespread applications of purposeful, construct-based evaluation.

FINAL THOUGHTS

Consistent with Salas and Cannon-Bowers (2001), it appears that the state of training research has never been more active or as conceptually well founded as it is today. All of this comes at an opportune time as the training industry itself is evolving even more rapidly. Successful organizations are investing increasingly more in employee training and development, the potential if not the very form of instructional delivery is changing as e-learning explodes, and training and development is even becoming an integral mechanism for restructuring organizations. The advancements in theory and research over the past 15 years should provide the foundation for training guidelines and principles that will ensure more effective and more efficient trainee learning maintained over time.

REFERENCES

Alliger, G. M., & Janak, E. A. (1989). Kirkpatrick's levels of training criteria: Thirty years later. *Personnel Psychology, 42,* 331–342.

Alliger, G. M., Tannenbaum, S. I., Bennett, W., Traver, H., & Shortland, A. (1997). A meta-analysis on the relations among training criteria. *Personnel Psychology, 50,* 341–358.

Arthur, W., Day, E. A., Bennett, W., McNelly, T. L., & Jordan, J. A. (1997). Dyadic versus individual training protocols: Loss and reacquisition of a complex skill. *Journal of Applied Psychology, 82,* 783–791.

Arvey, R. A., Salas, E., & Gialluca, K. A. (1992). Using task inventories to forecast skills and abilities. *Human Performance, 5,* 171–190.

Azevedo, R., & Bernard, R. M. (1995). A meta-analysis of the effects of feedback in computer based instruction. *Journal of Educational Computing Research, 13*(2), 111–127.

Baldwin, T. T., & Ford, J. K. (1988). Transfer of training: A review and directions for future research. *Personnel Psychology, 41,* 63–105.

Baldwin, T. T., & Magjuka, R. J. (1997). Training as an organizational episode: Pretraining influences on trainee motivation. In J. K. Ford, S. W. J. Kozlowski, K. Kraiger, E. Salas, & M. Teachout (Eds.), *Improving training effectiveness in work organizations* (pp. 99–127). Mahwah, NJ: Erlbaum.

Baldwin, T. T., Magjuka, R. J., & Loher, B. T. (1991). The perils of participation: Effects of choice of training on trainee motivation and learning. *Personnel Psychology, 44,* 260–267.

Bassi, L. J., Benson, G., & Cheney, S. (1998). *The top ten trends.* Alexandria, VA: American Society for Training and Development.

Bassi, L. J., & Van Buren, M. E. (1999). *The 1999 ASTD State of the Industry Report.* Washington, DC: American Society for Training and Development.

Bhawuk, D. P. S., & Brislin, R. W. (2000). Cross-cultural training: A review. *Applied Psychology: An International Review, 49,* 162–191.

Black, J. S., & Mendenhall, M. (1990). Cross-cultural training effectiveness: A review and theoretical framework for future research. *American Management Review, 15,* 113–136.

Bowden, R., & Merritt, R., Jr. (1995). The adult learner challenge: Instructionally and administratively. *Education, 115,* 426–432.

Brennan, M., & Anderson, C. (2001). *The U.S. corporate elearning market forecast and analysis, 2000–2005.* Framingham, MA: IDC.

Brislin, R. W., & Bhawuk, D. P. S. (1999). Cross-cultural training: Research and innovations. In J. Adamopoulos & Y. Kashima (Eds.), *Social psychology and cultural context* (pp. 205–216). Thousand Oaks, CA: Sage.

Brislin, R. W., Cushner, K., Cherrie, C., & Yong, M. (1986). *Intercultural interactions: A practical guide.* Beverly Hills, CA: Sage.

Broad, M. L., & Newstrom, J. W. (1992). *Transfer of training: Action-packed strategies to ensure high payoff from training investments.* Reading, MA: Addison-Wesley.

Brown, K. G. (2001). Using computers to deliver training: Which employees learn and why. *Personnel Psychology, 54,* 271–296.

Brown, K. G., & Ford, J. K. (2002). Using computer technology in training: Building an infrastructure for active learning. In K. Kraiger (Ed.), *Creating, implementing, and maintaining effective training and development: State-of-the-art lessons for practice* (pp. 192–233). San Francisco: Jossey-Bass.

Brown, K. G., Milner, K. R., Ford, J. K., & Golden, W. (in press). Repurposing instructor-led training into web-based training: A case study and lessons learned. In B. Khan (Ed.), *Web-based training.* Englewood Cliffs, NJ: Educational Technology.

Buckingham, M., & Coffman, C. (1999). *First break all the rules: What the world's greatest managers do differently.* New York: Simon & Schuster.

Burns, H., & Parlett, J. W. (1991). *Intelligent tutoring systems: Evolutions in design.* Hillsdale, NJ: Erlbaum.

Byrne, J. A. (1995, October 23). Virtual B-schools. *Business Week, n3447,* 64–68.

Campbell, J. P. (1971). Personnel training and development. *Annual Review of Psychology, 22,* 565–602.

Cannon-Bowers, J. A. Rhodenizer, L., Salas, E., & Bowers, C. A. (1998). A framework for understanding pre-practice conditions and their impact on learning. *Personnel Psychology, 51,* 291–320.

Cannon-Bowers, J. A., & Salas, E. (Eds.). (1998). *Making decisions under stress: Implications for individual and team training.* Washington, DC: American Psychological Association.

Cannon-Bowers, J. A., Salas, E., Blickensderfer, E., & Bowers, C. A. (1998). The impact of cross-training and workload on team functioning: A replication and extension of initial findings. *Human Factors, 40,* 92–101.

Cannon-Bowers, J. A., Salas, E., Tannenbaum, S. I., & Mathieu, J. E. (1995). Toward theoretically based principles of training effectiveness: A model and initial empirical investigations. *Military Psychology, 7,* 141–164.

Cannon-Bowers, J. A., Tannenbaum, S. I., Salas, E., & Volpe, C. E. (1995). Defining team competencies and establishing team training requirements. In R. Guzzo, & E. Salas (Eds.), *Team effectiveness and decision making in organizations* (pp. 333–380). San Francisco: Jossey-Bass.

Catalanello, R., & Kirkpatrick, D. (1968). Evaluating training programs: The state of the art. *Training and Development Journal, 22*(5), 2–9.

Clark, R. E. (1994). Media will never influence learning. *Educational Technology Research and Development, 42,* 21–29.

Colquitt, J. A., LePine, J. A., & Noe, R. A. (2000). Towards an integrative theory of training motivation: A meta-analytic path analysis of 20 years of research. *Journal of Applied Psychology, 85,* 678–807.

Colquitt, J. A., & Simmering, M. S. (1998). Consciousness, goal orientation, and motivation to learn during the learning process: A longitudinal study. *Journal of Applied Psychology, 83,* 654–665.

Cronbach, L. J., & Snow, R. E. (1977). *Aptitudes and instructional methods.* New York: Irvington.

Cushner, K., & Brislin, R. W. (1996). *Intercultural interactions: A practical guide* (2nd ed.). Thousand Oaks, CA: Sage.

Dalton, M. (1999). *Learning tactics inventory: Facilitator's guide.* San Francisco: Jossey-Bass/Pfeiffer.

Decker, P. J., & Nathan, B. R. (1985). *Behavior modeling training.* New York: Praeger.

Deshpande, S. P., & Viswesvaran, C. (1992). Is cross-cultural training of expatriate managers effective: A meta analysis. *International Journal of Intercultural Relations, 16,* 295–330.

Detterman, D. K. (1993). The case for the prosecution: Transfer as an epiphenomenon. In D. K. Detterman & R. J. Sternberg (Eds.), *Transfer on trial: Intelligence, cognition, and instruction* (pp. 1–24). Norwood, NJ: Ablex.

Dick, W., & Carey, L. (1996). *The systematic design of instruction* (4th ed.). New York: Longman.

Dubois, D. A. (2002). Leveraging hidden expertise: Why, when, and how to use cognitive task analyses. In K. Kraiger (Ed.), *Creating, implementing, and maintaining effective training and development: State-of-the-art lessons for practice* (pp. 80–114). San Francisco: Jossey-Bass.

Dweck, C. S. (1986). Motivational processes affecting learning. *American Psychologist, 41,* 1040–1048.

Facteau, J. D., Dobbins, G. H., Russell, J. E. A., Ladd, R. T., & Kudisch, J. D. (1995). The influence of general perceptions of the training environment on pretraining motivation and perceived training transfer. *Journal of Management, 21,* 1–25.

Fisher, S. L., & Ford, J. K. (1998) Differential effects of learner effort and goal orientation on two learner outcomes. *Personnel Psychology, 51,* 397–420.

Ford, J. K., & Kraiger, K. (1995). The application of cognitive constructs and principles to the instructional systems of model training: Implications for needs assessment, design, and transfer. In C. L. Cooper & I. T. Robertson (Eds.), *International review of industrial and organizational psychology* (Vol. 10, pp. 1–48). Chichester, England: Wiley.

Ford, J. K., Quiñones, M. A., Sego, D. J., & Sorra, J. S. (1992). Factors affecting the opportunity to perform trained tasks on the job. *Personnel Psychology, 45,* 511–527.

Ford, J. K., Smith, E. M., Weissbein, D. A., Gully, S. M., & Salas, E. (1998). Relationships of goal-orientation, metacognitive activity, and practice strategies with learning outcomes and transfer. *Journal of Applied Psychology, 83,* 218–233.

Ford, J. K., & Weissbein, D. A. (1997). Transfer of training: An updated review and analysis. *Performance Improvement Quarterly, 10*(2), 22–41.

Foxon, M. J. (1993). A process approach to the transfer of training: Pt. 1. The impact of motivation and supervisor support on transfer maintenance. *The Australian Journal of Educational Technology, 9*(2), 130–143.

Foxon, M. J. (1994). A process approach to the transfer of training: Pt. 2. Using action planning to facilitate the transfer of training. *The Australian Journal of Educational Technology, 10*(1), 1–18.

Gagne, R. M. (1962). Military training and principles of learning. *American Psychologist, 17,* 83–91.

Gagne, R. M., Briggs, L. J., & Wager, W. W. (1992). *The principles of instructional design* (4th ed.). Fort Worth, TX: Harcourt Brace Jovanovich.

Gagne, R. M., & Medsker, K. L. (1996). *The conditions of learning.* Fort Worth, TX: Harcourt-Brace.

Gephart, M. A., Marsick, V. J., Van Buren, M. E., & Spiro, M. S. (1996). Learning organizations come alive. *Training and Development, 50,* 56–66.

Georghiades, P. (2000). Beyond conceptual change learning in science education: Focusing on transfer, durability and metacognition. *Educational Research, 42,* 119–139.

Ghodsian, D., Bjork, R., & Benjamin, A. (1997). Evaluating training during training: Obstacles and opportunities. In M.A. Quiñones & A. Ehrenstein (Eds.) *Training for a rapidly changing workplace: Applications of psychological research* (pp. 63–88). Washington, DC: American Psychological Association.

Gick, M. L., & Holyoak, K. J. (1987). The cognitive basis of knowledge transfer. In S. M. Cormier & J. D. Hagman (Eds.), *Transfer of learning: Contemporary research and applications* (pp. 9–46). San Diego, CA: Academic Press.

Goldstein, I. L. (1980). Training in work organizations. *Annual Review of Psychology, 31,* 229–272.

Goldstein, I. L., & Ford, J. K. (2001). *Training in organizations: Needs assessment, development, and evaluation* (4th ed.). Belmont, CA: Wadsworth.

Goldstein, A. P., & Sorcher, M. (1974). *Changing supervisor behavior.* New York: Pergamon Press.

Gollwitzer, P. M. (1999). Implementation intentions: Strong effects of simple plans. *American Psychologist, 54,* 493–503.

Gopher, D., Weil, M., & Bareket, T. (1994). Transfer of skill from a computer game trainer to flight. *Human Factors, 36,* 387–405.

Guzzo, R. A., & Dickson, M. W. (1996). Teams in organizations: Recent research on performance and effectiveness. *Annual Review of Psychology, 47,* 307–338.

Haccoun, R. R., & Hamtiaux, T. (1994). Optimizing knowledge tests for inferring acquisition levels in single group training evaluation designs: The internal referencing strategy. *Personnel Psychology, 47,* 593–604.

Hall, B. (1997). *Web-based training cookbook.* New York: Wiley.

Harrison, J. K. (1992). Individual and combined effects of behavior modeling and the culture assimilator in cross-cultural management training. *Journal of Applied Psychology, 77,* 952–962.

Harrison, R., & Hopkins, R. L., (1967). The design of cross-cultural training: An alternative to the university model. *Journal of Applied Behavioral Science, 3,* 431–460.

Hesketh, B. (1997a). Dilemmas in training for transfer and retention. *Applied Psychology: An International Review, 46,* 317–339.

Hesketh, B. (1997b). Whither dilemmas in training for transfer. *Applied Psychology: An International Review, 46,* 380–386.

Hicks, W. D., & Klimoski, R. (1987). The process of entering training programs and its effect on training outcomes. *Academy of Management Journal, 30,* 542–552.

Holding, D. H. (1991). Transfer of training. In J. E. Morrison (Ed.), *Training for performance: Principles of applied human learning* (pp. 93–125). Chichester, England: Wiley.

Holton, E. F., III. (1996). The flawed four-level evaluation model. *Human Resource Development Quarterly, 7,* 5–21.

Howell, W. C., & Cooke, N. J. (1989). Training the human information processor: A review of cognitive models. In I. L. Goldstein (Ed.), *Training and development in organizations* (pp. 121–182). San Francisco: Jossey-Bass.

Industry report 1997. (1997, October). *Training, 34*(10), 56.

Jentsch, F., & Bowers, C. (1998). Evidence for the validity of PC-based simulations in studying aircrew coordination. *International Journal of Aviation Psychology, 8,* 243–260.

Jeppesen, J. (2002). Creating and maintaining the learning organization. In K. Kraiger (Ed.), *Creating, implementing, and maintaining effective training and development: State-of-the-art lessons for practice* (pp. 302–330). San Francisco: Jossey-Bass.

Jonassen, D., & Tessmer, M. (1996/1997). An outcomes-based taxonomy for instructional systems design, evaluation, and research. *Training Research Journal, 2,* 11–46.

Kirkpatrick, D. L. (1976). Evaluation of training. In R. L. Craig (Ed.), *Training and development handbook: A guide to human resource development* (2nd ed., pp. 18.1–18.27). New York: McGraw-Hill.

Kirkpatrick, D. L. (1994). *Evaluating training programs: The four levels*. San Francisco: Berrett-Koehler.

Knowles, M. S. (1990). *The adult learner* (4th ed.). Houston, TX: Gulf.

Kochanski, J. (1997). Competency-based management. *Training and Development, 51*(10), 41–44.

Kozlowski, S. W. J., & Salas, E. (1997). An organizational systems approach for the implementation and transfer of training. In J. K. Ford, S. W. J. Kozlowski, K. Kraiger, E. Salas, & M. Teachout (Eds.), *Improving training effectiveness in work organizations* (pp. 247–287). Hillsdale, NJ: Erlbaum.

Kraemer, A. (1973). *Development of a cultural self-awareness approach to instruction in intercultural communication* (Technical Rep. No. 73-17). Arlington, VA: HumRRO.

Kraiger, K. (1995, August). *Paradigms lost: Applications and misapplications of cognitive science to the study of training.* Invited address for Science Weekend at the Annual Meeting of the American Psychological Association, Toronto, CN.

Kraiger, K. (2002). Decision-based evaluation. In K. Kraiger (Ed.), *Creating, implementing, and maintaining effective training and development: State-of-the-art lessons for practice* (pp. 331–375). San Francisco: Jossey-Bass.

Kraiger, K., Ford, J. K., & Salas, E. (1993). Application of cognitive, skill-based, and affective theories of learning outcomes to new methods of training evaluation. *Journal of Applied Psychology, 78,* 311–328.

Kraiger, K., Salas, E., & Cannon-Bowers, J. A. (1995). Measuring knowledge organization as a method for assessing learning during training. *Human Factors, 37,* 804–816.

Krendl, K. A., Ware, W. H., Reid, K. A., & Warren, R. (1996). Learning by any other name: Communications research traditions in learning and media. In D. H. Jonassen (Ed.), *Handbook of research for educational communications and technology* (pp. 93–111). New York: Macmillan.

Kulik, C. C., & Kulik, J. A. (1991). Effectiveness of computer-based instruction: An updated analysis. *Computers in Human Behavior, 7,* 75–94.

Landis, D., & Bhagat, R. (Eds.). (1996). *Handbook of intercultural training*. Newbury Park, CA: Sage.

Latham, G. P. (1988). Human resource training and development. *Annual Review of Psychology, 39,* 545–582.

Lee, J. A. (1966). Cultural analysis in overseas operations. *Harvard Business Review, 44*(5), 106–114.

Lee, S. H., & Pershing, J. A. (1999). Effective reaction evaluation in evaluating training programs. *Performance Improvement, 38*(8), 32–39.

London, M., & Moore, E. M. (1999). Continuous learning. In D. R. Ilgen & E. D. Pulakos (Eds.), *The changing nature of performance* (pp. 119–153). San Francisco: Jossey-Bass.

Lord, R. G., & Maher, K. J. (1991). Cognitive theory in industrial/organizational psychology. In M. D. Dunnette & L. M. Hough (Eds.), *Handbook of industrial and organizational psychology* (2nd ed., Vol. 2, pp. 1–62). Palo Alto, CA: Consulting Psychologists Press.

Loughner, P., & Moeller, L. (1998). The use of task analysis procedures by instructional designers. *Performance Improvement Quarterly, 11*(3), 79–101.

Machin, A. M. (2002). Planning, managing, and optimizing transfer of training. In K. Kraiger (Ed.), *Creating, implementing, and maintaining effective training and development: State-of-the-art lessons for practice* (pp. 263–301). San Francisco: Jossey-Bass.

Marks, M. A. (1999). A test of the impact of collective efficacy in routine and novel performance environments. *Human Performance, 12,* 259–309.

Martocchio, J. J., & Judge, T. A. (1997). Relationship between conscientiousness and learning in employee training: Mediating influences of self-deception and self-efficacy. *Journal of Applied Psychology, 82,* 764–773.

Marx, R. D. (1982). Relapse prevention for managerial training: A model of maintenance of behavior change. *Academy of Management Review, 7,* 433–441.

Mathieu, J. E., Martineau, J. W., & Tannenbaum, S. I. (1993). Individual and situational influences on the development of self-efficacy: Implication for training effectiveness. *Personnel Psychology, 46,* 125–147.

Maurer, T. J., & Tarulli, B. A. (1994). Investigation of perceived environment, perceived outcome, and person variables in relationship to voluntary development activity by employees. *Journal of Applied Psychology, 79,* 3–14.

Mayer, R. E., Moreno, R., Boire, M., & Vagge, S. (1998). Maximizing constructivist learning from multimedia communications by minimizing cognitive load. *Journal of Educational Psychology, 91,* 638–643.

McGehee, W., & Thayer, P. W. (1961). *Training in business and industry*. New York: Wiley.

McLinden, D. J. (1995). Proof, evidence, and complexity: Understanding the impact of training and development in business. *Performance Improvement Quarterly, 8*(3), 3–18.

Meister, J. (1998). Ten steps to creating a corporate university. *Training and Development, 52*(11), 38–43.

Morgan, B. B., Jr., Glickman, A. S., Woodard, E. A., Blaiwes, A. S., & Salas, E. (1986). *Measurement of team behaviors in a Navy environment* (Technical Rep. No. 86-014). Orlando, FL: Naval Training Systems Center.

Morgan, R. B., & Casper, W. (2001). Examining the factor structure of participant reactions to training: A multi-dimensional approach. *Human Resource Development Quarterly.*

Nelson, T. O., & Leonesio, R. (1988). Allocation of self-paced study time and the "labor-in-vain effect." *Journal of Experimental Psychology: Learning, Memory, & Cognition, 14,* 676–686.

Newell, A., & Simon, H. H. (1972). *Human problem-solving*. Englewood Cliffs, NJ: Prentice-Hall.

Newstrom, J. W. (1986). Leveraging management development through the management of transfer. *Journal of Management Development, 5*(5), 33–45.

Noe, R. A. (1986). Trainees' attributes and attitudes: Neglected influences on training effectiveness. *Academy of Management Review, 11,* 736–749.

Noe, R. A. (2002). *Employee training and development* (2nd ed). Boston: McGraw-Hill.

Noe, R. A., & Colquitt J. A. (2002). Planning for training impact: Principles of training effectiveness. In K. Kraiger (Ed.), *Creating, implementing, and maintaining effective training and development: State-of-the-art lessons for practice* (pp. 53–79). San Francisco: Jossey-Bass.

Noe, R. A., & Schmitt, N. (1986). The influence of trainee attitudes on training effectiveness: Test of a model. *Personnel Psychology, 39,* 497–523.

Noe, R. A., & Wilk, S. L. (1993). Investigation of the factors that influence employees' participation in development activities. *Journal of Applied Psychology, 78,* 291–302.

O'Brien, G. E., Fiedler, F. E., & Hewett, T. (1970). The effects of programmed culture training upon the performance of volunteer medical teams in Central America. *Human Relations, 24,* 209–231.

Peters, L. H., O'Connor, E. J., & Eulberg, J. R. (1985). Situational constraints: Sources, consequences and future considerations. *Research in Personnel and Human Resource Management, 3,* 79–114.

Pfeffer, J., & Sutton, R. I. (2000). *The knowing-doing gap: How smart companies turn knowledge into action.* Boston: Harvard Business School Press.

Phillips, J. M., & Gully, S. M. (1997). Role of goal orientation, ability, need for achievement, and locus of control in the self-efficacy and goal-setting process. *Journal of Applied Psychology, 82,* 792–802.

Quiñones, M. (1995). Pretraining context effects: Training assignment as feedback. *Journal of Applied Psychology, 80,* 226–238.

Quiñones, M. A. (1997). Contextual influences on training effectiveness. In M. A. Quiñones & A. Ehrenstein (Eds.), *Training for a rapidly changing workplace* (pp. 177–200). Washington, DC: American Psychological Association.

Rasker, P. C., Post, W. M., & Schraagen, J. M. C. (2000). The effects of two types of intra-team feedback on developing a shared mental model in command and control teams. *Ergonomics, 43,* 1167–1189.

Ree, M. J., & Earles, J. A. (1991). Predicting training success: Not much more than *g. Personnel Psychology, 44,* 321–332.

Reingold, J. (1999, October 20). Corporate America goes to school. *Business Week, n3549,* 66–72.

Robinson, D. G., & Robinson, J. C. (1995). *Performance consulting: Moving beyond training.* San Francisco: Barrett-Koehler.

Rothwell, W. J., & Kazanas, H. C. (1990). Planned OJT is productive OJT. *Training and Development, 44*(10), 53–56.

Rouiller, J. Z., & Goldstein, I. L. (1993). The relationship between organizational transfer climate and positive transfer of training. *Human Resource Development Quarterly, 4,* 377–390.

Russell, T. L. (1999). *No significant difference phenomenon.* Raleigh: North Carolina State University.

Ryder, J. M., & Redding, R. E. (1991). Integrating cognitive task analysis into instructional systems development. *Educational Technology Research and Development, 41,* 75–96.

Saari, L. M., Johnson, T. R., McLaughlin, S. D., & Zimmerle, D. M. (1988). A survey of management and education practices in U.S. companies. *Personnel Psychology, 41,* 731–743.

Sackett, P. R., & Mullen, E. J. (1993). Beyond formal experimental design: Towards an expanded view of the training evaluation process. *Personnel Psychology, 46,* 613–627.

Salas, E., Bowers, C. A., & Rhodenizer, L. (1998). It is not how much you have but how you use it: Toward a rational use of simulation to support aviation training. *International Journal of Aviation Psychology, 8,* 197–208.

Salas, E., Burke, C. S., & Cannon-Bowers, J. A. (2002). Tips and guidelines for designing and delivering team training. In K. Kraiger (Ed.), *Creating, implementing, and maintaining effective training and development: State-of-the-art lessons for practice* (pp. 234–259). San Francisco: Jossey-Bass.

Salas, E., & Cannon-Bowers, J. A. (1997). Methods, tools, and strategies for team training. In M. A. Quiñones & A. Ehrenstein (Eds.), *Training for a rapidly changing workplace: Applications of psychological research* (pp. 249–280). Washington, DC: American Psychological Association.

Salas, E., & Cannon-Bowers, J. A. (2000). Designing training systems systematically. In E. A. Locke (Ed.), *The Blackwell handbook of principles of organizational behavior* (pp. 43–59). Malden, MA: Blackwell.

Salas, E., & Cannon-Bowers, J. B. (2001). The science of training: A decade of progress. *Annual Review of Psychology, 52,* 471–499.

Schank, R. C., & Joseph, D. M. (1998). Intelligent schooling. In R. J. Sternberg & W. M. Williams (Eds.), *Intelligence, instruction, and assessment: Theory into practice* (pp. 43–65). Mahwah, NJ: Erlbaum.

Schmidt, R. A., & Bjork, R. A. (1992). New conceptualizations of practice: common principles in three paradigms suggest new concepts for training. *Psychological Science, 3,* 207–217.

Schmidt, A. M., & Ford, J. K. (2001, April). *Promoting active learning through Metacognitive Instruction.* Symposium presented at the annual meeting of the Society for Industrial-Organizational Psychology, San Diego, CA.

Schraagen, J. M., Chipman, S. F., & Shalin, V. L. (2000). *Cognitive task analysis.* Mahwah, NJ: Erlbaum.

Shebilske, W. L., Regian, J. W., Arthur, W., Jr., & Jordan, J. A. (1992). A dyadic protocol for training complex skills. *Human Factors, 34,* 369–374.

Shippman, J. S., Ash, R. A., Battista, M., Carr, L., Eyde, L. D., Hesketh, B., Kehoe, J., Pearlman, K., & Sanchez, J. I. (2000).

The practice of competency modeling. *Personnel Psychology, 53,* 703–740.

Simon, S. J. & Werner, J. M. (1996). Computer training through behavior modeling, self-paced, and instructional approaches: A field experiment. *Journal of Applied Psychology, 81,* 648–659.

Smith, E. M., Ford, J. K., & Kozlowski, S. W. J. (1997). Building adaptive expertise: Implications for training design strategies. In M. A. Quiñones & A. Ehrenstein (Eds.), *Training for a rapidly changing workforce* (pp. 89–118). Washington, DC: American Psychological Association.

Smith-Jentsch, K. A., Zeisig, R. L., Acton, B., & McPherson, J. A. (1998). Team dimensional training: A strategy for guided team self-correction. In J. A. Cannon-Bowers & E. Salas (Eds.), *Making decision under stress: Implications for individual and team training* (pp. 271–297). Washington, DC: American Psychological Association.

Steele-Johnson, D., & Hyde, B. G. (1997). Advanced technologies in training: Intelligent tutoring systems and virtual reality. In M. A. Quiñones & A. Ehrenstein (Eds.), *Training for a rapidly changing workplace: Applications of psychological research* (pp. 225–248). Washington, DC: American Psychological Association.

Sternberg, R. J., & Grigorenko, E. L. (1997). Are cognitive styles still in style? *American Psychologist, 52,* 700–712.

Stevens, C. K., & Gist, M. E. (1997). Effects of self-efficacy and goal orientation training on negotiation skill maintenance: What are the skill mechanisms? *Personnel Psychology, 50,* 955–978.

Stewart, E. (1966). The simulation of cultural differences. *Journal of Communication, 16,* 291–304.

Stout, R. J., Cannon-Bowers, J. A., & Salas, E. (1996/1997). The role of shared mental models in developing team situational awareness: Implications for team training. *Training Research Journal, 2,* 85–116.

Sundstrom, E., McIntyre, M., Halfhill, T., & Richards, H. (2000). Work groups: From the Hawthorne studies to work teams of the 1990s and beyond. *Group Dynamics, 4*(1), 44–67.

Swezey, R. W., & Salas, E. (1992). Guidelines for use in team-training development. In R. W. Swezey & E. Salas (Eds.), *Teams: Their training and performance* (pp. 219–245). Norwood, NJ: Ablex.

Tannenbaum, S. I. (1997). Enhancing continuous learning: Diagnostic findings from multiple companies. *Human Resource Management, 36,* 437–452.

Tannenbaum, S. I. (2002). A strategic view of organizational training and learning. In K. Kraiger (Ed.), *Creating, implementing, and maintaining effective training and development: State-of-the-art lessons for practice* (pp. 10–52). San Francisco: Jossey-Bass.

Tannenbaum, S. I., & Alliger, G. A. (2000). *Knowledge management: Clarifying the key issues.* Austin, TX: IHRIM Press.

Tannenbaum, S. I., Mathieu, J. E., Salas, E., & Cannon-Bowers, J. A. (1991). Meeting trainees' expectations: The influence of training fulfillment on the development of commitment, self-efficacy, and motivation. *Journal of Applied Psychology, 76,* 759–769.

Tannenbaum, S. I., & Woods, S. B. (1992). Determining a strategy for evaluating training: Operating within organizational constraints. *Human Resource Planning, 15*(2), 63–81.

Tannenbaum, S. I., & Yukl, G. (1992). Training and development in work organizations. *Annual Review of Psychology, 43,* 399–441.

Tennyson, R. D., & Elmore, R. L. (1997). Learning theory foundations for instructional design. In R. D. Tennyson (Ed.), *Instructional design: International perspectives: Vol. 1. Theory, research, and models* (pp. 55–78). Mahwah, NJ: Erlbaum.

Thayer, P. W., & Teachout, M. S. (1995). *A climate for transfer model* (Rep. No. AL/HR-TP-1995-0035). Brooks Air Force Base, TX: Technical Training Research Division, Armstrong Laboratory.

Toney, R. J., & Ford, J. K. (2001, April). *Leveraging the capabilities of Web-based training to foster active learning.* Symposium presented at the annual meeting of the Society for Industrial-Organizational Psychology, San Diego, CA.

Towler, A. J., & Dipboye, R. L. (2001, April). *Development of a learning preference measure.* Poster presented at the annual meeting of the Society for Industrial-Organizational Psychology, San Diego, CA.

Tracey, J. B., Tannenbaum, S. I., & Kavanagh, M. J. (1995). Applying trained skills on the job: The importance of work environment. *Journal of Applied Psychology, 80,* 239–252.

Twitchell, S., Holton, E. F., III, & Trott, J. R., Jr. (2001). Technical training evaluation practices in the United States. *Performance Improvement Quarterly, 13*(3), 84–109.

Van Buren, M. E. (2001). *State of the industry: Report 2001.* Washington, DC: American Society for Training and Development.

Volpe, C. E., Cannon-Bowers, J. A., Salas, E., & Spector, P. E. (1996). The impact of cross-training on team functioning: An empirical investigation. *Human Factors, 38,* 87–100.

Warr, P., & Allen, C. (1998). Learning strategies and occupational training. In C. L. Cooper & I. T. Robertson (Eds.), *International Review of Industrial and Organizational Psychology, 13,* 83–121.

Warr, P., & Bunce, D. (1995). Trainee characteristics and the outcomes of open learning. *Personnel Psychology, 48,* 347–376.

Weaver, C. A., III, & Kelemen, W. L. (1997). Judgments of learning at delays: Shift in response patterns or increased metamemory accuracy? *Psychological Science, 8,* 318–321.

Wedman, J., & Tessmer, M. (1993). Instructional designers' decisions and priorities: A survey of design practice. *Performance Improvement Quarterly, 6*(2), 43–57.

Weldon, D. E., Carlston, D. E., Rissman, A. K., Slobodin, L., & Triandis, H. C. (1975). A laboratory test of effects of culture assimilator training. *Journal of Personality and Social Psychology, 32,* 300–310.

Wexley, K. N. (1984). Personnel training. *Annual Review of Psychology, 35,* 519–551.

Whalen, T., & Wright, D. (2000). *The business case for web-based training.* Norwood, MA: Artech House.

Wiener, E. L., Kanki, B. G., & Helmreich, R. L. (Eds.). (1993). *Cockpit resource management.* San Diego, CA: Academic Press.

Williams, T. C., & Zahed, H. (1996). Computer-based training versus traditional lecture: Effect on learning and retention. *Journal of Business and Psychology, 11,* 297–310.

Wilson, M. A., & Zalewski, M. A. (1994). An expert system for abilities-oriented job analysis. *Computers in Human Behavior, 10,* 199–207.

Yang, C., & Moore, D. M. (1995). Designing hypermedia systems for instruction. *Journal of Educational Technology Systems, 24,* 3–30.

CHAPTER 9

Strategic Industrial and Organizational Psychology and the Role of Utility Analysis Models

JOHN W. BOUDREAU AND PETER M. RAMSTAD

The beginning of the twenty-first century poses an interesting paradox for industrial and organizational (I/O) psychology and strategic human resources (HR) management. Leading I/O psychology journals, especially in the United States, have reduced attention to utility analysis at a time when the quantitative measurement of human capital is receiving unprecedented attention.

First, the good news: The accounting and management professions recognize that traditional corporate measurement systems must be enhanced to account for intangibles in a knowledge-based economy (Brookings Institute, 2000; Canibano, Garcia-Ayuso, & Sanchez, 2000; Lev, 1997). Strategic HR management writers have noted the importance of understanding the value of human capital (e.g., Boudreau & Ramstad, 1999; Lepak & Snell, 1999). Consulting firms increasingly offer products designed to measure or demonstrate the relationship between HR programs and financial value (Fitz-enz, 2000; Grossman, 2000; Stamps, 2000). Yet, much of this focus is on developing new measures with rela-

tively less attention to frameworks for decision support. As Boudreau (1998) noted, there is disturbing evidence that financial analysts face significant difficulties in using HR measures (Eccles & Mavrinac, 1995; Mavrinac & Seisfeld, 1997; Welbourne & Andrews, 1996). Who better than professionals in I/O psychology to offer solutions drawing on the long heritage of measurement development?

Now, the bad news: I/O psychology has largely missed the opportunity to frame and inform this growing and important debate. The last decade has actually seen a decrease in attention to utility analysis, in contrast to the increasing amount of research in the 1980s and early 1990s that began with the resurgence of interest prompted by work by Cascio, Schmidt and their colleagues (Cascio & Silbey, 1979; Schmidt, Hunter, McKenzie, & Muldrow, 1979). Boudreau's (1991) review identified more than 40 studies in the area, including 28 studies published between 1979 and 1990 focusing solely on the issue of estimating *SDy*, the standard deviation of employee performance in dollars! Since 1991 there has been a noticeable decrease in attention to utility analysis. For this chapter, we searched for research since 1991. Articles on utility analysis have appeared in many outlets, and there has even emerged a journal entitled *Human Resource Costing and*

The authors thank Wendy Boswell and Benjamin Dunford for helpful assistance in preparing this chapter.

Accounting, published by the Personnel Economics Institute in Stockholm, Sweden. Yet, we identified only 13 articles in *Personnel Psychology* and *Journal of Applied Psychology.*

Does this pattern reflect the irrelevance of utility analysis to I/O psychology and the measurement of human capital and human resources? We will suggest a different conclusion based on the convergence between utility-analysis research issues and unresolved strategic HR management issues. These issues are traditionally addressed by I/O psychology, and create an unprecedented opportunity for integrative research that draws on the best of these fields. However, such integration requires a new emphasis in utility analysis and I/O psychology research, as well as a perspective on HR strategy that better encompasses the logic of utility analysis.

The original working title of this chapter was "Cost-Benefit Analysis for I/O Psychological Interventions." Typically, such chapters discuss how to estimate the payoff from I/O interventions, after the fact. We believe that integrating the tools and paradigms of I/O psychology with emerging models of strategic HR management is much more fundamental than refining cost-benefit techniques. Such an integration actually suggests that utility analysis logic may be most valuable in identifying opportunities for strategic I/O psychology contributions *before* interventions are chosen. Thus, this integration will draw heavily upon not only I/O psychology principles, but on elements of organizational strategy (Porter, 1985) as well; hence the inclusion of "Strategic Industrial/Organizational Psychology" in the title.

We will review developments in utility analysis research since 1991, but we will take as a departure point the fundamental idea of decision support. *Decision support* is also a familiar theme in utility analysis, and has been repeatedly emphasized (Arvey & Murphy, 1998; Boudreau, 1991; Boudreau & Ramstad, 1999; Boudreau, Sturman, & Judge, 1994; Cascio, 1996, 2000; Skarlicki, Latham, & Whyte, 1996). Here, we use the framework to highlight the key I/O and strategy linkages, and to suggest future integrative research.

Then, we will take a perspective that is more prescriptive, showing how the logic and methods of utility analysis actually provide the mechanisms for I/O psychology to become more strategic, and to assist strategic HR management in becoming more operationally rigorous. As it turns out, the kernels of this integration existed in the utility analysis logic all along, but has been largely unrecognized. We will address the "criterion problem" in *SDy* research (Arvey & Murphy, 1998, p. 161) from a decision-based perspective, as an alternative to the traditional I/O focus on measurement and statistical assumptions, and show how the decision-based perspective reveals opportunities to capitalize on the links between

human capital and organizational success. We will present a model, HC BRidge (HC BRidge™ is a trademark of the Boudreau-Ramstad Partnership), that links human capital and, organizational performance, and show how it suggests new directions for I/O research on utility analysis estimation, acceptance, and decision making. We will then address *SDy* measurement from the strategic perspective, to show how *SDy* addresses a fundamental gap in HR strategy.

UTILITY ANALYSIS AS A DECISION PROCESS: A REVIEW SINCE 1991

Several authors have described utility analysis research since 1991, each summarizing the basic utility-analysis equation, the continuing debate regarding measurement, and recent enhancements to the utility model (e.g., Cabrera & Raju, 2001). Although each review took a different approach, they all arrived at a similar conclusion—that a return to the fundamental process of decision making is essential to advancing the field.

Boudreau (1991, 1996) proposed that utility analysis measurement was founded on two premises: (a) Measures will lead to more rational and productive choices about people; and (b) measures will convince others to support and invest in HR management programs. Landy (1989) noted that a significant gap was the lack of information on how managers actually use information in making decisions. Boudreau et al. (1994) suggested that future selection research should focus on how recruiters, managers, and employees make actual decisions throughout the selection process. Many have suggested that drawing on theories of decision making and decision processes is key to enhancing the relevance of utility analysis research (Boudreau, 1991, 1996; Highhouse, 1996; Skarlicki et al., 1996). Boudreau and Ramstad (1997) noted that "metrics are not neutral" because they convey values, priorities, and an underlying strategic framework, suggesting that the strategic framework used to organize and articulate measurement linkages was key to understanding decisions.

The Importance of Decision Science: Talentship

Human resource metrics are commonly evaluated by asking key decision makers if they like the HR measures, or if the HR measures seem businesslike. Yet, it would seem rather ludicrous to assess the financial analysis framework by asking whether business leaders liked it (in fact, if they miss their numbers, they are likely to hate it!). Why do HR and I/O focus so strongly on client opinions about measures, while finance focuses on the outcomes of the measures? The finance profession has created a system that is so logically connected to important organizational outcomes, and so clearly able to improve important decisions about financial capital, that it is an accepted metaphor for the business organization, even when its message is unpleasant (Boudreau & Ramstad, 1997). Information is valuable if it improves important decisions in an uncertain world (Bazerman, 1998; Bierman, Bonnini, & Hausman, 1991). Similarly, the crucial outcome of any human-capital information system is its ability to enhance decisions, in this case decisions about human capital (Boudreau, 1995). The logic, richness, and relevance of our frameworks for understanding human capital are the key. The professional practice of accounting is essential for organizations, but it is the decision science of finance that draws on accounting measurements to support decisions about financial capital. Similarly, the professional practice of HR management is essential, but the decision science of human capital will integrate HR management practices and measures to create a decision framework for talent. We have coined the term *talentship* to refer to this emerging decision science (Boudreau & Ramstad, 2000, 2002). Thus, as finance is to accounting, so talentship is to HR management. This chapter will not develop the decision science of talentship, but we propose to show how I/O psychology and utility analysis can play a significant role. Later, we will expand on talentship and the lessons to be learned from established decision sciences. First, we review utility analysis research using a decision-based perspective.

A Decision-Process Lens

We will organize our review of the utility analysis literature according to a seven-step decision process: (a) learn, assess, and sense patterns; (b) identify and gather appropriate data; (c) analyze and identify key messages; (d) design summaries and prescriptions; (e) present summaries and prescriptions; (f) influence key human capital decisions; and (g) effect execution and behavior change.

Learn, Assess, and Sense Patterns

This stage reflects how individuals perceive talent issues and decide to attend to them. In the field, we encounter this as the inklings that certain talent issues are important: For example, the HR manager who says, "We seem to be outsourcing all the work of our nonexempt employees to cut costs, but those folks are pretty important to our competitiveness, and we can do a better job of nurturing their contributions internally, than an outside company. The cost reductions of outsourcing are

tangible, and I can't demonstrate with numbers, but I think we're throwing out the baby with the bath water." This is a fertile area for I/O psychology to play a key role in helping to understand how problems are identified in the first place, long before data are gathered and models are applied. How do decision makers learn which patterns to attend to?

There is little research in the utility analysis area per se on these issues. Research questions would include what cues are most salient to different organizational decision makers, and what factors contribute to their decisions to attend to them. This is important, because the lack of well-accepted paradigms for human capital decisions probably leads to a wide variety of attention patterns. For example, some may focus on cost reduction, whereas others focus on complaints from key managers; still others take their initial cues from news stories or reports of best practices. These different starting points may significantly affect later stages of the process.

A frequently mentioned body of research in this area has to do with fads, fashions, and the issue of technical versus administrative decisions. It has been noted (Boudreau, 1996; Skarlicki et al., 1996) that the literature on diffusion of new practices may be useful in understanding the *impact* of utility analysis, and we will return to that later. The same literature may help understand the pre-impact stages of decision making. Johns (1993) and Abrahamson (1991, 1996) questioned the assumption of rational cost-benefit analysis in adopting innovations, suggesting that such decisions are driven by fashions and fads. I/O research might fruitfully explore whether decision makers rely on the imitation of recognized industry leaders or gurus as their starting point for decisions, rather than on a rational examination of the decision issue. Johns's (1993) technical versus administrative distinction is also useful, because it suggests why decision makers may approach human capital through analysis or through opinion, and this significantly affects the information they attend to. Another rich source of ideas can be found in the persuasion literature. Boudreau (1996) noted that persuasion models (e.g., Perloff, 1993; Petty & Cacioppo, 1984; Quinn, Hildebrandt, Rogers, & Thompson, 1991; Reardon, 1991) offer insights into factors affecting the reactions of utility-analysis receivers and senders. These theories suggest what variables may affect the cues that are relevant at the early stages of decisions, and how to predict and influence them.

A fascinating example of this phenomenon can be found in emerging research on the cognitive processes underlying the much-touted finding that objective financial measures are associated with managers' self-reports of their firms' numbers or patterns of HR practices (e.g., Becker & Huselid, 1998; Huselid, 1995). Recent results indicate that when students and managers are told that hypothetical firms have strong financial performance, their subsequent estimates of the prevalence of HR practices are higher (Gardner, Wright, & Gerhart, 2000). These tantalizing, if preliminary, data suggest how mental maps may affect the prior assumptions of decision makers, and it seems likely that such mental maps also affect how decision makers attend to cues that initially structure their data gathering.

Identify and Gather Appropriate Data: Extensions and New Applications of Utility Models

This stage includes deciding what model will guide data gathering, and the adoption of one model over another. Today, there are many models available, each implying a particular array of necessary data. Model design and choice have received a great deal of attention in the utility analysis literature. Prior to 1991, the selection utility framework evolved from a focus on variance explained; to calculating the expected standardized increase in criterion scores, given a certain validity and selection ratio; to translating those standardized values into dollar values, with offsetting costs (Boudreau, 1991; Schmidt & Hunter, 1998). The selection utility model was extended to encompass recruitment, employee flows, financial and economic considerations, labor market effects on offer acceptance patterns, and so on (e.g., Boudreau, 1983; Boudreau & Rynes, 1985). Each embellishment presented new implications for data gathering and analysis. Perhaps the resulting complexity is a drawback of utility analysis (Rauschenberger & Schmidt, 1987). We will return to this issue later. Here, we will summarize the extensions and data requirements of the utility analysis model since 1991, and then examine the emerging research on the determinants of choices among decision models.

Extending Utility Models to Downsizing and Internal Movement.   Utility analysis models have been extended to encompass elements of employee retention and internal movement. Figure 9.1 depicts the underlying concepts. Traditional models focused primarily on the quality of employees hired into a job (the top box of Figure 9.1). Subsequently, the number of employees leaving the job was included. Boudreau and Berger (1985) introduced parameters reflecting the number and quality of employees who leave the organization, suggesting that the workforce at any time is a function of those retained from before, and those added. This is shown in the bottom half of Figure 9.1. Each arrow represents a flow of employees, value, and associated costs. See Boudreau (1991) and Boudreau and Berger (1985) for details. They also noted that this concept could be extended by the consideration of movement between jobs as simultaneous

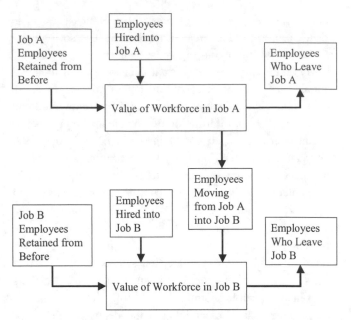

Figure 9.1   Acquisition, separation, and internal movement utility. *Source:* Adapted from Boudreau and Berger (1985).

internal turnover from the source job, and *internal selection* to the destination job.

Mabon (1996, 1998) applied this logic to downsizing decisions. He showed that the true value of downsizing depends significantly on the correlation among pay, tenure, and employee value. For example, if highly paid employees are also the most valuable, layoffs designed to maximize cost reduction with minimum headcount reductions (laying off the highest paid employees) may have unseen but devastating effects on overall value. Barrick and Alexander (1991) applied Markov movement and survival probabilities to account for employees who leave the work groups that they are selected into, but do not leave the organization.

Extending the Utility Model to Reflect Probationary Hiring.   DeCorte (1994, 1997, 1998b) applied the Boudreau-Berger retention model to a probationary period, during which acquired employees may be dismissed if performance is not satisfactory. Applying this model requires that decision makers estimate the proportion of new hires expected to survive the probationary period, as well as the costs of training and maintaining new employees, and the average expected value of those who survive the probationary period. By assuming that predictor scores and performance ratings have a linear bivariate-normal distribution, DeCorte derived the predicted success rate from the performance cutoff score, and the average value of the surviving group from the correlation between performance ratings and selection scores, along with an estimate of the average dollar value of the applicant population.

Results suggest when unsatisfactory employees can be dismissed after probation, the overall attained workforce value can be enhanced. Paradoxically, the incremental utility of a more valid selection is *lower* with a probationary period, because the probationary period provides the opportunity to correct selection mistakes from less valid, and presumably less costly, alternative predictors. This also means that the traditional selection utility model will overestimate utility when selection mistakes can be systematically corrected through later dismissal.

DeCorte (1998b) also noted that it is possible to estimate optimal criterion and test score cutoff levels that can include both an optimal *immediate rejection* level and an optimal *immediate acceptance* level (for those whose initial qualifications are so high that additional screening is not optimal). The notion of optimizing rather than simply evaluating results is intriguing. Rather than using utility models merely to estimate the value of alternatives, decision makers might calculate optimal decision parameters, and then attempt to achieve them. For example, DeCorte (1998b) noted that one optimal solution required hiring 66 new employees to eventually end up with 17, which might at first have seemed an excessive probationary turnover rate. The utility model used (in this case, choosing optimization rather than simple evaluation) determines the kind of data gathered and the decision approach, again showing the importance of approaching utility analysis through a decision framework.

Updating the Classification Problem. In making a *classification* decision, one is not merely selecting applicants for a single position but instead assigning applicants to one of several different positions. This issue has been discussed since the early days of utility analysis (Brogden, 1949), but since 1991 there have been some new developments. Alley and Darbyk (1995) and DeCorte (1998a) provide methods to calculate the expected benefits of personnel classification decisions when it is assumed that selection criteria are equally correlated and equally valid, that equal numbers are to be assigned to each classification, and that the jobs are all equally important. DeCorte (2000a) relaxed the assumptions of equal validities, equal correlations, and equal assignments, and added the assumption of an infinitely large applicant set. Results suggest that the benefits of testing applied to classification may be significantly higher than for using tests for more typical one-position selection. With enhanced computing power, one can envision optimally combining multiple predictors to assign applicants among multiple positions. Labor shortages and flexible roles may mean that classification better fits the reality of selection than does the more studied situation in which applicants are selected for one job. For example, organizations might systematically consider each applicant's most appropriate role, rather than simply the applicant's fitness for a particular assignment. Again, the choice of the decision model fundamentally changes the entire process.

Utility Analysis for Pay Decisions. The Boudreau and Berger (1985) acquisition-retention framework has been used to evaluate pay strategies through their effect on employee movement. Klass and McClendon (1996) examined the decision to lead, lag, or match the market. Like Rich and Boudreau (1987) and Sturman (2000), Klass and McClendon gathered parameter information from published studies, and simulated effects on employee-separation and offer-acceptance patterns. Results for bank tellers suggested that a lag policy produced higher payoffs, although leading the market (paying higher than the average) did enhance retention and attraction of top candidates. The authors noted that these results did not advocate for a particular pay policy, and showed how simulated reductions in citizenship behavior due to low pay might change the results. Boudreau, Sturman, Trevor, and Gerhart (1999) also examined compensation utility using the Boudreau and Berger model. Like Klass and McClendon, they simulated effects on retention patterns, but focused on a different pay element—performance-based pay. Their simulation, based on earlier results on compensation and turnover from a large private-sector organization (Trevor, Gerhart, & Boudreau, 1997), suggested that the payoff from performance-based pay is significantly higher when performance variability has large dollar values, with payoff actually being negative when applied to low-variability employee populations. These applications suggest that choosing to examine pay decisions through the lens of a model of employee attraction and retention might yield very different conclusions from an analysis using simply market compensation comparisons or costs.

Utility Analysis Applied to Training, Quality Circles, and Employee Day Care. Applications of utility analysis to decisions other than employee selection, retention, and pay suggest further embellishments of the utility framework. Morrow, Jarrett, and Rupinski (1997) estimated the utility of a variety of training programs and populations in a single organization over a four-year period. They estimated traditional utility parameters (e.g., effect size, number trained, duration of effect, and dollar value of variability in performance), along with a new parameter designed to reflect the proportion of relevant job skills affected by a particular training program. The study is unique in estimating the utility of many programs in one organization. Barrick and Alexander (1992) found a positive effect of a one-year quality-circle intervention at a large bank in the Midwestern United States, using utility calculated as the combined effects on turnover, absenteeism, and overtime. Kossek and Grace (1990) estimated a positive utility effect for a day-care center, using reduced turnover and absence and enhanced public relations.

Some Black Boxes in the Utility Model. Boudreau et al. (1994) summarized a number of factors that might alter selection utility values or explain decision-maker reactions to utility analysis, including (a) existing predictors that will be retained, when adding new ones (see also Burke & Frederick, 1986; Raju & Burke, 1986); (b) temporal changes in validity; (c) multidimensionality in criteria that may make performance ratings used alone less representative of all valued outcomes; (d) employee movement between positions; (e) multiattribute criterion definitions; and (f) unacknowledged costs, such as increased training, pay, or bureaucracy (see also Jones & Wright, 1992). Russell, Colella, and Bobko (1993) argued for a strategy-utility link, with examples showing that the timing of utility benefits may significantly affect their value. For example, if a start-up organization must show a profit within a year or go out of business, projected utility gains beyond one year have little strategic value. Such short time windows can also be accommodated by increasing the discount rate on future returns (Boudreau, 1983), but the more direct decision link suggested by Russell et al. may be more understandable.

The Confidence Interval and Potential Variability in Utility Estimates. Sturman's (2000) computer-simulation evidence indicated that applying suggested adjustments to the traditional utility model, in combination, can produce substantial reductions (sometimes in excess of 90%). He noted the need to consider the situational context when estimating utility, and the fact that if line managers or other constituents are aware of the potential effects of such adjustments, they may be understandably skeptical about unadjusted utility values. Variability in utility estimates had been examined prior to 1991 (e.g., Alexander & Barrick, 1987; Rich & Boudreau, 1987), but recently DeCorte (2000b) returned to this issue, noting that the expected average standardized criterion score of those selected—traditionally estimated using the selection ratio and validity coefficient—is actually the limiting case that assumes infinitely many applicants are available. DeCorte (1998a, 1998b, 2000b) provided formulas to calculate a point estimate and confidence interval that reflect a finite number of applicants. Russell (1998) noted that the typical assumption that the validation criterion (usually performance ratings) and the dollar value of employees have a correlation of 1.0 is likely to be violated (e.g., DeNisi, 1996). Using a correction

formula from McNemar (1962), he showed that even when observed sample correlations are high, the range of possible unobserved true correlations can be very large. For example, the true correlation between employee value and selection-test scores can range from -0.02 to $+1.00$, even when the true correlation between the test scores and performance ratings is .70 and the true correlation between performance and employee dollar value is also .70. Becker and Huselid (1992) derived a similar result for regression analysis, showing that a measured regression coefficient will overstate the true regression coefficient the higher the predictor correlations and the lower the reliabilities (p. 230). This suggests that decision makers and researchers should incorporate wider confidence intervals into their utility assessments as they consider the risk and return to I/O intervention investments.

Summary. Recent years have seen new utility analysis applications, but also new cautions and adjustments. With the work prior to 1991, a wide array of models and parameters is available. In one way, this bodes well for future utility analysis applications. The enhanced computing power and mathematical logic of new models, and their application to a wider variety of HR interventions, suggests that more precise and sophisticated analysis is feasible for many more decision makers. On the other hand, the sheer volume of parameters and models can be daunting to even the most motivated and informed user. This highlights the importance of understanding the processes that do (and should) guide decision makers to choose one model or analytical approach versus another. Little research explains how to improve decision makers' ability to understand and appropriately choose among this increasing set of options, or when richer utility models are actually likely to enhance the ultimate human capital decision. We turn to this issue next.

Identify and Gather Appropriate Data: The Processes of Choosing an Analysis Approach

This stage of the process involves choosing which analysis approach will be used. Each new application, more precise model, or way to overcome limitations, implicitly or explicitly suggests that the prior absence of these embellishments may explain the failure to use or believe utility analysis results. This is a different question than the persuasive effect or acceptance of utility analysis *after* the model has been applied and results are presented, which has received much attention that we will discuss later. Here we focus on research examining why utility analysis is not more widely applied and reported, and the potential effects at the point at which decision makers choose what frameworks they will use.

Macan and Highhouse (1994) surveyed American HR professionals and psychologists who reported that their managers were seldom aware that HR activities could be justified in dollar terms, despite their interest in the impact of HR on the bottom line. Florin-Thuma and Boudreau (1987) provided an early study that actually examined the views of managers who had chosen not to implement performance feedback. They found that managers had underestimated how far employee performance fell below standards, and thus underestimated the potential insights from analyzing performance feedback. After receiving the utility analysis, these same managers reported finding the results compelling, in part because they corrected misconceptions about the impact of the performance problem. Several authors have noted the persuasive value of involving decision makers in the early stages of utility-model development. Advocates of multiattribute utility (MAU) approaches, for example, derive key dimensions directly from the users (e.g., Roth, 1994; Roth & Bobko, 1997). How to induce or encourage that involvement remains relatively unexamined.

Roth, Segars, and Wright (2000) provide one of the most explicit treatments of the decision to adopt utility models. They proposed that utility analysis acceptance is affected in part by processes in the pre-use stage, prior to conducting the utility analysis. They use *image theory* to suggest how decision makers may evaluate analysis approaches according to their *value image* (criteria for moral correctness), *trajectory image* (the goals of the decision), and *strategic image* (the tactics for achieving the goals). They note the possible effects of prior decision-maker experience or success with decision models, including whether the models match broad screening criteria such as awareness, confidence, and political or emotional factors. Results from Macan and Highhouse (1994) support the premise that familiarity with utility analysis affects impressions of it. This stage of the process remains relatively unexplored, yet may provide fertile ground for understanding how to enhance decision quality, and may explain the adoption patterns of analytical models.

Analyze the Data and Identify the Key Messages: The Array of Alternatives to Utility Analysis

This stage of the decision process involves applying the chosen model, analyzing the data as the model directs, and determining the implications or messages in the analysis. Certainly, the earlier review of emerging utility model embellishments is relevant here, because those models imply certain key messages. While attention to developments regarding utility analysis models is important, decision makers are now faced with an array of alternatives that goes well

beyond utility analysis models. This growing array of choices presents an important context as decision makers interpret the data they gather, and provide a perspective on the advantages and limitations of utility analysis models generally. In Table 9.1 we summarize the available measurement alternatives discussed in this section. We discuss traditional and utility analysis methods throughout this chapter, so we focus on the alternatives beginning with the third row of Table 9.1.

Financial Efficiency Measures of Human Resource Operations. This category includes systems for calculating the costs of HR programs and HR departments, as well as an array of various dollar- or time-based ratios for different HR processes such as staffing, compensation, labor relations, and so on. These approaches focus on dollar-based indicators of HR operations, and compare those standardized indicators across organizations. Perhaps the most visible examples include products from the Saratoga Institute, as described in the work of Fitz-enz (1995, 1997). The primary focus is on the efficient use of resources, as embodied in input-output ratios such as the time to fill vacancies, turnover rates, turnover costs, compensation budgets compared to total expenses, and the like. Some elements of *behavioral costing* (Cascio, 2000) also fit into this category (e.g., the cost savings from reducing turnover or absenteeism). Compared to utility analysis, this approach can be quite compelling because of its fairly direct connection to accounting outcomes. Accounting emphasizes efficiency and cost control, and these approaches can identify where HR programs can achieve visible cost reductions. The ability to compare such ratios to those of other organizations allows HR professionals to identify potential improvement targets. Compared to utility analysis, this approach has the advantage of providing a standard approach to gathering and reporting data (in fact, the Saratoga Institute offers computer programs that automatically extract information from databases such as PeopleSoft and SAS to produce the standard ratios). It does not require understanding the bivariate linearity assumptions underlying utility analysis, and it does not require estimates of the value of employee performance variability.

Of course, this is also the drawback, because such efficiency-focused systems are generally poor at reflecting implications for the value of employees. It seems likely that they will create a focus on cost reduction, perhaps rejecting more expensive alternatives that may have significant payoffs beyond their additional costs. For example, cost per hire can be reduced by cutting the number of selection activities, but such reductions may well reduce validity and subsequent workforce quality. In fact, valuable I/O interventions that show high utility will generally increase the cost-per-hire and

TABLE 9.1   HR Measurement Alternatives

Measurement Approach	Illustrative Measurements	References	Observations
Traditional evaluation of HR programs	New-hire skills, trainee knowledge, changes in attitudes, turnover levels	Textbooks on experimental design, as well as research reports of program effects	A rich source of information on program effects, but statistical results are not easily translated to reflect organizational goals. Statistical presentations may be daunting to many organizational constituents.
Utility analysis for specific programs	Knowledge, skills, performance assessments, transformed to dollar values and offset with estimated costs	Boudreau (1991); Boudreau & Ramstad (2001, this chapter); Cascio (2000)	Wide array of approaches estimating the payoff from HR program investments. Useful logic and rigor, but the complexity and assumptions may reduce credibility and usefulness.
Financial efficiency measures of HR operations	Cost per hire, time to fill, training costs	Cascio (2000); Fitz-enz (1995, 1997)	Compelling explicit dollar-value calculations and comparisons, but may overemphasize human capital cost relative to value.
HR activity and best practice indices	"100 Best Companies to Work For," human capital benchmarks	Becker & Huselid (1998); Delery & Doty (1996); Huselid, Jackson, & Schuler (1997); Ichniowski et al. (1997)	Focus on specific HR activities provides a useful link to specific actions. Tantalizing results showing that HR practices correlate with financial outcome measures. Causal mechanisms and direction may be unclear, leading to incorrect conclusions and actions.
Multiattribute utility (MAU)	ProMES applied to HR programs, specific MAU models built for particular organizations	Roth (1994); Roth & Bobko (1997)	Useful method for explicating the underlying value dimensions. Can incorporate nonlinearities and non-dollar outcomes. The participant requirements can be daunting. Generally rely heavily on self-reported and subjective parameters.
HR dashboard or balanced scorecard	How the organization or HR function meets goals of "customers, financial markets, operational excellence, and learning"	Becker et al. (2001); Kaplan & Norton (1992)	Vast array of HR measures can be categorized. Balanced scorecard is well known to business leaders. Software can allow users to drill or cut HR measures to support their own analysis questions. Potential for naive users to misinterpret or misanalyze the information.
Financial statement augmentation	Supplements to annual reports (e.g., Skandia and ABB); human capital navigator	Skandia Corporation (1996); Sveiby (1997)	Reporting human capital factors with standard financial statements raises the visibility of HR. A vast array of human resource and human capital measures can be reported. The link between reported measures and organizational and investor outcomes remains uninvestigated. Information overload can result without a logic framework.
Financial statement reconciliation	HR accounting, intangible Asset measurement, "putting human capital on the balance sheet"	Bassi et al. (2000); Flamholtz (1999); Lev & Zarowin (1999)	Reliance on standard financial statements or accounting logic may be compelling to financial analysts. Acknowledges the limitations of financial analysis to account for human capital. May be limited in its ability to inform decisions about HR program investments.
Intellectual capital and knowledge management	Patents, networks, information system investments, knowledge stocks and flows	Argote & Ingram (2000); Crossan et al. (1999); Hall et al. (2000); Sveiby (1997)	Useful specific focus on both stocks and flows of knowledge. Multidisciplinary array of measures may be more credible to those outside the I/O psychology discipline. Focus on relationships with financial outcomes may be compelling. Less informative regarding the effects of HR programs on intellectual capital, with recent exceptions (Collins, Smith, & Stevens, 2001).
Causal chain analysis	Path models linking employee attitudes to service behavior to customer responses to profit	Boudreau & Ramstad (1999); Rucci et al. (1998); Schneider et al. (1996)	Useful logic linking employee variables to financial outcomes. Valuable for organizing and analyzing diverse data elements. Danger of focusing on one path to the exclusion of other explanatory variables.

time-to-fill. Efficiency-based measures, no matter how financially compelling, cannot explicitly reflect employee value. Moreover, such indices provide little guidance as to the associations between interventions or practices and outcomes.

Human Resource Activity and Best Practice Indexes. These approaches directly measure HR activities, such as merit pay, teams, valid selection, training, and so on, and their association with changes in financial outcomes, such as profits and shareholder value creation (e.g., Becker & Huselid, 1998; Delery & Doty, 1996; Huselid, 1995; Huselid, Jackson, & Schuler, 1997). As Gerhart, Wright, and McMahan (2000) have noted, this approach is also reflected in research on the performance of individual plants or facilities (e.g., Arthur, 1994; Ichniowski, Shaw, & Prennushi, 1997; MacDuffie, 1995; Youndt, Snell, Dean, & Lepak, 1996). It has produced measurement methods to assess the existence of a particular combination of HR practices, such as high-performance work systems, deemed appropriate across a wide variety of organizations (e.g., Pfeffer, 1998). Some results have been striking, with evidence that increasing sophistication in HR practices may have very significant associations with ultimate financial outcomes (Becker & Huselid, 1998). We noted earlier some of the emerging controversy regarding the reliability of survey measures of HR practices. However, there is no doubt that these results have appropriately received significant attention from both researchers and practitioners. It is also not surprising to see the emergence of commercial products and their associated marketing, suggesting that financial performance might improve by measuring a firm's HR activities, comparing them to the activities that have been most strongly associated with financial outcomes, and then adjusting the array of activities to fit this best-practice index. Researchers in this field are generally quite clear that general causal inferences are not warranted by much of the existing research (Cappelli & Neumark, 2001). Still, it seems likely that such best-practice indices offer tempting alternatives to decision makers and potentially influence their interpretation of utility analysis data.

Compared to utility analysis, the *best-practice* approach more directly incorporates recognizable financial outcomes. In fact, it can use virtually any financial outcome as a dependent variable. This approach also better reflects the idea of bundles of HR practices that work synergistically together (Ichniowski et al., 1997; MacDuffie, 1995). This is an important limitation of utility analysis. Yet, to understand these relationships will require more focused examination of the mediating effects between interventions and financial outcomes, and how they vary across organizations (e.g., Gerhart et al., 2000). Later, we will suggest how utility analysis research might inform these questions. However, for decision makers faced with demands to show tangible relationships between HR practices and financial outcomes, HR activity indices may seem a much more direct approach than utility analysis.

Multiattribute Utility (MAU) Analysis. Deficiencies in dollar-value payoff functions have long been noted, and their possible omission of the value dimensions of important constituents (e.g, Boudreau, 1991). Dimensions such as diversity and legal exposure do not appear in utility analysis models, and might well offset utility gains in certain situations (Roth, 1994; Roth & Bobko, 1997). Multiattribute utility (MAU) techniques have been proposed to incorporate these additional attributes into decision models. Generally, MAU involves identifying a set of important attributes, scaling the attribute levels so that they can be combined, and then combining them into an overall index based on the importance of each attribute to the decision. Utility analysis calculations are often imposed on existing situations while MAU approaches offer significant early involvement of decision makers, potentially producing greater understanding and acceptance of the underlying logic and eventual decisions. MAU explicates many decision elements, making them available for study. Such approaches can also reflect nonlinear relationships, and a large and diverse array of nonmonetary outcomes, which is difficult in traditional utility analysis. Systems for implementing MAU analysis are well known. Roth and Bobko (1997) present an example of the steps and associated research propositions.

Multiattribute utility approaches may be daunting, because they require decision makers to define attributes, construct measures, estimate weights and scaling algorithms, construct the utility functions, and then interpret them to make the decision. It is also important to note that the value of MAU analysis hinges on the ability of participants to understand and articulate the important attribute-outcome relationships. Utility analysis relies on explicit assumptions about statistical distributions, linear relationships, and so on that are not obvious to decision makers. Accordingly, utility analysis might allow a level of sophistication not attained with MAU. Thus, MAU analysis draws attention to important limitations in the outcomes contained in utility analysis models—the myopia of relying solely on linearity and dollar values. However, it also points out the importance of assuring that decision makers have the capacity and mental models to understand the necessary relationships between attributes and outcomes. We will return later to the integration of utility analysis with such mental maps.

Human Resource Balanced Scorecards or Dashboards. Kaplan and Norton (1992, 1996a, 1996b) suggested that traditional "financial-perspective" measures tended to lag organizational performance, and proposed to extend organizational measurement systems by adding a "customer perspective," which measures customer satisfaction, market share, and so on; an "internal-process" perspective, which measures intermediate value processes such as cycle time, quality, and cost; and a "learning-and-growth" perspective, which measures the systems, organizational procedures, and people that contribute to competitive advantage. It has been suggested (e.g., Cabrera & Cabrera, 1999) that the results of HR activities might be linked to elements of such a scorecard or dashboard. The concept of a *balanced scorecard* has achieved great popularity in many organizations, and has spawned significant organizational efforts to create HR measures aligned with each of the four perspectives just described and to categorize existing HR measures into the four categories (Becker et al., 2001; Donnelly, 2000). Like efficiency measures and financial statement reconciliation or augmentation (discussed next), such approaches have the advantage of tying HR measures to measurement systems that are familiar to line managers. However, this approach also shares the drawback of adopting a measurement logic not specifically developed to deal with human capital and I/O interventions. There are at least two pitfalls in attempts to apply the scorecard approach to HR measurement: (a) relegating HR measures to the learning-and-growth category, rather than integrating the effects of such interventions with strategic outcomes; and (b) applying the four quadrants only to the HR function, by calculating HR-function financials (e.g., HR program budgets), customers (e.g., HR client satisfaction surveys), operational efficiency (e.g., the yield rates of recruitment sources), and learning and growth (e.g., the qualifications of HR professionals). Despite the appearance of a strategic linkage, both pitfalls lead to measurement systems with little link to organizational outcomes, and often little relevance to key decisions.

The balanced scorecard framework is useful in that it highlights the importance of intervening variables, such as HR management I/O psychology processes, in understanding financial success. Scorecards or dashboards are now commonly augmented by software that allows decision makers to drill down or cut the data based on a wide variety of variables, creating cross-tabulations, correlations, and regression analyses based on the unique preferences of individual analysts. For example, HR scorecards routinely allow training costs to be broken down by locations or by course, and linked to trainee turnover. This array of scorecard analysis options is impressive, but remains vulnerable to the same risks of MAU techniques from which they are derived. Specifically, they provide broad frameworks, leaving decisions about details to the user, which presumes a high-quality

analytical logic among users. If users are not sophisticated, such approaches risk creating a false sense of expertise about the connection between talent and strategic success. For example, Gascho, Marlys, and Salterio (2000) placed 58 first-year master's of business administration (MBA) students in the role of a hypothetical senior executive of a company that had implemented the balanced scorecard. Subjects gave performance evaluations to managers in each of two hypothetical divisions, after viewing different arrays of divisional performance information. Results suggested that measures used in common by the two divisions were much more influential than the division-unique measures developed using the balanced scorecard. The authors noted that existing traditional financial measures are already common across units, so this may suggest that scorecard measures, often designed to be unique to units, may receive less attention.

Utility analysis incorporates some elements of scorecards (e.g., program outcomes related to learning), and may provide useful logic to guide scorecard users confronted with the information overload that results from a vast array of analysis options. However, utility analysis research has not addressed these questions to date.

Financial Statement Augmentation and Reconciliation.
Accounting scholars increasingly suggest that traditional financial statement ratios are less informative to investors. For example, Lev and Zarowin (1999, p. 362) present data showing that "overall results indicate a weakening of the association between market values and accounting information (earnings, cash flows, and book values) over the past 20 years." This pattern was most evident in firms with increasing expenditures for research and development (R&D), while even high-technology firms with large but *stable* R&D investment levels showed far less decline. Evidence like this has prompted a wide variety of proposals to augment financial statements with more information about intangible assets. In traditional accounting, such expenditures (e.g., the costs of a new organizational design, training programs, hiring of R&D employees, general R&D) are subtracted as expenses when they are incurred, even if their benefits will accrue over time. It has been suggested that financial reporting might treat such expenditures more like other assets, such that only a portion of the cost is counted as depreciation in each period and the rest is listed as an asset. A similar argument was first made in human resource accounting more than 25 years ago, and continues today (see Flamholtz, 1999). We refer to such approaches as *financial statement reconciliation* in Table 9.1, because they attempt to reconcile the difference between organizational value, as seen through traditional financial statements, and the financial market valuation of the organization.

The desire to put people on the balance sheet, so to speak, has led to another approach which we call "financial statement augmentation" in Table 9.1. It involves the reporting of human capital factors alongside traditional financial information, including several often-cited examples (e.g., Skandia Corporation, 1996). Skandia produces more than 100 metrics in their intellectual capital report (Edvinsson & Malone, 1997), including replacement and acquisition costs, development of cross-functional teams, external relationships, information technology investments, and adoption of industry quality standards. As Liebowitz and Wright (1999) note, many of the measures are quantitative, but many are also very subjective. As yet, there is no generally accepted method of reflecting investments in people in financial reports, so it is up to the user to develop theories about the relationships to organizational performance. Moreover, these approaches provide little guidance about the connection between such augmented financial reports and investor responses. The focus on firm-level numbers also limits the applicability to investments in HR programs. Still, because such approaches acknowledge and augment traditional financial reports, they are likely to have credibility with those who rely on such reports.

Existing research in this area consists of policy-capturing studies with mixed results as to the importance of intangible factors in the decisions of investment managers (e.g., Bassi et al., 2000; Eccles & Mavrinac, 1995). We know little about the mental models used by such analysts to relate reported human capital numbers to predicted organizational value. The logic of utility analysis might assist such decision makers in understanding the connections between human capital investments and outcomes. The historically rich tradition of cognitive research in I/O psychology could also be useful in articulating such mental models. This would require utility analysis research to change its perspective from estimating the value of programs, to identifying how the logic of utility analysis might inform the interpretation of firm-level patterns. Later, we will describe a model to guide the search for such bridge elements.

Intellectual Capital and Knowledge Management. The increased attention to intangibles and the associated importance of R&D have led to increased measurement of knowledge and intellectual capital (Boudreau, in press; Dzinkowski, 2000). A recurring theme in this research is the notion that intellectual capital exists at several levels, such as individuals, teams, organizations, customers, and external constituents (Nahapiet & Ghosal, 1998), and that its measurement must incorporate not only the *stock* (amount that exists at a particular time) but also the *flow* (movement from one period to another) of intellectual capital among these constituents and across these levels (Argote & Ingram, 2000; Boudreau, in press; Crossan et al., 1999). Intellectual-capital models describe useful processes for tracking and measuring knowledge stocks and flows, but they are generally less informative regarding how I/O practices might enhance them (although Collins et al., 2001, have explored this). Utility analysis research could benefit by considering criteria such as knowledge stocks and flows, and intellectual-capital research might use utility analysis logic to examine how I/O and HR programs enhance intellectual capital. Boudreau (in press) provides a detailed review of knowledge measures.

Causal-Chain Analysis. This approach focuses on measuring the links between HR management programs and organizational outcomes. Perhaps the best-known example is the work by Sears, Roebuck & Co., a large U.S. retailer, in which empirical connections were uncovered among the attitudes of store associates, their on-the-job behaviors, the responses of store customers, and the financial performance of the stores (Rucci, Kirn, & Quinn, 1998), based on the general connections among service, value, and profit (Heskett, Jones, Loveman, Sasser, & Schlesinger, 1994). This notion has also been reflected in employee attitude surveys that reflect strategic goals (Schneider, Ashworth, Higgs, & Carr, 1996) and in the work of scholars studying the connections between HR practices and manufacturing-plant performance (MacDuffie, 1995). Decision makers find such approaches attractive because they offer tangible and logical structures and data to understand the intervening links between interventions and business outcomes, a feature that is generally lacking in existing utility models. Even when measurement of every linkage is not possible, the logic of the connections may be compelling. Research on reactions to utility models might investigate whether decision makers apply such mental models. Moreover, comparisons between empirical outcomes from causal-chain models and utility analysis may help assess utility accuracy. In turn, the statistical logic of utility analysis can offer causal-chain research a basis for ensuring that relevant variables and assumptions are included.

Summary. Decision makers have many tools to define how they will use, analyze, and interpret data. Each tool has advantages; some are likely to be more compelling than utility analysis, but there are also significant future research opportunities in examining how decision processes differ depending on the approaches used. All of the measurement methods highlight the need for high-quality logical frameworks linking investments to outcomes, yet few frameworks exist. Utility analysis can help articulate the actual or perceived links between human capital investments and organizational outcomes.

Design Summaries and Prescriptions

How should the results of analyses be presented, and what conclusions should be drawn? Boudreau (1983, 1991) suggested that presentations might include *break-even analysis,* which calculates the minimum threshold for one or more parameters necessary to achieve an acceptable payoff. Florin-Thuma and Boudreau (1987) presented utility analysis results compared to the prior estimates of managers, demonstrating where the model and the prior estimates agreed and diverged. *Persuasion theories* suggest useful frameworks and options regarding communication design (e.g., adopting a position at odds with that expected by receivers, using credible outside sources, tailoring the richness of the message to the involvement and expertise of the audience, choice of distribution channel, etc.), as Boudreau (1996) and Skarlicki et al. (1996) have noted. Roth et al. (2000) suggested some interesting design implications from image theory, including designs that are explicitly made compatible with value, trajectory, and strategic images. Macan and Highhouse (1994) reported that HR managers and I/O psychologists used several methods to present program effects (e.g., logic and anecdotes; legal issues; total quality, etc.). We have seen relatively little systematic research in utility analysis regarding key variables in presentation design. Far more attention has been given to examining the effects of utility analysis results, which we discuss next.

Present Summaries and Prescriptions: Utility Analysis Acceptance

Cascio (1996) suggested that we must focus on communication if we are to enhance the impact of utility analysis. Rauschenberger and Schmidt (1987, p. 55) noted that "communicating utility analysis research to organizational decision makers is perhaps the most pressing current issue in utility analysis." Research on the presentation of utility analysis consists of a few studies of utility analysis acceptance.

The Futility of Utility Analysis?   Latham and Whyte (1994) found that utility analysis actually *reduced* managers' reported support for a hypothetical selection program. "These troubling results have stimulated a great deal of discussion" (Borman, Hanson, & Hedge, 1997, p. 321), and spurred a recent stream of research addressing user acceptance and reaction to utility analysis, so we review them in detail. The Latham and Whyte study provided a hypothetical selection utility analysis to 143 experienced managers. They noted

Mintzberg's (1975) suggestion that actual managers may underemphasize analytical input, and Johns's (1993) findings that technical merit may not always determine the adoption of HR innovations. The study did not intend to test these theories, and explicitly eschewed formal hypotheses. Instead, it asked whether managers are more likely to adopt a psychologist's recommended selection procedure when that advice is accompanied by (a) explanations of standard validation procedures; (b) standard validation plus an expectancy table based on past experience with another organization; (c) validation plus utility analysis showing significant financial benefits; and (d) validation plus both expectancy tables and utility analysis. The experience of a psychologist who delivered the information (1 year vs. 10 years since receiving a doctorate) was also varied. Managers responded to an eight-item scale tapping their confidence in the effectiveness of the program, ability to justify it to others, and willingness to implement the program. Analyses revealed only one significant difference—condition c produced significantly *lower* ratings than condition a. While this is a tantalizingly counterintuitive effect, the negative effect of utility analysis was apparently mitigated by the addition of the expectancy table. No effects of consultant experience were observed, although for condition c the more experienced consultant was associated with preferences that were notably *lower* than for the inexperienced consultant. The authors noted the artificial setting and the reliance on textbook explanations of utility analysis.

Potential Motivational Explanations.   Whyte and Latham (1997) replicated the original study, while contrasting two written hypothetical summaries of validation results that were stated either to be supported by a psychologist, or to have come from a hypothetical trusted advisor. A third condition combined the written summary with a video presentation by a psychologist recommending utility analysis and the opportunity to question him (although none chose to do so). Acceptance and confidence ratings were slightly (but significantly) higher with the trusted advisor versus the control condition, but greatly and significantly *lower* in the expert-utility condition. Cronshaw (1997), the expert in the study, suggested this may have reflected perceptions that he was persuading or selling the intervention, that his actions may have been seen as coercive or self-motivated, and that these factors may have reduced audience commitment. He concluded that "it is not utility analysis *per se* that imperils I/O psychologists, but the intemperate way that it is often used" (p. 614). I/O psychologists have a significant role to play in articulating a strategic linkage between such investments and organizational outcomes. Approaching the task through collaboration with business leaders seems likely to produce greater perceived objectivity and actual contextual rigor, as we will describe later.

Information Complexity. Carson, Becker, and Henderson (1998) proposed that information that is easier to understand will be more persuasive, noting that Latham and Whyte (1994) confounded length and complexity with utility analysis. Carson et al. replicated the Latham and Whyte experiment with the same validity-only and validity-plus-utility conditions, but added two simplified explanations of these conditions. They did not replicate the Latham and Whyte finding of reduced acceptability in the utility analysis condition. The simplified utility description not only was easier to understand, but it received nonsignificantly higher ratings than the simplified validity-only scenario. A second study that added a utility scenario describing the derivation of SDy again failed to replicate the Latham-Whyte findings, but found that both revised utility-analysis scenarios received higher acceptability ratings than the Latham-Whyte utility- and validity-only conditions. Although this is somewhat supportive of simplified utility analysis, Carson et al. (1998) noted that even the highest ratings achieved in both their study and Latham and Whyte was below 30 on a scale from 8 to 40. There is much to learn about generating acceptance for I/O psychology and HR interventions among managers. We will return to this later.

Effects of Framing. Hazer and Highhouse (1997) presented 179 managers with a scripted dialogue between an HR manager and a company president describing utility analysis for a trial HR program, varying (a) the SDy estimation method (40% of salary vs. the Cascio-Ramos estimate of performance in dollars [CREPID]); (b) framing in terms of the loss from discontinuing versus the equivalent gain by continuing the program; and (c) HR program as selection versus training. Managers rated the credibility and usefulness of the information. Only the SDy manipulation was significant (although it accounted for less than 5% of variance), with managers favoring the utility analysis estimating SDy as 40% of salary. A post hoc test suggested that framing had the usual effect (framing as cost avoidance resulted in more likely implementation), but only for those who incorrectly understood how benefits were calculated. The authors noted that these results are consistent with some principles of persuasion (e.g., Petty & Cacioppo, 1984), and that they may reflect a number of possible underlying cognitive processes that should be tested further.

Considering Alternative Audiences. Utility analysis research largely omits the perspectives of constituents other than HR or line managers, even though financial-management

and HR-accounting research has focused on investors and shareholders. Perhaps more important, how might utility analysis affect *employees,* the recipients of I/O psychology interventions? Employees seldom decide whether to adopt programs, but it may well be important that employees understand the logic of program success. For example, suppose the utility of a training program rests on the effect of training on employees' knowledge of customers. Employees may be well suited to support or refute the connection. While training may enhance knowledge, which may correlate with sales, employees may be able to explain why, and thus to enhance both the accuracy and persuasiveness of utility presentations. Moreover, I/O psychology programs may be more effective if target employees understand the logic (e.g., "we are training you in customer knowledge because we have found that it seems to relate strongly to sales"). Employee *line-of-sight* (Boswell, 2000) and how it relates to utility analysis remains unexplored. Research on applicant reactions to selection procedures and trainee perceptions of the value of training is also relevant here. Would applicants find testing more palatable, or trainees find training more motivating, if they knew the logic that was used to justify them?

Summary. Attention to managerial reactions to utility analysis is a welcome step toward examining cognitive processes in utility analysis, rather than attention only to "mathematical modeling and psychometric measurement" (Roth et al., 2000, p. 10). Several authors (e.g., Boudreau, 1996; Carson et al., 1998; Macan & Highhouse, 1994; Skarlicki et al., 1996) have suggested that theories of persuasive information processing may provide rich hypotheses, particularly the concepts underlying dual-process theories that describe when decisions are made systematically versus peripherally. Roth et al. (2000) noted the need for clearer constructs regarding comprehension, information processing, and reactions. Thus, cognitive responses have been studied at the presentation and acceptance stage of the decision process— but clearly, these cognitive processes are likely to be important at all stages. Extending this work to reflect theories of persuasive communication and message design seems promising. These same theories could be directed toward a variety of constituents beyond HR and line managers, including employees, investors, labor organizations, regulatory agencies, and so on. This requires addressing the substantive basis for reactions to I/O and HR investments. Persuasion theory may direct our attention to general attributes of the situation, audience, or message that affect acceptance, but it cannot tell us the nature of the skepticism that seems to characterize reactions to utility analysis (recall the relatively low acceptance ratings of Latham and colleagues as well as Carson et al.).

Researchers will need to better describe the particular mental maps that managers and others use to connect investments in I/O and HR practices with organizational success. Essentially, we need to ask not only "What variables correlate with acceptance?" but also "How does the logic of our cost-benefit analyses compare to the logic of those receiving such analyses?" Answers to this question will help explain not only the somewhat tepid response of decision makers who are relatively unfamiliar with utility analysis (Carson et al.; Latham & Whyte, 1994), but also the apparent difficulty in understanding and disbelief in the size of utility analysis results among those who have used utility analysis (Macan & Highhouse).

Influence Actual Decisions and Behaviors

Very little research exists on how utility analysis changes actual decisions, program implementations, or other behaviors. This stage of the decision process is both critical and difficult to study. This is obviously very different from utility analysis acceptance, or intentions to adopt hypothetical programs. Investigating actual decision behaviors of managers requires a much deeper understanding of organizational context. Florin-Thuma and Boudreau (1987) offered an early attempt to map the decision processes of managers in a small retail frozen yogurt shop. They documented the initial decision not to provide employee feedback (by having employees weigh each serving). They then gathered serving and inventory data and compared the managers' estimates of decision attributes to the empirical results. When entered into the utility equation, even the managers' own estimates supported the value of providing feedback. Even so, managers had significantly underestimated the performance deviations (over-speed serving) and thus the value of feedback to store performance. Their underestimate of the problem apparently led them initially to dismiss the feedback intervention. Morrow et al. (1997) gathered utility estimates for several training programs, even those in an actual organization. They noted that the utility analysis seemed more acceptable for having been based on assumptions suggested by the organization's leaders, but that ultimately the organization decided against training programs, even those that had shown returns of more than 100%. They observed that "training managers, based on the results of the managerial course evaluations concluded that [the needs of] individual participants must be considered . . . and the core curriculum was discontinued" (p. 115).

Thus, we remain largely ignorant about the influence of utility analysis in organizations, although preliminary results suggest the value of more study. It may be useful to distinguish decisions about HR *policies,* reflecting the design of programs (e.g., incentive pay), from those concerning HR *practices,* reflecting the actual execution and application

(e.g., whether pay actually varies by performance; Gerhart, Wright, & MacMahan, 2000; Huselid & Becker, 2000). Theories of the diffusion of innovations (e.g., Abrahamson, 1996; Johns, 1993) may also be instructive, suggesting that HR innovations are affected by fads, fashions, and an administrative mindset. Research examining actual decisions would be informative, but it will be difficult to achieve experimentally controlled use of different decision-support systems in actual organizations. As an interim step, we would encourage researchers to collect data on the prior beliefs of employees and managers about the connections between interventions and organizational outcomes, and then to compare them to the empirical results (e.g., Florin-Thuma & Boudreau, 1987).

Conclusions

We have proposed a seven-step decision process as a framework for utility analysis research: (a) learn, assess, and sense patterns; (b) identify and gather appropriate data; (c) analyze and identify key messages; (d) design summaries and prescriptions; (e) present summaries and prescriptions; (f) influence key human capital decisions; and (g) effect execution and behavior change. Certainly, the legacy of the 1980s has continued, and steps b and c have received a good deal of attention, extending utility analysis and applying it to new areas (e.g., selection with a probationary period; classification, compensation, and employee day care). Perhaps due to repeated cautions to avoid making utility overly complex and unusable, we have seen a surge in research to uncover factors that affect managerial reactions and acceptance, reflecting steps d and e. We see much less attention to the initial sensing processes that lead to decision model choices (step a), although there are some promising frameworks, such as persuasion theory and the technical-versus-administrative distinction. Finally, only very limited research addresses the effects of utility analysis or other decision models on actual decisions and behaviors in organizations, including constituents other than line managers (steps f and g).

We have also noted that research examining the effect of utility analysis on actual decisions has generally focused on describing acceptance patterns, identifying attributes that enhance or detract from the persuasive impact of messages. This is likely to provide useful general insights into ways to make utility analysis more convincing or acceptable, but focusing only on persuasion implies that utility messages are correct. The accuracy of utility analysis results remains unclear, as indicated by the continuing debate about the structure of utility models, and examples of adjustments that might vastly reduce reported utility estimates (Sturman, 2000).

Moreover, focusing on persuasion suggests that a crucial hurdle is to convince others. This assumption is understandable. For decades, the profession of HR management has noted that it lacks respect (Guest & Peccei, 1994; Skinner, 1981), and that pattern persists (Wright, MacMahan, Snell, & Gerhart, 2001). However, learning how to convince decision makers may tell us little about the subjective and objective connections between investments in human capital and organizational outcomes.

Understanding the connections between HR and strategic success is key. A recurring theme in all of the decision stages is that understanding such connections is essential for utility analysis to achieve greater acceptability and accuracy. Yet, it is often overlooked that such connections may reveal the underlying logical gaps that justify the skepticism. For example, a framework that articulates these connections could help identify attributes that must be included in MAU analysis. Finally, describing and understanding the connections between investments in human capital and organizational success will be necessary to interpret the results of qualitative research describing actual decisions in organizations.

What is needed is a rich and reliable framework for making conceptual connections between talent and organizational success. These connections are the basis for ensuring not only that managers understand the importance of HR work, but also that HR is actually working on things that matter. In short, I/O psychology must take a more strategic perspective, looking beyond single HR programs and individual-level outcomes, and encompassing the strategic processes and outcomes of the organization (Boudreau & Ramstad, 2001, 2002). We believe that I/O psychology has much to contribute to strategy, especially through the lens of utility analysis, and that strategy provides a valuable alternative perspective for I/O psychologists and HR professionals. This suggests a perspective that is more normative than the largely descriptive work that has been done so far. By examining the development and diffusion of the most successful decision-support systems in organizations (e.g., financial and market analysis), we can identify useful principles to guide descriptive research on decision-model adoption and effects, as well as prescriptive research to make future utility analysis and human capital decision models more useful.

LEARNING FROM SUCCESSFUL DECISION-SUPPORT SYSTEMS

We can enhance human capital measurement by examining the features of successful decision-support models in other areas, such as finance. Virtually everyone analyzes organizations using the logic and measures of finance. This is true even when analyzing resources such as human capital, as the history of utility analysis vividly illustrates. As Boudreau and Ramstad (1998, 2002) noted, the success of financial and marketing systems reflects their fundamental focus on enhancing decisions about an important resource (financial capital or customers). In the same way, we have seen that the value of utility analysis and other HR measurement systems lies in their ability to enhance decisions about human capital, including decisions by employees, managers, and I/O and HR professionals. Yet, the answer is not simply to adopt financial ratios and apply them to HR programs. Rather, the key is to understand how successful measurement systems have evolved, and search for general principles.

The Need for a Decision Science for HR: Talentship

Both finance and marketing are *decision sciences* that evolved from a professional practice. Marketing evolved as a decision science from the professional practice of sales. Finance evolved as a decision science from the professional practice of accounting. Both sales and accounting are important processes. They have professional standards and best practices, and they produce important data to assess organizational performance. However, accounting and sales do not in themselves provide a decision science. For example, accounting can provide the numbers that describe the volatility and return on corporate bonds. However, it is the science of finance that applies portfolio theory to those numbers, to support decisions about the appropriate mix of financial instruments to optimize risk and return for an organization, and about the appropriate deployment of financial capital to investments. Similarly, the sales process generates important data on sales of products to particular customers. However, it is the science of marketing that developed and applies the theory of customer segmentation and product life cycles to support decisions about advertising, product placement, and so on. *Finance* is the decision science that improves organizational performance by enhancing decisions about financial capital. *Marketing* is the decision science that improves organizational performance by enhancing decisions about customer capital.

Today, the field of HR management is characterized by a strong professional practice. The professional practice of HR management, supported by a wide variety of research, tools, best practices, and the like, has evolved significantly over the past several years, and with it the stature of the HR function and professionals. Yet, as we have seen, we still lack a decision framework that connects talent and strategic organizational value. Utility analysis, and other frameworks from I/O psychology and other social sciences, can form the basis of a decision science for talent that will evolve from the professional practice of human resources. We have coined the term *talentship* to capture the distinction between the decision science of talent and the professional practice of HR management. Talentship is to human resources as finance is to accounting and as marketing is to sales. *Talentship* is the decision science that improves organizational performance by enhancing decisions that impact or depend on human capital. Talentship will build on HR management practices and measures, but it will go beyond the professional practice to create tools and frameworks that enhance decisions. Note that the domain of decisions is purposefully broad, including not only decisions made by I/O psychologists and HR professionals, but also individual decisions by employees about their own talent (e.g., whether to take a certain training course or career opportunity), as well as decisions by line managers regarding the talent under their stewardship.

Boudreau and Ramstad (1997) suggested that human capital measurement could learn three important lessons from the evolution of finance and marketing: (a) Reveal the value linkages; (b) focus on the constraints; and (c) intangibility does not prevent measurement.

Reveal the Value Linkages.   The first lesson—reveal the value linkages—is illustrated by Pfeffer's (1998, p. 359) suggestion, "ask yourself the last time the finance or controller's staff, or better yet, internal audit, had to measure its contribution to the bottom line," noting that "measurement systems embody an implicit theory of how the function or the firm operates" (p. 362). The financial system concentrates on articulating the links between decisions about financial capital and organizational outcomes, rather than proposing or defending internal programs recommended by the finance department. Contrast this with the overwhelming focus of utility analysis on acceptance by managers, or the value of particular functional HR programs. Throughout this chapter we have seen that this focus has left gaps in our ability to articulate the logical maps between human capital and organizational outcomes. Although this logic is implied in the structure of utility analysis models (e.g., $r_{x,y}$ relates variation in selection attributes to dollar-valued organizational results, SDy translates variability among employees or applicants into organizational outcomes), the *links* that articulate the connection are generally missing.

Focus on the Constraints.   The second lesson—focus on the constraints—is rooted in the value of information. The importance of decisions depends on the value of the resource being managed. Boudreau and Ramstad (1997) noted management systems have achieved prominence in different eras (agriculture, transportation, industrial) in part because they focused on a constrained resource. For example, the financial analysis system (e.g., income statements, balance sheets, etc.) predated the Security and Exchange Commission's (SEC's) regulations in effect today. Johnson and Kaplan (1987, pp. 6–18) describe how financial models evolved to provide decision support systems necessary to optimize the use of a particular resource (money) at a particular time (the start of the Industrial Revolution). In addition, they show how financial management systems resulted from the Industrial Revolution's demand for external capital. Financial analysis achieved prominence when it did in part because it dealt with an important *constrained* resource, at a time when the knowledge about how to manage that resource was very rare or nonexistent. Several years later, during the Great Depression, the SEC implemented legislation (U.S. SEC Acts of 1933 and 1934) to regulate this information at precisely the time when capital was most constrained and labor was most abundant. Boudreau and Ramstad (1997) noted that today organizations routinely lay off capital by giving it back to shareholders in the form of stock repurchases. Today's key constraint is increasingly organizational talent. We shall show later how the principle of constraints is important to future research on SDy.

Intangibility Does Not Prevent Measurement.   The third lesson—intangibility does not prevent measurement—reflects the synergy between measurement and decision making. In marketing, for example, a *brand* is intangible, residing primarily in the minds of customers. Yet, organizations systematically manage their brands with measures such as the amount and quality of shelf space, customer awareness, repeat purchases, and so on. These measures did not precede the notion of brands. Rather, organizations perceived the general value of their brands by informally observing customer behavior with crude measurement systems. Sales records might have been organized by sales representative or region, with one salesperson or region generating higher sales. Over time, such higher sales might be attributed to advertising in that region, or to the extra client calls made by the salesperson. A hypothesis might have evolved to explain this link, suggesting that customer awareness was a key driver of sales. Measures of customer awareness would develop and verify this relationship across many regions and salespeople. Eventually, customer awareness was more finely defined to include brand awareness, and more sophisticated measures emerged. The give and take between the professional practice of sales, which generated the data, and the decision science of marketing, which created the theory of brands, eventually led to enhancements in both the professional practice and the decision science, driven by enhanced measures.

I/O Psychology and Talentship

I/O psychology might find particular optimism in the analogy to consumer brands, because so much of I/O psychology is devoted to measuring intangible constructs (e.g., personality, attitudes, cognitions). The lessons from marketing suggest that improved measurement will result from a closer synergy between measures and the decision systems they support. Yet, I/O psychology, HR management, and utility analysis are at an early stage in this process, compared to finance and marketing. We have seen tantalizing evidence that familiarity with utility analysis methods leads to perceptions that they are less costly and less complicated (Macan & Highhouse, 1994, p. 431). However, we have yet to see a research agenda specifically building on the potential synergy between measures and decisions. I/O can contribute to the development of talentship—the human capital decision science. Utility analysis and the broader field of I/O psychology seem well positioned to contribute to the development of the measurement systems that will evolve to address the critical constraint of this era: human capital. The logic and assumptions of utility analysis provide one useful framework for defining such systems. However, this will require that I/O psychology research and measurement more strongly integrate with principles of strategic organizational value. Our decision-based review of the utility analysis literature, and the three lessons from successful decision-support systems described here, reveal a consistent theme: the need to articulate the elements that bridge human capital and organizational success. An articulated logic reveals the key constraints and provides both the measures and the logic to clarify the intangible. Next, we describe a framework that articulates the bridge between human capital investments and organizational strategic success.

THE STRATEGIC HUMAN CAPITAL BRIDGE (HC BRidge) FRAMEWORK

Articulating the Links Between I/O and HR Investments and Organizational Success

Changing the focus of utility analysis research from measurement to strategic value connections requires articulating the links between I/O interventions and organizational success. This fundamental dilemma for organizational researchers will require solutions that go beyond I/O psychology, HR management, and utility analysis. Yet, I/O psychology has an important role in constructing the framework, and the need for it is evident in utility analysis research.

Roth et al. (2000) noted that the utility acceptance process might best be studied through case studies or open-ended interviews deeply examining prior values, decision processes, perceptions of costs and benefits, and environmental factors. We agree that qualitative analysis is promising, and suggest that research go further, to examine not just acceptance but decision logic. A framework for articulating and evaluating the previously held mental maps of decision makers is needed to assess not only acceptance, but where decision processes can be improved.

Rauschenberger and Schmidt (1987) recognized the need for articulation, urging that "the practitioner develop a definition of utility appropriate for the organizational decision makers who will be expected to understand and use it," and noting that "different organizational decision makers within the *same* organization may require different definitions of utility" (p. 54). Recognizing the perspective of decision makers is clearly important. However, that should not imply that the value of our frameworks is judged solely on the basis of acceptance. The more appropriate focus for I/O psychology is to discover and articulate a logical framework linking talent to organizational success that is a useful tool for common understanding. For example, finance professionals do not strive merely to have line managers accept their models of how financial capital relates to business success. Instead, finance professionals educate their counterparts in a professionally developed decision science about financial capital. Similarly, for I/O psychology and HR management, the ultimate goal is to enhance decisions, even if that requires correcting constituents' understanding of the links between talent and organization success.

Gerhart, Wright, McMahan, and Snell (2000) suggested that the interrater reliability of the reported number of HR practices may be so low as to make existing estimates of the HR-practice and firm-performance relationship implausible. Controversy persists (Gerhart, Wright, & MacMahan, 2000; Huselid & Becker, 2000) regarding how to identify knowledgable respondents and discern how firm size and diversity affect the ability of decision makers to grasp key relationships. All parties seem to agree on the need to understand the variables that mediate between HR practices and strategic success. Morrow et al. (1997) alluded to this when they noted that "training can have a large [yet] unimportant effect in a decision-making context. . . . [T]he relevance of the criteria to the job must be measured and controlled in order for effect sizes to be comparable in an organizational context" (p. 94).

Our proposal goes beyond assessing the empirical relation between utility estimates and actual productivity increases (Schmidt, Hunter, Outerbridge, & Trattner, 1986). Such evidence will benefit from a logical framework to explain the intervening processes. Our proposal also extends beyond simply involving recipients in defining utility parameters, or identifying the assumptions that will persuade the audience. Evidence of the value of participation is mixed (Latham, Erez, & Locke, 1988; Roth et al., 2000), but participation will be enhanced by more explicitly describing the mental models used by managers and leaders, and comparing these mental models to evidence about how HR and I/O investments actually link to organizational performance. A systematic decision science may actually uncover fallacies in managerial assumptions (e.g., Florin-Thuma & Boudreau, 1987). Typically, managers encounter such logic only when they are being sold on the value of an HR or I/O program. As Cronshaw (1997) and Latham and Whyte (1994) suggest, such situations can engender distrust rather than learning. Human resources and I/O psychology must articulate these linkages independent of persuasion attempts.

The need for an articulated linking framework is also apparent in studies that have invoked the idea of a strategic perspective on utility analysis. The recurring theme is to "illuminate the middle ground" (Boudreau & Ramstad, 1997) in ways that are tangible, articulated, and subject to discussion and refutation by key constituents. Cabrera and Cabrera (1999) proposed that balanced scorecards articulate hypotheses about how the elements of an organization connect to create value. Jones and Wright (1992) suggested considering the larger bureaucratic and organizational costs. Russell et al. (1993) presented several hypothetical examples indicating how the timing of the returns from I/O interventions may well affect their strategic value depending on the strategic context, such as whether an operation is likely to fail with or without the added value derived from enhanced human capital.

Russell (1998) used the notion of *value distance,* first suggested in 1967, to capture the number of processes between individual performance and the customer experience (e.g., the toothpaste maker at Proctor & Gamble is very distant, while the owner-operator of a one-man tailor shop is quite proximal). Russell correctly observes that value distance might affect the relevance of correlations based on performance ratings, as parameters in calculating the value of I/O interventions. In fact, we next suggest that articulating this concept with the benefit of recent work on strategy, business processes, and value chains from the strategy literature, offers precisely the map for understanding that is currently lacking. For an illustration of the usefulness of value chains, see Webb and Gile (2001).

From Black Box to Bridge: The HC BRidge Strategic Human Capital Framework

An increasingly common theme in strategic HR management research is the need to reveal what is within the black box, so to speak, between HR practices and strategic organizational outcomes (e.g., Becker & Gerhart, 1996; Chadwick & Cappelli, 1999; Dyer & Shafer, 1999; McMahan, Virick, & Wright, 1999). Inspired by the tantalizing evidence noted earlier, that HR practices associate with firm-level financial outcomes, researchers have begun to insert selected intervening variables into studies of this relationship (e.g., attitudes, turnover, etc.). We propose that systematic integration of principles from I/O psychology and strategy research holds the promise to go to the next step: to move beyond simply acknowledging the black box and instead to articulate and test a rich and detailed framework of linking elements—in essence, to move from a black box to a bridge. As we have seen, the lessons from disciplines such as marketing and finance suggest the importance and power of such frameworks for advancing theory-building, measurement, and management influence. We must develop a decision science that specifies a rich and logical set of connections between talent and strategic success.

Figure 9.2 contains the model we have proposed to articulate business strategies tangibly enough to connect them to human capital and human resource investments. It is based on causal-chain analysis and value distance, as it specifies linking elements between I/O and HR investments and organizational success. Some of these links have been proposed before (e.g., Becker & Huselid, 1998; Boudreau, 1998; Boudreau & Ramstad, 1997; Cascio, 1996; Fitz-enz, 2000). A more detailed application of the HC BRidge framework to the strategic challenges of the Internet can be found in Boudreau, Dunford, and Ramstad (2001). Here, we concentrate on the three major anchor points of the framework.

Impact identifies whether and how elements of strategic success (e.g., uniqueness, growth, profitability) link with

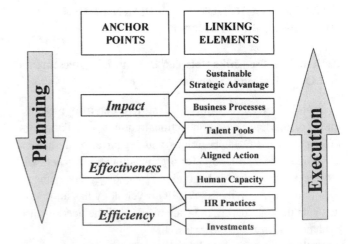

Figure 9.2 HC BRidge™ Framework. *Source:* Copyright 2000 by Boudreau and Ramstad. All rights reserved.

talent pools. We use the term *talent pools,* rather than *jobs,* to focus on contribution rather than administration. For example, in a theme park a key talent pool would consist of those who have significant customer contact. This includes jobs such as characters and amusement ride hosts, but also includes store clerks, groundskeepers, and even parking lot attendants. There is no particular job of customer contact, yet these workers comprise a talent pool whose work collectively (and perhaps collaboratively) affects customer experience.

Effectiveness connects HR practices to talent pools. This anchor point encompasses familiar I/O questions about the impact of interventions on ability, attitudes, and motivation, which are subelements of Human Capacity in Figure 9.2. However, it also articulates whether and how that capacity produces aligned actions that contribute to the effectiveness of the talent pool.

Efficiency links the resources expended to the resulting HR practices and I/O interventions. As noted previously, many traditional HR measurement approaches concentrate primarily on efficiency. Efficiency measures are useful, but must be embedded within the contexts of *impact* and *effectiveness* to avoid misinterpretation.

HC BRidge and Utility Analysis

The HC BRidge framework clarifies the progress and potential of utility-model development. Using Figure 9.2, we can see that early utility analysis work observed a link between *HR practices* and *aligned actions* (e.g., test scores and job performance ratings) and then extrapolated directly to *strategic success* by translating into dollar values. Figure 9.2 suggests that this approach provided only limited explanations regarding how *aligned actions* create *talent pools,* which in turn support key *business processes* such as quality, speed, innovation, logistics, and production, which lead to sustainable *strategic success.* It should be no surprise that asking raters to combine these links in a single translation from performance to dollar values (*SDy* estimation) has presented a daunting task, as we will discuss shortly. Modifications of the early utility model have included embellishments to reflect additional HR practices (e.g., recruiting, training, retention, and pay), but utility models generally retained the same logical leap from an observed performance criterion to dollar values. For example, adjusting utility estimates in line with traditional business measurement systems (e.g., financial adjustments) recognized the connection but did not articulate intervening processes.

Thus, the HC BRidge model suggests untapped opportunities in utility analysis and I/O research, focusing on articulating how HR practices connect to aligned actions and key

business processes. For example, the CREPID *SDy* estimation process (and others) weighs performance dimensions according to their perceived importance, but provides little guidance or investigation into the factors leading to perceived importance. We find that HC BRidge helps experts articulate the links among performance dimensions, business processes, and the value or uniqueness of the organization's competitive position. It seems likely that such articulation will produce utility estimates that are more understandable and credible to decision makers, and allow a much richer diagnosis of managers' thought processes.

For example, applying the HC BRidge framework to the case of Encyclopedia Britannica, Boudreau and colleagues (2001) focused on how talent linked to sources of sustainable uniqueness on the Internet. This analysis revealed the fallacy of the typical assumption that Britannica's future rested mostly on maximizing the performance of Web technicians, and purging the organization of so-called old-economy talent (e.g., door-to-door sales staff). The Web technician talent pool, and its associated aligned actions, were indeed important, but provided no *unique* source of value. A unique and competitively differentiating Web experience required drawing on Britannica's traditional strength in finding and presenting distinctive information. Paradoxically, this uniqueness required elements of the old-economy talent pools, such as information specialists and former door-to-door salespeople. Utility analysis of selection tests or training for Web technicians at Britannica would likely have shown a positive return, even while failing to acknowledge the combination of old-economy and new-economy talent necessary to achieve unique strategic value. This might explain managers' skepticism, if utility analysis showing significant value from enhanced selection for Web technicians, but the managers recognize the simultaneous need to transform their old-economy talent.

This has fundamental implications for utility analysis and I/O research. As we have shown, prior utility analysis research has focused primarily on measurement limitations, including demographic characteristics of raters or performance ratings in a single job. Consider how future investigations might differ if based on a framework like that shown in Figure 9.2. Researchers would elicit a list of specific talent pools, specific key business processes affected by those talent pools, and the specific elements of strategic advantage they might affect. Reactions to utility analysis might be examined as a function of the logical connections that are omitted and included. High utility values may seem unbelievable until a specific connection between human capacity (e.g., enhanced knowledge) is traced to its effect on aligned actions (e.g., fewer errors), key business processes (e.g., solving customer problems the first time), and competitive advantage (e.g., unique levels of customer satisfaction). Such an analysis would also allow I/O researchers to better diagnose the nature of constituent reactions (some constituents may perceive different links than others) and pinpoint where greater measurement or communication efforts are needed.

Finally, the HC BRidge framework suggests departures from traditional approaches to I/O interventions. It may be much more important to identify the most critical talent pools *before* focusing on the value of particular programs. Traditionally, utility analysis—and I/O psychology research more generally—takes the intervention as the point of departure. Having identified the intervention, attention focuses on understanding its effects on employees in a particular job. Yet, the definition of *SDy* in utility analysis reveals that *variation* in employee value is a key factor in effectiveness, and is independent of the intervention. Thus, it may be more fruitful to assess the economic potential of talent first, and then apply I/O interventions where they can have the greatest strategic effect. This reverses the traditional approach and elevates the economic analysis of talent pools to a prominent position. Training research recognizes the importance of needs analysis, yet training utility analysis is typically seen merely as evaluation, after the fact. Future research might fruitfully focus on how to use utility-analysis logic to diagnose the high-potential opportunities. Those opportunities might be defined by the relative *SDy* levels among talent pools, which brings us to the *strategic* relevance of *SDy*.

THE STRATEGIC RELEVANCE OF *SDy* IN DEFINING PIVOTAL TALENT POOLS

One can certainly forgive those readers who approach this section on *SDy* with trepidation. This parameter—the standard deviation of employee performance in dollars—has been the object of significant technical debate and psychometric measurement attention. However, the frequency of *SDy* measurement research has recently diminished considerably. Boudreau (1991) described how pre-1991 research embodied vigorous debate and attention to measuring *SDy*, characterized as the Achilles' heel of utility analysis. *SDy* was very subjective, whereas other utility elements were more tangible. It has been suggested (e.g, Arvey & Murphy, 1998; Boudreau, 1991) that further research on *SDy* and the logic used by its estimators may never make utility analysis estimates extremely precise. Boudreau suggested that, lacking an objective criterion to evaluate *SDy* estimates, convergence around one accepted estimation method was unlikely, and noted how infrequently *SDy* estimation differences actually affected the correct decision.

We will review recent *SDy* research shortly, but first we propose a different and more strategic perspective suggested by the HC BRidge framework. As we noted earlier, *SDy* is of significant potential value, as a powerful link between I/O psychology and strategic HR management. This is also generally true of utility analysis. Demonstrating the point using *SDy* is perhaps the strongest test, because traditional *SDy* research epitomizes the fixation on measurement and parameter definition that has so often limited the relevance of utility analysis. Thus, here we will redefine the *SDy* debate to focus on a seldom-acknowledged issue, yet an issue that is fundamental to I/O psychology, HR management, and strategy. That issue is how to identify the key talent pools—those that are most critical to organizational success.

In Figure 9.2, this issue arises in the Talent Pools parameter. This is a critical connection point in linking I/O and HR to strategic success. Research and practice in business strategy typically focuses on the model elements above Talent Pools, defining the elements of strategic success and the business processes that support it but seldom specifying which talent is critical and why. Analogously, research and practice in HR and I/O psychology typically focus on the model elements below Talent Pools, with theories and measures of HR practices, resulting human capacity (capability, opportunity, and motivation), and aligned actions (performance, turnover, or other behaviors), but seldom evaluating whether they are strategically the most critical (Boudreau & Ramstad, 2002). Despite this gap, there is tantalizing evidence to show how several disciplines could contribute to this issue. I/O psychology has long acknowledged that the effect of psychological interventions depends on the target employee population. Larger *SDy* values imply greater potential utility because of larger employee performance variations (Boudreau, 1991). The issue is also touched upon in the evaluation of jobs in setting pay policies (higher-paid positions carry greater importance due to greater responsibility, knowledge, etc.; cf. Milkovich & Newman, 1999); training evaluation (cf. Kirkpatrick's 1994 notion that training-intervention effects depend on the link from reactions to learning to behaviors to results); and in employee surveys tied to strategic services (e.g., Schneider et al., 1996).

Yet, average pay, job results, or service levels are clearly not adequate proxies for employee impact. Logistics experts are extremely important to Wal-Mart or Federal Express, but less important to SUN or Cisco Systems; yet all four companies might employ them at similar market pay levels. Accounts of unsung heroes in lower-paid jobs abound, including the trash sweepers at Disney (Boudreau, 1998; Boudreau & Ramstad, 1999), the information specialists at Brittanica.com (Boudreau et al., 2001), the repair technicians at Xerox (Brown & Duguid, 2000), and the store associates at Sears (Rucci et al., 1998).

These positions carry low pay, low-complexity job descriptions, and sometimes significant value distance from customers. They would probably receive low *SDy* estimates. Yet performance differences in such roles can produce pivotal effects on highly important business processes.

Human resource strategy writers routinely refer to concepts such as *core competencies* and *key employees* (Nonaka & Takeuchi, 1995; Porter 1996; Prahalad & Hamel, 1990; Treacy & Wiersema, 1997; Ulrich, 1996), generally noting that *core* or *key* refers to proximity to organizational goals. The emerging resource-based view suggests that which roles are pivotal will vary (Teece, Pisano, & Shuen, 1997), particularly with strategic events (Barnett, Greve, & Park, 1994; Barney, 1992). Lepak and Snell (1999) addressed this issue specifically, describing an "HR architecture" differentiated by employee uniqueness and value; but we have no accepted measures to differentiate employees by their value. Key employees may indeed merit different HR treatment, but identifying which employees are key and why remains elusive. Godfrey and Hill (1995) noted that many of the critical constructs in emerging strategy theories remain unobservable. It is precisely this unobservability that creates a powerful nexus for integrating principles from I/O psychology, HR management, and strategy. *SDy* provides a good example.

An overlooked principle in defining key talent is the distinction between *average value* and *variability in value,* something that utility analysis explicitly recognizes. When strategy writers describe critical jobs or roles, they typically emphasize the average level of value (e.g., the general influence, customer contact, uniqueness, or power of certain jobs). Yet variation interacts with average importance to determine the talent where HR practices can have the greatest effect. The HC BRidge model suggests (Boudreau et al., 2001; Boudreau & Ramstad, 1997) that roles are *pivotal* when variability in performance affects critical resources (Barney, 1992) or constrained business processes (Porter, 1996). An important question for I/O and HR strategy is not which talent has the greatest *average* value, but rather in which talent pools does performance *variation* create the biggest strategic impact.

For example, consider Federal Express's Asia-Pacific operations. The average strategic value of pilots is very high. Pilot shortages could potentially halt shipping operations, pilots are highly paid, and their job description requires high intelligence and qualifications. Using the HC BRidge framework to connect talent to strategy, it is clear that variation in pilot performance and among pilot job applicants is relatively small. The high levels of certification and training required by law to apply or take a pilot position essentially create a very narrow distribution. Average impact is high; variability in impact is low. Thus, investments in HR practices to enhance poor pilot performance would produce little strategic benefit.

Now, consider the couriers at Federal Express Asia-Pacific. Courier job descriptions traditionally reflect driving and picking up packages. Performance variation among couriers is probably much larger than among pilots, in part because their low pay and relatively low stature means that they receive much less attention than more visible and strategic talent pools, such as pilots. Variation in driving performance may actually be relatively small, but when the courier role is connected to strategy, it becomes clear that couriers significantly affect on-time delivery and customer satisfaction. For example, one aligned action (see Figure 9.2) involved a common customer request: If the courier can wait just 15 minutes, the customer will have 20 more boxes to ship. What is the correct action? It depends, of course, on whether waiting will delay the shipments already collected enough to miss the deadline to be loaded on the last flight to the United States. On this performance dimension, couriers may vary widely, with high-performing couriers and dispatchers working together to make more appropriate decisions, and the difference could often be worth thousands of dollars. The strategic variability in courier performance is higher than for pilots, but both traditional strategy analysis, and even *SDy* estimates based on job descriptions that reflect only driving, would miss this.

What are the implications for utility analysis, I/O and HR research, *SDy*, and strategy? The logic of *SDy* suggests defining key human resources, based on performance variation. In the HC BRidge model, talent pools are composed of *pivotal roles,* meaning that organizational outcomes pivot significantly on variation in worker quality. Thus, *SDy* estimation not only is important to evaluate I/O interventions after the fact, but is even more important to identify which talent pools are most important prior to such interventions. I/O psychology has typically estimated *SDy* on single jobs, while HR strategy has struggled with differential importance across talent pools. There may be great promise in future research that actually measures the Impact (see Figure 9.2) of performance variability across different talent pools, even if such measurements are never used to evaluate an intervention.

Research on *SDy*

Research on *SDy* measurement has continued, strongly reflecting questions of accuracy, but more recently emphasizing how more-accurate *SDy* estimates might enhance credibility and influence with decision makers. Arvey and Murphy (1998) proposed that *SDy* may not be such a critical parameter, and questioned the continued investment in *SDy* estimation research, stating, "Rather than focusing so much attention on the estimation of *SDy*, we suggest that utility researchers should focus on understanding exactly what *Y* represents" (p. 162), supporting our suggestion to better articulate the links between human capital and organizational value.

Estimating SDy more directly

Researchers have suggested ways to simplify SDy estimation, to tie it more closely to observable performance elements or to its underlying assumptions. Cesare, Blankenship, and Giannetto (1994) found that in social services, archival supervisory job performance and worth ratings were linearly related ($r = .67$), supporting a basic utility assumption. Raju, Cabrera, and Lezotte (1996) developed a utility model in which performance is viewed as categorical rather than continuous. Raju, Burke, and Normand (1990) suggested that more practical SDy estimates might begin with observed performance standard deviations that are then transformed using subjective estimates of the relative range of performance ratings versus actual employee value, and finally multiplied by the estimated slope of the employee-performance value function. They suggest a number of ways to estimate the slope, such as average salary. Morrow et al. (1997) calculate, this slope as the "fully-loaded cost of employment including benefits and overhead" (p. 98). Raju et al. (1990) suggested that shifting subjective judgment from SDy to these two new factors may enhance the quality of utility analysis estimates, which has been debated (Judeisch, Schmidt, & Hunter, 1993; Raju, Burke, Normand, & Lezotte, 1993; Schmidt & Hunter, 1998). However, there is agreement that the performance transformation requires expert judgment, and the choice of slope-scaling factors (e.g., compensation, sales, full employment costs) remains a challenge for which we have little research and few tools.

Judiesch, Schmidt, and Mount (1992) showed that SDy estimates were consistent with the proposition that raters anchor on average value, and estimate the 15th and 85th percentiles by multiplying by SDp—the ratio of SDy to average value. They compared estimated SDp to actual output or sales, or to proxies obtained from prior research on similar job titles. After adjustments, the average SDp values from subjective percentile estimates were similar to the output- or sales-based estimates, and estimated and output-based ratings correlated at .70. However, SDp is a percentage, not a dollar value. So, like Raju et al. (1990), Judiesch et al. (1992) recommended multiplying SDp by an "objective estimate of average revenue value" (p. 247), proposing taking the ratio of total payroll for the job divided by total payroll for the organization, multiplied by total organization revenue, and divided by the number of employees. They noted that while this is consistent with some labor market assumptions, unique factors in any particular firm may render this estimate incorrect, a problem that plagues all estimation based on average wages. They proposed "allowing senior executives to adjust the relative value of the job upward or downward if they judged that relative wages did not accurately reflect the relative value of jobs" (p. 247). Thus, both approaches rely on subjective judgments about the value of human capital, emphasizing the importance of articulating the underlying mental models, as we noted earlier.

With regard to estimating SDp, Hunter, Schmidt, and Judiesch (1990) examined jobs for which sales or output quantity was judged to be the primary indicator of value, focusing on studies with actual output counts or using variability in compensation for jobs judged to have a very strong link between compensation and sales (attorneys, physicians, and dentists). They specifically reported findings for a wide variety of routine blue-collar jobs; routine clerical jobs; crafts (radar mechanics, cooks, repairpersons, welders, handcrafters, and drillers); life insurance sales agents; retail and industrial sales; and professionals. Jobs of higher complexity had higher SDp levels, suggesting that job complexity might provide a simple rule of thumb for estimating SDp. Hunter et al. (1990) found that sales jobs had SDp levels far higher than their complexity scores would indicate, suggesting that "other constructs may be required for sales jobs" (p. 37). This is correct, as many other factors may influence the value of performance variation, even in jobs with objective output measures. For example, salespeople may achieve high sales at the expense of essential paperwork that would help improve future products, or production workers may achieve high output at the expense of helping others. This would lower the actual value of workers achieving high sales or output, biasing SDp levels upward. Observed sales might also underestimate SDp if those who achieve low current sales also alienate customers, affecting future sales. Cesare et al. (1994) and Judiesch et al. (1992) found that approximately 50% of the variability in estimated SDp was due to nonoutput factors or error, so even if estimates converge toward actual values, there is still much to be explained. The aligned-action element of the HC BRidge model can help articulate these complexities. Using general rules of thumb (such as job complexity) has merit, but can be enhanced by better understanding of the other constructs involved.

Becker and Huselid (1992) proposed measuring SDy by directly correlating or regressing unit financial performance on individual performance ratings. Their results from performance ratings of 335 retail-store supervisors in 117 locations suggested that the ratio of SDy to average salary ranged from 74% to 100% of salary. The authors noted that this requires special conditions in which unit-level outcomes and performance appraisals are available (where it may be possible to forego SDy completely by directly observing how HR practices and unit performance relate). They also noted the dangers of reverse causation and unmeasured factors (e.g., a downturn in the local economy would lower *SDy* even with no change in performance levels and variability), and that with multiple supervisors per store, *SDy* based on individual performance might overstate individual managers' contributions. Cesare et al. (1994) found supervisors' dollar-valued performance estimates were not related to archival employee performance ratings, but were correlated with factors such as the supervisors' own self-worth estimates. They called for training raters on what factors to consider. Again, establishing the logical links explaining the relationship between store outcomes and supervisor performance would be essential to such training.

Identifying the Factors That Influence SDy Estimates

A second research theme is how demographic and situational factors affect *SDy* estimates. Bobko, Shetezer, and Russell (1991) varied the anchor sequence (50th, then 85th, and vice versa) and the frame (faculty members' leaving versus being acquired) in a survey of search committee members at universities. They found that framing affected *SDy* (calculated as the difference between the percentile estimates), resulting in higher *SDy* values for acquisitions than losses. They suggested different *SDy* estimation methods for different purposes (e.g., selection vs. retention), that "multiple values of *SDy* exist, and the choice depends upon the researcher/practitioner's purpose in generating a dollar utility estimate" (p. 184), and that their respondents noted the difficulty of translating intangible faculty contributions into dollars—all of which reinforces the need for better articulation of logical connections, noted earlier.

Roth, Pritchard, Stout, and Brown (1994) examined what information judges used to make *SDy* estimates, and the judges' demographic background. Their subjects estimated the value of employees at the 15th, 50th, 85th, and 97th performance percentiles, and the variable costs associated with those percentiles, in a sample of 159 insurance agents, supervisors, and managers. They found that variable costs increased with the performance percentiles, but that costs as a percentage of value were higher at lower percentiles. Costs were 123% of the value of the 15th percentile, suggesting that 15th-percentile employees actually represent a net loss, a rare finding when subjects estimate only dollar values, not costs. Subjects rated the importance of 14 factors in their decisions, giving very similar ratings to all of them, although *work performance* and *initiative* were rated significantly higher. This approach has promise, but little theory or context was available to guide the choice of factors. Figure 9.2 would suggest

articulating relationships between *aligned actions* and *business processes* might be an appropriate starting point.

Conclusions

As Boudreau (1991) and recent reviewers (Arvey & Murphy, 1998) noted, we may be no closer to understanding whether *SDy* captures variability in employee value, and journal editors may have tired of such attempts. Even when performance and output are closely tied, value estimates and actual output are seldom correlated greater than .70. Observed job-specific *SDy* estimates apparently reflect the combined effect of performance in the target job with other factors of production, suggesting the need to identify other factors and their effects. Boudreau (1991, pp. 649–650) noted the dangers of focusing solely on jobs, because similar job titles such as computer programmer or sales associate may encompass very different tasks and different relationships to the value-creation systems of organizations. Hunter et al. (1992, p. 236) suggested that "in many jobs there is very little relationship between wages and output for individual employees." Increasingly, organizations have broadened pay ranges and job classes, to better reward and motivate employee behaviors beyond traditional job titles. Job titles become less homogenous, and average pay for a job title becomes a less specific proxy for value. The logical link between employee variability and value is the essential element of *SDy*. We need more theory and research on this link.

Research on factors influencing *SDy* estimates has also produced intriguing results but the studied factors vary widely, ranging from salary and performance, to supervising subordinates and community relations, to rater demographic characteristics (Roth, Pritchard, Stout, & Brown, 1994, p. 439). Raters apparently adopt varying approaches, and researchers have few frameworks to identify explanatory variables. Future research might benefit from focusing on the fundamental question posed by Arvey and Murphy (1998): "understanding exactly what Y represents" (p. 165), perhaps using linking models like that shown in Figure 9.2.

FINAL THOUGHTS

The title of this chapter includes "strategic industrial and organizational psychology," perhaps a counterintuitive phrase for a review of utility analysis. Even I/O psychologists often find utility analysis research excessively focused on the esoterica of models and measurement. Yet we have shown that utility analysis is inextricably connected to strategic human capital research. Research that aims to predict and explain utility analysis and its effects inevitably confronts the need to understand the key logical perceptions and processes linking human capital to sustainable strategic advantage.

Thus, we examined utility models through a decision-process lens, revealing the value of future research focused on decision processes, rather than exclusively on refining models and estimates. This will enhance our understanding of how and when model enhancements are important. Utility analysis research risks atrophy without such a research agenda. Focusing on decisions also revealed that the primary cognitive task underlying utility analysis is to link investments in human capital to organizational success. Even the debate about *SDy* measurement rests on this fundamental question.

Hence, we proposed the HC BRidge framework in Figure 9.2, depicting the elements that bridge investments in human capital and organizational strategic success. Future research will likely embellish and alter this framework, but we believe that the fundamental value of this linking logic will be consistent. The elements of Figure 9.2 are implied in virtually all utility models, so it may help assess the contribution of future utility-model enhancements. Such a framework also provides a valuable template for research on the cognitive connections that decision makers must make to link investments in I/O and HR programs with changes in human capacity and then with performance and organizational outcomes. These linkages are central to the task of identifying key talent, and they reveal new ways in which I/O psychology may inform HR strategy and vice versa. For example, *SDy*, one of the most esoteric of utility parameters, represents a core concept in identifying which talent is strategically key.

These linking elements, whether represented by the HC BRidge framework or by the future frameworks that will develop, have implications for many areas of strategic I/O psychology, even beyond utility analysis. I/O processes such as job analysis, test development, performance measurement, reward design, and training are significantly important to strategic success. Utility analysis has long been the sole vehicle for translating I/O programs to strategy. By taking a more strategic perspective on utility, we actually begin to develop a more strategic perspective on I/O.

REFERENCES

Abrahamson, E. (1991). Managerial fads and fashion: The diffusion and rejection of innovations. *Academy of Management Review, 16,* 586–612.

Abrahamson, E. (1996). Management fashion. *Academy of Management Review, 21*(1), 254–285.

Alexander, R. A., & Barrick, M. R. (1987). Estimating the standard error of projected dollar gains in utility analysis. *Journal of Applied Psychology, 72,* 475–479.

Alley, W. E., & Darbyk, M. M. (1995). Estimating the benefits of personnel selection and classification: An extension of the Brogden table. *Educational and Psychological Measurement, 55,* 938–958.

Argote, L., & Ingram, P. (2000). Knowledge transfer: A basis for competitive advantage in firms. *Organizational Behavior and Human Decision Processes, 82*(1), 150–169.

Arthur, J. B. (1994). Effects of human resource systems on manufacturing performance and turnover. *Academy of Management Journal, 37*(3), 670–687.

Arvey, R. D., & Murphy, K. R. (1998). Performance evaluation in work settings. *Annual Review of Psychology, 49,* 141–168.

Barnett, W. P., Greve, H. R., & Park, D. Y. (1994). An evolutionary model of organizational performance. *Strategic Management Journal, 15,* 11–28.

Barney, J. B. (1992). Integrating organizational behavior and strategy formulation research: A resource based analysis. *Advances in Strategic Management, 8,* 39–61.

Barrick, M. R., & Alexander, R. A. (1991). Assessing the utility of stochastic employee movements. *Decision Sciences, 22,* 171–180.

Barrick, M. R., & Alexander, R. A. (1992). Estimating the benefits of a quality circle intervention. *Journal of Organizational Behavior, 13*(1), 73–80.

Bassi, L. J., Lev, B., Low, J., McMurrer, D. P., & Seisfeld, G. A. (2000). Measuring corporate investments in human capital. In M. M. Blair & T. A. Kochan (Eds.), *The new relationship: Human capital in the American corporation* (pp. 334–381). Washington, DC: Brookings Institution.

Bazerman, M. (1998). *Judgment in managerial decision making* (4th ed.). New York: Wiley.

Becker, B., & Gerhart, B. (1996). The impact of human resource management on organizational performance: Progress and prospects. *Academy of Management Journal, 39*(4), 779–801.

Becker, B. E., & Huselid, M. A. (1992). Direct estimates of Sdy and the implications for utility analysis. *Journal of Applied Psychology, 77*(3), 227–233.

Becker, B. E., & Huselid, M. A. (1998). High performance work systems and firm performance: A synthesis of research and managerial implications. *Research in Personnel and Human Resource Management, 16,* 53–101.

Becker, B. E., Huselid, M. A., & Ulrich, D. (2001). *The HR Scorecard: Linking people, strategy and performance.* Boston: Harvard Business School Press.

Bierman, H., Jr., Bonnini, C. P., & Hausman, W. H. (1991). *Quantitative analysis for business decisions.* Burr Ridge, IL: Richard Irwin.

Bobko, P., Shetzer, L., & Russell, C. (1991). Estimating the standard deviation of professors' worth: The effects of frame and presentation order in utility analysis. *Journal of Occupational Psychology, 64,* 179–188.

Borman, W., Hanson, M., & Hedge, J. (1997). Personnel selection. *Annual Review of Psychology, 48,* 299–337.

Boswell, W. R. (2000). *Aligning employees with the organization's strategic objectives: Out of line of sight out of mind.* Unpublished doctoral dissertation, Cornell University, Ithaca, New York.

Boudreau, J. W. (1983). Economic considerations in estimating the utility of human resource productivity improvement programs. *Personnel Psychology, 36*(3), 551–576.

Boudreau, J. W. (1991). Utility analysis for decisions in human resource management. In M. D. Dunnette & L. M. Hough (Eds.), *Handbook of industrial and organizational psychology* (Vol. 2, pp. 621–745). Palo Alto, CA: Consulting Psychologists Press.

Boudreau, J. W. (1995, August). *"So what?": HR measurement as a change catalyst.* Paper presented at the national meeting of the Academy of Management, Vancouver, British Columbia, Canada.

Boudreau, J. W. (1996). The motivational impact of utility analysis and HR measurement. *Journal of Human Resource Costing and Accounting, 1*(2), 73–84.

Boudreau, J. W. (1998). Strategic human resource management measures: Key linkages and the PeopleVANTAGE model. *Journal of Human Resource Costing and Accounting, 3*(2), 21–40.

Boudreau, J. W. (in press). Strategic knowledge measurement and management. In S. E. Jackson, M. Hitt, & A. S. DeNisi (Eds.), *Managing knowledge for sustained competitive advantage.* New York: Jossey-Bass/Pfeiffer.

Boudreau, J. W., & Berger, C. J. (1985). Decision-theoretic utility analysis applied to employee separations and acquisitions [Monograph]. *Journal of Applied Psychology, 70,* 581–612.

Boudreau, J. W., Dunford, B. B., & Ramstad, P. M. (2001). The human capital impact on e-business: The case of encyclopedia Britannica. In N. Pal & J. M. Ray (Eds.), *Pushing the digital frontier* (pp. 192–221). New York: Amacom.

Boudreau, J. W., & Ramstad, P. M. (1997). Measuring intellectual capital: Learning from financial history. *Human Resource Management, 36*(3), 343–356.

Boudreau, J. W., & Ramstad, P. M. (1999). Human resource metrics: Can measures be strategic? In P. M. Wright, L. D. Dyer, J. W. Boudreau, & G. T. Milkovich (Eds.), *Research in personnel and human resources management* (Suppl. 4, pp. 75–98). Greenwich, CT: JAI Press.

Boudreau, J. W., & Ramstad, P. M. (2000, May). *"Talentship" and the Human Capital Value Proposition.* Paper presented to the Center for Advanced Human Resources (CAHRS) Sponsor Meeting. Cornell University, Ithaca, New York.

Boudreau, J. W., & Ramstad, P. M. (2001). *Strategic I/O psychology.* Professional development workshop presented at the Society for Industrial and Organizational Psychology national meeting, San Diego, CA.

Boudreau, J. W., & Ramstad, P. M. (2002). *From "professional business partner" to "strategic talent leader": "What's next" for human resource management.* CAHRS Working Paper No. 02-10. Ithaca, NY: Cornell University.

Boudreau, J. W., & Rynes, S. L. (1985). Role of recruitment in staffing utility analysis. *Journal of Applied Psychology, 70,* 354–366.

Boudreau, J. W., Sturman, M. C., & Judge, T. A. (1994). Utility analysis: What are the black boxes and do they affect decisions? In N. Anderson & P. Herriot (Eds.), *Assessment and selection in organizations: Methods and practice for recruitment and appraisal* (pp. 77–96). New York: Wiley.

Boudreau, J. W., Sturman, M. C., Trevor, C. O., & Gerhart, B. A. (1999). *The value of performance-based pay in the war for talent* (CAHRS Working Paper No. 99-06). Ithaca, NY: Cornell University.

Brogden, H. E. (1949). When testing pays off. *Personnel Psychology, 2,* 171–183.

Brookings Institute (2000). *Understanding intangible sources of value: Human capital sub group report.* Retrieved http://www brook.edu/es/research/projects/intangibles/doc/sub_hcap.htm

Brown, J. S., & Duguid, P. (2000). *The social life of information.* Boston: Harvard Business School Press.

Burke, M. J., & Frederick, J. T. (1986). A comparison of economic utility estimates for alternative *SDy* estimation procedures. *Journal of Applied Psychology, 71,* 334–339.

Cabrera, E. F., & Cabrera, A. (1999, August). *Strategic utility analysis.* Paper presented at the Academy of Management national meeting, Chicago, IL.

Cabrera, E. F., & Raju, N. S. (2001). Utility analysis: Current trends and future directions *International Journal of Selection and Assessment, 9*(1), 1–11.

Canibano, L., Garcia-Ayuso, M., & Sanchez, P. (2000). Accounting for intangibles: A literature review. *Journal of Accounting Literature, 19,* 102–130.

Cappelli, P., & Neumark, D. (2001). Do "high-performance" work practices improve establishment-level outcomes? *Industrial and Labor Relations Review, 54*(4), 737–775.

Carson, K. P., Becker, J. S., & Henderson, J. A. (1998). Is utility really futile? A failure to replicate and an extension. *Journal of Applied Psychology, 83*(1), 84–96.

Cascio, W. F. (1996). The role of utility analysis in the strategic management of organizations. *Journal of Human Resource Costing and Accounting, 1*(2), 85–95.

Cascio, W. F. (2000). *Costing human resources: The financial impact of behavior in organizations* (4th ed.). Cincinnati, OH: South-Western College.

Cascio, W. F., & Sibley, V. (1979). Utility of the assessment center as a selection device. *Journal of Applied Psychology, 64,* 107–118.

Cesare, S. J., Blankenship, M. H., & Giannetto, P. W. (1994). A dual focus of *SDy* estimations: A test of the linearity assumption and multivariate application. *Human Performance, 7*(4), 235–255.

Chadwick, C., & Capelli, P. (1999). Alternatives to generic strategy typologies in strategic human resource management. In P. M. Wright, L. D. Dyer, J. W. Boudreau, & G. T. Milkovich (Eds.), *Research in personnel and human resource management* (Suppl. 4, pp. 1–29). Greenwich, CT: JAI Press.

Collins, C., Smith, K. G., & Stevens, C. K. (2001). *Human resource practices, knowledge creation capability and performance in high technology firms.* Unpublished manuscript.

Cronshaw, S. F. (1997). Lo! The stimulus speaks: The insider's view on Whyte and Latham's "the futility of utility analysis." *Personnel Psychology, 50*(3), 611–615.

Crossan, M. M., Lane, H. W., & White R. E. (1999). "An organizational learning framework: From intuition to institution." *Academy of Management Review, 24*(3), 522–537.

DeCorte, W. (1994). Utility analysis for the one-cohort selection-retention decision with a probationary period. *Journal of Applied Psychology, 79*(3), 402–411.

DeCorte, W. (1997). Utility analysis for the probationary selection decision to obtain a fixed quota of successful selectees. *Journal of Organizational Behavior, 18*(1), 67–82.

DeCorte, W. (1998a). An analytic procedure to estimate the benefits of a particular type of personnel classification decision. *Education and Psychological Measurement, 58*(6), 929–943.

DeCorte, W. (1998b). Estimating and maximizing the utility of sequential selection decisions with a probationary period. *British Journal of Mathematical & Statistical Psychology, 51,* 101–121.

DeCorte, W. (2000a). Estimating the classification efficiency of a test battery. *Education and Psychological Measurement, 60*(1), 73–85.

DeCorte, W. (2000b). Using order statistics to assess the sampling variability of personnel selection utility estimates. *Journal of Applied Statistics, 27*(6), 703–713.

Delery, J. E., & Doty, D. H. (1996). Modes of theorizing in strategic human resource management: Tests of universalistic, contingency, and configurational predictions. *Academy of Management Journal, 39,* 802–835.

DeNisi, A. S. (1996). *Cognitive approach to performance appraisal: A program of research.* New York: Routledge.

Donnelly, G. (2000, March). Recruiting, retention and returns. *CFO Magazine,* 68–74.

Dyer, L., & Shafer, R. A. (1998). From human resource strategy to organizational effectiveness: Lessons from research on organizational agility. In P. M. Wright, L. D. Dyer, J. W. Boudreau, & G. T. Milkovich (Eds.), *Research in personnel and human resource management* (Suppl. 4, pp. 145–174). Greenwich, CT: JAI Press.

Dzinkowski, R. (2000). The measurement and management of intellectual capital: An introduction. *Management Accounting, 78,* 32–36.

Eccles, R. G., & Mavrinac, S. C. (1995). Improving the corporate disclosure process. *Sloan Management Review, 36*(4), 11–25.

Edvinsson, L., & Malone, M. (1997). *Intellectual capital.* Cambridge, MA: Harvard Business School Press.

Fitz-enz, J. (1995). *How to measure human resources management.* New York: McGraw Hill.

Fitz-enz, J. (1997). *The eight practices of exceptional companies: How great organizations make the most of their human assets.* New York: Amacom.

Fitz-enz, J. (2000). *The ROI of human capital: Measuring the economic value of employee performance.* New York: Amacom.

Flamholtz, E. G. (1999). *Human resource accounting* (3rd ed.). Boston: Kluwer.

Florin-Thuma, B. C., & Boudreau, J. W. (1987). Performance feedback utility in a small organization: Effects on organizational outcomes and managerial decision processes. *Personnel Psychology, 40,* 693–713.

Gardner, T. M., Wright, P. M., & Gerhart, B. A. (2000). *The HR-firm performance relationship: Can it be in the mind of the beholder?* (CAHRS Working Paper No. 00-02). Ithaca, NY: Cornell University.

Gerhart, B. A., Wright, P. M., & McMahan, G. C. (2000). Measurement error and estimates of the HR–firm performance relationship: A response to Becker & Huselid. *Personnel Psychology, 53*(4), 855–873.

Gerhart, B. A., Wright, P. M., McMahan, G. C., & Snell, S. (2000). Measurement error in research on human resources and firm performance: How much error is there and how does it influence effect size estimates? *Personnel Psychology, 53*(4), 803–834.

Godfrey, P. C., & Hill, C. W. L. (1995). The problem of unobservables in strategic management research. *Strategic Management Journal, 16,* 519–533.

Grossman, R. J. (2000). Measuring up. *HRMagazine, 45*(1), 28–35.

Guest, D., & Peccei, R. (1994). The nature and causes of effective human resource management, *British Journal of Industrial Relations, 32*(2), 219–242.

Hall, B., Jaffe, A., & Trajtenberg, M. (2000). Social capital, intellectual capital, and the organizational advantage. *Academy of Management Review, 23*(2), 242–266.

Hazer, J. T., & Highhouse, S. (1997). Factors influencing managers' reactions to utility analysis: Effects of SD_y method, information frame, and focal intervention. *Journal of Applied Psychology, 82*(1), 104–112.

Heskett, J. L., Jones, T. O., Loveman, G. W., Sasser, W. E., Jr., & Schlesinger, L. A. (1994). Putting the service-value-profit chain to work. *Harvard Business Review, 72,* 164–174.

Highhouse, S. (1996). The utility estimate as a communication device: Practical questions and research directions. *Journal of Business and Psychology, 11*(1), 85–100.

Hunter, J. E., Schmidt, F. L., & Judiesch, M. K. (1990). Individual differences in output variability as a function of job complexity. *Journal of Applied Psychology, 75,* 28–42.

Huselid, M. A. (1995). The impact of human resource management practices on turnover, productivity, and corporate financial performance. *Academy of Management Journal, 38*(3), 635–672.

Huselid, M. A., & Becker, B. E. (2000). Comment on *Measurement error in research in human resource decisions and firm performance: How much error is there and how does it influence effect size estimates? Personnel Psychology, 53*(4), 835–854.

Huselid, M. A., Jackson, S. E., & Schuler, R. S. (1997). Organizational characteristics as predictors of personnel practices. *Personnel Psychology, 42,* 727–786.

Ichniowski, C., Shaw, K., & Prennushi, G. (1997). The effects of human resource management practices on productivity: A study of steel finishing lines. *American Economic Review, 87*(3), 291–313.

Johns, G. (1993). Constraints on the adoption of psychology-based personnel practices: Lessons from organizational innovation. *Personnel Psychology, 46,* 569–612.

Johnson, H. T., & Kaplan, R. S. (1987). *Relevance lost.* Boston: Harvard Business School Press.

Jones, G. R., & Wright, P. M. (1992). An economic approach to conceptualizing the utility of human resource management practices. *Research in Personnel and Human Resources Management, 10,* 271–299.

Judiesch, M. K., Schmidt, F. L., & Hunter, J. E. (1993). Has the problem of judgment in utility analysis been solved? *Journal of Applied Psychology, 78*(6), 903–911.

Judiesch, M. K., Schmidt, F. L., & Mount, M. K. (1992). Estimates of the dollar value of employee output in utility. *Journal of Applied Psychology, 77*(3), 234–250.

Kaplan, R. S., & Norton, D. P. (1992, January/February). The balanced scorecard—measures that drive performance. *Harvard Business Review, 70,* 71–79.

Kaplan, R. S., & Norton, D. P. (1996a). Using the balanced scorecard as a strategic management system. *Harvard Business Review,* January/February, 75–85.

Kaplan, R. S., & Norton, D. P. (1996b). Linking the balanced scorecard to strategy. *California Management Review, 39*(1), 53–79.

Kirkpatrick, D. (1994). *Evaluating training programs: The four levels.* San Francisco: Barrett-Koehler.

Klass, B. S., & McClendon, J. A. (1996). To lead, lag, or match: Estimating the financial impact of pay level policies. *Personnel Psychology, 49,* 121–142.

Kossek, E. E., & Grace, P. (1990). Taking a strategic view of employee child care assistance: A cost-benefit model. *Human Resource Planning, 13*(3), 189–192.

Landy, F. (1989). *Psychology of work behavior* (4th ed.). Pacific Grove, CA: Brooks/Cole.

Latham, G. P., Erez, M., & Locke, E. A. (1988). Resolving scientific disputes by the joint design of crucial experiments by the antagonists: Application to the Erez-Latham dispute regarding participation in goal setting. *Journal of Applied Psychology, 73*(4), 753–772.

Latham, G. P., & Whyte, G. (1994). The futility of utility analysis. *Personnel Psychology, 47*(1), 31–47.

Lepak, D. P., & Snell, S. A. (1999). The human resource architecture: Toward a theory of human capital allocation and development. *The Academy of Management Review, 24*(1) 34–48.

Lev, B. (1997, February). *The boundaries of financial reporting and how to extend them.* Working paper presented at the OECD Conference "Industrial Competitiveness in the Knowledge Based Economy," Stockholm, Sweden.

Lev, B., & Zarowin, P. (1999). The boundaries of financial reporting and how to extend them. *Journal of Accounting Research, 37,* 353–385.

Liebowitz, J., & Wright, K. (1999). Does measuring knowledge make "cents"? *Expert Systems with Applications, 17,* 99–103.

Lipe, M. G., & Salterio, S. E. (2000). The balanced scorecard: Judgmental effects of common and unique performance measures. *The Accounting Review, 75*(3), 283–298.

Mabon, H. (1996, Spring). The cost of downsizing in an enterprise with job security. *Journal of Human Resource Costing and Accounting, 1,* 35–62.

Mabon, H. (1998). Utility aspects of personality and performance. *Human Performance, 11*(2/3), 289–304.

Macan, T. H., & Highhouse, S. (1994). Communicating the utility of HR activities: A survey of I/O and HR professionals. *Journal of Business and Psychology, 8*(4), 425–436.

MacDuffie, J. P. (1995). Human resource bundles and manufacturing performance: Organizational logic and flexible production systems in the world auto industry. *Industrial and Labor Relations Review, 48*(2), 197–221.

Mavrinac, S., & Seisfeld, G. A. (1997). Measures that matter: An exploratory investigation of investors' information needs and value priorities. In *Enterprise value in the knowledge economy: Measuring performance in the age of intangibles.* Cambridge, MA: Ernst & Young Center for Business Innovation.

McMahan, G. C., Virick, M., & Wright, P. M. (1998). Alternative theoretical perspectives for strategic human resource management revisited: Progress, problems and prospects. In P. M. Wright, L. D. Dyer, J. W. Boudreau, & G. T. Milkovich (Eds.), *Research in personnel and human resource management* (Suppl. 4, pp. 99–122). Greenwich, CT: JAI Press.

McNemar, Q. (1962). *Psychological statistics.* New York: Wiley.

Milkovich, G. T., & Newman, J. M. (1999). Compensation (6th ed.) Boston: Irwin/McGraw-Hill.

Mintzberg, H. (1975). The manager's job: Folklore and fact. *Harvard Business Review, 53,* 49–61.

Morrow, C. C., Jarrett, M. Q., & Rupinski, M. T. (1997). An investigation of the effect and economic utility of corporate-wide training. *Personnel Psychology, 50,* 91–119.

Nahapiet, J., & Ghosal, S. (1998). Social capital, intellectual capital, and the organizational advantage. *Academy of Management Review, 23*(2), 242–266.

Nonaka, I., & Takeuchi, H. (1995). *The knowledge-creating company: How Japanese companies create the dynamics of innovation.* New York: Oxford University Press.

Perloff, R. M. (1993). *The dynamics of persuasion.* Hillsdale, NJ: Erlbaum.

Petty, R. E., & Cacioppo, J. T. (1984). The effects of involvement on responses to argument quantity and quality: Central and peripheral routes to persuasion. *Journal of Personality and Social Psychology, 46,* 69–81.

Pfeffer, J. (1998). *The human equation.* Boston: Harvard Business School Press.

Porter, M. E. (1985). *Competitive advantage: Creating and sustaining superior performance.* New York: Free Press.

Porter, M. E. (1996). What is strategy? *Harvard Business Review, 74*(6), 61–77.

Prahalad, C. K., & Hamel, G. (1990). The core competence of the corporation. *Harvard Business Review, 68,* 79–91.

Quinn, R. E., Hildebrandt, H. W., Rogers, P. S., & Thompson, M. P. (1991). A competing values framework for analyzing presentational communication in management contexts. *The Journal of Business Communication, 28,* 213–232.

Raju, N. S., & Burke, M. J. (1986). Utility analysis. In R. A. Berk (Ed.), *Performance assessment: Methods and applications* (pp. 186–202). Baltimore: Johns Hopkins.

Raju, N. S., Burke, M. J., & Normand, J. (1990). A new approach for utility analysis. *Journal of Applied Psychology, 75,* 3–12.

Raju, N. S., Burke, M. J., Normand, J., & Lezotte, D. V. (1993). What would be if what is wasn't? Rejoiner to Judiesch, Schmidt, and Hunter. *Journal of Applied Psychology, 78*(6), 912–916.

Raju, N. S., Cabrera, E. F., & Lezotte, D. V. (1996, April). *Utility analysis when employee performance is classified into two categories: An application of three utility models.* Paper presented at the Annual Meeting of the Society for Industrial and Organizational Psychology, San Diego, CA.

Rauschenberger, J. M., & Schmidt, F. L. (1987). Measuring the economic impact of human resource programs. *Journal of Business and Psychology, 2*(1), 50–59.

Reardon, K. K. (1991). *Persuasion in practice.* Newbury Park, CA: Sage.

Rich, J. R., & Boudreau, J. W. (1987). The effects of variability and risk in selection utility analysis: An empirical comparison. *Personnel Psychology, 40,* 55–84.

Roth, P. L. (1994). Multiattribute utility analysis using the Promes approach. *Journal of Business and Psychology, 9*(1), 69–80.

Roth, P. L., & Bobko, P. (1997). A research agenda for multiattribute utility analysis in human resource management. *Human Resource Management Review, 7*(3), 341–368.

Roth, P. L., Pritchard, R. D., Stout, J. D., & Brown, S. H. (1994). Estimating the impact of variable costs on *SDy* in complex situations. *Journal of Business and Psychology, 8*(4), 437–454.

Roth, P., Segers, A., & Wright, P. (2000). *The acceptance of utility analysis: Designing a model.* Paper presented at the Academy of Management Annual Meeting, Toronto, Ontario, Canada.

Rucci, A. J., Kirn, S. P., & Quinn, R. T. (1998). The employee-customer-profit chain at Sears. *Harvard Business Review, 76*(1), 83–97.

Russell, C. J. (1998). *Maybe they shouldn't believe, or why personnel selection is like a peanut butter sandwich: Value distance as a source of ambiguity in utility estimates.* Paper presented at the national meeting of the Society of Industrial and Organizational Psychology, Dallas, TX.

Russell, C., Colella, A., & Bobko, P. (1993). Expanding the context of utility: The strategic impact of personnel selection. *Personnel Psychology, 46,* 781–801.

Schmidt, F. L., & Hunter, J. E. (1998). The validity and utility of selection methods in personnel psychology: Practical and theoretical implications of 85 years of research findings. *Psychological Bulletin, 124*(2), 262–274.

Schmidt, F. L., Hunter, J. E., McKenzie, R. C., & Muldrow, T. W. (1979). Impact of valid selection procedures on work-force productivity. *Journal of Applied Psychology, 64,* 609–626.

Schmidt, F. L., Hunter, J. E., Outerbridge, A. N., & Trattner, M. H. (1986). The economic impact of job selection methods on size, productivity, and payroll costs of the federal work force: An empirically based demonstration. *Personnel Psychology, 39,* 1–30.

Schneider, B., Ashworth, S. D., Higgs, A. C., & Carr, L. (1996). Design, validity and use of strategically focused employee attitude surveys. *Personnel Psychology, 49,* 695–705.

Skandia Corporation (1996). Power of Innovation—Skandia Navigator. *Skandia's 1996 Interim Report,* 10–11.

Skarlicki, D. P., Latham, G. P., & Whyte, G. (1996). Utility analysis: Its evolution and tenuous role in human resource management decision making. *Revue Canadienne des Sciences de l'Administration, 13*(1), 13–21.

Skinner, W. (1981). Big hat, no cattle: Managing human resources. *Harvard Business Review, 59*(5), 106–114.

Stamps, D. (2000). Measuring minds. *Training, 37,* 76–82.

Sturman, M. C. (2000). Implications of utility analysis adjustments for estimates of human resource intervention value. *Journal of Management, 26*(2), 281–299.

Sveiby, K. E. (1997). *The new organizational wealth.* San Francisco: Barrett-Koehler.

Teece, D. J., Pisano, G., & Shuen, A. (1997). Dynamic capabilities and strategic management. *Strategic Management Journal, 18,* 509–533.

Treacy, M., & Wiersema, F. (1997). *The discipline of market leaders.* Reading, MA: Addison-Wesley.

Trevor, C. O., Gerhart, B., & Boudreau, J. W. (1997). Voluntary turnover and job performance: Curvilinearity and the moderating influences of salary growth and promotions. *Journal of Applied Psychology, 82*(1), 44–61.

Ulrich, D. (1996). *Human resource champions*. Boston: Harvard Business Review.

Webb, J., & Gile, C. (2001). Reversing the value chain. *The Journal of Business and Strategy, 22,* 13–17.

Welbourne, T. M., & Andrews, A. O. (1996). Predicting the performance of initial public offerings: Should human resource management be in the equation? *Academy of Management Journal, 39*(4), 891–919.

Whyte, G., & Latham, G. (1997). The futility of utility analysis revisited: When even an expert fails. *Personnel Psychology, 50*(3), 601–610.

Wright, P. M., MacMahan, G. C., Snell, S., & Gerhart, B. A. (2001). Comparing line and HR executives' perceptions of HR effectiveness: Services, roles and contributions. *Human Resource Management, 40*(2), 111–123.

Youndt, M. A., Snell, S. A., Dean, J. W., & Lepak, D. P. (1996). Human resource management, manufacturing strategy, and firm performance. *Academy of Management Journal, 39*(4), 836–867.

PART TWO

ORGANIZATIONAL PSYCHOLOGY

CHAPTER 10

Motivation

TERENCE R. MITCHELL AND DENISE DANIELS

Motivation is a core construct. To understand why people behave the way they do in organizations, one must know something about motivation. It is not the only cause of behavior or always the most important one, but it is usually part of the picture. Motivation is a component of most human activity, and the literature on the topic is vast. O'Reilly (1991) in his Annual Review article said that it is the "most frequently researched topic in micro organization behavior" (p. 431), and Cooper and Robertson (1986) estimated that the topic of motivation and related issues fills one third of our journal space. Pinder's (1998) book is the best overall recent source on the topic, and recent reviews by Kanfer (1994), Mitchell (1997), and Ambrose and Kulik (1999) give good but slightly narrower perspectives.

Given what is available, we have decided to approach this review with a few clear objectives. First, we cover the motivational landscape. We believe that most major approaches to the topic have a corner of the truth. Some of the time, or for some of the people or to some degree the motivational approach discussed in an article, makes an important contribution to behavior. On some occasions, people's needs are key, or their goals, their friends at work, rewards, or the task at hand. We cover these different points of view.

Second, we highlight some of the variables that differentiate when, where, and how certain motivational factors operate. We discuss issues related to time, the extent to which these motivational mechanisms are malleable or changeable, and what factors are needed to use these strategies in the workplace. We close with a discussion of the

implications of what we have reviewed for theory, research, and practice.

BACKGROUND

As an introduction to the concept of motivation, we shall use a context with which many of us are familiar: the selection and subsequent performance of graduate students. Universities often use some sort of cutoff point on standardized test scores such as the GRE or GMAT to select students. Suppose a university admits three students who all score from 680 to 690. We then observe their behavior and performance over time, and we note that (a) the three individuals differ substantially among each other with an agreed-upon rank order and (b) each individual has ups and downs as well. Because ability (as assessed by our standardized tests) is seen as relatively similar for all three students, we are likely to attribute the variance within and across the three individuals at least partly to their motivation.

Definition

The previous example points out some important aspects of motivation. First, motivation varies across and within individuals. Second, it seems to combine with ability to produce behavior and performance. Because abilities are often seen as innate or accomplished through arduous and lengthy training and development activities, we often view motivation as discretionary or willful—something that one chooses to expend. Pinder's (1998) initial simple definition is "the energy a person expends in relation to work" (p. 1), whereas Dowling and Sayles (1978) maintain that "motivation means an inner desire to make an effort" (p. 16). Examining what constitutes this "energy" or "inner desire" leads to a more detailed description of motivation.

Most recent authors have associated motivation with three general psychological processes (Bandura, 1986; Ford, 1992; Kanfer, 1990; Mitchell, 1982; Pinder, 1998). First, there is an arousal component. Most researchers see arousal as caused by a need or desire for some object or state that is at least partially unfulfilled or below expectation. This discrepancy initiates action. Second, there is a directional component. Personal goals are universally seen as providing direction. Locke (1997) suggested that goal directedness is "a cardinal attribute of the actions of all living organisms" (p. 376). Third, there is an intensity dimension. Some needs are more important than others. Some goals are more difficult to attain than others.

What are the results of these three processes? In terms of specific behavior, four things are usually mentioned. First, motivation focuses attention on particular issues, people, task elements, and so on. It has a riveting directional aspect.

Second, motivation produces effort. People work harder when they are motivated. Third, motivation results in persistence. The higher the motivation, the longer we will sustain our effort. Fourth, motivation results in what we call *task strategies,* patterns of behavior produced to reach a particular goal.

In summary, motivation is an internal set of processes—what we call a hypothetical construct. It is complex in that it involves multiple processes and multiple behaviors. It is personal; different people have different needs and different things that they think are important. Furthermore, it is goal directed. Goals (and goal discrepancies) are seen as major goads to attention and action, whereas goal difficulty and importance are associated with motivational intensity. Goals are clearly the major psychological mechanism associated with motivation.

The Big Picture

Given the complexity just described above, some sort of big picture is necessary as a guide to the rest of this review. Figure 10.1 presents such an overview. This diagram captures some, but not all, of the complexity and detail involved in understanding motivation. It suggests that both individual

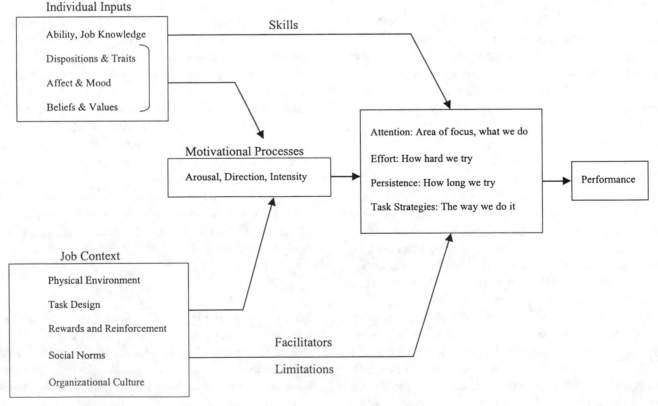

Figure 10.1   An overall model of motivation.

attributes and the context in which one works influence motivational processes. Abilities and skills combine with motivation and the enabling or limiting aspects of the environment to produce task-relevant behaviors. Over time and contexts these behaviors contribute to individual performance.

Some other important distinctions should be mentioned. First, note that motivation differs from behavior. The psychological state is motivation; the outcome or result of that state is behavioral (e.g., effort). Second, note that behavior differs from performance. The latter is an outside standard that is determined by the organization and usually assessed by others. Third, note that personal factors and the work setting can influence behavior either directly or through motivation. For example, your actual ability can influence your behavior, and knowledge of your ability can influence your motivation, which can influence your behavior. Task interdependencies can influence your actual behaviors as well as your motivation to engage in these behaviors. Finally, note that behavior is caused by multiple factors: personal, social, technological, and contextual. Thus, motivation may play a huge role in determining some behaviors, whereas ability or technology may be important for others (Ford, 1992).

It is important to point out that motivation is dynamic and unfolds over time. Motivational processes lead to intentions that result in behavior. However, the mechanisms driving that behavior, such as need discrepancies or goal level currently attained, change over time. Things happen while we are engaged in a particular task (e.g., successes and failures, social input) that may increase or decrease subsequent motivation (Kuhl, 1984). People often decide to exert more or less effort at the moment, while they are involved in an activity, or to switch to another activity. This "on-line" motivational process is receiving increased attention in the literature (e.g., Frese & Zapf, 1994), and we will cover it in more detail in our review.

Our Coverage

We made a number of decisions with respect to this review. First, we wanted to provide broad coverage. Most of the major theories are reviewed (we have omitted the job design and social influence—i.e., teams and culture—work because they are covered in other chapters in this volume). We try to summarize the prevailing wisdom (mostly through the use of narrative summaries and meta-analyses, which are available for almost every topic) and then concentrate on what has been written in the last few years. Second, our major focus is on work-related issues and the field of organizational behavior. Finally, as mentioned earlier, we try to highlight dimensions or aspects of motivational topics that help us to sort out

the complexity of when, where, and how a particular factor is operating or is important.

MOTIVATION IN THE ORGANIZATIONAL BEHAVIOR LITERATURE

Before we begin our review of motivation in the organizational behavior literature, we need to provide an organizing framework for the various theoretical approaches that we will be discussing. Because there is no agreed-upon integrative theory of motivation (although some have been suggested; e.g., Locke, 1997) and very few middle-range theories, we consequently have no universally accepted way of presenting the various approaches to motivation. When reviewing research for this chapter, we categorized articles according to the major theoretical positions that they represented (e.g., goal setting, rewards and reinforcement, dispositions and traits, etc.). We then began to see some contrasts or tensions that were represented. For example, some theoretical approaches are internal to the individual (cognitive approaches, dispositional approaches), whereas others are clearly more external (task design, reinforcement). Some theoretical approaches are more cognitive in nature (self-regulation, expectancy theory, goal setting, self-efficacy), whereas others have very little to do with cognitions (genetic disposition, emotion, affect). Some are more distal or distant from the immediate causes of action and reflect one's accumulated history (e.g., needs). Others are more proximal or directly associated with behavior (e.g., goals). The more we looked, the more we realized that nearly every theoretical approach had an alternative that was in tension with it. Although these alternative approaches did not necessarily contradict one another, each provided a different lens through which to view motivation. We decided to organize our review around these various tensions. Figure 10.2 provides a schematic of these contrasts in the literature.

The first contrast we make is between internally and externally focused motivational theories. Internally focused theories can be broken down into those that are more cognitive or "thoughtful" (including goals, self-efficacy, expectancy) and those that are not controlled at a cognitive level. The thoughtful motivational theories differ from one another in terms of those that are focused on the cognitive processes that occur before a task is undertaken and those that occur while one is actually working on a task. We differentiate between these two theoretical approaches as those that are *proactive* and *on-line,* respectively. In contrast, the nonrational theories can be distinguished as those that are *hot* in nature, or more in

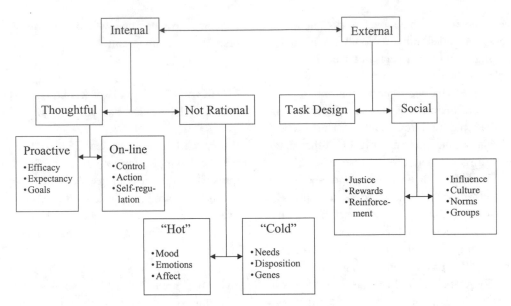

Figure 10.2   Overview of motivation tensions.

the moment (i.e., mood, emotions, affect), compared with those that are *cold* and less malleable (i.e., needs, genes, personality).

At the other end of the spectrum, the external theories of motivation focus on aspects of the situation that influence the amount of effort that one is likely to put forth. The external theoretical approaches can be separated into those that are focused on the task itself (job design theories, covered elsewhere) and those that are focused on the social aspects of the situation. In this latter category there is a contrast between the culture and norms of the group (covered elsewhere in this volume), which create expectations for performance and motivation, and the perceived fairness of the outcomes that one receives (a perception that is socially determined). We recognize that these external approaches have an impact on internal processes. But the reason we differentiate them is that the focus of the theory is on how these external factors operate on the person (e.g., job design) rather than the internal state (e.g., goals).

In this section we review the literature in each of these theoretical categories, with particular emphasis on advances that have been made since Kanfer's (1990) handbook chapter. For each theory we review what we know, as well as the new directions that research is taking, and highlight what we do not yet know as important areas for future research. We begin our review with those theories that are more internal—that is, theories focused on the thoughts, feelings, or personality of the individual. We then move to the external theories of motivation, which focus on outcomes such as reinforcement and justice.

The first category consists of theories that are thoughtful: those that are more internal to the individual and are based on a cognitive approach to understanding human behavior (see Figure 10.2). We begin with theories that are more proactive in that they entail judgments about future performance, including expectancy, self-efficacy, and goal setting. We then move to the more on-line or in-the-moment approaches to understanding motivation, including control theory, action theory, and self-regulation.

Expectancy Theory

Expectancy theory is one of the earliest cognitive approaches to understanding motivation. It was first articulated by Vroom (1964), who suggested that people tend to make rational decisions about whether to exert effort based on their perceptions of whether their effort will lead to outcomes that they value. The theory is sometimes referred to as *VIE theory*, referencing its three major constructs: valence, instrumentality, and expectancy. Expectancy is a probability assessment reflecting an individual's belief that a given level of effort will lead to a given level of performance. Instrumentality refers to the subjective assessment that a given performance level will result in one or more secondary outcomes, such as pay or promotion. Finally, valence refers to the value that an individual places on a given secondary outcome. Vroom (1964) argued that individuals subjectively combine these three constructs, summing across outcomes, to determine the extent to which they should exert a particular level of effort. He referred to this as *motivational force*.

What We Know

Many studies have been directed at refining expectancy theory and trying to assess its validity. Much of this research seems to support Vroom's (1964) ideas. For example, expectancy theory has been shown consistently to predict job effort and occupational choice, accounting for 5% to 30% of the variance in these criteria (Mitchell, 1997). However, numerous reviews have also highlighted important methodological problems associated with the tests of the theory. For example, the theory relies on an explicit mathematical model of motivational force, but it is clear that people seldom make such mental calculations. Perhaps the biggest area of debate surrounding expectancy theory is whether it should be used to predict outcomes within subjects or between subjects (see Pinder, 1998, for a concise review). Although both methods have provided evidence in support of expectancy theory (Westaby, 1999), a large majority of the research shows that the theory predicts outcomes better within subjects than it does between subjects (see VanEerde & Thierry, 1996).

New Directions

Expectancy theory initially generated a substantial amount of research and debate, but it is no longer doing so. Its lack of direct influence on the motivational field today may be attributed to the rise of other cognitive theories, during what has been referred to as the cognitive revolution in the field of organizational behavior (Ilgen, Major, & Tower, 1994). In particular, the current emphasis on goal setting, self-efficacy, and self-regulation may have subsumed some of the major concepts within VIE theory. As Locke and Latham (1990) pointed out, "In practice, many expectancy measures are probably equivalent to self-efficacy measures, or at least partially so" (p. 68). It is to the theory of self-efficacy that we now turn our attention.

Self-Efficacy

The concept of self-efficacy is a relative newcomer to the field of motivation. It was developed by Bandura (1986, 1997) in the context of his work on social cognitive theory and defined by Wood and Bandura (1989) as "beliefs in one's capabilities to mobilize the motivation, cognitive resources, and courses of action needed to meet given situational demands" (p. 408). Most of the research on self-efficacy has focused on one of two things: (a) understanding the mechanisms through which self-efficacy influences performance and (b) understanding its antecedents in order to know how better to change self-efficacy (and ultimately performance) in the workplace.

What We Know

There is substantial research demonstrating a link between self-efficacy and performance. The results from two separate meta-analyses indicate that the link between self-efficacy and performance is strong, with a mean $r = .37$ in one (Hysong & QuiÑones, 1997) and $r = .38$ in the other (Stajkovic & Luthans, 1998). As Gist and Mitchell (1992) noted, "People who think they can perform well on a task do better than those who think they will fail" (p. 183).

There has been some debate in the literature about whether self-efficacy truly has a generative component; that is, does it actually cause high levels of motivation and subsequent performance, or are the correlations between self-efficacy and performance due simply to the fact that people are pretty good at assessing their own ability levels and predicting their future performance levels? Chen, Casper, and Cortina (1999) reported in their meta-analyses that mental ability and conscientiousness are both related to self-efficacy (corrected r of approximately .20) and that self-efficacy partially mediates the relationships between ability and conscientiousness and subsequent performance. Self-efficacy is also highly correlated with past performance. Because of this, Vancouver, Thompson, and Williams (1999) suggested that perhaps self-efficacy is simply a by-product of past performance that by itself contributes nothing to motivation and future performance. This issue is difficult to tease out statistically; examining the effect of self-efficacy on performance by controlling for past performance may overcorrect for the problem because self-efficacy is likely to be at least partly responsible for past performance as well (Bandura, 1997). If all of the work on the relationship between self-efficacy and performance were correlational in nature, we would be at an impasse over how to understand self-efficacy's role in the motivational process. However, thanks to the programmatic research on the Pygmalion/golem effect conducted by Eden (e.g., 1992) over the past decade, we can present a causal picture of the effects of self-efficacy on performance.

The *Pygmalion effect* refers to the idea that communicating high expectations can improve self-efficacy, which in turn improves performance. Its opposite is the *golem effect,* in which low expectations are communicated and self-efficacy and performance decrease as a result. Eden and his colleagues have shown that self-efficacy can be manipulated and that doing so influences performance (Eden, 1992). Telling Israeli Defense Force candidates that they would do well in Special Forces resulted in increases in volunteering (Eden & Kinnar, 1991); self-efficacy training for the unemployed increased their job-search skills and activities, as well as the likelihood of finding a job (Eden & Aviram, 1993); and having positive expectations for military trainees initially low in ability raised their self-efficacy and subsequent scores on a physical fitness test (Oz & Eden, 1994). There have been two recent meta-analyses of Pygmalion effects. McNatt (2000) reported an average corrected *d* (average difference between experimental and control groups) of .62, and Kiernan and Gold (1998) reported an average of .76. Both papers reported that these effects are relatively strong, and both suggest that men and people in the military are more susceptible than women and nonmilitary subjects.

There are multiple mechanisms through which self-efficacy works. Those with higher self-efficacy tend to exert more effort and to persist at a task longer than those with lower self-efficacy (Bandura, 1997). In addition, self-efficacy helps individuals focus their attention and reduce distractions (Kanfer & Ackerman, 1996). Those with higher self-efficacy tend to choose more difficult goals and commit to those goals than do low self-efficacy individuals (Locke & Latham, 1990). Self-efficacy may also encourage people to seek feedback (Tsui & Ashford, 1994) and to choose more efficient task strategies (Wood, George-Falvy, & Debowski, 1999).

Because self-efficacy appears to be an important influence on motivation and performance, quite a bit of research has focused on understanding its antecedents, as well as on implementing effective training programs for improving self-efficacy. Bandura (1982) suggested that self-efficacy is developed through four mechanisms: enactive mastery, vicarious experience, verbal persuasion, and physiological arousal. More recent research suggests that the effects of these types of experience on self-efficacy are moderated by who or what is providing the information, as well as by an individual's belief in his or her ability as a state or trait variable. Parsons and his colleagues found that the self-efficacy of military trainees learning to pilot helicopters was strongly influenced by negative peer feedback at the beginning of their training program, but by the end of the training program it was more likely to be affected by feedback from the task itself and from supervisors (Parsons, Fedor, & Herold, 1999). Martocchio (1994) showed that people who believe that ability does not change (trait) have lower self-efficacy and higher anxiety than do those who view ability as something that can be acquired with experience (state). In addition, those who have a state view of ability have higher affect, higher goals, and higher performance than do those who hold to a trait view of ability (Tabernero & Wood, 1999).

Building on these ideas, Stevens and Gist (1997) conducted a study in which they trained MBA students on negotiation skills. They showed that mastery-oriented training (which assumes a state view of ability and focuses on enhancing task competence) led to more skill-maintenance

activities, more planned effort, and more positive affect than did performance-oriented training (which assumes a trait view of ability and focuses on demonstrating high task performance). In addition, they showed that mastery training overcame the effects of initial low self-efficacy; that is, low self-efficacy subjects in the mastery-oriented training condition performed at the same level as did their high self-efficacy counterparts.

New Directions

Three areas of research are relatively new in the self-efficacy field. First, recently there has been quite a bit of effort to understand the similarities and differences among self-efficacy and related constructs. Second, there has been interest in the concept of group efficacy. Finally, some research has highlighted some of the negative effects of high self-efficacy. We discuss each of the areas next.

Mitchell (1997) pointed out that self-efficacy is similar to concepts discussed by others using other terms, including personal agency beliefs (Ford, 1992), personal efficacy (Gurin & Brim, 1984), capacity beliefs (Skinner, Wellborn, & Connell, 1990), and perceived competence (Deci, 1980). Self-efficacy has been differentiated from self-esteem, which tends to be a stable value judgment that people make about themselves (Pinder, 1998); and although low self-efficacy on a given task may influence self-esteem, it does not necessarily do so. Brockner (1988) introduced the idea of task-related self-esteem, which is similar to the concept of self-efficacy. Confidence is another construct that has much in common with self-efficacy. Trafimow and Sniezek (1994) did studies of performance estimation for items on a general knowledge test. They found that subjects' general confidence (a trait measure) was positively related to their item confidence (similar to self-efficacy). Some confusion has arisen over the difference between self-efficacy and expectancy. Both constructs are subjective estimates of personal capability, but expectancy relates to a particular performance level on a given task, and self-efficacy is broader in that it can cover multiple performance levels. From a practical perspective, however, the operational measures for expectancy and self-efficacy are often indistinguishable.

More recently, Eden forwarded his conceptualization of *means efficacy,* which he defined as a person's belief in the tools available to do the job (Eden & Granat-Flomin, 2000). Eden differentiated means efficacy from self-efficacy in that the former is based on beliefs about factors external to the individual, and the latter is more about internal factors (Eden, 1996). He suggested that self-efficacy together with means efficacy make up a construct referred to as subjective efficacy, which is a better estimate of future performance than is either means efficacy or self-efficacy alone. Self-efficacy has traditionally been understood to include some component of means efficacy (cf. Gist & Mitchell, 1992), but this new distinction between internal and external sources of efficacy may be useful.

The last constructs we address in this section are *role-breadth self-efficacy* (RBSE; Parker, 1998) and *global,* or *general, self-efficacy* (GSE). RBSE is a more global construct than is self-efficacy, which is always related to a given task. RBSE relates to people's judgments about their ability to carry out the broader and more proactive roles on the job (beyond the technical requirements). Parker (1998) found that RBSE can be influenced by job-enrichment activities. GSE is broader yet, in that it assesses people's beliefs in their capabilities to perform a wide variety of tasks. It is a more trait-like, dispositional variable than is self-efficacy (Eden, 1999). At this point, exactly how GSE differs from self-esteem or other more general constructs is unclear.

A number of researchers have begun examining the concept of *group efficacy.* Guzzo and his colleagues conducted an excellent review of the various ways in which group efficacy can be conceptualized and measured (Guzzo, Yost, Campbell, & Shea, 1993). Like self-efficacy, group efficacy is consistently related to group performance (Mulvey & Klein, 1998; Prussia & Kinicki, 1996). In addition to its impact on performance, group efficacy has been shown to predict job satisfaction and organizational commitment (Riggs & Knight, 1994) and to moderate the impact of long hours and work overload on experienced physical and psychological strain (Jex & Bliese, 1999). Group efficacy may be a better predictor of group performance than individuals' self-efficacy. Feltz and Lirgg (1998) found that team efficacy was related to a hockey team's win record, but individual efficacy was not. The antecedents of group efficacy appear similar to those of individual self-efficacy: Enactive mastery, vicarious experience, and verbal persuasion have all been shown to influence group efficacy. Group efficacy appears to have its strongest effects on performance in certain circumstances. For example, Gibson (1999) found group efficacy to be most strongly related to performance when there was low uncertainty and high collectivism and when people worked interdependently. More research is needed to understand how group and individual efficacy interact. That is, what happens when an individual has a high (low) level of self-efficacy, but the group has low (high) collective efficacy?

Most of what we have reviewed to this point highlights the positive impact of efficacy on performance. However, there are situations in which high self-efficacy or group efficacy may have a detrimental impact. When initial self-efficacy

estimates are too high and performance does not match expectations, people tend to become discouraged and use avoidance strategies (Stone, 1994). Those with high levels of self-efficacy may be more likely to reject negative feedback (Nease, Mudgett, & QuiÑones, 1999). This may in turn make it more likely for them to fall prey to escalation of commitment and have decreased performance (Goltz, 1999). Whyte (1998) argued that in a group context, overly high group efficacy may be the instigating factor causing groupthink, which may lead to performance decrements. Gibson and Holzinger (1998) supported this notion. They found that in some situations group efficacy was actually negatively related to group effectiveness. They attributed this unexpected finding to the way in which they measured group efficacy: namely, by asking the group to make a collective estimation of efficacy. They suggest that this measure was likely influenced by group-induced attitude polarization, in which group members' individual estimates were swayed by the input from their peers.

Although there are some potential downsides to high levels of self-efficacy and group efficacy, in general the research supports the idea that efficacy is an important component of motivation and a strong predictor of performance. Furthermore, research supports the idea that self-efficacy is malleable and provides several demonstrated ways of improving it. One of the ways in which self-efficacy influences performance is through its influence on self-set goals.

Goal Setting

The theory of goal setting is quite easily the single most dominant theory in the field: Over a thousand articles and reviews have been published on the topic in a little over 30 years (Mitchell, Thompson, & George-Falvy, 2000). Rather than reviewing all of this research we focus on the basic premises of goal setting and then turn our attention to the current areas of interest and future research directions.

What We Know

Goal setting is based on the idea that most of human behavior is the result of a person's consciously chosen goals and intentions. Locke and Latham (1990) provided an excellent and extensive summary and review of the goal-setting literature. Their conclusion, backed up by a plethora of persuasive evidence is that goal setting works. Indeed, the research is uniform in its verdict that difficult and specific goals result in higher levels of performance than do easy or vague, "do your best" goals. In addition to the importance of difficult and specific goals, the goal-setting research is also clear that several other factors are necessary for goal setting to work. First, in order for goal setting to impact performance, feedback that enables people to gauge their progress toward goal attainment is required (Erez, 1977). Second, goal commitment is necessary for a goal to have motivational effects (Tubbs, 1994). Finally, ability and knowledge are important; giving someone a specific and difficult goal, providing feedback, and ensuring commitment will not result in increased performance if that individual does not have the requisite skills and abilities to perform the task.

Goal setting influences performance through four mechanisms (Locke, Shaw, Saari, & Latham, 1981). Compared with those who do not have goals, individuals with goals are more likely to (a) focus their attention and action toward the accomplishment of the goal, (b) exert more effort, (c) persist on tasks even in the face of failure, and (d) develop strategies that aid in accomplishing the goal. More recent research in the area of goals typically focuses on extending these traditional findings by understanding the various antecedents and consequences of goal setting, explicating the various moderating factors of the goal-performance relationship, and expanding the application of goal setting to the group level (Mitchell, 1997).

Research on self-set goals has tried to explain why people set the goals that they do. This is particularly important to understand because the evidence shows a linear relationship between goal difficulty and performance: The more difficult the goal, the higher the performance level will be as long as goal commitment remains high (Locke, 1997). Two different meta-analyses of goal difficulty—Mento, Steel, and Karren (1987) and Wright (1990)—reported similar effect sizes for the effects of goal difficulty on performance ($d = .58$ and $.55$, respectively).

An excellent review of the antecedents of goal setting by Wofford, Goodwin, and Premack (1992) found that the major determinants of an individual's goal level were past performance and ability. External factors such as providing a performance bonus also increase goal difficulty (Wood, Atkins, & Bright, 1999). After demonstrating that individuals with high task-specific self-esteem chose more difficult goals under piece-rate than hourly payment plans, Moussa (1996) concluded that these internal and external factors interact with each other. In a group context, collective efficacy has also been shown to influence group goal difficulty (Mulvey & Klein, 1998). In addition, self-efficacy, expectancy of goal attainment, and task difficulty were the best predictors of an individual's goal commitment (Wofford et al., 1992).

The performance consequences of goals are also clear: Goals increase performance, whether it is individual performance (Locke & Latham, 1990), group performance

(Durham, Knight, & Locke, 1997; O'Leary-Kelly, Martocchio, & Frink, 1994; Wegge, 1999; Weingart, 1992), or organizational performance (Thompson, Hochwarter, & Mathys, 1997). Pritchard's PROMES system shows promise as an application of goal setting principles designed to increase individual and group performance (Pritchard, 1995). Other outcomes of goal setting have also been explored. For example, Ludwig and Geller (1997) found that participative goals among pizza delivery drivers not only increased performance on a targeted behavior (complete stops at intersections) but also generalized to other driving behaviors that had not been targeted (turn signal and safety belt use). Goals have been used to reduce accidents and improve safety in the construction industry (Cooper, Phillips, Sutherland, & Makin, 1994). Brunstein, Schultheiss, and Grassmann (1998) demonstrated that goals that are congruent with an individual's personal dispositions can increase well-being and life adjustment. Although increased performance is arguably the most important outcome of goal setting, it is not the only outcome.

Perhaps the most commonly studied moderator of the goal-performance relationship is goal commitment. Tubbs (1994) defined goal commitment as the force or strength of attachment to a personal goal. Work throughout the early 1990s focused on the appropriate measures of goal commitment (Hollenbeck, Williams, & Klein, 1989; Wright, O'Leary-Kelly, Cortina, Klein, & Hollenbeck, 1994).

Early goal-setting research assumed that goal commitment was necessary for assigned goals to work (Locke & Latham, 1990). A meta-analysis by Donovan and Radosevich (1998) challenged the moderating role of goal commitment on the relationship between goal difficulty and performance. Their work found that the interaction effect of goal difficulty and commitment on performance was low. However, the number of studies they examined was small (12), and their work did not capture the perspective over time. Another meta-analysis (Klein, Wesson, Hollenbeck, & Agle (1999), using a larger sample (83 studies), found evidence for a stronger moderating effect of goal commitment on the relationship between goal difficulty and performance (mean corrected r of $.23$), and this effect of commitment on performance was stronger for difficult goals than for easy goals.

Like the research on goals themselves, the emphasis in goal-commitment research over the past decade has been on the antecedents and consequences of goal commitment. Locke and Latham (1990) suggested that goal commitment can be strengthened with monetary incentives that are tied to goal attainment (assuming that the goal is not impossible). Wright (1992) found this to be the case with easy goals, but with difficult goals Wright found that making incentives dependent on goal attainment actually led to lower commitment (rejection of goal). In contrast, Lee, Locke, and Phan (1997) found no effect of incentives on commitment. Clearly, more research is needed in this area to determine what the relationships between commitment and incentives are. In addition to incentives, the specificity of goals has been examined as an antecedent of goal commitment. Wright and Kacmar (1994) found that specific goals were more likely to result in goal commitment on an anagram task than were vague goals. Normative information may also influence goal commitment. Martin and Manning (1995) found performance increases in high-commitment subjects when they had information that others performed a task well. In addition, Hinsz, Kalnbach, and Lorentz (1997) found that using outrageous anchors to increase self-set goals did not reduce goal commitment.

A couple of studies indicate that individual differences may influence goal commitment. Hollenbeck et al. (1989) found that students' need for achievement and locus of control influenced their commitment. Barrick, Mount, and Strauss (1993) found that sales representatives with high conscientiousness were more likely to be committed to sales goals. Situational constraints and leader-member exchange have also been found to influence goal commitment (Klein & Kim, 1998). Finally, goal commitment can be impaired if people are allowed to set their own goals and then are assigned goals instead (Austin, 1989).

Task complexity appears to be another moderator of the goal-performance relationship. For the last two decades research has been accumulating that indicates that goal effects are less strong, or even detrimental, to performance on complex tasks (Wood, Mento, & Locke, 1987). Other research has indicated that goal setting is not as effective when a task is novel but has a stronger relationship to performance when a task becomes well learned (Mitchell, Hopper, Daniels, George-Falvy, & James, 1994). Research by Kanfer, Ackerman, Murtha, Dugdale, and Nelson (1994) showed that goals helped performance during spaced practice but hurt performance during massed practice on their air traffic controller task. One explanation for these various results may be that the primary mechanisms through which goal setting works—attention, effort, and persistence—may not be effective for accomplishing tasks that are complex or novel. In these cases, developing task strategies may be more effective—working smarter, not harder (Wood & Locke, 1990). Understanding how to use goals to improve strategy is a newer area of goal-setting research. One lab study found that the type of goal assigned can influence goal strategy (Audia, Kristof-Brown, Brown, & Locke, 1996). Another study showed that goals can help on explicit learning of

complex tasks (DeShon & Alexander, 1996). Finally, George-Falvy (1996) showed that participatively set goals may be more effective than assigned goals on complex tasks because they encourage effective strategy development.

Interest in applying goal setting to the group level has increased dramatically during the past decade. The basic findings in this area are very similar to individual-level goal setting; a meta-analysis by O'Leary-Kelly et al. (1994) confirmed that group goals have a strong and positive effect on performance. Several studies have shown that more difficult goals result in higher performance than do easier goals (Durham et al., 1997; Weingart, 1992). In addition, these studies found that group goals influence performance through their effect on effort, planning, and tactics.

As with individual-level goal-setting research, there has been much attention to the goal commitment construct at the group level. In particular, research has focused on how goal commitment is related to group cohesion. In terms of assigned goals, Podsakoff, MacKenzie, and Ahearne (1997) conducted two studies demonstrating that goal acceptance moderates the relationship between group cohesion and performance. With self-set goals, however, more cohesive groups are more likely to self-select more difficult goals (Klein & Mulvey, 1995).

New Directions

More and more recent research in goal setting has been examining how individual-difference factors such as conscientiousness, goal orientation, and emotion influence the goal-performance relationship. Several studies have highlighted the link between conscientiousness and both self-set goals and goal commitment (Barrick et al., 1993; Gellatly, 1996), emphasizing that individuals with higher levels of conscientiousness are more likely to self-select difficult goals and to be committed to difficult goals.

Numerous recent studies have also focused on the relationship between one's goal orientation (as defined by Dweck, 1986) and performance. Briefly, Dweck (1986) described two different goal orientations that people have: learning-goal-oriented individuals are more concerned with mastering the task, and therefore set goals related to learning, whereas performance-goal-oriented individuals are more interested in performing well on the task and therefore self-set goals related to task outcome, regardless of mastery level. VandeWalle (1999) reviewed this literature and found that a learning-goal orientation is related to higher self-set goals, seeking training, and feedback-seeking behavior. A study by Harackiewicz, Barron, Carter, Lehto, and Elliot (1997) found that students with a *workmastery* achievement motivation (i.e., learning-goal orientation) were more likely to adopt mastery goals and be more interested in course material, whereas students with *competitiveness* achievement motivation (i.e., performance-goal orientation) were more likely to set performance goals and work-avoidance goals and had less intrinsic interest in course material. Similarly, Colquitt and Simmering (1998) found that having a learning-goal orientation was related to the motivation to learn and to performance in a management course. Those with a learning-goal orientation are also more likely to use more complex learning strategies than their performance-goal orientation counterparts (Fisher & Ford, 1998). In a study where the subjects' goal orientation was manipulated, those with learning-goal orientations had higher self-efficacy, self-set goals, and intrinsic motivation on complex tasks, whereas those with performance-goal orientations had higher levels of the same constructs on simple tasks (Hoover, Johnson, & Schmidt, 1998). One potential reason for these effects is that those with learning-goal orientations tend to see ability as malleable, whereas those with performance-goal orientations view ability as immutable (Button, Mathieu, & Zajac, 1996). Other research has demonstrated that viewing ability as malleable lowers anxiety but leads to increases in self-efficacy, satisfaction, goals, and ultimately performance (Martocchio, 1994; Tabernero & Wood, 1999).

Although the impact of goal orientation on self-set goals is clear, their impact on performance is not. Whereas some studies have found that learning-goal orientations lead to higher performance (e.g., Tabernero & Wood, 1999; Vande-Walle, 1999), others have found no difference in performance between learning- and performance-goal-oriented individuals (Hoover et al., 1998), and still others have found performance-goal-oriented individuals to have higher performance (Harackiewicz et al., 1997). Preliminary evidence seems to indicate that these disparate findings might be explained by the type of task: A learning-goal orientation is more likely to lead to increases in performance when the task is complex, whereas a performance-goal orientation is more likely to improve performance if the task is simple (Winters & Latham, 1996). Regardless of what future research will determine on this issue, it is clear that the study of individual differences is making its mark in the goal-setting literature.

Emotions have also been examined recently for their relationship to the goal-setting process. For example, Brunstein et al. (1998) conducted two studies using a thematic apperception test (TAT) to measure students' need orientations. They also asked these students to list the goals toward which they were working. When the students' goals were congruent with their need orientations (e.g., focused on task achievement for students high on need for achievement), the students had better emotional well-being; incongruency between one's goals and need orientation on the other hand was associated with declining emotional well-being. Anticipated emotion and framing also appear to impact the goal-performance relationship. Roney, Higgins, and Shah (1995) found that when performance goals on an anagram task were framed positively (21 out of 25 right), subjects had better persistence and higher task performance than when the goal was framed negatively (4 of 25 wrong). Another study of sales persons' goals found that anticipated emotions associated with goal achievement helped predict behavior and sales (Brown, Cron, & Slocum, 1997). Finally, Brunstein, Dangelmayer, and Schultheiss (1996) found that individuals' perceptions of their significant others' support of personal goals was positively related not only to goal achievement but also to relationship satisfaction and mood 1 month later. An interesting picture of the relationship between affect and goals is emerging, but we have quite a bit of work to do in this area fully to understand the various connections between the goal-setting process and emotion.

The overwhelming evidence for goal setting is positive; that is, goal setting works to improve performance across a variety of contexts and on numerous tasks (Pritchard, 1995). However, whereas we know quite a bit about the relationship between goals and quantifiable task-performance outcomes, we do not necessarily have a clear picture of the effects of goals on affect, extrarole behaviors, performance quality, complex or novel tasks, and interdependent tasks to name a few. For example, we know that goal achievement can lead to feelings of satisfaction (Thomas & Mathieu, 1994), but we know little about the affective consequences of failure to reach a goal (Pinder, 1998). Research by Brunstein and Gollwitzer (1996) concluded that failure to achieve goals can lead to lowered motivation and performance on future tasks, particularly if the goal is relevant to the person's self-definition and if he or she ruminates on the failure. Some tantalizing research indicates that specific goals in conjunction with bonuses for goal attainment may have a negative impact on employees' extrarole behaviors (Wright, George, Farnsworth, & McMahan, 1993). Incentives can also decrease performance when they are linked with goals that are viewed as unattainable (Lee et al., 1997). We know that quantity and quality goals sometimes interfere with each other (Gilliland & Landis, 1992); however, goals can improve creativity when people work alone and expect their work to be evaluated (Shalley, 1995). We know that goals can decrease performance on complex or novel tasks (Mitchell et al., 1994; Wood et al., 1987), that they may increase anxiety (Wegge, 1999), that they may hinder cooperation and decrease performance on interdependent tasks

(Mitchell & Silver, 1990), and that this effect appears to increase as the group size increases (Seijts & Latham, 2000). Are there other negative impacts of goals? How do we balance the clear positive performance outcomes associated with goal setting with some of these potential downsides? In what situations are these negative outcomes associated with goal setting most likely to be observed? Although none of these downsides are likely to call into question the fundamental findings of goal setting, these areas of research are worth pursuing to understand more fully the boundary conditions of the theory. There is still fertile theoretical ground to be explored in the field of goal setting.

The last issue we address in the area of goals is one that has received relatively little attention until recent years: What happens after a person selects a goal and begins working toward it? More than 50 years ago Lewin recognized that there are two stages to the motivational process: *goal setting* and *goal striving* (Lewin, Dembo, Festinger, & Sears, 1944). What we have discussed up to now pertains mostly to the first aspect of this process. Goal setting is by nature forward looking; it anticipates performance levels that are to be achieved in the future. The goal-striving or in-the-moment aspect of motivation has not been examined in anywhere near the same depth as has the more proactive and forward-looking goal setting. This is not to say, however, that it has been ignored. Several researchers have begun to examine this concept, though often under different rubrics, including action theory (Wilpert, 1995), control theory (Carver & Scheier, 1990; Klein, 1989), and self-regulation theory (Kanfer & Ackerman, 1989). Although there is no consensus in the literature on what to call this active-processing component of goal achievement, we refer to this body of work as *on-line motivation*.

On-Line Motivation

Most of the researchers in the area of on-line motivation focus on the motivational process after a goal has been accepted. Work by Gollwitzer (1999) and Bargh (1999; Bargh & Gollwitzer, 1994) suggests that people move toward their goals by utilizing *implementation intentions*, or strategies about when, where, and how goal attainment will be reached. This concept of implementation intentions appears to be very similar to the goal-setting mechanism of strategy development. Indeed, recent research by Diefendorff and Lord (2000) shows that there are two outcomes associated with planning. The first is intellectual—planning leads to conscious strategy development; the second is volitional—planning leads to increased persistence and confidence and decreased distractibility. Both of these effects are captured in the concept of implementation intentions. Diefendorff and

Lord also showed that the intellectual effects of planning occur before the task is undertaken, whereas the volitional effects are in the moment, frequently in response to changes in the environment.

Further research on implementation intentions indicates that they cause action initiation to become automatic when the appropriate situation arises (Gollwitzer, 1999). That is, implementation intentions effectively create instant habits, or automatic scripts, that are called up given the appropriate environmental prime. It is here that the on-line motivation research appears to diverge a bit from the goal-setting research. Whereas goal setting assumes that most human behavior is consciously goal directed, on-line motivational researchers have found evidence that there is much less under volitional control than we may realize. Bargh and Chartrand (1999) argued that most of daily life is driven by nonconscious mental processes, which free up cognitive capacity for conscious self-regulation. Wegner and Wheatley (1999) demonstrated that people perceive behavior to be conscious and willful more frequently than it actually is. In other words, although we may believe that much of our behavior is conscious and goal directed, it is possible that we are really on autopilot most of the time, behaving in ways that are consistent with cognitive scripts developed long before the situation we are currently encountering.

Action and control theorists have emphasized the feedback loop process through which people compare their current state with their *referent standard,* or goal (Klein, 1989). Control theory assumes that when there are discrepancies between one's current state and goal, individuals want to resolve those discrepancies by moving closer to the goal (Carver & Scheier, 1990). Consistent with the concept of implementation intentions, control theories posit the recall of automatic scripts for frequently encountered situations (Klein, 1989). When a novel or unexpected situation is encountered, however, more conscious cognitive processing occurs. Work on self-regulation by Kanfer and Ackerman (1989) proposed that given a fixed amount of cognitive capacity, performance is likely to decrease when more cognitive processing is required.

Goal-setting theorists have not received control theory warmly. One of the major areas of disagreement between the two theories relates to the nature of human beings: Do we seek to reduce feedback-loop discrepancies as control theorists propose, or are we actively involved in setting goals that require us to stretch (create discrepancies) as goal-setting theorists argue? Phillips, Hollenbeck, and Ilgen (1996) found that most people set positive discrepancies for themselves, even after a task is well learned. While this finding does not negate the value that control theory has added to the field, it does raise the question of where one's goals (or referent standards) come from. Control theorists suggest that people have goal hierarchies and that goals at one level are determined by higher order goals, which are in turn determined by yet higher order goals. Locke (1991) argued that this explanation simply "pushes the tension-reduction problem back a step further" (p. 13).

There do appear to be a few philosophical and methodological differences between goal setting and action-control theory, but they are remarkably similar in much of their content. Rather than focusing on areas of disagreement between the two approaches, theoretical development might be better served if researchers viewed goal setting as applicable to the preaction phase of human behavior and parts of control theory as more applicable to the on-line active processing phase of human behavior.

Like the "thoughtful" theories of motivation, those approaches that we have labeled "not rational" examine motivation from a perspective that is internal to the individual. Unlike the thoughtful theories, however, this not-rational approach focuses on who people are (including traits and dispositions) and what they feel and need, rather than on what they think and believe. These approaches to motivation are not irrational in any sense, but they do not emphasize the cognitive approach to understanding human motivation and behavior that marked the theories of the previous section. Within this not-rational grouping, research can be further subdivided into "hot" and "cold" categories. The hot theories focus more on transitory mood states and emotions, which have a more direct and proximal impact on motivation and performance. The cold theories emphasize dispositions, genetic traits, and needs—more stable, indirect, and distal influences on motivation and performance.

Hot Theories: Mood, Emotion, Affect

Before we move into a discussion of what we know about mood, emotion, and affect, it is important that we define these terms. We borrow from George and Brief (1996) the definition of *mood* as a pervasive and generalized affective state, which is influenced by situational factors but is not directed at specific targets. Mood is distinct from *emotion,* which is directed at someone or something. *Affect,* on the other hand, is generally agreed to include components of both mood and emotion (Weiss & Brief, in press). Thus, we can think of affect as being a more general term for feelings, and we can think of mood and emotion as particular kinds of feelings: The first is a more generalized overall feeling state, and the second is a more intense feeling that is directed at some target.

What We Know

Historically, the prevailing paradigm in psychology has swung back and forth between a cognitive and behaviorist approach to understanding human behavior. Neither of these perspectives has done much to encourage research on feelings. Consequently, since the 1930s affect has played a very minor role in the study of organizational behavior (Pinder, 1998). Recently, however, there have been some hopeful signs that the study of affect is beginning to take a more prominent place in our understanding of human motivation.

In 1996 two major theoretical pieces were published that served both to focus attention on the underemphasized area of affect and to provide others with a foundation for future research. The first, Weiss and Cropanzano's chapter on affective events theory, proposed a close link between singular, discrete events on the job and one's emotions at any given moment. That is, they suggested that moods and emotions can and do fluctuate widely in a relatively short span of time and that this has some important implications for on-the-job behavior. The second piece, by George and Brief, reviewed research suggesting that mood can enhance or decrease ongoing motivation.

There is a growing body of literature showing that affect can influence cognitive processes and performance on some tasks. For example, positive affect has been shown to improve memory recall (Isen, Shalker, Clark, & Karp, 1978), improve creativity (Estrada, Isen, & Young, 1997), facilitate decision making (Staw & Barsade, 1993), increase prosocial behaviors (George, 1991), encourage coping behavior in the face of stressful events (Aspinwall & Taylor, 1997), and increase the use of constructive approaches to conflict resolution (Carnevale & Isen, 1986). Research by Mitchell et al. (1994) showed that mood influenced self-efficacy judgments once a task was well learned. Another study demonstrated that psychological well-being predicts job performance (Wright & Cropanzano, 2000). Psychological well-being is defined as an individual's propensity to feel positive emotion but not feel negative emotion (Cropanzano & Wright, 1999); that is, it can be thought of as the propensity for being in a "good mood." Finally, research by Erez, Isen, and Purdy (1999) induced a positive mood in subjects and found a corresponding increase in persistence and performance on an anagram task; this relationship was mediated by an increase in the subjects' valence, instrumentality, and expectancy perceptions, suggesting a link between affect and other motivational constructs.

Weiss and Brief (in press) conducted a review of affect at the workplace and concluded that for most of the past century the study of affect in organizations was equivalent to the study of job satisfaction. Job satisfaction includes not only an affective component (cf. Locke, 1976) but also a belief component (Weiss, Nicholas, & Daus, 1999). Because job satisfaction incorporates both feeling and thought, it should be a better predictor of motivation and performance than a construct including only one or the other. Indeed, two different meta-analyses seem to support this notion. Kraus (1995) reviewed 88 different studies that examined the link between attitude and behavior, where attitude is defined as incorporating affect and belief concepts. He found that attitude consistently predicted future behavior (mean $r = .38$). Williams, Gordon, McManus, McDaniel, and Nguyen (2000) reported a meta-analysis showing that pay satisfaction is positively related to commitment and performance ($r = .37$ and .10, respectively) and negatively related to intent to leave and turnover ($r = -.24$ and $-.12$). Until very recently (cf. Judge, Thoresen, Bono, & Patton, 2001), however, industrial and organizational (I/O) psychologists have by and large dismissed the relationship between job satisfaction and job performance. Judge et al. attributed this dismissal in large part to the meta-analysis by Iaffaldano and Muchinsky (1985) that found a very weak relationship between the two constructs.

For the apparently weak relationship between job satisfaction and performance, one explanation is that job satisfaction and task behavior do not correspond in their target and action elements (Kraus, 1995). That is, job satisfaction is too general and global to predict a very specific action such as performance on a given task. Another explanation is that affect and job satisfaction may predict performance at the individual, within-persons level but not at the between-persons level. This is consistent with findings by Fisher and Noble (2000), who showed that people experience more positive affect than is usual when they are performing better than usual for them and less positive affect when they are performing worse than usual for them, and that this is true on a moment-to-moment basis (i.e., not aggregated over time). Other explanations are reviewed in Weiss and Brief (in press). Most of these relate to the levels at which the satisfaction-performance relationship has been measured. The argument is that examining the relationship at an aggregate, group level would be more appropriate and lead to stronger findings.

A final explanation is forwarded by Judge, Thoresen, Bono and Patton (2001), who conducted a meta-analysis of the relationship between job satisfaction and performance on 312 independent samples (combined $N = 54,417$). Using newer analysis techniques than those used by Iaffaldano and Muchinsky (1985), they reported a mean corrected correlation between job satisfaction and job performance of .30. They suggested that previous findings of a null relationship

between the two constructs were based on limitations in analyses and on misinterpretation of findings.

The research to date is clear that affect has an influence on certain kinds of performance and that this influence is both direct and indirect through the mediating effect of cognitive motivational constructs. It is also clear that affect has been understudied. In the next section we look at some areas that future research on the hot area of affect should explore.

New Directions

One issue that is not well understood relates to the sequence of events surrounding mood, emotion, motivation, and performance. For example, some research has found that affect is influenced by and follows performance (Locke & Latham, 1990). Other research has found that affect influences performance (e.g., Erez et al., 1999). Most likely there is a reciprocal relationship between affect and performance, in which some types of emotion and mood are more likely to be antecedent to performance-related constructs and other types are more likely to be consequences of them. Some of the discrepancy in findings in this area may be due to the time frame used in measuring affect. Weiss and Cropanzano (1996) suggested that the impact of affect is immediate: It influences a person in the moment. The influence of some kinds of affect is also much stronger than rational analysis at a given moment in time (Loewenstein, 1996). Therefore, research that examines affect and other constructs needs to take a more immediate, moment-by-moment perspective, rather than a cumulative one. The use of experience sampling and mood diaries (e.g., Weiss et al., 1999) should be encouraged to tease out some of these relationships.

In general, the research on affect has focused very narrowly on only a few moods and emotions, and most of these moods and emotions have been positive in nature. A couple of intriguing studies have examined the influence of negative affect on work-related outcomes, but these are the exception. For example, George (1990) found that negative affect was a stronger predictor than positive affect of whether prosocial behaviors would be exhibited. Raghunathan and Pham (1999) showed that different kinds of negative moods led to different kinds of decision making: Sadness resulted in high-risk and high-reward preferences, whereas anxiety led to low-risk and low-reward choices. Recent research has also begun to examine the links between anger or frustration and violence on the job. Negative affect is not the only area that needs to be studied. The negative effects of the expression of positive emotions are also worthy of future study. A good review by Morris and Feldman (1996) examined some of the dysfunctional effects of emotional labor and showed that when there is a discrepancy between felt and expressed emotion, there can be high personal and social costs. Overall, we still know little about the motivational influences of a wide variety of affective states, including envy, fear, guilt, depression, love, compassion, pride, and gratitude, to name a few. Future research needs to help us understand the spectrum of mood and emotion and how these influence both motivation and performance.

Although we do not know as much about the more transient hot theories, we do know quite a bit about the more stable theories of individual difference (i.e., the cold theories), to which we now turn our attention. At a broad level, individual differences can be thought of as stable internal characteristics that make each individual unique in behavior and attitude (Ozer & Reise, 1994). In this category are both need theories and dispositional theories. Dispositional theories can be further divided into those that are affective and those that are nonaffective. Although affective dispositions are similar to the hot theories (which, after all, include "affect"), they differ in that they are more long-term and stable individual characteristics. In the following section we review what we know as well as new directions of research for these theories of individual difference.

Need Theories

What We Know

Most need theorists and researchers agree that needs are an unobservable force (some category of "wants") internal to the person, which creates a tension when the need is not being met. People try to reduce or eliminate this tension through some action. Because this tension directs attention, effort, and persistence, needs are thought to be motivating.

One of the most prominent need theories is Maslow's (1943) need hierarchy, which posits five categories of human needs arranged in hierarchical order. While Maslow's (1943) theory is quite possibly the most well known theory of motivation in popular culture today, it is garnering little research attention. This is largely because the early research related to this theory (most of which was conducted in the 1950s and 1960s) was not able to demonstrate a strong link between people's need levels and their subsequent behavior. Early findings also provoked questions about many of the underlying assumptions of the theory (e.g., people move from lower to higher levels and move only when a need is filled).

Another early need-theory approach to human motivation was McClelland's (1961) focus on need for achievement, need for power, and need for affiliation. For the purposes of

organizational researchers, the most fruitful area of study flowing from McClelland's (1961) theory has focused on the need for achievement. Achievement motivation emphasizes the need to achieve success and avoid failure. Those with a high need for achievement have an approach-oriented tendency to select tasks with an intermediate level of difficulty—those on which they are likely to succeed about 50% of the time. On the other hand, those with a high fear of failure are characterized by having avoidance-oriented tendencies. The concept of approach and avoidance orientations has lead to more recent research, which while not explicitly need theory, certainly has its roots in these concepts.

New Directions

Perhaps one of the best examples of new research that draws from need theory ideas is work by Kanfer and her colleagues (Kanfer, Ackerman, & Heggestad, 1996; Kanfer & Heggestad, 1997, 2000). Drawing on their research on the self-regulatory process, Kanfer et al. (1996) proposed that differences in self-regulatory ability might be due to individual differences in terms of motivational skills. Further research indicated that these skills are influenced by motivational traits that fall into two primary trait clusters: achievement and anxiety (Kanfer & Heggestad, 1997). These two trait clusters are remarkably similar to McClelland's ideas of approach and avoidance orientations. And like the research surrounding McClelland's theory, Kanfer and Heggestad (1997) showed support for the idea that ideally motivated employees have high-achievement and low-anxiety traits. More recently, Kanfer and her colleagues have focused on the development of two versions of the Motivational Trait Questionnaire (MTQ), which measures three motivational traits that fall into the two primary trait clusters: competitive excellence and personal mastery (both achievement traits) and achievement anxiety (Kanfer & Heggestad, 2000).

Several others have conducted research that is also consistent with these findings. VanEerde (2000) developed a model that views procrastination in the larger context of self-regulation: The tendency to procrastinate results from an avoidance orientation toward unattractive long-term goals and the simultaneous approach orientation toward attractive short-term goals. Bateman and Crant (1993) studied an approach-oriented personality trait referred to as the *proactive personality,* which is demonstrated by those who "show initiative, take action and persevere" (cited in Parker & Sprigg, 1999, p. 926). Their findings indicate that this individual difference can moderate the relationship between job demands and job control when predicting strain. That is, people with a proactive personality are less likely to experience strain when the demands of the job are high, as long as control over managing those demands is also high.

Although most current research on individual differences does not directly assess needs as Maslow, McClelland, and others originally conceptualized them, some new trends indicate that need-theory concepts are being examined in other theoretical contexts.

Dispositions

While we were reviewing the literature for this chapter, it became apparent that although the topic of personality and disposition was not the single biggest area of review (goal setting has that distinction), it is the fastest growing area of research in the field of motivation. Researchers are currently paying great attention to individual differences, and there is every indication that this will continue to be the case for the foreseeable future. As Mount and Barrick (1998) stated, "Understanding individual differences and their implications for behavior at work is one of the central tenets of our field, and personality characteristics are central to understanding individual differences" (p. 851). Dispositions can be categorized into both nonaffective and affective dispositions, as we discuss next.

What We Know

Beginning with several reviews and meta-analyses in the early 1990s (Barrick & Mount, 1991; Tett, Jackson, & Rothstein, 1991), it became quickly apparent that the topic of personality was garnering attention. Prior to this time, individual differences were seen largely as secondary in importance to the situation (Mitchell, 1979) or to a person's ability in causing behavior. While it is true that the relationship between personality and performance is moderated by situational strength (Liu & Weiss, 2000), these meta-analyses demonstrated that if personality is viewed using a consistent conceptualization, such as the Big Five, there are clear relationships between certain personality traits and job performance (cf. Hogan, Hogan, & Roberts, 1996). In particular, there appears to be a consistent link between conscientiousness and performance across a variety of different jobs.

Research throughout the 1990s has confirmed the ability of conscientiousness to predict not only performance but also other on-the-job behaviors. For example, conscientiousness has been shown to be positively related to selection and performance appraisal ratings (Dunn, Mount, Barrick, & Ones, 1995), training performance (Martocchio & Judge, 1997), students' classroom performance (Mone, Moss, & White, 1999), sales levels (Barrick, Stewart, & Piotrowski,

2000; Vinchur, Schippmann, Switzer, & Roth, 1998) truck driver performance and retention (Barrick & Mount, 1996), and group performance (Neuman & Wright, 1999). The conscientiousness-performance relationship has also been confirmed in a meta-analysis using a sample of 36 studies only from the European Community (Salgado, 1997). This research found conscientiousness and emotional stability to be valid predictors of job performance across a variety of occupations. Although conscientiousness predicts many job related outcomes, it does not necessarily predict everything. One recent study found no link between conscientiousness levels of Home Depot employees and the integrity or safety behaviors of these workers (Fallon, Avis, Kudisch, Gornet, & Frost, 1998).

The conscientiousness-performance connection appears robust across time, place, and job types, but some of the other Big Five traits appear to be connected with performance only in certain contexts or on certain jobs (cf. Dunn et al., 1995). Extraversion, for example, is consistently related to sales performance (Barrick et al., 2000; Vinchur et al., 1998), but it is not necessarily related to performance in other occupations. In some jobs, emotional stability shows connections with performance (Barrick & Mount, 1996; Salgado, 1997), and in some group contexts agreeableness is linked with performance (Neuman & Wright, 1999). In general, none of these effects are as large or as consistent as the conscientiousness-performance relationship.

Because the connection between personality and performance has been clearly established, more recent research has begun to look at the mechanisms through which personality has its impact on performance. Clearly, personality is a relatively distal influence on performance; what are the more proximal influences? Several studies have recently examined some of the mediating factors between personality and performance. Martocchio and Judge (1997) found that employees' conscientiousness levels were related to their self-efficacy, which was positively related to their learning. Similarly, Mone et al. (1999) found that self-efficacy mediated the relationship between Big Five traits and psychology students' classroom performances. They found that personal goals, goal commitment, and behavioral strategies were also mediators. Finally, Barrick et al. (2000) found that two motivational orientations, status striving and accomplishment striving, mediated the relationship between extraversion and conscientiousness and the performance of 164 telemarketing sales representatives. These motivational orientations appear to have much in common with McClelland's need conceptualization, as well as with Kanfer's motivational traits.

In contrast to the nonaffective dispositions, affective dispositions have reflected the tendency for an individual to be in a more positive or negative state of mind. Some people appear consistently happier than others, regardless of circumstances. Watson and Clark (1984) referred to this tendency as positive affectivity (PA) and to the opposite (consistent distress, unhappiness, or other negative emotions) as negative affectivity (NA). There are numerous specific measures of dispositional affect, but in general they appear to fall into these two categories.

Although the concept of affect is relatively short-term, affective dispositions are not. Several lines of evidence seem to indicate that they are indeed dispositional. First, affective dispositions can predict attitudes and performance over time. Steel and Rentsch (1997) found that job satisfaction measured at one point in time controlled about 20% of the variance in job satisfaction measures taken 10 years later. Similarly, Wright and Staw (1999) conducted a longitudinal study with social welfare employees and found that happiness dispositions were good predictors of performance over time. A second stream of research identified the genetic basis for positive and negative affectivity. Arvey and Bouchard's twin research found evidence of a genetic cause of job satisfaction (Arvey, Bouchard, Segal, & Abraham, 1989; Bouchard, Arvey, Keller, & Segal, 1992) and of attitudes (Arvey & Bouchard, 1994).

In reviewing the literature, we believe that core self-evaluations can be considered a positive affective disposition. The concept of core self-evaluations has been developed by Judge and his colleagues as a higher order or broad personality construct in which self-esteem, generalized self-efficacy, locus of control, and neuroticism (reverse scored) all load onto it. Like other studies examining the long-term effect of PA, core self-evaluations predict job and life satisfaction (Judge, Locke, Durham, & Kluger, 1998) as well as task motivation and performance (Erez & Judge, 2001), and these relationships are stable over time. In one study, core job evaluations measured in childhood and early adulthood were linked to job satisfaction measured in middle adulthood (Judge, Bono, & Locke, 2000). Like measures of nonaffective disposition, core self-evaluations seem to have their impact on performance through self-regulatory mechanisms such as activity level, goal setting, and goal commitment (Erez & Judge, 2001).

New Directions

In some ways, all of the research in the area of dispositions is something of a new direction. However, at least two topics in this field stand out as needing more attention before researchers can draw any firm conclusions. First, there is no clarity about whether the personality-performance findings discussed earlier are consistent across cultures. While Salgado's (1997) European meta-analysis concluded that conscientiousness predicted performance in the European Union, as it does in the United States, there is no evidence demonstrating this link in non-Western cultures. A cross-cultural study examining several personality scales between the United States and India found that whereas the scales themselves exhibited similar psychometric properties across the two groups, Indian respondents reported lower self-esteem and internal locus of control than did their U.S. counterparts (Ghorpade, Hattrup, & Lackritz, 1999). The authors attributed this in part to India's collectivistic culture, in which esteeming the self is viewed as self-aggrandizement. But this also means that assuming similarities of personality traits across cultures may be inappropriate. More comparative studies must be conducted before researchers can say anything with confidence on this topic.

A second topic that is currently generating quite a bit of research is the area of genetic influence on personality, including the effects of evolutionary psychology (Buss, Haselton, Shackelford, Bleske, & Wakefield, 1998). As previously discussed, Arvey and Bouchard (1994) showed that there is a heritable component to affective dispositions. And the genetic research is also clear that nonaffective dispositions including work values (Keller, Bouchard, Arvey, Segal, & Dawes, 1992) and Big Five traits including extraversion and neuroticism (Viken, Rose, Kaprio, & Koskenvuo, 1994) also have high heritability coefficients (up to .50). More recent research in psychology has turned toward understanding behavior from an evolutionary perspective. Nicholson (1997) argued persuasively for a gene-based understanding of personality and behavior including gender differences, in-group/out-group, and status seeking. Because of the strong genetic influence that has been documented for so many individual differences, it would seem a relatively short step for an evolutionary psychology perspective to be applied in this domain.

Up to this point our review of motivation theories has centered on those that emphasize internal attributes of the individual. Now we shift conceptual gears away from these internal theories of motivation and toward those theories that focus on external aspects of the task or situation. It is apparent in Figure 10.2 that the external approaches have an initial tension between what we call task or job design and more social approaches to understanding motivation. Two external elements that people focus on when working are the task itself and their social, interactive context. As mentioned, job design is covered elsewhere in this volume. However, it is important to say that tasks have motivational properties and that many people exert large amounts of effort and persist for a long time when working on tasks that they find enriching and intrinsically satisfying.

There is also a distinction within the social category between an outcome orientation and a social-influence orientation. The outcome-oriented theories (justice, reinforcement) suggest that our evaluations of our outcomes and social comparisons are important, whereas the social-influence approaches argue that much of our motivation comes from trying to fulfill the explicit and implicit expectations of those around us (team pressure, norms, social influence, culture). These latter topics are also covered elsewhere in this volume, but again it is important to point out that motivation can be strongly influenced by the perceived expectations of others.

Reinforcement and equity-justice approaches to motivation have a focus on outcomes, or what a person receives as a result of his or her behavior. Although both approaches share an outcomes orientation to motivation, they differ significantly in terms of their underlying assumptions about human behavior. Reinforcement looks at behavior as a function of its consequences and virtually ignores the psychological mechanisms that might mediate environmental stimuli and behavior. Reinforcement has also traditionally been concerned with learning; that is, reinforcement has been examined as a way to improve how and what people learn. Equity and justice approaches, on the other hand, examine a person's perceptions of fairness as a determinant of motivation. Clearly, psychological and perceptual characteristics are key for these approaches.

Reinforcement

As it was originally conceptualized, reinforcement theory, or behavior modification, does not really fit in a discussion of motivation. That is, reinforcement purists would argue that there is no such thing as motivation as an unobservable psychological process (cf. Skinner, 1990). On the other hand, reinforcement works, and it has provided the basis for many organizational practices from pay to discipline. Komaki, Coombs, and Schepman (1991) described reinforcement theory as a motivation theory emphasizing the consequences of behavior. At a very basic level, reinforcement theory is based on the idea that some behavioral consequences increase the likelihood that a behavior will be exhibited again, whereas other behavioral consequences decrease the likelihood that the behavior will be exhibited. The implications for managers are that they should reward behavior that they would like repeated, and make sure that undesirable behavior is not rewarded.

What We Know

In 1964 Vroom wrote, "without a doubt the law of effect or principle of reinforcement must be included among the most substantiated findings of experimental psychology and is at the same time among the most useful findings for applied psychology concerned with control of human behavior" (quoted in Luthans & Stajkovic, 1999, p. 13). While organizational behavior theory and practice have changed substantially over the past several decades, the idea that reinforcement influences performance continues to be demonstrated today. Reinforcement programs have been shown to decrease absenteeism (e.g., Landau, 1993), increase safety behaviors (e.g., Sulzer-Azarof, Loafman, Merante, & Hlavacek, 1990), increase procedure-following behaviors (Welsh, Luthans, & Sommer, 1993), and increase the friendly behaviors of customer service representatives (Brown & Sulzer-Azarof, 1994).

By definition, a reinforcer is anything that increases the frequency of the demonstration of a desired behavior. Reinforcement theory also argues that reinforcers need to be presented consistently and in a timely manner. In practice, organizations reward desired behavior with two primary types of reinforcement: (a) financial, including pay for performance, merit pay, profit sharing, and gain sharing, and (b) nonfinancial, including feedback and recognition (Luthans & Stajkovic, 1999). Both types of reinforcement appear to have positive organizational impacts, based on the results of three meta-analyses conducted within the last decade.

The first, a meta-analysis of financial incentives on performance presented by Kluger and DeNisi (1996), shows an averaged effect size of .41 (with substantial variation across studies), suggesting a moderate effect. In addition, the types of incentives and the type of task had moderating effects. For example, negative or discouraging incentives (too hard to attain) had negative effects on performance. A more recent analysis by Jenkins, Mitra, Gupta, and Shaw (1998) reported an average weighted r of .34 between financial incentives and performance quantity, with slightly stronger effects in field studies than in lab studies. It is important to note that this research did not find any relationship between financial incentives and performance quality. Finally, a review and meta-analysis conducted by Stajkovic and Luthans (1997) showed that the effect of using a systematic reinforcement approach increased performance. The average d across different organizations and different types of reinforcement was .51 (a 17% increase), suggesting a reliable and moderate positive effect. Although this last meta-analysis found similar performance effects for nonfinancial and financial reinforcement, the practical importance of financial reinforcement is seen in many organizational compensation systems, which seek to enhance employee motivation. Reinforcement is not the only viable theoretical approach to understanding compensation (see Bartol & Locke, in press, for a good review of others), but it is clearly important in helping us understand the compensation-performance link.

New Directions

The meta-analyses on reinforcement just cited confirm that reinforcement theory has something to add to our knowledge of motivation. However, much of the organizational research on reinforcement has examined the link between financial incentives and desired behaviors. More recent work has been highlighting the importance of nonfinancial reinforcers. Although research shows that reinforcement can be an effective motivational tool, some have criticized the emphasis on external reinforcement in many organizations. In part this is due to the difficulty of accurately assessing individual-level performance in organizations, which is a necessary precursor to implementing financial incentives such as merit pay (Campbell, Campbell, & Chia, 1998). But there have also been questions about the effectiveness of external incentive rewards in general. For example, Heath (1997) documented what he referred to as the *extrinsic incentives bias,* or the tendency that people have to believe that others are more motivated than themselves by extrinsic incentives, and less motivated by intrinsic incentives such as learning new things. In a similar vein, Beer and Katz (1998) asked a sample of executives from 30 countries to respond to a questionnaire assessing their perceptions of financial incentives. Their results indicated that these executives did not find incentives to be particularly motivating. Thus, it would appear that even though most of us believe that external incentive rewards can be reinforcing (especially for other people), we also tend to value work-related outcomes that are not financial. This is consistent with Luthans and Stajkovic's (1999) work showing that nonfinancial reinforcement has performance effects similar to those of financial reinforcement. Researchers may want to examine the work-related implications of these findings, particularly in relation to organizational compensation and reward systems.

Historically, reinforcement research has focused on those consequences that encourage certain desired behaviors. That is, reinforcement research has typically examined the effects of reinforcement. However, the theory of operant conditioning includes the application of punishment in order to decrease undesirable behaviors. The concept of punishment has not been well examined in the organizational behavior literature. Some recent grounded research using an interview methodology examined how managers think and feel about punishing subordinates (Butterfield, Trevino, & Ball, 1996). Among other things, this research emphasized that punishment in organizational contexts is common and that managers feel that its instrumentality varies: It works only sometimes. Other research by Liden and his colleagues demonstrated that different kinds of punishments are more likely depending on the role of the person instigating the punishment. That is, managers' and groups' disciplinary decisions were more severe than were individual group members' decisions (Liden et al., 1999). Although we know much about what kinds of reinforcements are effective, we do not know as much about punishment.

Justice

The topic of organizational justice, or people's perceptions of fairness in organizations, has received substantial interest over the past decade (Cropanzano & Greenberg, 1997). Justice perceptions are based on what a person receives in an organizational context, including tangible outcomes as well as less tangible interpersonal factors. Because justice perceptions are determined almost exclusively in relation to others ("How much did so-and-so get?" or "Was I treated fairly?") we consider it within the social category of motivational theories.

What We Know

The major organizing framework in the justice literature is the distinction between distributive and procedural justice. Distributive-justice judgments relate to people's evaluations of their outcomes, whereas judgments about procedural justice relate to people's perceptions of how fairly they were treated in a given process. Both types of justice have important implications for organizations; however, whereas distributive justice was the focus of much of the early work in this area, more recent research has focused more on procedural justice issues.

The theory surrounding distributive justice developed from Adams's (1965) work on *equity theory.* In brief, this theory predicts that people will evaluate the fairness of their situation in an organization based on a comparison of the ratio of their own inputs and outcomes with some referent's ratio of inputs and outcomes. When these ratio comparisons are not equal, people are motivated to change the situation by either modifying their inputs and outcomes, changing their referent other, distorting their perceptions, or quitting.

Adams's (1965) equity theory predicts that people will be motivated to create a situation of equity or fairness. Recent research examining the psychological processes underlying this fairness motive has shown two interesting phenomena. First, work by Thierry (1998) demonstrated that outcomes, particularly in relation to pay, communicate information that influences people's self-concepts. For example, those who are paid more tend to believe that their performance is better than others and that they have more control over organizational outcomes than do others. Second, research examining how people form justice judgments has shown that even mild personal experiences of injustice have a much stronger influence on impressions of justice than do reports from others of more severe injustice (Lind, Kray, & Thompson, 1998). These research findings would seem to indicate that justice judgments are very personal. Not only are these judgments likely to be based on people's own personal experiences, but their motives for making them are at least in part to enhance or preserve their self-concepts.

The research testing equity theory has been generally supportive across a variety of contexts. We know, for example, that outcomes that are perceived as unfair can lead to poor performance (Greenberg, 1988), increased turnover and absenteeism (Schwarzwald, Koslowsky, & Shalit, 1992), and lowered commitment to the organization (Schwarzwald et al., 1992). However, the effects of *positive inequity* (i.e., situations in which a person is overrewarded relative to referent others) do not appear to be as strong as those of *negative inequity* (i.e., a person is underrewarded relative to others). For example, Bloom (1999) found that higher pay dispersion on professional baseball teams (a recipe for higher inequity perceptions) led to lower individual performance for those on the low end of the pay scale. Those at the high end of the pay scale actually had higher performance; however, this effect was not enough to offset the lowered performance of the underpaid players, and the overall impact of higher pay dispersion led to lower team performance. Others have found similar results across a range of organizational contexts (e.g., Greenberg, 1988).

Research on equity theory expanded substantially with the introduction of the concept of procedural justice. That is, was the process for making a distributive decision fair? Several criteria appear to be involved in making an evaluation of procedural fairness. Thibaut and Walker (1975) identified voice as an important determinant of whether a procedure was considered fair. This is consistent with research showing that people who have choice in determining which task to engage in are more likely to view the process as fair (Cropanzano & Folger, 1991). Leventhal (1980) proposed that fair procedures are those that meet six different criteria: consistently

applied, free from bias, accurate, correctable, representative of all concerns, and based on prevailing ethical standards. Subsequent research has supported these criteria for procedural justice and has shown a link between them and satisfaction (Taylor, Tracy, Renard, Harrison, & Carrol, 1996)

When processes are perceived as fair, the benefits to the organization are high. Procedural justice has been shown to influence the acceptance of human-resources interventions ranging from pay systems (Schaubroeck, May, & Brown, 1994), to smoking bans (Greenberg, 1994), to parental leave policies (Grover, 1991), to disciplinary actions (Ball, Trevino, & Sims, 1994). When people believe that the process was fair, they are more likely to cooperate with those in authority, even when the outcome may be less than positive for them personally (Tyler & DeGoey, 1995). Greenberg (1990) showed that theft as a response to pay cuts can be minimized with processes that are perceived as fair. Commitment and job satisfaction can be enhanced with procedural justice (Takeuchi, Tekleab, & Taylor, 2000), which is at least one of the mechanisms through which participation in goal setting affects satisfaction (Roberson, Moye, & Locke, 1999). Higher perceptions of procedural justice lead to lower levels of turnover (Dailey & Kirk, 1992) and lower likelihood of litigation (Bies & Tyler, 1993). Perhaps most widely researched is the relationship between procedural justice and organizational citizenship behaviors (OCBs).

A large number of studies have shown that procedural justice is an antecedent of OCBs (for a review, see Morgeson, 1999). This relationship is mediated by satisfaction (Moorman, 1991) and perceived organizational support (Moorman, Blakely, & Niehoff, 1998), and this is especially true for reciprocation-wary employees—those who believe that they may be exploited by others (Lynch, Eisenberger, & Armeli, 1999). Another recent study seems to indicate that procedural justice has its strongest influence on employees who feel that they have been treated unfairly in the past (Taylor, Masterson, Renard, & Tracy, 1998). In other words, processes that are procedurally just may have their biggest impact on those employees who are currently most dissatisfied.

An interesting finding is that subordinates appear to play a role in the extent to which procedural justice is used. Two studies have shown that employees who are assertive (Korsgaard, Roberson, & Rymph, 1998) or who use supervisor-focused impression management tactics (Dulebohn & Ferris, 1999) can increase the procedural justice behaviors on the part of their managers. Finally, it appears that it is possible to train leaders in procedural justice. Skarlicki and Latham (1997) showed that union leaders who had been trained in organizational justice principles were perceived by their union members as more fair and that these union members exhibited increased OCBs directed toward the union and fellow union members.

Although procedural justice is clearly important, it may not be any more or less important than distributive justice. Brockner and Wisenfeld (1996) found that when distributive justice is high, procedural justice does not control much variance in the evaluation of exchanges. On the other hand, when procedural justice is high, distributive outcomes do not control much variance. A more recent study by Skarlicki, Folger, and Klimiuk (2000) found similar results: When procedural justice was high, distributive justice was unrelated to performance; however, with low procedural justice, distributive justice became predictive of performance. Apparently, employees are concerned about justice, but either procedural or distributive justice will do. Two meta-analyses have been conducted recently between justice constructs and various organizational attitudes and behaviors (Bartle & Hayes, 1999; Colquitt, Conlon, Wesson, Porter, & Ng, 2001). Both papers report strong and significant relationships between both procedural and distributive justice and attitudes (e.g., job satisfaction and trust). Corrected mean rs ranged from .48 to .68. There are also positive but less strong effects on types of organizational citizenship behaviors (r from .15 to .32) and on performance ($r = .15$ in both papers).

Other theoretical work in the area of equity theory has highlighted an individual difference factor related to equity perceptions, namely, *equity sensitivity*. Huseman, Hatfield, and Miles (1987) developed a measure for this construct, which has been tested in a variety of settings. The research on equity sensitivity suggests that people can be categorized along a continuum as benevolents, equity sensitives, or entitleds (King, Miles, & Day, 1993). *Benevolents* are defined as having a higher tolerance for negative inequity, and they have been shown to have relatively high levels of satisfaction regardless of reward condition. *Equity sensitives* are most likely to conform to the predictions of equity theory, showing aversion to both conditions of under- and overreward. *Entitleds,* on the other hand, prefer situations of positive inequity, or overreward. They tend to value tangible extrinsic outcomes more than they value the intrinsic work outcomes.

New Directions

A new concept in this area that is currently generating quite a bit of research is that of interactional justice, or the idea that how decision makers in the organization treat people is important in determining equity perceptions. Two aspects of interactional justice are discussed in the literature: the extent to which people believe that they have been treated with dignity and respect and the extent to which people believe that they

have been given appropriate information about the procedures that affect them (Cropanzano & Greenberg, 1997). There is some debate over whether interactional justice is a subset of procedural justice or whether it is a third category of justice distinct from distributive and procedural justice. While social aspects of procedural justice are highly related to interactional justice (Konovsky & Cropanzano, 1991), there is also evidence that procedural and interactional fairness have different antecedents (Schminke, Ambrose, & Cropanzano, 2000).

Regardless of its position in the nomological net, perceptions of interactional justice do have positive outcomes. In particular, such perceptions increase OCBs (Moorman, 1991), particularly supervisor-focused OCBs (Skarlicki et al., 2000), and decrease retaliation behaviors (Greenberg, 1994). A recently developed and validated interpersonal treatment scale shows that this measure is related to satisfaction with supervisor, job satisfaction, and turnover intentions (Donovan, Drasgow, & Munson, 1998).

Another new direction in the justice literature relates to retaliation and violence in response to perceptions of inequity. In the early 1990s Greenberg (1993) demonstrated that people are likely to act in ways that harm the organization in response to unfair treatment. Similarly, Skarlicki and Folger (1997) showed that the interaction of low distributive, procedural, and interactional justice led to retaliation behaviors including taking supplies, damaging equipment, calling in sick, or leaving a mess. Although equity theory does a good job of explaining negative behaviors based on restitution (e.g., theft), it does not do as well in explaining retaliatory behaviors, which have no clear positive outcome for the individual engaging in them. Such destructive behavior makes more sense when viewed through the lens of the psychological contract (Rousseau & Greller, 1994) or of social exchange literatures (Greenberg & Scott, 1996). Essentially, employees who are treated in ways that do not meet their expectations view their situation as a violation of the psychological contract that they have with the organization and tend to react negatively toward the organization as a result (Morrison & Robinson, 1997). It may help to think of these negative behaviors as being the opposite of OCBs (cf. Pawar & Eastman, 1999): When employees are treated fairly, they engage in OCBs; when they are treated unfairly, they engage in deviant and destructive behaviors.

Summary: Overall Perspective

Our review of the literature is now complete. As promised, the field of motivation is vast and complex. One can focus on the person or the context, proximal or distal factors, organizational or social outcomes, thoughtful or more routinized activities, or cognitive or more emotional processes. Based on our narrative review and the meta-analyses we uncovered, it is clear that all of these perspectives have some validity. As a result, there are some underlying principles about which most researchers agree.

First, goals are a major factor on the motivational landscape. Almost every approach to this topic includes goals. We humans are goal setters and goal seekers. We also prefer pleasure to pain and will seek positive outcomes and states and avoid negative ones. Third, we prefer mastery and control to uncertainty and ambiguity. Mastery and control are direct antecedents of our expectations, confidence, and efficacy. We also prefer interesting, stimulating, and satisfying to boring, stressful, and repetitious activities. In addition, we are constantly involved in social interaction and social comparison. We want to have a positive view of ourselves and be liked by others and be treated fairly. The social context is a major source of such information. Finally, we are all unique with genetic and personal backgrounds that shape our wants, desires, and reactions to events. These individual differences play a crucial role in understanding motivation and variation in motivation.

DISCUSSION

Given these different principles and perspectives it seems unlikely that a general theory of motivation will emerge. More likely, orientations will evolve around different perspectives. Ambrose and Kulik (1999), for example, suggested that we should focus on classes of behavior such as effort or citizenship behaviors. Mitchell (1997) discussed how different theories could be grouped around the motivational processes of arousal, attention and direction, and intensity and persistence. Others have suggested that we should focus either on the intention/choice activities (prior to action) or the actual on-line behavioral activities (Wilpert, 1995).

The idea of tensions, which we presented in this paper, incorporates some of these orientations. Included are the internal-external, task-social, thoughtful–not rational, hot-cold and prechoice-on-line distinctions. Presumably, elements of the person and context will help to determine the extent to which one or the other (or both) side of these dichotomies is operating.

But after doing this review, a number of other "perspectives" occurred to us. Different theories come to mind based on the type of questions we ask. Here are four such questions:

1. What is the underlying dynamic? It seemed to us that we could classify theories according to an overall theme. More specifically, some theories clearly revolve around

discrepancy ideas. Needs are activated based on this idea, as are feelings of injustice. In addition, there is the discrepancy between one's goal and one's current level of goal attainment. Supposedly, such discrepancy states are unpleasant and aversive, and we strive to reduce them.

Another theme might be called a pull orientation. We wish to please others (conform to social norms), and we are attracted to positive rewards, outcomes, and the attainment of goals. Motivation in this sense seems to be centered in the external context. A contrasting theme might be labeled a push orientation. Theories that focus on our genes, personality, expectancies, efficacy, and self-set goals could be seen as fitting this description. These factors help to shape our preferences, expectations, and orientations.

2. What is the effect of time? Obviously, people and contexts change over time. Tasks become easier, activities become routinized, groups become cohesive, goals are attained, rewards change, and so on. We suspect that different motivational theories and principles operate as these changes take place.

A different way to think about time is to look at the orientation of the theories themselves. All of the theories are meant to predict behavior that will follow one's current motivational state. However, the information that they use or the constructs that they employ are time related and time dependent. For example, both reinforcement theory and equity theory use information from the past. Reinforcement histories supposedly influence current action, as does our assessment of our past outcomes relative to the outcomes of others. Fairness judgments are based on past actions and activities.

Some approaches are more in the moment and are not particularly reflective in nature. Our personalities (consistent and persistent behavioral tendencies) seem to emerge in context. Our moods are fleeting and variable. In addition, social, interpersonal interaction and the social context can change constantly over short periods of time. Such changes in mood or context can lead to very different norms or personality traits being salient.

Finally, much of what we do is motivated by anticipation. Expectancies, self-efficacy, and goals are reflections of what we think we will do, can do, and want to do with respect to upcoming activities (Daniels & Mitchell, 1995). These constructs suggest that what we do now is partially determined by our view of the future.

3. How malleable are these states? Both internal and external motivational orientations vary in terms of how easy it is to influence the underlying motivational process. Internally, our genes and personality are hard to change. Our mood

may be partly personal and partly contextual. While mood may change frequently, it is not exactly under personal or external control. On the other hand, goals, expectancies, and efficacy appear to be much more malleable.

Looking at external factors presents a similar picture. Changing the design of jobs often involves a major change in how tasks get done. New technology or methods may be needed. Social norms are also hard to change, but perhaps less so than redesigning tasks. On the other hand, new reward or reinforcement practices can be adopted somewhat more readily. Thus, it may be tougher to change a person's reaction to work through job design than it would be to change that same person's reinforcement expectations.

4. How easy are these theories to use or implement? An earlier paper by Mitchell (1997) examined this question in detail. Some theories, such as goal setting or equity, require ongoing monitoring, assessment, feedback, and revisions and are individually focused. Many resources are needed. Job design or social norms, on the other hand, are implemented and put in place and persist over time with less need to monitor and maintain them. They are also focused on everyone, not individuals. Selection strategies designed to bring in people with certain needs or traits focus on attributes that persist over time and do not usually require monitoring or feedback.

Not all theories are equally effective, however. Goal setting may require huge amounts of resources to do well, but the goal setting–performance relationships are strong. Job design, on the other hand, has a less strong impact on performance. Nor are all theories equally appropriate to particular jobs or people. Thus, before choices are made about which approach or approaches to use, one needs to assess the context, resources needed, and outcomes desired (Mitchell, 1997).

CONCLUSIONS

The field of motivation is still vibrant and interesting. We researchers have confidence about the meaning of the construct and how it operates. We have a good idea of the mechanisms that create and sustain it. Recently, the areas of affect, goal setting (especially self-regulation and on-line behavior), individual differences, and justice have captured our attention, whereas need theories and expectancy theory have received less attention.

There are also areas in need of more research. How do thoughtful processes become more routine? What mechanisms are involved with the allocation of effort and time over

tasks? How do emotions such as anger and guilt (e.g., over injustice) influence constructs such as goal acceptance or self-efficacy? How do distal constructs such as personality influence more proximal states such as expectancies or goal commitment? How does the task and social context influence one's mood? Answering these and many other questions requires more research.

In closing, we want to point out that practical issues are important as well. More field and longitudinal research is needed to assess the effects of individual motivational interventions and combinations of interventions. We need better diagnostic models and theories evolving from applications. Such research will help us answer the important questions of when and where particular motivational interventions work as well as why they work.

REFERENCES

Adams, J. S. (1965). Inequity in social exchange. In L. Berkowitz (Ed.), *Advances in experimental social psychology* (Vol. 2, pp. 267–299). New York: Academic Press.

Ambrose, M. L., & Kulik, C. T. (1999). Old friends, new faces: Motivation research in the 1990s. *Journal of Management, 25,* 231–292.

Arvey, R. D., & Bouchard, T. J., Jr. (1994). Genetics, twins, and organizational behavior. *Research in Organizational Behavior, 16,* 47–82.

Arvey, R. D., Bouchard, T. J., Jr., Segal, N. L., & Abraham, L. M. (1989). Job satisfaction: Environmental and genetic components. *Journal of Applied Psychology, 74,* 187–192.

Aspinwall, L. G., & Taylor, S. E. (1997). A stitch in time: Self-regulation and proactive coping. *Psychological Bulletin, 121,* 417–436.

Audia, G., Kristof-Brown, A., Brown, K. G., & Locke, E. A. (1996). Relationship of goals and micro-level work processes to performance on a multi-path manual task. *Journal of Applied Psychology, 81,* 483–497.

Austin, J. T. (1989). Effects of shifts in goal origin on goal acceptance and attainment. *Organizational Behavior and Human Decision Processes, 44,* 415–435.

Ball, G. A., Trevino, L. K., & Sims, H. P., Jr. (1994). Just and unjust punishment: Influences on subordinate performance and citizenship. *Academy of Management Journal, 37,* 299–322.

Bandura, A. (1982). Self-efficacy mechanism in human agency. *American Psychologist, 37,* 122–147.

Bandura, A. (1986). Social foundations of thought and action: A social cognitive theory. Englewood Cliffs, NJ: Prentice-Hall.

Bandura, A. (1997). *Self-efficacy: The exercise of control.* New York: W. H. Freeman.

Bargh, J. A. (1999). The cognitive monster. In S. Chaiken & Y. Trope (Eds.), *Dual process theories in social psychology* (pp. 361–382). New York: Guilford Press.

Bargh, J. A., & Chartrand, T. L. (1999). The unbearable automaticity of being. *American Psychologist, 54,* 462–479.

Bargh, J. A., & Gollwitzer, P. M. (1994). Environmental control of goal-directed action: Automatic and strategic contingencies between situations and behavior. *Nebraska Symposium on Motivation, 41,* 71–124.

Barrick, M. R., & Mount, M. K. (1991). The Big Five personality dimensions and job performance: A meta-analysis. *Personnel Psychology, 44,* 1–26.

Barrick, M. R., & Mount, M. K. (1996). Effects of impression management and self-deception on the predictive validity of personality constructs. *Journal of Applied Psychology, 81,* 261–272.

Barrick, M. R., Mount, M. K., & Strauss, J. P. (1993). Conscientiousness and performance of sales representations: Test of the mediating effects of goal setting. *Journal of Applied Psychology, 78,* 715–722.

Barrick, M. R., Stewart, G. L., & Piotrowski, M. (2000). *Personality and performance: Test of the mediating effects of motivation.* Presented at the 15th Annual Conference of the Society for Industrial and Organizational Psychology, New Orleans, LA.

Bartle, S., & Hayes, B. C. (1999, April). *Organizational justice and work outcomes: A meta-analysis.* Paper presented at the Annual Meeting of the Society for Industrial and Organizational Psychology, Atlanta, GA.

Bartol, K. M., & Locke, E. A. (in press). Incentives and motivation. In S. Rynes & B. Gerhart (Eds.), *Compensation in Organizations: Progress and prospects.* San Francisco: New Lexington Press.

Bateman, T. S., & Crant, J. M. (1993). The proactive component of organizational behavior: A measure and correlates. *Journal of Organizational Behavior, 14,* 103–118.

Beer, M., & Katz, N. (1998, August). *Do incentives work? The perceptions of senior executives from thirty countries.* Paper presented at the National Meetings of the Academy of Management, San Diego, CA.

Bies, R. J., & Tyler, T. R. (1993). The "litigation mentality" in organizations: A test of alternative psychological explanations. *Organizational Science, 4,* 352–366.

Bloom, M. (1999). The performance effects of pay dispersion on individuals and organizations. *Academy of Management Journal, 42,* 25–40.

Bouchard, T. J., Jr., Arvey, R. D., Keller, L. M., & Segal, N. L. (1992). Genetic influences on job satisfaction: A reply to Cropanzano and James. *Journal of Applied Psychology, 77,* 89–93.

Brockner, J. (1988). *Self-esteem at work: Research, theory and practice.* Lexington, MA: Lexington Books.

Brockner, J., & Wisenfeld, B. M. (1996). An integrative framework for explaining reaction to decisions: Interactive effects of outcomes and procedures. *Psychological Bulletin, 120,* 189–208.

Brown, C. S., & Sulzer-Azarof, B. (1994). An assessment of the relationship between customer satisfaction and service friendliness. *Journal of Organizational Behavior Management, 14,* 55–75.

Brown, S. P., Cron, W. L., & Slocum, J. W., Jr. (1997). Effects of goal directed emotions on sales person volitions, behavior and performance: A longitudinal study. *Journal of Marketing, 61,* 39–50.

Brunstein, J. C., Dangelmayer, G., & Schultheiss, O. C. (1996). Personal goals and social support in close relationships: Effects on relationship mood and marital satisfaction. *Journal of Personality and Social Psychology, 71,* 1006–1019.

Brunstein, J. C., & Gollwitzer, P. M. (1996). Effects of failure on subsequent performance: The importance of self-defining goals. *Journal of Personality and Social Psychology, 70,* 395–408.

Brunstein, J. C., Schultheiss, O. C., & Grassmann, R. (1998). Personal goals and emotional well-being: The moderating role of motive dispositions. *Journal of Personality and Social Psychology, 75,* 494–508.

Buss, D. M., Haselton, M. G., Shackelford, T. K., Bleske, A. L., & Wakefield, J. C. (1998). Adaptations, exaptations, and spandrels. *American Psychologist, 53*(5), 533–548.

Butterfield, K. D., Trevino, L. K., & Ball, G. A. (1996). Punishment from the manager's perspective: A grounded investigation and inductive model. *Academy of Management Journal, 39,* 1479–1512.

Button, S. B., Mathieu, J. E., & Zajac, D. M. (1996). Goal orientation in organizational research: A conceptual and empirical foundation. *Organizational Behavior and Human Decision Processes, 67,* 26–48.

Campbell, D. J., Campbell, K. M., & Chia, H. B. (1998). Merit pay, performance appraisal and individual motivation: An analysis and alternative. *Human Resource Management, 37,* 131–146.

Carnevale, P. J., & Isen, A. M. (1986). The influence of positive affect and visual access on the discovery of integrative solutions in bilateral negotiation. *Organizational Behavior and Human Decision Processes, 37,* 1–13.

Carver, C. S., & Scheier, M. F. (1990). Origins and functions of positive and negative affect: A control-process view. *Psychological Review, 97,* 19–35.

Chen, G., Casper, W. J., & Cortina, J. M. (1999). *Meta-analytic examination of the relationship among cognitive ability, conscientiousness, self-efficacy and task performance.* Paper presented at the annual conference of the Society for Industrial and Organizational Psychology, New Orleans, LA.

Colquitt, J. A., Conlon, D. E., Wesson, M. J., Porter, C. O. L. H., & Ng, K. Y. (2001). Justice at the millennium: A meta-analytic review of 25 years of organizational justice research. *Journal of Applied Psychology, 86,* 425–445.

Colquitt, J. A., & Simmering, M. J. (1998). Conscientiousness, goal orientation and motivation to learn during the learning process; a longitudinal study. *Journal of Applied Psychology, 83,* 654–665.

Cooper, C. L., & Robertson, I. T. (1986). Editorial forward. In C. L. Cooper & I. T. Robertson (Eds.), *International review of industrial and organizational psychology* (pp. ix–xi), Chichester, England: Wiley.

Cooper, M. D., Phillips, R. A., Sutherland, V. J., & Makin, P. J. (1994). Reducing accidents using goal setting and feedback: A field study. *Journal of Occupational and Organizaitonal Psychology, 67,* 219–241.

Cropanzano, R., & Folger, R. (1991). Procedural justice and worker motivation. In R. M. Steers & L. W. Porter (Eds.), *Motivation and work behavior* (5th ed., pp. 131–143). New York: McGraw-Hill.

Cropanzano, R., & Greenberg, J. (1997). Progress in organizational justice: Tunneling through the maze. In C. L. Cooper & I. T. Robertson (Eds.), *International review of industrial and organizational psychology.* New York: Wiley.

Cropanzano, R., & Wright, T. A. (1999). A 5-year study of change in the relationship between well-being and job performance. *Consulting Psychology Journal: Practice and Research, 51,* 252–265.

Dailey, R. C., & Kirk, D. J. (1992). Distributive and procedural justice as antecedents of job dissatisfaction and intent to turnover. *Human Relations, 45,* 305–317.

Daniels, D., & Mitchell, T. R. (1995, August). *Differential effects of self-efficacy, goals and expectations on task performance.* Paper presented at the 55th Annual Meeting of the Academy of Management, Vancouver, BC, Canada.

Deci, E. L. (1980). *The psychology of self-determination.* Lexington, MA: Lexington.

DeShon, R. P., & Alexander, R. A. (1996). Goal setting effects on implicit and explicit learning of complex tasks. *Organizational Behavior and Human Decision Processes, 65,* 18–36.

Diefendorff, J. M., & Lord, R. G. (2000). *The volitional effects of planning on performance and goal commitment.* Paper presented at the annual meeting of the Society for Industrial and Organizational Psychology, New Orleans, LA.

Donovan, J. J., & Radosevich, D. J. (1998). The moderating role of goal commitment on the goal difficulty-performance relationship: A meta-analytic review and critical reanalysis. *Journal of Applied Psychology, 83*(2), 308–315.

Donovan, M. A., Drasgow, F., & Munson, L. J. (1998). The perceptions of fair interpersonal treatment scale: Development and validation of a measure of interpersonal treatment in the workplace. *Journal of Applied Psychology, 83,* 683–692.

Dowling, W. F., & Sayles, L. R. (1978). *How managers motivate: The imperatives of supervision.* New York: McGraw Hill.

Dulebohn, J. H., & Ferris, G. R. (1999). The role of influence tactics in perceptions of performance evaluations' fairness. *Academy of Management Journal, 42*(3), 288–303.

Dunn, K. S., Mount, M. K., Barrick, M. R., & Ones, D. S. (1995). Relative importance of personality and general mental ability in managers' judgments of applicant qualifications. *Journal of Applied Psychology, 80,* 500–509.

Durham, C. C., Knight, D., & Locke, E. A. (1997). Effect of leader role, team-set goal difficulty, efficacy and tactics on team performance. *Organizational Behavior and Human Decision Processes, 72,* 203–231.

Dweck, C. S. (1986). Motivational processes affecting learning. *American Psychologist, 41,* 1040–1048.

Eden, D. (1992). Leadership expectations: Pygmalion effects and other self-fulfilling prophecies in organizations. *Leadership Quarterly, 3*(4), 271–305.

Eden, D. (1996). *From self efficacy to measure efficacy: Internal and external sources of general and specific efficacy.* Paper presented at the 1996 Academy of Management Meeting, Cincinnati, OH.

Eden, D. (1999, August). *The impact of self-efficacy on work motivation theory and research.* Paper presented at the Academy of Management Annual Meeting, Chicago.

Eden, D., & Aviram, A. (1993). Self-efficacy training to speed reemployment: Helping people to help themselves. *Journal of Applied Psychology, 78,* 352–360.

Eden, D., & Granat-Flomin, R. (2000). *Augmenting means efficacy to improve service performance among computer users: A field experiment in the public sector.* Paper presented at the Annual Conference of the Society for Industrial and Organizational Psychology, New Orleans, LA.

Eden, D., & Kinnar, J. (1991). Modeling galatea: Boosting self-efficacy to increase volunteering. *Journal of Applied Psychology, 76,* 770–780.

Erez, A., Isen, A. M., & Purdy, C. (1999). *The influence of positive-affect on expectancy motivation: Integrating affect and cognition into motivation theories.* Paper presented at the 1999 Academy of Management Annual Meetings, Chicago, IL.

Erez, A., & Judge, T. A. (2001). Relationship of core self-evaluations to goal setting, motivation, and performance. *Journal of Applied Psychology, 86,* 1270–1279.

Erez, M. (1977). Feedback: A necessary condition for the goal setting-performance relationship. *Journal of Applied Psychology, 62,* 624–627.

Estrada, C. A., Isen, A. M., & Young, M. J. (1997). Positive affect improves creative problem solving and influences reported source of practice satisfaction in physicians. *Motivation and Emotion, 18,* 285–299.

Fallon, J. D., Avis, J. M., Kudisch, J. D., Gornet, T. P., & Frost, A. (1998, April). *Conscientiousness as a predictor of productive and counterproductive behaviors.* Paper presented at the annual meeting of the Society for Industrial and Organizational Psychology, Dallas, TX.

Feltz, D. L., & Lirgg, C. D. (1998). Perceived team and player efficacy in hockey. *Journal of Applied Psychology, 83,* 557–564.

Fisher, C. D., & Noble, C. S. (2000). *Emotion and the "Illusory Correlation" between job satisfaction and job performance.* Paper presented at the 2nd Conference on Emotions in Organisational Life, Toronto, Ontario, Canada.

Fisher, S. L., & Ford, J. K. (1998). Differential effects of learner effort and goal orientation on two learning outcomes. *Personnel Psychology, 51*(2), 397–418.

Ford, M. E. (1992). *Motivating humans: Goals, emotions and personal agency beliefs.* Newbury Park, CA: Sage.

Frese, M., & Zapf, D. (1994). Action as the core of work psychology. In M. D. Dunnette, L. M. Hough, & H. Triandis (Eds.), *Handbook of industrial and organizational psychology* (Vol. 4, pp. 271–340). Palo Alto, CA: Consulting Psychologist Press.

Gellatly, I. R. (1996). Conscientiousness and task performance: Test of a cognitive process model. *Journal of Applied Psychology, 81,* 474–482.

George, J. M. (1990). Personality, affect and behavior in groups. *Journal of Applied Psychology, 75,* 107–116.

George, J. M. (1991). State or trait: Effects of positive mood on prosocial behavior at work. *Journal of Applied Psychology, 76,* 299–307.

George, J. M., & Brief, A. P. (1996). Motivational agendas in the workplace: The effects of feelings on focus of attention and work motivation. *Research in Organizational Behavior, 18,* 75–109.

George-Falvy, J. (1996, August). *Effects of task complexity and learning stage on the relationship between participation in goal setting and task performance.* Paper presented at the 56th Annual Meeting of the Academy of Management, Cincinnati, OH.

Ghorpade, J., Hattrup, K., & Lackritz, J. R. (1999). The use of personality measures in cross-cultural research: A test of three personality scales across two countries. *Journal of Applied Psychology, 84*(5), 670–679.

Gibson, C. B. (1999). Do they do what they believe they can? Group efficacy and group effectiveness across tasks and cultures. *Academy of Management Journal, 42,* 138–152.

Gibson, C. B., & Holzinger, I. W. (1998). *Team goals, efficacy and effectiveness: Investigating the differential impact of a team goal setting intervention on self-efficacy, group efficacy, individual effectiveness and team effectiveness.* Presented at Academy of Management Annual Meeting, San Diego, CA.

Gilliland, S. W., & Landis, R. S. (1992). Quality and quantity goals in a complex decision task: Strategies and outcomes. *Journal of Applied Psychology, 77,* 672–681.

Gist, M. E., & Mitchell, T. R. (1992). Self-efficacy: A theoretical analysis of its determinants and malleability. *Academy of Management Review, 17,* 183–211.

Gollwitzer, P. M. (1999). Implementation intentions: Strong effects of simple plans. *American Psychologist, 54*(7), 493–503.

Goltz, S. M. (1999). *Self-efficacy's mediating role in success bred recommitment of resources to a failing course of action.* Paper presented at the Society for Industrial and Organizational Psychology Annual Meeting, Atlanta, GA.

Greenberg, J. (1988). Equity and workplace status: A field experiment. *Journal of Applied Psychology, 73,* 606–613.

Greenberg, J. (1990). Employee theft as a reaction to underpayment inequity: The hidden cost of pay cuts. *Journal of Applied Psychology, 75,* 561–568.

Greenberg, J. (1993). Stealing in the name of justice: Informational and interpersonal moderators of theft reactions to underpayment inequity. *Organizational Behavior and Human Decision Processes, 54,* 81–103.

Greenberg, J. (1994). Using socially fair treatment to promote acceptance of work site smoking ban. *Journal of Applied Psychology, 79,* 288–297.

Greenberg, J., & Scott, K. S. (1996). Why do workers bite the hands that feed them? Employee theft as a social exchange process. In B. M. Staw & L. L. Cummings (Eds.), *Research in organizational behavior* (Vol. 18, pp. 111–156). Greenwich, CT: JAI Press.

Grover, S. L. (1991). Predicting the perceived fairness of parental leave policies. *Journal of Applied Psychology, 76,* 247–255.

Gurin, P., & Brim, O. G., Jr. (1984). Change of self in adulthood: The example of sense of control. In P. B. Baltes & O. G. Brim, Jr. (Eds.), *Life-span development and behavior* (Vol. 6, pp. 281–334). New York: Academic Press.

Guzzo, R. A., Yost, P. R., Campbell, R. J., & Shea, G. P. (1993). Potency in groups. *British Journal of Social Psychology, 32,* 87–105.

Harackiewicz, J. M., Barron, K. E., Carter, S. M., Lehto, A. T., & Elliot, A. J. (1997). Predictors and consequences of achievement goals in the college classroom: Maintaining interest and making the grade. *Journal of Personality and Social Psychology, 73,* 1284–1295.

Heath, C. (1997, August). *On the social psychology of agency relationships: Lay theories of motivation overemphasize extrinsic rewards.* Paper presented at the 1997 Academy of Management Annual Meeting, Boston.

Hinsz, V. B., Kalnbach, L. R., & Lorentz, N. R. (1997). Using judgmental anchors to establish challenging self-set goals without jeopardizing commitment. *Organizational Behavior and Human Decision Processes, 71*(3), 287–308.

Hogan, R., Hogan, J., & Roberts, B. W. (1996). Personality measurement and employment decisions. *American Psychologist, 51,* 469–477.

Hollenbeck, J. R., Williams, C. R., & Klein, H. J. (1989). An empirical examination of the antecedents of commitment to difficult goals. *Journal of Applied Psychology, 74,* 18–23.

Hoover, P., Johnson, D. S., & Schmidt, A. (1998). *Goal orientation effects on motivation: When tasks are dynamically complex.* Paper presented at the Society for Industrial and Organizational Psychology Annual Conference, Dallas, TX.

Huseman, R. C., Hatfield, J. D., & Miles, E. W. (1987). A new perspective on equity theory: The equity sensitive construct. *Academy of Management Review, 12,* 222–234.

Hysong, S. J., & QuiÑones, M. A. (1997, April). *The relationship between self efficacy and performance: A meta-analyses.* Paper presented at 12th Annual Conference of the Society for Industrial and Organizational Psychology, St. Louis, MO.

Iaffaldano, M. T., & Muchinsky, P. M. (1885). Job satisfaction and job performance: A meta-analyses. *Psychological Bulletin, 97,* 251–273.

Ilgen, D. R., Major, D. A., & Tower, S. L. (1994). The cognitive revolution in organizational behavior. In J. Greenberg (Ed.), *Organizational behavior: The state of the science* (pp. 1–22). Hillsdale, NJ: Erlbaum.

Isen, A. M., Shalker, T. E., Clark, M., & Karp, L. (1978). Affect, accessibility of material in memory, and behavior: A cognitive loop? *Journal of Personality and Social Psychology, 36,* 1–12.

Jenkins, G. D., Jr., Mitra, A., Gupta, N., & Shaw, J. D. (1998). Are financial incentives related to performance: A meta-analytic review of empirical research. *Journal of Applied Psychology, 83,* 777–787.

Jex, S. M., & Bliese, P. D. (1999). Efficacy beliefs as a moderator of the impact of work related stressors: A multi-level study. *Journal of Applied Psychology, 84,* 349–361.

Judge, T. A., Bono, J. E., & Locke, E. A. (2000). Personality and job satisfaction: The mediating role of job characteristics. *Journal of Applied Psychology, 85*(2), 237–249.

Judge, T. A., Locke, E. A., Durham, C. C., & Kluger, A. N. (1998). Dispositional effects on job and life satisfaction: The role of core evaluation. *Journal of Applied Psychology, 83,* 17–34.

Judge, T. A., Thoresen, C. J., Bono, J. E., & Patton, G. K. (2001). The job satisfaction-job performance relationship: A qualitative and quantitative review. *Psychological Bulletin, 127,* 376–407.

Kanfer, R. (1990). Motivation theory and industrial and organizational psychology. In M. D. Dunnette & L. M. Hough (Eds.), *Handbook of industrial and organizational psychology* (pp. 75–170). Palo Alto, CA: Consulting Psychologist Press.

Kanfer, R. (1994). Work motivation: New directions in theory and research. In C. L. Cooper & I. T. Robertson (Eds.), *Key reviews in managerial psychology* (pp. 1–53). New York: Wiley.

Kanfer, R., & Ackerman, P. L. (1989). Motivation and cognitive abilities: An integrative/aptitude–treatment interaction approach to skill acquisition [Monograph]. *Journal of Applied Psychology, 74,* 657–690.

Kanfer, R., & Ackerman, P. L. (1996). A self-regulatory skills perspective to reducing cognitive interference. In I. G. Sarason & B. R. Sarason (Eds.), *Cognitive interference theories: Methods and findings* (pp. 153–171). New York: Erlbaum.

Kanfer, R., Ackerman, P. L., & Heggestad, E. D. (1996). Motivational skills and self-regulation for learning: A trait perspective. *Learning and Individual Differences, 8*(3), 185–209.

Kanfer, R., Ackerman, P. L., Murtha, T. C., Dugdale, B., & Nelson, L. (1994). Goal setting, conditions of practice and task performance: A resource allocation perspective. *Journal of Applied Psychology, 79,* 826–835.

Kanfer, R., & Heggestad, E. D. (1997). Motivational traits and skills: A person-centered approach to work motivation. *Research in Organizational Behavior, 19,* 1–56.

Kanfer, R., & Heggestad, E. (2000). Individual differences in trait motivation: Development of the Motivational Trait Questionnaire (MTQ). *International Journal of Educational Research, 33,* 751–776.

Keller, L. M., Bouchard, T. J., Jr., Arvey, R. D., Segal, N. L., & Dawes, R. V. (1992). Work values: Genetic and environmental influences. *Journal of Applied Psychology, 77,* 79–88.

Kiernan, N. M., & Gold, M. A. (1998, August). *Pygmalion in work organizations.* Paper presented at the Annual Meeting of the Academy of Management, San Diego, CA.

King, W. C., Jr., Miles, E. W., & Day, D. D. (1993). A test and refinement of the equity sensitivity construct. *Journal of Organizational Behavior, 14,* 301–317.

Klein, H. J. (1989). An integrated control theory model of work motivation. *Academy of Management Review, 14,* 150–172.

Klein, H. J., & Kim, J. S. (1998). A field study of the influence of situational constraints, leader member exchange and goal commitment on performance. *Academy of Management Journal, 41,* 88–95.

Klein, H. J., & Mulvey, P. W. (1995). Two investigations of the relationships among group goals, goal commitment, cohesion and performance. *Organizational Behavior and Human Decision Processes, 61,* 44–53.

Klein, H. J., Wesson, M. J., Hollenbeck, J. R., & Agle, B. J. (1999). Goal commitment and the goal setting process: Conceptual clarification and empirical synthesis. *Journal of Applied Psychology, 84,* 885–896.

Kluger, A. N., & DeNisi, A. (1996). The effects of feedback interventions on performance: A historical review, a meta-analysis, and a preliminary feedback intervention theory. *Psychological Bulletin, 119,* 254–284.

Komaki, J., Coombs, T., & Schepman, S. (1991). Motivational implications of reinforcement theory. In R. M. Steers & L. W. Porter (Eds.), *Motivation and work behavior* (pp. 87–107). New York: McGraw Hill.

Konovsky, M. S., & Cropanzano, R. (1991). The perceived fairness of employee drug testing as a predictor of employee attitudes and job performance. *Journal of Applied Psychology, 76,* 698–707.

Korsgaard, M. A., Roberson, L., & Rymph, R. D. (1998). What motivates fairness? The role of subordinate assertive behavior on managers' interactional fairness. *Journal of Applied Psychology, 83,* 731–744.

Kraus, S. J. (1995). Attitudes and the prediction of behavior: A meta-analysis of the empirical literature. *Personality and Social Psychology Bulletin, 21*(1), 58–75.

Kuhl, J. (1984). Volitional aspects of achievement motivation and learned helplessness: Toward a comprehensive theory of action control. In B. A. Maher (Ed.), *Progress in experimental personality research* (Vol. 13, pp. 119–170). New York: Academic Press.

Landau, J. C. (1993). The impact of a change in an attendance control system on absenteeism and tardiness. *Journal of Organizational Behavior Management, 13,* 51–70.

Lee, T. W., Locke, E. A., & Phan, S. H. (1997). Explaining the assigned goal-incentive interaction: The role of self-efficacy and personal goals. *Journal of Management, 23,* 541–559.

Leventhal, G. S. (1980). What should be done with equity theory? In K. J. Gergen, M. S. Greenberg, & R. H. Willis (Eds.), *Social exchanges: Advances in theory and research* (pp. 27–55). New York: Plenum.

Lewin, K., Dembo, T., Festinger, L., & Sears, P. S. (1944). Level of aspiration. In J. M. Hunt (Ed.), *Personality and the behavioral disorders* (Vol. 1, pp. 333–378). New York: Ronald.

Liden, R. C., Wayne, S. J., Judge, T. A., Sparrowe, R. T., Kraimer, M. L., & Franz, T. M. (1999). Management of poor performance: A comparison of manager, group member, and group disciplinary decisions. *Journal of Applied Psychology, 84*(6), 835–850.

Lind, E. A., Kray, L., & Thompson, L. (1998). The social construction of injustice: Fairness judgments in response to own and others' unfair treatment by authorities. *Organizational Behavior and Human Decision Processes, 75*(1), 1–22.

Liu, C., & Weiss, H. M. (2000). *Interactive effects of personality and situational strength on goal behaviors.* Purdue University. West Lafayette, Indiana.

Locke, E. A. (1976). The nature and causes of job satisfaction. In M. D. Dunnette (Ed.), *Handbook of industrial and organizational psychology* (pp. 1297–1349). Chicago: Rand McNally.

Locke, E. A. (1991). Goal theory versus control theory: Contrasting approaches to understanding work motivation. *Motivation and Emotion, 15,* 9–28.

Locke, E. A. (1997). The motivation to work: What we know. *Advances in Motivation and Achievement, 10,* 375–412.

Locke, E. A., & Latham, G. P. (1990). *A theory of goal setting and task performance.* Englewood Cliffs, NJ: Prentice Hall.

Locke, E. A., Shaw, K. N., Saari, L. M., & Latham, G. P. (1981). Goal setting and task performance: 1969–1980. *Psychological Bulletin, 90,* 125–152.

Loewenstein, G. (1996). Out of control: Visceral influences on behavior. *Organizational Behavior and Human Decision Processes, 65,* 272–292.

Ludwig, T. D., & Geller, E. S. (1997). Assigned versus participatory goal setting and response generalization. Managing injury control among professional pizza deliverers. *Journal of Applied Psychology, 82,* 253–261.

Luthans, F., & Stajkovic, A. D. (1999). Reinforce for performance: The need to go beyond pay and even rewards. *Academy of Management Executive, 13*(2), 49–57.

Lynch, P. D., Eisenberger, R., & Armeli, S. (1999). Perceived organizational support: Inferior versus superior performance by wary employees. *Journal of Applied Psychology, 84*(4), 467–483.

Martin, B. A., & Manning, D. J., Jr. (1995). Combined effects of normative information and task difficulty on the goal commitment-performance relationship. *Journal of Management, 21*(1), 65–81.

Martocchio, J. J. (1994). Effects of conceptions of ability on anxiety, self-efficacy, and learning in training. *Journal of Applied Psychology, 79,* 819–825.

Martocchio, J. J., & Judge, T. A. (1997). Relationship between conscientiousness and learning in employee training: Mediating influences of self deception and self efficacy. *Journal of Applied Psychology, 82,* 764–773.

Maslow, A. H. (1943). A theory of human motivation. *Psychological Review, 50,* 370–396.

McClelland, D. C. (1961). *The achieving society.* Princeton, NJ: Van Nostrand.

McNatt, D. B. (2000). Ancient Pygmalion joins contemporary management: A meta-analysis of the result. *Journal of Applied Psychology, 85*(2), 314–322.

Mento, A. J., Steel, R. P., & Karren, R. J. (1987). A meta-analytic study of the effects of goal setting on task performance: 1966–1984. *Organizational Behavior and Human Decision Processes, 39,* 52–83.

Mitchell, T. R. (1979). Organizational behavior. *Annual Review of Psychology, 30,* 243–281.

Mitchell, T. R. (1982). Motivation: New directions for theory, research and practice. *Academy of Management Review, 7,* 80–88.

Mitchell, T. R. (1997). Matching motivational strategies with organizational contexts. *Research in Organizational Behavior, 19,* 57–149.

Mitchell, T. R., Hopper, H., Daniels, D., George-Falvy, J., & James, L. R. (1994). Predicting self-efficacy and performance during skill acquisition. *Journal of Applied Psychology, 79*(4), 506–517.

Mitchell, T. R., & Silver, W. S. (1990). Individual and group goals when workers are interdependent: Effects on task strategies and performance. *Journal of Applied Psychology, 75,* 185–193.

Mitchell, T. R., Thompson, K., & George-Falvy, J. (2000). Goal setting: Theory and practice. In C. L. Cooper & E. A. Locke (Eds.), *Industrial and organizational psychology: Linking theory with practice* (pp. 216–249). Oxford, England: Blackwell.

Mone, M. A., Moss, M. C., & White, L. A. (1999, August). *The mediating role of task cognition and strategies in the relationship between the Big Five personality dimensions and achievement.* Presented at the Academy of Management annual meeting, Chicago.

Moorman, R. H. (1991). Relationship between organizational justice and organizational citizenship behaviors: Do fairness perceptions influence employee citizenship? *Journal of Applied Psychology, 76,* 845–855.

Moorman, R. H., Blakely, G. L., & Niehoff, B. P. (1998). Does perceived organizational support mediate the relationship between procedural justice and organizational citizenship behavior? *Academy of Management Journal, 41,* 351–357.

Morgeson, F. P. (1999). *Understanding prosocial constructs in organizational behavior theory and research: Toward a role theory conceptualization.* Presented at the Academy of Management annual meeting, Chicago.

Morris, J. A., & Feldman, D. C. (1996). The dimensions, antecedents and consequences of emotional labor. *Academy of Management Review, 21,* 986–1010.

Morrison, E. W., & Robinson, S. L. (1997). When employees feel betrayed: A model of how psychological contract violation develops. *Academy of Management Review, 22,* 226–256.

Mount, M. K., & Barrick, M. R. (1998). Five reasons why the "Big Five" article has been frequently cited. *Personnel Psychology, 51*(4), 849–858.

Moussa, F. M. (1996). Determinants and process of the choice of goal difficulty. *Group and Organization Management, 21,* 414–438.

Mulvey, P. W., & Klein, H. J. (1998). The impact of perceived loafing and collective efficacy on group goal process and group performance. *Organizational Behavior and Human Decision Processes, 74,* 62–87.

Nease, A. A., Mudgett, B. O., & QuiÑones, M. A. (1999). Relationships among feedback sign, self-efficacy, and acceptance of performance feedback. *Journal of Applied Psychology, 84*(5), 806–814.

Neuman, G. A., & Wright, J. (1999). Team effectiveness: Beyond skills and cognitive ability. *Journal of Applied Psychology, 84,* 376–389.

Nicholson, N. (1997, August). *Hunter-gatherers of the organization: The challenge of evolutionary psychology for management theory and practice.* Paper presented at the annual meetings of the Academy of Management, Boston.

O'Leary-Kelly, A. M., Martocchio, J. J., & Frink, D. D. (1994). A review of the influence of group goals on group performance. *Academy of Management Journal, 37,* 1285–1301.

O'Reilly, C. A., III. (1991). Organizational behavior: Where we've been, where we're going. *Annual Review of Psychology, 42,* 427–458.

Oz, S., & Eden, D. (1994). Restraining the golem: Boosting performance by changing the interpretations of low scores. *Journal of Applied Psychology, 79,* 744–754.

Ozer, D. J., & Reise, S. P. (1994). Personality assessment. *Annual Review of Psychology, 45,* 357–388.

Parker, S. K. (1998). Enhancing role breadth self-efficacy: The roles of job enrichment and other organizational interventions. *Journal of Applied Psychology, 83*(6), 835–852.

Parker, S. K., & Sprigg, C. A. (1999). Minimizing strain and maximizing learning: The role of job demands, job control, and proactive personality. *Journal of Applied Psychology, 84*(6), 925–939.

Parsons, C. K., Fedor, D. B., & Herold, D. M. (1999). *The development of training based self-efficacy in a multidimensional feedback environment.* Paper presented at the Society for Industrial and Organizational Psychology annual meeting, Atlanta, GA.

Pawar, B. S., & Eastman, K. K. (1999, August). *A common conceptual space for employee extra-role behaviors.* Paper presented at the Academy of Management annual meeting, Chicago.

Phillips, J. M., Hollenbeck, J. R., & Ilgen, D. R. (1996). Prevalence and prediction of positive discrepancy creation: Examining a discrepancy between two self-regulation theories. *Journal of Applied Psychology, 81,* 498–511.

Pinder, C. G. (1998). *Work motivation in organizational behavior.* Upper Saddle River, NJ: Prentice-Hall.

Podsakoff, P. M., MacKenzie, S. B., & Ahearne, M. (1997). Moderating effects of goal acceptance on the relationship between group cohesiveness and productivity. *Journal of Applied Psychology, 82,* 974–983.

Pritchard, R. D. (1999). *Productivity measurement and improvement: Organizational case studies.* New York: Praeger.

Prussia, G. E., & Kinicki, A. J. (1996). A motivational investigation of group effectiveness using social-cognitive theory. *Journal of Applied Psychology, 81,* 187–198.

Raghunathan, R., & Pham, M. T. (1999). All negative moods are not equal: Motivational influences of anxiety and sadness on decision making. *Organizational Behavior and Human Decision Processes, 79,* 56–77.

Riggs, M. L., & Knight, P. A. (1994). The impact of perceived group success—failure on motivational beliefs and attitudes: A causal model. *Journal of Applied Psychology, 79,* 755–766.

Roberson, Q. M., Moye, N. A., & Locke, E. A. (1999). Identifying a missing link between participation and satisfaction: The mediating role of procedural justice perceptions. *Journal of Applied Psychology, 84*(4), 585–593.

Roney, C. R. R., Higgins, E. T., & Shah, J. (1995). Goals and framing: How outcome focus influences motivation and emotion. *Journal of Personality and Social Psychology, 21,* 1151–1160.

Rousseau, D. M., & Greller, M. M. (1994). Human resource practices: Administrative contract makers. *Human Resource Management, 33*(3), 385–401.

Salgado, J. F. (1997). The five factor model of personality and job performance in the European Community. *Journal of Applied Psychology, 82*(1), 30–43.

Schaubroeck, J., May, D. R., & Brown, F. W. (1994). Procedural justice explanations and employee reactions to economic hardship: A field experiment. *Journal of Applied Psychology, 79,* 455–460.

Schminke, M., Ambrose, M. L., & Cropanzano, R. S. (2000). The effects of organizational structure on perceptions of procedural fairness. *Journal of Applied Psychology, 85*(2), 294–304.

Schwarzwald, J., Koslowsky, M., & Shalit, B. (1992). A field study of employees' attitudes and behaviors after promotion decisions. *Journal of Applied Psychology, 77,* 511–514.

Seijts, G. H., & Latham, G. P. (2000). The effects of goal setting and group size on performance in a social dilemma. *Canadian Journal of Behavioral Science, 32,* 104–116.

Shalley, C. E. (1995). Effects of coaction, expected evaluation and goal setting on creativity and productivity. *Academy of Management Journal, 38,* 483–503.

Skarlicki, D. P., & Folger, R. (1997). Retaliation in the workplace: The roles of distributive, procedural, and interactional justice. *Journal of Applied Psychology, 82,* 434–445.

Skarlicki, D. P., Folger, R., & Klimiuk, J. (2000, April). *Which quid for what quo pro? Applying advances in organizational justice research to understand the relationship between fairness and job performance.* Paper presented at the annual meeting of the Society for Industrial and Organizational Psychology, New Orleans, LA.

Skarlicki, D. P., & Latham, G. P. (1997). Leadership training in organizational justice to increase citizenship behavior within a labor union: A replication. *Personnel Psychology, 50,* 617–633.

Skinner, B. F. (1990). Can psychology be a science of mind? *American Psychologist, 45,* 1206–1211.

Skinner, B. F., Wellborn, J. G., & Connell, J. P. (1990). What it takes to do well in school and whether I've got it: A process model of perceived control and children's engagement and achievement in school. *Journal of Educational Psychology, 82,* 22–32.

Stajkovic, A. D., & Luthans, F. (1997). A meta-analysis of the effects of organizational behavior modification on task performance, 1975–1995. *Academy of Management Journal, 40,* 1122–1149.

Stajkovic, A. D., & Luthans, F. (1998). Self-efficacy and work related performance: A meta analysis. *Psychological Bulletin, 124,* 240–261.

Staw, B. M., & Barsade, S. G. (1993). Affect and managerial performance: A test of the sadder-but-wiser vs. happier-and-smarter hypotheses. *Administrative Science Quarterly, 38,* 304–331.

Steel, R. P., & Rentsch, J. R. (1997). The dispositional model of job attitude revisited: Findings of a 10 year study. *Journal of Applied Psychology, 82,* 873–879.

Stevens, C. K., & Gist, M. E. (1997). Effects of self-efficacy and goal-orientation training on negotiation skill maintenance: What are the mechanisms? *Personnel Psychology, 50,* 955–978.

Stone, D. N. (1994). Overconfidence in initial self-efficacy judgments: Effects on decision processes and performance. *Organizational Behavior and Human Decision Processes, 59,* 452–474.

Sulzer-Azarof, B., Loafman, B., Merante, R. J., & Hlavacek, A. C. (1990). Improving occupational safety in a large industrial plant: A systematic replication. *Journal of Organizational Behavior Management, 12,* 99–120.

Tabernero, C., & Wood, R. E. (1999). Implicit theories versus the social construal of ability in self-regulation and performance on a complex task. *Organizational Behavior and Human Decision Processes, 78,* 104–127.

Takeuchi, R., Tekleab, A. G., & Taylor, M. S. (2000). *Procedural justice interventions: Restoring psychological contract violations and effects.* Paper presented at the annual meeting of the Society for Industrial and Organizational Psychology, New Orleans, LA.

Taylor, M. S., Masterson, S. S., Renard, M. K., & Tracy, K. B. (1998). Managers' reactions to procedurally just performance management systems. *Academy of Management Journal, 41,* 568–579.

Taylor, M. S., Tracy, K. B., Renard, M. K., Harrison, J. K., & Carrol, S. J. (1996). Due process in performance appraisal: A quasi-experiment in procedural justice. *Administrative Science Quarterly, 40,* 495–523.

Tett, R. P., Jackson, D. N., & Rothstein, M. (1991). Personality measures as predictors of job performance: A meta-analysis review. *Personnel Psychology, 44,* 703–742.

Thibaut, J., & Walker, L. (1975). *Procedural justice: A psychological analysis.* Hillsdale, NJ: Erlbaum.

Thierry, H. (1998). The reflection theory on compensation. In M. Erez, U. Kleinbeck, & H. Thierry (Eds.), *Work motivation in the context of a globalizing economy.* Hillsdale, NJ: Erlbaum.

Thomas, K. M., & Mathieu, J. E. (1994). Role of causal attributions in dynamic self-regulation and goal processes. *Journal of Applied Psychology, 79,* 812–818.

Thompson, K. R., Hochwarter, W. A., & Mathys, N. J. (1997). Stretch targets: What makes them effective? *Academy of Management Executive, 11*(3), 48–60.

Trafimow, D., & Sniezek, J. A. (1994). Perceived expertise and its effect on confidence. *Organizational Behavior and Human Decision Processes, 57,* 290–302.

Tsui, A. S., & Ashford, S. J. (1994). Adaptive self-regulation: A process view of managerial effectiveness. *Journal of Management, 20,* 93–121.

Tubbs, M. E. (1994). Commitment and the role of ability in motivation: Comment on Wright, O'Leary-Kelly, Cortina, Klein & Hollenbeck. *Journal of Applied Psychology, 79,* 804–811.

Tyler, T. R., & DeGoey, P. (1995). Collective restraint in social dilemmas: Procedural justice and social identification effects on support for authorities. *Journal of Personality and Social Psychology, 69,* 482–497.

Vancouver, J., Thompson, C. M., & Williams, A. A. (1999). *The changing signs in the relationships between self-efficacy, personal goals and performance.* Paper presented at the Academy of Management annual meeting, Chicago.

VandeWalle, D. (1999). *Goal orientation comes of age for adults: A literature review.* Paper presented at the Academy of Management annual meeting, Chicago.

VanEerde, W. (2000). Procrastination: Self-regulation in initiating aversive goals. *Applied Psychology: An International Review, 49,* 372–389.

VanEerde, W., & Thierry, H. (1996). Vroom's expectancy models and work-related criteria: A meta-analysis. *Journal of Applied Psychology, 81,* 575–586.

Viken, R. J., Rose, R. J., Kaprio, J., & Koskenvuo, M. (1994). A developmental genetic analysis of adult personality: Extraversion and neuroticism from 18 to 59 years of age. *Journal of Personality and Social Psychology, 66,* 722–730.

Vinchur, A. J., Schippmann, J. S., Switzer, F. S., III, & Roth, P. L. (1998). A meta-analytic review of predictors of job performance for sales people. *Journal of Applied Psychology, 83,* 586–597.

Vroom, V. H. (1964). *Work and motivation.* New York: Wiley.

Watson, D., & Clark, L. A. (1984). Negative affectivity: The disposition to experience negative emotional states. *Psychological Bulletin, 96,* 465–490.

Wegge, J. (1999, June). *Participation in group goal setting: Some novel findings and a comprehensive theory as a new ending to an old story.* Third International Conference on Work Motivation, Sydney, Australia.

Wegner, D. M., & Wheatley, T. (1999). Apparent mental causation: Sources of the experience of will. *American Psychologist, 54*(7), 480–492.

Weingart, L. R. (1992). Impact of group goals, task component complexity, effort and planning on group performance. *Journal of Applied Psychology, 77,* 682–693.

Weiss, H. M., & Brief, A. P. (in press). Affect at work: An historical perspective. In R. L. Payne & C. L. Cooper (Eds.), *Emotions at work: Theory, research, and applications in management.* Chichester, England: Wiley.

Weiss, H. M., & Cropanzano, R. (1996). Affective Events Theory: A theoretical discussion of the structure, causes and consequences of affective experiences at work. In B. M. Staw & L. L. Cummings (Eds.), *Research in organizational behavior* (Vol. 18, pp. 1–74). Greenwich, CT: JAI Press.

Weiss, H. M., Nicholas, J. P., & Daus, C. S. (1999). An examination of the joint effects of affective experiences and job beliefs on job satisfaction and faviations in affective experiences over time. *Organizational Behavior and Human Decision Processes, 78,* 1–24.

Welsh, D. H. B., Luthans, F., & Sommer, S. M. (1993). Organizational behavior modification goes to Russia: Replicating an experimental analysis across cultures and tasks. *Journal of Organizational Behavior Management, 13,* 15–30.

Westaby, J. D. (1999). *Identifying motivational attributes underlying stable organizational attitudes: Using multiple methods to compare expectancy theory and reasons theory.* Working Paper, Columbia University, New York.

Whyte, G. (1998). Recasting Janis's groupthink model: The key role of collective efficacy in decision fiascos. *Organizational Behavior and Human Decision Processes, 73*(2/3), 185–209.

Williams, M. L., Gordon, R. E., III, McManus, J., McDaniel, M., & Nguyen, N. (2000, April). *A meta-analysis of the antecedents and consequences of pay satisfaction.* Paper presented at the annual meeting of the Society for Industrial and Organizational Psychology, New Orleans, LA.

Wilpert, B. (1995). Organizational behavior. *Annual Review of Psychology, 46,* 59–90.

Winters, D., & Latham, G. (1996). The effects of learning versus outcome goals on a simple versus a complex task. *Group and Organization Management, 21,* 236–250.

Wofford, J. C., Goodwin, V. L., & Premack, S. (1992). Meta-analysis of the antecedents of personal goal level and of the antecedents and consequences of goal commitment. *Journal of Management, 18,* 595–615.

Wood, R. E., Atkins, P. W. B., & Bright, J. E. H. (1999). Bonuses, goals, and instrumentality effects. *Journal of Applied Psychology, 84*(5), 703–720.

Wood, R. E., & Bandura, A. (1989). Social-cognitive theory of organizational management. *Academy of Management Review, 14,* 361–384.

Wood, R. E., George-Falvy, J., & Debowski, S. (2001). Motivation and information search on complex tasks. In M. Erez, U. Klienbeck, & H. Thierry (Eds.), *Work motivation in the global context of a Globalizing Economy* (pp. 27–48). Mahwah, NJ: Erlbaum.

Wood, R. E., & Locke, E. A. (1990). Goal setting and strategy effects on complex tasks. In B. M. Staw & L. L. Cummings (Eds.), *Research in organizational behavior* (Vol. 12, pp. 73–110). Greenwich, CT: JAI Press.

Wood, R. E., Mento, A. J., & Locke, E. A. (1987). Task complexity as a moderator of goal effects: A meta-analysis. *Journal of Applied Psychology, 72,* 416–425.

Wright, P. M. (1990). Operationalization of goal difficulty as a moderator of the goal difficulty—performance relationship. *Journal of Applied Psychology, 75,* 227–234.

Wright, P. M. (1992). A theoretical examination of the constraint validity of operationalizations of goal difficulty. *Human Resource Management Review, 2,* 275–298.

Wright, P. M., George, J. M., Farnsworth, S. R., & McMahan, G. C. (1993). Productivity and extra-role behavior: The effects of goals and incentives on spontaneous helping. *Journal of Applied Psychology, 78,* 374–381.

Wright, P. M., & Kacmar, K. M. (1994). Goal specificity as a determinant of goal commitment and goal change. *Organizational Behavior and Human Decision Processes, 59,* 242–260.

Wright, P. M., O'Leary-Kelly, A. M., Cortina, J. M., Klein, H. J., & Hollenbeck, J. R. (1994). On the meaning and measurement of goal commitment. *Journal of Applied Psychology, 79,* 795–803.

Wright, T. A., & Cropanzano, R. (2000). Psychological well being and job satisfaction as predictors of job performance. *Journal of Occupational Health Psychology, 5*(1), 84–94.

Wright, T. A., & Staw, B. M. (1999). Affect and favorable work outcomes: Two longitudinal tests of the happy-productive worker thesis. *Journal of Organizational Behavior, 20,* 1–23.

CHAPTER 11

Job Attitudes

CHARLES L. HULIN AND TIMOTHY A. JUDGE

In this chapter we discuss portions of the theoretical and empirical literature on job satisfaction. Job satisfaction is an application of the original conceptual definitions of social attitudes, although the deviations that job attitudes have taken from these beginnings are as important as the direct linear connections. We discuss theoretical models of antecedents of job satisfactions. Our discussion of these theoretical models emphasizes constructs (e.g., frames of reference, organizational withdrawal) rather than individual variables as manifestations of the constructs (e.g., local unemployment, turnover); there are more individual variables that may be regarded as antecedents or consequences of job attitudes than can be reasonably discussed in this chapter. We focus our discussion on three general areas: theoretically necessary breadth of measures of constructs, the strength and generality of the job satisfaction–job behavior relationship, and new directions of job attitude research.

We discuss differences and similarities between social attitudes and job satisfactions in terms of their relations with individual job behaviors and general behavioral constructs. Differences between social attitudes and job satisfactions

may tell us as much about social attitudes as it does about job satisfactions. The differences may also suggest questions about the ecological validity of investigations of social attitudes that have studied a limited range of (student) populations, settings, and content or targets of the attitudes.

We address the departure of the study of job attitudes from the original tripartite definitions of social attitudes that emphasized *cognitive* and *affective,* and *behavioral* elements of attitude space (Campbell, 1963; Thurstone, 1928). We have focused job satisfaction on judgment-based, cognitive evaluations of jobs on characteristics or features of jobs and generally ignored affective antecedents of evaluations of jobs and episodic events that happen on jobs. The issues are not the narrow questions about affect or emotions as *influences* on job attitudes versus affective responses as *components* of a tripartite conception of attitudes. The issue is the cognitive emphasis that has ignored systematic consideration of affect and emotion as causes, components, or consequences of job satisfactions (Weiss & Brief, in press).

DEFINITION AND NATURE OF JOB SATISFACTION

Job satisfactions are multidimensional psychological responses to one's job. These responses have cognitive (evaluative), affective (or emotional), and behavioral components.

The authors thank Marcus Crede, Reeshad Dalal, Pat Laughlin, Andy Miner, and Howard Weiss for their discussions of the social and job attitude literature and recent theoretical developments. Their contributions improved the final product.

Job satisfactions refer to internal cognitive and affective states accessible by means of verbal—or other behavioral—and emotional responses. The multidimensional responses can be arrayed along good-bad, positive-to-negative continua. They may be quantified using assessment techniques that assess evaluations of features or characteristics of the job, emotional responses to events that occur on the job, and behavioral dispositions, intentions, and enacted behaviors.

Our definition is consistent with definitions of social attitudes offered by Campbell (1963), Eagley and Chaiken (1993), Fishbein (1980), Fishbein and Ajzen (1972, 1975), Thurstone (1928), Triandis (1980), and others. These definitions stress the role of cognitive evaluations in social attitudes but also include affect and behaviors as components of attitudes. Eagley and Chaiken (1993), for example, defined attitude as a psychological tendency that is expressed by evaluating a particular entity with some degree of favor or disfavor. However, they include overt and covert cognitive, affective, and behavioral classes of responding in the term *evaluating*.

The original tripartite definition of attitudes comprising cognitive, affective, and behavioral elements has eroded in industrial and organizational (I/O) psychology until we are left with assessments of attitudes as cognitive evaluations of social objects. This change seems to have occurred almost by default, perhaps as a result of the zeitgeist in American psychology that has led to the adoption of theoretical positions favoring cognitions even in the absence of definitive data (Zajonc, 1980, 1984).

We acknowledge that affective reactions have an evaluative component. Affective responses are more than evaluations, however. Further, all evaluative judgments are not affect, although affect may influence cognitive evaluations. Evaluations of an object very likely modestly influence emotional responses to the object; the two types or responses are not the same.

Cranny, Smith, and Stone (1992) stated that "Although a review of published works shows that constitutive definitions of the construct vary somewhat from one work to the next, there appears to be general agreement that job satisfaction is an *affective (that is emotional) reaction* [italics added] to a job that results from the incumbent's comparison of actual outcomes with those that are desired (expected, deserved, and so on)" (p. 1). This definition appears to assume that comparisons of actual outcomes with those desired from a job will reflect variance due to *emotional* reactions, and these emotional reactions can be captured using structured, paper-and-pencil measures of judgments and evaluations. There is little doubt that until very recently this was the generally agreed-upon definition; comparisons between job outcomes and desired outcomes were treated as a reasonable basis for measurement of job attitudes.

As a result of the focus of research on satisfaction as a stable individual difference variable, we have a good picture of a network of relations with job attitudes, assessed as cognitive evaluations of job characteristics, as its core construct. These relations are useful and reliable (Roznowski & Hulin, 1992). This network may, however, be a biased view of a broader construct of job attitudes that also includes affective or emotional reactions.

Measurement of job affect creates problems for researchers. Affective reactions are likely to be fleeting and episodic—that is, state variables rather than consistent chronic, traitlike variables (Diener & Larsen, 1984; Tellegen, Watson, & Clark, 1999; Watson, 2000). Measurement of affect should reflect its statelike, episodic nature.

Triandis (1980), Fishbein (1980), Eagley and Chaiken (1993), and others have included affective responses in the assessments of social attitudes. Emotional or affective responses to objects or entities assessed as stable variables have typically not improved predictions of behavioral intentions or behaviors. One may regard social and job attitudes as "acquired behavioral dispositions" (Campbell, 1963) without treating relations with behavioral intentions or behaviors as the touchstone of the usefulness of an affective component of attitudes. Further, typical assessments of affect as stable, chronic responses may not adequately reflect true affect or emotional responses to objects.

Weiss and Cropanzano (1996) and George (1989) argued that affect and mood on the job are important components of job attitudes and potentially important predictors of some job behaviors. The possibility that on-the-job affect will spill over, more generally than do job attitudes, to nonjob behaviors that reflect emotional well-being cannot be overlooked. Testing a theory that includes affect, however, requires assessments that capture the dynamic, within-person manifestations of affect and emotional reactions. Otherwise we become enmeshed in a methodological stalemate (Larsen & Csikszentmihalyi, 1983) in which researchers attempt to study propositions of newly developed theories with methods and analyses appropriate only to the needs of an older generation of theoretical models. Weiss, Nicholas, and Daus (1999); Totterdell (2000); Miner (2001); Miner, Glomb, and Hulin (2001); and Ilies and Judge (in press) assessed affective responses on the job using assessments and analyses that handle the within-person and multilevel demands of conceptualizations and assessments of affect as a dynamic variable. These conceptual and empirical efforts are reviewed at the end of this chapter.

CONCEPTUAL SIMILARITY AND EMPIRICAL DIFFERENCES BETWEEN SOCIAL AND JOB ATTITUDES

If we define attitudes as psychological tendencies expressed by cognitive, affective, and behavioral evaluations of a particular entity, then in the study of job satisfaction different aspects of the job or the job as a whole become the target of the evaluations. The conceptual overlap between social attitudes and job satisfactions is apparent. Empirical differences are also apparent. Relations between social attitudes and behaviors and between-job satisfactions and behaviors are an important difference. At the risk of oversimplification, social attitudes are typically weakly related to specific behaviors (Campbell, 1963; Eagley & Chaiken, 1993; Fishbein, 1980; Fishbein & Ajzen, 1972, 1974, 1975; Wicker, 1969); job attitudes are generally reliably and moderately strongly related to relevant job behaviors. Reasons for the lack of reliable relations between social attitudes and behaviors have been discussed by Campbell (1963), Doob (1947), Fishbein and Ajzen (1974), Hull, (1943), and Thurstone (1928). Eagley and Chaiken (1993), on the other hand, concluded that the relationship between attitudes and behaviors is reliable if a number of other variables are taken into consideration.

Doob (1947), Hull (1943), Thurstone (1928), and Fishbein and Ajzen (1974) have argued that when we identify individuals' attitudes toward an object, we have only identified their general orientation toward the object; we have not identified if or how they may choose to enact a specific behavior regarding that object. Their attitude will, however, correspond to the centroid of a broad behavioral construct comprising many specific behaviors. Correlations between general attitudes toward an object and specific, isolated behaviors toward that construct are subject to many sources of variance having much to do with behavioral thresholds, distributions, base rates, opportunities, norms, and so on that may overwhelm any underlying relationship between an attitude and a behavioral orientation toward the object. To assess attitude-behavior correspondence properly, we need to assess the correspondence between a general attitude toward the object and the general value, positive or negative, of a broad family of enacted behaviors (Fishbein, 1980; Fishbein & Ajzen, 1972, 1974).

Fishbein and Ajzen (1974, 1975) further argued we need to distinguish among attitudes toward an object, attitudes toward a behavior, and behavioral intentions to carry out that act. The first two constructs predict the last, but behavioral intentions establish the correspondence between attitudes and an act. Relations between attitudes toward acts and behavioral intentions are generally high; relations between attitudes toward an object and intentions to engage in specific behaviors related to that object are occasionally moderately large but are generally modest. Intentions, however, are related to behaviors. This argument shifted the focus from studies of general attitudes and a variety of relevant behaviors to analyses of the antecedents and of specific behavioral intentions. In this research strategy, every behavior requires the analysis of a different, behavioral intention. Behavioral intentions are the idiot savants of social and I/O psychology; they do one thing very well, but that is all they do. Dawes and Smith (1985) referred to relations between intentions and behaviors as a reductio ad absurdum.

Job Satisfaction and Job Behaviors

Research on relations between job satisfaction and specific behaviors has generated a set of generally positive results. Job attitudes are reliably related to a variety of specific job behaviors (Hulin, 1991; Roznowski & Hulin, 1992). Relations between multiple-act behavioral families and general job satisfaction are stronger and theoretically more useful than are relations between general job satisfaction and specific behaviors (Fisher & Locke, 1992; Roznowski & Hulin, 1992). Nonetheless, the general finding is that a wide variety of important specific behaviors are consistently related to job satisfactions. If one has an applied goal predicting a specific behavior, then a measure of intentions to engage in that behavior during the time period of interest is the predictor of choice. However, if corrections for attenuation, sampling variance, and restrictions due to base rates of infrequent behaviors are applied to the observed relations between general job attitudes (satisfactions) and specific job behaviors, the resulting estimates of population correlations are sizable and useful and may provide a better basis for understanding the attitude-behavior nexus (Hulin, 1991, 2001).

Fisher and Locke (1992), Hulin (1991), and Roznowski and Hulin (1992) noted that empirical relations between general attitudes and specific behaviors may be poor estimates of theoretical population correlations involving general job attitudes and the underlying behavioral propensity that generated the observed behavioral manifestation. An empirical correlation of $-.12$, for example, is consistent with a general unifactor model in which job satisfaction has a loading of $-.6$ and a continuously distributed absence propensity has a loading of .5 on the same factor. These loadings generate a theoretical correlation of $-.30$, but after the correlation is degraded for influences of absence distributions and other statistical influences (but not unreliability), the empirical correlation between satisfaction and absences over a short period of time may be trivially small and a poor guide to the theoretical value.

Roznowski and Hulin (1992) concluded that after an individual joins an organization, a vector of scores on a well-constructed, validated set of job satisfaction scales is the most informative data an organizational psychologist or manager can have about an individual employee and his or her likely behaviors. As evidence for this they cited a range of empirical relations between job satisfactions and specific job behaviors that include the following:

- Attendance at work (Scott & Taylor, 1985; Smith, 1977),
- Turnover decisions (Carsten & Spector, 1987; Hom, 2001; Hom, Katerberg, & Hulin, 1979; Hulin, 1966b, 1968; Miller, Katerberg, & Hulin, 1979; Mobley, Horner, & Hollingsworth, 1978),
- Decisions to retire (Hanisch & Hulin, 1990, 1991; Schmitt & McCune, 1981),
- Psychological withdrawal behaviors (Roznowski, Miller, & Rosse, 1992),
- Prosocial and organizational citizenship behaviors (Bateman & Organ, 1983; Farrell, 1983; Roznowski et al., 1992),
- Prounion representation votes (Getman, Goldberg, & Herman, 1976; Schriesheim, 1978; Zalesny, 1985), and
- Prevote unionization activity (Hamner & Smith, 1978).

Attendance at work, psychological withdrawal, and prosocial behaviors appear to be manifestations of a general family of responses labeled *work withdrawal* that reflect attempts to withdraw from, or become involved with, the quotidian work tasks that make up a job. Turnover and retirement decisions are manifestations of a family of behaviors labeled *job withdrawal* (Hanisch & Hulin, 1990, 1991). Voting patterns in union representation elections and prevote activity may be manifestations of a family of behaviors that represent *formal attempts to change the characteristics of a work situation* (Hulin, 1991). A focus on general behavioral families, rather than on individual behavioral manifestations of the underlying constructs, should generate more reliable relations and greater understanding of the behavioral responses to job satisfactions.

Generally, job satisfactions are reliably related to many job behaviors and to the more general behavioral families. This contrasts with a *lack* of general and reliable relations between social attitudes and specific behaviors (Fishbein & Ajzen, 1974; Wicker, 1969). These general satisfaction–specific job behavior relations, for all their applied importance, should not blind us to the theoretically more meaningful and empirically

stronger relations between general job attitudes and general behavioral constructs (Fisher & Locke, 1992; Hanisch, Hulin, & Roznowski, 1998; Hulin, 1991; Roznowski & Hansich, 1990; Roznowski & Hulin, 1992).

There are many conceptual similarities between social attitudes and job satisfactions. There are also important differences between these constructs as studied. Job attitudes, qua evaluations of the job, may be more salient and accessible for workers than the social attitudes typically assessed in social attitude research. Having a dissatisfying job that may occupy the majority of one's waking hours is nearly inescapable from first awakening until the return home. A job is not something we think of only occasionally as most do about religion, capital punishment, an honor system on campus, or donating blood. We experience jobs on a nearly constant basis during our working hours; stress caused by job dissatisfaction is our constant companion. Individuals are also aware of strongly positive job attitudes or job affect throughout the day. The salience and importance of jobs and job attitudes may ensure that job attitudes and job behaviors are more nearly congruent than are many social attitudes and social behaviors.

Job attitudes are also highly personal; one's job intimately involves the self. Job satisfactions represent evaluations of the respondent's own job, the activity that serves to identify us, not an evaluation of an abstract concept or object as social attitudes typically are. We are what we do. We no longer wear our occupations as our names as people did in the past—Archer, Baker, Bowman, Brewer, Butcher, Carpenter, Cartwright, Clark, Cook, Cooper, Dalal, Farrier, Fletcher, Hunter, Judge, Mason, Miller, Miner, Porter, Sawyer, Scribner, Shoemaker, Smith, Squire, Tailor, Tanner, Tinker, Wagner, Weaver, and so on—but our jobs remain major sources of our self-identities. We are defined privately and socially by what we do (Green, 1993; Hulin, 2001). Work is a source of autonomy. In individualist cultures, autonomy is among the most strongly held values. In the United States and other individualist cultures, our autonomy often rests on the foundation of a job, the money it provides, the goods that can be purchased with that money, and the value of "standing on one's own two feet." Attitudes toward that part of ourselves that one evaluates in a standard job attitude scale cannot be divorced from the individual respondent whose attitudes are being assessed. This degree of personal investment in the attitude object is typically absent from social attitudes assessed in most attitude studies.

Summary

Reliable relations between job satisfactions and job behaviors may reflect the unavoidability of feelings about jobs and the salience of jobs to most employees. If we cannot avoid the negative feelings engendered by a job, we avoid as much of the job as we can; we engage in work withdrawal. Job attitudes, if strong enough, may lead to *job withdrawal* in the form of retirement or quitting. Voting in favor of union representation is an attempt to change the nature of one's job permanently. Positive job attitudes are less likely to engender withdrawal behaviors or attempts to change the work situation.

Job Satisfaction and Job Performance

Recent evidence suggests that job satisfaction is meaningfully related to job performance. Judge, Thoresen, Bono, and Patton (2001) provided an updated meta-analysis of this literature. Their meta-analysis addressed several potential problems with an earlier meta-analysis (Iaffaldano & Muchinsky, 1985) that reported a nonsignificant relationship. Iaffaldano and Muchinsky (1985) combined results from specific facets of job satisfaction. Their estimated .17 correlation between satisfaction and performance was based on the average of the correlations between specific job satisfaction facets and job performance. This approach is not an appropriate estimate of the relationship between *overall* job satisfaction and job performance. The average relationship aggregated across job satisfaction facets is not the same as the relationship involving the overall construct. Facets of job satisfaction are part of a hierarchical construct of overall job satisfaction; the facets are manifestations of a general construct. A composite of the facets or other estimate of the shared variance among the facets is a stronger basis for the relation between general job attitudes and job performance. Using this approach, Judge et al. estimated the corrected correlation to be .30.

An important area for research is the nature of job performance (Borman, 1991; Campbell, 1992). It is a broad construct, not a behavior. Job performance comprises many specific behaviors typically measured through a subjective supervisory evaluation. That job performance is composed of many behaviors is an advantage in terms of its psychometric breadth. It is a disadvantage in terms of isolating its antecedents, consequences, and correlates. Research on job satisfaction–job performance relationships will continue, but we are unlikely to understand the nature of the relationship without a knowledge of the myriad behaviors comprised by job performance and how these behaviors combine and interact with exogenous factors to generate overall job performance. Judge et al. (2001) found similar correlations regardless of the gross nature of the measure of job performance (supervisory evaluations, objective output, etc.), but even objective output is a result of many behaviors by an employee, technological influences, group contributions, feedback from managers, and opportunities.

Teasing apart the causal nature of satisfaction-performance relationships, investigating mediators and moderators of the relationship, and disaggregating performance to understand what specific behaviors are typically comprised by it may be illuminating. Some job behaviors may result from job satisfaction. Others may cause job satisfaction. Still others may be both causes and effects of job satisfaction. If job performance is disaggregated, behavioral families can be reconstructed, as have behavioral families in the withdrawal area, to highlight relations with antecedents and advance theoretical understanding. Some researchers have already begun to break job performance down into behavioral families in theoretical (Borman & Motowidlo, 1997; Campbell, 1992) and empirical (Scullen, 1998) studies.

THEORETICAL MODELS OF JOB ATTITUDES

In the following sections we do not review every theory on the formation of job satisfaction. For example, Herzberg's (1967) two-factor theory is one of the best known job satisfaction theories, but we do not review it here. Numerous reviews have effectively laid the theory to rest (e.g., Hulin & Smith, 1967; Korman, 1971; Locke, 1969; Wernimont, 1966), and we see little reason to till further in what is essentially barren ground. We also do not review the social information approach to job attitudes. This approach to attitude formation accounts for attitudes in information-impoverished laboratory conditions. It has not been applied extensively to account for attitudes on organizational employees in normal working situations.

The Cornell Model

The Cornell model of job attitudes (Hulin, 1991; Smith, Kendall, & Hulin, 1969) was the theoretical foundation of a series of studies of job and retirement attitudes. Two products of this research effort were the Job Descriptive Index (JDI), the most widely used measure of job satisfaction in use today (Cranny et al., 1992, p. 2; DeMeuse, 1985) and the Retirement Descriptive Index (RDI). A modified version of the Cornell model is depicted in Figure 11.1. This figure depicts sources of influence on frames of reference and how they might influence the *costs* of work-role membership and the *value* of work-role outcomes to job incumbents, with hypothesized effects on relations between job inputs, job outcomes, and job attitudes.

The Cornell model is differentiated from other theories of job attitudes by the influences of frames of reference on evaluations of job outcomes, as initially formulated (Smith et al.,

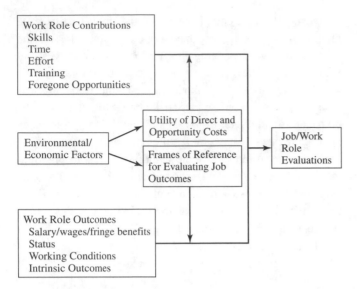

Figure 11.1   Cornell model of job attitudes.

1969), and also on job inputs, as modified by Hulin (1991) incorporating March and Simon's (1958) input-outcome economic model of job attitudes. The frame of reference on standards for evaluating job outcomes was adapted from Helson's (1948, 1964) work on adaptation-level theory. The concept of frames of reference as generated and modified by individuals' experiences was used to account in part for differences in job satisfactions of individuals on objectively identical jobs. Some employees working on objectively unpleasant jobs, with few positive outcomes, express positive evaluations of their work and working conditions, whereas some employees on objectively highly desirable jobs evaluate their jobs quite negatively.

Data supporting the influence of frames of reference were provided by Kendall (1963) and Hulin (1966a). Kendall (1963) reported an analysis of data from employees of 21 organizations located in 21 different communities. Significant negative correlations between community prosperity and job satisfactions were obtained. Hulin (1966a) extended Kendall's (1963) study on a sample of 1,950 employees working in 300 different communities employed by the same organization, doing the same work at the same wage rates. The results confirmed the effects on job satisfactions of frames of reference indexed by economic conditions of communities, the extent of substandard housing, and productive farming in the area. There were consistent negative correlations between economic conditions in communities (scored positively) and job attitudes and positive correlations between percentage of substandard housing and job attitudes. These results were interpreted as meaning that prosperous communities with few slums and the jobs of other workers in the community influenced employees' frames of reference for evaluating work, working conditions, and pay;

prosperous conditions lead to higher frames of reference and lower job satisfactions. Workers living in poor communities tend to evaluate their jobs positively because the alternative might be a worse job or no job at all.

Summary

The Cornell model highlights the influence of factors exogenous to the individual and the organization on job attitudes and how these factors are translated into effects on evaluations of jobs through their influence on individual differences. This inclusion of factors that characterize broader social and economic settings of organizations and jobs emphasizes limitations of the study of employees removed from their social and economic contexts.

Thibaut and Kelley's Comparison Level Model of Satisfaction

Thibaut and Kelley's (1959) comparison level model was developed to account for satisfactions an individual derived from a dyadic relationship or membership in a group. The core of the model is comparisons of outcomes from a focal role with outcomes directly or vicariously experienced by the individual in past dyadic roles. The distribution of role outcomes establishes the *comparison level (CL)*. Roles that provide outcomes less than the CL are dissatisfying; those with role outcomes greater than the CL are satisfying. Generalizing Thibaut and Kelley's (1959) model to job satisfactions assumes that group or dyadic membership and work roles are analogous (for the formation of attitudes) and that the influences of other roles are from outcomes directly or vicariously experienced.

A second comparison level, *comparison level for alternatives* (CL_{ALT}), is also important in the Thibaut and Kelley (1959) model. CL_{ALT} refers to the outcomes one could receive from the best alternative role available to the person. These alternative role outcomes seem to be conceptually related to opportunity costs of holding a given job. The difference between the outcomes from the current role and CL_{ALT} determines the likelihood of the individual changing roles. These relationships hypothesized by Thibaut and Kelley (1959) are shown in Table 11.1.

The situations depicted in Table 11.1 show the relations among current role outcomes, CL, comparisons for alternatives, CL_{ALT}, satisfaction, and likely role withdrawal behaviors. The $>$ and $<$ symbols indicate situations in which the outcomes from the focal role are greater or less than CL and CL_{ALT}, respectively. Satisfaction is influenced by CL,

TABLE 11.1 Relations Between CL, CL_{ALT}, Satisfaction, and Behavior

Current Role Outcomes	CL	CL_{ALT}	Satisfaction	Behavior
Situation A	>	>	Satisfied	Stay
Situation B	>	<	Satisfied	Leave
Situation C	<	>	Dissatisfied	Stay
Situation D	<	<	Dissatisfied	Leave

Note. CL = comparison level. CL_{ALT} = comparison level for alternatives. > and < indicate situations in which the outcomes from the focal role are greater than or less than CL and CL_{ALT}, respectively.

behavior by CL_{ALT}. We would add that withdrawal from a role does not mean only quitting. Leaving a relationship may take many forms (Hanisch & Hulin, 1990, 1991; Simon, 1975).

The relations among CL, CL_{ALT}, satisfactions, and role withdrawal are complex. The empirical literature suggests that satisfaction is correlated with job withdrawal—leaving a job—operationalized by a number of behaviors. However, local economic conditions may reduce job withdrawal through the operation of CL_{ALT} because there are few alternatives available with superior outcomes. We expect relations between job attitudes and organizational withdrawal, both work and job (Hanisch & Hulin, 1990, 1991; Hulin, 1991). The specific withdrawal behaviors enacted may differ depending on situational constraints (Hanisch, Hulin, & Seitz, 1996).

Summary

Thibaut and Kelley's (1959) comparison level model highlights interactions of factors exogenous to the individual or the job in the formation of job attitudes and as influences on job behaviors. The basis for CL and satisfactions are outcomes from past roles; the bases for withdrawal behaviors are outcomes from currently available alternative work roles. Past roles and currently available alternative roles are exogenous factors that limit relationships between endogenous factors and job satisfactions and constrain the effectiveness of organizational interventions designed to influence job attitudes or control organizational withdrawal behaviors.

Value-Percept Model

Locke (1976) defined *values* as that which one desires or considers important. His value-percept model holds that job satisfaction results from the attainment of important values. The model expresses job satisfaction as follows: Satisfaction = (want − have) × importance, or

$$S = (V_c - P) \times V_i,$$

where S is satisfaction, V_c is value content (amount wanted), P is the perceived amount of the value provided by the job, and V_i is the importance of the value to the individual. Locke hypothesized that discrepancies between what is desired by the person and what is received from the job are dissatisfying only if the job attribute is important to the individual. A discrepancy between the pay level desired and the pay provided, for example, is assumed to be more dissatisfying to individuals who value pay highly than to those who value pay to a lesser degree. Because individuals consider multiple facets when evaluating their job satisfaction, the cognitive calculus is repeated for each job facet. Overall satisfaction is estimated by aggregating across all contents of a job weighted by their importance to the individual.

What one desires (V_c, or want) and what one considers important (V_i, or importance) are conceptually distinct; in practice, people may not distinguish the two. An individual who values a job attribute is likely to desire it. Dachler and Hulin (1969) found strong relations between satisfaction with a job facet and the rated importance of that facet. They also reported that the strength of the relationship varied by method of assessing both satisfaction and importance.

Wainer (1976) discussed the general issue of weighting (multiplying by importance or other variables) and combining correlated facets of any general construct. As long as the facets are correlated, linear restraints make improvement in the weighted linear combination over a unit weighting of standardized scores of the facets unlikely. The reliability of weighted discrepancy scores generated by multiplying a difference between two unreliable variables by a third unreliable variable may be problematical. Despite the theoretical information in importance, empirical gains from weighting deficiencies by importance may not be realized (Mikes & Hulin, 1968).

Rice, Gentile, and McFarlin (1991) found that facet importance moderated the relationships between facet amount and facet satisfaction. They also found, however, that facet importance did not moderate the relationship between facet satisfaction and overall job satisfaction. Simple aggregations of facet satisfactions may predict overall satisfaction because facet importance (intensity) is already reflected in each facet extensity (satisfaction score). Another issue is that without substantial individual differences in values, Locke's (1976) theory loses its cogency. Job satisfaction would be related to value attainment; weighting discrepancies by small differences in values would not improve the relationship of value attainment with overall satisfaction. Although individuals are likely to differ in what they value in a job, some attributes are generally more valued than are others. Cross-cultural research on populations of workers differing substantially in values can address this issue.

Summary

The value-percept model expresses job satisfactions in terms of employees' values and job outcomes. The model highlights the role of individual differences in values and job outcomes, but its use of weighting may be inappropriate unless weighting variables are measured with very high reliability. The model also ignores influences from exogenous factors, costs of holding a job, or current and past social, economic, or organizational conditions external to the individual-job nexus.

Job Characteristics Model

The job characteristics model (JCM) argues that enrichment of specified job characteristics is the core factor in making employees satisfied with their jobs. The model, formulated by Hackman and Oldham (1976), focuses on five core job characteristics that make work challenging and fulfilling and make jobs that provide them more satisfying and motivating than jobs that provide them to a lesser degree:

1. *Task identity*—degree to which one can see one's work from beginning to end,
2. *Task significance*—degree to which one's work is seen as important and significant,
3. *Skill variety*—extent to which job allows employees to perform different tasks,
4. *Autonomy*—degree to which employee has control and discretion for how to conduct his or her job, and
5. *Feedback*—degree to which the work itself provides feedback concerning how the employee is performing the job.

The JCM has received direct and indirect support. When individuals are asked to evaluate the importance of different facets of work such as pay, promotion opportunities, coworkers, and so forth, the nature of the work itself consistently emerges as the most important job facet (Jurgensen, 1978). This is not surprising because job satisfaction researchers have known for some time that of the major job satisfaction facets—pay, promotion opportunities, coworkers, supervision, the overall organization, and the work itself—satisfaction with the work itself is generally the facet most strongly correlated with overall job satisfaction (e.g., Rentsch & Steel, 1992) or the factor regarded as the most important (Herzberg, Mausner, Peterson, & Capwell, 1957). That work satisfaction is the facet of job satisfaction that correlates most strongly with overall satisfaction, and is the facet with the strongest correlations with outcomes, suggests this focus of the theory—the nature of the work itself—is on a solid foundation.

Meta-analyses of relationships between workers' reports of job characteristics and job satisfaction have produced generally positive results (Fried & Ferris, 1987; Loher, Noe, Moeller, & Fitzgerald, 1985). Frye (1996) reported a true score correlation of .50 between perceptions of job characteristics and job satisfaction.

Growth need strength (GNS) is a component of the model that accounts for individual differences in receptiveness to challenging job characteristics. According to Hackman and Oldham (1976), GNS is employees' desire for personal development, especially as it applies to work. High GNS employees want their jobs to contribute to their personal growth; work characteristics are especially important to individuals who score high on GNS. The relationship between work characteristics and job satisfaction is stronger for high-GNS employees (average $r = .68$) than for low-GNS employees (average $r = .38$; Frye, 1996). However, task characteristics are related to job satisfaction even for those who score low on GNS.

Despite empirical support, there are limitations with the theory. Adding the dimensions may produce a better result than the complex weighted formulation of Hackman and Oldham (1976; see earlier comments with respect to weighting in the value-percept model). A serious limitation with the JCM is that most of the studies have used self-reports of job characteristics, which has garnered a well-deserved share of criticisms (Roberts & Glick, 1981).

Another limitation concerns the GNS construct. It is not clear what this construct measures; little construct validity evidence is available. Are other individual differences involved in the job characteristics–job attitude relationship? Empirical research by Turner and Lawrence (1965) and a review by Hulin and Blood (1968) highlighted the role of differences in cultural background in reactions to job characteristics. Is GNS a reflection of cultural background? Of personality traits such as conscientiousness? In the research on the JCM, the construct validity of GNS has been neglected.

In addition, the directions of causal arrows linking job satisfaction and perceptions of job characteristics are not clear. The relationship between perceptions of job characteristics and job satisfaction may be bidirectional (James & Jones, 1980; James & Tetrick, 1986) or perhaps from satisfaction to perceptions of task characteristics; the latter hypothesis cannot be rejected (Hulin & Roznowski, 1984). Finally, there is little evidence that GNS mediates the relationship between job characteristics and outcomes as proposed.

Summary

The JCM hypothesizes that job satisfactions depend on characteristics of the work itself and, like the value-percept model, that the roots of job satisfactions lie within the individual and the job. GNS may be influenced by individuals' cultural backgrounds, as these lead to individual differences in need configurations; other influences are minimized.

Disposition Influences

The earliest writings on job satisfaction recognized the importance of dispositional influences on job satisfaction. Hoppock (1935) found that questions about levels of emotional adjustment substantially separated satisfied and dissatisfied employees. This replicated earlier results by Fisher and Hanna (1931). Weitz (1952) developed a *gripe index* to take into account individuals' tendencies to feel negatively, or positively, about many aspects of their lives to gauge more accurately relative dissatisfaction with one's job. Smith (1955) found that individuals prone to poor emotional adjustment were more susceptible to feelings of monotony. The Cornell model was based in part on the idea that there existed very satisfied garbage collectors and very dissatisfied executives and that these so-called anomalous satisfaction levels could be explained.

However, of the thousands of studies published on the topic of job satisfaction prior to 1985, few considered individual differences as the sources of job satisfactions. Even fewer focused on personality. As Staw and Ross (1985) commented, "Rarely . . . are job attitudes formulated as having an endogenous source of variance, one that is reflective of the ongoing state of the person as opposed to being a product of the situation" (p. 469). This may overstate the case given the role of individual frames of reference in the Cornell model of job satisfaction. Nevertheless, these origins of job satisfaction were untilled ground until the mid-1980s.

This state of affairs began to change with the publication of two seminal studies by Staw and colleagues, a study by Arvey and colleagues, and an integrative piece by Adler and Weiss (1988) on the benefits of developing and using personality measures designed specifically to be applied to normal, working adults as opposed to residents of Minnesota mental hospitals or their visitors. Staw and Ross (1985) exploited the National Longitudinal Surveys (NLS) database and found that measures of job satisfaction were reasonably stable over time (over 2 years, $r = .42$; over 3 years, $r = .32$; over 5 years, $r = .29$). They also found that job satisfaction showed modest stability even when individuals changed both employers and occupations over a 5-year period ($r = .19$, $p < .01$). Finally, the authors found that prior job satisfaction was a stronger predictor of current satisfaction ($b = .27$, $t = 14.07$, $p < .01$) than changes in pay ($b = .01$, $t = 2.56$, $p < .01$) or changes in status ($b = .00$). The Staw and Ross (1985)

study has been criticized (e.g., Davis-Blake & Pfeffer, 1989; Gerhart, 1987; Gutek & Winter, 1992; Newton & Keenan, 1991) on the grounds that it is difficult to establish a dispositional basis of job satisfaction without measuring dispositions. Also, job quality and characteristics may not change with a change of job. Correlations of satisfaction levels across time and jobs may reflect relative consistency in jobs as much as they do stable individual dispositions; those who are able to secure a good, high-quality job at one time are likely to do the same later, even after a change in jobs.

Staw, Bell, and Clausen (1986) corrected this deficiency by exploiting a unique longitudinal data set in which psychologists rated children on a number of characteristics, 17 of which the authors argued assessed affective disposition ("cheerful," "warm," and "negative"). Staw et al. reported results showing that affective disposition assessed at ages 12 to 14 correlated .34 ($p < .05$) with overall job satisfaction assessed at ages 54 to 62.

In a similarly provocative study, Arvey, Bouchard, Segal, and Abraham (1989) found significant consistency in job satisfaction levels in 34 pairs of monozygotic twins reared apart from early childhood. The intraclass correlation (ICC) of the general job satisfaction scores of the twin pairs was .31 ($p < .05$). This correlation may have been observed because the twins with similar dispositions selected themselves, or were selected, into similar environments by organizations because of genetic influence on ability. Arvey et al. (1989) attempted to eliminate this explanation by controlling for job level, using the Dictionary of Occupational Titles (DOT) scales to classify jobs on four dimensions. Controlling for the DOT scales had little effect on the correlation (ICC = .29). The implication of the study is that individuals are born with characteristics that predispose them to be satisfied with a job. Heritability of job satisfaction is very likely indirect, operating through heritability in personality or other dispositions. This is not a revolutionary conclusion from the perspective of 2001. In 1989, however, when little research had been published on the heritability of personality, it was a revolutionary finding.

The Staw et al. (1986) and Arvey et al. (1989) studies are as significant for the stimulus they provided as for their substantive findings. Judge and Hulin (1993) attempted to develop an improved measure of the dispositional influence on job satisfaction. Drawing from Weitz's (1952) gripe index, which asked individuals to indicate their satisfaction with a list of objectively neutral objects common to everyday life (your telephone number, your first name, $8\frac{1}{2}" \times 11"$ paper), Judge and Hulin (1993) found that employees' responses to neutral objects were correlated with job satisfaction, a finding replicated by Judge and Locke (1993). Judge and Hulin (1993) also found that after controlling for job satisfaction, the scores on this instrument had an independent path to job turnover 4 months after the initial assessment. Despite favorable psychometric evidence for the measure (Judge & Bretz, 1993), this line of research did little to advance the literature. It is unclear what construct this measure assesses. Across several studies (Judge & Hulin, 1993; Judge & Locke, 1993; Judge, Locke, Durham, & Kluger, 1998), the adapted Weitz (1952) measure was consistently correlated with job satisfaction, but the correlations rarely exceeded .30.

While Judge, Hulin, Locke, and others were studying affective predispositions as assessed by the Weitz (1952) measure, other researchers were investigating a different measure: positive affectivity (PA) and negative affectivity (NA). PA characterizes individuals predisposed to experience joviality, self-assurance, and attentiveness. NA characterizes individuals predisposed to experience fear, sadness, guilt, and hostility (Watson, 2000). Several studies have related both PA and NA to job satisfaction (e.g., Agho, Mueller, & Price, 1993; Brief, Butcher, & Roberson, 1995; Levin & Stokes, 1989; Necowitz & Roznowski, 1994; Watson & Slack, 1993).

Despite apparent validity advantages to the trait PA-NA taxonomy (relative to the Weitz measure), limitations are apparent. First, Watson and colleagues argued that trait PA-NA are independent dimensions. For example, Watson (2000) commented, "Positive and negative moods do, in fact, vary more or less independently of one another" (p. 27). However, it is not clear that PA-NA should be characterized as this statement implies. The rotation of axes within the traditional mood circumplex (Tellegen et al., 1999) suggested that mood or emotion may be scored as independent PA and NA traits or as hedonic tone versus activation or arousal. Tellegen et al. (1999) derived a three-level hierarchical structure with "a general bipolar Happiness-Versus-Unhappiness dimension, the relatively independent PA and NA dimensions at the level below it, and dis-

crete emotions at the base" (p. 297). The bandwidth (Cronbach & Gleser, 1957) and systematic heterogeneity arguments (Humphreys, 1985; Roznowski & Hanisch, 1990) suggest the use of hedonic tone, but the issue is not resolved.

A second limitation is that PA-NA scores are confounded with current affect. Indeed, advocates of the PA/NA dimensions argue that they assess "mood dispositional" (Watson, 2000) tendencies. Job experiences may affect mood assessments as much as they are influenced by stable individual differences. Recent research by Weiss et al. (1999); Miner et al. (2001); and Miner (XXX) found modest relations between averages of mood assessed in near real time using event signal methods (ESM) and job satisfactions assessed within a few months or weeks of mood assessments.

In a different approach to dispositional influences on job attitudes, Judge, Locke, and Durham (1997) focused on core self-evaluations, fundamental beliefs individuals hold about themselves, their functioning, and the world. Core self-evaluations are hierarchical with a broad, general trait comprising specific traits. Judge et al. argued that core self-evaluations are assessed by traits that meet three criteria: (a) an evaluation focus (the degree to which a trait involves evaluation, as opposed to description); (b) fundamentality (in Cattell's, 1965 personality theory, fundamental or source traits underlie surface traits); and (c) breadth or scope (according to Allport, 1961, cardinal traits are broader in scope than are secondary traits). Judge et al. identified four specific traits based on these evaluative criteria: (a) self-esteem, (b) generalized self-efficacy, (c) neuroticism, and (d) locus of control. Judge et al.'s hypothesized model linking core self-evaluations to job satisfaction is provided in Figure 11.2. As the figure shows, this model also includes core self-evaluations of reality (global beliefs about their broader environment) and of others (beliefs about the motives and behaviors of others).

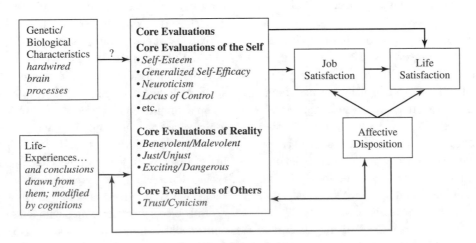

Figure 11.2   Core self-evaluation model of job attitudes.

Two primary studies and one meta-analysis have related core self-evaluations to job satisfaction. Judge et al. (1998) found that core self-evaluations had a true-score total effect of .48 on job satisfaction across three samples when both constructs were self-reported by the focal individuals and .37 when core self-evaluations were measured independently (by a significant other). Judge et al. determined that evaluations of the world and of others added little or no variance beyond core self-evaluations. These evaluations have been dropped from subsequent tests of the theory. Judge, Bono, and Locke (2000) found that core self-evaluations correlated .41 ($p <$ .01) with job satisfaction when both constructs were self-reported and .19 ($p <$ .05) when core self-evaluations were reported by significant others. Judge and Bono (2001) completed a meta-analysis of 169 independent correlations (combined $N = 59,871$) between each of the four core traits and job satisfaction. When the four meta-analyses were combined into a single composite measure, the overall core trait correlated .37 with job satisfaction.

Some limitations of these studies should be recognized. In the two primary studies, sizable discrepancies between correlations derived from self-ratings of core evaluations and core ratings of focal individuals provided by significant others raise questions about the best summary of the relation with job satisfactions. The reliance on relations among self-report measures as an empirical basis for an area of study is a problem that eventually must be solved by I/O psychology in general. In tests of this theory, self-reports are further confounded with evaluations of job and self. If jobs are a fundamental part of the self, evaluations of the job (i.e., job attitudes) and evaluations of the self may be expected to be related. One is part of the other.

Because core self-evaluations research is less extensive than PA-NA research in the job satisfaction literature, and because PA-NA researchers argue that PA can be equated with extraversion and NA with neuroticism (Brief, 1998; Watson, 2000), one might ask what either taxonomy adds beyond the Big Five personality model (Goldberg, 1990), which has considerable support in the personality literature (see McCrae & Costa, 1997). Which of these typologies should be used? A summary of recent meta-analytic reviews of the traits just presented is provided in Table 11.2. The correlations between the Big Five traits and job satisfaction are from Judge, Heller, and Mount's (2001) meta-analysis of 335 correlations from 163 independent samples. The correlations between the core self-evaluations traits and job satisfaction are from the Judge and Bono (2001) study of 169 independent correlations. The correlations involving PA, NA, and affective disposition are from Connolly and Viswesvaran's (2000) meta-analysis of 27 articles. The results reveal that PA-NA and one core self-

TABLE 11.2 Meta-Analytic Estimates of the Relationship of Personality to Job Satisfaction

Trait	Mean r	Mean ρ
Big Five traits		
Neuroticism	−.24	−.29[a]
Extraversion	.19	.25[a]
Openness to Experience	.01	.02
Agreeableness	.13	.17
Conscientiousness	.20	.26
Core self-evaluations traits		
Self-esteem	.20	.26[a]
Generalized self-efficacy	.38	.45[a]
Locus of control	.24	.32[a]
Emotional stability	.20	.24[a]
Positive and negative affectivity		
Positive affectivity	.41	.49[a]
Negative affectivity	−.27	−.33[a]
Affective disposition		
Ad hoc measures of affective disposition	.29	.36[a]

Note. Mean r = average uncorrected correlation. Mean ρ = average corrected correlation.
[a]80% credibility intervals exclude zero.

evaluation generally has higher correlations with job satisfaction than do the Big Five traits. The correlations involving generalized self-efficacy and positive affectivity are particularly strong. However, the number of correlations involved in the meta-analyses of these particular traits was small, and the variability of the correlations was large. The variability in the assessment of PA/NA as a state, a trait, or something in between adds ambiguity to these results.

Judge and Heller (2001) found that of the three taxonomic structures (the five-factor model, PA-NA, and core self-evaluations), core self-evaluations were the most useful predictor of job satisfaction, cognitive evaluations of the job. Altogether, the three frameworks explained 36% of the variance in self-reported job satisfaction and 18% of the variance when using reports by significant others. Judge and Heller further showed that these frameworks could be reduced to three sets of factors for the purposes of predicting job satisfaction: (a) core self-evaluations/neuroticism (all four core traits plus NA), (b) extraversion (including PA), and (c) conscientiousness. Their results showed that when these three factors were related to job satisfaction, however, only the first factor consistently influenced job satisfaction across studies.

Core self-evaluations may be more strongly related to job satisfaction, job performance, and other organizationally relevant outcomes because they represent a broader concept compared, for example, with neuroticism. There are predictive advantages with broader rather than narrower bandwidth measures of psychological constructs (Cronbach & Gleser, 1957; Humphreys, 1985). The neuroticism measures heavily sample anxiety, stress proneness, and psychosomatic items and undersample depressive tendencies and negative self-concept. The latter seem to be more relevant to most work attitudes and behaviors than are the former (work stress would be an exception). Core self-evaluations may be similar, in concept and in measurement, to emotional stability; they may add something beyond neuroticism to the understanding of job satisfaction.

Summary

The issue seems to be *which* individual dispositional traits are best suited to provide insights into job satisfaction. Dispositional sources of job satisfaction have been mapped only partially. Other traits derived from other taxonomies and other state variables may also prove useful.

Person-Environment Fits

The various person-environment fit models of job attitudes are closely related to the dispositional approaches reviewed earlier. These person-environment fit models go beyond the hypothesized simple main effects of personal characteristics on job attitudes and beyond the interactions between personal values and the importance of these values hypothesized by the value-percept model. Person-environment models were developed following the seminal work of Paterson (Paterson & Darley, 1936). Shaffer's work (Shaffer, 1953) expanded the person-environment fit construct and combined it with Murray's (1943) needs to generate a multidimensional person-environment fit model that attempted to account for job satisfactions of job incumbents with different constellations of needs working on jobs that provide different outputs assumed to be differentially satisfying to those with different needs.

As with the other models discussed in this section, some empirical evidence of the validity of the model has been presented (Shaffer, 1953). Need satisfactions were correlated .44 with overall job satisfaction, and satisfaction of the highest strength needs was correlated most strongly with job satisfaction. Porter's (1961) need satisfaction model of job attitudes was basically a person-environment fit model in which job satisfaction was calculated by discrepancies between "How much is there now?" and "How much should there be?" The first question reflects what the environment provides, and the second reflects what the person wants. The fit between person and environment determines job satisfaction.

Dawis (1992) provided a contemporary statement of person-environment fit models and research. Person-environment fit models of job satisfactions offer an opportunity to blend job attitude research with vocational psychology that emphasizes patterns of vocational reinforcers and basic needs or desires of

individual job incumbents. Such an approach requires valid representations of the needs of individuals and the reinforcements available from different occupational groupings of jobs. In spite of the impressive developmental work represented by Holland's (1985) RIASEC (*R*ealistic, *I*nvestigative, *A*rtistic, *S*ocial, *E*nterprising, *C*onforming) circumplex model of vocational preferences, this approach that combines two research traditions has not advanced the research area greatly in the past several years; nor does its promise seem to have been realized in terms of gains in understanding the antecedents of job attitudes. For these gains to be realized a theoretically sound, multivariate empirical basis for characterizing vocations and individuals is required where there is a conceptual match between the entries in the vectors describing individuals and vocations. Our knowledge of vocations gained from the RIASEC model is impressive, but the match between these occupational groupings and multivariate descriptions of individuals provided, for example, by the Big Five personality theory, may be problematical. The original need-theoretic approach emphasized by Paterson (e.g., Paterson & Darley, 1936) and the other researchers at Minnesota did not survive critical theoretical or empirical analyses. This need-based approach appears to have suffered the same fate as Maslow's need hierarchy model (Maslow, 1943); independent empirical investigations of its basic validity are not convincing.

Summary

Person-environment fit models emphasize complex multivariate interactions between person and environmental characteristics as determinants of job satisfactions. The conceptual advantages of these models do not seem to have been translated into significant gains in our understanding of the antecedents of job satisfactions. Empirical investigations have generated support for this approach, but it is not clear whether there are gains beyond the insights offered by simpler main-effect models of personality antecedents.

COMPARISONS OF THEORETICAL APPROACHES

In Figures 11.3 through 11.6 we attempt to summarize graphically the structures of the job satisfaction models just discussed. There is much similarity among the models. Job outcomes are typically judged in relation to a set of standards. There are a number of hypothesized influences on the standards involved in evaluating job outcomes. These influences range from economic-environmental influences that affect employees' frames of reference for evaluating specific job outcomes to personality, core self-evaluations, and perhaps

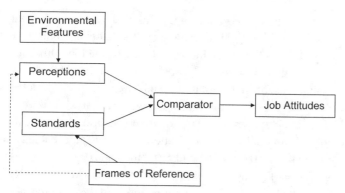

Figure 11.3 Graphical depiction of structure of Cornell model of job attitudes.

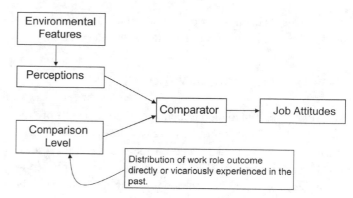

Figure 11.5 Graphical depiction of structure of Thibaut-Kelley model of job attitudes.

biological factors. Job outcomes (and perhaps inputs) and standards are processed through a comparator, and the result of these cognitive processes is an evaluation of one's job, job satisfaction.

The graphical representations of the different theories highlight the similarities in their structures more than might be apparent in the verbal descriptions. The theories are not redundant in terms of their hypothesized influences on the standards. Nor are they unique. A comprehensive study comparing these models would be difficult because of the number, range, sources, and levels (individual to social, economic, and community) of variables involved in the models. Subsets of the different influences could be studied, but comparisons of complete models using appropriate random effects designs will be difficult.

One way of summarizing these models of job attitudes is to highlight the sources of the influences on job attitudes. The JCM and Locke's value-percept model emphasize the influence of job characteristics and hypothesize that the influence of each job characteristic is moderated by the values or GNS of the employees. Core self-evaluations and the other

dispositional models stress direct influences from person and other micro variables. Both the Cornell model and the Thibaut and Kelley model, the most macro of the models, include substantial influences of variables external to the person-job nexus. Both are relatively balanced in terms of their hypothesized influences of job and person characteristics on job attitudes. Only the Thibaut and Kelley model and the Cornell model emphasize variables external to the individual and his or her job.

The structure and content of the theoretical explanations of the formation of job attitudes are also similar in terms of what is omitted: Not one of these theories that links a variety of antecedents and satisfactions through the mechanism of cognitive evaluations and comparisons of one's standards and job outcomes (or inputs) includes on-the-job affect or emotions. Affect has been deemphasized so much that this component of attitude space, as an antecedent or consequence, has nearly disappeared. We do not imply that cognitive evaluations of one's job are free of feelings. We do, however, suggest that assessments and inclusions of affect, assessed using methods that capture this dynamic source of variance, might provide

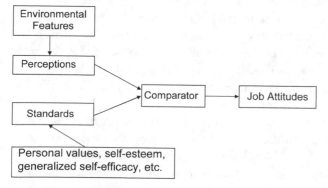

Figure 11.4 Graphical depiction of Locke's value-percept model of job attitudes.

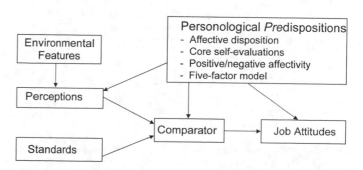

Figure 11.6 Graphical depiction of generalized dispositional/personological model of job attitudes.

unique insights in our attempts to understand job attitudes and predict important behaviors. This idea is developed next.

NEW THEORETICAL DEVELOPMENTS

The cognitive, affective, and behavioral components of attitudes may have kept attitude research as one of the most active research areas in social science for the past several decades. Whatever the current research emphasis in social science—behaviors, cognitions, or emotions—attitudes, as originally defined, met the criteria for relevant research. The deemphasis of an affect component of social attitudes has been paralleled by a similar treatment of affect or emotions in job attitudes. Weiss and Brief (in press) noted the neglect of affect in the history of job satisfaction research. Weiss and Cropanzano (1996) have also drawn attention to the field's neglect of affect and proposed a theory of job attitudes that emphasizes affect on an equal footing with cognitive evaluations, hypothesizes different antecedents for cognitive evaluations versus affect, and hypothesizes different sets of behaviors as consequences of individual differences in affect as contrasted with cognitive evaluations.

Called affective events theory (AET), this theory emphasizes links between job events and job affect and hypothesizes links between job affect and job behaviors that are independent of the links between traditional job attitudes (cognitive evaluations of jobs) and job behaviors. AET hypothesizes links between job affect and spontaneous, short-term behaviors, such as work withdrawal and organizational citizenship behaviors, rather than the more reasoned long-term behaviors that have been related to job satisfactions, such as turnover or retirement. These two families of behaviors are identified by Weiss and Cropanzano (1996) as affect- and judgment-driven behaviors. Figure 11.7 depicts a simplified, graphical version of AET.

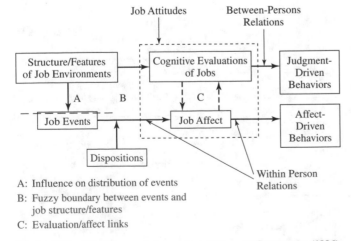

A: Influence on distribution of events
B: Fuzzy boundary between events and
   job structure/features
C: Evaluation/affect links

Figure 11.7 Affective events theory from Weiss and Cropanzano (1996).

Affect is defined conceptually as individuals' emotional reactions to their jobs and to the events that happen on their jobs. It refers to how an individual feels on the job. This contrasts with the cognitive representation of job attitudes—evaluations of stable features and characteristics of jobs. How we feel in the morning when we arrive at work is very likely a relatively stable part of our personalities and dispositions. Empirically, the correlations between adjacent days ranged from .50 to .65 depending on the scale (PA, NA, or hedonic tone) across 12 days in two studies (Miner, 2001; Miner et al., 2001). These morning, preworkday, feelings are very likely influenced by longer than normal commuting delays caused by heavy traffic or construction, an incident of road rage, a blizzard in April, an overnight gas price increase, a warm sunny day in February, and other positive and negative exogenous factors. These feelings are further modified by events that occur on the job during the day. An argument with a coworker, unexpected praise from a supervisor, or a comment by someone about the availability of jobs and starting salaries at another organization will influence our feelings on the job (Miner et al., 2001). These events and the changes in affect that they trigger may be ephemeral but may have long-term influences on how we evaluate our jobs. Feelings and affect levels triggered by job events, for all their ephemerality, however, may have consequences for behaviors on the job—(not) helping our coworkers, getting somebody to cover for us so we can attend a meeting called by our supervisor, or how long we spend on the phone with a customer needing assistance (Miner, 2001). Within a framework of stable evaluations of one's job, it is possible to feel anger, frustration, elation, and unhappiness while on a job one evaluates positively and to feel these emotions in one day and to respond behaviorally, both positively and negatively, to episodes of positive and negative affect.

AET is differentiated from other current approaches by (a) the distinctions between job structure or features and job events, although job features (e.g., HR policies) are likely to influence *distributions* of job events; (b) an emphasis on affect as a component of job attitudes; and (c) the hypothesized independent links between job affect and affect-driven behaviors, on the one hand, and among job satisfactions, cognitive evaluations of jobs, and judgment-driven behaviors on the other. Dispositions are hypothesized to moderate the link between events and affect.

Job features and job events should be treated as fuzzy sets. Features differentiating between these two sets of variables would be permanence, frequency, and predictability—job events being more transient and less predictable than stable job features. A subset of job events that becomes sufficiently frequent and predictable may cross the boundary between features and events. Affect- and judgment-driven behaviors are fuzzy sets; judgment-driven and affect-driven behaviors do not yield crisp classification of all job behaviors into one category or the other. The fuzziness of the boundaries does not invalidate AET as a useful framework. All classes of events in social science have a degree of fuzziness.

Job affect is inherently dynamic. We should expect significant within-person cofluctuations in affect and exogenous events. Job events serve as stochastic shocks to an underlying affect level and cycle. Job events are individually unpredictable and infrequent; their influence contributes to the dynamic nature of job affect. Organ and Ryan (1995) illustrated this problem by noting that predictions of organizational citizenship behaviors (OCBs) from affective states "will somehow have to reckon with the problem of *detecting discrete episodes of OCB* [italics added] (rather than subjective reactions that presumably reflect aggregations or trends of OCB over time) *and the psychological states antecedent to or concurrent with those episodes* [italics added]" (p. 781). This problem has been addressed, and partially solved, by event signal methods (ESM), or momentary ecological assessments, and multilevel statistical analyses that combine within- and between-person effects (Bryk & Raudenbush, 1992).

Totterdell (1999) and Weiss et al. (1999) addressed the demands of studying affect levels as dynamic variables. Miner et al. (2001) assessed affect on the job using palmtop computers to administer mood checklists at four random times during the workday. The within-person, dynamic nature of affect and mood on the job is highlighted by the intraclass correlations that revealed that approximately 60% of the variance in mood or job affect scores resided within persons; approximately 40% of the variance in mood scores could be attributed to between-person differences. This within-person variance would be treated as error in most studies of job attitudes. Relations involving within-person differences and other variables would be impossible to study if affect assessments were aggregated and studied as stable, between-person individual differences. Near real-time assessments of job affect permit analyses of within-person relations between negative and positive job events and mood on the job after controlling for mood assessed at the beginning of each work day (Miner et al.).

One important aspect of this new approach to job attitudes is the possibility of within-person relations between, say, affect and behaviors, which are independent of affect-behavior relations found between individuals. One example of this is the negative relationship between exercise and blood pressure found in the medical literature. When the assessment is made between individuals, those who exercise more have lower blood pressure. However, the same relationship assessed within individuals is positive; those who are exercising have higher blood pressures than those who are not exercising.

Miner (2001) has found that between individuals, those with more positive affect levels are more likely to exhibit citizenship and helping behaviors. Within persons the relationship is negative; individuals report lower levels of affect while they are helping coworkers.

AET offers a new approach to the study of job attitudes. It emphasizes a source of variance in job attitudes that has been largely ignored for 40 years. It represents more than adding a variable (affect) to the study of job attitudes. Appropriate definitions of affect and within-person relations require changed research directions and methods. Analyses of affective events, affect, and the on-the-job consequences of affect may answer some questions about job attitudes and behaviors on the job that are unanswered by the traditional studies of relations between cognitive evaluations and job performance.

MEASUREMENT OF JOB ATTITUDES

Cognitive Evaluations

Much satisfaction research has been based on homegrown, unvalidated measures consisting generally of a collection of Likert-type items that ask the respondents to evaluate their pay, the work they do, their supervision, and so on. Some scales have been based on collections of items asking respondents how satisfied they were with different features of their jobs. Other scales have been based on items asking about how well the respondents' jobs fulfilled their needs. The JDI (Smith et al., 1969) modified by Roznowski (1989), the Job Diagnostic Survey (JDS; Hackman & Oldham, 1976), the Minnesota Satisfaction Questionnaire (MNSQ; Dawes, Dohm, Lofquist, Chartrand, & Due, 1987; Weiss, Dawis, England, & Lofquist, 1967), and the Index of Organizational Reactions (IOR; Dunhan & Smith, 1979; Dunham, Smith, & Blackburn, 1977) represent significant exceptions to this use of unvalidated scales purporting to assess job attitudes. The JDI appears to be the most widely applied measure of job satisfaction in use today (Cranny et al., 1992, p. 2; DeMeuse, 1985); the JDS, MNSQ, and IOR have been used collectively on an additional several thousands of employees. These four standardized, validated instruments together may account for a slight majority of the research on job satisfaction.

These standardized instruments have been evaluated psychometrically; they converge dimensionally with each other when they assess satisfaction with similar job characteristics (Dunham et al., 1977), are related to appropriate individual differences and job characteristics, and have reasonable levels of temporal stability or internal consistency. The four instruments, however, differ substantially. The MNSQ assesses the extent to which jobs are evaluated as providing need fulfillment of a number of basic needs. The JDS assesses the degree to which jobs provide core characteristics (responsibility, task feedback, task significance, etc.) to the employee. The IOR asks respondents to evaluate job features and scores these into eight facets of job satisfaction (work itself, the organization, career future and security, pay, etc.). The JDI assesses five facets of job satisfaction (work itself, pay, promotional opportunities and policies, supervision, coworkers) by asking respondents to describe their jobs in terms of the presence or absence of 72 characteristics of the work itself, coworkers, and so on. A complete evaluation of the psychometric properties of all available scales requires more space than we have available.

Investigators interested in research on job attitudes have access to several standardized and validated measures that provide information on different aspects of individuals' job attitudes. Despite the dimensional convergence, the instruments are not equivalent; the use of one rather than another will generate marginally to significantly different results. The choice of a measure of job attitudes in any study is not an irrelevant detail. The widespread use of the JDI may reflect the extensive psychometric research that accompanied its initial publication (Smith et al., 1969) and that has appeared in the decades since (e.g., Balzer et al., 1997; Hanisch, 1992; Roznowski, 1989). The five scales that compose the JDI also have been used extensively as antecedents and outcomes of varying levels of job attitudes in studies ranging from community characteristics and their effects on job attitudes (Kendall, 1963) to longitudinal studies of the effects of sexual harassment (Glomb, Munson, Hulin, Bergman, & Drasgow, 1999). This database provides researchers with the evidence necessary to evaluate the properties and functioning of this set of scales and may account for its wide use.

Job Affect, Mood, and Emotions

Job affect or emotions experienced on the job present a different set of conceptual and assessment problems. Job affect and emotions are influenced by events that occur on the job. Individual job events are likely to be infrequent and difficult to predict. Praise from a supervisor, an overheard conversation in the hallway about a coworker's evaluation, a just-in-time delivery that was not quite in time, or a surly customer are all job events and are generally unpredictable. Yet they do occur, and their occurrences may trigger job emotions. Assessment of emotions on the job, carried out in near real time several times during a workday are necessary to tap into event-affect-behavior cycles and capitalize on the dynamic state nature of affect.

The dynamic nature of job affect makes it difficult to use research practices that rely on one-shot, paper-and-pencil

assessments of employees' attitudes. Palm top computers, however, can signal the research participants, present items with clickable response formats, store the data, and maintain an acceptable degree of data security. Items can be sampled randomly at each signal from the pool of items defining the content of the scales. Such sampling may reduce respondents' tendencies to focus on specific emotions that have been assessed at previous signals. These devices can control the timing of the response within temporal intervals desired by the researcher as opposed to a signal and diary method in which researchers have no such control; diaries can be completed by the participants any time during the observation period. Several studies of affect and mood that have used ESM or signal contingent methods at work (Alliger & Williams, 1993; Fisher, 2000; Totterdell, 1999, 2000; Weiss et al., 1999; Zohar, 1999) generally support the hypothesized importance of affect and mood at work and document the promise of ESM to generate assessments of emotions and affect at work.

Another issue that must be resolved is the specification of the content of affect and emotion assessments. Should on-the-job affect be assessed as PA and NA, two orthogonal dimensions, or as a bipolar hedonic tone dimension ranging from negative to positive and an orthogonal arousal or activation dimension? These different rotations of the mood-emotion circumplex (Tellegen et al., 1999) are shown in Figure 11.8. Either the PA-NA rotation, indicated by dotted axes, or the hedonic tone-arousal rotation, indicated by solid lines, adequately account for the correlations among affective or emotional terms and responses. Although these may be mathematically equivalent rotations, the use of one rather than the other has significant implications for the study of job affect.

The potential contributions of affect to understanding variance in job satisfactions may not be realized until the rotation

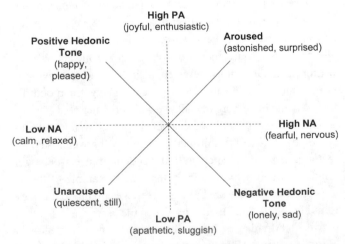

Figure 11.8 Mood-emotion circumplex from Tellegen, Watson, & Clark (1999). PA = positive affectivity; NA = negative affectivity.

of axes in the mood circumplex that is used to define the mood and affect dimensions is resolved. Our interpretation of the evidence suggests that the hedonic tone-arousal rotation is most useful and that the arousal dimension appears to contribute relatively little to the study of mood and affect at work (Miner et al., 2001).

Palm top computers and repeated event signaled assessments of employees' affect at work should extend our database of job attitudes and add to our knowledge of affect, mood, emotion and social attitudes in general. The use of ESM in populations of working individuals will correct problems of reliance on relatively uncontrolled assessment methods and permit generalizations to broader populations. Both developments should contribute to information about job and social attitudes.

SUMMARY

There is much overlap between job satisfactions and social attitudes, but the conceptual similarities between attitudes and job satisfactions mask important differences. If the roots of attitude theory had been in job attitudes rather than in traditional social attitudes, the theories of attitude-behavior relations would be different. The reliable relations between job attitudes and job behaviors may be the general, ecologically valid finding; the lack of relations between typically studied social attitudes and behaviors may represent the anomaly to be explained. Hulin (2001) commented on the general importance and ecological validity of the study of work behaviors, attitudes, and motivations for general questions about human behaviors as opposed to the more restricted studies of social behaviors of college sophomores. The study of social attitudes might have progressed down different avenues than it did if the attitude database had comprised the many studies documenting relations between job satisfactions and job behaviors.

The strong personal relevance of job attitudes as opposed to the often-problematical relevance—and abstraction—of frequently studied social attitudes is one possible explanation for the reliably observed satisfaction-behavior relations. The accessibility of job attitudes as opposed to the accessibility of attitudes to religion in the abstract or donating blood is also likely involved in the differences in attitude-behavior relations between social and job attitudes.

Not all job behaviors are related to job attitudes. Job behaviors, as any set of behaviors, are multiply determined. They are subject to constraints due to environmental, organizational, and technological variables, as well as group processes. These influences on behaviors may overwhelm the influence on behaviors from individuals' job attitudes. However, when variance in behaviors is largely under the control of individuals, we find reliable and often substantial relations between satisfactions and behaviors. The greater the influences on behaviors that are due to variables not under the control of individuals and the further removed the "behavioral" criterion is from the individual, the less likely we are to find substantial correlations.

The theoretical models of antecedents of job attitudes include influences on job attitudes ranging from macroeconomic conditions, to alternative jobs available to the individual, to microlevel influences of personality and affective dispositions. These models have not been evaluated and compared in a unified study that would permit the untangling and disaggregating of overlapping and redundant sets of antecedents. The competing models, each with some supporting evidence, and some with a great deal of supporting evidence, represent an unresolved problem with job satisfaction research. Given the practical importance of job attitudes as predictors of job behaviors ranging from tardiness to voting in NLRB-sponsored union representation elections, the theoretical importance of the models of job attitudes as guides for organizational interventions to improve job attitudes, and the theoretical importance that job satisfaction research may have for social attitude research and theory, resolution of the contradictions in the competing models is an important priority in this area.

New theories of job attitudes that stress affect and emotions experienced on the job, in addition to the traditional job satisfactions qua cognitive evaluations of jobs, have raised important questions and suggested unexplored areas for empirical research and conceptual development. Research in these areas has produced promising results that suggest relatively neglected variables beyond the popular cognitive domain may contribute much to our knowledge of job satisfactions, their antecedents, and their consequences.

REFERENCES

Adler, S., & Weiss, H. M. (1988). Recent developments in the study of personality and organizational behavior. In C. L. Cooper & I. T. Robertson (Eds.), *International review of industrial and organizational psychology* (pp. 307–330). Chichester, England: Wiley.

Agho, A. O., Mueller, C. W., & Price, J. L. (1993). Determinants of employee job satisfaction: An empirical test of a causal model. *Human Relations, 46,* 1007–1027.

Alliger, G. M., & Williams, K. J. (1993). Using signal-contingent experience sampling methodology to study work in the field:

A discussion and illustration examining task perceptions and mood. *Personnel Psychology, 46,* 525–549.

Allport, G. W. (1961). *Pattern and growth in personality.* New York: Holt, Rinehart, & Winston.

Arvey, R. D., Bouchard, T. J., Segal, N. L., & Abraham, L. M. (1989). Job satisfaction: Environmental and genetic components. *Journal of Applied Psychology, 74,* 187–192.

Balzer, W. K., Kihm, J. A., Smith, P. C., Irwin, J. L., Bachiochi, P. D., Robie, C., Sinar, E. F., & Parra, L. F. (1997). *Users' manual for the Job Descriptive Index (JDI, 1997 revision) and the Job In General scales.* Bowling Green, OH: Bowling Green State University.

Bateman, T. S., & Organ, D. W. (1983). Job satisfaction and the good soldier: The relationship between affect and employee "citizenship." *Academy of Management Journal, 26,* 587–595.

Borman, W. C. (1991). Job behavior, performance, and effectiveness. In M. D. Dunnette & L. M. Hough (Eds.), *Handbook of industrial and organizational psychology* (2nd ed., Vol. 2, pp. 445–505). Palo Alto, CA: Consulting Psychologist Press.

Borman, W. C., & Motowidlo, S. J. (1997). Task performance and contextual performance: The meaning for personnel selection research. *Human Performance, 10,* 99–109.

Brief, A. P. (1998). *Attitudes in and around organizations.* Thousand Oaks, CA: Sage.

Brief, A. P., Butcher, A., & Roberson, L. (1995). Cookies, disposition, and job attitudes: The effects of positive mood inducing events and negative affectivity on job satisfaction in a field experiment. *Organizational Behavior and Human Decision Processes, 62,* 55–62.

Byrk, A. S., & Raudenbush, S. W. (1992). *Hierarchical linear models: Applications and data analysis methods.* Newbury Park, CA: Sage.

Campbell, D. T. (1963). Social attitudes and other acquired behavioral dispositions. In S. Koch (Ed.), *Psychology: A study of a science* (Vol. 6, pp. 94–171). New York: McGraw-Hill.

Campbell, J. P. (1992). Modeling the performance prediction problem in industrial and organizational psychology. In M. D. Dunnette & L. M. Hough (Eds.), *Handbook of industrial and organizational psychology* (2nd ed., Vol. 1, pp. 687–732). Palo Alto, CA: Consulting Psychologists Press.

Carsten, J. M., & Spector, P. W. (1987). Unemployment, job satisfaction, and employee turnover: A meta-analytic test of the Muchinsky model. *Journal of Applied Psychology, 72,* 374–381.

Cattell, R. B. (1965). *The scientific analysis of personality.* Baltimore: Penguin.

Connolly, J. J., & Viswesvaran, C. (2000). The role of affectivity in job satisfaction: A meta-analysis. *Personality and Individual Differences, 29,* 265–281.

Cranny, C. J., Smith, P. C., & Stone, E. F. (1992). *Job satisfaction.* New York: Lexington.

Cronbach, L. J., & Gleser, G. C. (1957). *Psychological tests and personnel decisions.* Urbana: University of Illinois Press.

Dachler, H. P., & Hulin, C. L. (1969). A reconsideration of the relationship between satisfaction and judged importance of environmental and job characteristics. *Organizational Behavior and Human Decision Processes, 4,* 252–266.

Davis-Blake, A., & Pfeffer, J. (1989). Just a mirage: The search for dispositional effects in organizational research. *Academy of Management Review, 14,* 385–400.

Dawes, R. V., Dohm, T. E., Lofquist, L. H., Chartrand, J. M., & Due, A. M. (1987). *Minnesota Occupational Classification System III.* Minneapolis: Department of Psychology, University of Minnesota.

Dawes, R. M., & Smith, T. L. (1985). Attitude and opinion measurement. In G. Lindzey & E. Aronson (Eds.), *The handbook of social psychology* (3rd ed., pp. 509–566). New York: Random House.

Dawis, R. V. (1992). Person-environment fit and job satisfaction. In C. J. Cranny, P. C. Smith, & E. F. Stone (Eds.), *Job satisfaction* (pp. 69–88). New York: Lexington.

DeMeuse, K. P. (1985). A compendium of frequently used measures in industrial-organizational psychology. *The Industrial-Organizational Psychologist, 2,* 53–59.

Diener, E., & Larsen, R. J. (1984). Temporal stability and cross-situational consistency of affective, behavioral, and cognitive responses. *Journal of Personality & Social Psychology, 47,* 871–883.

Doob, L. W. (1947). The behavior of attitudes. *Psychological Review, 54,* 135–156.

Dunham, R. B., & Smith, F. J. (1979). *Organizational surveys: An internal assessment of organizational health.* Glenview, IL: Scott-Foresman.

Dunham, R. B., Smith, F. J., & Blackburn, R. S. (1977). Validation of the Index of Organizational Reactions with the JDI, the MSQ, and Faces Scales. *Academy of Management Journal, 20,* 420–432.

Eagley, A. H., & Chaiken, S. (1993). *The psychology of attitudes.* New York: Harcourt.

Farrell, D. (1983). Exit, voice, loyalty, and neglect as responses to job dissatisfaction: A multidimensional scaling study. *Academy of Management Journal, 26,* 596–607.

Fishbein, M. (1980). A theory of reasoned action: Some applications and implications. In H. Howe & M. M. Page (Eds.), *Nebraska symposium on motivation: Beliefs, attitudes, and values* (pp. 65–116). Lincoln: University of Nebraska Press.

Fishbein, M., & Ajzen, I. (1972). Attitudes and opinions. *Annual Review of Psychology, 81,* 487–544.

Fishbein, M., & Ajzen, I. (1974). Attitudes towards objects as predictors of single and multiple behavioral criteria. *Psychological Review, 81,* 59–74.

Fishbein, M., & Ajzen, I. (1975). *Belief, attitudes, intentions, and behavior: An introduction to theory and research.* Reading, MA: Addison-Wesley.

Fisher, C. (2000). Mood and emotions while working: Missing pieces of job satisfaction? *Journal of Organizational Behavior, 21,* 185–202.

Fisher, C. D., & Locke, E. A. (1992). The new look in job satisfaction research and theory. In C. J. Cranny, P. C. Smith, & E. F. Stone (Eds.), *Job satisfaction* (pp. 165–194). New York: Lexington.

Fisher, V. E., & Hanna, J. V. (1931). *The dissatisfied worker.* New York: Macmillan.

Fried, Y., & Ferris, G. R. (1987). The validity of the job characteristics model: A review and meta-analysis. *Personnel Psychology, 40,* 287–322.

Frye, C. M. (1996). *New evidence for the Job Characteristics Model: A meta-analysis of the job characteristics-job satisfaction relationship using composite correlations.* Paper presented at the 11th Annual Meeting of the Society for Industrial and Organizational Psychology, San Diego, CA.

George, J. M. (1989). Mood and absence. *Journal of Applied Psychology, 74,* 317–324.

Gerhart, B. (1987). How important are dispositional factors as determinants of job satisfaction? Implications for job design and other personnel programs. *Journal of Applied Psychology, 72,* 366–373.

Getman, J. G., Goldberg, S. B., & Herman, J. B. (1976). *Union representation elections: Law and reality.* New York: Russell Sage.

Glomb, T. M., Munson, L. J., Hulin, C. L., Bergman, M. E., & Drasgow, F. (1999). Structural equation models of sexual harassment: Longitudinal explorations and cross-sectional generalizations. *Journal of Applied Psychology, 84,* 14–28.

Goldberg, L. R. (1990). An alternative "description of personality": The Big-Five factor structure. *Journal of Personality and Social Psychology, 59,* 1216–1229.

Green, A. (1993). *Wobblies, pilebutts, and other heroes.* Urbana: University of Illinois Press.

Gutek, B. A., & Winter, S. J. (1992). Consistency of job satisfaction across situations: Fact or framing artifact? *Journal of Vocational Behavior, 41,* 61–78.

Hackman, J. R., & Oldham, G. R. (1976). Motivation through the design of work: Test of a theory. *Organizational Behavior and Human Performance, 16,* 250–279.

Hamner, W., & Smith, F. J. (1978). Work attitudes as predictors of unionization activity. *Journal of Applied Psychology, 63,* 415–421.

Hanisch, K. A. (1992). The Job Descriptive Index revisited: Questions about the question mark. *Journal of Applied Psychology, 77,* 377–382.

Hanisch, K. A., & Hulin, C. L. (1990). Retirement as a voluntary organizational withdrawal behavior. *Journal of Vocational Behavior, 37,* 60–78.

Hanisch, K. A., & Hulin, C. L. (1991). General attitudes and organizational withdrawal: An evaluation of a causal model. *Journal of Vocational Behavior, 39,* 110–128.

Hanisch, K. A., Hulin, C. L., & Roznowski, M. A. (1998). The importance of individuals' repertoires of behaviors: The scientific appropriateness of studying multiple behaviors and general attitudes. *Journal of Organizational Behavior, 19,* 463–480.

Hanisch, K. A., Hulin, C. L., & Seitz, S. T. (1996). Mathematical/computational modeling of organizational withdrawal processes: Benefits, methods, and results. In G. Ferris (Ed.), *Research in personnel and human resources management* (Vol. 14, pp. 91–142). Greenwich, CT: JAI Press.

Helson, H. (1948). Adaptation-level as a basis for a quantitative theory of frames of reference. *Psychological Review, 55,* 297–313.

Helson, H. (1964). *Adaptation-level theory.* New York: Harper & Row.

Herzberg, F. (1967). *Work and the nature of man.* Cleveland, OH: World Book.

Herzberg, F., Mausner, B., Peterson, R. O., & Capwell, D. F. (1957). *Job attitudes: A review of research and opinions.* Pittsburgh, PA: Psychological Services of Pittsburgh.

Holland, J. L. (1985). *Making vocational choices* (2nd ed.). Englewood Cliffs, NJ: Prentice-Hall.

Hom, P. W. (2001). The legacy of Hulin's work on turnover thinking and research. In J. M. Brett & F. D. Drasgow (Eds.), *Psychology of work: Theoretically based empirical research* (pp. 169–188). Mahwah, NJ: Erlbaum.

Hom, P. W., Katerberg, R., & Hulin, C. L. (1979). A comparative examination of three approaches to the prediction of turnover. *Journal of Applied Psychology, 64,* 280–290.

Hoppock, R. (1935). *Job satisfaction.* New York: Harper.

Hulin, C. L. (1966a). The effects of community characteristics on measures of job satisfaction. *Journal of Applied Psychology, 50,* 185–192.

Hulin, C. L. (1966b). Job satisfaction and turnover in a female clerical population. *Journal of Applied Psychology, 50,* 280–285.

Hulin, C. L. (1968). The effects of changes in job satisfaction levels on turnover. *Journal of Applied Psychology, 52,* 122–126.

Hulin, C. L. (1991). Adaptation, persistence, and commitment in organizations. In M. D. Dunnette & L. M. Hough (Eds.), *Handbook of industrial and organizational psychology* (2nd ed., Vol. 2, pp. 445–505). Palo Alto, CA: Consulting Psychologist Press.

Hulin, C. L. (2001). Lessons from I/O psychology. In J. M. Brett & F. D. Drasgow (Eds.), *Psychology of work: Theoretically based empirical research* (pp. 3–22). Mahwah, NJ: Erlbaum.

Hulin, C. L., & Blood, M. R. (1968). Job enlargement, individual differences, and work responses. *Psychological Bulletin, 69,* 41–55.

Hulin, C. L., & Roznowski, M. (1984). Productivity and the organization. In J. W. C. Chow, J. R. Dewald, & M. J. Hopkins (Eds.), *Productivity: Confronting the crisis.* Edmonton, Saskatchewan, Canada: Decho.

Hulin, C. L., & Smith, P. A. (1967). An empirical investigation of two implications of the Two-Factor Theory of job satisfaction. *Journal of Applied Psychology, 51,* 396–402.

Hull, C. L. (1943). *Principles of behavior: An introduction to behavior theory.* New York: Appleton-Century-Crofts.

Humphreys, L. G. (1985). General intelligence: An integration of factor, test, and simplex theory. In B. B. Wolman (Ed.), *Handbook of intelligence: Theories, measurement, and applications* (pp. 201–224). New York: Wiley.

Iaffaldano, M. T., & Muchinsky, P. M. (1985). Job satisfaction and job performance: A meta-analysis. *Psychological Bulletin, 97,* 251–273.

Ilies, R., & Judge, T. A. (in press). Understanding the dynamic relationship between personality, mood, and job satisfaction: A field experience sampling study. *Organizational Behavior and Human Decision Processes.*

James, J. R., & Tetrick, L. E. (1986). Confirmatory analytic tests of three causal models relating job perceptions to job satisfaction. *Journal of Applied Psychology, 71,* 77–82.

James, L. R., & Jones, A. P. (1980). Perceived job characteristics and job satisfaction: An examination of reciprocal causation. *Personnel Psychology, 33,* 97–135.

Judge, T. A., & Bono, J. E. (2001). Relationship of core self-evaluations traits—self-esteem, generalized self-efficacy, locus of control, and emotional stability—with job satisfaction and job performance: A meta-analysis. *Journal of Applied Psychology, 86,* 80–92.

Judge, T. A., Bono, J. E., & Locke, E. A. (2000). Personality and job satisfaction: The mediating role of job characteristics. *Journal of Applied Psychology, 85,* 237–249.

Judge, T. A., & Bretz, R. D. (1993). Report on an alternative measure of affective disposition. *Educational and Psychological Measurement, 53,* 1095–1104.

Judge, T. A., & Heller, D. (2001). *The dispositional sources of job satisfaction: An integrative test.* Working paper, University of Florida, Gainesville, Florida.

Judge, T. A., Heller, D., & Mount, M. K. (2001). *Personality and job satisfaction: A meta-analysis.* Paper presented at the Society for Industrial and Organizational Psychology Annual Meetings, San Diego, CA.

Judge, T. A., & Hulin, C. L. (1993). Job satisfaction as a reflection of disposition: A multiple source casual analysis. *Organizational Behavior and Human Decision Processes, 56,* 388–421.

Judge, T. A., & Locke, E. A. (1993). Effect of dysfunctional thought processes on subjective well-being and job satisfaction. *Journal of Applied Psychology, 78,* 475–490.

Judge, T. A., Locke, E. A., & Durham, C. C. (1997). The dispositional causes of job satisfaction: A core evaluations approach. *Research in Organizational Behavior, 19,* 151–188.

Judge, T. A., Locke, E. A., Durham, C. C., & Kluger, A. N. (1998). Dispositional effects on job and life satisfaction: The role of core evaluations. *Journal of Applied Psychology, 83,* 17–34.

Judge, T. A., Thoresen, C. J., Bono, J. E., & Patton, G. K. (2001). The job satisfaction-job performance relationship: A qualitative and quantitative review. *Psychological Bulletin, 127,* 376–407.

Jurgensen, C. E. (1978). Job preferences (What makes a job good or bad?). *Journal of Applied Psychology, 50,* 479–487.

Kendall, L. M. (1963). *Canonical analysis of job satisfaction and behavioral, personal background, and situational data.* Unpublished doctoral dissertation, Cornell University. Ithaca, NY.

Korman, A. K. (1971). Environmental ambiguity and locus of control as interactive influences on satisfaction. *Journal of Applied Psychology, 55,* 339–342.

Larsen, R., & Csikszentmihalyi, M. (1983). The experience sampling method. In H. T. Reis (Ed.), *Naturalistic approaches to studying social interaction.* San Francisco: Jossey-Bass.

Levin, I., & Stokes, J. P. (1989). Dispositional approach to job satisfaction: Role of negative affectivity. *Journal of Applied Psychology, 74,* 752–758.

Locke, E. A. (1969). What is job satisfaction? *Organizational Behavior and Human performance, 4,* 309–336.

Locke, E. A. (1976). The nature and causes of job satisfaction. In M. D. Dunnette (Ed.), *Handbook of industrial and organizational psychology* (pp. 1297–1343). Chicago: Rand McNally.

Loher, B. T., Noe, R. A., Moeller, N. L., & Fitzgerald, M. P. (1985). A meta-analysis of the relation of job characteristics to job satisfaction. *Journal of Applied Psychology, 70,* 280–289.

March, J. G., & Simon, H. A. (1958). *Organizations.* New York: Wiley.

Maslow, A. H. (1943). A theory of human motivation. *Psychological Review, 50,* 370–396.

McCrae, R. R., & Costa, P. T., Jr. (1997). Personality trait structure as a human universal. *American Psychologist, 52,* 509–516.

Mikes, P. S., & Hulin, C. L. (1968). The use of importance as a weighting component of job satisfaction. *Journal of Applied Psychology, 52,* 394–398.

Miller, H. E., Katerberg, R., & Hulin, C. L. (1979). Evaluation of the Mobley, Horner, and Hollingsworth model of employee turnover. *Journal of Applied Psychology, 64,* 509–517.

Miner, A. G. (2001). *Antecedents, behavioral outcomes, and performance implications of mood at work: An experience sampling study.* Unpublished doctoral dissertation, University of Illinois at Urbana-Champaign.

Miner, A. G., Glomb, T. M., & Hulin, C. L. (2001, April). *Mood at work: Experience sampling using palmtop computers.* Symposium conducted at the meeting of the Society for Industrial and Organizational Psychology, San Diego, CA.

Mobley, W. H., Horner, S. O., & Hollingsworth, A. T. (1978). An evaluation of precursors of hospital employee turnover. *Journal of Applied Psychology, 63,* 408–414.

Murray, H. A. (1943). *Thematic apperception test.* Cambridge, MA: Harvard University Press.

Necowitz, L. B., & Roznowski, M. (1994). Negative affectivity and job satisfaction: Cognitive processes underlying the relationship and effects on employee behaviors. *Journal of Vocational Behavior, 45,* 270–294.

Newton, T., & Keenan, T. (1991). Further analyses of the dispositional argument in organizational behavior. *Journal of Applied Psychology, 76,* 781–787.

Organ, D. W., & Ryan, K. (1995). A meta-analytic review of attitudinal and dispositional predictors of organizational citizenship behavior. *Personnel Psychology, 48,* 775–802.

Paterson, D. G., & Darley, J. G. (1936). *Men, women, and jobs.* Minneapolis: University of Minnesota Press.

Porter, L. W. (1961). A study of need satisfactions in bottom and middle management jobs. *Journal of Applied Psychology, 45,* 1–10.

Rentsch, J. R., & Steel, R. P. (1992). Construct and concurrent validation of the Andrews and Withey job satisfaction questionnaire. *Educational and Psychological Measurement, 52,* 357–367.

Rice, R. W., Gentile, D. A., & McFarlin, D. B. (1991). Facet importance and job satisfaction. *Journal of Applied Psychology, 76,* 31–39.

Roberts, K. H., & Glick, W. (1981). The job characteristics approach to task design: A critical review. *Journal of Applied Psychology, 66,* 193–217.

Roznowski, M. (1989). Examination of the measurement properties of the Job Descriptive Index with experimental items. *Journal of Applied Psychology, 74,* 805–814.

Roznowski, M., & Hanisch, K. A. (1990). Building systematic heterogeneity into job attitudes and behavior measures. *Journal of Vocational Behavior, 36,* 361–375.

Roznowski, M., & Hulin, C. (1992). The scientific merit of valid measures of general constructs with special reference to job satisfaction and job withdrawal. In C. J. Cranny, P. C. Smith, & E. F. Stone (Eds.), *Job satisfaction* (pp. 123–163). New York: Lexington.

Roznowski, M., Miller, H. E., & Rosse, J. G. (1992). *On the utility of broad-band measures of employee behavior: The case for employee adaptation and citizenship.* Paper presented at the annual meeting of the Academy of Management, Las Vegas, NV.

Schmitt, N., & McCune, J. T. (1981). The relationship between job attitudes and the decision to retire. *Academy of Management Journal, 24,* 795–802.

Schriesheim, C. (1978). Job satisfaction, attitudes toward unions, and voting an a union representation election. *Journal of Applied Psychology, 63,* 548–552.

Scott, K. D., & Taylor, G. S. (1985). An examination of conflicting findings on the relationship between job satisfaction and absenteeism: A meta-analysis. *Academy of Management Journal, 28,* 599–612.

Scullen, S. E. (1998). *Toward greater understanding of the construct validity on managerial performance ratings.* Unpublished doctoral dissertation. Iowa City, IA: University of Iowa, Iowa City, IA.

Shaffer, R. H. (1953). Job satisfaction as related to need satisfactions in work. *Psychological Monographs: General and Applied, 67*(364).

Simon, P. (1975). Fifty ways to leave your lover. In *still crazy after all these years.*

Smith, F. J. (1977). Work attitudes as predictors of attendance on a specific day. *Journal of Applied Psychology, 62,* 16–19.

Smith, P. C. (1955). The prediction of individual differences in susceptibility to industrial monotony. *Journal of Applied Psychology, 39,* 322–329.

Smith, P. C., Kendall, L. M., & Hulin, C. L. (1969). *Measurement of satisfaction in work and retirement.* Chicago: Rand-McNally.

Staw, B. M., Bell, N. E., & Clausen, J. A. (1986). The dispositional approach to job attitudes: A lifetime longitudinal test. *Administrative Science Quarterly, 31,* 437–453.

Staw, B. M., & Ross, J. (1985). Stability in the midst of change: A dispositional approach to job attitudes. *Journal of Applied Psychology, 70,* 469–480.

Tellegen, A., Watson, D., & Clark, L. A. (1999). On the dimensionality and hierarchical structure of affect. *Psychological Science, 10,* 297–303.

Thibaut, J. W., & Kelley, H. H. (1959). *The social psychology of groups.* New York: Wiley.

Thurstone, L. L. (1928). Attitudes can be measured. *American Journal of Sociology, 33,* 529–554.

Totterdell, P. (1999). Mood scores: Mood and performance in professional cricketers. *British Journal of Psychology, 90,* 317–332.

Totterdell, P. (2000). Catching moods and hitting runs: Mood linkage and subjective performance in professional sports teams. *Journal of Applied Psychology, 85,* 848–859.

Triandis, H. C. (1980). Values, attitudes, and interpersonal behavior. In H. Howe & M. M. Page (Eds.), *Nebraska symposium on motivation: Beliefs, attitudes, and values* (Vol. 27, pp. 195–259). Lincoln: University of Nebraska Press.

Turner, A. N., & Lawrence, P. R. (1965). *Industrial jobs and the worker.* Cambridge, MA: University of Harvard Press.

Wainer, H. (1976). Estimating coefficients in linear models: It don't make no nevermind. *Psychological Bulletin, 83,* 213–217.

Watson, D. (2000). *Mood and temperament.* New York: Guilford Press.

Watson, D., & Slack, A. K. (1993). General factors of affective temperament and their relation to job satisfaction over time. *Organizational Behavior and Human Decision Processes, 54,* 181–202.

Weiss, H. M., & Brief, A. P. (in press). Affect at work: An historical perspective. In R. L. Payne & C. L. Cooper (Eds.), *Emotions at work: Theory, research, and applications in management.* Chichester, England: Wiley.

Weiss, H. M., & Cropanzano, R. (1996). Affective events theory: A theoretical discussion of the structure, causes and consequences of affective experiences at work. *Research in Organizational Behavior, 19,* 1–74.

Weiss, H. M., Dawis, England, & Lofquist, (1967).

Weiss, H. M., Nicholas, J. P., & Daus, C. S. (1999). An examination of the joint effects of affective experiences and job satisfaction and variations in affective experiences over time. *Organizational Behavior and Human Decision Processes, 78,* 1–24.

Weitz, J. (1952). A neglected concept in the study of job satisfaction. *Personnel Psychology, 5,* 201–205.

Wernimont, P. F. (1966). Intrinsic and extrinsic factors in job satisfaction. *Journal of Applied Psychology, 50,* 41–50.

Wicker, A. W. (1969). Attitudes versus actions: The relationship of verbal and overt behavioral responses to attitude objects. *Journal of Social Issues, 25,* 41–78.

Zajonc, R. B. (1980). Feeling and thinking: Preferences need no inferences. *American Psychologist, 35,* 151–175.

Zajonc, R. B. (1984). On the primacy of affect. *American Psychologist, 39,* 117–123.

Zalesny, M. D. (1985). Comparison of economic and noneconomic factors in predicting faculty vote preference in a union representation election. *Journal of Applied Psychology, 70,* 243–256.

Zohar, D. (1999). When things go wrong: The effect of daily work hassles on effort, exertion and negative mood. *Journal of Occupational and Organizational Psychology, 72,* 265–283.

CHAPTER 12

Leadership Models, Methods, and Applications

BRUCE J. AVOLIO, JOHN J. SOSIK, DONG I. JUNG, AND YAIR BERSON

What a difference a decade made in the field of leadership research. Whereas the emphasis in the leadership literature during the 1980s was on contingency models and examining the initiation of structure and consideration in every imaginable context, the focus in the 1990s and beyond shifted to some of the more colorful aspects of leadership including charismatic, transformational, visionary, unethical, and inspiring (Hughes, Ginnett, & Curphy, 1999). Some other giant leaps involved examining shared leadership in teams, global leadership, strategic leadership, and followership.

Changes in emphasis with leadership research and theory have brought the field to a point where it is once again taking off in some new directions. Sensing this "time between times," we focus our attention on emerging streams of research while also reviewing relevant prior literature (see Bass, 1990; Chemers, 1997; House & Aditya, 1997; Yukl, 1998; Zaccaro & Klimoski, 2001, for additional reviews).

Halfway through most conferences on leadership, someone stands up and says, "Never has a construct been studied so much that we know so little about." Unfortunately, this comment is not only obsolete—it is also wrong! We have learned an enormous amount about what constitutes leadership, where it comes from, how it can be measured, what contributes to its being ethical or unethical, how people see it differently and why, how the context alters its interpretation, and what happens when it is substituted for or replaced.

Here we define leadership as a social influence process that can occur at the individual, dyadic, group, or strategic level, where it can be shared within a top management team. We embrace Katz and Kahn's (1978) definition of organizational leadership as being "the influential increment over and above mechanical compliance with the routine directives of the organization" (p. 528) and Bryman's (1996) synthesis of earlier definitions of leadership: "The common elements in these definitions imply that leadership involves a social influence process in which a person steers members of the group toward a goal" (p. 2).

AREAS REQUIRING FURTHER EXPLORATION

With all of the money spent on leadership development in organizations, one would think we now know a lot about this area. Unfortunately, that is not the case. We know very little about standard leadership training interventions and how they directly or indirectly impact leadership development (Avolio, 1999; McCauley, 2001). We also know very little about how planned and unplanned live events affect leader development (Avolio, 1999; Zaccarro, Mumford, Connelly, Marks, & Gilbert, 2000).

We also know very little about how to develop leaders to lead others when they are distant. For example, is the articulation of a vision and its diffusion affected by how distant the leader works from followers? How does one build a coherent unit when everyone, including the leader, works virtually, or through technology, versus face to face? How is the management of impressions different when a leader has contact with staff through technology?

Moving from individual- to group-level leadership, what constitutes collective or shared leadership, and how does it emerge in teams? As organizations delevel and become more network oriented, there is more opportunity for collective or shared leadership to emerge in groups. Today, more people are working on project teams that cut across traditional organizational boundaries in business-to-business (B2B) settings. How can shared leadership within and between organizational boundaries be measured and effectively developed? What constitutes the criteria for effective development at individual, group, and strategic levels? For individual development, should the criteria include changes in moral perspective? For teams, is it a coherent and shared mental model? At the strategic level, is it the efficient diffusion of a company's mission or vision across levels, or how well a new-enterprise information technology (IT) system is utilized? Or is it simply how people in an organization identify with its culture and mission (Day, 2001)?

Even relatively small companies are now globally positioned. How will leaders address the challenges of working with a culturally diverse workforce that brings to work differences in values, traditions, customs, and beliefs about what constitutes effective leadership? What implications does the diversification of work teams have for male and female leadership? How will these cultural differences affect how we define, measure, develop, and sustain leadership?

What constitutes strategic leadership, and how does it impact on individual, group, and organizational effectiveness? Should we view strategic leadership as an individual-level or as a group-level phenomenon, such as in top management teams? Should the concept of strategic leadership be studied only at the pinnacle of organizations? What happens to strategic leadership when it is examined in a flattened, networked organization, or in several organizations that work in alliance? How should we include the context in the study of strategic leadership (Zaccaro & Klimoski, 2001)?

What are the cognitive processes that inhibit leaders and followers from achieving their best results? Are there more effective strategies for developing mental models in leaders and followers that can accelerate levels of development and trust in each other? How resilient are these mental models, and to what extent are they developed and structured differently across cultures? How does the context affect what leaders and followers think, and what influence does it play in mediating and moderating the effects of leadership on motivation and performance?

A neglected construct in leadership research has been followership. What have we learned so far about what constitutes exemplary followership, and how does it differ from exemplary leadership? Does followership vary as a consequence of the context? For example, does exemplary followership differ in a strong versus in a weak context (see Mischel, 1973)? How does the leader's creation of networks among followers shape their development (Chan & Drasgow, 2001)? Do the capabilities and motivations of followers set certain limits on a leader's developmental potential?

Can the context shape the effects of leadership, or should we consider the context as part of leadership in organizations? With many leaders and followers linked together through technology, what exactly does the local context mean, if one has daily contact with followers at distance that spans continents, cultures, and time zones? How does the level of leadership in terms of context affect what we should and should not include in our leadership theories? Presently, most models of leadership have ignored the issue of level and how it shapes what constitutes leadership (Zaccaro & Klimoski, 2001). Examples to the contrary include work by Hambrick and Mason (1984), who discussed large-scale leadership of collectives, as well indirect and mediated leadership.

Today, it is not uncommon to find four distinctly different generations of employees in the workforce. How do their experiences and values shape how leaders need to lead in organizations? Generations X and Y are said to be more challenging and less accepting of authority. If this is true, how do we develop them into leadership roles, and what changes in leadership are required for current and future leaders to remain effective?

All of the challenges just cited make the measurement of leadership at all levels in organizations more complex and also more interesting. They pose giant challenges for the field, some of which are already being pursued, and which we review later.

In sum, we have attempted to highlight major themes and significant trends that have led us to the current state of leadership studies. Our vision for the field of leadership is that it will become less model specific and much more integrated across subdisciplines, or even transdisciplinary. Too often, leadership authors have drilled down so deeply on critiquing individual models of leadership that they have failed to consider how one model may be integrated with another. At a minimum, future theoretical work on leadership must include the following elements: a multilevel view ranging from the mental models of leaders and followers through to strategic and collective leadership of large organizational entities; an integration of the context into how we define and measure leadership at each of these levels; the incorporation of time; the basic idea that leadership and its impact represent an emergent process; what mediating factors are directly influenced by leadership; a more exacting choice of relevant dependent variables as opposed to convenient performance measures; how technology mediates leadership close up and at a distance; and how cultural differences affect how leaders and followers lead and follow.

Major Trends and Future Directions

Lowe and Gardner (2000) reviewed the last 10 years of research published in the journal *Leadership Quarterly* and highlighted where the field has been and where it is heading. Other papers included in that same issue pointed to new directions in the leadership field, including several themes that we pursue in this chapter: strategic leadership, e-leadership, collective leadership, and leadership development. To the extent that the *Leadership Quarterly* contains a representative sampling of what has and perhaps will be published, some of the past trends in leadership research identified by Lowe and Gardner offer a basis for launching our discussion.

Lowe and Gardner (2000) reported nearly an equivalent emphasis in articles published on theory and research over the last decade in the *Leadership Quarterly,* i.e., 46% vs. 55%, respectively. This pattern points to a field in transition, as new theoretical perspectives entered the field in the 1980s and 1990s, shaping directions in research. Lowe and Gardner also reported that most articles were still published by American authors, supporting House and Aditya's (1997) claim that 98% of leadership research still originates in North America. However, some giant steps are being made to promote and include research from other cultures.

Lowe and Gardner (2000) identified several trends that have shaped the field of leadership studies during the 1990s. These included work on transformational leadership (Avolio, 1999; Bass, 1998; Bass & Avolio, 1993, 1994) and neo-charismatic leadership theories based on House's (1977) theory of charismatic leadership, as well as Burns (1978) and Bass (1985; see also Bass & Steidlmeier, 1999; Bryman, 1993; Conger & Hunt, 1999; Conger & Kanungo, 1987, 1998; House & Shamir, 1993). Lowe and Gardner also pointed to renewed interest in cross-cultural leadership research, which received a tremendous boost from House and his associates' Global Leadership and Organizational Behavior Effectiveness study (GLOBE) project, as well as other cross-cultural research.

Another driving force behind the transformation of leadership research and theory during the 1990s involved the emphasis on levels of analysis in theory building, research design, and measurement (Dansereau, Alutto, & Yammarino,

1984; Dansereau, Yammarino, & Markham, 1995; Dansereau & Yammarino, 1998; Klein & House, 1995). A levels-of-analysis frame of reference provided a huge leap toward more sophisticated multilevel models of leadership that now include the context in which leadership is embedded. Today, work on levels of analysis has dramatically shaped the conceptualization of how leadership is defined, measured across research streams, and within context over time (Brass, 2001; House & Aditya, 1997; Zaccaro & Klimoski, 2001). The context now being examined includes a broad range of constructs such as the nature and level of change, the medium through which leaders and followers interact, the cultures in which each are embedded, the organization level, the type of work group or unit, and the network. Future research on leadership now needs to standardize approaches to examining individual, dyadic, group, and larger collective phenomena (Lowe & Gardner, 2000). We envision that all future research will allocate greater attention to defining the level at which leadership is investigated, as well as the levels at which various models are tested and hold across different contexts (Zaccaro & Banks, 2001).

House and Aditya (1997) noted an emerging trend over the previous decade regarding the focus on strategic leadership. However, there is still a thin base of research on what constitutes strategic leadership, as well as strategic change in organizations (Boal & Hoojberg, 2000; Lowe & Gardner, 2000). Moreover, much of the research in this area has been based on case analyses, cross-sectional designs, and small samples, and it lacks a strong and coherent theoretical base.

Ironically, we know very little about how leadership actually changes people, units, organizations, and larger collectives (Burns, personal communication, November 2000; Yukl, 1999). We need to examine how leadership affects fundamental change in individuals, groups, and organizations. How can we evaluate such change while also taking into consideration the context in which leadership is embedded? What criteria can we use for assessing change at the individual, group, organizational, and even community levels? For example, can we measure behavioral or attitudinal change at each of these respective levels? What does the performance domain look like when we cut across these levels and examine change over time? Surprisingly, we know very little about the leadership of CEOs across all types and sizes of organizations. Nonetheless, some authors have attributed between 20% and 40% of organizational effectiveness to executive leadership (Ireland & Hitt, 1999).

Prior research has not explored how shared or collective leadership associated with top management teams contributes to an organization's adaptability and effectiveness (Elron, 1997). However, several studies have produced a positive relationship between strategic leadership and firm performance, but in most cases prior research has not examined how the context moderates or mediates strategic leadership performance (Finklestein & Hambrick, 1996). Demonstrating the importance of the context, Waldman, Ramirez, House, and Puranam (2001) showed that executives who were rated by followers as more charismatic had little impact on firm performance under stable environmental conditions, but under unstable or uncertain conditions charismatic leadership significantly predicted financial performance.

A major decision for organizations about leadership deals with its succession (Lauterbach, Vu, & Weisberg, 1999). Organizations that rely on internal networks enjoy smooth transitions and the continuation of strategy. Yet, selecting a new leader who comes from the same stock as the previous one may result in staying the course when radical change is required (Hambrick & Mason, 1984). The area of leadership and succession, particularly at the tops of organizations, deserves more attention in the literature.

A number of questions highlight the need for future research on the context in which leadership is observed and interpreted, including the following: Are the same leadership styles differentially effective as we move up the organizational hierarchy? How does the legacy left by a former leader affect his or her successor's ability to maintain and enhance organizational performance? How do strategic leadership styles vary in terms of their impacts across different sectors of the economy? Are some strategic leadership styles generic and equally effective across all sectors? As the world of work becomes more complex, can leadership at the top be more effectively shared; if so, what are optimal strategies for developing and deploying shared leadership? How will strategic leadership change after inserting advanced IT in organizations in which every employee is connected to the CEO?

Leadership and Creating Meaning

Smircich and Morgan (1982) provided an alternative definition of leadership, which has not been thoroughly explored and may have even greater relevance as leaders lead at a distance from followers in today's global economy. They stated that "leadership is realized in the process whereby one or more individuals succeeds in attempting to frame and define the reality of others" (p. 258). Are there differences in how leaders create impressions and use impression-management strategies to influence followers to support their positions? How do different types of leaders use impression-management strategies to create the meaning that they want their followers to derive from a particular situation, and will the creation of meaning work differently across cultures? For example, W. L. Gardner and Avolio (1998)

argued that charismatic versus noncharismatic leaders use different impression-management styles to gain commitment and trust from followers. How do these differences extend across cultures?

Smircich and Morgan (1982) related the management of meaning to a number of important areas including the emergence of leadership: "They emerge as leaders because of their role in framing experience in a way that provides a viable basis for actions" (p. 258). Simply put, leaders define the situation in which followers find themselves, shaping their range of perceived and actual choices. Charismatic leaders frequently emerge in times of crisis because they offer a viable alternative interpretation to resolve the crisis while managing an impression of confidence and an ability to inspire followers to pursue a solution (Conger & Kanungo, 1998).

The management of meaning has direct relevance to studying strategic leadership. Such leaders usually do not have direct contact with all followers and therefore must manage the meaning of events at a distance—and in today's organizations through advanced IT. Strategic leaders have a mandate to define the current and future reality of their organizations (Ireland & Hitt, 1999). However, we know that many strategic leaders lose their mandate when their framing of reality does not make sense to followers, lacks credibility, or ultimately does not contribute to success. Indeed, according to Howard (2001), somewhere between 30% and 50% of CEOs are prematurely ousted from their jobs.

To make sense of each follower's future requires the leader to develop a relationship through which followers come to identify with the leader's vision (Shamir, House, & Arthur, 1993). According to Shamir and his associates, to energize followers, leaders must successfully link the follower's self-concept to the collective thinking or concept of the group. This creates a sense of alignment around the vision to move forward. Visions represent one of the highest forms of managing meaning (Awamleh & Gardner, 1999; Graen & Uhl-Bien, 1995) and could be examined in terms of their diffusion through organizations as being an outcome of successful leadership. Specifically, all other things being equal, the extent to which a vision is wired into each employee's thinking and behavior could be used as a criterion measure of leadership effectiveness in an organization.

In sum, Smircich and Morgan (1982) stated that "leadership as a phenomenon depends upon the existence of people who are prepared to surrender their ability to define their reality for others" (p. 270). The way leaders transform reality for followers is a fertile area for future research (Yukl, 1999), including differences in followers' willingness to surrender their interpretations of reality or to share in the responsibility of creating the interpretation of the future.

Leadership Substitutes

Whereas leaders are said to influence how followers derive meaning from events, another line of research argues that we attribute too much meaning to leaders as the central causes of events. Followers erroneously attribute events or performance outcomes to the influence of a leader when in fact it is due to the context (Kerr & Jermier, 1978). This may be particularly evident with charismatic leaders, who emerge during times of crisis (Beyer, 1999). Meindl, Ehrlich, and Dukerich (1985) argued that people use leadership as a way of explaining or interpreting what goes on in organizations when they do not fully understand the cause of events. In these cases, using a levels-of-analysis framework in the design of models and methods can facilitate a better understanding of what causes what over time.

Although the literature on leadership substitutes provides an interesting perspective on how the context can moderate the impact of leadership on follower perceptions and performance, the weight of evidence shows that substitutes for leadership do not substitute as predicted by Kerr and Jermier (1978). Podsakoff, Niehoff, MacKenzie, and Williams (1993) were unable to find sufficient evidence to support J. P. Howell, Dorfman, and Kerr's (1986) claim that leadership substitutes moderate the relationship between leader behaviors and various intermediate process and outcome measures. Podsakoff, MacKenzie, and Fetter (1993) examined effects of substitutes for leadership with a sample of professional employees. The authors concluded that a substantial portion of the variance in perceptions and performance was shared by *both* leadership behaviors and substitutes. All substitutes for leadership independently influenced at least one of the criterion measures, accounting for 30% to 40% of the variance in employee attitudes, 18% to 23% in employee role perceptions, and 7% in performance. Podsakoff, MacKenzie, and Bommer (1995) concluded that "although the notion that subordinate, task, and organizational characteristics moderate the effects of a leader's behavior seems intuitively appealing, the weight of empirical evidence does not support it" (p. 381). However, these same substitutes added to leadership can augment the prediction of employee role perceptions, job attitudes, and performance. Podsakoff et al. reported that the total variance explained in employee attitudes and in role performance by leadership and its substitutes (e.g., task feedback, professional orientation, rewards outside of the leader's control, etc.) were 35% and 33%.

We now turn to addressing some of the issues just mentioned by focusing on the individual, later returning to the strategic context in which individual leadership is observed and developed.

Implicit Leadership Theory

Calder (1977), as well as Mitchell (1979), argued that leadership was not directly observable. Observer ratings were based in part on attributions, thus introducing some degree of error or bias into all leadership ratings (Lord, Binning, Rush, & Thomas, 1978; Rush, Phillips, & Lord, 1981). Summarizing a long line of research on implicit notions of leadership, Lord and Maher (1991) defined leadership as a process perceived by others and then labeled leadership. Calder's (1977) work provided the basis for a cognitive revolution in leadership research that continues to emerge and have a significant influence on the field of leadership research and theory today. Much of this research is based on the work of Lord and his associates. Early experimental research by Rush, Thomas, and Lord (1977) demonstrated that college students exposed to the same experimental leadership conditions interpreted leadership behaviors differently. Phillips and Lord (1981) attributed those differences to a cognitive categorization process that uses contextual and behavioral cues to classify leadership behaviors. Each observer comes to the situation with a pre-existing mental structure, which results in observed behaviors being encoded based on the rater's categorization process. Differences in category systems or implicit theories (e.g., between men and women leaders) can result in an encoding and recall of behavior that is different for men and women.

Lord, Foti, and DeVader (1984) suggest that perceptions of leadership are based on hierarchically organized categories, which are each represented by a prototype. Prototypes are formed based on experiences with individuals or events. A prototypical category might be the use of a political or military leader. Traits that people associate with prototypical categories become important facets of how perceivers construct their categories and prototypes (Mischel, 1973). Observed leadership behavior is then categorized more or less automatically based on prototypical matching between an observer's implicit theory of leadership and actual behavior.

Work on implicit leadership theory (ILT) clearly has implications for leadership research as it moves across different cultures. ILT also has implications for theory development as we examine how followers internalize leadership messages and identify with a leader's vision within and between cultures. Work on ILT has implications for leadership development as well. ILT also affects whether an individual sees himself or herself as a leader worthy of development.

In sum, the work by Lord and his associates has demonstrated the importance of viewing leadership as being in the eye of the beholder. This stream of research has implications for examining biases in leadership measurement, for developing new theories that capture how leaders manage the meaning of events for followers, and the development of leadership itself. Other issues deserving closer scrutiny include the following: To what extent are changes in generational views of leadership being shaped by the media exposure on the topic? How can leaders build trust when they are so overexposed in the media? Does the generation now entering the workforce come with different expectations about what constitutes trusted leadership?

INTEGRATING SEVERAL STREAMS OF LEADERSHIP RESEARCH

The emergence of leadership research in the early 1900s was based on the idea that certain traits predisposed an individual to emerge as a leader (Bass, 1990). Up until published reviews by Mann (1959) and Stogdill (1948), trait theories of leadership dominated the literature. However, conclusions drawn from early reviews set a new direction for leadership research focusing on leadership style or behaviors, which lasted the next 40 years. Indeed, the shift away from personality research and leadership was unfortunate, given that Kenny and Zaccaro (1983) later reported that 48% to 82% of the variance in leadership emergence was accounted for by the leader's attributes. Ironically, Stogdill (1974) reported that personality attributes such as surgency, emotional stability, conscientiousness, and agreeableness were all positively related to leadership effectiveness (Hogan, Curphy, & Hogan, 1994). Yet it was Stogdill's review that led to a near abandonment of research on traits.

Lord, DeVader, and Alliger (1986) argued that many previous authors misinterpreted Mann and Stogdill's reviews, and raised several concerns. First, both Mann and Stogdill examined the relationship between leadership emergence and personality, limiting the scope of research reviewed. Second, although there were a number of consistent significant relationships between leadership traits and emergence, Mann commented on the lack of relationships. Lord et al. conducted a meta-analysis of the literature reviewed by Mann, reporting that many of the relationships between personality and leadership emergence had been underestimated. They concluded that traits (e.g., intelligence, masculinity-femininity, and dominance) were associated with leadership perceptions to a much greater extent than had been reported.

Howard (2001) discussed the importance of examining not only which traits predicted leadership success and effectiveness but also those traits that predicted failures. Hogan, Raskin, and Fazzini (1990) focused on what caused leadership failures after finding that 60% to 70% of employees reported that their worst or most stressful aspect of their job

was their supervisor. Earlier work by McCall and Lombardo (1983) and by Hellervik, Hazucha, and Schneider (1992) reported that managers who failed exhibited a number of personality flaws including being overly controlling, irritable, and exploitative. These results parallel findings reported by Kaplan, Drath, and Kofodimos (1991). Many bright, hard-working managers fail because they are arrogant, abrasive, selfish, and lacking what Goleman (1998) called *emotional intelligence*.

Judge, Bono, Ilies, and Werner (2000) completed a meta-analysis of 94 studies examining the relationship among the Big Five personality traits, leadership emergence, effectiveness, and transformational leadership. Judge et al. reported a multiple R of .47 with the Big Five traits predicting leadership effectiveness. Extraversion was most consistently and positively correlated with leadership emergence and effectiveness. Extraversion, conscientiousness, and openness to experience were consistently correlated with leadership effectiveness. Judge and Bono (2000) examined the relationship between transformational leadership and the Big Five personality factors. Results based on over 200 organizations indicated that agreeableness was the strongest predictor of transformational leadership, followed by extraversion. Openness to experience was also positively related to transformational leadership; however, this relationship disappeared when effects of other personality traits were statistically controlled. Overall, the multiple-R value between the Big Five personality traits and transformational leadership was .40.

The Big Five personality traits have also been linked as antecedents to leadership emergence in autonomous teams (Taggar, Hackett, & Saha, 1999). Earlier research on antecedents of leadership found that the leader's interests, energy, verbal fluency, confidence, and independence were each predictors of leadership success (reported in Bass, 1990).

In sum, one of the main conclusions from this literature is that personality does indeed matter and, like attributes of the context, must be taken into consideration when predicting leadership emergence and effectiveness. The accumulated research in this area indicates that there are certain attributes one might want to take into consideration when making selection decisions. Some of these attributes may also prove to be quite effective in predicting whether a more or less successful candidate will succeed at current leadership in an organization (McCauley, 2001).

Male and Female Leaders

Over the last decade, many attributes associated with effective management have been associated with women (Helgesen, 1990; Rosener, 1995). Changes in organizational structure and a greater emphasis on inclusion have led to calls for managers to be more collaborative, cooperative, participative, empathetic, nurturing, and developmentally oriented. These qualities have been traditionally associated with "female advantages" (Rosener, 1995), as well as with transformational leadership (Maher, 1997). The conventional wisdom suggests that men and women differ in terms of leadership styles and behaviors. The literature on sex role types indicates that men tend to be seen as more task oriented, whereas women are viewed as more relationship oriented. Men have been shown to be less comfortable working for a female leader, while also viewing her success as being due more to luck than to capability (Forsyth & Forsyth, 1984). As noted later, however, these effects may disappear when organizational context factors are controlled (Eagly & Johannesen-Schmidt, 2000). Hollander and Neider (1978) reported that female respondents tended to cite more incidents of bad leadership being associated with male leaders, while citing an equivalent number of good incidents for male and female leaders. Eagly, Karau, and Makhijani (1995) concluded from their meta-analysis of the literature that women who exhibited a more masculine style were perceived as less effective than were women who used a feminine style. Women using a feminine style were also seen as less effective than men, who exhibited a masculine style.

Men and women can lead equally effectively (Eagly et al., 1995; Powell, 1993), but may differ in terms of how they lead (Adler, 1996; Eagly & Johnson, 1990; Parker & Ogilvie, 1996). However, Kanter (1977) argued that individual differences in terms of personality were probably more important than gender in determining how male and female leaders performed in managerial roles.

Many books written for the general public contend that women's leadership styles are different than men's (Helgesen, 1990; Loden, 1985; Rosener, 1995). Rosener labeled the style of women as being interactive and that of men as being command and control oriented. Nonetheless, much of the research on this topic has not reported reliable male-female differences (Bartol & Martin, 1986; Eagly & Johannesen-Schmidt, 2000; Eagly, Karu, Miner, & Johnson, 1994). Eagly et al. (1994) reported that men generally scored higher than women on motivation to manage others in a more hierarchical manner. Eagly and Johannesen-Schmidt (2000) conducted a meta-analysis of literature comparing male to female leadership styles. Most differences were relatively small, but there was a tendency for women to be more interpersonally oriented, less autocratic, and more participative.

Comparisons of male and female leaders on transformational leadership behavior have also produced small but significant differences. Bass, Avolio, and Atwater (1996)

reported that women were rated more transformational than were their male counterparts. Ross and Offermann (1997) reported that military cadets' ratings of their commanding officers' transformational leadership were positively correlated with being seen as more nurturing and feminine and were negatively correlated with attributes such as aggressiveness and masculinity. Hackman, Furniss, Hills, and Peterson (1992) reported a positive relationship between ratings of transformational leadership and communal qualities assessed by Bem's (1974) sex role inventory. Eagly and Johannesen-Schmidt (2000) examined the normative database ($N = 9,000$ raters) for the Multifactor Leadership Questionnaire (MLQ) Form 5X (see Avolio, Bass, & Jung, 1999), reporting that female leaders were rated higher on two aspects of transformational leadership: attributed charisma and individualized consideration. Male leaders were rated higher on all aspects of negative, or less effective, leadership.

Eagly and Johannesen-Schmidt (2000) suggested that some gender-stereotypic role differences may disappear as the specific characteristics of those organizational roles are controlled. For example, Moskowitz, Suh, and Desaulniers (1994) reported that agentic behavior traditionally associated with men was more controlled by the status of the interacting partners (e.g., any boss with a follower), whereas communal behaviors were more controlled by gender regardless of organizational roles.

In sum, literature comparing male and female leaders has generally reported relatively few differences in terms of leadership style. Future research needs to take a closer look at how the organizational and cultural contexts affect these results, especially at more senior levels. A more precise comparison of men and women leaders needs to take into account other variables that may be correlated with gender differences including level, tenure, and experience (Yukl, 1998).

Leadership Knowledge, Skills, and Ability

A thin base of literature links leadership ability to behavior and performance (Mumford, Zaccaro, Harding, Jacobs, & Fleishman, 2000). Mumford et al. argued that leadership involves a complex form of social problem solving in which a leader's performance is associated with his or her ability to sense the need for change, identify goals, construct viable solution paths, and do so by understanding the complexity of the internal and external environment. Complex problem-solving skills, social judgment skills (Goleman, 1998), and knowledge (Simonton, 1994) have all been linked to effectiveness.

Leaders frequently need to generate solutions to multiple, rapidly unfolding problems by coming up with the best alternative solutions in the shortest period of time (Day, 2001;

Mintzberg, 1973). Leaders need skills and abilities to develop and implement solutions with followers, peers, or supervisors operating in complex, dynamic contexts. To do so, leaders need the social skills that come with some of the traits identified earlier (House & Baetz, 1979; Yukl & Van Fleet, 1992; Zaccaro, 1996). Moreover, effective leaders must also have the skills to persuade followers—often in very difficult, complex social situations—to accept and support their proposed solutions (Conger & Kanungo, 1998).

Leaders need a certain knowledge set in order to come up with solutions required to address challenges and opportunities (Mumford et al., 2000). For example, Simonton (1984, 1990) reported that charismatic leaders had a rather unique set of career experiences that provided them with the experiential knowledge to solve problems confronting their followers. Ironically, although the acquisition of knowledge and skills is clearly important to leadership effectiveness, the area has been downplayed in the leadership literature; however, some exceptions exist (Jacobs & Jaques, 1987). Leaders who accumulate knowledge characterized by a broader and longer time perspective are expected to be more successful as they ascend to higher level positions in organizations (Jaques, 1977). Similarly, tacit experience and knowledge were shown to have significant, positive relationships with leadership effectiveness and performance (Sternberg & Wagner, 1993).

There are several important issues to consider in this emerging area of interest. First, how does the accumulation of life experiences shape the knowledge and implicit or schematic structures of leaders through the development of intelligence, tacit knowledge, wisdom, or perspective-taking capacity? How do such experiences impact the leader's development and performance? How can we use these measures in the selection of leaders? For example, it seems highly feasible to use the Sternberg's work on tacit knowledge as one means of determining who is more or less able to lead.

Summarizing Attributes of Successful and Unsuccessful Leaders

Research comparing successful and unsuccessful leaders has been synthesized in two excellent reviews of this literature. Hogan et al.'s (1994) review presents the Big Five model of personality as a convenient way to summarize individual differences associated with leader effectiveness. Their review reveals a consistent association between leader success and surgency (e.g., dominance, extraversion, sociability), conscientiousness (e.g., integrity, responsibility), agreeableness (e.g., diplomacy, cooperativeness), and emotional stability (e.g., self-confidence, positive mood, emotional control).

Additional leader attributes associated with success were provided by Kirkpatrick and Locke's (1991) review. These included drive, honesty and integrity, self-confidence, cognitive ability, and knowledge. Leaders may also be unsuccessful because of personality defects or character flaws (e.g., Kaplan et al., 1991; Kets de Vries, 1988). Leaders who lack intelligence, good social skills, decisiveness, self-confidence, self-esteem, self-confidence, hubris, honesty, and ambition often fail. This stream of research parallels evidence reported in the popular press indicating that CEOs of Fortune 500 companies failed because of personal problems such as self-deception, decision gridlock, and passive leadership (Sellers, 1999). Again, such attributes could be used to prescreen when selecting future leaders in organizations.

The selection of managers based on leadership attributes has been a longstanding concern in the literature. Identifying the set of characteristics of effective leaders as well as developing the selection tools to assess them has hampered progress, although recent work has moved the field forward considerably. Extensive research on managerial abilities and specifically the definition and characterization of leadership in terms of complex social problem-solving skills, as well as attributes repeatedly linked to effectiveness, now provide a firmer basis for developing new selection tools (Marshall-Mies et al., 2000).

The Development of Moral and Immoral Leadership

Ethics and character of leaders have gained increased research attention over the last decade (e.g., Bass & Steidlmeier, 1999; Hollander, 1995; Kanungo & Mendonca, 1996). This emerging literature highlights prosocial motives, morality, and trustworthiness as being important determinants of effective leader-follower relations. For example, the charismatic leadership literature has distinguished constructive versus destructive leaders (Avolio, 1999; Bass & Steidlmeier, 1999; Conger & Kanungo, 1998; House & Howell, 1992), who differ on prosocial versus self-centered motives paralleling higher and lower stages of moral development (Kuhnert & Lewis, 1987). Prosocial leaders are empathetic, self-sacrificing, trustworthy, individually considerate, and focused on building collective missions, whereas self-centered leaders are self-aggrandizing, dominating, exploitative, and manipulative and promote compliance through fear (Bass & Steidlmeier, 1999; O'Connor, Mumford, Clifton, Gessner, & Connelly, 1995).

Overall, the literature on leadership attributes and individual differences has produced a wealth of information regarding the identification and development of effective leadership. Nonetheless, most of this literature still applies to middle- to lower-level leaders. Future research needs to examine the personal attributes and life experiences of more senior.

Leadership Styles and Behaviors

Unlike the limited amount of work on knowledge, skills, and problem-solving capability, there has been an extensive research on differences in leadership styles and behaviors (Hughes et al., 1999; Yukl, 1998). Much of this emerged following the disappointing conclusions reported by Mann and Stogdill's reviews of leadership traits. This led to a stream of research on the people versus production styles of leaders, as well as on initiation of structure and consideration generated in research conducted at the University of Michigan and Ohio State University (Bass, 1990). At Ohio State University researchers measured nine behavioral constructs, which initially included initiation, membership, representation, integration, organization, domination, communication, recognition, and production orientation. Leaders were rated on how frequently they displayed behaviors associated with each construct (Hemphill & Coons, 1957; Stogdill, 1963). Factor analyses resulted in a clustering of constructs into four categories labeled consideration, initiation of structure, production emphasis, and sensitivity (Bass, 1990). These early results led to the development of two-factor theories of leadership, which dominated the literature well into the 1980s— for example in Fiedler's (1967) contingency model, Blake and Mouton's (1964) managerial grid, Hershey and Blanchard's (1969) situational leadership theory, and more recent work by Graen and his colleagues on leader-member exchange (LMX) theory (Fiedler, 1967; Graen, Novak, & Sommerkamp, 1982). Preceding this period, work by Hemphill (1949) focused on examining what the situation demanded of leaders. The outgrowth of focusing on the situation led to other contingency models such as Vroom and Yetton's (1973) normative decision-making model, and House and Mitchell's (1974) path-goal theory.

(Non)Contingent Rewards and Punishment

Other research on leadership styles included how leaders used rewards and punishment to influence follower motivation and performance. Podsakoff and Todor (1985) examined the relationship between the use of contingent reward and punishment behaviors on follower motivation. They reported that group cohesion, drive, and productivity were all related positively to leader-contingent reward behavior. Contingent punishment was also positively related to group drive and productivity, whereas noncontingent reward and punishment produced equivocal results. Their findings supported earlier arguments by Hunt and Osborn (1980), as well as House and Mitchell's (1975) path-goal theory of leadership, indicating that noncontingent versus contingent rewards were less likely to produce positive motivational effects.

Podsakoff, Todor, and Skov (1982) demonstrated that the impact of using contingent or noncontingent rewards depends on the nature of the context. For example, both low and high performers were equally dissatisfied with the use of noncontingent punishment; however, there were no effects on performance. The use of contingent rewards has been associated with higher follower satisfaction, advancement opportunities, and performance over a large number of samples, levels, and cultures (Bass, 1998; Lowe, Kroeck, & Sivasubramaniam, 1996).

Fiedler's Contingency Theory

Additional work on leadership styles and behaviors based on Fiedler's (1967) contingency model of leadership has generated considerable controversy over the last 30 years (Schriesheim, Tepper, & Tetrault, 1994). Part of the controversy stems from Fiedler's measurement of relational- versus task-focused leadership, using what he called the least preferred coworker (LPC) scale. According to Fiedler's theory, leaders are categorized according to their scores on the LPC scale as being more task oriented than people oriented. Fiedler then classified the context in terms of those situations being more or less favorable using the following three dimensions: leader-member relations, task structure, and position power. Fiedler argued that task-oriented leaders were more effective in highly favorable and unfavorable situations, whereas relationship-oriented leaders were more effective in the middle range.

A third aspect of the controversy concerns Fiedler's insistence that leader effectiveness is based on changing the situation versus the leader. Fiedler argued in favor of changing the context to match the leader's preferred style. Unfortunately, research on the leader-match process has produced both support (see Peters, Hartke, & Pohlmann, 1985; Strube & Garcia, 1981) and discrepancies for his model (e.g., Jago & Ragan, 1986).

Schriesheim et al. (1994) examined 147 empirical studies that used Fiedler's contingency model and concluded that both high- and low-LPC leaders demonstrated effective performance depending on the context. Schriesheim et al. (1994) concluded that not all of the predictions in Fiedler's model held up; however, altering the situation may indeed be one way of enhancing the impact of leadership on performance. Fiedler's early emphasis on the context balanced off the emphasis on behavior and attributes in the literature.

Leader Style, Relationships, and Leader-Member Exchange Theory

The roots of LMX theory can be traced to the work of Dansereau, Graen, and Haga (1975), which was originally referred to as vertical dyad linkage (VDL) theory. Graen et al. (1982) extended this work into what is now called LMX theory by focusing on exchanges and relationships that were not necessarily vertical.

Reviews by Gerstner and Day (1997) showed that the LMX scale was correlated with a broad range of variables, including follower satisfaction, performance, and turnover. However, controversy also surrounds this construct's measurement. Schriesheim, Castro, and Cogliser (1999) pointed to problems with how the LMX construct was defined, measured, and analyzed. They also criticized LMX research for not examining the level of analysis to assess relationships. However, there were important findings produced by LMX research, which has led to new streams of research focusing on individualized leadership, trust-building in teams, and cross-cultural research (Graen & Uhl-Bien, 1995; Schriesheim et al., 1999).

A main concern about LMX theory is how it has changed over time in terms of what constitutes LMX. Schriesheim et al. (1999) indicated that Graen and his colleagues have continued to define LMX as the quality of exchange between a leader and followers; however, what constitutes the quality of that exchange has varied. For example, Schriesheim et al. examined 13 studies published by Graen and his colleagues over a period of 10 years, concluding that there were 18 sub-dimensions describing the quality of LMX (trust, competence, motivation, assistance and support, understanding, latitude, authority, information, influence in decision making, communications, confidence, consideration, talent, delegation, innovativeness, expertise, control of organizational resources, and mutual control). Schriesheim et al. reviewed 37 dissertations and research papers reporting that there were 11 different theoretical definitions associated with LMX and 35 different sub content elements, and concluded that "a decade after the inception of LMX theory, there was still so much disagreement as to the basic definition of the construct as well as no clear or consistent direction provided about where or how to proceed in developing the theory" (p. 76). Alternatively, we might also describe LMX as changing with the times. From 1972 to 2001 organizations became flatter, more networked, technologically connected, and arranged in strategic alliances configured in B2B models. Leaders and followers now interact more at a distance through technology, and followers instead of leaders are often the experts in

work processes. How these global changes are affecting the exchanges between leaders and followers remains an interesting domain for future research.

Taken together, the research on leadership styles and behaviors has identified a number of styles that consistently show up differentiating more or less effective leadership. Recently, this literature was significantly extended on the order of a giant leap as leadership research began to examine more the behaviors and styles of charismatic and transformational leaders.

Transformational, Charismatic, and Visionary Theories

Much effort in leadership research before the late 1980s did not focus on what constituted charismatic or inspirational leadership. A giant step toward understanding these profound forms of leadership was taken in the 1980s based on work by House (1977) and Burns (1978). House and Shamir (1993) highlighted the need to integrate charismatic, transformational, and visionary theories of leadership because all overlap with each other and appear to evolve in the same direction. A distinguishing characteristic of these theories builds on the relationship between leaders and followers discussed earlier in LMX theory. Charismatic leaders transform the needs, values, and aspirations of followers from individual to collective interests. They ask followers to consider the greater good of their group, organization, community, or society above and beyond their own self-interests (Bass, 1985; Bennis & Nanus, 1985; Conger & Kanungo, 1987; Tichy & Devanna, 1986). Earlier theories covered in this review focused attention on the tangible exchanges that occur between leaders and followers, as opposed to examining how trusting a leader motivates followers to extraordinary efforts and performance. The focus shifted to symbolic leadership, building identification with the leader's cause or vision, challenging followers to think differently, inspiring followers to extraordinary efforts, and building enough confidence in followers for them to lead (House & Shamir, 1993). Charismatic theories highlighted the importance of behaviors that were originally discussed by House (1977) and Burns (1978), and later by Bass (1985), Bennis and Nanus (1985), Tichy and Devanna (1986), and Conger and Kanungo (1987). Leaders who are transformational or charismatic have produced higher levels of effort, satisfaction, and performance (Avolio, 1999; Bass, 1998).

Podsakoff, MacKenzie, Moorman, and Fetter (1990) explored some of the internal mechanisms affected by transformational leadership. They examined how transactional and transformational leadership impacted the trust that followers had in their leaders, as well as how trust influenced organizational citizenship behaviors. Their results provided evidence to support Bass's (1985) contention that transformational leadership activates higher order needs through the development of trust, leading followers to exhibit extra-role behaviors in addition to in-role behaviors that honor transactional agreements.

Bass and Avolio (1997) addressed some of the issues concerning the need for integrating various models of charismatic-transformational leadership, developing a model referred to as a *full range theory of leadership.* Bass and Avolio chose the label "full range" to expand the thinking in the field of what constitutes the broadest possible range of leadership beliefs, values, perspectives, and styles. As Yukl (1999) noted, "Although no single theory should be expected to include all aspects of leadership behavior, use of the label 'full range leadership theory' by Bass (1996) invites critical evaluation of completeness" (p. 290). Yukl's criticism challenges the field of leadership exactly as Bass and Avolio had intended in choosing the term 'full range.'

In a critique of the charismatic-transformational leadership literature, Yukl (1999) highlighted the importance of examining how transformational versus transactional leadership influences followers through instrumental, compliance, personal identification, and internalization citing Kelman's (1958, 1974) theoretical work as a basis. Yukl pointed out that "the theory would be stronger if the essential influence processes were identified more clearly and used to explain how each type of behavior affects each type of mediating variable and outcome" (p. 287). House and Shamir (1993) provided some useful suggestions for pursuing several lines of research recommended by Yukl. For example, if a follower associates his or her self-concept with a leader's vision or values, one would expect higher levels of identification. Leaders who appeal to the ideological values of their followers would have followers whose images of themselves were linked to the leader's mission and vision. By implicating the follower's working self-concept, House and Shamir argued, a charismatic leader is making certain identities maintained by followers more salient, resulting in greater motivational potential.

Yukl (1999) described work on transformational leadership as following in the footsteps of earlier heroic theories of leadership (Calder, 1977). The effective leader is described as influencing followers to sacrifice and exert exceptional effort. Yukl argued that leadership should also be viewed as reciprocal or shared. More recent discussions of transformational leadership address some of Yukl's concerns (see Avolio, 1999; Sivasubramaniam et al., 2002). However, many leadership researchers still have difficulty viewing leadership as a collective phenomenon.

A final area of concern raised by Yukl (1999) relates to whether it is possible to have a simultaneous occurrence of transformational and charismatic leadership: "In fact, the developing and empowering behaviors associated with transformational leadership seem to make it less likely that followers will attribute extraordinary qualities to the leader" (p. 299). He argued that more empowered and developed followers are less likely to be dependent on their leader, apparently making the assumption that dependence is a necessary condition for charismatic leadership, which would contradict the theory and results in this area (Bass, 1998). Dependence is not a precondition for transformational leadership; nor do we suspect it is for leaders who are socialized charismatic leaders. Nevertheless, examining the power-dependence dynamics between charismatic-transformational leaders and their follower is an important area for leadership research to explore (see Xin & Tsui, 1996).

In sum, work on charismatic and transformational leadership has opened new and exciting areas for leadership researchers to pursue. Most of the work in this area is relatively new, and there is still much to be learned about these complex leadership phenomena.

Measurement Issues Pertaining to Leadership

Leadership has been measured primarily by survey methods (Beyer, 1999; Bryman, Stephens, & Campo, 1996), focusing more on the individual than on interactions between the individual and the situation (Beyer, 1999). Leadership theories, such as Fiedler's contingency model (Fiedler, 1967), include concepts that were developed using factor analysis or other quantitative methods. These techniques provide stable factors that are easy to replicate across multiple studies.

The development of the MLQ (Avolio et al., 1999; Bass & Avolio, 1990) is used here as an example for both the utility and the challenges and limitations of using quantitative methodology. Bass (1985) developed the MLQ and included scales of transformational and transactional leadership. Extensive research on the MLQ over the last 15 years provided both support and criticism (e.g., Bycio, Hackett, & Allen, 1995) concerning its factor structure. These criticisms have led to modifications both in the number of scales used and in item wording. Avolio et al. conducted a comprehensive validation study of the MLQ on 14 diverse samples using confirmatory factor analysis and reported strong support for the original model offered by Bass (1985), as compared to eight other models.

Use of the MLQ demonstrates the utility of quantitative approaches to the measurement of leadership. Nevertheless, critics of quantitative research (e.g., Bryman et al., 1996) argue that these methods are not sufficient when used alone. Surveys typically fail to take into consideration how the context influences leadership, which is a major shortcoming of leadership research.

Implicit Leadership Theory and Leadership Measurement

Critics of survey methodology (e.g., Podsakoff & Organ, 1986) argue that questionnaires require raters to report a specific behavior, yet raters have to recall, weigh, and infer information to respond. In order to simplify this cognitive process, respondents fall back on their implicit models of leadership, which can bias their observations and responses to surveys (Lord & Maher, 1991). Eden and Leviatan (1975) argued that a respondent's reliance on attributions could lead to biases such as specific response patterns throughout a questionnaire that can distort evaluations.

In the last decade a growing number of studies have used qualitative research methods. Bryman et al. (1996) used qualitative methods to show that charisma was exhibited less frequently than instrumental (transactional) behaviors among British police officers. Beyer and Browning (1999) conducted intensive interviews and collected archival and ethnographic data to demonstrate the impact of a charismatic leader on the emergence of the U.S. semiconductor industry. Berson, Avolio, Shamir, and Popper (2001) analyzed the content of videotaped visions reporting a relationship between transformational leadership scores and the optimistic content of visions coded by raters.

Qualitative evidence can offer a more holistic perspective of leadership, helping to explain why differences in ratings exist, rather than simply showing differences. Qualitative strategies such as grounded theory (Glaser & Strauss, 1967) allow for theory development and the inclusion of multiple levels of analysis, including the context in which leadership is observed (Hunt & Ropo, 1995). Nevertheless, qualitative inquiry also has its disadvantages, such as replicating previous measurements (Reissman, 1993) and comparing data collected from different places.

The Utility of Triangulation for Assessing Leadership

Jick (1979) suggested triangulation using quantitative and qualitative measures of the same phenomenon as a method for boosting validity. Triangulation fosters the use of innovative methods, facilitates the examination of new aspects of theories, and allows synthesis and critical comparison between different theories. Whereas quantitative methods allow for better generalizations based on systematic observation, qualitative measures are superior in the vividness and density of information that they provide on phenomena (Weiss, 1968). For example, Berson and Avolio (2000a) examined the utility of triangulation for measuring the relationship between visionary leadership and organizational performance. They reported that how frequently the vision was expressed was less important to organizational performance than was the vision's content.

Triangulating unobtrusive evidence with quantitative and qualitative data provides further support for using triangulation (Webb, Campbell, Schwartz, & Sechrest, 1966). Unobtrusive data can help confirm patterns in quantitative data that are more prone to measurement bias. For example, Berson and Avolio (2000b) used internal correspondence to confirm that a business unit whose managers were rated low in trust was facing shutdown. Interview data revealed that employees did not trust their managers, describing them as weak and helpless, even though followers were unaware of the impending shutdown. The triangulation of survey, interview, and unobtrusive data helped explain why these managers were rated so low on trust.

Leadership research has moved from relying solely on quantitative methods to adding in qualitative methods (e.g., Bryman et al., 1996; Hunt & Ropo, 1995). However, as Bryman et al. concluded, the use of qualitative methods is rare and is frequently done as an addendum to quantitative measurement. Triangulation may be an effective method for testing some of the more complex and controversial aspects of neo-charismatic theories of leadership.

Defining Leadership Effectiveness

As Yukl (1998) suggested, measuring leadership effectiveness has varied from one study to another, often reflecting a researcher's philosophy and implicit assumptions toward leadership. As such, the choice of what constitutes leadership effectiveness has been somewhat arbitrary, potentially affecting the predictive validity of models (Lowe et al., 1996). Looking at prior research on leadership and effectiveness, we classified three different sets of measures: (a) perceived (subjective or process-oriented) versus actual (objective or outcome-oriented) measures; (b) short-term versus long-term measures; and (c) leadership effectiveness measures derived from above (i.e., performance evaluation by superiors) versus below (i.e., performance evaluation of and by followers). Observational measures used in prior research include perceived leader effectiveness, satisfaction, commitment, and loyalty, whereas actual performance was by profit, sales increases, and percentage of goals met.

The time frame also can have several important implications when measuring leadership effectiveness because some leaders may be seen as ineffective in the short term, although they are highly effective leaders over time. For example, we can speculate that while transactional leaders are more likely to be rated as effective in the short run, a transformational leader may be perceived by followers to be more effective over a longer period of time (Nahavandi, 2000). A careful selection of criterion measures is required to uncover this potentially important distinction between the two different leadership styles. Finally, a number of previous studies have demonstrated that a leader and his or her effectiveness tend to be defined and evaluated differently depending on the source of information such as subordinates, peers, and superiors (Atwater & Yammarino, 1997; Facteau, Facteau, Schoel, Russell, & Poteet, 1998; Yammarino & Atwater, 1997).

In our literature review we found that prior studies have used perceived and actual measures of leadership effectiveness evenly. Although it is beyond the scope of this chapter to present a detailed breakdown for each category, a large number of leadership studies measured actual performance. Finally, most leadership studies used more immediate or short-term outcomes such as followers' efforts, commitments, and supervisory ratings, rather than longer term measures such as sales increase, stock prices, and a firm's financial performance because longer term measures are more likely to be contaminated by extraneous factors such as economic conditions and other variables that are beyond leader's personal control (Yukl, 1998). Similarly, a large percentage of prior leadership studies used performance measures obtained from below. Given the popularity of 360-degree feedback for performance evaluation (Atwater, Ostroff, Yammarino, & Fleenor, 1998), future research needs to incorporate all rating sources of leadership effectiveness.

Reciprocal and Shared Leadership

House and Aditya (1997) commented that "there is some speculation, and some preliminary evidence, to suggest that concentration of leadership in a single chain of command may be less optimal than shared leadership responsibility among two or more individuals in certain task environments. . . . [L]eadership involves collaborative relationships that lead to collective action grounded in shared values of people who work together to effect positive change" (p. 457). They referred to collective leadership in their review of the leadership literature, borrowing the term *peer leadership* from work published by Bowers and Seashore (1966), stating, "It is also possible that some of the specific leader behaviors required to enact generic functions can be distributed

throughout the entire work group or work unit being managed. Thus, several individuals would enact the same specific leaders' behaviors contemporaneously" (p. 458). As House and Aditya noted, "The research by Bowers and Seashore (1966) clearly demonstrates that the exercise of leaders' behaviors can be shared by members of work units, as well as conducted by formal work unit managers" (p. 459).

Several authors have described leadership as being a collective social influence process (Bales, 1954; Bowers & Seashore, 1966; House & Aditya, 1997) or as coleadership (Pearce & Sims, 2000). For example, while summarizing the Harvard Laboratory Studies on leadership, Bales (1954) suggested that the term *coleadership* might be beneficial for groups to allocate the task and relational leadership roles to different individuals. Research on self-managing teams (Manz & Sims, 1987, 1993) has helped to move the leadership field toward recognizing the importance of leadership *by* the team versus leadership *of* the team by a single individual (Sivasubramaniam et al., 2002). However, most prior research on leadership in teams at all organizational levels has assessed the leadership of a single individual leading a team (Cohen, Chang, & Ledford, 1997). Although several authors have introduced the concept of distributed or collective leadership *within* teams (Katzenbach, 1997; Kozlowski, Gully, Salas, & Cannon-Bowers, 1996; Manz & Sims, 1993; Pearce & Sims, 2000), there have been few attempts to examine leadership as a group-level construct. Dunphy and Bryant (1996) concluded that future research must include leadership *by* the team and *of* the team when modeling effectiveness.

Yukl (1998) stated, "The extent to which leadership can be shared . . . [,] the success of shared leadership[,] and the implications for the design of organizations are important and interesting questions that deserve more research. As yet, we have only begun to examine these research questions" (p. 504). For instance, Pearce and Sims (2000) examined the contribution of vertical and shared leadership to the rated effectiveness in change management teams, concluding that shared leadership independently contributed to predicting team effectiveness above and beyond vertical leadership.

Burns (1997) extended his work on individual transformational leadership to include a focus on *collective leadership*. He argued for "the existence of webs of potential collective leadership" (p. 1). He then suggested that "the initiator [i.e., leader] may continue as a single dominating 'leader' à la Castro, but more typically she will merge with others in a series of participant interactions that will constitute collective leadership. . . . I see crucial leadership acts in the collective process" (pp. 2–3). Similar to Burns's extensions to transformational leadership, Bass (1998) noted that "transformational leadership could be shared among the team members. . . . Instead of motivation being supplied by identification of members with an idealized, charismatic leader, similar motivation would be supplied by identification with the team. . . . Inspiration would come from a sharing of mutually articulated goals" (p. 157).

Sivasubramaniam et al. (2000) reported that perceptions of collective transformational leadership in student teams predicted team potency and group performance over a three-month period of time. Pearce (1997) reported that shared leadership was related to group potency, citizenship, and group effectiveness. Mankin, Cohen, and Bikson (1996) argued that the role of leadership will change in technology-mediated groups and that leadership may emerge more as a shared construct initiated within a team. Preliminary evidence to support their position comes from Weisband, Schneider, and Connolly (1995). Group members interacting through computer-mediated systems instead of face to face participated more equally.

In sum, by advancing leadership as a shared process, we can position researchers to explore from a cognitive, behavioral, and contextual perspective an alternative and more complex form of leadership relevant to today's web-based, virtual organizations.

EMERGING AREAS IN LEADERSHIP THEORY AND RESEARCH

Leadership Development: Born/Made

We now explore an area of leadership where more has been written than perhaps in any other area. Unfortunately, volume does not correlate with quality. Numerous popular books profess to have the solution to developing high potential leadership. However, as House and Aditya (1997) concluded, "That management training and development efforts will result in improved management appears to be taken as an article of faith by many organizations, professional management associations and consultants. Yet, despite the immense amount of investment in management training on the part of corporations and government, there is little evidence that such training results in more effective management behavior" (p. 459). Because only 10% of all leadership development programs are evaluated beyond participants' satisfaction with the program, it is premature to say that leadership development can or cannot be developed. For example, Burke and Day (1986) completed a meta-analysis of 70 different management training studies and concluded that there were positive and negative effects for knowledge development. House and Aditya (1997) cited preliminary evidence supporting the positive effects of training that were associated with use of Graen's LMX.

Leadership Development in Context

When evaluating leadership development, it is important to consider how the context promotes or inhibits the transfer of training effects. For example, supervisory training not supported by the management culture of the organization has resulted in higher role conflict and stress and lower job performance (Fleishman, Harris, & Burtt, 1955; House, 1960; Sykes, 1962).

Most leadership training fails to recognize that leadership constitutes a complex interaction between leaders, followers, and the context (Day, 2000; Fiedler, 1996). Day made a useful distinction between leader development and leadership development. Leader development has the primary goal of enhancing an individual's capacity and potential (H. Gardner, 1983, 1985). Day provided specific examples focusing on areas such as self-awareness, self-regulation, and self-motivation, citing the work of McCauley (2000, 2001). Leadership development focuses on the interaction of the leader within a social-organizational context, an area repeatedly neglected in past leadership development research (Fiedler, 1996; Zaccaro & Klimoski, 2001). Day concluded that "leadership development can be thought of as an integration strategy by helping people understand how to relate to others, coordinate their efforts, build commitments, and develop extended social networks by applying self-understanding to social and organizational imperatives" (p. 10).

Starting with the context, individuals can be developed based on their job assignments and responsibilities. Challenging new assignments can be strategically used to develop the potentials of leaders (McCauley & Brutus, 1998). What leaders learn from both positive and negative experiences on the job represents a fruitful area for future research. Indeed, many companies such as Coca Cola, General Electric, and Citibank strategically utilize work assignments as a way of building individual and collective leadership potential. Research done by McCauley, Ruderman, Ohlott, and Morrow (1994) showed that challenging work assignments are correlated with on-the-job learning, but such learning has not been empirically linked to leader or leadership development. Thus, does leadership develop differentially over time as one moves through various stages of life (Erikson, 1968; Kuhnert & Lewis, 1987)?

Self-Concept and Leadership Development

The manner in which a leader views himself or herself, behaves, and influences followers may stem from an awareness of the leader's self-concept or identity (Hanges, Lord, & Dickson, 2000), self-goals, possible selves (Lord, Brown, & Freiberg, 1999; Sosik, 2000), self-awareness, self-regulation

(W. L. Gardner & Avolio, 1998; Sosik & Dworakivsky, 1998), familial issues (Simonton, 1994), maturation (Erikson, 1968), dependence versus independence (Conger, 1999), defense mechanisms, and repression of a shadow self (Kets de Vries, 1988). To develop fully, leaders must develop self-awareness and acceptance to understand how to interact with followers (Goleman, 1998; Kets de Vries, 1988).

360-Degree Survey Feedback and Leadership Development

One of the central features of most leader development programs is the use of 360-degree feedback systems (Waldman & Atwater, 1998). However, relatively little is known about their impact on creating leader self-awareness and development (Atwater, Waldman, Atwater, & Cartier, 2000). Atwater and her associates offered some positive evidence for the impact of upward feedback on leader development, as did Hegarty (1974). However, why feedback had a positive impact had not been determined in prior research. As Atwater and her associates argued, improvements could stem from an awareness of self-other rating differences, from highlighting dimensions of leadership that focus one's efforts, from motivational pride to close the gap between self-other ratings, or from some combination of factors. On the negative side, Kluger and DeNisi (1996) reported that in over one third of the cases of providing feedback, performance was actually reduced after feedback.

Atwater et al. (2000) reported that in an organization where cynicism was higher, the level of positive change following feedback was lower: "This finding suggests that cynicism may have contributed to the ratings of leadership that supervisors received after the initial feedback, rather than cynicism being related to concurrent ratings of leadership at Time 1" (p. 287).

Impact of Leadership Training

Although only a small number of studies have examined how training can impact neo-charismatic or transformational leadership development, several results are worth noting. Avolio and Bass (1998) reported the results of a field study of community leaders that went through a 1-year training intervention, using the full-range leadership model. There were significant and positive changes in followers' evaluations of transformational leadership for those participants who created leadership development plans that were independently coded as having clear, specific, and measurable goals.

Crookall (1992) conducted a training study with prison shop supervisors to compare transformational to situational leadership training. Group 1 received a transformational training program, whereas Group 2 received situational training and Group 3 received no training. Both trained groups pre- to posttraining intervention improved on the order of 10% to 50% depending on the criterion measures. Transformational leadership training had a more positive impact on personal growth and performance while improving inmates' respect for supervisors, skills development, and good citizenship behaviors. Barling, Weber, and Kelloway (1996) examined the impact of transformational leadership training with bank managers in a field experiment conducted in a large financial institution. Using a coaching model, they reported that certain aspects of transformational leadership improved as well as managerial performance. Dvir, Eden, Avolio, and Shamir (2002) completed a true field experiment with Israeli platoon commanders randomly assigned to two versions of transformational leadership training. Both programs involved 3 days of training. The newer or experimental transformational leadership program also included a 3-hr booster session approximately 1 month after the close of the first session. The booster session was used to coach individual commanders on leadership development and self-reflection. Results showed significant differences in what was learned about transformational leadership, changes in transformational behavior, and performance effects, which were all in the predicted direction. Transformational leadership ratings increased over time for the group going through the experimental transformational leadership program. Six months following the close of training, groups going through the experimental transformational leadership training had significantly higher performance.

A growing body of evidence suggests that transformational leadership can be developed using in vitro methods. We have also learned that some leadership styles may be learned in vivo. For example, Klonsky (1983) reported that parental warmth, discipline, and achievement demands predicted the type of leadership behaviors observed among high school students. Cox and Cooper (1989) reported that many successful British CEOs experienced an early loss of a parent or were separated from them at an early age. Avolio and Gibbons (1988) used life history interviews of executives and concluded that those who were evaluated as more transformational had parents who set high standards and encouraged them to do their best, came from family circumstances that were challenging, and learned from parents to deal more effectively with disappointment and conflict. Zacharatos, Barling, and Kelloway (2000) examined relationships between parental leadership style and the leadership of children based on self, peer, and supervisor ratings. Results showed that perceptions of one's father's transformational leadership had a significant relationship with self and other transformational leadership ratings.

There is a shift occurring in the field of leadership development where research and practice are focusing more on how people learn within their work context to be more effective leaders (McCauley, 2001; Moxley & O'Connor-Wilson, 1998). Work on coaching and mentoring is a popular emerging area. Coaching has typically been described like mentoring as a longer-term process that focuses on both the context and the individual (Day, 2000; Kilburg, 1996). Like other areas of leader and leadership development, however, there is still very little research to support the effectiveness of coaching (Day, 2000; Kilburg, 1996). There is also a thin literature base demonstrating the effectiveness of mentoring programs (Day, 2000). Research comparing formal to informal mentoring programs concluded that there are more positive benefits for informal mentoring relationships (Ragins & Cotton, 1999). Additional research indicates that gender and racial differences need to be explored in terms of the effectiveness of mentoring and coaching.

Thus, the collective evidence suggests that leaders and leadership can and are developed over time, both in natural settings as well as in workshops. After nearly 60 years of research on leadership development, the field is finally getting around to answering a question that represents one of the core reasons for studying leadership: Can we develop it over time?

Examining Leadership Across Cultures

Culture is a part of the social context in which leadership is embedded, and it is expected to moderate and mediate leader and follower interactions. Culture is a mindset that emerges through social interaction and is transmitted and diffused through the interaction among individuals (Hofstede, 1980, 1983; Triandis, 1994). Over the years, studies have examined a broad range of questions concerning the linkage between leadership and culture: Are certain leader behaviors and styles culturally universal? Do theories of leadership developed in the United States generalize to other cultural settings? House, Hanges, Agar, and Quintanilla (1995) argued that answers to these questions could provide organizations with a strategic advantage for developing a diverse range of future leaders (for additional reviews see House, Wright, & Aditya, 1997; Peterson & Hunt, 1997).

Single-Culture and Single-Country Research to Multiculture and Multicountry Research

Single-culture and *single-country* research aims to replicate specific leadership theories or models in other cultural settings. For example, Shamir, Zakay, Breinin, and Popper (1998) examined charismatic leadership behavior and its

effects on followers' attitudes and leadership effectiveness in the Israeli military. *Multiculture* and *multicountry* research examines arguments concerning whether a particular leadership theory, model, or style generalizes across cultures. The GLOBE project initiated by House and his international research team (Den Hartog, House, Hanges, Ruiz-Quintanilla, & Dorfman, 1999) represents this second category of cross-cultural leadership research. Preliminary evidence cited earlier showed that attributes associated with charismatic leadership were universal (Bass, 1997).

A third category of cross-cultural leadership research has examined the effects of cultural diversity within group or team settings, testing how differences in ethnicity of leaders and followers affected the perceptions and outcomes of leadership within those groups and teams. This research examines how certain styles of leadership affect followers' motivation, effectiveness, and performance when followers are ethnically or culturally different from their leader or when in culturally heterogeneous groups (Hooijberg & DiTomaso, 1996). Such research has compared how different leadership styles displayed within different ethnic groups within a single culture affected follower perceptions, motivation, and performance (Jung & Avolio, 1999).

Cultural Values and Leadership

Over the last two decades, cross-cultural research has focused primarily on four cultural dimensions (see Hofstede, 1980, 1993). These dimensions included power distance, uncertainty avoidance, individualism/collectivism, and masculinity/femininity. These four cultural dimensions have been used to identify potential boundary conditions for leadership theories that have been applied across cultures (Dorfman, 1996). For example, a leadership theory that argues for a democratic leader as an ideal style of leadership may not generalize to cultures where an unequal distribution of power is accepted as the norm (Dorfman & Howell, 1988; Jung, Bass, & Sosik, 1995).

Key Results of Research on Cross-Cultural Leadership

Early cross-cultural leadership studies focused on task- and relationship-oriented leadership styles. This research included a wide range of samples from the Philippines and China (Bennett, 1977), Japan (Misumi, 1985; Misumi & Peterson, 1985), India (Sinha, 1984), New Zealand (Anderson, 1983), Mexico (Ayman & Chemers, 1991), and Israel (Fleishman & Simmons, 1970), among many other cultures and nations, and has reached two general conclusions: (a) The most effective leadership styles are a combination of high relationship- and high task-oriented leadership, and (b) although general patterns of leadership are similar across cultures, specific behaviors and attitudes expressed by leaders appear to differ across cultures (Bass, 1997).

Prior cross-cultural research has also tested social identity and LMX theory. Pelled and Xin (1997) investigated the effect of leader-member demographic similarity on followers' organizational attachment to Mexican organizations, with leaders coming from a high power distance culture. They reported that Mexican employees, who had a small age gap with their superior, were less likely to be absent and were more attached to their organization. These same followers exhibited lower commitment to their work while expressing higher levels of comfort working for a younger supervisor. Farh, Tsui, Xin, and Cheng (1998) examined the effects of relational demography and personal network ties called *Guanxi* in China on leader-follower relationships and reported that demographic similarities among leaders and followers had a positive impact on follower trust in the leader.

Recent cross-cultural leadership research has focused on testing neo-charismatic models of leadership. For instance, Shamir et al. (1998) reported mixed support for the relationship between charismatic leadership and Israeli followers' attitudes toward their respective leader. Only one of three charismatic behaviors (emphasizing units' collective identity) was positively related to followers' identification with and trust in the leader, whereas the other two behaviors (i.e., supportive behavior and ideological emphasis) were either unrelated or negatively related.

Contrary to the Shamir et al. (1998) results, the majority of cross-cultural research on charismatic-transformational leadership has supported the hierarchy of leadership effectiveness styles comprising Bass and Avolio's (1994) model of leadership. Koh, Terborg, and Steers (1991) reported that transformational leadership of Singaporean school principals had significant add-on effects to transactional leadership in predicting organizational commitment, citizenship behavior, and teacher satisfaction. Similar augmentation effects have been reported in a wide variety of samples, including Canadian (Boyd, 1988; J. M. Howell & Avolio, 1993), Mexican (Dorfman & Howell, 1988; Echavarria & Davis, 1994), Italian (Bass & Avolio, 1994), and Danish (Den Hartog, Van Muijen, & Koopman, 1994). Overall, the positive effects that transformational leadership has on follower's motivation and performance have been well documented in other cultural settings, including Austria (Geyer & Steyrer, 1998), Israel (Popper, Mayseless, & Castelnovo, 2000), and Korea (Cho, 1999; Jung, Butler, & Baik, 2000).

Results of multiculture and multicountry research are equally interesting. For example, Dorfman and Howell (1988)

reported different effects associated with charismatic leadership when comparing Mexican versus American employees. Charismatic leadership had a strong positive relationship with both Mexican and American employee satisfaction levels; however, the relationships were much stronger for American versus Mexican employees. Dorfman et al. (1997) reported that among six leadership behaviors examined across five countries, leader supportiveness, contingent reward, and charisma had universally positive relationships with followers' level of satisfaction, whereas participative, directive, and contingent punishment had positive relationships in only two cultures.

Fu and Yukl (2000) compared the perceived effectiveness of influence tactics in the United States and China, reporting that American and Chinese managers favored different influence tactics. American managers rated rational persuasion and exchange as more effective styles compared with their Chinese counterparts. Chinese managers rated coalition building, upward appeals, and gifts as more effective than did American managers. Rao, Hashimoto, and Rao (1997) examined influence tactics employed in Japan and reported that Japanese managers used many of the same influence tactics as did their American counterparts but differed on behaviors.

Valikangas and Okumura (1997) examined differences in follower motivation, comparing leaders in the United States and Japan. They concluded that leadership in the United States was based on followers' *utility expectations* (i.e., a "right" agency will result in the "right" outcomes). Leadership in Japan was based on *identity expectations* (i.e., a "right" group or corporate identity will result in "right" behaviors among followers).

How do people in different cultures perceive their ideal leaders? Using an attribute-rating task in which people rated a list of attributes according to how well each attribute fit their prototype of leaders, Gerstner and Day (1994) examined leadership prototypes across eight countries. Gerstner and Day reported that *to be determined* was a prototypical attribute of leaders in Western countries, whereas *intelligence* was considered highly prototypical in Asia. Den Hartog et al. (1999) reported that a number of attributes associated with charismatic-transformational leadership were considered "ideal" attributes of leadership across 62 different countries. The following leadership attributes were endorsed across cultures: encouraging, positive, motivational, confidence builder, dynamic, and foresight. On the other hand, being a loner, noncooperative, ruthless, nonexplicit, irritable, and dictatorial were seen as negative facets of leadership (Conger & Hunt, 1999).

Brodbeck et al. (2000) reported differences in leadership prototypes across 22 European countries. Their sample included middle-level managers ($N = 6,052$), who rated 112 traits and behaviors in terms of how well they represented outstanding business leadership. Some leadership concepts were culturally endorsed and grouped according to the values representing a cluster of nations. Interpersonal directness and proximity were more strongly associated with outstanding leadership in Nordic countries versus Near East and Central European countries. Autonomy was associated with outstanding leadership in Germanic countries. Wofford, Lovett, Whittington, and Coalter (1999) argued that differences in leadership prototypes may be a function of the type of organization from which raters are pooled. For example, with raters coming from the United States and Mexico, Wofford et al. (1999) reported that differences in leadership prototypes in their investigation were due to the type of institutions from which participants were sampled, as well as to their national cultures. Xin (1997) reported that different impression-management tactics were used by Asian American and Caucasian American managers. Specifically, Asian American managers used more job-focused (e.g., pointing out past accomplishments to my supervisor) and more supervisor-focused (e.g., offering to do things for my supervisor that are not formally required) impression-management tactics and less self-disclosure (e.g., expressing my feeling to my supervisor). Jung and Avolio (1999) reported that Asian Americans generated more ideas when they worked with a transformational leader in a brainstorming task, whereas Caucasian Americans performed better when working with a transactional leader. Asian Americans also performed better when they worked alone than when they worked as a group generating ideas requiring radical changes.

A common theme running through many cross-cultural studies of leadership concerns how cultural values moderate or mediate relationships between a leader and his or her followers. Support for both cultural-universal and culture-specific aspects of leadership have been provided in prior research. However, several important issues must be addressed to advance the field. First, Hunt and Peterson (1997) pointed out the need to define and measure leadership constructs in a similar way across different studies. Leadership has been measured based on various methods, including the use of influence tactics (e.g., Fu & Yukl, 2000), prototype attributes (e.g., Brodbeck et al., 2000), charismatic and transformational leadership behaviors (Shamir et al., 1998), and motivational differences (Valikangas & Okumura, 1997). Second, there has been insufficient attention to defining the level of analysis at which cultural differences should be examined (Hunt & Peterson, 1997). For example, different types of leadership effectiveness and outcome measures have been compared across different levels of analysis in organizations, making it difficult to discern the impact of

cultural differences reported in this literature. Third, there has been a high degree of variance in the quality of methods used by different researchers. For example, some researchers hired professionals to translate and back-translate their survey instruments to ensure functional and conceptual equivalence, whereas others did not use professional translation. Fourth, by and large, culture has generally been included in studies as either a moderator or mediator variable (Hunt & Peterson, 1997). Most prior research has not treated culture as a fundamental variable that drives the relationship between leaders and followers (House, Wright, & Aditya, 1997). Finally, the majority of cross-cultural research has relied on quantitative, survey-based research designs, and more qualitative, unobtrusive research methods are now needed to examine how culture shapes leadership.

Strategic Leadership Research

Beginning with Barnard (1938), research on strategic leadership has concentrated on identifying best practices that contribute to firm success. Recent research has focused on internal firm characteristics (Hoskisson, Hitt, Wan, & Yiu, 1999), either in the form of agency contracts (Jensen & Meckling, 1976) or by focusing on a firm's unique resources. Both approaches take into consideration the role of leaders as representing strategic assets for the firm.

Strategic leadership researchers have argued that organizations become a reflection of their top managers (Hambrick & Mason, 1984; Klimoski & Koles, 2001). Hambrick (1989) emphasized the importance of strategic leadership but also recognized that its impact may be more indirect. Moreover, top managers face ambiguous environments and often experience information overload (March & Simon, 1959). Under these conditions, successful leadership is determined by the frame of reference used by decision makers, which includes their personal background, experiences, education, and other biographical characteristics. Strategic leadership helps to coordinate and maintain organizational systems, while readying it for adaptive change.

Beginning with Kotter (1982) and Hambrick and Mason (1984), strategic leadership research has focused on personal and background characteristics of executives related to firm success. According to Hambrick and Mason, personal characteristics together with environmental constraints and organizational factors constitute the leader's "discretion" (Cannella & Monroe, 1997). The amount of discretion employed by top managers moderates the relationship between their strategic choices and organizational outcomes. Cannella and Monroe criticized the overreliance on using biographical data as predictors of strategic performance. They argued that strategic leadership theory relies too much on descriptive variables to explain choices that executives make while providing little guidance on how to include the *process* of leadership in its research designs. Here is where some of the work on the neo-charismatic theories of leadership (e.g., Bass, 1985; House, 1995) may contribute to strategic leadership theory by focusing on how the leader's think, behave, and are affected by the context.

Integrating Transformational and Strategic Leadership

The neo-charismatic theories of leadership focus on interpersonal processes between leaders and followers (House & Aditya, 1997). These theories focus on the process of leadership within organizations, although they could also be applied to leadership across organizations. Transformational or charismatic leaders have followers who emulate them and perform beyond expectations (Avolio, 1999; Bass, 1985). Their followers may be more open to shifts in their worldview and to accepting new values and changes in thinking and strategy (Boal & Bryson, 1988). Transformational leaders often convey their ideas using a strategic vision for the organization that includes strategic goals presented in a future-oriented optimistic framework (Berson et al., 2001). As noted by Zaccaro and Banks (2001), "a fundamental requirement of organizational leadership is setting the direction for collective effort on behalf of organizational progress" (p. 181).

The turbulence that characterizes today's environment dictates constant transformation and even radical change for organizations. The process of radical change begins with a strategic vision that leaders have for their organization. A vision is an outline of a strategic and lofty action plan or a guideline to the "new way of doing things" following the transformation (Nutt & Backoff, 1997). A comprehensive vision can help to align the views of multiple stakeholders, which is critical to change and success (Nutt & Backoff, 1997).

Although it seems that strategic leaders would benefit from a charismatic or transformational style, strategic leadership theorists have taken a different position on this issue. They argue that charisma may narrow the executive's information processing orientation, thereby restricting the range of strategic choices (Finkelstein & Hambrick, 1996). Specifically, Finkelstein and Hambrick suggested that charismatic leaders are more likely to receive filtered and distilled information from their followers and may be less aware of information that contradicts their visions. This occurs when followers are threatened by the charismatic leader's ability to "see the future" and are hesitant to offer ideas that conflict with their leader's vision. Alternatively, Cannella and Monroe (1997) argued that charismatic-transformational leadership could

actually help strategic leaders implement their organization's strategy. Indeed, Brass and Krackhadt (1999) suggested that the high social intelligence characterizing transformational or charismatic leaders allows them to estimate the social capital, or the potential influence that is available to a leader based solely on the characteristics and the structure of a social setting. Transformational or charismatic leaders can both analyze the environment and enforce norms that help them accomplish instrumental objectives, such as strategy implementation without restricting the flow of information.

Berson and Avolio (2000b) examined the contribution of transformational leadership to the dissemination of strategic goals. Their findings indicated that senior executives rated more transformational were also more effective disseminators of strategic goals than were nontransformational executives. Transformational leaders exhibited a prospector strategy, which emphasized innovation and risk taking (Miles & Snow, 1978). Absence of transformational leadership at the top created confusion and a lack of alignment with regard to the dissemination of strategic goals across subsequent organizational levels.

Several researchers have offered models of organizational life cycles (e.g., Mintzberg, 1980; Quinn & Cameron, 1983) that included formation, development, maturity, and decline. In the strategic management literature (e.g., Zanetti & Cunningham, 2000) authors have highlighted certain strategic implications for each stage of an organization's life cycle with implications for leadership research. The new genre of leadership, specifically transformational leadership (Avolio, 1999; Bass, 1985), offers a range of leadership behaviors that could be examined in relationship to organizational life cycles. Strategic leadership theory can also benefit from studies that examine the cognitive and emotional characteristics of effective strategists. Boal and Hooijberg (2001) offered several avenues for future research emphasizing social capital, cognitive complexity, and managerial wisdom as a basis for examining how strategic leaders think and link their thinking to action.

In sum, the strategic management and leadership literatures are beginning to converge in ways that lay the groundwork for an interesting line of research projects. How CEOs and top management teams in organizations affect employee motivation and performance is now being researched in ways that will advance both areas.

E-Leadership and Its Distribution in Organizations

Leadership within the context of advanced information technology (AIT) has become a strategic asset for organizations (Avolio, Kahai, & Dodge, 2000). Such leadership may be termed *e-leadership*. It can involve one-to-one, one-to-many, and within- and between-group and collective interactions via AIT. Sociotechnical systems theory (e.g., Trist, 1993) suggests that organizational effectiveness is a function of how well the leadership and AIT systems are aligned with each other and the external environment. This theoretical framework suggests several important implications for e-leadership research within and between organizations.

Several intraorganizational issues are relevant to e-leadership. First, e-leadership and technology can be viewed as system components that interact and evolve over time, providing structures that guide action in organizations using AIT. Avolio et al. (2000) identified adaptive structuration theory (AST; DeSanctis & Poole, 1994) as a useful theoretical framework for examining the interaction between technology and leadership. AST proposes that AIT affects human interaction by providing structures (e.g., rules, resources) stemming from the AIT, task, environment, emergent structures, and the group. People also influence the interpretation and use of AIT (i.e., adoption, resistance, or rejection). Leaders are also part of the sociotechnical system who "make meaning" by promoting technology adoption while considering the impact of existing organizational norms and culture on the use of this technology.

Leadership can promote successful adaptations to technological change, or it can restrict new AIT development, implementation, and adoption. Oz and Sosik (in press) surveyed 159 chief information officers and reported that passive leadership in AIT project teams was the main factor contributing to project failure. Vandenbosch and Ginzberg (1997) suggested that the adoption and derived benefits of groupware technology by organizations have fallen short of expectations because of the absence of leadership that fosters a cooperative culture. Leadership can restrict new AIT use to such an extent that it has little, if any, impact on organizational effectiveness. For example, autocratic leadership may repel attempts at collaboration enabled by groupware systems (Kahai, Sosik, & Avolio, 1997). Similarly, using LMX theory, a leader who has created an in-group versus an out-group among followers may inhibit collaboration using groupware due to a lack of trust (Avolio et al., 2001). Successful implementation and integration of AIT may require a significant transformation in the leadership system in advance of, during, and after the insertion of the new technology.

The IT revolution has influenced how new organizational systems need to be structured by leaders to adapt in the e-business context. Organic structures, shaped by massive enterprise-wide information systems, collaborative work flows, and geographically distant or temporally removed teams, are required to achieve flexibility and openness in the current work environment (Oz, 2000).

Leaders today often make decisions that have relatively little historical base in the midst of rapidly changing technological environments (Sheehy & Gallagher, 1996). As such, more disciplined analytical models of decision making, which dominated the strategic management literature (e.g., Stevenson, Pearce, & Porter, 1985), may have been modified to include models placing greater value on experimentation and continuous learning (Hedlund & Rolander, 1990).

Comprehensive enterprise-wide information systems have promoted collaborative sharing of information across organizational stovepipes, causing shifts in power dynamics and networking (Postmes, Spears, & Lea, 2000; Sheehy & Gallagher, 1996). Widespread availability of information on company intranets and the Internet provide followers with increased online networking opportunities via chat rooms, e-mail, and message boards, offering them alternative channels of information to those provided within traditional management hierarchies. These trends offer leaders an unprecedented opportunity to empower their followers to build more intelligent communities. However, AIT can also present leaders and followers with the challenges of information overload, followers' receiving messages that are discrepant with their leaders, and social isolation.

Applications of E-Leadership Between Organizations

The proliferation of B2B and business-to-customer (B2C) transactions highlights the role of e-leadership as a between-systems concept (Avolio et al., 2000). For example, Ford, General Motors, Chrysler, Nissan, and Renault are partnering to develop a vast electronic supply chain network that will link their business transactions (Baer & Davis, 2001). This B2B initiative will require effective information and collaborative leadership that can harness technology to support virtual teams working across time zones and diverse cultures. Current leadership models need to incorporate macrolevel variables that span organizations, such as culture congruence and technology compatibility, which play a critical role in defining interorganizational leadership.

Another interorganizational issue relevant to e-leadership is the deployment of B2C technologies that link organizations to their customers via supply chains and enterprise information systems. Internet-mandated changes in business have prompted organizations such as Charles Schwab and Company to develop customer-centric strategies that implement personalized and customized technologies meeting each customer's needs. The deployment and adaptation of such customer-centric systems pose significant challenges to both researchers and practitioners because our current models of leadership do not take into full consideration customers as constituents in the leadership system.

The Internet and other forms of AIT have enabled new models for interacting within and between organizations (e-business) and with customers and suppliers (e-commerce; O'Mahoney & Barley, 1999). The new business models highlight fundamental differences to leading in a digitized world that must now be researched. Studies of leadership in computer-mediated environments provide a foundation for examining how leaders influence social interactions within and between organizations. Early work on group support systems (GSSs) focused on how facilitation (e.g., George, Dennis, & Nunamaker, 1992) and emergent (e.g., Harmon, Schneer, & Hoffman, 1995) or appointed leadership (e.g., Lim, Raman, & Wai, 1994) influenced group processes (e.g., consensus, communication content) and outcomes (e.g., decision quality, satisfaction). Evidence indicated that the type of facilitation and leadership had an impact in GSS contexts and highlighted the potential for GSS structures or processes (e.g., anonymity) to substitute for or moderate leadership effects on group processes and outcomes (George, Easton, Nunamaker, & Northcraft, 1990; Ho & Raman, 1991).

Over the last decade, a series of research studies have systematically manipulated and measured effects of various leadership styles, including directive, participative, transactional, and transformational approaches, on various process and outcome variables collected in GSS contexts. Participative (directive) leadership for groups solving a less (more) structured task led to more solution proposals (Kahai et al., 1997). Transformational leadership has been linked with higher levels of group potency (Sosik, Avolio, & Kahai, 1997), more questioning and supportive comments (Sosik, 1997), and more creative outcomes in terms of elaboration and originality (Sosik, Kahai, & Avolio, 1998) versus transactional leadership. Anonymity moderated the impact of leadership style on GSS performance depending on whether the group used the GSS to brainstorm or to complete a task report (Sosik et al., 1997). Anonymity also interacted with leadership to influence motivation levels of GSS users (Sosik, Kahai, & Avolio, 1999).

Several findings of GSS research are relevant for building new models of e-leadership. First, research on relational development in groupware contexts (Walther, 1995) suggests that groups may shift from task to relational communication over time. Second, group history creates an embedded social structure that may influence the subsequent adoption and effective

use of GSS technology (Weisband et al., 1995). Third, there may be differences in national and organizational cultures affecting the use of AIT. For example, collectivistic cultures may find collaborative technologies more useful than individualistic ones. Finally, whereas anonymity may enhance group identification of GSS users (Lea & Spears, 1992), it may make it difficult for users to judge the credibility of an idea in high power distance cultures (Dennis, Hilmer, & Taylor, 1998).

Relevant Models and Methods for E-Leadership

Several leadership models are relevant to examining e-leadership. Given that GSS process structure may neutralize leader efforts (Ho & Raman, 1991) and GSS anonymity may enhance effects of transformational leadership on group potency (Sosik et al., 1997), substitutes for leadership theory (Kerr & Jermier, 1978) may be a useful framework for examining how the context affects measurement of e-leadership. LMX theory (Graen & Uhl-Bien, 1995) may provide some insight on how dyadic relationships emerge in virtual contexts or how in-groups and out-groups differ in terms of trust, commitment, and motivation when interacting virtually. Theories of shared leadership (e.g., Avolio, 1999) may be helpful to understanding how team member perceptions influence trust and subsequent team interaction (e.g., efficacy, cohesion) and outcomes (e.g., creativity, satisfaction). Neo-charismatic theories (Conger & Kanungo, 1998; W. L. Gardner & Avolio, 1998) and social distance (Shamir, 1995) focusing on self-perceptions and self-presentation are relevant to examining how AIT influences leaders working at a distance virtually with followers.

What's Next With E-Leadership?

At the individual level of analysis, work is needed examining how leader-follower virtual interactions influence follower perceptions of leadership, the effectiveness of impression-management strategies (W. L. Gardner & Avolio, 1998), and perceptions of social distance (Shamir, 1995). At the group level, we need to examine shared leadership (Sivasubramaniam et al., 2000); interactions among leadership, AIT structural features, and task type (Sosik et al., 1997); the use of AIT within and between multicultural teams; how e-leadership transforms team processes and outcomes over time (Walther, 1995); and which forms of AIT best support e-leadership (Avolio et al., 2000). At the organizational level, work is required on culture and structural influences of AIT, on their interaction with leadership, and on the subsequent transformation of technology and leadership into an integrated system that works.

In sum, organizations are dramatically changing with the integration of AIT. B2B and B2C models of e-commerce have enabled Web-based dot-com organizations, such as Amazon.com, to change the fundamentals of business. Such organizations possess structures, cultures, and human resources that are vastly different from traditional bricks-and-mortar organizations. A critical research question is, How does the integration of technology into organizations affect our models, measures, and development of leadership?

CONCLUSION: NEW LEADERS IN NEW ORGANIZATIONAL CONTEXTS

Projected workplace trends toward increased diversity, multiple generations, teaming, innovation, environmental turbulence, global competition, and AIT suggest that certain attributes may be required for leaders to adapt to and fit in with these trends. Increased diversity will require leaders to possess a cultural intelligence characterized by tolerance, empathy, and cooperativeness to appreciate differences among followers. Leaders will need integrative complexity to synthesize multiple perspectives into coherent solutions (Simonton, 1994). Leading followers from the baby boom, generation X, and Internet generation cohorts will require leaders to appreciate cross-generational differences. Adapting to information-based team environments will require leaders to understand a collectivistic orientation (Jung et al., 1995), systems thinking (Mumford et al., 2000), and capacities for filtering large amounts of information coming from computer networks (Avolio et al., 2000). Dealing with environmental turbulence and global competition will require leaders to be adaptable (Mann, 1959), resilient to stress (Goleman, 1998), fully knowledgeable of competitors and their products (Kirpatrick & Locke, 1991), and capable of solving complex problems quickly (Zaccaro et al., 2000).

How are leaders being selected and prepared for these changes? Based on the available evidence, the answer is probably not well. Leadership failure rates range from 50% to 60%, costing organizations billions of dollars each year (Hogan et al., 1994). To reduce failure rates will require a better integration of the various lines of leadership research. For example, there is a need for research to examine the intersection of trait-based (e.g., Kirkpatrick & Locke, 1991), skill-based (Mumford et al., 2000), behavior-based (e.g., Avolio, 1999; Bass, 1998), and situational (e.g., Fiedler, 1967) leadership theories to develop profiles of successful and unsuccessful leaders. Such profiles could help researchers focus on

converging toward, rather than diverging from, understanding leadership processes and outcomes within the new and emerging organizational realities. With this level of integration and awareness of the context, we can begin to examine leadership as a total system, which includes the leader, followers, emerging context, and time in our assessments of leadership potential and effectiveness.

In sum, now where hierarchies are less clear, more leaders will likely emerge without position power (Huxam & Vangen, 2000). How leaders acquire, utilize, distribute, and replenish their influence and power is even more interesting today, given the seismic shift in organizations, the workforce, and the environmental context. How followers will play a role in the leadership dynamic may represent one of the most significant and important frontiers for research in the future. It is also likely that there will be far fewer followers and more leaders needing to figure out how to share leadership. Shared leadership also represents a new frontier for leadership researchers, especially shared leadership across time, distance, organizations, and cultures in the form of virtual teams.

REFERENCES

Adler, N. J. (1996). Global women political leaders: An invisible history, an increasingly important future. *Leadership Quarterly, 7,* 133–161.

Anderson, L. (1983). Management of the mixed-cultural work group. *Organizational Behavior and Human Decision Processes, 31,* 303–330.

Atwater, L. E., Ostroff, C., Yammarino, F., & Fleenor, J. (1998). Self-other agreement: Does it really matter? *Personnel Psychology, 51*(3), 577–598.

Atwater, L. E., Waldman, D., Atwater, D., & Cartier, J. (2000). An upward feedback field experiment: Supervisors' cynicism, follow-up and commitment to subordinates. *Personnel Psychology, 53,* 275–297.

Atwater, L. E., & Yammarino, F. J. (1997). Self-other rating agreement: A review and model. *Research in Personnel and Human Resource Management, 15,* 121–174.

Avolio, B. J. (1999). *Full leadership development: Building the vital forces in organizations.* Thousand Oaks, CA: Sage.

Avolio, B. J., & Bass, B. M. (1998). You can drag a horse to water but you can't make it drink unless it is thirsty. *Journal of Leadership Studies, 5,* 4–17.

Avolio, B. J., Bass, B. M, & Jung, D. I. (1999). Re-examining the components of transformational and transactional leadership using the Multifactor Leadership Questionnaire. *Journal of Occupational and Organizational Psychology, 72,* 441–461.

Avolio, B. J., & Gibbons, T. C. (1988). Developing transformational leaders: A life span approach. In J. A. Conger, R. N. Kanungo, and associates (Eds.), *Charismatic leadership: The elusive factor in organizational effectiveness* (pp. 276–308). San Francisco: Jossey-Bass.

Avolio, B. J., Kahai, S. S., & Dodge, G. (2000). E-leading in organizations and its implications for theory, research and practice. *Leadership Quarterly, 11,* 615–670.

Awamleh, R., & Gardner, W. L. (1999). Perceptions of leader charisma and effectiveness: The effects of vision content, delivery, and organizational performance. *Leadership Quarterly, 10,* 345–374.

Ayman, R., & Chemers, M. M. (1991). The effect of leadership match on subordinate satisfaction in Mexican managers: Some moderating influences of self-monitoring. *Journal of Applied Psychology, 68,* 338–341.

Baer, M., & Davis, J. (2001, February 20). Some assembly required. *Business 2.0,* 76–85.

Bales, R. F. (1954). In conference. *Harvard Business Review, 32,* 44–50.

Barling, J., Weber, T., & Kelloway, E. K. (1996). Effects of transformational leadership training on attitudinal and financial outcomes. *Journal of Applied Psychology, 81,* 827–832.

Barnard, C. I. (1938). *The functions of the executive.* Cambridge, MA: Harvard University Press.

Bartol, K. M., & Martin, D. C. (1986). Women and men in task groups. In R. D. Ashmore & F. K. Del Boca (Eds.), *The social psychology of female-male relations* (pp. 259–310). San Diego, CA: Academic Press.

Bass, B. M. (1985). *Leadership and performance beyond expectations.* New York: Free Press.

Bass, B. M. (1990). *Bass and Stogdill's handbook of leadership.* New York: Free Press.

Bass, B. M. (1996). *A new paradigm of leadership: An inquiry into transformational leadership.* Alexandria, VA: U.S. Army Research Institute for the Behavioral Sciences.

Bass, B. M. (1997). Does the transactional-transformational paradigm transcend organizational and national boundaries? *American Psychologist, 22,* 130–142.

Bass, B. M. (1998). *Transformational leadership: Industry, military, and educational impact.* Mahwah, NJ: Erlbaum.

Bass, B. M., & Avolio, B. J. (1990). *Transformational leadership development: Manual for the multifactor leadership questionnaire.* Palo Alto, CA: Consulting Psychologists Press.

Bass, B. M., & Avolio, B. J. (1993). Transformational leadership: A response to critiques. In M. M. Chemers & R. Ayman (Eds.), *Leadership research and theory: Perspectives and directions* (pp. 49–80). New York: Academic Press.

Bass, B. M., & Avolio, B. J. (1994). *Improving organizational effectiveness through transformational leadership.* Thousand Oaks, CA: Sage.

Bass, B. J., & Avolio, B. J. (1997). *Revised manual for the Multi-Factor Leadership Questionnaire.* Palo Alto, CA: Mindgarden.

Bass, B. M., Avolio, B. J., & Atwater, L. (1996). The transformational and transactional leadership of men and women. *Applied Psychology: An International Review, 45,* 5–34.

Bass, B. M., & Steidlmeier, P. (1999). Ethics, character, and authentic transformational leadership behavior. *Leadership Quarterly, 10,* 181–217.

Bem, S. L. (1974). The measurement of psychological androgyny. *Journal of Consulting and Clinical Psychology, 42,* 155–162.

Bennett, M. (1977). Testing management theories cross-culturally. *Journal of Applied Psychology, 62,* 578–581.

Bennis, W. G., & Nanus, B. (1985). *Leaders: The strategies for taking charge.* New York: Harper and Row.

Berson, Y., & Avolio, B. J. (2000a, April). *An exploration of critical links between transformational and strategic Leadership.* Paper presented at the annual meeting of the Society of Industrial and Organizational Psychology, New Orleans, LA.

Berson, Y., & Avolio, B. J. (2000b). *Using triangulation in the measurement of transformational leadership.* Unpublished manuscript.

Berson Y., Avolio, B. J., Shamir, B., & Popper, M. (2001). The relationships between leadership style, vision content, and contextual influences. *Leadership Quarterly, 12,* 53–74.

Beyer, J. M. (1999). Taming and promoting charisma to change organizations. *Leadership Quarterly, 10,* 307–330.

Beyer, J. M., & Browning, L. D. (1999). Transforming an industry in crisis: Charisma, routinization, and supportive cultural leadership. *Leadership Quarterly, 10,* 483–520.

Boal, K. B., & Hooijberg, R. (2000). Strategic leadership research: Moving on. *Leadership Quarterly, 11*(4), 515–549.

Bowers, D. G., & Seashore, S. E. (1966). Predicting organizational effectiveness with a four-factor theory of leadership. *Administrative Science Quarterly, 11,* 238–263.

Boyd, J. (1988). *Leadership extraordinary: A cross national military perspective on transactional versus transformational leadership.* Unpublished doctoral dissertation, Nova University, Fort Lauderdale, Florida.

Brass, D. J. (2001). Social capital and organizational leadership. In J. S. Zaccaro & R. J. Klimoski (Eds.), *The nature of organizational leadership: Understanding the imperatives confronting today's leaders* (pp. 132–152). San Francisco: Josey-Bass.

Brass, D. J., & Krackhadt, D. (1999). The social capital of 21st century leaders. In J. G. Hunt, G. E. Dodge, & L. Wong (Eds.), *Out-of-the-box leadership: Transforming the 21st century army and other top performing organizations* (pp. 179–194) Greenwich, CT: JAI Press.

Brodbeck, F. C., Frese, M., Akerblom, S., Audia, G., et al. (2000). Cultural variation of leadership prototypes across 22 European countries. *Journal of Occupational and Organizational Psychology, 73*(1), 1–29.

Bryman, A. S. (1993). *Charisma and leadership in organizations.* London: Sage.

Bryman, A. S. (1996). The importance of context: Qualitative research and the study of leadership. *Leadership Quarterly, 7,* 353–370.

Bryman, A. S., Stephens, M., & Campo, C. A. (1996). The importance of context: Qualitative research and the study of leadership. *Leadership Quarterly, 7*(3), 353–370.

Burke, M. J., & Day, R. R. (1986). A cumulative study of the effectiveness of managerial training. *Journal of Applied Psychology, 71,* 232–265.

Burns, J. M. (1978). *Leadership.* New York: Harper and Row.

Burns, J. M. (1997). *Empowerment for change.* Unpublished manuscript, University of Maryland, Kellogg Leadership Studies, College Park, MD.

Bycio, P., Hackett, R. D., & Allen, J. S. (1995). Further assessments of Bass's (1985) conceptualization of transactional and transformational leadership. *Journal of Applied Psychology, 80,* 468–478.

Calder, B. J. (1977). An attribution theory of leadership. In B. M. Staw & G. R. Salancik (Eds.), *New directions in organizational behavior* (pp. 179–204). Chicago: St. Clair.

Cannella, A. A., & Monroe, M. J. 1997. Contrasting perspectives on strategic leaders: Toward a more realistic view of top managers. *Journal of Management, 23,* 213–238.

Chan, K. Y., & Drasgow, F. (2001). Toward a theory of individual differences in leadership: Understanding the motivation to lead. *Journal of Applied Psychology, 86,* 481–498.

Chandler, A. (1962). *Strategy and structure.* Cambridge, MA: MIT Press

Chemers, M. M. (1997). *An integrative theory of leadership.* Mahwah, NJ: Erlbaum.

Cho, G. (1999). *Antecedents and consequences of leadership trust: An application of follower-centered approach to leadership.* Unpublished doctoral dissertation, State University of New York, Buffalo, NY.

Cohen, S. G., Chang, L., & Ledford, G. E. (1997). A hierarchical construct of self management leadership and its relationship to quality of work life and perceived group effectiveness. *Personnel Psychology, 50,* 275–308.

Conger, J. A. (1999). Charismatic and transformational leadership in organizations: An insider's perspective on these developing streams of research. *Leadership Quarterly, 10,* 145–179.

Conger, J. A., & Hunt, J. G. (1999). Overview charismatic and transformational leadership: II. Taking stock of the present and future. *Leadership Quarterly, 10,* 121–127.

Conger, J. A., & Kanungo, R. N. (1987). Toward a behavioral theory of charismatic leadership in organizational settings. *Academy of Management Review, 12,* 637–647.

Conger, J. A., & Kanungo, R. N. (1998). *Charismatic leadership in organizations.* Thousand Oaks, CA: Sage.

Cox, C. J., & Cooper, C. L. (1989). The making of the British CEO: Childhood, work, experience, personality, and management style. *Academy of Management Executive, 3,* 241–245.

Crookall, P. S. (1992). *Leadership in the prison industry: A study of the effect of training prison shop foreman in situational and transformational leadership on inmates' productivity and personal growth.* Unpublished doctoral dissertation, University of Western Ontario, London, Ontario, Canada.

Dansereau, F., Alutto, J. A., & Yammarino, F. J. (1984). *Theory testing in organizational behavior: The varient approach.* Englewood Cliffs, NJ: Prentice Hall.

Dansereau, F., Graen, G., & Haga, J. (1975). A vertical dyad linkage approach to leadership within formal organizations: A longitudinal investigation of the role making process. *Organizational Behavior and Human Performance, 36,* 46–78.

Dansereau, F., & Yammarino, F. J. (1998). *Leadership: The multiple-level approaches contemporary and alternative.* Greenwich, CT: JAI Press.

Dansereau, F., Yammarino, F. J., & Markham, S. E. (1995). Leadership: The multiple-level approaches. *Leadership Quarterly, 6,* 97–109.

Day, D. V. (2000). Leadership development: A review in context. *Leadership Quarterly, 11,* 581–615.

Day, D. V. (2001). Assessment of leadership outcomes. In J. S. Zaccaro & R. J. Klimoski (Eds.), *The nature of organizational leadership: Understanding the imperatives confronting today's leaders* (pp. 384–412). San Francisco: Josey-Bass.

Den Hartog, D., House, R. J., Hanges, P. J., Ruiz-Quintanilla, A., & Dorfman, P. (1999). Culture specific and cross-culturally generalizable implicit leadership theories: Are attributes of charismatic/transformational leadership universally endorsed? *Leadership Quarterly, 10,* 219–257.

Den Hartog, D., Van Muijen, J., & Koopman, P. (1994, July). *Transactional versus transformational leadership: An analysis of the MLQ in the Netherlands.* Paper presented at the 23rd International Congress of Applied Psychology, Madrid, Spain.

Dennis, A. R., Hilmer, K. M., & Taylor, N. J. (1998). Information exchange and use in GSS and verbal group decision-making: Effects of minority interest. *Journal of Management Information Systems, 14,* 61–88.

DeSanctis, G., & Poole, M. S. (1994). Capturing the complexity of technology use: Adaptive structuration theory. *Organization Science, 5,* 121–147.

Dorfman, P. W. (1996). International and cross-cultural leadership. In B. J. Punnett & O. Shenkar (Eds.), *Handbook for international management research* (pp. 267–349). Cambridge, MA: Blackwell.

Dorfman, P. W., & Howell, J. P. (1988). Dimensions of national culture and effective leadership patterns: Hofstede revisited. *Advances in International Comparative Management, 3,* 127–150.

Dorfman, P. W., & Howell, J. P., Hibino, S., Lee, J. K., Tate, U., & Bautista, A. (1997). Leadership in Western and Asian countries: Commonalities and differences in effective leadership processes across cultures. *Leadership Quarterly, 8,* 233–274.

Dunphy, D., & Bryant, B. (1996). Teams: Panaceas or prescriptions for improved performance? *Human Relations, 49,* 677–699.

Dvir, T., Eden, D., Avolio, B. J., & Shamir, B. (2002). Impact of transformational Leadership training on follower development and performance: A field experiment. *Academy of Management Journal.*

Eagly, A. H., & Johannesen-Schmidt, M. C. (2000). *The leadership styles of women and men.* Unpublished manuscript.

Eagly, A. H., & Johnson, B. (1990). Gender and the emergence of leaders: A meta-analysis. *Psychological Bulletin, 108,* 233–256.

Eagly, A. H., Karau, S., & Makhijani, M. (1995). Gender and the effectiveness of leaders: A meta-analysis. *Psychological Bulletin, 111,* 3–22.

Eagly, A. H., Karu, S. J., Miner, J. B., & Johnson, B. T. (1994). Gender and motivation to manage in hierarchic organizations: A meta-analysis. *Leadership Quarterly, 5,* 135–159.

Echavarria, N., & Davis, D. (1994, July). *A test of Bass's model of transformational and transactional leadership in the Dominican Republic.* Paper presented at the 23rd International Congress of Applied Psychology, Madrid, Spain.

Eden, D., & Leviatan, U. (1975). Implicit leadership theory as a determinant of the factor structure underlying supervisory behavioral scales. *Journal of Applied Psychology, 60,* 736–741.

Elron, E. (1997). Top management teams with multinational corporations. Effects of cultural heterogeneity. *Leadership Quarterly, 8,* 393–412.

Erikson, E. A. (1968). *Identity, youth, and crisis.* New York: W. W. Norton.

Facteau, C., Facteau, J., Schoel, L., Russell, J., & Poteet, M. (1998). Reactions of leaders to 360-degree feedback from subordinates and peers. *Leadership Quarterly, 9,* 427–448.

Farh, J., Tsui, A. S., Xin, K., & Cheng, B. (1998). The influence of relational demography and Guanxi: The Chinese case. *Organization Science, 9,* 471–488.

Fiedler, F. E. (1967). *A theory of leadership effectiveness.* New York: McGraw-Hill.

Fiedler, F. E. (1996). Research on leadership selection and training: One view of the future. *Administrative Science Quarterly, 41,* 241–250.

Finkelstein, S., & Hambrick, D. C. (1996). *Strategic leadership: Top executives and their effects on organizations.* St. Paul, MN: West.

Fleishman, E. A., Harris, E. F., & Burtt, H. E. (1955). *Leadership and supervision in industry.* Columbus, OH: Ohio State University, Bureau of Educational Research.

Fleishman, E. A., & Simmons, J. (1970). Relationship between leadership patterns and effectiveness ratings among Israeli foremen. *Personnel Psychology, 23,* 169–172.

Forsyth, D. R., & Forsyth, N. M. (1984). *Subordinate's reactions to female leaders.* Paper presented at the Eastern Psychological Association Convention, Baltimore.

Fu, P. P., & Yukl, G. (2000). Perceived effectiveness of influence tactics in the United States and China. *Leadership Quarterly, 11,* 251–266.

Gardner, H. (1983). *Frames of mind: The theory of multiple intelligences.* New York: Basic Books.

Gardner, H. (1985). *The mind's new science: A history of the cognitive revolution.* New York: Basic Books.

Gardner, W. L., & Avolio, B. A. (1998). The charismatic relationship: A dramaturgical perspective. *Academy of Management Review, 23,* 32–58.

George, J. F., Dennis, A. R., & Nunamaker, J. F. (1992). An experimental investigation of facilitation in an EMS decision room. *Group Decision and Negotiations, 1,* 57–70.

George, J. F., Easton, G., Nunamaker, J. F., & Northcraft, G. (1990). A study of collaborative group work with and without computer-based support. *Information Systems Research, 1,* 394–415.

Gerstner, C. R., & Day, D. (1994). Cross-cultural comparison of leadership prototypes. *Leadership Quarterly, 5,* 121–134.

Gerstner, C. R., & Day, D. V. (1997). Meta-analytic review of leader-member exchange theory: Correlates and construct issues. *Journal of Applied Psychology, 82,* 827–844.

Geyer, A., & Steyrer, J. (1998). Transformational leadership and objective performance in banks. *Applied Psychology: An International Review, 47,* 397–420.

Glaser, B., & Strauss, A. (1967). *The discovery of grounded theory: Strategies of qualitative research.* London: Wiedenfeld and Nicholson.

Goleman, D. (1998). *Working with emotional intelligence.* New York: Bantam Books.

Graen, G. B., Novak, M. A., & Sommerkamp, P. (1982). The effects of leader-member exchange and job design on productivity and job satisfaction: Testing a dual attachment model. *Organizational Behavior and Human Performance, 30,* 109–131.

Graen, G. B., & Uhl-Bien, M. (1995). Relationship based approach to leadership: Development of leader-member exchange (LMX) theory of leadership over 25 years. Applying a multi-level multi-domain perspective. *Leadership Quarterly, 68,* 219–247.

Hackman, M. R., Furniss, A. H., Hills, M. J., & Peterson, R. J. (1992). Perceptions of gender role characteristics and transformational and transactional leadership behavior. *Perceptual and Motor Skills, 75,* 311–319.

Hambrick, D. C. (1989). Guest editor's introduction: Putting top managers back in the strategy picture. *Strategic Management Journal, 10,* 5–15.

Hambrick, D. C., & Mason, P. (1984). Upper echelons: The organization as a reflection of its top managers. *Academy of Management Review, 9,* 193–206.

Hanges, P. J., Lord, R. G., & Dickson, M. W. (2000). An information-processing perspective on leadership and culture: A case study for connectionist architecture. *Applied Psychology: An International Review, 49,* 133–161.

Harmon, J., Schneer, J. A., & Hoffman, L. R. (1995). Electronic meetings and established decision groups: Audioconferencing effects on performance and structural stability. *Organizational Behavior and Human Decision Processes, 61,* 138–147.

Hedlund, G., & Rolander, D. (1990). Action in heterarchies: New approaches to managing the MNC. In C. Barlett & G. Hedlun (Eds.), *Managing the global firm* (pp. 15–45). London: Routledge.

Hegarty, W. (1974). Using subordinate ratings to elicit behavioral changes in supervisors. *Journal of Applied Psychology, 59,* 764–766.

Helgesen, S. (1990). *The female advantage: Woman's way of leadership.* New York: Doubleday/Currency.

Hellervik, L. W., Hazucha, J. F., & Schneider, R. J. (1992). Behavior change: Models, methods, and review of evidence. In M. D. Dunnette & L. M. Hough (Eds.), *Handbook of industrial and organizational psychology* (2nd ed., Vol. 3, pp. 823–896). Palo Alto, CA: Consulting Psychologists Press.

Hemphill, J. K. (1949). The leader and his group. *Educational Research Bulletin, 28,* 225–229, 245–246.

Hemphill, J. K., & Coons, A. E. (1957). Development of the leader behavior questionnaire. In R. M. Stogdill, & A. E. Coons (Eds.), *Leader behavior: Its description and measurement* (pp. 27–35). Columbus: Ohio State University, Bureau of Business Research.

Ho, T. H., & Raman, K. S. (1991). The effect of GSS and elected leadership on small group meetings. *Journal of Management Information Systems, 8,* 109–133.

Hofstede, G. (1980). *Cultural consequences: International differences in work related values.* Beverly Hills, CA: Sage.

Hofstede, G. (1993). Cultural constraints in management theories. *Academy of Management Executive, 7,* 81–94.

Hogan, R., Curphy, G. J., & Hogan, J. (1994). What we know about leadership, effectiveness and personality. *American Psychologist, 49,* 493–504.

Hogan, R., Raskin, R., & Fazzini, D. (1990). The dark side of charisma. In K. E. Clark & M. B. Clark (Eds.), *Measures of leadership* (pp. 343–354). West Orange, NJ: Leadership Library of America.

Hollander, E. P. (1995). Ethical challenges in the leader-follower relationship. *Business Ethics Quarterly, 5,* 54–65.

Hollander, E. P., & Neider, L. L. (1978). *Critical incidents and rating scales comparing "good-bad" leadership.* Paper presented at the American Psychological Association Convention, Toronto, Canada.

Hooijberg, R., & DiTomaso, N. (1996). Leadership in and of demographically diverse organization. *Leadership Quarterly, 7,* 1–20.

Hoskisson, R. E., Hitt, M. A., Wan, W. P., & Yiu, D. (1999). Theory and research in strategic management: Swings of a pendulum. *Journal of Management, 25,* 417–456.

House, R. J. (1960). *An experiment in the use of selected methods of improving the effectiveness of communication training for management.* Unpublished doctoral dissertation, Ohio State University, Columbus.

House, R. J. (1977). A 1976 theory of charismatic leadership. In J. G. Hunt & L. L. Larson (Eds.), *Leadership: The cutting edge* (pp. 189–207). Carbondale, IL: Southern Ilinois University Press.

House, R. J. (1995). Leadership in the twenty first century. In A. Howard (Ed.), *The changing nature of work* (pp. 411–450). San Francisco: Jossey-Bass.

House, R. J., & Aditya, R. N. (1997). The social scientific study of leadership: Quo Vadis? *Journal of Management, 23,* 409–473.

House, R. J., & Baetz, M. L., (1979). Leadership: Some empirical generalizations and new research directions. *Research in Organizational Behavior, 1,* 341–423.

House, R. J., Hanges, P., Agar, M., & Quintanilla, A. R. (1995). *The global leadership and organizational behavior effectiveness research program.* Unpublished manuscript, University of Pennsylvania, Philadelphia.

House, R. J., & Howell, J. M. (1992). Personality and charismatic leadership. *Leadership Quarterly, 3,* 81–108.

House, R. J., & Mitchell, T. R. (1975). Path-goal theory of leadership. *Journal of Contemporary Business, 3,* 81–97.

House, R. J., & Shamir, B. (1993). Towards an integration of transformational, charismatic and visionary theories of leadership. In M. Chemers & R. Ayman (Eds.), *Leadership: Perspectives and research directions* (pp. 81–107). New York: Academic Press.

House, R. J., Wright, N. S., & Aditya, R. N. (1997). Cross-cultural research on organizational leadership: A critical analysis and a proposed theory. In P. C. Earley & M. Erez (Eds.), *New perspectives on international industrial/organizational psychology* (pp. 535–625). San Francisco, CA: Jossey-Bass.

Howard, A. (2001). Identifying, assessing, and selecting senior leaders. In J. S. Zaccaro & R. J. Klimoski (Eds.), *The nature of organizational leadership: Understanding the imperatives confronting today's leaders* (pp. 305–346). San Francisco: Josey-Bass.

Howell, J. M., & Avolio, B. J. (1993). Transformational leadership, transactional leadership, locus of control, and support for innovation: Key predictors of consolidated business unit performance. *Journal of Applied Psychology, 78,* 891–902.

Howell, J. P., Dorfman, P. W., & Kerr, S. (1986). Moderator variables in leadership research. *Academy of Management Review, 11,* 88–102.

Hughs, R. L., Ginnett, R. C., & Curphy, G. J. (1999). *Leadership: Enhancing the lessons of experience* (3rd ed.). New York: McGraw-Hill.

Hunt, J. G., & Osborn, R. N. (1980). A multiple-influence approach to leadership for managers. In P. Hersey & J. Stinson (Eds.), *Perspectives in leader effectiveness* (pp. 47–62). Columbus: Ohio University, Center for Leadership Studies.

Hunt, J. G., & Peterson, M. F. (1997). Two scholars' views of some nooks and crannies in cross-cultural leadership. *Leadership Quarterly, 8*, 343–354.

Hunt, J. G., & Ropo, A. (1995). Multi-level leadership: Grounded theory and mainstream theory applied to the case of General Motors. *Leadership Quarterly, 6*, 379–412.

Huxam, C., & Vangen, S. (2000). Leadership in the shaping and implementation of collaboration agendas: How things happen in a (not quite) joined-up world. *Academy of Management Journal, 43*, 1159–1175.

Ireland, R. D., & Hitt, M. A. (1999). Achieving and maintaining strategic competitiveness in the twenty-first century: The role of strategic leadership. *Academy of Management Executive, 13*, 43–57.

Jacobs, T. O., & Jaques, E. (1987). Leadership in complex system. In J. A. Zeidner (Ed.), *Human productivity enhancement: Vol. 2. Organizations, personnel, and decision-making* (pp. 201–245). New York: Praeger.

Jago, A. G., & Ragan, J. W. (1986). The trouble with Leader Match is that it doesn't match Fiedler's contingency model. *Journal of Applied Psychology, 71*, 555–559.

Jaques, E. (1977). *A general theory of bureaucracy*. London: Heinemann.

Jensen, M. C., & Meckling, W. (1976). Theory of the firm: Managerial behavior, agency costs and ownership structure. *Journal of Financial Economics, 3*, 305–360.

Jick, T. D. (1979). Mixing qualitative and quantitative methods: Triangulation in action. *Administrative Science Quarterly, 24*, 602–611.

Judge, T. A., & Bono, J. E. (2000). Personality and transformational leadership. *Journal of Applied Psychology, 85*, 751–765.

Judge, T. A., Bono, J. E., Ilies, R., & Werner, M. (2000). *Personality and leadership: A review*. Unpublished manuscript, University of Iowa, Iowa City, Iowa.

Jung, D., & Avolio, B. (1999). Effects of leadership style and followers' cultural orientation on performance in group and individual task conditions. *Academy of Management Journal, 42*, 208–218.

Jung, D., Bass, B., & Sosik, J. (1995). Bridging leadership and culture: A theoretical consideration of transformational leadership and collectivistic cultures. *Journal of Leadership Studies, 2*, 3–18.

Jung, D., Butler, M., & Baik, K. (2000, April). *Effects of transformational leadership on group members' collective efficacy and perceived performance*. Paper presented at the Society for Industrial and Organizational Psychology conference, New Orleans, LA.

Kahai, S. S., Sosik, J. J., & Avolio, B. J. (1997). Effects of leadership style and problem structure on work group process and outcomes in an electronic meeting system environment. *Personnel Psychology, 50*, 121–146.

Kanter, R. M. (1977). *Men and women of the corporation*. New York: Basic Books.

Kanungo, R. N., & Mendonca, M. (1996). *Ethical dimensions in leadership*. Beverly Hills, CA: Sage.

Kaplan, R. E., Drath, W. H., & Kofodimos, J. R. (1991). *Beyond ambition: How driven managers can lead better and live better*. San Francisco: Jossey-Bass.

Katz, D., & Kahn, R. L. (1978). *The social psychology of organizations* (2nd ed.). New York: Wiley.

Katzenbach, J. R. (1997). *Teams at the top: Unleashing the potential of both teams and individual leaders*. Boston: Harvard Business School Press.

Kelman, H. C. (1958). Compliance, identification, and internalization: Three processes of attitude change. *Journal of Conflict Resolution, 2*, 51–56.

Kelman, H. C. (1974). Further thoughts on processes of compliance, identification, and internalization. In J. T. Tedeschi (Ed.), *Perspectives on social power* (pp. 125–171). Chicago: Aldine.

Kenny, D. A., & Zaccaro, S. J. (1983). An estimate of variance due to traits in leadership. *Journal of Applied Psychology, 68*, 678–685.

Kerr, S., & Jermier, J. M. (1978). Substitutes for leadership: Their meaning and measurement. *Organizational Behavior and Human Performance, 22*, 375–403.

Kets de Vries, M. F. R. (1988). Prisoners of leadership. *Human Relations, 41*, 261–280.

Kilburg, R. R. (1996). Toward a conceptual understanding and definition of executive coaching. *Consulting Psychology Journal: Practice and Research, 48*, 134–144.

Kirkpatrick, S. A., & Locke, E. A. (1991). Leadership: Do traits matter? *Academy of Management Executive, 5*, 48–60.

Klein, K. J., & House, R. J. (1995). On fire: Charismatic leadership and levels of analysis. *Leadership Quarterly, 6*, 183–198.

Klimoski, R. J., & Koles, K. L. K. (2001). The chief executive officer and top management team interface. In J. S. Zaccaro & R. J. Klimoski (Eds.), *The nature of organizational leadership: Understanding the imperatives confronting today's leaders* (pp. 219–269). San Francisco: Jossey-Bass.

Klonsky, B. G. (1983). The socialization and development of leadership ability. *Genetic Psychology Monographs, 108*, 97–135.

Kluger, A., & DeNisi, A. (1996). The effects of feedback interventions on performance: A historical review, a meta-analysis and preliminary feedback theory. *Psychological Bulletin, 119*, 254–284.

Koh, W., Terborg, J., & Steers, R. (1991, August). *The impact of transformational leadership on organizational commitment, organizational citizenship behavior, teacher satisfaction and student performance in Singapore*. Paper presented at the Academy of Management Annual Meeting, Miami, FL.

Kotter, J. P. (1982). *The general managers*. New York: Free Press.

Kozlowski, S. W. J., Gully, S. M., Salas, E., & Cannon-Bowers, J. A. (1996). Team leadership and development: Theories, principles, and guidelines for training leaders and teams. In M. M. Beyerlein, D. A. Johnson, & S. T. Beyerlein (Eds.),

Advances in interdisciplinary studies of work teams (pp. 253–291). Greenwich, CT: JAI Press.

Kuhnert, K. W., & Lewis, P. (1987). Transactional and transformational leadership: A constructive/developmental analysis. *Academy of Management Review, 12,* 648–657.

Lauterbach, B., Vu, J., & Weisberg, J. (1999). Internal versus external successions and their effect on firm performance. *Human Relations, 12,* 1485–1504.

Lea, M., & Spears, R. (1992). Paralanguage and social perception in computer-mediated communication. *Journal of Organizational Computing, 2,* 321–341.

Lim, L., Raman, K. S., & Wei, K. (1994). Interacting effects of GDSS and leadership. *Decision Support Systems, 12,* 199–211.

Loden, M. (1985). *Feminine leadership or how to succeed in business without being one of the boys.* New York: Time Books.

Lord, R. G., Binning, J. F., Rush, M. C., & Thomas, J. C. (1978). The effect of performance cues and leader behavior on questionnaire ratings of leadership behavior. *Organizational Behavior and Human Performance, 21,* 27–39.

Lord, R. G., Brown, D. J., & Freiberg, S. J. (1999). Understanding the dynamics of leadership: The role of follower self-concepts in the leader/follower relationship. *Organizational Behavior and Human Decision Processes, 78,* 167–203.

Lord, R. G., Foti, R. J., & DeVader, C. L. (1984). A test of leadership categorization theory: Internal structure, information processing, and leadership perceptions. *Organizational Behavior and Human Performance, 34,* 343–378.

Lord, R. G., DeVader, C. L., & Allinger, G. M. (1986). A meta-analysis of the relationship between personality traits and leadership perceptions: An application of validity generalization procedures. *Journal of Applied Psychology, 71,* 402–410.

Lord, R. D., & Maher, K. J. (1991). *Leadership and information processing: Linking perceptions and performance.* Boston: Unwind Hyman.

Lowe, K. B., & Gardner, W. L. (2000). Ten years of the *Leadership Quarterly*: Contributions and challenges for the future. *Leadership Quarterly, 11,* 459–514.

Lowe, K. B., Kroeck, K. G., & Sivasubramaniam, N. (1996). Effectiveness correlates of transformational and transactional leadership: A meta-analytic review. *Leadership Quarterly, 7,* 385–425.

Maher, K. J. (1997). Gender-related stereotypes of transformational and transactional leadership. *Sex Roles, 37,* 209–225.

Mankin, D., Cohen, S. G., & Bikson, T. K. (1996). *Teams and technology.* Boston: Harvard Business School Press.

Mann, R. D. (1959). A review of the relationships between personality and performance in small groups. *Psychological Bulletin, 56,* 241–270.

Manz, C. C., & Sims, H. P., Jr. (1987). Leading workers to lead themselves: The external leadership of self-managing work teams. *Administrative Science Quarterly, 32,* 106–128.

Manz, C. C., & Sims, H. P., Jr. (1993). *Business without bosses: How self-managing teams are building high performance companies.* New York: Wiley.

March, J. C., & Simon, H. A. (1959). *Organizations.* New York: Wiley.

Marshall-Mies, J. C., Fleishman, E. A., Martin, J. A., Zaccaro, S. J., Baughman, W. A., & McGee, M. L. (2000). Development and evaluation of cognitive and metacognitive measures for predicting leadership potential. *Leadership Quarterly, 11,* 135–153.

McCall, M. W., & Lombardo, M. M. (1983). *Off the track: Why and how successful executives get derailed.* Greensboro, NC: Center for Creative Leadership.

McCauley, C. D. (2000, April). *A systematic approach to leadership development.* Paper presented at the 15th Annual Conference of the Society for Industrial and Organizational Psychology, New Orleans, LA.

McCauley, C. D. (2001). Leader training and development. In J. S. Zaccaro & R. J. Klimoski (Eds.), *The nature of organizational leadership: Understanding the imperatives confronting today's leaders* (pp. 347–383). San Francisco: Jossey-Bass.

McCauley, C. D., & Brutus, S. (1998). *Management development through job experiences: An annotated bibliography.* Greensboro, NC: Center for Creative Leadership.

McCauley, C. D., Ruderman, M. N., Ohlott, P. J., & Morrow, J. E. (1994). Assessing the developmental components of managerial jobs. *Journal of Applied Psychology, 79,* 544–560.

Meindl, J. R., Ehrlich, S. B., & Dukerich, J. M. (1985). The romance of leadership. *Administrative Science Quarterly, 30,* 521–551.

Miles, R. E., & Snow, C. C. (1978). *Organizational strategy, structure and process.* New York: McGraw-Hill.

Mintzberg, H. (1973). *The nature of managerial work.* New York: Harper and Row.

Mintzberg, H. (1980). *The nature of managerial work.* Englewood Cliffs, NJ: Prentice Hall.

Mischel, W. (1973). Toward a cognitive social learning reconceptualization of personality. *Psychological Review, 80,* 252–283.

Misumi, J. (1985). *The behavioral science of leadership: An interdisciplinary Japanese research program.* Ann Arbor, MI: University of Michigan Press.

Misumi, J., & Peterson, M. (1985). The performance-maintenance (PM) theory of leadership: Review of a Japanese research program. *Administrative Science Quarterly, 30,* 198–223.

Mitchell, T. R. (1979). Organizational behavior. *Annual Review of Psychology, 30,* 243–281.

Moskowitz, D. W., Suh, E. J., & Desaulniers, J. (1994). Situational influences on gender differences in agency and communication. *Journal of Personality and Social Psychology, 66,* 753–761.

Moxley, R. S., & O'Connor-Wilson, P. (1998). A systems approach to leadership development. In C. D. McCauley, R. S., Moxley, & E. Van Velsor (Eds.), *The Center for Creative Leadership hand-*

book of leadership development (pp. 217–241). San Francisco: Jossey-Bass.

Mumford, M. D., Zaccaro, S. J., Harding, F. D., Jacobs, T. O., & Fleishman, E. A. (2000). Leadership skills for a changing world: Solving complex social problems. *Leadership Quarterly, 11,* 11–35.

Nahavandi, A. (2000). *The art and science of leadership.* Upper Saddle River, NJ: Prentice Hall.

Nutt, P. C., & Backoff, R. W. (1997). Facilitating transformational change. *Journal of Applied Behavioral Science, 33,* 490–508.

O'Connor, J., Mumford, M. D., Clifton, T. C., Gessner, T. L., & Connelly, M. S. (1995). Charismatic leaders and destructiveness: A historiometric study. *Leadership Quarterly, 6,* 529–558.

O'Mahoney, S., & Barley, S. R. (1999). Do digital communications affect work and organization? The state of our knowledge. *Research in Organizational Behavior, 21,* 125–161.

Oz, E. (2000). *Management information systems.* Cambridge, MA: Course Technology.

Oz, E., & Sosik, J. J. (2000). Why information system projects are abandoned: A leadership and communication theory and exploratory study. *Journal of Computer Information Systems, 41*(1), 66–78.

Parker, P. S., & Ogilvie, D. T. (1996). Gender, culture, and leadership: Toward a culturally distinct model of African-American women executives' leadership strategies. *Leadership Quarterly, 7,* 189–214.

Pearce, C. L. (1997). *The determinants of change management team effectiveness: A longitudinal study.* Unpublished doctoral dissertation, University of Maryland, College Park.

Pearce, C. L., & Sims, H. P., Jr. (2000). *Vertical vs. shared leadership as predictors of the longitudinal effectiveness of change.* Unpublished manuscript.

Pelled, L. H., & Xin, K. R. (1997). Birds of a feather: leader-member demographic similarity and organizational attachment in Mexico. *Leadership Quarterly, 8,* 433–450.

Peters, L. H., Hartke, D. D., & Pohlmann, J. T. (1985). Fiedler's contingency theory of leadership: An application of the meta-analysis procedures of Schmidt and Hunter. *Psychological Bulletin, 97,* 274–285.

Peterson, M. F., & Hunt, J. G. (1997). International perspectives on international leadership. *Leadership Quarterly, 8,* 203–232.

Phillips, J. S., & Lord, R. G. (1981). Causal attributions and perceptions of leadership. *Organizational Behavior and Human Performance, 28,* 143–163.

Podsakoff, P. M., MacKenzie, S. B., & Bommer, W. H. (1995). Meta-analysis of the relationships between Kerr and Jermier's substitutes for leadership and employee job attitudes, role perceptions, and performance. *Journal of Applied Psychology, 81,* 380–399.

Podsakoff, P. M., Mackenzie, S. B., & Fetter, R. (1993). Substitutes for leadership and the management of professionals. *Leadership Quarterly, 4,* 1–44.

Podsakoff, P. M., MacKenzie, S. B., Moorman, R. H., & Fetter, R. (1990). Transformational leader behaviors and their effects on follower's trust in leader, satisfaction, and organizational citizenship behaviors. *Leadership Quarterly, 1,* 107–142.

Podsakoff, P. M., Niehoff, B. P., MacKenzie, S. B., & Williams, M. L. (1993). Do substitutes for leadership really substitute for leadership? An empirical examination of Kerr and Jermier's situational leadership model. *Organizational Behavior and Human Performance, 54,* 1–44.

Podsakoff, P. M., & Organ, D. W. (1986). Self-reports in organizational research: Problems and prospects. *Journal of Management, 12,* 31–41.

Podsakoff, P. M., & Todor, W. D. (1985). Relationships between leader reward and punishment behavior and group process and productivity. *Journal of Management, 11,* 55–73.

Podsakoff, P. M., Todor, W. D., & Skov, R. B. (1982). Effects of leader contingent and noncontingent reward and punishment behaviors on subordinate performance and satisfaction. *Academy of Management Journal, 25,* 810–821.

Popper, M., Mayseless, O., & Castelnovo, O. (2000). Transformational leadership and attachment. *Leadership Quarterly, 11,* 267–289.

Postmes, T., Spears, R., & Lea, M. (2000). The formation of group norms in computer-mediated communication. *Human Communication Research, 26,* 341–371.

Powell, G. (1993). *Women and men in management* (2nd ed.). Newbury Park, CA: Sage.

Quinn, R., & Cameron, K. (1983). Organizational life cycles and shifting criteria of effectiveness: Some preliminary evidence. *Management Science, 29,* 33–51.

Ragins, B. R., & Cotton, J. L. (1999). Mentor functions and outcomes: A comparison of men and women in formal and informal mentoring relationships. *Journal of Applied Psychology, 84,* 529–550.

Rao, A., Hashimoto, K., & Rao, A. (1997). Universal and culturally specific aspects of managerial influence: A study of Japanese managers. *Leadership Quarterly, 8,* 295–312.

Reissman, C. K. (1993). *Narrative analysis.* Newbury Park, CA: Sage.

Rosener, J. B. (1995). *America's competitive secret: Utilizing women as management strategy.* New York: Oxford University Press.

Ross, S. M., & Offermann, L. R. (1997). Transformational leaders: Measurement of personality attributes and work group performance. *Personality and Social Psychology Bulletin, 23,* 1078–1086.

Rush, M. C., Phillips, J. S., & Lord, R. G. (1981). Effects of a temporal delay in rating on leader behavior descriptions: A laboratory investigation. *Journal of Applied Psychology, 66,* 442–450.

Rush, M. C., Thomas, J. C., & Lord, R. G. (1977). Implicit leadership theory: A potential threat to the internal validity of leader behaviors. *Organizational Behavior and Human Performance, 20,* 93–110.

Schriesheim, C. A., Castro, S. L., & Cogliser, C. C. (1999). Leader-member exchange (LMX) research: A comprehensive review of theory, measurement and data analytic practices. *Leadership Quarterly, 10,* 63–113.

Schriesheim, C. A., Tepper, B. J., & Tetrault, L. A. (1994). Least preferred co-worker score, situational control, and leadership effectiveness. A meta-analysis of contingency model performance predictions. *Journal of Applied Psychology, 79,* 561–573.

Sellers, P. (1999, June 21). CEOs in denial. *Fortune, 139,* 80–82.

Shamir, B. (1995). Social distance and charisma. *Leadership Quarterly, 6,* 19–47.

Shamir, B., House, R., & Arthur, M. (1993). The motivational effects of charismatic leadership: A self-concept based theory. *Organization Science, 4,* 1–17.

Shamir, B., Zakay, E., Breinin, E., & Popper, M. (1998). Correlates of charismatic leader behavior in military units: Subordinates' attitudes, unit characteristics, and superiors' appraisals of leader. *Academy of Management Journal, 41,* 384–409.

Sheehy, N., & Gallagher, T. (1996). Can virtual organizations be made real? *Psychologist, 9,* 159–162.

Simonton, D. K. (1984). *Genius, creativity, and leadership: Historic inquiries.* Cambridge, MA: Harvard University Press.

Simonton, D. K. (1990). Personality and politics. In L. A. Pervin (Ed.), *Handbook of personality: Theory and research* (pp. 670–692). New York: Guilford Press.

Simonton, D. K. (1994). *Greatness: Who makes history and why.* New York: Guilford Press.

Sinha, J. B. P. (1984). A model of effective leadership styles in India. *International Studies of Management and Organization, 14,* 86–98.

Sivasubramaniam, N., Jung, D. I., Avolio, B. J., & Murry, W. D. (2001). A longitudinal model of the effects of team leadership and group potency on group performance. *Group and Organization Management, 27*(1), 66–96.

Smircich, L., & Morgan, G. (1982). Leadership: The management of meaning. *Journal of Applied Behavioral Science, 18,* 257–273.

Sosik, J. J. (1997). Effects of transformational leadership and anonymity on idea generation in computer-mediated groups. *Group and Organization Management, 22,* 460–487.

Sosik, J. J. (2000). Meaning from within: Possible selves and personal meaning of charismatic and non-charismatic leaders. *Journal of Leadership Studies, 7,* 3–17.

Sosik, J. J., Avolio, B. J., & Kahai, S. S. (1997). Effects of leadership style and anonymity on group potency and effectiveness in a group decision support system environment. *Journal of Applied Psychology, 82,* 89–103.

Sosik, J. J., & Dworakivsky, A. C. (1998). Self-concept based aspects of the charismatic leader: More than meets the eye. *Leadership Quarterly, 9,* 503–526.

Sosik, J. J., & Godshalk, V. M. (2000). The role of gender in mentoring: Implications for diversified and homogenous mentoring relationships. *Journal of Vocational Behavior, 57,* 20.

Sosik, J. J., Kahai, S. S., & Avolio, B. J. (1998). Transformational leadership and dimensions of group creativity: Motivating idea generation in computer-mediated groups. *Creativity Research Journal, 11,* 111–121.

Sosik, J. J., Kahai, S. S., & Avolio, B. J. (1999). Leadership style, anonymity, and creativity in group decision support systems: The mediating role of optimal flow. *Journal of Creative Behavior, 33,* 1–30.

Sternberg, R. J., & Wagner, R. K. (1993). The g-ocentric view of intelligence and job performance is wrong. *Current Directions in Psychological Science, 2,* 1–5.

Stevenson, W. B., Pearce, J. L., & Porter, L. W. (1985). The concept of "coalition" in organizational theory and research. *Academy of Management Review, 10,* 256–268.

Stogdill, R. M. (1948). Personality factors associated with leadership: A survey of the literature. *Journal of Personality, 25,* 35–71.

Stogdill, R. M. (1963). *Manual for the leader behavior description questionnaire—for XII.* Columbus: Ohio State University, Bureau of Business Research.

Stogdill, R. M. (1974). *Handbook of leadership.* New York: Free Press.

Strube, M. J., & Garcia, J. E. (1981). A meta-analytic investigation of Fiedler's contingency model of leadership effectiveness. *Psychological Bulletin, 90,* 307–321.

Sykes, A. J. M. (1962). The effects of a supervisory training course in changing supervisor's perceptions and expectations of the role of management. *Human Relations, 15,* 227–243.

Taggar, S., Hackett, R., & Saha, S. (1999). Leadership emergence in autonomous work teams: Antecedents and outcomes. *Personnel Psychology, 52,* 899–926.

Tichy, N. N., & Devanna, M. A. (1986). *The transformational leader.* New York: Wiley.

Triandis, C. H. (1994). Cross-cultural industrial and organizational psychology. In M. D. Dunnette & L. Hough (Eds.), *Handbook of industrial and organizational psychology* (pp. 103–172). Palo Alto, CA: Consulting Psychologists Press.

Trist, E. L. (1993). A socio-technical critique of scientific management. In E. Trist & H. Murray (Eds.), *The social engagement of social science: A Tavistock anthology* (pp. 580–598). Philadelphia: University of Pennsylvania Press.

Valikangas, L., & Okumura, A. (1997). Why do people follow leaders? A study of a U.S. and a Japanese change program. *Leadership Quarterly, 8,* 313–337.

Vandenbosch, B., & Ginzberg, M. J. (1997). Lotus notes and collaboration: Plus ca change. *Journal of Management Information Systems, 13,* 65–81.

Waldman, D. A., & Atwater, L. E. (1998). *The power of 360-degree feedback: How to leverage performance evaluations for top productivity.* Houston, TX: Gulf.

Waldman, D. A., Ramirez, G., House, R., & Puranam, P. (2001). Does leadership matter? CEO leadership attributes and profitability under conditions of perceived environmental uncertainty. *Academy of Management Journal, 44,* 134–143.

Walther, J. B. (1995). Related aspects of computer mediated communication: Experimental observations over time. *Organization Science, 6,* 196–203.

Webb, E. J., Campbell, D. T., Schwartz, R. D., & Sechrest, L. (1966*). Unobtrusive measures: Non-reactive research in the social sciences.* Chicago: Rand-McNally.

Weisband, S., Schneider, S. K., & Connolly, T. (1995). Computer-mediated communication and social information: Status salience and status differences. *Academy of Management Journal, 38,* 1124–1151.

Weiss, R. S. (1968). Issues in holistic research. In S. Howard, G. Becker, D. Riesman, & R. Weiss (Eds.), *Institutions and the person* (pp. 342–350). Chicago: Aldine.

Wofford, J. C., Lovett, S., Whittington, J. L., & Coalter, T. M. (1999, August). *Implicit leadership theory and culture: The case of Mexico and the US.* Paper presented at the Academy of Management conference, Chicago.

Xin, K. R. (1997). Asian-American managers: An impression gap? *Journal of Applied Behavioral Science, 33,* 335–355.

Xin, K. R., & Tsui, A. S. (1996). Different strokes for different folks? Influence tactics by Asian-American and Caucasian-American managers. *Leadership Quarterly, 7,* 109–132.

Yammarino, F., & Atwater, L. (1997). Do managers see themselves as others see them? Implications of self-other rating agreement for human resources management. *Organizational Dynamics, 25*(4), 35–44.

Yukl, G. (1998). *Leadership in organizations* (4th ed.). Englewood Cliffs, NJ: Prentice Hall.

Yukl, G. (1999). An evaluation of conceptual weaknesses in transformational and charismatic leadership theories. *Leadership Quarterly, 10,* 285–305.

Yukl, G., & Van Fleet, D. D. (1992). Theory and research on leadership in organizations. In M. D. Dunnette (Eds.), *Handbook of industrial and organizational psychology* (Vol. 3, pp. 147–197). Palo Alto, CA: Consulting Psychologist Press.

Zaccaro, S. J. (1996). *Models and theories of executive leadership: Conceptual/empirical review and integration.* Alexandria, VA: U.S. Army Research Institute for the Behavioral and Social Sciences.

Zaccaro, S. J., & Banks, D. J. (2001). Leadership, vision and organizational effectiveness. In J. S. Zaccaro & R. J. Klimoski (Eds.), *The nature of organizational leadership: Understanding the imperatives confronting today's leaders* (pp. 181–218). San Francisco: Jossey-Bass.

Zaccaro, S. J., & Klimoski, R. J. (2001). *The nature of organizational leadership: Understanding the imperatives confronting today's leaders.* San Francisco: Jossey-Bass.

Zaccaro, S. J., Mumford, M. D., Connelly, M., Marks, M., & Gilbert, J. A. (2000). Assessment of leader abilities. *Leadership Quarterly, 11,* 37–64.

Zacharatos, A., Barling, J., & Kelloway, E. K. (2000). Development and effects of transformational leadership in adolescents. *Leadership Quarterly, 11,* 211–226.

Zanetti, L. A., & Cunningham, R. B. (2000). Perspectives on public-sector strategic management. In J. Rabin, G. J. Miller, & W. B. Hildreth (Eds.), *Handbook of strategic management.* New York: Marcel Dekker.

CHAPTER 13

Theories and Practices of Organizational Development

JOHN R. AUSTIN AND JEAN M. BARTUNEK

From its roots in action research in the 1940s and 1950s (Collier, 1945), and building on Lewin's insight that "there is nothing so practical as a good theory" (Lewin, 1951, p. 169), organizational development has explicitly emphasized both the practice and the scholarship of planned organizational change. Ideally, at least, research is closely linked with action in organizational development initiatives, and the solution of practical organizational problems can lead to new scholarly contributions (Pasmore & Friedlander, 1982; Rapoport, 1970).

Despite this more or less implicit expectation, there have been many disconnects between practitioners' and academics' approaches to contributing new knowledge. For example, action research as it was originally conceived became more and more practice and solution oriented and less focused on making a scholarly contribution (Bartunek, 1983). Some recent approaches to organizational development, such as many large-group interventions, have been implemented primarily by practitioners, with little academic investigation of their success. Some theories of change formulated by academics are not at all feasible to implement.

It is easy enough for academics to suggest that practitioners' work is not sufficiently novel and thought-out to contribute to scholarly understandings of change. However, it is also the case that many new methods of accomplishing planned organizational change have been developed by people who were focusing in particular on practice contributions (e.g., team building, sociotechnical systems, and large-group interventions, to name just a few). It is through practice that organizational improvement actually takes place. Another way to put this is that organizational development practitioners have a substantial knowledge base from which it is valuable for academics to draw, albeit one that is sometimes more tacit than explicit, just as practitioners may draw from academics' knowledge (e.g., Cook & Brown, 1999).

It is not only with respect to organizational development that there are separations between academic and practitioner approaches to organizational knowledge. Rynes, Bartunek, and Daft (2001), introducing a special research forum on academic-practitioner knowledge transfer in the *Academy of Management Journal,* referred to the "great divide" between academics and practitioners in organizational research. But they also argued that there are many reasons—academic, economic, and practical—why it is important that more explicit links be developed between academics and practitioners. For example, corporate universities are becoming more prominent, and training organizations such as the American Society for Training and Development are gaining substantially in membership.

A recent Swedish law mandated that universities collaborate with their local communities in generating research (Brulin, 1998). Many work organizations are outsourcing some knowledge-generation activities to academics. Given organizational development's history, the development of understanding and appreciation of both academic and practitioner contributions is particularly crucial.

Several reviews of organizational development and change have been presented prior to this chapter (recent ones include Armenakis & Bedeian, 1999; Porras & Robertson, 1992; Weick & Quinn, 1999). These reviews have made important scholarly contributions to the understanding of such topics as variables involved in planned organizational change; the content, context, and processes of organizational change; and the degree to which such change is constant or sporadic. But prior reviews have not explicitly incorporated both practitioner and academic knowledge about organizational development. In contrast to these prior approaches, we focus on the kinds of emphases that characterize practitioner and academic knowledge regarding organizational development and do this using both academic and practitioner literatures. In so doing, we hope to break down some of the barriers that typically exist between organizational development practice and scholarship.

We divide the chapter into several sections. First we briefly compare contemporary and earlier organizational development emphases. Organizational development is an evolving field, and its emphases today are not the same as its initial emphases (Mirvis, 1990). The state of the field at the present time has implications for the types of knowledge needed by practitioners and academics.

Second, we use a distinction introduced by Bennis (1966) and modified by Porras and Robertson (1992) to distinguish different types of conceptual emphases between practice and academic scholarship on change. Third, on the basis of this distinction we situate organizational development within larger literatures on organizational change. Although in its early days organizational development was often seen to represent the majority of approaches to "planned change" in organizations, it is now recognized as one of many approaches to planned change. We situate it within various "motors" of change as these were described by Van de Ven and Poole (1995).

Fourth, we describe some contemporary organizational development interventions and the motors in practice that we see as important in them. Finally, we describe barriers to enhanced links between academics and practitioners and then suggest some strategies that may be used to reduce these barriers. This latter approach is in the spirit of the force field analysis approach developed originally by Lewin (1951) and

used often by practitioners (Schmuck, Runkel, Saturen, Martell, & Derr, 1972).

We believe that the kinds of knowledge—or knowing, as Cook and Brown (1999) put it—of organizational development practice do not always link as well as they might with academic scholarship on change. But developing greater links is crucially important because at its core organizational development involves the promotion of change. In their interviews with a number of organizational development "thought leaders," Worley and Feyerherm (2001) found numerous recommendations for increased collaboration between organizational development practitioners and other change-related disciplines.

Our focus is on the theoretical and practical knowledge underlying today's organizational development practice. Worley and Varney (1998) remind us that the practice requires skill competencies as well as knowledge competencies. Skill competencies include managing the consulting practice, analysis, and diagnosis; designing and choosing appropriate interventions; developing client capability; and evaluating organizational change. In this chapter we examine the theories of change that inform the application of these skills. Detailed consideration of these skill competencies is beyond the scope of this chapter but can be found in other resources (Cummings & Worley, 2000; French & Bell, 1999).

ORGANIZATION DEVELOPMENT TODAY, NOT YESTERDAY

Early approaches to organizational development centered primarily on the implementation of humanistic ideals at work. The types of values emphasized included personal development, interpersonal competency, participation, commitment, satisfaction, and work democracy (French & Bell, 1999; Mirvis, 1988). The focus generally was within the workplace.

Over time, however, there has been a shift in emphases. In comparison to its early formulations, organizational development pays much more attention to the larger environment in which the business operates and aims at helping businesses accomplish their strategic objectives, in part through organizational alignment with the larger environment (e.g., Bunker & Alban, 1996; Church & Burke, 1995; Mirvis, 1988, 1990; Seo, Putnam, & Bartunek, 2001).

Early approaches placed considerable emphasis on individual and group development (e.g., Harrison, 1970), and although the terms *"whole organization"* was used, the types of change fostered by organizational development often focused more on the group (e.g., team building) or on other organizational subunits. Given the organizational environment of the 1980s and beyond, individual development and group development have been less emphasized unless they are treated within the context of large systems change and the adjustment of an organization to its larger environment. Such adjustment often involves radical departure from the organization's prior strategic emphases (Nadler, Shaw, & Walton, 1995) and is sometimes referred to as *organizational transformation* (e.g., Nadler et al., 1995; Quinn & Cameron, 1988; Tichy & Devanna, 1986; Torbert, 1989) or *radical organizational culture change* (e.g., Cameron & Quinn, 1999).

Despite the shifts that have occurred in the understanding of organizational development's focus, there remains an emphasis on organizational development as humanistically oriented—as concerned about the people who make up an organization, not just the strategic goals of the organization. Thus, for example, Church, Waclawski, and Seigel (1999) defined organizational development as the process of promoting positive, humanistically oriented, large-system change. By humanistic they mean that the change is "about improving the conditions of people's lives in organizations" (p. 53). Beer and Nohria (2000) included organizational development within the category of capacity-building interventions in organizations, not as primarily economically oriented.

This shift in emphasis locates organizational development within the context of multiple types of organizational change efforts (Van de Ven & Poole, 1995). It cannot be discussed entirely separately from types of change that, at first glance, seem far removed from its emphases. However, there are still important distinctions between the practice knowledge and academic knowledge of organizational development and other types of planned change.

THE CONCEPTUAL KNOWLEDGE OF ORGANIZATIONAL DEVELOPMENT

Contemporary as well as past approaches to organizational development are based on more or less explicit assumptions about (1) the processes through which organizations change and (2) the types of intervention approaches that lead to change. These two phrases, which seem quite similar, actually represent two different conceptual approaches: one that is more likely to be addressed by academic writing on organizational development and one that is more likely to be addressed by practitioner writing. We use them to frame approaches to change that are presented primarily for academics and primarily for practitioners.

In 1966 Bennis distinguished between *theories of change* and *theories of changing*. Theories of change attempt to answer the question of how and why change occurs. Theories of changing attempt to answer the question of how to generate change and guide it to a successful conclusion. Porras and Robertson (1987, p. 4) expanded on Bennis's notion, relabeling the two different approaches as *change process theory* and *implementation theory*. (Although the categories are essentially the same, we will use Porras and Robertson's terms because they are much easier to distinguish.)

Porras and Robertson (1987, 1992) described change process theory as explaining the dynamics of the change process. This approach centers around the multiple types of variables involved in the accomplishment of planned change. In contrast, they described implementation theory as "theory that focuses on activities change agents must undertake in effecting organizational change" (p. 4). They included strategy, procedure, and technique theories as examples of implementation approaches.

Porras and Robertson's focus was primarily on organizational development interventions as explicitly defined. As noted earlier, however, the understanding of dynamics of change has been widened well beyond organizational development (e.g., Weick & Quinn, 1999; Van de Ven & Poole, 1995). Porras and Robertson also asserted that change process theory should inform implementation theory; that is, the findings of academic research should inform practice. There is awareness now that organizational development practice should also have an impact on academic knowledge (Rynes et al., 2001).

In this chapter we expand on the understandings of change process theory and implementation theory. We describe an array of change process theories using the model developed by Van de Ven and Poole (1995) for that purpose. We also describe several implementation models and suggest possible links between them and change process models.

We noted that academic writing tends to focus more on change process theory whereas practitioner writing focuses more on implementation theory. There has been relatively little interaction between the two types of theories; to some extent they occupy separate intellectual spaces and are held in more or less separate "communities of practice" (J. S. Brown & Duguid, 1991, 1999; Tenkasi, 2000). Change process theories tend to draw from empirical work grounded in academic fields such as psychology, sociology, economics, and anthropology. Implementation theories tend to draw from practitioner-oriented experiential work; they may emerge from the same academic disciplines as change process theories but do not make the connections explicit. It is hoped that this chapter suggests useful connections between the two.

Change Process Theories

Porras and Robertson (1992) concluded their review of organizational change and development research with a call for increased attention to theory in change research. Through attention to the variety of ways organizations might change, this call has been answered.

Researchers have approached the task of understanding organizational change from a dizzying array of perspectives. In their interdisciplinary review of about 200 articles on change, Van de Ven and Poole (1995) identified four ideal types of change theories. They labeled them as life cycle, evolution, dialectic, and teleology and located organizational development primarily within the teleological framework. These four types are distinguished by their underlying generative mechanisms, or *motors*. Van de Ven and Poole suggested that most change theories can be understood within one motor or in a combination of motors.

We found evidence of extensive theory development pertinent to organizational development based on each change motor. In the following sections we summarize recent change research categorized by primary underlying motor of change. With Van de Ven and Poole (1995) we recognize that most change theories capture elements from different motors, although one motor is typically primary.

The Teleological Motor

The teleological motor describes organizational change as the result of purposeful social construction by organization members. The motor of development is a cycle of goal formation, implementation, evaluation, and modification. Organizational change is goal driven; impetus for change emerges when actors perceive that their current actions are not enabling them to attain their goals, and the focus is on processes that enable purposeful activity toward the goals. The teleological motor can be found in most contemporary theories of organizational change. For example, recent extensions of evolutionary theories and institutional theories—evolutionary innovation and institutional agency—have adopted a teleological motor. Change leadership theories rely on the teleological motor as well. In the following we summarize some teleological change theories that have emerged or reemerged during the prior decade.

Strategic Change.   Rajagopalan and Spreitzer (1996) observed that strategic change deals primarily with teleological change. Underlying most strategic change theories is the understanding that planned change triggered by goal-oriented managers can trigger change in both an organization

and its environment. Following this teleological logic, several researchers have sought to understand the role of leadership in generating organizational change (Nutt & Backoff, 1997). Bass's transformational leadership framework (Bass, 1985; Bass & Avolio, 1994) posits that organizational change emerges as the result of leaders' attempts to develop their followers and transform follower goals to match more closely those of the organization. Other researchers view organizational change as the end result of cognitive development of organizational leaders (Hooijberg, Hunt, & Dodge, 1997; Torbert, 1991).

Cognitive Framing Theories.   Several studies emphasize the importance of cognitive change by managers in creating organizational change. Reconceptualization of the context then leads to further cognitive change in a continuing iterative process (Barr, Stimpert, & Huff, 1992; Bartunek, Krim, Necochea, & Humphries, 1999; Weick, 1995). Gioia and Chittipeddi (1991) found that managerial efforts to communicate a planned change built cognitive consensus, which further enabled the change.

Change Momentum.   Studies of change momentum within organizations have relied on the evolutionary motor to explain selection of organizational routines, which in turn create inertial forces (Amburgey, Kelly, & Barnett; 1993; Kelly & Amburgey, 1991). Jansen (2000) proposed a new conceptualization of momentum that focuses on teleological processes of change. She distinguished between inertia, the tendency of a body at rest to stay at rest or a body in motion to stay in motion, and momentum, the force or energy associated with a moving body. Evolutionary change theories deal primarily with inertia. However, momentum is a teleological theory. The force that keeps a change moving is goal driven and purposeful. Jansen found that change-based momentum, defined as the perception of the overall energy associated with pursuing some end state, fluctuated in a systematic way throughout a change process.

Theories of Innovation.   Several researchers consider how individual attempts at innovation combine with environmental characteristics to generate organizational change (C. M. Ford, 1996; Glynn, 1996). Glynn proposed a theoretical framework for how individual intelligence combines with organizational intelligence to generate creative ideas. These ideas are then implemented provided that certain enabling conditions (adequate resources and support, incentives and inducements) are present. This process presents a model of organizational change that is driven by individual cognitions and collective sense-making processes within the organization. Oldham and Cummings (1996) and Drazin and Schoonhoven (1996) reported evidence of multilevel influences on organizational innovation driven by individual creative action. Amabile, Conti, Coon, Lazenby, and Herron (1996) built from an individual level of creativity to identify group- and organization-level constraints on individual creativity and subsequent organization-level innovation.

Taken together, research on innovation and creativity reveals a complex mix of predictors of organizational change. At the center of these predictors is the teleological assumption of goal-driven, purposeful action. As Orlikowski and Hofman (1997) noted, the specific decisions and immediate strategies may be unplanned improvisations, but they are guided by a goal-driven theme. Recent theorizing on organizational innovation highlights the interaction between purposeful action, sense making, organizational settings, and environmental jolts to trigger organizational change (Drazin, Glynn, & Kazanjian, 1999).

Organizational development in recent years reflects many of these approaches. As noted earlier, there is much greater emphasis now on accomplishing strategic ends (Bartunek et al., 1999; Jelinck & Litterer, 1988) and on the role of leadership in these processes (Nadler & Tushman, 1989). There has also been some attention paid to cognitive framing of different participants in a merger process (Marks & Mirvis, 2001). As part of the understanding of change processes, questions have been raised about resistance to change (e.g., Dent & Goldberg, 1999).

The Life Cycle Motor

The life cycle motor envisions change as a progression through a predetermined sequence of stages. The ordering of the stages does not change, but the speed of progress and the triggers that lead to advancement through the process vary. Van de Ven and Poole (1995) noted that the "trajectory to the final end state is preconfigured and requires a specific historical sequence of events" (p. 515).

Whereas life cycle models of organizational change proliferated in the 1970s and 1980's (Quinn & Cameron, 1983), we found little continued theoretical development of this motor since 1995. One exception is in the area of entrepreneurship, where theorists continue to use a life cycle motor to understand the development and failure of new ventures (Hanks, Watson, Jansen, & Chandler, 1994), including self-organized transitions (Lichtenstein, 2000a, 2000b). Variations of the life cycle model, especially in conjunction with the teleological motor, are apparent in recent research on punctuated

equilibrium. It emerges as a motor in several contemporary organizational development approaches discussed in the next section, such as transforming leadership (Torbert, 1989) and advanced change theory (Quinn, Spreitzer, & Brown, 2000).

Punctuated Equilibrium. The evolution-revolution framework of organizational change (Greiner, 1972) has formed the foundation of many recent organizational change theories (Mezias & Glynn, 1993) that have been used to describe dynamics in organizations. Greiner described the typical life cycle of an organization as consisting of extended evolutionary periods of incremental change interspersed with short revolutionary periods. This framework provides the basis for recent theories of strategic redirection (Doz & Prahalad, 1987), transformation (Laughlin, 1991), punctuated equilibrium (Tushman & Romanelli, 1985), and change archetypes (Greenwood & Hinings, 1993). During reorientations large and important parts of the organization—strategy, structure, control systems, and sometimes basic beliefs and values—change almost simultaneously in a way that leads to very different organizational emphases.

Whereas Tushman and Romanelli (1985) suggested the effectiveness of punctuated equilibrium approaches to change, others suggested some cautions in the use of this approach. Previously established competencies may be threatened by transformations (Amburgey et al., 1993). In addition, Sastry (1997) found that reorientation processes increased the risk of organizational failure unless evaluation processes were suspended for a trial period after the reorientation. However, certain change processes may enable successful reorientations. Mezias and Glynn (1993), for example, suggested that previously established routines may guide reorientations in such a way that competencies are not destroyed.

Questions have also been raised about how frequent true reorientations of the type suggested by Tushman and Romanelli are. Cooper, Hinings, Greenwood, and Brown (1996) recently suggested that instead of true reorientations, the types of change that typically occur involve one layer of orientation placed on top of another layer that represents the prior orientation. Reger, Gustafson, DeMarie, and Mullane (1994) also suggested that changes may often include this type of middle ground.

As noted earlier, punctuated equilibrium theories (Gersick, 1991; Tushman & Romanelli, 1985) emphasize the life cycle motor (the normal interspersing of evolutionary and revolutionary periods) but combine it with the teleological motor. Organizational actors, especially leaders, purposefully respond to environmental conditions that require a particular type of change in order to achieve effectiveness.

The Dialectic Motor

The dialectic motor describes organizational change as the result of conflict between opposing entities. New ideas and values must directly confront the status quo. This motor builds from the Hegelian process of a thesis and antithesis coming into direct conflict. There are then several paths that may be taken, including separating the thesis and antithesis, attempting to create a synthesis of them, and attempting to embrace the differing perspectives (e.g., Baxter & Montgomery, 1996; Seo et al., 2001). Some argue that achieving a synthesis that appears to close off change may be less productive than developing organizational capacity to embrace conflicting approaches (cf. Bartunek, Walsh, & Lacey, 2000).

The dialectic motor often drives cognitive and political change theories and plays a prominent role in schematic change theories and communicative change models. It also forms the basis for a number of organizational development approaches outlined in the next section.

Schematic Change. Schematic models of change build from an understanding of individual cognitive processing to understand how changes occur in shared schemas. Schemas are cognitive frameworks that provide meaning and structure to incoming information (Mitchell & Beach, 1990). Organizational change is categorized by the level of change in the shared schemas. First order change occurs within a shared schema and second order change involves change in the shared schema (Watzlawick, Weakland, & Fisch, 1974).

Change in schemas typically occurs through a dialectic process triggered by the misalignment of a schema in use with the context (e.g., Labianca, Gray, & Brass, 2000). If a situation does not fit within an expected schematic framework, the person shifts to an active processing mode (Louis & Sutton, 1991). In this mode, the individual uses environmental cues to generate a new schema or modify an existing one. The direct comparison of the schema (thesis) to the context (antithesis) creates the change.

This schematic dialectic is applied to organizational change through change in shared schemas. Bartunek (1984) proposed that organizational schema change required a direct conflict between the current schema and the new schema. Such conflict between schemata underlies large-scale organizational changes including major industry change (Bacharach, Bamberger, & Sonnenstuhl, 1996), organizational breakup (Dyck & Starke, 1999), organizational identity change (Dutton & Dukerich, 1991; Reger et al., 1994), and organizational responses to new economic systems (Kostera & Wicha, 1996).

Communicative Change Theories. Drawing from notions of social construction (Berger & Luckmann, 1966) and structuration (Giddens, 1984), several theorists have begun to consider change as an element of social interaction. Change is recognized and generated through conversation and other forms of communication (J. D. Ford, 1999a; J. D. Ford & Ford, 1995). Organizations consist of a plurality of perspectives that are revealed through conversation (Hazen, 1994) that form the context for all organizational action. When different perspectives meet through conversation, either a synthesized perspective is generated or one perspective is spread. New and old perspectives coexist within the organization at the same time as the newer synthesized understanding diffuses through multiple conversations (Gilmore, Shea, & Useem, 1997). Whether the end result is synthesis or diffusion is partially determined by the significance of the perspectives and interaction to the identities of the participants (Gergen & Thatchenkery, 1996). Significant organizational change typically requires new organizational language that results from the conversational dialectic (Barrett, Thomas, & Hocevar, 1995) and that realigns discordant narratives and images (Faber, 1998).

The Evolutionary Motor

The evolutionary motor focuses on change in a given population over time. It involves a continuous cycle of variation, selection, and retention. Evolutionary theories of organizational change focus on environmental conditions that create inertial pressures for organizational change. Change theories built around this motor begin with the assumption that one must understand the environmental setting of an organization in order to understand the dynamics of change. Organizations evolve based on their ability to respond and adapt to these powerful external forces. In the early 1990s the evolutionary motor was most evident in population ecology models. However, it is also the driving force of change in recent research on the rate of organizational change and in theories of institutional change.

Internal Change Routines. Research on organizational routines applies variation, selection, and retention to intraorganizational processes by considering how individual actions are selected and retained within the population of organization members.

Nelson and Winter (1982; see also Feldman, 2000) proposed that organizations develop routines, or patterns of action, that drive future action. Routines become more developed and complex as they are used. Routines that involve changing current routines are called modification routines. Like other organizational routines, modification routines can be relatively stable over time, leading the organization to approach organizational change in a consistent manner. Well-developed routines of organizational change enable an organization to adjust to different demands for change by modifying the content of the change but using a consistent process to manage the change (Levitt & March, 1988).

Experience with a certain type of change enables an organization to refine its routines for implementing that type of change. As a result, the organization develops expertise with that type of change and may be more likely to initiate similar changes in the future. For example, in their study of the Finnish newspaper industry, Amburgey et al. (1993) found that experience with a certain type of organizational change increased the likelihood that a newspaper would initiate a similar type of change again. They argued that this process occurs because the organization develops competence with the change type. Thus, costs of change are lowered and the organization is likely to see the change as a solution to an increasing number of problems.

Hannan and Freeman (1984) used the notion of organizational routines to explain how organizations attempt to increase the reliability of their actions and enable organizations to create conditions of stability in relatively unstable environments. They posited that these routines institutionalize certain organizational actions and create organizational inertia, which hinders the organization's ability to change. Kelly and Amburgey (1991) extended this model by showing that the same routinization processes that create inertia can also create momentum. Routines that institutionalize a certain rate of change create conditions that encourage change consistent with those routines. While disruptions in routines brought about by organizational change can destroy competencies (Levitt & March, 1988), that same organizational change can create competencies that make future organizational change more effective (Amburgey & Miner, 1992).

S. L. Brown and Eisenhardt (1997) found that organizations establish an internal pacing mechanism to operate in a constantly changing environment. For example, managers plan to release new versions of their products every nine months or set goals targeting a certain amount of income that needs to come from new products each year. While organizations continue to respond to environmental changes, they may devote a larger percentage of their resources to developing internal capabilities to change regardless of industry pressures.

Institutional Change.   Institutional theory is often associated with stability rather than with change. Organizations grow more similar over time because the institutional environment provides resources to organizations that con-

form to institutional norms that create barriers to innovations (North, 1990; Zucker, 1987). However, as Greenwood and Hinings (1996) noted, theories of stability are also theories of change.

Institutional theory proposes that organizational actions are determined by the ideas, values, and beliefs contained in the institutional environment (Meyer & Rowan, 1977). Strong institutional environments influence organizational change by legitimating certain changes and organizational forms (DiMaggio & Powell, 1991). In order for an organizational change to be successful, it needs to be justified within the institutional system of values (D'Aunno, Sutton, & Price, 1991). In addition, broader institutional forces sometimes trigger organizational change (Greenwood & Hinings, 1993) or provide comparisons that in turn prompt such change (Fligstein, 1991; Greve, 1998).

Institutional change theories rely on the evolutionary motor to understand the dynamics of change. Isomorphic pressures on organizations act as a selection and retention process for validating organizational changes. However, institutional theorists emphasize that organizational actors play a part in creating the institutional forces that restrain them (DiMaggio & Powell, 1991; Elsbach & Sutton, 1992; Oliver, 1991; Suchman, 1995). Thus, institutional models of change have begun to build teleological motors into theories of institutional change by considering the strategic actions of institutional actors (Bloodgood & Morrow, 2000; Johnson, Smith, & Codling, 2000). For example, Creed, Scully, and Austin (forthcoming) illustrated how organizational activists selectively use available institutional logics to legitimate controversial changes in workplace benefits policies.

Summary of Change Process Research

Change process theory continues to develop and evolve. During the past decade new approaches to understanding change processes have emerged from each change motor identified by Van de Ven and Poole. Contemporary theorizing frequently draws from multiple motors with comparatively great attention to the teleological motor. Attempts to understand such multilevel issues as institutional agency, innovation, and temporal pacing of organizational change require that researchers build links between theories of individual change and theories of organizational change. Interactions between research on individual resistance to change, organizational-level political pressures, and institutional constraints can lead to further clarification of change process at each level. Thus, multilevel theorizing can expand our understanding of change processes and may lead to the identification of additional change motors.

Samples of Contemporary Interventions in Organizational Development

Several approaches to intervention characterize contemporary organizational development. It is neither possible nor desirable to give a complete list here. In this section, however, we identify some organizational development interventions that have been prominent since the early 1990s. We start at this date in order to capture trends present since Porras and Robertson's (1992) review of the field. (Some of these, however, were developed in advance of 1990.) All the approaches we summarized have been used in a number of countries around the globe.

Our review includes articles published in both academic and practitioner journals. It is not meant to be exhaustive, but illustrative of the theories that have drawn the most attention in the 1990s. These approaches include appreciative inquiry, learning organizations, and large-scale interventions. We also discuss employee empowerment. There is no one universally accepted method of accomplishing empowerment, but it is a more or less explicit goal of much organizational development work as well as an expected means through which organizational development efforts achieve their broader ends.

Appreciative Inquiry

Cooperrider and Srivastva (1987) introduced appreciative inquiry as a complement to other types of action research. Since then appreciative inquiry has emerged as a widely used organizational development intervention. Since 1995, articles about appreciative inquiry have dominated practitioner journals such as the *OD Practitioner* and *Organization Development Journal* (e.g., Sorenson, Yaeger, & Nicoll, 2000). Appreciative inquiry builds from several important assumptions. First, social systems are socially constructed; people create their own realities through dialogue and enactment. Second, every social system has some positive working elements, and people draw energy for change by focusing on positive aspects of the system. Third, by focusing on building consensus around these positive elements and avoiding discussion of the negative aspects of the system, a group will create momentum and energy toward increasing the positives there.

Recent writings on appreciative inquiry highlight the social constructionist focus on dialogue as a way to enact a reality. Most articles and books on appreciative inquiry use case studies and frameworks for appreciative discussions to help practitioners lead appreciative inquiry interventions (Barrett, 1995; Bushe & Coetzer, 1995; Cooperrider, 1997; Rainey, 1996; Srivastva & Cooperrider, 1999). Driving these case studies is the

observation that by focusing on the positive elements about "what is," participants create a desire to transform the system. In a recent critique of appreciative inquiry, Golembiewski (1998) argued for a more balanced examination of the benefits of this type of intervention and increased attention to how appreciative inquiry might connect with other approaches and theories of change.

Appreciative inquiry is playing an increasingly important global role. It has been successful as an approach to global consultation efforts (e.g., Barrett, 1995; Barrett & Peterson, 2000), in part because it emphasizes appreciation of different approaches. Mantel and Ludema (2000), for example, described how appreciative inquiry creates new language that supports multiple positive ways of accomplishing things. This is particularly important in a global setting in which people are operating out of very different perspectives on the world (Tenkasi, 2000).

Large-Group Interventions

As noted at the beginning of this chapter, the primary conceptual basis for organizational development has been action research. As it was originally designed, action research customarily begins by searching out problems to be addressed. However, Bunker and Alban (1996) recounted that by the 1970s some concern had been raised about this approach; Ronald Lippitt believed that starting with problems caused organization members to lose energy and to feel drained and tired. (Similarly, appreciative inquiry starts with positive, rather than negative, features of an organization.)

Lippitt saw problem solving as past oriented. He believed that focusing on the future, rather than the past, would be more motivating. Thus, he began to engage organization members in thinking about their preferred futures (Lippitt, 1980). Attention to a future organization member's desire is a first major emphasis of many large-group interventions. A second emphasis is on gathering "the whole system," or, if the whole system is not possible, representatives of a large cross section of the system (at least 10% of it), to contribute to future planning. One reason for the prominence of large-group interventions is recent emphasis on organizational transformation. Many (though not all) large-group interventions are designed to help accomplish transformation, based on the expectation that in order to transform a system, sufficient numbers of organization members with power to affect transformational processes must participate in change efforts. Filipczak (1995) noted that the typical aims of large-group interventions include such foci as changing business strategies, developing a mission or vision about where the company is headed in the next century, fostering a more participative environment, and initiating such activities as self-directed work teams or reengineering the organization.

A wide variety of large-group interventions have been developed in recent years (e.g., Bunker & Alban, 1997; Holman & Devane, 1999; Weber & Manning, 1998). A list of many of these, along with very brief summary descriptions of each, is presented in Table 13.1. To give a more concrete sense of the different types of large-group interventions, we briefly introduce two of the interventions currently in practice: the search conference and workout.

TABLE 13.1 Summary Listing of Large-Group Interventions

Intervention	Summary Description
Future Search	A 3-day conference aimed at helping representatives of whole systems envision a preferred future and plan strategies and action plans for accomplishing it.
Real-time strategic change	Conference aimed at enabling up to 3,000 organizational members consult on major issues facing their organization.
Open Space Technology	A loosely structured meeting that enables groups of organization members ranging in size from a small group to 1,000 individuals develop their own agendas in relationship to prespecified organizational concerns.
Search Conferences	Participative events that enable a diverse group of organization members to identify their desired future and develop strategic plans to implement to accomplish this future.
Participative design workshops	Workshops based on the search conference model in which groups of employees participate democratically in designing, managing, and controlling their own work.
Simu-real	Workshops in which organizational members work on real problems in simulated settings that enable them to learn how their organization approaches tasks and to determine what they would like to change.
Workout	Meetings in which groups of employees brainstorm ways to solve an organizational problem. Managers typically must accept or reject solutions in a public forum at the conclusion of the meeting.
Conference model	A series of conferences through which organization members study the correspondence between their own work and their desired future and develop new designs for work.
ICA strategic planning process†	A method designed to maximize the participation of community members in change processes that affect them by means of focused conversation, workshops, and event planning.

Note. Descriptions of the interventions are taken from Bunker and Alban (1996) and Weber and Manning (1998).
†ICA stands for The Institute of Cultural Affairs.

Search Conferences.   Search conferences represent one of the oldest forms of large-group interventions. They were originally developed in England by Emery and Trist (1973) in the 1960s, and have been further developed by Emery and Purser (1996). They have been used in a number of different countries (e.g., Babüroglu, Topkaya, & Ates, 1996; Emery, 1996).

Search conferences basically take place in two- to three-day offsite meetings in which 20 to 40 organizational members participate. Participants are chosen based on their knowledge of the system, their diversity of perspectives, and their potential for active participation.

Search conferences involve several phases, each of which includes multiple components. First the participants pool their perceptions of significant changes in their environment that affect their organization. Next they focus attention on the past, present, and future of their organization, ending with the generation of a shared vision based on participants' ideals for a more desirable future. The intent is to develop long-term strategies that enhance the system's capacity to respond to changing environmental demands. In the final phase they work on next steps, action plans, and strategies for dealing with the environment.

The conference structure is explicitly democratic, and participants are fully responsible for the control and coordination of their own work. All data collected are public. The expectation is that as diverse participants begin to see mutually shared trends in their environment, they will recognize a common set of challenges facing the organization and its members and will also recognize that these common challenges will require cooperation.

Workout.   Workout is a process developed at General Electric that was aimed at helping employees address and solve problems without having to go through several hierarchical levels. It has been successful enough at GE that its use has been expanded to many other organizations.

Workout sessions involve several steps (Bunker & Alban, 1996). First, a manager introduces the problem on which a group with expertise pertinent to the problem will work. Then the manager leaves, and the employees work together for approximately two days on the problem. The manager returns, and the employees report proposals regarding how to solve the problems. On the spot, the manager must accept the proposals, decline them, or ask for more information. If the manager requests more information, the process that will follow in order to reach a decision must be specified.

No blaming or complaining is allowed. Employees who do not like something are responsible for developing a recommended action plan and then volunteering to implement it.

Learning Organizations

The idea that organizations and their members learn has been present for decades. However, most scholarly attention to learning focused on learning as an adaptive change in behavioral response to a stimulus, particularly the learning of routines (e.g., Levitt & March, 1988). Learning was not necessarily viewed as desirable for the organization.

In the 1970s, however, Argyris and Schön (1978) introduced learning in a positive way, as a means of improving organizations. Argyris and Schön and others (e.g., Feldman, 2000) argued that learning must include both behavioral and cognitive elements and involve the capacity to challenge routines, not simply enact them. This formulation was the basis for the learning organization, which in recent years has been one of the most popular business concepts. Communities of researchers and practitioners who study and practice learning organizations have emerged and grown rapidly (Easterby-Smith, 1997; Tsang, 1997).

More than any other written works, Peter Senge's (1990) best-selling book, *The Fifth Discipline,* and the workbooks that have followed, *The Fifth Discipline Fieldbook* (Senge, Kleiner, Roberts, Ross, & Smith, 1994) and *The Dance of Change,* (Senge et al., 1999), have been responsible for bringing the learning organization into the mainstream of business thinking (Seo et al., 2001). For Senge (1990), a learning organization is "an organization that is continually expanding its capacity to create its future" and for which "adaptive learning must be joined by generative learning, learning that enhances our capacity to create" (p. 14). Senge described five different "disciplines" as the cornerstone of learning organizations: (a) *systems thinking,* learning to understand better the interdependencies and integrated patterns of our world; (b) *personal mastery,* developing commitment to lifelong learning and continually challenging and clarifying personal visions; (c) *mental models,* developing reflection and inquiry skills to be aware, surface, and test the deeply rooted assumptions and generalizations that we hold about the world; (d) *building shared vision,* developing shared images of the future that we seek to create and the principles and guiding practices by which to get there; and (e) *team learning,* group interaction that maximizes the insights of individuals through dialogue and skillful discussion and through recognizing interaction patterns in teams that undermine learning. The workbooks describe ways to accomplish these disciplines and challenges to sustain the momentum of learning. For example, Senge et al. (1994) described "left-hand column" and "ladder of inference" methods to help increase the ability to recognize one's mental models. They described dialogue as a way in which group members can think together to foster team learning, and they described ways in which people might draw forth their own personal visions as a way of developing personal mastery.

The learning organization envisioned and promoted by Senge and his colleagues is only one of the many versions of learning organization currently available, although most other authors owe at least some of their approach to Senge's work (e.g., Garvin, 1993; Lipshitz, Popper, & Oz, 1996; Nevis, DiBella, & Gould, 1995; Watkins & Marsick, 1994). For example, Nevis et al. (1995) defined a learning organization as one that is effective at acquiring, sharing, and utilizing knowledge. Garvin (1993) viewed systematic problem solving and ongoing experimentation as the core of a learning organization.

We mentioned several intervention tools aimed at facilitating the development of learning organizations. An additional tool, learning histories, is particularly important. *Learning histories* are extended descriptions of major organizational changes that are designed to help organizations reflect on and learn from their previous experiences (Bradbury & Clair, 1999; Kleiner & Roth, 1997, 2000; Roth & Kleiner, 2000). They include an extensive narrative of processes that occur during a large-scale change event in an organization. The narrative is composed of the people who took part in or were affected by the change. They also include an analysis and commentary by "learning historians," a small group of analysts that includes trained outsiders along with insider members of the organization. The analysts identify themes in the narrative, pose questions about its assumptions, and raise "undiscussable" issues surfaced by it. Thus, learning histories are ways for organization members to reflect on events that happened and learn about underlying processes in their organizations from this reflection.

Empowerment

Although there has not been agreement on standard intervention processes to develop employee empowerment, there is little doubt that achieving empowerment is a major emphasis of much organizational development and similar consulting. It has been emphasized since Peter Block's (1987) influential book *The Empowered Manager.*

There is considerable variation in how empowerment is understood. For example, Ehin (1995) described empowerment as a frame of reference that incorporates deep, powerful, and intimate values about others, such as trust, caring, love, dignity, and the need for growth. In the context of work teams, Mohrman, Cohen, and Mohrman (1995) described empowerment as the capability of making a difference in the attainment of individual, team, and organization goals, and they suggested that it includes adequate resources and knowledge of the organization's direction. Thomas and Velthouse (1990), followed by Spreitzer (1996), focused on empowerment in terms of cognitive variables (task assessments) that determine motivation in individual workers.

Just as there are multiple definitions of empowerment, there are multiple mechanisms in organizations that may be used to help foster it. These may include structural factors (Spreitzer, 1996) and attempts to redesign particular jobs so that they include more of the individual task components that make up empowerment (Thomas & Velthouse, 1990). Most frequently, the means by which empowerment is discussed as being fostered in organizations is through participation in organizational decision making (e.g., Hardy & Leiba-Sullivan, 1998) and enhancement of the organizational mechanisms (e.g., knowledge, resources, or teams) that help employees participate in decision making (Bowen & Lawler, 1992).

The types of interventions we have described appreciative inquiry, the various large-group interventions, and learning organizations—all include empowerment of employees as central components. In all of these interventions it is groups of employees as well as managers who contribute to both organizational assessment (e.g., through appreciative inquiry and through various learning exercises, including the construction of learning histories) and organizational change (e.g., through planning solutions such as in workout sessions, and in reflecting future planning for the organization). Empowerment is both a means by which these interventions take place and an expected outcome of them.

Implementation Theories

Implementation theories address how actions generate change and what actions can be taken to initiate and guide change. Porras and Robertson distinguished types of implementation based on whether they focused on intervention strategy, procedure, or technique. Similar to the approach taken by Van de Ven and Poole (1995), we focus on four "motors" of change—four primary implementation approaches that are expected to accomplish the desired change. These motors come primarily from literature written for practitioners rather than literature written for academics. They are participation, self-reflection, action research, and narrative. Participation and action research have been cornerstones of organizational development practice for decades (French & Bell, 1999). However, what they mean in practice has evolved. Self-reflection and narrative, while implicit in some earlier organizational development work, have become much more prominent recently. It is not surprising that

these methods play prominent roles in the organizational development interventions describe dearlier.

Participation

Participation in organizational change efforts and, in particular, participation in decision making, formed the earliest emphases of organizational development (French & Bell, 1999). Such participation is still viewed as important, but the ways in which such participation is understood and takes place have expanded, and there is greater awareness that employees do not always wish to participate in change efforts (Neumann, 1989).

Earlier rationales for participation often centered on the expectation that employees were more likely to accept decisions in which they had participated. Now, however, the rationale for participation is somewhat different, as expectations of the role of employees in participation expand. In particular, there is now much more explicit emphasis on employees participating in *inquiry* about their organizations and contributing necessary *knowledge* that will foster the organization's planning and problem solving. This is illustrated in the roles of employees in the various large-scale interventions, as various participants are expected to reflect on and contribute knowledge about the organization's past as well as its future (e.g., in search conferences). It is also illustrated in the expectation that employees contribute to learning processes in their organizations, for example, through the various exercises designed to foster their own capacity and in their contribution to learning histories. Creative new means of participation such as GE's workout sessions give employees much more responsibility for solving problems and acknowledge much more employee knowledge than was often the case in the past.

Self-Reflection

The growing interest in large-scale transformation in organizations has been accompanied by a similar interest in leadership of organizational transformation and thus in the development of leaders who can blend experience and reflection in order to create lasting organizational change. Torbert (1999) and Quinn et al. (2000) suggested that a primary means by which leaders accomplish this is through self-reflection and self-inquiry.

Torbert (1999) suggested that leaders need to develop the ability to reflect while acting so that they can respond to changing conditions and develop new understandings in the moment. Individual transformation involves an awareness that transcends one's own interests, preferences, and theories, enabling more holistic understanding of patterns of action and thought. Transformational leaders determine the appropriate method of transformation by cultivating a strong understanding of the context, including tradition, vision, and organization and individual capabilities. The exercise of transforming leadership affects the organization's capacity for transformation. In a longitudinal study of CEOs, Rooke and Torbert (1998) found that five CEO's that scored as transforming leaders based on Torbert's developmental scale supported 15 progressive organizational transformations, whereas five CEO's that did not score as transforming leaders supported no organizational transformations.

Advanced change theory (Quinn et al., 2000) proposed that by modeling a process of personal transformation, change agents enable deeper organizational change. This process demands that change agents be empowered to take responsibility for their own understanding (Spreitzer & Quinn, 1996) and develop a high level of cognitive complexity (Denison, Hooijberg, & Quinn, 1995). This generally requires a change in values, beliefs, or behaviors, which is generated by an examination of internal contradictions. The leader creates opportunities for reflection and value change through intervention and inquiry. The leader is constantly shifting perspectives and opening up values and assumptions for questioning. The more skilled organization leaders are at generating deep personal cognitive change, the more likely it is that the leaders will support or create deep organizational change.

Action Research

Action research consists of a set of theories of changing that work to solve real problems while also contributing to theory. While the original models of action research emphasized the solution of problems, models of action research developed in later years include a wider array of emphases. In particular, many contemporary action research models propose that change can be triggered through a process of direct comparison between action and theory.

Participatory Action Research.   Participatory action research was developed largely by Whyte (1991) and his colleagues. It refers to a process of systematic inquiry in which those experiencing a problem in their community or workplace participate with researchers in deciding the focus of knowledge generation, in collecting and analyzed data, and in taking action to manage, improve, or solve their problem.

Action Science.   Dialectic change theories envision change as the outcome of conflict between a thesis and antithesis. Action science focuses on how to bring the thesis and antithesis into conflict. Argyris and Schön's (1974) Model II learning and Argyris, Putnam, and Smith's (1985) action science model provide a common base for dialectic action science methods. Change is triggered by calling attention to discrepancies between action and espoused values. Highlighting differences between *"theories in use"* and *"espoused theories"* generates the impetus for change. Argyris focused on processes that enable double-loop learning and awareness of underlying values guiding action. Individuals work to expose the mental models driving their action and to identify the values and actions through which they influence their context.

Several other writers have expanded this approach to change by highlighting the importance of understanding how action is embedded in a broader system of values and meaning. For example, Nielsen (1996) called for "tradition-sensitive" change dialectic strategies in which the change agent directly links the change with biases in the shared tradition system.

Action Learning.   Action learning, like action science, has a goal of changing behavior by comparing behaviors and theories. In an action science intervention, the individual compares theories in use with espoused theories. In an action learning intervention, the dialectic is between theoretical knowledge and personal experience. Revans (1980) outlined a process in which action learning groups work to understand social theories and ideas by applying them to a real situation. Participants use the theory to understand the logical implications of their experience and use the experience to internalize, refine, and make sense of the theory. Because of its group emphasis, action learning focuses on interpersonal interactions and their effects on project outcomes (Raelin, 1997).

Cooperative Inquiry.   Cooperative inquiry was developed primarily by Reason and his colleagues (e.g., Reason, 1999). Cooperative inquiry is an inquiry strategy in which those involved in the research are both coresearchers and cosubjects. It includes several steps. First, a group of people chooses an issue to explore and develop one or more means by which they will explore it. Then they carry out the agreed-upon action and report on its outcomes. Through this action and reflection they become more fully immersed in their experience and are led to ask new questions. Finally, they reconsider their original questions in light of their experience.

Action Inquiry.   Action inquiry (or developmental action inquiry) has been developed primarily by Torbert and his collaborators (e.g., Torbert, 1999). Briefly, it is concerned with developing researchers' capacities in real time to increase their attention by turning to its origin, to create communities of inquiry, and to act in an objectively timely manner. This is a manner in which they become increasingly able to get multiple types of feedback from their actions that can increase their ability to act and to achieve personal congruity.

Narrative-Rhetorical Intervention

Narrative interventions highlight the role that rhetoric and writing can play in generating organizational change. This approach to change finds its theoretical roots in sense making (Weick, 1995) and interpretive approaches to organizations (Boje, 1991). Organizational actors partially create their reality through the retrospective stories that they tell about their experience and through future-oriented stories that they create as a pathway for action. Convergence of narratives by organization members drives collective sense making (Boyce, 1995).

Organizational change can be generated through sharing of stories and building consensus around new images of the future (e.g., J. D. Ford, 1999b) in which the stories shift. The stories thus offer a goal toward which organization actors can work, and the role of the change agent is to assist organization members in reconceiving their understandings (Frost & Egri, 1994) by creating new stories. J. D. Ford and Ford (1995) identified four types of conversations that drive change: initiative, understanding, performance, and closure. Initiative conversations start a change process; understanding conversations generate

awareness; performance conversations prompt action; and closure conversations acknowledge an ending.

Several current organizational development practices rely on a narrative theory of changing. Appreciative inquiry draws on narrative organizational development theories by challenging organization members to generate local theories of action. Barry (1997) identifies strategies from narrative therapy that can enable organizational change. These include influence mapping, problem externalization, identifying unique outcomes, and story audiencing. Using the case of a high-technology research organization, O'Connor (2000) illustrated how stories told during a strategic change link the change with the past to highlight anticipated future problems and accentuate how the past and present differ.

THE CONNECTION BETWEEN IMPLEMENTATION THEORIES AND CHANGE PROCESS THEORIES

It is possible to construct a rough map of the links between particular implementation motors, interventions, and change processes, especially as implementation motors would likely occur in the interventions described earlier. Such a rough map is depicted in Table 13.2. It indicates that implementation strategies have been developed primarily for the teleological motor, as this is expressed in its multiple forms. However, at least one organizational development intervention potentially applies to each of the other change process motors.

TABLE 13.2   Possible Relationships Between Change Process Models and Implementation Models as Expressed in Contemporary Intervention Approaches

	Implementation Models			
	Participation	Reflection	Action Research	Narrative
	Often used in appreciative inquiry, large-group interventions, learning organizations, empowerment	Often used in appreciative inquiry, large-group interventions, learning organizations	Often used in learning organizations, empowerment	Often used in appreciative inquiry, large-group intervention, learning organizations
Change Process Motors				
Teleological (e.g., strategy, cognitive framing, change momentum, continuous change)	X	X	X	
Life cycle (e.g., punctuated equilibrium/transformation)		X	X	
Dialectic (e.g., schema change, communication change)			X	X
Evolutionary (e.g., internal change routines, institutional change)			X	

Possible ways of implementing each change process model by means of one or more of the implementation approaches are indicated by **X**.

THE DIVIDE BETWEEN IMPLEMENTATION THEORIES AND CHANGE PROCESS THEORIES

The fact that some organizational development interventions are applicable to the different change process theories means that they represent *potential* means for fostering these different types of change. It does not mean that authors who describe the different types of change motors reference organizational development work or that the implementation models reference the change process theories. In most cases there is no explicit connection between them. To the contrary, we believe that there is a fairly strong divide between those who focus on change process models and those who focus on particular interventions and their underlying implementation models.

To test whether this appeared to be true, we took a closer look at where change process theories were being published and where implementation models and descriptions of interventions were published during the 1990s. We examined 209 articles published since 1990 whose central ideas involved change process theory and implementation theory (this list of articles is available from the primary author). We only included articles that had obvious implications for change process or implementation theories.

Table 13.3 provides a summary of our findings. It shows that for the most part there is a segregation between journals publishing theories of change processes and journals publishing implementation theories. Only a few journals consistently published both types of change research work. Those that appeared often in our investigation include *Organization Science, Journal of Management Studies,* and the *Strategic Management Journal* (although with a larger sample some others also fit into this category).

We sorted the journals into three groupings and sought to understand whether there were any fundamental difference among the groupings. The first, and perhaps most obvious, difference is that journals that published implementation theory articles had a larger percentage of authors with nonacademic affiliations (Table 13.1, column 3). While a majority of the implementation theory articles were written by authors with academic affiliations, virtually all of the change process theory articles were written by authors with academic affiliations. Second, a comparison of citations within the articles shows that while implementation theory articles referenced change process theory articles, authors of change process theory articles rarely cited implementation theory articles. The findings suggest a low level of interaction between these two approaches to change theorizing. In particular, academic scholars are paying comparatively little attention to practices through which change is facilitated. The overlap of the two knowledge networks is created by the journals that publish both types of work and by a few individual researchers who publish in both theoretical areas. In general, there is relatively little information passing from one knowledge network to the other. Several knowledge transfer barriers limit the knowledge flows between these two networks. Attempts to create more integration between change process and implementation models need to find ways around these barriers.

Barrier 1: Different Knowledge Validation Methods

We found a wide array of knowledge validation strategies in the change process theory and implementation theory literatures. These are the methods used to convey the significance and legitimacy of authors' theories and conclusions. They

TABLE 13.3   Change and Organizational Development Theory in the 1990s

Journal	No. of Articles	% Implementation Theory	% Authors with Academic Affiliation
Academy of Management Journal	8	0	100
Administrative Science Quarterly	10	0	100
Academy of Management Review	16	13	93
Organization Studies	13	23	82
Strategic Management Journal	16	44	100
Organization Science	12	50	100
Journal of Management Studies	6	50	100
Journal of Organizational Change Management	18	72	89
Organization Development Journal	21	81	56
Journal of Applied Behavioral Science	14	86	57
OD Practitioner	34	88	29
Leadership and Organization Development	18	94	77
Other journal articles	15	47	
Books and book chapters	13	46	
Total	**209**	**50**	**82**

include appeals to previous research, clear and logical research designs, appeals to the authors' expertise, and use of detailed cases. An author's choice of knowledge validation strategy is determined by the targeted audience of the article and the author's own understanding of what determines knowledge validity.

Examination of the articles reveals strong norms of homogeneity within journals and within articles. Authors tend to cite other articles that employ similar knowledge validation methods, and journals tend to favor a certain knowledge validation method. This homogeneity enables clear progression of research because it makes it easy for the reader to understand how the current article builds from previous similar work. However, it can also hinder knowledge transfer between knowledge networks. References to previous work are typically limited to work in journals that employ similar strategies for legitimating knowledge.

Method variety within a journal provides one potential pathway around this knowledge transfer barrier. For example, a few journals, such as *Organization Science,* publish research using a wide range of methods. However, this diversity at the level of the journal is not mirrored at the article level. Authors still tend to reference other research using similar methodologies.

Epistemological understanding about knowledge may act as a larger barrier to knowledge transfer than methodological homogeneity. Many change process articles use a hypothesis-testing format to identify generalizable knowledge about organizational change. Writers of these articles attempt to persuade the reader of the legitimacy of their theory and conclusions by highlighting links with previous research findings and carefully describing the methodology and analysis of the study.

Implementation articles, on the other hand, often do not attempt to generalize their findings. These authors provide detailed descriptions of the context of the study that readers can use to link the article and theory to their own situation. The contextual approach of implementation fits an expertise-based epistemology. That is, expertise is developed through experience in similar situations; practitioners can gain expertise by reading detailed cases and attempting to connect those cases with their personal experience. The detailed descriptions in case-based articles enable readers to determine whether and how the theory is applicable to their situations and how it contributes to their expertise.

Epistemological differences between change process and implementation articles are similar to Geertz's (1983) distinction between *"experience-near"* and *"experience-far"* concepts. People use experience-near concepts to explain what they experience and to describe the experience to others. The goal is to communicate a sense of the immediate context. Specialists use experience-far concepts to map their observations and categorize them as part of a larger abstract body of knowledge. Academics often dismiss experience-near approaches as not rigorous enough; practitioners often dismiss experience-far approaches as not applicable to many contexts.

Barrier 2: Different Goals and Audiences

The journals included in our review have differing goals and audiences. The grouping of journals according to their tendency to publish change process or implementation theory articles is consistent with the journal audience. Thus, journals geared toward managers or organizational development practitioners offer more guidance on how to affect change. For example, the mission of the *OD Practitioner* is to present information about state-of-the-art approaches to organizational development diagnosis and intervention. The articles in the *OD Practitioner* include well-developed implementation theories that are supported by case studies, appeals to practice, and connections with previous articles and books regarding similar issues.

As one example, the *OD Practitioner* sponsored a recent special issue on appreciative inquiry, which is becoming a widely adopted organizational development intervention technique (Sorenson et al., 2000). Yet we found comparatively little acknowledgement of appreciative inquiry in more academically oriented research and writings on organizational change and development. The academic silence and practitioner enthusiasm about appreciative inquiry illustrates the significance of the practitioner/academic theoretical divide. As Golembiewski (1998) noted, appreciative inquiry challenges several assumptions of previous research on resistance to change (Head, 2000). Academic theorizing about change would benefit from more attention to the questions raised by appreciative inquiry practitioners. But as long as theoretical discussions of appreciative inquiry remain limited to practitioner-oriented journals, the theoretical implications risk being ignored by those developing and testing change process theories.

The journals with a mix of change process and implementation theories may provide some insight into the barriers between academic-practitioner knowledge transfer. We suggest some characteristics of these journals that may offer guidance on this issue. The *Strategic Management Journal* included several change-related articles that have a strong teleological element (Barr et al., 1992; Fombrun & Ginsberg, 1990; Gioia & Chittipeddi, 1991; Greve, 1998; Simons, 1994). As would be expected in a strategy journal, the primary focus is on managerial action. Discussions of research results lead naturally into implications for practicing managers or change agents. Although the research designs in *Strategic Management Journal* are similar to those reported in *Academy of Management Journal* and *Administrative Science Quarterly,* the teleological, planned-change focus is similar to that of the practitioner journals such as the *OD Practitioner* and the *Harvard Business Review.* This mix may provide a template for communicating practitioner experience to academic researchers. *Organization Science* also publishes both change process and implementation articles. Several *Organization Science* articles provide implementation theories grounded in change process research (e.g., Bate, Khan, & Pye, 2000; Denison et al., 1995: Kimberly & Bouchikhi, 1995; Kuwada, 1998). The result is an emergent understanding of the process underlying change and how it can be influenced. These journals have an academic audience but may provide a channel for practitioner-developed theory because of their close affiliation with managerial concerns and their willingness to publish innovative process-driven work.

Barrier 3: Different Theoretical Antecedents

Some change process theories have recently paid more attention to implementation. This convergence is occurring as change process theorists build teleological motors into their existing models, since the teleological motor offers a natural common ground for integrating change process and implementation models. However, the similarity of converging approaches can be overlooked if the writers are unaware of each other's work. This is particularly the case when there are differing theoretical antecedents behind the change process theories.

One illustration of this barrier is found in recent work on institutional agency and dialectic action research. Foster (2000) showed how both streams of research have addressed the issue of how actors can initiate and guide change in existing institutional structures. Institutional theorists have used this line of inquiry to expand understanding of institutional change theories (Barley & Tolbert, 1997), whereas action research theorists have focused on improving change agent effectiveness in changing broad tradition systems (Nielsen, 1996).

Despite the similarity of interest, neither stream of research is drawing on the insights of the other stream. Institutional theorists struggle to identify skills and strategies that enable change to the institutional structure (Fligstein, 1997). Building from individual cognitive theories, action research writers have identified successful strategies for institutional change (Argyris et al., 1985). Recent action research work has explicitly tied actor strategies with changes in the tradition system (Austin, 1997; Nielsen, 1996), which is similar to the institu-

tional structure. This recent focus of action research on tradition systems considers how change agents are constrained by pressure to connect their change strategy with widely held social values. Building from sociological theories of organizational fields, institutional researchers have outlined a process of isomorphism and legitimation that offers insight into what strategies will fit within a given field (DiMaggio & Powell, 1991; Greenwood & Hinings, 1996).

Further indication of the importance of theoretical commonalities for information transfer is shown through linkages between communicative change theories and narrative organizational development theories. Articles in these two areas of inquiry have more cross-referencing than any other set of change process theories and implementation theories. These fields draw from the same theoretical roots: social constructionism and social cognition. Recent articles (J. D. Ford, 1999b; O'Connor, 2000) acknowledge and build on previous work in both fields. Their common roots may enable easy transfer of research by providing a common language and understanding of acceptable method of inquiry. Schematic change theory and action research theories also have substantial overlap. However cross-referencing is more pronounced in schematic change theory than in action research. Both change theories, communicative and schematic, use the dialectic motor. The close linkages with change process models suggest that the dialectic motor, like the teleological motor, may provide a fruitful framework for future integration of change process theories and implementation theories.

STRATEGIES FOR OVERCOMING BARRIERS TO KNOWLEDGE TRANSFER

A sense-making approach to knowledge transfer (Weick, 1979, 1995) assumes that individuals actively select information from their environment and make determinations about its relevance and meaning. Individuals compare the new information with their current cognitions and attempt to integrate it into their personal schemas or reject it as irrelevant. The barriers to knowledge transfer identified earlier cause individuals to reject the new information as irrelevant. Individuals do not see how the information fits within their schemas because the information does not fit their perception of valid knowledge validation methods or because it builds from an unknown theoretical tradition. For the information to be accepted and used, it must be linked in some way with the receiving individual's conception of relevant knowledge.

The notion of idea translation (Czarniawska & Joerges, 1996) provides some insights on how the sense-making process between change process theories and implementation theories is being limited. Czarniawska and Joerges proposed that ideas do not simply move unchanged from one local setting to another, but are transformed when moved into a new setting. They further proposes that ideas are ambiguous: They are given meaning through their connection with other logics, through action taken on them, and through the ways in which they are translated for new settings. Translation includes interpretation and materialization. Interpretation occurs when the idea is connected with other already-understood words and values. Understanding of the idea depends on what words and values the idea is connected with in this stage. The same idea will be interpreted differently by different individuals. The communicator can guide this stage in translation by offering suggested words and values to use to understand the new idea. Materialization occurs when individuals act on the new idea. It becomes embedded in a complex of ideas motivating the action, and this leads to further transformation of the idea as feedback may lead to its modification or rejection. The communicator has less control over this part of the process.

Change and organizational development theorists translate ideas through interpretation when they connect their work with widely known words, stories, and values. As an example, a change process theory may be translated into an implementation theory when the writer presents the planned, purposeful action of managers engaged in the change process. An implementation theory may inform a change process theory when the writer describes how a particular approach, such as action research, affected the outcome of the change process (e.g., a particular transformation attempt). Change process and implementation theorists translate ideas through materialization when they report on results of theoretically motivated change attempts. Through their description of the action, the theory is "made real" and is subsequently transformed.

There are some excellent templates for how translation between change process theory and implementation theory would look in practice. We describe some of them below.

Same-Author Translation

Writers may translate their own research for a new audience. Because the translation process changes the content of the idea, it may include subtle shifts. Eisenhardt and Brown's work on change pacing is one illustration of this type of translation. S. L. Brown and Eisenhardt developed a theory of change (1997) published in an academic journal. In subsequent publications, a *Harvard Business Review* article (Eisenhardt & Brown, 1998a) and a book (Eisenhardt & Brown, 1998b), they translated their change theory for a managerial audience. In the process of translation, their theory was transformed into an implementation theory. In their 1997 article S. L. Brown and Eisenhardt focused attention at the organization level of analysis to learn how organizations

continuously change. They used a multiple-case inductive research method to develop a theory of continuous organizational change that identifies the significance of limited structure and extensive communication, experimental "probes" to attempt to understand the future, and transition processes that link the present with the future. These organizational practices combine to enable change through flexible sense-making processes. In their later journal article and book, Eisenhardt and Brown shifted their focus to managerial action. They built from their theory of change and recommended specific strategies for managing change in markets that are continually shifting. These recommendations include strategies for establishing performance metrics, generating transitions, and understanding and establishing rhythms. Taken together, the strategies provide an implementation theory based on organizational temporal rhythms and heedful engagement with the constantly shifting market. The authors illustrated their points with stories demonstrating how managers at well-known technology companies have enabled their companies to prosper in chaotic environments.

This translation process subtly changed the idea of time pacing. The focus moved from the organization level to the strategic, managerial level. The shift to managerial action provides a more explicit teleological focus to the theory. The translation also involves a different writing style that relies less on reporting the methodology and more on story telling. This changes the goal behind the writing from generalizability to contextualizing. The methodology in the 1997 article indicates limitations of the theory, whereas the stories in subsequent articles invite readers to find the commonality between the story and their own contexts. One aspect that made this translation easier to accomplish was that the academic methodology employed was iterative case analysis. Stories were already present in the initial data collection process, so the raw data for the translation were ready to be used.

Multiple-Author Translation

Multiple-author translation is more common than is same-author translation. This process is used regularly in the *Academy of Management Executive,* where, for example, there is a section devoted to research translations. In multiple-author translation, a researcher builds from other researchers' work and translates it for a new audience. An illustration of this approach is Jansen's (2000) research on change momentum. Jansen developed and tested a momentum change theory based on the concepts of energy flows and movement momentum. She observed that most academic theories of change that referred to momentum were actually confusing momentum with inertia. Several implementation theorists have identified the importance of generating energy in order to move a change forward (Jick, 1995; Katzenbach, 1996; Kotter, 1995; Senge et al., 1999). Jansen translated the momentum idea into a change process theory and showed how it complements other evolutionary and teleological change theories. By referring to the implementation theory articles, Jansen invited other researchers to draw from them.

Multiple-author translation is less direct than same-author translation. It remains unclear how influential the initial idea is to the translation process. The translator claims credit for the idea because it is new to the targeted audience, and uses appeals to previous writings on the idea to legitimate it. Appeals to practitioner articles show that the idea has managerial relevance, and appeals to academic research show that the idea has empirical validity. Translation is enabled if both appeals are included within the same article. Linking the practitioner with the academic research implies a link and thus a translation process between the two.

Common Language Translation

Another method of idea translation is to present implementation and change process theories side by side within the same article and show their commonalities (and, sometimes, differences). This is a common strategy for review articles, especially articles dealing with organizational learning and learning organizations (e.g., Easterby-Smith, 1997; Miller, 1996; Tsang, 1997). The advantage of this strategy is that it explicitly calls attention to a stream of research of which the reader may be unaware and legitimates it by showing its links with research that has already been validated by the audience. This strategy invites the audience to continue the translation process by including the newly translated research in their own work.

The common strategy for language translation is the most direct strategy. It requires the author explicitly to link the ideas and explain that link using a rhetorical style suited to the audience. Whereas the single-author translation strategy requires the author to have a working understanding of how to communicate a single idea to multiple audiences, the common-language translation strategy requires the author to have an understanding of how to communicate diverse ideas to a single audience. This chapter is an example of common language translation.

Translating Implementation Theory to Change Process Theory

There are not as many examples of the explicit translation of practice work (implementation) to inform change process models as there are of translations from change process models to implementation models. However, some methods are being developed that may begin to address this gap.

The major method is one in which an individual member of an organization who is working to change it also studies the change or works in combination with an external researcher to study the change and to communicate about it to a scholarly audience. The first way this might happen involves insiders conducting their own action research projects (Coghlan, 2001; Coghlan & Brannick, 2001). When insiders then write about these projects for an external audience, they are translating their work for people who are likely to understand them from a slightly different perspective. A second way is through organizational members writing together with external researchers to describe and analyze a change process for a scholarly audience (Bartunek, Foster-Fishman, & Keys, 1996; Bartunek et al., 1999). This type of approach is referred to as *insider-outsider team research* (Bartunek & Louis, 1996). It is a kind of multiple-author approach, but one in which practitioners and academics are working jointly, rather than sequentially and independently, to make the work accessible to multiple audiences.

CONCLUSION

Research in organizational change and development has been increasing. Calls for more attention to theorizing about change processes have certainly been heeded. In addition, the variety of intervention types and underlying implementation models is considerably greater today than it was only a decade ago.

But to a large extent theorizing and practice, change process models and implementation models, have been developing separately. There are significant gaps between the two theoretical knowledge networks, even as there are potential overlaps in the work in which they are engaged. Whether or not the two groups are aware of it, the limited information flow between practitioners working from and further developing implementation theories and academics refining change process models limits the development of both types of theorizing. The barriers to knowledge transfer that we have identified—different knowledge validation standards, goals and audience, and theoretical antecedents—lead us to believe that successful connections between change process models and implementation models require a translation process. On some occasions such translation processes have been demonstrated, and those demonstrations provide a model for what might be done.

It is customary in chapters of this type to comment on the state of theorizing in a given field. There are some areas that could clearly use further conceptual development in terms of both change process and implementation models. These include downsizing, mergers and acquisitions, and nonlinear changes in mature organizations. On the whole, however, as the review here has made evident, there are abundant examples of change process theories, many of which address phenomena that are pertinent to the practice of organizational development. There are also a growing number of implementation models. As shown in Table 13.2, there are multiple potential overlaps between the two types of approaches. Thus, the current state of theorizing seems to us to be one that has the potential for the development of much more explicit links and connections between change process and implementation theories in ways that would benefit both. Such potential has not been realized as yet. However, the translation efforts we have described suggest that the means exists to begin to accomplish this after more concerted efforts are made, and that this accomplishment will be of considerable value to both the theory and the practice of organizational development.

Because of its dual interest in theory development and practical application, organizational development can play an important role in the translation of research to practice and in developing research questions informed by practice. For this to happen, academics and practitioners alike would benefit from increased attention to translation rather than expecting the audience to do the translation on its own. To take this theorizing to the next level, it would be useful for scholars and practitioners to ask questions like the following: What can appreciative inquiry practice teach us about strategic change? or How is action research similar to institutional agency? How can an understanding of life cycles affect the use of narrative strategies in organization change? If organizational development practitioners and organizational scholars can learn to ask—and answer—these questions, they will make a contemporary contribution to theory and practice that is consistent with organizational development's original ideals.

REFERENCES

Amabile, T. M., Conti, R., Coon, H., Lazenby, J., & Herron, M. (1996). Assessing the work environment for creativity. *Academy of Management Journal, 39,* 1154–1184.

Amburgey, T. L., Kelly, D., & Barnett, W. P. (1993). Resetting the clock: The dynamics of organizational change and failure. *Administrative Science Quarterly, 38,* 51–73.

Amburgey, T. L., & Miner, A. S. (1992). Strategic momentum: The effects of repetitive, positional, and contextual momentum on merger activity. *Strategic Management Journal, 13,* 335–348.

Argyris, C., Putnam, R., & Smith, D. M. (1985). *Action science: Concepts, methods and skills for research and intervention.* San Francisco: Jossey-Bass.

Argyris, C., & Schön, D. (1974). *Theory in practice: Increasing professional effectiveness.* San Francisco: Jossey-Bass.

Argyris, C., & Schön, D. (1978). *Organizational learning: A theory of action perspective.* Reading, MA: Addison-Wesley.

Armenakis, A. A., & Bedeian, A. G. (1999). Organizational change: A review of theory and research in the 1990s. *Journal of Management, 25,* 293–315.

Austin, J. R. (1997). A method for facilitating controversial social change in organizations: Branch Rickey and the Brooklyn Dodgers. *Journal of Applied Behavioral Science, 33*(1), 101–118.

Babüroglu, O., Topkaya, S., & Ates, O. (1996). Post-search follow-up: Assessing search conference based interventions in two different industries in Turkey. *Concepts and Transformation, 1,* 31–50.

Bacharach, S. B., Bamberger, P., & Sonnenstuhl, W. J. (1996). The organizational transformation process: The micropolitics of dissonance reduction and the alignment of logics of action. *Administrative Science Quarterly, 41*(3), 477–506.

Barley, S. J., & Tolbert, P. S. (1997). Institutionalization and structuration: Studying the links between action and institution. *Organization Studies, 18,* 93–117.

Barr, P. S., Stimpert, J. L., & Huff, A. S. (1992). Cognitive change, strategic action, and organizational renewal. *Strategic Management Journal, 27,* 489–510.

Barrett, F. J. (1995). Creating appreciative learning cultures. *Organizational Dynamics, 24,* 36–49.

Barrett, F. J., & Peterson, R. (2000). Appreciative learning cultures: Developing competencies for global organizing. *Organization Development Journal, 18*(2), 10–21.

Barrett, F. J., Thomas, G. F., & Hocevar, S. P. (1995). The central role of discourse in large-scale change: A social construction perspective. *Journal of Applied Behavioral Science, 31,* 352–372.

Barry, D. (1997). Telling changes: From narrative family therapy to organizational change and development. *Journal of Organizational Change Management, 10*(1), 30–46.

Bartunek, J. M. (1983). How organization development can develop organizational theory. *Group and Organization Studies, 8,* 303–318.

Bartunek, J. M. (1984). Changing interpretive schemes and organizational restructuring: The example of a religious order. *Administrative Science Quarterly, 36,* 187–218.

Bartunek, J. M., Foster-Fishman, P., & Keys, C. (1996). Using collaborative advocacy to foster intergroup collaboration: A joint insider/outsider investigation. *Human Relations, 49,* 701–732.

Bartunek, J. M., Krim, R., Necochea, R., & Humphries, M. (1999). Sensemaking, sensegiving, and leadership in strategic organizational development. In J. Wagner (Ed.), *Advances in qualitative organizational research* (Vol. 4, pp. 37–71). Greenwich: JAI Press.

Bartunek, J. M., & Louis, M. R. (1996). *Insider-outsider team research.* Thousand Oaks, CA: Sage.

Bartunek, J. M., Walsh, K., & Lacey, C. A. (2000). Dynamics and dilemmas of women leading women. *Organization Science, 11,* 589–610.

Bass, B. M. (1985). *Leadership and performance beyond expectations.* New York: Free Press.

Bass, B. M., & Avolio, B. J. (1994). *Improving organizational effectiveness through transformational leadership.* Thousand Oaks, CA: Sage.

Bate, P., Khan, R., & Pye, A. (2000). Towards a culturally sensitive approach to organization structuring: Where organization design meets organization development. *Organization Science, 11*(2), 197–211.

Baxter, L. A., & Montgomery, B. M. (1996). *Relating: Dialogues and dialectics.* New York: Guilford Press.

Beer, M., & Nohria, N. (2000). Breaking the code of change. *Harvard Business Review, 78*(3), 122–141.

Bennis, W. G. (1966). *Changing organizations.* New York: McGraw-Hill.

Berger, P., & Luckmann, T. (1966). *The social construction of reality.* New York: Anchor Books.

Block, P. (1987). *The empowered manager: Positive political skills at work.* San Francisco: Jossey-Bass.

Bloodgood, J. M., & Morrow, J. L. (2000). Strategic organizational change within an institutional framework. *Journal of Managerial Issues, 12*(2), 208–226.

Boje, D. (1991). The storytelling organization: A study of story performance in an office-supply firm. *Administrative Science Quarterly, 36*(1), 106–126.

Bowen, D. E., & Lawler, E. E. (1992, spring). The empowerment of service workers: What, why, how, and when. *Sloan Management Review,* 31–39.

Boyce, M. E. (1995). Collective centering and collective sensemaking in the stories of one organization. *Organization Studies, 16*(1), 107–137.

Bradbury, H., & Clair, J. (1999). Promoting sustainable organizations with Sweden's natural step, *Academy of Management Executive, 13*(4), 63–74.

Brown, J. S., & Duguid, P. (1991). Organizational learning and communities-of-practice: Toward a unified view of working, learning, and innovation. *Organization Science, 2,* 40–57.

Brown, J. S., & Duguid, P. (1999). Organizing knowledge. *Reflections: The Sol Journal, 1*(2), 28–42.

Brown, S. L., & Eisenhardt, K. M. (1997). The art of continuous change: Linking complexity theory and time-paced evolution in relentlessly shifting organizations. *Administrative Science Quarterly, 42,* 1–34.

Brulin, G. (1998). The new task of Swedish universities: Knowledge formation in interactive cooperation with practitioners. *Concepts and Transformation, 3,* 113–128.

Bunker, B. B., & Alban, B. T. (1997). *Large group interventions.* San Francisco: Jossey-Bass.

Bushe, C., & Coetzer, G. (1995). Appreciative inquiry as a team development intervention. *Journal of Applied Behavioral Science, 31,* 13–30.

Cameron, K. S., & Quinn, R. E. (1999). *Diagnosing and changing organizational culture.* Reading, MA: Addison-Wesley.

Church, A. H., & Burke, W. W. (1995). Practitioner attitudes about the field of Organization Development. In W. A. Pasmore & R. W. Woodman (Eds.), *Research in organization development and change* (Vol. 8, pp. 1–46). Greenwich, CT: JAI Press.

Church, A. H., Waclawski, J., & Seigel, W. (1999). Will the real O.D. practitioner please stand up? *Organization Development Journal, 17*(2), 49–59.

Coghlan, D. (2001). Insider action research projects: Implications for practising managers. *Management Learning, 32,* 49–60.

Coghlan, D., & Brannick, T. (2001). *Doing action research in your own organization.* London: Sage.

Collier, J. (1945). United States Indian Administration as a laboratory of ethnic relations. *Social Research, 12,* 275–276.

Cook, S. D. N., & Brown, J. S. (1999). Bridging epistemologies: The generative dance between organizational knowledge and organizational knowing. *Organization Science, 10,* 381–400.

Cooper, D., Hinings, B., Greenwood, R., & Brown, J. (1996). Sedimentation and transformation in organizational change: The case of Canadian law firms. *Organization Studies, 17,* 623–647.

Cooperrider, D. L. (1997). Resources for getting appreciative inquiry started: An example OD proposal. *OD Practitioner, 28*(1), 28–33.

Cooperrider, D. L., & Srivastva, S. (1987). Appreciative inquiry in organizational life. In R. W. Woodman & W. A. Pasmore (Eds.), *Research in organization development* (Vol. 1, pp. 129–169). Greenwich, CT: JAI Press.

Creed, W. E. D., Scully, M., & Austin, J. R. (forthcoming). Clothes make the person? The tailoring of legitimating accounts and the social construction of identity. *Organization Science.*

Cummings, T., & Worley, C. (2000). *Organization development and change* (7th ed.). Cincinnati, OH: Southwestern College Publishing.

Czarniawska, B., & Joerges, B. (1996). Travel of ideas. In B. Czarniawska & G. Sevon (Eds.), *Translating organizational change* (pp. 13–48). New York: Walter De Gruyter.

D'Aunno, T., Sutton, R. I., & Price, R. H. (1991). Isomorphism and external support in conflicting institutional environments: A study of drug abuse treatment units. *Academy of Management Journal, 34,* 636–661.

Denison, D. R., Hooijberg, R., & Quinn, R. E. (1995). Paradox and performance: Toward a theory of behavioral complexity in managerial leadership. *Organization Science, 6*(5), 524–540.

Dent, E. B., & Goldberg, S. G. (1999). Challenging resistance to change. *Journal of Applied Behavioral Science, 35,* 25–41.

DiMaggio, P. J., & Powell, W. W. (1991). The iron cage revisited: Institutional isomorphism and collective rationality in organizational fields. In W. W. Powell & P. J. DiMaggio (Eds.), *The new institution in organizational analysis,* (pp. 63–82). Chicago: University of Chicago Press.

Doz, Y. L., & Prahalad, C. K. (1987). A process model of strategic redirection in large complex firms: The case of multinational corporations. In A. Pettigrew (Ed.), *The management of strategic change* (pp. 63–83). Oxford, UK: Blackwell.

Drazin, R., Glynn, M. A., & Kazanjian, R. K. (1999). Multilevel theorizing about creativity in organizations: A sensemaking perspective. *Academy of Management Review, 24,* 286–307.

Drazin, R., & Schoonhoven, C. B. (1996). Community, population, and organization effects on innovation: A multi-level perspective. *Academy of Management Journal, 39,* 1065–1083.

Dutton, J. E., & Dukerich, J. M. (1991). Keeping an eye on the mirror: Image and identity in organizational adaptation. *Academy of Management Journal, 34,* 517–554.

Dyck, B., & Starke, F. A. (1999). The formation of breakaway organizations: Observations and a process model. *Administrative Science Quarterly, 44*(4), 792–822.

Easterby-Smith, M. (1997). Disciplines of organizational learning: Contributions and critiques. *Human Relations, 50,* 1085–1113.

Ehin, C. (1995). The quest for empowering organizations: Some lessons from our foraging past. *Organization Science, 6,* 666–670.

Eisenhardt, K. M., & Brown, S. L. (1998a). Time pacing: Competing in markets that won't stand still. *Harvard Business Review, 76*(2), 59–69.

Eisenhardt, K. M., & Brown, S. L. (1998b). *Competing on the edge: Strategy as structured chaos.* Cambridge, MA: Harvard Business School Press.

Elsbach, K. D., & Sutton, R. I. (1992). Acquiring organizational legitimacy through illegitimate actions: A marriage of institutional and impression management theories. *Academy of Management Journal, 35,* 699–738.

Emery, F., & Trist, E. (1973). *Towards a social ecology.* New York: Plenum.

Emery, M. (1996). The influence of culture in search conferences. *Concepts and Transformation, 1,* 143–164.

Emery, M., & Purser, R. (1996). *The search conference.* San Francisco, CA: Jossey-Bass.

Faber, B. (1998). Toward a rhetoric of change: Reconstructing image and narrative in distressed organizations. *Journal of Business and Technical Communication, 12*(2), 217–237.

Feldman, M. S. (2000). Organizational routines as a source of continuous change. *Organization Science, 11,* 611–629.

Filipczak, B. (1995, September). *Critical mass: Putting whole systems thinking into practice. Training,* 33–41.

Fligstein, N. (1991). The structural transformation of American industry: An institutional account of the causes of diversification in the largest firms, 1919–1979. In W. W. Powell & P. J. DiMaggio (Eds.), *The new institution in organizational analysis,* (pp. 311–336). Chicago: University of Chicago Press.

Fligstein, N. (1997). Social skill and institutional theory. *American Behavioral Scientist, 40*(4), 397–405.

Fombrun, C. J., & Ginsberg, A. (1990). Shifting gears: Enabling change in corporate aggressiveness. *Strategic Management Journal, 11,* 297–308.

Ford, C. M. (1996). A theory of individual creative action in multiple social domains. *Academy of Management Review, 21,* 1112–1142.

Ford, J. D. (1999a). Conversations and the epidemiology of change. In W. A. Pasmore & R. W. Woodman (Eds.), *Research in organizational change and development* (Vol. 12, pp. 1–39). Greenwich, CT: JAI Press.

Ford, J. D. (1999b). Organizational change as shifting conversations. *Journal of Organizational Change Management, 12,* 480–500.

Ford, J. D., & Ford, L. W. (1995). The role of conversations in producing intentional change in organizations. *Academy of Management Review, 20,* 541–570.

Foster, P. C. (2000, August). *Action learning and institutional change processes.* Paper presented at the Annual Academy of Management Meeting. Toronto, Ontario, Canada.

French, W. L., & Bell, C. H. (1999). *Organization Development* (6th ed.). Englewood Cliffs, NJ: Prentice Hall.

Frost, P., & Egri, C. (1994). The shamanic perspective on organizational change and development. *Journal of Organizational Change Management, 7,* 7–23.

Garvin, D. A. (1993, July-August). Building a learning organization. *Harvard Business Review,* 78–91.

Geertz, C. (1983). *Local knowledge: Further essays in interpretive anthropology.* New York: Basic Books.

Gergen, K., & Thatchenkery, T. (1996). Organization science as social construction: Postmodern potentials. *Journal of Applied Behavioral Science, 32,* 356–377.

Gersick, C. J. G. (1991). Revolutionary change theories: A multilevel exploration of the punctuated equilibrium paradigm. *Academy of Management Review, 16,* 10–36.

Giddens, A. (1984). *The constitution of society.* Berkley: University of California Press.

Gilmore, T., Shea, G., & Useem, M. (1997). Side effects of corporate cultural transformations. *Journal of Applied Behavioral Science, 33,* 174–189.

Gioia, D. A., & Chittipeddi, K. (1991). Sensemaking and sensegiving in strategic change initiation. *Strategic Management Journal, 12,* 433–448.

Glynn, M. A. (1996). Innovative genius: A framework for relating individual and organizational intelligences to innovation. *Academy of Management Review, 21,* 1081–1111.

Golembiewski, R. T. (1998). Appreciating appreciative inquiry: Diagnosis and perspectives on how to do better. In R. W. Woodman & W. A. Pasmore (Eds.), *Research in organizational change and development* (Vol. 11, pp. 1–45). Greenwich, CT: JAI Press.

Greenwood, R., & Hinings, C. R. (1993). Understanding strategic change: The contributions of archetypes. *Academy of Management Journal, 36,* 1052–1081.

Greenwood, R., & Hinings, C. R. (1996). Understanding radical organizational change: Bringing together the old and the new institutionalism. *Academy of Management Review, 21*(4), 1022–1054.

Greiner, L. (1972, July-August). Evolution and revolution as organizations grow. *Harvard Business Review,* 37–46.

Greve, H. R. (1998). Managerial cognition and the mimetic adoption of market positions: What you see is what you do. *Strategic Management Journal, 19,* 967–988.

Hanks, S., Watson, C., Jansen, E., & Chandler, G. (1994). Tightening the life cycle construct: A taxonomic study of growth stage configurations in high-technology organizations. *Entrepreneurship Theory and Practice, 18,* 5–29.

Hannan, M. T., & Freeman, J. (1984). Structural inertia and organizational change. *American Sociological Review, 49,* 149–164.

Hardy, C., & Leiba-O'Sullivan, S. (1998). The power behind empowerment: Implications for research and practice. *Human Relations, 51,* 451–483.

Harrison, R. (1970). Choosing the depth of organizational intervention. *Journal of Applied Behavioral Science, 6,* 181–202.

Hazen, M. (1994). Multiplicity and change in persons and organizations. *Journal of Organizational Change Management, 6,* 72–81.

Head, T. C. (2000). Appreciative inquiry: Debunking the mythology behind resistance to change. *OD Practitioner, 32*(1), 27–32.

Holman, P., & Devane, T. (Eds.). (1999). *The change handbook: Group methods for shaping the future.* San Francisco: Berrett-Koehler.

Hooijberg, R., Hunt, J. G., & Dodge, G. (1997). Leadership complexity and development of the leaderplex model. *Journal of Management, 23,* 375–408.

Jansen, K. J. (2000, August). A longitudinal examination of momentum during culture change. Paper presented at the Annual Academy of Management Meeting, Toronto, Ontario, Canada.

Jelinek, M., & Litterer, J. A. (1988). Why OD must become strategic. In W. A. Pasmore & R. W. Woodman (Eds.), *Research in organizational change and development* (Vol. 2, pp. 135–162). Greenwich, CT: JAI Press.

Jick, T. D. (1995). Accelerating change for competitive advantage. *Organizational Dynamics, 24*(1), 77–82.

Johnson, G., Smith, S., & Codling, B. (2000). Microprocesses of institutional change in the context of privatization. *Academy of Management Review, 25,* 572–580.

Katzenbach, J. R. (1996). Real change leaders. *McKinsey Quarterly,* (1), 148–163.

Kelly, D., & Amburgey, T. L. (1991). Organizational inertia and momentum: A dynamic model of strategic change. *Academy of Management Journal, 34,* 591–612.

Kimberly, J. R., & Bouchikhi, J. (1995). The dynamics of organizational development and change: How the past shapes the present and constrains the future. Organization Science, *6,* 9–18.

Kleiner, A., & Roth, G. (1997). How to make experience your company's best teacher. *Harvard Business Review, 75*(5), 172–177.

Kleiner, A., & Roth, G. (2000). *Oil change: Perspectives on corporate transformation.* New York: Oxford University Press.

Kostera, M., & Wicha, M. (1996). The "divided self" of Polish state-owned enterprises: The culture of organizing. *Organization Studies, 17*(1), 83–105.

Kotter, J. P. (1995). Leading change: Why transformation efforts fail. *Harvard Business Review, 73*(2), 59–67.

Kuwada, K. (1998). Strategic learning: The continuous side of discontinuous strategic change. *Organization Science, 9,* 719–736.

Labianca, G., Gray, B., & Brass, D. J. (2000). A grounded model of organizational schema change during empowerment. *Organization Science, 11,* 235–257.

Laughlin, R. C. (1991). Environmental disturbances and organizational transitions and transformations: Some alternative models. *Organization Studies, 12,* 209–232.

Levitt, B., & March, J. G. (1988). Organizational learning. *Annual Review of Psychology, 14,* 319–340.

Lewin, K. (1951). *Field theory in social science.* New York: Harper and Row.

Lichtenstein, B. B. (2000a). Self-organized transition: A pattern amid the chaos of transformative change. *Academy of Management Executive, 14*(4), 128–141.

Lichtenstein, B. B. (2000b). Emergence as a process of self-organizing: New assumptions and insights from the study of non-linear dynamic systems. *Journal of Organizational Change Management, 13,* 526–544.

Lippitt, R. (1980). *Choosing the future you prefer.* Washington, DC: Development Publishers.

Lipshitz, R., Popper, M., & Oz, S. (1996). Building learning organizations: The design and implementation of organizational learning mechanisms. *Journal of Applied Behavioral Science, 32,* 292–305.

Louis, M. R., & Sutton, R. I. (1991). Switching cognitive gears: From habits of mind to active thinking. *Human Relations, 44,* 55–76.

Mantel, J. M., & Ludema, J. D. (2000). From local conversations to global change: Experiencing the Worldwide Web effect of appreciative inquiry. *Organization Development Journal, 18*(2), 42–53.

Marks, M. L., & Mirvis, P. H. (2001). Making mergers and acquisitions work: Strategic and psychological preparation. *Academy of Management Executive, 15*(2), 80–92.

Meyer, J. W., & Rowan, B. (1997). Institutionalized organizations: Formal structure as myth and ceremony. *American Journal of Sociology, 82,* 340–363.

Mezias, S. J., & Glynn, M. A. (1993). The three faces of corporate renewal: Institution, revolution, and evolution. *Strategic Management Journal, 14,* 77–101.

Miller, D. (1996). A preliminary typology of organizational learning: Synthesizing the literature. *Journal of Management, 22,* 485–505.

Mirvis, P. H. (1988). Organizational development: Pt. 1. An evolutionary perspective. In W. A. Pasmore & R. W. Woodman (Eds.), *Research in organizational change and development* (Vol. 2, pp. 1–57). Greenwich, CT: JAI Press.

Mirvis, P. H. (1990). Organizational development: Pt. 2. A revolutionary perspective. In W. A. Pasmore & R. W. Woodman (Eds.), *Research in organizational change and development* (Vol. 4, pp. 1–66). Greenwich, CT: JAI Press.

Mitchell, T. R., & Beach, L. R. (1990). "Do I love thee? Let me count" toward an understanding of intuitive and automatic decision making. *Organizational Behavior and Human Decision Processes, 47,* 1–20.

Mohrman, S., Cohen, S., & Mohrman, A. (1995). *Designing team-based organizations.* San Francisco: Jossey-Bass.

Nadler, D. A., Shaw, R. B., & Walton, A. E. (1995). *Discontinuous change: Leading organizational transformation.* San Francisco: Jossey-Bass.

Nadler, D. A., & Tushman, M. L. (1989). Organizational frame bending: Principles for managing reorientation. *Academy of Management Executive, 3,* 194–204.

Nelson, R. R., & Winter, S. G. (1982). *An evolutionary theory of economic change.* Cambridge, MA: Belknap Press.

Neumann, J. E. (1989). Why people in don't participate in organizational change. In R. W. Woodman & W. A. Pasmore (Eds.), *Research in organizational change and development* (Vol. 3, pp. 181–212). Greenwich, CT: JAI Press.

Nevis, E. C., DiBella, A. J., & Gould, J. M. (1995, winter). Understanding organizations as learning systems. *Sloan Management Review, 36,* 73–85.

Nielsen, R. P. (1996). *The politics of ethics.* New York: Oxford University Press.

North, D. C. (1990). *Institutions, institutional change and economic performance.* New York: Cambridge University Press.

Nutt, P. C., & Backoff, R. W. (1997). Transforming organizations with second-order change. In W. A. Pasmore & R. W. Woodman (Eds.), *Research in organizational change and development* (Vol. 10, pp. 229–274). Greenwich, CT: JAI Press.

O'Connor, E. S. (2000). Plotting the organization: The embedded narrative as a construct for studying change. *Journal of Applied Behavioral Science, 36,* 174–192.

Oldham, G. R., & Cummings, A. (1996). Employee creativity: Personal and contextual factors at work. *Academy of Management Journal, 39,* 607–634.

Oliver, C. (1991). Strategic responses to institutional processes. *Academy of Management Review, 16,* 145–179.

Orlikowski, W. J., & Hofman, D. J. (1997). An improvisational model for change management: The case of groupware technologies. *Sloan Management Review, 38*(2), 11–21.

Pasmore, W. A., & Friedlander, F. (1982). An action-research program for increasing employee involvement in problem solving. *Administrative Science Quarterly, 27,* 343–362.

Porras, J. I., & Robertson, P. J. (1987). Organization development theory: A typology and evaluation. In R. W. Woodman & W. A. Pasmore (Eds.), *Research in organizational change and development* (Vol. 1, pp. 1–57). Greenwich, CT: JAI Press.

Porras J. I., & Robertson P. J. (1992). Organizational development: theory, practice, research. In M. D. Dunnette & L. M. Hough (Eds.), *Handbook of organizational psychology* (Vol. 3, pp. 719–822). Palo Alto, CA: Psychology Press.

Quinn, R. E., & Cameron, K. (1983). Organizational life cycles and the shifting criteria of effectiveness. *Management Science, 29,* 33–51.

Quinn, R. E., & Cameron, K. S. (1988). *Paradox and transformation: Toward a theory of change in organization and management.* Cambridge, MA: Ballinger.

Quinn, R. E., Spreitzer, G. M., & Brown, M. V. (2000). Changing others through changing ourselves: The transformation of human systems. *Journal of Management Inquiry, 9,* 147–164.

Raelin, J. A. (1997). Action learning and action science: Are they different? *Organizational Dynamics, 26*(1), 21–44.

Rainey, M. A. (1996). An appreciative inquiry into the factors of cultural continuity during leadership transition. *OD Practitioner, 28*(1), 34–42.

Rajagopalan, N., & Spreitzer, G. M. (1996). Toward a theory of strategic change: A multi-lens perspective and integrative framework. *Academy of Management Review, 22,* 48–79.

Rapoport, R. N. (1970). Three dilemmas in action research. *Human Relations, 23,* 488–513.

Reason, P. (1999). Integrating action and reflection through cooperative inquiry. *Management Learning, 30,* 207–226.

Reger, R. K., Gustafson, L. T., DeMarie, S. M., & Mullane, J. V. (1994). Reframing the organization: Why implementing total quality is easier said than done. *Academy of Management Review, 19,* 565–584.

Revans, R. (1980). *Action Learning.* London: Blond and Briggs.

Rooke, D., & Torbert, W. R. (1998). Organizational transformation as a function of CEO's developmental stage. *Organization Development Journal, 16,* 11–28.

Roth, G., & Kleiner, A. (2000). *Car launch: The human side of managing change.* New York: Oxford University Press.

Rynes, S. L., Bartunek, J. M., & Daft, R. L. (2001). Across the Great Divide: Knowledge creation and transfer between practitioners and academics. *Academy of Management Journal, 44,* 340–356.

Sastry, M. A. (1997). Problems and paradoxes in a model of punctuated organizational change. *Administrative Science Quarterly, 42,* 237–275.

Schmuck, R. A., Runkel, P. J., Saturen, S. L., Martell, R. T., & Derr, C. B. (1972). *Handbook of organization development in schools.* Palo Alto, CA: National Press Books.

Senge, P. (1990). *The fifth discipline: The art and practice of the learning organization*. New York: Doubleday/Currency.

Senge, P., Kleiner, A., Roberts, C., Ross, R., & Smith, B. (1994). *The fifth discipline fieldbook: Strategies for building a learning organization*. New York: Doubleday/Currency.

Senge, P., Kleiner, A., Roberts, C., Roth, G., Ross, R., & Smith, B. (1999). *The dance of change: The challenges to sustaining momentum in learning organizations*. New York: Doubleday/Currency.

Seo, M., Putnam, L., & Bartunek, J. M. (2001). Tensions and contradictions of planned organizational change. Unpublished manuscript, Boston College, Chestnut Hill, MA.

Simons, R. (1994). How new top managers use control systems as levers of strategic renewal. *Strategic Management Journal, 15,* 169–189.

Sorenson, P. F., Yaeger, T. F., & Nicoll, D. (2000). Appreciative inquiry 2000: Fad or important new focus for OD? *OD Practitioner, 32*(1), 3–5.

Spreitzer, G. M. (1996). Social structural characteristics of psychological empowerment. *Academy of Management Journal, 39,* 483–504.

Spreitzer, G. M., & Quinn, R. E. (1996). Empowering middle managers to be transformational leaders. *Journal of Applied Behavioral Science, 32,* 237–261.

Srivastva, S., & Cooperrider, D. L. (1999). *Appreciative management and leadership* (Revised edition). Euclid, OH: Williams Custom Publishing.

Suchman, M. (1995). Managing legitimacy: Strategic and institutional approaches. *Academy of Management Review, 20,* 571–610.

Tenkasi, R. V. (2000). The dynamics of cultural knowledge and learning in creating viable theories of global change and action. *Organization Development Journal, 18*(2), 74–90.

Thomas, K. W., & Velthouse, B. A. (1990). Cognitive elements of empowerment: An "interpretive" model of intrinsic task motivation. *Academy of Management Review, 15,* 666–681.

Tichy, N. M., & Devanna, M. A. (1986). *The transformational leader*. New York: Wiley.

Torbert, W. R. (1989). Leading organizational transformation. In R. W. Woodman & W. A. Pasmore (Eds.), *Research in organizational change and development* (Vol. 3, pp. 83–116). Greenwich, CT: JAI Press.

Torbert, W. R. (1991). *The power of balance: Transforming self, society, and scientific inquiry*. Newbury Park, CA: Sage.

Torbert, W. R. (1999). The distinctive questions developmental action inquiry asks. *Management Learning, 30,* 189–206.

Tsang, E. W. K. (1997). Organizational learning and the learning organization. *Human Relations, 50,* 73–89.

Tushman, M. L., & Romanelli, E. (1985). Organizational evolution: A metamorphosis model of convergence and reorientation. In L. Cummings & B. M. Staw (Eds.), *Research in organizational behavior* (Vol. 7, pp. 171–222). Greenwich, CT: JAI Press.

Van de Ven, A. H., & Poole, M. S. (1995). Explaining development and change in organizations. *Academy of Management Review, 20,* 510–540.

Watkins, K. E., & Marsick, V. J. (1994). *Sculpting the learning organization*. San Francisco: Jossey-Bass.

Watzlawick, P., Weakland, J. H., & Fisch, R. (1974). *Change: Principles of problem formation and problem resolution*. New York: W. W. Norton.

Weber, P. S., & Manning, M. R. (1998). A comparative framework for large group organizational change interventions. In R. W. Woodman & W. A. Pasmore (Eds.), *Research in organizational change and development* (Vol. 11, pp. 225–252). Greenwich, CT: JAI Press.

Weick, K. (1979). *The social psychology of organizing* (2nd ed.). Reading, MA: Addison-Wesley.

Weick, K. (1995). *Sensemaking in organizations*. Thousand Oaks, CA: Sage.

Weick, K., & Quinn, R. E. (1999). Organizational change and development. *Annual Review of Psychology, 50,* 361–386.

Whyte, W. F. (Ed.). (1991). *Participatory action research*. Newbury Park, CA: Sage.

Worley, C. G., & Feyerherm, A. E. (2001, April). *Founders of the field reflect on the future of OD*. Paper presented at the Western Academy of Management Conference, Sun Valley, Idaho.

Worley, C., & Varney, G. (1998, winter). A search for a common body of knowledge for master's level organization development and change programs. *Academy of Management ODC Newsletter,* 1–4.

Zucker, L. G. (1987). Institutional theories of organizations. *Annual Review of Sociology, 13,* 443–464.

CHAPTER 14

Work Groups and Teams in Organizations

STEVE W. J. KOZLOWSKI AND BRADFORD S. BELL

The last decade and a half has witnessed a remarkable transformation of organizational structures worldwide. Although there are economic, strategic, and technological imperatives driving this transformation, one of its more compelling aspects has been an ongoing shift from work organized around individual jobs to team-based work structures (Lawler, Mohrman, & Ledford, 1992, 1995). Increasing global competition, consolidation, and innovation create pressures that are influencing the emergence of teams as basic building blocks of organizations. These pressures drive a need for diverse skills, expertise, and experience. They necessitate more rapid, flexible, and adaptive responses. Teams enable these characteristics. In addition, organizations have globalized operations through expansion, mergers and acquisitions, and joint ventures—placing increased importance on cross-cultural and mixed culture teams. Advanced computer and communication technologies provide new tools to better link individuals with their team in real time and even enable teams to be *virtual*—distributed in time and space.

This ongoing transformation in the basic organization of work has captured the attention of researchers and is reflected by new theories of team functioning, a rapidly growing number of empirical studies, and numerous literature reviews written on the burgeoning research on teams. It is also reflected in a shift in the locus of team research. For most of its history, small group research has been centered in social psychology (McGrath, 1997). Over the last 15 years, however, group and team research has become increasingly centered in the fields of organizational psychology and organizational behavior. Indeed, Levine and Moreland (1990) in their extensive review of small group research concluded that "Groups are alive and well, but living elsewhere. . . . The torch has been passed to (or, more accurately, picked up by) colleagues in other disciplines, particularly organizational psychology" (p. 620).

We would like to acknowledge several colleagues who provided insightful comments on an initial outline or draft of this chapter. Our thanks to Neil Anderson, Murray Barrick, Jan Cannon-Bowers, Paul Goodman, Stan Gully, Cyn D. Fisher, Richard Hackman, John Hollenbeck, Susan Jackson, Michelle Marks, John Mathieu, Susan Mohamed, Greg Stewart, Anne Tsui, Eduardo Salas, Ruth Wageman, Wang Zhong-Ming, and Michael West. Thanks also to Richard Klimoski for his helpful editorial guidance throughout. We would also like to acknowledge the Air Force Office of Scientific Research for support (F49620-98-1-0363 and F49620-01-1-0283, S. W. J. Kozlowski and R. P. DeShon, Principal Investigators) that in part assisted the composition of this chapter. Although many sources provided inputs to this chapter, the views expressed are those of the authors.

Several literature reviews published over the last 15 years help to document this shift in locus, characterize differences brought to group and team research by an organizational perspective, and provide a fairly comprehensive assessment this vast body of research. Goodman, Ravlin, and Schminke (1987) sent a signal marking the shift in locus and highlighted one of the key distinctions between the small group literature, which pays relatively little attention to the group task and its technology, and the organizational literature, which views *what groups do* and *how they do it* as a critical characteristics. Similarly, Bettenhausen (1991) documented the emphasis in organizational research on task-driven processes in teams, relative to the small group focus on interpersonal attraction and interaction. Sundstrom, De Meuse, and Futrell (1990) presented an organizational systems perspective on teams that addressed both development and effectiveness—two issues rarely considered in concert. Hackman (1992) viewed groups as contexts for individual behavior, which is an important perspective because teams in part enact their context. Guzzo and Shea (1992) and Guzzo and Dickson (1996) reviewed team research in organizations. Sundstrom (1999) identified "best practices" for managing effective teams. Cohen and Bailey (1997) and Sundstrom, McIntyre, Halfhill, and Richards (2000) provided focused reviews of work team effectiveness based on field research during the periods of 1990–1996 and 1980–mid-1999, respectively. Finally, Gully (2000) presented an insightful assessment of team effectiveness research since 1985 that examines key boundary conditions. An examination of this body of work leads to the conclusion that there is an enormous wealth of information available on work teams in organizations. Nevertheless, answers to many fundamental questions remain elusive.

Our objective in this chapter is to provide an integrative perspective on work groups and teams in organizations, one that addresses primary foci of theory and research, highlights applied implications, and identifies key issues in need of research attention and resolution. Given the volume of existing reviews, our review is not intended to be exhaustive. Rather, it uses representative work to characterize key topics and focuses on recent work that breaks new ground to help move theory and research forward. Although our approach risks trading breadth for depth, we believe that there is much value in taking a more integrative view of the important areas of team research, identifying key research themes, and linking the themes and disparate topics closer together. To the extent that we identify new and necessary areas of theory development and research, the value of this approach should be evident.

The chapter is organized as follows. We begin by examining the nature of work teams. We define them, identify four critical conceptual issues—*context, work flow, levels,* and *time*—that serve as review themes and discuss the multitude of forms that teams may assume. We then shift attention to the heart of the review, examining key aspects of the creation, development, operation, and management of work teams. To accomplish our objectives of breadth and integration, we adopt a life cycle perspective to organize the review. Topics involved in the team life cycle include (a) team composition; (b) team formation, socialization, and development; (c) team processes and effectiveness; (d) team leadership and motivation; (e) and team continuance and decline. We characterize representative theory and research, identify thematic limitations, and highlight work that is beginning to push the boundaries on critical conceptual issues. We also address application concerns whenever possible. Finally, we close with a discussion that reflects back on the topics, considers the state of progress regarding our critical conceptual themes, and suggests directions for new research to foster continued progress and development.

THE NATURE OF WORK TEAMS AND GROUPS

What Is a Team?

Although some scholars distinguish work teams and work groups (Katzenbach & Smith, 1993), we make no such distinction and use the terms interchangeably. Others distinguish dyads or triads from larger teams. Although we acknowledge that intrateam processes increase in complexity with more team members, we do not highlight these distinctions in this chapter. Work teams and groups come in a variety of types and sizes, cutting across different contexts, functions, internal processes, and external links. However, several features provide a foundation for a basic definition. Work teams and groups are composed of two or more individuals who (a) exist to perform organizationally relevant tasks, (b) share one or more common goals, (c) interact socially, (d) exhibit task interdependencies (i.e., work flow, goals, outcomes), (e) maintain and manage boundaries, and (f) are embedded in an organizational context that sets boundaries, constrains the team, and influences exchanges with other units in the broader entity (Alderfer, 1977; Hackman, 1987; Hollenbeck et al., 1995; Kozlowski, Gully, McHugh, Salas, & Cannon-Bowers, 1996; Kozlowski, Gully, Nason, & Smith, 1999; Salas, Dickinson, Converse, & Tannenbaum, 1992).

We view teams from an organizational systems perspective. Teams are embedded in an open, yet bounded system composed of multiple levels. This broader system sets *top-down* constraints on team functioning. Simultaneously, team responses are complex *bottom-up* phenomena that emerge over time from individual cognition, affect, behavior, and interactions among members within the team context (Kozlowski & Klein, 2000). From this perspective, we assert that four conceptual issues are critical in efforts to investigate and understand work teams: (a) task or work flow interdependence, (b) contextual creation and constraint, (c) multilevel influences, and (d) temporal dynamics. We briefly introduce these issues in the following discussion and use them as a basis to identify both the strengths and limitations of extant research.

The centrality of task interdependence is one issue that clearly distinguishes the work teams and small group literatures (Goodman et al., 1987). In the organizational literature, *technology*—and the tasks it entails—denotes the means by which system inputs are transformed or converted to outputs; technology is not equipment or support systems (e.g., McGrath & Hollingshead, 1994). Technology and its associated tasks create a structure that determines the flow of work and links across team members. Interactions among work team members are substantially influenced by this work flow structure (Steiner, 1972; Van de Ven, Delbecq, & Koenig, 1976), which links individual inputs, outcomes, and goals. Thus, it has a critical influence on team processes essential to team effectiveness. In contrast, laboratory tasks in small-group research are often pooled or additive, thereby minimizing the necessity for task-driven interaction among team members (McGrath, 1997). From an organizational systems perspective, the task work flow sets interaction requirements and constraints that must be considered in team theory, research, and practice.

Teams are embedded in an organizational context, and the team itself enacts a context for team members. The broader organizational context characterized by technology, structure, leadership, culture, and climate constrains teams and influences their responses. However, teams also represent a proximal context for the individuals who compose them. Team members operate in a bounded interactive context that they in part create by virtue of their attributes, interactions, and responses. Team-level normative expectations, shared perceptions, and compatible knowledge are generated by and emerge from individual interactions. Dynamic team processes in part create contextual structure that constrains subsequent team processes. Thus, the team context is a joint product of both top-down and bottom-up influences.

Organizations, teams, and individuals are bound together in a multilevel system. Teams do not behave, individuals do; but, they do so in ways that create team-level phenomena. Individuals are nested within teams, and teams in turn are linked to and nested in a larger multilevel system. This hierarchical nesting and coupling, which is characteristic of organizational systems, necessitates the use of multiple levels—individual, team, and the higher-level context—in efforts to understand and investigate team phenomena. However, many of the theoretical, measurement, and data analytic issues relevant to a multilevel perspective on teams are often neglected in research and practice. These issues are especially important when researchers try to attribute individual characteristics to the team collective (e.g., team ability, team personality, team learning). Such generalizations necessitate precise multilevel theory and analyses to ensure the meaningfulness of the collective team-level constructs (Kozlowski & Klein, 2000). Unfortunately, there are many examples of such generalizations that lack the standing of true constructs.

Finally, time is an important characteristic of work teams (McGrath, 1990). Teams have a developmental life span; they form, mature, and evolve over time (Morgan, Salas, & Glickman, 1993). Team constructs and phenomena are not static. Many—indeed, most—team-level phenomena (e.g., collective efficacy, mental models, performance) emerge upwards from the individual to the team level and unfold via complex temporal dynamics (Kozlowski et al., 1999) that include not only linear but also cyclical and episodic aspects (Kozlowski, Gully, McHugh, et al., 1996; Marks, Mathieu, & Zaccaro, 2001). Although time is explicitly recognized in models of team development, it is largely neglected in many other areas of team research; yet time is relevant to virtually all team phenomena. It is impossible to understand team effectiveness without paying attention to the processes that unfold over time to yield it.

Types of Work Teams

Work-teams can assume a wide variety of different forms—they are not unitary entities. Many factors or contingencies relevant to effective team functioning vary across different types of teams, creating challenges for studying and understanding them. This fact is reflected in the many efforts to describe, classify, or otherwise distinguish differences among of teams. We consider some of the major distinctions in the following discussion and then comment on their theoretical and research value.

General Typologies

General typologies are an effort to distinguish a broad range of team types. For example, Sundstrom and colleagues (2000) integrated the Sundstrom et al. (1990) and Cohen and Bailey (1997) typologies to yield six team categories: (a) production,

(b) service, (c) management, (d) project, (e) action and performing, and (f) advisory. Production teams represent core employees who cyclically produce tangible products (e.g., automobile assembly) and vary on discretion from supervisor-led to semiautonomous to self-directed. Service teams engage in repeated transactions with customers (e.g., airline attendants) who have different needs, making the nature of the transactions variable. Senior managers of meaningful business units with primary responsibility for directing and coordinating lower level units under their authority comprise management teams. Project teams are temporary entities that execute specialized time-constrained tasks and then disband (e.g., new product development). Action and performing teams are composed of interdependent experts who engage in complex time-constrained performance events. Examples include aircrews, surgical teams, military units, and musicians.

More Specific Classifications

In addition to general typologies, researchers have identified more specific types of teams. For example, some scholars have distinguished crews from other types of work teams (e.g., Cannon-Bowers, Salas, & Blickensderfer, 1998). The key distinguishing characteristic is the capability and necessity for crews to form and be immediately prepared to perform together effectively (Ginnett, 1993). Thus, advocates of this distinction assert that crews—unlike more conventional teams—do not go through an identifiable developmental process (Arrow, 1998). Examples include aircrews, military combat units, and surgical teams. However, it is notable that crews are used for team tasks that necessitate high expertise, extensive training, and well-developed, standardized performance guidelines. Thus, although crews continually form, disband, and reform with new members as an integral part of their life cycles, the high level of prior socialization, trained knowledge, and explicit performance standards provide strong structural supports that substitute for an extended group development process.

Top management teams (TMT; Hambrick & Mason, 1984; Jackson, 1992a) represent another specific classification—one based on level in the organizational hierarchy. Because it is difficult to gain access to TMTs, much of the research on TMT effectiveness has focused on factors that can be gleaned through archival records. As a result, research has centered on TMT composition (e.g., heterogeneity of function, organizational tenure, team tenure, age, and education; team size) and the external environment (e.g., industry as a proxy for environmental turbulence, market characteristics), and their effects on organizational effectiveness (Eisenhardt & Schoonhoven, 1990; Finkelstein & Hambrick, 1990; Simons,

Pelled, & Smith, 1999; Smith et al., 1994; West & Anderson, 1996). Although the amount of empirical work in this area is relatively small compared to work team research in general, the area is active and growing. One troubling aspect of this growing area, however, is its relative independence of the broader work teams literature (Cohen & Bailey, 1997). This issue has been neglected and is in need of rectification.

More recently, the globalization of organizations and changing nature of work have yielded new team forms such as distinctions based on culture (cross-cultural, mixed-culture, and transnational teams; Earley & Erez, 1997) and collocation in time and space (virtual teams; Bell & Kozlowski, 2002). For example, the challenge of cross- and mixed-culture teams is to break through the barriers of different fundamental values, cultural assumptions, and stereotypes to successfully coordinate and jointly perform effectively. One of the biggest conceptual challenges in this area of work is dealing with the multiple levels—individual, group, organization, and culture—that are relevant to understanding such teams. Chao (2000), for example, presents a multilevel model of intercultural relationships that specifies how individual- and group-level interactions are affected by higher-level relationships. Essentially, interactions among individuals or groups of different cultures are affected by their cultural identities and by the relative standing of their cultures on factors important to the interaction. Variation in how groups deal with this higher-level link affects the quality of interaction and the potential for group effectiveness. Thus, Chao's model provides a basis to guide research on intercultural team interactions.

Bell and Kozlowski (2002) distinguish virtual teams from conventional face-to-face teams based on two features: (a) spatial distance—virtual team members are dispersed in space; and (b) technological mediation of information, data, and personal communication—virtual team members interact via advanced communications media. These two features enable diverse expertise—located worldwide—to be combined into a team that transcends the usual boundaries of space and time. As organizations and work continue to evolve, new types of work teams will be created and classified.

The Role of Typology in Understanding Teams

Although there is value in characterizing distinctions across different types of teams, description and classification are merely the first steps in comprehending the implications of such differences for effective team functioning. In our view, it is more useful to focus on the dimensions that underlie apparent differences in team classifications or typologies.

Surfacing such dimensions is key to identifying the varying factors or contingencies that determine the effectiveness of different types of teams. Identifying these contingencies will better enable researchers and practitioners to specify design and operational factors that promote team effectiveness for different teams.

Some scholars have made steps in this direction. Sundstrom et al. (1990), for example, identified three dimensions underlying the categories of their typology: (a) work team differentiation—the degree to which membership is inclusive, variable, or exclusive and the span of the team's life cycle; (b) external integration—the degree to which the team's task is entrained by (i.e., requires synchronization with) organizational pacers external to the team; and (c) work cycles—the general length of the team's task and the degree to which performance episodes are multiple, variable, repeatable, and novel.

Kozlowski et al. (1999) focused directly on dimensions rather than classification, proposing that five features—(a) task, (b) goals, (c) roles, (d) process emphasis, and (e) performance demands—distinguish teams ranging along a simple-to-complex continuum. Complex teams are characterized by (a) tasks that are externally driven, dynamic, and structured by explicit work flows; (b) common goals that necessitate specific individual contributions that may shift over a work cycle; (c) roles that are specified and differentiated such that they required specialized knowledge and skill; (d) a process emphasis that focuses on task-based roles, task interaction, and performance coordination; and (e) performance demands that require coordinated individual performance in real time, the capability to adapt to shifting goals and contingencies, and a capacity to continually improve over time. In contrast, simple teams are characterized by (a) tasks that are internally oriented, static, and unstructured in that they lack explicit work flows; (b) common goals that make no specific demands for individual contributions and that are fixed for the team's life cycle; (c) roles that are unspecified and undifferentiated, such that all team members possess essentially equivalent knowledge and skill; (d) a process emphasis that focuses on social roles, social interaction, normative behavior, and conflict; and (e) minimal performance demands that allow pooled or additive contributions to the group product. Similarly, Bell and Kozlowski (2002) characterized a continuum of team complexity ranging from simple to complex, based on the dimensions of (a) task environment, (b) external coupling, (c) internal coupling, and (d) work flow interdependence. The complex end of the continuum relative to the simple end is defined by tasks that are dynamic as opposed to static, external coupling that is tight rather than loose, and internal coupling that is

synchronous and strong in contrast to asynchronous and weak. Work flow interdependence ranges from complex to simple, as intensive, reciprocal, sequential, and pooled (see Van de Ven et al., 1976).

Looking across the dimensions described previously, we believe that the following features capture most of the unique characteristics that distinguish different team forms:

- The external environment or organizational context in terms of its (a) dynamics and (b) degree of required coupling.
- Team boundary permeability and spanning.
- Member (a) diversity and (b) collocation and spatial distribution.
- Internal coupling requirements.
- Work flow interdependence with its implications for (a) goal, (b) role, (c) process, and (d) performance demands.
- Temporal characteristics that determine the nature of (a) performance episodes and cycles and (b) the team life cycle.

We offer these features as a point of departure for a concerted effort to develop a definitive set of dimensions that characterize key contingencies essential for the effectiveness of different types of teams.

We believe that continuing efforts to better characterize dimensions that distinguish different types of teams can help pay big theoretical dividends. More to the point, we believe that focusing on typology and classification is misguided if such a focus is viewed as an end in itself; there is the danger of reifying classifications and failing to see underlying factors that account for apparent differences. Rather, by surfacing dimensions that distinguish teams, we will be better equipped to identify the critical contingencies relevant to effectiveness for different types of teams. Understanding what factors constrain and influence effectiveness for different types of teams will enable theoretical progress and better targeted interventions. This issue currently represents a major gap in theory and research, substantially limiting our ability to develop meaningful applications and interventions designed to enhance team effectiveness.

TEAM COMPOSITION

Events within teams often reflect the number and type of people who are its members. As a result, considerable research has focused on team composition—the nature and attributes of team members (for a review, see Jackson & Joshi, 2002). Team composition is of research and practical interest because the combination of member attributes can have a powerful influence on team processes and outcomes. A better understanding of such effects will help practitioners to select and construct more effective teams.

Moreland and Levine (1992) categorized team composition research along three dimensions. First, different characteristics of a team and its members can be studied, including size, demographics, abilities and skills, and personalities. Second, the distribution of a given characteristic within a group can be assessed. Measures of central tendency and variability are typically used, but special configurations are sometimes measured as well. Third, different analytical perspectives can be taken toward the composition of a team. Team composition can be viewed as a *consequence* of various social or psychological processes (e.g., socialization), as a *context* that moderates or shapes other behavioral or social phenomena, or as a *cause* that influences team structure, dynamics, or performance.

We review and discuss team composition issues along each of these three dimensions. First, we provide a brief review of research that has focused on different characteristics of teams and their members. Second, we discuss issues relating to levels of conceptualization and analysis in research on team composition. Finally, we discuss some practical implications that can emerge from a better understanding of team composition and its effects on team structure, dynamics, and performance.

Team Size

Researchers have offered recommendations concerning the best size for various types of teams. Katzenbach and Smith (1993) suggested that work teams should contain a dozen or so members, whereas Scharf (1989) suggested that seven was the best size. A variety of other such recommendations are easily found in the literature. Such recommendations are difficult to evaluate because they are often based on personal experiences rather than empirical evidence. However, it is also difficult to determine what constitutes appropriate team size from empirical research. Some research suggests that size has a curvilinear relationship with effectiveness such that having too few or too many members reduces performance (Nieva, Fleishman, & Reick, 1985), whereas other studies have found team size to be unrelated to performance (Hackman & Vidmar, 1970; Martz, Vogel, & Nunamaker, 1992) or have found that increasing team size actually improves performance without limit (Campion, Medsker, & Higgs, 1993).

These differing recommendations and results are probably due to the fact that appropriate team size is contingent on the task and the environment in which the team operates. For example, larger teams may have access to more resources such as time, energy, money, and expertise that may not only facilitate team performance on more difficult tasks but also can provide more slack if environmental conditions worsen (Hill, 1982). However, larger teams can also experience coordination problems that interfere with performance (e.g., Lantané, Williams, & Harkins, 1979) and motivation losses caused by a dispersion of responsibility (Sheppard, 1993). Overall, the question of the optimal group size is a complex one, and future research is needed to determine the impact of team size given specific team contingencies such as the nature of the team task and its consequent internal and external coupling demands.

Demographic

The extent to which team processes and outcomes are influenced by the homogeneity or heterogeneity of team member demographic characteristics has also been the focus of considerable attention, although it is difficult to determine whether team diversity is desirable. Studies have reported that diversity has positive (Bantel, 1994; Gladstein, 1984), negative (Haleblian & Finkelstein, 1993; Jackson et al., 1991; Pelled, Eisenhardt, & Xin, 1999; Wiersema & Bird, 1993), or even no effects on team effectiveness (Campion et al., 1993). These mixed findings have led reviewers to draw different conclusions regarding the effects of diversity: Bettenhausen (1991) concluded that groups composed of similar members perform better than do those composed of dissimilar members, whereas Jackson, May, and Whitney (1995) concluded that diversity tends to have a positive relationship with team effectiveness.

Argote and McGrath (1993) suggested that the effect of diversity on team outcomes is likely to depend on four factors. First, the effects of diversity probably depend on the nature of the team's task. Jackson et al. (1995), for example, concluded that the value of member heterogeneity for team performance is clearest in the domains of creative and intellective tasks. Second, the effects of diversity may depend on the particular outcomes studied. Research seems to suggest that diversity may have a positive effect on performance but a more negative effect on behavioral outcomes such as team member turnover. Third, research has shown that the impact of diversity may vary across time. Watson, Kumar, and Michaelsen (1993), for example, found that homogeneous groups displayed better initial performance than did heterogeneous groups, but these effects dissipated across time, and heterogeneous groups later performed better than more homogenous groups. Finally, the impact of diversity may depend on the attributes on which homogeneity-heterogeneity is assessed. Some research suggests that diversity in demographic characteristics may have negative consequences, but diversity in skills and expertise may have positive effects. Future research needs to examine these factors and how they may constrain or moderate the impact of diversity on team processes and outcomes.

Dispositions and Abilities

In addition to demographic diversity, researchers have also considered team composition effects of constructs like personality and cognitive ability on team effectiveness. Unlike demographic diversity, which is usually directly conceptualized and assessed as a team-level property (homogeneity-heterogeneity), personality and ability are fundamentally individual-level psychological characteristics. Such constructs necessitate models of emergence to guide conceptualization, measurement, and representation at the team level. Many potential representations are possible, including averages, highest or lowest, variance, and even complex configurations. In the absence of an explicit theoretical model of emergence to guide composition, "team personality" or "team ability" (or other such constructs) are of questionable construct validity, and research may yield spurious findings (Kozlowski & Klein, 2000).

Personality

The last decade has witnessed renewed interest in personality that has been extended to teams as researchers have examined the impact of team personality composition on team effectiveness. In general, this research has found a link between aggregate team member personality and team performance (Jackson, 1992a; Moreland & Levine, 1992). Consistent with individual-level research, team-level conscientiousness appears to be a fairly potent positive predictor of team effectiveness (Barrick, Stewart, Neubert, & Mount, 1998; Neuman, Wagner, & Christiansen, 1999; Neuman & Wright, 1999). Although conscientiousness has been most frequently studied, some research suggests that other Big Five personality factors, such as extraversion (Barry & Stewart, 1997) and agreeableness (Neuman & Wright, 1999), may also play a role in determining work team effectiveness.

Although team personality composition appears to be a relatively robust predictor of team effectiveness, research suggests that different compositions may be more or less effective, depending on the task and the amount of member interaction required for effective team performance. Research has found that team-level conscientiousness is more strongly related to effectiveness for performance and planning tasks than it is for creativity and decision-making tasks (Barry & Stewart, 1997; Neuman & Wright, 1999). In contrast, team-level extraversion seems to have a greater impact on team effectiveness for decision-making tasks than it does for performance or planning tasks, possibly because the former involve a greater degree of persuasion and personal influence (Barry & Stewart, 1997; Neuman & Wright, 1999). Similarly, LePine, Colquitt, and Erez (2000) found that team conscientiousness and openness did not predict team decision effectiveness. However, when decision rules were changed to require adaptability, conscientiousness became negative and openness positive predictors of decision effectiveness. Although the mechanisms by which team personality composition influences team performance require further investigation, it is clear that personality composition has important implications for team effectiveness.

Cognitive Ability

Among the factors studied in relation to work team effectiveness, one consistent predictor is team members' collective cognitive ability. Team members' average cognitive ability is related to team performance among military tank crews (Tziner & Eden, 1985), assembly and maintenance teams (Barrick et al., 1998), and service teams (Neuman & Wright, 1999). In addition, LePine, Hollenbeck, Ilgen, and Hedlund (1997) found that the performance of hierarchical decision-making teams was enhanced when both the leader and staff were high in cognitive ability.

A meta-analysis by Devine and Phillips (2000) found a positive relationship between average team cognitive ability and team performance of .19, which increased to .30 when a large outlier study was omitted. Moderator analyses suggested that the relationship between team-level cognitive ability and performance is fairly consistent across information-processing and behavioral tasks. However, team-level cognitive ability exhibited a considerably stronger relationship with team performance for unfamiliar tasks ($r = .36$) versus familiar tasks ($r = .12$), and the strength of the ability-performance relationship differed somewhat, depending on whether the lowest member score was used ($r = .25$) or the team average was utilized ($r = .30$). Although research in this area is promising, continued work is needed to identify those conditions under which team-level cognitive ability has more or less of an impact on team performance.

Theoretical and Empirical Issues

Levels of conceptualization, measurement, and analysis have tended to be either ignored or treated simply in much of the research on team composition. The dominant use of averaging or additive models to guide the aggregation of individual characteristics to the team level suggests the use of simple team tasks or a very limited conceptualization of the compositional construct at the higher level (Kozlowski & Klein, 2000). Such issues are critical for developing a sound understanding how team member attributes combine to form higher-level constructs and must be carefully articulated. Well-defined models of emergence need to guide the representation of individual-level characteristics at the team level. Kozlowski and Klein (2000) provide a differentiated typology of six different emergent processes; this typology was based on contextual constraints and interaction processes and addressed how lower-level phenomena manifest as higher-level phenomena. Such models can assist researchers in determining the most appropriate method for representing lower-level phenomena at higher levels. For example, when emergence is more continuous and linear, averaged or summed values are an appropriate method of representing lower-level phenomena at the team level. However, when emergence is more discontinuous and nonlinear, it is more appropriate to use dispersion or configural models to capture the emergent characteristic of the team. For example, conceptualizing team composition as a pattern of different but compatible personalities represents the use of a configural model (e.g., Stewart & Barrick, in press).

There has also been a relative lack of attention to the latent constructs that underlie variables of interest within research on team demographic composition. As a result, it is often difficult to determine precisely how or why variables such as team members' age, tenure, or demographics influence team processes and outcomes. Recent research on team personality and cognitive ability composition has placed greater attention on understanding these underlying constructs; however, additional research is needed to identify the mechanisms by which team composition has its effects.

Applied Issues

An understanding of team composition can serve as a valuable tool for selecting and constructing effective teams. Procedures could be designed to produce the optimal blend of employee characteristics (Driskell, Hogan, & Salas, 1987; Heslin, 1964; Jackson, 1992b), including hiring new workers or firing old ones, training current workers, or engaging the services of adjunct workers such as temporary employees or consultants (Klimoski & Jones, 1995; Moreland, Levine, & Wingert, 1996; Stevens & Campion, 1994).

Although past work provides some valuable information about how to manage team composition, researchers have often adopted a more-is-better approach (i.e., the additive model assumption) suggesting that the person with the highest score on a particular attribute (e.g., cognitive ability) or the most skilled individual should be selected for the team. However, recent research suggests that it may be more important to create an appropriate configuration of team member characteristics. For example, research by Stewart and Barrick (in press) suggests that if a team consists of a lot of extraverts, it may be better to hire a less extraverted person or even an introvert. Conversely, if a team has no extraverts, it may be important to hire highly extraverted applicants. To create an appropriate blend of team member characteristics, one will need to know what personality traits currently compose the team and the target team personality configuration before selecting a particular individual. One should also consider the team's task because it may be important to have a homogenous group of team members for some types of tasks and a heterogeneous team composition for others (Neuman & Wright, 1999).

Human resource systems such as selection, training, and performance appraisal must be conceptualized and managed at the team level (Schneider, Smith, & Sipe, 2000) to appropriately address composition issues. Focusing on the individual level alone will not provide the information needed to make effective decisions regarding team composition. Including the team level provides information concerning not only the team's current composition but also the team's tasks and processes that assist in the development of an appropriate combination of team member characteristics for the task at hand.

TEAM FORMATION, SOCIALIZATION, AND DEVELOPMENT

Formation

Teams may be formed anew, whereby all members are new to each other and to the team, or teams with a developmental history may have influxes and outflows of members that affect its composition and character. In either instance, development and newcomer socialization are relevant issues. Socialization has generally been seen as a mechanism for bringing new members into existing teams or groups. With few exceptions, much of this theory and research has focused on the socialization of individuals into the organization and—although that area is theoretically relevant—has paid relatively little attention to the work group or team as central to the socialization process; that is, the vast majority of work on socialization in work settings focuses on organizational influences, but is far less sensitive to the proximal social and work context within which socialization actually takes place. Although socialization is a critical aspect of team maintenance and continuance, we know relatively little about it in the team context.

Development tends to assume the formation of a brand-new team with no prior history. Much of the classic theory in this area also assumes no broader organizational context, work roles, or prescribed interactions. Consider, for example, Tuckman's (1965) classic model of group development, with its sequential stages of forming, storming, norming, and performing. Clinical and therapy groups, which provided the foundation for this model, have no prior history, no broader context, and are almost completely unstructured, save for a common goal: to "get well." Thus, the dominant focus in Tuckman's model is on the group's struggle to create structure to regulate their interpersonal interactions and to finally make progress toward the goal. Although this model—and the many, many others based on it—provides a useful contribution to our understanding of group development for simple teams, it provides little theoretical insight on skill development for work groups. As discussed in the prior section, work teams are subject to variety of structural features that drive interactions and exchanges among members. Interpersonal issues are relevant, but they do not dominate the developmental process; yet, with few exceptions (Gersick, 1988; Kozlowski et al., 1999; McGrath, 1990; Morgan et al., 1993), there are relatively few theories that are specifically targeted on work team development.

Socialization

Existing teams are governed by a relatively stable set of norms, role expectations, and shared systems of knowledge and meaning (e.g., group climate, mental models). These informal structures emerge through social and work-based interactions among members across a group's developmental history. Newcomers present a potential challenge to this stable structure and are thus subject to efforts by group members to assimilate the person to it. At the same time, newcomers are confronted by a novel and ambiguous social and work context. Although they want very much to "fit in" and "learn the ropes" and are generally prepared to accept guidance from the group, they may also seek to have the group accommodate to their needs, values, and capabilities. Thus, work group socialization is a process of mutual influence in which newcomers attempt to reduce uncertainty by learning about the work and group context, guided by group members who facilitate assimilation to existing norms, expectations, and meaning systems; at the same time, newcomers attempt to

exert influence on the group to accommodate to their unique attributes and needs (Anderson & Thomas, 1996; Moreland & Levine, 1982).

We find it interesting that even though researchers clearly recognize the centrality of the work group in the socialization process, the dominant perspective in the literature is characterized by a focus on *organizational* socialization—not on a primary process of *work group* socialization that occurs within a broader and more distal organizational context (Chao, Kozlowski, Major, & Gardner, 1994). Virtually all efforts to identify the relevant content of newcomer socialization make provision for learning about the work group and its social structure (e.g., Chao, O'Leary-Kelly, Wolf, Klein, & Gardner, 1994), but it is merely one part of a broader process. Moreover, early theory and research on organizational socialization can be characterized as accentuating the powerful influence that the organizational context exerted on newcomers in an effort to assimilate them; this was later followed by a shift in perspective that emphasized the proactive role that newcomers play in shaping their own socialization process. Missing is the sense of mutual influence as the group seeks to assimilate the newcomer, and the newcomer endeavors to adapt while seeking accommodation by the group. This lack of attention to mutual influence is a major shortcoming of the socialization literature and means that our knowledge of the process of team socialization is limited. There are, however, some notable exceptions.

Group and Team Socialization

Moreland and Levine (1982) detail a model of group socialization that focuses on membership processes—primarily applicable to autonomous voluntary groups who control their own membership and are not nested in a broader organizational context. Its major focus is on mutual decisions on the part of a newcomer and the group regarding joining, assimilation and accommodation, and continuance or withdrawal of membership. The model spans five phases: investigation, socialization, maintenance, resocialization, and remembrance. Difficulties in assimilation or accommodation may prompt the group to resocialize a newcomer. Resocialization failure leads to lower commitment and exit. Aspects of the model are potentially relevant to team socialization—in particular, its explicit attention to the group as the primary locus of socialization and mutual expectations as drivers of the process. Remarkably, although the model has been elaborated in several papers, it has generated relatively little research attention, and the little research that has been conducted has been limited to ad hoc laboratory groups. Thus, the utility of the model to work team socialization remains to be examined.

Basing their ideas on a focused review of the organizational socialization literature, Anderson and Thomas (1996) present a model that is explicitly focused on work group socialization and the mutual influence of the newcomer and the group on outcomes of the process. Thus, it is an effort to address the neglected issues noted previously. The model spans the socialization phases of anticipation, encounter, and adjustment, identifying potential characteristics of the newcomer and the group that may contribute to socialization as a process of mutual influence and adjustment. Although the model is too recent to have prompted research, the authors provide propositions that may serve as a point of departure for such efforts.

Direct Findings for Work Group Socialization

Although most socialization research has neglected explicit attention to the role of the work group, there are some exceptions; additionally, useful knowledge regarding team socialization can be gleaned from existing research. For example, as one aspect of their study, Chao, Kozlowski, et al. (1994) focused on how the quality of newcomer role development relations with their leader and team influenced role outcomes of ambiguity and conflict, with the role outcomes in turn expected to influence socialization effectiveness. Results indicated that newcomer role development quality predicted role outcomes. Moreover, role outcomes were better predictors of socialization effectiveness than were organizational tactics, especially over time. Chao, Kozlowski, et al. concluded that these findings supported the primacy of the work group—not the organization—as the locus of socialization.

Similarly, Major, Kozlowski, Chao, and Gardner (1995) examined the potential effects of leader and team relations on ameliorating the negative effects of unmet newcomer expectations on socialization outcomes. "Reality shock" is one of the major challenges for newcomers as they confront the unpleasant fact that their work expectations are largely unmet. An inability to resolve reality shock yields low commitment and satisfaction and generally leads to withdrawal. Major et al. reasoned that positive relationships with work group members would moderate the effects of reality shock, weakening its relationship with negative outcomes. They reported support for their proposition and concluded that high-quality interactions with work group members provided an important support for effective socialization.

Indirect Findings for Work Group Socialization

Results from research on socialization practices indicates that newcomers view supervisors and work group members as available and helpful socialization agents who are far more helpful than are formal socialization practices (Louis, Posner, & Powell, 1983). Research on newcomer information acquisition also indicates the importance of work group members in the processes of learning, understanding, and adjusting. Ostroff and Kozlowski (1992) hypothesized that newcomers have to resolve issues of their fit in the work group before they can turn attention to task and role issues. In support, the researchers reported that newcomers focused on acquiring group knowledge early on, later shifting to task and role issues. Organizational factors were of lowest priority. They also found that supervisors and social learning in the group context were the most effective newcomer strategies for learning about the role and group. Perhaps most important was that they reported that increasing newcomer reliance on the supervisor over time as a source of information was related to increases in newcomer satisfaction, commitment, and adjustment over time.

Role of the Group in Socialization

The previously reviewed research clearly indicates that group leaders and members are key players in newcomer socialization. Unfortunately, however, this research provides little insight about group characteristics and their precise role in the socialization process. Moreland and Levine (1989) provide several suggestions in this regard. For example, they suggest that groups with a longer developmental history present a more difficult socialization challenge to the newcomer because such groups will demand more assimilation and will resist accommodation efforts. There is some support for this notion. Katz (1982) reported that younger research and development (R&D) groups communicated more with outsiders and were more open to new ideas; older groups were more insular. Similarly, groups that are typified by stable membership present a more difficult socialization environment relative to groups with frequent personnel inflows and outflows. Furthermore, groups that are more successful are more likely to be insular, whereas groups experiencing performance problems may be more open to suggestions from newcomers with requisite knowledge and abilities. Groups can also apply deliberate socialization tactics. By controlling recruitment and selection, they can influence the quality of fit, thereby aiding assimilation. By encapsulating the newcomer—maximizing their time and energy commitment to the group—they tie the newcomer to the group, minimizing alternative commitments and enhancing socialization. There is, however, little solid support for the effectiveness of these tactics in realistic team situations. More theory and research are clearly needed on work team socialization.

Development

Classic Stage Models

Several models describe the developmental stages through which groups pass over their life span. The descriptive characteristics of these models are remarkably parallel to Tuckman's (1965) widely cited model of group development (Kozlowski et al., 1999). Tuckman reviewed the group literature, defined by therapy, T-group, natural, and laboratory group studies and proposed that groups go through the developmental stages of *forming, storming, norming,* and *performing.*

As team members first come together during the formation stage, they cautiously begin to explore the group and attempt to establish some social structure. They attempt to define the group task and to establish how they will accomplish it. As team members realize that defining the task is more difficult than they had expected it to be, they move to the storming stage. Members argue about what actions the group should take. Different factions may form as conflict progresses. As the group finally reconciles competing loyalties and responsibilities, it begins to firmly establish ground rules, roles, and status. During this norming stage, members reduce emotional conflict and become more cooperative, developing a sense of cohesion and common goals. As these normative expectations take hold, the group moves to the performing stage. Members are able to prevent group problems or to work through such problems when they arise. They become closely attached to the team and satisfied with its progress as they more toward their common goal.

Implications for Work Team Development

Although classic stage models of group development provide rich descriptions of social interaction processes, they have tended to focus on the simpler types of teams—those with tasks that have undefined workflows and internally driven processes. Thus, they focus primary attention on the interpersonal ambiguity and conflict that new group members endure as they attempt to create a social hierarchy with common norms to guide interactions among members.

This focus has several implications. First, the models have not been sensitive to the organizational context. When new teams form in organizations, members typically bring socialization and cultural knowledge that reduces much—but not all—of the social uncertainty present at group formation. Second, the models have a limited conceptualization of the task, its contingencies, dynamics, and the temporal constraints these factors set on team activities. The task is often viewed as a single incident of project planning, problem solving, or decision making that is determined by internal group dynamics; external contingencies are not acknowledged. There is no consideration of externally driven task dynamics, including variations in task complexity, difficulty, or tempo, and there is little recognition of multiple task episodes that cycle demands on the team. Third, the focus on unstructured task situations means that the models do not consider the development of task-relevant patterns of interaction and exchange among members that is dictated by work flow structure. Instead, group interaction is driven by interpersonal attractions and conflicts. Thus, the models tend to focus on self-insight and interpersonal processes rather than on specifying the task- and team-relevant knowledge and learning that accrue during development. Fourth, the models are collectively oriented, with the group or team conceptualized as a holistic entity. This is a relevant perspective when member contributions to team outcomes represent simple aggregations. However, when composition to the higher level is represented by more complex patterns, there is a need to better disentangle the individual, dyadic, and team-level contributions. Finally, the models provide only a general description of the particular issues that arise during development, the means by which they are addressed, and the results of the process. Thus, like the socialization literature, much of the literature on team development provides relatively little insight regarding the development of work teams. There are, however, some notable exceptions.

One of the points noted previously and a central theme in this chapter is the need to consider time, its dynamics, and its effects. Work teams are linked to an external context that sets the pace, tempo, and cycles of team activities (Kelly, Futoran, & McGrath, 1990), which may change over time necessitating adaptation; this has important implications for work team development, which is not necessarily a uniform series of fixed stages. Gersick (1988, 1989), for example, observed the developmental processes of 16 project teams (eight field and eight lab) with life cycles ranging from 1 week to 6 months and proposed a two-stage *punctuated equilibrium model* (PEM) of group development. Gersick's key conclusion is that group development is not dictated by a linear progression of stages. Rather, it is linked to an external deadline that paces progress. Early group interactions establish stable norms that pattern group activity though an initial period of inertia. At the halfway point, a significant transformation occurs—the punctuated equilibrium—as groups reorganize to focus on task completion. This model represents an important contribution to our understanding of group development because it acknowledges that the process is influenced by external temporal contingencies in addition to internal factors. It should also be noted that the PEM may be limited to project or problem-solving teams with a single fixed objective and limited life span, although these types of teams do capture a substantial segment of work groups in organizations.

Although the PEM is often regarded as a direct challenge to stage models of development (e.g., Guzzo & Shea, 1992), some scholars view the two perspectives as distinctive, yet complementary. Chang, Bordia, and Duck (in press) contrasted Wheelan's (1994) integrative model of group development—a classic stage model—with Gersick's PEM. Examining 25 student project groups, they concluded that the models are complementary depending on (a) what content is addressed and (b) what unit of analysis is used in regard to time. Content that focused on group processes and structure and more microtiming tended to support linear development, whereas content that focused on the groups' approach to their task and more macrotiming tended to support the PEM. These findings suggest that neither perspective alone is an adequate account of team development—we need broader, more integrative models.

Similarly, Morgan et al. (1993) formulated a model of work team development that integrated the Tuckman and Gersick models. The model was designed to apply to work teams operating in complex environments in which coordination is a central aspect of effective performance. Assumptions of the model are that (a) team development processes shift over time, (b) shifting processes form reciprocal process-outcome links such that intermediate outcomes serve as inputs for subsequent processes, and (c) team members acquire contextually grounded skills that lead to improvements in team effectiveness over time. This integration of Gersick and Tuckman yields a model with nine stages of development: preforming, forming, storming, norming, performing-I, reforming (punctuated equilibrium transition), performing-II, conforming, and de-forming. Another key feature of the model is the distinction made between task work (task-relevant knowledge and skill development) and teamwork (knowledge and skills that enhance the quality of team member interactions—i.e., coordination, cooperation, communication) that must be integrated in parallel as a central aspect of the developmental process. Research by Glickman et al. (1987) provides general support for the primary assumptions of the model and, in particular, the distinction between task work and teamwork skills and their necessary integration for team effectiveness.

More recently, Kozlowski and colleagues (1999) have proposed a normative model of *team compilation* that integrates team development with a performance perspective—that is, team performance and adaptability at any given point in time are viewed as dynamic consequences of a continuous developmental process. There are three key conceptual features of the theory. First, temporal dynamics are viewed in terms of both linear and cyclical time, representing the effects

of developmental processes and task episodes, respectively. Team capabilities improve developmentally prompting transition to more advanced phases of skill acquisition. Within a phase, variations in task episodes or cycles provide opportunities for learning and skill acquisition (see also Kozlowski, Gully, McHugh, et al., 1996; Kozlowski, Gully, Salas, & Cannon-Bowers, 1996). Second, developmental transitions prompt attention to different *content* that is the focus of new learning, different *processes* by which knowledge and skills are acquired, and different *outcomes* that capture current capabilities. Third, team compilation is viewed as an emergent multilevel phenomenon. Knowledge, skills, and performance outcomes compile successively upwards across focal levels from an individual self-focus to dyadic exchanges to an adaptive team network.

The model is formulated around four phase transitions, each with a distinct focal level and content, process, and outcome specifications. In Phase 1, individuals are focused on resolving their fit in social space through a socialization process; this yields outcomes of interpersonal knowledge and team orientation, providing a foundation for shared norms, goals, and climate perceptions. In Phase 2, individuals focus on acquiring task knowledge via skill acquisition processes with outcomes of task mastery and self-regulation skills. In Phase 3, the level shifts to dyads that must negotiate role relationships, identifying key role sets and routines to guide task-driven interactions. In Phase 4, the level shifts to the team as it creates a flexible network of role interdependencies that will enable continuous improvement and adaptability to novel and challenging demands. Although there are no direct tests of the model, it is synthesized from a substantial and diverse literature. DeShon, Kozlowski, Schmidt, Wiechmann, and Milner (2001) provide preliminary support for the basic proposition that developmental shifts in focal level from individual to team contribute to team performance adaptability.

Research Implications and Application Issues

Socialization

At no other point are employees as malleable and open to guidance as they are during their initial encounter with the organization and their work group. This provides an obvious opportunity to have a long-term influence on the shaping of new employees that has not gone unnoticed by organizations. Indeed, the vast majority of organizations make some formal effort to socialize newcomers to inculcate norms, goals, and values via training, induction, and orientation programs (Anderson, Cunningham-Snell, & Haigh, 1996). Yet the available evidence suggests that these formal efforts have only moderate and transitory effects, which are swamped by the more intense and proximal socialization processes that occur within work groups (Anderson & Thomas, 1996; Chao, Kozlowski, et al., 1994).

We know that team leaders and work group members play a critical role in newcomer socialization. Given this clear impact, some researchers have suggested that it may be a useful strategy to train team leaders and group members to be more effective socialization agents (Ostroff & Kozlowski, 1992). To our knowledge, no such efforts have been pursued and evaluated. Thus, for the most part, the effectiveness of this more local process is accidental, dependent on the mutual proaction of newcomers and their work groups. This issue has clear application potential that has not been sufficiently explored and leveraged.

Although the importance of the work group as a key agent in socialization is recognized implicitly by the literature, it has largely neglected the importance of newcomer socialization *to the group*. It is in the work group's vested interest to socialize newcomers. It helps to maintain existing norms, expectations, and shared systems of meaning; it enhances social and work interactions; and it is essential to long-term group functioning. Thus, although we know how and what newcomers try to learn from work group members, we know far less about the precise role of the group in the process. What group characteristics influence the process and how? What tactics do groups use to prompt assimilation and resist accommodation? What are the effects of different group characteristics and tactics—in interaction with newcomer characteristics and tactics—on the socialization process, group functioning, and group effectiveness? These are critical research questions that for the most part remain to be explored in future research. We believe that progress on elucidating work group socialization will necessitate another shift in research perspective in the socialization literature, one that takes a contextual approach—focusing on the newcomer in the group context, one that is sensitive to multiple levels—newcomers, dyadic relationships with group members, and the group as a whole—and one that models the emergent effects of newcomer assimilation and group accommodation processes on group responses across levels and over time.

Development

Like that of socialization, the formative period of team development offers an unprecedented opportunity to shape the nature and functioning of new teams. Unfortunately, unlike socialization, in which there is a growing empirical foundation, relatively little research addresses work team development. What we know about the process is largely based on extrapolations from case studies examining other types of teams (Tuckman, 1965) or on the relatively few observational studies of work team development—studies that tend to be based on very few teams. For the most part, the work team development process remains largely unexplored.

In some ways, the area of team development may be paralleling and lagging its socialization counterpart. Two decades ago, the socialization area was typified by classic descriptive theories that were primarily focused on voluntary groups. Empirical research was spotty and not of the highest quality. Then there was a period of theory development specifically targeted on organizational socialization; these theories subsequently stimulated many empirical advances. Today, socialization is a vibrant area of theory development and research. The team development area is like socialization was two decades ago. We are beginning to see the creation of new theories specifically focused on work team development that move beyond the classic descriptive models. Hopefully, these and other new theories will stimulate rigorous empirical research on work team development. For example, further research to validate and extend Gersick's model (1988) is needed. If the punctuated equilibrium is a universal phenomenon in project groups and other types of teams, surely interventions to accelerate the initial unproductive phase can be created to help improve the efficiency and effectiveness of the team development process. Similarly, research to validate the content, processes, and outcomes specified for the phases of team development by Kozlowski et al. (1999) would provide a foundation for creating interventions that promote team development at all stages of a team life cycle. For now, however, the process of team development—and its resulting quality—is largely taken as a matter of faith; leaders and teams are expected to muddle through and figure it out. From an applied perspective, one cannot help but marvel at the magnitude of the lost opportunity to influence long-term team effectiveness.

TEAM EFFECTIVENESS, PROCESSES, AND ENHANCEMENTS

From an organizational psychology perspective, team effectiveness is the core focus of theory and research on teams. All topics addressed in this chapter bear on team effectiveness in one way or another. There are literally thousands of articles addressing this topic—far too many for us to capture. Our intent, therefore, is to briefly characterize key aspects of models of team effectiveness and then to focus primary attention on those topics that uniquely distinguish the organizational approach from that of its progenitors—that is, on processes relevant to work-driven team member interactions, the nature of team performance, and interventions designed to enhance team processes and team performance.

Team Effectiveness

Most models of team effectiveness begin where most models of team development end. Models of team effectiveness generally assume mature teams that have completed a formative developmental process. Most models of team effectiveness are at least loosely formulated around an input-process-outcome (IPO) framework posited by McGrath (1964); inputs are the primary cause of processes that in turn mediate the effect of inputs on outcomes. *Inputs* represent various resources available to the team both internally (e.g., composition of knowledge, skills, and abilities, personalities, demographics, group structure, team design) and externally (e.g., rewards, training, organizational climate) at multiple levels (e.g., individual, group, organization). *Processes* represent mechanisms that inhibit or enable the ability of team members to combine their capabilities and behavior. Although the small group literature has generally focused on dysfunctional processes that yield process losses (Steiner, 1972), the focus of team effectiveness is on synergies that produce process gains (Hackman, 1987). At a global level, examples include coordination, cooperation, and communication (Tannenbaum, Beard, & Salas, 1992). *Outcomes* represent criteria to assess the effectiveness of team actions. *Team effectiveness* is generally conceived as multifaceted, with an emphasis on both internal (i.e., member satisfaction, team viability) and external (i.e., productivity, performance) criteria (Hackman, 1987). In practice, team effectiveness is broadly defined and assessed in various ways. It therefore lacks the precision of a theoretical construct; one must look to its specification for particular types of teams to determine its grounded meaning (Goodman et al., 1987). Space precludes an examination of specific models. Good exemplars, however, include Gladstein (1984), Hackman (1987), and Tannenbaum et al. (1992).

Relative to models of team development, team effectiveness models are more static in nature; this is due in large part to the assumed causal linkage inherent in the IPO heuristic and to the way that process is represented—by a box. Theorists do acknowledge linear time (McGrath, 1964), reciprocal linkages (Hackman, 1987), and feedback loops (Tannenbaum et al., 1992) to capture different temporal dynamics. Nevertheless, effectiveness criteria are generally treated as retrospective summaries, and designs to evaluate team effectiveness models tend to be based on cross-sectional, static data (Goodman et al., 1987). Time is relatively unappreciated in most perspectives on team effectiveness (Kozlowski et al., 1999). McGrath's (1991) time-interaction-performance (TIP) model is a rare exception in this regard.

Although the IPO framework lends structure to many models of team effectiveness, thereby creating a substantial degree of similarity across models, there are also some important differences. One key difference worth highlighting concerns whether processes are caused by input factors (i.e., mediators) or whether they are better conceptualized as contingencies (i.e., moderators) that affect the input-to-output link. The former point of view is more representative of the small group research perspective and is a major reason why that tradition has tended to focus on process losses that stem from natural patterns of group interaction (e.g., Steiner, 1972). In contrast, the latter point of view is more representative of a normative approach that conceptualizes processes as mechanisms that enable the group to fit patterns of interaction to team task design and work flows (e.g., Hackman, 1987). This latter perspective is interventionist in orientation and—whether it does or does not explicitly conceptualize processes as moderators—seeks to specify appropriate patterns of interaction and exchange and to intervene through training, leadership, or other techniques to improve the fit of team processes with task-driven requirements to enhance team effectiveness (e.g., Hackman, 1987; Kozlowski, Gully, McHugh, et al., 1996; Kozlowski et al., 1999; Kozlowski, Gully, Salas, et al., 1996; Tannenbaum et al., 1992); this naturally raises the question of what process mechanisms enable team effectiveness.

Team Processes

Just as in the effectiveness area, there is an extensive literature on team processes, the concept itself is so broadly defined as to be ill defined, and there is little convergence on a core set of processes. Much of the small-group literature primarily addresses "natural" group processes that unfold in voluntary groups that have no broader embedding context (i.e., the organization) and no task-driven interdependencies; hence, the focus on interpersonal processes involved in group attraction (e.g., cohesion) and divisiveness (e.g., conflict). Although such processes are certainly of relevance to work teams, other process mechanisms are more relevant to fitting team member interactions to task work flows. To organize our review of team processes, we focus on cognitive, affective-motivational, and behavioral mechanisms.

Cognitive Constructs and Mechanisms

Three primary cognitive mechanisms are represented in the literature: team mental models, transactive memory, and team learning. *Team mental models* are team members' shared, organized understanding and mental representation of knowledge about key elements of the team's task environment (Klimoski & Mohammed, 1994). Four content domains underlying team mental models have been proposed (Cannon-Bowers, Salas, & Converse, 1993): (a) equipment model—knowledge of equipment and tools used by the team; (b) task model—understanding about the work that the team is to accomplish, including its goals or performance requirements and the problems facing the team; (c) member model—awareness of team member characteristics, including representations of what individual members know and believe and their skills, preferences, and habits; and (d) teamwork model—what is known or believed by team members with regard to what are appropriate or effective processes.

Related to team mental models but at a much higher level of generality are conceptualizations of *team climate*. Team climate represents group-level shared perceptions of important contextual factors that affect group functioning and group outcomes via mediating climate perceptions. For example, Hofmann and Stetzer (1996) have demonstrated that team safety climate affects team safety behaviors and outcomes. Similarly, Anderson and West (1998) have developed the Team Climate Inventory as a tool to improve team innovation. Variations in the extent to which climate is shared at the team level has been shown to affect its link to team outcomes (González-Romá, Peiró, & Tordera, in press).

Team coherence (Kozlowski, Gully, McHugh, et al., 1996) is another variant of the team mental model construct. The main difference is that coherence does not assume that team members share all knowledge identically; rather, some knowledge specific to individuals is different but compatible or complementary. Team coherence is presumed to form on the basis of developmental processes that unfold over time, shared experiences, and leader facilitation. Complementary cognition and behavior—along with shared affect and climate perceptions—provide a foundation for essential teamwork capabilities. When a team is guided by a shared comprehension of its task situation and its corresponding goals, strategies, and role links, it is able to adapt to task variations and to maintain synchronicity without explicit directives (Kozlowski, Gully, McHugh, et al., 1996). This sharing represents an integration of task work and teamwork capabilities.

The general thesis of the shared mental model literature and its variants is that team effectiveness will improve if members have an appropriate shared understanding of the task, team, equipment, and situation (e.g., Cannon-Bowers et al., 1993; see March 2001 issue of *Journal of Organizational Behavior* for articles on shared cognition). Empirical research, however, has lagged behind work on conceptual

development (Mohammed & Dumville, 2001). Some early research used team mental models as a post hoc explanation for observed performance differences among teams, although more recent research has measured the construct more directly. For example, Mathieu, Heffner, Goodwin, Salas, and Cannon-Bowers (2000) examined the effect of shared mental convergence on team processes and performance using two-person, undergraduate teams performing a PC-based flight-combat simulation. Results indicated that teamwork and task work mental models related positively to team process and performance and that team processes fully mediated the relationship between shared mental models and performance. Minionis, Zaccaro, and Perez (1995) used concept maps to examine shared knowledge among team members in a computer-simulated tank exercise. Results indicated that shared mental models enhanced performance on collective tasks requiring member interdependence but did not affect tasks that could be completed without coordinated action. Using a similar paradigm, Marks, Zaccaro, and Mathieu (2000), indicated that the quality of team mental models positively influenced communication processes and performance. Thus, although empirical support is limited, emerging findings support the general thesis that appropriate team mental models have positive effects on team processes and effectiveness.

These research findings suggest that the development of team mental models is a promising leverage point for interventions to improve team effectiveness. Several methods for fostering the development of team mental models have been proposed, including team planning (Stout, Cannon-Bowers, Salas, & Milanovich, 1999), computer-based instruction (Smith-Jentsch, Milanovich, Reynolds, & Hall, 1999), and team self-correction training (Blickensderfer, Cannon-Bowers, & Salas, 1997). For example, team self-correction training involves the following elements: (a) event review, (b) error identification, (c) feedback exchange, and (d) planning for the future. Team self-correction can be enhanced through training in skills such as providing feedback, situational awareness, and assertiveness. Similarly, Kozlowski and colleagues (Kozlowski, Gully, McHugh, et al., 1996; Kozlowski, Gully, Salas, et al., 1996) posit that leaders can play a central role in developing team coherence by leading the team through an iterative four-step *learning cycle* that makes use of (a) goal setting, (b) performance monitoring, (c) error diagnosis, and (d) process feedback. Providing support for these perspectives, Marks et al. (2000) enhanced team mental models with leader prebriefs regarding effective strategies to use. Smith-Jentsch, Zeisig, Acton, and McPherson (1998) also used structured leader pre- and debriefs to enhance team mental models and performance.

Transactive memory is a group-level shared system for encoding, storing, and retrieving information—a set of individual memory systems that combines knowledge possessed by particular members with shared awareness of who knows what (Wegner, 1986; Wegner, Giuliano, & Hertel, 1985). It was introduced to explain how intimate relationships (i.e., dating couples) foster the development of shared memory. The development of transactive memory involves communicating and updating information each partner has about the areas of the other's knowledge. In essence, each partner cultivates the other as an external memory aid and in so doing becomes part of a larger system. The application of the concept to work teams involves a similar logic. Each team member keeps current on who knows what, channels incoming information to the appropriate person, and has a strategy for accessing the information (Mohammed & Dumville, 2001). In addition to knowing who is the expert in different knowledge areas, transactive memory also involves storing new information with individuals who have matching expertise and accessing relevant material from others in the system (Wegner, 1986, 1995).

Transactive memory is presumed to offer teams the advantage of cognitive efficiency. Through the encoding and information allocation processes, individual memories become progressively more specialized and are fashioned into a differentiated collective memory that is useful to the group. The knowledge specialization that individuals develop within a transactive memory system reduces cognitive load, provides access to an expanded pool of expertise, and decreases redundancy of effort (Hollingshead, 1998b). On the downside, however, the complexity of transactive memory can create confusion—especially when expertise is in dispute and important information falls through the cracks (Wegner, 1986). There is also the potential problem of time lags to acquire needed information. When performance is time critical, such lags are likely to adversely affect team effectiveness.

Like team mental models, empirical research on transactive memory lags behind theoretical development. Because the concept was introduced to explain the behavior of intimate couples, most research has examined dyads (e.g., Hollingshead, 1998a, 1998b). There is some work addressing transactive memory in work groups. Liang, Moreland, and Argote (1995) trained undergraduates to assemble a radio either individually or in groups. Trainees were later tested either with their original group or in a newly formed group. Evidencing stronger transactive memory systems, members of groups trained together specialized in remembering different aspects of the task, coordinated behaviors more effectively, and displayed greater trust in each other's expertise. Moreover, the effects of group training on task performance were mediated by the operation of transactive memory. Moreland (2000) conducted a follow-up using a similar design and task. Transactive memory was measured more directly through the complexity of group members' beliefs about one another's radio expertise, and the agreement and accuracy of those beliefs. Lewis (2000) has begun to validate field measures and to establish the link between transactive memory and team performance in organizational settings.

Although this area is still in its infancy, some research and practical recommendations can be offered. From a research perspective, most work on transactive memory has been conducted with couples in the laboratory using contrived tasks. Thus, future research needs to focus on work teams and how transactive memory emerges and is maintained in field contexts (Mohammed & Dumville, 2001). From a practical perspective, the nature of communication media in teams may be important for fostering and maintaining transactive memory. Hollingshead (1998b), for example, found that couples working via a computer conferencing system performed more poorly on a knowledge-pooling task than did couples who worked face-to-face. Those results and a follow-up suggest that both nonverbal and paralinguistic communication play an important role in the retrieval of knowledge in transactive memory systems. Finally, another line of research suggests that training intact teams may be useful for developing transactive memory systems (Moreland, 2000; Moreland, Argote, & Krishnan, 1998).

Team learning refers to relatively permanent changes in the knowledge of an interdependent set of individuals associated with experience and can be distinguished conceptually from individual learning. Argote, Gruenfeld, and Naquin (1999), for example, found that skilled individual learners will not necessarily result in a team that learns collectively. Edmonson's (1999) model of team learning suggests that psychological safety—a shared belief that the team is safe for interpersonal risk taking—contributes to team learning behaviors such as seeking feedback, sharing information, experimenting, asking for help, and talking about errors. These behaviors are then presumed to facilitate performance by allowing the team to shift directions as situations change and to discover unexpected implications of team actions.

Very little research has examined team learning. Argote, Insko, Yovetich, and Romero (1995) examined the effects of turnover and task complexity on group learning in a laboratory. They reported a group learning curve: The performance of groups making origami birds increased significantly over six periods, with the performance increase occurring at a decreasing rate. Turnover and task complexity were detrimental to performance, and the differences between turnover and no-turnover groups as well as between simple and complex task groups were amplified as groups gained experience over time. Edmonson (1999) examined team learning in an organizational context, reporting that team psychological safety positively affected learning behaviors, which in turn positively affected team performance. Cannon and Edmondson (2000) found that learning-oriented beliefs promoted group performance and that effective coaching, clear direction, and a supportive work context were antecedents of group learning.

Although this work is still in its formative stage, some research and practical recommendations may be noted. From a research perspective, much of the empirical work is weak. First—and most critically—learning or knowledge is rarely assessed directly. Instead, team learning is assumed from changes in team performance, behavior, or both. Thus, there is a clear need for research to directly measure changes in both individual and team knowledge, to clearly distinguish collective knowledge from individual knowledge, and to separate team learning from other team cognitive constructs (i.e., team mental models, transactive memory) and from team performance. Until these issues are addressed, the standing of team learning as a meaningful and useful construct remains murky. A second and related limitation is that many of the variables examined as having an impact on team learning such as turnover, may have impacts on team performance apart from affecting team learning. In other words, although turnover may affect the "collective" knowledge of the team, it also may influence communication patterns, induce socialization efforts, affect team mental models, and so forth, which may ultimately impact team performance. Thus, it is important for researchers to demonstrate that variables such as turnover and task complexity have an impact directly on team learning. Finally, besides Edmonson's work, there has been little effort to specify the process by which team learning occurs. What are the conditions that facilitate team learning? How is the process different from individual learning? How does team learning emerge from individual learning? There are levels of analysis issues that need to be explicitly addressed to better understand whether the process of learning is similar or different at the individual and team levels (Kozlowski & Klein, 2000).

Affective and Motivational Constructs and Mechanisms

There are four primary team process constructs or mechanisms that can be classified as affective, affectively related, or motivational in nature: (a) cohesion, (b) collective mood or group emotion, (c) collective efficacy, and (d) conflict and divisiveness. We address each of these processes in turn.

Team researchers have offered multiple definitions of *cohesion*. Festinger (1950) defined cohesiveness as "the resultant of all the forces acting on the members to remain in the group" (p. 274). Goodman et al. (1987) defined cohesion as the commitment of members to the group's task. Evans and Jarvis (1980) concluded that "member attraction to the group" (p. 360) is the most common definition of cohesion. Mixed results for the effects of cohesion on performance, however, have led researchers to suggest that it may be multidimensional. Gross and Martin (1952) described cohesion in terms of two underlying dimensions—task cohesion and interpersonal cohesion. Task cohesion is defined as a group's shared commitment or attraction to the group task or goal; it is thought to increase commitment to the task and to increase individual effort by group members on the task. Interpersonal cohesion is defined as the group members' attraction to or liking of the group (Evans & Jarvis, 1980). Interpersonal cohesion allows groups to have less inhibited communication and to effectively coordinate their efforts.

Research findings tend to support the multidimensional view. For example, a meta-analysis by Mullen and Copper (1994) distinguished three types of cohesion: (a) interpersonal cohesion, (b) task cohesion, and (c) group pride. They concluded that task cohesion is the critical element of group cohesion when the cohesion-performance relationship is examined and that interpersonal cohesion might do little more than cause members to exert only as much effort as required to remain in the group. Zaccaro and Lowe (1988) found that only task cohesion was important for an additive task; interpersonal cohesion had no impact. On a disjunctive task, however, Zaccaro and McCoy (1988) found that the best group performance occurred when groups had both high levels of task cohesion and interpersonal cohesion.

Although it has been observed that a cohesive group may engage its energies in high performance *or* its restriction (Seashore, 1954), most empirical research has supported a positive relationship between cohesion and group performance across a wide variety of team types (Evans & Dion, 1991; Greene, 1989; Hambrick, 1995; Katzenbach & Smith, 1993; Mullen & Copper, 1994; Smith et al., 1994). However, several important issues remain to be firmly resolved with respect to the effects of cohesion on team effectiveness. First, the relative impacts of task and interpersonal cohesion may depend on the effectiveness outcome being examined. For example, Mullen and Copper (1994) found that task cohesion had the largest impact on team performance, presumably because it increases task commitment. In contrast, Barrick et al. (1998) found that social cohesion positively affected ratings of team viability. Second, task type may operate as a moderator of cohesion effects. Gully, Devine, and Whitney (1995) suggested that cohesive groups perform well on interdependent tasks because they can coordinate better, whereas coordination is unimportant for more independent tasks. Research supports this suggestion and has found that cohesion has less of an effect when the team task is additive. In fact, some researchers have suggested that cohesion can be detrimental to additive tasks because it partially focuses group effort onto social development rather than on concentration just on the task (Lott & Lott, 1965).

Two practical recommendations can be offered for enhancing team cohesion. First, it may be important to have the right mix of individuals to enhance team cohesion. Barrick et al. (1998) found that teams high in extraversion and emotional stability had higher levels of social cohesion. Second, clear norms and goals may help teams to develop both task and interpersonal cohesion, although it is difficult to know precisely the direction of this relationship. Thus, using selection to manage group composition and team development to inculcate norms and goals may be useful ways to establish cohesive groups.

Collective mood or *group emotion* captures the idea of group affective tone (e.g., George, 1990). Barsade and Gibson (1998) argue that two approaches—top-down and bottom-up—can be used to understand group emotion. The top-down approach views the group as a whole and leads researchers to examine how the feeling and behaviors of individuals arise from group dynamics. It is characterized by four streams of research that treats group emotion as (a) powerful forces that dramatically shape individual emotional response (e.g., psychological effects of crowds); (b) social norms that prescribe emotional feelings and expression (e.g., sets of socially shared norms about how individuals should feel and how they should express those feelings in particular situations); (c) the interpersonal glue that keeps groups together (e.g., group cohesion); and (d) a window to viewing a group's maturity and development (e.g., group emotions have been used to understand the temporal development of groups). The bottom-up approach examines the ways in which individual level emotions combine at the team level to influence outcomes and is represented by three research foci: (a) mean-level affect, (b) affective homogeneity-heterogeneity, and (c) the effects of minimum-maximum team member affect on the group.

Shaw (1976) suggested that there is consistent evidence that group effectiveness, cohesiveness, morale, group motivation, and communication efficiency are positively related to the composition of such individual-level attributes as adjustment, emotional control, and emotional stability and negatively related to such attributes as depressive tendencies, neuroticism, paranoid tendencies, and pathology. Some researchers have suggested that affective homogeneity is beneficial because research has shown that similarity between individuals creates attraction (Schneider, 1987). Similar to the effects of group composition, it has been argued that teams with members who are more similar affectively will be more comfortable with each others' interpersonal interactions, thereby generating more cooperation, trust, social integration, and cohesion. These effects in turn should positively influence group outcomes. For example, George (1990) reported that positive and negative dispositional affectivity within groups related to group-level positive and negative affective tones, respectively. Her findings indicated that group-level positive affective tone is negatively related to group absenteeism, whereas group-level negative affective tone is associated with lower levels of prosocial behavior. Barsade, Ward, Turner, and Sonnenfeld (2000) examined the dispositional positive affective similarity among members of senior management teams and found that affective similarity has a positive effect on group outcomes. On the other hand, some group composition research has shown that affective heterogeneity can be beneficial for some outcomes such as creativity (Jackson, 1992b). Barsade and Gibson (1998) suggest that it may be good when the affective qualities of individuals complement one another (e.g., pessimist and optimist, low energy and high energy, etc.). Finally, it may be possible to take the idea of minority influence and examine it from an affective perspective. Barsade (1998) suggests that a single person can have a strong influence on group affect. For example, a person who has strong dispositional negative affect may infect the team with his or her negativity and the team's mood may become much more negative than would be expected from its mean-level dispositional affect.

Although the ideas regarding the effects of group emotion on team effectiveness are provocative, several important issues need to be resolved. First, more empirical support is needed. Most of Barsade's ideas are drawn from research on group composition and other topics. Barsade draws parallels suggesting that similar effects may occur when the compositional variable of interest is affect. However, aside from a few empirical studies, most of these issues remain unexamined. Research is clearly needed. Second, Barsade and Gibson (1998) make clear reference to top-down and bottom-up levels of analysis issues. It is important for research to address these issues with precision to better understand the impact of group-level affect on individual-level variables and vice versa (Kozlowski & Klein, 2000).

The potential practical implications of this work are tempered by the need for more basic research. For example, although there is some support for a relationship between dispositional affect and job skills (see Staw, Sutton, & Pelled, 1994, for a review), the research is not yet specific enough to be able to determine how this would transfer across different group contexts. Such research is necessary to determine the most effective ways of influencing group outcomes through affect. Is it best to control group affect by establishing norms, or will it be more effective to select team members based on affective individual differences? Similarly, managers may need to influence the impact of maximum and minimum group members because these members—through contagion—can have a strong influence on the affect of the group; or there may be a need to manage affective heterogeneity or homogeneity. Selection as a means to manage group composition may be a useful tool in this regard. However, far more research will have to be conducted before there is a sufficient foundation for specific practical recommendations.

Bandura's (1997) concept of *collective efficacy* is defined as a group's shared belief in its own collective ability to organize and execute courses of action required to produce given levels of attainment. Zaccaro, Blair, Peterson, and Zazanis (1995, p. 309) defined collective efficacy as "a sense of collective competence shared among members when allocating, coordinating, and integrating their resources as a successful, concerted response to specific situational demands." Shea and Guzzo (1987, p. 335) defined a similar construct, called *group potency,* as "the collective belief of a group that it can be effective." Although many scholars view these two constructs as similar, Guzzo, Yost, Cambell, and Shea (1993) asserted that collective efficacy is task specific and group potency is a more general shared belief about group effectiveness across multiple tasks. It is generally presumed that a well-developed structure and interactive or coordinative task processes are necessary or at least a sufficient condition for shared efficacy beliefs to develop (Paskevich, Brawley, Dorsch, & Widmeyer, 1999). In other words, there needs to be a common foundation to foster shared judgments of future effectiveness. Similar to individual-level efficacy, collective efficacy is hypothesized to influence what a group chooses to do, how much effort it will exert in accomplishing its goal, and what its persistence will be in the face of difficulty or failure (Bandura, 1986).

Some of the initial research examining the effects of collective efficacy has focused on physical tasks and the performance of sports teams. For example, Hodges and Carron (1992) found that triads high in collective efficacy improved their performance on a muscular endurance task following a failure experience, whereas triads low in collective efficacy experienced a performance decrement. In the field, Feltz and Lirgg (1998) found that ice hockey teams with higher levels of collective efficacy performed better. Similar results have been reported for work teams. Virtually all the studies that have examined this issue have found a positive relationship between collective efficacy and work team effectiveness

(e.g., Campion et al., 1993; Edmondson, 1999; Hyatt & Ruddy, 1997). Furthermore, a recent meta-analysis by Gully, Joshi, Incalcaterra, and Beaubein (in press) examining 256 effect sizes from 67 empirical studies concluded that team efficacy is a strong predictor of team performance ($\rho = .41$).

There are three important issues that need to be addressed by continuing research on collective efficacy: (a) levels of analysis concerns in measurement, (b) elucidation of the underlying process, and (c) examination of potential contextual moderators. First, Gist (1987) suggested three methods of assessing collective efficacy: (a) aggregating individual perceptions of *self*-efficacy, (b) averaging individuals' perceptions of *collective* efficacy, or (c) using consensual group responses to a single questionnaire. The third approach has been criticized because it ignores the variability that exists when beliefs are not shared (Bandura, 1997). A fourth approach, suggested by Lindsley, Brass, and Thomas (1995), has individual members estimate the group's belief that it can perform a specific task that contrasts with an individual's view about what he or she alone believes the group can do. Levels of analysis theorists recognize these alternatives as distinctly different conceptualizations of the higher-level construct relative to its individual-level origins (e.g., Chan, 1998). Thus, research needs to examine differences in meaning and effect among these different versions of collective efficacy. Second, research is needed to examine exactly how collective efficacy influences team performance. Paskevich et al. (1999) found that certain aspects of multidimensional collective efficacy were related strongly to task-based aspects of cohesion. Through what mechanisms does collectively efficacy develop and have impact? Is it analogous to individual self-efficacy, or are there distinctive mechanisms at the team level? Thus, research needs to elucidate the underlying process and to distinguish individual- and team-level effects. Third, it is likely that contextual factors such as the team task and culture, among others, may affect the link between collective efficacy and team effectiveness. For example, Gibson (1999) found that when task uncertainty was high, work was independent, and collectivism was low, group efficacy was not related to group effectiveness. However, when task uncertainty was low, work was interdependent, and collectivism was high, the relationship between group efficacy and group effectiveness was positive. Moreover, the recent meta-analysis conducted by Gully et al. (in press) reported that work flow interdependence moderated the relationship between team efficacy and team performance such that the relationship was stronger when interdependence was higher ($\rho = .45$) and weaker when interdependence was lower ($\rho = .34$).

Based on the supportive research findings, it is reasonable to assert that high collective efficacy is generally a desirable team characteristic. From a practical perspective, the relevant question is *How can collective efficacy be fostered?* Unfortunately, most research has examined the collective efficacy-performance relationship. There has been much less attention focused on the antecedents of collective efficacy, making it difficult to provide firm recommendations on how managers and organizations can build efficacy at the team level. However, one might assume that many of the factors shown to influence individual-level self-efficacy may be relevant—at least as a point of departure. Thus, future research should consider team-level goal orientation, regulatory focus (DeShon et al., 2001), attributional processes, and success-failure experiences, especially early in a team's life cycle.

Most of the process constructs and mechanisms discussed thus far are oriented toward forces that push team members together. Shared mental models, team learning, cohesion, and collective efficacy are forces for convergence; moreover, the image of a team as a "well-oiled machine" clearly characterizes our interest in those processes that yield synergy and the enhancement of team effectiveness. Yet it is also the case that teams are not always characterized by convergence. Indeed, *divergence, divisiveness,* and *conflict* are common phenomena in teams and organizations (Brown & Kozlowski, 1999). For example, Lau and Murnighan (1998) describe how demographic differences can split a group along "fault lines" into competing and divisive entities. Brown and Kozlowski (1999) present a dispersion theory that focuses on latent constructs (e.g., perceptions, values, beliefs). In their model, convergent and divergent processes can operate simultaneously within and across groups, affecting the nature of emergent collective constructs. Sheremata (2000) argues that groups and organizations are characterized by both centrifugal forces—which push the entity apart—and centripetal forces—which pull it back together.

Conflict is a manifestation of the processes underlying fault lines, divergence, and centrifugal forces. Work teams provide an interpersonal context in which conflict is likely; It must then be managed because it is often detrimental to team performance (Jehn, 1995). Marks et al. (2001) identified two conflict management strategies: (a) preemptive conflict management involves establishing conditions to prevent, control, or guide team conflict before it occurs; whereas (b) reactive conflict management involves working through task, process, and interpersonal disagreements among team members. Most research has focused on reactive conflict management strategies, such as identification of the parameters of conflict between team members, problem solving, compromising, openness and flexibility, and willingness to accept differences of opinion. Although it is more limited, there has been some work on preemptive conflict management such as

establishing norms for cooperative rather than competitive approaches to conflict resolution (Tjosvold, 1985), using team contracts or charters to specify a priori how team members agree to handle difficult situations (Smolek, Hoffman, & Moran, 1999), and developing team rules and norms about the nature and timing of conflict (Marks et al., 2001).

Recent research has shed light on several important aspects of intrateam conflict and provides promise for developing better conflict management in teams. Some research suggests that conflict may be beneficial for teams; it depends on the types of conflict and task. For example, Jehn (1995) found that for groups performing routine tasks, both task conflict (disagreement about task content) and relationship conflict (interpersonal incompatibilities) were detrimental. However, for groups performing nonroutine tasks, only relationship conflict was detrimental. In fact, at times, task conflict was beneficial for groups performing nonroutine tasks. Similarly, Amason (1996) found that higher levels of cognitive conflict (task based) and lower levels of affective conflict (relationship based) led to increased effectiveness in top management teams. Furthermore, research by Simons and Peterson (2000) found that top management teams low in interpersonal trust tended to attribute conflict to relationship-based issues, whereas top management teams high in interpersonal trust tended to attribute conflict to task-based disagreements. Thus, interpersonal trust may be an important variable to consider in managing conflict in teams.

Behavioral Constructs and Mechanisms

There are three primary topics that can be classified as observable process mechanisms that influence team effectiveness: (a) coordination, (b) cooperation, and (c) communication. We acknowledge at the outset that these three concepts are often ill defined and difficult to clearly separate. However, we argue that coordination involves a temporal component that is not an essential part of cooperation or collaboration and that communication is frequently a means to enable coordination or cooperation but is distinguishable from the other two.

Coordination can be defined as activities required to manage interdependencies with the team work flow. The notions of (a) integrating disparate actions together in concert with (b) temporal pacing or entrainment are central to the conceptualization of coordination (Argote & McGrath, 1993). Its essential elements and underlying processes include (Zalesny, Salas, & Prince, 1995) (a) goals (e.g., identifying goals through conflict and resolution), (b) activities and tasks (e.g., mapping goals to activities through leadership), (c) actors-team members (e.g., task assignment), and

(d) interdependencies (e.g., resource allocation, sequencing, and synchronization). Coordination is vital to group effectiveness in situations in which a successful outcome for the entire group is the end result of numerous contributions or efforts by all group members (i.e., integration) and in which successful contributions by one participant are contingent on a correct and timely contribution by another participant (i.e., temporal entrainment).

Several operationalizations have been used to capture team coordination behavior. Assessments consistent with the previously sketched conceptualization have focused on temporal response patterns and sequential analysis (Zalesny et al., 1995), such as using observer ratings of communication patterns (Brannick, Roach, & Salas, 1993), measuring the amount of time one team member waits for another before engaging in a joint effort (Coovert, Campbell, Cannon-Bowers, & Salas, 1995), and using Petri nets and artificial neural networks to model and analyze ongoing processes. This last technique can graph the interactions of team members over time, determining the flow of activities and communication.

Empirical research has established team coordination as an important correlate of team performance. For example, Guastello and Guastello (1998) reported that coordination rules were implicitly learned and then transferred successfully to new rules of similar difficulty. They also noted that team coordination may occur without verbal mediation or leadership actions and that coordination transfer was less positive to a task of greater difficulty. Stout, Salas, and Carson (1994) examined the effects of coordination on two-person team performance on a flight simulation task. Interactive processes that were examined included such behaviors as providing information in advance, making long- and short-term plans, asking for input, assigning tasks, and stepping in to help others. Coordination ratings positively predicted mission performance of the team when individual task proficiency was held constant.

Important concerns relevant to future research on coordination center on issues of levels and time. With respect to levels, it is important to identify coordinated team responses that represent a broad range of disparate and complex patterns of individual action and are not simply the sum of the responses of team members. Similarly, it is important to determine when the responses of individuals are part of a coordinated team response and when they are simply individual responses (Zalesny et al., 1995). Finally, a key issue concerns how to represent interactions of individual team members over time at higher levels of analysis. Recent theoretical work on the nature of emergent constructs—how higher-level phenomena emerge from the characteristics and interactions of individuals—offers some guidance in this regard (Kozlowski

& Klein, 2000). With respect to temporal issues, research must be sensitive to both the context and the temporal elements in which coordination occurs. Most theories assume that coordination is learned: *How does it develop and emerge at the team level over time* (Kozlowski et al., 1999)?

Cooperation can be defined as "the willful contribution of personal efforts to the completion of interdependent jobs" (Wagner, 1995, p. 152) and is often viewed as the opposite of conflict. Much of the research on cooperation and collaboration has been conducted in social psychology around issues of free riding and social loafing (Latané et al., 1979). This research has focused considerable energy on identifying factors that might eliminate uncooperative tendencies and instead induce cooperation in groups (Kerr & Bruun, 1983). We discuss such work later in this chapter in the section on leadership and motivation. Cooperation and collaboration have also been examined in the context of culture—specifically, in the difference between individualistic and collectivistic orientations.

Research suggests that cooperation is generally associated with team effectiveness. For example, Wagner (1995) reported that individualists are less apt—and collectivists more apt—to behave cooperatively. He also found that individualism-collectivism moderates relationships between group size, identifiability, and cooperation such that group size and identifiability have greater effects on the cooperation of individualists than they do on the cooperation of collectivists. Seers, Petty, and Cashman (1995) found that departments with greater team-member exchange had significantly higher efficiency as captured from archival records. Pinto and Pinto (1990) examined the effect of cross-functional cooperation in hospital project teams and found that cooperation positively predicted both task and psychosocial outcomes, such that teams high in cooperation relied more heavily on informal modes of communication than did low-cooperation teams. Finally, Smith et al. (1994) showed that cooperation in TMTs was positively related to return on investment and sales growth.

Most theoretical work that incorporates *communication* does so in the context of coordination and cooperation—that is, as noted previously, communication is seen as a means for enabling the more primary processes of coordination and cooperation. Communication can serve two important functions (Glickman et al., 1987) that aid task work and teamwork. Task work communication involves exchanging task-related information and developing team solutions to problems. Teamwork communication focuses on establishing patterns of interaction and enhancing their quality.

Research using content analysis has found that differences in communication patterns are related to differences in team performance (e.g., Foushee & Manos, 1981). Ancona and Caldwell (1992a, 1992b) found that external communication frequency was positively related to team performance. However, external communication was negatively associated with a team's assessment of its overall performance and with member ratings of team cohesion. Ancona (1990) reported that team leader strategies (e.g., probing) affected the types and frequency of external communication. Smith et al. (1994) reported that communication frequency was negatively related to TMT effectiveness, and they suggested that greater communication frequency may be indicative of high levels of conflict. Campion et al. (1993) found that communication between teams did not have a significant impact on productivity, member satisfaction, or managers' judgments of team performance. Waller (1999) indicated that frequency of information collection (e.g., request weather information) related to the performance of airline crews.

What are the compelling research issues for team communication? From our perspective, the *central* issue in team processes concerns the synergistic combination of individual contributions to team effectiveness. Communication is a primary means to enable more proximal factors like coordination and cooperation. Communication is a lens. Thus, research on communication type and frequency can be revealing of what team members are trying to coordinate, how much information they need, or how difficult it is to coordinate their activity. However, focusing solely on communication type and amount in the absence of attention to coordination and cooperation is incomplete. In addition, from a coordination perspective, focusing only on type and frequency ignores timing issues. When requests for information or assistance are made, how quickly others respond and the timing constraints imposed by the team task are likely to be critical issues in sorting out when communication is and is not helpful for team effectiveness.

Enhancing Team Effectiveness

Decision Effectiveness

Team decision effectiveness has been the subject of high-profile research streams in the 1990s. Sparked by major military catastrophes caused by breakdowns in team coordination processes, this work was undertaken to better understand team decision effectiveness and to develop interventions to promote it. Here we highlight two such efforts. Hollenbeck, Ilgen, and their colleagues (1995) developed a theory of decision making for hierarchical teams with distributed expertise, in which team members possess distinctive roles and have access to different decision-relevant information. This allows them to

make a decision recommendation that they pass on to a team leader, who then renders the team's decision. The research paradigm is temporally sensitive in that the leader makes decisions, gets feedback, and has to incorporate the feedback into subsequent decisions. Hollenbeck et al. (1995) introduced the theory and tested it in two research contexts, showing that team leaders are generally sensitive to the quality and accuracy of the advice they receive from team members and—over time—adjust accordingly. Hollenbeck, Colquitt, Ilgen, LePine, and Hedlund (1998) evaluated boundary conditions across different components of decision accuracy and member specialization. Finally, Phillips (1999) examined antecedents of hierarchical sensitivity—a core theoretical construct indicative of the leader's ability to accurately assess the validity of staff members' recommendations.

Cannon-Bowers, Salas, and their colleagues conducted a 7-year multidisciplinary research effort—the Team Decision Making Under Stress (TADMUS) program—that was designed to improve team training and the human factors of interface design for tactical decision-making teams (TDM; Cannon-Bowers & Salas, 1998). One of the key features of the TADMUS program was its active integration of theory development, basic research, field testing, and application. The program was driven by grounded theory, which was evaluated by basic laboratory research. Promising findings were subject to field testing to ensure generalization to the operational environment. Finally, proven techniques were implemented and institutionalized. In many ways, TADMUS represents an excellent example of the way in which theory and basic research can transition to effective organizational application.

Team Competencies and Performance

The relevance of team processes to enhancing team effectiveness is that they are presumed by the IPO framework to be proximal predictors of team performance outcomes. Hence, although there are other strategies relevant for improving team effectiveness—such as influencing the composition of team abilities via selection or improving processes via team design and leadership—direct enhancement of team processes via training is the most prevalent team effectiveness intervention (Cannon-Bowers & Salas, 1997). This strategy necessitates two foci: (a) specifying the competencies that underlie effective team performance and (b) designing and delivering training that improves these competencies, enhances team processes, and increases team effectiveness.

From a criterion perspective, team performance can be defined as a product or outcome of team action that satisfies external constituencies (Hackman, 1987). However, at the more specific level of identifying factors that constitute critical team performance dimensions, definitional challenges are encountered. As noted in our discussion of team typologies, it is very difficult to develop a common specification of team performance—it varies by the type of team. Constraints emanating from the team's context, its task, and their implications for internal and external links lead to different dimensions of performance being relevant for different types of teams. Thus, team performance specification and measurement must be grounded by the team context and task (Goodman et al., 1987). Rigorous, reliable, and valid measures of team performance are essential tools for enhancing team effectiveness (see Brannick, Salas, & Prince, 1997, for issues and measurement approaches).

It is also important to appreciate the orientation taken by researchers toward team performance in their efforts to enhance team effectiveness. The orientation has been much more targeted on processes than it has been on outcomes. Rather than treating team performance as a static, retrospective, summary variable intended to capture the outcome of many specific behaviors over an extended period of time, efforts to understand team performance for training purposes have tended to focus on what individuals and teams need to *do* to perform well. In other words, the focus has been on behaviors that have to be exhibited *over time* and on the underlying competencies that enable those behaviors. An important issue here is the need to distinguish between team-level performance outcomes and the individual-level actions and interactions that are the foundation for team-level performance (Kozlowski, Brown, Weissbein, Cannon-Bowers, & Salas, 2000). In this regard, researchers have generally distinguished between task work skills—individual job or technical skills—and teamwork skills—knowledge, skills, and attitudes (KSAs) that enable one to work effectively with others to achieve a common goal. Thus, at a general level team performance and teamwork competencies are easy to identify—they are the cognitive, affective-motivational, and behavioral process mechanisms described previously and the KSAs that enable them, respectively. Three relatively comprehensive efforts to identify teamwork competencies are described in the following discussion.

Fleishman and Zaccaro (1992) describe a taxonomy of team performance functions in an effort to be more specific than were previous classifications of group performance tasks. They synthesized seven major categories of team performance functions: (a) orientation (e.g., information exchange regarding member resources and constraints), (b) resource distribution (e.g., load balancing of tasks by members), (c) timing (e.g., activity pacing), (d) response coordination (e.g., timing and coordination of responses), (e) motivation

(e.g., balancing team orientation with individual competition), (f) systems monitoring (e.g., adjustment of team and member activities in response to errors and omissions), and (g) procedure maintenance (e.g., monitoring of general procedural-based activities). Note that these performance functions primarily implicate competencies that enhance coordination and cooperation.

Based on their extensive work with aircraft cockpit crews and TDM teams, Salas, Cannon-Bowers, and their colleagues synthesized a set of eight teamwork skill dimensions (Cannon-Bowers, Tannenbaum, Salas, & Volpe, 1995; Salas & Cannon-Bowers, 1997): (a) adaptability—competency to adjust strategies using compensatory behavior and reallocation of team resources; (b) shared situational awareness—possession of shared-compatible mental models of the team's internal and external environment used to arrive at a common understanding of the team situation and to derive appropriate strategies to respond; (c) performance monitoring and feedback—the capability to monitor teammate performance, give constructive feedback about errors, and make helpful suggestions for improvement; (d) leadership and team management—competencies to plan, organize, direct, motivate, and assess teammates; (e) interpersonal relations—skills to resolve conflict and engage cooperation; (f) coordination—competencies to integrate and synchronize task activities with other teammates; (g) communication—capability to clearly and accurately convey information and acknowledge its receipt; and (h) decision making—competencies to pool, integrate, and select appropriate alternatives and evaluate consequences.

In addition, they have also developed a typology for classifying team competencies and specifying essential knowledge (i.e., facts, concepts, relations), skills (i.e., cognitive-behavioral procedures), and attitudes (affective components of teamwork). The two-by-two typology is based on task and team dimensions. Each dimension is further distinguished by whether the competencies are specific or generic—resulting in four distinct classes of competencies appropriate for different types of teams. For example, *transportable competencies* (task and team generic) generalize across teams and are most appropriate for situations in which individuals are members of multiple project teams. In contrast, *context-driven competencies* (task and team specific) are appropriate for action teams with tight links to a dynamic external environment and complex internal work flows with a strong emphasis on coordination, knowledge of interlinked role demands, and adaptability (e.g., trauma teams, emergency response, TDM teams, aircrews). Specific competencies and KSAs for each of the four cells can then be mapped for different types of teams (Salas & Cannon-Bowers, 1997).

Based on an extensive review, Stevens and Campion (1994) developed a 35-item measure of the KSAs underlying effective teamwork behavior. Although it has been shown that certain personality traits evidence criterion-related validity, these authors concentrated on those KSAs that were more in line with traditional ability-based systems. They also selected attributes solely at the individual level of analysis because their focus was on selecting, training, and evaluating individuals for a team environment—not creating the best combination of team members. Finally, the authors rejected those KSAs that were team- or task-specific and instead focused on those skills related to the team- and task-generic component of the model proposed by Cannon-Bowers et al. (1995). Their search resulted in a final list of 10 interpersonal KSAs and four self-management KSAs. The interpersonal KSAs were then classified further into conflict resolution, collaborative problem solving, and communication KSAs. The self-management KSAs were also separated into two categories: goal setting and performance management KSAs and planning and task coordination KSAs. Work by Stevens and Campion (1994) and by others (e.g., Ellis, Bell, & Ployhart, 2000; McClough & Rogelberg, 1998) suggest that the measure is a valid predictor of team performance.

Team Training

A variety of direct interventions have been proposed to improve team performance and effectiveness. We touch on a few techniques that have received research attention, but we note that this is a huge area of practice—there are literally thousands of interventions. Some form of *team building* is perhaps the most ubiquitous team training technique and generally focuses on improving team skills in one or more of four areas (Salas, Rozell, Driskell, & Mullen, 1999): (a) goal setting—skills to set and achieve objectives; (b) interpersonal relations—skills to develop communication, supportiveness, and trust; (c) problem solving—skills for problem identification, solution generation, implementation, and evaluation; and (d) role clarification—skills to enhance understanding of others' role requirements and responsibilities. Although there are many testimonials touting the effectiveness of team-building techniques, solid empirical support for their efficacy is weak. A recent meta-analysis (Salas, Rozell, et al., 1999) indicated no significant overall effect for team building on team performance. There was a small positive effect for subjective measures of performance but no effect for objective indicators. Moreover, of the four components, only role clarification evidenced any contribution to team performance.

Although team building is oriented toward improving characteristics that emerge naturally during socialization and team development, team building is typically targeted at mature teams that have already developed strong informal structures and normative behavior patterns. It is quite a bit more difficult to change informal structure after it has jelled than it is to shape it during socialization and development. Thus, we believe that team-building techniques may have more potential for leveraging improvement if applied when team members are more malleable (e.g., Kozlowski et al., 1999; Kozlowski, Gully, Salas, et al., 1996).

Because of the enormous human and material consequences of team failure, the aviation and military communities have pioneered efforts to improve team effectiveness through training. On the aviation side, some form of *crew resource management* (CRM) training is in widespread use in both commercial and military aviation. Early CRM training focused on changing the teamwork attitudes of team members, whereas work in the 1990s shifted toward better definition, measurement, and training of team processes. On the military side, the TADMUS program developed and evaluated a variety of training techniques designed to improve the effectiveness of military TDM teams (see Cannon-Bowers & Salas, 1998). Although these are distinctive areas of research, the tasks of aviation cockpit crews and TDM teams share many underlying commonalities; consequently, key processes essential for team effectiveness and methodologies to design and deliver training exhibit a high degree of overlap across both areas. Key processes are defined by the eight dimensions of teamwork (described previously; Salas & Cannon-Bowers, 1997). Similarly, there is overlap in training techniques employed in both areas. Salas and Cannon-Bowers (1997), for example, identify six general training strategies for enhancing team processes and other essential KSAs: (a) task simulations, as a means to develop accurate performance expectations for various task demands; (b) role plays and behavior modeling, for building compatible KSAs; (c) team self-correction, in which team members monitor each other and provide corrective feedback; (d) team leader training, in which the leader guides the team through the self-correction process; (e) cross-training to instill crucial knowledge about the behavior and information needs of one's teammates; and (f) teamwork skill training to provide generic teamwork skills when members must work on across a variety of tasks or on many different teams. Research from TADMUS and extensive work on CRM provides an empirical foundation supporting the efficacy of these techniques.

Although research on team training will continue to advance, these systematic efforts to identify key team competencies (Salas & Cannon-Bowers, 1997), develop appropriate performance assessment technologies (Brannick et al., 1997), apply structured methodologies to design training (e.g., Salas,

Prince, et al., 1999), and evaluate training effectiveness (e.g., Salas, Fowlkes, Stout, Prince, & Milanovich, 1999) provide a model for team training research and practice for other types of teams.

Issues for Future Research on Team Training

We close this discussion on the use of training to enhance team effectiveness by identifying issues that need to be carefully considered in future research; these issues are organized around three themes: (a) what to train, (b) when to train, and (c) how to train.

What to Train?   There has been considerable progress in the 1990s on identifying important teamwork competencies and specifying their underlying KSAs. We note that virtually all of this work has been conducted on action teams that place the most complex and challenging demands on teamwork skills. The big question that remains is to what extent do these competencies—presumably in some modified form—apply to other types of teams that have much weaker demands for temporal entrainment and coordination? Thus, a key research issue is the generality of the competencies to other team types. A related issue concerns the assessment of team performance. Many research assessments rely on extensive observation during complex simulations or in-context performance (see Brannick et al., 1997). However, assessing individual and team contributions to team effectiveness in organizational environments is plagued by all of the problems that beset individual-level performance appraisal. This area is underresearched.

When to Train?   As we noted previously, much team training is remedial—targeted on mature teams rather than during team socialization and development when team members are more malleable and training can exert more leverage. There are well-developed descriptive (Morgan et al., 1993) and normative (Kozlowski, Gully, McHugh, et al., 1996; Kozlowski et al., 1999; Kozlowski, Gully, Salas, et al., 1996) models that specify developmental phases in which particular competencies are likely to be most pertinent to trainees and more malleable to the influence of interventions. However, there has been relatively little research to examine the efficacy of shifting the target of training to track developmental progress. DeShon et al. (2001) provide promising evidence that shifting regulatory focus from individual to team contributes to enhanced team performance adaptability. We believe that this area represents a research issue with the potential for considerable practical gain.

How to Train?   The development and evaluation of new techniques will probably continue to capture the attention of many researchers and practitioners. Emerging technologies are making it increasingly possible to push team training out of the classroom and into the workplace, making it more contextually grounded and resolving the ever-present gap between training and skill transfer. With the increasing penetration of computers into the workplace, we will witness the growth of web-based training, distance and distributed training, distributed interactive simulations, and other tools that take advantage of increased computing power, low cost, and enhanced connectivity. However, it is important to remember that these new tools are merely delivery media. How to use these advanced tools to good instructional effect is the critical research issue (Kozlowski et al., 2001).

A final issue concerns the level at which training should be delivered—individuals or intact teams? Much "team" training is really targeted on individual skill building. Can individual training improve team effectiveness? Focusing on the issue of *vertical transfer* (i.e., the extent to which individual actions propagate upwards to influence team performance), Kozlowski and colleagues (Kozlowski & Salas, 1997; Kozlowski et al., 2000) have argued that the nature of the teams' task should dictate the mode of delivery—individual or team. When team-level performance is based on *compilation* processes—work flows that emphasize distributed expertise, temporal entrainment, and synchronous coordination—training should be delivered to intact teams in actual performance settings (or very close approximations) because of the emphasis on integrating disparate actions. In contrast, when team-level performance is based on *composition* processes—work flows that emphasize additive individual contributions—training should be targeted at the individual level because it is more efficient and cost effective. Research on this issue is virtually nonexistent and represents an opportunity to refine team training delivery models.

TEAM LEADERSHIP AND MOTIVATION

Team Leadership

Most models of team effectiveness recognize the critical role of team leaders. Although there is certainly no shortage of leadership theories, examining this extensive literature is beyond the scope of this chapter (see Yukl & Van Fleet, 1992, for a comprehensive review). However, at the onset we note that the focus of many leadership theories is on traits, such as intelligence and originality (Bass, 1981; Fiedler, 1989), or on the frequency of leader's activities, such as telephone calls and scheduled meetings (McCall, Morrison, & Hannan, 1978). Relatively neglected is *what leaders should actually be doing to enhance team effectiveness*—their functional role—a perspective that we believe is more productive. In addition, many leadership theories focus on the individual level; there are relatively few attempts to examine the differences between leading in the team context and leading individuals. In this section, we examine the functional role of team leaders and discuss how leadership functions are sometimes shifted to team members through self-management. We conclude with practical recommendations for leading teams.

Functional Role of Team Leaders

Although there have been only a few efforts to specify the functional role of team leaders, there is reasonable consistency in the important leadership functions that need to be accomplished. Different labels have been used to describe these functions, but they can be grouped into two basic categories: (a) the development and shaping of team processes and (b) the monitoring and management of ongoing team performance (Fleishman et al., 1991; Hackman & Walton, 1986; Komaki, Desselles, & Bowman, 1989; Kozlowski, Gully, McHugh, et al., 1996; Kozlowski, Gully, Salas, et al., 1996; McGrath, 1962).

With respect to team development, leaders are often faced with the challenge of building a new team. In these situations, a leader's functional role is to develop individuals into a coherent, seamless, and well-integrated work unit (Kozlowski, Gully, McHugh, et al., 1996). In other instances, teams experience personnel outflows and inflows over time. As new replacement personnel are brought into the team, they need to be socialized and assimilated (Moreland & Levine, 1989). Leaders are critical to this newcomer assimilation process (Ostroff & Kozlowski, 1992). Developmental functions of team leaders focus on the enactment of *team orientation* and coaching to establish *team coherence* (Kozlowski, Gully, McHugh, et al., 1996). Team orientation includes factors with motivational implications, such as promoting shared goal commitment, creating positive affect, and shaping climate perceptions. Team coherence includes the development of linked individual goals, a repertoire of team task strategies, and compatible team member role expectations. The leader's developmental role is to establish and maintain coherence and integration among the members of the unit. Coherence then allows team members to self-manage during periods of intense task engagement.

A second major functional role of team leaders is to establish and maintain favorable performance conditions for the team. In this capacity, leaders engage in two types of behavior: monitoring and taking action (Hackman & Walton, 1986;

Kozlowski, Gully, McHugh, et al., 1996; Kozlowski, Gully, Salas, et al., 1996; McGrath, 1962). Monitoring involves obtaining and interpreting data about performance conditions and events that might affect them. Monitoring functions include vigilance, diagnosing group deficiencies, data-gathering skills, forecasting impending environmental changes, and information use in problem solving. For example, an effective leader should monitor whether the team has adequate material resources and should also forecast potential resource crises. Leaders also need to collect performance information and provide feedback. In doing so, they make team members aware of the consequences of their behaviors. When problems are discovered, leaders must gather information to determine the nature of the problem and take action to devise and implement effective solutions. A leader's actions can be designed to improve the present state of affairs, exploit existing opportunities, or to head off impending problems. Specific actions can include clarifying the direction of the team, strengthening the design of the group or its contextual supports, providing coaching or process assistance, or ensuring the group has adequate resources (Fleishman et al., 1991; Hackman & Walton, 1986; Komaki et al., 1989; Kozlowski, Gully, McHugh, et al., 1996; Kozlowski, Gully, Salas, et al., 1996; McGrath, 1962).

One important characteristic underlying these theoretical efforts to identify the key functional roles of team leaders is the assumption that the leader interacts directly with team members in the processes of team development and performance management. However, this assumption may not always hold true—especially with today's advanced technologies and the capability to have virtual teams composed of members who are spatially and temporally distributed (Bell & Kozlowski, 2002). In these environments, it may be necessary for teams to manage themselves in the absence of a formal leader. Considerable research has focused on self-managing teams, which we review in the next section.

Self-Managing Teams

Teams described as self-managing have several defining characteristics. They are given relatively whole work tasks and are allowed increased autonomy and control over their work (Hackman, 1986; Manz, 1992). In addition, the members of such teams are responsible for many traditional management functions, such as assigning members to various tasks, solving within-team quality and interpersonal problems, and conducting team meetings (Lawler, 1986). Self-managing teams often have leaders; however, their primary function is to enable self-management.

Many benefits have been attributed to self-managing teams, including increased productivity, better quality work, and improved quality of work life for employees, as well as decreased absenteeism and turnover (Cohen & Ledford, 1994; Lawler, 1986; Manz & Sims, 1987). Although research suggests that self-managing work teams can be quite effective (Neck, Stewart, & Manz, 1996; U.S. Department of Labor, 1993), they sometimes fail. It has been suggested that these failures are often linked to the behaviors of team leaders. For example, teams with leaders who are too actively involved in the team's activities or who are too autocratic may not develop a sense of autonomy and may feel powerless (Stewart & Manz, 1995). It has been suggested that the optimal leader for self-managing teams is one who displays passive involvement in the team's activities and a democratic power orientation. Such leaders lead through modeling and assisting—helping the team to develop self-direction and ownership for activities.

Recent research also suggests that the social context within a team and the team's task may moderate the effectiveness of self-managing teams. For example, Tesluk, Kirkman, and Cordery (2001) found that self leadership resulted in greater autonomy in work units that displayed a less cynical orientation toward change efforts. In work groups that had a more cynical attitude toward change efforts, a self-leadership management style had little impact on perceptions of team autonomy. Stewart and Barrick (2000) found that for teams engaged primarily in conceptual tasks, team self-leadership exhibited a positive relationship with performance. In contrast, for teams engaged primarily in behavioral tasks, there was a negative relationship between self-leadership and performance. However, the mechanisms underlying these differential effects were unclear and should be examined in future work.

Practical Applications

Research and theory on leadership has been conducted at multiple levels of analysis. Although some theories focus on specific characteristics of leaders or their followers (e.g., Bass, 1981), other theories such as leader-member exchange (LMX) focus on the dyadic relationships between a leader and a member (e.g., Dansereau, Graen, & Haga, 1975), and still other theories focus specifically on leadership in team contexts (e.g., Hackman & Walton, 1986; Kozlowski, Gully, McHugh, et al., 1996; Kozlowski, Gully, Salas, et al., 1996). Although the focal level differs across these theories, many of them provide recommendations that are presumed to be applicable in team settings. Indeed, many of the leader characteristics (e.g. intellectual stimulation, consideration) and leader-member exchange patterns (e.g., delegation) that have been shown to be effective in leading individuals should also be effective for leading individuals in the team context.

It is important, however, to recognize that team environments create a number of unique challenges for leaders. For example, team leaders must focus not only on developing individual skills but also on promoting the development of teamwork skills that underlie coordination, such as mutual performance monitoring, error detection, load balancing, and resource sharing (Kozlowski, Gully, McHugh, et al., 1996). Team leaders also must guide the development of a collective, team-level efficacy—the belief that the team can work together effectively to accomplish the task or goals set before it (Campion et al., 1993; Shea & Guzzo, 1987). Team leaders can also be instrumental in developing effective team mental models (Klimoski & Mohammed, 1994). Marks et al. (2000), for example, found that leader briefings that highlighted task strategies affected the development of team mental models, which in turn positively influenced team communication processes and team performance.

It is also important for team leaders to tailor their behavior based on the team's environment and task. The research by Stewart and Barrick (2000; discussed previously), for example, suggests that leaders should promote different levels of self-leadership depending on the team's task. Leaders may also need to adopt a different role when faced with the challenge of leading a virtual team. In these situations, it is often very difficult for leaders to monitor the performance of team members due to spatial and temporal separation. As a result, it may be critical for virtual team leaders to clearly define the team's objective, facilitate team members' understanding of their responsibilities, and create explicit structures that help the team manage its performance (Bell & Kozlowski, 2002).

Team Motivation

The majority of theory and research on motivation has been focused at the individual level. In fact, relatively little research has specifically examined motivation as it operates in team contexts or at the team level. Much of what we know about motivation in team contexts comes from research in the field of social psychology that has examined the productivity or process loss that often occurs when individuals work in groups. Although much of this work focuses on individual motivation and performance in the group context—not on team motivation and performance per se—researchers frequently extrapolate effects to the team level. Moreover, as we discuss in the following sections, many of these findings may not apply to teams as they typically exist in organizational settings, suggesting that researchers need to focus greater attention on the issue of motivation in work teams. In the following section, we provide a brief review of research on productivity loss in teams. We then examine some theories that have focused specifically on motivation in teams, and we conclude with practical recommendations for motivating teams.

Productivity Loss

A large body of research has shown that individuals tend to exert less effort when their efforts are combined rather than individual. This effect—referred to as *social loafing*—and similar phenomena (e.g., free rider and sucker effects) are considered to be robust and to generalize across tasks and work populations (Karau & Williams, 1993). However, research has also shown that there are numerous variables that moderate the tendency to engage in social loafing. For example, social loafing can be eliminated by having individuals work with close friends, increasing the identifiability of individual contributions, and providing clear performance standards. In fact, research suggests that many of the variables that eliminate social loafing also serve to enhance team performance. This effect is known as *social facilitation,* which results from the motivation to maintain a positive self-image in the presence of others—particularly when others are viewed as potential evaluators (Zajonc, 1965).

Research on social loafing and social facilitation have developed independently and offer rather conflicting views on the motivational effects of individuals working in teams. This apparent discrepancy, however, may be explained by the fact that traditional research on social loafing has often been conducted in artificial groups that do not conform to the definition of groups as involving individuals' mutual awareness and potential mutual interaction (McGrath, 1984). These studies have typically used pooled tasks in which team members provide independent and unidentifiable contributions to the team's performance. Recent research, however, has found that characteristics of teams in work organizations—such as team member familiarity, interaction, and communication—eliminate social loafing and may actually lead to social facilitation (Erez & Somech, 1996). Thus, the extent to which social loafing and related effects are important motivational phenomena in the context of work teams is open to question.

Theories of Team Motivation

Compared to research on individual-level motivation, relatively little work has directly considered the issue of motivation in teams. Indeed, there are no well-developed motivation theories that explicitly incorporate the team level. What is interesting, however, is that much of the work on this topic has focused on the issue of aligning individual-level and team-level sources of motivation. Weaver, Bowers,

Salas, and Cannon-Bowers (1997), for example, differentiated between individual-level motivation—referred to as *task work motivation*—and team-level motivation—referred to as *teamwork motivation.* They argued that team performance is enhanced when these individual-level and team-level sources of motivation are congruent not only with one another but also with the goals of the organization (Saavedra, Early, & Van Dyne, 1993).

Research on goals, feedback, and rewards has also considered congruence among individual-level and team-level sources of motivation. It has found that group goals—in addition to or instead of individual goals—are necessary or at least facilitative when the task is a group rather than an individual one (Matsui, Kakuyama, & Onglatco, 1987; Mitchell & Silver, 1990). Some research also suggests that it is important for team members to receive individual- and team-level performance feedback (Matsui et al., 1987). Team feedback by itself may be problematic when the good performance of one team member can compensate for the poor performance of a teammate (Salas et al., 1992). People performing poorly who only receive team feedback may not attempt to improve their performance if the team is succeeding. Finally, research suggests that the relative effectiveness of team-based (as compared to individual-based) rewards may depend on several factors, such as the degree of team interdependence (Wageman, 1995) and the characteristics of team members (e.g., individualism-collectivism; DeMatteo, Eby, & Sundstrom, 1998; Kirkman & Shapiro, 2000).

Overall, research suggests that individual-level and team-level sources of motivation should be congruent with one another and with other features of the organizational context. Despite these findings, we know relatively little about how motivation operates at the team level. Research has often produced mixed findings or has failed to examine potentially important contingency variables. As DeMatteo et al. (1998, p. 152) state in their review of team-based rewards, "Despite hundreds of studies examining group rewards, the conditions under which team rewards will be effective are unclear." To advance understanding, a multilevel theory of motivation is needed that will guide future research and serve as a tool for integrating and interpreting relevant research findings. Because the promising work in this area involves constructs relevant to models of regulatory activity (i.e., goals, feedback), we believe that a multilevel model of self- and team-regulation has the potential to provide this integration.

Practical Recommendations

Several authors have offered recommendations for enhancing team motivation. Sheppard (1993), for example, suggested that lost productivity can arise in teams when any one of the following three conditions is present: Individuals (a) perceive no value to contributing, (b) perceive no contingency between their contributions and achieving a desirable outcome, or (c) perceive the costs of contributing to be excessive. To overcome these effects, Sheppard provided three categories of solutions that correspond to each of the three sources of productivity loss. These include providing incentives for contributing, making contributions indispensable, and decreasing the costs associated with contributing, respectively. The Productivity Measurement and Enhancement System (ProMES; Pritchard, Jones, Roth, Stuebing, & Ekeberg, 1988) is a concrete example of how group-based feedback, goal setting, and incentives can be used to reduce productivity loss and enhance team performance.

Rewards and incentives—examined mainly in service teams—are among the most frequently studied factors designed to enhance team motivation in organizations. Effects for rewards have been mixed. Several studies have found that rewards have no significant relationship with team effectiveness (e.g., Campion et al., 1993; Gladstein, 1984), although a few studies have found rewards to have positive effects under certain conditions (Wageman, 1997). Wageman (1995) found that service technician groups with low task interdependence performed best with individual-based rewards, but groups with high interdependence performed best with group-based rewards. Pritchard and colleagues (1988) also found that incentives lead to a small increase in team productivity, although their ProMES intervention produced more substantial increases. Finally, Cohen, Ledford, and Spreitzer (1996) found that a nonmonetary reward—recognition by management—was positively associated with team ratings of performance, trust in management, organizational commitment, and satisfaction for both self-directed and traditionally managed groups in a telecommunications company. Overall, there is some evidence to suggest that group-based rewards can increase team effectiveness. However, research is needed to further examine the role of contingency variables—such as task structure and team composition—in the relationship between reward systems and work team effectiveness (DeMatteo et al., 1998).

Swezey and Salas (1992) conducted a review of research on individuals within teams or groups and identified several prescriptive guidelines that have relevance to team motivation. They offered several concrete suggestions for motivating teams, such as employing positive reinforcement techniques and developing a system of rewards for those who exhibit supportive behaviors toward teammates. As discussed previously, research has tended to show that team performance is enhanced when goals, feedback, rewards, and task interdependence

requirements are congruent with one another. Thus, to enhance team motivation, an organization should ensure that the work context is configured so that individual and team motivation are aligned and do not contradict each other.

CONTINUANCE AND DECLINE

Team Viability

Team effectiveness has often been defined as the quantity and quality of a team's outputs (e.g., Shea & Guzzo, 1987). This definition, however, overlooks the possibility that a team can "burn itself up" through unresolved conflict or divisive interaction, leaving members unwilling to continue working together (Hackman, 1987, p. 323). Thus, some researchers have argued that definitions of team effectiveness should also incorporate measures of team viability (Guzzo & Dickson, 1996; Sundstrom et al., 1990). Team viability refers to members' satisfaction, participation, and willingness to continue working together in the future. It can also include outcomes indicative of team maturity, such as cohesion, coordination, effective communication and problem solving, and clear norms and roles (Sundstrom et al., 1990). The major issue, however, is whether a team can sustain effective levels of performance over time.

Relatively little is known about long-term team viability, although theory (Katz, 1980) suggests that team continuance has a curvilinear relationship with team performance: Team effectiveness initially improves with time but declines with increasing group age. Katz (1982) suggests that decline begins 2–3 years into a team's existence. Research on R&D teams suggests that effectiveness peaks between 2–3 (Katz & Allen, 1988) and 4–5 years of group age (Pelz & Andrews, 1966), with marked decline after 5 years (Katz & Allen, 1988). Other work suggests decline as quickly as 16 months of group existence (Shepard, 1956). Although the mechanisms that cause team performance to fade over time are not well understood, several explanations have been offered. Hackman (1992) suggests that the increased cohesiveness that develops over time may lead to groupthink and other negative outcomes associated with the rejection of dissenting opinions. Continuance also tends to increase team member familiarity. It has been argued that familiarity may be beneficial early in a team's existence by fostering rapid coordination and integration of team members' efforts (Cannon-Bowers et al., 1995). However, familiarity may eventually become a liability as the lack of membership change contributes to stultification and entropy (Guzzo & Dickson, 1996). Similarly, Katz (1982) has suggested that communication within and between teams declines as teams age. Katz and Allen (1988), who examined 50 R&D teams, provided support for this suggestion, showing that declines in communication were associated with effectiveness declines over time. It is important to note that they also reported that the greatest communication decay was in those areas most central to team activities (e.g., for technical service teams, intrateam communication; for project teams, external communication). Thus, team communication appears to an important mediator of the effects of team continuance on team effectiveness. Additional research is needed to examine team viability over significant periods of time and to identify factors that can promote it.

Recommendations for Enhancing Team Viability

Although research suggests that team performance deteriorates given enough time, it may be possible to combat this trend. West and Anderson (1996) show that four factors—vision, participative safety, task orientation, and support for innovation—define a climate that predicts team innovativeness. It is also important for organizations to assess whether a group is using the energy and talents of its members well (rather than wasting or misapplying them), and to determine whether group interaction patterns that develop over time expand (rather than diminish) members' performance capabilities. For example, it has been suggested that although cohesion is detrimental when it is social or interpersonal in nature, it may be beneficial when it is task focused (Hackman, 1992). Team goals and rewards may be used to facilitate task-based cohesion (Zaccaro & Lowe, 1988), or interventions may be developed to maintain team communication over time.

Teams should also be provided ongoing assistance throughout their life cycles. Hackman (1987) suggests that this assistance can come in three forms. First, teams can be provided opportunities to renegotiate aspects of their performance situation. Second, process assistance should be provided as needed to promote positive group synergy. For example, it may be important to manage personnel inflows and outflows over the course of a team's life cycle. Just as stable membership can lead to dullness and entropy, the introduction of new members—properly managed—can renew and revitalize a team. And third, teams should be provided opportunities to learn from their experiences.

Finally, it may be possible to influence team viability through the selection of team members. Barrick et al. (1998) found that teams that have greater cognitive ability, that are more extraverted, and that are more emotionally stable are more likely to stay together in the future. They also found that the effects of extraversion and emotional stability on team viability were mediated by social cohesion. Teams that were more extraverted and emotionally stable had more positive group interactions, thus becoming more socially cohesive, which in turn enhanced the team's capability to maintain itself (Barrick et al., 1998). Clearly, the issue of team viability can benefit from additional research attention.

RESEARCH ISSUES AND RECOMMENDATIONS

At the beginning of this chapter, we noted that there was a wealth of material on work groups and teams in organizations. We have endeavored to cover the essence of the most relevant material in this review and have identified a multitude of issues in need of research attention. In this final section, we highlight what we regard as the major issues that ought to shape future work in the area. We begin with a reconsideration of our four themes—context, task interdependence, levels, and time—to provide a framework for a discussion of general theory and research issues. We then close with more specific recommendations for new research organized around the major topics addressed in the review.

Research Issues

Context

One of the key distinguishing characteristics of the organizational perspective on work groups and teams is appreciation of the fact that they are embedded in a broader system that sets constraints and influences team processes and outcomes. Yet, as one looks across this literature, it is clear that the effects of top-down, higher-level contextual factors on team functioning are neglected research issues. The importance of contextual influences is explicitly recognized theoretically—virtually every model of team effectiveness incorporates organizational contextual factors—yet context is not well represented in research. Beyond theoretical influences, we know relatively little about the effects of the organizational context on team functioning.

Context is also relevant as a product of bottom-up processes; that is, individual team members—by virtue of their cognition, affect, behavior, and mutual interaction processes—enact structural features (e.g., norms, expectations, roles) that serve as team generated contextual constraints. Again, contextual enactment is well represented in theory but represents just a small portion of the research base. For example, the strong influence of normative expectations on team functioning is an accepted truism in the literature, but knowledge of how such expectations develop is sketchy. There is relatively little work examining the formation of these bottom-up constraints (e.g., Bettenhausen & Murnighan, 1985).

We think that the field's relative lack of knowledge in this area is due in part to the prevalence of laboratory research on team effectiveness. This observation is not intended as a criticism of laboratory research on teams per se. Appropriately targeted laboratory research has and will continue to contribute much to our understanding of teams. However, it must be acknowledged that laboratory research, because of its synthetic nature, can contribute to our understanding of contextual influences in only very limited ways. Decomposing the effects of context is really the province of field research with its access to contextually rich research settings. Unfortunately, when contextual effects have been examined in field research on teams, there has been a tendency to focus on the effects of indirect support factors as opposed to more direct links to the organizational system. In other words, research has tended to conceptualize team contextual factors in terms of the provision of training or availability of rewards (e.g., Cohen & Bailey, 1997), which we would expect to be supportive of team functioning, instead of conceptualizing direct system links such as technology, structure, and other factors relevant to work flow input-output linkages; yet it is these latter factors that are most likely to operate as major constraints on team structure and process.

Team research needs to incorporate the effects of major organizational context factors specified in models of team effectiveness.

Task Interdependence

Recognition of the central importance of team task interdependence to team structure and process is a second key characteristic of the organizational perspective on work groups and teams. For the most part, this appreciation is reasonably well represented in both theory and research, which generally regard task interdependence either as a critical boundary condition or a moderator of effects (Gully et al., in press; Saavendra et al., 1993; Wageman, 1999). Given its demonstrated importance, new research that fails to consider the effects of task interdependence for the team phenomenon in question has little relevance to building knowledge in the work groups and teams literature. It is a feature that should be explicitly addressed—either as a boundary condition or a moderator—in all work on groups and teams.

We applaud the general recognition of the importance of task interdependence but assert that this focus only gets at half of the problem—intrateam links. We believe that research also has to attend to external system links and attend

to how the interface with relevant external factors affects intrateam links. In other words, external links to broader contextual demands such as goals, temporal pacers (deadlines), and environmental inputs can influence team internal interdependences. Moreover, task demands and related interdependencies are not necessarily steady states. Tasks can be conceptualized as episodic (Marks et al., 2001) and cyclical (Kozlowski, Gully, McHugh, et al., 1996; Kozlowski, Gully, Salas, et al., 1996), making the nature and form of internal interdependencies dynamic and unpredictable (Kozlowski et al., 1999).

Theorists and researchers need to be more sensitive to external influence on task interdependencies and to the dynamics and variations of task interdependencies.

Levels

Teams are composed of individuals and are embedded in a nested organizational systems structure. Teams do not think, feel, or behave; individuals do, but individuals think, feel, and behave in an interactive context that can shape their cognition, affect, and behavior such that it has emergent collective properties. These emergent properties evolve over time and are further constrained by higher-level contextual factors. A key implication of this organizational systems conceptualization is that team function and process must be regarded as multilevel phenomena (Kozlowski & Klein, 2000).

A multilevel conceptualization of team phenomena means that theory and construct definition, measurement procedures, and data analyses must be consistent with principles drawn from the levels of analysis perspective (Kozlowski & Klein, 2000). A levels perspective necessitates that constructs, data, and analyses be *aligned* with the level to which conclusions are to be drawn. For much of the research in this area, that level is the team, yet many studies that draw generalizations to the team level assess data or conduct analyses at the individual level. Such generalizations are flawed. In other instances, studies assess data at the individual level but aggregate to the team level in order to conduct analyses and draw conclusions. When this aggregation process is properly guided by a model of higher-level composition (Chan, 1998) or emergence (Kozlowski & Klein, 2000), we can have high confidence in the construct validity and meaningfulness of the higher-level construct that results from the process. When the process is done improperly—that is, with no validation of the underlying model for data aggregation—the result is misspecified constructs, faulty analyses, and flawed generalizations.

A very common example of this flawed procedure is to collect perceptions from individuals about team characteristics and then to blindly average the individual responses to create team-level representations. It is not the use of averages per se that is problematic. As long as conclusions regarding such aggregated characteristics are explicit about the fact that they are "averages of individual perceptions," there is no problem. However, researchers frequently treat averaged *variables* created by blind aggregation procedures as team-level *constructs,* imbued with parallel meaning drawn from their individual-level origins; this is a major flaw. Treating an average of individual perceptions as a team-level construct necessitates a theoretically driven justification. For averaged measures, this justification is generally based on an assumption that team members have *shared* perceptions of the characteristics in question. Sharedness is evaluated prior to aggregation by showing restricted within-group variance on the characteristics, thereby establishing the construct validity of the aggregated measure. In the absence of such careful procedures, many "team-level constructs" present in the literature lack the meaning attributed to them. The previously described example represents merely one model that may guide aggregation procedures. Other theoretically driven procedures are necessary for higher-level constructs that conform to alternative models of emergence (Kozlowski & Klein, 2000).

Research on team phenomena must be cognizant of and consistent with the principles of multilevel theory, data, and analyses.

Time

Despite McGrath's persistent calls for greater attention to time in team theory and research, it is perhaps the most neglected critical issue in this area. It is—with few exceptions—poorly represented in theory and is virtually ignored in research that is largely based on cross-sectional methodologies. Temporal concerns are most prominent in the area of team development—where time is generally viewed as a simple linear progression but is vitally relevant to all phases of team processes and performance. Theorists are beginning to become more sensitive to the effects of time across a broader range of team phenomena. For example, time is an explicit factor in McGrath's (1991) TIP model, Kelly et al. (1990) describe how temporal entrainment can pace and cycle team processes, and McGrath (1997) makes a persuasive case for the need to conceptualize team effectiveness as a dynamic and adaptive process—not a static outcome. Kozlowski and colleagues (1999) construct a model of team effectiveness that explicitly addresses developmental progression (i.e., linear time) and dynamic variation (i.e., cyclical entrainment) in the intensity of team tasks. The model considers implications for the emergence of team processes and development of flexible, adaptive

teams. Similarly, Marks et al. (2001) develop a temporally based theory of team processes. In their model, team performance emerges from episodic processes comprising transition-action sequences that unfold over time. We believe that these and other models are beginning to provide a sophisticated and expanded conceptualization of temporal impacts on team function and process. Such models provide guidance and points of departure for further efforts.

Why is time so neglected in research? We do not have a definitive answer to this question, but we suspect that pragmatic challenges have worked to relegate time to low priority when researchers make the inevitable trade-offs in data collection design. The challenge for addressing time in laboratory research is that the time frame is limited in duration. It is a commonly held belief that meaningful developmental processes or emergent phenomena cannot occur and be detected in the short duration of the typical laboratory experiment—so why bother? We think such beliefs are misguided. Many important team phenomena such as the initial establishment of norms (Bettenhausen & Murnighan, 1985), the effects of leaders (Marks et al., 2001), and the influence of regulatory focus (DeShon et al., 2001) can develop very quickly and exert persistent effects over time (Kelly et al., 1990). A focus on carefully targeted team phenomena—those that are expected theoretically to get established early and unfold quickly—can help the field to begin mapping the implications of temporal processes on team development and functioning. Similarly, the challenge for addressing time in field research is the necessity to extend data sampling over time, with consequent effects on sample attrition. Getting access to good field samples is always difficult; getting access over time compounds the challenge. Although cross-sectional designs are clearly more efficient, they by necessity can only treat temporally relevant phenomena like team processes as a box—a static representation of the essence by which teams create collective products. Longitudinal designs, although they are less efficient, will be far more revealing of the team phenomenon under investigation.

Team theory and research should explicitly address the implications of time for team phenomena.

Research Recommendations

As we covered substantive topics in this chapter, we identified a large number of issues in need of specific research attention to resolve conceptual and application ambiguities. We have no intention to summarize each of those recommendations; rather, in this last section, we highlight what we consider to be the more important issues that should shape future research on work teams in organizations.

The Nature of Teams

Organizational teams come in a wide range of varieties, with new forms being developed all the time. Such diversity illustrates the vibrancy of the team as a primary form of work organization, but it also creates challenges. Diversity in the nature of teams has made it difficult to develop useful general models and interventions applicable to all teams. Thus, it is vital that researchers identify the boundary conditions and critical contingencies that influence team functioning and processes for different types of teams. To accomplish this goal, we believe that researchers need to focus less attention on descriptive classification and more attention on the underlying dimensions and characteristics that are responsible for distinguishing different types of teams. There is relatively little theoretical value in efforts to create a team typology that does not also surface the factors responsible for differential classification. Moreover, identifying the underlying characteristics that distinguish different types of teams will help make more salient the contingencies that determine effectiveness across team types; this will enable both theoretical advances as well as better targeted interventions for enhancing team effectiveness.

Composition

Historically, research on team composition has tended to focus on manifest or descriptive characteristics—size and demographics. More recently, team researchers have started to examine team composition in terms of latent constructs—ability and personality. These lines of research have been largely independent. We believe that there is potential value from an integration of these areas. Demographic composition has demonstrated effects, but it is difficult to imagine that such effects occur without mediation by psychological characteristics. Combining these areas may help researchers better focus on identifying mediating characteristics relevant to both types of composition factors. A related issue is that composition research would benefit from more attention to contextual moderators that affect the composition-outcome linkage. In addition, the levels of analysis perspective can be profitably applied to this area of work. Indeed, it must be more prominently applied because a significant portion of team composition research neglects many basic principles of multilevel theory.

Understanding how to compose better teams is the key to leveraging selection as a tool for enhancing team effectiveness. Conventional selection methodology, with its focus on the individual as opposed to the team level, generally promotes a more-is-better perspective when it is applied to the team level: If conscientiousness promotes better individual

performance, then greater collective conscientiousness must be better for team performance. However, as we discussed previously with respect to levels issues, whether this assumption is true or not is dependent on the way in which the construct emerges at the team level: What is the meaning of team conscientiousness in the context of the team task? If it is additive, more *is* better. If it is configural, however, we need to identify the pattern or configuration of characteristics that create synergy in the team collective. We think that this idea—theoretically, empirically, and practically—is an interesting, exciting, and compelling research issue.

Formation, Socialization, and Development

Existing teams experience personnel outflows and inflows, necessitating a socialization process to acculturate newcomers to the existing informal structure. In other situations, teams are formed anew, necessitating a developmental process wherein all team members simultaneously contribute to the formation of informal structure. Although these are distinctive processes and literatures, we believe that some parallels allow the two literatures to mutually inform. For socialization, the primary issue is that research needs to be far more attentive to the effects of the work group on the process of individual socialization. Currently, the work group is viewed as one among many factors that affect the process rather than as the primary locus of socialization. In addition, although socialization theory conceptualizes the process as bidirectional, research typically examines it as unidirectional. Research needs to better capture processes by which the newcomer assimilates to the group, as well as processes by which the group accommodates to the newcomer. We need to better understand what insiders can do to facilitate socialization and then train them to do so.

With respect to team development—research is needed! Although a useful foundation is provided by classic stage models (e.g., Tuckman, 1965), we believe that there is a need to validate and extend newer models that have been specifically formulated for work teams. For example, Gersick's (1988) PEM was derived from descriptive data based on just eight project teams. Although there has been some research to evaluate the PEM and compare it with other models of group development (see Chang et al., in press), there is relatively little work of this type, and it tends to be limited to small sample sizes. The PEM has not been subjected to empirical substantiation on a large set of teams, nor on a diverse sample of team types. Although we believe that temporal entrainment is important to team development, we do not believe that it will manifest itself as a uniform punctuated equilibrium in all types of teams. Indeed, research indicates that the punctuated equilibrium transition can be quite variable

(Chang et al., in press), suggesting that other factors influencing temporal entrainment may be operating (Kelly et al., 1990); this would seem to be an important concern, but it has received no real research attention. Similarly, Morgan et al. (1993) have some limited evidence in support of their model but only from a small sample of teams. Kozlowski et al. (1999) synthesized a broad literature base for their normative model to support the content, processes, and outcomes that they proposed were relevant at different phases of development. However, efforts to examine model prescriptions are still preliminary (DeShon et al., 2001). If supported, the model was designed to provide a prescriptive foundation for creating interventions that would promote team development at all phases of the team life cycle. Thus, we assert that solid empirical research to validate, compare, and extend models of work team development is needed.

Team Effectiveness, Processes, and Enhancements

The critical focus of team effectiveness research has been on team processes that link team resources to team outcomes. Thus, conceptualizing team processes and developing interventions that enhance these processes have been dominant themes in this area. We organized our review around cognitive, affective-motivational, and behavioral process mechanisms.

One of the biggest challenges in the cognitive domain is the necessity to clearly disentangle team mental models, transactive memory, and team learning. Of the three areas, the team mental model literature is arguably the best developed in terms of conceptualization, measurement, and demonstrated effects. Although more work is clearly needed, this research has moved from preliminary to more mature in nature, making it far more advanced relative to the two other mechanisms. Transactive memory has potential utility for the cognitive domain—especially because it provides a means to address the notion of "compatible but different" knowledge at the team level. However, we need research that moves the concept out of the laboratory, into larger teams, and into meaningful work contexts to better gauge its potential. Finally, team learning should be regarded as a construct that is still at an early stage of conceptualization, definition, and development. Key issues include the need to clearly conceptualize the construct, develop measures to assess it directly, and distinguish it from individual learning and performance. In addition, team learning needs to be distinguished from the other cognitive mechanisms. Until these issues are addressed, team learning will remain an ambiguous concept.

With respect to affective-motivational process mechanisms, work on collective efficacy has demonstrated promise

as a contributor to team effectiveness. Key research issues include levels of analysis concerns in measurement, articulation of the underlying processes by which collective efficacy is formed and has effects, and examination of potential contextual moderators. The latter issue is also relevant to the cohesion-performance relationship. We need to see solid empirical demonstrations that collective mood or group emotion contribute to team effectiveness; currently, much of this work is purely conceptual. Finally, we need to see levels of analysis concerns—both conceptual and methodological—addressed in research on team conflict. Team conflict has tended to be assessed via individual-level perceptions that are averaged to the team level. What kind of higher-level construct is conflict? Is it shared by all team members, thereby necessitating evaluation of restricted within team variance? Is it a configuration of team member perceptions? If so, an average misspecifies the construct. We think that this work is promising but must better attend to basic levels of analysis principles.

As for behavioral mechanisms, research on team coordination needs to focus on issues of levels and time. If we are to conceptualize coordination as patterns of task interaction over time, we need to better distinguish the individual and collective levels and the emergence of team coordination. Recent work by Marks et al. (2001) provides a theoretical framework and a typology addressing team processes—with coordination as a key mechanism—that will be helpful for conceptualizing this issue. Finally, we regard communication as an enabler of coordination and cooperation processes. Thus, research on the type and amount of communication should be better integrated with an examination of coordination and cooperation to be more revealing of underlying processes.

Many types of interventions have the potential to enhance team processes, but team training is chief among them. There are three overarching issues in regard to team training research: content (what), timing (when), and techniques (how). The key research issue for training content is the extent to which the frameworks for teamwork competencies generalize from action teams to other, less complex team types. For timing, the primary concern is sorting out when it is most appropriate to deliver important teamwork skills. This necessitates increased research integration between the areas of training and team development. Advanced computer technologies and enhanced connectivity are creating a host of new training tools—web-based training, distance learning, distributed interactive simulation. Currently, these tools are primarily used as media to deliver content. The key research issue is how to best utilize these tools for good instructional effect. In addition, team training always raises the issue of the target for delivery—individuals or intact teams? Emerging theory has developed principles to guide this decision, but basic research is needed to establish the impact of delivery level on team effectiveness.

Leadership and Motivation

Leadership and motivation are distinct literatures but conceptually related areas; many leadership models are focused on motivating or influencing member behavior. Both literatures are huge, and yet both literatures have relatively little to say about leading and motivating teams. On the leadership side, the dominant presumption is that leadership effects "average out" across group members; this tends to result in theories that treat the group as an undifferentiated whole—or in theories that focus on individual influence that aggregates to the group level (there are, of course, exceptions). On the motivation side, theories are almost universally targeted at the individual level. What is the meaning and mechanisms of team-level motivation?

Both areas would benefit from theory development and research that are explicitly targeted at the team level. For leadership, efforts to further develop and validate the functional roles of team leaders are needed: What do leaders need to do to promote team effectiveness? There is potential to integrate the functional leadership approach with team self-management: How do teams create substitute mechanisms to fulfill leader functional roles? Team self-management research would benefit from additional efforts to map boundary conditions and moderators that influence its effectiveness as a technique.

For motivation, we need to see the development of true team-level theory. There is some limited work indicating that goals and feedback mechanisms operate at both the team and individual levels (DeShon et al., 2000). This suggests that goal-based motivational theories (e.g., goal-setting, self-regulation) have the potential to be generalized to the team level. Theory and research challenges relate to the development of multilevel theory—relating parallel theoretical mechanisms at different levels—and evaluation—keeping parallel mechanisms empirically distinct so that relative contributions can be disentangled. Although it is challenging, we believe that this would be a profitable point of departure for a team-level theory of motivation.

Continuance and Decline

As teams continue to increasingly form the basic building blocks of organizations, concerns will naturally emerge as to how to maintain their effectiveness over time. Remarkably, we know relatively little about the prospects of long-term effectiveness and the factors that may enhance or inhibit team longevity. Research on technological innovation in the 1970s suggested that mature teams become more insular, communicate less, and are less innovative than younger teams. However, although it is suggestive, empirical support is quite limited. We need basic research to examine the effects of group longevity on team processes and effectiveness over the long term.

Conclusion

Teams are alive and well and living in organizations. This reality is pushing the field of industrial and organizational psychology to shift from a science and practice that is primarily focused on the individual level—our traditional roots—to a field that encompasses multiple levels: individual, team, and organization. Because teams occupy the intersection of the multilevel perspective, they bridge the gap between the individual and the organizational system as a whole. They become a focal point. They challenge us to attend to the organizational context, team task, levels, and time. They challenge us to develop new theories, new methodologies, new measurement tools, and new applications—not to just attempt to dust off and generalize our current ones. This creates major challenges for many of our field's traditional methods (e.g., selection, appraisal, training), but it also creates opportunities for theoretical innovation and advances in practice. Our field has much to learn and much to do, but we are confident that industrial and organizational psychology is capable of meeting the challenge afforded by the organization of work around teams.

REFERENCES

Alderfer, C. P. (1977). Group and intergroup relations. In J. R. Hackman & J. L. Suttle (Eds.), *Improving the quality of work life* (pp. 227–296). Palisades, CA: Goodyear.

Amason, A. C. (1996). Distinguishing the effects of functional and dysfunctional conflict on strategic decision making: Resolving a paradox for top management teams. *Academy of Management Journal, 39,* 123–148.

Ancona, D. G. (1990). Outward bound: Strategies for team survival in the organization. *Academy of Management Journal, 33,* 334–365.

Ancona, D. G., & Caldwell, D. F. (1992a). Bridging the boundary: External activity and performance in organizational teams. *Administrative Science Quarterly, 37,* 634–665.

Ancona, D. G., & Caldwell, D. F. (1992b). Demography and design: Predictors of new product design team performance. *Organizational Science, 3,* 321–339.

Anderson, N., Cunningham-Snell, N. A., & Haigh, J. (1996). Induction training as socialization: Current practice and attitudes to evaluation in British organizations. *International Journal of Selection and Assessment, 4,* 169–183.

Anderson, N., & Thomas, H. D. C. (1996). Work group socialization. In M. A. West (Ed.), *Handbook of work group psychology* (pp. 423–450). Chichester, UK: Wiley.

Anderson, N., & West, M. A. (1998). Measuring climate for work group innovation: Development and validation of the team climate inventory. *Journal of Organizational Behavior, 19,* 235–258.

Argote, L., Gruenfeld, D., & Naquin, C. (2001). Group learning in organizations. In M. E. Turner (Ed.), *Groups at work: Advances in theory and research* (pp. 369–411). Mahwah, NJ: Erlbaum.

Argote, L., Insko, C. A., Yovetich, N., & Romero, A. A. (1995). Group learning curves: The effects of turnover and task complexity on group performance. *Journal of Applied Social Psychology, 25,* 512–529.

Argote, L., & McGrath, J. E. (1993). Group processes in organizations. Continuity and change. In C. L. Cooper & I. T. Robertson (Eds.), *International review of industrial and organizational psychology* (Vol. 8, pp. 333–389). New York: Wiley.

Arrow, H. (1998). Standing out and fitting in: Composition effects on newcomer socialization. In D. H. Gruenfeld (Ed.), *Composition. Research on managing groups and teams* (Vol. 1, pp. 59–80). Stamford, CT: JAI Press.

Bandura, A. (1986). *Social foundations of thought and action.* Englewood Cliffs, NJ: Prentice Hall.

Bandura, A. (1997). *Self-efficacy: The exercise of control.* New York: W. H. Freeman.

Bantel, K. A. (1994). Strategic planning openness: The role of top team demography. *Group and Organization Management, 19,* 406–424.

Barrick, M. R., Stewart, G. L., Neubert, J. M., & Mount, M. K. (1998). Relating member ability and personality to work-team processes and team effectiveness. *Journal of Applied Psychology, 83,* 377–391.

Barry, B., & Stewart, G. L. (1997). Composition, process, and performance in self-managed groups: The role of personality. *Journal of Applied Psychology, 82,* 62–78.

Barsade, S. G. (1998). *The ripple effect: Emotional contagion in groups.* Working paper.

Barsade, S. G., & Gibson, D. E. (1998). Group emotion: A view from top and bottom. In D. H. Gruenfeld and Colleagues (Eds.), *Composition. Research on managing groups and teams* (Vol. 1, pp. 81–102). Stamford, CT: JAI Press.

Barsade, S. G., Ward, A., Turner, J., & Sonnenfeld, J. (2000). To your heart's content: A model of affective diversity in top management teams. *Administrative Science Quarterly, 45,* 802–836.

Bass, B. M. (1981). *Stogdill's handbook of leadership.* New York: Free Press.

Bell, B. S., & Kozlowski, S. W. J. (2002). A typology of virtual teams: Implications for effective leadership. *Group and Organization Management, 27,* 12–49.

Bettenhausen, K. L. (1991). Five years of group research: What we have learned and what needs to be addressed. *Journal of Management, 17,* 345–381.

Bettenhausen, K. L., & Murnighan, J. K. (1985). The emergence of norms in competitive decision-making groups. *Administrative Science Quarterly, 30,* 350–372.

Blickensderfer, E., Cannon-Bowers, J. A., & Salas, E. (1997). Theoretical bases for team self-corrections: Fostering shared mental models. In M. M. Beyerlein & D. A. Johnson (Eds.), *Advances in interdisciplinary studies of work teams* (Vol. 4, pp. 249–279). Greenwich, CT: JAI Press.

Brannick, M. T., Roach, R. M., & Salas, E. (1993). Understanding team performance: A multimethod study. *Human Performance, 6,* 287–308.

Brannick, M. T., Salas, E., & Prince, C. (Eds.). (1997). *Team performance assessment and measurement: Theory, methods, and applications.* Mahwah, NJ: Erlbaum.

Brown, K. G., & Kozlowski, S. W. J. (1999, April). *Toward an expanded conceptualization of emergent organizational phenomena: Dispersion theory.* Symposium presented at the 14th Annual Conference of the Society for Industrial and Organizational Psychology, Atlanta, GA.

Campion, M. A., Medsker, G. J., & Higgs, A. C. (1993). Relations between work group characteristics and effectiveness: Implications for designing effective work groups. *Personnel Psychology, 46,* 823–850.

Cannon, M., & Edmondson, A. (2000, August). *Confronting failure: Antecedents and consequences of shared learning-oriented beliefs in organizational work groups.* Paper presented at the annual meeting of the Academy of Management Conference, Toronto, Ontario, Canada.

Cannon-Bowers, J. A., & Salas, E. (1997). A framework for developing team performance measures in training. In M. T. Brannick, E. Salas, & C. Prince (Eds.), *Team performance assessment and measurement: Theory, methods, and applications* (pp. 45–62). Mahwah, NJ: Erlbaum.

Cannon-Bowers, J. A., & Salas, E. (Eds.). (1998). *Making decisions under stress: Implications for individual and team training.* Washington, DC: American Psychological Association.

Cannon-Bowers, J. A., Salas, E., & Blickensderfer, E. L. (1998). Making fine distinctions among team constructs: Worthy endeavor or "Crewel" and unusual punishment? In R. Klimoski (Chair), *When is a work team a crew and does it matter?* Symposium presented at the 13th annual conference of the Society for Industrial and Organizational Psychology, Dallas, TX.

Cannon-Bowers, J. A., Salas, E., & Converse, S. A. (1993). Shared mental models in expert team decision making. In N. J. Castellan (Ed.), *Individual and group decision making* (pp. 221–246). Hillsdale, NJ: Erlbaum.

Cannon-Bowers, J. A., Tannenbaum, S. I., Salas, E., & Volpe, C. E. (1995). Defining team competencies and establishing team training requirements. In R. Guzzo & E. Salas (Eds.), *Team effectiveness and decision making in organizations* (pp. 333–380). San Francisco: Jossey-Bass.

Chan, D. (1998). Functional relations among constructs in the same content domain at different levels of analysis: A typology of composition models. *Journal of Applied Psychology, 83,* 234–246.

Chang, A., Bordia, P., & Duck, J. (in press). Punctuated equilibrium and linear progression: Toward a new understanding of group development. *Academy of Management Journal.*

Chao, G. T. (2000). Levels issues in cultural psychology research. In K. J. Klein & S. W. J. Kozlowski (Eds.), *Multilevel theory, research and methods in organizations* (pp. 308–346). San Francisco: Jossey-Bass.

Chao, G. T., Kozlowski, S. W. J., Major, D. A., & Gardner, P. (1994, April). *The effects of individual and contextual factors on organizational socialization and outcomes.* Paper presented at the 9th Annual Conference of the Society for Industrial and Organizational Psychology, Nashville, TN.

Chao, G. T., O'Leary-Kelly, A. M., Wolf, S., Klein, H. J., & Gardner, P. D. (1994). Organizational socialization: Its content and consequences. *Journal of Applied Psychology, 79,* 730–743.

Cohen, S. G., & Bailey, D. E. (1997). What makes teams work: Group effectiveness research from the shop floor to the executive suite. *Journal of Management, 23,* 239–290.

Cohen, S. G., & Ledford, G. E., Jr. (1994). The effectiveness of self-managing teams: A quasi-experiment. *Human Relations, 47,* 13–43.

Cohen, S. G., Ledford, G. E., & Spreitzer, G. M. (1996). A predictive model of self-managing work team effectiveness. *Human Relations, 49,* 643–676.

Coovert, M. D., Campbell, G. E., Cannon-Bowers, J. A., & Salas, E. (1995, May). *A methodology for team performance measurement system.* Paper presented at the 10th Annual Conference of the Society for Industrial and Organizational Psychology, Orlando, FL.

Dansereau, F., Graen, G., & Haga, W. J. (1975). A vertical dyad linkage approach to leadership within formal organizations: A longitudinal investigation of the role making process. *Organizational Behavior and Human Performance, 13,* 46–78.

DeMatteo, J. S., Eby, L. T., & Sundstrom, E. (1998). Team-based rewards: Current empirical evidence and directions for future research. In L. L. Cummings & B. Staw (Eds.), *Research in organizational behavior* (Vol. 20, pp. 141–183). Greenwich, CT: JAI Press.

DeShon, R. P., Kozlowski, S. W. J., Schmidt, A. M., Wiechmann, D., & Milner, K. A. (2001, April). *Developing team adaptability: Shifting regulatory focus across levels.* Paper presented at the 16th Annual Conference of the Society for Industrial and Organizational Psychology, San Diego, CA.

DeShon, R. P., Kozlowski, S. W. J., Wiechmann, D., Milner, K. R., Davis, C. A., & Schmidt, A. M. (2000, April). *Training and developing adaptive performance in teams and individuals.* Paper presented at the 15th Annual Conference of the Society for Industrial and Organizational Psychology, New Orleans, LA.

Devine, D. J., & Phillips, J. L. (2000, April). *Do smarter teams do better? A meta-analysis of team-level cognitive ability and team performance.* Paper presented at the 15th Annual Conference of the Society for Industrial and Organizational Psychology, New Orleans, LA.

Driskell, J. E., Hogan, R., & Salas, E. (1987). Personality and group performance. In C. Hendrick (Ed.), *Group processes and intergroup relations* (pp. 91–112). Newbury Park, CA: Sage.

Early, P. C., & Erez, M. (Eds.). (1997). *New perspectives on international industrial/organizational psychology.* San Francisco: New Lexington Press.

Edmonson, A. C. (1999). Psychological safety and learning behavior in work teams. *Administrative Science Quarterly, 44,* 350–383.

Eisenhardt, K. M., & Schoonhoven, C. B. (1990). Organizational growth: Linking founding team strategy, environment, and growth among U.S. semi-conductor ventures, 1978–1988. *Administrative Science Quarterly, 35,* 484–503.

Ellis, A., Bell, B. S., & Ployhart, R. E. (2000, April). *Team training: An application of Stevens and Campion's teamwork KSA's.* Paper presented at the 15th Annual Conference of the Society for Industrial and Organizational Psychology, New Orleans, LA.

Erez, M., & Somech, A. (1996). Is group productivity loss the rule or the exception? Effects of culture and group-based motivation. *Academy of Management Journal, 39,* 1513–1537.

Evans, C. R., & Dion, K. L. (1991). Group cohesion and performance: A meta-analysis. *Small Group Research, 22,* 175–186.

Evans, C. R., & Jarvis, P. A. (1980). Group cohesion: A review and re-evaluation. *Small Group Behavior, 11,* 359–370.

Feltz, D. L., & Lirgg, C. D. (1998). Perceived team and player efficacy in hockey. *Journal of Applied Psychology, 83,* 557–564.

Festinger, L. (1950). Informal social communication. *Psychological Review, 57,* 271–282.

Fiedler, F. E. (1989). The effective utilization of intellectual abilities and job-relevant knowledge in group performance: Cognitive resource theory and an agenda for the future. *Applied Psychology: An International Review, 38,* 289–304.

Finkelstein, S., & Hambrick, D. C. (1990). Top management team tenure and organizational outcomes: The moderating role of managerial discretion. *Administrative Science Quarterly, 35,* 484–503.

Fleishman, E. A., Mumford, M. D., Zaccaro, S. J., Levin, K. Y., Korotkin, A. L., & Hein, M. B. (1991). Taxonomic efforts in the description of leader behavior: A synthesis and functional interpretation. *Leadership Quarterly, 2*(4), 245–287.

Fleishman, E. A., & Zaccaro, W. J. (1992). Toward a taxonomy of team performance functions. In R. W. Swezey & E. Salas (Eds.),

Teams: Their training and performance (pp. 31–56). Norwood, NJ: Ablex.

Foushee, C. H., & Manos, K. L. (1981). Information transfer within the cockpit: Problems in intracockpit communications. In C. E. Billings & E. S. Cheaney (Eds.), *Information transfer problems in the aviation system* (NASA Tech. Paper No. 1875, pp. 63–71). Moffett Field, CA: NASA.

George, J. M. (1990). Personality, affect, and behavior in groups. *Journal of Applied Psychology, 75,* 107–116.

Gersick, C. J. G. (1988). Time and transition in work teams: Toward a new model of group development. *Academy of Management Journal, 31,* 9–41.

Gersick, C. J. G. (1989). Marking time: Predictable transitions in task groups. *Academy of Management Journal, 32,* 274–309.

Gibson, C. B. (1999). Do they do what they believe the can? Group efficacy and group effectiveness across tasks and cultures. *Academy of Management Journal, 42,* 138–152.

Ginnett, R. C. (1993). Crews as groups: Their formation and their leadership. In E. L. Wiener, B. G. Kanki, & R. L. Helmrich (Eds.), *Cockpit resource management* (pp. 71–98). San Diego, CA: Academic Press.

Gist, M. E. (1987). Self-efficacy: Implications for organizational behavior and human resource management. *Academy of Management Review, 17,* 183–211.

Gladstein, D. L. (1984). Groups in context: A model of task group effectiveness. *Administrative Science Quarterly, 29,* 499–517.

Glickman, A. S., Zimmer, S., Montero, R. C., Guerette, P. J., Campbell, W. J., Morgan, B. B., & Salas, E. (1987). *The evolution of teamwork skills: An empirical assessment with implications for training* (Tech. Rep. No. TR-87-016). Orlando, FL: Naval Training Systems Center.

González-Romá, V., Peiró, J. M., & Tordera, N. (in press). An examination of the antecedents and moderator influences of climate strength. *Journal of Applied Psychology.*

Goodman, P. S., Ravlin, E., & Schminke, M. (1987). Understanding groups in organizations. In L. L. Cummings & B. M. Staw (Eds.), *Research in organizational behavior* (Vol. 9, pp. 121–173). Greenwich, CT: JAI Press.

Greene, C. N. (1989). Cohesion and productivity in work groups. *Small Group Behavior, 20,* 70–86.

Gross, N., & Martin, W. E. (1952). On group cohesiveness. *American Journal of Sociology, 57,* 546–554.

Guastello, S. J., & Guastello, D. D. (1998). Origins of coordination and team effectiveness: A perspective from game theory and nonlinear dynamics. *Journal of Applied Psychology, 83,* 423–437.

Gully, S. M. (2000). Work team research: Recent findings and future trends. In M. Beyerlein (Ed.), *Work teams: Past, present, and future* (pp. 25–44). Dordrecht, The Netherlands: Kluwer.

Gully, S. M., Devine, D. J., & Whitney, D. J. (1995). A meta-analysis of cohesion and performance: Effects of levels of analysis and task interdependence. *Small Group Research, 26,* 497–520.

Gully, S. M., Incalcaterra, K. A., Joshi, A., & Beaubien, J. M. (in press). A meta-analysis of team-efficacy, potency, and performance: Interdependence and levels of analysis as moderators of observed relationships. *Journal of Applied Psychology.*

Guzzo, R. A., & Dickson, M. W. (1996). Teams in organization: Recent research on performance and effectiveness. *Annual Review of Psychology, 47,* 307–338.

Guzzo, R. A., & Shea, G. P. (1992). Group performance and intergroup relations in organizations. In M. D. Dunnette & L. M. Hough (Eds.), *Handbook of industrial and organizational psychology* (2nd ed., Vol. 3, pp. 269–313). Palo Alto, CA: Consulting Psychologist Press.

Guzzo, R. A., Yost, P. R., Campbell, R. J., & Shea, G. P. (1993). Potency in groups: Articulating a construct. *British Journal of Social Psychology, 32,* 87–106.

Hackman, J. R. (1986). The psychology of self-management in organizations. In M. S. Pollack & R. O. Perlogg (Eds.), *Psychology and work: Productivity change and employment* (pp. 85–136). Washington, DC: American Psychological Association.

Hackman, J. R. (1987). The design of work teams. In J. Lorsch (Ed.), *Handbook of organizational behavior* (pp. 315–342). New York: Prentice Hall.

Hackman, J. R. (1992). Group influences on individuals in organizations. In M. D. Dunnette & L. M. Hough (Eds.), *Handbook of industrial and organizational psychology* (Vol. 3, pp. 199–267). Palo Alto, CA: Consulting Psychologist Press.

Hackman, J. R., & Vidmar, N. (1970). Effects of size and task type on group performance and member reactions. *Sociometry, 33,* 37–54.

Hackman, J. R., & Walton, R. E. (1986). Leading groups in organizations. In P. S. Goodman (Ed.), *Designing effective work groups* (pp. 72–119). San Francisco: Jossey-Bass.

Haleblian, J., & Finkelstein, S. (1993). Top management team size, CEO dominance, and firm performance: The moderating roles of environmental turbulence and discretion. *Academy of Management Journal, 36,* 844–863.

Hambrick, D. C. (1995). Fragmentation and other problems CEOs have with their top management teams. *California Management Review, 37,* 110–127.

Hambrick, D. C., & Mason, P. A. (1984). Upper echelons: The organization as a reflection of its top managers. *Academy of Management Review, 9,* 193–206.

Heslin, R. (1964). Predicting group task effectiveness from member characteristics. *Psychological Bulletin, 62,* 248–256.

Hill, G. W. (1982). Group versus individual performance: Are N + 1 heads better than one? *Psychological Bulletin, 91,* 517–539.

Hodges, L., & Carron, A. V. (1992). Collective efficacy and group performance. *International Journal of Sport Psychology, 23,* 48–59.

Hofmann, D. A., & Stetzer, A. (1996). A cross-level investigation of factors influencing unsafe behaviors and accidents. *Personnel Psychology, 49,* 307–339.

Hollenbeck, J. R., Colquitt, J. A., Ilgen, D. R., LePine, J. A., & Hedlund, J. (1998). Accuracy decomposition and team decision making: Testing theoretical boundary conditions. *Journal of Applied Psychology, 83,* 494–500.

Hollenbeck, J. R., Ilgen, D. R., Sego, D. J., Hedlund, J., Major, D. A., & Phillips, J. (1995). Multilevel theory of team decision making: Decision performance in teams incorporating distributed expertise. *Journal of Applied Psychology, 80,* 292–316.

Hollingshead, A. B. (1998a). Retrieval processes in transactive memory systems. *Journal of Personality and Social Psychology, 74,* 659–671.

Hollingshead, A. B. (1998b). Communication, learning, and retrieval in transactive memory systems. *Journal of Experimental Social Psychology, 34,* 423–442.

Hyatt, D. E., & Ruddy, T. M. (1997). An examination of the relationship between work group characteristics and performance: Once more into the breech. *Journal of Applied Psychology, 50,* 553–585.

Jackson, S. E. (1992a). Consequences of group composition for the interpersonal dynamics of strategic issue processing. In P. Shrivastava, A. Huff, & J. E. Dutton (Eds.), *Advances in strategic management* (Vol. 8, pp. 345–382). Greenwich, CT: JAI Press.

Jackson, S. E. (1992b). Team composition in organizational settings: Issues in managing an increasingly diverse workforce. In S. Worchel, W. Wood, & J. Simpson (Eds.), *Group process and productivity* (pp. 138–173). Newbury Park, CA: Sage.

Jackson, S. E., Brett, J. F., Sessa, V. I., Cooper, D. M., Julin, J. A., & Peyronnin, K. (1991). Some differences make a difference: Individual dissimilarity and group heterogeneity as correlates of recruitment, promotions, and turnover. *Journal of Applied Psychology, 76,* 675–689.

Jackson, S. E., & Joshi, A. (2002). Research on domestic and international diversity in organizations: A merger that works. In N. Anderson, D. S. Ones, H. K. Sinangil, & C. Viswesvaran (Eds.), *Handbook of industrial, work and organizational psychology.* (Vol. 2, pp. 206–231). Thousand Oaks, CA: Sage.

Jackson, S. E., May, K. E., & Whitney, K. (1995). Understanding the dynamics of diversity in decision-making teams. In R. A. Guzzo & E. Salas (Eds.), *Team effectiveness and decision making in organizations* (pp. 204–261). San Francisco: Jossey-Bass.

Jehn, K. A. (1995). A multimethod examination of the benefits and detriments of intragroup conflict. *Administrative Science Quarterly, 40,* 256–282.

Karau, S. J., & Williams, K. D. (1993). Social loafing: A meta-analytic review and theoretical integration. *Journal of Personality and Social Psychology, 65,* 681–706.

Katz, R. (1980). Time and work: Toward an integrative perspective. *Research in Organizational Behavior, 2,* 81–127.

Katz, R. (1982). The effects of group longevity on communication and performance. *Administrative Science Quarterly, 27,* 81–104.

Katz, R., & Allen, T. J. (1988). Investigating the not invented here (NIH) syndrome: A look at the performance, tenure, and communication patterns of 50 R&D project groups. In M. L. Tushman & W. L. Moore (Eds.), *Readings in the management of innovation* (pp. 293–309). New York: Ballinger.

Katzenbach, J. R., & Smith, D. K. (1993). *The wisdom of teams: Creating the high performance organization.* Boston, MA: Harvard Business School Press.

Kelly, J. R., Futoran, G. C., & McGrath, J. E. (1990). Capacity and capability: Seven studies of entrainment of task performance rates. *Small Group Research, 21,* 283–314.

Kerr, N., & Bruun, S. (1983). The dispensability of member effort and group motivation losses: Free-rider effects. *Journal of Personality and Social Psychology, 44,* 78–94.

Kirkman, B. L., & Shapiro, D. L. (2000). Understanding why team members won't share: An examination of factors related to employee receptivity to team-based rewards. *Small Group Research, 31,* 175–209.

Klimoski, R. J., & Jones, R. (1995). Suppose we took staffing for effective group decision making seriously? In R. Guzzo & E. Salas (Eds.), *Team effectiveness and decision making in organizations* (pp. 291–332). San Francisco: Jossey-Bass.

Klimoski, R. J., & Mohammed, S. (1994). Team mental model: Construct or metaphor? *Journal of Management, 20,* 403–437.

Komaki, J. L., Desselles, M. L., & Bowman, E. D. (1989). Definitely not a breeze: Extending an operant model of effective supervision to teams. *Journal of Applied Psychology, 74,* 522–529.

Kozlowski, S. W. J., Brown, K. G., Weissbein, D. A., Cannon-Bowers, J., & Salas, E. (2000). A multi-level perspective on training effectiveness: Enhancing horizontal and vertical transfer. In K. J. Klein & S. W. J. Kozlowski (Eds.), *Multilevel theory, research, and methods in organizations* (pp. 157–210). San Francisco, CA: Jossey-Bass.

Kozlowski, S. W. J., Gully, S. M., McHugh, P. P., Salas, E., & Cannon-Bowers, J. A. (1996). A dynamic theory of leadership and team effectiveness: Developmental and task contingent leader roles. In G. R. Ferris (Ed.), *Research in personnel and human resource management* (Vol. 14, pp. 253–305). Greenwich, CT: JAI Press.

Kozlowski, S. W. J., Gully, S. M., Nason, E. R., & Smith, E. M. (1999). Developing adaptive teams: A theory of compilation and performance across levels and time. In D. R. Ilgen & E. D. Pulakos (Eds.), *The changing nature of work performance: Implications for staffing, personnel actions, and development* (pp. 240–292). San Francisco: Jossey-Bass.

Kozlowski, S. W. J., Gully, S. M., Salas, E., & Cannon-Bowers, J. A. (1996). Team leadership and development: Theory, principles, and guidelines for training leaders and teams. In M. Beyerlein, D. Johnson, & S. Beyerlein (Eds.), *Advances in interdisciplinary studies of work teams: Team leadership* (Vol. 3, pp. 251–289). Greenwich, CT: JAI Press.

Kozlowski, S. W. J., & Klein, K. J. (2000). A multilevel approach to theory and research in organizations: Contextual, temporal, and emergent processes. In K. J. Klein & S. W. J. Kozlowski (Eds.), *Multilevel theory, research, and methods in organizations: Foundations, extensions, and new directions* (pp. 3–90). San Francisco: Jossey-Bass.

Kozlowski, S. W. J., & Salas, E. (1997). An organizational systems approach for the implementation and transfer of training. In J. K. Ford, S. W. J. Kozlowski, K. Kraiger, E. Salas, & M. Teachout (Eds.), *Improving training effectiveness in work organizations* (pp. 247–287). Mahwah, NJ: Erlbaum.

Kozlowski, S. W. J., Toney, R. J., Mullins, M. E., Weissbein, D. A., Brown, K. G., & Bell, B. S. (2001). Developing adaptability: A theory for the design of integrated-embedded training systems. In E. Salas (Ed.), *Advances in human performance and cognitive engineering research* (Vol. 1, pp. 59–123). Amsterdam: JAI/Elsevier Science.

Lantané, B., Williams, K., & Harkins, S. (1979). Many hands make light the work: The causes and consequences of social loafing. *Journal of Personality and Social Psychology, 37,* 822–832.

Lau, D. C., & Murnighan, J. K. (1998). Demographic diversity and faultlines: The compositional dynamics of organizational groups. *Academy of Management Review, 23,* 325–340.

Lawler, E. E. (1986). *High involvement management.* San Francisco: Jossey-Bass.

Lawler, E. E., Mohrman, S. A., & Ledford, G. E. (1992). *Employee involvement and total quality management: Practices and results in Fortune 1000 companies.* San Francisco: Jossey-Bass.

Lawler, E. E., Mohrman, S. A., & Ledford, G. E. (1995). *Creating high performance organizations: Practices and results of employee involvement and total quality management in Fortune 1000 companies.* San Francisco: Jossey-Bass.

LePine, J. A., Colquitt, J. A., & Erez, A. (2000). Adaptability to changing task contexts: Effects of general cognitive ability, conscientiousness, and openness to experience. *Personnel Psychology, 53,* 563–593.

LePine, J. A., Hollenbeck, J. R., Ilgen, D. R., & Hedlund, J. (1997). Effects of individual differences on the performance of hierarchical decision-making teams: Much more than g. *Journal of Applied Psychology, 82,* 803–811.

Levine, J. M., & Moreland, R. L. (1990). Progress in small group research. *Annual Review of Psychology, 41,* 585–634.

Lewis, K. (2000, August). *Is performance all in their minds? The impact of transactive memory on knowledge-worker team performance.* Paper presented at the Annual Meeting of the Academy of Management, Toronto, Ontario, Canada.

Liang, D. W., Moreland, R., & Argote, L. (1995). Group versus individual training and group performance: The mediating role of transactive memory. *Personality and Social Psychology Bulletin, 21,* 384–393.

Lindsley, D. H., Brass, D. J., & Thomas, J. B. (1995). Efficacy-performance spirals: A multilevel perspective. *Academy of Management Review, 20,* 645–678.

Lott, A. J., & Lott, B. E. (1965). Group cohesiveness as interpersonal attraction: A review of relationships with antecedent and consequent variables. *Psychological Bulletin, 64,* 259–309.

Louis, M. R., Posner, B. Z., & Powell, G. N. (1983). The availability and helpfulness of socialization practices. *Personnel Psychology, 36,* 857–866.

Major, D. A., Kozlowski, S. W. J., Chao, G. T., & Gardner, P. D. (1995). Newcomer expectations and early socialization outcomes: The moderating effect of role development factors. *Journal of Applied Psychology, 80,* 418–431.

Manz, C. C. (1992). Self-leading work teams: Moving beyond self-management myths. *Human Relations, 45,* 1119–1140.

Manz, C. C., & Sims, H. P., Jr. (1987). Leading workers to lead themselves: The external leadership of self-managing work teams. *Administrative Science Quarterly, 32,* 106–128.

Marks, M. A., Mathieu, J. E., & Zaccaro, S. J. (2001). A temporally based framework and taxonomy of team processes. *Academy of Management Review, 26,* 356–376.

Marks, M. A., Zaccaro, S. J., & Mathieu, J. E. (2000). Performance implications of leader briefings and team interaction training for team adaptation to novel environments. *Journal of Applied Psychology, 85,* 971–986.

Martz, W. B., Jr., Vogel, R. R., & Nunamaker, J. F., Jr. (1992). Electronic meeting systems: Results from the field. *Decision Support Systems, 8,* 141–158.

Mathieu, J. E., Heffner, T. S., Goodwin, G. F., Salas, E., & Cannon-Bowers, J. A. (2000). The influence of shared mental models on team process and performance. *Journal of Applied Psychology, 85,* 273–283.

Matsui, T., Kakuyama, T., & Onglatco, L. U. (1987). The effects of goals and feedback on performance in groups. *Journal of Applied Psychology, 72,* 407–415.

McCall, M. W., Jr., Morrison, A. M., & Hannan, R. L. (1978). *Studies of managerial work: Results and methods* (Tech. Rep. No. 9). Greensboro, NC: Center for Creative Leadership.

McClough, A., & Rogelberg, S. (1998, April). *An exploration of Stevens and Campion's teamwork KSA instrument.* Paper presented at the 13th Annual Conference of the Society for Industrial and Organizational Psychology, Dallas, TX.

McGrath, J. E. (1962). *Leadership behavior: Some requirements for leadership training.* Washington, DC: U.S. Civil Service Commission.

McGrath, J. E. (1964). *Social psychology: A brief introduction.* New York: Holt, Rinehart, & Winston.

McGrath, J. E. (1984). *Groups: Interaction and performance.* Englewood Cliffs, NJ: Prentice Hall.

McGrath, J. E. (1990). Time matters in groups. In J. Galegher, R. Krout, & C. C. Egido (Eds.), *Intellectual teamwork* (pp. 23–61). Hillsdale, NJ: Erlbaum.

McGrath, J. E. (1991). Time, interaction, and performance (TIP): A theory of groups. *Small Group Research, 22,* 147–174.

McGrath, J. E. (1997). Small group research, that once and future field: An interpretation of the past with an eye toward the future. *Group Dynamics, 1,* 7–27.

McGrath, J. E., & Hollingshead, A. B. (1994). *Groups interacting with technology.* Thousand Oaks, CA: Sage.

Minionis, D. P., Zaccaro, S. J., & Perez, R. (1995, May). *Shared mental models, team coordination, and team performance.* Paper presented at the 10th Annual Meeting of the Society for Industrial and Organizational Psychology, Orlando, FL.

Mitchell, T. R., & Silver, W. S. (1990). Individual and group goals when workers are interdependent: Effects on task strategies and performance. *Journal of Applied Psychology, 75,* 185–193.

Mohammed, S., & Dumville, B. C. (2001). Team mental models in a team knowledge framework: Expanding theory and measurement across disciplinary boundaries. *Journal of Organizational Behavior, 22,* 89–106.

Moreland, R. L. (2000). Transactive memory: Learning who knows what in work groups and organizations. In L. Thompson, D. Messick, & J. Levine (Eds.), *Shared cognition in organizations: The management of knowledge* (pp. 3–31). Mahwah, NJ: Erlbaum.

Moreland, R. L., Argote, L., & Krishnan, R. (1998). Training people to work in groups. In R. S. Tindale, L. Heath, J. Edwards, E. J. Posavac, F. B. Bryant, Y. Suarez-Balcazar, E. Henderson-King, & J. Myers (Eds.), *Theory and research on small groups* (pp. 37–60). New York: Plenum Press.

Moreland, R. L., & Levine, J. M. (1982). Socialization in small groups: Temporal changes in individual-group relations. In L. Berkowitz (Ed.), *Advances in experimental social psychology* (Vol. 15, pp. 137–192). New York: Academic Press.

Moreland, R. L., & Levine, J. M. (1989). Newcomers and oldtimers in small groups. In P. B. Paulus (Ed.), *Psychology of group influence* (2nd ed., pp. 143–186). Hillsdale, NJ: Erlbaum.

Moreland, R. L., & Levine, J. M. (1992). The composition of small groups. In E. J. Lawler, B. Markovsky, C. Ridgeway, & H. A. Walker (Eds.), *Advances in group processes* (Vol. 9, pp. 237–280). Greenwich, CT: JAI Press.

Moreland, R. L., Levine, J. M., & Wingert, M. L. (1996). Creating the ideal group: Composition effects at work. In E. H. Witte & J. H. Davis (Eds.), *Understanding group behavior: Small group processes and interpersonal relations* (Vol. 2, pp. 11–35). Mahwah, NJ: Erlbaum.

Morgan, B. B., Salas, E., & Glickman, A. S. (1993). An analysis of team evolution and maturation. *Journal of General Psychology, 120,* 277–291.

Mullen, B., & Copper, C. (1994). The relation between group cohesiveness and performance: An integration. *Psychological Bulletin, 115*(2), 210–227.

Neck, C. P., Stewart, G. L., & Manz, C. C. (1996). Self-leaders within self-leading teams: Toward an optimal equilibrium. In M. Beyerlein, D. A. Johnson, & S. Beyerlein (Eds.), *Advances in interdisciplinary studies of work teams: Team leadership* (Vol. 3, pp. 43–65). Greenwich, CT: JAI Press.

Neuman, G. A., Wagner, S. H., & Christiansen, N. D. (1999). The relationship between work-team personality composition and the job performance in teams. *Group and Organization Management, 24,* 28–45.

Neuman, G. A., & Wright, J. (1999). Team effectiveness: Beyond skills and cognitive ability. *Journal of Applied Psychology, 84,* 376–389.

Nieva, V. F., Fleishman, E. A., & Reick, A. (1985). *Team dimensions: Their identity, their measurement, and their relationships* (Research Note 85-12). Washington, DC: U.S. Army, Research Institute for the Behavioral and Social Sciences.

Ostroff, C., & Kozlowski, S. W. J. (1992). Organizational socialization as a learning process: The role of information acquisition. *Personnel Psychology, 45,* 849–874.

Paskevich, D. M., Brawley, L. R., Dorsch, K. D., & Widmeyer, W. N. (1999). Relationship between collective efficacy and team cohesion: Conceptual and measurement issues. *Group Dynamics, 3,* 210–222.

Pelled, L. H., Eisenhardt, K. M., & Xin, K. R. (1999). Exploring the black box: An analysis of work group diversity, conflict, and performance. *Administrative Science Quarterly, 44,* 1–28.

Pelz, D. C., & Andrews, F. M. (1966). *Scientists in organizations: Productive climates for research and development.* Ann Arbor, MI: University of Michigan, Institute for Social Research.

Phillips, J. M. (1999). Antecedents of leader utilization of staff input in decision-making teams. *Organizational Behavior and Human Decision Processes, 77,* 215–242.

Pinto, M. B., & Pinto, J. K. (1990). Project team communication and cross-functional cooperation in new program development. *Journal of Product Innovation Management, 7,* 200–212.

Pritchard, R. D., Jones, S. D., Roth, P. L., Stuebing, K. K., & Ekeberg, S. E. (1998). Effects of group feedback, goal setting, and incentives on organizational productivity. *Journal of Applied Psychology, 73,* 337–358.

Saavedra, R., Earley, P. C., & Van Dyne, L. (1993). Complex interdependence in task-performing groups. *Journal of Applied Psychology, 78,* 61–72.

Salas, E., & Cannon-Bowers, J. A. (1997). Methods, tools, and strategies for team training. In M. A. Quinones & A. Ehrenstein (Eds.), *Training for a rapidly changing workplace: Applications of psychological research* (pp. 249–279). Washington, DC: American Psychological Association.

Salas, E., Dickinson, T. L., Converse, S. A., & Tannenbaum, S. I. (1992). Toward an understanding of team performance and training. In R. W. Swezey & E. Salas (Eds.), *Teams: Their training and performance* (pp. 3–29). Norwood, NJ: Ablex.

Salas, E., Fowlkes, J., Stout, R. J., Prince, C., & Milanovich, D. M. (1999). Does CRM training enhance teamwork skills in the cockpit? Two evaluation studies. *Human Factors, 41,* 326–343.

Salas, E., Prince, C., Bowers, C. A., Stout, R., Oser, R. L., & Cannon-Bowers, J. A. (1999). A methodology to enhance crew resource management training. *Human Factors, 41,* 161–172.

Salas, E., Rozell, D., Driskell, J. D., & Mullen, B. (1999). The effect of team building on performance: An integration. *Small Group Research, 30,* 309–329.

Scharf, A. (1989). How to change seven rowdy people. *Industrial Management, 31,* 20–22.

Schneider, B. (1987). The people make the place. *Personnel Psychology, 40,* 437–453.

Schneider, B., Smith, D. B., & Sipe, W. P. (2000). Personnel selection psychology: Multi level considerations. In K. J. Klein & S. W. J. Kozlowski (Eds.), *Multilevel theory, research, and methods in organizations* (pp. 91–120). San Francisco: Jossey-Bass.

Seashore, S. E. (1954). *Group cohesiveness in the industrial work group.* Ann Arbor, MI: University of Michigan, Institute for Social Research.

Seers, A., Petty, M. M., & Cashman, J. F. (1995). Team-member exchange under team and traditional management: A naturally occurring quasi-experiment. *Group and Organization Management, 20,* 18–38.

Shaw, M. E. (1976). *Group dynamics.* New York: McGraw-Hill.

Shea, G. P., & Guzzo, R. A. (1987). Groups as human resources. In K. M. Rowland & G. R. Ferris (Eds.), *Research in personnel and human resource management* (Vol. 5, pp. 323–356). Greenwich, CT: JAI Press.

Shepard, H. A. (1956). Creativity in R/D teams. *Research in Engineering, October,* 10–13.

Sheppard, J. A. (1993). Productivity loss in performance groups: A motivation analysis. *Psychological Bulletin, 113,* 67–81.

Sheremata, W. A. (2000). Centrifugal and centripetal forces in radical new product development under time pressure. *Academy of Management Review, 25,* 389–408.

Simons, T. L., Pelled, L. H., & Smith, K. A. (1999). Making use of difference: Diversity, debate, and decision comprehensiveness in top management teams. *Academy of Management Journal, 6,* 662–673.

Simons, T. L., & Peterson, R. S. (2000). Task conflict and relationship conflict in top management teams: The pivotal role of intragroup trust. *Journal of Applied Psychology, 85,* 102–111.

Smith, K. G., Smith, K. A., Olian, J. D., Smis, H. P., Jr., O'Bannon, D. P., & Scully, J. A. (1994). Top management team demography and process: The role of social integration and communication. *Administrative Science Quarterly, 39,* 412–438.

Smith-Jentsch, K. A., Milanovich, D. M., Reynolds, A. M., & Hall, S. M. (1999, April). *Fostering the development of shared teamwork knowledge structure through computer-based instruction.* Paper presented at the 14th Annual Conference of the Society for Industrial and Organizational Psychology, Atlanta, GA.

Smith-Jentsch, K. A., Zeisig, R. L., Acton, B., & McPherson, J. A. (1998). Team dimensional training: A strategy for guided team self-correction. In J. A. Cannon-Bowers & E. Salas (Eds.), *Making decisions under stress: Implications for individual and team training* (pp. 271–297). Washington, DC: American Psychological Association Press.

Smolek, J., Hoffman, D., & Moran, L. (1999). Organizing teams for success. In E. Sundstrom (Ed.), *Supporting work team effectiveness* (pp. 24–62). San Francisco: Jossey-Bass.

Staw, B. M., Sutton, R. I., & Pelled, L. H. (1994). Employee positive emotion and favorable outcomes at the workplace. *Organization Science, 5,* 51–71.

Steiner, I. D. (1972). *Group process and productivity.* New York: Academic Press.

Stevens, M. J., & Campion, M. A. (1994). The knowledge, skill, and ability requirements for teamwork: Implications for human resource management. *Journal of Management, 20,* 503–530.

Stewart, G. L., & Barrick, M. R. (2000). Team structure and performance: Assessing the mediating role of intrateam process and the moderating role of task type. *Academy of Management Journal, 43,* 135–148.

Stewart, G. L., & Barrick, M. R. (in press). Lessons learned from the person-situation debate: A review and research agenda. In D. B. Smith & B. Schneider (Eds.), *Personality and Organizations.* Mahwah, NJ: Erlbaum.

Stewart, G. L., & Manz, C. C. (1995). Leadership for self-managing work teams: A typology and integrative model. *Human Relations, 48,* 347–370.

Stout, R. J., Cannon-Bowers, J. A., Salas, E., & Milanovich, D. M. (1999). Planning, shared mental models, and coordinated performance: An empirical link is established. *Human Factors, 41,* 61–71.

Stout, R. J., Salas, E., & Carson, R. (1994). Individual task proficiency and team process behavior: What's important for team functioning. *Military Psychology, 6,* 177–192.

Sundstrom, E. (1999). Supporting work team effectiveness: Best practices. In E. Sundstrom (Ed.), *Supporting work team effectiveness: Best management practices for fostering high performance* (pp. 301–342). San Francisco: Jossey-Bass.

Sundstrom, E., DeMeuse, K. P., & Futrell, D. (1990). Work teams: Applications and effectiveness. *American Psychologist, 45,* 120–133.

Sundstrom, E., McIntyre, M., Halfhill, T., & Richards, H. (2000). Work groups from the Hawthorne studies to work teams of the 1990's and beyond. *Group Dynamics: Theory, Research, and Practice, 4,* 44–67.

Swezey, R. W., & Salas, E. (1992). Guidelines for use in team training development. In R. W. Swezey & E. Salas (Eds.), *Teams: Their training and performance* (pp. 219–245). Norwood, NJ: Ablex.

Tannenbaum, S. I., Beard, R. L., & Salas, E. (1992). Team building and its influence on team effectiveness: An examination of conceptual and empirical developments. In K. Kelley (Ed.), *Issues, theory, and research in industrial/organizational psychology* (pp. 117–153). Amsterdam: Elsevier.

Tesluk, P., Kirkman, B. L., & Cordery, J. L. (2001). *Effects of work unit cynicism on efforts to increase self-management in work groups: Implications for implementing high-involvement approaches.* Manuscript in preparation.

Tjosvold, D. (1985). Implications of controversy research for management. *Journal of Management, 11,* 21–37.

Tuckman, B. W. (1965). Developmental sequence in small groups. *Psychological Bulletin, 63,* 384–399.

Tziner, A., & Eden, D. (1985). Effects of crew composition on crew performance: Does the whole equal the sum of its parts? *Journal of Applied Psychology, 70,* 85–93.

U.S. Department of Labor. (1993). *High performance work practices and firm performance.* Washington, DC: Office of the American Workplace.

Van De Ven, A. H., Delbecq, A. L., & Koenig, R. (1976). Determinants of coordination modes within organizations. *American Sociological Review, 41,* 322–338.

Wageman, R. (1995). Interdependence and group effectiveness. *Administrative Science Quarterly, 40,* 145–180.

Wageman, R. (1997). Critical success factors for creating superb self-managing teams. *Organizational Dynamics, 26,* 49–61.

Wageman, R. (1999). Task design, outcome interdependence, and individual differences: Their joint effects on effort in task-performing teams [Commentary on Huguet et al., 1999]. *Group Dynamics, 3,* 132–137.

Wagner, J. A. (1995). Studies of individualism-collectivism: Effects on cooperation in groups. *Academy of Management Journal, 38,* 152–172.

Waller, M. J. (1999). The timing of adaptive group responses to nonroutine events. *Academy of Management Journal, 42,* 127–137.

Watson, W. E., Kumar, K., & Michaelsen, L. K. (1993). Cultural diversity's impact on interaction process and performance: Comparing homogenous and diverse task groups. *Academy of Management Journal, 36,* 590–602.

Weaver, J. L., Bowers, C. A., Salas, E., & Cannon-Bowers, J. A. (1997). Motivation in teams. In M. M. Beyerlein & D. A. Johnson (Eds.), *Advances in interdisciplinary studies of work teams* (Vol. 4, pp. 167–191). Greenwich, CT: JAI Press.

Wegner, D. M. (1986). Transactive memory: A contemporary analysis of the group mind. In B. Mullen & G. R. Goethals (Eds.), *Theories of group behavior* (pp. 185–208). New York: Springer-Verlag.

Wegner, D. M. (1995). A computer network model of human transactive memory. *Social Cognition, 13,* 319–339.

Wegner, D. M., Giuliano, T., & Hertel, P. (1985). Cognitive interdependence in close relationships. In W. J. Ickes (Ed.), *Compatible and incompatible relationships* (pp. 253–276). New York: Springer-Verlag.

West, M. A., & Anderson, N. R. (1996). Innovation in top management teams. *Journal of Applied Psychology, 81,* 680–693.

Wheelan, S. A. (1994). *Group processes: A developmental perspective.* Sydney, Australia: Allyn and Bacon.

Wiersema, M. F., & Bird, A. (1993). Organizational demography in Japanese firms: Group heterogeneity, industry dissimilarity, and top management team turnover. *Academy of Management Journal, 36,* 996–1025.

Yukl, G., & Van Fleet, D. D. (1992). Theory and research on leadership in organizations. In M. Dunnette & L. Hough (Eds.), *Handbook of I/O psychology* (Vol. 3, pp. 147–198). Palo Alto, CA: Consulting Psychologists Press.

Zaccaro, S. J., Blair, V., Peterson, C., & Zazanis, M. (1995). Collective efficacy. In J. Maddux (Ed.), *Self efficacy, adaptation, and adjustment* (pp. 305–328). New York: Plenum Press.

Zaccaro, S. J., & Lowe, C. A. (1988). Cohesiveness and performance on an additive task: Evidence for multidimensionality. *Journal of Social Psychology, 128,* 547–558.

Zaccaro, S. J., & McCoy, M. C. (1988). The effects of task and interpersonal cohesiveness on performance of a disjunctive group task. *Journal of Applied Social Psychology, 18,* 837–851.

Zajonc, R. B. (1965). Social facilitation. *Science, 149,* 269–274.

Zalesny, M. D., Salas, E., & Prince, C. (1995). Conceptual and measurement issues in coordination: Implications for team behavior and performance. In G. R. Ferris (Ed.), *Research in personnel and human resources management* (Vol. 13, pp. 81–115). Greenwich, CT: JAI Press.

CHAPTER 15

Customer Service Behavior

ANN MARIE RYAN AND ROBERT E. PLOYHART

Desatnick (1994) suggested that the twenty-first century is going to be either the era of customer sovereignty or the era of customer rebellion and revolt. The quality of service is driven in part by the behavior of the service provider. In this chapter, we examine influences on customer service behavior (hereafter referred to as CSB) and how traditional industrial/ organizational (I/O) psychology topics (i.e., selection, motivation) might be approached if the goal is enhancing CSB. We take the position that not all service situations are similar (i.e., the service provided in a doctor-patient relationship is not the same as that at a fast-food restaurant) and therefore a discussion of CSB requires a contingency perspective.

CSB is broadly defined as any activities of employees specifically directed toward affecting service quality (e.g., greeting or assisting customers, rectifying service failures). Note that there are many factors that influence a customer's experience of service and the ability of employees to deliver that service (e.g., amount of computer downtime, product quality, store physical layout, unrealistic customer expectations such as on-time flight departures in bad weather; e.g., K. A. Brown & Mitchell, 1993; Spencer, 1991). Also note that the quality of customer service depends upon what the customer desires—not just the level of service delivered (George & Jones, 1991). Our focus is on the behaviors in which employees engage for the specific purpose of enhancing customer perceptions of service quality.

Why focus on CSB in this Handbook, given the variety of behaviors individuals exhibit at work? First, service has been

and continues to be the major sector of growth in jobs (64.7% of all jobs; Statistical Abstracts of the United States, 1999) and services are said to account for three fourths of the gross national product (Spencer, 1991). Second, ever since Peters and Waterman's *In Search of Excellence* (1989), a focus on the customer has become a major component of organizational strategies, regardless of whether the organization is in the service or manufacturing sector. Poor service has been found to be a key reason for switching to competitors (Weitzel, Schwarzkopf, & Peach, 1989; Zemke & Schaaf, 1989). Third, customer service is one area in which researchers have strong evidence that employee affect and attitudes influence some bottom-line outcomes of great importance to organizations (e.g., customer satisfaction, repeat business); this is an area in which I/O psychologists have convincingly demonstrated that concern for the employee benefits the organization's goals.

There have been many excellent reviews on CSB-related research (e.g., Bowen & Schneider, 1988; Bowen & Waldman, 1999; Schneider & Bowen, 1992), and our goal is not to summarize or replicate those reviews. Indeed, the volume of literature on CSB is so great as to prevent a thorough review in the space allotted here. Instead, we focus our chapter on how some common variations in the nature of services affect CSB and the systems that I/O psychologists develop to promote positive CSB. In any workplace, I/O psychologists would advocate certain practices to predict, motivate, or teach desired behaviors. Our focus in this chapter is a contingency approach to the understanding, prediction, and influence of CSB; we hold that there are aspects of the service situation that should and do affect the choices one must make regarding how to bring about positive CSB. A one-size-fits-all approach to promoting CSB will not be successful. Contingency approaches to choosing human resources (HR) practices have been discussed in the strategic human resource management (HRM) literature (Delery & Doty, 1996; Huselid, 1995), and our chapter follows from that line of thinking. Others have noted the need for a consideration of the situation in deciding how to design systems to promote CSB (Bowen & Waldman, 1999; Jackson & Schuler, 1992). This chapter adds value to those suggestions in that it provides a more comprehensive examination of both aspects of services and I/O interventions. Our chapter has an intervention rather than a description focus; the goal is to discuss what appear to be the best ways to promote CSB and to higher quality service.

First, we describe aspects of services that may influence how one promotes CSB. This section lays the groundwork for the contingency perspective. Then we review the major research and practice areas and discuss their relation to the promotion of positive CSBs in the context of a contingency model. After discussing what is known about CSB and each intervention focus, we provide a table to illustrate how a contingency perspective might drive future research.

THE NATURE OF SERVICES

Researchers (e.g., Bowen & Schneider, 1988; P. Mills & Margulies, 1980; Schneider, 1990; Schneider & Bowen, 1985, 1992) have noted repeatedly that three continua recur in how services are distinguished from goods: the *intangibility* of services as contrasted with the tangibility of goods, the *simultaneity* of production and consumption of services as compared to separation of the production and consumption of goods, and the fact that many services involve *coproduction,* or active customer participation in the production of the service (e.g., providing information regarding medical symptoms or desired hairstyle). Schneider and colleagues (Bowen & Schneider, 1988; Schneider, 1990; Schneider & Bowen, 1985, 1992) have talked extensively about the implications of these distinctions for service management as compared to traditional manufacturing approaches; in this chapter we do not reiterate all the insights provided by these writings. However, they have noted that these are three aspects on which services can vary as well (e.g., some services are more tangible than are others, haircut vs. financial advice; customers may be more of a coproducer in some cases, Internet retailing vs. bricks and mortar). Variations on these three dimensions

can influence CSB and the interventions organizations undertake to promote CSB.

For example, Bowen and Schneider (1985) have noted that as intangibility increases, customers rely more on the service provider's behavior as an indicator of the quality of the service they are receiving. Yet intangibility makes it difficult to set specific goals or to prescribe specific behaviors for employees to demonstrate, leaving the organization with less control over employee behavior with more intangible services.

Another example is that the extent of coproduction may change the roles and behaviors of the employee (Bowen & Schneider, 1988; Legnick-Hall, 1996). Kelley, Donnelly, and Skinner (1990) noted that customers have expectations regarding what service employees should do and how they should behave (i.e., CSB) and what customers should do and how they should behave. A mismatch between customer and service provider expectations is likely to be problematic. For example, customers that do not understand what is expected of them (e.g., clearing own table, procedures for dropping off rental cars) require more from service employees, as do those customers who do not provide what is required (e.g., not reporting all symptoms to a doctor) or act inappropriately (e.g., angry and abusive airline passenger in a snowstorm delay; Kelley et al., 1990). Legnick-Hall (1996) noted that in addition to the importance of clarity of expectations, customer abilities and motivation to engage in coproduction are important influences on the outcome of the service encounter, and thereby may be important influences on an employee's CSB.

Besides these three oft-mentioned aspects of services, there are several other variations in services that we see as key influences on how organizations can manage CSB. A fourth distinction of importance is the *type of relationship* with customers that the employee has. Gutek and colleagues (Gutek, 1995; Gutek, Bhappu, Liao-Troth, & Cherry, 1999) have distinguished service relationships from service encounters. The former refers to cases in which a customer and employee expect to have repeated contact in the future (e.g., hairdresser, physician). Encounters are single interactions between a customer and service provider with no expectation of future interaction (e.g., fast-food cashier). They also describe pseudorelationships wherein customers have repeated contact with the same organizational location or unit (e.g., bank branch) but with different customer service providers. For purposes of simplicity, we do not consider this variant. How might this distinction change how we promote CSB? Gutek et al. (1999) noted that because of expected future interaction, providing good service is in one's self-interest in relationships, whereas individuals in encounters would not have the same motivations. Monitoring employees may be more essential to the promotion of high-quality service in encounters than it is in relationships (Gutek et al., 1999). Researchers (e.g., Bitner, Booms, & Mohr, 1994; Rafaeli, 1993) have also noted that employees look to customers for cues on how to behave (e.g., what type of transaction is desired, satisfaction, etc.). Thus, the nature of the relationship with the customer probably influences how employees decide to behave.

A fifth distinction is the extent to which a specific CSB to be exhibited is inherently discretionary. Many authors have described CSB as a form of prosocial (i.e., helping) behavior directed toward customers (George, 1991; George & Bettenhausen, 1990). Debate exists, however, as to whether one should consider these prosocial behaviors to be role prescribed (George, 1991) or outside formal role requirements (Morrison, 1997). Bettencourt and Brown (1997) distinguished *extrarole* CSBs (e.g., going beyond the call of duty) from *role-prescribed* CSBs (e.g., greet and say thank-you). Bettencourt, Gwinner, and Meuter (2001) further described service-oriented citizenship behaviors as taking three forms: loyalty behaviors, as employees act as representatives of firms; participation, as service employees provide information back to the organization regarding customer needs; and service delivery behaviors, conscientiously performing the activities surrounding delivering service. In any particular organization, these forms of citizenship behaviors may be considered more or less as role requirements. Whether a CSB is role-prescribed or extrarole results in different implications for interventions to promote CSBs. For example, Morrison (1997) noted that with discretionary behaviors, organizations must create an environment where employees *desire* to engage in the CSB.

Another dimension to consider is the extent to which the roles and expectations associated with a service interaction are *standard* or common versus *customized* (Bitner et al., 1994; Rogelberg, Barnes-Farrell, & Creamer, 1999). For example, Bitner et al. (1994) indicated that certain types of interactions (being seated in a restaurant) are repeated frequently so that there are standard scripts that employees and customers will know to follow. They note that when there is more unfamiliarity with what should occur or when there is interference with the standard script, there may be greater differences in employee and customer expectations. Also, Kelley et al. (1990) noted that customization requires greater coproduction because the customer must convey what he or she wants. In some cases, latitude in determining the extent of customization may be provided to the customer contact employee (Lovelock, 1983); for example, some customer service employees are essentially order takers, others create the service experience within their own determination (professor teaching), and others have tremendous control (surgeon, hairdresser; Lovelock, 1983). Differences in the standardization of service will influence how to best promote CSB.

One final dimension noted by several researchers as influencing how to promote CSB is the *nature of the customer contact*. For example, is the service delivered face-to-face, by telephone, e-mail, mail, or other means (Bowen, 1986; Rogelberg et al., 1999)? Bowen (1986) noted that customer physical presence is desirable when service production and delivery are absolutely inseparable (dentistry), there are marketing advantages (add-on sales are possible), and when it allows the customer to be more involved in the production of the service (customer will perform more service tasks). The physical presence of the customer is potentially an important situational determinant of CSB. The level or amount of customer contact that an individual has (constant vs. sporadic) is also a concern. For example, K. A. Brown and Mitchell (1993) noted that tellers, who have high amounts of customer contact, felt their performance was more hindered by social obstacles (coworker behaviors, workplace disruptions) than did account representatives who spent less time in contact with customers.

Note that these dimensions likely covary (e.g., intangibility may be related to coproduction). Also, there are other typologies of services and other distinctions among service situations that may influence CSBs and the systems developed to support those behaviors (e.g., duration of contact episode, P. Mills & Margulies, 1980; supply and demand for the service, Lovelock, 1983; internal vs. external customer, George, 1990; see also Albrecht & Zemke, 1985; Zeithaml, Berry & Parasuraman, 1993). Further, a strategic approach to human resources (Schuler & Jackson, 1987) would involve fitting HR practices to business strategy (i.e., chosen market segments such as high-end customers, aspects of service promoted such as speed or affordability, etc.). Although we cannot consider all these possibilities here, the dimensions noted should illustrate the usefulness of a contingency approach to the promotion of CSB. In each section that follows on various I/O topics, we end with a presentation of research questions based on a consideration of these dimensions.

THE CONCEPTUALIZATION AND MEASUREMENT OF CUSTOMER SERVICE PERFORMANCE

Defining and measuring customer service performance is perhaps more difficult than for other types of employee performance. Part of the difficulty arises from the fact that the nature of customer service (i.e., intangible, simultaneous production and consumption, coproduction) makes it difficult to use objective measures (e.g., Bowen & Schneider, 1988); another part of the difficulty arises because service quality ultimately lies in the eyes of the customer (R. L. Oliver, 1981; Parasuraman, Zeithaml, & Berry, 1985). A third difficulty is that what is viewed as good CSB likely varies greatly depending upon situational factors (e.g., busyness, professional level of CSB provider; e.g., doctor vs. waiter). Thus, the provision of high-quality service is very much a dynamic, interactive, and largely subjective experience (Boulding, Kalra, Staelin, & Zeithaml, 1993).

Further complicating the conceptualization and measurement of customer service is the diffuse ways in which it has been examined in the research literature. Some studies have focused on customer perceptions of service quality, whereas others have examined supervisory ratings of employee service behaviors; some research discusses service satisfaction, whereas other research discusses service quality; certain researchers focus on the emotional aspects of service, and others focus on the more technical features; some research focuses on the employee, and others focus on the customer. In this section, we review the major ways in which service performance has been conceptualized and operationalized at the individual level.

Conceptualization

Customer service performance is not conceptualized the same way in the I/O and service management literatures. In the I/O literature, employee service performance is generally defined as involving the types of behaviors in which an employee engages to satisfy a customer's expectations. For example, J. Hogan, Hogan, and Busch (1984) note that customer service requires three behaviors: (a) treating customers with tact, courtesy, and consideration; (b) perceiving customer needs; and (c) providing accurate and pleasant communication. A meta-analysis conducted by Frei and McDaniel (1998), building from the development of Personnel Decisions International's (PDI's) Servicefirst Inventory (Fogli & Whitney, 1991), considered customer service to be composed of four dimensions: (a) active customer relations, (b) polite customer relations, (c) helpful customer relations, and (d) personalized customer relations. They further suggest that CSB is composed of friendliness, reliability, responsiveness, and courteousness. Thus, the I/O literature tends to conceptualize service performance as an employee performing specific behaviors in particular ways to increase customer perceptions of service—that is, the conceptualization of service performance is what is done (or should be done) on the job, as defined by a job analysis.

In the service management literature, however, the focus is on customer service performance from the customer's perspective. The two most common definitions of customer service performance are those reflecting satisfaction and quality,

and the extant literature has tended to treat these concepts as separate. According to Parasuraman et al. (1985), "perceived service quality is a global judgment, or attitude, relating to the superiority of the service, whereas satisfaction is related to a specific transaction" (p. 16). This definition is consistent with others in the marketing literature (e.g., Hunt, 1979; R. L. Oliver, 1981). In these definitions, satisfaction or quality is usually defined according to the customer's perceptions. Thus—at least in the marketing literature—it is the customer's perceptions of satisfaction with specific service transactions that accumulate over time into perceptions of service quality (R. L. Oliver, 1981; Parasuraman et al., 1985).

In this literature, service quality lies in the judgment of the customer regarding how well the service *received* met the service *expected* (e.g., Gronroos, 1982; R. C. Lewis & Booms, 1983; Parasuraman, Berry, & Zeithaml, 1991b; R. A. Smith & Houston, 1982). Although the conceptualization of service quality as a customer's comparison between expectations and perceived service is relatively simple, the actual description of this psychological process is not. Multiple forms of expectancies may exist, each type of expectancy may be multiply determined, and each type of expectancy has different implications for deriving quality perceptions (e.g., Cadotte, Woodruff, & Jenkins, 1987). R. L. Oliver (1981) discussed several theories—such as adaptation-level theory and opponent-process theory—that can be used to account for how expectancies regarding service are formed and change.

Parasuraman et al. (1991b) and Zeithaml et al. (1993) argued that customer expectations have multiple, changing levels (see also Parasuraman, Zeithaml, & Berry, 1994b). The desired level reflects what customers expect should happen, and the adequate level reflects what they find minimally acceptable. For example, when visiting a fast-food restaurant we might expect the service to be fast (desired level), but we might recognize that the lunch hour rush will require an acceptable 10-min wait (adequate level). Thus, the desired level is to some degree higher than the adequate level. The area between these two levels is known as the *zone of tolerance,* and it is within this zone that service quality should be perceived as moderate or better. Parasuraman et al. (1991b) further note that the boundaries of the zone of tolerance (i.e., desired and adequate levels) are variable over time and situations. They also argued that the zones differ for different dimensions of service (we discuss these dimensions shortly). Finally, they suggested that several factors influence how these levels might change. Specifically, the adequate and desired levels may increase when the customer has experience with the service, when there are several perceived alternatives, when the service is required in an emergency situation, when personal or situational factors make the service particularly important, and when there is a service failure (see Zeithaml et al., 1993).

Boulding et al. (1993) have provided perhaps the most complete model of expectancy formation, suggesting there are two completely different types of expectancies. *Will expectancies* reflect what a customer thinks will most likely happen in the service. *Should expectancies* reflect what a customer ideally wants to happen. Notice that this is similar to the adequate and desired levels of expectancies in Parasuraman et al. (1991b), except that Boulding et al. (1993) state that these are two different types of expectancies and not simply different levels for the same expectancy. Will and should expectancies are determined by two factors: the current service delivery and expectancies formed as a result of previous interactions.

The process model described by Boulding et al. (1993) was generally supported by their data. What is innovative about this model is that it attempts to capture and explain the dynamic, ever-changing *process* of forming perceptions of service quality. The model is considerably more complex than are previous conceptualizations of service quality, but it also probably better reflects the customer's actual psychological processes. Unfortunately, in practice it is somewhat difficult to measure all of the necessary constructs to adequately assess the model.

Although limited research has examined how service quality perceptions are formed, considerable research has examined the structure and content of service quality perceptions. Nearly all research in this area has used variations of the SERVQUAL dimensions identified by Parasuraman et al. (1985; see also Parasuraman, Zeithaml, & Berry, 1988; Parasuraman, Berry, & Zeithaml, 1991a). The first dimension, *tangibles*, refers to the physical appearance of the store and service personnel. *Responsiveness* reflects the service provider's attentiveness and readiness to provide prompt service for a customer. *Assurance* is whether the service provider is competent and is capable of using this competence to instill confidence and trust in the customer. *Empathy* is how well the service employee can understand the customer's needs and expectations and provide customized, individualized attention in a caring way. *Reliability* reflects whether the service provider can provide the service correctly the first time, as promised, or quickly fix problems that may arise. Of these five dimensions, research suggests that the reliability dimension is the most important across most service jobs (e.g., Parasuraman et al., 1991a; Parasuraman et al. 1988). Parasuraman et al. (1988) and Parasuraman et al. (1991a) suggest that these dimensions form the basic structure of quality perceptions, but more dimensions may need to be added depending on the service context of a particular study (e.g., Carman, 1990). Nonetheless, the dimensions identified by Parasuraman et al. (1985) appear to be endorsed by most individuals who conduct research on customer service (e.g., George & Jones, 1991; B. R. Lewis & Mitchell, 1990; Parasuraman et al., 1988; Schneider &

Bowen, 1995). It is also important to recognize that research efforts conducted independent of the Parasuraman et al. (1985) framework and based on job analyses have identified similar dimensions (J. Hogan et al., 1984). Thus, as a basic structure describing the common elements of service quality, the Parasuraman et al. (1991a) dimensions appear to be reasonably well supported.

A key distinction between the I/O and service management literatures becomes apparent when we consider Boulding et al.'s (1993) model of how perceptions are formed and the SERVQUAL dimensions. Customer perceptions are based on the behavior and appearance of the service provider, the quality and price of the product (if present), and possibly even the layout of the store (Dodds & Monroe, 1985; Garvin, 1987; Zeithaml, 1987). Thus, customer service performance is only partly determined by behavior in the marketing conceptualization, whereas behavior is the focus of the I/O conceptualization. Obviously, these different foci indicate that multiple criteria can be considered as indicators of customer service performance—assessments of CSB (ratings by supervisors or by customers) and global evaluations of service quality (which are based on but not necessarily commensurate with behaviors; e.g., service quality can be low because of the huge demand for services, not the specific behaviors of the customer service provider). Four of the five SERVQUAL dimensions do focus on behavior, but the Boudling et al. (1993) model as well as other work suggests that the performance evaluations on these dimensions are reflective of issues other than just whether the customer service provider demonstrates specific behaviors (e.g., expectations based on past experiences, the environment, product features).

There are a few additional considerations that must be addressed in adequately conceptualizing customer service performance. First is the issue of coproduction and customer participation. Kelley et al. (1990) developed a framework for analyzing customer participation in service production and delivery that was an expansion of a basic framework by Gronroos (1982). Kelley et al.'s essential point was that the performance of the service provider may often be a function of the service provider's behavior, the customer's behavior, and their interaction.

Second, service context may affect the conceptualization of performance. Using a classification system described by Lovelock (1983), Kelley et al. (1990) note that service quality may differ when the service is directed towards people, involves intangible or tangible things, or requires a high degree of customization. Gutek et al. (1999) described how customers may expect different behaviors from customer service providers in relationships versus in encounters, and thus the effectiveness of a single behavior may be positive or negative depending on the service context. At the end of this section on performance, we speculate on other ways in which context might influence conceptualizations of performance.

Measurement

A great deal of the research conducted during the last 12 years has used some variation of the SERVQUAL measure (B. R. Lewis & Mitchell, 1990; Parasuraman et al., 1988). The SERVQUAL instrument contains paired expectancy items and perception items that are completed by customers. For example, an expectancy item is *These firms should be dependable* and its corresponding perception item is *XYZ is dependable,* where XYZ refers to the specific organization. Scoring SERVQUAL involves computation of a difference score, such that each expectancy is subtracted from its corresponding perception rating to create the quality score for a specific service dimension. Quality scores (i.e., difference scores) are then summed within service dimension to create the dimension score (e.g., tangibles, reliability, etc.).

In one of the first major critiques of SERVQUAL, Carman (1990) argued that in contrast to claims that the instrument provides a comprehensive assessment for any service context, the instrument will often need to be customized to a particular setting and it must be administered separately for each service function. He also noted that the measurement of expectations posed serious practical and conceptual problems (i.e., length of survey, little variance) and that an importance weight should be assigned to each item (i.e., some customers may consider empathy more important than reliability and vice versa). Similar critiques of the SERVQUAL instrument were advanced by Babakus and Boller (1992), and Finn and Lamb (1991), who conducted confirmatory factor analyses and did not find the hypothesized factor structure.

In response to these critiques and to further refine the instrument, Parasuraman et al. (1991a) recommended assigning importance weights to each of the scales (not items) and noted some problems with the dimensionality of the measure, but overall they concluded that it provided a sufficient measure of service quality. Further questions and critiques of the measure (see Buttle, 1996, and A. M. Smith, 1995, for reviews) raised other issues regarding practical and psychometric difficulties with measuring expectancies (e.g., Babakus & Mangold, 1992; Cronin & Taylor, 1992; Teas, 1993)—especially because several researchers have found that the perception-only portion of the SERVQUAL is more predictive than the service quality measure is (i.e., perception-expectancy; Babakus & Boller, 1992; Cronin & Taylor, 1992; Parasuraman et al., 1991a). To better assess the different levels of expectancies (i.e., adequate and desired), Parasuraman, Zeithaml, and Berry (1994a) compared three different response formats for

expectancy: (a) measures of desired expectancy, adequate expectancy, and perceived service; (b) direct measures of service adequacy and service superiority; and (c) direct measures of service superiority only. Their study found that all three versions produced similar properties but argued that when it is practically feasible, the three-measure version will provide greater diagnostic potential. Of course, on more theoretical grounds, if expectancies are composed of both adequate and desired levels, then the three-measure version is also the only one consistent with the underlying theory.

A second and related criticism surrounds the use of a difference score in the original SERVQUAL conceptualization (Babakus & Boller, 1992; T. J. Brown, Churchill, & Peter, 1993). For example, T. J. Brown et al. (1993) note that difference scores are often unreliable and have restricted variance. Parasuraman et al. (1994a) argue that the reliabilities of the SERVQUAL dimensions usually meet minimum standards for internal consistency and that the difference scores have practical diagnostic value, although as we have noted, the perception-only aspect of SERVQUAL usually predicts better than the difference score does.

Third, the dimensionality of SERVQUAL continues to be an area of debate (e.g., Carman, 1990; Parasuraman et al., 1994b). However, unless researchers administer the quality measure to customers from within the same industry, it may not be surprising that factor structures differ. Couple this fact with the rather small sample sizes used in most of these studies, along with the analysis of difference scores, and many of the factor interpretation problems are understandable. To date, these issues have not been adequately addressed. Also, some recent research has questioned the test-retest reliability of the SERVQUAL instrument (Lam & Woo, 1997).

More general questions regarding customer service performance remain. There is a need to develop a consensus regarding the definition of the criterion space in terms of both content and sources of information. Within the I/O psychology literature, relatively few studies (e.g., Weekley & Jones, 1997) have used customers as part of the criterion development process. Instead, customer service performance is often measured via supervisory ratings of employee behaviors on dimensions identified through a job analysis (J. Hogan et al., 1984), based on the SERVQUAL measure, or merely an overall customer service performance dimension. A comparison of popular models of performance (e.g., Campbell's model, 1990) to the dimensions of SERVQUAL and other approaches to assessing customer service performance is needed so that a clearer conceptualization of service performance results.

Research is needed on how the source of evaluation (customer or supervisor) affects the evaluation because it is quite possible that the same behavior can be seen as effective by one source and ineffective by the other. For example, a server who gives patrons free drinks may foster favorable customer ratings but negative supervisory ratings when this behavior is forbidden by company policy. Furthermore, we need to understand the extent to which evaluations by different sources are driven more or less by the actual behaviors of employees versus other factors (e.g., product quality affecting customer ratings but not supervisor ratings).

Research on performance consistency would also be helpful. Because of the nature of the customer service construct, not only is the mean or modal level of service performance important, but the variance across customers is also of considerable interest.

Finally, we believe that a very fruitful area for research will be to interject more psychological theory and research into the measurement of service performance. For example, theories about relationships from social psychology may be useful for better conceptualizations of performance in service relationships. Theories of impression formation may be helpful for understanding customer perceptions. Cognitive and decision-making research might better inform how people form normative standards and compare these standards to actual service treatment.

As noted earlier, we believe a contingency perspective that considers the various dimensions that distinguish the nature of service is a necessary perspective to promoting CSB. To truly understand customer service performance, future researchers must consider how the service context affects the conceptualization and measurement of performance. Table 15.1 provides an indication of how consideration of the situation can influence research on this topic. The table serves to illustrate how a contingency perspective might be applied, but it is not exhaustive regarding potential effects of the service situation on how performance should be conceptualized and measured.

SELECTION AND CSB

Despite the wealth of research on service management, there is surprisingly little *published* research on the selection of customer service employees (Schneider & Schechter, 1991); this does not suggest that organizations are not concerned with the selection of service employees or that consulting companies and test developers are not devoting attention to service employee selection, but rather it suggests that little of this work has been published in scientific journals (Hurley, 1998). Indeed, there are many proprietary instruments designed for the prediction of customer service (e.g., Servicefirst, Customer Service Inventory, Hogan Personality Inventory, etc.), but, again, little of the research surrounding the development of

TABLE 15.1 Performance

Nature of Service	Research Questions
Intangibility	• Intangibility means that performance will ultimately be judged based on the impressions of others (e.g., ratings). Is there greater agreement between supervisor and customer perceptions for more tangible service situations? • Will CSB have more weight in performance evaluations than do other aspects of the service situation for more intangible services?
Simultaneity	• Simultaneity means that the evaluation of CSB may not be disentangled from the evaluation of the product (e.g., waiter's behavior and meal consumed). How does increased simultaneity affect the extent to which performance evaluations are based on CSB vs. aspects of the service itself, the organizational environment, etc.?
Coproduction	• In coproduction, an employee's performance is in part constrained by the customer. How does the extent of coproduction influence the role of actual CSB in performance evaluations? How do supervisor evaluations in situations of high coproduction account for the customer's performance?
Relationship vs. encounters	• Do different employee behaviors produce different levels of effectiveness in relationships vs. encounters? For example, in a relationship situation, taking the time to get to know the customer may be critical; in an encounter, trying to get to know the customer may in fact result in worse performance because it violates the customer's expectations. • Are dimensions weighted differently in evaluating performance in relationships vs. encounters (e.g., reliability, empathy)?
Role-prescribed vs. extrarole	• How can extrarole CSBs best be included in models of customer service performance? Are extrarole CSBs weighted the same as role-prescribed CSBs in performance evaluations by customers? By supervisors?
Standard vs. customized service	• As the service becomes more customized, does agreement between customer and supervisory perceptions in evaluations decrease? Does agreement among customers in evaluations of performance decrease? • Is employee performance more variable in custom than it is in standard situations?
Nature and level of customer contact	• Are traditional performance appraisal procedures more amenable to service contexts that contain low customer contact? Do different dimensions of performance get more weight in evaluations in situations in which the customer is physically present?

these instruments has been published. Thus, this appears to be one domain in which practice has far outpaced research. In this section we focus primarily on research that has been published.

As discussed previously, the provision of customer service relies primarily on the service provider's identifying and meeting the customer's expectations. Many customer service jobs are primarily interpersonal and nontechnical, requiring dealing with people with diverse backgrounds, interests, values, and goals. The service provider must therefore possess the knowledge, skill, ability, and other (KSAO) characteristics necessary for dealing with what are often stressful, demanding, and ambiguous social situations (George & Jones, 1991). It is not surprising, then, that most attempts to select service providers have focused on KSAOs unrelated to cognitive ability.

Indeed, the vast majority of published research indicates that certain personality constructs are required for the provision of excellent service. For example, J. Hogan et al. (1984) developed a measure of service orientation, which is a predisposition to behave in a friendly, pleasant, and empathic manner when interacting with other people and is comprised of items reflecting adjustment (neuroticism), sociability, and likeability. The current Hogan Personality Inventory (HPI; R. Hogan & Hogan, 1992) manual reports on validation studies with their service orientation measure. For a criterion of supervisory ratings of overall job performance, most of the validities are around .30. Subsequent to the J. Hogan et al. (1984) study, there have been many demonstrations of links between specific personality traits or personality composites and supervisor ratings of customer service performance (Day & Silverman, 1989; Hurley, 1998; Mount, Barrick, & Stewart, 1998; Rosse, Miller, & Barnes, 1991), as well as self-ratings of citizenship behavior (Bettencourt et al., 2001).

In a slightly different conceptualization of service orientation, Saxe and Weitz (1982) developed a measure called the selling orientation-customer orientation (SOCO). The SOCO scale was designed for use with salespersons who use a blend of marketing (meeting customer demands) and selling (creating customer demands) practices. Of interest here is that the dimensions assessed by the SOCO measures are many of the same dimensions of service orientation (e.g., empathy, sensitivity) but are placed within a sales context. Saxe and Weitz found the SOCO scale was related to sales performance ($r = .40$). Similar results have been found with buyers (Michaels & Day, 1985).

Not all studies find relationships between personality and customer service performance, however (Rogelberg et al., 1999). Hurley (1998) reviewed 13 published studies linking personality (broadly defined) and customer service from 1971 to 1996. He found that extraversion, agreeableness, and adjustment were the primary personality correlates of overall customer service. Frei and McDaniel (1998) performed a meta-analysis of service orientation measures and found an average observed validity of .24; after corrections for range restriction and criterion unreliability, the mean validity was .50. Of particular interest was the lack of correlation between the service orientation measures and cognitive ability ($r = -.06$). However, the service orientation measures were related to agreeableness ($r = .43$), emotional stability ($r = .37$), and conscientiousness ($r = .42$). Relationships with openness ($r = .07$) and extraversion ($r = .07$) were near zero, contradicting Hurley's (1998) conclusion that extraversion was a useful predictor.

Thus, the research to date suggests that service orientation is a strong predictor of supervisory ratings of service performance, and that service orientation is primarily composed of emotional stability, agreeableness, and conscientiousness. Data on relations between extraversion and service performance are less clear. One implication of these findings is that the prediction of supervisory ratings of overall service performance is likely to be greatest when the personality composite called customer service orientation is used rather than individual personality traits (Hough & Schneider, 1996). Many popular customer service inventories are inherently multidimensional because items are only retained if they have meaningful relations with criteria (e.g., R. Hogan & Hogan, 1992; Paajanen, Hansen, & McLellan, 1993). However, composite measures of service orientation may enhance prediction at the cost of understanding—unless test developers map the composite service orientation measure back onto traditional personality constructs.

The prediction of customer service has also been undertaken with measures other than personality tests. First, paper-and-pencil situational judgment tests (SJTs), which present applicants with work situations and then ask them how they would respond, have been found to be predictive of customer service performance. For example, Weekley and Jones (1999) found validities of .16 and .19 for an SJT with ratings of overall service performance. Video-based SJTs, in which applicants are presented with service situations on video and then respond using a paper-and-pencil format, have shown correlations with service performance in the .20s (uncorrected; Weekley & Jones, 1997). More interesting is that when the scoring key was based on customers' judgments, the validity increased to .33. Another approach is high-fidelity testing, such that the physical or psychological features of the job are reproduced in the selection test. High-fidelity tests would include customer service call simulations (e.g., A. E. Mills & Schmitt, 2000) and computerized tests that simulate handling of customer inquiries and accounts (Wiechmann, 2000).

Other approaches that are lower fidelity include biodata instruments and structured interviews designed to predict customer service performance. Schneider and Schechter (1991) used paper-and-pencil tests, a structured interview, and a work simulation to predict the service performance of telephone sales and service personnel. Of these methods, they found that the interview was the strongest predictor of service performance. Thus, although the research focus has been on personality testing in selecting for CSB, there are many other selection tools that might be helpful in assessing whether one is likely to be successful at customer service.

There are several research questions related to selecting for CSB that need to be addressed. Although most researchers have focused on overall service orientation, little is known about the relative merits of this approach. For example, would specific trait measures be better predictors than an overall measure of service orientation would if performance is conceptualized as multidimensional? Is effective service performance dependent on a person's predisposition for service, or can appropriate training and reward structures produce similar results? Does something equivalent to a knowledge or skill for customer contact exist, and if so, how is it best acquired? Bettencourt et al. (2001) demonstrated that attitudes, personality, and knowledge each contributed to the prediction of service-oriented citizenship behaviors. Such broader frameworks would aid in selection system design.

Second, it is important to recognize that most of the previously presented studies have predicted overall customer service performance assessed via supervisory ratings. Although the supervisor's perspective is clearly an important one, it is a limited perspective. For example, in many service contexts, the supervisor may not observe the majority of the employee's interactions with customers (Gronroos, 1982). Similarly, customers may have very negative impressions of the employee's service even though the employee performed in an organizationally approved manner (e.g., not giving customers free refills of soda). Nearly all of the validity information presented previously is specific to supervisory ratings of service performance.

Almost all of this research has focused on individual-level selection and the prediction of individual-level performance. However, in many service settings, such as retail and food service, employees work as individuals *and* as part of a team. For example, a waitress may have not only her own tables to cover but also those of a coworker if he is falling behind. Thus, personality constructs related to teamwork (see Barrick, Stewart, Neubert, & Mount, 1998; Neuman & Wright, 1999) may also be important, even though they are not always part of service orientation.

KSAOs other than personality traits may also relate to providing good customer service and should be considered more fully in research. For example, cognitive ability may be needed to learn information related to products and services. Although in practice these considerations are probably made, research has not addressed the relative importance of various KSAOs to the provision of customer service.

Finally, how context factors into the personality-service relationship needs to be more closely examined. The same KSAOs would not be required for a service provider interacting with customers over the phone as would be necessary for someone working face-to-face with customers. Similarly, the demands and expectations of the customer may change the predictive validity of various personality constructs. For example, KSAOs relating to fostering long-term relations (e.g., empathy) may be most important in a service *relationship* because the customer expects the employee to remember his or her information and preferences. However, KSAOs such as extraversion may be most important in a service *encounter* because the customer may have only self-interest as a primary goal, with no concern for the service provider (e.g., Gutek et al., 1999). Table 15.2 illustrates how a contingency approach might influence research questions in this area.

TABLE 15.2   Selection

Nature of Service	Research Questions
Intangibility	• Is the relationship between personality or service orientation and customer service stronger as the service becomes more intangible?
Simultaneity	• How do the personalities of the customer and service provider interact? Are those who possess more of certain traits (e.g., agreeableness) able to work with a greater diversity of customers?
Coproduction	• Are flexibility and adaptability better determinants of performance in coproduction situations than they are in other customer service settings?
Relationship vs. encounters	• Is there a difference in the KSAO requirements of relationships vs. encounters? For example, relationships require KSAOs that reflect a willingness and ability to maintain social relations and foster harmonious interactions with relatively few customers. Encounters require KSAOs that reflect a willingness and ability to deal with many customers in a short-term setting, with no real need to develop social relations.
Role-prescribed vs. extrarole	• Does service orientation (or do more basic traits) predict extrarole behaviors and prescribed CSBs equally well?
Standard vs. customized service	• Does the provision of customized service place greater demands on the job knowledge and technical competencies of employees than the provision of standard service does—that is, will cognitive ability and job knowledge have stronger relations with service performance in customized rather than standard settings?
Nature and level of customer contact	• Are personality and service orientation better predictors for face-to-face service jobs than they are for ones without the customer physically present? Does the amount of customer contact (i.e., continuous vs. sporadic) moderate the validities of customer orientation measures?

SERVICE CLIMATE AND EMPLOYEE ATTITUDES

Schneider and colleagues (Schneider, Gunnarson, & Niles-Jolly, 1994) have been the leaders in researching *service climate,* defined as employee perceptions of what the organization rewards and supports concerning customer service. Researchers have identified how a climate for service relates to more positive customer perceptions of service, and they have examined what defines and creates a more positive service climate (e.g., Burke, Rupinski, Dunlap & Davison, 1996; Paradise-Tornow, 1991; Schneider, Wheeler, & Cox, 1992; Schneider, White, & Paul, 1998; Tornow & Wiley, 1991). In general, there is a consensus that a climate for service is a key element in motivating positive CSB by employees. There are a number of methodological and theoretical issues that have been raised by researchers in the area (e.g., justification of data aggregation, Schneider et al., 1998; controlling for unit size and location, Burke et al., 1996; strength of climate as a moderator of the relation between climate and outcomes, Schneider, Salvaggio & Subirats, 2000). However, these issues are not unique to the study of service climates; they relate to studies of climate in general and therefore are not reviewed here.

In addition to the link between service climate and customer perceptions of service quality, several other relationships have been the focus of linkage research. Researchers have examined the link between a climate for service and a climate for employee well-being (Abramis & Thomas, 1990; Schneider et al., 1998). The suggestion has been made that a strong concern for customers by employees will not exist without a strong organizational concern for employees. As Schneider and Bowen (1992) noted, a climate for employee well-being does not presuppose a climate for service—one can have well-treated employees and not have policies that promote service excellence. However, there is some evidence of a link between the two.

A third focus has been the establishment of links between customer perceptions of service and employee perceptions of organizational climate (not service climate but general employee attitudes; e.g., Rucci, Kirn, & Quinn, 1998; Ryan, Schmit, & Johnson, 1996; Schmit & Allscheid, 1995; Schneider & Bowen, 1985; Schneider, Parkington, & Buxton, 1980; Thompson, 1996; Tornow & Wiley, 1991; Wiley, 1991, 1996). The rationale for these links is that customers are affected by the mindset of employees (Ulrich, Halbrook, Meder, Stuchlik, & Thorpe, 1991); employees who feel negatively about the organization and the job will transmit that affect in serving customers, thereby influencing customer perceptions of the organization and the service received. Note that employee climate for service perceptions is more strongly related to customer opinions than it is to employee well-being perceptions (Brooks, 2000).

Finally, several researchers have linked service climate perceptions of employees to organizational outcomes such as profits, sales dollars, and customer retention (Burke et al., 1996; Heskett, Jones, Loveman, Sasser, & Schlesinger, 1994; Schneider & Bowen, 1985; Schneider et al., 1980; Schneider, White, & Paul, 1997; Thompson, 1996; Tornow & Wiley, 1991; Weitzel et al., 1989). Although the finding of a link between service climate and customer satisfaction or customer quality ratings is quite consistent, relations to profits and other financial measures are sometimes found and sometimes not; this is likely because many other factors influence such variables (e.g., costs of goods), because in some cases customer satisfaction is negatively related to financial performance (e.g., busy stores with high sales may keep customers waiting and be less friendly; Wiley, 1991), and because financial indicators may lag behind service indicators and connections may not be apparent in single-shot or short-term studies (Schneider, 1991).

In sum, a climate for service as well as a general positive workplace climate appear to influence service quality—presumably, partly through a direct influence on CSB. (As indicated earlier, service quality measures reflect more than CSB.) However, several researchers have noted that the relationship between employee perceptions of the way the organization functions and customer perceptions of service quality are not unidirectional (Ryan et al., 1996; Schneider et al., 1998)—that is, customers provide information on service quality that is often shared with employees, and that information influences employee perceptions. Also, Schneider, Ashworth, Higgs, and Carr (1996) noted that after a service practice is improved across the organization (e.g., all employees are provided with feedback on customer satisfaction), the relationship of that practice to outcomes will no longer be present, although presumably there will have been improvement in customer satisfaction across the board. One final caveat is that potential time lags remain a relatively unexplored issue It is difficult to determine how long it takes for organizational service climate to affect customers or for customers to affect the organization's climate (Schneider et al., 1998); it is also unknown how long effects might persist (Schneider et al., 1998). The few studies over time (Ryan et al., 1996; Schneider et al., 1998) do not indicate lag effects, but these were limited in scope.

In general, recommendations for improving service include promoting a service climate (see Ahmed & Parasuraman, 1994; Schneider, Chung, & Yusko, 1993; Schneider et al., 1994, for discussions of issues in developing a service climate) and treating employees well so as to enhance their job satisfaction.

A strong climate for service is created via emphasizing and rewarding positive CSB, logistical and operational support, appropriate staffing of positions, quality training programs focused on CSB, and communication and cooperation (Schneider et al., 1993; Schneider et al., 1994; Schneider et al., 1992). Also, employee predispositions to be satisfied (Judge, 1993) might be considered in selection for customer service positions.

Two other topic areas deserve mention in a discussion of employee attitudes and CSB. Although most of the research on employee attitudes linked to customer outcomes has concentrated on traditional employee survey concepts (e.g., working conditions, supervision), some researchers have begun to apply social justice theories to the customer service arena. Most of the research has concentrated on the customer's feelings of being treated fairly (e.g. Blodgett, Granbois, & Walters, 1993; Blodgett, Hill, & Tax, 1997; Goodwin & Ross, 1992; A. K. Smith, Bolton, & Wagner, 1999) rather than on how employee justice perceptions influence CSB. However, Bettencourt and Brown (1997) found that workplace fairness perceptions of tellers were positively related to engagement in both extrarole and role-prescribed CSBs (as evaluated by managers), with the fairness of performance evaluations and pay policies being key predictors of extrarole behaviors. Thus, we would expect future research linking attitudes to CSB to also include a focus on more specific theoretical frameworks such as justice theory.

One other area of research on employee attitudes deserves separate mention as important in the customer service arena. The literature on stress perceptions contains many studies of employees in boundary-spanning roles such as customer service providers (Boles & Babin, 1996; Singh, Goolsby, & Rhoads, 1994; Singh, Verbeke, & Rhoads, 1996; Spencer, 1991; Weatherly & Tansik, 1993). Stressors of particular concern for customer service providers include role ambiguity and conflict (i.e., between demands of customers and management or between demands of different customers; Bowen & Waldman, 1999; Hartline & Ferrell, 1996; Shamir, 1980; Weatherly & Tansik, 1993), interpersonal conflicts with customers (Bowen & Waldman, 1999; Shamir, 1980), constraints on emotions (Rafaeli, 1993; Shamir, 1980), and unusual hours and work-family conflict (Boles & Babin, 1996). In terms of our set of service dimensions, we might expect certain types of customer service positions to provide different stressors (e.g., role ambiguity may vary with intangibility and customization; interpersonal conflict and emotional constraint will vary with the nature and level of customer contact) and therefore require different types of support systems and different stress management interventions.

TABLE 15.3   Climate and Attitudes

Nature of Service	Research Questions
Intangibility	• Does service intangibility moderate the influence of service climate on CSB, such that a stronger relation is observed for more intangible services? • Does service intangibility moderate the relation of employee and customer perceptions of service such that a stronger relation exists for more tangible services?
Simultaneity	• Is the link between employee attitudes and organizational outcomes stronger in more simultaneous production and consumption situations than it is in those that are less simultaneous?
Coproduction	• Does the extent of the role of the customer in production of the service influence whether a reciprocal influence of customer attitudes on employee attitudes is observed?
Relationship vs. encounters	• Does service climate play a greater role than individual differences do in CSBs exhibited in encounters vs. relationships? • Are employee perceptions negatively related to outcomes such as profit and productivity in encounters and positively related in relationships (Brooks, 2000)?
Role-prescribed vs. extrarole	• Is extrarole CSB exhibition more influenced by service climate than role-prescribed CSB exhibition is (Brooks, 2000; Morrison, 1997)?
Standardization vs. customization	• Do service climate and employee attitudes have a greater influence on CSB in customized vs. standard service situations? • Does customization result in greater stress (George & Jones, 1991)?
Nature and level of customer contact	• Are employee and customer perceptions of service more highly related in situations of customer physical presence and in situations of greater customer contact?

How does a contingency approach suggest differences in how one could or should implement findings on climate and attitudes? Table 15.3 lists some research questions. Aspects of service might moderate the relations between employee perceptions of service climate and customer perceptions of service climate, as well as between employee attitudes and customer perceptions more generally and between employee attitudes and organizational outcomes.

MOOD, EMOTIONS, AND CSB

An important component of the customer service experience is the affect or emotions expressed toward or in the presence of customers (George, 1990, 1995; Rafaeli & Sutton, 1987, 1989). Measures of emotional display in customer service settings examine whether a greeting or smile was provided and eye contact made with the customer. Note that mood is related to emotion but is seen as a more general feeling

(George & Brief, 1996). The rationale for a relation between employee affective displays and customer responses is that of emotional contagion (Hatfield, Cacioppo, & Rapson, 1994), which argues that individuals absorb the affective states of those with whom they interact. Researchers have demonstrated that employee positive affect is related to CSB and to customer perceptions of service quality (Kelley & Hoffman, 1997). George (1991) demonstrated that those who experienced positive moods at work (i.e., in the last week) were more likely to engage in role-prescribed prosocial behavior or customer service behaviors, as well as in helpful behaviors that were not role prescribed (e.g., helping coworkers; see also George, 1990). Researchers have noted that both the affect displayed by individual employees and the emotional expression of the group may be relevant to customer service (affective tone, George, 1990, 1995; emotional front, Pugh, 1999; Rafaeli & Sutton, 1989). For example, group positive affective tone has been found to be positively related to customer service performance (George, 1995).

Hochschild (1979, 1983) defined emotional labor as expressing socially desirable emotions as a role requirement. Several writers have commented that emotional labor involves not only acting in prescribed ways (smiling) but also suppressing emotions (anger at unreasonable customers; Ashforth & Humphrey, 1993, 1995; Grandey, 2000; Hoobler, Duffy, & Tepper, 2000). Also, emotions displayed in a service encounter may be genuine rather than acted—that is, the employee may be highly empathic (Ashforth & Humphrey, 1993; Rogers, Clow, & Kash, 1994; Tolich, 1993).

If an organization wanted to influence customer service behavior by enhancing positive mood or regulating emotions, what action might it take? George (1991) notes that those with higher positive affectivity (trait) could be selected, or the physical surrounding, the nature of social interactions, and other situational characteristics might be manipulated to positively affect mood. Others have suggested that hiring highly empathic individuals may lead to greater responsiveness to customer needs (Rogers et al., 1994). Emotional display rules can be developed and employees can be trained in their execution (Ashforth & Humphrey, 1993; Rogers et al., 1994; Tolich, 1993) and monitored and rewarded for performing them.

However, researchers have noted potential negative effects of prescribing emotional regulation (Grandey, 2000; Hochschild, 1979; Hoobler et al., 2000; Rafaeli, 1993). Research suggests that acting rather than displaying genuine emotion might lead to strain (Pugliesi, 1999; Rafaeli, 1993; Schaubroeck & Jones, 2000). Insincerely executed emotional displays (e.g., the *have a nice day* delivered in a bored monotone) can harm rather than improve customer perceptions of service. We found a fair amount of unpublished research that examines the positive and negative consequences of emotional regulation in customer service settings by considering models of regulation put forth by emotion theorists. A greater connection of basic and applied research will aid efforts to understand how to create positive affective situations for customers without undue strain and other negative effects on employees.

A contingency approach is helpful for determining best ways for organizations to influence emotional displays and affective tone as well as the negative effects of emotional regulation. (See Table 15.4.) For example, Hoobler et al. (2000) noted that engaging in emotional suppression as a means of regulating emotion may have negative rather than positive effects on customer perceptions in long duration or repeated interactions with the same customers; in situations that do not concern one-time encounters, it may be better to train employees to regulate emotion via reappraisal rather than suppression. Affect may be more important in terms of influencing CSB and customer perceptions in certain types of service contexts (e.g., more intangible services, physically present customers). Emotion may be easier for employees to regulate if they are in continual customer

TABLE 15.4   Emotions

Nature of Service	Research Questions
Intangibility	• Does group affective tone have a greater effect on customer perceptions when the service is more intangible?
Simultaneity	• Does employee affect have a greater influence on organizational outcomes when the production and consumption are more simultaneous?
Coproduction	• Does the extent of customer involvement in production influence the difficulty of regulating emotions?
Relationship vs. encounters	• Is emotional regulation more difficult in relationships than in encounters (Hoobler et al., 2000)? • Does emotional display have more of an impact on customer perceptions in relationships than in encounters?
Role-prescribed vs. extrarole	• Is role-prescribed emotional display less strongly related to customer perceptions of service quality than extrarole emotional display? • Is positive affect positively related to engaging in extrarole CSBs (George, 1990, 1991)? • Do employees view role-prescribed emotional display rules as stressors?
Standard vs. customized service	• Is emotional regulation easier in standard than in customized service situations?
Nature and level of customer contact	• Is emotional regulation more difficult with physically present customers than it is on the phone or with electronically present customers? • Is emotional regulation more difficult for those with more customer contact?

contact (i.e., get into and stay in a role) as opposed to occasional customer interactions; or it may be more difficult to regulate emotion when there is no break from customer interaction.

TRAINING AND SOCIALIZATION OF CSB

Training is considered critical to the success of service organizations. Desatnick (1994) noted that among 16 top service providers, one common theme was that all devoted considerable resources to training. Schneider and Bowen (1992, 1995) describe two types of customer service training: formal and informal. *Informal* training is primarily directed toward orienting the new employee into the climate and culture of the organization through interactions with coworkers. *Formal* training involves designing and delivering programs and exercises whereby the individual is taught how to be a better service provider. Schneider and Bowen (1995) note that both types of training send employees the signal that service is important and valued, and thus both contribute to fostering a service climate.

Socialization is seen as a critical way to influence CSB. Researchers have noted that newcomer success on the job is related to seeking and being provided with information on how to do the job effectively (Bauer & Green, 1998). Because service employees often have some discretion in how they perform their job duties and organizations have less control over CSBs, employees must learn what is considered appropriate behavior. However, the role ambiguity associated with many customer service positions makes this process more difficult. Kelley (1992) found that socialization affected both motivation (direction and effort) and service climate, and it is through these constructs that socialization influenced employee service orientation. Thus, socialization may not always have a direct effect on CSB but may do so indirectly through introducing and reinforcing a service climate.

Researchers have discussed tactics that organizations might use to socialize newcomers (Ashforth & Saks, 1996; Jones, 1986; Van Maanen & Schein, 1979), typically labeling them as (a) *institutionalized socialization,* which is collective, formal, and sequential, and encourages newcomers to passively accept preset roles; and (b) *individualized socialization,* which is individual and informal and should allow newcomers to adopt unique approaches to their roles. In terms of service situations, whether an organization chooses to employ institutionalized or individualized socialization tactics should vary with features of the service context requiring innovative customer service providers or consistent and standard service.

Morrison's (1993) work on newcomer information seeking also may indicate some important issues in socialization of those with customer service roles. For example, she found that role clarity was related to the frequency with which newcomers sought information about job requirements, role behaviors, and performance feedback. For service providers, the availability and sources of such information likely vary with aspects of the service context (e.g., standardization of the service, customers as coproducers).

Formal training programs are also seen as critical for service organizations, and they may present special challenges compared to entry-level training for other jobs because the content of training is often more interpersonal than it is technical in nature. Schneider and Bowen (1992) note three categories of service training content: (a) technical skills (how to use the cash register), (b) interpersonal and customer relation skills (how to interact with difficult customers or how to identify customer expectations), and (c) knowledge concerning cultural values and norms. Thus, the relative importance of these three skill categories in a given setting should be reflected in training content. Our contingency approach suggests that training needs analyses will indicate different needs depending upon the service context.

Factors facilitating transfer of training may also vary more in their influence in service settings than for other jobs. Yelon and Ford (1999) argued that the nature of a task makes a substantial difference in the process of transfer and presented a model of training transfer that fits well with our contingency approach. They contrasted *closed skills,* in which the circumstances when they are used as well as how they are performed are standard (e.g., checking in an airline passenger) to *open skills,* in which the skills have to be adapted to varying circumstances and there is no one right way to perform (e.g., rerouting passengers from a canceled flight). They also note that skill performance can vary from heavily supervised situations to very autonomous work settings. Yelon and Ford argue that most training transfer research has focused on supervised, closed skills. Although there are cases in which CSBs may be supervised and require the use of closed skills, we have noted earlier that many service settings will require CSBs that are the result of more open skills and also will be performed in unsupervised settings. Yelon and Ford propose different approaches to training transfer for these different situations. For teaching closed skills, they suggest using high-fidelity simulation training, specifying conditions for use of the skill, and providing incentives for adhering to a set procedural checklist. For autonomous open skill situations, they recommend training how to modify procedures and suggest varying the conditions of practice. Transfer of training in service contexts may be difficult because customers are a large part of the service context—that is, employees may be trained in certain skills, but individual differences in customer behavior may uniquely affect the proper application of those skills.

There are many research issues related to CSB socialization and training. Table 15.5 provides some questions based on our contingency approach. As we noted in the sections on performance and selection, I/O psychologists need to better understand the relative importance of technical, interpersonal, and cultural KSAOs for each of the service contexts to

better understand where training should be focused. Also, relative to that for technical skills, effective training for interpersonal skills, emotional regulation, and so forth has not been as well-researched. The best methods to teach CSB may vary by context factors (e.g., formal training with practice may be more appropriate for standardized service situations, but customized services may require more intensive and individualized training as well as greater time spent on observational learning).

MOTIVATING CSB

Much has been written regarding the application of motivational theories and techniques in efforts to enhance CSB (e.g., behavior management techniques, Crowell, Anderson, Abel, & Sergio, 1988; Luthans & Waldersee, 1992; Wilson, Boni, & Hogg, 1997; self-regulation, Waldersee & Luthans, 1994; providing bonuses and recognition programs, Bowen & Waldman, 1999; Desatnick & Detzel, 1993; T. R. Oliver, 1993; Zemke & Schaaf, 1989; monitoring and control systems such as secret shoppers, customer satisfaction surveys, and electronic monitoring of calls, Shell & Allgeier, 1992; Zeithaml, Berry, & Parasuraman, 1988). Space precludes a detailed review here. Although many of these efforts have reported some positive outcomes, it is also clear that the usefulness of traditional motivational tools such as clarifying expectations, goal-setting, providing feedback, and recognizing and rewarding positive behaviors has been less than what was expected by many customer service researchers.

Why are there difficulties in applying motivational tools to CSB? Morrison (1997) argues that traditional approaches may prove challenging to implement because it is difficult to monitor service quality, providing extrinsic incentives for CSB can undermine intrinsic motivation, and prescribing behaviors can limit flexibility and be viewed negatively by customers. Because intangibility, simultaneity, and coproduction result in idiosyncratic situations and unpredictable customer behavior, management cannot resort to typical means of controlling and monitoring behavior such as goal setting or developing rules and procedures (Bowen, Siehl, & Schneider, 1989; Jackson & Schuler, 1992; Schneider, 1990). Further, Bowen and Waldman (1999) noted that because customer satisfaction is seen as linked to a group of employees rather than to one individual's performance, the focus of rewards for CSB may be more appropriately linked to the group level.

Thus, although the practitioner literature recommends that precise performance standards for CSB are essential (e.g., Desatnick, 1994) and that management should train and reinforce these standards, empirical researchers do not all

TABLE 15.5   Training

Nature of Service	Research Questions
Intangibility	• As intangibility increases, does formal training become a less effective means of influencing performance? • Do newcomers engage in more information-seeking behaviors with intangible than with tangible service positions?
Simultaneity	• As simultaneity increases, does formal training become a less effective means of influencing performance?
Coproduction	• As coproduction increases, is training on interpersonal sensitivity more important to overall performance? • As coproduction increases, do the conditions that facilitate training transfer change? • With greater coproduction, is the customer a greater source of socialization information? • Do newcomers engage in more information-seeking behaviors in situations of greater coproduction? • Should organizations employ more individualized than institutionalized socialization in situations of greater coproduction?
Relationship vs. encounters	• Different training content and KSAOs may need to be trained in relationship and encounter contexts. For example, negotiation training may be more important for relationship contexts, whereas diversity training may be more important for encounter contexts. • Is the customer a greater source of socialization information in relationships than it is in encounters?
Role-prescribed vs. extrarole	• Is informal socialization more important than formal training in situations in which CSB is considered extrarole?
Standard vs. customized service	• As the service becomes more customized, does formal training on technical skills become more critical to effective performance? • With greater customization, is the customer a greater source of socialization information? • With greater customization, should organizations employ more individualized than institutionalized socialization?
Nature and level of customer contact	• As the level of customer contact increases, do different types of interpersonal skills need to be trained? Is refresher training more important for jobs with less frequent customer contact?

agree. Recommended approaches to motivating CSB do not rely as heavily on defining expected behaviors. For example, a climate for service can be the substitute for management control systems (Bowen & Schneider, 1988; Bowen et al., 1989). Morrison recommends relying on propositions of social exchange to encourage positive CSB. George and Jones (1991) suggest that monitoring and reward systems should not be tied to the demonstration of specific behaviors because good customer service will mean varying behaviors to meet what the customer desires.

Researchers have also noted specific influences on motivation and behavior that may be strong in service contexts. For those involved in service relationships rather than just service encounters, other rewards may accrue as they would from any interpersonal relationship. For example, Beatty, Mayer, Coleman, Reynolds, and Lee (1996) documented how successful sales associates felt rewarded by the affection of long-term customers and the feelings of self-worth and accomplishment from helping their customers. They note that the customer service literature does not discuss, as a reward, the friendships and social connections developed as part of a service relationship.

Also, Rafaeli (1993) has noted that customers and coworkers have a more immediate, constant, and powerful influence over CSB than do formal policies, management control systems, or training programs. If management control of CSB is limited, to what extent can or should management attempt to influence *customer* behavior and thereby influence CSBs shown by employees? For example, clarifying for customers what are appropriate service expectations, forewarning of slowdowns, posting signs with such messages as *no shirt, no service* or *no refunds without a receipt* can have an impact on CSB by influencing the customer's expectations and behavior (Rafaeli, 1993).

Table 15.6 provides several ideas regarding how a contingency approach might suggest which motivational techniques would work best in each type of service setting. For example, the more intangible, simultaneous, coproduced, or customized the service, the less effective will be reward systems and other motivational techniques that rely on precisely defining expected behaviors. More research is needed on current motivational theories in service settings, such as work on the application of self-regulation research to CSB and the nature of influences on customer service self-efficacy.

DESIGN OF CUSTOMER SERVICE JOBS

Studies of how job design can facilitate CSB have primarily focused on the role of discretion or empowerment, although a few have been concerned with other job characteristics

TABLE 15.6   Motivation

Nature of Service	Research Questions
Intangibility	• Is intangibility negatively related to the ability to prescribe expectations? • Is intangibility negatively related to the ability to monitor CSB? • Do employees feel CSBs are less recognized and rewarded when intangible services are delivered?
Simultaneity	• Is simultaneity positively associated with self-monitoring?
Coproduction	• Does greater coproduction result in less prescription of expectations and greater difficulty in monitoring service quality? • Do employees in coproduction situations feel more negatively about the recognition and rewarding of their CSBs?
Relationship vs. encounters	• Does the specification of expectations have less of an influence on performance in relationships than it does in encounters? • Because of self-interest, is there less need for external rewards of CSB in relationships than there is in encounters? • Is the monitoring of CSB more important to ensuring good service in encounters than it is in relationships (Gutek et al., 1999)?
Role-prescribed vs. extrarole	• As social exchange principles underlie the motivation of extrarole CSBs, what is the relative influence of exchange with the organization vs. exchange with the customer in determining whether a positive CSB will be demonstrated?
Standard vs. customized service	• Are customized service situations more difficult to monitor than are standardized situations in terms of service quality? • Are techniques like goal setting more effective in standardized vs. customized situations?
Nature and level of customer contact	• Is the specification of expectations and monitoring and rewarding performance more difficult for physically present customers than it is for virtual customers? • Does the effectiveness of goal setting and traditional reward and recognition programs vary with the level of customer contact on the job?

(Campion & McClelland, 1991, 1993; Rogelberg et al., 1999). Campion and McClelland (1993) found that task enlargement appeared to have costs for customer service, based on employee self-reports; however, knowledge enlargement (adding understanding of procedures or rules) led to better customer service, based on employee and manager reports. Rogelberg et al. (1999) found that job characteristics (e.g., autonomy) accounted for a significant amount of variance in CSB.

Many researchers have discussed empowerment as a means of enhancing customer service quality (Bowen & Lawler, 1992; Fulford & Enz, 1995; Kelley, 1993; Morrison, 1997; Sparks, Bradley, & Callan, 1997; Weaver, 1994; Zeithaml et al., 1988; Zemke & Schaaf, 1989). Jackson and Schuler (1992) argued that intangibility, simultaneity, and coproduction require the job be enriched so that service firms practicing greater autonomy will be more effective. However, most researchers have also cautioned about potential negative effects of empowerment on CSB. For example, Sparks et al. (1997) showed that customer evaluations depended on the service provider's communication style—that is, empowerment in and of itself was not a positive influence. Kelley (1993) noted that although empowering employees may have positive effects on customer satisfaction and service quality, it is important to understand what determines when employees will exercise the discretion they have been given. Bowen and Lawler (1992) discuss the costs of empowering service employees, including the possibility of inconsistency in service delivery and recovery situations, too great or inappropriate giveaways, and poor decisions. Finally, Hartline and Ferrell (1996) found that empowered service employees experienced greater role conflict and ambiguity.

Several authors have advocated a contingency approach to empowerment (Bowen & Lawler, 1992; Schneider & Bowen, 1992). For example, if the organizational strategy is to provide quick and reliable service, a nonempowered employee who goes by the book may be what the customer wants. The positive effects of empowerment on an individual's job attitudes (e.g., increased job satisfaction, Fulford & Enz, 1995; reduction in role ambiguity, Singh, 1993, but see also Hartline & Ferrell, 1996) may be accompanied by positive effects on customer satisfaction, or they may be accompanied by negative outcomes in service quality, depending upon aspects of the situation.

Bowen and Lawler (1992) point directly to two of our contingency variables—encounter versus relationship and predictability of the service situation—as important factors in deciding whether to empower workers. They advocate greater empowerment in relationship situations than in situations in which ties to the customer are only for short transactions. They also suggest that if there is unpredictability in the types of requests, empowerment is appropriate; if expectations of customers are simple and predictable, then one can use a less empowered approach and have more policies and rules. We expand the notion of a contingency approach to empowerment and job design in service settings by suggesting other propositions to explore in Table 15.7.

DIRECTIONS

Throughout this chapter we have identified many research questions to be addressed and have emphasized the need to consider the service context in applying HR tools and strategies. A few areas that we have not mentioned are also likely to be future foci. First, many customer service settings involve working in teams (i.e., interdependency in delivering

TABLE 15.7 Job Design

Nature of Service	Research Questions
Intangibility	• Is empowerment more effective with more intangible than tangible services?
Simultaneity	• Is empowerment more effective with more simultaneous services?
Coproduction	• Is empowerment more effective with greater levels of coproduction?
Relationship vs. encounters	• Does empowerment have more positive effects on CSB and customer perceptions in relationships than it does in encounters (Bowen & Lawler, 1992)?
Role-prescribed vs. extrarole	• Are empowered employees more likely to engage in extrarole CSBs than are nonempowered employees?
Standard vs. customized service	• Does empowerment have more of an effect on CSB and customer perceptions in customized than it does in standard situations (Bowen & Lawler, 1992)?
Nature and level of customer contact	• Does autonomy have more positive and more negative effects in customer-present situations? • Does empowerment result in less consistent service in jobs with sporadic customer contact?

the service)—such as a cafeteria line food service or a health care setting in which a nurse records information before the patient sees a doctor. The chapter on teams elsewhere in this volume (see chapter by Kozlowski & Bell in this volume) highlights many important issues that should be considered in the customer service context, and we expect that an increased focus on teams in this setting will improve our understanding both of teams and of CSB.

Second, we have mentioned several times that the customer influences CSB. Greater attention to how those outside the organization influence the behavior and attitudes of those in the organization would be productive. Note that many traditional HR practices have an internal focus. Greater incorporation of the customer into job analyses for selection, training needs assessments, performance evaluations, reward and recognition systems, and other areas should proceed thoughtfully so as to ultimately lead to greater gains in CSB.

Third, given the increased use of the Internet, customer service behaviors in a virtual environment should be the focus of more research. Finally, the contingency approach to CSB treats organizational differences as important. Although we are aware of no data on this issue, an important question is to what extent research conducted at the individual level is conditional on higher level phenomena. For example, is validity generalization less likely in service organizations? Several of our research questions suggest that these types of issues may be quite important, although there are far too few studies to make any conclusive statements. An integration of micro- and macroapproaches will help us to fully understand CSB.

This chapter began with a discussion of the prevailing view that service is poor and needs to be improved. The chapter discussed how applications of basic principles from I/O psychology might enhance CSB. Most of the existing I/O research is from an industrial rather than service world. Adapting principles derived from industrial to service contexts offers a future of considerable challenge. We hope that this chapter highlights directions from which this journey may begin.

REFERENCES

Abramis, D. J., & Thomas, C. (1990). Effects of customer service communication on employees' satisfaction. *Psychological Reports, 67,* 1175–1183.

Ahmed, I., & Parasuraman, A. (1994). Environmental and positional antecedents of management commitment to service quality: A conceptual framework. *Advances in Service Marketing and Management, 3,* 69–93.

Albrecht, K., & Zemke, R. (1985). *Service America: Doing business in the new economy.* Homewood, IL: Dow Jones-Irwin.

Ashforth, B. E., & Humphrey, R. H. (1993). Emotional labor in service roles: The influence of identity. *Academy of Management Review, 18,* 88–115.

Ashforth, B. E., & Humphrey, R. H. (1995). Emotion in the workplace: A reappraisal. *Human Relations, 48,* 97–125.

Ashforth, B. E., & Saks, A. M. (1996). Socialization tactics: Longitudinal effects on newcomer adjustment. *Academy of Management Journal, 39,* 149–178.

Babakus, E., & Boller, G. W. (1992). An empirical assessment of the SERVQUAL scale. *Journal of Business Research, 24,* 253–268.

Babakus, E., & Mangold, W. G. (1992). Adapting the SERVQUAL scale to hospital services: An empirical investigation. *Health Services Research, 26,* 767–786.

Barrick, M. R., Stewart, G. L., Neubert, M. J., & Mount, M. K. (1998). Relating member ability and personality to work-team processes and team effectiveness. *Journal of Applied Psychology, 83,* 377–391.

Bauer, T. N., & Green, S. G. (1998). Testing the combined effects of newcomer information seeking and manager behavior on socialization. *Journal of Applied Psychology, 83,* 72–83.

Beatty, S. E., Mayer, M., Coleman, J. E., Reynolds, K. E., & Lee, J. (1996). Customer-sales associate retail relationships. *Journal of Retailing, 72,* 223–247.

Bettencourt, L. A., & Brown, S. W. (1997). Contact employees: Relationships among workplace fairness, job satisfaction and prosocial service behaviors. *Journal of Retailing, 73,* 39–61.

Bettencourt, L. A., Gwinner, K. P., & Meuter, M. L. (2001). A comparison of attitude, personality, and knowledge predictors of service-oriented organizational citizenship behaviors. *Journal of Applied Psychology, 86,* 29–41.

Bitner, M. J., Booms, B. H., & Mohr, L. A. (1994). Critical service encounters: The employee's viewpoint. *Journal of Marketing, 58,* 95–106.

Blodgett, J. G., Granbois, D. H., & Walters, R. G. (1993). The effects of perceived justice on complainants' negative word-of-mouth behavior and repatronage intentions. *Journal of Retailing, 69,* 399–428.

Blodgett, J. G., Hill, D. J., & Tax, S. S. (1997). The effects of distributive, procedural, and interactional justice on postcomplaint behavior. *Journal of Retailing, 73,* 185–210.

Boles, J. S., & Babin, B. J. (1996). On the front lines: Stress, conflict, and the customer service provider. *Journal of Business Research, 37,* 41–50.

Boulding, W., Kalra, A., Staelin, R., & Zeithaml, V. A. (1993). A dynamic process model of service quality: From expectations to behavioral intentions. *Journal of Marketing Research, 30,* 7–27.

Bowen, D. E. (1986). Managing customers as human resources in service organizations. *Human Resource Management, 25,* 371–383.

Bowen, D. E., & Lawler, E. E. (1992). The empowerment of service workers: What, why, how, and when. *Sloan Management Review, 33,* 31–39.

Bowen, D. E., & Schneider, B. (1985). Boundary-spanning-role employees and the service encounter: Some guidelines for management and research. In J. A. Czpepiel, M. R. Soloman, & C. Suvrenant (Eds.), *The service encounter* (pp. 127–147). Lexington, MA: D.C. Heath.

Bowen, D. E., & Schneider, B. (1988). Services marketing and management: Implications for organizational behavior. *Research in Organizational Behavior, 10,* 43–80.

Bowen, D. E., Siehl, C., & Schneider, B. (1989). A framework for analyzing customer service orientations in manufacturing. *Academy of Management Review, 14,* 75–95.

Bowen, D. E., & Waldman, D. A. (1999). Customer-driven employee performance. In D. R. Ilgen & E. D. Pulakos (Eds.), *The changing nature of performance* (pp. 154–191). San Francisco: Jossey-Bass.

Brooks, S. M. (2000, August). *Diagnosing the value chain: A summary of linkage research dynamics.* Paper presented at the annual meeting of the Academy of Management, Toronto, Canada.

Brown, K. A., & Mitchell, T. R. (1993). Organizational obstacles: Links with financial performance, customer satisfaction, and job satisfaction in a service environment. *Human Relations, 46,* 725–757.

Brown, T. J., Churchill, G. A., & Peter, J. P. (1993). Improving the measurement of service quality. *Journal of Retailing, 69,* 127–139.

Burke, M. J., Rupinski, M. T., Dunlap, W. P., & Davison, H. K. (1996). Do situational variables act as substantive causes of relationships between individual difference variables? Two large-scale tests of "common cause" models. *Personnel Psychology, 49,* 573–598.

Buttle, F. (1996). SERVQUAL: Review, critique, research agenda. *European Journal of Marketing, 30,* 8–32.

Cadotte, E. R., Woodruff, R. B., Jenkins, R. L. (1987). Expectations and norms in models of consumer satisfaction. *Journal of Marketing Research, 24,* 305–314.

Campbell, J. P. (1990). Modeling the performance prediction problem in industrial and organizational psychology. In M. D. Dunnette & L. M. Hough (Eds.), *Handbook of industrial and organizational psychology* (2nd ed., Vol. 1, pp. 687–732). Palo Alto, CA: Consulting Psychologists Press.

Campion, M. A., & McClelland, C. L. (1991). Interdisciplinary examination of the costs and benefits of enlarged jobs: A job design quasi-experiment. *Journal of Applied Psychology, 76,* 186–198.

Campion, M. A., & McClelland, C. L. (1993). Follow-up and extension of the interdisciplinary costs and benefits of enlarged jobs. *Journal of Applied Psychology, 78,* 339–351.

Carman, J. M. (1990). Consumer perceptions of service quality: An assessment of the SERVQUAL dimensions. *Journal of Retailing, 66,* 33–55.

Cronin, J. J., & Taylor, S. A. (1992). Measuring service quality: A reexamination and extension. *Journal of Marketing, 56,* 55–68.

Crowell, C. R., Anderson, D. C., Abel, D. M., & Sergio, J. P. (1988). Task clarification, performance feedback, and social praise: Procedures for improving the customer service of bank tellers. *Journal of Applied Behavior Analysis, 21,* 65–71.

Day, D. V., & Silverman, S. B. (1989). Personality and job performance: Evidence of incremental validity. *Personnel Psychology, 42,* 25–36.

Delery, J. E., & Doty, D. H. (1996). Modes of theorizing in strategic human resources management: Tests of universalistic, contingency, and configurational performance predictions. *Academy of Management Journal, 39,* 802–835.

Desatnick, R. L. (1994). Managing customer service for the 21st century. *Journal for Quality and Participation, 17,* 30–35.

Desatnick, R. L., & Detzel, D. H. (1993). *Managing to keep the customer.* San Francisco: Jossey-Bass.

Dodds, W. B., & Monroe, K. B. (1985). The effect of brand and price information on subjective product evaluations. In E. Hirschman & M. Holbrook (Eds.), *Advances in consumer research* (Vol. 12, pp. 85–90). Provo, UT: Association for Consumer Research.

Finn, D. W., & Lamb, C. W. (1991). An evaluation of the SERVQUAL scales in a retail setting. In R. H. Holman, D. Brinberg, & R. J. Lintz (Eds.), *Advances in consumer research* (pp. 111–115). Provo, UT: Association for Consumer Research.

Fogli, L., & Whitney, K. (1991, August). *Service first: A test to select service oriented personnel.* Symposium presented at the annual meeting of the American Psychological Association, San Francisco.

Frei, R. L., & McDaniel, M. A. (1998). Validity of customer service measures in personnel selection: A review of criterion and construct evidence. *Human Performance, 11,* 1–27.

Fulford, M. D., & Enz, C. A. (1995). The impact of empowerment on service employees. *Journal of Managerial Issues, 7,* 161–175.

Garvin, D. A. (1987). Competing on the eight dimensions of quality. *Harvard Business Review, 65,* 101–109.

George, J. M. (1990). Personality, affect, and behavior in groups. *Journal of Applied Psychology, 75,* 107–116.

George, J. M. (1991). State or trait: Effects of positive mood on prosocial behaviors at work. *Journal of Applied Psychology, 76,* 299–307.

George, J. M. (1995). Leader positive mood and group performance: The case of customer service. *Journal of Applied Social Psychology, 25,* 778–794.

George, J. M., & Bettenhausen, K. (1990). Understanding prosocial behavior, sales performance, and turnover: A group-level analysis in a service context. *Journal of Applied Psychology, 75,* 698–709.

George, J. M., & Brief, A. P. (1996). Motivational agendas in the workplace: The effects of feelings on focus of attention and work motivation. In B. W. Staw & L. L. Cummings (Eds.), *Research in organizational behavior* (Vol. 18, pp. 75–107). Greenwich, CT: JAI Press.

George, J. M., & Jones, G. R. (1991). Towards an understanding of customer service quality. *Journal of Managerial Issues, 3,* 220–238.

Goodwin, C., & Ross, I. (1992). Consumer responses to service failures: Influence of procedural and interactional fairness perceptions. *Journal of Business Research, 25,* 149–163.

Grandey, A. A. (2000). Emotion regulation in the workplace: A new way to conceptualize emotional labor. *Journal of Occupational Health Psychology, 5,* 95–110.

Gronroos, C. (1982). *Strategic management and marketing in the service sector.* Helsingfors: Swedish School of Economics and Business Administration.

Gutek, B. A. (1995). *The dynamics of service: Reflections on the changing nature of customer/provider interactions.* San Francisco: Jossey-Bass.

Gutek, B. A., Bhappu, A. D., Liao-Troth, M. A., & Cherry, B. (1999). Distinguishing between service relationships and encounters. *Journal of Applied Psychology, 84,* 218–233.

Hartline, M. D., & Ferrell, O. C. (1996). The management of customer-contact service employees: An empirical investigation. *Journal of Marketing, 60,* 52–70.

Hatfield, E., Cacioppo, J. T., & Rapson, R. L. (1994). *Emotional contagion.* New York: Cambridge University Press.

Heskett, J. L., Jones, T. O., Loveman, G. W., Sasser, W. E., & Schlesinger, L. A. (1994). Putting the service-profit chain to work. *Harvard Business Review, 72,* 164–174.

Hochschild, A. R. (1979). Emotion work, feeling rules, and social structure. *American Journal of Sociology, 85,* 551–575.

Hochschild, A. R. (1983). *The managed heart.* Berkeley: University of California Press.

Hogan, J., Hogan, R., & Busch, C. M. (1984). How to measure service orientation. *Journal of Applied Psychology, 69,* 167–173.

Hogan, R., & Hogan, J. (1992). *Manual for the Hogan Personality Inventory*. Tulsa, OK: Hogan Assessment Systems.

Hoobler, J. M., Duffy, M. K., & Tepper, B. J. (2000, August). *Emotion regulation in emotional labor performance*. Paper presented at the annual meeting of the Academy of Management, Toronto, Canada.

Hough, L. M., & Schneider, R. J. (1996). Personality traits, taxonomies, and applications in organizations. In K. R. Murphy (Ed.), *Individual differences and behavior in organizations* (pp. 3–30). San Francisco: Jossey-Bass.

Hunt, K. (1979). *Conceptualization and measurement of consumer satisfaction and dissatisfaction*. Cambridge, MA: Marketing Science Institute.

Hurley, R. F. (1998). Customer service behavior in retail setting: A field study of the effect of service provider personality. *Journal of the Academy of Marketing Science, 26,* 115–127.

Huselid, M. A. (1995). The impact of human resources management practices on turnover, productivity, and corporate financial performance. *Academy of Management Journal, 38,* 635–672.

Jackson, S. E., & Schuler, R. S. (1992). HRM practices in service-based organizations: A role theory perspective. In T. A. Swartz, D. E. Bowen, & S. W. Brown (Eds.), *Advances in services marketing and management* (Vol. 1, pp. 123–157). Greenwich, CT: JAI Press.

Jones, G. R. (1986). Socialization tactics, self-efficacy, and newcomers' adjustments to organizations. *Academy of Management Journal, 29,* 262–279.

Judge, T. A. (1993). Does affective disposition moderate the relationship between job satisfaction and voluntary turnover? *Journal of Applied Psychology, 78,* 395–401.

Kelley, S. W. (1992). Developing customer orientation among service employees. *Journal of the Academy of Marketing Science, 20,* 27–36.

Kelley, S. W. (1993). Discretion and the service employee. *Journal of Retailing, 69,* 104–126.

Kelley, S. W., Donnelly, J. H., & Skinner, S. J. (1990). Customer participation in service production and delivery. *Journal of Retailing, 66,* 315–335.

Kelley, S. W., & Hoffman, K. D. (1997). An investigation of positive affect, prosocial behaviors and service quality. *Journal of Retailing, 73,* 407–427.

Lam, S. S. K., & Woo, K. S. (1997). Measuring service quality: A test-retest reliability investigation of SERVQUAL. *Journal of the Market Research Society, 39,* 381–397.

Legnick-Hall, C. A. (1996). Customer contributions to quality: A different view of the customer-oriented firm. *Academy of Management Review, 21,* 791–824.

Lewis, R. C., & Booms, B. H. (1983). The marketing aspects of service quality. In L. L. Berry, G. L. Shostack, & G. Upah (Eds.), *The marketing aspects of service quality* (pp. 99–107). Chicago: American Marketing Association.

Lewis, B. R., & Mitchell, V. W. (1990). Defining and measuring the quality of customer service. *Marketing Intelligence and Planning, 8,* 11–17.

Lovelock, C. H. (1983). Classifying services to gain strategic marketing insights. *Journal of Marketing, 47,* 9–20.

Luthans, F., & Waldersee, R. (1992). A micro-management approach to quality service: Steps for implementing behavioral management. In T. A. Swartz, D. E. Bowen, & S. W. Brown (Eds.), *Advances in services marketing and management* (Vol. 1, pp. 277–296). Greenwich, CT: JAI Press.

Michaels, R. E., & Day, R. L. (1985). Measuring customer orientation of salespeople: A replication with industrial buyers. *Journal of Marketing Research, 22,* 443–446.

Mills, A. E., & Schmitt, N. (2000, April). *Traditional tests and telephone simulations: Minority and majority performance*. Paper presented at annual meeting of the Society for Industrial and Organizational Psychologists, New Orleans, LA.

Mills, P., & Margulies, N. (1980). Toward a core typology of service organizations. *Academy of Management Review, 5,* 255–266.

Morrison, E. W. (1993). Longitudinal study of the effects of information seeking on newcomer socialization. *Journal of Applied Psychology, 78,* 173–183.

Morrison, E. W. (1997). Service quality: An organizational citizenship behavior framework. In D. B. Fedor & S. Ghosh (Eds.), *Advances in the management of organizational quality* (Vol. 2, pp. 211–249). Greenwich, CT: JAI Press.

Mount, M. K., Barrick, M. R., & Stewart, G. L. (1998). Five-factor model of personality and performance in jobs involving interpersonal interactions. *Human Performance, 11,* 145–165.

Neuman, G. A., & Wright, J. (1999). Team effectiveness: Beyond skills and cognitive ability. *Journal of Applied Psychology, 84,* 376–389.

Oliver, R. L. (1981). Measurement and evaluation of satisfaction processes in retail settings. *Journal of Retailing, 57,* 25–48.

Oliver, T. R. (1993). Recognize and reward exemplary service behavior. In R. L. Desatnick & D. H. Detzel (Eds.), *Managing to keep the customer* (pp. 149–175). San Francisco: Jossey-Bass.

Paajanen, G. E., Hansen, T. L., & McLellan, R. A. (1993). *PDI employment inventory and PDI customer service inventory manual*. Minneapolis, MN: Personnel Decisions Incorporated.

Paradise-Tornow, C. A. (1991). Management effectiveness, service quality, and organizational performance in banks. *Human Resource Planning, 14,* 129–140.

Parasuraman, A., Berry, L. L., & Zeithaml, V. A. (1991a). Refinement and reassessment of the SERVQUAL scale. *Journal of Retailing, 67,* 420–451.

Parasuraman, A., Berry, L. L., & Zeithaml, V. A. (1991b). Understanding customer expectations of service. *Sloan Management Review, 32,* 39–48.

Parasuraman, A., Zeithaml, V. A., & Berry, L. L. (1985). A conceptual model of service quality and its implications for future research. *Journal of Marketing, 49,* 41–50.

Parasuraman, A., Zeithaml, V. A., & Berry, L. L. (1988). SERVQUAL: A multiple-item scale for measuring consumer perceptions of service quality. *Journal of Retailing, 64,* 12–40.

Parasuraman, A., Zeithaml, V. A., & Berry, L. L. (1994a). Alternative scales for measuring service quality: A comparative assessment based on psychometric and diagnostic criteria. *Journal of Retailing, 70,* 201–230.

Parasuraman, A., Zeithaml, V. A., & Berry, L. L. (1994b). Reassessment of expectations as a comparison standard in measuring service quality: Implications for further research. *Journal of Marketing, 58,* 111–124.

Peters, T. J., & Waterman, R. H. (1989). *In search of excellence: Lessons from America's best-run companies.* New York: HarperCollins.

Pugh, S. D. (1999, April). *Exploring the employee-customer link: How work group emotional fronts impact customers.* Paper presented at the annual meeting of the Academy of Management, Chicago, IL.

Pugliesi, K. (1999). The consequences of emotional labor: Effects on work stress, job satisfaction, and well-being. *Motivation and Emotion, 23,* 125–154.

Rafaeli, A. (1993). Dress and behavior of customer contact employees: A framework for analysis. *Advances in Service Marketing and Management, 2,* 175–211.

Rafaeli, A., & Sutton, R. I. (1987). Expression of emotion as part of the work role. *Academy of Management Review, 12,* 23–37.

Rafaeli, A., & Sutton, R. I. (1989). The expression of emotion in organizational life. *Research in Organizational Behavior, 11,* 1–42.

Rogelberg, S. G., Barnes-Farrell, J. L., & Creamer, V. (1999). Customer service behavior: The interaction of service predisposition and job characteristics. *Journal of Business and Psychology, 13,* 421–435.

Rogers, J. D., Clow, K. E., & Kash, T. J. (1994). Increasing job satisfaction of service personnel. *Journal of Services Marketing, 8,* 14–26.

Rosse, J. G., Miller, H. E., & Barnes, L. K. (1991). Combining personality and cognitive ability predictors for hiring service-oriented employees. *Journal of Business and Psychology, 5,* 431–445.

Rucci, A. J., Kirn, S. P., & Quinn, R. T. (1998). The employee-customer-profit chain at Sears. *Harvard Business Review, 76,* 82–97.

Ryan, A. M., Schmit, M. J., & Johnson, R. (1996). Attitudes and effectiveness: Examining relations at the organizational level. *Personnel Psychology, 49,* 853–882.

Saxe, R., & Weitz, B. A. (1982). The SOCO scale: A measure of the customer orientation of salespeople. *Journal of Marketing Research, 19,* 343–351.

Schaubroeck, J., & Jones, J. R. (2000). Antecedents of workplace emotional labor dimensions and moderators of their effects on physical symptoms. *Journal of Organizational Behavior, 21,* 163–183.

Schmit, M. J., & Allscheid, S. P. (1995). Employee attitudes and customer satisfaction: Making theoretical and empirical connections. *Personnel Psychology, 48,* 521–536.

Schneider, B. (1990). The climate for service: An application of the climate construct. In B. Schneider (Ed.), *Organizational climate and culture* (pp. 383–412). San Francisco: Jossey-Bass.

Schneider, B. (1991). Service quality and profits: Can you have your cake and eat it, too? *Human Resource Planning, 14,* 151–158.

Schneider, B., Ashworth, S. D., Higgs, C. A., & Carr, L. (1996). Design, validity, and use of strategically focused employee attitude surveys. *Personnel Psychology, 49,* 695–705.

Schneider, B., & Bowen, D. E. (1985). Employee and customer perceptions of service in banks: Replication and extension. *Journal of Applied Psychology, 70,* 423–433.

Schneider, B., & Bowen, D. E. (1992). Personnel/human resources management in the service sector. In G. R. Ferris & K. M. Rowland (Eds.), *Research in personnel and human resources management* (Vol. 10, pp. 1–30). Greenwich, CT: JAI Press.

Schneider, B., & Bowen, D. E. (1995). *Winning the service game.* Boston: Harvard Business School.

Schneider, B., Chung, B., & Yusko, K. P. (1993). Service climate for service quality. *Current Directions in Psychological Science, 2,* 197–200.

Schneider, B., Gunnarson, S. K., & Niles-Jolly, K. (1994). Creating the climate and culture of success. *Organizational Dynamics, 23,* 17–29.

Schneider, B., Parkington, J. J., & Buxton, V. M. (1980). Employee and customer perceptions of service in banks. *Administrative Science Quarterly, 25,* 252–267.

Schneider, B., Salvaggio, A. N., & Subirats, M. (2000, April). *Climate strength: A new direction for climate research.* Poster presented at the annual meeting of the Society for Industrial and Organizational Psychology, New Orleans, LA.

Schneider, B., & Schechter, D. (1991). Development of a personnel selection system for service jobs. In S. Brown, E. Hummesson, B. Edvardsoon, & B. Gustavsoon (Eds.), *Service quality* (pp. 217–235). Lexington, MA: Lexington Books.

Schneider, B., Wheeler, J. K., & Cox, J. F. (1992). A passion for service: Using content analysis to explicate service climate themes. *Journal of Applied Psychology, 77,* 705–716.

Schneider, B., White, S. S., & Paul, M. C. (1997). Relationship marketing: An organizational perspective. *Advances in Services Marketing and Management, 6,* 1–22.

Schneider, B., White, S. S., & Paul, M. C. (1998). Linking service climate and customer perceptions of service quality: Test of a causal model. *Journal of Applied Psychology, 83,* 150–163.

Schuler, R. S., & Jackson, S. E. (1987). Linking competitive strategies with human resource management practices. *Academy of Management Executive, 1,* 207–220.

Shamir, B. (1980). Between service and servility: Role conflict in subordinate service roles. *Human Relations, 33,* 741–756.

Shell, R. L., & Allgeier, R. G. (1992). A multi-level incentive model for service organizations. *Applied Ergonomics, 23,* 43–48.

Singh, J. (1993). Boundary role ambiguity: Facets, determinants, and impacts. *Journal of Marketing, 57,* 11–31.

Singh, J., Goolsby, J. R., & Rhoads, G. K. (1994). Behavioral and psychological consequences of boundary spanning burnout for customer service representatives. *Journal of Marketing Research, 31,* 558–569.

Singh, J., Verbeke, W., & Rhoads, G. K. (1996). Do organizational practices matter in role stress processes? A study of direct and moderating effects for marketing-oriented boundary spanners. *Journal of Marketing, 60,* 69–86.

Smith, A. K., Bolton, R. N., & Wagner, J. (1999). A model of customer satisfaction with service encounters involving failure and recovery. *Journal of Marketing Research, 36,* 356–372.

Smith, A. M. (1995). Measuring service quality: Is SERVQUAL now redundant? *Journal of Marketing Management, 11,* 257–276.

Smith, R. A., & Houston, M. J. (1982). Script-based evaluations of satisfaction with services. In L. L. Berry, G. L. Shostack, & G. Upah (Eds.), *The marketing aspects of service quality* (pp. 59–62). Chicago: American Marketing Association.

Sparks, B. A., Bradley, G. L., & Callan, V. J. (1997). The impact of staff empowerment and communication style on customer evaluations: The special case of service failure. *Psychology and Marketing, 14,* 475–493.

Spencer, J. L. (1991). *The role of the airline service employee: Relationships among management practices, social support, key characteristics of the service role and performance.* Unpublished doctoral dissertation, Columbia University, New York.

Statistical Abstracts of the United States. (1999). Retrieved December 2001, from www.census.gov/statab.

Teas, R. K. (1993). Expectations, performance evaluation and consumers' perceptions of quality. *Journal of Marketing, 57,* 18–34.

Thompson, J. W. (1996). Employee attitudes, organizational performance, and qualitative factors underlying success. *Journal of Business and Psychology, 11,* 171–196.

Tolich, M. B. (1993). Alienating and liberating emotions at work. *Journal of Contemporary Ethnography, 22,* 361–381.

Tornow, W. W., & Wiley, J. W. (1991). Service quality and management practices: A look at employee attitudes, customer satisfaction, and bottom-line consequences. *Human Resource Planning, 14,* 105–116.

Ulrich, D., Halbrook, R., Meder, D., Stuchlik, M., & Thorpe, S. (1991). Employee and customer attachment: Synergies for competitive advantage. *Human Resource Planning, 14,* 89–104.

Van Maanen, J., & Schein, E. H. (1979). Toward a theory of organizational socialization. In B. M. Staw (Ed.), *Research in organizational behavior* (Vol. 1, pp. 209–264). Reading, MA: Addison-Wesley.

Waldersee, R., & Luthans, F. (1994). The impact of positive and corrective feedback on customer service performance. *Journal of Organizational Behavior, 15,* 83–95.

Weatherly, K. A., & Tansik, D. A. (1993). Managing multiple demands: A role-theory examination of the behaviors of customer contact service workers. *Advances in Services Marketing and Management, 2,* 279–300.

Weaver, J. J. (1994). Want customer satisfaction? Satisfy your employees first. *HR Magazine, February,* 110, 112.

Weekley, J. A., & Jones, C. (1997). Video-based situational testing. *Personnel Psychology, 50,* 25–49.

Weekley, J. A., & Jones, C. (1999). Further studies in situational tests. *Personnel Psychology, 52,* 679–700.

Weitzel, W., Schwarzkopf, A. B., & Peach, E. B. (1989). The influence of employee perceptions of customer service on retail store sales. *Journal of Retailing, 65,* 27–39.

Wiechmann, D. (2000). *Applicant reactions to novel selection tools.* Unpublished masters thesis Michigan State University, Department of Psychology, East Lansing.

Wiley, J. W. (1991). Customer satisfaction and employee opinions: A supportive work environment and its financial cost. *Human Resource Planning, 14,* 117–128.

Wiley, J. W. (1996). Linking survey results to customer satisfaction and business performance. In A. I. Kraut (Ed.), *Organizational surveys: Tools for assessment and change* (pp. 88–116). San Francisco: Jossey-Bass.

Wilson, C., Boni, N., & Hogg, A. (1997). The effectiveness of task clarification, positive reinforcement and corrective feedback in changing courtesy among police staff. *Journal of Organizational Behavior Management, 17,* 65–99.

Yelon, S., & Ford, J. K. (1999). Pursuing a multidimensional view of transfer. *Performance Improvement Quarterly, 12,* 58–78.

Zeithaml, V. A. (1987). Characteristics affecting the acceptance of retailing technologies: A comparison of elderly and nonelderly consumers. *Journal of Retailing, 63,* 49–69.

Zeithaml, V. A., Berry, L. L., & Parasuraman, A. (1988). Communication and control processes in the delivery of service quality. *Journal of Marketing, 52,* 35–48.

Zeithaml, V. A., Berry, L. L., & Parasuraman, A. (1993). The nature and determinants of customer expectations of service. *Journal of the Academy of Marketing Science, 21,* 1–12.

Zemke, R., & Schaaf, D. (1989). *The service edge: 101 companies that profit from customer care.* New York: New American Library.

PART THREE

THE WORK ENVIRONMENT

CHAPTER 16

Changes in Workers, Work, and Organizations

WAYNE F. CASCIO

The characteristics, beliefs, and attitudes of workers have changed dramatically over the past several decades, largely in response to social trends, rapid advances in computer technology, and organizational restructuring. The nature of work—namely, how we work, where we work, and when we work—has also changed. Changes in workers and work, along with the economic implications of globalization, have combined to spawn new forms of organizations.

This chapter will address each of these issues. To provide some perspective on the youngest generation of workers, we will begin by examining just a few of the social, political, and economic trends that have influenced them. This generation was born in the early 1980s:

- They have no meaningful recollection of the Reagan era, and probably do not even know that he had ever been shot.

- Black Monday, 1987, is as significant to them as the Great Depression.

- There has only been one pope.

- They were 11 when the Soviet Union broke apart and they do not remember the Cold War.

- Tiananmen Square means nothing to them.

- Their lifetimes have always included the fact of AIDS.

- As far as they know, stamps have always cost about 33 cents.

- Roller-skating has always meant "inline" for them.

- They have no idea that Americans were ever held hostage in Iran.

- The Vietnam War is as ancient history to them as World War I, World War II, and the Civil War.

- There has always been MTV.

- They have always had an answering machine.
- Bottle caps have always been screw-off and plastic.
- They were born about the time that Sony introduced the Walkman.
- Popcorn has always been cooked in the microwave.

It's not just the young generation. Many of us have changed the ways that we live and work, largely because of new technology. Do any of the following describe your own habits?

- You have a list of 15 phone numbers to reach your family of three.
- You chat several times a day with a stranger from South Africa, yet you haven't spoken with your next door neighbor this year.
- You get an extra phone line so you can get phone calls.
- You call your son's beeper to let him know it's time to eat. He e-mails you back from his bedroom, "What's for dinner?"
- Your reason for not staying in touch with family is that they do not have e-mail addresses.
- You start tilting your head sideways to smile. :-)

Whether young or old, all of us have lived through the downsizing phenomenon that has been so common since the mid-1980s. It has become the preferred route to improve corporate efficiency, despite longitudinal research that questions its efficacy (Cascio, Morris, & Young, 1997; Cascio & Young, in press; Morris, Cascio, & Young, 1999). Thus *Newsweek* magazine wrote: "Firing people has gotten to be trendy in corporate America, in the same way that building new plants and being considered a good corporate citizen gave you bragging rights 25 years ago" (February 26, 1996, p. 4). Concurrently with this comment, *The New York Times* reported that more than 43 million jobs had been extinguished since 1979, that the rate of job loss hit a peak of 3.4 million a year in 1992, and and that it has remained that high ever since. Almost two out of every three Americans either had a close family member or friend who had lost a job, or had lost one personally (Uchitelle & Kleinfeld, 1996). In 2001, companies in the United States announced layoffs of 1.96 million workers ("Shadow of Recession," 2002).

Restructuring, including downsizing, often leads to predictable effects—diminished loyalty from employees. In the wave of takeovers, mergers, downsizings, and layoffs, thousands of workers have discovered that years of service mean little to a struggling management or a new corporate parent. This leads to a rise in stress and a decrease in satisfaction, commitment, intentions to stay, and perceptions of an organization's trustworthiness, honesty, and caring about its employees (Gutknecht & Keys, 1993; Kleinfeld, 1996; Schweiger & DeNisi, 1991). Indeed, our views of hard work, loyalty, and managing as a career will probably never be the same.

Companies counter that today's competitive business environment makes it difficult to protect workers. Understandably, organizations are streamlining in order to become more competitive (by cutting labor costs) and to become more flexible in their response to the demands of the marketplace. However, the rising disaffection of workers at all levels has profound implications for employers. Said a victim of three corporate downsizings in four years: "A job is just an opportunity to learn some new skills that you can then peddle elsewhere in the marketplace" ("Working Scared," 1993). This is quite a change from the world of work that dominated the first 85 years of the twentieth century. In that world, many people were proud to say that they had worked for one or two companies their entire careers. Today, labor experts predict that new workers entering the labor market will hold 7 to 10 jobs in their lifetimes. In fact, some 10% of the American workforce actually switch occupations every year (Henkoff, 1996).

At the same time, jobs are relatively plentiful in America. The national unemployment rate was 5.8% in 2002 (U.S. Bureau of Labor Statistics, 2002). Investments by venture capitalists in start-up companies, which rose 150% between 1998 and 1999 (Sommer, 2000), also have lead to the high demand for people. Given the wide availability of jobs and the increasing mobility of labor, employee retention has become a major issue in American organizations, and new strategies to retain workers are becoming popular. We will consider such strategies in a later section.

Labor shortages add further complication to the staffing plans of employers. Thus the U.S. Bureau of Labor Statistics estimates that between 1998 and 2008 total employment will increase by 14%. Over that same period, however, the supply of workers is expected to grow by only 12%. This will result in a shortage of 10 million workers. Why is this happening? To a large extent, it reflects the decreased birth rate of the late 1960s and the early 1970s, combined with the aging of the baby boom generation (those born between 1946 and 1964; Bernstein, 2002). The baby boom generation currently accounts for 78 million people and 55% of the workforce (Fisher, 1996).

CHANGES IN THE PSYCHOLOGICAL CONTRACT

Downsizing and other forms of restructuring have altered the psychological contract that binds workers and employers. To put the changes into perspective, consider some features of the old contract and how they have changed to reflect the realities of today's workplaces (for more on this, see Rousseau, 1995, 1996):

Old Psychological Contract	New Psychological Contract
Stability, predictability	Change, uncertainty
Permanence	Temporariness
Standard work patterns	Flexible work
Valuing loyalty	Valuing performance and skills
Paternalism	Self-reliance
Job security	Employment security
Linear career growth	Multiple careers
One-time learning	Life-long learning

Stability and predictability characterized the old psychological contract. In the 1970s, for example, workers held an average of three to four jobs during their working lives. Change and uncertainty, however, are hallmarks of the new psychological contract. As we noted previously, workers will soon hold 7–10 jobs during their working lives. Job-hopping no longer holds the same stigma as it once did. Thus interviewers used to regard with skepticism a job candidate who had held more than two jobs in three years. Today, workers in high-technology jobs often tout the fact that they have held two jobs in the past three years as a badge of honor, an indication that they are on the cutting edge of their fields. Beyond that, the massive downsizing of the workforce has made job mobility the norm, rather than the exception. This has led workers operating under the new psychological contract to expect temporary employment relationships. Permanent employment relationships, with few exceptions (e.g., tenured college professors), no longer exist.

Another major change in the psychological contract has been the shift from standard work patterns to flexible work patterns. For all of the emphasis on the so-called new economy, however, most jobs are still modeled on the clock-punching culture of the industrial past. Middle-income parents are now logging 260 more hours a year on the job than they did a decade ago. In the aggregate, Americans are now working more hours than the Japanese ("Flexibility," 2000). For many of them, however, 9:00 A.M. to 5:00 P.M. is not working anymore. Time is employees' most precious commodity. They want the flexibility to control their own time—where, when, and how they work. They want balance in their lives between work and leisure. Flexibility in schedules is the key, as organizations strive to retain talented workers in a hot job market.

Small business owners in particular are finding that flexibility on hours is a cheap benefit that allows them to compete with large companies whose schedules may be more rigid. As a result, many are hiring members of a group once shunned by employers—mothers of young children. "We're learning that the trade-off if they have to leave work for something child-related is loyalty in return for that flexibility," says Susan Lyon, president of Lyon & Associates, a small advertising and marketing firm in San Diego (R. Johnson, 2000).

Despite the fact that only 53% of U.S. employers offer flextime to their employees ("What Employers Are Offering," 2000), a recent poll found 56% of managers reporting that employees with flexible schedules are more productive per hour. That kind of positive buzz is what is driving work redesign processes to enhance flexibility at companies such as Ernst & Young, Hewlett-Packard, Bank of America, and Lucent Technologies (Conlin, 2000).

Effects on Reactions to Organizations

In years past, employers strove mightily to instill loyalty to the company among their employees. Downsizing and restructuring have changed all of that, at least for the foreseeable future. For most of the 1990s, downsizing set the tone for the modern employment contract. As companies frantically restructured to cope with slipping market share or heightened competition, they tore up old notions of paternalism. They told employees, "Don't expect to spend your life at one company anymore. You are responsible for your own career, so get all the skills you can and prepare to change jobs, employers, even industries. As for the implicit bond of loyalty that might have existed before, well, forget it," said employers. "In these days of fierce global competition, loyalty is an unaffordable luxury" ("We Want You to Stay," 1998).

Today, after several years of tight labor markets, employers have changed their tune. Now, it's "Don't leave. We need you. Work for us—you can build a career here." Employers are going to great lengths to persuade employees that they want them to stay for years. According to a recent survey, employees are less loyal to their companies, and they tend to put their own needs and interests above those of their employers. More often they are willing to trade off higher wages and benefits for flexibility and autonomy, job characteristics that allow them to balance their lives on and off the job. Almost 9 out of every 10 workers live with family members, and nearly half care for dependents, including children, elderly parents, or ailing spouses (A. A. Johnson, 1999). Among employees who switched jobs in the last five years, pay and benefits rated in the bottom half of 20 possible reasons that they did so. Factors rated highest were nature of work, open communication, and effect on personal and/or family life. When it comes to loyalty, each employee is behaving as if he or she is the chief executive officer (CEO) of "Me, Inc." In some cases, tightly knit groups of employees (coworkers, former colleagues, classmates, or friends) decide to stay or leave en masse, behaving as if they are the CEOs of "We, Inc." That phenomenon has been termed the *pied piper effect,* as top performers at the heart of these networks convince others to follow them (Wysocki, 2000). Paternalism on the part of the company has given way to self-reliance on the part of the employee or groups of employees.

Another change in the psychological contract is the shift from *job security,* the knowledge that one would always have a job with a given employer, to *employment security,* having skills that some employer in the labor market is willing to pay for. This is why the concepts of lifelong learning and multiple careers are so important to employees. Obsolescence is the enemy. Opportunities for workplace training and continual professional development are prized commodities as employees strive to keep themselves marketable.

Effects on Reactions to Work

Do these changes in the psychological contract imply that Americans are not as committed as they once were to work as a central activity in their lives? Data from the annual *General Social Survey* (a multitopic survey administered to roughly 1,500 adult, English-speaking men and women) suggests that the answer is no (National Research Council, 1999). The following item from the survey was asked in 1973 and again in 1996: "If you were to get enough money to live as comfortably as you would like for the rest of your life, would you continue to work, or would you stop working?" In 1973, 69% of Americans said they would continue to work. In 1996, 68% said they would continue to work—virtually no change.

In the same survey, respondents were asked to look at a card and rank the top four of five job characteristics (the job characteristic not chosen as one of the four most important was coded as 5). The five items that were ranked were high income (income), no danger of being fired (job security), short working hours with lots of free time (hours), chances for advancement (promotions), and work is important and gives a feeling of accomplishment (intrinsic).

In 1973, the average ranking (calculated across all respondents) was as follows:

1. Intrinsic.
2. Promotions.
3. Income.
4. Job security.
5. Hours.

What is most striking is that this basic ordering, despite some minor fluctuations, has remained remarkably stable since then. The rank order of these characteristics has remained virtually the same, with intrinsic aspects of work being the job characteristics most preferred by Americans in general, and short hours the least preferred. Job security still ranks fourth.

Although there appears to be continuity in the centrality of work in the lives of Americans and in the characteristics of jobs that they seek, this is not to imply that dramatic changes are not occurring in the world of work. Business trends that seem immutable and unstoppable are driving much of the change. In the next section we will consider four such trends: globalization, new technology, electronic (e-) commerce, and demographic changes and increasing diversity.

GLOBALIZATION

The global village is getting smaller every day. Markets in every country have become fierce battlegrounds where both domestic and foreign competitors fight for market share, and foreign competitors can be formidable. For example, Coca-Cola earns more than 80% of its revenues from outside the United States. The 500 largest firms in the world employ more than 47 million people, they gross more than $14,000 billion in revenues and $667 billion in profits, and the total value of their assets is about $46,000 billion ("The World's Largest Corporations," 2001).

These few examples suggest that cross-cultural exposure, if not actual interaction, has become the norm. In the world of business, globalization is a defining characteristic of the twenty-first century. *Globalization* refers to commerce without borders, along with the interdependence of business operations in different locations.

Signs of Globalization

In this emerging economic order, foreign investment by the world's leading corporations is a fact of modern organizational life. More than 800 multinational companies have regional headquarters in Hong Kong alone (Kraar, 1997). Today, foreign investment is viewed not just as an opportunity for U.S. companies investing abroad but also as an opportunity for other countries to develop subsidiaries in the United States and elsewhere. Indeed, a single marketplace has been created by factors such as the following (Cascio, 2003):

- Satellite dishes in the world's most remote areas, which beam live television feeds from CNN and MTV. Internet booksellers like Amazon.com provide 24-hour-a-day supermarkets for consumers everywhere.
- Global telecommunications enhanced by fiber optics, satellites, and computer technology (Revzin, Waldman, & Gumbel, 1990).

- Giant multinational corporations such as Gillette, Unilever, and Nestlé, which have begun to lose their national identities as they integrate and coordinate product design, manufacturing, sales, and services on a worldwide basis.
- Growing free trade among nations (exemplified by the 1993 North American Free Trade Agreement [NAFTA] among Mexico, the United States, and Canada).
- Financial markets' being open 24 hours a day around the world.
- Foreign control of more than 15% of U.S. manufacturing assets and employment of more than 8 million U.S. workers (6% of the U.S. workforce).
- The emergence of global standards and regulations for trade, commerce, finance, products, and services.

Companies compete just about everywhere, especially when economic conditions give them a substantial price advantage. As an example, consider Hong Kong's airline, Cathay Pacific.

The airline's computer center has moved to Sydney, Australia, where the land costs only 1% what a comparable site in Hong Kong would cost. Its revenue-accounting back office has been shifted to Guangzhou, China, and even some of its aircraft maintenance is now done in Xiamen on the South China coast, where labor costs only 10% to 20% of Hong Kong rates. The labor-intensive part of Cathay Pacific's reservations, such as special meals for passengers, is handled out of Bombay, India (Kraar, 1997).

As a consequence of this onslaught of cross-cultural exposure and interaction, it might appear that the world's cultures are growing more homogenous—but don't be fooled. A quote from T. Fujisawa, cofounder of Honda Motor Company, suggests otherwise: "Japanese and American management is 95% the same, and differs in all important respects" (Adler, Doktor, & Redding, 1986, p. 301). In other words, while organizations are becoming more similar in terms of structure and technology, people's behavior within those organizations continues to reveal culturally based differences (Adler et al., 1986).

The Backlash Against Globalization

In no small part, the booming U.S. economy of recent years has been fueled by globalization. Open borders have allowed new ideas and technology to flow freely around the globe, accelerating productivity growth and allowing U.S. companies to be more competitive than they have been in decades. Yet there is a growing fear on the part of many people that globalization benefits big companies instead of average

citizens—of America or any other country ("Backlash," 2000). In the public eye, multinational corporations are synonymous with globalization. In all of their far-flung operations, therefore, they bear responsibility to be good corporate citizens, to preserve the environment, to uphold labor standards, to provide decent working conditions and competitive wages, to treat their employees fairly, and to contribute to the communities in which they operate. Such behaviors will make a strong case for continued globalization.

Implications for Work, Workers, and Organizations

As every advanced economy becomes global, a nation's most important competitive asset becomes the skills and cumulative learning of its workforce. Globalization, almost by definition, makes this true. Virtually all developed countries can design, produce, and distribute goods and services equally well and equally fast. Every factor of production other than workforce skills can be duplicated anywhere in the world. Capital moves freely across international boundaries, seeking the lowest costs. State-of-the-art factories can be erected anywhere. The latest technologies move from computers in one nation, up to satellites parked in space, and back down to computers in another nation—all at the speed of electronic impulses. It is all fungible—capital, technology, raw materials, information—all except for one thing, the most critical part, the one element that is unique about a nation or a company: its workforce. A workforce that is knowledgeable and skilled at doing complex things keeps a company competitive and attracts foreign investment (Reich, 1990).

In fact, the relationship forms a virtuous circle: well-trained workers attract global corporations, which invest and give the workers good jobs; the good jobs, in turn, generate additional training and experience. We must face the fact that, regardless of the shifting political winds in Tokyo, Berlin, Washington, Beijing, or Budapest, the shrunken globe is here to stay. Does this imply that cultural nuances in different countries and regions of the world will become less important? Hardly. To put this issue into perspective, let us consider the concept of culture.

Triandis (1998) emphasizes that *culture* provides implicit theories of social behavior that act like a computer program, controlling the actions of individuals. He notes that cultures include unstated assumptions, the way the world is. These assumptions influence thinking, emotions, and actions without people's noticing that they do. Members of cultures believe that their ways of thinking are obviously correct and need not be discussed. Expatriate managers, and Americans working for foreign-owned companies, ignore them at their peril. To help put cultural differences into perspective, consider a typology of cultural differences: the theory of vertical and horizontal individualism and collectivism.

Vertical and Horizontal Individualism and Collectivism

Triandis (1998) notes that vertical cultures accept hierarchy as a given, whereas horizontal cultures accept equality as a given. Individualistic cultures emerge in societies that are complex (many subgroups with different attitudes and beliefs) and loose (relatively few rules and norms about what is correct behavior in different types of situations). Collectivism emerges in societies that are simple (individuals agree on beliefs and attitudes) and tight (many rules and norms about what is correct behavior in different types of situations).

Triandis (1998) argues that these syndromes (shared patterns of attitudes, beliefs, norms, and values organized around a theme) constitute the parameters of any general theory about the way culture influences people. Crossing the cultural syndromes of individualism and collectivism with the cultural syndromes of vertical and horizontal relationships yields a typology of four kinds of cultures.

Additional culture-specific attributes define different kinds of individualism or collectivism. According to Triandis (1998), the following four may be the universal dimensions of these constructs:

1. *Definition of the self:* autonomous and independent from groups (individualists), versus interdependent with others (collectivists).
2. *Structure of goals:* priority given to personal goals (individualists), versus priority given to in-group goals (collectivists).
3. *Emphasis on norms versus attitudes:* attitudes, personal needs, perceived rights, and contracts determine social behavior (individualists), versus norms, duties, and obligations as determinants of social behavior (collectivists).
4. *Emphasis on relatedness versus rationality:* collectivists emphasize *relatedness* (giving priority to relationships and taking into account the needs of others), whereas individualists emphasize *rationality* (careful computation of the costs and benefits of relationships).

There are many implications and patterns of variation of these important differences with respect to organizational issues and globalization. Two of them are *goal-setting and reward systems* (individual vs. team- or organization-wide), and *communications* (gestures, eye contact, and body language in high-context cultures, vs. precision with words in low-context cultures). Two others are *performance feedback* (where characteristics of the culture—vertical-horizontal or individualist-collectivist—interact with the objectives, style, frequency, and inherent assumptions of the performance-feedback process), and *assessment practices* (preferences for different approaches, possible variation in validity across cultures). Finally, there are implications for training and development (e.g., language training for expatriates, along with training to avoid culture shock that results from repeated disorientation experienced by individuals in a foreign land whose customs and culture differ from one's own; Cascio, 1998). This is just a brief overview. There are many other behavioral implications of globalization, such as work motivation across cultures (Erez, 1997), leadership (House, Wright, & Aditya, 1997), and decision making in multinational teams (Ilgen, LePine, & Hollenbeck, 1997).

TECHNOLOGY

It is no exaggeration to say that modern technology is changing the ways we live and work. The information revolution will transform everything it touches—and it will touch everything. Information and ideas are key to the new creative economy, because every country, every company, and every individual depends increasingly on knowledge. People are cranking out computer programs and inventions, while lightly staffed factories churn out the sofas, the breakfast cereals, the cell phones. The five fastest growing occupations in the United States are all computer-related, according to projections by the Bureau of Labor Statistics. That agency also projects that by 2005, the percentage of workers employed in industry will fall below 20%, the lowest level since 1850. Meanwhile the share of U.S. capital spending devoted to information technology has more than tripled since 1960, from 10% to more than 35% (Coy, 2000).

As an example, consider Buckman Laboratories, a specialty chemical company that operates in 90 countries and sells more than 1,000 products. It has enjoyed sales growth of 250% over the past 10 years, and fully 35% of its total sales come from products less than five years old. The company's success comes from putting its talent in the field, so that salespeople can provide rapid, customized solutions whenever a customer encounters a problem. To facilitate the sharing of knowledge, the company hosts a private, Internet-based forum where anyone can pose a question or offer an answer. The company expects and encourages employees at all levels to use the forums. To ensure accessibility, the forums are held in multiple languages, with translation assistance provided (Fulmer, 1999). State-of-the-art technology, including high-speed data transfer, facilitates such forums, but it is not cheap. Chief executive officer Bob Buckman believes the

$90,000 per month cost (roughly 3.5% of revenues) is well worth it. While a large company like Buckman Laboratories may well be able to absorb such an expense, smaller companies find it to be prohibitive.

In the information economy, the most important intellectual property is not software or music. It is the intellectual capital that resides in people. When assets were physical things like coal mines, shareholders truly owned them. When the most vital assets are people, however, there can be no true ownership. The best that corporations can do is to create an environment that makes the best people want to stay. Therein lies a key challenge in managing human resources, and we shall examine it further in a later section.

Impact of New Technology on Work, Workers, and Organizations

Where we work, when we work, and how we communicate are being revolutionized as a seamless web of electronic communications media—e-mail, voice mail, cellular telephones, laptop computers with modems, hand-held organizers, video conferencing, and interactive pagers make teamwork and mobility a reality. Not only is work becoming seamless as it moves among home, office, and telephone, but it also is becoming endless as it rolls through a 24-hour day ("Power Gizmos," 1997). Technology facilitates the rapid diffusion of information and knowledge. It is the engine that enables new ways of organizing and new organizational forms.

As an example, consider the *virtual workplace,* in which workers and managers operate remotely from each other. Without information and knowledge, workers in virtual workplaces would become disconnected and ineffective. Fortunately, technology and enlightened management practices can ensure that this does not happen. One such technology that enables virtual work arrangements is known as groupware. *Groupware* refers to computer-based systems that are designed explicitly to support groups of people working together. This is what enables virtual interactions (Ishii, Kobayashi, & Arita, 1994). The goal of groupware technology is simple: to promote and improve interaction among individuals (Aannestad & Hooper, 1997). This is collaborative empowerment.

Technology also has important implications for how we interact in organizational settings. For example, a key issue is *performance management.* When workers and managers operate remotely from each other, managers often ask, "If I can't see them, how do I know that they are working?" The key to resolving that dilemma is to shift from managing based on time to managing based on results (Cascio, 2000a). A second issue is *career management,* as workers in virtual work arrangements become similar to expatriate workers in

that both can easily become out of sight, out of mind (so to speak) and miss out on important office conversations, informal meetings, and desirable assignments. It will be important to use technology to ensure that such workers remain in the loop. A related implication is a potential lack of social interaction with managers and coworkers. Teleworkers often report that they suffer from feelings of isolation and loneliness. Mix-and-match programs that provide the opportunity to come into the office several days a week can help.

Perhaps the most central use of technology in the management of people is an organization's *human resources information system (HRIS).* Indeed, as technology integrates with traditionally labor-intensive human resource (HR) activities, HR professionals are seeing improvements in response time and efficiency of the report information available. Dozens of vendors offer HRIS applications ranging from benefits enrollment to applicant tracking, time and attendance records, training and development, payroll, pension plans, and employee surveys (HRIS Buying Guide, 2000). Such systems are moving beyond simply storing and retrieving information to include broader applications such as report generation, succession planning, strategic planning, career planning, employee self-service applications (e.g., benefits enrollment), and evaluating HR policies and practices (Geutal, 2001). In that sense, today's HRISs are tools for management control and decision making.

E-COMMERCE

Consider this forecast:

> The Internet will change the relationship between consumers and producers in ways more profound than you can yet imagine. The Internet is not just another marketing channel; it's not just another advertising medium; it's not just a way to speed up transactions. The Internet is the foundation for a new industrial order. The Internet will empower consumers like nothing else ever has. . . . The Web will fundamentally change customers' expectations about convenience, speed, comparability, price, and service. (Hamel & Sampler, 1998)

Whether it's business-to-business (B2B) or business-to-consumer (B2C), e-commerce is taking off. As an example, consider Boise Office solutions, the office products subsidiary of paper giant Boise Cascade Corporation. Some 30 percent of its $2.5 billion in annual sales are online, and that's expected to rise to 45 percent within a year. The result? Savings of at least $585,000 a year so far, and each percentage point rise in online sales is expected to add $100,000 in additional savings (Hof & Hamm, 2002).

In the automobile industry, consider this scenario from former Ford Motor Company CEO Jac Nasser ("At Ford," 2000). He pictures the day when a buyer hits a button to order a custom-configured Ford Mustang online, transmitting a slew of information directly to the dealer who will deliver it, the finance and insurance units who will underwrite it, the factory that will build it, the suppliers that provide its components, and the Ford designers brainstorming future models. To buyers it will mean getting just what they ordered, delivered right to their doorstep in days. Although there are plenty of risks associated with this scenario, e-commerce is encouraging the reinvention of manufacturing, and it would be foolish to underestimate the ultimate outcome.

The extent of the online revolution is noteworthy, for the number of Internet users worldwide is still rising—by 48% in 2000 and 27% in 2001, to more than 500 million people today (Hof & Hamm, 2002). At present, both B2B and B2C transactions comprise only about 2% of commercial and retail transactions. While that may seem small, consider that even as venture funding of Internet companies fell 71% in 2001, Internet trade between businesses rose 73% to $496 billion, and online retail spending rose 56% to $112 billion, in the worst retail year in a decade (Hof & Hamm, 2002). The Internet is still in its infancy, and many experts expect that eventually it will be a major factor in pricing. The idea is that prices will be driven downward as B2B online markets allow an endless number of suppliers to bid competitively for contracts with big manufacturers.

Impact on Work, Workers, and Organizations

Retail e-commerce sites, so the thinking goes, will cut consumer prices by pitting a multitude of sellers against one another, allowing Web-surfing buyers to identify quickly the lowest possible price for any good. Web-based search engines will provide buyers with more information—and bargaining power—about products than ever before. Whether those predictions come to pass will depend on several factors, the most important of which is how much economic activity finally does move online (Blackmon, 2000). While advocates make the future of e-commerce sound irresistible, the fact is that there is a lack of face-to-face interaction with customers. This is an important issue, at least for some people and some types of products. In addition, the speed of change will not go away. If anything, workers in e-businesses will have to accelerate their responses to the speed of change in order to remain competitive. This will be an ongoing challenge. In addition, consider one inescapable fact—all of the people who make e-commerce possible are knowledge workers. The organizations they work for still have to address the human resource challenges of attracting, retaining, and motivating them to perform well.

DEMOGRAPHIC CHANGES AND INCREASING CULTURAL DIVERSITY

Employers are facing a chronic shortage of skilled help. The number as well as the mix of people available to work are changing rapidly. The U.S. Bureau of Labor Statistics projects that there will be a 6.5% decrease in the population of 35- to 44-year-olds between 2000 and 2006 (Bernstein, 2002; "The Shrinking Workforce," 2000). As far as the mix is concerned, the U.S. Census Bureau projects that over the next 50 years, non-Hispanic whites will comprise a slim majority of the U.S. population. Latin Americans will make up nearly a quarter of the population, with Asians, African Americans, and, to a much lesser extent, Native Americans, comprising the rest. In fact, the Latin American population in the United States will continue to grow at a rate at least 6 times faster than the general population and reach 35 million, surpassing the number of African Americans sometime after 2000 ("America's Changing Complexion," 2000; Tsacounis, 2002). The Latino population will reach 50–60 million by 2020, and 90–100 million by 2040 (Day, 1996). Currently, female participation has jumped to 60% from 50% two decades ago, and the long-term trend toward earlier retirement has recently been reversed. Only 10% want to stop working altogether when they retire from their jobs (Coy, 2000; "Most in Survey," 2000).

Given the demographic changes that are taking place, the business case for diversity is clear. For example, a recent study of diversity commissioned by the cable television industry found that people of color have $650 billion in spending power and represent 20% of all cable subscribers, generating $6.7 billion in cable-subscriber revenue. The report concluded that racial bias, by any measure, is simply a bad business practice for the cable television industry or any other enterprise ("Update," 1999).

In another study, Covenant Investment Management (2000) recently evaluated the stock market performance, as well as the records of advancement of women and non-White employees, of the largest 500 companies traded on the New York Stock Exchange. For the 100 companies that rated lowest on the study's advancement ranking, the average stock market return was 7.9%. For the 100 companies that rated highest on the study's advancement ranking, the average stock market return was 18.3%. That was 2.5 times higher than the return of firms that did not emphasize the advancement of women and minorities.

Implications for Work, Workers, and Organizations

These trends have two key implications for decision makers: (a) The reduced supply of workers will make finding and keeping employees a top priority, and (b) the task of managing a culturally diverse workforce, of harnessing the motivation and efforts of a wide variety of workers, will present a continuing challenge to organizations and their managers. The organizations that thrive will be the ones that embrace the new demographic trends instead of fighting them. Said leading economist R. Hokanson, "The ingenuity of businesses will be tested again and again as labor force developments over the next ten years represent new challenges, as well as the continuation of existing ones" (as cited in Armas, 2000). In the next several sections we will consider what leading organizations are doing to find and retain talent.

THE ART OF FINDING TALENT

In a recent paper, Cascio (2000b) examined what leading companies are doing to find and retain talent in the tight labor markets that they face. Much of the material in the following sections comes from this source. Thus, the International Franchise Association found in a recent survey that 95% of its members ranked labor as their biggest challenge. The labor shortage has emerged as the number-one headache for franchisees. In some cases it is curbing growth and expansion possibilities, and in others it is forcing operators to reduce their business hours for lack of staff (Morse, 2000). Among high-technology firms worldwide, it is estimated that 800,000 jobs will go begging this year alone. This has forced employers to use creative recruitment tactics in order to attract competent staff. The following sections describe some of these tactics.

Cisco Systems

Cisco Systems, located in the heart of the Silicon Valley, makes routers for the Internet and high-end networking gear. Cisco's recruiters target *passive job seekers,* people who are happy and successful where they are. Since this group is not very accessible, Cisco had to learn how to lure them. It began by holding focus groups with ideal recruitment targets, such as senior engineers and marketing professionals from competitors, to find out how they spend their free time (lots of movies), what Web sites they visit, and how they feel about job hunting (they hate it). Then the real work started.

Cisco learned how to reach potential applicants through a variety of routes not usually used in recruiting, such as infiltrating art fairs, microbrewery festivals, and even home-and-garden shows. In Silicon Valley, the first-time home buyers that such shows attract tend to be young achievers at successful technology companies. Cisco recruiters work the crowds, collecting business cards from prospects and speaking to them informally about their careers.

The way the company uses help-wanted ads in the newspaper has also changed dramatically. Rather than listing specific job openings, the company runs ads featuring its Internet address and an invitation to apply at Cisco. Directing all job seekers to its Web site is a major benefit. There it can post hundreds of job openings and detailed information about each one. Since most prospects visit Cisco's Web site from their jobs, Cisco can even determine where they work.

Relying again on focus groups, Cisco sought to learn how happily employed people could be enticed to interview for a job. The response: "I'd do it if I had a friend who told me he had a better opportunity at Cisco than I have at my present employer." So the company launched its "Make Friends @ Cisco" program to help prospects make a pal at Cisco who could describe what it's like to work there. Although the program is advertised only in local movie theaters, Cisco receives about 150 requests each week from applicants wishing to be introduced to a friend who works at the company. About a third of new hires now come through the program (Nakache, 1997).

To accelerate and standardize online resume submission, Cisco uses a tool called "Profiler" on its employment Web page. Profiler asks applicants to provide educational and employment information by choosing appropriate selections from a series of pull-down menus. Because most people log on to Profiler from work (peak usage of Cisco's employment page occurs between 10:00 A.M. and 3:00 P.M.), they risk being caught in the act by a boss who is just dropping by. To deal with this, there is an "Oh No! My Boss Is Coming" button, which quickly fills the screen with "Seven Habits of a Successful Employee." The employment page also includes a virtual tour of the company's campus in Silicon Valley. The entire kit gets prominent play on the company's home page, thus ensnaring curious passers-by (Nakache, 1997).

The company diligently measures the outcomes of its recruiting efforts. For example, Cisco's cost per hire is only $6,556, versus an industry average of $10,800. Its in-house staff of recruiters has remained steady at about 100, even as the company's annual rate of hiring rose from 2,000 to 8,000 people.

The most important statistic, however, is 45 days. This is the average time it takes Cisco to fill an open job—down from 113 days three years ago. (Indeed, a study by iLogos.com found that, on average, using the Internet shaves 20 days off a company's hiring cycle.) That's precious time for any company.

How avidly does Cisco pursue candidates online? It has software that tracks where visitors to its Web site go after leaving. It then places employment banner ads on those sites.

Home Depot

The Home Depot, which sells everything from hardware to lumber to plumbing supplies for home-improvement projects, automated its hiring and promotion system as one part of the settlement of a sex discrimination lawsuit (Daniels, 2000). In 2001 the company's revenues were $52.3 billion. Since 1979 it has gone from four stores in Atlanta to 1,301 in four countries, with more than 230,000 associates (as employees are called) (Pascual, 2001; Sellers, 2001). Recruiting and hiring are everyday activities for this company.

At a cost of $10 million, the company installed computer kiosks in every store. Computerized staffing would help ensure that a broader pool of applicants, including women, would be considered for jobs. Job seekers' applications go into a company-wide network. Since the system was introduced into all 900 Home Depot stores in 1998, the number of female managers has increased by 30% and the number of minority managers by 28%.

Rather than feeling displaced by the system, hiring managers are happy to get help from the computerized system, which handles initial screening. Applicants, who apply at kiosks in stores or by calling a toll-free number, are given a 40- to 90-minute basic skills test that helps weed out unqualified applicants before live interviews. Managers say that has meant better candidates, which, in turn, has helped reduce turnover by 11%. Other retailers, such as Target, Publix supermarkets, and Hollywood Video, have also automated their application processes, but where the Home Depot breaks new ground is in using its system for promotion decisions as well as for initial hiring decisions. Here is how the promotion system works.

Employees are required to register for jobs they might want in the future, and they are encouraged to update their profiles regularly at the kiosks sitting in employee break rooms. Imagine that a cashier wants to become an assistant manager. What the cashier doesn't know is that he needs to work first as a sales associate. The computer will point that out, along with some helpful hints about what to do each step of the way. Managers can interview and promote only people who have registered an interest in the position, and they must interview at least three people. This new way of doing things is not negotiable, and five managers have been dismissed for not using the system, according to a Home Depot lawyer.

The system is networked, so that if someone applies to a Home Depot in Atlanta the application could potentially go to any store within commuting distance. That means store managers have a bigger pool of applicants to choose from, and many say it provides them with great candidates they might never have considered before.

GE Medical Systems

This company invents and makes computerized tomography (CT) scanners, magnetic resonance imagers, and other biomedical equipment that requires some of the most demanding software coding and electrical engineering anywhere. It is an innovation powerhouse, with more than 80% of its equipment sales coming from products no more than three years old. The company competes for talent with the likes of Intel, Cisco Systems, Microsoft, and Hewlett-Packard, and hires about 500 technical workers a year.

What is remarkable about GE Medical is that last year it cut its cost of hiring by 17%, reduced the time needed to fill a position by between 20% and 30%, and cut in half the percentage of new hires that do not work out (Stewart, 1998). How did it do this? By doing four things well:

1. Developing detailed staffing plans.
2. Rigorously measuring the performance of outside recruiters (e.g., *first-pass yield,* the percentage of resumes that result in interviews; *second-pass yield,* the percentage of interviews that result in offers). The company then limited its relationships with outside recruiters to those that scored highest on first- and second-pass yields.
3. Having summer interns grade their programs and their bosses (former summer interns are twice as likely to accept a job offer as other candidates). Bosses who get low grades do not get interns, but do get training to improve their performance.
4. Focusing major attention on employee referrals.

In terms of employee referrals, fully 10% of them result not just in an interview, but in a hire. In comparison, only 1% of people whose resumes come into GE Medical are even called for an interview. Nothing else—not headhunters and not internships—even comes close to that kind of yield. The company doubled the number of employee referrals by taking three easy steps:

1. The program is simple and rewarding—no complex forms and no bureaucracy. The referring employee receives a small goodie like a gift certificate at a local retail store simply for referring a qualified candidate.

2. The company pays the referring employee $2,000 if the person he or she refers is hired, and $3,000 if the new hire is a software engineer. That may seem like a lot of money, but the more often GE pays it, the more money it saves, because it replaces a $15,000 to $20,000 headhunter's fee.

3. The company begins asking new employees for referrals almost from their first day on the job. If the new employee comes, say, from Motorola, for the first 3 months he or she is still one of Motorola's and remembers everyone there. Nine months later, he or she is one of GE's. That, of course, is the goal.

Employee Referrals at MasterCard

In 1995 employee referrals accounted for less than 10% of all new hires, but by 1999 that number had zoomed to almost 40%. MasterCard pays current employees $1,000 for referrals of hourly workers, and $2,000 to $3,000 for referrals of professionals.

What makes this program different, however, is that MasterCard pays its employees *immediately* for anyone hired from their referrals. Initially there was concern that some employees might make bad referrals just to get the money. That concern ended when one employee pointed out that it was employees' responsibility to make the referral, and then it was the responsibility of HR and the hiring manager to make the decision to hire. It's their fault if a bad hiring decision was made, so why punish the employee?

By changing the program to pay the employee immediately upon the hire of a candidate he or she referred, MasterCard generated good will among its employees, and within a year it quadrupled the number of referrals from present employees. Subsequent research revealed that the referral program pays for itself nearly tenfold in terms of the savings in recruitment and retention costs, and that has helped convince some very skeptical upper managers of the value of the program (Leonard, 1999).

Recruiting From Online Resumes: Pros and Cons

It is estimated that more than one million people will transmit their resumes over the Internet this year. Is this a recruiting bonanza for employers? In one sense, yes, for employers can scan online job boards using keywords to identify candidates with the educational background, training accomplishments, and workplace experience that they need.

On the other hand, there are some very serious privacy concerns for job seekers, and employee-relations concerns for employers, that should be recognized (Useem, 1999). Resumes posted at one site can be traded or sold to other sites,

they can be stolen by unscrupulous headhunters or duplicated and reposted by roving *spiders,* and current employers can locate them as well. The Internet is so vast that many people think their resumes are safe there. Think again, for a number of factors can wrest control from a job seeker. Spidering technologies are one of the most common.

Dispatched at night by job boards looking to populate themselves with candidates, these programs creep like robots through other sites and return laden with resumes. Even private, password-secured sites are not immune to these programs. The result? A resume posted on a handful of sites can end up quickly plastered across a dozen—and a runaway resume can be hard to stop. Many job boards do not even allow candidates the option of removing outdated versions.

A second problem is with unscrupulous recruiters, thousands of small-time headhunters who, looking for a quick commission, harvest resumes from the Internet and send them to employers in bulk—without consulting the candidates. There is a shadowy new subspecies of HR professional known as a *salvager.* In the name of protecting company secrets, some corporations have begun to assign HR staff members to patrol cyberspace in search of wayward workers. Their objective is to reassign employees who are circulating their resumes online (and who therefore have one foot out the electronic door) off of sensitive projects. Fair enough, but such a practice can also be viewed as an invasion of an employee's privacy and right to search for a job that might make better use of his or her skills. In short, such a practice can easily create an employee-relations disaster. Perhaps it was concerns such as these that led the European Central Bank to post technology-based job vacancies on its Web site, but then require that all job applications be mailed in on paper ("Work Week," 2000).

The next step after recruiting candidates for jobs is to select those whose level of predicted performance is highest. With a diverse pool of candidates that differ along a variety of dimensions, there will likely be high levels of variability among candidates. It is especially important, therefore, to use staffing methods that have the highest levels of validity in predicting job performance. The next section identifies the most successful ones.

STAFFING METHODS: WHICH ONES WORK BEST?

Schmidt and Hunter (1998) published an exhaustive meta-analysis (i.e., quantitative cumulation of research results) that summarized the results of thousands of empirical research studies in personnel selection over 85 years and millions of employees. Specifically, the meta-analysis summarized the track records of 19 different selection procedures for predicting job performance and training performance.

The criterion in question was overall job performance, typically measured by using supervisory ratings of job performance, although other measures, such as production and sales records, were also used. The same article also presented the validity of paired combinations of general mental ability (GMA) and the other 18 selection procedures. Expressed in terms of the average validity (correlation coefficient expressed on a scale from -1 to $+1$) for predicting overall job performance, the top five methods are as follows:

- Work sample tests (.54).
- GMA tests (.51).
- Structured employment interviews ($-.51$).
- Peer ratings (.49).
- Job knowledge tests (.48).

Although work sample tests yield the highest validity (.54), their primary application is with experienced employees (e.g., in making promotion decisions) rather than with inexperienced applicants. In combination, however, the top three pairs of predictors are a GMA test plus a work sample test (mean validity of .63), a GMA test plus an integrity test (mean validity of .65), and a GMA test plus a structured interview (mean validity of .63). An advantage of the latter two combinations is that they can be used both for entry-level selection and for the selection of experienced employees. The five poorest predictors are assigning points to training and experience (.11), years of education (.10), interests (.10), graphology (.02), and age ($-.01$).

The research evidence for the validity of GMA measures for predicting job performance is stronger than for any other method (Schmidt & Hunter, 1998). General mental ability (also known as *cognitive ability*) predicts job-related learning, the acquisition of job knowledge on the job (Schmidt & Hunter, 1992; Schmidt, Hunter, & Outerbridge, 1986), and performance in job training programs (Hunter & Hunter, 1984; Ree & Earles, 1992). However, this is not to imply that GMA is the only predictor worth considering.

Integrity tests are used in industry to hire employees with reduced probability of counterproductive job behaviors, such as drinking or drugs on the job, fighting on the job, stealing from the employer, sabotaging equipment, and other undesirable behaviors (Schmidt & Hunter, 1998). They do predict these behaviors, but they also predict evaluations of overall job performance (Ones, Viswesvaran, & Schmidt, 1993). Even though their validity is lower, integrity tests produce

a larger increment in validity (.14) and a larger percentage of increase in validity (and utility) than do work samples. This is because there is zero correlation between integrity tests and GMA (vs. .38 for work samples). In terms of basic personality traits, integrity tests have been found to measure mostly conscientiousness, but also some components of agreeableness and emotional stability (Ones, 1993). The overall conclusion from this research is that the methods firms use to hire and promote employees make an important, practical difference in terms of work performance and overall productivity

Thus far we have been speaking of job performance as if it was a unidimensional construct. This actually an oversimplification, as the next section demonstrates.

Performance: What Is It?

Performance is what an organization hires one to do, and to do well (Campbell, Gasser, & Oswald, 1996). Current theories of job performance suggest that the performance domain is multifaceted and is likely to include dimensions that are not highly or even positively correlated with each other (Borman & Motowidlo, 1993; Campbell, McCloy, Oppler, & Sager, 1993).

On the basis of a thorough review of the literature on job performance, Campbell et al. (1993) developed a comprehensive model that included eight basic components of job performance. Although many people erroneously use the term *performance* in the singular, and focus exclusively on job-specific task proficiency, Campbell et al. moved beyond that narrow view. They argued that components of performance in any job can be clustered into some subset of these eight general factors, which are as follows:

1. *Job-specific task proficiency:* the degree to which the individual can perform the core substantive or technical tasks that are central to his or her job.

2. *Non–job-specific task proficiency:* performance behaviors that are not specific to one's job (e.g., serving on committees or task forces).

3. *Written and oral communication task proficiency:* proficiency in writing or speaking, independent of the correctness of the subject matter.

4. *Demonstration of effort:* the degree to which individuals commit themselves to all job tasks, work at high levels of intensity, and keep working when it is cold, wet, or late.

5. *Maintenance of personal discipline:* the degree to which the individual avoids negative behaviors, such as alcohol

and substance abuse at work, law or rule infractions, and excessive absenteeism.

6. *Facilitation of peer and team performance:* the degree to which the individual supports his or her peers, helps them with job problems, and acts as a de facto trainer. It also encompasses how well an individual facilitates group functioning by being a good model, keeping the group goal-directed, and reinforcing participation by the other group members.

7. *Supervision and leadership:* all of the behaviors directed at influencing the performance of subordinates through face-to-face interpersonal interaction and influence—goal setting, teaching effective methods, modeling appropriate behaviors, and rewarding or punishing as appropriate. The distinction between this factor and facilitation of peer and team performance is a distinction between peer leadership and supervisory leadership.

8. *Management and administration:* the major elements in management that are distinct from supervision, such as articulating goals for the unit or enterprise, organizing people and resources to work on the goals, monitoring progress, helping to solve problems or overcome crises that stand in the way of goal accomplishment, controlling expenditures, and obtaining resources.

Campbell et al. (1993) emphasized that not all eight factors are present in every job, that the eight factors are not independent of one another, and that general cognitive ability may correlate to some extent with each one. However, noncognitive abilities might be more valid predictors of some of the factors. The point is simply that the term *performance* is a multifaceted construct that extends beyond factor 1—job-specific task proficiency. Different types of predictors, cognitive and noncognitive, are likely to differ in their ability to predict different aspects of performance. Different aspects of performance, in turn, are more important in some jobs than in others (e.g., mechanical performance vs. project management or retail sales).

If we consider the forces that are shaping the new world of work—speed of change; globalization; increasing cultural diversity of customers and employees; technology; mergers, acquisitions, and cross-border alliances; and greater need for self-reliance—a compelling case can be made for retaining workers. Having a diverse cadre of well-trained, committed employees is a competitive advantage. Why? Because it encourages employers to invest in training and development opportunities that address the very forces that are shaping the new world of work. In our next section, therefore, we will examine alternative strategies that firms are using to increase employee retention.

THE ART OF RETAINING TALENT

Employee Retention: Market-Based Strategies

We noted earlier that after employees are hired, the best that organizations can do is to create an environment that makes the best people want to stay. However, one set of retention strategies takes a contrarian view. Such strategies are market driven (Cappelli, 2000). They are based on a new reality: that the market, not an individual organization, ultimately will determine the movement of that organization's employees. According to this theory, managers can make organizations as pleasant and rewarding places to work in as possible, and they can fix problems that may push people to leave. What they cannot do, however, is to counter the pull of the market. They cannot shield their employees from attractive opportunities and aggressive recruiters. In the past, many organizations sought to keep employee turnover as low as possible. The new goal is to influence who leaves and when.

Thus, Prudential now enables its business-unit managers to develop highly targeted retention programs and to create cost-effective contingency plans for filling potential gaps in skills. It also provides the means to measure the impact of HR decisions, a capability that is crucial to managing people effectively in this rapidly shifting labor market. Prudential's "Building Management Capability" program integrates recruiting, retention, and training efforts to make an honest assessment of how long the company would like employees to stay on board.

Such an analysis inevitably reveals that different groups of employees warrant very different retention efforts. The firm wants to keep some employees, such as a top product designer or a front-line employee who is deeply respected by customers, indefinitely. It wishes to retain others, such as employees with specific skills that are currently in short supply, or members of a team who are installing a new information system, for shorter, well-defined periods. Finally, according to the market-driven approach, there will be some employees for whom investments in retention do not make sense—for example, those whose jobs require little training, or those whose skills are not in demand in the broader market (Cappelli, 2000).

Once an organization knows which employees it wishes to retain and for how long, it can use a number of mechanisms to encourage them to stay. The key is to resist the temptation to use the mechanisms across the board for all employees. Instead, it is important to tailor programs to retention requirements for various employees and to the level of demand for them in the marketplace. The next section describes some possible mechanisms for increasing employee retention.

Compensation

Some organizations offer pay packages weighted toward unvested stock options, signing bonuses paid in stages rather than in lump sums, or deferred signing bonuses. Burger King, for example, offers workers a signing bonus but withholds payment until they have been on the job 3 months. Three months may not seem like a long time, but in the fast-food business, where annual turnover averages 300%, it's an eternity. All such pay-based incentives use golden handcuffs, so to speak, to try to lock in valued employees. The problem with them is that they are easy for outsiders to match—via "golden hellos" (Cappelli, 2000).

Job Design

By thinking carefully about which tasks to include in which jobs, companies can exert considerable influence over retention rates. Thus, to improve its retention of drivers, United Parcel Service (UPS) redesigned its jobs. In the delivery business, drivers are particularly important because they know the idiosyncrasies of the routes and they have direct relationships with customers. When UPS studied the reasons its drivers left, it found that much of the turnover could be traced to the tedious and exhausting task of loading packages at the beginning of a run. It therefore unbundled the loading task from the drivers' job and assigned it to a new group of workers.

Of course, employee turnover in the new loading jobs is an eye-popping 400% per year, but that doesn't matter. With high hourly wages, low skill requirements, and minimal learning requirements, the loading jobs are fairly easy to fill. The lesson from this is that UPS did not attempt to decrease turnover. Rather, it targeted the specific skills it wanted to retain. For employees without those skills, it allowed the revolving door to spin freely (Cappelli, 2000).

Social Ties

Loyalty to companies may be disappearing, but loyalty to colleagues is not. Whether a company builds social ties through golf leagues, Friday-afternoon socials, or closely knit teams to carry out particular projects, the broad objective is to create a sense of community within a larger organization. Psychologists have long known that teams build commitment (Huszczo, 1996). Team members work hard because they do not want to let other team members down. The more accountable a team is for its performance, the greater the peer pressure on members to make sacrifices for the team. Team-based incentives, in particular, help create the sense that the

fate of the community relies on the performance of its members. This engenders greater worker commitment.

Job Customization

Consider this scenario: Key employees undertake a formal assessment of their work and nonwork goals, and how those goals might best be achieved in the context of the company's operations. The assessments form the basis for individual employment agreements, which might be created using cafeteria-style programs similar to those used in allocating employee benefits. Each employee is allocated a set amount of money to purchase options in such areas as career development and balancing work and personal life. The amount available to allocate would depend on the importance of the employee to the company. Does this sound far-fetched? Such individualized deals clearly raise concerns over the issue of fairness, they have implications for employee morale, and perhaps they raise legal concerns as well, but they are consistent with a market-based approach to employee retention (Cappelli, 2000).

Employee Retention: Supportive Organizational Practices

In contrast to the market-based strategies just described, some organizations have built organizational cultures, management practices, and HR strategies that encourage employees to stay. In the following sections we will consider six company examples of such strategies.

SAS Institute

SAS Institute, located in Cary, North Carolina, is the largest privately owned software company in the world. It also is an anachronism. Here's what *Fast Company* magazine had to say about the company: "In an era of relentless pressure, this place is an oasis of calm. In an age of frantic competition, this place is methodical and clearheaded. In a world of free agency, signing bonuses, and stock options, this is a place where loyalty matters more than money" (Fishman, 1999, p. 87).

In a world of outsourcing and contracting out, SAS Institute outsources and contracts out almost nothing. Day-care workers, on-site health professionals, food-service workers, and even most security guards are all SAS Institute employees. In an era of managed care, SAS offers a full indemnity health plan, with low deductibles. In almost every respect, SAS Institute seems like a throwback to an earlier era, to a time when there were long-term attachments between companies and their people, and large, progressive organizations offered generous, inclusive benefits in an effort to enhance the welfare of their workforces (O'Reilly & Pfeffer, 2000). The company employs about 5,400 people (about half of them work at company headquarters in Cary), but it operates on a worldwide basis. It has 40 sales offices in the United States, and 68 offices around the world. More than 80% of the *Fortune 500* companies use SAS software. SAS Institute spends 30% of its revenues on research and development of new products, about twice the average for the software industry. Annual revenues in 2001 were $113 billion (SAS Institute, 2002).

Here are just a few more of the company's practices. It offers a 35-hour work week, lots of coaching and internal training, open-job posting with almost all promotions from within the company, personal autonomy for workers, competitive pay, bonuses, and a company contribution of 15% of each employee's pay toward retirement. The company is characterized by an egalitarian approach to management, all people are treated with dignity and respect, and there is a strong belief in the power of intrinsic, internal motivation. In a nutshell, the company's philosophy is a simple one: Treat your people well and they will treat your customers well. Customers, in turn, will be good to the company (Goodnight, 2000).

In the more than 25 years since the company's founding, employee turnover has never exceeded 5% (Fishman, 1999). In addition to building and maintaining customer relationships, consider the economic benefits of such a low turnover rate (O'Reilly & Pfeffer, 2000). If the average turnover in the software industry is 20% (a conservative estimate) and SAS Institute's is 3%, the difference is 17%. Given the size of SAS's workforce (5,400 employees), this means that about 925 fewer people per year leave SAS than other companies in the industry. Using a conservative estimate of the average salary per employee of $60,000 per year, and 1.5 times salary as the fully loaded cost of turnover, SAS Institute is saving more than $100 million per year from its lower turnover. Those savings can then be reinvested in the company and in the employees who work for it. SAS Institute is listed among the top 10 places to work in America by *Fortune* and *Working Mother* magazines and, not surprisingly, it has about 200 applicants for each job opening (Goodnight, 2000). The company's business model, which is based on the assumption of long-term relationships with employees and customers, its generous benefits, and its supportive organizational culture all contribute to its amazing ability to attract and retain talent.

Here is a sampling of what four other leading companies are doing to create the kind of place that workers want to return to each and every day, along with a key lesson from each company's experience (Stein, 2000).

Capital One Financial

Lesson: *Pinpoint your competitive advantage as a business, then integrate it into your recruiting and retention strategy.* Capital One is a business based on numerical analysis. It issues credit cards to subprime borrowers with damaged credit histories. In the past three years its revenues are up 220%, and its profits are up 190%. It has grown from 5,900 to 15,000 employees, yet its annual turnover rate is less than 10%.

In 1998 the company administered 4–5 hours of cognitive and noncognitive tests (e.g., measures of values, temperament, personality) to each of its 1,600 employees, from call-center operators to senior executives. Through statistical analysis of the data it identified the most valid predictors of job performance, and today administers just two tests (one cognitive and one noncognitive) to applicants to get an accurate forecast of how they will perform on the jobs that they are applying for.

As a result of HR research, the company also found that candidates recruited through the company's internal referral program performed better and had longer tenure with the company. Today Capital One awards up to $2,500 to employees who refer successful applicants. Not surprisingly, present employees refer almost 45% of new hires.

Southwest Airlines

Lesson: *Get it right from the start. Invest in the hiring process, and hire very selectively.* This company uses a behavior-based, conversational style of interviewing designed to put people at ease by giving them a chance to talk about themselves in job-relevant situations. The questions—focusing on common sense, judgment, and decision-making skills—are designed to figure out how a candidate will fit into Southwest's famous, customer-focused culture. Where did the questions come from? The firm's HR director, whose official job title is "vice president of people," spent 10 years analyzing the behavior of Southwest's own employees. Last year, Southwest hired 5,000 new employees out of 160,000 applicants, of whom fully 70,000 were interviewed.

The time and money invested in the hiring process have resulted in a turnover rate of only 9.6% (6.0% for upper management), by far the lowest in the industry. It has also enabled Southwest to maintain a strong, unified culture in the face of enormous growth (more than 34,000 employees), and to groom management talent from within (Southwest Airlines,

2002). Fewer than five outsiders hold senior management positions, and many began their careers in entry-level jobs. President and chief operating officer Coleen Barrett, for example, started out in 1971 as former CEO Herb Kelleher's legal secretary.

Home Depot

Lesson: *Allow all employees, no matter how junior, to have decision-making authority. In a service industry, that provides an edge over competitors.* With 230,000 employees, Home Depot's culture is built from the inside out. More than 90% of non–entry-level jobs are filled internally, and only about 12 of the company's 400 department heads came from outside the company. The company calls its sales staff "associates." As company founders Bernie Marcus and Arthur Blank wrote in *Built to Last* (their history of the company), "'Associate' implies an equal as opposed to a wage slave. We value what the salesperson on the store floor says just as much—sometimes more—than what the district manager says. . . . The salesperson touches the customer more" (Collins & Porras, 1994, p. 218).

Home Depot's stock-purchase plan allows all employees to buy stock at any time for a 15% discount off the company's stock price, set once a year. The payoff: Home Depot's employee turnover is as much as 20% lower than the average in the retail industry.

Cisco Systems

Lesson: *Do everything you can, from day one, to make new employees feel welcome.* In this age of mergers and acquisitions, no one does a better job of integrating new businesses—and acclimatizing new employees—than Cisco. In 2000, for example, Cisco acquired more than 20 companies, and lost only 7% of its own nearly 31,000 employees. How does the company do it?

To begin, Cisco will not consider acquiring a company unless that company's culture, management practices, and pay systems are similar to its own. Then it focuses on making the first impression as positive as possible. When new employees arrive, they find the e-mail, telephone, and other systems they need already up and running. An orientation session teaches them how to navigate the company Web site, with its data on benefits and regulations; describes the elements of Cisco's culture; and suggests how to succeed within it. A transition team is assigned to each new acquisition to ensure that the honeymoon period is sweet. That means assigning a sponsor—who definitely does not act like a boss—to each new employee.

By the time CEO John Chambers delivers his regular quarterly chat, new hires feel like part of the Cisco family. Given that every employee gets stock options, a share price that rose 916% from 1997 through 1999 and is poised to rise again, probably smoothes any remaining rough edges.

RESPONSES OF FIRMS TO CHANGES IN WORK AND WORKERS

In today's world of fast-moving global markets and fierce competition, the windows of opportunity are often frustratingly brief. Three-C (command, control, compartmentalization) logic dominated industrial society's approach to organizational design throughout the nineteenth and twentieth centuries, but trends such as the following are accelerating the shift toward new forms of organization for the 21st (Colvin, 2000; Kiechel, 1993):

- Smaller companies that employ fewer people.
- The shift from vertically integrated hierarchies to networks of specialists.
- Technicians, ranging from computer-repair specialists to radiation therapists, replacing manufacturing operatives as the worker elite.
- Pay tied less to a person's position or tenure in an organization and more to the market value of his or her skills.
- A change in the paradigm of doing business from making a product to providing a service, often by part-time or temporary employees.
- Outsourcing of activities that are not core competencies of a firm (e.g., payroll).
- The redefinition of work itself: constant learning, more higher-order thinking, less nine-to-five mentality.

The fact is that these changes in work and workers are manifested in rethinking how we organize work and link people together and to organizations. This has led to a radical reconceptualization of twenty-first-century organizations.

THE TWENTY-FIRST-CENTURY ORGANIZATION

We begin this section by identifying key characteristics of the twenty-first-century organization, and show how they differ from previous versions. Then we will assess the fit of the new form with the types of changes in work and workers that we have discussed so far. Driven by new technologies, particularly the Internet, the organization is undergoing a radical transformation that is nothing less than a new Industrial Revolution (Byrne, 2000a; Colvin, 2000). This time around, the revolution is reaching every corner of the globe and, in the process, rewriting the rules laid down by Alfred P. Sloan, Jr. (the legendary chairman of General Motors), Henry Ford, and other Industrial-Age giants. The twenty-first-century organizations that emerge will, in many ways, be the polar opposite of the organizations that helped shape them.

Many factors are driving change, but none is more important than the rise of Internet technologies. Like the steam engine or the assembly line, the Internet has already become an advance with revolutionary consequences, most of which we have only begun to feel. The Internet gives everyone in the organization, from the lowliest clerk to the chairman of the board, the ability to access a mind-boggling array of information—instantaneously, from anywhere. Instead of seeping out over months or years, ideas can be zapped around the globe in the blink of an eye. That means that the twenty-first-century organization must adapt itself to management via the Web. It must be predicated on constant change, not stability; organized around networks, not rigid hierarchies; built on shifting partnerships and alliances, not self-sufficiency; and constructed on technological advantages, not bricks and mortar.

The organizational chart of the large-scale enterprise had long been defined as a pyramid of ever-shrinking layers leading to an omnipotent CEO at its apex. The twenty-first-century corporation, in contrast, is far more likely to look like a web: a flat, intricately woven form that links partners, employees, external contractors, suppliers, and customers in various collaborations. The players will grow more and more interdependent, and managing this intricate network will be as important as managing internal operations.

In contrast to factories of the past 100 years that produced cookie-cutter products, the company of the future will tailor its products to each individual by turning customers into partners and giving them the technology to design and demand exactly what they want. Mass customization will result in waves of individualized products and services, as well as huge savings for companies, which no longer will have to guess what and how much customers want.

Intellectual capital will be critical to business success. The advantage of bringing breakthrough products to market first will be shorter than ever because technology will let competitors match or exceed them almost instantly. To keep ahead of the steep new-product curve, it will be crucial for businesses to attract and retain the best thinkers. Companies will need to build a deep reservoir of talent—including both employees and free agents—to succeed in this new era. Attracting and retaining top talent, however, will require more than just huge paychecks. Organizations will need to create the kinds of cultures and reward systems that keep the best minds engaged. The old command-and-control hierarchies are fast crumbling in favor of organizations that empower vast numbers of people and reward the best of them as if they were owners of the enterprise.

It's Global

In the beginning, the *global company* was defined as one that simply sold its goods in overseas markets. Later, global companies assumed a manufacturing presence in numerous countries. The company of the future will call on talent and resources—especially intellectual capital—wherever they can be found around the globe, just as it will sell its goods and services around the globe. Indeed, the very notion of a headquarters country may no longer apply as companies migrate to places of greatest advantage. The new global corporation might be based in the United States but do its software programming in Sri Lanka, its engineering in Germany, and its manufacturing in China. Every outpost will be connected seamlessly by the Internet so that far-flung employees and freelancers can work together in real time.

It's About Speed

All this work will be done in an instant. "The Internet is a tool, and the biggest impact of that tool is speed," says Andrew S. Grove, chairman of Intel Corporation. That means the old, process-oriented company must revamp radically. With everything from product cycles to employee turnover on fast-forward, there is simply not enough time for deliberation or bureaucracy.

The twenty-first-century organization will not have one ideal form. Some will be completely virtual, wholly dependent on a network of suppliers, manufacturers, and distributors for their survival; others will be less so. Some of the most successful companies will be very small and very specialized. Others will be gargantuan in size, scope, and complexity. Table 16.1 presents a summary of these changes.

Many firms are experimenting with new forms of organization. Our next section examines three such new organizational forms.

New Forms of Organization

One example of a new organizational form that is evolving from these changes is the *virtual organization,* in which teams of specialists come together to work on a project—as in the movie industry—and disband when the project is finished (Cascio, 2002). Virtual organizations are already quite popular in consulting, in legal defense, and in sponsored research. They are multisite, multiorganizational, and dynamic (Snow,

TABLE 16.1 What a Difference a Century Can Make: Contrasting Views of the Corporation

Characteristic	20th Century	21st Century
Organization	The pyramid	The Web or network
Focus	Internal	External
Style	Structured	Flexible
Source of strength	Stability	Change
Structure	Self-sufficiency	Interdependencies
Resources	Atoms–physical assets	Bits-information
Operations	Vertical integration	Virtual integration
Products	Mass production	Mass customization
Reach	Domestic	Global
Financials	Quarterly	Real-time
Inventories	Months	Hours
Strategy	Top-down	Bottom-up
Leadership	Dogmatic	Inspirational
Workers	Employees	Employees + free agents
Job expectations	Security	Personal growth
Motivation	To compete	To build
Improvements	Incremental	Revolutionary
Quality	Affordable best	No compromise

Source: Reprinted from the August 28, 2000, issue of *Business Week* by special permission. Copyright © 2000 by The McGraw-Hill Companies, Inc.

Lipnack, & Stamps, 1999). At a macro level, a virtual organization consists of a grouping of units of different firms (e.g., other businesses, consultants, contractors) that have joined in an alliance to exploit complementary skills in pursuing common strategic objectives (Dess, Rasheed, McLaughlin, & Priem, 1995). The objectives often focus on a specific project, such as a defined objective in research and development, a multifaceted and complex consulting project, or a legal case involving multiple issues (Igbaria & Tan, 1998).

In the entertainment industry, virtual organizations are common. For example, in making a movie, the producer, the director, the film editors, the workers who construct and deconstruct movie sets, the special-effects specialists, the actors, the actresses, and scores of people who provide indirect services collaborate to make the movie. All of these individuals, independent contractors, companies, and consultants (some of whom have overlapping memberships) work intensely on a temporary basis to complete a specific project. When the project is over—poof!—they split up again to pursue their own interests and peddle their talents elsewhere. That is the essence of a virtual organization. It is a temporary collaboration. In fact, one observer has referred to this phenomenon as an "organizational tent," as opposed to a conventional organization, referred to as an "organizational palace" (Hedberg, 2000).

More common in the information age, however, is the virtual workplace in which employees operate remotely from each other and from managers (Cascio, 2000a). They work anytime, anywhere—in real space or in cyberspace. The widespread availability of e-mail, teleconferencing, faxes, and intranets

(within-company information networks) facilitates such arrangements. Compelling business reasons, such as reduced real estate expenses, increased productivity, higher profits, improved customer service, access to global markets, and environmental benefits, drive their implementation. Jobs in sales, marketing, project engineering, and consulting seem to be best suited for virtual workplaces because individuals in these jobs already work with their clients by phone, or at the clients' premises. Such jobs are service and knowledge oriented, are dynamic, and evolve according to customer requirements.

A third example of a new organizational form is the *modular corporation*. The basic idea is to focus on a few core competencies—those a company does best, such as designing and marketing computers or copiers—and to outsource everything else to a network of suppliers (Spee, 1995; Tully, 1993). If design and marketing are core competencies, then manufacturing or service units are modular components. They can be added or taken away with the flexibility of switching parts in a child's Lego set. Does the modular corporation work? As an example, consider Dell Computer.

Dell Computer: The Modular Corporation in Action

Dell prospers by remaining perfectly clear about what it is and what it does. "We are a really superb product integrator. We're a tremendously good sales-and-logistics company. We're not the developer of innovative technology" (Topfer, 2000, p. 100). CEO Michael Dell believes his company can grow at a rapid rate by focusing on its core business. Grow it has, from $3.4 billion in sales in fiscal 1995 to $25.3 billion in 2000 (McWilliams, 2000).

Dell sells IBM-compatible personal computers (PCs) in competition with Compaq, Apple, and IBM. While others rely primarily on computer stores or dealers, however, Dell sells directly to consumers, who read about the products on the company's Web page, in newspaper ads, or in catalogues. Buyers either order online or call a toll-free number and place their orders with a staff of well-trained salespeople.

Dell doesn't build countless identical computers, flood them out to retailers, and hope you like what you see. Instead, it waits until it has your custom order (and your money), then orders components from suppliers and assembles the parts. At its OptiPlex factory in Austin, Texas, 84% of orders are built, customized, and shipped within 8 hours. Some components, like the monitor or speakers, may be sent directly from the supplier to your home (never passing through Dell) and arrive on your doorstep at the same time as everything else (O'Reilly, 2000). In 1999, for example, Dell custom-assembled more than 25,000 different computer configurations for buyers ("At Ford," 2000). By eliminating intermediaries—and the retailer's typical 13% markup—Dell can charge lower prices than its rivals.

Modular companies are flourishing in two industries that sell trendy products in a fast-changing marketplace: apparel (Nike and Reebok are modular pioneers) and electronics. Such companies work best when they accomplish two objectives: (a) collaborating smoothly with suppliers and (b) choosing the right specialty. Companies need to find loyal, reliable vendors they can trust with trade secrets, and they need the vision to identify what customers will want, not just what the company is technically good at. For example, Dell deals with hundreds of suppliers, but about 90% of its parts and components come from the same two dozen companies. It works closely with them to make sure the parts are designed for snap-in assembly and for just-in-time delivery (O'Reilly, 2000).

CONCLUSIONS

Implications for Organizations

If people are so critical to business success in the twenty-first-century organization, what will it take to attract and retain the best? According to John T. Chambers, CEO of Cisco Systems:

> The reason people stay at a company is that it's a great place to work. It's like playing on a great sports team. Really good players want to be around other really good players. Secondly, people like to work for good leadership. So creating a culture of leaders that people like is key. And the third is, are you working for a higher purpose than an IPO or a paycheck? Our higher purpose is to change the way the world works, lives, and plays. (as cited in Byrne, 2000b, p. 212)

The forces that are shaping today's world of work will not go away. To capitalize on them, organizations must be prepared to embrace the many dimensions of diversity and to make staffing and promotion decisions that use valid predictors to identify the best talent for the work to be done. Speed of change will make the adoption of new technology, and perhaps rapid restructuring, essential so as not to miss out on fast-breaking opportunities. To accomplish all of that successfully will require particular emphasis on the delivery of training and development when and where it is needed. Since teamwork and cross-functional collaboration will become more important in agile organizations, reward and incentive systems will need to be aligned closely with that focus. Rather than individual rewards, team-based or organization-wide rewards such as profit sharing or gain sharing will probably be more suitable in linking work design, organizational objectives, and rewards tightly together for effective performance. Finally, consider some implications of the new pattern of loyalty to vision, mission, supervisors, or teams. It is true that organizations are finding today's employees more difficult to manage—but they are also finding them to be highly motivated and committed to tasks they value (Rousseau & Wade-Benzoni, 1995). The most effective leaders will be those who inspire people to excel and to commit to the vision or mission that they articulate, and who create work environments in which creativity and innovation can thrive at all levels.

Implications for People

Recognize that employment relationships tend to be relatively brief. If the average tenure of 25- to 34-year-olds is 2.7 years (less so for those who work in information technology), always emphasize employment security for yourself. This will require a personal commitment to lifelong learning, coupled with a willingness to reinvent yourself as often as is necessary, in order to keep up with evolving changes in the world of work. Manage your own knowledge rather than waiting to see what your company will do to train and retrain you.

A second implication is that diversity in many dimensions (race, ethnicity, gender, age, religion, cultural identity) is a fact of modern organizational life. Rather than viewing diversity as a problem, look at it as an opportunity to learn from others and to capitalize on new markets and new customers. After all, as the saying goes, "When you look for the good in others, you discover the best in yourself."

A third implication is that downsizing, restructuring, and organizational mobility will be with us for the foreseeable future. Prepare yourself mentally and in terms of marketable skills and knowledge for this possibility. Take advantage of self-assessment opportunities to learn about your strengths and areas for development. Maintain a network of contacts that you can tap for possible job leads as the need arises.

In some ways, the changes that we have been describing, along with their implications for organizations and for people, represent a sort of brave new world. On the other hand, every career is a journey, and even the longest journey begins with the first step. Don't be afraid to take steps now to prepare yourself and your organization for the challenging journey ahead.

REFERENCES

Aannestad, B., & Hooper, J. (1997, November). The future of groupware in the interactive workplace. *HRMagazine*, 37–42.

Adler, N. J., Doktor, R., & Redding, S. G. (1986). From the Atlantic to the Pacific century: Cross-cultural management reviewed. *Journal of Management, 12*, 295–318.

America's changing complexion. (2000, August 28). *Business Week,* 79.

Armas, G. (2000, December 18). Some states scrambling to plug worker "brain drain." *The Denver Post,* pp. 2A, 16A.

Backlash: Behind the anxiety over globalization. (2000, April 24). *Business Week,* 38–43, 202.

Bernstein, A. (2002, May 20). Too many workers? Not for long. *Business Week,* 126–130.

Blackmon, D. A. (2000, July 17). Price buster: E-commerce hasn't had an impact on the economy's overall price structure. Yet. *The Wall Street Journal,* pp. R12, R26.

Borman, W. C., & Motowidlo, S. J. (1993). Expanding the criterion domain to include elements of contextual performance. In N. Schmitt & W. Borman (Eds.), *Personnel selection in organizations* (pp. 71–98). San Francisco: Jossey-Bass.

Byrne, J. A. (2000a, August 28). Management by web. *Business Week,* 84–96.

Byrne, J. A. (2000b, August 28). Visionary vs. visionary. *Business Week,* 210–214.

Campbell, J. P., Gasser, M. B., & Oswald, F. L. (1996). The substantive nature of job performance variability. In K. R. Murphy (Ed.), *Individual differences and behavior in organizations* (pp. 258–299). San Francisco: Jossey-Bass.

Campbell, J. P., McCloy, R. A., Oppler, S. H., & Sager, C. E. (1993). A theory of performance. In N. Schmitt & W. Borman (Eds.), *Personnel selection in organizations* (pp. 35–70). San Francisco: Jossey-Bass.

Cappelli, P. (2000, January/February). A market-driven approach to retaining talent. *Harvard Business Review,* 103–111.

Cascio, W. F. (1998). The theory of vertical and horizontal individualism and collectivism: Implications for international human resource management. In J. L. Cheng & R. B. Peterson (Eds.), *Advances in international and comparative management* (pp. 87–103). Greenwich, CT: JAI Press.

Cascio, W. F. (2000a). Managing a virtual workplace. *Academy of Management Executive, 13*(3), 81–90.

Cascio, W. F. (2000b, September). *Recruiting and retaining top talent in a tight labor market.* Paper presented at the Frankfurter Allgemaine Zeitung Conference on Employment, Kronberg, Germany.

Cascio, W. F. (2002). The virtual organization. In C. L. Cooper & W. W. Burke (Eds.), *The new world of work* (pp. 203–221). Oxford, UK: Blackwell.

Cascio, W. F. (2003). *Managing human resources: Productivity, quality of work life, profits* (6th ed.). Burr Ridge, IL: McGraw-Hill/Irwin.

Cascio, W. F., Morris, J. R., & Young, C. E. (1997). Financial consequences of employment-change decisions in major U.S. corporations. *Academy of Management Journal, 40*(5), 1175–1189.

Cascio, W. F., & Young, C. E. (in press). Financial consequences of employment-change decisions in major U.S. corporations: 1982–2000. In K. P. DeMeuse & M. L. Marks (Eds.), *Resizing the organization.* San Francisco: Jossey-Bass.

Collins, J. C., & Porras, J. (1994). *Built to last: Successful habits of visionary companies.* New York: Harper Business.

Colvin, G. (2000, March 6). Managing in the info era. *Fortune,* F6–F9.

Conlin, M. (2000, September 20). Nine to 5 isn't working anymore. *Business Week,* 94–98.

Covenant Investment Management. (2000). Retrieved September 21, 2001, from www.villagelife.org

Coy, P. (2000, August 28). The creative economy. *Business Week,* 76–82.

Daniels, C. (2000, April 3). To hire a lumber expert, click here. *Fortune,* 267–270.

Day, J. (1996). *Population projections of the United States by age, sex, race, and Hispanic origin: 1995 to 2050.* Washington, DC: U.S. Bureau of the Census.

Dess, G. G., Rasheed, A. M. A., McLaughlin, K. J., & Priem, R. L. (1995). The new corporate architecture. *Academy of Management Executive, 9*(3), 7–18.

Erez, M. (1997). A culture-based model of work motivation. In P. C. Earley & M. Erez (Eds.), *New perspectives on international industrial and organizational psychology* (pp. 193–242). San Francisco: New Lexington Press.

Fisher, A. (1996, September 30). Wanted: Aging baby-boomers. *Fortune,* 204.

Fishman, C. (1999, January). Sanity, Inc. *Fast Company,* 87–95.

Flexibility: The answer to burnout. (2000, September 20). *Business Week,* 162.

At Ford, e-commerce is job 1. (2000, February 28). *Business Week,* 74–78.

Fulmer, W. E. (1999). *Buckman laboratories (A)* [Case No. N9-899-175]. Boston: Harvard Business School.

Geutal, H. G. (2001, August). *HR and the Internet age: The brave new world of eHR.* Paper presented at the Society for Human Resource Management Thought Leaders conference, Washington, DC.

Gutknecht, J. E., & Keys, J. B. (1993). Mergers, acquisitions, and takeovers: Maintaining morale of survivors and protecting employees. *Academy of Management Executive, 7*(3), 26–36.

Hamel, G., & Sampler, J. (1998, December 7). The E-Corporation. *Fortune,* 80–92.

Hedberg, B. (2000, September). *Organizing in the new economy, between inside and outside.* Proceedings of the 5th annual telework workshop, Stockholm, Sweden.

Henkoff, R. (1996, January 15). So you want to change your job. *Fortune,* 52–56.

Hof, R. D., & Hamm, S. (2002, May 13). How e-biz rose, fell, and will rise anew. *Business Week,* 64–72.

House, R. J., Wright, N. S., & Aditya, R. N. (1997). Cross-cultural research on organizational leadership: A critical analysis and a proposed theory. In P. C. Earley & M. Erez (Eds.), *New perspectives on international industrial and organizational psychology* (pp. 535–625). San Francisco: New Lexington Press.

HRIS Buying Guide. (2000, April). *HR Magazine,* 181–200.

Hunter, J. E., & Hunter, R. F. (1984). Validity and utility of alternative predictors of job performance. *Psychological Bulletin, 96,* 72–98.

Huszczo, G. E. (1996). *Tools for team excellence.* Palo Alto, CA: Davies-Black.

Igbaria, M., & Tan, M. (Eds.). (1998). *The virtual workplace.* Hershey, PA: Idea Group.

Ilgen, D. R., LePine, J. A., & Hollenbeck, J. R. (1997). Effective decision making in multinational teams. In P. C. Earley & M. Erez (Eds.), *New perspectives on international industrial and organizational psychology* (pp. 377–409). San Francisco: New Lexington Press.

Ishii, H., Kobayashi, M., & Arita, K. (1994). Interactive design of seamless collaboration media. *Communications of the ACM, 37*(8), 83–97.

Johnson, A. A. (1999, February). *Strategic meal planning: Work-life initiatives for building strong organizations.* Paper presented at the conference on Integrated Health, Disability, and Work/Life Initiatives, New York.

Johnson, R. (2000, September 19). Employers now vie to hire moms with young children. *The Wall Street Journal,* p. B2.

Kiechel, W., III. (1993, May 17). How we will work in the year 2000. *Fortune,* 38–52.

Kleinfeld, N. R. (1996, March 4). The company as family no more. *The New York Times,* pp. A1, A8–A11.

Kraar, L. (1997, May 26). The real threat to China's Hong Kong. *Fortune,* 85–94.

Leonard, B. (1999, August). Employee referrals should be cornerstone of staffing efforts. *HR News,* 54.

Lewis, G. (1993, April 17). *Working scared* [Television broadcast]. New York: National Broadcasting Company.

McWilliams, G. (2000, August 31). System upgrade. *The Wall Street Journal,* pp. A1, A8.

Morris, J. R., Cascio, W. F., & Young, C. E. (1999, Winter). Downsizing after all these years: Questions and answers about who did it, how many did it, and who benefited from it. *Organizational Dynamics,* 78–87.

Morse, D. (2000, August 22). Labor shortage has franchisees hustling for workers. *The Wall Street Journal,* p. B2.

Most in survey want to keep working after retiring. (2000, September 29). *The Denver Post,* p. 8A.

Nakache, P. (1997, September 29). Cisco's recruiting edge. *Fortune,* 275, 276.

National Research Council. (1999). *The changing nature of work: Implications for occupational analysis.* Washington, DC: National Academy Press.

Ones, D. S. (1993). *The construct validity of integrity tests.* Unpublished doctoral dissertation, University of Iowa, Iowa City.

Ones, D. S., Viswesvaran, C., & Schmidt, F. L. (1993). Comprehensive meta-analysis of integrity test validities: Findings and implications for personnel selection and theories of job performance. *Journal of Applied Psychology Monograph, 78,* 679–703.

O'Reilly, B. (2000, February 7). They've got mail! *Fortune,* 101–112.

O'Reilly, C. A., III., & Pfeffer, J. (2000). *Hidden value: How great companies achieve extraordinary results with ordinary people.* Boston: Harvard Business School Press.

Pascual, N. (2001, November 26). Tidying up at Home Depot. *Business Week,* 102–104.

Power gizmos to power business. (1997, November 24). *Business Week,* 190.

Ree, M. J., & Earles, J. A. (1992). Intelligence is the best predictor of job performance. *Current Directions in Psychological Science, 1,* 86–89.

Reich, R. B. (1990, January/February). Who is us? *Harvard Business Review,* 53–64.

Revzin, P., Waldman, P., & Gumbel, P. (1990, February 1). World view: Ted Turner's CNN gains global influence and a "diplomatic" role. *The Wall Street Journal,* pp. A1, A10.

Rousseau, D. M. (1995). *Psychological contracts in organizations: Written and unwritten agreements.* Newbury Park, CA: Sage.

Rousseau, D. M. (1996). Changing the deal while keeping the people. *Academy of Management Executive, 10*(1), 50–59.

Rousseau, D. M., & Wade-Benzoni, K. A. (1995). Changing individual-organizational attachments. In A. Howard (Ed.), *The changing nature of work* (pp. 290–322). San Francisco: Jossey-Bass.

SAS Institute. (2002). Retrieved June 18, 2002, from www.SAS.com

Schmidt, F. L., & Hunter, J. E. (1992). Development of causal models of processes determining job performance. *Current Directions in Psychological Science, 1,* 89–92.

Schmidt, F. L., & Hunter, J. E. (1998). The validity and utility of selection methods in personnel psychology: Practical and theoretical implications of 85 years of research findings. *Psychological Bulletin, 124,* 262–274.

Schmidt, F. L., Hunter, J. E., & Outerbridge, A. M. (1986). The impact of job experience and ability on job knowledge, work sample performance, and supervisory ratings of job performance. *Journal of Applied Psychology, 71,* 432–439.

Schweiger, D. M., & DeNisi, A. S. (1991). Communication with employees following a merger: A longitudinal field experiment. *Academy of Management Journal, 34,* 110–135.

Sellers, P. (2001, March 19). Exit the builder, enter the repairman. *Fortune,* 86–88.

Shadow of recession. (2002, February 9). Retrieved February 9, 2002, from www.CBSmarketwatch.com

The shrinking workforce. (2000, January 10). *Business Week,* 8.

Snow, C. C., Lipnack, J., & Stamps, J. (1999). The virtual organization: Promises and payoffs, large and small. In C. L. Cooper & D. M. Rousseau (Eds.), *The virtual organization* (pp. 15–30). New York: Wiley.

Sommer, R. (2000). *Retaining intellectual capital in the 21st century.* Alexandria, VA: Society for Human Resource Management.

Southwest Airlines. (2002). Retrieved June 18, 2002, from www.southwest.com

Spee, J. C. (1995, March). Addition by subtraction: Outsourcing strengthens business focus. *HRMagazine,* 38–43.

Stein, N. (2000, May 29). Winning the war to keep talent. *Fortune,* 132–138.

Stewart, T. (1998, February 16). In search of elusive tech workers. *Fortune,* 171–172.

The tech slump. (2000, December 18). *Business Week,* 54–58.

Topfer, M. (2000, October 16). Former vice-chairman of Dell, as quoted in Morris, B. Can Michael Dell escape the box? *Fortune,* 92–110.

Triandis, H. C. (1998). Vertical and horizontal individualism and collectivism: Theory and research implications for international comparative management. In J. L. Cheng & R.B. Peterson (Eds.), *Advances in international and comparative management* (pp. 7–35). Greenwich, CT: JAI Press.

Tsacounis, S. (2002, April 11). *Staffing in a changing workforce environment: The nature of today's workforce.* Workshop presented at the Annual Conference of the Society for Industrial and Organizational Psychology, Toronto.

Tully, S. (1993, February 8). The modular corporation. *Fortune,* 106–108, 112–114.

Uchitelle, L., & Kleinfeld, N. R. (1996, March 3). On the battlefield of business, millions of casualties. *The New York Times,* 1, 14–16.

Update. (1999, June 21). *Broadcasting and Cable Magazine,* 40.

U.S. Bureau of Labor Statistics. (2002). Retrieved June 17, 2002, from www.stats.bls.gov

Useem, J. (1999, May 24). Read this before you put a resume online. *Fortune,* 290, 292.

We want you to stay. Really. (1998, June 22). *Business Week,* 67–72.

What employers are offering their employees. (2000). *Workplace Visions, 4,* 3.

Work Week. (2000, August 22). *The Wall Street Journal,* p. A1.

The world's largest corporations: The global 500 by the numbers. (2001, July 23). *Fortune,* 232–234, F1–F24.

Wysocki, B., Jr. (2000, March 30). Yet another hazard of the new economy: The Pied Piper effect. *The Wall Street Journal,* pp. A1, A16.

CHAPTER 17

Work Design

FREDERICK P. MORGESON AND MICHAEL A. CAMPION

Although the design of work has an enormous impact on organizational success and individual well-being, interest in the topic appears to be waning in industrial and organizational (I/O) psychology circles (Campion, 1996). The apparent decline of interest in work design research is troubling for a number of reasons. First, work design resides at the intersection of industrial and organizational psychology, and thus represents an important synthesis between these two domains. Not only does work design theory draw heavily from motivational theories in organizational psychology, it also incorporates such central industrial psychology topics as the analysis of jobs and their requirements, as well as the linkage between jobs and human resource systems.

Second, work design has great practical significance to organizations as they try to attain such diverse outcomes as efficiency and satisfaction. Third, a major part of every manager's job involves the design of a subordinate's work. Finally, the nature of work has a profound influence on those performing it, and attention to the design aspects of work can yield insight into individual outcomes. The reduced research interest in recent times is all the more surprising given the resurgent interest in work design in organizations. Although

assuming a variety of different names (e.g., just-in-time manufacturing, lean manufacturing, six-sigma, reengineering, total quality management), they all involve aspects of work design.

The purpose of this chapter is to review the research literature on work design. Our focus is primarily on the content and structure of jobs individuals perform (Oldham, 1996), but, where appropriate, extends to the design of work around teams. A broadened focus on work design enables us not only to capture the range of research conducted under the auspices of job design, but also to consider the natural evolution from jobs to teams as important work design elements. We will concentrate primarily on research that has appeared in the I/O literature (because of space constraints), but readers should recognize that a number of different disciplines have also investigated work design issues (e.g., industrial engineering, operations management, ergonomics).

This chapter is organized around an integrated work design framework (Figure 17.1) and is divided into seven primary sections. First, we review the major work design perspectives that have been investigated in the I/O psychology literature. This provides needed background on the history and theoretical

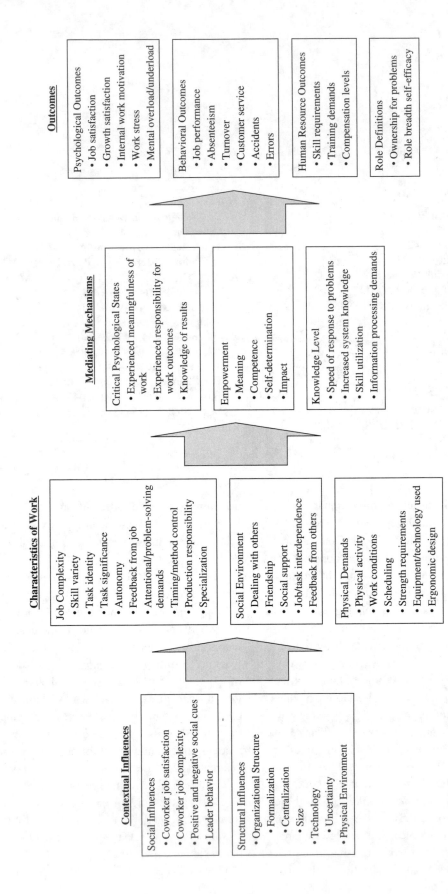

Figure 17.1 An integrated work design framework.

underpinnings of work design research. Second, we examine the variety of contextual influences on work, which includes social and structural factors. Third, we examine characteristics of work that have been identified in the literature. This includes questions about the structure of work, whether incumbent self-reports of work characteristics reflect objective properties of the job or subjective perceptions, and potential measurement concerns.

Fourth, we identify the range of mediating mechanisms assumed to underlie work design effects. This helps explain how work design influences outcomes. Fifth, we examine the empirical relationships between work design features and affective, behavioral, human resource, and role-definition outcomes. We then discuss how work redesign impacts outcomes and consider the evidence for individual differences in work design. Sixth, using the previous review of the literature, we discuss the work design framework highlighted in Figure 17.1. Seventh, we discuss several trends that are likely to influence work design in the future.

MAJOR WORK DESIGN PERSPECTIVES

This section will serve to introduce the major perspectives on work design. Critical evaluation of these approaches will be presented in subsequent sections where the major issues in work design research are reviewed.

Scientific Management

The works of Smith (1776) and Babbage (1835) serve as the foundation for contemporary work design theory. These theorists discussed how the division of labor could increase worker efficiency and productivity. They noted that breaking work into discrete jobs enables specialization and simplification, allowing workers to become highly skilled and efficient at performing particular tasks. Additional efficiency gains occur because (a) workers do not switch between tasks as much; (b) distractions are reduced due to the presence of fewer work elements; and (c) workers recognize a variety of small ways to continue to increase efficiency.

The first systematic attempt documented in the literature to design jobs utilizing these principles occurred in the early part of the twentieth century through the efforts of Taylor (1911) and Gilbreth (1911). Dubbed *scientific management* by Taylor, these efficiency-oriented approaches focused on principles such as specialization and simplification as means of easing staffing difficulties and lowering training requirements. Critical to these approaches is the notion that management should decide how to divide and design work, and then

institute control mechanisms (e.g., training, incentive systems, supervision) to ensure work is completed in accordance with management's wishes. Although the problems associated with scientific management have been well documented, many of its principles still underlie modern work design (Cherns, 1978; Wall & Martin, 1987).

Job Enrichment Approaches

One of the problems with designing work to maximize efficiency is that it commonly ends up being repetitive, tedious, and boring. Partly as a reaction to the reductionistic nature of efficiency-oriented work design, and partly as an acknowledgment of human potential and higher order needs, organizational theorists began to focus on the characteristics that could enhance worker satisfaction and provide for intrinsic needs (e.g., Herzberg, Mausner, & Snyderman, 1959; Likert, 1961; McGregor, 1960). Two primary theoretical models have been developed under the auspices of job enrichment: Herzberg's *motivator-hygiene theory* and Hackman and Oldham's *job characteristics theory.*

Motivator-Hygiene Theory

Motivator-hygiene theory (Herzberg et al., 1959) codified how work could serve to motivate employee behavior. In brief, this theory distinguished between aspects of work that are satisfying and motivating (*motivators*) and those that are dissatisfying (*hygiene factors*). Such things as recognition, achievement, and advancement are intrinsic to the work and were termed motivators. Such things as salary, company policies, and working conditions are external to the work itself and were considered to be hygiene factors. According to motivator-hygiene theory, only job changes that impacted motivators would improve satisfaction and motivation. Changes aimed at hygiene factors would reduce dissatisfaction, but would not effect satisfaction or motivation. Although research generally failed to confirm this and other key aspects of this theory (Locke & Henne, 1986), it remains important because it represents an early attempt to understand how the content of work can impact worker motivation and marks the beginning of interest in job enrichment.

Job Characteristics Theory

Although motivator-hygiene theory stimulated research and served as the foundation for a number of work redesign efforts (Herzberg, 1976), it was beset by a number of significant weaknesses (Oldham, 1996). Research by Turner and Lawrence (1965) and Hackman and Lawler (1971) sought to address these weaknesses and understand how job characteristics are related to individual reactions to work. This research directly led to the job characteristics theory, most fully articulated by Hackman and Oldham (1975, 1976, 1980).

The job characteristics approach suggested that five job characteristics produce critical psychological states in the job holder, and ultimately result in a set of positive work outcomes. First, *skill variety* involves the use of a wide variety of the worker's skills and abilities. Second, *task identity* involves the extent to which the worker feels he or she is responsible for a meaningful and whole part of the work. Third, *task significance* involves the impact the job has on the lives of others. Together, these three job characteristics are presumed to increase the meaningfulness of work.

Fourth, *autonomy* involves the amount of freedom and independence an individual has in terms of carrying out his or her work assignment. This was expected to increase experienced responsibility for work outcomes. Fifth, *feedback* concerns the extent to which the job duties provide knowledge of the results of the job incumbent's actions. This was expected to provide knowledge concerning the results of work activities. It is important to note that this feedback explicitly refers to feedback obtained directly from the job itself. This differs, however, from the manner in which Hackman and Lawler (1971) conceptualized feedback. They posit that feedback can come from the task itself, or it may come from supervisors or coworkers. This difference becomes important later when we discuss the social environment of work.

These five job characteristics are presumed to influence the psychological states. The psychological states are posited to directly influence four outcomes: (a) internal work motivation, (b) growth satisfaction, (c) general satisfaction, and (d) work effectiveness. It was hypothesized that there are three moderators of the job characteristics–critical psychological states relationship and the critical psychological states–outcomes relationship. The most commonly examined moderator has been *growth need strength (GNS)*. It was suggested that individuals high in GNS (e.g., the need for personal accomplishment) would react more favorably to enriched work. The two other moderators (individual knowledge and skill and context satisfaction) have been much less frequently studied.

Job characteristics theory and the motivational approach it represents rose to become the dominant approach for research on job attitudes (Staw, 1984). Although some aspects of the model have failed to accumulate research support and there have been a number of criticisms (Roberts & Glick, 1981), these job characteristics have generally been found to have positive relationships with a variety of affective outcomes, and smaller relationships to behavioral outcomes

(Fried & Ferris, 1987; Loher, Noe, Moeller, & Fitzgerald, 1985).

Sociotechnical Systems Theory

The sociotechnical systems approach arose from work conducted at the Tavistock Institute in Great Britain that focused on the use of autonomous groups to accomplish work (Trist & Bamforth, 1951). This perspective suggested that organizations are composed of people interacting with each other and a technical system to produce products or services. This interaction had a reciprocal and dynamic influence on the operation and appropriateness of the technology as well as on the behavior of the people that operate it (Pasmore, Francis, Haldeman, & Shani, 1982). Given the interdependence between human and technical systems, sociotechnical systems theory suggested that productivity and satisfaction could be maximized via joint optimization. In other words, optimal organizational functioning would occur only if the social and technical systems were designed to fit each other (Trist, 1981).

For sociotechnical design to be appropriate, however, Cummings (1978) suggested that three conditions must be satisfied. First, there must be adequate task differentiation such that the tasks performed are autonomous and form a self-completing whole. This suggests a certain minimum of interdependence within the tasks themselves. Second, employees must have adequate boundary control, so they can influence and control transactions within the task environment. Finally, employees must be able to control the immediate task environment so they can regulate their behavior and convert raw materials into finished product.

If these conditions for self-regulation are satisfied, Cherns (1978) discussed how to design work according to sociotechnical principles. First, the design process must be congruent with the design outcomes. For example, if increased participation and empowerment is one of the hoped-for outcomes of the work design, the process by which the work is designed should be participative and involve key stakeholders. Second, it is important to identify which tasks and objectives are essential, and that no more than is absolutely necessary be specified. Such minimal critical specification enables flexibility and the ability to respond to unanticipated circumstances. Third, the possibility of unexpected events suggests that if variance cannot be eliminated, it should be controlled as close as possible to its origin, suggesting that work be designed with sufficient autonomy or control. Fourth, in order to control variance at its source, workers must be multifunctional, have some level of control over boundary tasks, and have access to enough information to make decisions. Finally, from an organizational perspective, sociotechnical systems theory suggests that organizational systems should be congruent with the work design chosen. For example, if teams are employed, it might be important to have a compensation system that is based, in part, on team performance.

As these design principles suggest, the sociotechnical approach has a great deal in common with the job enlargement approach (Rousseau, 1977). It focuses on such things as autonomy, task feedback, and completing a whole piece of work. It differs largely by focusing on the team level of analysis. In addition, although sociotechnical systems theory has a relatively long history, its key principles have not been completely tested and validated (e.g., such as joint optimization and controlling variance at its source). In fact, some have suggested that "it remains exceedingly difficult to specify propositions of the theory that are empirically disconfirmable" (Hackman, 1981, p. 80). Notwithstanding the foregoing, the sociotechnical approach is important because it formalized a focus on the group level of analysis and still exerts a strong influence on contemporary work design research and theory.

Social Information Processing Perspective

The social information processing approach of Salancik and Pfeffer (1978) arose from dissatisfaction with the need-satisfaction and expectancy models of motivation and job attitudes. Its importance for work design comes from the fact that it called attention to the effects of context and the consequences of past choices as opposed to individual predispositions and rational decision-making processes.

The theoretical model was developed by Salancik and Pfeffer (1978) and subsequently examined in a number of studies in the 1970s and 1980s. The fundamental premise of the social information processing perspective is that individuals adapt their attitudes, behavior, and beliefs to their social context as well as their past and present behavior and situation. This implies that the characteristics of work are not given but are constructed from social information. It also suggests the perception of job characteristics and reaction to work redesign may be influenced by factors outside the objective features of work.

As summarized by Pfeffer (1981), the social information processing approach has four basic premises:

> First, the individual's social environment may provide cues as to which dimensions might be used to characterize the work environment. . . . Second, the social environment may provide information concerning how the individual should weight the various dimensions—whether autonomy is more or less important than variety of skill, whether pay is more or less important than social

usefulness or worth. Third, the social context provides cues concerning how others have come to evaluate the work environment on each of the selected dimensions. . . . And fourth, it is possible that the social context provides direct evaluation of the work setting along positive or negative dimensions, leaving it to the individual to construct a rationale to make sense of the generally shared affective reaction. (Pfeffer, 1981, p. 10)

Thus, the social environment impacts individuals in two ways. First, it helps individuals construct meaning about uncertain organizational features and events. It emphasizes what the socially acceptable beliefs and norms are, as well as the permissible forms of action given the organization's broader context. Second, the social environment directs attention by making certain information more salient. This provides information about expectations for individual behavior as well as the likely consequences of behavior. Generally speaking, research has found that social cues influence perceptions of and reactions to work, although there has been some debate about the magnitude of those effects (Kilduff & Regan, 1988).

Interdisciplinary Model of Job Design

Recognizing that work design research in I/O psychology was focused almost exclusively on motivationally oriented approaches, Campion (1988, 1989; Campion & Thayer, 1985) outlined an interdisciplinary model of job design. This perspective suggested that different scientific disciplines have produced several distinct approaches to job design and that research in each approach has been conducted relatively independently of other approaches. The interdisciplinary job design perspective highlights this fact and suggests that there are at least four basic approaches, each focusing on a distinct set of outcomes.

Grounded in classical industrial engineering research, the *mechanistic model* evolved largely to deal with the pressures for efficiency that arose during the Industrial Revolution. This approach recommended increased simplification, specialization, and repetition of work. These changes were intended to result in increased efficiency, easier staffing, reduced training costs, and lowered compensation requirements.

Proceeding primarily from research in organizational psychology, the *motivational model* evolved in response to job dissatisfaction, the deskilling of industrial jobs, and alienation of workers that resulted from the overapplication of the mechanistic model. The approach usually provides job-enriching recommendations such as increasing the variety of tasks performed or the autonomy with which they are executed. The intended benefits of this model include increased job satisfaction, intrinsic motivation, retention, and customer service.

Based on human factors and experimental psychology research, the *perceptual model* arose from increases in technological complexity and a shift in many jobs from manually performing work to operating and monitoring. This approach is primarily concerned with reducing the information-processing requirements of work in order to reduce the likelihood of errors, accidents, and mental overload.

Emerging from ergonomics and medical sciences research, the *biological model* sought to alleviate physical stresses of work. Reductions in physical requirements and environmental stressors, and increased consideration of postural factors, are common recommendations. Taking these factors into account when designing jobs can reduce physical discomfort, physical stress, and fatigue.

CONTEXTUAL INFLUENCES ON WORK DESIGN

In virtually all its incarnations, both the mechanistic (e.g., Taylor, 1911) and motivational (e.g., Herzberg et al., 1959; Turner & Lawrence, 1965) approaches to work design have suggested that the primary influence on work design outcomes were aspects of the work itself. That is, it was long thought that features of the work were the main determinant of affective (e.g., satisfaction) and behavioral (e.g., job performance) outcomes. There is reason to believe, however, that there might be other influences. We examine both social and structural influences.

Social Influences

Spurred on by the social information processing model of Salancik and Pfeffer (1978), a host of researchers have examined the influence social information might have on work design perceptions and outcomes. The first research was conducted in laboratory settings and served to demonstrate that social information could impact task perceptions and task satisfaction. Although some found stronger effects for task enrichment (Weiss & Shaw, 1979), others suggested that social cues were more important for affective outcomes (O'Reilly & Caldwell, 1979; S. E. White & Mitchell, 1979). Of course, in this lab research the strength of task and social cue manipulations are experimentally controlled. Thus, discussions about relative importance in fixed effects designs are not warranted.

Using a more extensive and complex within-subjects design, Griffin, Bateman, Wayne, and Head (1987) found that enriched tasks, coupled with positive social information cues, were the most motivating. Unenriched tasks, coupled with negative social information cues, were the least

motivating. This suggests that both objective facets of the work environment and social information determine perceptions and affect. Similarly, Seers and Graen (1984) found that including both task and leadership characteristics improved prediction of performance and satisfaction outcomes.

To test congruency model predictions, Pierce, Dunham, and Blackburn (1979) conducted a field study looking at the relative impact of social system design (organic or mechanistic) and job design on job satisfaction. They found that workers had the highest satisfaction when they had complex jobs in organic organizational structures (i.e., participative, with few rules). Interestingly, the second highest levels of satisfaction were from workers who had complex jobs in mechanistic organizational structures. This suggests that features of the work itself are more important than social system factors for affective reactions.

In a field experiment, Griffin (1983) directly examined the relative impact of social cues and task changes. He found that social cues had a greater impact on social outcomes (e.g., friendship opportunities, dealing with others) and that the task manipulation had a greater effect on task characteristics. Both social cues and task changes impacted intrinsic, extrinsic, and overall satisfaction, although the task changes had a larger effect. Only the task changes, however, impacted productivity.

Other research has sought to define the range of situations under which social information can influence work design. Caldwell and O'Reilly (1982) found that an individual's job satisfaction is related to perceptions of task characteristics. Adler, Skov, and Salvemini (1985) reached a similar conclusion when they found that manipulating job satisfaction affects perceptions of task scope. Using an equity theory perspective, Oldham and colleagues (Oldham, Kulik, Ambrose, Stepina, & Brand, 1986; Oldham & Miller, 1979; Oldham et al., 1982) have sought to understand the consequences of different social comparisons in the workplace. Oldham et al. (1982) found that individuals do make comparisons to others in the work setting, and they tend to select more complex jobs as their referent. Oldham et al. (1986) then found that employees who felt disadvantaged relative to their referents were typically less satisfied and less internally motivated but that employees who felt advantaged or equitable relative to their referents performed at higher levels, were absent less frequently, and withdrew from the organization less frequently.

Two final studies in this area deserve attention. First, Vance and Biddle (1985) not only looked at the influence of social cues on task attitudes, but they also investigated the timing of the social cues. They found that task-related attitudes were influenced by social cues, but the impact of those social cues was lessened with experience with the task. This suggests that social cues were more important before subjects had the opportunity to acquire many objective cues. Second, Kilduff and Regan (1988) found that although positive and negative cues impacted perceptions of task characteristics, they had no influence on actual behavior. They concluded that although ratings of tasks were responsive to information cues, actual behavior was responsive to direct experience with the task.

Several conclusions can be drawn based on this research. First, task perceptions and attitudes are influenced by social information. Second, workers do actively compare their jobs and situations to those of others. Third, the impact of social information seems to be less than that of objective task characteristics. Finally, the influence of social information appears to be strongest for attitudes, whereas objective task characteristics impact both attitudes and behavior.

Structural Influences

There are ample reasons to believe that structural factors such as organizational structure, technology, and the physical environment will impact work design and reactions to work design. After all, work exists within a larger organizational system and many aspects of these systems influence the ways in which it is designed. For example, organizations that are highly decentralized are likely to design work to be more autonomous. Because of this, researchers have sought to understand the mechanisms through which structural factors impact work design.

In terms of organizational structure, Pierce and Dunham (1978a) found that such things as formalization and centralization were negatively related to perceptions of several job characteristics (e.g., autonomy, variety, feedback, and identity). Similarly, Rousseau (1978a) found negative relationships between several aspects of departmental structure (size, centralization, and formalization) and job characteristics and satisfaction.

In addition, Rousseau (1978b) found that job characteristics such as variety and autonomy mediated the relationship between the technological and structural context of the organization and employee outcomes like satisfaction and motivation. Evidence for mediation has been supported in a number of different studies (e.g., Brass, 1981; Oldham & Hackman, 1981; Pierce, 1979). For example, Oldham and Hackman (1981) found that job characteristics mediated the relationship between organizational structure and the employee reactions of growth, pay, and supervisory satisfaction. It should be recognized, however, that many of these tests for mediation have been methodologically weak because of problems with common method bias.

Oldham and Brass (1979) examined how the physical environment affected job characteristics. In this quasi-experiment, workers at a newspaper organization moved from a traditional office setting to an open-plan office arrangement (i.e., offices with no interior walls or partitions). Even though there were no changes to the jobs themselves, moving to a new office decreased the perception of several job characteristics (e.g., task significance, task identity). As in other studies, Oldham and Brass found that the job characteristics mediated the relationship between the physical setting and reduced worker satisfaction and motivation. They suggested that the physical setting influences employee motivation and satisfaction by changing perceptions of specific job characteristics.

In a direct test of the relative influence of job design, structure, technology, and leader behavior, Pierce, Dunham, and Cummings (1984) found that job design (particularly autonomy and variety) was the primary predictor of employee attitudes and behavior and that technology was the second most important. They suggested that job design is most important because it is much closer to the worker and is experienced on a more direct and regular basis.

Finally, Wright and Cordery (1999) examined how elements of the technical context can interact with job design and influence job satisfaction and intrinsic motivation. Specifically, they suggested that in high-uncertainty environments (as indexed by elements of the technological system), enhanced employee decision control would be associated with positive employee outcomes. As predicted, they found that individuals high in production uncertainty and job control were more satisfied and intrinsically motivated than those low in production uncertainty and high in job control. In addition, those low in production uncertainty and job control were more satisfied and intrinsically motivated than those high in production uncertainty and low in job control. These results suggest that one of the key factors to consider when designing work is to make the level of autonomy or control congruent with the demands of the work itself.

CHARACTERISTICS OF WORK

A large body of research has investigated the ways in which work can be described and the issues that arise when attempting to describe work. This section begins with a discussion of the structure of work, followed by a consideration of whether objective features or subjective perceptions of work are being measured in work design research, and concludes with a consideration of potential measurement problems in the research literature.

Structure of Work

Perhaps one of the most important aspects to designing and redesigning work revolves around understanding its structure. This entails identifying the important dimensions of work and understanding what implications this has for work design. Until recently this has had a relatively narrow focus, but two different lines of research have expanded our understanding of the nature of work. The first involves the measurement of job characteristics identified by Hackman and Oldham (1975), and the second concerns a broader research literature that seeks to understand the dimensions upon which work can be described.

Dimensionality of Motivational Job Characteristics

The bulk of the research in this area centers on the job characteristics model of Hackman and Oldham (1975, 1976) and their Job Diagnostic Survey (JDS; see Table 17.1). As previously noted, they suggested that jobs could be described in terms of skill variety, task identity, task significance, autonomy, and feedback from the job. A large number of studies have examined and attempted to replicate this five-factor structure (Birnbaum, Farh, & Wong, 1986; Dunham, Aldag, & Brief, 1977; Fried & Ferris, 1986; Griffin, Moorhead, Johnson, & Chonko, 1980; Harvey, Billings, & Nilan, 1985; Idaszak & Drasgow, 1987; Pierce et al., 1979; Pokorney, Gilmore, & Beehr, 1980).

Although some support has been found (e.g., Lee & Klein, 1982), more studies have reported inconsistent factor solutions. For example, Dunham (1976) found that a single dimension (reflecting job complexity) was the most parsimonious representation of five job characteristics. Using a larger and more diverse sample, Dunham et al. (1977) found two-, three-, four-, and five-factor solutions, depending on the sample. Green, Armenakis, Marbert, and Bedeian (1979) also failed to find the a priori factor structure and suggested that because the format and content of some items are relatively complex, the ability levels of questionnaire respondents may be responsible for the idiosyncratic factor-analytic results.

Concurrently with the work of Hackman and Oldham (1975), Sims, Szilagyi, and Keller (1976) developed the Job Characteristics Inventory (JCI; see Table 17.2). The resultant six factors (Variety, Autonomy, Feedback, Dealing With Others, Task Identity, and Friendship) were composed of items principally taken from the work of Hackman and Lawler (1971). As such, these factors are quite similar in character to those in the JDS (the JCI does not measure task significance). Notable differences between the two include the use of simpler 5-point Likert scales and more items per

TABLE 17.1   Job Diagnostic Survey

Scale	Items
Skill Variety	1. How much *variety* is there in your job? That is, to what extent does the job require you to do many different things at work, using a variety of your skills and talents? 2. The job requires me to use a number of complex or high-level skills. 3. The job is quite simple and repetitive (R).
Task Identity	1. To what extent does your job involve doing a *"whole"* and *identifiable piece of work?* That is, is the job a complete piece of work that has an obvious beginning and end? Or is it only a small *part* of the overall piece of work, which is finished by other people or by automatic machines? 2. The job is arranged so that I can do an entire piece of work from beginning to end. 3. The job provides me the chance to completely finish the pieces of work I begin.
Task Significance	1. In general, how *significant* or *important* is your job? That is, are the results of your work likely to significantly affect the lives or well-being of other people? 2. This job is one where a lot of other people can be affected by how well the work gets done. 3. The job itself is very significant and important in the broader scheme of things.
Autonomy	1. How much *autonomy* is there in your job? That is, to what extent does your job permit you to decide *on your own* how to go about doing the work? 2. The job gives me considerable opportunity for independence and freedom in how I do the work. 3. The job gives me a chance to use my personal initiative or judgment in carrying out the work.
Feedback From Job	1. To what extent does *doing the job itself* provide you with information about your work performance? That is, does the actual *work itself* provide clues about how well you are doing–aside from any "feedback" co-workers or supervisors may provide? 2. Just doing the work required by the job provides many chances for me to figure out how well I am doing. 3. After I finish a job, I know whether I performed well.

Source: Based on Hackman and Oldham (1980), with Idaszak and Drasgow's (1987) revised items.

scale. Pierce and Dunham (1978b) directly compared the four common dimensions in the JCI and the JDS and found that the JCI was psychometrically superior (in terms of internal consistency and dimensionality). This is likely due, in part, to the larger number of items and simplified ratings scales. Likewise, Griffin (1981) found that JCI dimensionality was stable over time, and Griffin et al. (1980) found that JCI dimensionality was consistent across samples. Finally, although Brief and Aldag (1978) reported satisfactory levels of internal consistency in a sample of registered nurses, they noted some confounding between Friendship and Dealing With Others (it is interesting to note that these two dimensions were not

TABLE 17.2   Job Characteristics Inventory (JCI)

Scale	Items
Variety	1. How much variety is there in your job? 2. How repetitious are your duties? 3. How similar are the tasks you perform in a typical work day? 4. The opportunity to do a number of different things. 5. The amount of variety in my job.
Autonomy	1. How much are you left on your own to do your own work? 2. To what extent are you able to act independently of your supervisors in performing your job function? 3. To what extent are you able to do your job independently of others? 4. The opportunity for independent thought and action. 5. The freedom to do pretty much what I want on my job. 6. The control I have over the pace of my work.
Feedback	1. To what extent do you find out how well you are doing on the job as you are working? 2. The opportunity to find out how well I am doing on my job. 3. The feeling that I know whether I am performing my job well or poorly. 4. To what extent do you receive information from your supervisor on your job performance? 5. The feedback from my supervisor on how well I'm doing.
Dealing With Others	1. To what extent is dealing with other people a part of your job? 2. How much of your job depends upon your ability to work with others? 3. The extent of feedback you receive from individuals other than your supervisor.
Task Identity	1. How often do you see projects or jobs through to completion? 2. The opportunity to do a job from the beginning to end (i.e., the chance to do a whole job). 3. The opportunity to complete work I start. 4. The degree to which the work I'm involved with is handled from beginning to end by myself.
Friendship	1. To what extent do you have the opportunity to talk informally with other employees while at work? 2. The opportunity in my job to get to know other people. 3. The opportunity to develop close friendships in my job. 4. How much opportunity is there to meet individuals whom you would like to develop friendship with? 5. Friendship from my co-workers. 6. The opportunity to talk to others on my job. 7. Meeting with others in my work.

Source: Based on Sims, Szilagyi, and Keller (1976).

included in the studies conducted by Pierce & Dunham, 1978b; Griffin, 1981; or Griffin et al., 1980). Nonetheless, it appears that the task dimensions measured by the JCI to be reasonably well established (Aldag, Barr, & Brief, 1981).

Given the ubiquity of the JDS and the inconsistent factor-structure findings, additional research has been conducted to understand the reasons for these results. Following up on the work of Green et al. (1979), Harvey et al. (1985) focused on the impact of two possible methodological issues in the JDS: (a) the use of negatively worded items and (b) the use of different response formats. They found that the use of three different response formats in the JDS added substantial amounts of construct-irrelevant variance to the measurement of job characteristics. In all cases, confirmatory factor analyses revealed that the inclusion of method factors increased the fit of factor models to the data.

To directly test the effect negatively worded items have on the factor structure of the JDS, Idaszak and Drasgow (1987) rewrote negatively worded items. This revised JDS was then administered to a sample of printing-company employees. The authors were able to replicate the five-factor structure and eliminated the previously found method factor. Interestingly, however, this revised measure did not improve the prediction of various outcomes (e.g., internal motivation, satisfaction; Cordery & Sevastos, 1993; Kulik, Oldham, & Langner, 1988).

One possible explanation for the effect of negatively worded items is that they create a more cognitively complex task for respondents when they make their ratings. This would suggest that respondents with higher ability levels would be able to make more accurate ratings and more faithfully reproduce the a priori factor structure. In fact, Fried and Ferris (1986) found just such an effect using a large sample of jobs and respondents. They found that management and staff, young people, and highly educated employees were able to produce the hypothesized five-factor structure. Nonmanagerial personnel, older respondents, and those with a lower level of education were unable to do so.

This corresponds to propositions in job analysis that as a judgment task increases in complexity (e.g., the need to mentally reverse negatively worded items, high reading demands, etc.), mental demands are increased (Morgeson & Campion, 1997). A corresponding increase in ability may enable more accurate responding. This conclusion should be tempered by the fact that Cordery and Sevastos (1993) were unable to find a similar relationship between educational level and responses to negatively worded items. The Cordery and Sevastos sample, however, did not have as great a range in educational level as did that of Fried and Ferris (1986).

The Dimensions of Work

Although the preceding research is suggestive of the role that methodological factors can play in the measurement of this set of job characteristics, it does not address the fundamental question of whether these dimensions are an adequate representation of the world of work (Roberts & Glick, 1981).

In fact, there is relatively little empirical evidence that the constructs developed by researchers are actually related to the categories job incumbents use when they think about their jobs (Taber, Beehr, & Walsh, 1985). Fortunately, research has been conducted that seeks to clarify and identify other possible dimensions of work.

Stone and Gueutal (1985) suggested that because most job characteristics are based on a narrow set of a priori formulations (i.e., the work of Turner & Lawrence, 1965), it is an open question as to whether job incumbents actually experience or view work in the same way. Using multidimensional scaling, they identified three dimensions: (a) Job Complexity, (b) Serves the Public, and (c) Physical Demand. The Job Complexity dimension subsumed virtually all the measures typically assessed in measures like the JDS and JCI. This is consistent with Dunham's (1976) finding only one dimension when factor-analyzing the JDS, Oldham and Miller's (1979) and Oldham et al.'s (1986) use of the JDS as a measure of job complexity, and Loher et al.'s (1985) meta-analytic conclusion that the JDS is likely a measure of job complexity. The Serves the Public dimension reflected interacting with and serving customers and the public. The Physical Demand dimension reflected physical strength requirements, health hazards, responsibility for equipment, and physical activity in the job. Notably, these last two dimensions are typically unmeasured in most work design surveys.

Earlier research by Dunham (1977) and Schneider, Reichers, and Mitchell (1982) further supports these findings. Dunham (1977) found that a job-complexity measure (based on combining the scales in the JDS) had the strongest relationships to estimated General Aptitude Test Battery (GATB) scores that reflect cognitive abilities (e.g., intelligence, verbal aptitude) and had the weakest relationships to physical abilities (e.g., manual and finger dexterity). Schneider et al. (1982) also examined how individual job characteristics were related to GATB scores. They discovered two clusters of GATB scores, one containing so-called white-collar abilities (verbal, numerical, clerical) and one containing blue-collar abilities (physical). Only the white-collar aptitudes were consistently related to job variety and autonomy. Taber et al. (1985) found that the traditional set of social science variables converged with only one of three important job evaluation dimensions. Although motivationally oriented job-characteristics measures converged with a mental demands dimension, they failed to reflect the physical demands and working conditions of the job. Finally, Campion (1989) found that cognitive skill requirements (e.g., quantitative, verbal, spatial, and general learning ability) were positively related to motivational job characteristics.

In total, this evidence suggests that the most commonly used measures of job characteristics are tapping into a work complexity–mental demands dimension and failing to measure other important aspects of work. Work conducted since the mid-1980s has sought to expand our understanding of these other work aspects. Recognizing the parochial nature of contemporary work design research, Campion (1988; Campion & Thayer, 1985) developed the Multimethod Job Design Questionnaire (MJDQ) to explicitly include other views of work in addition to the commonly measured motivational perspective (see Table 17.3). Because it includes multiple views of work, it is possible that the MJDQ might act as a general measure of work (Edwards, Scully, & Brtek, 1999).

To investigate just such a possibility, Edwards et al. (1999, 2000) recently examined the MJDQ in an attempt to determine its underlying structure. Although Campion (1988; Campion & Thayer, 1985) suggested a four-factor model (corresponding to the four distinct job design approaches), Edwards et al. (1999) conducted confirmatory factor analyses and found little support for this model. Following a series of exploratory factor analyses, Edwards et al. (1999) suggested that a 10-factor model best fit the data, achieved discriminant validity, and produced adequate reliabilities. These factors can be grouped according to their broader work design approach. As such, the *motivational approach* included feedback, skill, and reward scales; the *mechanistic approach* included specialization and task-simplicity scales; the *biological approach* included physical ease, work conditions, and work-scheduling scales; and the *perceptual-motor approach* included ergonomic design and cognitive simplicity scales. Although this represents a more comprehensive description of work, it is still limited because these 10 scales do not fully represent the dimensions relevant to each work design approach. Because some of the items from the MJDQ are the sole indicators of a given work dimension (e.g., a single item is used to represent autonomy), they cannot be used to form scales. Additional items would need to be developed so these dimensions of work could be measured.

Other research conducted over the past 20 years has sought to clarify and refine a host of work characteristics long neglected in the bulk of work design research. Some of this work has been conducted in order to understand the demands of increased technological sophistication in highly automated manufacturing environments (Martin & Wall, 1989; Wall & Jackson, 1995; Wall, Jackson, & Davids, 1992; Wall, Jackson, & Mullarkey, 1995), whereas other work has sought to address deficiencies in existing work design conceptualizations (Brass, 1981; Kiggundu, 1981, 1983; Seers & Graen, 1984; Wong & Campion, 1991). What follows is a discussion of the major groupings of work characteristics identified.

Wall et al. (1992) and Wall et al. (1995) have further clarified three aspects of work autonomy and responsibility

TABLE 17.3   Multimethod Job Design Questionnaire (MJDQ)

Scale	Items
Motivational	1. *Autonomy:* The job allows freedom, independence, or discretion in work scheduling, sequence, methods, procedures, quality control, or other decision making.
	2. *Intrinsic job feedback:* The work activities themselves provide direct and clear information as to the effectiveness (e.g., quality and quantity) of your job performance.
	3. *Extrinsic job feedback:* Other people in the organization, such as managers and co-workers, provide information as to the effectiveness (e.g., quality and quantity) of your job performance.
	4. *Social interaction:* The job provides for positive social interaction such as team work or co-worker assistance.
	5. *Task/goal clarity:* The job duties, requirements, and goals are clear and specific.
	6. *Task variety:* The job has a variety of duties, tasks, and activities.
	7. *Task identity:* The job requires completion of a whole and identifiable piece of work. It gives you a chance to do an entire piece of work from beginning to end.
	8. *Ability/skill-level requirements:* The job requires a high level of knowledge, skills, and abilities.
	9. *Ability/skill variety:* The job requires a variety of knowledge, skills, and abilities.
	10. *Task significance:* The job is significant and important compared with other jobs in the organization.
	11. *Growth/learning:* The job allows opportunities for learning and growth in competence and proficiency.
	12. *Promotion:* There are opportunities for advancement to higher level jobs.
	13. *Achievement:* The job provides for feelings of achievement and task accomplishment.
	14. *Participation:* The job allows participation in work-related decision making.
	15. *Communication:* The job has access to relevant communication channels and information flows.
	16. *Pay adequacy:* The pay on this job is adequate compared with the job requirements and with the pay in similar jobs.
	17. *Recognition:* The job provides acknowledgment and recognition from others.
	18. *Job security:* People on this job have high job security.
Mechanistic	1. *Job specialization:* The job is highly specialized in terms of purpose, tasks, or activities.
	2. *Specialization of tools and procedures:* The tools, procedures, materials, and so forth used on this job are highly specialized in terms of purpose.
	3. *Task simplification:* The tasks are simple and uncomplicated.
	4. *Single activities:* The job requires you to do only one task or activity at a time.
	5. *Skill simplification:* The job requires relatively little skill and training time.
	6. *Repetition:* The job requires performing the same activity(ies) repeatedly.
	7. *Spare time:* There is very little spare time between activities on this job.
	8. *Automation:* Many of the activities of this job are automated or assisted by automation.
Biological	1. *Strength:* The job requires fairly little muscular strength.
	2. *Lifting:* The job requires fairly little lifting and/or the lifting is of very light weights.
	3. *Endurance:* The job requires fairly little muscular endurance.
	4. *Seating:* The seating arrangements on this job are adequate (e.g., ample opportunities to sit, comfortable chairs, good postural support, etc.).
	5. *Size differences:* The work place allows for all size differences between people in terms of clearance, reach, eye height, leg room, and so forth.
	6. *Wrist movement:* The job allows the wrists to remain straight without excessive movement.
	7. *Noise:* The work place is free from excessive noise.
	8. *Climate:* The climate at the work place is comfortable in terms of temperature and humidity and it is free of excessive dust and fumes.
	9. *Work breaks:* There is adequate time for work breaks given the demands of the job.
	10. *Shift work:* The job does not require shift work or excessive overtime.
Perceptual-motor	1. *Lighting:* The lighting in the work place is adequate and free from glare.
	2. *Displays:* The displays, gauges, meters, and computerized equipment on this job are easy to read and understand.
	3. *Programs:* The programs in the computerized equipment on this job are easy to learn and use.
	4. *Other equipment:* The other equipment (all types) used on this job is easy to learn and use.
	5. *Printed job materials:* The printed materials used on this job are easy to read and interpret.
	6. *Work place layout:* The work place is laid out so that you can see and hear well to perform the job.
	7. *Information input requirements:* The amount of information you must attend to in order to perform this job is fairly minimal.
	8. *Information output requirements:* The amount of information you must put out on this job, in terms of both action and communication, is fairly minimal.
	9. *Information processing requirements:* The amount of information you must process, in terms of thinking and problem solving, is fairly minimal.
	10. *Memory requirements:* The amount of information you must remember on this job is fairly minimal.
	11. *Stress:* There is relatively little stress on this job.
	12. *Boredom:* The chances of boredom on this job are fairly small.

Source: Based on Campion (1988).

TABLE 17.4   Wall, Jackson, and Mullarkey (1995) Measure

Scale	Items
Timing control	1. Do you decide on the order in which you do things? 2. Do you decide when to start a piece of work? 3. Do you decide when to finish a piece of work? 4. Do you set your own pace of work?
Method control	1. Can you control how much you produce? 2. Can you vary how you do your work? 3. Do you plan your own work? 4. Can you control the quality of what you produce? 5. Can you decide how to go about getting your job done? 6. Can you choose the methods to use in carrying out your work?
Monitoring demand	1. Does your work need your undivided attention? 2. Do you have to keep track of more than one process at once? 3. Do you have to concentrate all the time to watch for things going wrong? 4. Do you have to react quickly to prevent problems' arising?
Problem-solving demand	1. Are you required to deal with problems which are difficult to solve? 2. Do you have to solve problems which have no obvious correct answer? 3. Do you need to use your knowledge of the production process to help prevent problems' arising in your job? 4. Do the problems you deal with require a thorough knowledge of the production process in your area? 5. Do you come across problems in your job you have not met before?
Production responsibility	1. Could a lapse of attention cause a costly loss of output? 2. Could an error on your part cause expensive damage to equipment or machinery? 3. Could your alertness prevent expensive damage to equipment and machinery? 4. Could your alertness prevent a costly loss of output? 5. If you failed to notice a problem, would it result in a costly loss of production?

(see Table 17.4). *Timing control* reflects the opportunity to determine the scheduling of work. *Method control* refers to the choice of how to carry out tasks. *Production responsibility* concerns the extent to which an individual can make errors that can result in costly losses of output. These aspects of autonomy and responsibility more precisely specify the kind of freedom and independence individuals have in carrying out their work assignments and the accountability they face if something goes wrong.

Wall et al. (1992) found that increased operator control improved job performance. The improved performance resulted primarily from a reduction in equipment downtime that resulted from frequent but less serious operating problems. They forwarded two explanations for why increased autonomy worked in this sample. First, operators can quickly respond to problems when they arise, and do not need to wait

for others to solve the problem. Second, because they are given autonomy, operators can increase their understanding of how problems arise, and then use that knowledge to anticipate and prevent problems. What this suggests, however, is that only certain types of jobs will receive performance benefits of increased job autonomy.

The second group of work characteristics involves the mental demands of work (Martin & Wall, 1989; Wall & Jackson, 1995; Wall et al., 1995). *Attentional demand* concerns the degree to which constant monitoring of work is required. *Problem-solving demand* reflects the active cognitive-processing requirements of a job. The identification of these two demands is important because it helps clarify how work design can actually impact the information-processing requirements of work. Karasek (1979; Karasek et al., 1998) also focused on the psychological demands of work, including mental workload, constraints on task completion, and conflicting demands.

There is evidence, however, that increasing these two groups of work characteristics does not always have positive outcomes. Martin and Wall (1989) found that strain reactions were the worst when jobs were high in attentional demand and production responsibility. There was no relationship, however, between these job characteristics and job satisfaction, job-related enthusiasm, or contentment. Karasek (1979) suggested that high psychological demands produced mental strain and job dissatisfaction when coupled with low levels of decision latitude (i.e., autonomy and variety). When high levels of psychological demands were coupled with high levels of decision latitude, however, there were generally positive effects on worker outcomes.

The final group of work characteristics concerns the *social context* of work. Long thought to be important for work design (e.g., Trist & Bamforth, 1951), the social context has been investigated by a variety of researchers (Brass, 1981; Corbett, Martin, Wall, & Clegg, 1989; Kiggundu, 1981, 1983; van der Vegt, Emans, & van de Vliert, 1998; Wong & Campion, 1991), thereby addressing the criticism that the interpersonal-social aspect of work has been missing from job characteristics conceptualizations (Seers & Graen, 1984).

A commonly investigated social aspect of work has been *job and task interdependence*. This is the connectedness of jobs such that the performance of one job depends on the successful performance of another (Kiggundu, 1983). Tasks are interdependent when the inputs, processes, or outputs of one task affect or depend on the inputs, processes, or outputs of other tasks within the same job. Kiggundu (1981) differentiated between initiated and received task interdependence. *Initiated task interdependence* is the extent to which work flows from one job to other jobs. *Received task interdependence* is the extent to which a job is affected by work from other jobs. Kiggundu (1983; see Table 17.5) found that

TABLE 17.5   Task Interdependence

Scale	Items
Initiated task interdependence	1. To what extent does your job have an impact on the work of other people outside your work group? That is, does your job feed into the jobs of other people? 2. To what extent do the jobs of your section or work group depend on the performance of your job? 3. How much effect does your job have on the performance of the rest of the jobs in your section? 4. To what extent does your job require you to provide help or advice that other people must have to be able to do their jobs? 5. To what extent does your job require you to provide other people with support services that they need to do their work? 6. What percentage of your time do you spend giving help or advice other people need to do their work? 7. What percentage of your job activities go on to affect other peoples' work? 8. How many hours a day do you spend providing support services other people need to do their jobs? 9. Other people's work depends directly on my job. 10. Unless my job gets done, other sections cannot do their work. 11. Unsatisfactory performance of my job would delay the work performance of other people. 12. I provide other people with the help or advice they need to do their work. 13. I provide other people with materials, tools, or supplies which they need to do their work. 14. I provide other people with information they need to do their work. 15. I provide support services which other people need to do their work.
Received task interdependence	1. How much does your job require support services provided by other people? 2. To what extent do you depend on other people's work to obtain the tools, materials, or equipment necessary to do your job? 3. To what extent do you receive the information you need to do your job from other people? 4. What percentage of your job activities are affected by the work of other people? 5. Give the number of people whose work affects the activities of your job. 6. How long would it take your job performance to be affected by performance changes in other peoples' work? 7. For what percentage of your job performance are you dependent on support services provided by other people? 8. I spend a great deal of time on contacts with other people that help me get my work done. 9. My job cannot be done unless other sections do their work. 10. I depend on other people's work for information I need to do my work. 11. I depend on other people's work for materials, tools, or supplies that I need to do my job. 12. My job depends on the work of many different people for its completion. 13. Most of my job activities are affected by the work activities of other people.

Source: Based on Kiggundu (1983).

initiated task interdependence was positively related to motivational outcomes, but that received task interdependence was unrelated to motivational outcomes.

Wong and Campion (1991) found that a measure of task interdependence could enhance the prediction of the motivational value of jobs. They found that the motivational design of tasks was only modestly related to the motivational design of the jobs. Prediction was improved, however, by consideration of the interdependencies among tasks. Specifically, as interdependencies among tasks increased, the motivational value of the job also increased, but only up to a point. Very high levels of interdependence were associated with lower ratings of the motivational design of the jobs. It may be that extreme levels of interdependence result in narrow jobs with limited stimulation. Similarly, Corbett et al. (1989) found that high levels of interdependence (in terms of method uniformity, workflow rigidity, synchronicity, and low levels of slack) were negatively related to intrinsic job satisfaction.

This focus on various types of interdependence, however, does not address other aspects of the social environment. Fortunately, research conducted in the stress literature has emphasized the importance of *social support* (Johnson & Hall, 1988; Karasek et al., 1998). Social support can come from coworkers or supervisors and might serve to buffer workers from a number of negative outcomes. Some research conducted within the social information processing framework has indirectly examined this aspect of the social environment. For example, Seers and Graen (1984) found that the quality of leader-subordinate relationships was related to performance and satisfaction outcomes. Finally, the work of Hackman and Lawler (1971) suggested that feedback from others (e.g., coworkers, leaders) represents an important aspect of work.

Summary

Although there has been a great deal of research into the various components of work, a definitive statement about the structure of work has yet to be made. The research reviewed here has investigated these work dimensions in piecemeal fashion, and factor analyses (or any other data reduction techniques) are necessarily limited by the kinds of variables that are measured and the variance between jobs in the convenience samples typically used. Looking across this body of research, however, reveals some relatively consistent patterns.

Given the evidence discussed earlier, it appears that work can be described in terms of three higher order factors, which, in turn, are composed of a number of lower order factors. This is illustrated in Figure 17.1. Job complexity is composed of all the traditional motivational job features, from those identified by Hackman and Oldham (1975), to those more recently investigated by Wall and colleagues. Increases in job control, autonomy, variety, and other features tend to increase the complexity of work, thereby increasing the mental demands required to perform the work (Campion, 1989). The social environment appears to be another important domain of work, consisting of various interdependencies and the feedback from, support of, and interaction with others (e.g., customers, coworkers, leaders). Finally, physical demands consist of the physical activities, equipment, and technology used, working conditions, and scheduling issues associated with work.

This organizing scheme converges to a remarkable extent with the Data, People, and Things worker functions developed by Fine (1955) and used in the *Dictionary of Occupational Titles (DOT)*. The *data* function concerns information-processing or mental demands (ranging from synthesizing to comparing), the *people* function concerns working with others (ranging from mentoring to taking instructions), and the *things* function concerns working with equipment or tools (ranging from setting up to handling). Job complexity is similar to the data function, the social environment is similar to the people function, and physical demands correspond to the things function. Although the DOT is being replaced by the Occupational Information Network (O*NET; Peterson et al., 2001), there is also evidence from the O*NET for this kind of tripartite structure (Jeanneret, Borman, Kubisiak, & Hanson, 1999; see also the chapter by Sackett and Laczo in this volume).

Objective Characteristics Versus Subjective Perceptions

One question that has arisen when considering these dimensions of work concerns the validity of job incumbents' self-reports. That is, when job incumbents provide ratings about their jobs, do these ratings reflect objective properties of the job, or are they fundamentally subjective perceptions that may or may not be isomorphic with the actual job duties and responsibilities (Shaw, 1980)? As we have seen, a variety of factors can impact work design perceptions. Although early work in this area suggested that employee perceptions "are causal in affecting the reactions of employees to their work" (Hackman & Lawler, 1971, p. 269), it has always been assumed that these perceptions converge with an objective reality. In fact, Hackman and Oldham (1975) suggested that their JDS provides a measure of objective job dimensions when completed by job incumbents. In any event, it is presumed that objective task properties are related to perceived task properties (Taber & Taylor, 1990). This question has been investigated in two different ways.

Convergent Validity

The first way researchers have investigated this question is by examining the convergence between different sources of job information. This includes convergence between job incumbent self-reports and ratings made by others (e.g., supervisors, observers, job analysts) as well as convergence with published job information (e.g., job analysis databases). Presumably, ratings made by individuals who are not currently performing the job would be less subject to biases or perceptual distortions, and convergence with existing job analysis databases would reflect convergence to a more objective reality.

A large number of studies have investigated this issue (Algera, 1983; Birnbaum et al., 1986; Brass, 1981; Brief & Aldag, 1978; Gerhart, 1988; Gould, 1979; Griffin, 1981; Hackman & Lawler 1971; Hackman & Oldham, 1975; Hackman, Pearce, & Wolfe, 1978; Jenkins, Nadler, Lawler, & Cammann, 1975; Kiggundu, 1980; Oldham, 1976; Oldham, Hackman, & Pearce, 1976; Spector, Dwyer, & Jex, 1988; Spector & Jex, 1991; Stone, 1975, 1976; Stone & Porter, 1975, 1978). Several have found relatively strong relationships between employee and supervisory ratings. For example, Oldham et al. found job-level correlations between supervisors and employees up to .85. Hackman and Lawler also found relatively high convergence between employees, supervisors, and researchers on the job dimensions of variety and autonomy (correlations in the .80s and .90s). Lower convergence was found with respect to feedback and dealing with others.

Others have found smaller convergence. For example, Birnbaum et al. (1986) found moderate to low correlations between incumbents and supervisors, ranging from .20 to .62. Again, variety and autonomy evidenced the highest convergence. Hackman and Oldham (1975) examined convergence between employees and supervisors, employees and observers, and supervisors and observers. The median correlations at the job level were .51, .63, and .46, respectively. Although there was moderate convergence across the sources, some job dimensions had low or negative relationships.

Several researchers (Campion, 1989; Dunham, 1977; Gerhart, 1988; Rousseau, 1982; Schneider et al., 1982; Taber et al., 1985) have investigated the convergence between incumbent perceptions of job characteristics and other job information (e.g., job analysis databases, job evaluation systems). They found modest convergence among these sources, again suggesting that incumbent self-reports are anchored in some level of objective reality. Spector and Jex (1991) compared employee perceptions to DOT-derived complexity ratings, as well as ratings made by independent raters. Although they found moderate convergence between DOT measures and independent raters, there was smaller convergence between employee perceptions and the other two sources of information. Spector, Fox, and Van Katwyk (1999) found very little convergence between incumbent ratings and job analyst or supervisor ratings. Only 4 of 10 comparisons were significant, and the strongest correlation was .27.

In their meta-analysis of job design research, Fried and Ferris (1987) concluded that there was moderate to good overlap between incumbent ratings of job characteristics and those made by others. Spector (1992) conducted a more focused meta-analysis of 16 convergence studies, separating studies that assessed individual-level (where the incumbent was the unit of analysis) versus aggregate-level (where the job was the unit of analysis) convergence. In general, convergence was greater at the job level, which might be expected given that idiosyncratic differences between incumbents would be eliminated by aggregating. At the job level, the mean correlation was .59, with autonomy and variety evidencing the highest relationships (.71 and .74, respectively). At the individual level, however, convergence was considerably lower. The mean correlation was .22, with autonomy and variety again evidencing the highest relationships (.30 and .46, respectively). Across both the individual and aggregate levels, however, incumbents and observers generally fail to convergence in their ratings of feedback. Given this evidence, Spector (1992) suggested that a conservative lower bound estimate of 10–20% was the amount of variance that could be attributed to the objective job environment.

However, there are three additional points to understand with respect to the studies that demonstrate convergence among different sources. First, higher levels of convergence at the aggregate level may be inflated because of aggregation bias (James, 1982). Correlations computed at the job level will typically be much higher than those computed at the individual level, regardless of actual levels of convergence. This increased convergence at the job level results from increased reliability, which is a function of the number of respondents and the correlations between respondents and between job variance.

Second, because convergence is indexed through correlations between different sources, it reflects patterns of covariance. That is, when a job incumbent rates autonomy high, so too does his or her supervisor. Issues of covariance, however, are independent of the absolute level of agreement across raters. In other words, although incumbents and supervisors may evidence distinct patterns of covariation in their ratings, the correlation between their ratings does not index the extent to which raters make similar mean-level ratings (Kozlowski & Hattrup, 1992). This suggests that high convergence may not reflect high agreement. This is an issue that is beginning to receive research attention (Sanchez, Zamora, & Viswesvaran, 1997).

Third, a lack of convergence may be due to real changes workers make in their jobs. Some workers may expand their jobs so that they integrate additional task elements into their roles (Ilgen & Hollenbeck, 1991). For example, Campion and McClelland (1993) found that incumbents often made their work more mechanistic. Such job crafting (Wrzesniewski & Dutton, 2001) would attenuate the relationship between self-reports and other-reports because workers may change their jobs in ways known only to them.

Manipulation of Job Properties

The other way researchers have sought to determine whether self-reports of job characteristics reflect objective reality or are simply subjective perceptions has been to alter or modify aspects of work, and then look for corresponding changes in incumbent perceptions. To the extent that job incumbents recognize objective changes in their work, we can be confident that their perceptions are anchored in reality. It is important to recognize, however, that such changes can provide only an approximate estimate of the degree to which variance in incumbent perceptions is caused by objective differences in jobs. This is due to the fact that the manipulated job characteristics in the literature tend not to be representative of the full range of characteristics in the work environment (i.e., a true random-effects design; Taber & Taylor, 1990). Nonetheless, both laboratory (Farh & Scott, 1983; Ganster, 1980; Gardner, 1986; Griffin et al., 1987; Jackson & Zedeck, 1982; Kilduff & Regan, 1988; Kim, 1980; O'Reilly & Caldwell, 1979; Terborg & Davis, 1982; Umstot, Bell, & Mitchell, 1976; Weiss & Shaw, 1979; S. E. White & Mitchell, 1979) and field (Billings, Klimoski, & Breaugh, 1977; Campion & McClelland, 1991, 1993; Champoux, 1978; Frank & Hackman, 1975; Griffeth, 1985; Griffin, 1983; Lawler, Hackman, & Kaufman, 1973; Luthans, Kemmerer, Paul, & Taylor, 1987; Morgeson & Campion, 2002; Orpen, 1979) studies have examined how changes in job properties were perceived by incumbents.

Although many of the laboratory studies have been conducted under the auspices of testing the social information processing approach to work design, one aspect of these studies has been to manipulate task characteristics and look for corresponding changes in perceptions. Research participants are randomly assigned to one of two conditions, one with an enriched task and one with an unenriched task. Without fail, research participants identify the enriched task as higher on motivational properties. In other research, within-subject designs have been employed in which the same research participant performs both enriched and unenriched tasks (e.g., Griffin et al., 1987; Terborg & Davis, 1982; Umstot et al., 1976). Again, strong differences have been found between the task-enrichment conditions. Although there are a number of concerns with this research (see Taber & Taylor, 1990), it does serve to illustrate a key point: Individuals' perceptions of work design are influenced by objective differences between tasks.

The method used in field studies has also been relatively consistent. Typically, two groups are identified, one whose job is redesigned and the other whose job is left alone. Several studies have found that job incumbents perceive their jobs as having increased in motivational job properties following a redesign (Griffeth, 1985; Griffin, 1983; Luthans et al., 1987; Orpen, 1979). Billings et al. (1977) found that those closest to the change reported differences in task variety, importance, and interdependence, but some of these changes in perceptions actually occurred before the actual technological change occurred. This suggests that something else in the environment is partly responsible for task perceptions. Although not as uniform as the laboratory research, the field research also suggests that incumbent perceptions are anchored in objective features of the task.

Measurement Concerns

Common Method Variance

It has long been recognized that data collected through a single method can lead to problems with *common method variance* (Campbell & Fiske, 1959; Cook & Campbell, 1979; Fiske, 1982). When data are collected with the same instrument, there can be spurious covariation among responses. As a result, observed correlations reflect shared method and trait variance (Spector, 1992). Because this can inflate observed relationships between various job dimensions and outcome measures, work design research that relies on self-reported survey questionnaires has been heavily criticized (Roberts & Glick, 1981; Schwab & Cummings, 1976).

Salancik and Pfeffer (1977) suggest that consistency and priming are the underlying causal mechanisms for common method variance. *Consistency* refers to the tendency of individuals to remember and maintain consistency with prior responses; whereas *priming* refers to the influence a questionnaire can have in orienting an individual's attention to certain responses. Thus, when responding to a job design questionnaire, the respondent may attempt to maintain logical consistency between various items. For example, because there is an intuitive relationship between having job autonomy and internal work motivation, if a respondent rates autonomy

as high, he or she may also feel that internal work motivation should be rated highly, if only to maintain consistency. Priming effects are likely to occur as well because most work design questionnaires collect information on a relatively narrow set of motivational job features (e.g., autonomy, variety) that, in turn, can influence or direct subsequent responding. Such psychological processes can have a profound influence on self-reported beliefs, attitudes, intentions, and behaviors because they can result in self-generated validity (Feldman & Lynch, 1988; Tourangeau & Rasinski, 1988).

There has been a good deal of debate as to the magnitude of common method variance effects in organizational research. Some have downplayed its influence (Fried & Ferris, 1987; Spector, 1987), whereas others have been very critical (Buckley, Cote, & Comstock, 1990; Mitchell, 1985; Roberts & Glick, 1981). For example, in examining previous studies, Buckley et al. (1990) estimated mean variance due to common method variance at more than 21%, with a range of 3.6 to 56.3%.

Two studies provide more direct evidence concerning the extent of common method variance in work design research. The first is a meta-analysis conducted by Crampton and Wagner (1994). They investigated the degree to which self-report methods have produced percept-percept inflation in organizational behavior research. One of the broad categories they investigated was termed *job scope* and included most of the job characteristics typically assessed in work design research (e.g., autonomy, variety, task identity, and so on). They found statistically significant levels of inflation in relationships between self-reported job scope and job satisfaction.

The second study was conducted by Glick, Jenkins, and Gupta (1986). They used structural equation modeling to investigate the relative influence of job characteristics and method effects on outcome measures. They found that the impact of method effects depended on the outcome measure they were trying to predict. For example, job characteristics accounted for two-thirds of the variance in job satisfaction when method effects are not removed, but the predicted variance dropped to 2% when method effects are removed. A similar, although not as great, decrease was observed for challenge satisfaction (from 77% to 15%). The ability of job characteristics to predict effort, on the other hand, actually increased when method effects were removed (from 19% to 20%). This suggests that common method variance is more likely to bias affective outcomes than behavioral outcomes.

In total, this evidence suggests that common method variance is a problem in work design research. Because of this, a variety of strategies have been used to avoid it. For example, researchers have (a) varied survey-question order (e.g., Campion, 1988; Spector & Michaels, 1983); (b) collected data from multiple sources (e.g., supervisors and incumbents; Algera, 1983; Campion & McClelland, 1991; Glick et al., 1986; Johns, 1978; Oldham et al., 1976); (c) used separate subsamples per job (Campion, 1988); (d) collected data longitudinally (Campion & McClelland, 1993); and (e) used archival measures (e.g., objective productivity; Griffin, 1983). It would be good scientific practice to engage in some of these strategies to avoid the problems associated with common method variance.

Levels of Analysis

A final measurement concern in the work design literature concerns level of analysis issues. Although work design theorizing has typically occurred at the job level, the majority of empirical tests have occurred at the individual level. Thus, in many instances, the level of measurement and the level of theory are different. By itself, this is not necessarily a problem. Differences in level of measurement and level of theory are common, and choosing a level for empirical testing should be guided by one's theoretical model (Klein, Dansereau, & Hall, 1994; Morgeson & Hofmann, 1999). Individuals could be considered informants about their jobs and therefore the best judge of a job's properties.

When data are analyzed at the individual level, however, one is dealing with the perceptions of incumbents, and it is unclear how much these perceptions agree with the perceptions of other incumbents in the same job (the convergence research reviewed previously did not examine within-job convergence). Although some degree of variability would be expected, work design theories rely on the assumption that there is a high level of agreement among incumbents. There is reason to believe there is a lack of convergence in a large amount of work design research.

For example, much empirical work design research has been conducted with a single job title. Given that incumbents are performing the same job, one would expect there to be little variability in reports about various job characteristics. If there is no variance in job characteristics, then it is statistically impossible for these characteristics to be significantly related to any other variable. However, this research typically finds significant relationships with a host of measures, including satisfaction and motivation. This suggests that there is variance within a job and that this within-job variability is responsible for many significant results. Because this is inconsistent with work design theory, caution should be exercised in interpreting findings based on a single job.

It is likely there are both job-level and individual-level influences on work design outcomes. For example, workers will perceive the amount of autonomy designed into the job itself similarly, but some workers are also likely to be given greater discretion depending on their relationships with their supervisors. Thus, the amount of autonomy reported by an incumbent will be a function of both individual- and job-level factors. Existing work design theory, however, does not clearly identify individual versus job-level sources of variation in job design.

Another level of analysis issue concerns when data should be aggregated from the individual to the job level. First, theorizing should refer to the job, not the individual. Most work design theory does refer to the job (or team) level. Second, the measures should reference the job, not the individual (Morgeson & Hofmann, 1999). This will indicate that ratings should be made about the job, not individual reactions to the job. Third, empirical support for aggregation to the job level should always be provided. This would include the calculation of interrater reliability via the intraclass correlation (Bartko, 1976) as well as an examination of interrater agreement (James, Demaree, & Wolf, 1984). If the r_{wg} statistic is used (James et al., 1984), a normal or negatively skewed distribution should be assumed, not a rectangular distribution.

MEDIATING MECHANISMS IN WORK DESIGN

A key conceptual question in work design concerns the underlying psychological mechanisms through which work design influences affective and behavioral outcomes. Because the bulk of the research in I/O psychology has focused on motivationally oriented work design, our discussion will focus primarily on motivational models and the psychological mechanisms presumed to underlie their effects. The reader should be aware, however, that other job design models postulate different underlying mechanisms (e.g., the perceptual model of job design has its impact because it reduces information-processing demands).

Hackman and Lawler (1971) suggested that jobs must (a) allow workers to feel responsible for a meaningful and identifiable part of the work, (b) provide outcomes that are intrinsically meaningful, and (c) provide feedback about performance success. Hackman and Oldham (1976, pp. 256–257) labeled these *critical psychological states* and suggested they mediate between characteristics of the work and outcomes. Thus, changes in work design influence affective and behavioral outcomes because they alter these critical psychological states. Unfortunately, there has been mixed support for the intervening role played by the psychological states (Fried & Ferris, 1987; Johns, Xie, & Fang, 1992; Oldham, 1996). This had led some to suggest that the Hackman and Oldham (1976) model is "too simple and tightly linked to capture a rather complex phenomenon" (Oldham, 1996, p. 41).

Recent work in the area of psychological empowerment (Conger & Kanungo, 1988; Spreitzer, 1995; Thomas & Velthouse, 1990), however, may provide a more parsimonious description of the motivational benefits of enlarged work. These researchers suggest that empowerment is an active motivational state characterized by four distinct cognitions: (a) meaning, (b) competence, (c) self-determination, and (d) impact (Spreitzer, 1995). The motivational work characteristics highlighted earlier would seem to be logically related to the experience of empowerment (Gagne, Senecal, & Koestner, 1997; Kraimer, Seibert, & Liden, 1999).

This was recently examined by Liden, Wayne, and Sparrowe (2000) in a study that assessed the extent to which empowerment mediated the relationship between motivational job characteristics, leadership, and quality of coworker relationships and work outcomes. Although not solely testing work design factors, Liden et al. (2000) found that some of the empowerment dimensions partially mediated the relationship between work design and satisfaction, commitment, and job performance.

There are, however, potential discriminant validity problems with the notion that work design increases psychological empowerment. This is due to the fact that at least one popular measure of empowerment utilizes the job characteristic of autonomy as an indicator of empowerment (Spreitzer, 1995). Thus, at some level it is unclear the extent to which motivational features of work (e.g., autonomy) are separable from the psychological experience of work.

All of the preceding formulations have relied on motivational explanations for how work design impacts affective and behavioral outcomes. In other words, they suggest that work design enhances work satisfaction and job performance by encouraging greater effort. Wall and Jackson (1995), however, offer a knowledge-based explanation. They suggest that changes in work design may improve organizational outcomes because increases in such things as autonomy not only tap into the existing knowledge of the workforce but also allow further learning on the job. In essence, there are logistical advantages associated with greater job control. If workers have the knowledge and authority to deal with problems as they arise, they are likely to be able to respond more quickly to the problem. In addition, greater job control promotes workers' understanding of the work system, thereby enhancing learning. If they learn more about the system, they are better able to anticipate and avoid problems (Wall et al., 1992). Similarly, autonomy can facilitate learning and development, and this increased knowledge can have beneficial effects on job performance (Parker, Wall, & Jackson, 1997).

Such a knowledge-based explanation is given further support in the research of Campion and McClelland (1993). They distinguished between task enlargement and knowledge enlargement and examined the effects of both on a variety of outcomes. *Task enlargement* involved adding requirements for doing other tasks on the same product, whereas *knowledge enlargement* involved adding requirements to the job for understanding procedures or rules relating to different products. They found that simply increasing the tasks resulted in a variety of negative outcomes over time (e.g., more mental overload, lower job efficiency). Increasing the knowledge component of the work, however, resulted primarily in benefits over time (e.g., satisfaction, less mental overload, better customer service). This converges with research that suggests that mental demands account for the effects of motivational job design (Campion, 1988; Campion & Thayer, 1985). This work thus offers initial evidence that knowledge-based explanations may be able to extend our understanding of the mechanisms that mediate between work design and outcomes.

OUTCOMES OF WORK DESIGN

Three distinct bodies of research have considered the outcomes of work design. The first includes correlations with psychological, behavioral, human resource, and role definition outcomes. The second involves experimental and quasi-experimental research that examines how actual changes to jobs impact outcomes. The third involves how individual differences moderate the relationships found in cross-sectional studies.

Psychological and Behavioral Outcomes

Two meta-analytic reviews summarized the job design research conducted prior to the mid-1980s. Fried and Ferris's (1987) meta-analysis was based on correlational data for between 3 and 22 samples (depending on dependent measure). They corrected for sampling error, predictor and criterion unreliability, and range restriction. They reported the 90% credibility value (CV), which is the estimated true validity above which 90% of all values in the distribution lie. They found that the five job characteristics outlined by Hackman and Oldham (1975) demonstrated moderate to strong relationships with psychological outcomes. For example, job feedback demonstrated the strongest relationship with overall job satisfaction (90% CV = .43), autonomy demonstrated the strongest relationship with growth satisfaction (90% CV = .71), and skill variety demonstrated the strongest relationship with internal work motivation (90% CV = .52). In another meta-analytic study, Loher et al. (1985) found similar results, estimating that the true correlation between each of the five job characteristics and job satisfaction to be .39.

Weaker relationships were found between job characteristics and behavioral measures. For example, task identity demonstrated the strongest relationship with job performance (90% CV = .13; eight samples) and autonomy demonstrated the strongest relationship with absenteeism (90% CV = −.29; three samples). These results, however, are based on a small number of studies.

Rentsch and Steel (1998) examined how job characteristics relate to absence over an almost 6-year period. In general, they found that skill variety, task identity, and autonomy were negatively related to both absence frequency and amount of lost time, with correlations in the low −.20 range. Liden et al. (2000) found no significant bivariate relationship between a summary measure of four of Hackman and Oldham's (1975) job characteristics and job performance ($r = .08$). They did, however, find a significant relationship between a modified version of the autonomy scale (relabeled *self-determination*) and job performance ($r = .16$). The form and magnitude of these relationships are consistent with the meta-analytic findings of Fried and Ferris (1987), suggesting generally small relationships between motivational job characteristics and behavioral outcomes.

Other Outcomes

Other research has examined outcomes of work design that extend beyond traditional attitudinal and behavioral measures. Campion (1988, 1989; Campion & Berger, 1990) has focused on the range of different outcomes from each work design model (i.e., mechanistic, motivational, perceptual, and biological). What is different about this research is that it not only identifies benefits associated with the work design approach, it also identifies the costs. In essence, the costs represent the loss of benefits that would have been attained if an alternative model had been chosen. For example, designing work according to the mechanistic model typically yields efficiency gains, easier staffing, and reduced training demands, yet tends to decrease satisfaction and motivation. Designing work according to the motivational model tends to increase satisfaction, intrinsic motivation, and retention, yet also increases training costs, the likelihood of errors, and work stress. Designing work according to the perceptual model tends to reduce errors, accidents, and mental overload, but it often creates boring and monotonous work. Finally, designing work according to the biological model tends to increase physical comfort and reduce physical stress and fatigue, but implementing this design often requires modifying equipment that has financial costs and may lead to inactivity on the job.

Finally, Parker (1998; Parker et al., 1997) has examined how role definitions are affected by work design, finding that enhanced autonomy not only increased employee ownership for problems, but employees also recognized a wider range of skills and knowledge as important for their roles. Parker outlined the concept of *role breadth self-efficacy,* which is the extent to which individuals feel confident that they are able to carry out broader and more proactive roles. She found that job enrichment increased role breadth self-efficacy. It was suggested that this occurred because increased control over the work environment motivates workers to try out and master new tasks. Success then increases self-efficacy.

Work Redesign Interventions

A large amount of work design research has been cross-sectional in nature. This is problematic because it severely limits the kinds of causal conclusions one can reach. Coupled with the fact that much of the cross-sectional research is plagued with common method bias, research on work redesign interventions offers the opportunity to determine how actual changes to jobs impact worker outcomes. As such, work redesign research allows us to have a more veridical understanding of the work design phenomena discussed throughout this chapter.

Many studies suggest that when interventions are guided by motivational approaches, job satisfaction increases. Positive results have been found for a variety of different jobs, including telephone service representatives, keypunchers, clerks, and operators (Ford, 1969); insurance keypunchers (Hackman, Oldham, Janson, & Purdy, 1975); government clerks (Graen, Scandura, & Graen, 1986; Orpen, 1979); university receptionists (Griffeth, 1985); garment manufacturers (Coch & French, 1948); telephone installers, connectors, and engineers (Ford, 1969); product inspectors (Mather & Overbagh, 1971); technicians, salespersons, engineers, and supervisors (Paul, Robertson, & Herzberg, 1968); clinical research information systems workers (Morgeson & Campion, 2002); machine shop workers (Griffin, 1983); insurance paperwork processors (Campion & McClelland, 1991, 1993); and blue-collar petrochemical workers (Ondrack & Evans, 1987). These positive results, however, should be tempered by other research that has been less than supportive (Bishop & Hill, 1971; Frank & Hackman, 1975; Griffin, 1991; Lawler et al., 1973; Locke, Sirota, & Wolfson, 1976; Luthans et al., 1987).

Other change efforts not guided by the motivational approach have also been studied. These changes have typically occurred when new technology, operating procedures, or work locations are implemented. As one might imagine, these types of changes have had a number of different effects on employee outcomes. For example, Billings et al. (1977)

examined the implications of a change from batch to mass production in the dietary department of a hospital. Although decreases in satisfaction and attendance were expected because of negative changes to work characteristics, none were found. Hackman et al. (1978) investigated the installation of office automation. They found that when motivational job characteristics were increased, internal work motivation (i.e., positive internal feelings when performing effectively) and satisfaction increased. When motivational job characteristics were decreased, internal work motivation and satisfaction decreased.

In the Oldham and Brass (1979) study mentioned earlier, although there were no objective changes to the work, perceptions of job characteristics changed and satisfaction and motivation decreased. Wall, Clegg, Davies, Kemp, and Mueller (1987) studied the shift from manual to automated assembly. They found little evidence that increased automation results in deskilling of work. Wall, Corbett, Martin, Clegg, and Jackson (1990) examined the impact of increased operator control. They found that increased control resulted in reduced levels of downtime, particularly for high-variance technologies. Increases in job satisfaction and reductions in job pressure were also observed. Finally, Morgeson and Campion (2002) conducted a longitudinal quasi-experiment in which jobs were differentially changed in terms of their motivational and mechanistic properties. They found that satisfaction, efficiency, training requirements, and work simplicity could be differentially affected, depending on the changes made to the jobs.

Individual Differences in Work Design

Individuals differ in terms of the attitudes and beliefs they hold, what they value, and how they respond to their environment. Research has investigated how these individual differences may influence responses to work design.

Early Research

Turner and Lawrence (1965) initiated research into individual differences. They found evidence that urban versus rural background moderated the relationship between job characteristics and satisfaction, with those from rural backgrounds responding more positively to enriched work. At about the same time, other researchers (Blood & Hulin, 1967; Hulin & Blood, 1968) investigated alienation from middle-class norms and found limited evidence for the moderator among blue-collar respondents. Others also found significant moderating effects for job involvement (Ruh, White, & Wood, 1975) and need for achievement (Steers, 1975). Additional research on such things as community size (Shepard, 1970) and Protestant work ethic (Stone, 1975, 1976), however, found little to no evidence (J. K. White, 1978).

Growth Need Strength

The most commonly studied moderator of the work design–work outcome relationship is *growth need strength (GNS)*, which is the preference or need individuals have for stimulating and challenging work. The basic premise is that motivation and satisfaction will result from a fit between the task characteristics and the needs of the employees, such that the relationship between motivating job design and job satisfaction will be strongest for high GNS individuals, although the validity of such need-based explanations has been questioned (Salancik & Pfeffer, 1977).

Meta-analytic studies have summarized this research and have reached optimistic conclusions about the moderating role of GNS. For example, Fried and Ferris (1987) suggested that GNS moderated the relationship between motivational job design and job performance, although they found that only five studies had actually examined this relationship. After conducting a meta-analysis of 28 studies, Loher et al. (1985) concluded that GNS was useful as a moderating variable of the job design–job satisfaction relationship. Unfortunately, this conclusion was based on comparing correlations for high- and low-GNS workers. As we have come to understand, comparing subgroup correlations is analytically inferior to more sophisticated regression techniques (Stone & Hollenbeck, 1984).

More recent research, however, has reached less optimistic conclusions. Using a large sample of jobs and respondents (876 jobs, 6,405 total respondents), Tiegs, Tetrick, and Fried (1992) comprehensively tested the moderating influence of GNS and context satisfaction. They found virtually no support for any moderating effect. Similarly, Rentsch and Steel (1998) found no moderating effect of competence or need for achievement, suggesting that growth needs do not act as moderators.

Other Individual Differences

Campion (1988) investigated whether preferences for work designed from each of four different job design models would moderate responses to jobs designed from those models, but found only limited support. Another possibility is that employee ability levels influence reactions to job redesign efforts. If the cognitive ability required by the job is beyond that which the individuals possess, they may react less positively to the change. For example, Schneider et al. (1982) and

Dunham (1977) found significant relationships between motivational characteristics of jobs and various ability requirements. From the multidisciplinary perspective, Campion (1989) found that motivational job design has a positive relationship with a wide range of mental ability requirements and that jobs designed from a mechanistic or a perceptual perspective were negatively related to mental ability requirements. Although it remains an important research question, there is a dearth of research specifically investigating the moderating role of employee abilities (Fried & Ferris, 1987).

Other researchers have hypothesized that the quality of interpersonal relationships at work may moderate the impact of job design on job attitudes, arguing that when workers enjoy satisfying relationships on the job it minimizes the detrimental impact of negative job design. For example, Fretz and Leong (1982) had results that were generally in the predicted direction but most relationships were not significant. In addition, Oldham (1976) studied the moderating role of supervisory and coworker satisfaction on the relationship between job design and intrinsic motivation. Although he concluded there were significant moderating effects, this was based on analyses of the top and bottom third of employees and a non-statistical comparison of subgroup correlations. Other studies have also found mixed (Abdel-Halim, 1979; Johns et al., 1992; Oldham et al., 1976) or negative results, leaving the role of interpersonal context as a moderator in question.

Finally, recent research has examined whether negative affectivity (the stable tendency to experience negative emotions) and positive affectivity (the stable tendency to experience positive emotions) are related to incumbent perceptions of job characteristics. This research has been prompted by suggestions that negative affectivity may seriously bias self-report measures (Brief, Burke, George, Robinson, & Webster, 1988; Burke, Brief, & George, 1993). In directly testing the impact of negative and positive affectivity on job characteristics ratings, both Munz, Huelsman, Konold, and McKinney (1996) and Spector et al. (1999) found little evidence that negative affect had any impact on ratings.

Summary

The weight of the evidence suggests that there may be some individual differences in how motivational work design relates to outcomes. The meaningfulness of these differences, however, is questionable for three reasons. First, much of the early work design research that found evidence for moderation employed inappropriate analytic techniques. Subgroup analyses were commonly conducted in which samples were divided into the top and bottom thirds on the measure of interest (e.g., GNS). Correlations between job design measures

and outcomes for each group were then compared and differences in the magnitude of these correlations were offered as evidence for moderation. It is doubtful that more rigorous analytic techniques (i.e., moderated multiple regression) would yield the same conclusions.

Second, in most instances in which jobs are being designed for multiple employees, it is best to design jobs in accordance with the average or typical employee. If jobs are tailored to the individual preferences of each current incumbent, the jobs may not be well suited to the future incumbents who might possess different preferences. Furthermore, redesigning the job for each new employee is impractical, and predicting the preferences of future employees is likely to become more difficult with changes in labor market demographics.

Third, the relationships between the job design models and their outcomes tend to be positive for all employees, even if they differ in magnitude between employees. For example, although some employees may respond more positively to the motivational approach than others, the relationship is rarely negative. That is, typically all employees respond positively to motivating work, but some respond more positively than others (J. W. White, 1978). Research on GNS is a good illustration. Even those employees low in GNS showed small increases in job satisfaction in response to motivating job characteristics (Loher et al., 1985). In addition, there is evidence that people generally prefer work that is designed to be motivating. Campion and McClelland (1991) found that individuals generally preferred jobs designed from the motivational perspective and not the perceptual perspective (i.e., job design that seeks to reduce the information-processing requirements of work), but were ambivalent about jobs designed from the mechanistic or biological perspectives.

AN INTEGRATED WORK DESIGN FRAMEWORK

As this chapter has illustrated, a wide range of issues have been investigated in work design. Although the results have been informative, there exists no overall framework integrating this research. Figure 17.1 provides an integrative framework that summarizes the issues that have been investigated in the literature. It is not a formal model in the sense that it provides testable hypotheses. Instead, it is a heuristic device that quickly and economically conveys the major work design factors that have been investigated.

Contextual Influences

Contextual influences define the leftmost side of the model. These include the range of social factors identified in the testing of social information processing theory, such as coworker job satisfaction and job complexity, as well as leader behavior. Although these social influences have commonly been viewed as biasing factors in the perception of work characteristics, they may instead represent important inputs into the social environment of work.

Structural influences such as organizational structure, technology, and the physical environment are the other main types of contextual influence. These factors have been much less widely studied, but they are likely to serve as important boundary conditions for the design of work. For example, the range of possible work design choices will be limited by the formalization and centralization of the organization or the primary technology that is used. These structural influences do not dictate the design of work—they just place important limits on it.

Characteristics of Work

The characteristics of work constitute the next major element in the model. The bulk of the evidence from the research conducted in the work design literature and elsewhere suggests that work can be divided into three major components: (a) job complexity, (b) social environment, and (c) physical demands. The *job complexity* dimension reflects the range of motivational job characteristics commonly investigated (e.g., variety, autonomy), as well as more recently discussed characteristics of mental demands, types of job control, specialization, and work responsibility. In essence, increases in these work features tend to make work more complex to perform, thereby increasing the mental demands place on the worker.

The *social environment* dimension has received less research attention than job complexity, but recent research on job and task interdependence has begun to address this gap. More work is clearly needed into other features of the social environment, such as how feedback from others and social support relate to important work design outcomes. The *physical demands* dimension has been all but ignored in contemporary work design research. This is unfortunate, because such things as physical activity, working conditions, the technology used, and ergonomic design have been shown to have important relationships to worker outcomes. Clearly, more research is needed to integrate physical demands into work design research.

Mediating Mechanisms

There is considerable evidence that the aforementioned characteristics of work are directly related to outcome measures. There is at least some reason to believe, however, that several factors mediate between work characteristics and outcomes.

The critical psychological states outlined by Hackman and Oldham (1975) has received only limited support as a mediating mechanism. Psychological empowerment has been forwarded as another possible mediating mechanism, and appears to offer a more parsimonious account of the motivational benefits of enriched work.

Knowledge-based explanations for the benefits of enriched work have only recently been forwarded, but they provide a compelling alternative perspective. It may be that positive outcomes (particularly behavioral outcomes) are simply due to increased knowledge of the organizational system and the ability to anticipate and respond to problems more quickly. Although not discussed in the literature, two other knowledge-level mechanisms become apparent. First, jobs might be designed or redesigned to better take advantage of the skills possessed by employees. Second, work complexity is directly related to the information-processing demands of the work. It may be that positive relationships between work characteristics and behavioral outcomes are due to their shared relationship with mental ability.

Outcomes

A host of psychological, behavioral, human resource, and role-definition outcomes has been investigated in the work design literature. Such psychological outcomes as job satisfaction and internal work motivation have been very heavily researched, whereas mental overload and underload have received less research attention. Relatively few of the behavioral outcomes have been studied, and only absenteeism has been found to be a consistent work design outcome. It seems clear that work design has some fairly predictable human resource outcomes, with skill requirements, training demands, and compensation levels all being related to different forms of work design.

ADDITIONAL ISSUES IN WORK DESIGN THEORY AND PRACTICE

Although a great deal of work design research has been conducted over the past 40 years, many issues still remain unresolved and other issues have only recently emerged. In this section we consider some of the remaining challenges to work design theory and practice.

The Changing Nature of Work

The dramatic technological changes and competitive pressures organizations experienced in the 1980s and 1990s have prompted many to discus how the nature of work in organizations has changed (Howard, 1995). Although proclamations about the death of the job are likely premature, the trend toward increased autonomy and the implementation of team-based structures clearly has implications for work design. As decision-making responsibility is pushed to lower levels in the organization, job complexity will increase, with a concomitant increase in skill requirements for workers.

Increases in autonomy are likely to be related to increased job crafting. The freedom to make decisions about what tasks are performed and in what sequence will enable workers to define their jobs idiosyncratically (Wrzesniewski & Dutton, 2001). If a worker defines his or her job differently, however, understanding the factors that predict how the job will be redefined then become a key issue. For example, when will a worker expand his or her role beyond the formal job requirements? This is an important area for future work design research.

Increased skill requirements also highlight the importance of two new areas of work design. First, the importance of knowledge level as the mediating mechanism between work design and outcomes becomes more salient. The heightened production responsibility in autonomous settings suggests that performance gains will occur only if workers are able to increase and exercise their knowledge of the work process. Such decision control can also help buffer negative stress reactions. Second, the expansion of worker role definitions and the efficacy workers have in their capacity for expanding their roles is critical for success in autonomous settings.

Another important change in the nature of work is a shift away from manufacturing-based organizations, where goods are produced using physical labor, to knowledge-based organizations, where services are provided. Although the work design literature has extensively studied manufacturing and entry-level work, very little research has examined knowledge-based work of higher level employees. This is a serious omission, because the importance of the factors outlined in Figure 17.1 are likely to be different for different types of work.

Tensions in Work Design

When work is designed or redesigned, there are inherent tensions between different work design approaches. For example, changes aimed at increasing the satisfying aspects of work often make it less efficient. Similarly, changes aimed at making work more efficient generally make it less satisfying and motivating (Campion, 1988; Campion & Thayer, 1985). Until recently, it was thought that these kinds of trade-offs were impossible to resolve (Campion & McClelland, 1993).

Recent research suggests that it may be possible to eliminate (or at least minimize) these trade-offs (Edwards et al., 2000; Morgeson & Campion, in press).

As noted in the discussion of work redesign, most redesign efforts could be classified as either attempting to increase the motivational properties of work, or altering the technical or physical environment (typically to make work more efficient). Morgeson and Campion (2002) conducted a longitudinal quasi-experiment that sought to increase both satisfaction and efficiency in jobs at a pharmaceutical company. They found that when jobs were designed to increase only satisfaction or only efficiency, the common trade-offs were present (e.g., increased or decreased satisfaction, training requirements). When jobs were designed to increase both satisfaction and efficiency, however, these trade-offs were reduced.

Morgeson and Campion (2002) suggested that a work design process that explicitly considers both motivational and mechanistic aspects of work is key to avoiding the trade-offs. Edwards et al. (2000) provide another possible explanation. They found that the negative relationship typically found between motivational and mechanistic design is almost entirely due to a negative relationship between skill demands and task simplicity. Thus, as task simplicity increases, skill usage decreases, leading to the common trade-offs between motivational and mechanistic design. However, they also found that task simplicity and specialization, two key components of a mechanistic approach, were negatively related. This suggests that different aspects of mechanistic approaches are not necessarily consistent with one another. For example, task specialization may actually require high levels of certain skills. Thus, it may be possible to avoid the common trade-offs by increasing task specialization because it makes work more efficient while at the same time increasing skill utilization (which makes work more motivating).

CONCLUSION

As this review has indicated, a large amount of research has been conducted under the auspices of work design. Yet the majority of the research has centered on the model developed by Hackman and Oldham (1975, 1976). This has had a curiously narrowing effect. Some topics have been investigated in great detail (e.g., the five-factor structure of the JDS), whereas other topics have been all but neglected (e.g., non-motivational explanations for the effect of work design). This chapter has sought to highlight some of these less researched areas and to develop a model to include the range of topics that have been investigated.

TABLE 17.6   Work-Design Research Needs

1. Investigation of a greater variety of structural variables and how they impact work design.
2. Examination of a more diverse set of work characteristics (particularly social environment and physical demands).
3. Articulation and testing of more sophisticated mediational mechanisms (beyond motivational explanations).
4. Linking work design to bottom-line organizational outcomes (e.g., productivity, quality, safety, customer service).
5. Focus on redesign research in which changes are made to jobs (either experimental or quasi-experimental).
6. Redesign interventions should attempt to achieve multiple competing goals (e.g., satisfaction and efficiency) while minimizing the trade-offs.
7. Articulation of techniques or processes about how to actually design and redesign jobs.
8. A better understanding of the relationship between objective job design and perceived job design.
9. Integration of work design research into job analysis research.
10. Investigation of a wider range of moderators of the work design–outcomes relationship (e.g., personality, ability).
11. Examination of new job configurations (e.g., composite careers, virtual organizations, telecommuting) and how work design models apply to these ways of organizing work.
12. Greater understanding of the link between job and team design.

Here we summarize a range of issues needing additional research attention. This list is summarized in Table 17.6. Research is needed in each phase of the work design process highlighted in Figure 17.1. For example, more research is needed to understand the structural influences on work design. This would seem to be all the more important given the increased emphasis on the strategic implications of human resource management. A more diverse set of work characteristics also need to be investigated. Job complexity measures are well established; more work is needed with respect to the social environment and physical demands. In terms of mediating mechanisms, more sophisticated explanations are needed beyond that offered by motivational models. The knowledge-level explanation is a good start that requires additional research. This approach may also profit from a linkage to the extensive literature on ability-based job performance explanations.

Much more research is needed on the bottom-line outcomes that organizations value (e.g., productivity, quality improvements, safety, customer service). This evidence has been lacking, and one possible reason has been the relatively weak correlational designs typically employed. More rigorous longitudinal work redesign research is needed to demonstrate that changes to work can produce changes in outcomes. These redesign interventions should also attempt to achieve multiple goals, such as improving the motivational and mechanistic properties of work. Although some work has shown that this can be done, additional research is needed to determine whether the work design trade-offs noted earlier

can be entirely avoided. Research is also needed into the process through which jobs are redesigned. If changes are going to be made to jobs, how exactly should they be made?

We need a better understanding of the relationship between objective work design and perceptions of work design. Job analysis has been troubled by the lack of a true score (Morgeson & Campion, 2000). Is there a true score for jobs on work design measures? Also, work design is naturally aligned with job analysis. Tighter linkages between the two are important because work design factors are critically important to many human resource outcomes.

A wider range of moderators of the work design–outcomes relationship should be investigated. Research into GNS has not yielded much support. Other important individual differences could include ability and personality. Research should investigate whether existing work design models apply to newer job configurations, such as telecommuting, virtual organizations, and composite careers. What are the implications of these new forms of work organization for work design? Finally, we need a better understanding of the link between job and team design. How can an organization designed around jobs be redesigned around teams?

REFERENCES

Abdel-Halim, A. A. (1979). Individual and interpersonal moderators of employee reactions to job characteristics: A reexamination. *Personnel Psychology, 32,* 121–137.

Adler, S., Skov, R. B., & Salvemini, N. J. (1985). Job characteristics and job satisfaction: When cause becomes consequence. *Organizational Behavior and Human Decision Processes, 35,* 266–278.

Aldag, R. J., Barr, S. H., & Brief, A. P. (1981). Measurement of perceived task characteristics. *Psychological Bulletin, 90,* 415–431.

Algera, J. A. (1983). "Objective" and perceived task characteristics as a determinant of reactions by task performers. *Journal of Occupational Psychology, 56,* 95–107.

Astrand, P. O., & Rodahl, K. (1977). *Textbook of work physiology: Physiological bases of exercise* (2nd ed.). New York: McGraw-Hill.

Babbage, C. (1835). *On the economy of machinery and manufactures.* London: Knight.

Barnes, R. M. (1980). *Motion and time study: Design and measurement of work* (7th ed.). New York: Wiley.

Bartko, J. J. (1976). On various intraclass correlation reliability coefficients. *Psychological Bulletin, 83,* 762–765.

Billings, R. S., Klimoski, R. J., & Breaugh, J. A. (1977). The impact of a change in technology on job characteristics: A quasi-experiment. *Administrative Science Quarterly, 22,* 318–339.

Birnbaum, P. H., Farh, J. L., & Wong, G. Y. Y. (1986). The job characteristics model in Hong Kong. *Journal of Applied Psychology, 71,* 598–605.

Bishop, R. C., & Hill, J. W. (1971). Effects of job enlargement and job change on contiguous but nonmanipulated jobs as a function of workers status. *Journal of Applied Psychology, 55,* 175–181.

Blood, M. R., & Hulin, C. L. (1967). Alienation, environmental characteristics, and worker responses. *Journal of Applied Psychology, 51,* 284–290.

Brass, D. J. (1981). Structural relationships, job characteristics, and worker satisfaction and performance. *Administrative Science Quarterly, 26,* 331–348.

Brief, A. P., & Aldag, R. J. (1978). The job characteristic inventory: An examination. *Academy of Management Journal, 21,* 659–670.

Brief, A. P., Burke, M. J., George, J. M., Robinson, B. S., & Webster, J. (1988). Should negative affectivity remain an unmeasured variable in the study of job stress? *Journal of Applied Psychology, 73,* 193–198.

Buckley, M. R., Cote, J. A., & Comstock, S. M. (1990). Measurement errors in the behavioral sciences: The case of personality/attitude research. *Educational and Psychological Measurement, 50,* 447–474.

Burke, M. J., Brief, A. P., & George, J. M. (1993). The role of negative affectivity in understanding relations between self-reports of stressors and strains: A comment on the applied psychology literature. *Journal of Applied Psychology, 78,* 402–412.

Caldwell, D. F., & O'Reilly, C. A. (1982). Task perceptions and job satisfaction: A question of causality. *Journal of Applied Psychology, 67,* 361–369.

Campbell, D. T., & Fiske, D. W. (1959). Convergent and discriminant validation by the multitrait-multimethod matrix. *Psychological Bulletin, 56,* 81–105.

Campion, M. A. (1988). Interdisciplinary approaches to job design: A constructive replication with extensions. *Journal of Applied Psychology, 73,* 467–481.

Campion, M. A. (1989). Ability requirement implications of job design: An interdisciplinary perspective. *Personnel Psychology, 42,* 1–24.

Campion, M. A. (1996). *Reinventing work: A new area of I/O research and practice.* Presidential address presented at the meeting of the Society for Industrial and Organizational Psychology, San Diego, CA.

Campion, M. A., & Berger, C. J. (1990). Conceptual integration and empirical test of job design and compensation relationships. *Personnel Psychology, 43,* 525–553.

Campion, M. A., & McClelland, C. L. (1991). Interdisciplinary examination of the costs and benefits of enlarged jobs: A job design quasi-experiment. *Journal of Applied Psychology, 76,* 186–198.

Campion, M. A., & McClelland, C. L. (1993). Follow-up and extension of the interdisciplinary costs and benefits of enlarged jobs. *Journal of Applied Psychology, 78,* 339–351.

Campion, M. A., & Thayer, P. W. (1985). Development and field evaluation of an interdisciplinary measure of job design. *Journal of Applied Psychology, 70,* 29–43.

Champoux, J. E. (1978). A serendipitous field experiment in job design. *Journal of Vocational Behavior, 12,* 364–370.

Cherns, A. (1978). The principles of sociotechnical design. *Human Relations, 29,* 783–792.

Coch, L., & French, J. R. P. (1948). Overcoming resistance to change. *Human Relations, 11,* 512–532.

Conger, J. A., & Kanungo, R. N. (1988). The empowerment process: Integrating theory and practice. *Academy of Management Review, 13,* 471–482.

Cook, T. D., & Campbell, D. T. (1979). *Quasi-experimentation: Design and analysis issues for field settings.* Chicago: Rand McNally.

Corbett, J. M., Martin, R., Wall, T. D., & Clegg, C. W. (1989). Technological coupling as a predictor of intrinsic job satisfaction: A replication study. *Journal of Organizational Behavior, 10,* 91–95.

Cordery, J. L., & Sevastos, P. P. (1993). Responses to the original and revised job diagnostic survey: Is education a factor in responses to negatively worded items? *Journal of Applied Psychology, 78,* 141–143.

Crampton, S. M., & Wagner, J. A. (1994). Percept-percept inflation in microorganizational research: An investigation of prevalence and effect. *Journal of Applied Psychology, 79,* 67–76.

Cummings, T. G. (1978). Self-regulating work groups: A sociotechnical synthesis. *Academy of Management Review, 3,* 625–634.

Dunham, R. B. (1976). The measurement and dimensionality of job characteristics. *Journal of Applied Psychology, 61,* 404–409.

Dunham, R. B. (1977). Relationships of perceived job design characteristics to job ability requirements and job value. *Journal of Applied Psychology, 62,* 760–763.

Dunham, R. B., Aldag, R. J., & Brief, A. P. (1977). Dimensionality of task design as measured by the job diagnostic survey. *Academy of Management Journal, 20,* 209–223.

Edwards, J. R., Scully, J. A., & Brtek, M. D. (1999). The measurement of work: Hierarchical representation of the multimethod job design questionnaire. *Personnel Psychology, 52,* 305–334.

Edwards, J. R., Scully, J. A., & Brtek, M. D. (2000). The nature and outcomes of work: A replication and extension of interdisciplinary work-design research. *Journal of Applied Psychology, 85,* 860–868.

Farh, J. L., & Scott, W. E. (1983). The experimental effects of autonomy on performance and self-reports of satisfaction. *Organizational Behavior and Human Performance, 31,* 203–222.

Feldman, J. M., & Lynch, J. G. (1988). Self-generated validity and other effects of measurement on belief, attitude, intention, and behavior. *Journal of Applied Psychology, 73,* 421–435.

Fine, S. A. (1955). A structure of worker functions. *Personnel and Guidance Journal, 34,* 66–73.

Fiske, D. W. (1982). Convergent-discriminant validation in measurements and research strategies. In D. Brinberg & L. H. Kidder (Eds.), *New directions for methodology of social and behavioral science: Forms of validity in research* (pp. 77–92). San Francisco: Jossey-Bass.

Fogel, L. J. (1967). *Human information processing.* Englewood Cliffs, NJ: Prentice Hall.

Ford, R. N. (1969). *Motivation through the work itself.* New York: American Management Association.

Frank, L. L., & Hackman, J. R. (1975). A failure of job enrichment: The case of the change that wasn't. *Journal of Applied Behavioral Science, 11,* 413–436.

Fretz, B. R., & Leong, F. T. (1982). Vocational behavior and career development, 1981: A review. *Journal of Vocational Behavior, 21,* 123–163.

Fried, Y., & Ferris, G. R. (1986). The dimensionality of job characteristics: Some neglected issues. *Journal of Applied Psychology, 71,* 419–426.

Fried, Y., & Ferris, G. R. (1987). The validity of the job characteristics model: A review and meta-analysis. *Personnel Psychology, 40,* 287–322.

Gagne, M., Senecal, C. B., & Koestner, R. (1997). Proximal job characteristics, feelings of empowerment, and intrinsic motivation: A multidimensional model. *Journal of Applied Social Psychology, 27,* 1222–1240.

Ganster, D. C. (1980). Individual differences and task design: A laboratory experiment. *Organizational Behavior and Human Performance, 26,* 131–148.

Gardner, D. G. (1986). Activation theory and task design: An empirical test of several new predictions. *Journal of Applied Psychology, 71,* 411–418.

Gerhart, B. (1988). Sources of variance in incumbent perceptions of job complexity. *Journal of Applied Psychology, 73,* 154–162.

Gilbreth, F. B. (1911). *Motion study.* London: Constable and Company.

Glick, W. H., Jenkins, G. D., & Gupta, N. (1986). Method versus substance: How strong are underlying relationships between job characteristics and attitudinal outcomes? *Academy of Management Journal, 29,* 441–464.

Gould, S. (1979). Age, job complexity, satisfaction, and performance. *Journal of Vocational Behavior, 14,* 209–223.

Graen, G. B., Scandura, T. A., & Graen, M. R. (1986). A field experimental test of the moderating effects of growth need strength on productivity. *Journal of Applied Psychology, 71,* 484–491.

Grandjean, E. (1980). *Fitting the task to the man: An ergonomic approach* (3rd ed.). London: Taylor and Francis.

Green, S. B., Armenakis, A. A., Marbert, L. D., & Bedeian, A. G. (1979). An evaluation of the response format and scale structure of the job diagnostic survey. *Human Relations, 32,* 181–188.

Griffeth, R. W. (1985). Moderation of the effects of job enrichment by participation: A longitudinal field experiment. *Organizational Behavior and Human Decision Processes, 35,* 73–93.

Griffin, R. W. (1981). A longitudinal investigation of task characteristics relationships. *Academy of Management Journal, 24,* 99–113.

Griffin, R. W. (1983). Objective and social sources of information in task redesign: A field experiment. *Administrative Science Quarterly, 28,* 184–200.

Griffin, R. W. (1991). Effects of work redesign on employee perceptions, attitudes, and behaviors: A long-term investigation. *Academy of Management Journal, 34,* 425–435.

Griffin, R. W., Bateman, T. S., Wayne, S. J., & Head, T. C. (1987). Objective and social factors as determinants of task perceptions and responses: An integrated perspective and empirical investigation. *Academy of Management Journal, 30,* 501–523.

Griffin, R. W., Moorhead, G., Johnson, B. H., & Chonko, L. B. (1980). The empirical dimensionality of the job characteristic inventory. *Academy of Management Journal, 23,* 772–777.

Hackman, J. R. (1981). Sociotechnical systems theory: A commentary. In A. H. Van de Ven & W. F. Joyce (Eds.), *Perspectives on organization design and behavior* (pp. 76–87). New York: Wiley.

Hackman, J. R., & Lawler, E. E. (1971). Employee reactions to job characteristics. *Journal of Applied Psychology Monograph, 55,* 259–286.

Hackman, J. R., & Oldham, G. R. (1975). Development of the job diagnostic survey. *Journal of Applied Psychology, 60,* 159–170.

Hackman, J. R., & Oldham, G. R. (1976). Motivation through the design of work: Test of a theory. *Organizational Behavior and Human Performance, 16,* 250–279.

Hackman, J. R., & Oldham, G. R. (1980). *Work redesign.* Reading, MA: Addison-Wesley.

Hackman, J. R., Oldham, G., Janson, R., & Purdy, K. (1975). A new strategy for job enrichment. *California Management Review, 17,* 57–71.

Hackman, J. R., Pearce, J. L., & Wolfe, J. C. (1978). Effects of changes in job characteristics on work attitudes and behaviors: A naturally occurring quasi-experiment. *Organizational Behavior and Human Performance, 21,* 289–304.

Harvey, R. J., Billings, R. S., & Nilan, K. J. (1985). Confirmatory factor analysis of the job diagnostic survey: Good news and bad news. *Journal of Applied Psychology, 70,* 461–468.

Herzberg, F. (1976). *The managerial choice.* Homewood, IL: Dow Jones-Irwin.

Herzberg, F., Mausner, B., & Snyderman, B. B. (1959). *The motivation to work.* New York: Wiley.

Howard, A. (1995). *The changing nature of work.* San Francisco: Jossey-Bass.

Hulin, C. L., & Blood, M. R. (1968). Job enlargement, individual differences, and worker responses. *Psychological Bulletin, 69,* 41–55.

Idaszak, J. R., & Drasgow, F. (1987). A revision of the job diagnostic survey: Elimination of a measurement artifact. *Journal of Applied Psychology, 72,* 69–74.

Ilgen, D. R., & Hollenbeck, J. R. (1991). The structure of work: Job design and roles. In M. D. Dunnette & L. M. Hough (Eds.), *Handbook of industrial and organizational psychology* (2nd ed., Vol. 2, pp. 165–207). Palo Alto, CA: Consulting Psychologists Press.

Jackson, S. E., & Zedeck, S. (1982). Explaining performance variability: Contributions of goal setting, task characteristics, and evaluative contexts. *Journal of Applied Psychology, 67,* 759–768.

James, L. R. (1982). Aggregation bias in estimates of perceptual agreement. *Journal of Applied Psychology, 67,* 219–229.

James, L. R., Demaree, R. G., & Wolf, G. (1984). Estimating within-group interrater reliability with and without response bias. *Journal of Applied Psychology, 69,* 85–98.

Jeanneret, P. R., Borman, W. C., Kubisiak, U. C., & Hanson, M. A. (1999). Generalized work activities. In N. G. Peterson, M. D. Mumford, W. C. Borman, P. R. Jeanneret, & E. A. Fleishman (Eds.), *An occupational information system for the 21st century: The development of O*NET* (pp. 105–125). Washington, DC: American Psychological Association.

Jenkins, G. D., Nadler, D. A., Lawler, E. E., & Cammann, C. (1975). Standardized observations: An approach to measuring the nature of jobs. *Journal of Applied Psychology, 60,* 171–181.

Johns, G. (1978). Attitudinal and nonattitudinal predictors of two forms of absence from work. *Organizational Behavior and Human Performance, 22,* 431–444.

Johns, G., Xie, J. L., & Fang, Y. (1992). Mediating and moderating effects in job design. *Journal of Management, 18,* 657–676.

Johnson, J. V., & Hall, E. M. (1988). Job strain, work place social support, and cardiovascular disease: A cross-sectional study of a random sample of the Swedish working population. *American Journal of Public Health, 78,* 1336–1342.

Karasek, R. A. (1979). Job demands, job decision latitude, and mental strain: Implications for job redesign. *Administrative Science Quarterly, 24,* 285–308.

Karasek, R. A., Brisson, C., Kawakami, N., Houtman, I., Bongers, P., & Amick, B. (1998). The job content questionnaire (JCQ): A instrument for internationally comparative assessment of psychosocial job characteristics. *Journal of Occupational Health Psychology, 3,* 322–355.

Kiggundu, M. N. (1980). An empirical test of the theory of job design using multiple job ratings. *Human Relations, 33,* 339–351.

Kiggundu, M. N. (1981). Task interdependence and the theory of job design. *Academy of Management Review, 6,* 499–508.

Kiggundu, M. N. (1983). Task interdependence and job design: Test of a theory. *Organizational Behavior and Human Performance, 31,* 145–172.

Kilduff, M., & Regan, D. T. (1988). What people say and what they do: The differential effects of informational cues and task design.

Organizational Behavior and Human Decision Processes, 41, 83–97.

Kim, J. S. (1980). Relationships of personality to perceptual and behavioral responses in stimulating and nonstimulating tasks. *Academy of Management Journal, 23,* 307–319.

Klein, K. J., Dansereau, F., & Hall, R. J. (1994). Levels issues in theory development, data collection, and analysis. *Academy of Management Review, 19,* 105–229.

Kozlowski, S. W. J., & Hattrup, K. (1992). A disagreement about within-group agreement: Disentangling issues of consistency versus consensus. *Journal of Applied Psychology, 77,* 161–167.

Kraimer, M. L., Seibert, S. E., & Liden, R. C. (1999). Psychological empowerment as a multidimensional construct: A test of construct validity. *Educational and Psychological Measurement, 59,* 127–142.

Kulik, C. T., Oldham, G. R., & Langner, P. H. (1988). Measurement of job characteristics: Comparison of the original and the revised job diagnostic survey. *Journal of Applied Psychology, 73,* 462–466.

Lawler, E. E., Hackman, J. R., & Kaufman, S. (1973). Effects of job redesign: A field experiment. *Journal of Applied Psychology, 3,* 49–62.

Lee, R., & Klein, A. R. (1982). Structure of the job diagnostic survey for public sector occupations. *Journal of Applied Psychology, 67,* 515–519.

Liden, R. C., Wayne, S. J., & Sparrowe, R. T. (2000). An examination of the mediating role of psychological empowerment on the relations between the job, interpersonal relationships, and work outcomes. *Journal of Applied Psychology, 85,* 407–416.

Likert, R. (1961). *New patterns of management.* New York: McGraw-Hill.

Locke, E. A., & Henne, D. (1986). Work motivation theories. In C. L. Cooper & I. T. Robertson (Eds.), *International review of industrial and organizational psychology* (Vol. 1, pp. 1–35). Chichester, UK: Wiley.

Locke, E. A., Sirota, D., & Wolfson, A. D. (1976). An experimental case study of the successes and failures of job enrichment in a government agency. *Journal of Applied Psychology, 61,* 701–711.

Loher, B. T., Noe, R. A., Moeller, N. L., & Fitzgerald, M. P. (1985). A meta-analysis of the relation of job characteristics to job satisfaction. *Journal of Applied Psychology, 70,* 280–289.

Luthans, F., Kemmerer, B., Paul, R., & Taylor, L. (1987). The impact of a job redesign intervention on salespersons' observed performance behaviors. *Group and Organization Studies, 12,* 55–72.

Martin, R., & Wall, T. D. (1989). Attentional demand and cost responsibility as stressors in shopfloor jobs. *Academy of Management Journal, 32,* 69–86.

Mather, J. R., & Overbagh, W. B. (1971). Better inspection performance through job enrichment. In J. R. Mather (Ed.), *New perspectives in job enrichment* (pp. 79–89). New York: Van Nostrand Reinhold.

McCormick, E. J. (1976). *Human factors in engineering and design* (3rd ed.). New York: McGraw-Hill.

McGregor, D. (1960). *The human side of enterprise.* New York: McGraw-Hill.

Meister, D. (1971). *Human factors: Theory and practice.* New York: Wiley.

Mitchell, T. R. (1985). An evaluation of the validity of correlational research conducted in organizations. *Academy of Management Review, 10,* 192–205.

Morgeson, F. P., & Campion, M. A. (1997). Social and cognitive sources of potential inaccuracy in job analysis. *Journal of Applied Psychology, 82,* 627–655.

Morgeson, F. P., & Campion, M. A. (2000). Accuracy in job analysis: Toward an inference-based model. *Journal of Organizational Behavior, 21,* 819–827.

Morgeson, F. P., & Campion, M. A. (2002). Avoiding tradeoffs when redesigning work: Evidence from a longitudinal quasi-experiment. *Personnel Psychology, 55,* 589–612.

Morgeson, F. P., & Hofmann, D. A. (1999). The structure and function of collective constructs: Implications for multilevel research and theory development. *Academy of Management Review, 24,* 249–265.

Munz, D. C., Huelsman, T. J., Konold, T. R., & McKinney, J. J. (1996). Are there methodological and substantive roles for affectivity in job diagnostic survey relationships? *Journal of Applied Psychology, 81,* 795–805.

Oldham, G. R. (1976). Job characteristics and internal motivation: The moderating effect of interpersonal and individual variables. *Human Relations, 29,* 559–569.

Oldham, G. R. (1996). Job design. *International Review of Industrial and Organizational Psychology, 11,* 33–60.

Oldham, G. R., & Brass, D. J. (1979). Employee reactions to an open-plan office: A naturally occurring quasi-experiment. *Administrative Science Quarterly, 24,* 267–284.

Oldham, G. R., & Hackman, J. R. (1981). Relationships between organizational structure and employee reactions comparing alternative frameworks. *Administrative Science Quarterly, 26,* 66–83.

Oldham, G. R., Hackman, J. R., & Pearce, J. L. (1976). Conditions under which employees respond positively to enriched work. *Journal of Applied Psychology, 61,* 395–403.

Oldham, G. R., Kulik, C. T., Ambrose, M., Stepina, L. P., & Brand, J. F. (1986). Relations between job facet comparisons and employee reactions. *Organizational Behavior and Human Decision Processes, 38,* 28–47.

Oldham, G. R., & Miller, H. E. (1979). The effect of significant other's job complexity on employee reactions to work. *Human Relations, 32,* 247–260.

Oldham, G. R., Nottenburg, G., Kassner, M. W., Ferris, G., Fedor, D., & Masters, M. (1982). The selection and consequences of job comparisons. *Organizational Behavior and Human Performance, 29,* 84–111.

Ondrack, D. A., & Evans, M. G. (1987). Job enrichment and job satisfaction in Greenfield and redesign QWL sites. *Group and Organization Studies, 12,* 5–22.

O'Reilly, C. A., & Caldwell, D. F. (1979). Informational influence as a determinant of perceived task characteristics and job satisfaction. *Journal of Applied Psychology, 64,* 157–165.

Orpen, C. (1979). The effects of job enrichment on employee satisfaction, motivation, involvement, and performance: A field experiment. *Human Relations, 32,* 189–217.

Parker, S. K. (1998). Enhancing role breadth self-efficacy: The roles of job enrichment and other organizational interventions. *Journal of Applied Psychology, 83,* 835–852.

Parker, S. K., Wall, T. D., & Jackson, P. R. (1997). That's not my job: Developing flexible employee work orientations. *Academy of Management Journal, 40,* 899–929.

Pasmore, W., Francis, C., Haldeman, J., & Shani, A. (1982). Sociotechnical systems: A North American reflection on empirical studies of the seventies. *Human Relations, 35,* 1179–1204.

Paul, W. J., Robertson, K. B., & Herzberg, F. (1968). Job enrichment pays off. *Harvard Business Review, 42,* 61–78.

Peterson, N. G., Mumford, M. D., Borman, W. C., Jeanneret, P. R., Fleishman, E. A., Campion, M. A., Levin, K. Y., Mayfield, M. S., Morgeson, F. P., Pearlman, K., Gowing, M. K., Lancaster, A., & Dye, D. (2001). Understanding work using the occupational information network (O*NET): Implications for practice and research. *Personnel Psychology, 54,* 451–492.

Pfeffer, J. (1981). Management as symbolic action: The creation and maintenance of organizational paradigms. In L. L. Cummings & B. M. Staw (Eds.), *Research in organizational behavior* (Vol. 3, pp. 1–52). Greenwich, CT: JAI Press.

Pierce, J. L. (1979). Employee affective responses to work unit structure and job design: A test of an intervening variable. *Journal of Management, 5,* 193–211.

Pierce, J. L., & Dunham, R. B. (1978a). An empirical demonstration of the convergence of common macro- and micro-organization measures. *Academy of Management Journal, 21,* 410–418.

Pierce, J. L., & Dunham, R. B. (1978b). Research notes. *Academy of Management Journal, 21,* 123–128.

Pierce, J. L., Dunham, R. B., & Blackburn, R. S. (1979). Social systems structure, job design, and growth need strength: A test of a congruency model. *Academy of Management Journal, 22,* 223–240.

Pierce, J. L., Dunham, R. B., & Cummings, L. L. (1984). Sources of environmental structuring and participant responses. *Organizational Behavior and Human Performance, 33,* 214–242.

Pokorney, J. J., Gilmore, D. C., & Beehr, T. A. (1980). Job diagnostic survey dimensions: Moderating effect of growth needs and correspondence with dimensions of job rating form. *Organizational Behavior and Human Performance, 26,* 222–237.

Rentsch, J. R., & Steel, R. P. (1998). Testing the durability of job characteristics as predictors of absenteeism over a six-year period. *Personnel Psychology, 51,* 165–190.

Roberts, K. H., & Glick, W. (1981). The job characteristics approach to task design: A critical review. *Journal of Applied Psychology, 66,* 193–217.

Rousseau, D. M. (1977). Technological differences in job characteristics, employee satisfaction, and motivation: A synthesis of job design research and sociotechnical systems theory. *Organizational Behavior and Human Performance, 19,* 18–42.

Rousseau, D. M. (1978a). Measures of technology as predictors of employee attitude. *Journal of Applied Psychology, 63,* 213–218.

Rousseau, D. M. (1978b). Characteristics of departments, positions, and individuals: Contexts for attitudes and behavior. *Administrative Science Quarterly, 23,* 521–540.

Rousseau, D. M. (1982). Job perceptions when working with data, people and things. *Journal of Occupational Psychology, 55,* 43–52.

Ruh, R. A., White, J. K., & Wood, R. R. (1975). Job involvement, values, personal background, participation in decision making, and job attitudes. *Academy of Management Journal, 18,* 300–312.

Salancik, G. R., & Pfeffer, J. (1977). An examination of need-satisfaction models of job attitudes. *Administrative Science Quarterly, 22,* 427–456.

Salancik, G. R., & Pfeffer, J. (1978). A social information processing approach to job attitudes and task design. *Administrative Science Quarterly, 23,* 224–253.

Sanchez, J. I., Zamora, A., & Viswesvaran, C. (1997). Moderators of agreement between incumbent and non-incumbent ratings of job characteristics. *Journal of Occupational and Organizational Psychology, 70,* 209–218.

Schneider, B., Reichers, A. E., & Mitchell, T. M. (1982). A note on some relationships between the aptitude requirements and reward attributes of tasks. *Academy of Management Journal, 25,* 567–574.

Schwab, D. P., & Cummings, L. L. (1976). A theoretical analysis of the impact of task scope on employee performance. *Academy of Management Review, 1,* 23–35.

Seers, A., & Graen, G. B. (1984). The dual attachment concept: A longitudinal investigation of the combination of task characteristics and leader-member exchange. *Organizational Behavior and Human Performance, 33,* 283–306.

Shaw, J. B. (1980). An information-processing approach to the study of job design. *Academy of Management Review, 5,* 41–48.

Shepard, J. M. (1970). Functional specialization, alienation, and job satisfaction. *Industrial and Labor Relations Review, 23,* 207–219.

Sims, H. P., Szilagyi, A. D., & Keller, R. T. (1976). The measurement of job characteristics. *Academy of Management Journal, 19,* 195–212.

Smith, A. (1776). *An inquiry into the nature and causes of the wealth of nations.* London: W. Strahan and T. Cadell.

Spector, P. E. (1987). Method variance as an artifact in self-reported affect and perceptions at work: Myth or significant problem? *Journal of Applied Psychology, 72,* 438–443.

Spector, P. E. (1992). A consideration of the validity and meaning of self-report measures of job conditions. In C. L. Cooper & I. T. Robertson (Eds.), *International review of industrial and organizational psychology* (Vol. 7, pp. 123–151). New York: Wiley.

Spector, P. E., Dwyer, D. J., & Jex, S. M. (1988). Relation of job stressors to affective, health, and performance outcomes: A comparison of multiple data sources. *Journal of Applied Psychology, 73,* 11–19.

Spector, P. E., Fox, S., & Van Katwyk, P. T. (1999). The role of negative affectivity in employee reactions to job characteristics: Bias effect or substantive effect? *Journal of Occupational Psychology, 72,* 205–218.

Spector, P. E., & Jex, S. M. (1991). Relations of job characteristics from multiple data sources with employee affect, absence, turnover intentions, and health. *Journal of Applied Psychology, 76,* 46–53.

Spector, P. E., & Michaels, C. E. (1983). A note on item order as an artifact in organizational surveys. *The British Psychological Society,* 35–36.

Spreitzer, G. M. (1995). Psychological empowerment in the workplace: Dimensions, measurement, and validation. *Academy of Management Journal, 38,* 1442–1465.

Staw, B. M. (1984). Organizational behavior: A review and reformulation of the field's outcome variables. In M. R. Rosenzweig & L. W. Porter (Eds.), *Annual review of psychology* (Vol. 35, pp. 627–666). Palo Alto, CA: Annual Reviews.

Steers, R. M. (1975). Effects of need for achievement on the job performance-job attitude relationship. *Journal of Applied Psychology, 60,* 678–682.

Stone, E. F. (1975). Job scope, job satisfaction, and the protestant ethic: A study of enlisted men in the U.S. Navy. *Journal of Vocational Behavior, 7,* 215–234.

Stone, E. F. (1976). The moderating effect of work-related values on the job scope-job satisfaction relationship. *Organizational Behavior and Human Performance, 15,* 147–167.

Stone, E. F., & Gueutal, H. G. (1985). An empirical derivation of the dimensions along which characteristics of jobs are perceived. *Academy of Management Journal, 28,* 376–396.

Stone, E. F., & Hollenbeck, J. R. (1984). Some issues associated with the use of moderated regression. *Organizational Behavior and Human Performance, 34,* 195–213.

Stone, E. F., & Porter, L. W. (1975). Job characteristics and job attitudes: A multivariate study. *Journal of Applied Psychology, 60,* 57–64.

Stone, E. F., & Porter, L. W. (1978). On the use of incumbent-supplied job-characteristics data. *Perceptual and Motor Skills, 46,* 751–758.

Taber, T. D., Beehr, T. A., & Walsh, J. T. (1985). Relationships between job evaluation ratings and self-ratings of job characteristics. *Organizational Behavior and Human Decision Processes, 35,* 27–45.

Taber, T. D., & Taylor, E. (1990). A review and evaluation of the psychometric properties of the job diagnostic survey. *Personnel Psychology, 43,* 467–500.

Taylor, F. W. (1911). *The principles of scientific management.* New York: W. W. Norton.

Terborg, J. R., & Davis, G. A. (1982). Evaluation of a new method for assessing change to planned job redesign as applied to Hackman and Oldham's job characteristic model. *Organizational Behavior and Human Performance, 29,* 112–128.

Thomas, K. W., & Velthouse, B. A. (1990). Cognitive elements of empowerment: An interpretive model of intrinsic task motivation. *Academy of Management Review, 15,* 666–681.

Tiegs, R. B., Tetrick, L. E., & Fried, Y. (1992). Growth need strength and context satisfactions as moderators of the relations of the job characteristics model. *Journal of Management, 18,* 575–593.

Tourangeau, R., & Rasinski, K. A. (1988). Cognitive processes underlying context effects in attitude measurement. *Psychological Bulletin, 103,* 299–314.

Trist, E. L. (1981). The sociotechnical perspective. In A. H. Van de Ven & W. F. Joyce (Eds.), *Perspectives on organization design and behavior* (pp. 19–75). New York: Wiley.

Trist, E. L., & Bamforth, K. M. (1951). Some social and psychological consequences of the longwall method of coal-getting. *Human Relations, 4,* 3–38.

Turner, A. N., & Lawrence, P. R. (1965). *Industrial jobs and the worker.* Boston: Harvard University Press.

Umstot, D. D., Bell, C. H., & Mitchell, T. R. (1976). Effects of job enrichment and task goals on satisfaction and productivity: Implications for job design. *Journal of Applied Psychology, 61,* 379–394.

van der Vegt, G., Emans, B., & van de Vliert, E. (1998). Motivating effects of task and outcome interdependence in work teams. *Group and Organization Management, 23,* 124–143.

Vance, R. J., & Biddle, T. F. (1985). Task experience and social cues: Interactive effects on attitudinal reactions. *Organizational Behavior and Human Decision Processes, 35,* 252–265.

Wall, T. D., Clegg, C. W., Davies, R. T., Kemp, N. J., & Mueller, W. S. (1987). Advanced manufacturing technology and work simplification: An empirical study. *Journal of Occupational Behavior, 8,* 233–250.

Wall, T. D., Corbett, M., Martin, R., Clegg, C. W., & Jackson, P. R. (1990). Advanced manufacturing technology, work design, and performance: A change study. *Journal of Applied Psychology, 75,* 691–697.

Wall, T. D., & Jackson, P. R. (1995). New manufacturing initiatives and shopfloor job design. In A. Howard (Ed.), *The changing nature of work* (pp. 139–174). San Francisco: Jossey-Bass.

Wall, T. D., Jackson, P. R., & Davids, K. (1992). Operator work design and robotics system performance: A serendipitous field study. *Journal of Applied Psychology, 77,* 353–362.

Wall, T. D., Jackson, P. R., & Mullarkey, S. (1995). Further evidence on some new measures of job control, cognitive demand and production responsibility. *Journal of Organizational Behavior, 16,* 431–455.

Wall, T. D., & Martin, R. (Eds.). (1987). *Job and work design.* New York: Wiley.

Weiss, H. M., & Shaw, J. B. (1979). Social influences on judgments about tasks. *Organizational Behavior and Human Performance, 24,* 126–140.

White, J. K. (1978). Individual differences and the job quality— worker response relationship: Review, integration, and comments. *Academy of Management Review, 3,* 267–280.

White, S. E., & Mitchell, T. R. (1979). Job enrichment versus social cues: A comparison and competitive test. *Journal of Applied Psychology, 64,* 1–9.

Wong, C., & Campion, M. A. (1991). Development and test of a task level model of motivational job design. *Journal of Applied Psychology, 76,* 825–837.

Wright, B. M., & Cordery, J. L. (1999). Production uncertainty as a contextual moderator of employee reactions to job design. *Journal of Applied Psychology, 84,* 456–463.

Wrzesniewski, A., & Dutton, J. E. (2001). Crafting a job: Revisioning employees as active crafters of their work. *Academy of Management Review, 26,* 179–201.

CHAPTER 18

Stress in Organizations

SABINE SONNENTAG AND MICHAEL FRESE

Stress in organizations is a widespread phenomenon with far-reaching practical and economic consequences. A report published by the National Institute for Occupational Safety and Health (1999) in the United States summarized findings from various surveys on organizational stress and found that between 26 and 40% of all surveyed workers experienced their work as very stressful. Similarly, 28% of the workers in the European Union reported that their work causes stress (Levi & Lunde-Jensen, 1996). In Japan, the percentage is even higher than either of these (Harnois & Gabriel, 2000).

Experiencing organizational stress is related to health problems and their associated costs. A study based on more than 46,000 U.S. employees showed that health care costs were 46% higher for workers who experienced high levels of stress (Goetzel et al., 1998). Moreover, organizational stress is assumed to be related to increased absenteeism. For example, estimates from the U.S. and England suggest that about the half of all lost days within organizations are related to workplace stress (Cooper, Liukkonen, & Cartwright, 1996;

Elkin & Rosch, 1990). Absenteeism costs organizations billions of dollars per year (Cox, Griffiths, & Rial-Gonzáles, 2000). In the long run, stress might lead to disabilities. Data from the Netherlands show that 30% of all cases of disability pensions are due to stress-related disorders (Van der Hek & Plomp, 1997), and similar findings exist for other countries. Moreover, mortality rates were found to be related to occupational groups—that is, to work-specific stressors (Fletcher, 1991).

Because of this practical relevance of workplace stress, there is an enormous and still ongoing research activity within the field of organizational stress (Beehr, 1995). Findings from past research have been summarized in previous review chapters and journal articles (Beehr & Newman, 1978; Danna & Griffin, 1999; Ganster & Schaubroeck, 1991; Kahn & Byosiere, 1992; McGrath, 1976; Sullivan & Bhagat, 1992). Many researchers criticized organizational stress studies for methodological weaknesses (Frese & Zapf, 1988; Kasl, 1978). Their main concerns referred to the following issues: The overwhelming majority of the empirical studies are cross-sectional in nature and do not allow inferences on causality. In many studies the independent and dependent measures share common method variance and overlap in content. Most studies focus on bivariate, linear

We are grateful to Paul Spector and Doris Fay for their helpful comments and suggestions on an earlier version of this chapter.

relationships and neglect possible moderator and nonlinear effects.

Nevertheless, over the years researchers witnessed methodological improvements in organizational stress studies (Beehr, 1998; Kahn & Byosiere, 1992), particularly during the past 10 years; the improvements include (a) a better operationalization of basic concepts that allow a better test of theoretical models (e.g., Edwards & Harrison, 1993; Wall, Jackson, Mullarkey, & Parker, 1996); (b) an increasing number of studies that use objective measures of stressors (Greiner, Ragland, Krause, Syme, & Fisher, 1997; Melamed, Ben-Avi, Luz, & Green, 1995); (c) a steady increase in longitudinal studies, with many of them using a structural equation modeling approach for data analysis (e.g., Bakker, Schaufeli, Sixma, Bosveld, & van Dierendonck, 2000; Dormann & Zapf, 1999; Schonfeld, 1992); (d) exploration of curvilinear effects (e.g., de Jonge & Schaufeli, 1998; Dollard, Winefield, Winefield, & de Jonge, 2000; Warr, 1990); and (e) use of innovative approaches such as multilevel designs (e.g., Jex & Bliese, 1999) and growth curve models (e.g., Barnett & Brennan, 1997; Garst, Frese, & Molenaar, 2000).

This chapter reviews research on stress in organizations and its practical implications. It aims at an extension of previous reviews by focusing more strongly on methodologically sound—although not perfect—studies. This gives us the opportunity to examine more deeply the processes and consequences associated with organizational stress. Specifically, we address the question of whether methodologically improved studies contribute to a better understanding of organizational stress. Most of the more recent review chapters and articles have exclusively looked at health and well-being consequences of organizational stress (Danna & Griffin, 1999; Ganster & Schaubroeck, 1991; Kahn & Byosiere, 1992). We broaden the view by including performance and other organizational behavior issues (e.g., organizational commitment and absenteeism).

In the first section of this chapter, we describe the stress concept and give an overview of stressors and stress reactions. In the second section, we present theories of organizational stress. The third section is devoted to empirical findings in organizational stress research. We describe the empirical evidence of main and moderator effects on the relationship between stressors and individual health and well-being. We summarize research findings on the relationship between stress and performance. In addition, we refer to the effects of stress on other aspects of organizational behavior. In the fourth section, we describe stress management interventions. In conclusion, we suggest a few research questions for the future.

THE STRESS CONCEPT

Overview of Conceptualizations of Stress

On the most general level, one can differentiate between four stress concepts: (a) the stimulus concept, (b) the response concept, (c) the transactional concept, and (d) the discrepancy concept. The stimulus concept focuses on situational conditions or events. Within this conceptualization, certain stimuli are stressful—for example, high time pressure, interpersonal conflict at work, or accidents. However, the stimulus concept is problematic because not all individuals react in a uniform manner to the same stressor. Nearly every situational condition or every event may evoke strain in some individuals. Although the stimulus conceptualization leads to conceptual problems, many researchers agree that there are subsets of stimuli that evoke strain in most individuals (Brief & George, 1995; Kahn & Byosiere, 1992).

The reaction concept focuses on physiological reactions as the crucial constituent of stress—that is, stress exists if an individual shows a specific reaction pattern regardless of situational characteristics (Selye, 1956). However, this conceptualization also has its shortcomings. It does not take into account that very different situations can result in the same physiological responses and that an individual's coping efforts may have an effect on that individual's reactions, thus altering the stress response.

Another class of concepts refers both to the situation and to the person when defining stress. The transactional concept brought forward by Lazarus (1966) assumes that stress results from a transaction between the individual and the environment, including the individual's perceptions, expectations, interpretations, and coping responses. In terms of operationalization and measuring stress in empirical studies, this concept has not yet fully developed its potential. Often, proponents of the transactional concept actually rely in their research practice exclusively on verbal responses or physiological measures of strain as indicators of stress. By doing so, they implicitly apply the reaction concept. The discrepancy concept describes stress as an incongruity between an individual's desires and the environment (Edwards, 1992); in operationalizing such a discrepancy, however, researchers face great difficulties.

Thus, *stress* is a broad term that conveys a variety of meanings. To avoid ambiguity, we refer to *stressors* and *stress reactions* or *strain* throughout this chapter. We use the terms *strains* and *stress reactions* synonymously.

Stressors

Stressors are conditions and events that evoke strain (Kahn & Byosiere, 1992). Stressors can be single events such as critical

TABLE 18.1   Overview of Stressors in Organizational Life

Physical stressors
Task-related job stressors
Role stressors
Social stressors
Work-schedule-related stressors
Career-related stressors
Traumatic events
Stressful change processes

life events or traumatic experiences, and they can also be chronic problems that continue over a longer period of time. The latter often are microstressors, so-called daily hassles (Kanner, Coyne, Schaefer, & Lazarus, 1981)—for example, daily difficulties with finishing one's work in time or daily problems in dealing with difficult clients.

Stressors can be grouped into the categories *physical stressors, task-related job stressors, role stressors, social stressors, work-schedule-related stressors, career-related stressors, traumatic events,* and *stressful change processes* (Table 18.1).

Physical stressors refer to aversive physical working conditions, including noise, dirt, heat, vibrations, chemical, or toxic substances. They also include poor ergonomic conditions at the workplace and accidents. Physical stressors have psychological effects (Seeber & Iregren, 1992). *Task-related* job stressors appear while the employee is doing a task; these stressors include high time pressure and work overload, high complexity at work, monotonous work, and disruptions (e.g., caused by an unexpected computer shutdown). *Role stressors* fall into role ambiguity and role conflict. *Social stressors* express themselves in poor social interactions with direct supervisors, coworkers, and others. These stressors include interpersonal conflicts at the workplace, (sexual) harassment, and mobbing or bullying (Zapf, Knorz, & Kulla, 1996). Additionally, having to deal with extremely difficult customers can also be conceptualized as social stressor. *Work-schedule-related stressors* stem from working time arrangements. The most prominent and well-researched stressors in this category are night and shift work. Additionally, long working hours and overtime belong to this category (Sparks, Cooper, Fried, & Shirom, 1997). *Career-related stressors* include job insecurity and poor career opportunities. *Traumatic stressors* are single events such as the exposure to disasters, major accidents, or extremely dangerous activities. Soldiers, police personnel, and firefighters are assumed to be particularly prone to the exposure of traumatic stressors (Corneil, Beaton, Murphy, Johnson, & Pike, 1999). *Organizational change* can also be regarded as a stressor. Examples include mergers, downsizing, or the implementation of new technologies. They are stressful because they

may result in other stressors such as job insecurity, overtime, and conflicts.

These categories make sense intuitively but largely lack an explicit theoretical foundation. There are only a few theoretically derived taxonomies of stressors. These taxonomies cover parts of potential stressors. Probably the most prominent taxonomy is the delineation of role stressors from role theory (Katz & Kahn, 1978). Role stressors comprise role overload, role conflict, and role ambiguity. Role overload occurs when individuals have to do too much or too complicated work, role conflict refers to situations with conflicting role expectations, and role ambiguity refers to situations with unclear role expectations. Many studies have been conducted on this successful model. Jackson and Schuler (1985) and Tubbs and Collins (2000) meta-analyzed findings from these studies and showed clear relationships between role stressors and impaired well-being.

Semmer (1984) and Leitner, Volpert, Greiner, Weber, and Hennes (1987) proposed a taxonomy of stressors based on action theory (cf. Frese & Zapf, 1994; Hacker, 1998). This taxonomy clusters stressors on the basis of how they disturb the regulation of goal-oriented action. Specifically, this taxonomy differentiates between regulation obstacles, regulation uncertainty, and overtaxing regulations. Regulation obstacles such as interruptions or organizational constraints make action regulation more difficult—if not impossible. Regulation uncertainty refers to uncertainties about how to reach the goal and includes stressors such as lack of appropriate feedback, role conflicts, and role ambiguity. In the case of overtaxing regulation, the speed and intensity of the regulation is the major problem. Typical examples are time pressure and requirement to concentrate. This taxonomy has been successfully used in some studies (e.g., Frese, 1985; Greiner et al., 1997; Leitner, 1993).

There is a long and ongoing debate on objective versus subjective approaches to the study of work stress (Frese & Zapf, 1988; Frese & Zapf, 1999; Kasl, 1998; Perrewé & Zellars, 1999; Schaubroeck, 1999). Often, subjective approaches have been linked to the use of self-report measures, whereas measures not using self-report were labeled objective. However, the distinction between objective and subjective approaches is not such a simple one. Frese and Zapf (1988) suggested another distinction: Objective approaches focus on events, processes, and workplace characteristics that are not related to the job holder's perceptions and that exist regardless of the individual's cognitive and emotional reactions. Subjective approaches in contrast refer to events, processes, and workplace characteristics as perceived and appraised by the job holder. This debate is particularly important with respect to practical implications: It makes sense to redesign jobs when strains can be attributed to objective stressors and not only to appraisal processes.

Stress Reactions

Stress in organizations affects both the individual and the organization (e.g., increased turnover rates). Individuals can be affected at the physiological, affective, and behavioral level, and in their leisure time and family life. Stressors affect individuals and organizations within different time frames; stress reactions can occur immediately (short-term reactions) or may take longer time to develop (long-term reactions). Table 18.2 gives an overview of stress reactions.

With respect to physiological responses, stress has an effect on the *cardiac system*. For example, individuals in so-called high-strain jobs (i.e., job with high demands and low job control, cf. Karasek, 1979) show blood pressure higher than that of individuals in other types of jobs (Schwartz, Pickering, & Landsbergis, 1996). Furthermore, the heart rate increases in stress situations (Frankenhaeuser & Johansson, 1976). Moreover, experiencing a stressful work situation is associated with increased levels of cholesterol and other metabolic and hemostatic risk factors for cardiovascular disease (Vrijkotte, van Doornen, & de Geus, 1999).

The cardiac system is partly affected by hormones. Stress affects the excretion of *hormones* such as catecholamines and corticosteroids (e.g., cortisol). With respect to catecholamines, it is well documented that the excretion of epinephrine (adrenaline) and norepinephrine (noradrenaline) increases as stress increases (Aronsson & Rissler, 1998; Frankenhaeuser, 1979; Frankenhaeuser & Johansson, 1976). The excretion of catecholamines seems to increase most when stressful working conditions are combined with inflexible working arrangements (Johansson, Aronsson, & Lindström,

1978; Melin, Lundberg, Soederlund, & Granqvist, 1999). With increasing work demands, the excretion of cortisol increases (Aronsson & Rissler, 1998). This increase in cortisol is most prominent when stress becomes chronic (Schulz, Kirschbaum, Prüssner, & Hellhammer, 1998). These physiological reactions—particularly the excretion of catecholamines and effects on the cardiac system—help in mobilizing additional effort for completing work assignments and upholding performance (Lundberg & Frankenhaeuser, 1978). However, when experienced repeatedly and over a longer period of time, these physiological reactions may contribute to the development of illnesses, including coronary heart diseases.

Stress also has an effect on the *immune functioning* (Herbert & Sheldon, 1993). Experiencing high levels of stress is detrimental to an individual's immune system. Although the exact underlying processes are still unclear, stress is associated with an increased risk of physical illnesses in the long run. Individuals experiencing high work stress are more likely to develop cardiovascular problems (Schnall, Landsbergis, & Baker, 1994) or musculoskeletal diseases (Bongers, de Winter, Kompier, & Hildebrandt, 1993). The experience of stress is associated with *affective reactions*. In the short term, mood disturbances can occur (Zohar, 1999). Such affective reactions seem to result mainly from specific aversive events and stressful achievement settings (Pekrun & Frese, 1992; Weiss & Cropanzano, 1996). In the long run, well-being and mental health can suffer. Evidence from longitudinal studies suggests that stressful work situations are associated with an increased level of depressive symptoms (Schonfeld, 1992), psychosomatic complaints (Frese, 1985; Parkes, Menham, & Rabenau, 1994) and other distress symptoms (Leitner, 1993). Burnout is another long-term stress reaction. It is characterized by emotional exhaustion, depersonalization (cynicism), and reduced personal accomplishment (Maslach & Jackson, 1981). Burnout has been largely studied in human service and educational occupations, but there is increasing evidence that often members of other occupational groups also react with burnout symptoms to stressful work situations (Maslach, Schaufeli, & Leiter, 2001).

Stressors can also have negative effects on the *behavioral level*. For example, in stressful situations attention is narrowed and working memory capacity is reduced. Moreover, reduced performance accuracy can be observed (Searle, Bright, & Bochner, 1999). When confronted with a stressor, individuals often increase their effort (Hockey, 1997). As a consequence, overall performance does not necessarily suffer from stressful situations (Tafalla & Evans, 1997). Moreover, it has been observed that stressors in the work situation are related to violence such as sabotage, interpersonal aggression, and hostility (Chen & Spector, 1992).

TABLE 18.2   Overview of Stress Reactions

	Short-Term Reactions	Long-Term Reactions
Experienced by the individual		
Physical	Physiological reactions	Physical illness
Affective	Disturbed mood	Poor well-being
Behavioral	Cognitive reactions	and mental health
	Increased effort	problems
	Performance decrease[a]	
	Accidents	
Experienced by larger organizational units		
	Interpersonal conflicts	Increased turnover
		Absence rates
Experienced outside work		
	Slow unwinding	Poor well-being
	Spillover of disturbed	in other life
	mood to private life	domains
		Physical illness

[a]Performance decrease was mainly found in laboratory but not in field studies.

Stressors encountered at work are also related to other aspects of organizational behavior. There is clear evidence that individuals who experience stressors are less committed to the organization (Mathieu & Zajac, 1990). Stressors are associated with turnover intentions (Chen & Spector, 1992) and actual turnover.

Stress experienced at work can also become obvious *outside the work situation*. Mood disturbances associated with stressful working situations generalize to the individual's private life (Doby & Caplan, 1995; Repetti, 1993; Totterdell, Spelten, Smith, Barton, & Folkard, 1995). There is increasing evidence from time sampling studies that mood experienced in one domain (e.g., work) spills over to another domain (e.g., family; e.g., Williams & Alliger, 1994).

Moreover, experiencing a stressful work situation has effects on unwinding processes. For example, Frankenhaeuser (1981) examined adrenaline excretion rates during periods of high workload and showed that adrenaline excretion rates remained elevated during leisure time in the evening. This high level of adrenaline excretion during the evening makes it difficult for individuals to unwind and recover from their stressful work situations (cf. also Meijman, Mulder, & Van Dormolen, 1992, for similar findings).

Additionally, stress reactions might not be limited to the person who him- or herself is exposed to the stressful situation. For example, an observational study showed that mothers' behavior towards their preschool children differed between stressful and unstressful workdays (Repetti & Wood, 1997).

THEORIES ON ORGANIZATIONAL STRESS

Theories can be differentiated in models that describe the stress process itself and models that explain stress reactions—that is, the relationship between stressors and strains. The first type of model describes what happens when an individual is exposed to a stressor, whereas the second type of model specifies configurations of stressors that are associated with strains. Typically, this second type of model neglects process aspects.

It is beyond the scope of this chapter to provide an exhaustive presentation of all theories and models. Instead, we concentrate on those models that have been influential in past theorizing and empirical research and on those that offer promising prospects for future research and practice. Interested readers may refer to Cooper (1998) and Kahn and Byosiere (1992) for descriptions of more models.

Theoretical Models Focusing on the Stress Process

These models aim at a detailed description of what happens during the stress process. Major models in the area are the transactional stress model (Lazarus, 1966; Lazarus & Folkman, 1984) and (other) cybernetic models (Edwards, 1992).

The Transactional Stress Model

One the most prominent stress models is the transactional model by Lazarus (1966; Lazarus & Folkman, 1984). Lazarus and Folkman define psychological stress as "a particular relationship between the person and the environment that is appraised by the person as taxing or exceeding his or her resources and endangering his or her well-being" (p. 19). Thus, Lazarus and Folkman assume that cognitive appraisals play a crucial role in the stress process. Appraisal processes refer to an individual's categorization and evaluation of an encounter with respect to this individual's well-being. Specifically, primary and secondary appraisal can be differentiated. By primary appraisal, encounters are categorized as irrelevant, benign-positive, or stressful. Stress appraisals comprise harm-loss, threat, and challenge. By secondary appraisals, individuals evaluate what can be done in the face of the stressful encounter—that is, they tax their coping options. On the basis of primary and secondary appraisals, individuals start their coping processes that can stimulate reappraisal processes.

To arrive at a better understanding of the stress process and how it develops over time, Lazarus (1991) suggested putting more emphasis on an intra-individual analysis of the stress phenomenon—for example, by studying the same persons in different contexts over time. A few studies followed such an approach (Folkman, Lazarus, Dunkel-Schetter, DeLongis, & Gruen, 1986); the majority of empirical studies in the area of organizational stress, however, did not adopt such a process perspective, but rather treated stressful situations and individuals' reactions to the situations as stable. Moreover, it has been questioned whether a focus on individual processes offers much to the understanding of workplace stress (Brief & George, 1995).

Cybernetic Model

Edwards (1992) proposed a cybernetic model of organizational stress (for a related model, cf. Cummings & Cooper, 1979, 1998). Edwards summarized earlier approaches to stress that implicitly assumed cybernetic principles (e.g., Kahn, Wolfe, Quinn, Snoek, & Rosenthal, 1964; McGrath, 1976) and explicitly built on Carver and Scheier's (1982) work on cybernetics as a general theory of human behavior. Crucial components in Carver and Scheier's model are an input function, a reference value, a comparator, and an output function. The input function refers to perceptions of one's own state or of situational features in the environment. The reference value comprises the individual's desires, values, or goals. The comparator compares the input function with the reference value. The output function refers to behavior that is activated when a discrepancy between the input function and the reference value is detected.

Edwards (1992) defines stress as "a discrepancy between an employee's perceived state and desired state, provided that the presense of this discrepancy is considered important by the employee" (p. 245). Thus, stress occurs when the comparison between an individual's perception and his or her desire results in a discrepancy. The perception is assumed to be influenced by the physical and social environment, personal characteristics of the individual, the individual's cognitive construction of reality, and social information. The discrepancy between perception and desires (i.e., stress), affects two outcomes: the individual's well-being and his or her coping efforts. Additionally, reciprocal effects between well-being and coping are assumed. Moreover, coping may have an effect on the person and the situation, the individual's desires, and the duration of the stressful situation and the importance attached to it. The effects of the discrepancy on well-being and coping efforts are moderated by additional factors such as the importance of the discrepancy and its duration.

Although there is empirical research on isolated aspects of the cybernetic model (e.g., on the effects of discrepancies between perceptions and desires on well-being (cf. Edwards, 1991), to our knowledge, no study on organizational stress has yet examined the cybernetic framework as a whole. One reason is that it is difficult to examine the crucial assumptions of this model in one single study. Such a study must include separate measures of perceptions, desires, importance, duration, well-being, and coping. The greatest challenge will be to design nonconfounded measures of individual perception, objective characteristics of the environment, the individual's cognitive construction of reality, and social information processes.

Theoretical Models on the Relationship Between Stressful Situations and Strains

These models specify the configuration of workplace factors that are associated with strains—that is, stress reactions. Major models include the person-environment fit theory (Harrison, 1978), job demand-job control model (Karasek, 1979), the vitamin model (Warr, 1987) and the effort-reward imbalance model (Siegrist, 1996).

Person-Environment Fit Theory

Person-environment (P-E) fit theory assumes that stress occurs because of an incongruity between the individual and the environment (for an overview, cf. Edwards, 1998; Harrison, 1978). Thus, it is neither the person nor the situation alone that causes stress experiences and strains. There are two types of incongruity between an individual and the environment. The first type refers to the fit between the demands of the environment and the abilities and competencies of the persons. The second type refers to the fit between the needs of the person and supplies from the environment.

At the conceptual level, P-E fit theory differentiates between the objective and the subjective person as well as between the objective and the subjective environment (Harrison, 1978). *Objective person* and *objective environment* refer to the individual needs, abilities, and competencies and to environmental supplies and demands as they actually exist—that is, independent of the person's perceptions. *Subjective person* and *subjective environment* refer to the individual's perceptions. Therefore, fit can refer to the congruence between (a) objective environment and objective person, (b) subjective environment and subjective person, (c) subjective and objective environment (i.e., contact with reality) and (d) subjective and objective person (i.e., accuracy of self-assessment).

The theory argues that the objective person and environment affect the subjective person and environment and that incongruity between the subjective environment and the subjective person produces strain. Strain increases as demands exceed abilities and as needs exceed supplies. When abilities exceed demands, strain may increase, decrease, or remain stable. Similarly, when supplies exceed needs, strain may increase, decrease, or remain stable. The exact picture of the relationships depends of the content and importance of the dimension in question.

In a classic study, French, Caplan, and Harrison (1982) explicitly tested P-E fit theory. Indeed, P-E misfit was associated with psychological, physical, and biological strains. Subsequent studies on P-E fit resulted in similar findings and identified a needs-supplies incongruity as the strongest predictor of strain (Edwards, 1991). However, many of these studies have been criticized for methodological shortcomings, particularly the operationalization of P-E fit as a difference score (Edwards, 1995). More recent studies—most of them published after 1990—overcame these problems by examining three-dimensional relationships of the person and environment with strain measures. These studies partially confirmed the basic assumption of P-E fit theory—that is, that strain increases as fit between the person and his or her work environment decreases (Edwards, 1996; Edwards & Harrison, 1993). These studies also pointed to complex patterns including curvilinear relationships; taken together, the studies do provide some empirical support for the P-E fit model. However, longitudinal studies are still missing. Therefore, a final conclusion about this model would be premature.

Job Demand-Job Control Model

The job demand-job control model differentiates between two basic dimensions of work place factors—namely, job demands and job decision latitude (Karasek, 1979). Job demands are the workload demands put on the individual. Job decision latitude refers to the employee's decision authority and his or her skill discretion. Karasek combined the two dimensions of job demands and job decision latitude in a two-by-two matrix of jobs: jobs low on demands and low on decision latitude (*passive* jobs), jobs low on demands and high on decision latitude (*low-strain* jobs), jobs high on demands and low on decision latitude (*high-strain* jobs) and jobs high on demands and high on decision latitude (*active* jobs).

With respect to stress reactions, Karasek (1979) states that the combination of high demands and low decision latitude in the high-strain jobs is most detrimental for people's health and well-being. The combination of high demands and high decision latitude in the active jobs, however, are assumed to produce little harm for the individual. Stated differently, the model basically assumes that high decision latitude attenuates the negative effects of high demands.

During the past two decades, the job demand-job control model stimulated a large amount of empirical research. There is substantial (although not unequivocal) support for the model. We discuss findings from this research in more detail later in this chapter. A theoretical critique is given by Kasl (1996).

Vitamin Model

Warr (1987) proposed a vitamin model to specify the relationships between stressors and employee health and well-being. The vitamin model claims nonlinear relationships develop between work characteristics and individual outcomes. Drawing an analogy to the effects of vitamins on the human body, Warr assumes that there are two types of work characteristics. First, some features of the work situation have a constant effect on the individual—that is, they have an effect that increases up to a certain point, but then any added increase of the level of this work characteristic does not have any further effects (neither beneficial nor detrimental effects). Warr likens these effects to characteristics to vitamin C. Examples are salary, safety, and task significance. For example, people need the vitamin of salary up to a certain point. Therefore, people's well-being increases with having more income; at a certain level, however, any additional salary increase will not have any further increase

of people's well-being. Second, other work features have a curvilinear relationship between the level of this work characteristic and well-being. Warr likens these to the vitamin D, which is positive to a certain dose, but then every further increase has a negative effect. Examples of these work features are job autonomy, social support, and skill utilization. For example, a low degree of job autonomy is detrimental to well-being. Therefore, up to a certain level, job autonomy increases well-being. If job autonomy is further increased, job autonomy becomes negative because people are overwhelmed with the responsibilities that job autonomy implies.

In terms of stress, this model implies that a specific amount of job autonomy, job demands, social support, skill utilization, skill variety, and task feedback is beneficial for the individual, but a very high level of these job characteristics creates a stressful situation. In contrast, high levels of salary, safety, and task significance do not show this detrimental effect.

Empirical studies on the vitamin model are still rare, and support for the curvilinear relationships between workplace factors and strain variables is mixed. Some studies did not find any significant curvilinear relationship (e.g., Parkes, 1991), whereas others gave support to the vitamin model (e.g., de Jonge & Schaufeli, 1998; Warr, 1990). Warr found curvilinear relationships between job demands and several strain measures such as job-related anxiety, job-related depression, and low job satisfaction; a curvilinear relationship was also found between autonomy and job satisfaction. De Jonge and Schaufeli (1998) found evidence for curvilinear relationships between job demands, job autonomy, and social support on the one hand and employee well-being on the other hand.

Effort-Reward Imbalance Model

A variant of a P-E fit model is Siegrist's (1996) effort-reward imbalance model. Basically, the effort-reward imbalance model assumes that a lack of reciprocity between costs and rewards are experienced as stressful and result in strains. More specifically, the model states that the degree to which an individual's efforts at work are rewarded or not is crucial for that person's health and well-being. Effort may be the response to both extrinsic and intrinsic demands. Extrinsic demands refer to obligations and demands inherent in the situation. Intrinsic demands result from a high need for control or approval. Rewards comprise money, esteem, and status control, such as job stability, status consistency, and career advancement. In essence, the model assumes that situations in which high efforts do not correspond to high rewards result in emotional distress situations—particularly high autonomic arousal.

A number of studies showed that a combination of high effort and low reward predicted self-reported health complaints, cardiovascular risk factors, and manifestations of coronary heart disease (Bosma, Peter, Siegrist, & Marmot, 1998; de Jonge, Bosma, Peter, & Siegrist, 2000; Peter, Geissler, & Siegrist, 1998; for a summary cf. Siegrist, 1998). Most interesting is that a longitudinal study with blue-collar workers showed that experiencing an effort-reward imbalance was associated with 6.15 times the risk of developing coronary heart disease 6.5 years later (Siegrist, Peter, Junge, Cremer, & Seidel, 1990; cf. also the similar results by Bosma et al., 1998).

Comparison of Models

Unfortunately, there are few empirical studies that directly compare different models; this is unfortunate because only a direct comparison can tell which theories are superior. Moreover, modern analysis methods—like structural equation analysis—allow and encourage such comparisons. For example, Elsass and Veiga (1997) tested the job demand-job control model and the P-E fit model with the same sample. Their data supported the P-E fit model, but not the job demand-job control model. Similarly, de Jonge et al. (2000) compared the job demand-job control model and the effort-reward imbalance model. These authors also reported better fit indexes for the effort-reward imbalance model than for the job demand-job control model. This might suggest that the P-E fit and the effort-reward imbalance models are superior to the job demand-job control model in explaining employee well-being. In the future, more such analyses are needed.

EMPIRICAL EVIDENCE

Main Effects of Stressful Situations on Individual Well-Being and Health

There is consistent evidence that perceived stressors at work are related to indicators of poor health and well-being (for meta-analyses, cf. Jackson & Schuler, 1985; Lee & Ashforth, 1996). However, most of these studies are cross-sectional in nature and based on same-source self-report measures. Many researchers criticized these predominant features of organizational stress research (Frese & Zapf, 1988; Kasl, 1978; Zapf, Dormann, & Frese, 1996). Cross-sectional designs allow no inference about causality, empirical relationships between stressors and strains might be due to third variables such as social class or negative affectivity, and strains may affect stressors—for example, in the sense of the drift hypothesis. A drift hypothesis implies that individuals with poor health are unable to retain favorable working conditions

in the long run, whereas healthier individuals are promoted into better—that is, less stressful—jobs (Frese, 1985). Health and well-being might also affect the perception of stressors because individuals with poor health overestimate the stressfulness of their jobs (Zapf, 1989). Additionally, same-source measures often used in organizational stress research share common method variance and therefore may result in an overestimation of true relationships.

Evidence From Studies With Objective Measures of Stressors

To examine whether the relationship between stressors and strains can be primarily explained by the use of self-report measures and the associated methodological problems, studies are needed in which stressors are assessed by non-self-report measures. There is an increasing number of such studies. In some of these studies, researchers inferred objective stressors from occupational titles and similar information. Analyses revealed significant relationships between stressful jobs and poor health and well-being. For example, Tsutsumi, Theorell, Hallqvist, Reuterwall, and de Faire (1999) reported increased odd ratios of plasma fibrinogen concentrations—a physiological indicator assumed to be associated with coronary heart disease—in study participants working in highly demanding jobs.

Other researchers assessed objective stressors by means of observations. These studies also showed association between objective stressors and impaired health and well-being. For example, Frese (1985) found correlations of $r = .18$ and $r = .19$ between observer ratings of psychological stressors and psychosomatic complaints. Melamed et al. (1995) measured monotony with observational ratings and found that short-cycle and medium–cycle repetitive work was significantly associated with psychological distress, particularly in women. Greiner et al. (1997) reported increased odd ratios of psychosomatic complaints in observed high-stress jobs.

In summary, these findings show that stressors at work are related to poor health and well-being—even when objective measures of stressors are used. Often the correlations between objective stressor measures and strains are smaller in size than are the correlations between self-report measures of stressors and strains (cf. Frese, 1985), but they do not break down completely; this suggests that common method variance inflates the relationships between self-reported stressors and self-reported strains, but it does not fully explain the empirical relationship between organizational stressors and strains. For methodological reasons, the correlations found between objective stressors and self-reported strains present the lower boundary of the stressor-illness relationships (Frese, 1993).

Evidence From Longitudinal Studies

To arrive at a clearer picture about the causal processes between stressors and strains, longitudinal studies are needed. Although they do not solve all the methodological problems (Zapf, Dormann, et al., 1996), they at least allow researchers to rule out some of the alternative interpretations. Table 18.3 gives an overview over longitudinal studies published between 1981 and 2000 that meet the following criteria: (a) data collection on work-related stressors and strains and (b) control for initial level of strains in the analyses.

Table 18.3 shows the number of time lags, the time interval between the various measurement points, sample size, type of stressors assessed, type of strains assessed, results with respect to lagged effects, concurrent effects, reverse effects (i.e., effects of strains on stressors), and nonsignificant findings. Most of the studies assessed data at two measurement points. Time lags ranged between 1 month and 180 months, with most studies using time lags of 12 months or less. A wide range of stressors were assessed, including workload, social stressors, and job insecurity. Also strain measured covered a large variety of indicators, including physiological measures, distress symptoms, depression, psychosomatic complaints, and physical illnesses. Most researchers analyzed their data with variants of cross-lagged panel correlations (CLPC), multiple regression analyses, or structural equation approaches (e.g., LISREL).

We discuss the study findings separately for concurrent, lagged, and reverse effects. Concurrent effects refer to synchronous effects of stressors (Time 2) on strain (Time 2) with controlling for strain (Time 1). Lagged effects imply effects of stressors (Time 1) on strain (Time 2) when controlling for strain (Time 1). Reverse effects refer to effects of strains (Time 1) on stressors (Time 2) with controlling for stressors (Time 1; drift hypothesis).

Most studies that examined *concurrent effects* focused on psychological strains (exceptions: Howard, Cunningham, & Rechniter, 1986; Spector, Chen, & O'Connell, 2000, which looked at physiological strain). About half of the studies found concurrent effects of all measured stressors on strains. The other half of the studies found support for relationships between some combinations of stressors and strains. Stressors with concurrent effects on strains included workload, role conflicts, and role ambiguity. Strains affected were depressive symptoms, burnout, and fatigue spillover into leisure time.

There was no systematic pattern of stressor-strain relationships for which concurrent effects were found.

Studies that addressed *lagged effects* of stressful work situations examined both psychological and physical strain symptoms. Psychological symptoms included strains such as distress, anxiety, depressive symptoms, and exhaustion. Physical symptoms included mainly (psycho)somatic health complaints, cardiovascular disease, and other illnesses. Lagged effects of stressors on psychological strain symptoms appeared in more than half of the studies, at least for some of the stressors or strains tested. Significant effects were more often found when stressors such as high demands and high workload were examined (as opposed to social stressors), when the time lag was relatively short (not longer than 12 months), and when no concurrent effects were tested simultaneously.

There is rather strong evidence that stressors at work have a lagged effect on physical strain symptoms, particularly (psycho)somatic health complaints (Carayon, 1993; Frese, 1985; Leitner, 1993; Parkes et al., 1994; for an exception, cf. Mauno & Kinnunen, 1999). Stressors have lagged effects on cardiovascular disease, particularly in men (Hibbard & Pope, 1993; Karasek, Baker, Marxner, Ahlbom, & Theorell, 1981). However, stressors seems to have none or only a minor lagged effect on other illnesses such as cancer (Hibbard & Pope, 1993). Taken together, these longitudinal studies suggest that there are lagged effects of stressors on strains, particularly if the time lag between two measurement points does not exceed 12 months.

Most of the studies tested either concurrent or lagged effects. The majority of these studies found evidence for an effect of stressors on strains, at least for some of the stressor or strain indicators. There are only a few studies that analyzed both lagged and concurrent effects within the same data set (Glickman, Tanaka, & Chan, 1991; Kohn & Schooler, 1982; Moyle, 1998; Roy & Steptoe, 1994; Schonfeld, 1992; Wolpin, Burke, & Greenglass, 1991). All these studies found concurrent effects (at least for some of the indicators). However, half of the studies failed to find lagged effects when concurrent effects were present. Only Wolpin et al. (1991), Schonfeld (1992), and Moyle (1998) reported lagged effects in the presence of concurrent effects. These findings indicate that individuals develop distress reactions to stressful situations rather quickly; this implies that having experienced stressful work situations in the past may have little effect on one's psychological well-being unless the stressful situation continues into the present. We assume, however, that the situation is different for physical symptoms. More studies on physical indicators are needed that examine concurrent and lagged effects simultaneously.

TABLE 18.3 Longitudinal Studies on Stressors, Well-Being, and Health

Study	Number of Waves	Time Lags	Sample Size	Statistical Procedure	Stressors	Strains	Third Variables	Lagged Main Effects	Concurrent Main Effects	Reverse Effects	Effects Tested But Not Found
Bakker, Schaufeli, Sixma, Bosveld, & van Dierendonck (2000)	2	60	207	LISREL	Patient demands	Burnout	—	Not tested	Patient demands ↗ emotional exhaustion; effects on other burnout components are mediated by emotional exhaustion	Depersonalization ↗ patient demands	—
Begley & Czajka (1993)	2	3	82	Multiple regression	Experienced stressfulness of organizational change	Job displeasure	Age, gender, marital status, education, organizational tenure, NA, organizational commitment	Not tested	Experienced stressfulness ↗ job displeasure	Not tested	—
Bromet, Dew, Parkinson, & Schulberg (1988)	2	12	322–325	Multiple regression, Logistic regression	Job demands	Affective disorders, alcohol-related problems, distress symptoms	Age, coworker support, friendship support	Job demands ↗ affective disorders; Job demands ↗ distress symptoms (p < .10)	Not tested	Not tested	No effect of job demands on alcohol-related problems
Carayon (1993)	2	12	122	CRPC	Workload	Daily life stress, physical health complaints	Not tested in CLPC	Workload ↗ physical health complaints	Not tested	No reverse effects	No lagged effect of workload on daily life stress
Chapman, Mandryk, Frommer, Edye, & Ferguson (1990)	3	36 + 24	2,634	Multiple regression	Quantitative demands, qualitative demands, outside stress	Systolic blood pressure, diastolic blood pressure	Age, education, weight, fitness, alcohol consumption, family history, etc.	Young women: Quantitative demands ↗ diastolic blood pressure	** chronicity scores: mixture of lagged and concurrent effects	Not tested	No effects on systolic blood pressure; no effects for men; no effects for all women together
Daniels & Guppy (1994)	2	1	244	Multiple regression	Various stressors	Well-being	No	Not tested	Stressors ↗ well-being	Not tested	
Dormann & Zapf (1999)	3	4 + 8	202	LISREL	Social stressors	Depressive symptoms	—	No effect of social stressors	Not tested	Not tested	No effect of social stressors
Frese (1985)	2	16	53–79	CLPC	Psychological stressors	Psychosomatic complaints	Not tested in CLPC	Psychological stressors ↗ psychosomatic complaints	Not tested	No reverse effects	No effect when observational measure of stressors was used

Study	Waves	Time lag	N	Method	Stressors	Strains	Controls	Results	Stressors → strains	Strains → Stressors	Notes
Garst, Frese, & Molenaar (2000)	6	4, 10, 12, 12, 24	448	Growth curve model	Job insecurity, time pressure, organizational problems, social stressors, uncertainty	Depression, psychosomatic complaints, irritation, worrying	Not in growth curve model	Uncertainty ↗ depression, psychosomatic complaints, irritation, worrying; social stressors ↗ psychosomatic complaints, worrying			No lagged effects of job insecurity
Glickman, Tanaka, & Chan (1991)	2	17	2,506	LISREL	Work load and economic strain	Distress	Age, life events	No lagged effect of workload and economic strain on distress	Workload and economic strain ↗ distress	Distress ↗ workload and economic strain (lagged)	No lagged effect of workload and economic strain on distress
Hibbard & Pope (1993)	2	180	2,157	Prospective design	Work stress	Ischiamic heart disease (IHD), malignancy, stroke, death	Age, education, self-reported health, marital and parental roles	Men: work stress ↗ IHD	Not tested	Not applicable	No effects for women; no effects on malignancy, stroke, or death
Howard, Cunningham, & Rechnitzer (1986)	2	24	217	Multiple regression	Role ambiguity	Systolic blood pressure, diastolic blood pressure, cholesterol, triglycerides, uric acids	Hardiness		Type A individuals: change in role ambiguity ↗ systolic blood pressure, diastolic blood pressure, triglycerides		No effects for Type B individuals; no effects on cholesterol and uric acids
Karasek, Baker, Marxner, Ahlbom, & Theorell (1981)	2	72	1,461	Logistic regression	Job demands	Cardiovascular disease	Age, intelligence, discretion, personal schedule freedom, education, smoking, overweight	Job demands ↗ cardiovascular disease	Not tested	Not applicable	—
Kohn & Schooler (1982)	2	120	687	LISREL	Time pressure, heaviness, dirtiness, hours of work	Distress	—	No lagged effects on distress	Dirtiness ↗ distress; hours of work ↗ distress	Distress ↗ time pressure (concurrent); distress ↗ heaviness (lagged)	No effects of time pressure and heaviness on distress; no lagged effects of dirtiness and hours of work on distress

(Continued)

TABLE 18.3 (*Continued*)

Study	Number of Waves	Time Lags	Sample Size	Statistical Procedure	Stressors	Strains	Third Variables	Lagged Main Effects	Concurrent Main Effects	Reverse Effects	Effects Tested But Not Found
Lee & Ashforth (1993)	2	8	169	LISREL	Role stress	Emotional exhaustion (EE); depersonalization, personal accomplishment	No	Lagged effects not testable effect of role	Role stress ↗ emotional exhaustion; stress on depersonalization and personal accomplishment mediated by EE	Not tested	
Leitner (1993)	3	12 + 12	222	CLPC	Barriers in work process	Psychosomatic complaints, irritation, strain, depression, anxiety, somatic symptoms	—	Barriers ↗ psychosomatic complaints, irritation, strain, depression, somatic symptoms, illness	Not tested	No reverse effect	No effect on anxiety or illness
Mauno & Kinnunen (1999)	2	12	219	LISREL	Job insecurity	Exhaustion, somatic symptoms, spillover into parenthood	No	Women: job insecurity ↗ exhaustion; job insecurity ↗ spillover	Not tested	No reverse effects	No effects for men; no effects on somatic symptoms
Mohr (2000)	2	84	62–65	Partial correlations	Job insecurity	Irascibility, anxiety, psychosomatic complaints, depression	—	Not tested	Job insecurity ↗ anxiety; job insecurity ↗ psychosomatic complaints	Not tested	No effects on irascibility and depression
Moyle (1998)	3	7 + 5	148	LISREL	Demands	Distress (GHQ)	Neuroticism	Demands ↗ distress	Demands ↗ distress	Distress ↗ demands	
Moyle & Parkes (1999)	3	2.5 + 6	85	Multiple regression	Demands relocation	Distress (GHQ)	Not entered into regression equation before other variables	Not tested	Demands ↗ distress	Not tested	Relocation per se does not affect distress
Muntaner, Tien, Eaton, & Garrison (1991)	2	12	11,789	Prospective	Psychological demands, physical demands	Psychotic disorders (delusions, schizophrenia, psychotic affective)	—	Physical demands ↗ delusions, psychological demands ↗ schizophrenia	Not tested	Not applicable/ not tested	No effects on psychotic-affective disorders, no effect of psychological demands on delusions, effect of physical demands on schizophrenia marginally significant (↗)

Study	Waves	Time lag	N	Analysis	Chronic stressors	Distress symptoms	Coping	Chronic stressors	Chronic stressors	Reverse effects	Other
Nelson & Sutton (1990)	3	6 + 3	91	Multiple regression			—	↗ distress symptoms (3-month time lag)	Not tested	Not tested	—
Newton & Keenan (1990)	2	24	247	Multiple regression	Role conflict, role ambiguity, quantitative high load, qualitative low load	Job dissatisfaction, anxiety, anger, frustration, hostility	—	Not tested	Δ role conflict ↗ job dissatisfaction, anxiety, frustration, anger, hostility; Δ role ambiguity ↗ job dissatisfaction, anxiety, anger, frustration, hostility; Δ quantitative high load ↗ anxiety; Δ quantitative high load ↗ job dissatisfaction, anger; Δ qualitative low load ↗ job dissatisfaction, anger, frustration, hostility	Not tested	Quantitative high load has no effect on frustration or hostility; qualitative low load has no effect on anger
Noor (1995)	2	8	180	Multiple regression	Role overload	GHQ scores, happiness	Age, NA	Not tested	Role overload ↗ GHQ scores	Not tested	No effect on happiness
Parkes (1991)	2	4	147	Multiple regression	Demands (i.e., time pressure)	Anxiety	Age, gender, discretion, locus of control, social dysfunctioning	Demands ↗ anxiety	Not tested	Not tested	—
Parkes, Menham, & von Rabenau (1994)	2	2	180	Multiple regression	Demands	Somatic symptoms	Gender, age, neuroticism	Demands ↗ somatic symptoms	Not tested	Not tested	—
Revicki, Whitley, Gallary, & Allison (1993)	3	12 + 12	369 (1st time lag); 192 (2nd time lag)	Multiple regression	(low) Role clarity	Depressive symptoms	Age, gender, marital status, other strain symptoms	No effects	Not tested	Not tested	No effects
Roy & Steptoe (1994)	4	3 + 3 + 3	48	Multiple regression	Daily stressors	Depression	NA, social support	No lagged effects	Daily stressors ↗ depression for all three time lags	No reverse effects	No lagged effects

(Continued)

TABLE 18.3 (*Continued*)

Study	Number of Waves	Time Lags	Sample Size	Statistical Procedure	Stressors	Strains	Third Variables	Lagged Main Effects	Concurrent Main Effects	Reverse Effects	Effects Tested But Not Found
Rydstedt, Johansson, & Evans (1998)	2	18	52	Multiple regression	Workload	Perceived effort, fatigue spillover, intake of stress-related drugs	Gender	Not tested	Delta-workload ↗ perceived efforts, fatigue spillover	Not tested	
Schonfeld (1992)	2	Approx. 6	255	LISREL	Episodic and chronic stressors	Depressive symptoms	No control variables in LISREL models	Stressors ↗ depressive symptoms	Stressors ↗ depressive symptoms; concurrent models fits the data better than lagged model	No reverse effects	
Shirom, Westman, Shamai, & Carel (1997)	2	24–36	665	Multiple regression	Overload	Cholesterol triglycerides	Age, body mass index, emotional reactivity, burnout, fatigue	Women; Overload ↗ cholesterol	Not tested		No effects in men; no effect on triglycerides
Siegrist, Peter, Junge, Cremer, & Seidel (1990)	2	66	263	Logistic regression	Status inconsistency, job insecurity, work pressure	Ischiamic heart disease (IHD)	Age, body mass index, blood pressure, cholesterol, coping	Status inconsistency ↗ IHD, job insecurity ↗ IHD, work pressure ↗ IHD	Not tested	Not applicable	—
Spector, Chen, & O'Connell (2000)	2	Approx. 12	110	Partial Korr	Interpersonal conflict constraints, role ambiguity, role conflict, workload	Anxiety, frustration, job satisfaction, physical symptoms	NA	Not tested	All stressors ↗ anxiety and frustration, role ambiguity and role conflict ↘ satisfaction	Not tested	No effect on physical symptoms
Tang & Hammontree (1992)	2	6	60	Multiple regression	Stressors in police jobs	Illness	Hardiness	Stressors ↗ illness	Not tested	Not tested	—
Wolpin, Burke, & Greenglass (1991)	2	12	262	Multiple regression	Various stressors	Burnout, job satisfaction	—	Stressors ↗ job satisfaction	Stressors ↗ job satisfaction, stressors ↗ burnout	Not tested	No lagged effects on burnout
Zapf & Frese (1991)	2	16	89	CLPC	Social stressors	Psychosomatic complaints, irritation, strain, anxiety, depression	Not in CLPC	No lagged effects	Not tested	No reverse effects	No lagged effects

Note. Time lags refer to months. CLPC = cross-lagged panel correlation. NA = negative affectivity.

A growing number of studies have tested *reverse effect*. These studies addressed the question of whether strains lead to an increase in stressors as suggested in the drift hypothesis (cf. Zapf, Dormann, et al., 1996). In 9 out of 12 studies, no such reverse effects were found (Carayon, 1993; Frese, 1985; Garst et al., 2000; Leitner, 1993; Mauno & Kinnunen, 1999; Moyle, 1998; Roy & Steptoe, 1994; Schonfeld, 1992; Zapf & Frese, 1991). Three studies reported reverse effects for (some of the) strain symptoms on (some of the) stressors (Bakker et al., 2000; Glickman et al., 1991; Kohn & Schooler, 1982). It is interesting to note that in most of the studies that found such reverse effects, both types of effects were present—effects of stressors on strains *and* effects of strains on stressors. This suggests that—at least for some individuals—experiencing organizational stress may be linked to a negative spiral: Stressors increase strain, which in turn increases stressors. Moyle (1998) and Garst et al. (2000), however, found an effect opposite to the drift hypotheses (a sort of refuge model). People with high strain eventually received workplaces that had fewer demands and stressors.

In summary, there is good and increasing evidence that stressors at work have a causal effect on health and well-being. The support for concurrent effects is stronger than for lagged effects, at least for psychological strains. Consistent lagged effects were mainly found for physical strain symptoms. This implies that an individual's present work situation seems to be more relevant for developing psychological disturbances, whereas an individual's past work situation may also have long-term effects on his or her physical health and well-being. Clearly more research is needed that examines concurrent versus lagged effects more systematically. Moreover, more attention should be paid to the time intervals at which data are gathered (cf. Dormann & Zapf, 1999). Differential effects of different stressors and different models of stressor-strain relationships should be examined (Frese & Zapf, 1988; Garst et al., 2000).

The Role of Resources

Stressors do not necessarily have a negative effect on the individual. The degree to which a stressful work situation affects the individual might be contingent on the availability of resources. Hobfoll (1998) defines resources as "objects, conditions, personal characteristics, and energies that are either themselves valued for survival, directly or indirectly, or that serve as a means of achieving these ends" (p. 54). With respect to organizational stress, resources refer to conditions within the work situation and to individual characteristics that can be used to attain goals. Both with respect to the advancement of stress theory and practical implications, it is highly relevant to establish whether these resources buffer (i.e., moderate) the effects of stressors on strains.

Resources at work most often studied were control at work and social support. Individual resources are coping styles, locus of control, self-efficacy, and competence. Additionally, we shall briefly refer to other factors such as Type A behavior pattern, hardiness, and sense of coherence.

Control at Work

Control at work refers to an individual's opportunity to influence one's activities in relation to a higher-order goal (Frese, 1989). P. R. Jackson, Wall, Martin, and Davids (1993) differentiated between control over timing and methods to do the work. Many studies addressed the question of whether high control at work buffers the negative effects of a stressful work situation on an individual's health and well-being. Most of these studies have been conducted within the framework of Karasek's (1979) job demand-job control model.

Epidemiological studies on cardiovascular diseases an as outcome variable tended to confirm the major assumptions of Karasek's model (for reviews, cf. Kristensen, 1995; Schnall et al., 1994; Theorell & Karasek, 1996). Individuals in high-strain jobs often suffered from cardiovascular illnesses. Moreover, in about half of the studies, high-strain jobs were associated with cardiovascular risk factors such as high blood pressure and smoking (Schnall et al., 1994).

With respect to other outcomes including psychological well-being and mental health, the findings are less conclusive. Several reasons for these inconsistent findings can be mentioned. *First,* there are many studies that did not explicitly test the interaction effect but that compared high demands-low control subgroups (i.e., high-strain jobs) with high demands-high control subgroups (i.e., active jobs). This comparison often revealed significant differences in health and well-being between high-strain jobs and active jobs (e.g., Eriksen & Ursin, 1999; Landsbergis, 1988). Theorell and Karasek (1996) have recently suggested that this procedure be used in general (for a critique, cf. Kasl, 1996).

In a qualitative review of empirical studies on the job demand-job control model published between 1979 and 1997, Van der Doef and Maes (1999) examined whether individuals in high-strain jobs experience poorer psychological well-being than do individuals in other jobs. Their review revealed that in 28 of the 41 studies with general psychological well-being as dependent variable, individuals in high-strain jobs indeed showed the lowest well-being scores. For job-related well-being such as job satisfaction, burnout, and job-related mood as dependent variables, a similar picture emerged. Strictly speaking, such a comparison between high-strain jobs and other jobs examines the main effects of job demands and job control—not the hypothesized interaction effect. When testing the interaction effect with the more appropriate moderated regression analysis, the job demand-job control model was supported less frequently. Some researchers reported support for the model (Fox, Dwyer, & Ganster, 1993; Sargent & Terry, 1998), whereas others did not (Landsbergis, 1988; Schaubroeck & Fink, 1998).

In the aforementioned review by Van der Doef and Maes (1999), 8 of 31 studies showed (partial) evidence for the interaction effect. An additional seven studies confirmed the interaction effect for subgroups of individuals, dependent on their personality, type of organization, and hierarchical position. A more recent study found support for the postulated interaction effect when using a multilevel analysis approach (Van Yperen & Snijders, 2000). It is noteworthy that significant interaction effects were also found in longitudinal studies (Parkes et al., 1994; Sargent & Terry, 1998).

A *second* reason for failing to find the postulated interaction effect between demands and control may lie in the operationalization of the core variables. For example, Wall et al. (1996) argued that Karasek's (1979) measure of decision latitude (used in many studies) is a conglomerate of many aspects of control such as decision over working methods, decision over scheduling of one's tasks, aspects of skill use, and task variety. Probably only proper job control attenuates the negative effects of high demands, whereas skill use and task variety do not. Wall et al. (1996) tested this assumption explicitly and found the hypothesized interaction effect for a relatively narrow job control measure but not for the broader decision latitude measure (for similar findings, cf. De Croon, Van der Beek, Blonk, & Frings-Dresen, 2000; Sargent & Terry, 1998).

A *third* reason for the inconsistent findings on the job demand-job control model lies in the effects of additional variables such as social support or self-efficacy. For example, Johnson and Hall (1988) incorporated social support into the model. This extended demand-control-support model showed social support to buffer the negative effects of the combination of high demands and low control. Stated differently, the detrimental effects of a high-strain job unfolded only when social support was low but not when social support was high. Thus, a three-way interaction was found.

Van der Doef and Maes (1999) suggested that field studies that tested the hypothesized three-way interaction—and that controlled for main effects and two-way interactions—resulted in inconclusive findings. For example, Parkes et al. (1994) reported support for the demand-control-support model. Most studies found no evidence for a three-way interaction between demands, control, and support (Dollard et al., 2000; Furda et al., 1994; Melamed, Kushnir, & Meir, 1991; for

a summary, cf. Van der Doef & Maes, 1999). Some authors even reported findings that cast doubt on the predictions of the demands-control-support model (Landsbergis, Schnall, Deitz, Friedman, & Pckering, 1992; Schaubroeck & Fink, 1998). Recent research suggests even more complex interactions and stresses the importance of coping (Daniels, 1999).

Fourth, Warr (1987) and Frese (1989) have argued that at work it should be very difficult to find interaction effects of stressors and control: Control implies that people can do something about the stressors. If people are bothered by stressors, they reduce the stressors; but they can only reduce stressors if they have control. If stressors continue to exist, it may be because they are noncontrollable by definition. Because noncontrollability and stressors are intertwined, it is difficult to show an interaction effect. It should be much easier to find an interaction effect if people are confronted with a new situation, such as in an experiment.

Fifth, experimental research tends to support the job demand-job control model. In such experiments, interaction effects of perceived demands and perceived control on dependent measures such as anxiety, task satisfaction, and subjective task performance were found (Jimmieson & Terry, 1997; Perrewé & Ganster, 1989), although there is also disconfirming evidence (Perrewé & Ganster, 1989; Searle et al., 1999). There is a large body of literature on the learned helplessness paradigm (Seligman, 1975), which also posits an interaction effect of stressors and control. Experimental research in this tradition has repeatedly replicated the interaction effects of bad events and noncontrol on reduction in well-being (Peterson, Maier, & Seligman, 1993).

In summary, there is strong empirical evidence for the additive main effect of job demands and job control. Individuals in high-strain jobs show the lowest well-being scores and suffer most from illnesses. However, the interaction effect has received far less support. Adequate operationalization of job control may be crucial for finding significant interaction effects. Experimental findings tended to support the helplessness concept with its interaction effects of stressors and noncontrol. In all, Karasek's (1979) model has contributed to a fair amount of empirical controversy that has been fruitful. Given the previous arguments and the experimental findings, the fact that noncontrol and stressors produce at least additive effects and that a number of field studies find an interaction effect after all, we tend to think that Karasek's model has not done that badly.

Social Support and Work Group Factors

Social support is important for protecting an individual's health and well-being. It can be characterized as resources provided by others (Cohen & Syme, 1985) and comprises emotional, informational, and instrumental (i.e., tangible) support (House, 1981). In general, the literature assumes that the beneficial effect of social support works both via main and interaction effects. A recent meta-analysis based on a total of 68 effect sizes addressed the main effect and has shown that social support is negatively associated with strains (Viswesvaran, Sanchez, & Fisher, 1999). We find it interesting that social support was also negatively related to stressors at work.

With respect to the interaction effect, Cohen and Wills (1985) pointed out that social support functions only as a buffer in the stressor-strain relationship if the available support matches "the specific need elicited by a stressful event" (p. 314). A number of cross-sectional studies suggest that social support buffers the negative effects of stressors (for a review, cf. Kahn & Byosiere, 1992).

Longitudinal studies are needed to arrive at a conclusion about causality. Dormann and Zapf (1999) reviewed 10 longitudinal studies published between 1985 and 1999 that examined the interaction effect of social support. Three of these studies found no moderator effects. In some of the other studies, moderator effects missed the conventional significance level or were only significant for a small part of all the effects tested. Thus, the evidence for an across-the-board moderator effect of social support is not very strong. A closer look at some of the recently published studies suggests that there might be specific mechanisms underlying the stress-buffering potential of social support. For example, in correspondence to the stress matching hypothesis (Cohen & Wills, 1985), Frese (1999) found the strongest effects for social stressors and socially related aspects of psychological dysfunctioning. Dormann and Zapf (1999) found a lagged moderator effect of social support only with an 8-month time lag, but neither for shorter nor for longer time lags. More research is needed that examines in more detail how the effects of social support unfold over time.

Moreover, there is increasing evidence that social support does not have unequivocal positive effects. A number of authors reported that a high degree of social support or related variables increased the relationship between stressors and strain symptoms (Schaubroeck & Fink, 1998). Peeters, Buunk, and Schaufeli (1995) showed that a high level of instrumental social support may induce feelings of inferiority that are detrimental to an individual's well-being.

In addition to social support, group work factors such as group cohesion or team climate play a role when it comes to stress in organizations. First, research suggests that individuals who work in teams experience better well-being than do individuals working in no team or a pseudoteam (Carter & West, 1999). Second, group cohesion and favorable team climates were found to be associated with team members' well-being (Carter & West, 1998; Sonnentag, Brodbeck,

Heinbokel, & Stolte, 1994; for an overview, cf. Sonnentag, 1996). Third, work group factors such as psychological safety (Edmondson, 1999) or collective efficacy (Schaubroeck, Lam, & Xie, 2000) might buffer the negative effects of stressors. However, empirical studies are still rare (for a related recent study, cf. Bliese & Britt, 2001). Forth, there is increasing evidence that emotional contagion occurs in work groups (Bakker & Schaufeli, 2000; Totterdell, Kellett, Techmann, & Briner, 1998). Emotional contagion refers to processes by which an individual's mood is transmitted to other persons—for example, other team members. On the one hand, this phenomenon implies that a stressful events can influence more persons than simply those directly faced with the stressor. On the other hand, other team members' positive moods can serve as a resource when another member is confronted with a stressful situation. Linking group work factors to stress issues seems to be a fruitful avenue for future research.

Coping Styles

A favorable coping style can be a core resource for bolstering an individual's health and well-being. Lazarus and Folkman (1994) defined coping as "constantly changing cognitive and behavioral efforts to manage specific external and/or internal demands that are appraised as taxing or exceeding the resources of the person" (p. 141). They differentiated between problem-focused and emotion-focused forms of coping. Problem-focused coping includes problem-solving behaviors that aim directly to change the stressor, other aspects of the environment, or one's own behavior. Emotion-focused coping refers to attempts to manage cognitions or emotions directly (for a critique and extension, cf. Semmer, 1996).

Problem-focused coping has been found to be positively related to mental health and well-being, whereas emotion-focused coping and an additional style of avoidance coping were often found to be associated with poorer well-being (Guppy & Weatherston, 1997; Hart, Wearing, & Headey, 1995; Leiter, 1991; Sears, Urizar, & Evans, 2000).

With respect to moderator effects, empirical findings are less conclusive. Many studies did not find the hypothesized moderator effects of coping on the relationship between stressors and strains (e.g., Ingledew, Hardy, & Cooper, 1997). Most studies that found a moderator effect of coping identified problem-solving coping as a favorable coping style, whereas emotion-focused coping turned out to be an unfavorable coping style (Parkes, 1990). This implies that individuals who approach the stressors directly or engage in other problem-solving behaviors are better off than individuals who concentrate on the management of their emotions and cognitions.

Authors like Perrez and Reicherts (1992) have argued that coping behavior should match the situation in order to be effective. A recent study in a hospital setting supports this assumption (de Rijk, Le Blanc, Schaufeli, & de Jonge, 1998). Problem-focused coping was found to be only superior in situations in which nurses could exert control over their work situations. In low-control situations, attempts of problem-focused coping were negatively associated with individuals' well-being.

Locus of Control

Locus of control (Rotter, 1966)—an individual difference concept—refers to whether individuals see themselves as primarily able to control their lives and their major experiences (internal locus of control) or whether individuals think that other people or forces beyond themselves (e.g., luck) determine what happens to them (external locus of control). At the most general level, it is assumed that individuals with an internal locus of control exert more direct action against the stressor than do those with an external locus of control. Therefore, it is expected that they will suffer less from work-related stressors (Cohen & Edwards, 1989). Indeed, individuals with an internal locus of control experience better mental health than do individuals with an external locus of control (for reviews, cf. Glass & McKnight, 1996; Kahn & Byosiere, 1992). Such a positive effect of an internal locus of control was also confirmed in longitudinal studies (Daniels & Guppy, 1994; Newton & Keenan, 1990).

Additionally, it was tested whether a high internal locus of control buffers the negative effects of a stressful work situation. Findings from cross-sectional studies seem to support such a moderator effect (for a review, cf. Kahn & Byosiere, 1992). However, results from longitudinal studies are less conclusive. For example, in the study by Newton and Keenan (1990), only a small portion of the tested moderator effects reached their significance level. Longitudinal studies by Parkes (1991) and Daniels and Guppy (1994) reported more complex three-way interactions between stressors in the work situation, job control, and locus of control.

Taken together, research suggests that locus of control has a main effect on well-being. However, longitudinal studies did not provide evidence for a simple moderator effect of locus of control on the relationship between stressors and strains.

Self-Esteem, Self-Efficacy, and Competence

Self esteem and self-efficacy are important for an individual's health and well-being. There is consistent empirical evidence for a main effect of self esteem and self-efficacy (for reviews,

cf. Kahn & Byosiere, 1992; Sonnentag, 2002). Evidence for a moderator effect of self-esteem is weak (Jex & Elacqua, 1999). With respect to self-efficacy, there is more evidence—although not unequivocal—for a moderator effect. Some studies show that the relationship between stressful work situations and poor well-being is stronger for individuals low on self-efficacy than for individuals high on self-efficacy (Jex & Bliese, 1999; VanYperen, 1998). There are additional studies that reported this moderator effect for some but not all of the studied stressor or strain measures (Bhagat & Allie, 1989; Jex & Elacqua, 1999). Jex and Gudanowski (1992) and Saks and Ashforth (2000) did not find an interaction effect for self-efficacy. Parker and Sprigg (1999) provide evidence that proactive personality—a concept closely related to self-efficacy—attenuates the stressor-strain relationship, particularly when job control is high. Also recent work by Schaubroeck and his coworkers suggests a more complex picture with three-way interactions between stressors, job control, and self-efficacy (Schaubroeck, Lam, & Xie, 2000; Schaubroeck & Merritt, 1997).

Because self-efficacy is an individual's belief that he or she is competent, the issue of subjective competence can be discussed within the self-efficacy framework. Surprisingly, we know of no studies on objective competence and skills as resources in the stress process. This is all the more surprising because skills needed at work should be the prime candidates for dealing with stressors.

Other Person Factors

In the past, researchers paid attention to the Type A behavior pattern as one important individual difference variable in explaining negative effects of stressful work situations, particularly with respect to cardiovascular diseases. Type A individuals are competitive, hostile, impatient, and hard driving. Ganster and Schaubroeck (1991) and Kahn and Byosiere (1992) summarized the findings of studies on Type A behavior pattern. There is some support for a main effect of Type A behavior on strain. More specifically, the hostility component was found to be closely related to physiological reactivity (Ganster, Schaubroeck, Sime, & Mayes, 1991). In contrast, the evidence for a moderator effect of Type A behavior pattern is weak (Kahn & Byosiere, 1992). More recent longitudinal studies are inconclusive. Type A behavior enhanced the relationship between stressors and strains in one study (Moyle & Parkes, 1999), whereas it attenuated this relationship in another study (Newton & Keenan, 1990).

Hardiness is another individual difference variable assumed to moderate the stressor-strain relationship. Hardiness comprises the dimensions commitment, control, and challenges

(Kobasa, Maddi, & Kahn, 1982). There is some evidence for a main effect of hardiness on individual health, but support for a moderator effect was found only in some studies (e.g., Howard et al., 1986) but not in others (e.g., Tang & Hammontree, 1992).

Sense of coherence (Antonovsky, 1991) is a concept closely related to hardiness. Its central aspects are perceived comprehensibility, manageability, and meaningfulness of the environment. Recently, researchers included sense of coherence as a potential moderator in studies on work-related stress. Cross-sectional research suggests that sense of coherence can attenuate the negative impact of high-strain jobs (Söderfeldt, Söderfeldt, Ohlson, Theorell, & Jones, 2000). Longitudinal tests are needed to substantiate this effect.

Conclusions About Moderator Effects

Methodological reasons make it difficult to detect moderator effects, particularly in nonexperimental studies. Moderated regression analysis is a conservative procedure that makes it hard to establish moderator effects. Thus, the field of moderators in stress research may very well have to deal with a large Type II error (i.e., not finding in research what exists in reality). First, main effects are entered first into the regression equation, and therefore not much variance remains to be explained by the interaction term. This problem is enhanced in longitudinal studies in which the initial level of the strain measure (i.e., the dependent variable) is also entered into the regression equation as a control variable. Because individual strain measures are fairly stable over time, a large proportion of the variance of the dependent variable is already explained. Thus, there is little variance left to be explained by the interaction effect. Second, most stress studies rely on relatively small sample sizes; this implies that the studies do not have enough power for detect the moderator effects even if they exist (Aiken & West, 1991).

Consequently, empirical findings on moderator effects are mixed. There are some studies—including those using longitudinal designs—that speak for a moderator effect of control, social support, and coping styles. Cross-sectional findings on a moderator effect of self-efficacy are encouraging. However, support for a moderator effect of locus of control, Type A behavior, or hardiness are weak.

If we analyze these findings in the light of methodological problems associated with the test of moderator effects, it seems warranted to continue research in this area. However, we think that the following recommendations may make it more likely to find moderator effects: First, more attention should be paid to a match between specific stressors and specific moderators (cf. Cohen & Wills, 1985). For example, it is plausible to assume that social support, which provides

additional information on role requirements, will attenuate the negative impact of role ambiguity but not the negative impact of high time pressure. Second, large sample sizes are needed for ensuring sufficient power for detecting effects. Third, design issues are important as well. Given the power issues involved, one can select workplaces with the extremes of stressors (high vs. low stressors) and resources (e.g., very high vs. very low control) and test for interactions within such a design (Aiken & West, 1991). Fourth, it is necessary to understand better whether the resources have an impact on stressors (and vice versa). One reason may be that, for example, control at work leads to a reduction of certain stressors (particularly those that match the control). If this is the case, then we would know why resources are sometimes negatively related to stressors. One way to deal with the problem of confounding between resources and stressors is to study people who are new in their jobs. Finally, we suggest combining experimental and field studies to a larger extent, attempting to simulate in the experiment the same types of stressors and resources that are studied in the field.

In summary, research on resources has revealed main effects of resources on health an well-being; this implies that the availability of resources is helpful and beneficial in itself and across a wide range of situations. Additionally, there is some—although not unequivocal—evidence that certain resources can attenuate the negative effects of stressors on health and well-being. Particularly important are control at work, social support, coping styles, and self-efficacy.

Stress and Performance

Stress in organizations may influence not only individual health and well-being but may also influence performance. Performance refers to individuals' actions that are relevant for organizational goals (Campbell, McCloy, Oppler, & Sager, 1993). Borman and Motowidlo (1993) differentiated between task and contextual performance. Task performance refers to in-role behaviors that contribute to the organization's technical core. Contextual performance refers to extra-role, discretionary behaviors that do not directly contribute to an organization's technical core but that are assumed to support its broader organizational, social, and psychological environment.

There are several contradictory assumptions about how stressors in organizations affect performance. It is plausible to assume that stressors have a negative linear effect on performance. Such a negative effect can be explained by direct and indirect effects. The direct effect implies that stressors—particularly situational constraints—make task accomplishment more difficult, if not impossible. For example, if a task has to be accomplished with specific technical equipment and this equipment is not available because of a computer breakdown, task performance will suffer directly. Moreover, stressors may indirectly affect performance—for example, by decreasing alertness or motivation, which in turn negatively affects performance.

There is a long tradition in conducting laboratory studies on the task performance effects of stressors (Postman & Bruner, 1948). These studies show that the exposure to stressors leads to cognitive reactions such as narrowed attention (including a focus on salient cues) and reduced working memory capacity (Baddeley, 1972; Hamilton, 1982; for summaries, cf. Hockey, 1986; Wickens, 1996). A reduced working memory capacity is associated with a speed-accuracy trade-off when working under stressful conditions—particularly under time pressure (Hockey, 1986; Lulofs, Wennekens, & van Houtem, 1981). Moreover, narrowed attention and reduced working memory capacity have an impact on decision-making strategies. More specifically, they result in simpler decision strategies, recognition rather than analytical strategies, and less complete mental simulations (Klein, 1996). Recent studies suggest that the effects of stressors on performance are mediated by fatigue (Hockey, Maule, Vlough, & Bdzola, 2000; Lorist et al., 2000).

Some of these effects of stressors were also found in more realistic simulations of work environments. For example, simulated workload resulted in a performance decrease in some studies (Glaser, Tatum, Nebeker, Sorenson, & Aiello, 1999; Jimmieson & Terry, 1999) but not in all (Shaw & Weekley, 1985). When using a mail-sorting task, Searle et al. (1999) found that high job demands (i.e., high workload) were associated with an increase in performance attempts but also with a reduction in performance accuracy, particularly in situations with low control.

In contrast to these findings from laboratory and simulation studies, findings from field studies are far less consistent. With respect to task performance, some stressors were found to be related to impaired performance, whereas others were not. For example, in a study on secretaries' job performance, Spector, Dwyer, and Jex (1988) reported a negative relationship between secretaries' perceptions of constraints and ambiguity with supervisory performance ratings. No significant relationships, however, between secretaries' perceptions of workload or conflict and supervisory performance ratings emerged. Similarly, Beehr, Jex, Stacy, and Murray (2000) found negative relationships between specific stressors (i.e., acute stressful events, chronic occupation-specific stressors and workload variability) and an objective financial performance measure of door-to-door book sellers but found a *positive* relationship between role overload and job performance. In a classic study of engineers and scientists, Andrews and

Farris (1972) reported that experienced time pressure increased subsequent performance. One of the best studies (Jones et al., 1988) showed that stressors at work increase the likelihood of errors and that an organization-wide stress management program and changes in management of the hospitals reduced malpractice. All these results point to the need to develop a more specific theory of how stressors are related to performance.

Evidence from meta-analyses suggests that there is no substantial relationship between role stressors such as role ambiguity or role conflict and job performance, at least when job performance is assessed by objective measures or supervisory-peer ratings (Jackson & Schuler, 1985; Tubbs & Collins, 2000). Findings from field studies on the performance effects of situational constraints are inconclusive as well. Some studies found performance-deteriorating effects of situational constraints, whereas others did not (for a summary, cf. Jex, 1998).

There are several explanations for the lack of substantial linear relationships between stressors and job performance in field studies. First, one might assume a curvilinear relationship between stressors and performance; this would imply that the performance effects of stressors are not uniform across all degrees of stressor intensity. For example, similarly to the Yerkes-Dodson Law (1908) on the relationship between arousal and performance, performance might increase as stressors increase up to a moderate degree; when stressors become too high, however, performance might decrease. Studies that tested the assumed curvilinear relationship between stressors and performance failed to find such a relationship, however (e.g., Jamal, 1985; Westman & Eden, 1996). Second, the relationship between stressors and job performance might be moderated by other variables. Such moderator variables might include individual competence (Payne, 1991) or work commitment (Jamal, 1985). Until now, however, empirical evidence for the existence of such moderator effects is weak (for a summary, cf. Jex, 1998). Third, the performance measures used in most of the field studies might be too global for showing a performance-deterioration effect of work stressors. For example, a study by Kjellberg, Sköldström, Andersson, and Lindberg (1996) suggests that specific performance measures such as reaction times show decrements under stress in a field setting.

Fourth, possibly there is essentially no—or no large—effect of stressors on performance in field settings. This interpretation would contradict findings from laboratory studies that showed stressors to impair basic cognitive processes. However, impairment of basic cognitive processes may not necessarily translate into a decrease in overall job performance in real-life work settings. Individuals are able to compensate for the effects of stressors—for example, by switching to different task strategies (Sperandio, 1971). Hockey (2000) offers an additional explanation for the inconsistency between laboratory and field study results: Many laboratory tasks are relatively simple, trivial, and underlearned. If stressors occur in such a situation, study participants have few possibilities to switch to different strategies, be it because of a lack of skills in the specific task, or because of the restrictions of the laboratory setting. Real-life work tasks, however, are usually well-learned and complex. If stressors occur in these real-life situations, individuals often possess the necessary skills to pursue different strategies. Moreover, in organizational settings, goal attainment has high priority; this implies that task performance must be protected, if necessary, at the expense of increased effort or neglect of subsidiary activities. Klein (1996) additionally argues that some of the cognitive strategies affected by stressors in laboratory settings play a minor role in real-life settings. For example, analytical decision strategies suffer from time pressure, but such strategies are rarely used in natural decision making; therefore, the negative impact of performance is limited.

There are a few studies that examined the relationship between stressors and contextual performance. For example, Motowidlo, Packard, and Manning (1986) reported negative relationships between the intensity and frequency of stressful events on the one hand and interpersonal aspects of job performance of nurses on the other hand. Kruse (1995, cited in Jex, 1998) tested whether situational constraints were related to organizational citizenship behavior (OCB) and reported negative relationships between situational constraints and three aspects of OCB. These findings suggest that in stress situations, individuals assign priority to maintain task performance at the expense of discretionary behaviors such as contextual performance. However, a longitudinal study by Fay and Sonnentag (in press) suggests that the experience of stressors at work can even have an enhancing effect on extrarole performance and personal initiative. Similarly, Bunce and West (1994) reported that health care professionals responded with innovations to the experience of stressors at work.

Taken together, laboratory studies showed that stressors impair basic cognitive processes. However, as field studies indicate, this impairment does not necessarily result in a decrease in overall job performance. In particular, workload was found to be associated with higher job performance. These findings suggest that individuals spend more effort, prioritize the most relevant tasks, and use compensatory strategies for upholding their performance under stressful situations. It remains unclear whether and how such a performance management strategy is associated with health or well-being effects. It might be that such an approach exhausts an individual's resources in the long run and therefore affects an individual's health and well-being in a negative way.

Stress and Other Aspects of Organizational Behavior

Organizational stress is related to low organizational commitment, high turnover rates, and—under specific conditions—increased levels of absenteeism. *Organizational commitment* refers to an individual's bond or link to the organization (Mowday, Porter, & Steers, 1982). It comprises attitudinal, normative, and continuance aspects (Allen & Meyer, 1990). In a meta-analysis on organizational commitment, Mathieu and Zajac (1990) reported mean weighted corrected correlations between role stressors (role overload, role conflict, role ambiguity) and various aspects of organizational commitment ranging between $r = -.206$ and $r = -.271$. Thus, individuals perceiving a more stressful work situation reported lower organizational commitment.

There is clear meta-analytic evidence that work-related strains including impaired health are positively related to *absence behavior* (Farrell & Stamm, 1988; Martocchio, Harrison, & Berkson, 2000). However, this does not necessarily imply that stressors at work are related to absenteeism. Stressors may overlap with strain and strain may overlap with absenteeism, but strain may not be the mediator between stressors and absenteeism. A variance decomposition idea explains how such a relationship may appear. There is common variance between stressors and strain and between strain and absenteeism. But the two common variance fields do not overlap. Thus, it is that part of strain that is not related to stressors that may contribute to absenteeism. As a matter of fact, the data on the relationship between stressors and absenteeism are inconclusive. Cross-sectional studies found weak and often nonsignificant relationships between work stressors and absence data (Chen & Spector, 1992; Hemingway & Smith, 1999; Peter & Siegrist, 1997). Some studies revealed positive relationships between stressors and absenteeism (e.g., Kristensen, 1991), whereas others showed negative relationships (e.g., North, Syme, Feeney, Shipley, & Marmot, 1996).

Also longitudinal studies resulted in inconsistent findings. Tang and Hammontree (1992) found that work stress in police officers was a significant predictor of self-reported absence; they also found this to be true when they controlled for prior absence (time lag was 6 months). Vahtera, Kivimäki, Pentti, and Theorell (2000) analyzed absence data from more than 500 Finnish municipal employees over a period of 7 years. They found that initially healthy employees who experienced high psychological job demands in 1990 had a 21% higher risk of long absence spells (more than 3 days) than did employees with low psychological job demands in 1990. For physical demands, the risk of long absence spells was even 66% higher. The experience of downsizing and perceived job insecurity also increased the risk of absence spells (Kivimäki et al., 1997).

Smulders and Nijhuis (1999) collected data on absence frequency and rate of 1,755 male employees of a Dutch technical maintenance company. In their analyses, Smulders and Nijhuis controlled for employee health and absenteeism in the 1st year of their study. Results showed that high job demands were not associated with higher absence frequency or absence rate during the following 3 years. Contrary to what one might expect, high demands predicted a *lower* absence rate, particularly when the Poisson regression method was used. Similarly, a natural experiment (Parkes, 1982) found lower absence rates in high-demand work settings.

These cross-sectional and longitudinal findings suggest that the relationship between stressful work situations and absenteeism does not follow a simple pattern. First, it might be that the relationship is contingent on moderator variables. In line with the job demand-job control model (Karasek, 1979), one might argue that job control is such a moderator. However, although there is some support for this assumption (e.g., Dwyer & Ganster, 1991), most empirical studies did not confirm the hypothesized interaction effect of job control on the demands-absenteeism relationship (Smulders & Nijhuis, 1999; Vahtera, Pentti, & Uutela, 1996).

Moreover, person factors such as organizational or professional commitment might play a role in the stressor-absenteeism relationship. It might be that in stressful work situations, absenteeism increases in employees with low commitment but decreases in highly committed employees. Data reported by Jamal (1984) partially supported this assumption. Gender might also play a role. For example, Melamed et al. (1995) found substantial correlations between objective monotony and sickness absence in women but not in men.

Additionally, a study by Peter and Siegrist (1997) suggests that it is not the stressfulness of a situation per se that affects an employee's absence behavior. In accordance with the effort-reward-imbalance model, the authors found that status incongruity (i.e. a mismatch between effort and career achievements) was positively related with both short-term and long-term absenteeism in middle managers, whereas effort alone (i.e. time pressure and interruptions) was not related to absenteeism. These findings can be explained in the context of a psychological contract interpretation (Rousseau, 1995): Stressors increase absenteeism if employees feel that their efforts are not rewarded adequately. Longitudinal studies are needed that explicitly test this assumption.

Stressful work situations are positively related to *turnover intentions* and *turnover behavior*. There is rather consistent evidence from numerous studies that stressors in the work

situation are positively related to intentions to quit the organization and to job search behavior (Cavanaugh, Boswell, Roehling, & Boudreau, 2000; Chen & Spector, 1992; Gupta & Beehr, 1979). With respect to actual turnover behavior, a recent meta-analysis by Griffeth, Hom, and Gaertner (2000) reported effect sizes ranging from $\rho = .10$ to $\rho = .21$ (corrected for measurement error in the predictors and sampling error) between stressors and turnover behavior.

Taken together, there is empirical support for the assumption that stressors in the work situation are related to low organizational commitment, turnover intentions, and turnover behavior. However, with respect to organizational commitment and turnover intentions, the issue of causality remains unclear. Although it makes intuitive sense to assume that experiencing a stressful work situation increases the intention to quit the organization, individuals who plan to leave the organization might *perceive* more stressors than do their coworkers who in fact experience the same work situation but intend to stay. Longitudinal studies are needed in this area.

In general, research in this area suggests that organizational stress is detrimental not only to individuals' health and well-being; it can also harm the organization by increasing turnover rates and—possibly, although it has not been proven—absenteeism.

STRESS INTERVENTIONS

Stress prevention can be achieved with different sorts of programs (Ivancevich & Matteson, 1988; Murphy, 1988; Murphy, 1996; Theorell, 1993). In the United States, stress interventions are often only directed at the individual in the sense of stress management programs. In Europe, there has been a bit more emphasis on job-oriented stress interventions such as job restructuring (which increases the resources control and skills; Cooper & Payne, 1992). Table 18.4 displays

TABLE 18.4   Stress Interventions in Organizations

	Individual	Organizational
Stressor reduction	Reduction of individual stressor (e.g., time pressure)	Reduction of stressor (e.g. organizational problems)
Resource increase	Competence training	Participation in decision making, health circles
Strain reduction	Relaxation, stress immunization, training, respites (vacations, leisure time)	Rest periods
Lifestyle changes	Antismoking program; exercise program	Nonsmoking buildings; salient staircases vs. salient elevators

organizational and personal approaches to stressors, strains, and resources. Although the differentiation in various approaches is convenient, in many cases multiple approaches are combined—for example, institutional resource enhancement and individual stress-management programs (cf. Kompier, Aust, Van den Berg, & Siegrist, 2000; Kompier, Cooper, & Geurts, 2000).

Stressor Reduction

Stressors can be reduced by individuals or by institutions (or some combination). Examples for the latter are reduction of noise, change of assembly line speed in accordance with the circadian rhythm, reduction of interruptions at work. *Individual stressor reduction* is often an outgrowth of stress management programs that alert people to the fact that they can change certain parts of their work environment. However, individual stressor reduction often presupposes a certain amount of control over work (or in general, a certain amount of resources). Certainly, people have an impact on what the job looks like—including the stressors and the resources (Ilgen & Hollenbeck, 1991). As discussed previously, we do not know of any studies, however, that have examined how resources affect stressors or vice versa. These studies are necessary to understand how people as individuals change stressors.

Institutional stressor reduction approaches may take many different forms. A general stressor reduction approach (or better exposure time reduction) is to decrease the number of working hours, which seems to have positive effects, as reported in some company reports (Kompier, Aust, et al., 2000) and in a meta-analysis (Sparks, Cooper, Fried, & Shirom, 1997). Other institutional approaches reduce specific stressors that are suspected to be problematic. For example, an organization may reduce noise and may ensure a better flow of material, thereby reducing organizational problems—or there may be a reduction of time pressure, task ambiguity, or task difficulty. Such institutional stressor reduction approaches are useful, although problems may arise if such an approach is used singly and not in combination with other approaches: First, reducing stressors may sometimes lead to a reduction of challenges. If there is high qualitative overload, one may be tempted to reduce overload by decreasing the cognitive demands of a job. This can, however, reduce not only overload but also challenges and resources. A case in point was the effort to reduce external disturbances in secretaries by introducing central typing pools. In this case, interruptions and disturbances—stressors about which secretaries frequently complain—were reduced, but this also reduced control over how and when to do a job and reduced a clear and reliable relationship between a secretary and his or her boss. Second, because technological and organizational changes are quite frequent and increasingly rapid, research is too slow to tell us which stressors are particularly problematic and need to be taken care of. Therefore, reduction of stressors should be accompanied by an increase in resources.

Increase in Resources

Two important resources at work are control at work and competencies or skills. Resources in the sense of control or participation in decision making help individuals to have an influence on how to do their work and to increase or reduce stressors appropriately. Stressors that come about through new technology can best be addressed when resources are given to influence one's work. Thus, restructuring work by increasing job content and responsibilities often has a stress-preventive function as well. At least two careful studies on the effects of *institutionally increasing* control have been done (Jackson, 1983; Wall & Clegg, 1981). Jackson (1983) used a four-group Solomon control group design to study the effects of enhanced participation (increase of group meetings) in decision making that she hypothesized to increase power, information, and social support. An increase of participation in decision making decreased emotional stress, absence frequency, and turnover intention. Wall and Clegg (1981) showed that increase in autonomy and control by introducing semiautonomous work groups led to short- and long-term (12 months after the study was ended) increases in mental health. Unfortunately, this effect could not be replicated in another study (Wall, Kemp, Jackson, & Clegg, 1986).

Increasing *individual competence and skills* is also an aspect of resources, although it has not been typically discussed as a stress prevention technique. Without the necessary skills it is not possible to use control (Frese, 1989). Three arguments speak for the importance of competence as a resource in the stress process. First, working smarter, not harder is a good description of what superworkers—that is, excellent performers—do (Frese & Zapf, 1994; Sonnentag, 2000); because working smart implies using efficient rather than inefficient action strategies, this means that employees experience less stress when working smart. Second, it follows from the P-E fit model (cf. our discussion of this model earlier in this chapter) that people can increase the fit by developing their competence to deal with environmental demands. When a person is supposed to produce a certain number of products, development of skills helps him or her to actually do that—the P-E fit will be high and strain low. Third, self-efficacy is intimately related to competence. Bandura (1997) has argued for the strain-reducing function of self-efficacy in various domains and has shown that self-efficacy (e.g., via mastery experiences that increase the competence to deal with difficult situations) plays an important role in the strain reduction process.

An additional resource is social support (mainly by supervisors; Frese, 1999), which may be increased by management training. However, to our knowledge, the strain-reducing nature of management training has not been shown yet.

Combination of Stressor Reduction and Increase in Resources

In general, Elkin and Rosch (1990) suggested that the following interventions can be used to decrease stress: task and work environment redesign, flexible work schedules, participation in management, analysis of work roles, establishment of goals, social support, cohesive teams, fair employment policies, and shared rewards. More specifically, Bunce and West (1996) showed that an approach encouraging people to innovatively deal with work stressors led to a reduction of strain (this finding was also replicated by Bond & Bunce, 2000). Bunce and West's concept increased the subjective resources to deal with stressors because it encouraged innovative approaches. It is similar to the German concept of health circles (quality circles applied to health issues) that discuss stressors and work problems that can potentially lead to ill health (Beermann, Kuhn, & Kompier, 1999; Slesina, 1994). A program on reduction of burnout with a similar element of suggesting innovative approaches to deal with the stressors has also been suggested by Van Dierendonck, Schaufeli, and Buunk (1998). They combined their approach to changing the workplace with enhancing the individual's realistic orientation toward investments and outcomes so that the impression of equity was increased. Van Dierendonck et al. (1998) found their training to reduce emotional exhaustion, although it did not positively affect depersonalization and personal accomplishment.

Strain Reduction

Individually oriented strain reduction programs belong to the most frequently used programs in business; as a matter of fact, in some reviews, individual strain reduction programs are the only ones discussed in presentations of evidence on stress management. A large body of studies exists, and reviews find clear and positive effects. Stress management programs attempt to influence employees to interpret a situation not as stressful but as a challenge. They also teach a person to improve one's coping strategies and to reduce strain (stress

immunization or relaxation techniques). Because there are excellent reviews (e.g., Bamberg & Busch, 1996; Murphy, 1996; Van der Klink, Blonk, Schene, & Van Dijk, 2001), we do not need to discuss studies on stress management in detail.

Two techniques stand in the foreground (Murphy, 1996): relaxation techniques and cognitive-behavioral techniques (cf. also Bellarosa & Chen, 1997). Relaxation is most often based on progressive muscle relaxation (Jacobson, 1938) as well as meditation and biofeedback. By and large, progressive muscle relaxation has been shown to be effective (e.g., Murphy, 1996). It is particularly effective for psychophysiological outcomes; for other outcomes, the effect size for cognitive-behavioral techniques is higher (Van der Klink et al., 2001).

Cognitive-behavioral techniques are based on cognitive therapy for depression (Beck, 1967; Whisman, 1998), on rational-emotive therapy (Ellis, 1962), and on stress immunization or stress inoculation (Meichenbaum, 1985). Cognitive therapy has been shown to be a highly useful procedure for depressive individuals in clinical trials (Robinson, Berman, & Neimeyer, 1990) and in stress management for working populations (Bamberg & Busch, 1996; Murphy, 1996; Van der Klink et al., 2001). Most studies do not really differentiate in detail between cognitive and rational-emotive therapy, and a combination is usually preferred. Similar positive effects appear for rational-emotive therapy. Rational-emotive therapy works by helping the person to use rational self-instructions. For example, a person might have a tendency to exaggerate a given stress situation and catastrophize when something goes wrong. Alternative self-instructions are then trained (for example, it is not catastrophic if something goes wrong because mistakes happen to most people). Stress inoculation training is "designed to impart skills to enhance resistance to stress" and its objective is "to prepare the individual to respond more favorably to negative stress events" (Saunders, Driskell, Johnston, & Salas, 1996, p. 171). Stress inoculation works via three phases: First, conceptualization and education; second, skill acquisition and rehearsal; and third, application and follow-through (Saunders et al., 1996). The first phase—conceptualization and education—teaches people to have a more sophisticated view of the nature of stress. Second—acquisition and rehearsal—provides a stronger repertoire of coping skills and rehearses them either in vivo (e.g., role-play) or in guided imagery. Third—application and follow-through—works also via role play and guided imagery to deal with the real-life threats and stressors. A meta-analysis of 37 studies showed that performance anxiety was strongly affected ($r = .509$), state anxiety was also affected ($r = .373$), and—finally—there was also a positive performance effect (r = .296; Saunders et al., 1996).

One meta-analysis of 16 work-related stress management studies found an average effect size of 0.41 (Bamberg & Busch, 1996). A second, more recent meta-analysis (Van der Klink et al., 2001) found somewhat different effect sizes for 18 cognitive-behavioral studies (d = .68), 17 relaxation studies (d = .35), and 8 so-called multimodel approaches (acquisition of passive and active coping skills; d = .51). Thus, stress management programs increase health by about a half of a standard deviation. The study by Murphy (1996) corroborates these results by showing that published reports on 64 stress management interventions show on average between 59% (for job and organizational outcome measures) and 68% (for physiological and biochemical outcome variables) positive and significant results. Furthermore, those interventions that used a combination of approaches (e.g., relaxation and cognitive-behavioral techniques) tended to lead to the best results. Murphy (1996) and Van der Klink et al. (2001) also reported results for more disturbed individuals and for remedial interventions to be better than results for normal employees or preventive approaches; this implies that clinical studies show better results than does stress management training for unselected working populations. An additional constraint of most stress management programs is that they presuppose that the employees can actually do something about their stress levels (i.e., have at least some measure of control at work). Employees with a high degree of control at work and with higher status jobs showed better success in stress management interventions than did low-control or low-status job employees (Van der Klink et al., 2001). For this reason, stress management programs are probably less useful for blue-collar workers than for white-collar workers and managers.

Thus, in general, a positive picture on stress management programs appears. However, a number of caveats are in order: First, it is quite plausible that negative or zero effects do not find their way into the journals (Murphy, 1996). Second, the better studies with randomized control groups showed a lower degree of success than did the studies without a control group (Murphy, 1996). Finally, reviews find clear nonspecific effects; this points to the importance of using control groups in stress intervention studies. For these reasons, a certain degree of skepticism has to prevail. On the positive side, stress management programs are often effective in increasing life expectancy—for example, if given to heart disease patients (34% reduction in cardiac mortality; Dusseldorp, Van Elderen, Maes, Meulman, & Kraaij, 1999).

Digressing somewhat from the general theme of strain reduction, it is useful to look at Van der Klink et al.'s (2001) comparison of individual stress management approaches to organizational changes with the aim to reduce stress and increase resources. Organizational changes had a nonsignificant effect size that was significantly lower than was the effect size for individually oriented approaches. Unfortunately, they could only include five samples from four organizational intervention studies; these studies showed widely differing effect sizes, from a negative effect size of −.20 (Landsbergis & Vivona-Vaughan, 1995) to a positive effect size of .50 (Jones et al., 1988). Moreover, one study had 1,375 participants (Heaney, Price, & Rafferty, 1995), whereas the other studies included only very small groups of participants. Thus, the field of organizational intervention does not provide sufficient data yet to make a meta-analysis feasible. Moreover, it is necessary to study moderators of the effect; for example, Landsbergis and Vivona-Vaughan (1995) explained their negative effects with lack of management commitment to stress management and with obstacles in the implementation of the intervention strategies.

An institutional approach to reducing strain is to provide rest periods. Whereas stress management is a modern topic and full of new research, the study of rest periods is an older topic, with only a few studies appearing each year (Graf, Rutenfranz, & Ulich, 1970). It is well-known that the recovery is fastest after short periods of work and that the first few minutes of a rest period are most important for recovery. Graf et al. (1970) suggests, therefore, that 5% of the work time should be taken as rest periods. Because rest periods are anticipated, performance is higher if there are rest periods (Graf et al., 1970). Therefore, there is usually no decrement in overall performance in spite of the time needed for rest periods (Galinsky, Swanson, Sauter, Hurrell, & Schleifer, 2000; Graf et al., 1970). At the same time, stress effects are smaller when rest periods are interspersed in work (Galinsky et al., 2000). Evidence in the literature suggests that rest periods should be organizationally prescribed and supervised but should not be self-taken (concealed breaks) because people tend to take less frequent and too short rest periods when left to their own decisions (Graf et al., 1970; Henning, Sauter, Salvendy, & Krieg, 1989). Employees also want to cluster rest periods and add them at the end or at the beginning of the workday rather than interspersing them into their workday at regular intervals. We think that the issue of rest periods should be taken more seriously again in the literature on stress interventions than it is at the moment.

Additionally, to strain reduction programs individuals may *initiate strain reduction by themselves* during vacation and other leisure time periods (for a recent review on respites from work, cf. Eden, 2001). Research has shown that during vacations, burnout decreases—particularly when an individual is satisfied with his or her vacations (Westman & Eden, 1997). Researchers even reported that military reserve service results in a decline in burnout and that psychological detachment from work increased this effect (Etzion, Eden, & Lapidot, 1998). Similarly, leisure time activities pursued during evenings of normal workdays can reduce strain. For example, a diary study revealed that specific activities such as low-effort activities, physical activities, and social activities had a positive impact on a person's well-being, whereas work-related activities performed during leisure time had a negative impact (Sonnentag, 2001). These studies suggest that psychological detachment from work during vacation or leisure time periods is crucial for strain reduction to occur.

Lifestyle Changes

Individually oriented lifestyle change programs attempt to improve diet, to support healthy living (e.g., reducing alcohol and tobacco consumption), and to increase physical exercise. Employee assistance programs (EAP) are a case in point: They often target alcoholism or other addictions, but they can also be broad-based and include exercise and stress management programs; they experienced a tremendous growth in companies during the 1970s and 1980s (Matteson & Ivancevich, 1987). Breslow and Enstrom (1980) have shown that men who used seven positive habits (sleeping 7–8 hours, eating breakfast almost every day, never or rarely eating between meals, being near height-adjusted weight, never smoking, moderate or no use of alcohol, and regular physical activity) had a lower mortality rate across 10 years than did those who followed zero to three practices. Exercise- and health-promoting programs at work have been quite successful in decreasing anxiety (Long & Van Stavel, 1995), in reducing cardiovascular mortality after myocardial infarction (O'Connor et al., 1989), and in enhancing general well-being (Ivancevich & Matteson, 1988). A dramatic example of the success of a wellness program for cardiovascular fitness is the one used by the New York Telephone Company that saved the organization $2.7 million in reduced absenteeism and treatments costs in 1 year alone (Cartwright, Cooper, & Murphy, 1995). More specific psychological programs— for example, toward the coronary-prone Type A behavior pattern—also proved to be effective in reducing coronary recurrences (Nunes & Kornfeld, 1987).

Surprisingly, *institutional approaches* such as building architecture have not been studied to our knowledge as potential stress interventions. Office buildings may make it easier or harder to use the stairs, for example, by making either the staircase or the lift salient. It is surprising that a relatively small amount of daily physical activities, such as walking stairs, walking to work, doing small errands on foot, or bicycling to work have an enormously positive effect on mortality ratios. An example is the study by Pfaffenberger, Hyde, Wing, and Hsieh (1986) who showed that people using up 500 to 2,000 kcal per week had a reduced mortality rate within the 16 years of study in comparison to men who did not do any physical exercises. The reduced mortality rate was even more pronounced for those using 2,000 kcal per week. Burning 2,000 kcal per week is equivalent to walking, for example, 35 km per week or climbing three flights of stairs 70 times per week; this speaks for the importance of encouraging light sports in the office building by building adequate, aesthetically pleasing, and salient staircases and by encouraging employees to use the stairs.

Conclusion on Stress Interventions

Taken together, the literature on stress intervention concepts and studies suggests a number of conclusions. First, stress intervention studies go under very different names and are presented in very different disciplines and journals. Stress management studies are done by clinicians or clinical work psychologists and are mainly published in the *Journal of Occupational Health Psychology* or the *International Journal of Stress Management*. Lifestyle changes are reported in sports psychology and in medical journals. Rest period studies appear in human factors journals, mainly ergonomics and new technology journals. Stressor reduction and resource enhancement is done by job enrichment and job design professionals and appear in *Academy of Management Journal, Human Relations,* and other outlets. Social resource enhancement—for example, social support increase—is really part of teaching management skills and appear, for example, in *Leadership Quarterly*. Obviously many articles also appear in the more general journals, such as *Journal of Applied Psychology, Journal of Organizational Behavior,* and *Applied Psychology: An International Review;* we think that it pays to pull these diverse areas together and gain by using theories across different intervention domains. The best developed areas of stress interventions are rest periods (although the literature in this area is quite old), stress management techniques, and lifestyle changes. These areas are easier to study because they can be studied experimentally (particularly rest periods) and only imply changes of individuals. Organizational approaches have been studied much less frequently because they are more difficult to study; there is a need to look at moderators (e.g., how well the program is supported by management and how well it is implemented), and these studies are much more risky because many aspects cannot be controlled by the change agent.

Second, nearly every review of the field speaks about the importance of doing more studies in the area of organizational changes. We can only repeat this call. Most authors assume that it makes sense to combine structural and institutional changes with individually oriented approaches, at least for blue-collar workers (e.g., Bamberg & Busch, 1996; Ivancevich, Matteson, Freedman, & Phillips, 1990; Kompier, Cooper, et al., 2000; Murphy, 1996).

Third, practically every review on stress intervention techniques has called for better designed studies in this area. Because there seems to be a relationship between effect size and study design (Murphy, 1996), this issue needs to be taken seriously. Undoubtedly, better research has been done within the last 15–20 years—particularly in the area of stress management and lifestyle changes.

Forth, one issue of improving design is related to the fact that there are nonspecific effects of stress management. A notreatment control group does not actually account for nonspecific effects; it is therefore necessary to include pseudotreatment control into designs because merely thinking about stress at work and self-reflecting may actually enhance health outcomes as well.

Fifth, most studies only look at short-term changes, but we need to be able to produce long-term changes with stress interventions. Both in the areas of job interventions and in stress management, there are hypotheses in the literature that the effects are mainly short term.

Sixth, by and large, more process-oriented research on stress interventions needs to be done (Bunce, 1997). This can be done by developing manuals as well as by checking how much trainers conform to the theoretically proposed procedures, how much of the effect was due to the specific program, and how much of the effect was due to general effects. Good examples for such an approach exist in the clinical psychology—particularly cognitive therapy—approaches to depression (e.g., Castonguay, Hayes, Goldfried, & DeRubeis, 1995; DeRubeis et al., 1990; Hollon, DeRubeis, & Evans, 1987).

Seventh, research on respites from work stress is a promising area of research (Eden, 2001). More studies are needed that examine the specific features—predictors as well as short- and long-term consequences—of successful respite periods.

Eighth, some authors have confronted emotion-focused versus problem-focused approaches of stress interventions (e.g., Bond & Bunce, 2000). We agree with Keinan and Friedland (1996; p. 269) that a simple comparison cannot be made and leads to inconclusive results and that the following issues need to be considered: (a) Emotion-focused strategies may be

better in situations that allow little control and other resources; (b) the long-term effectiveness of emotion-focused strategies may be lower than that for problem-focused approaches; (c) a combination of emotion- and problem-focused strategies is probably superior to either one of them alone.

Finally, more research is needed that pits different approaches against each other. One of the most important issues is whether there are general and specific effects of an intervention (Bunce, 1997; Murphy, 1996). Trainer characteristics also need to be studied more frequently. For example, one study surprisingly showed that less well-trained trainers were more effective in stress management than were experienced trainers (Saunders et al., 1996). Another surprising finding of the meta-analysis by Van der Klink et al. (2001) that needs to be studied in more detail is that there is an inverse relationship between number of sessions and effect size.

OVERALL CONCLUSIONS

Empirical research summarized in this chapter shows that organizational stress has detrimental effects on individual health and well-being. Moreover, stress interventions—particularly those aimed at individual stress management—have been found to have beneficial effects.

Researchers have criticized past empirical studies on organizational stress for their methodological shortcomings (Frese & Zapf, 1988; Kasl, 1978; Sullivan & Bhagat, 1992). During the past decade, an increasing number of studies followed a more rigorous research methodology (e.g., objective measures of stressors, longitudinal designs, test of curvilinear effects). We are convinced that this improved methodology has contributed to substantial progress within organizational stress research. Specifically, we observed progress with respect to the following issues:

First, objective stressors—and not just the perception of stressors—are related to indicators of poor health and well-being. This implies that the well-documented empirical relationship between stressors and strains can not be fully explained by common method variance and overlap in content between independent and dependent variables.

Second, stressors have a causal effect on health and well-being with concurrent effects that are stronger than lagged effects. There are *additional* reverse effects of strains on stressors. However, these effects seem to be relatively weak.

Third, resources are important for an individual's health and well-being. The main effects of resources such as control at work, social support, and self-efficacy are stronger than their buffer effects.

Fourth, there are curvilinear effects of stressors on strains. However, it seems that compared to the linear effects, these curvilinear effects are of minor importance.

Fifth, better designed studies with objective measures report smaller correlations than do studies with subjective measures (cf. also Zapf, Dormann, et al., 1996); it may appear that this points to actually low impact rates of stressors on strain and that the effect of stressors at work is rather small. We think that this would be a mistake (Frese & Zapf, 1988) because (a) no study ever measures all stressors at work; (b) objective measures of stressors underestimate the relationship between stressors and strains because observers' errors decrease the correlations; (c) strain is caused by many factors (stressors at work, biological and psychological predispositions, stressors outside work, etc.)—every one of which can only have a certain amount of influence; (d) there is a selection effect of most studies on stress at work (healthy workers effect) because ill people have a lower probability to be in the sample; (e) there are moderators that may increase the relationships; (f) finally, low correlations often appear to be of less practical importance than is actually the case, as shown by Abelson (1985), Frese (1985), and Rosenthal and Rubin (1982).

Sixth, there are some studies that use natural experiments in stress research (e.g., Parkes, 1982). Kasl (1978) has called for more studies making use of natural experiments, and we can only repeat the suggestion here again.

As a whole, the recent advancements made in organizational stress research demonstrate that it pays to invest in a better research methodology. However, to make real progress in a field it is not sufficient to focus only on research methodology. It is necessary to also invest in theory development and to make sure to address the most relevant research questions (Brief & George, 1995). For deepening the understanding of the process of how and when organizational stress affects the individual and the larger organization, we suggest the following avenues for future research:

First, there is a clear need for a direct comparison between competing theoretical models. Such comparisons are still very rare (for an exception, cf. de Jonge et al., 2000). Such comparisons will be helpful for advancing theory about organizational stress because they will show which specific assumptions within one model make it superior to a competing model.

Second, researcher should pay more attention to the impact of specific stressors and specific resources on specific strains. Such a specificity hypothesis (Broadbent, 1985) implies that specific stressors are related to specific symptoms but not to others. Empirical tests of this hypothesis are still rare (Hesketh & Shouksmith, 1986; Steen, Firth, & Bond, 1998). For a resource to be effective as a stress buffer, it is crucial that the resource matches the specific requirements of the stressor (Cohen & Wills, 1985). Here, researchers have to specify more explicitly which resources are most helpful in a specific stressful situation.

Third, aspects of time should be taken much more seriously within organizational stress research. When studying the effects of stressors longitudinally, researchers should pay more attention to the time lags between the first and subsequent measurement points. Until now it seems that the time lags have been chosen rather arbitrarily or for convenience reasons. As the Dormann and Zapf (1999) study illustrated, some effects are found only for a limited set of time lags. Researchers need to spell out more clearly within which time frame they expect specific strain symptoms to develop. Frese and Zapf (1988) have differentiated the following models based on time and stress exposure effects: (a) stress reaction model that implies an ill-health reaction to the stressor, which is reduced when the stressor is reduced; (b) accumulation model, in which the effect is not reduced even if the stressor no longer present; (c) dynamic accumulation model, in which the effects increase ill health further even when individuals are no longer exposed to the stressors; (d) adjustment model, in which people learn to cope with the stressor and ill health is reduced even though the people are still exposed to the stressors; (e) sleeper effect model, in which the ill health appears after the stressor disappears, as in the case of posttraumatic stress disorder. We think that it is useful to explicitly test different models, taking into consideration exposure time and differential timing effects (cf. also Garst et al., 2000).

Fourth, more attention to time aspects is also necessary for testing interaction effects. It is necessary to examine in more detail at which point in time in the stress process resources are most helpful. For example, resources might act as powerful stress buffers only early in the stress process.

Fifth, researchers should explicitly address the mediating processes in the stressor-strain relationship; this refers both to mediators at the physiological level and to mediators at the emotional and cognitive level (i.e., appraisals).

Sixth, there should be more studies on stress and performance. Laboratory studies suggest that stressors have a negative effect on basic cognitive processes. However, in field study settings, the effects of stressors on job performance are less obvious. It seems that individuals uphold their performance by increasing effort. This increased work effort might have detrimental long-term effects on health and well-being, however. It is interesting to note that there are only a few field studies that simultaneously examined the effects of stressors on performance and on health and well-being. Research on the health effects of organizational stress and research on the performance effects of organizational stress are separate research areas, particularly in field studies. By focusing exclusively on health and well-being or on performance effects, researchers get to know only one side of the coin. We suggest further advancing organizational stress research by looking simultaneously at the impact of stressors on performance *and* on health and well-being. Such studies could identify the health and well-being costs of upholding high performance in stressful situations. Moreover, such studies could shed light on the performance requirements under which strain symptoms occur. It is also useful to address the role of resources by examining which resources let people uphold performance without impairing health and well-being.

Taken together, organizational stress research has benefited from methodologically more sophisticated studies. It has become obvious that organizational stress affects individual health and well-being in a negative way. Individuals, however, have a broad range of ways of dealing with stress so that both their health and performance do not suffer necessarily. Despite this research progress, there remain many questions to be answered by future research.

REFERENCES

Abelson, R. P. (1985). A variance explanation paradox: When a little is a lot. *Psychological Bulletin, 97,* 129–133.

Aiken, L. S., & West, S. G. (1991). *Multiple regression: Testing and interpreting interactions.* Newbury Park, CA: Sage.

Allen, N. J., & Meyer, J. P. (1990). The measurement of antecedents of affective, continuance and normative commitment to the organization. *Journal of Occupational Psychology, 63,* 1–18.

Andrews, F. M., & Farris, G. F. (1972). Time pressure and performance of scientists and engineers: A five-year panel study. *Organizational Behavior and Human Performance, 8,* 185–200.

Antonovsky, A. (1991). The structural sources of salutogenic strenghts. In C. L. Cooper & R. Payne (Eds.), *Personality and stress: Individual differences in the stress process* (pp. 67–104). Chichester, England: Wiley.

Aronsson, G., & Rissler, A. (1998). Psychophysiological stress reactions in female and male urban bus drivers. *Journal of Occupational Health Psychology, 3,* 122–129.

Baddeley, A. D. (1972). Selective attention and performance in dangerous environments. *British Journal of Psychology, 63,* 537–546.

Bakker, A. B., & Schaufeli, W. B. (2000). Burnout contagion processes among teachers. *Journal of Applied Social Psychology, 30,* 2289–2308.

Bakker, A. B., Schaufeli, W. B., Sixma, H. J., Bosveld, W., & van Dierendonck, D. (2000). Patient demands, lack of reciprocity, and burnout: A five-year longitudinal study among general practitionars. *Journal of Occupational Behavior, 21,* 425–441.

Bamberg, E., & Busch, C. (1996). Betriebliche Gesundheitsförderung durch Streßmanagementtraining: Eine Metaanalyse (quasi-)experimenteller Studien (Work oriented improvements in health through stress-management training: A metaanalysis of quasi-experimental studies). *Zeitschrift für Arbeits- und Organisationspsychologie, 40,* 127–137.

Bandura, A. (1997). *Self-efficacy: The exercise of control.* New York: Freeman.

Barnett, R. C., & Brennan, R. T. (1997). Change in job conditions, change in psychological distress, and gender: A longidtudinal study of dual-earner couples. *Journal of Organizational Behavior, 18,* 253–274.

Beck, A. T. (1967). *Depression: Causes and treatment.* Philadelphia: University of Pennsylvania Press.

Beehr, T. A. (1995). *Psychological stress in the workplace.* New York: Routledge.

Beehr, T. A. (1998). Research on occupational stress: An unfinished enterprise. *Personnel Psychology, 51,* 835–844.

Beehr, T. A., Jex, S. M., Stacy, B. A., & Murray, M. A. (2000). Work stressors and coworker support as predictors of individual strain and job performance. *Journal of Organizational Behavior, 21,* 391–405.

Beehr, T. A., & Newman, J. E. (1978). Job stress, employee health, and organizational effectiveness: A facet analysis, model, and literature review. *Personnel Psychology, 31,* 665–699.

Beermann, B., Kuhn, K., & Kompier, M. A. J. (1999). Germany: Reduction of stress by health circles. In M. A. J. Kompier & C. L. Cooper (Eds.), *Preventing stress, improving productivity: European case studies in the workplace* (pp. 222–241). London: Routledge.

Begley, T. M., & Czajka, J. M. (1993). Panel analysis of the moderating effects of commitment on job satisfaction, intent to quit, and health following organizational change. *Journal of Applied Psychology, 78,* 552–556.

Bellarosa, C., & Chen, P. Y. (1997). The effectiveness and practicality of occupational stress management interventions: A survey of subject matter expert opinions. *Journal of Occupational Health Psychology, 2,* 247–262.

Bhagat, R. S., & Allie, S. M. (1989). Organizational stress, personal life stress, and symptoms of life strains: An examination of the moderating role of sense of competence. *Journal of Vocational Behavior, 35,* 231–253.

Bliese, P. D., & Britt, T. W. (2001). Social support, group consensus and stressor-strain relationships: Social context matters. *Journal of Organizational Behavior, 22,* 425–436.

Bond, F. W., & Bunce, D. (2000). Mediators of change in emotion-focused and problem-focused worksite stress management interventions. *Journal of Occupational Health Psychology, 5,* 156–163.

Bongers, P. M., de Winter, C. R., Kompier, M. A. J., & Hildebrandt, V. H. (1993). Psychosocial factors at work and musculoskeletal diseases. *Scandinavian Journal of Work Environment and Health, 19,* 297–312.

Borman, W. C., & Motowidlo, S. J. (1993). Expanding the criterion domain to include elements of contextual performance. In

N. Schmitt & W. Borman (Eds.), *Personnel selection in organizations* (pp. 71–98). New York: Jossey-Bass.

Bosma, H., Peter, R., Siegrist, J., & Marmot, M. (1998). Two alternative job stress models and the risk of coronary heart disease. *American Journal of Public Health, 88,* 68–74.

Breslow, L., & Enstrom, J. E. (1980). Persistence of health habits and their relationship to mortality. *Preventive Medicine, 9,* 469–483.

Brief, A. P., & George, J. M. (1995). Psychological stress and the workplace: A brief comment on Lazarus' outlook. In R. Crandall & P. L. Perrewé (Eds.), *Occupational stress: A handbook* (pp. 15–19). Washington, DC: Taylor & Francis.

Broadbent, D. E. (1985). The clinical impact of job design. *British Journal of Clinical Psychology, 24,* 33–44.

Bromet, E. J., Dew, M. A., Parkinson, D. K., & Schulberg, H. C. (1988). Predictive effects of occupational and marital stress on the mental health of a male workforce. *Journal of Organizational Behavior, 9,* 1–13.

Bunce, D. (1997). What factors are associated with the outcome of individual-focused worksite stress management interventions? *Journal of Occupational and Organizational psychology, 70,* 1–17.

Bunce, D., & West, M. (1994). Changing work environments: Innovative coping responses to occupational stress. *Work and Stress, 8,* 319–331.

Bunce, D., & West, M. A. (1996). Stress management and innovation at work. *Human Relations, 49,* 209–232.

Campbell, J. P., McCloy, R. A., Oppler, S. H., & Sager, C. E. (1993). A theory of performance. In E. Schmitt &W. C. Borman (Eds.), *Personnel selection in organizations* (pp. 35–70). San Francisco: Jossey-Bass.

Carayon, P. (1993). A longitudinal test of Karasek's job strain model among office workers. *Work and Stress, 7,* 299–314.

Carter, A. J., & West, M. A. (1999). Sharing the burden: Teamwork in health care settings. In R. L. Payne & J. Firth-Cozens (Eds.), *Stress in health professionals: Psychological and organisational issues* (pp. 191–202). Chichester, England: Wiley.

Carter, S. M., & West, M. A. (1998). Reflexivity, effectiveness, and mental health in BBC-TV production teams. *Small Group Research, 29,* 583–601.

Cartwright, S., Cooper, C. L., & Murphy, L. R. (1995). Diagnosing a healthy organization: A proactive approach to stress in the workplace. In L. R. Murphy, J. J. J. Hurrell, S. L. Sauter, & C. W. Puryear Keita (Eds.), *Job stress interventions* (pp. 217–233). Washington, DC: American Psychological Association.

Carver, C. S., & Scheier, M. F. (1982). Control theory: A useful conceptual framework for personality—social, clinical, and health psychology. *Psychological Bulletin, 92,* 111–135.

Castonguay, L. G., Hayes, A. M., Goldfried, M. R., & DeRubeis, R. J. (1995). The focus of therapist interventions in cognitive therapy for depression. *Cognitive Therapy & Research, 19,* 485–503.

Cavanaugh, M. A., Boswell, W. R., Roehling, M. V., & Boudreau, J. W. (2000). An empirical examination of self-reported work stress among U.S. managers. *Journal of Applied Psychology, 85,* 65–74.

Chapman, A., Mandryk, J. A., Frommer, M. S., Edye, B. V., & Ferguson, D. A. (1990). Chronic perceived work stress and blood pressure among Australian government employees. *Scandinavian Journal of Work, Environment and Health, 16,* 258–269.

Chen, P. Y., & Spector, P. E. (1992). Relationships of work stressors with aggression, withdrawal, theft and substance use: An exploratory study. *Journal of Occupational and Organizational Psychology, 65,* 177–184.

Cohen, S., & Edwards, J. R. (1989). Personality characteristics as moderators of the relationship between stress and disorder. In R. W. J. Neufeld (Ed.), *Advances in the investigation of psychological stress* (pp. 235–283). New York: Wiley.

Cohen, S., & Syme, S. L. (1985). *Social support and health.* New York: Academic Press.

Cohen, S., & Wills, T. A. (1985). Stress, social support, and the buffering hypothesis. *Psychological Bulletin, 98,* 310–357.

Cooper, C. (Ed.). (1998). *Theories of organizational stress.* New York: Oxford University Press.

Cooper, C. L., Liukkonen, P., & Cartwright, S. (1996). *Stress prevention in the workplace: Assessing the costs and benefits to organisations.* Dublin, Ireland: European Foundation for the Improvement of Living and Working Conditions.

Cooper, C. L., & Payne, R. L. (1992). International perspectives on research into work, well-being, and stress management. In J. C. Quick, L. R. Murphy, & J. J. J. Hurrell (Eds.), *Stress and well-being at work* (pp. 348–368). Washington, DC: American Psychological Association.

Corneil, W., Beaton, R., Murphy, S., Johnson, C., & Pike, K. (1999). Exposure to traumatic incidents and prevalence of posttraumatic stress symptomatology in urban firefighters in two countries. *Journal of Occupational Health Psychology, 4,* 131–141.

Cox, T., Griffiths, A., & Rial-Gonzáles, E. (2000). *Research on work-related stress.* Luxembourg: European Agency for Safety and Health at Work.

Cummings, T., & Cooper, C. L. (1979). A cybernetic theory of occupational stress. *Human Relations, 32,* 395–418.

Cummings, T. G., & Cooper, C. L. (1998). A cybernetic theory of organizational stress. In C. L. Cooper (Ed.), *Theories of organizational stress* (pp. 101–121). New York: Oxford University Press.

Daniels, K. (1999). Coping and the job demands-control-support model: An exploratory study. *International Journal of Stress Management, 6,* 125–144.

Daniels, K., & Guppy, A. (1994). Occupational stress, social support, job control, and psychological well-being. *Human Relations, 47,* 1523–1544.

Danna, K., & Griffin, R. W. (1999). Health and well-being in the workplace: A review and synthesis on the literature. *Journal of Management, 25,* 357–384.

De Croon, E. M., Van der Beek, A. J., Blonk, R. W. B., & Frings-Dresen, M. H. W. (2000). Job stress and psychosomatic health complaints among Dutch truck drivers: A re-evaluation of Karasek's interactive job demand-control model. *Stress Medicine, 16,* 101–107.

de Jonge, J., Bosma, H., Peter, R., & Siegrist, J. (2000). Job strain, effort-reward imbalance and employee well-being: A large-scale cross-sectional study. *Social Science and Medicine, 50,* 1317–1327.

de Jonge, J., & Schaufeli, W. B. (1998). Job characteristics and employee well-being: A test of Warr's vitamin model in health care workers using structural equation modelling. *Journal of Organizational Behavior, 19,* 387–407.

de Rijk, A. E., Le Blanc, P. M., Schaufeli, W. B., & de Jonge, J. (1998). Active coping and need for control as moderators of the job demand-control model: Effects on burnout. *Journal of Occupational and Organizational Psychology, 71,* 1–18.

DeRubeis, R. J., Evans, M. D., Hollon, S. D., Garvey, M. J., Grove, W. M., & Tuason, V. B. (1990). How does cognitive therapy work? Cognitive change and symptom change in cognitive therapy and pharmacotherapy for depression. *Journal of Consulting and Clinical Psychology, 58,* 862–869.

Doby, V. J., & Caplan, R. D. (1995). Organizational stress as threat to reputation: Effects on anxiety at work and at home. *Academy of Management Journal, 38,* 1105–1123.

Dollard, M. F., Winefield, H. R., Winefield, A. H., & de Jonge, J. (2000). Psychosocial job strains and productivity in human service workers: A test of the demand-control-support model. *Journal of Occupational and Organizational Psychology, 73,* 501–510.

Dormann, C., & Zapf, D. (1999). Social support, social stressors at work, and depressive symptoms: Testing for main and moderating effects with structural equations in a three-wave longitudinal study. *Journal of Applied Psychology, 84,* 874–884.

Dusseldorp, E., Van Elderen, T., Maes, S., Meulman, J., & Kraaij, V. (1999). A meta-analysis of psychoeducational programs for coronary heart disease patients. *Health Psychology, 18,* 506–519.

Dwyer, D. J., & Ganster, D. C. (1991). The effects of job demands and control on employee attendance and satisfaction. *Journal of Organizational Behavior, 12,* 595–608.

Eden, D. (2001). Vacations and other respites: Studying stress on and off the job. In C. L. Cooper & I. T. Robertson (Eds.), *International review of industrial and organizational psychology.* Chichester, England: Wiley.

Edmondson, A. (1999). Psychological safety and learning behavior in work teams. *Administrative Science Quarterly, 44,* 350–383.

Edwards, J. R. (1991). Person-job fit: A conceptual integration, literature review, and methodological critique. In C. L. Cooper & I. T. Robertson (Eds.), *International review of indsutrial and organizational psychology* (pp. 283–357). Chichester, England: Wiley.

Edwards, J. R. (1992). A cybernetic theory of stress, coping, and well-being in organizations. *Academy of Management Review, 17,* 238–274.

Edwards, J. R. (1995). Alter natives to difference scores as dependent variables in the study of congruence in organizational research. *Organizational Behavior and Human Decision Processes, 64,* 307–324.

Edwards, J. R. (1996). An examination of competing versions of the person-environment fit approach to stress. *Academy of Management Journal, 39,* 292–339.

Edwards, J. R. (1998). Cybernetic theory of stress, coping, and well-being. In C. L. Cooper (Ed.), *Theories of organizational stress* (pp. 122–152). Oxford, England: Oxford University Press.

Edwards, J. R., & Harrison, R. V. (1993). Job demands and worker health: Three-dimensional re-examination of the relationship between person-environment fit and strain. *Journal of Applied Psychology, 78,* 626–648.

Elkin, A. J., & Rosch, P. J. (1990). Promoting mental health at the workplace: The prevention side of stress management. *Occupational Medicine: State of the Art Review, 5,* 739–754.

Ellis, A. (1962). *Reason and emotion in psychotherapy.* New York: Lyle Stuart.

Elsass, P. M., & Veiga, J. F. (1997). Job control and job strain: A test of three models. *Journal of Occupational Health Psychology, 2,* 195–211.

Eriksen, H. R., & Ursin, H. (1999). Subjective health complaints: Is coping more important than control? *Work and Stress, 13,* 238–252.

Etzion, D., Eden, D., & Lapidot, Y. (1998). Relief from job stressors and burnout: Reserve service as a respite. *Journal of Applied Psychology, 83,* 577–585.

Farrell, D., & Stamm, C. L. (1988). Meta-analysis of the correlates of employee absence. *Human Relations, 41,* 211–227.

Fay, D., & Sonnentag, S. (in press). Rethinking the effects of stressors: A longitudinal study on personal initiative. *Journal of Occupation Health Psychology.*

Fletcher, B. C. (1991). *Work, stress, disease and life expectancy.* Chichester, England: Wiley.

Folkman, S., Lazarus, R. S., Dunkel-Schetter, C., DeLongis, A., & Gruen, R. (1986). The dynamics of a stressful encounter: Cognitive appraisal, coping, and encounter outcomes. *Journal of Personality and Social Psychology, 50,* 992–1003.

Fox, M. L., Dwyer, D. J., & Ganster, D. C. (1993). Effects of stressful job demands and control on physiological and attitudinal outcomes in a hospital setting. *Academy of Management Journal, 36,* 289–318.

Frankenhaeuser, M. (1979). Psychoneuroendicrine approaches to the study of emotion as related to stress and coping. In R. A. Dienstbier (Ed.), *Nebraska Symposium on Motivation 1978* (pp. 123–161). Lincoln: University of Nebraska Press.

Frankenhaeuser, M. (1981). Coping with stress at work. *International Journal of Health Services, 11,* 491–510.

Frankenhaeuser, M., & Johansson, G. (1976). Task demand as reflected in catecholamine excretion and heart rate. *Journal of Human Stress, 2,* 15–23.

French, J. R. P. Jr., Caplan, R. D., & Harrison, R. V. (1982). *The mechanisms of job stress and strain*. Chichester, England: Wiley.

Frese, M. (1985). Stress at work and psychosomatic complaints: A causal interpretation. *Journal of Applied Psychology, 70,* 314–328.

Frese, M. (1989). Theoretical models of control and health. In S. L. Sauter, J. J. Hurrell Jr., & C. L. Cooper (Eds.), *Job control and worker health* (pp. 107–128). Chichester, England: Wiley.

Frese, M. (1993). *Stress factors and health: A multicausal relationship.* Paper presented at the work and health: Scientific basis of progress in the working environment. European Commission Health and Safety at work. Copenhagen, Denmark.

Frese, M. (1999). Social support as a moderator of the relationship between work stressors and psychological dysfunctioning: A longitudinal study with objective measures. *Journal of Occupational Health Psychology, 4,* 179–192.

Frese, M., & Zapf, D. (1988). Methodological issues in the study of work stress: Objective vs. subjective measurement and the question of longituydinal studies. In C. L. Cooper & R. Payne (Eds.), *Causes, coping, and consequences of stress at work* (pp. 375–411). New York: Wiley.

Frese, M., & Zapf, D. (1994). Action as the core of work psychology: A German approach. In H. C. Triandis, M. D. Dunnette, & L. M. Hough (Eds.), *Handbook of industrial and organizational psychology* (2nd ed., Vol. 4, pp. 271–340). Palo Alto, CA: Consulting Psychologists Press.

Frese, M., & Zapf, D. (1999). On the importance of the objective environment in stress and attribution theory: Counterpoint to Perrewé and Zellars. *Journal of Organizational Behavior, 20,* 761–765.

Furda, J., de Jonge, J., Le Blanc, P., Meijman, T., Schreurs, P., & Scheenen, J. (1994). Het Demand-control-support model in relatie tot gezondheidsklachten en herstelklachten [The demand-control-support model in relation to health complaints and recovery complaints: A longitudinal study]. *Gedrag en Organisatie, 7,* 225–238.

Galinsky, T. L., Swanson, N. G., Sauter, S. L., Hurrell, J. J., & Schleifer, L. M. (2000). A field study of supplementary rest breaks for data-entry operators. *Ergonomics, 43,* 622–638.

Ganster, D. C., & Schaubroeck, J. (1991). Work stress and employee health. *Journal of Management, 17,* 235–271.

Ganster, D. C., Schaubroeck, J., Sime, W. E., & Mayes, B. T. (1991). The nomological validity of the Type A personality among employed adults. *Journal of Applied Psychology, 76,* 143–168.

Garst, H., Frese, M., & Molenaar, P. C. M. (2000). The temporal factor of change in stressor-strain relationships: A growth curve model on a longitudinal study in East Germany. *Journal of Applied Psychology, 85,* 417–438.

Glaser, D. M., Tatum, B. C., Nebeker, D. M., Sorenson, R. C., & Aiello, J. R. (1999). Workload and social support: Effects on performance and stress. *Human Performance, 12,* 155–176.

Glass, D. C., & McKnight, J. D. (1996). Perceived control, depressive symptomatology, and professional burnout: A review of the evidence. *Psychology and Health, 11,* 23–48.

Glickman, L., Tanaka, J. S., & Chan, E. (1991). Life events, chronic strain, and psychological distress: Longitudinal causal models. *Journal of Community Psychology, 19,* 283–305.

Goetzel, R. Z., Anderson, D. R., Whitmer, R. W., Ozminkowski, R. J., Dunn, R. L., & Wasserman, J. (1998). The relationship between modifiable health risks and health care expenditures. *Journal of Occupational and environmental Medicine, 40,* 843–854.

Graf, O., Rutenfranz, J., & Ulich, E. (1970). Arbeitszeit und Arbeitspausen [Work time and work breaks]. In A. Mayer & B. Herwig (Eds.), *Betriebspsychologie* (2nd ed., Vol. 9, pp. 244–277). Goettingen, Germany: Hogrefe.

Greiner, B. A., Ragland, D. R., Krause, N., Syme, S. L., & Fisher, J. M. (1997). Objective measurement of occupational stress factors: An example with San Francisco urban transit operators. *Journal of Occupational Health Psychology, 2,* 325–342.

Griffeth, R. W., Hom, P. W., & Gaertner, S. (2000). A meta-analysis of antecedents and correlates of employee turnover: Update, moderator tests, and research implications for the next millennium. *Journal of Management, 26,* 463–488.

Guppy, A., & Weatherston, L. (1997). Coping strategies, dysfunctional attitudes and psychological well-being in white collar public sectors employees. *Work and Stress, 11,* 58–67.

Gupta, N., & Beehr, T. A. (1979). Job stress and employee behaviors. *Organizational Behavior and Human Performance, 23,* 373–387.

Hacker, W. (1998). *Allgemeine Arbeitspsychologie: Psychische Regulation von Arbeitstätigkeiten* [General work psychology: Psychological regulation of work actions]. Bern, Switzerland: Huber.

Hamilton, V. (1982). Cognition and stress: An information processing model. In L. Goldberger & S. Breznitz (Eds.), *Handbook of stress: Theoretical and clinical aspects* (pp. 105–120). New York: Free Press.

Harnois, G., & Gabriel, P. (2000). *Mental health and work: Impact, issues and good practices*. Geneva, Switzerland: International Labour Organisation.

Harrison, R. V. (1978). Person-environment fit and job stress. In C. L. Cooper & R. Paye (Eds.), *Stress at work* (pp. 175–205). New York: Wiley.

Hart, P. M., Wearing, A. J., & Headey, B. (1995). Police stress and well-being: Integrating personality, coping and daily work experiences. *Journal of Occupational and Organizational Psychology, 68,* 133–156.

Heaney, C. A., Price, R. H., & Rafferty, J. (1995). Increasing coping resources at work: A field experiment to increase social support, improve work team functioning, and enhance employee mental health. *Journal of Organizational Behavior, 16,* 335–352.

Hemingway, M. A., & Smith, C. S. (1999). Organizational climate and occupational stressors as predictors of withdrawal behaviours and injuries in nurses. *Journal of Occupational and Organizational Psychology, 72,* 285–299.

Henning, R. A., Sauter, S. L., Salvendy, G., & Krieg, E. F. (1989). Microbreak length, performance, and stress in a data entry task. *Ergonomics, 32,* 855–864.

Herbert, T. B., & Sheldon, C. (1993). Stress and immunity in humans: A meta-analytic review. *Psychosomatic Medicine, 55,* 364–379.

Hesketh, B., & Shouksmith, G. (1986). Job and non-job acitivities, job satisfaction and mental health among veterinarians. *Journal of Organizational Behavior, 7,* 325–339.

Hibbard, J. H., & Pope, C. R. (1993). The quality of social roles as predictors of morbidity and mortality. *Social Science and Medicine, 36,* 217–225.

Hobfoll, S. E. (1998). *Stress, culture, and community: The psychology and physiology of stress.* New York: Plenum.

Hockey, G. R., Maule, A. J., Vlough, P. J., & Bdzola, L. (2000). Effects of negative mood states on risk in everyday decision making. *Cognition and Emotion, 14,* 823–856.

Hockey, G. R. J. (1986). Changes in operator efficiency as a function of environmental stress, fatigue, and circadian rhythms. In K. R. Boff, L. Kaufman, & J. P. Thomas (Eds.), *Handbook of perception and human performance* (Vol. 2, pp. 44-1–44-49). Washington, DC: National Academy Press.

Hockey, G. R. J. (1997). Compensatory control in the regulation of human performance under stress and high workload: A cognitive-energetical framework. *Biological Psychology, 45,* 73–93.

Hockey, G. R. J. (2000). Work environments and performance. In N. Chmiel (Ed.), *Work and organizational psychology: A European perspective* (pp. 206–230). Oxford, England: Blackwell.

Hollon, S. D., DeRubeis, R. J., & Evans, M. D. (1987). Causal mediation of change in treatment for depression: Discriminating between nonspecificity and noncausality. *Psychological Bulletin, 102,* 139–149.

House, J. S. (1981). *Work stress and social support.* Reading, MA: Addison-Wesley.

Howard, J. H., Cunningham, D. A., & Rechniter, P. A. (1986). Personality (hardiness) as a moderator of job stress and coronary risk in Type A individuals: A longitudinal study. *Journal of Behavioral Medicine, 9,* 229–245.

Ilgen, D. R., & Hollenbeck, J. R. (1991). The structure of work: Job design and roles. In M. D. Dunnette & L. M. Hough (Eds.), *Handbook of industrial and organizational psychology* (2nd ed., Vol. 2, pp. 165–207). Palo Alto, CA: Consulting Psychologists Press.

Ingledew, D. K., Hardy, L., & Cooper, C. L. (1997). Do resources bolster coping and does coping buffer stress? An organizational study with longitudinal aspect and control for negative affectivity. *Journal of Occupational Health Psychology, 2,* 118–133.

Ivancevich, J. M., & Matteson, M. T. (1988). Promoting the individual's health and well-being. In C. L. Cooper & R. Payne (Eds.), *Causes, coping and consequences of stress at work* (pp. 267–299). Chichester, England: Wiley.

Ivancevich, J. M., Matteson, M. T., Freedman, S. M., & Phillips, J. S. (1990). Worksite stress management interventions. *American Psychologist, 45,* 252–261.

Jackson, P. R., Wall, T. D., Martin, R., & Davids, K. (1993). New measures of job control, cognitive demand, and production responsibility. *Journal of Applied Psychology, 78,* 753–762.

Jackson, S. E. (1983). Participation in decision making as a strategy for reducing job-related strain. *Journal of Applied Psychology, 68,* 3–19.

Jackson, S. E., & Schuler, R. S. (1985). A meta-analysis and conceptual critique of research on role ambiguity and role conflict in work settings. *Organizational Behavior and Human Performance, 33,* 1–21.

Jacobson, E. (1938). *Progressive relaxation.* Chicago: University of Chicago Press.

Jamal, M. (1984). Job stress and job performance controversy: An empirical assessment. *Organizational Behavior and Human Performance, 33,* 1–21.

Jamal, M. (1985). Relationship of job stress to job performance: A study of managers and blue collar workers. *Human Relations, 38,* 409–424.

Jex, S. M. (1998). *Stress and job performance: Theory, research, and implications for managerial practice.* Thousand Oaks, CA: Sage.

Jex, S. M., & Bliese, P. D. (1999). Efficacy beliefs as a moderator of the impact of work-related stressors: A multilevel study. *Journal of Applied Psychology, 84,* 349–361.

Jex, S. M., & Elacqua, T. C. (1999). Self-esteem as a moderator: A comparison of global and organization-based measures. *Journal of Occupational and Organizational Psychology, 72,* 71–81.

Jex, S. M., & Gudanowski, D. M. (1992). Efficacy beliefs and work stress: An exploratory study. *Journal of Occupational Behavior, 13,* 509–517.

Jimmieson, N. L., & Terry, D. J. (1997). Responses to an in-basket activity: The role of work stress, behavioral control, and informational control. *Journal of Occupational Health Psychology, 2,* 72–83.

Jimmieson, N. L., & Terry, D. J. (1999). The moderating role of task characteristics in determining responses to a stressful work simulation. *Journal of Organizational Behavior, 20,* 709–736.

Johansson, G., Aronsson, G., & Lindström, B. O. (1978). Social psychological and neuroendocrine stress reactions in highly mechanised work. *Ergonomics, 21,* 583–599.

Johnson, J. V., & Hall, E. M. (1988). Job strain, workplace social support and cardiovascular disease: A cross-sectional study of a random sample of the Swedish working population. *American Journal of Public Health, 78,* 1335–1342.

Jones, J. W., Barge, B. N., Steffy, B. D., Fay, L. M., Kunz, L. K., & Wuebker, L. J. (1988). Stress and medical malpractice:

Organizational risk assessment and intervention. *Journal of Applied Psychology, 73,* 727–735.

Kahn, R. L., & Byosiere, P. (1992). Stress in organizations. In M. D. Dunnette & L. M. Hough (Eds.), *Handbook of industrial and organizational psychology* (2nd ed., Vol. 3, pp. 571–650). Palo Alto, CA: Consulting Psychologists Press.

Kahn, R. L., Wolfe, D. M., Quinn, R. P., Snoek, J. D., & Rosenthal, R. A. (1964). *Organizational stress: Studies in role conflict and ambiguity.* New York: Wiley.

Kanner, A. D., Coyne, J. C., Schaefer, C., & Lazarus, R. S. (1981). Comparison of two modes of stress measurement: Daily hassles and uplifts versus major life events. *Journal of Behavioral Medicine, 4,* 1–39.

Karasek, R. (1979). Job demands, job decision latitude, and mental strain: Implications for job redesign. *Administrative Science Quarterly, 24,* 285–306.

Karasek, R., Baker, D., Marxner, F., Ahlbom, A., & Theorell, T. (1981). Job decision latitude, job demands, and cardiovascular disease: A prospective study of Swedish men. *American Journal of Public Health, 71,* 694–705.

Kasl, S. V. (1978). Epidemiological contributions to the sutdy of work stress. In C. L. Cooper & R. Pane (Eds.), *Stress at work* (pp. 3–48). Chichester, England: Wiley.

Kasl, S. V. (1986). Stress and disease in the workplace: A methodological commentary on the accumulated evidence. In M. F. Cataldo & T. J. Coates (Eds.), *Health and industry: A behavioral medicine perspective* (pp. 52–85). New York: Wiley.

Kasl, S. V. (1996). The influence of the work environment on cardiovascular health: A historical, conceptual, and methodological critique. *Journal of Occupational Health Psychology, 1,* 42–56.

Kasl, S. V. (1998). Measuring job stressors and studying the health impact of the work environment: An epidemiologic commentary. *Journal of Occupational Health Psychology, 3,* 390–401.

Katz, D., & Kahn, R. L. (1978). *The social psychology of organizations* (2nd ed.). New York: Wiley.

Keinan, G., & Friedland, N. (1996). Training effective performance under stress: Queries, dilemmas, and possible solutions. In J. E. Driskell & E. Salas (Eds.), *Stress and human performance* (pp. 257–277). Mahwah, NJ: Erlbaum.

Kivimäki, M., Vahtera, J., Thomson, L., Griffiths, A., Cox, T., & Pentti, J. (1997). Psychosocial factors predicting employee sickness absence during economic decline. *Journal of Applied Psychology, 82,* 858–872.

Kjellberg, A., Sköldström, B., Andersson, O., & Lindberg, L. (1996). Fatigue effects of noise on aeroplane mechanics. *Work and Stress, 10,* 62–71.

Klein, G. (1996). The effect of acute stressors on decision making. In J. E. Driskell & E. Salas (Eds.), *Stress and human performance* (pp. 49–88). Mahwah, NJ: Erlbaum.

Kobasa, S. C., Maddi, S. R., & Kahn, S. (1982). Hardiness and health: A prospective study. *Journal of Personality and Social Psychology, 42,* 168–177.

Kohn, M. L., & Schooler, C. (1982). Job conditions and personality: A longitudinal assessment of their reciprocal effects. *American Journal of Sociology, 87,* 1257–1286.

Kompier, M. A. J., Aust, B., Van den Berg, A.-M., & Siegrist, J. (2000). Stress prevention in bus drivers: Evaluation of 13 natural experiments. *Journal of Occupational Health Psychology, 5,* 11–31.

Kompier, M. A. J., Cooper, C. L., & Geurts, S. A. E. (2000). A multiple case study approach to work stress prevention in Europe. *European Journal of Work and Organizational Psychology, 9,* 371–400.

Kristensen, T. S. (1991). Sickness absence and work strain among Danish slaughterhouse workers: An analysis of absence from work regarded as coping behavior. *Social Science and Medicine, 32,* 15–27.

Kristensen, T. S. (1995). The demand-control-support model: Methodological challenges for future research. *Stress Medicine, 11,* 17–26.

Landsbergis, P. A. (1988). Occupational stress among health care workers: A test of the job demands-control model. *Journal of Occupational Behavior, 9,* 217–239.

Landsbergis, P. A., Schnall, P. L., Deitz, D., Friedman, R., & Pckering, T. (1992). The patterning of psychological attributes and distress by "job strain" and social support in a sample of working men. *Journal of Behavioral Medicine, 15,* 379–405.

Landsbergis, P. A., & Vivona-Vaughan, E. (1995). Evaluation of an occupational stress intervention in a public agency. *Journal of Organizational Behavior, 16,* 29–48.

Lazarus, R. S. (1966). *Psychological stress and the coping process.* New York: Springer.

Lazarus, R. S. (1991). Psychological stress in the workplace. *Journal of Social Behavior and Personality, 6,* 1–13.

Lazarus, R. S., & Folkman, S. (1984). *Stress, appraisal, and coping.* New York: Springer.

Lee, R. T., & Ashforth, B. E. (1993). A longitudinal study of burnout among supervisors and managers: Comparisons between the Leister and Maslach (1988) and Golembiewski et al. (1986) models. *Organizational Behavior and Human Decision Processes, 54,* 369–398.

Lee, R. T., & Ashforth, B. E. (1996). A meta-analytic examination of the correlates of the three dimensions of job burnout. *Journal of Applied Psychology, 81,* 123–133.

Leiter, M. P. (1991). Coping patterns as predictors of burnout: The function of control and escapist coping patterns. *Journal of Organizational Behavior, 12,* 123–144.

Leitner, K. (1993). Auswirkungen von Arbeitsbedingungen auf die psychosoziale Gesundheit [Effects of working conditions on psycho-social health]. *Zeitschrift für Arbeitswissenschaft, 47,* 98–107.

Leitner, K., Volpert, W., Greiner, B., Weber, W.-G., & Hennes, K. (1987). *Analyse psychischer Belastung in der Arbeit: Das*

RHIA-Verfahren, Handbuch [Analysis of mental stressors at work: The RHIA instrument and manual]. Cologne, Germany: TÜv Rheinland.

Levi, L., & Lunde-Jensen, P. (1996). *A model for assessing the costs of stressors at national level: Socio-economic costs of work stress in two EU member states*. Dublin, Ireland: European Foundation for the Improvement of Living and Working Conditions.

Long, B. C., & Van Stavel, R. (1995). Effects of exercise training on anxiety: A meta-analysis. *Journal of Applied Sport Psychology, 7,* 167–189.

Lorist, M. M., Klein, M., Nieuwenhuis, S., de Jong, R., Mulder, G., & Meijman, T. F. (2000). Mental fatigue and task control: Planning and preparation. *Psychophysiology, 37,* 614–625.

Lulofs, R., Wennekens, R., & van Houtem, J. V. (1981). Effect of physical stress and time pressure on performance. *Perceptual and Motor Skills, 52,* 787–793.

Lundberg, U., & Frankenhaeuser, M. (1978). Psychophysiological reactions to noise as modified by personal control over noise intensity. *Biological Psychology, 6,* 55–59.

Martocchio, J. J., Harrison, D. A., & Berkson, H. (2000). Connections between lower pack pain, interventions, and absence from work: A time based meta-analysis. *Personnel Psychology, 53,* 595–624.

Maslach, C., & Jackson, S. E. (1981). The measurement of experienced burnout. *Journal of Organizational Behavior, 2,* 99–113.

Maslach, C., Schaufeli, W. B., & Leiter, M. P. (2001). Job burnout. *Annual Review of Psychology, 52,* 397–422.

Mathieu, J. E., & Zajac, D. M. (1990). A review and meta-analysis of the antecedents, correlates, and consequences of organizational commitment. *Psychological Bulletin, 108,* 171–194.

Matteson, M. T., & Ivancevich, J. M. (1987). *Controlling work stress*. San Francisco, CA: Jossey-Bass.

Mauno, S., & Kinnunen, U. (1999). Job insecurity and well-being: A longitudinal study among male and femal employees in Finland. *Community, Work & Family, 2,* 147–171.

McGrath, J. E. (1976). Stress and behavior in organizations. In M. D. Dunnette (Ed.), *Handbook of industrial and organizational psychology*. Chicago: Rand McNally.

Meichenbaum, D. (1985). *Stress inoculation training*. New York: Pergamon.

Meijman, T. F., Mulder, G., & Van Dormolen, M. (1992). Workload of driving examiners: A psychophysiological field study. In H. Kragt (Ed.), *Enhancing industrial performances* (pp. 245–260). London: Taylor & Francis.

Melamed, S., Ben-Avi, I., Luz, J., & Green, M. S. (1995). Objective and subjective work monotony: Effects on job satisfaction, psychological distress, and absenteeism in blue-collar workers. *Journal of Applied Psychology, 80,* 29–42.

Melamed, S., Kushnir, T., & Meir, E. I. (1991). Attenuating the impact of job demands: Additive and interactive effects of perceived control and social support. *Journal of Vocational Behavior, 39,* 40–53.

Melin, B., Lundberg, U., Soederlund, J., & Granqvist, M. (1999). Psychological and physiological stress reactions of male and female assembly workers: A comparison between two difference forms of work organization. *Journal of Organizational Behavior, 20,* 47–61.

Mohr, G. B. (2000). The changing significance of different stressors after the announcement of bankruptcy: A longitudinal investigation with special emphasis on job insecurity. *Journal of Organizational Behavior, 21,* 337–359.

Motowidlo, S. J., Packard, J. S., & Manning, M. R. (1986). Occupational stress: Its causes and consequences on job performance. *Journal of Applied Psychology, 71,* 618–629.

Mowday, R. T., Porter, L. W., & Steers, R. M. (1982). *Employee-organizational linkages*. New York: Academic Press.

Moyle, P. (1998). Longitudinal influences of managerial support on employee well-being. *Work and Stress, 12,* 29–49.

Moyle, P., & Parkes, K. (1999). The effects of transition stress: A relocation study. *Journal of Organizational Behavior, 20,* 625–646.

Murphy, L. R. (1988). Workplace interventions for stress reduction and prevention. In C. L. Cooper & R. Payne (Eds.), *Causes, coping and consequences of stress at work* (pp. 301–339). Chichester, England: Wiley.

Murphy, L. R. (1996). Stress management in work settings: A critical review of health effects. *American Journal of Health Promotion, 11,* 112–135.

Muntaner, C., Tien, A. Y., Eaton, W. W., & Garrison, R. (1991). Occupational characteristics and the occurence of psychotic disorders. *Social Psychiatry and Psychiatric Epidemiology, 26,* 273–280.

National Institute for Occupational Safety and Health. (1999). *Stress . . . at work* (DHHS Publication No. 99-101). Cincinnati, OH: Author.

Nelson, D. L., & Sutton, C. (1990). Chronic work stress and coping: A longitudinal study and suggested new directions. *Academy of Management Journal, 33,* 859–869.

Newton, T. J., & Keenan, A. (1990). The moderating effect of the Type A behavior pattern and locus of control upon the relationship between change in job demands and change in psychological strain. *Human Relations, 43,* 1229–1255.

Noor, N. M. (1995). Work and family roles in relation to women's well-being: A longitudinal study. *British Journal of Social Psychology, 34,* 87–106.

North, F. M., Syme, S. L., Feeney, A., Shipley, M., & Marmot, M. (1996). Psychosocial work environment and sickness absence among British civil servants: The Whitehall II study. *American Journal of Public Health, 86,* 332–340.

Nunes, E. V., Frank, K. A., & Kornfeld, D. S. (1987). Psychologic treatment for the Type A behavior pattern and for coronary heart disease: A meta-analysis of the literature. *Psychosomatic Medicine, 48,* 159–173.

O'Connor, G. T., Buring, J. E., Yusuf, S., Goldhaber, S. Z., Olmstead, E. M., Paffenbarger, R. S., & Hennekens, C. H. (1989). An overview of randomized trials of rehabilitation with exercise after myocardial infarction. *Circulation, 80,* 234–244.

Parker, S. K., & Sprigg, C. A. (1999). Minimizing strain and maximizing learning: The role of job demands, job control, and proactive personality. *Journal of Applied Psychology, 84,* 925–939.

Parkes, K. R. (1982). Occupational stress among nurses: A natural experiment. *Journal of Applied Psychology, 67,* 784–796.

Parkes, K. R. (1990). Coping, negative affectivity, and the work environment: Additive and interactive predictors of mental health. *Journal of Applied Psychology, 75,* 399–409.

Parkes, K. R. (1991). Locus of control as moderator: An explanation for additive versus interactive findings in the demand-discretion model of work stress. *British Journal of Psychology, 82,* 291–312.

Parkes, K. R., Menham, C. A., & Rabenau, C. V. (1994). Social support and the demand-discretion model of job stress: Tests of additive and interactive effects in two samples. *Journal of Vocational Behavior, 44,* 91–113.

Payne, R. (1991). Individual differences in cognition and the stress process. In C. L. Cooper & R. Payne (Eds.), *Personality and stress: Individual differences in the stress process* (pp. 181–204). New York: Wiley.

Peeters, M. C. W., Buunk, B. P., & Schaufeli, W. B. (1995). Social interactions and feelings of inferiority among correctional officers: A daily event-recording approach. *Journal of Applied Social Psychology, 25,* 1073–1089.

Pekrun, R., & Frese, M. (1992). Emotions in work and achievement. In C. L. Cooper & I. T. Robertson (Eds.), *International review of industrial and organizational psychology* (Vol. 7, pp. 153–200). Chichester, England: Wiley.

Perrewé, P. L., & Ganster, D. C. (1989). The impact of job demands and behavioral control on experienced job stress. *Journal of Organizational Behavior, 10,* 213–229.

Perrewé, P. L., & Zellars, K. L. (1999). An examination of attributions and emotions in the transactional approach to the organizational stress process. *Journal of Organizational Behavior, 20,* 739–752.

Perrez, M., & Reicherts, M. (1992). A situation-behavior approach to stress and coping. In M. Perrez & M. Reicherts (Eds.), *Stress, coping, and health* (pp. 17–38). Seattle, WA: Hogrefe and Huber.

Peter, R., Geissler, H., & Siegrist, J. (1998). Associations of effort-reward imbalance at work and reported symptoms in different groups of male and female public transport workers. *Stress Medicine, 14,* 175–182.

Peter, R., & Siegrist, J. (1997). Chronic work stress, sickness absence, and hypertension in middle managers: General or specific sociological explanations. *Social Science and Medicine, 45,* 1111–1120.

Peterson, C., Maier, S. F., & Seligman, M. E. P. (1993). *Learned helplessness: A theory for the age of personal control.* New York: Oxford University Press.

Pfaffenberger, R. S., Hyde, R. T., Wing, A. L., & Hsieh, C.-C. (1986). Physical activity, all-cause mortality, and longevity of college alumni. *New England Journal of Medicine, 314,* 605–613.

Postman, L., & Bruner, J. S. (1948). Perception under stress. *Psychological Review, 55,* 314–323.

Repetti, R. L. (1993). Short-term effects of occupational stressors on daily mood and health complaints. *Health Psychology, 12,* 125–131.

Repetti, R. L., & Wood, J. (1997). Effects of daily stress at work on mothers' interactions with preschoolers. *Journal of Family Psychology, 11,* 90–108.

Revicki, D. A., Whitley, T. W., Gallary, M. E., & Allison, E. J. J. (1993). Impact of work environment characteristics on work-related stress and depression in emergency medicine residents: A longitudinal study. *Journal of Community and Applied Social Psychology, 3,* 273–284.

Robinson, L. A., Berman, J. S., & Neimeyer, R. A. (1990). Psychotherapy for the treatment of depression: A comprehensive review of controlled outcome research. *Psychological Bulletin, 108,* 30–49.

Rosenthal, R., & Rubin, D. B. (1982). A simple, general purpose display of magnitude of experimental effect. *Journal of Educational Psychology, 74,* 166–169.

Rotter, J. B. (1966). Generalized expectancies for internal versus external control of reinforcement. *Psychological Monographs: General and Applied, 80,* 1.

Rousseau, D. M. (1995). *Psychological contracts in organizations: Understanding written and unwritten agreements.* Thousand Oaks, CA: Sage.

Roy, M. P., & Steptoe, A. (1994). Daily stressors and social support availability as predictors of depressed mood in male firefighters. *Work and Stress, 8,* 210–219.

Rydstedt, L. W., Johansson, G., & Evans, G. W. (1998). A longitudinal study of workload, health and well-being among male and female urban bus drivers. *Journal of Occupational and Organizational Psychology, 71,* 35–45.

Saks, A. M., & Ashforth, B. E. (2000). The role of dispositions, entry stressors, and behavioral plasticity theory in predicting newcomers' adjustment to work. *Journal of Organizational Behavior, 21,* 43–62.

Sargent, L. D., & Terry, D. J. (1998). The effects of work control and job demands on employee adjustment and work performance. *Journal of Occupational and Organizational Psychology, 71,* 219–236.

Saunders, T., Driskell, J. E., Johnston, J. H., & Salas, E. (1996). The effects of stress inoculation training on anxiety and performance. *Journal of Occupational Health Psychology, 1,* 170–186.

Schaubroeck, J. (1999). Should the subjective be the objective? On studying mental processes, coping behavior, and actual exposures in organizational stress research. *Journal of Organizational Behavior, 20,* 753–760.

Schaubroeck, J., & Fink, L. S. (1998). Facilitating and inhibiting effects of job control and social support on stress outcomes and role behavior: A contingency model. *Journal of Organizational Behavior, 19,* 167–195.

Schaubroeck, J., Lam, S., & Xie, J. L. (2000). Collective efficacy versus self-efficacy in coping responses to stressors and control: A cross cultural study. *Journal of Applied Psychology, 85,* 512–525.

Schaubroeck, J., & Merritt, D. E. (1997). Divergent effects of job control on coping with work stressors: The key role of self-efficacy. *Academy of Management Journal, 40,* 738–754.

Schnall, P. L., Landsbergis, P. A., & Baker, D. (1994). Job strain and cardiovascular disease. *Annual Review of Public Health, 15,* 381–411.

Schonfeld, I. S. (1992). A longitudinal study of occupational stressors and depressive symptoms in first-year female teachers. *Teaching & Teaching Education, 8,* 151–158.

Schulz, P., Kirschbaum, C., Prüssner, J., & Hellhammer, D. (1998). Increased free cortisol secretion after awakening in chronically stressed individuals due to work overload. *Stress Medicine, 14,* 91–97.

Schwartz, J. E., Pickering, T. G., & Landsbergis, P. A. (1996). Work-related stress and blood pressure: Current theoretical models and considerations from a behavioral medicine perspective. *Journal of Occupational Health Psychology, 1,* 287–310.

Searle, B. J., Bright, J. E. H., & Bochner, S. (1999). Testing the 3-factor model of occupational stress: The impact of demands, control and social support on a mail sorting task. *Work and Stress, 13,* 268–279.

Sears, S. F. J., Urizar, G. G. J., & Evans, G. D. (2000). Examining a stress-coping model of burnout and depression in extension agents. *Journal of Occupational Health Psychology, 5,* 56–62.

Seeber, A., & Iregren, A. (1992). Behavioural effects of contaminated air: Applying psychology in neurotoxicology [Special issue]. *Applied Psychology: An International Review, 41*(3).

Seligman, M. E. P. (1975). *Helplessness: On depression, development and death.* San Francisco, CA: Freeman.

Sclye, H. (1956). *The stress of life.* New York: McGraw-Hill.

Semmer, N. (1984). *Streßbezogene Tätigkeitsanalyse* [Stress-related job-analysis]. Weinheim, Germany: Beltz.

Semmer, N. (1996). Individual differences, work stress and health. In M. J. Schabracq, J. A. M. Winnubst, & C. L. Cooper (Eds.), *Handbook of work and health psychology* (pp. 51–86). Chichester, England: Wiley.

Shaw, J. B., & Weekley, J. A. (1985). The effects of objective work-load variations of psychological strain and post-work-load performance. *Journal of Management, 11,* 87–98.

Shirom, A., Westman, M., Shamai, O., & Carel, R. S. (1997). Effects of work overload and burnout on cholesterol and triglycerides levels: The moderating effects of emotional reactivity among male and female employees. *Journal of Occupational Health Psychology, 2,* 275–288.

Siegrist, J. (1996). Adverse health effects of high effort/low reward conditions. *Journal of Occupational Health Psychology, 1,* 27–41.

Siegrist, J. (1998). Adverse health effects of effort-reward imbalance at work: Theory, empirical support, and implications for prevention. In C. L. Cooper (Ed.), *Theories of organizational stress* (pp. 190–204). Oxford, England: Oxford University Press.

Siegrist, J., Peter, R., Junge, A., Cremer, P., & Seidel, D. (1990). Low status control, high effort at work and ischemic heart disease: Prospective evidence from blue-collar men. *Social Science and Medicine, 31,* 1127–1134.

Slesina, W. (1994). Gesundheitszirkel: Der "Düsseldorfer Ansatz" [Health circles: The Düsseldorf approach]. In G. Westermeyer & B. Bähr (Eds.), *Betriebliche Gesundheitszirkel* (pp. 25–34). Göttingen, Germany: Verlag für Angewandte Psychologie.

Smulders, P. G. W., & Nijhuis, F. J. N. (1999). The job demands-job control model and absence behavior: Results of a 3-year longitudinal study. *Work and Stress, 13,* 115–131.

Söderfeldt, M., Söderfeldt, B., Ohlson, C.-G., Theorell, T., & Jones, I. (2000). The impact of sense of coherence and high-demand/low-control job environment on self-reported health, burnout and psychophysiological stress indicators. *Work and Stress, 14,* 1–15.

Sonnentag, S. (1996). Work group factors and individual well-being. In M. A. West (Ed.), *Handbook of work group psychology* (pp. 345–367). Chichester, England: Wiley.

Sonnentag, S. (2000). Expertise at work: Experience and excellent performance. In C. L. Cooper & I. T. Robertson (Eds.), *International review of industrial and organizational psychology* (pp. 223–264). Chichester, England: Wiley.

Sonnentag, S. (2001). Work, recovery activities, and individual well-being: A diary study. *Journal of Occupational Health Psychology, 6,* 196–210.

Sonnentag, S. (2002). Performance, well-being and self-regulation. In S. Sonnentag (Ed.), *The psychological management of individual performance: A handbook in the psychology of management in organizations* (pp. 405–423). Chichester, England: Wiley.

Sonnentag, S., Brodbeck, F. C., Heinbokel, T., & Stolte, W. (1994). Stressor-burnout relationship in software development teams. *Journal of Occupational and Organizational Psychology, 67,* 327–341.

Sparks, K., Cooper, C., Fried, Y., & Shirom, A. (1997). The effects of hours of work on health: A meta-analytic review. *Journal of Occupational and Organizational Psychology, 70,* 391–408.

Spector, P. E., Chen, P. Y., & O'Connell, B. J.. (2000). A longitudinal study of relations between job stressors and job strains while controlling for prior negative affectivity and strains. *Journal of Applied Psychology, 85,* 211–218.

Spector, P. E., Dwyer, D. J., & Jex, S. M. (1988). Relation of job stressors to affective, health, and performance outcomes: A comparison of multiple data sources. *Journal of Applied Psychology, 73,* 11–19.

Sperandio, J. C. (1971). Variation of operator's strategies and regulating effects on workload. *Ergonomics, 14,* 571–577.

Steen, N., Firth, H. W. B., & Bond, S. (1998). Relation between work stress and job performance in nursing: A comparison of models. *Structural Equation Modeling, 5,* 125–142.

Sullivan, S. E., & Bhagat, R. S. (1992). Organizational stress, job satisfaction, and job performance: Where do we go from here? *Journal of Management, 18,* 353–374.

Tafalla, R. J., & Evans, G. W. (1997). Noise, physiology, and human performance: The potential role of effort. *Journal of Occupational Health Psychology, 2,* 148–155.

Tang, T. L. P., & Hammontree, M. L. (1992). The effects of hardiness, police stress, and life stress on police officers' illness and absenteeism. *Public Personnel Management, 21,* 493–510.

Theorell, T. (1993). Medical and physiological aspects of job interventions. In C. L. Cooper & I. T. Robertson (Eds.), *International review of industrial and organizational psychology* (Vol. 8, pp. 173–192). Chichester, England: Wiley.

Theorell, T., & Karasek, R. A. (1996). Current issues relating to psychosocial job strain and cardiovascular disease research. *Journal of Occupational Health Psychology, 1,* 9–26.

Totterdell, P., Kellett, S., Techmann, K., & Briner, R. B. (1998). Evidence of mood linkage in work groups. *Journal of Personality and Social Psychology, 74,* 1504–1515.

Totterdell, P., Spelten, E., Smith, L., Barton, J., & Folkard, S. (1995). Recovery from work shifts: How long does it take? *Journal of Applied Psychology, 80,* 43–57.

Tsutsumi, A., Theorell, T., Hallqvist, J., Reuterwall, C., & de Faire, U. (1999). Association between job characteristics and plasma fibrinogen in a normal working population: A cross sectional analysis in referents of the SHEEP study. *Journal of Edidemiology and Community Health, 53,* 348–354.

Tubbs, T. C., & Collins, J. M. (2000). Jackson and Schuler (1985) revisited: A meta-analysis of the relationships between role ambiguity, role conflict, and job performance. *Journal of Management, 26,* 155–169.

Vahtera, J., Kivimäki, M., Pentti, J., & Theorell, T. (2000). Effect of change in the psychosocial work environment on sickness absence: A seven year follow up of initially health employees. *Journal of Epidemiology and Community Health, 54,* 484–493.

Vahtera, J., Pentti, J., & Uutela, A. (1996). The effect of objective job demands on registered sickness absence spells: Do personal, social and job related resources act as moderators? *Work and Stress, 10,* 286–308.

Van der Doef, M., & Maes, S. (1999). The job demand-control (-support) model and psychological well-being: A review of 20 years of empirical research. *Work and Stress, 13,* 87–114.

Van der Hek, H., & Plomp, H. N. (1997). Occupational stress management programmes: A practical overview of published effect studies. *Occupational Medicine, 47,* 133–141.

Van der Klink, J. J. L., Blonk, R. W. B., Schene, A. H., & Van Dijk, F. J. H. (2001). The benefits of interventions for work-related stress. *American Journal of Public Health, 91,* 270–276.

Van Dierendonck, D., Schaufeli, W. B., & Buunk, B. P. (1998). The evaluation of an individual burnout intervention program: The role of inequity and social support. *Journal of Applied Psychology, 83,* 392–407.

VanYperen, N. W. (1998). Informational support, equity and burnout: The moderating effect of self-efficacy. *Journal of Occupational and Organizational Psychology, 71,* 29–33.

VanYperen, N. W., & Snijders, T. A. B. (2000). A multilevel analysis of the demands-control model: Is stress at work determined by factors at the group level of the individual level? *Journal of Occupational Health Psychology, 5,* 182–190.

Viswesvaran, C., Sanchez, J. I., & Fisher, J. (1999). The role of social support in the process of work stress: A meta-analysis. *Journal of Vocational Behavior, 54,* 314–334.

Vrijkotte, T. G. M., van Doornen, L. J. O., & de Geus, E. J. C. (1999). Work stress and metabolic and hemostatic risk factors. *Psychosomatic Medicine, 61,* 796–805.

Wall, T. D., & Clegg, C. W. (1981). A longitudinal study of group work redesign. *Journal of Occupational Psychology, 2,* 31–49.

Wall, T. D., Jackson, P. R., Mullarkey, S., & Parker, S. K. (1996). The demands-control model of job strain: A more specific test. *Journal of Occupational and Organizational Psychology, 69,* 153–166.

Wall, T. D., Kemp, N. J., Jackson, P. R., & Clegg, C. W. (1986). Outcomes of autonomous workgroups: A long-term field experiment. *Academy of Management Journal, 29,* 280–304.

Warr, P. B. (1987). *Work, unemployment, and mental health.* Oxford, England: Oxford University Press.

Warr, P. B. (1990). Decision latitude, job demands, and employee well-being. *Work and Stress, 4,* 285–294.

Weiss, H. M., & Cropanzano, R. (1996). Affective events theory: A theoretical discussion of the structure, causes and consequences of affective experiences at work. In B. M. Staw & L. L. Cummings (Eds.), *Research in organizational behavior* (Vol. 18, pp. 1–74). Stamford, CT: JAI Press.

Westman, M., & Eden, D. (1996). The inverted-U relationship between stress and performance: A field study. *Work and Stress, 10,* 165–173.

Westman, M., & Eden, D. (1997). Effects of a respite from work on burnout: Vacation relief and fade-out. *Journal of Applied Psychology, 82,* 516–527.

Whisman, M. A. (1998). Mediators and moderators of change in cognitive therapy of depression. *Psychological Bulletin, 114,* 248–265.

Wickens, C. D. (1996). Designing for stress. In J. E. Driskell & E. Salas (Eds.), *Stress and human performance* (pp. 279–295). Mahwah, NJ: Erlbaum.

Williams, K. J., & Alliger, G. M. (1994). Role stressors, mood spillover, and perceptions of work-family conflict in employed parents. *Academy of Management Journal, 37,* 837–868.

Wolpin, J., Burke, R. J., & Greenglass, E. R. (1991). Is job satisfaction an antecedent of a consequence of psychological burnout? *Human Relations, 44,* 193–209.

Zapf, D. (1989). *Selbst- und Fremdbeobachtung in der psychologis-chen Arbeitsanalyse: Methodische Probleme bei der Erfassung von Stress am Arbeitsplatz* [Self and expert observation in psychological job analysis: Methodological problems in the measurement of stressors at work]. Göttingen, Germany: Hogrefe.

Zapf, D., Dormann, C., & Frese, M. (1996). Longitudinal studies in organizational stress research: A review of the literature with reference to methodological issues. *Journal of Occupational Health Psychology, 1,* 145–169.

Zapf, D., & Frese, M. (1991). Soziale Stressoren am Arbeitsplatz [Social stressors at the workplace]. In S. Greif, E. Bamberg, &

N. Semmer (Eds.), *Psychischer Stress am Arbeitsplatz* (pp. 168–184). Göttingen, Germany: Hogrefe.

Zapf, D., Knorz, C., & Kulla, M. (1996). On the relationship be-tween mobbing factors, and job content, social work environ-ment, and health outcomes. *European Journal of Work and Organizational Psychology, 5,* 215–237.

Zohar, D. (1999). When things go wrong: The effect of daily work hassles on effort, exertion and negative mood. *Journal of Occu-pational and Organizational Psychology, 72,* 265–283.

CHAPTER 19

Judgment and Decision Making

TERRY CONNOLLY AND LISA ORDÓÑEZ

The research domain generally referred to by the term *judgment and decision making* (JDM) is vast and ill bounded. It is, however, reasonably easy to identify the core concerns and issues it covers, even if one is unsure of the remote boundaries. The field has generally been concerned with choices made after some degree of deliberation: Choosing to take a particular job is included; choosing to remove one's hand from a hot burner is not. The deliberation involved includes some prediction or anticipation of two distinct sorts: prediction of the possible consequences of alternative actions, and prediction of one's evaluative reactions to these consequences. What will or might happen if I do A or B? And will I like these outcomes or not? Selection of an action is often preceded by significant inferential effort, as when medical diagnosis precedes selection of a treatment. Substantial creative effort may be invested in generating action alternatives.

The term *judgment* is often used, imprecisely, to refer to several distinct parts of this process. The physician might use the phrase "In my medical judgment . . ." as a preface to a statement of what disease she thinks the patient is suffering

from (diagnostic inference); what future course she expects the disease to follow (prediction or prognosis); what treatment she is recommending (decision); or what tradeoffs among risks, side effects, and prospects the patient will prefer (preferential prediction). Other topics often included under the JDM rubric include problem solving (viewing the physician as trying to solve the puzzle of the patient's symptoms); information search (ordering tests, conducting exploratory surgery); memory (recall of earlier cases or symptom patterns); and dynamic decision making (as when the physician makes multiple interventions over time as the patient responds to or fails to respond to treatments). JDM and its terminology, in short, are not neatly defined.

Given this inclusive and open-ended definition of the field and its constituent topics, we make no claim of comprehensiveness for this chapter, nor for the relative emphasis among the topics we have included. Our general goal has been to provide the reader with an introduction to the central issues in JDM, but we have been highly selective as to topics and relative emphasis. We have treated lightly or left out altogether many topics conventionally included in JDM surveys, in part by conscious (if inevitably biased) assessment of interest and research potential, in part by simple oversight. Our biases are generally toward actual or potential application rather than toward theory building per se. We note methodological issues only where they seem special to, or especially serious for, JDM. Finally, we have allowed ourselves a little scope for speculation on where the field might develop next—less in the spirit of confident prediction than in the hope that it will spur our imaginations and those of others.

In this age of rapid and convenient electronic literature searches, we saw little point in stuffing this chapter full of exemplary citations on each topic. Other useful sources include two collections of papers sponsored by the Judgment and Decision Making Society: Goldstein and Hogarth (1997), addressing theoretical issues, and Connolly, Arkes, and Hammond (2000), for more emphasis on applications. Recent review articles of note include Dawes (1998); Mellers, Schwartz, and Cooke (1998); and Highhouse (2001).

NORMATIVE-PRESCRIPTIVE VERSUS BEHAVIORAL-DESCRIPTIVE THEMES IN JUDGMENT AND DECISION MAKING

Perhaps more than other areas of the human sciences, JDM research includes elements of both description and prescription, of trying to discover what people actually do when they form judgments and make decisions and of advising them on how they might do these things better. The advice-giving theme can be traced to mathematicians of the eighteenth century French court who offered advice on such matters as the fair price for gambles (Bernstein, 1996; Stigler, 1986). The roots of the descriptive theme are more widely scattered but were well established by the time of two landmark review papers (Edwards, 1954, 1961) that substantially launched behavioral interest in decision making.

The two themes seem to be built into the subject matter. If one starts, for example, with an interest in how a doctor makes a particular difficult diagnosis (e.g., Einhorn, 1974), one would probably investigate the types of diagnostic information that the doctor collects, the way she puts it together into an overall judgment, her ability to reproduce the same judgment on repeated cases, and so on. But it would be hard not to ask the evaluative questions: How well is she doing? Are her diagnoses correct? How well could anyone, or a computer, do in making this diagnosis from this information? How might she be helped to do it better?

Conversely, a decision analyst might be able to show that, given specified preferences and probability estimates, a manager would be well advised to make a given set of investments. This still leaves open the manager's ability to state appropriate preferences and to assess required probabilities—and to generate enough faith in the entire analysis to be prepared to take action based on it. Thus, serious descriptive work on decisions often reaches important normative questions, while intendedly prescriptive studies rise or fall on the realism with which they represent the psychology of the decision maker.

This interplay of descriptive and prescriptive issues is a central source of interest to many JDM researchers. However, it has also led to what many see as an undue interest in decision errors. A major research program of the 1970s and 1980s, associated with Kahneman and Tversky (see the later section on heuristics and biases), assumes that observed decision behavior is generated by a reasonably small number of cognitive rules of thumb or *heuristics,* mental shortcuts that generally produce reasonable (and quick) results. These heuristics were demonstrated by showing that people generate systematic "errors" in specific, carefully constructed situations. The errors were defined as a deviation between what a subject did and the conclusions derived from some optimal rule—for example, a subject's probability estimate when given some information and the estimate that would be generated by Bayes's theorem in the same situation. This investigation of errors took on something of a life of its own (Edwards & von Winderfeldt, 1986; Jungermann, 1983), ignoring the facts that (a) the errors existed only if the optimal rule was, in fact, appropriate and accepted, and (b) there was little effort to assess the generality of the errors.

None of this is to suggest that humans are immune to decision error. Most of us, drawing on scientific evidence and personal experience alike, are happy to accept any help that is offered in our important life decisions. It is not clear, however, how common serious decision errors actually are. How might one assess an overall decisional batting average for the typical human, other than citing casual evidence suggesting that it is close to neither 0 nor 1,000? Without an agreement on what constitutes decision error and an overall estimate of its frequency, one cannot assess how serious the biases caused by heuristic use might be. We argue only that when presented with a normative recommendation, it is always wise to ask if its assumptions are descriptively accurate and that when presented with a descriptive analysis of some decision maker, it is always interesting to ask how well he or she is doing.

INFERENCE PROCESSES

The Lens Model

Brunswik (1952) illustrated his discussion of visual perception with a diagram that has come to be called the *lens model* (Figure 19.1). He argued that our skill at estimating some physical quantity such as the weight or distance of an object is the result of our ability to combine various imperfect "cues" to the quantity being estimated. For example, cues for distance include image brightness and sharpness, binocular disparity, parallax, and so on. None of the cues is perfectly correlated with actual distance, but a skilled perceiver can make use of the multiplicity and redundancy of cues to achieve highly valid estimates. The "lens" terminology simply draws attention to the similarity between the process of cue generation and integration and the diverging rays of light from an object being brought into focus by a convex lens.

Hammond (1955) proposed that the same model might be used to represent judgment processes. For example, the variable of interest might be a job applicant's ability at some task, as reflected in cues such as scores on some predictive tests, reports from previous employers, and claimed experience in similar jobs. The judge's task would be to combine these imperfect cues into an overall judgment of the candidate's ability and thus into a prediction of the candidate's performance on the job.

The great value of the lens model is that it draws our attention simultaneously to the judge (represented on the right-hand side as combining cues onto a judgment) and to the environment (represented on the left-hand side as some underlying state of interest spinning off imperfect cues). Achieving good accuracy requires both that the cues be reasonably informative about the underlying variable and that the judge use these cues in an effective way. In fact, the mathematical relationships among the cue validities and utilizations

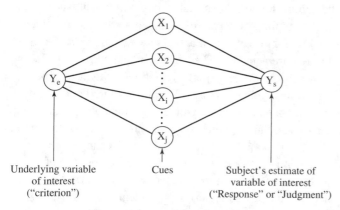

Figure 19.1 Brunswik's lens model.

and overall achievement have been helpfully analyzed in the so-called *lens model equation* (Tucker, 1964). The model also draws attention to one of Brunswik's methodological precepts, the call for "representative design" (Brunswik, 1955). In essence, this requires that cue sets presented to subjects retain the cue ranges and intercorrelations found in some specified environment. Specifically, representative design forbids use of factorial crossing of cue values because this procedure destroys naturally occurring cue intercorrelations. This will disrupt the judge's normal judgment policy and may, in the limit, produce cue sets that the judge finds incredible. Consider, for example, the reaction of an employer to a set of applicant records in which there was no relationship among test scores, undergraduate grade-point average, and quality of references. At least some of these applicants would probably be rejected as erroneous or fraudulent.

Multiple-Cue Probability Learning Studies

In more or less complete violation of representative design precepts, a large body of research has emerged that broadly addresses subjects' abilities to learn to use probabilistic information. The general format is to present the subject with a (long) series of trials in each of which several cues are presented and the subject is asked to predict the value of some criterion variable to which the cues are related. After the subject makes an estimate, he or she is told the correct answer before proceeding to the next trial. Such a format lends itself to endless variations in task characteristics: number of cues presented, their validity, the functional form of their relationship to the underlying variable that the subject is to estimate, the quality of feedback presented, whether the task is embedded in a meaningful verbal context, whether learning aids are provided, and so on.

The evidence from dozens of such studies is that except for the simplest versions, these *multiple-cue probability learning* (MCPL) tasks are very hard to learn. "Simple" generally means one or two cues, strongly and linearly related to the criterion, under conditions of low feedback error. For example, Slovic (1974) used a task with one linear cue that correlated .80 with the criterion and found subject estimates approaching maximum possible performance in the last of 100 trials. However, when the cue validity was −.80, learning after 100 trials was less than half this level. Deane, Hammond, and Summers (1972), using a three-cue task, found reasonable learning after 150 trials when all three relationships were positive, but almost no learning when the relationships were U-shaped. Learning improves somewhat when the subjects are warned about possible nonlinearities

(Earle, 1970). Two-cue interactions are learned only if helpful verbal cues are provided (Camerer, 1981). Even after reaching high levels of performance under low-error feedback, subjects' performances rapidly decline when feedback error levels are increased (Connolly & Miklausich, 1978). In short, as Klayman (1988) suggested, learning from outcome feedback is "learning the hard way."

In many real-world tasks, of course, feedback is probably much *less* helpful than is the outcome feedback provided in these MCPL laboratory tasks. A human resources (HR) professional trying to learn the task of predicting candidates' potentials from application materials receives feedback only after significant delay (when the applicant has been hired and on the job for some time); under high error (supervisor ratings may introduce new sources of error); and, crucially, only for those applicants actually hired (see Einhorn, 1980, on the inferential problems facing waiters who believe that they can spot good tippers). Laboratory MCPL tasks show excruciatingly slow learning of simple tasks under relatively good outcome feedback. Real-world tasks are almost certainly more difficult, and real-world feedback almost certainly less helpful, than are the laboratory conditions. It thus seems unlikely that outcome feedback is the key to learning real-world tasks of this sort, and interest in laboratory MCPL studies seems to have largely subsided in recent years.

Policy Capturing

Policy capturing, also known as *judgment analysis* (Stewart, 1988), is the process of developing a quantitative model of a specific person making a specific judgment. The general form of such a model is an equation, often first-order linear, relating the judgments, J, to a weighted sum of the information "cues," x_i. Hundreds of such studies have been conducted, dating at least to Wallace (1923) who modeled expert judges of corn. Hammond and Adelman (1976) studied judgments of handgun ammunition; Slovic (1969) studied stockbrokers; Phelps and Shanteau (1978) studied hog judges; and Doyle and Thomas (1995) studied audiologists. In addition, policy capturing has been commonly used for organizational applications, such as decisions concerning salary raises (Sherer, Schwab, & Heneman, 1987), alternative work arrangements (Powell & Mainiero, 1999), and applicant ratings and recommended starting salaries (Hitt & Barr, 1989). Policy capturing is thus a very widely used procedure.

It is also fair to say that the technique has been widely abused and that many of the findings are hard to assess or interpret. The basic approach is so simple and obvious that it is easy to overlook some important subtleties that vitiate the final conclusions. We shall sketch some of these points here;

see Stewart (1988) and A. Brehmer and Brehmer (1988) for a fuller discussion.

Suppose one were interested in modeling the judgment process of a university department head who is selecting candidates for graduate school. The department head reads an applicant's file, writes a merit score between 0 and 100 on the cover, and moves to another file. At a later stage the files are rank ordered, and applicants are admitted in descending order of merit score until all the places are filled. How might one model the department head's judgment process?

A first step is to establish what information she is collecting from each file: the *cues*. Simply asking her what cues she is using may be misleading: It is possible that she is biased toward (or against) women, minorities, left-handers, or scrabble players and is either unaware of the fact or chooses not to admit it. Second, how does she code this information? What counts as a "strong" GPA or an "acceptable" letter of reference? Significant work may be needed to translate the department head's inspection of the file into a set of scale scores representing the cues that she discovers and the scores in it. Stewart (1988) provided helpful practical advice on this process, and A. Brehmer and Brehmer (1988) discussed common failures. Doyle and Thomas (1995) reported an exemplary study in identifying the cues used by audiologists in assessing patients for hearing aids. Once cues and judgments have been identified and scored, estimation of a standard multiple linear regression model is straightforward. Interpretation, however, may not be. In particular, the interpretation of the relative weights given to each cue is conceptually difficult (see Stevenson, Busemeyer, & Naylor, 1991).

One subtle (and, in our view, unsolved) problem in policy capturing is how to meet Brunswik's goal of representative design. This goal plainly prohibits constructing simple orthogonal designs among the cues: Such independence destroys patterns of cue intercorrelations on which expert judges may rely. Cue ranges and intercorrelations should reflect those found in some relevant environment, such as the pool of applicants or patients with whom the expert regularly deals. A sample of recent actual cases would appear to meet this requirement, but even here complexities arise. If one wishes to compare expert predictions with actual performance, then only the subset of applicants hired or admitted is relevant—and this subset will have predictably truncated cue ranges and intercorrelations compared to the entire pool. Changes in pool parameters arising from changes in the employment rate, prescreening, self-selection into or out of the pool, or even of educational practices may all affect the modeled judgment. The underlying problem of what exactly defines the environment that the sample of cases is intended to represent is a conceptually subtle and confusing one.

Given these methodological worries, some caution is needed in summaries of research findings. Common generalizations (A. Brehmer & Brehmer, 1988; Slovic & Lichtenstein, 1971) include the following: (a) Judges generally use few cues, and their use of these cues is adequately modeled by simple first-order linear models; (b) judges describe themselves as using cues in complex, nonlinear, and interactive ways; (c) judges show modest test-retest reliabilities; and (d) interjudge agreement is often moderate or low, even in areas of established expertise. In light of the methodological shortcomings just noted, we propose that such broad generalizations be taken as working hypotheses for new applications, not as settled fact.

Heuristics and Biases

Edwards (1968) ran the following simple experiment. He showed subjects two book bags containing 100 poker chips. Bag A contained mainly red chips, Bag B mainly black. He randomly chose one of the bags, drew out a small sample of chips, and showed them to the subjects. He then asked the subjects for their estimate of how likely it was that he was drawing from Bag A. He found that subjects, initially persuaded that the probabilities were 50/50 before seeing the sample, generally revised their estimates in the direction suggested by the sample (i.e., toward A if the sample was mainly red chips) but not as far as would be required by Bayes's theorem. Edwards (1968) labeled the phenomenon *conservatism*. It involves three elements: a well-structured probabilistic task (e.g., sampling from two known populations); a sensible normative model for how the task should be performed (Bayes's theorem); and an observation that actual behavior is systematically biased with regard to this normative model.

The dominant paradigm for research on judgment under uncertainty through the 1970s and 1980s, the so-called heuristics and biases paradigm (Tversky & Kahneman, 1981), was founded on observations of systematic errors of this sort: probabilistic tasks in which human behavior deviated systematically from a normative rule. The paradigm was, however, more than a simple catalog of errors. Tversky and Kahneman (1981) argued that the observed errors were manifestations of cognitive rules of thumb or heuristics that, though generally effective and low-cost, can be misleading in certain unusual circumstances. Thus, for example, we might be well guided as to the relative popularity among our acquaintances of various hobbies by noting the ease or difficulty with which we could bring examples to mind (the availability heuristic). We would likely be misled, however, about embarrassing or illegal hobbies, whose practitioners might well take pains to conceal their interest. Similarly, dramatic causes of death are judged

to be commoner than less dramatic ones (Slovic, Fischhoff, & Lichtenstein, 1979), and easily found words as more likely than those more difficult to search for (Tversky & Kahneman, 1973). (We discuss examples of heuristics and biases in prediction research more fully in the following section on simple prediction.)

Work in this paradigm has declined in recent years. First, whatever the theoretical intentions, much of it became an ever-growing catalog of errors, with modest or no theoretical underpinnings that might allow prediction of when a particular heuristic would be evoked or error displayed. Second, there was growing doubt about the appropriateness of some of the normative models invoked to demonstrate that errors had been made. Third, it became clear that at least some of the claimed errors were actually the result of subjects' working successfully on problems other than the one the experimenter intended. (See Jungerman, 1983, and Gigerenzer, 1991, for extended critiques of the heuristics and biases approach.) Research interest in documenting our shortcomings seems to have declined. Increasingly, researchers are exploring the actual mechanisms that account for our performance, including the sometimes excellent performance of experts in real settings. (See Goldstein & Hogarth, 1997, and Connolly et al., 2000, for recent samplings of the literature.)

PREDICTION

Simple Prediction

There is evidence that, in making predictions, we use a variety of the heuristics discussed earlier. We will discuss three such heuristics: anchoring and adjustment, availability, and representativeness.

Imagine that an organization wants to predict sales for the coming quarter. A common approach would be to start with current sales as an initial estimate (the anchor), and then make an adjustment to account for market trends, new incentives, and so on. While this anchor-and-adjust heuristic may provide a reasonable estimate, research indicates that two potential problems may arise. First, the anchor may not be appropriate: If a new motivation program is applied to only a subset of salespeople, then the average of this group's sales should be used as an anchor, rather than the average of all salespeople. Second, adjustment from the anchor may not be sufficient: The predicted value may be too close to the anchor of average sales. Bolger and Harvey (1993) found that decision makers used an anchor-and-adjust strategy for predicting events over time (e.g., sales) and that their adjustments were insufficient.

Another method for making predictions uses the availability heuristic: The likelihood of an event is judged by how easily instances come to mind through either memory or imagination. This heuristic is generally reasonable because frequent events will tend to be noticed and remembered more than will less frequent events. A manager may predict how likely a particular employee is to be late for work based on recollections of past episodes. However, availability may lead to biased predictions when we selectively attend to information that is available (e.g., a vivid or recent event) instead of considering historical-statistical data systematically. For instance, people who had recently experienced an accident or a natural disaster estimated similar future events as more likely than those who had not experienced these events (Kunreuther et al., 1978). Similarly, managers conducting performance appraisals can produce biased evaluations (either positive or negative) when they rely on memory alone: Vivid episodes and events within three months prior to the evaluation are overweighted relative to other information (Bazerman, 1998).

A third heuristic used in prediction is representativeness, in which the likelihood of an event is judged by its similarity to a stereotype of similar events. Thus, a manager might predict the success of an employee by how similar he is to other known successful employees. Again, while this is generally a good initial estimate, using the representativeness heuristic can lead to systematic biases. First, people have a tendency to make nonregressive predictions from unreliable predictors. For example, Tversky and Kahneman (1974) attempted to teach Israeli flight instructors that positive reinforcement promotes learning faster than does negative reinforcement. The flight instructors objected, citing examples of poor performance following praise and improved performance after reprimands. The instructors were attributing fluctuations in performance to interventions alone and not recognizing the effect of chance elements. Those trainees who received praise had performed at a level above their average performance, whereas those who were reprimanded had performed below their average. Statistically, both groups should tend to perform closer to their average performance on subsequent flights. Thus, the flight instructors falsely concluded that praise hurts and reprimands help because they predicted, by representativeness, that performance should be similar to the previous episode instead of regressing their predictions of performance to the mean. A parallel fallacy arises when we predict that the best performing salesperson this year will be the top performer the following year.

Another bias that has been attributed to using the representativeness heuristic is the tendency to neglect base rates or the prior probabilities of outcomes (Kahneman & Tversky,

1973). Imagine that a company knows that a small percentage (e.g., 1%) of its employees is using illegal drugs. The company conducts a random drug test in order to determine which employees are using drugs and are subject to termination. The test is relatively accurate, being correct 90% of the time; that is, the test will be incorrect only 10% of the time when either a drug user tests negative (false negative) or a nonuser tests positive (false positive). Should the company fire employees who test positive for drugs? Most would say yes because the probability of being a drug user given the positive test result should be representative of the accuracy of the test (somewhere around 90%). The true answer is that it is very unlikely that this person is a drug user: Although the test is relatively accurate, it is not very diagnostic in this situation because the probability that a person who tests positive is a drug user is only 8.3%. The reason for this counterintuitive probability is that we neglect the influence of the base rate of drug users. Because the probability of being a drug user is so low, most of the people testing positive will not be drug users. For example, imagine that there were 1,000 employees in this company: 10 (1%) would be drug users, and 990 would be nonusers. Because the test is 90% accurate, 9 of the 10 drug users will test positive. However, 99 (10%) of the nonusers would also test positive (the false positives). Thus, of the 108 people who test positive, only 9 (8.3%) will be drug users. Note that even if the accuracy of the test in this example is increased to 99%, the probability that an individual who receives a positive test result is actually a drug user is still only 50%. This drug-testing example is an adaptation of the well known cab problem from Kahneman and Tversky (1973).

There are other potential difficulties in making predictions. In some situations, our judgments are overconfident. Experiments demonstrating overconfidence often ask difficult almanac questions in which subjects either choose between two options (e.g., "Which river is longer, the Tigris or the Volga?") or state a range of values in which they are 90% confident a true value lies (e.g., "How long is the Tigris river?"). Klayman, Soll, Gonzalez-Vallejo, and Barlas (1999) found a general overconfidence for almanac questions, but the overconfidence was much higher for subjective confidence intervals than for the two-choice questions (approximately 45% versus 5%). They found significant differences between individuals, but overconfidence was stable across individuals answering questions from different domains (e.g., prices of shampoo and life expectancies in different countries). A person who was overconfident in one domain was likely to be overconfident in another. Overconfidence has been found in many, though not all, contexts (Yates, 1990). There is evidence that it declines with experience (Keren, 1987) and with instructions to think of ways in which an estimate might be wrong (Fischhoff, 1982). Overconfidence and its control have obvious implications in such organizational contexts as hiring, estimating timelines and costs, and developing business strategies.

There are also problems with learning from experience to make better predictions. The hindsight bias (Fischhoff & Beyth, 1975) hinders us in learning from our mistakes. In retrospect, we believe that we knew all along what was going to happen and are unable to recover fully the uncertainty we faced before the event. This impedes learning the real relationships between decisions and outcomes that are necessary for good predictions. Unfortunately, warning people of this bias does not help (Fischhoff, 1977). In addition, we may not seek the necessary information to test our beliefs because we have a tendency to seek confirming evidence (also known as the confirmation bias; Wason, 1960) rather than disconfirming evidence. (See the section on information search, information purchase.) Finally, the structure of the environment may not readily provide information to test relationships because some information is naturally hidden. For example, personnel selection is often based on HR test scores whose correlations with future job performance may be low. This will be true even for valid predictors of performance. We hire only applicants with high scores, so the variance of test scores for those hired is low, and any variation in job performance will likely be due to other factors (e.g., motivation, training, random elements). We generally do not observe the performance of those we do not hire—data essential to testing the validity of our predictions.

Idea Generation

Before an outcome's likelihood can be assessed, it must first be identified as a possibility. There is good evidence that we do not routinely generate many of the possible outcomes that may flow from our actions (Gettys & Fisher, 1979), and numerous remedial techniques have been proposed. One popular approach, group brainstorming, was first proposed in a nonacademic book (Osborn, 1953) as a way to generate as many ideas as possible. The participants were encouraged to improve, combine, and piggyback off other ideas without criticism in order to generate more ideas than could be generated when working individually. While this approach is intuitively appealing, subsequent research (McGrath, 1984) has shown that compared to brainstorming groups, the same number of individuals working alone (called nominal groups) produce more ideas with the same level of quality. Diehl and Stroebe (1987) concluded that the main reason appears to be production blocking: Because only one group member can talk at a time, the other members may forget

their ideas, construct counterarguments, and so on in the meantime.

In the 1980s computerized technology was developed to aid group brainstorming and decision-making processes (fortunately ignoring the evidence discussed earlier!). One popular system consists of several networked computers with a common main screen that can be seen by all in the room (Connolly, 1997; Nunamaker, Dennis, Valacich, Vogel, & George, 1991). Group members type ideas on their computers and interact by passing files between machines. All members can thus be productive simultaneously, while drawing stimulation from reading and adding to one another's files. This form of interaction appears to overcome the problems of face-to-face brainstorming. Electronic brainstorming (EBS) groups can outperform equivalent nominal groups (Valacich, Dennis, & Connolly, 1994), at least when the EBS groups are large (approximately eight or more). It is not entirely clear why large EBS groups enjoy this advantage in idea generation (Connolly, 1997). Anonymity provided by the EBS system increases the number of ideas produced (Connolly, Jessup, & Valacich, 1990) and the number of controversial ideas (Cooper, Gallupe, Pollard, & Cadsby, 1998), but may decrease satisfaction with the task (Connolly et al., 1990).

It is interesting to note that businesses continue to use face-to-face group brainstorming even though the literature clearly shows that it is inferior to both nominal groups and EBS. One reason may be its strong intuitive appeal. Paulus, Dzindolet, Poletes, and Camacho (1993) found that subjects predicted future performance and perceived actual performance as better in face-to-face brainstorming groups than in nominal groups, when in fact performance was superior in the latter. Another reason for the popularity of face-to-face brainstorming is the lack of access to EBS equipment. There is also some evidence that the performance of face-to-face groups can be raised to that of nominal groups by using highly trained facilitators (Oxley, Dzindolet, & Paulus, 1996).

PREFERENCES

Values, Goals, Objectives

The idea of preference is fundamental to the idea of purposive choice: We prefer some possible outcomes to others and try to select actions accordingly. This is not the same as the claim that people "have" values (or preferences, goals, purposes, desires, etc.), in the sense that they can instantaneously say which of two real or imagined states they prefer at a given moment. As Fischhoff (1991) pointed out, some researchers (e.g., economists, opinion pollsters) behave as though people have fully articulated preferences for all possible objects and states of being, whereas others (e.g., decision analysts) suppose that we have only a few, basic values and must derive or construct preferences from these for most unfamiliar choices. An articulated values theorist might study a series of hiring decisions with a view to inferring the relative importance that a particular HR manager gives to different candidate attributes, such as experience, age, and gender. In the same context a basic values theorist might work with the manager to improve the accuracy or consistency with which her values are applied to future hiring decisions. (Indeed, it is possible to imagine doing both studies with the same manager, first capturing her "policy" from a series of earlier decisions and then applying them routinely to subsequent decisions as a form of decision aiding.)

Whichever view of valuing one assumes, there is plenty of evidence to indicate that the process can be imperfectly reliable and precise. Preferences for alternative medical treatments can shift substantially (for both patients and physicians) when the treatments are described in terms of their mortality rates rather than their survival rates (McNeil, Pauker, & Tversky, 1988). Subjects asked how much they would be prepared to pay to clean up one, several, or all the lakes in Ontario offered essentially the same amount of money for all three prospects (Kahneman, Knetch, & Thaler, 1986). Simonson (1990) found that people's preferences for different snacks changed markedly from what they predicted a week ahead to what they chose at the time of consumption. Strack, Martin, and Schwartz (1988) found that students' evaluation of their current life satisfaction was unrelated to a measure of their dating frequency when the two questions were asked in that order, but strongly related ($r = .66$) when the dating question was asked first. Apparently, the evaluation of one's life overall is affected by the aspects one is primed to consider. MBA students' ratings of their satisfaction with and the fairness of potential salary offers were markedly influenced by the offers received by other students in their class (Ordóñez, Connolly, & Coughlan, 2000). As these examples suggest, measures of preferences for real-life entities are sensitive to issues of framing, timing, order, context, and a host of other influences. It is unclear whether the problems are primarily those of imperfect measurement or of imperfect development of the respondents' values and preferences themselves.

A common assumption of basic values researchers is that complex value structures are organized in the form of hierarchies or value trees (e.g., Edwards & Newman, 1982). The HR manager, for example, might consider a candidate's attractiveness in terms of a few high-level goals, such as job knowledge, motivation, and growth potential, and assign some importance to each. At a lower level these attributes

would be decomposed, so that "job knowledge" might include scores for formal education, job experience, and recent training, and so on. Such trees help to connect high-level values to lower level operational measures. More complex interconnections among value elements are also possible (see, e.g., Keeney, 1992).

Utilities and Preferences

The term utility is used in two different ways in JDM. In the formal, mathematical sense (Coombs, Dawes, & Tversky, 1970), utilities are simply a set of real numbers that allow reconstruction or summary of a set of consistent choices. The rules for consistency are strict but appear to be perfectly reasonable. For example, choices must be transitive, meaning that if you choose A over B and B over C, then you must also choose A over C. Situations in which thoughtful people wish to violate these rules are of continuing interest to researchers (Allais, 1953; Ellsberg, 1961; Tversky, 1969). Utilities, in this sense, are defined in reference to a set of choices, not to feelings such as pain and pleasure.

A very powerful formulation of this choice-based view of utility (von Neumann & Morgenstern, 1947) relies on the idea of probabilistic "in-betweenness." Suppose A is (to you) the "best" in some choice set, and C is the "worst." You like B somewhere in between. Von Neumann and Morgenstern (1947) suggested that you would be prepared to trade B for a suitable gamble, in which you win (get A) with probability p and lose (get C) with probability $(1 - p)$. You could make the gamble very attractive by setting p close to 1.0 or very unattractive by setting it close to 0.0 so that because you value B in between A and C, one of these gambles should be worth the same to you as B itself. The value of p at which this happens is your "utility" for B, and this expresses your preference for B in an unambiguous way.

The beauty of this approach is that it allows a decision maker to evaluate every outcome on a decision tree by the same metric: an equivalent (to her) best/worst gamble. Further, if some of these outcomes are uncertain, their utility can be discounted by the probability of getting them—their "expected utility." If I value some outcome at 0.7 (i.e., as attractive to me as a best-worst gamble with .7 to win, .3 to lose), then I would value a toss-up at that same outcome at $(.5 \times .7)$ or .35. This provides a tight logic for expected utility as a guide to complex choices.

It is not clear how closely this formal view of utility conforms with the experience or anticipation of pleasure, desire, attractiveness, or other psychological reactions commonly thought of as reflecting utility or disutility. Indeed, the introduction of a gambling procedure for measurement gives many people problems because it seems to involve elements of risk as well as outcome preferences. Many people turn down bets such as (.5 to win $10, .5 to lose $5), despite their positive expected value (EV): $(.5 \times \$10) + (.5 \times -\$5) = \$2.50$, in the example. Why? One possibility is declining marginal utility: The $10 gain offers only a modest good feeling, whereas the $5 loss threatens a large negative feeling, so the 50-50 chance between the two is overall negative. This is referred to as *risk aversion,* although it may have little connection to the actual churn of feeling that the gambler experiences while the coin is in the air.

The psychology of risk—what is seen as risky, how risk is talked about, how people feel about and react to risk—is a vast topic, beyond the scope of this brief chapter. Many studies (e.g., Fischhoff, Lichtenstein, Slovic, Derby, & Keeney, 1981; Peters & Slovic, 1996) raise doubts about our ability to assess different risks and show very large inconsistencies in our willingness to pay to alleviate them (Zeckhauser & Viscusi, 1990). Public policies toward risk are hampered by large discrepancies between expert and lay judgments of the risks involved (Fischhoff, Bostrom, & Quadrel, 1993; Slovic, 1987, 1993). The notion of risk aversion or risk tolerance as a stable personality characteristic guiding behavior across a range of situations finds little empirical support (Lopes, 1987). This rich and important literature is only imperfectly summarized by proposing a negatively accelerated utility function!

Comparison Processes

The ideas we have reviewed to this point all associate preference or value with an outcome in isolation from others. That is, they suppose that a specific outcome has a specific utility to a specific decision maker. Both casual reflection and careful research show that this assumption is false. One's feelings about a $3,000 pay raise, for example, might shift significantly if one discovered that a rival had made more, or less; if one expected nothing, or $5,000; or if it was given for merit rather than as a cost of living adjustment. Comparison processes of various sorts influence the value we attach to options and outcomes.

Relatively recently, theories of preference have attempted to integrate the emotions of regret and disappointment through the use of comparisons. Regret theory (Bell, 1982; Loomes & Sugden, 1982) posits that the utility of a risky option depends not only on outcomes and associated probabilities but also on comparisons between the outcomes of the chosen and unchosen options. The modified utility function is the expected utility of the option considered in isolation plus a regret-rejoice component that adjusts for comparison with what might have been if another option had been selected. A recruiter feels good about the success of a new employee she

has selected; perhaps she feels an additional pleasure when she learns that the rejected candidate is performing poorly at another firm. Thus, the feeling of regret (rejoicing) occurs when you would have been better (worse) off if you had made another choice. Studies have shown that anticipated regret leads to regret-minimizing choices (Josephs, Larrick, Steele, & Nisbett, 1992; Ritov, 1996; Zeelenberg, Beattie, van der Pligt, & de Vries, 1996), changes attitudes about behavior (Parker, Stradling, & Manstead, 1996), and changes future behavior (Richard, van der Pligt, & de Vries, 1996). Anticipation of regret about poor outcomes has been used to explain why consumers purchase higher priced but well-known brands (Simonson, 1992) and why they are reluctant to trade equivalent lottery tickets, even with an added cash incentive (Bar-Hillel, 1996).

Where regret theory compares outcomes across alternatives, disappointment theory (Bell, 1985; Loomes & Sugden, 1986) compares outcomes across different states of nature. In the hiring example, the recruiter whose chosen candidate turns in a poor performance feels bad both because of the poor performance itself and because she is disappointed in her expectations of a good performance. As with regret theory, disappointment theory adjusts the basic expected utility of an option according to the comparisons across the different possible outcomes. Finally, decision affect theory (Mellers, Schwartz, Ho, & Ritov, 1997; Mellers, Schwartz, & Ritov, 1999) integrates both disappointment and regret feelings with the utility of an option in order to determine the overall anticipated pleasure of an option.

Regret, disappointment, and decision affect theories all start with the basic expected utility of an outcome and make an adjustment to reflect comparisons with other outcomes, real or imagined. Comparisons are also central to equity theory (Adams, 1965; Walster, Berscheid, & Walster, 1973), in which an outcome's value is modified by the recipient's judgment of whether it was fair. According to equity theory, equity is achieved when the ratio of outputs (e.g., salary, benefits, rewards, punishment) to inputs (e.g., hours worked, effort, organizational citizenship behaviors) are the same for all individuals being considered. Thus, in order to determine if equity is achieved, a comparison other (e.g., a coworker) is required. Early studies investigated equity theory by placing subjects in an experimental work context in which they received payment for the amount of work completed. Subjects were informed about the pay given to other similar workers. Research results have strongly supported equity theory predictions (Greenberg, 1982). Equity imbalance was restored in a manner consistent with equity theory: Underpaid workers decreased their performance (i.e., lowered their inputs), whereas overpaid workers increased their performance (increasing inputs). In an interesting field study (Greenberg, 1988), workers were temporarily reassigned to offices that were either of higher or lower status than their regular offices. Consistent with equity theory, those assigned to higher status offices increased their performance, whereas those in lower status offices decreased their performance.

Choice Rules

In almost every practical choice situation, each of the options being considered has a number of features, attributes, or dimensions that affect its worth to the decision maker. A job, for example, might be defined in terms of such dimensions as salary, location, interest of work, promotion possibilities, and so on. Researchers have proposed a number of alternative models to describe the process by which decision makers choose between such multiattribute alternatives.

Multiattribute utility theory (MAUT) models suppose that what people do (or, in the prescriptive use, should do) is to evaluate each attribute of each alternative, add the resulting utilities into an overall utility for each alternative, and choose the alternative with the highest total. This is referred to as a compensatory model, in the sense that an improvement on one attribute can compensate for or trade off against a loss on another. (We discuss decision-aiding procedures for making these tradeoffs in the following section.) Some authors (e.g., Edgell & Geisler, 1980) have proposed modifications of the basic MAUT models, called random utility models, to reflect the fact that subjects' preferences are not always stable from one occasion to another.

Conjunctive models reflect preferences of the screening type, such as an army physical examination. A candidate with flat feet, for example, would be rejected regardless of how well he or she scores on other measures of physical fitness. These models are thus noncompensatory, in the sense that more on one attribute may not make up for less on another: Any low attribute value makes the entire alternative low value. An early conjunctive model, the *satisficing* rule, was proposed by Simon (1955). Simon argued that in real settings MAUT procedures make unrealistic demands on a decision maker's time and attention. Instead, decision makers search for an alternative that is acceptable on all important dimensions and stop their search with the first such alternative. Note that this again introduces an element of probabilism into the choice, in that the order in which alternatives are considered may determine which of several acceptable options is found first. (Simon, 1955, also argued that aspiration levels may change as search proceeds, adding a second element of probabilism.)

Lexicographic (dictionary-like) models rely on sequential comparisons between alternatives. Options are compared first on the most important attribute, and if they differ, the winning option is chosen. If they tie, the next most important attribute is considered, and so on, until a winner is found. Another version of this, called the elimination by aspects (EBA) model, selects an attribute (or "aspect") at random and eliminates from consideration any option that fails to reach threshold on this attribute. The process continues until only one option remains, and it is then chosen. (Note that neither of these processes is compensatory: Overall attractive options may be eliminated by a loss on an early comparison.)

Additive difference models (Tversky, 1969) assume that the decision maker compares alternatives along one dimension at a time, storing the sum of the differences favoring one alternative over the other. Probabilistic versions of this rule have also been proposed, in which comparison terminates when one alternative reaches some threshold of cumulative advantage over the other.

A number of authors (Beach & Mitchell, 1978; Payne, Bettman & Johnson, 1993) have suggested that the combination rule that a decision maker uses represents a tradeoff between effort and accuracy. The fully compensatory MAUT rule allows the fullest consideration of all attributes and values, but requires extensive information-processing effort. Other rules are less effortful, but do not guarantee that the best option will be chosen.

DECIDING: (A) SINGLE CHOICE EVENTS

Subjective Expected Utility Theory

The previous section discussed preferences among riskless options. However, selecting among risky options in which outcomes occur with some probability is even more difficult. For example, a firm may have to select between a set of new products to develop, each with probabilities of profits and losses. One of the simplest ways of placing a value on a risky proposition is by calculating its EV, which is the sum of each outcome multiplied by its associated probability (i.e., EV = $\Sigma p_i x_i$). A new product with a 75% chance of making $15 million in profits and a 25% chance of failing, with a loss of a million in development costs would have an EV = .75*($15M) + .25*($ − 1M) = $11.75M in expected profits. This is the amount of money the firm would make on average if they repeatedly marketed new products with these probability-outcome characteristics. Clearly, such a calculation would be an imperfect guide to decision making in any single case.

It can be easily shown that our preferences for risky propositions are not always consistent with an EV model. For example, how much would you pay for a gamble in which you flip a coin until the first head appears (on the *n*th flip) and pays $(\$2)^n$? If you get two tails followed by a head, you would receive $2^3 = \$8$. Most people offer less than $4 to play this game. However, this game actually has an infinite EV, and according to the EV model you should be willing to pay as much as you are able. The EV for the game is $\Sigma p_i x_i = \Sigma (1/2)^n 2^n = (1/2)2 + (1/4)4 + (1/8)8 + \cdots (1/\infty)\infty = 1 + 1 + 1 \ldots$ that continues infinitely and, thus, leads to an infinite EV.

Daniel Bernoulli (1738/1954) used the previous example (known as the *St. Petersburg paradox*) to infer that people do not value a prospect in terms of the objective value of the outcomes, but on the subjective values or utilities. Thus, people value propositions based on the expected utility rather than expected value. This model also explains why you might prefer $50 for sure over an equal EV gamble with a 50% chance winning $100 and otherwise $0 in a single play (the EV model predicts that you will be indifferent between the gamble and the sure thing, as noted earlier). Thus, the model of value is changed from EV with the purely objective values of probability (p) and outcome value (x) to the expected utility with the subjective outcome value or utility [$u(x)$ in EU $= \Sigma p_i u(x_i)$].

Later, Savage (1954) went one step further and proposed subjective values of both probability (i.e., subjective probability $s[p]$) and outcome in subjective expected utility (SEU) theory (SEU $= \Sigma s[p_i]u[x_i]$). This model provides a way of placing value not only on risky events with monetary outcomes but also on uncertain events based on the degree of belief that a monetary outcome or nonmonetary event will occur. SEU expanded the application of decision theory to include a much broader range of decisions.

Prospect Theory

Although expected utility theory (EUT) provides a good normative model of choice, several studies have demonstrated the theory's weaknesses as a descriptive model of valuation and choice. The empirical violations of the axioms call into question the general applicability of EUT. For example, Tversky (1969) showed that in certain problems people consistently violate the transitivity axiom. The Allais paradox (1953) is a famous demonstration of how another EUT axiom (called independence) is violated by many people. Imagine that you have to decide which of two new products to develop:

Product A   will make $1 million in profits for sure
Product B   10% chance of making $5 million in profits
             89% chance of making $1 million in profits
             1% chance of making no profit (i.e., breaking even)

Which would you choose? Most would select Product A. Now, imagine you faced a different set of new products: which would you select to develop?

Product C   11% chance of making $1 million in profits
             89% chance of making no profit
Product D   10% chance of making $5 million in profits
             90% chance of making no profit

Most would select Product D. However, the selection of both Products A and D violates EUT. Notice that selecting A over B implies the EU(A) > EU(B), which can be rewritten as:

$$1.0U(1M) > .1U(5M) + .89U(1M) + .01U(0M), \quad (19.1)$$

which simplifies to

$$.11U(1M) > .1U(5M) + .01U(0M). \quad (19.2)$$

However, selecting D over C implies

$$.1U(5M) + .9U(0M) > .11U(1M) + .89U(0M), \quad (19.3)$$

which simplifies to the following statement, directly contradicting Equation 19.2:

$$.11U(1M) < .1U(5M) + .01U(0M). \quad (19.4)$$

Prospect theory (Kahneman & Tversky, 1979) was developed to model how risky propositions are valued while accommodating decision behavior such as the Allais paradox. The model uses the same general form as EUT but modifies the outcome value and probability functions to be more psychologically descriptive. A value of a prospect is defined as $\Sigma v(x_i)\pi(p_i)$ where $v(\cdot)$ and $\pi(\cdot)$ are the value and decision weight functions, respectively.

The decision weight function, while similar to the subjective probability function of SEU, introduces new psychological features to subjective probability. One feature is that low probabilities are overweighted and high probabilities are underweighted. For example, Lichtenstein, Slovic, Fischhoff, Layman, and Combs (1978) showed that people tend to judge low-probability health risks (e.g., botulism) more likely than the objective values but tend to underestimate higher probability health risks (e.g., heart disease). Another feature of the decision weight function is that it is nonlinear. Objective probabilities sum linearly, as in deriving Equations 19.2 and 19.4 from 19.1 and 19.3 in the examples above (e.g., .90 − .89 = .01). However, decision weights are nonadditive (e.g., $\pi[.9] - \pi[.89] \neq \pi[.01]$), accounting for the selection of Products A over B and D over C.

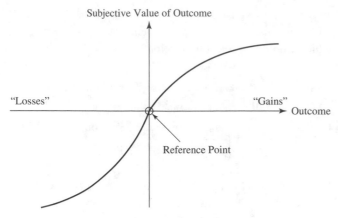

Figure 19.2 Prospect theory's value function.

In a second modification of EUT, prospect theory proposed a value function that was a significant departure from the previous utility functions (Figure 19.2). Most earlier utility functions defined subjective value with respect to overall wealth. The prospect theory value function defines value with respect to a reference point (or the status quo). Second, the value function for the domain of losses (relative to the reference point) is steeper than is that for gains. This leads to a result called *loss aversion* in which losses are more painful than equal magnitude gains are pleasurable. Finally, the value function is concave (risk averse) above the reference point and convex (risk seeking) below it. Because identical options can often be described in terms of different reference points, this raises the possibility that different ways of describing the same problem may shift choices from risk seeking to risk averse. This general framing problem is discussed in the following section.

Framing

To illustrate framing, consider the following options described by Hogarth (1987). He presented MBA subjects with a riskless option and a risky option, as follows:

> Imagine that you have just learned that the sole supplier of a crucial component is going to raise prices. The price increase is expected to cost the company $6 million. Two alternative plans have been formulated to counter the effect of the price increase. The anticipated consequences of these plans are as follows:
>
> One group was given Set I and asked to select between Plans A and B:
>
> Plan A the company will save $2 million
>
> Plan B 1/3 probability that $6 million will be saved
>
> 2/3 probability that nothing will be saved

Another group of people were asked to select between Plans C and D in Set II:

Plan C the company will lose $4 million

Plan D 1/3 probability that there will be no loss

2/3 probability that the company will lose $6 million

Notice that the information in the two formulations is identical and that Plan A = Plan C and Plan B = Plan D. However, information is framed differently in the two choice sets: it is framed positively (i.e., money saved) in Plans A and B and negatively (i.e., money lost) in Plans C and D. Framing of the information is similar to the "glass half-empty/half-full" description of optimistic/pessimistic perspectives.

The majority of subjects select the riskless option (Plan A) over the risky option (Plan B) in Set I but select the risky option over the riskless option (Plan D over C) in Set II, resulting in a reversal of preferences. According to prospect theory, risk attitudes are not simply a characteristic of the individual decision maker but depend on the context in which options are evaluated. Because of the differing shapes of the value functions for the domains of gains and losses, people are risk averse when options are framed positively and risk seeking when options are framed negatively.

Another type of framing, attribute framing, has been shown for riskless options. For example, Levin and Gaeth (1988) showed that subjects evaluated ground beef more favorably when it was described as 75% lean than as 25% fat (although this advantage drastically diminished after consumers tasted the beef). The credit card lobby insists on using the label "cash discount" rather than "credit card surcharge" for gas stations that charge higher prices when customers use their credit cards instead of cash (Thaler, 1980).

Non-SEU Models of Decision Making

Most of the decision models discussed to this point have been variants on the expected value or expected utility model. They assume that a decision maker's overall evaluation of some option is formed by an evaluation of the possible outcomes flowing from the option, discounting these evaluations to reflect the uncertainty of their occurrence, and then adding these discounted evaluations together to form the overall evaluation. From EV to prospect theory, the guiding spirit is evaluate, discount, and add. In this section we look briefly at three models that do not follow this format.

Image theory (Beach, 1990, 1993) sees the decision maker as concerned with maintaining consistency among three mental images: a value image (summarizing her values and beliefs about rightness); a trajectory image (summarizing her goals and a path to their attainment); and a strategic image (a set of plans that guide tactical behavior toward the goals). The theory emphasizes screening of decision options for compatibility with the decision maker's value image, and selection of options to maintain consistency between the strategic and trajectory images. Actual comparative evaluation of options against one another (the "profitability test") occurs only in the relatively rare case in which several options survive screening. Much of the research to date has focused on this screening process (Beach, 1998), with major emphasis on the number of "violations" an option must incur before it is rejected. There has been relatively little research on the nature and stability of the images themselves (Dunegan, 1993).

A second nontraditional decision model is presented by Lopes (1987, 1995) under the somewhat ungainly title of the *security-potential/aspiration* (SP/A) model. The core intuition guiding the model is that assessment of an uncertain prospect such as a gamble generates a conflict between the downside or worst-case outcomes and the upside or best-case outcomes. Some individuals (security-minded) tend to be primarily concerned with the downside possibilities, whereas others (potential-minded) tend to be primarily concerned with the upside possibilities. For example, offered a choice between two gambles of equal expected value, one with outcomes tightly clustered and the other with gambles widely distributed, the security-minded person will prefer the tight clustering (because the possibility of large losses is smaller) whereas the potential-minded person will prefer the wide distribution (because the possibility of large gains is larger). This basic balancing act is modified by the subject's aspiration level, a level of gain or loss that the subject hopes to do better than. This very brief sketch conveys none of the elegance and scope of Lopes's argument, nor of its remarkable consistency with a wide range of data, both from choices between gamble and from verbal protocols collected while making those choices. The SP/A model is presented as a full alternative to prospect theory and, indeed, does a better job of accommodating some parts of the evidence than prospect theory does (Schneider, 1992).

The third non-SEU model we consider has emerged from what is called the *naturalistic decision making* (NDM) movement, which has been concerned with studying expert decision makers in their natural settings. These settings are often complex, time-pressured, highly uncertain, high-stakes and dynamic, and thus unfriendly to thoughtful, deliberative decisions (Orasanu & Connolly, 1993). Instead, researchers (Cannon-Bowers & Salas, 1998; Kline, 1993) have found that choice in such settings often turns on rapid assessment of the situation followed by rapid selection of an action that matches the situation demands. These recognition-based or recognition-

primed decisions (RPD; Cohen & Freeman, 1997) thus emphasize thinking much less, and rapid assessment-action matching much more, than does conventional decision making. Indeed, these expert performances, though often highly effective, may address phenomena rather different from what has conventionally been called decision making. It is not surprising that experts doing what they know how to do use mental processes quite different from those used by others trying to find a course of action when they do not know what to do. Work on RPD thus reminds us that effective expert performance may not rely on reflective decision processes of the conventional sort.

Signal Detection Theory

An important model of decision making that has been largely ignored in JDM research goes by the name of signal detection theory (SDT). The name reflects the roots of the model, which was in guiding early radar operators in deciding whether a given display included a "signal" (e.g., a real target) hidden in the "noise" on the radar screen. The SDT approach is driven by practical prescriptive goals of improving decision making and is only indirectly concerned with the psychology of the decision maker. The approach is, however, of great generality for many applied problems, from assessing cracks in aircraft wings to detecting breast cancer, and from evaluating job candidates to testing for AIDS, drug use, or lying.

SDT (Getty, Pickett, D'Orsi, & Swets, 1988; Swets, 1988) considers a diagnostic situation, one in which repetitive choices must be made between two alternatives. An evidence system of some kind produces probabilistic information of imperfect accuracy to guide the choices. For example, a test for some specific disease might produce a numerical score: If the score is high, the patient is likely to have the disease; if it is low, he or she is unlikely to have it. What should you, the physician, do with a given score? Because the test is imperfect, there is a possibility of an error either way. If you act as though the disease is present when it is not (a false positive), you incur costs of wasteful, painful, and perhaps dangerous treatments and patient distress. If you act as though the disease is absent when it is actually present (false negative), you incur costs of failing to treat real disease. You need to set a threshold on the test score at which you will act. The threshold requires consideration of how likely the disease is to start with (the base rate) and of the costs and benefits of the two different sorts of error you might make.

The evidence system offers the decision maker a set of choices, which can be summarized in a plot of false-positive probabilities versus true-positive probabilities, called a received operating characteristic (ROC) another echo of SDT's

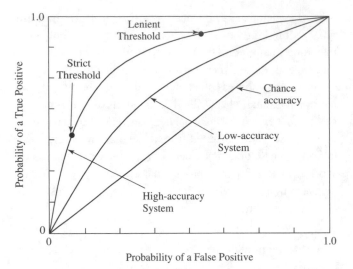

Figure 19.3   Diagnostic systems in signal detection theory.

roots in radar curve (Figure 19.3). The decision maker may decide to set a very strict threshold, insisting on a very high test score so that the chance of a false positive is small. The price she pays is that she will miss many true positives. Using the same system, she could choose a lax threshold, acting even when test scores were quite low. Doing this would push the true-positive probability higher, but only at the cost of more false alarms. The ROC curve is thus a summary of the evidence system's accuracy. A highly accurate system would offer very high true-positive probabilities with small false-positive probabilities. A completely useless system would offer identical probabilities of each. Anything that pushes the ROC up and to the left (higher true-positive probability for the same false-positive probabilities) represents an improvement in accuracy and offers the decision maker a better range of options at which to set the threshold. Curve A thus offers a better menu of choices than does Curve B, and one research goal is to improve existing diagnostic systems in this way.

Independently of this improvement, it is possible to help the decision maker set appropriate thresholds so as to make the best choice from those offered by the ROC curve. (Consider, e.g., if you would want to use the same threshold on an HIV test for screening blood donations and for evaluating real patients. A false positive on the first case merely wastes a pint of good blood. In the second case, it would erroneously lead a patient to believe that he or she had a life-threatening disease.)

An excellent example of the SDT approach is given in Getty et al. (1988), in which the problem is improving the diagnosis of malignant breast cancers from mammograms. The authors were able to devise a checklist and scoring system of features that the radiologists were to score from each image,

and this led to significant improvement in the accuracy of the evidence system (ROC curve). The enhanced procedure offered real improvements over the existing methods. For 1,000 cases with a cancer prevalence of 32% (the population that their study addressed), they estimated that the improved procedure would identify an additional 42 malignancies (with no additional false positives), 82 fewer false-positives (with no additional missed malignancies), or various blends in between. Given the seriousness of the disease, and of both sorts of error, the enhancement offered by the SDT analysis is clearly significant.

DECIDING: (B) MULTIPLE RELATED EVENTS

Information Search, Information Purchase

One common way in which decisions are linked sequentially is when the outcomes of an earlier decision provide (part of) the information environment for a later decision. A doctor deciding on what laboratory tests to order for a patient is setting up the information environment in which she will make her subsequent diagnostic and treatment decisions. Similarly, a new product manager ordering a market survey is gathering information on which to base a later decision on whether to launch the product. In a shorter time frame these acquisition and use processes merge.

Research on these processes has varied in how explicit the cost of acquiring information is. Russo and Dosher (1983) recorded the subject's eye movements to study which items of information he or she extracts from a decision table and in what order. The cost of an information item is the cognitive effort involved in attending to an item. A related methodology is the information board (Payne, 1976), in which decision-relevant information is displayed to the subject in a matrix of small envelopes that may be removed and opened. A computer-based analog called *Mouselab* has been extensively used (Payne et al., 1993) to explore underlying cognitive processes such as the combination rule being used by the subject.

Information cost is somewhat more explicit in work such as Wason (1960, 1968; Wason & Johnson-Laird, 1972), in which the subject makes an explicit request of the experimenter to turn over a card based on whether an exemplar fits some unknown rule. In Wason and Johnson-Laird's (1972) experiment, for example, subjects were shown four cards displaying E, K, 4, and 7. They were told that each card had a letter on one side and a number on the other and were asked which cards they would turn over to test the rule, "If a card has a vowel on one side it has an even number on the other side." Only 4% of their subjects selected E and 7, the correct choice. Almost half chose E and 4—an error because the obverse of the 4 card cannot invalidate the rule, and thus produces, at best, evidence consistent with the rule but not testing it. This common finding has been interpreted as a general bias toward confirmatory search: seeking evidence that will confirm, rather than test, one's initial beliefs. However, a penetrating analysis by Klayman and Ha (1987) suggests that such search patterns are better understood as examples of a positive test strategy, a generally appropriate heuristic that fails only in relatively rare situations, such as the four-card problem.

Explicit treatments of sampling cost flow easily from the Bayesian inference task discussed earlier (see the section on heuristics and biases). Instead of being presented with a sample of poker chips drawn from the selected bag, subjects are allowed to buy them, at a fixed monetary cost per chip, before making their bet on which bag was selected—a bet for which they can win money. Findings from many such studies (see Einhorn & Hogarth, 1981, for a review) include the following:

1. Partial sensitivity to normatively relevant variables (e.g., Pitz, 1968, found increased buying when cost per chip was reduced and diagnosticity was increased, and Snapper & Peterson, 1971, found some sensitivity to variations in information quality).

2. Sensitivity to normatively irrelevant variables, such as information order (Fried & Peterson, 1969) and total information available (Levine, Samet, & Brahlek, 1975).

3. Substantial losses (e.g., Kleiter & Wimmer, 1974), which persist with little or no learning over repeated trials (e.g., Wallsten, 1968).

4. Both over-purchase and under-purchase (e.g., Hershman & Levine, 1970; largely parallel results are reported in an alternative, regression-based model of information purchase by Connolly and colleagues; see Connolly, 1988, for an overview).

The evidence from both Bayesian and regression models of information purchase suggests that subjects routinely and persistently make costly errors in balancing the costs and benefits of their information purchases. This should not be surprising. Optimal information purchase requires the subject to make accurate assessments of how accurate the different sources are, to select the best subset, and to combine the information acquired in an optimal way. Extensive evidence suggests that all three subtasks are quite difficult. It is thus likely that serious nonoptimalities will be found when the balance must be struck in practical settings. This is consistent with the reluctance of patients to seek second and third medical opinions before undertaking major courses of treatment, which, in our terms, represents a major underpurchase of decision-relevant information. It is also consistent with the huge body of evidence (Guion, 1975) on the predictive uselessness of unstructured job interviews—which are, nonetheless, still very widely used and represent a huge overpurchase of decision-irrelevant information. Wherever information costs and benefits need to be brought into balance, then, there is good reason to suspect significant departures from optimality (March & Feldman, 1981).

Sunk Costs and Escalation of Commitment

One important way in which a series of decisions over time can be linked is when nonrecoverable costs incurred at an earlier stage influence decisions at a later stage. The prescriptive advice on such matters is clear: The costs are sunk and should play no part in the later decisions. Equally clearly, many of us violate such advice. We finish the indifferent restaurant meal, sit through to the end of bad movies, and remain in failed relationships so as not to "waste" the money spent on the restaurant bill or movie ticket or the time "invested" in the relationship. We fall, in short, into the sunk cost trap.

Arkes and Blumer (1985) reported 10 small experiments in which sunk cost effects were demonstrated. Although most used a scenario format (and are thus open to the criticism that they involved the subjects in no real decisions), Experiment 2 made clever use of actual theater-ticket buying decisions to investigate sunk cost effects. Of patrons buying season tickets for a university theater, one third were given a modest discount, and one third a substantial discount, from the normal price. Patrons paying full price subsequently attended significantly more of the performances than did those who received discounts, although the effect faded later in the theater season. Arkes and Blumer interpreted this as evidence that the larger sunk costs of the full-price patrons influenced their later attendance decisions.

Similar effects have been reported in organizational (e.g., Staw & Ross, 1989) and other (Brockner, Shaw, & Rubin, 1979) contexts. In a typical organizational study, Staw, Barsade, and Koput (1997) found that loan officers at banks were more likely to continue funding and extending problem loans when they had been responsible for the initial decision than when they took over responsibility for the loan after its initiation. A related effect in the persuasion literature, the *foot-in-the-door technique,* involves winning compliance to a large request by first obtaining compliance to a smaller one (Freedman & Fraser, 1966). More subjects agreed to put up a large lawn sign when they had earlier been asked to sign a petition on the same subject than when subjects were approached directly with the large request.

Despite such apparently robust demonstrations, there is some confusion as to what phenomena are appropriately included in sunk cost effects, and an embarrassing range of partially conflicting explanations has been offered. One setting in which escalating commitment has been demonstrated in scenario studies is in continuing to fund partially completed projects (e.g., Staw, 1976). However, when degree of project completion and expenditure are independently manipulated (Garland, 1990; Conlon & Garland, 1993), only the former factor shows an effect. Public use of sunk cost arguments by public officials may reflect either the entrapment of the speaker or the calculation that sunk cost arguments will persuade the audience. Staw and Hoang (1995) claim to have demonstrated sunk cost effects in their finding that basketball players drafted early (and expensively) into the NBA thereafter are played more and traded at higher prices than their performance appears to justify. The result could, however, simply reflect the failure of their performance model to capture what a player is worth to a team. It is thus somewhat unclear just what is to be included as a sunk cost effect, or how reliably such effects can be reproduced.

One account of the sunk cost effect has been offered in terms of prospect theory's loss function. The initial cost is taken as a loss (below the reference point), thus putting the decision maker into a region of risk seeking. Continuing the project now offers a risky project with some hope of gain, while abandonment forces acceptance of a certain loss (Thaler, 1980). Arkes (1996) argued instead for a quite general aversion to waste, a category mistakenly expanded to include partially completed projects or previously incurred costs. Staw (1976) and Aronson (1984) offered accounts based on self-justification, whereas Kiesler (1971) saw behavioral commitment as the central mechanism. Brockner (1992) presented a multitheoretical perspective.

Overall, then, the sunk cost effect and its relatives seem obviously worrying and possibly widespread. There is, however, a suggestion that we may be lumping together several rather different effects, each driven by a complex psychology of its own.

Dynamic Decision Making

Dynamic decision problems are those in which the decision maker may act repeatedly on an environment that responds to his or her actions and also changes independently over time, both endogenously and exogenously (Edwards, 1962). An example might be a senior manager's efforts to improve low morale in an organization. She may, over a period of months, try a number of different interventions, scaling up successes and abandoning failures. Over the same period various factors internal and external to the organization may also affect morale. Clearly, such problems set decision makers extraordinary challenges.

They have also proved difficult for researchers, partly because of their inherent complexity and partly because of the experimenter's partial lack of control. Complexity implies difficulty in deriving optimal strategies. Lack of control arises from the fact that the problem facing the decision maker at time t is partially the consequence of his or her earlier decisions, as well as of the experimental conditions imposed. On the positive side, the growing availability of computers has helped both in the creation of realistically complex experimental environments and in the analysis of strategic alternatives. Some examples of the sorts of studies this allows include the following:

1. *Simulated medical diagnosis.* Kleinmuntz and Kleinmuntz (1981) created a diagnostic task in which simulated doctors attempted to treat simulated patients on the basis of their initial symptoms and of the results of any tests the doctor chose to order. They could also act at any point to administer "treatments" that might or might not improve the patient's health. Health fluctuated, over the 60 time periods of each trial, both in response to the doctor's interventions and to the preset (downward) course of the disease. The simulated strategies explored included Bayesian revision, a heuristic hypothesis-testing strategy, and a simple trial and error approach. The computationally intensive Bayesian strategy yielded only modest improvements over the heuristic strategy in this environment, and even the simplistic trial and error approach did well on some cases. Further simulation results are reported in Kleinmuntz (1985), and experimental results with real subjects are in Kleinmuntz and Thomas (1987).

2. *Artificial worlds.* A number of European researchers (see Mahon, 2000, for a review) have explored dynamic decision problems with the aid of simulated worlds: fire fighting in simulated forests (B. Brehmer, 1990), economic development in a simulated third-world country (Reither, 1981), control of a simulated smallpox epidemic (Hesse, 1982), and so on. Funke (1995) provided an extensive review, with studies classified as to the person, task, and systems factors each examined. Typical findings are those of B. Brehmer (1990) from his simulated fire-fighting task. Subjects initially perform quite poorly but can learn this complex task with repeated play. Feedback delays impede learning substantially. Opportunities to offset feedback delay by decentralizing decision making were mainly ignored.

3. *Systems dynamics.* A group strongly associated with MIT (Diehl & Sterman, 1993; Paich & Sterman, 1993; Sterman, 1987, 1989) base their dynamic decision-making tasks on feedback dynamics models in which coupled feedback processes make response over time extremely nonintuitive to most subjects. For example, in Sterman (1987) subjects faced a capital budgeting task in which there was significant lag between ordering new equipment and having it available to meet increased demand. Most subjects in this task generated very large and costly oscillations, despite instruction in system linkages

As this sampling suggests, empirical studies of dynamic decision tasks are difficult. The tasks themselves are quite complex, even if they are greatly oversimplified versions of real-world analogs. Amateur subjects are thus easily overwhelmed, whereas expert subjects object to the unreality of the tasks. Findings thus tend to be task specific and difficult to aggregate over different studies. Progress, clearly, is being made, but there are important challenges in this area.

MULTIPLE DECISION MAKERS

Group decision making is significantly more complex than are decisions made by individuals. Several new issues arise: combining multiple beliefs and preferences, social interaction of decision makers, and conflict and cooperation. In this section we examine research that addresses these issues in terms of group decision making for certain and uncertain outcomes, technology designed specifically to aid group decision making, and negotiation between two parties.

Group Decision Making

Two new phenomena have been discovered in group decision making: groupthink and the risky shift. Janis (1972) defined *groupthink* as "a mode of thinking that people engage in when they are deeply involved in a cohesive in-group, when the members' strivings for unanimity override their motivation to realistically appraise alternative courses of action" (p. 9). A classic case example is the failed Bay of Pigs invasion, in which the American military sent Cuban exiles to overthrow the dictator Fidel Castro. These groupthink decisions are characterized by highly cohesive groups that are under high stress from an external threat and have low self-esteem due to an earlier failure or decision difficulty. Several other attributes may also contribute to groupthink: an illusion of invulnerability, collective rationalization, belief in the inherent morality of the group, insulation, lack of impartial leadership, direct pressure on dissenters, stereotypes of out-groups, and lack of a decision-making procedure. However, note that merely increasing group familiarity alone is not sufficient to cause groupthink: Watson, Michaelsen, and Sharp (1991) found that groups who spent more than 30 hours on decision-making tasks were more effective than were individual decision makers.

The *risky shift* (Stoner, 1961) is the tendency for decisions made by groups to be more risk seeking than would be predicted by the individual members' risk preferences. However, as Bazerman (1998) pointed out, most of the studies finding the risky shift used Stoner's (1961) Choice Dilemma Questionnaire (CDQ) method. Other studies using different methodologies have found either no shift or a cautious shift (i.e., more risk averse).

Are groups better or worse decision makers than individuals? The answer depends on the situation and decision to be made (and, of course, on the criteria for "good"; in many settings a technically inferior decision to which the whole group is agreed may be an excellent choice). There is no clear pattern of group effects in either reducing or increasing decision biases. The hindsight bias was reduced slightly with groups compared to individuals (Stahlberg, Eller, Maass, & Frey, 1995), although Bukszar and Connolly (1988) found no effect. However, groups were even more affected than individuals by the representativeness heuristic in a base-rate (cab) problem (Argote, Seabright, & Dyer, 1986). And groups, like individuals, appear to be biased in their information search (Schulz-Hardt, Dieter, Luethgens, & Moscovici, 2000). Tindale (1993) argued that group effectiveness depends on the demonstrability of the solution. If there is a solution that one or more members of the group can demonstrate as the correct answer, then the group will usually adopt this solution. However, if the solution cannot be easily demonstrated (as in the cab problem), then the group decides by majority rule (Tindale & Davis, 1985). Because most individuals neglect base rates in situations such as the cab problem, the majority will also fall prey to this bias. Tindale (1993) presented data in which decision biases are reduced or enhanced with groups as compared to individuals.

Kerr, MacCoun, and Kramer (1996) reviewed studies investigating decision biases at both the individual and the group level. They also concluded that the strength of decision biases can either be lower, equal to, or higher for groups as compared to individuals depending on the type of decision, the initial values of the individuals, and how individual values are aggregated into group decisions. They organized the various results into a formal model of group decision making called the *social decision scheme* (SDS) model (Davis, 1973; see the special issue of *Organizational Behavior and Human*

Decision Processes, 1999, on this topic). This model provides a framework for answering the question about how individual values are aggregated into a group decision and what decisions will emerge given different decision rules such as "majority wins," "truth wins," or "equiprobability," in which every option has an equal probability of being selected as long as it has a single advocate. For example, Whyte and Sebenius (1997) found that groups did not debias individual estimates that were improperly and inappropriately anchored. Using SDS methodology, the authors showed that group estimates were based on the majority point of view that was biased before group discussion began.

Although it is unclear whether groups are better or worse at making decision than individuals, there are certain conditions in which groups can increase decision-making quality. Several studies of heterogeneous groups (in terms of many attributes such as personalities, gender, attitudes, and experience) indicate that heterogeneity is positively related to creativity and decision effectiveness (Jackson, May, & Whitney, 1995). Guzzo and Waters (1982) found that the quality of group decisions and the number of diverse alternatives increased when expression of emotion was delayed until alternative solutions were discussed. They suggested that early expression of emotions may reduce the group energy and narrow the range of accepted ideas. Under time pressure, quality of decisions generally decline; task cohesion can help groups maintain decision quality at a level comparable to low time pressure situations (Zaccaro, Gualtieri, & Minionis, 1995).

Group Decision Support Systems

Given the difficulties with decision making in general, research has been conducted on group decision support systems (GDSS) to ease the added complexity of group decision making. GDSSs usually takes the form of computerized, networked systems that aid in idea generation and decision making. A brief summary of key findings follows, but a more detailed account can be found in Hollingshead and McGrath (1995). In general, groups using GDSS versus unaided groups demonstrate more equal participation and increased focus on the task but also interact less, take longer, and have lower overall consensus and decreased satisfaction with the process and the decision (Hollingshead & McGrath, 1995; McLeod, 1992). GDSS provides a unique environment in which group members can interact anonymously. Jessup, Connolly, and Tansik (1990) showed that anonymous members using GDSS tended to be more critical, more probing, and more likely to generate comments or ideas than when individual contributions were identified.

Which is better for group decision-making task performance: face-to-face interaction or GDSS? The answer depends on the task. GDSSs are better for idea generation: Group members can simultaneously submit ideas, which reduces the problem of idea production being blocked while listening to others or waiting for a turn to speak. However, face-to-face interactions appear to be superior for problem-solving and conflict-resolution situations. It is interesting to note that Hollingshead and McGrath (1995) suggested that some of the benefits of GDSSs may stem from the structured aspects of the decision-making process rather than from the GDSS itself. Note that Archer (1990) found no differences in decision quality between GDSS and face-to-face when the decision process phases of a complex business situation were organized and managed in a rational manner.

Much of the work in GDSS concerns the technology itself, and research on the behavioral impacts on group decision performance is still in the early stages. The limited research that has been conducted has largely used ad hoc teams. Work needs to be done on intact groups that have had experience working and making decisions together. In addition, there is evidence that simply structuring the decision-making task can improve performance. There may be other features that GDSSs can provide to improve decision making that cannot achieved in any other context.

Negotiation

Negotiation is the process in which people determine "what each side shall give and take or perform and receive in a transaction between them" (Thompson, 1990, p. 516). There is a vast literature in the field of negotiation, and our review here is cursory. For further information on the psychological aspects of the negotiation process, see Thompson (1990) and Bazerman, Curhan, Moore, and Valley (2000). We will focus on dyadic negotiations; however, there is also an extensive literature in multiparty negotiations and coalition formations that we do not discuss here (see Miller & Komorita, 1986; Murnighan, 1986, for reviews).

Early social psychological work in the 1960s and 1970s focused primarily on individual differences or situational characteristics. The extensive literature on individual differences has shown little effect on negotiations (Thompson, 1990). The research on situational variables provided primarily descriptive accounts and did not use clear standards of rationality as a basis of evaluating performance (Bazerman et al., 2000). In economics, the game theoretic approach attempted to go beyond describing behavior and defined optimal behavior in negotiations. Unfortunately, this line of research suffers from two main disadvantages (Bazerman, 1998): It (a) requires that all possible strategies be defined with associated outcomes, which is either difficult or impossible to perform, and (b) makes the dubious assumption of rationality on the part of the negotiator. More recently, researchers have examined the interaction between individual differences and contextual variables. For example, Kray, Thompson, and Galinsky (2001) examined how men and women adopt different bargaining strategies after stereotypes about effective negotiators are activated. When stereotypes are activated implicitly, men are more assertive than women and prevail in a distributive negotiation. However, women are more assertive (and more successful negotiators) than men when stereotypes are activated explicitly.

The 1980s through 1990s used the behavioral decision research (BDR) as a framework. Raiffa (1982), in his decision analytic approach, shifted the attention away from prescriptions of optimal strategies to descriptions of actual negotiation behavior. Rather than propose optimal bargaining solutions based on objective facts of a negotiation, this type of research examines the perceptions of the situation, the other party, and the self. Thus, the new format was not to present a normative picture of negotiations but to describe behavior and, at times, demonstrate the systematic deviations from the rational negotiator. In the 1990s a social cognitive perspective was developed, and the focus was on the negotiator as information processor (Thompson, Peterson, & Kray, 1995).

Many of the findings in this field have taken the heuristics and biases results (e.g., framing and overconfidence) and found them in a negotiation context. A great deal of evidence indicates that the framing of a negotiation has strong implications for negotiations. For example, in a labor-management salary negotiation (Bazerman, 1984), a raise from $10 to $11/hr can been seen by labor as a gain of $1 or as a loss of $1 if the union demanded $12/hr. Likewise, management can view $11/hr as a loss of $1, compared to the previous salary, or as a gain of $1, compared to the union's demands. The greater impact of losses over equal magnitude gains (i.e., "loss aversion") results in a reluctance to trade concessions (Ross & Stillinger, 1991), creating a barrier to conflict resolution. Neale and Bazerman (1985) showed that negotiators with positive frames were more likely to make concessions and were more successful than those with negative frames (however, negatively framed negotiators earned on average more per transaction when an agreement was reached). Real estate agents have been shown to anchor on the list price of a house and insufficiently adjust when assessing the value of a home (Northcraft & Neale, 1987); conflict management experts fall prey to the availability bias and do not search sufficiently for necessary information (Pinkley, Griffith, & Northcraft, 1995); and student negotiators were overconfident in believing that their offer will be accepted in final arbitration (Bazerman & Neale, 1982).

In addition, new biases have been found that are unique to the negotiation context. One well-known bias, the fixed-pie

assumption, occurs because the negotiators assume that they must distribute a fixed pie (Bazerman, Magliozzi, & Neale, 1985) instead of searching for integrated solutions that increase joint payoffs. This belief in the mythical fixed pie can also lead to the incompatibility bias (Thompson & Hastie, 1990; Thompson & Hrebec, 1996), in which negotiators falsely assume that their interests are incompatible with those of their opponents. Bazerman (1998) gave an example of a labor-management negotiation in which both sides value increased training programs: Management would gain workforce flexibility, labor would gain job security. However, because of the incompatibility bias, they settle for a less-than-optimal arrangement because they do not realize that they have common interests and negotiate as if a compromise must be reached. In addition, the fixed-pie assumption can lead to devaluing any concession made by the opponent (Ross & Stillinger, 1991): If management is offering more job training, it must not be too costly or must be benefiting them in some way.

Recent research augments the BDR perspective and adds an emphasis on social psychological variables, such as the importance of relationships, egocentrism, and emotions. Ethics, the mode of communication, and cross-cultural issues have also received more attention recently.

CONCLUSION

As this selective survey of JDM connections to industrial and organizational (I/O) psychology has, we hope, made clear, we see the linkage between the two fields as having accomplished significant work, but as having a potential for much more. As Highhouse (2001) pointed out, there are many topics in I/O psychology that seem to fall naturally into the JDM domain: personnel selection and placement, job choice, performance assessment, feedback provision and acceptance, compensation, resource planning, strategic forecasting, and others. The two disciplines have, however, remained largely isolated, despite the clear potential for collaboration. Our hope is that the present chapter may contribute something to stimulate this linkage.

It may help a little if we clarify what we see as the current state of development of JDM. The mere name of the discipline makes an implicit claim: that there is sufficient commonality across different decision situations for a general theory of decisions to make some sense. We would assess the evidence to date on this point as mixed. Weather forecasters do have *something* to say to heart surgeons, and hog judges have *something* to say to HR practitioners; but it would be absurd to claim that we have a successful general theory of judgment and decision that embraces all four territories as mere applications. Any general claims require extensive local tinkering before they bring much insight to specific practical applications.

In our view the best contributions that JDM can currently make to I/O issues is as a fertile source of interesting hypotheses and as a provider of frameworks and instruments. For example, we would not read the literature on overconfidence in lab problems as supporting strong predictions that managers will be overconfident in predicting hiring needs. It does, we think, make such a hypothesis worth exploring. It also suggests how the relevant research could be conducted. In return, such research would inform JDM of the boundary conditions on its findings: When, for example, does overconfidence generalize, when is it bounded, what mechanisms are successful in minimizing it? It is this two-way enrichment of one another's disciplines that we see as the potential for an enhanced collaboration between JDM and I/O. Our fond hope is that this chapter may do something to facilitate the interchange.

REFERENCES

Adams, J. S. (1965). Inequity in social exchange. In L. Berkowitz (Ed.), *Advances in experimental social psychology* (Vol. 2, pp. 267–299). New York: Academic Press.

Allais, M. (1953). Le comportement de l'homme rationnel devant le risque: Critique des postulats et axiomes de l'ecole Americaine [Rational man's behavior in the presence of risk: Critique of the postulates and axioms of the American school]. *Econometrica, 21,* 503–546.

Archer, N. P. (1990). A comparison of computer conferences with face-to-face meetings for small group business decisions. *Behaviour and Information Technology, 9,* 307–317.

Argote, L., Seabright, M., & Dyer, L. (1986). Individual versus group use of base-rate and individuating information. *Organizational Behavior and Human Decision Processes, 38,* 65–75.

Arkes, H. R. (1996). The psychology of waste. *Journal of Behavioral Decision Making, 9,* 213–224.

Arkes, H. R., & Blumer, C. (1985). The psychology of sunk cost. *Organizational Behavior and Human Decision Processes, 35,* 124–140.

Aronson, E. (1984). *The social animal.* San Francisco: W. H. Freeman.

Bar-Hillel, M. (1996). Why are people reluctant to exchange lottery tickets? *Journal of Personality and Social Psychology, 70,* 17–27.

Bazerman, M. H. (1984). The relevance of Kahneman and Tversky's concept of framing to organizational behavior. *Journal of Management, 10,* 333–343.

Bazerman, M. H. (1998). *Judgment in managerial decision making.* New York: Wiley.

Bazerman, M. H., Curhan, J. R., Moore, D. A., & Valley, K. A. (2000). Negotiation. *Annual Review of Psychology, 51,* 279–314.

Bazerman, M. H., Magliozzi, T., & Neale, M. A. (1985). Integrative bargaining in a competitive market. *Organizational Behavior and Human Decision Processes, 35,* 294–313.

Bazerman, M. H., & Neale, M. A. (1982). Improving negotiation effectiveness under final offer arbitration: The role of selection and training. *Journal of Applied Psychology, 67,* 543–548.

Beach, L. R. (1990). *Image theory: Decision making in personal and organizational contexts.* Chichester, UK: Wiley.

Beach, L. R. (1993). Broadening the definition of decision making: The role of prechoice screening of options. *Psychological Science, 4,* 215–220.

Beach, L. R. (1998). *Image theory: Theoretical and empirical foundations.* Mahwah, NJ: Erlbaum.

Beach, L. R., & Mitchell, T. R. (1978). A contingency model for the selection of decision strategies. *Academy of Management Review, 3,* 439–449.

Bell, D. E. (1982). Regret in decision making under uncertainty. *Operations Research, 30,* 961–981.

Bell, D. E. (1985). Disappointment in decision making under uncertainty. *Operations Research, 30,* 961–981.

Bernoulli, D. (1954). Exposition of a new theory on the measurment of risk (L. Sommer, trans.). *Econometrica, 22,* 23–36. (Original work published 1738)

Bernstein, P. L. (1996). *Against the gods: The remarkable story of risk.* New York: Wiley.

Bolger, F., & Harvey, N. (1993). Context-sensitive heuristics in statistical reasoning [Special Issue: The cognitive psychology of reasoning]. *Quarterly Journal of Experimental Psychology: Human Experimental Psychology, 46A,* 779–811.

Brehmer, A., & Brehmer, B. (1988). What have we learned about human judgment from thirty years of policy capturing? In B. Brehmer & C. R. B. Joyce (Eds.), *Human judgment: The SJT view* (pp. 75–114). Amsterdam: North-Holland.

Brehmer, B. (1990). Strategies in real-time, dynamic decision making. In R. M. Hogarth (Ed.), *Insights in decision making: A tribute to Hillel J. Hogarth* (pp. 262–279). Chicago: University of Chicago Press.

Brockner, J. (1992). The escalation of commitment to a failing course of action: Toward theoretical progress. *Academy of Management Review, 17,* 39–61.

Brockner, J., Shaw, M. C., & Rubin, J. Z. (1979). Factors affecting withdrawal from an escalating conflict: Quitting before it's too late. *Journal of Experimental Social Psychology, 15,* 492–503.

Brunswik, E. (1952). *The conceptual framework of psychology.* Chicago: University of Chicago Press.

Bukszar, E., & Connolly, T. (1988). Hindsight bias and strategic choice: Some problems in learning from experience. *Academy of Management Journal, 31,* 628–641.

Camerer, C. (1981). *The validity and utility of expert judgment.* Unpublished doctoral dissertation, University of Chicago, Graduate School of Business.

Cannon-Bowers, J. A., & Salas, E. (Eds.). (1998). *Decision making under stress: Implications for training and simulation.* Washington, DC: American Psychological Association.

Cohen, M. S., & Freeman, J. T. (1997). Understanding and enhancing critical thinking in recognition-based decision making. In R. Flin & L. Martin (Eds.), *Decision making under stress: Emerging themes and applications* (pp. 161–169). Aldershot, UK: Ashgate.

Conlon, D. E., & Garland, H. (1993). The role of project completion information in resource allocation decisions. *Academy of Management Journal, 36,* 402–413.

Connolly, T. (1988). Studies of information-purchase processes. In B. Brehmer & C. R. B. Joyce (Eds.), *Human judgment: The SJT view* (pp. 75–114). Amsterdam: North-Holland.

Connolly, T. (1997). Electronic brain storming: Science meets technology in the group meeting room. In S. Kiesler (Ed.), *Culture of the internet* (pp. 263–276). Mahwah, NJ: Erlbaum.

Connolly, T., Arkes, H. R., & Hammond, K. R. (Eds.). (2000). *Judgment and decision making: An interdisciplinary reader* (2nd ed.). New York: Cambridge University Press.

Connolly, T., Jessup, L. M., & Valacich, J. S. (1990). Effects of anonymity and evaluative tone on idea generation in computer-mediated groups. *Management Science, 36,* 689–703.

Connolly, T., & Miklausich, V. M. (1978). Some effects of feedback error in diagnostic decision tasks. *Academy of Management Journal, 21,* 301–307.

Coombs, C. H., Dawes, R. M., & Tversky, A. (1970). *Mathematical psychology: An elementary introduction.* Englewood Cliffs, NJ: Prentice Hall.

Cooper, W. H., Gallupe, R. B., Pollard, S., & Cadsby, J. (1998). Some liberating effects of anonymous electronic brainstorming. *Small Group Research, 29,* 147–178.

Davis, J. H. (1973). Group decision and social interaction: A theory of social decision schemes. *Psychological Review, 80,* 97–125.

Dawes, R. M. (1998). Behavioral decision making and judgment. In D. T. Gilbert & S. T. Fiske (Eds.), *The handbook of social psychology* (4th ed., Vol. 2, pp. 497–548). Boston: McGraw-Hill.

Deane, D. H., Hammond, K. R., & Summers, D. A. (1972). Acquisition and application of information in complex inference tasks. *Journal of Experimental Psychology, 92,* 20–26.

Diehl, E., & Sterman, J. D. (1993). Effects of feedback complexity on dynamic decision making. *Organizational Behavior and Human Decision Processes, 62,* 198–215.

Diehl, M., & Stroebe, W. (1987). Productivity loss in brainstorming groups: Toward the solution of a riddle. *Journal of Personality and Social Psychology, 53,* 497–509.

Doyle, J., & Thomas, S. A. (1995). Capturing policy in hearing-aid decisions by audiologists. *Medical Decision Making, 15,* 58–64.

Dunegan, K. J. (1993). Framing, cognitive modes, and image theory: Toward an understanding of a glass half full. *Journal of Applied Psychology, 78,* 491–503.

Earle, T. C. (1970). Task learning, interpersonal learning, and cognitive complexity. *Oregon Research Institute Bulletin, 10*(2).

Edgell, S. E., & Geisler, W. S. (1980). A set-theoretic random utility model of choice behavior. *Journal of Mathematical Psychology, 22,* 265–278.

Edwards, W. (1954). The theory of decision making. *Psychological Bulletin, 51,* 380–417.

Edwards, W. (1961). Behavioral decision theory. *Annual Review of Psychology, 12,* 473–498.

Edwards, W. (1962). Dynamic decision making and probabilistic information processing. *Human Factors, 4,* 59–73.

Edwards, W. (1968). Conservatism in human information processing. In B. Kleinmuntz (Ed.), *Formal representation of human judgment* (pp. 17–52). New York: Wiley.

Edwards, W., & Newman, J. R. (1982). *Multiattribute evaluation.* Beverley Hills, CA: Sage.

Edwards, W., & von Winterfeldt, D. (1986). On cognitive illusions and their implications. In H. R. Arkes & K. R. Hammond (Eds.), *Judgment and decision making: An interdisciplinary reader* (pp. 642–679). Cambridge, UK: Cambridge University Press.

Einhorn, H. J. (1974). Expert judgment: Some necessary conditions and an example. *Journal of Applied Psychology, 59,* 562–571.

Einhorn, H. J. (1980). Learning from experience and suboptimal rules in decision making. In T. S. Walsten (Ed.), *Cognitive processes in choice and decision behavior* (pp. 1–20). Hillsdale, NJ: Erlbaum.

Einhorn, H. J., & Hogarth, R. M. (1981). Behavioral decision theory: Processes of judgment and choice. *Annual Review of Psychology, 32,* 53–88.

Ellsberg, D. (1961). Risk, ambiguity, and the Savage axioms. *Quarterly Journal of Economics, 75,* 643–669.

Fischhoff, B. (1977). Cognitive liabilities and product liability. *Journal of Products Liability, 1,* 207–220.

Fischhoff, B. (1982). Debiasing. In D. Kahneman, P. Slovic, & A. Tversky (Eds.), *Judgment under uncertainty: Heuristics and biases* (pp. 422–444). Cambridge, UK: Cambridge University Press.

Fischhoff, B. (1991). Value elicitation: Is there anything in there? *American Psychologist, 46,* 835–847.

Fischhoff, B., & Beyth, R. (1975). "I knew it would happen": Remembered probabilities of once-future things. *Organizational Behavior and Human Decision Processes, 13,* 1–16.

Fischhoff, B., Bostrom, A., & Quadrel, M. J. (1993). Risk perception and communication. *Annual Review of Public Health, 14,* 183–203.

Fischhoff, B., Lichtenstein, S., Slovic, P., Derby, S. L., & Keeney, R. L. (1981). *Acceptable risk.* Cambridge, UK: Cambridge University Press.

Freedman, J. L., & Fraser, S. C. (1966). Compliance without pressure: The foot-in-the-door technique. *Journal of Personality and Social Psychology, 4,* 195–202.

Fried, L. S., & Peterson, C. R. (1969). Information seeking: Optional versus fixed stopping. *Journal of Experimental Psychology, 80,* 525–529.

Funke, J. (1995). Experimental research on complex problem solving. In P. Frensch & J. Funke (Eds.), *Complex problem solving: The European perspective* (pp. 243–268). Hillsdale, NJ: Erlbaum.

Garland, H. (1990). Throwing good money after bad: The effect of sunk costs on the decision to escalate commitment to an ongoing project. *Journal of Applied Psychology, 75,* 728–731.

Getty, D. J., Pickett, R. M., D'Orsi, C. J., & Swets, J. A. (1988). Enhanced interpretation of diagnostic images. *Investigative Radiology, 23,* 240–252.

Gettys, C. F., & Fisher, S. D. (1979). Hypothesis plausibility and hypothesis generation. *Organizational Behavior and Human Decision Processes, 24,* 93–110.

Gigerenzer, G. (1991). How to make cognitive illusions disappear: Beyond "heuristics and biases." In W. Stroebe & M. Hewstone (Eds.), *European review of social psychology* (Vol. 2, pp. 83–115). Chichester, UK: Wiley.

Goldstein, W. M., & Hogarth, R. M. (Eds.). (1997). *Research on judgment and decision making: Currents, connections, and controversies.* New York: Cambridge University Press.

Greenberg, J. (1982). Approaching equity and avoiding inequity in groups and organizations. In J. Greenberg & R. L. Cohen (Eds.), *Equity and justice in social behavior* (pp. 389–435). New York: Academic Press.

Greenberg, J. (1988). Equity and workplace status: A field experiment. *Journal of Applied Psychology, 73,* 606–613.

Guion, R. M. (1975). Recruiting, selection, and job placement. In M. D. Dunnette (Ed.), *Handbook of industrial and organizational psychology* (pp. 777–828). Chicago: Rand-McNally.

Guzzo, R. A., & Waters, J. A. (1982). The expression of affect and the performance of decision-making groups. *Journal of Applied Psychology, 67,* 67–74.

Hammond, K. R. (1955). Probabilistic functioning and the clinical method. *Psychological Review, 62,* 255–262.

Hammond, K. R., & Adelman, L. (1976). Science, values and human judgment. *Science, 194,* 389–396.

Hershman, R. L., & Levine, J. R. (1970). Deviations from optimal information purchase strategies in human decision making. *Organizational Behavior and Human Performance, 5,* 313–329.

Hesse, F. W. (1982). Effects of semantic context on problem solving. *Zeitschrift fur Experimentelle und Angewandte Psychologie, 29,* 62–91.

Highhouse, S. (2001). Judgment and decision making research: Relevance to industrial and organizational psychology. In N. Anderson, D. S. Ones, H. K Sinangil, & C. Viswesvaran (Eds.), *Handbook of industrial, work, and organizational psychology* (Vol. 1, pp. 314–332). Beverly Hills, CA: Sage.

Hitt, M. A., & Barr, S. H. (1989). Managerial selection decision models: Examination of cue processing. *Journal of Applied Psychology, 74,* 53–61.

Hogarth, R. M. (1987). *Judgement and choice: The psychology of decision* (2nd ed.). London: Wiley.

Hollingshead, A. B., & McGrath, J. E. (1995). Computer-assisted groups: A critical review of the empirical research. In R. A. Guzzo & E. Salas (Eds.), *Team effectiveness and decision making in organizations* (pp. 46–78). San Francisco: Jossey-Bass.

Jackson, S. E., May, K. E., & Whitney, K. (1995). Understanding the dynamics of diversity in decision-making teams. In R. A. Guzzo & E. Salas (Eds.), *Team effectiveness and decision making in organizations* (pp. 204–261). San Francisco: Jossey-Bass.

Janis, I. L. (1972). *Victims of groupthink.* Boston: Houghton-Mifflin.

Jessup, L. M., Connolly, T., & Tansik, D. A. (1990). Toward a theory of automated group work: The deindividuating effects of anonymity. *Small Group Research, 21,* 333–348.

Josephs, R. A., Larrick, R. P., Steele, C. M., & Nisbett, R. E. (1992). Protecting the self from negative consequences of risky decisions. *Journal of Personality and Social Psychology, 55,* 710–717.

Jungermann, H. (1983). The two camps on rationality. In R. W. Scholz (Ed.), *Decision making under uncertainty* (pp. 63–86). Amsterdam: Elsevier.

Kahneman, D., Knetch, J., & Thaler, R. (1986). Fairness and the assumptions of economics. *Journal of Business, 59,* S285–S300.

Kahneman, D., & Tversky, A. (1973). On the psychology of prediction. *Psychological Review, 80,* 237–251.

Kahneman, D., & Tversky, A. (1979). Prospect theory: An analysis of decision under risk. *Econometrica, 47,* 263–291.

Keeney, R. L. (1992). *Value-focused thinking.* Cambridge, MA: Harvard University Press.

Keren, G. (1987). Facing uncertainty in the game of bridge: A calibration study. *Organizational Behavior and Human Decision Processes, 39,* 98–114.

Kerr, N. L., MacCoun, R. J., & Kramer, G. P. (1996). Bias in judgment: Comparing individuals and groups. *Psychological Review, 103,* 687–719.

Kiesler, C. A. (1971). *The psychology of commitment.* New York: Academic Press.

Klayman, J. (1988). On the how and why (not) of learning from outcomes. In B. Brehmer & C. R. B. Joyce (Eds.), *Human judgment: The SJT view* (pp. 115–162). Amsterdam: North-Holland.

Klayman, J., & Ha, Y.-W. (1987). Confirmation, disconfirmation, and information in hypothesis-testing. *Psychological Review, 94,* 211–222.

Klayman, J., Soll, J. B., Gonzalez-Vallejo, C., & Barlas, S. (1999). Overconfidence: It depends on how, what, and whom you ask.

Organizational Behavior and Human Decision Processes, 79, 216–247.

Kleinmuntz, D. (1985). Cognitive heuristics and feedback in a dynamic decision environment. *Management Science, 31,* 680–702.

Kleinmuntz, D., & Kleinmuntz, B. (1981). Systems simulation decision strategies in simulated environments. *Behavioral Science, 26,* 255–270.

Kleinmuntz, D., & Thomas, J. (1987). The value of action and inference in dynamic decision making. *Organizational Behavior and Human Decision Processes, 39,* 341–364.

Kleiter, G. D., & Wimmer, H. (1974). Information seeking in a multistage betting game. *Archiv fur Psychologie, 126,* 213–230.

Kline, G. A. (1993). A recognition-primed decision (RPD) model of rapid decision making. In G. A. Klein, J. Orasanu, R. Calderwood, & C. E. Zsambok (Eds.), *Decision making in action: Models and methods* (pp. 138–147). Norwood, NJ: Ablex.

Kray, L. J., Thompson, L., & Galinsky, A. (2001). Battle of the sexes: Gender stereotype confirmation and reactance in negotiations. *Journal of Personality and Social Psychology, 80,* 942–958.

Kunreuther, H., Ginsberg, R., Miller, L., Sagi, P., Slovic, P., Borkin, B., & Katz, N. (1978). *Disaster insurance protection: Public policy lessons.* New York: Wiley.

Levin, I. P., & Gaeth, G. J. (1988). How consumers are affected by the framing of attribute information before and after consuming the product. *Journal of Consumer Research, 15,* 374–378.

Levine, J. M., Samet, M. G., & Brahlek, R. E. (1975). Information seeking with limitations on available information and resources. *Human Factors, 17,* 502–513.

Lichtenstein, S., Slovic, P., Fischhoff, B., Layman, M., & Combs, B. (1978). Perceived frequency of lethal events. *Journal of Experimental Psychology: Human Learning and Memory, 4,* 551–578.

Loomes, G., & Sugden, R. (1982). Regret theory: An alternative theory of rational choice under uncertainty. *Economic Journal, 92,* 805–824.

Loomes, G., & Sugden, R. (1986). Disappointment and dynamic inconsistency in choice under uncertainty. *Review of Economic Studies, 53,* 271–282.

Lopes, L. L. (1987). Between hope and fear: The psychology of risk. In L. Berkowitz (Ed.), *Advances in experimental social psychology* (Vol. 20, pp. 255–295). San Diego: Academic Press.

Lopes, L. L. (1995). Algebra and process in the modeling of risky choice. *The Psychology of Learning and Motivation, 32,* 177–220.

Mahon, G. S. (2000). *The performance of highly active problem solving strategies in novel decision environments.* Unpublished doctoral dissertation, University of Arizona, Tucson, AZ.

March, J. G., & Feldman, M. (1981). Information in organizations as signal and symbol. *Administrative Science Quarterly, 26,* 171–186.

McGrath, J. E. (1984). *Groups: Interaction and performance.* Englewood Cliffs, NJ: Prentice Hall.

McLeod, P. L. (1992). An assessment of the experimental literature on the electronic support of group work: Results of a meta-analysis. *Human Computer Interaction, 7,* 257–280.

McNeil, B. J., Pauker, S. G., & Tversky, A. (1988). On the framing of medical decisions. In D. E. Bell & H. Raiffa (Eds.), *Decision making: Descriptive, normative, and prescriptive interactions* (pp. 562–568). Cambridge, UK: Cambridge University Press.

Mellers, B. A., Schwartz, A., & Cooke, A. D. J. (1998). Judgment and decision making. *Annual Review of Psychology, 49,* 447–477.

Mellers, B. A., Schwartz, A., Ho, K., & Ritov, I. (1997). Decision affect theory: Emotional reactions to the outcomes of risky options. *Psychological Science, 8,* 423–429.

Mellers, B. A., Schwartz, A., & Ritov, I. (1999). Emotion-based choice. *Journal of Experimental Psychology: General, 128,* 332–345.

Miller, C. E., & Komorita, S. (1986). Coalition formation in organizations: What laboratory studies do and do not tell us In R. J. Lewicki, B. H. Sheppard, & M. H. Bazerman (Eds.), *Research on negotiation in organization* (Vol. 1, pp. 117–138). Greenwich, CT: JAI Press.

Murnighan, K. (1986). Organizational coalitions: Structural contingencies and the formation process. In R. J. Lewicki, B. H. Sheppard, & M. H. Bazerman (Eds.), *Research on negotiation in organization* (Vol. 1, pp. 155–174). Greenwich, CT: JAI Press.

Neale, M. A., & Bazerman, M. H. (1985). The effects of framing and negotiator overconfidence on bargaining behaviors and outcomes. *Academy of Management Journal, 28,* 34–49.

Northcraft, G. B., & Neale, M. A. (1987). Experts, amateurs, and real estate: An anchoring-and-adjustment perspective on property pricing decisions. *Organizational Behavior and Human Decision Processes, 39,* 84–97.

Nunamaker, J. F., Dennis, A. R., Valacich, J. S., Vogel, D. R., & George, J. F. (1991). Electronic meeting systems to support group work. *Communications of the ACM, 34,* 40–61.

Orasanu, J., & Connolly, T. (1993). The reinvention of decision making. In G. A. Klein, J. Orasanu, R. Calderwood, & C. E. Zsambok (Eds.), *Decision making in action: Models and methods* (pp. 3–20). Norwood, NJ: Ablex.

Ordóñez, L. D., Connolly, T., & Coughlan, R. (2000). Multiple reference points in pay satisfaction assessment. *Journal of Behavioral Decision Making, 13,* 329–344.

Osborn, A. F. (1953). *Applied imagination.* New York: Scribner's.

Oxley, N. L., Dzindolet, M. T., & Paulus, P. B. (1996). The effects of facilitators on the performance of brainstorming groups. *Journal of Social Behavior and Personality, 11,* 633–646.

Paich, M., & Sterman, D. (1993). Boom, bust, and failures to learn in experimental markets. *Management Science, 39,* 1439–1458.

Parker, D., Stradling, S. G., & Manstead, A. S. R. (1996). Modifying beliefs and attitudes to exceeding the speed limit: An intervention study based on the theory of planned behavior. *Journal of Applied Social Psychology, 26,* 1–19.

Paulus, P. B., Dzindolet, M. T., Poletes, G., & Camacho, L. M. (1993). Perception of performance in group brainstorming: The illusion of group productivity. *Personality and Social Psychology Bulletin, 19,* 78–89.

Payne, J. W. (1976). Task complexity and contingent processing in decision making: An information search and protocol analysis. *Organizational Behavior and Human Performance, 16,* 366–387.

Payne, J. W., Bettman, J. R., & Johnson, E. J. (1993). *The adaptive decision maker.* Cambridge, UK: Cambridge University Press.

Peters, E., & Slovic, P. (1996). The role of affect and worldviews as orienting dispositions in the perception and acceptance of nuclear power. *Journal of Applied Social Psychology, 26,* 1427–1453.

Phelps, R. H., & Shanteau, J. (1978). Livestock judges: How much information can an expert use? *Organizational Behavior and Human Performance, 21,* 209–219.

Pinkley, R. L., Griffith, T. L., & Northcraft, G. B. (1995). "Fixed pie" a la mode: Information availability, information processing, and the negotiation of suboptimal agreements. *Organizational Behavior and Human Decision Processes, 62,* 101–112.

Pitz, G. F. (1968). Information seeking when available information is limited. *Journal of Experimental Psychology, 76,* 25–34.

Powell, G. N., & Mainiero, L. A. (1999). Managerial decision making regarding alternative work arrangements. *Journal of Occupational and Organizational Psychology, 72,* 41–56.

Raiffa, H. (1982). *The art and science of negotiation.* Cambridge, MA: Harvard University Press.

Reither, F. (1981). About thinking and acting of experts in complex situations. *Simulation and Games, 12,* 125–140.

Richard, R., van der Pligt, J., & de Vries, N. (1996). Anticipated regret and time perspective: Changing sexual risk-taking behavior. *Journal of Behavioral Decision Making, 9,* 185–199.

Ritov, I. (1996). Probability of regret: Anticipation of uncertainty resolution in choice. *Organizational Behavior and Human Decision Processes, 66,* 228–236.

Ross, L., & Stillinger, C. (1991). Barriers to conflict resolution. *Negotiation Journal, 7,* 389–404.

Russo, J. E., & Dosher, B. A. (1983). Strategies for multi-attribute choice. *Journal of Experimental Psychology: Learning, Memory, and Cognition, 9,* 676–696.

Savage, L. J. (1954). *The foundations of statistics.* New York: Wiley.

Schneider, S. L. (1992). Framing and conflict: Aspiration level contingency, the status quo, and current theories of risky choice. *Journal of Experimental Psychology: Learning, Memory, & Cognition, 8,* 1040–1057.

Schulz-Hardt, S., Dieter, F., Luethgens, C., & Moscovici, S. (2000). Biased information search in group decision making. *Journal of Personality and Social Psychology, 78,* 655–669.

Sherer, P. D., Schwab, D. P., & Heneman, H. G. (1987). Managerial salary-raise decisions: A policy approach. *Personnel Psychology, 40,* 27–38.

Simon, H. A. (1955). A behavioral model of rational choice. *Quarterly Journal of Economics, 69,* 99–118.

Simonson, I. (1990). The effect of purchase quantity and timing on variety-seeking behavior. *Journal of Marketing Research, 32,* 150–162.

Simonson, I. (1992). The influence of anticipating regret and responsibility on purchase decisions. *Journal of Consumer Research, 19,* 105–118.

Slovic, P. (1969). Analyzing the expert judge: A descriptive study of a stockbroker's decision processes. *Journal of Applied Psychology, 53,* 255–263.

Slovic, P. (1974). Hypothesis testing in the learning of positive and negative linear functions. *Organizational Behavior and Human Decision Processes, 11,* 368–376.

Slovic, P. (1987). Perception of risk. *Science, 236,* 280–285.

Slovic, P. (1993). Perceived risk, trust, and democracy. *Risk Analysis, 13,* 675–682.

Slovic, P., Fischhoff, B., & Lichtenstein, S. (1979). Rating the risks. *Environment, 21,* 14–20.

Slovic, P., & Lichtenstein, S. (1971). Comparison of Bayesian and regression approaches to the study of information processing in judgment. *Organizational Behavior and Human Performance, 6,* 649–744.

Snapper, K. J., & Peterson, C. R. (1971). Information seeking and data diagnosticity. *Journal of Experimental Psychology, 87,* 429–433.

Stahlberg, D., Eller, F., Maass, A., & Frey, D. (1995). We knew it all along: Hindsight bias in groups. *Organizational Behavior and Human Decision Processes, 63,* 46–58.

Staw, B. M. (1976). Knee-deep in the Big Muddy: A study of escalating commitment to a chosen course of action. *Organizational Behavior and Human Performance, 16,* 27–44.

Staw, B. M., Barsade, S. G., & Koput, K. (1997). Escalation at the credit window: A longitudinal study of bank executives' recognition and write-off of problem loans. *Journal of Applied Psychology, 82,* 130–142.

Staw, B. M., & Hoang, H. (1995). Sunk costs in the NBA: Why draft order affects playing time and survival in professional basketball. *Administrative Science Quarterly, 40,* 474–494.

Staw, B. M., & Ross, J. (1989). Understanding behavior in escalation situations. *Science, 246,* 216–220.

Sterman, J. D. (1987). Testing behavioral simulation models by direct experiment. *Management Science, 33,* 1572–1592.

Sterman, J. D. (1989). Misperceptions of feedback in dynamic decision making. *Organizational Behavior and Human Decision Processes, 43,* 301–335.

Stevenson, M. K., Busemeyer, J. R., & Naylor, J. C. (1991). Judgment and decision making. In M. D. Dunnette & L. M. Hough (Eds.), *Handbook of industrial and organizational psychology* (2nd ed.) (pp. 283–374). Palo Alto, CA: Consulting Psychologists' Press.

Stewart, T. R. (1988). Policy analysis: Procedures. In B. Brehmer & C. R. B. Joyce (Eds.), *Human judgment: The SJT view,* (pp. 41–74). Amsterdam: North-Holland.

Stigler, S. M. (1986). *The history of statistics: The measurement of uncertainty before 1900.* Cambridge, MA: Belknap.

Stoner, R. A. F. (1961). *A comparison of individual and group decisions involving risk.* Unpublished master's thesis, MIT Press, School of Industrial Management.

Strack, F., Martin, L. L., & Schwartz, N. (1988). Priming and communication: Social determinants of information use in judgments of life satisfaction. *European Journal of Social Psychology, 18,* 429–442.

Swets, J. A. (1988). Measuring the accuracy of diagnostic systems. *Science, 240,* 1285–1293.

Thaler, R. H. (1980). Toward a positive theory of consumer choice. *Journal of Economic Behavior and Organization, 1,* 39–60.

Thompson, L. (1990). Negotiation behavior and outcomes: Empirical evidence and theoretical issues. *Psychological Bulletin, 108,* 515–532.

Thompson, L., & Hastie, R. (1990). Social perception in negotiation. *Organizational Behavior and Human Decision Processes, 47,* 98–123.

Thompson, L., & Hrebec, D. (1996). Lose-lose agreements in interdependent decision making. *Psychological Bulletin, 120,* 396–409.

Thompson, L., Peterson, E., & Kray, L. (1995). Social context in negotiation: An information-processing perspective. In R. Kramer & D. Messick (Eds.), *Negotiation as a social process* (pp. 5–36). New York: Sage.

Tindale, R. S. (1993). Decision errors made by individuals and groups. In N. J. Castellan, Jr. (Ed.), *Individual and group decision making: Current issues* (pp. 109–124). Hillsdale, NJ: Erlbaum.

Tindale, R. S., & Davis, J. H. (1985). Individual and group reward allocation decisions in two situational contexts: The effects of relative need and performance. *Journal of Personality and Social Psychology, 48,* 1148–1161.

Tucker, L. R. (1964). A suggested alternative formulation in the developments by Hursch, Hammond, and Hursch, and by Hammond, Hursch, and Todd. *Psychological Review, 71,* 528–530.

Tversky, A. (1969). Intransitivity of preferences. *Psychological Review, 76,* 31–48.

Tversky, A., & Kahneman, D. (1973). Availability: A heuristic for judging frequency and probability. *Cognitive Psychology, 5,* 207–232.

Tversky, A., & Kahneman, D. (1974). Judgment under uncertainty: Heuristics and biases. *Science, 185,* 1124–1131.

Tversky, A., & Kahneman, D. (1981). The framing of decisions and the psychology of choice. *Science, 211,* 453–458.

Valacich, J. S., Dennis, A. R., & Connolly, T. (1994). Idea generation in computer-based groups: A new ending to an old story. *Organizational Behavior and Human Decision Processes, 57,* 448–467.

von Neumann, J., & Morgenstern, O. (1947). *Theory of games and economic behavior* (2nd rev. ed.). Princeton, NJ: Princeton University Press.

Wallace, H. (1923). What is in the corn judge's mind? *Journal of the American Society of Agronomy, 15,* 300–304.

Wallsten, T. S. (1968). Failure of predictions from subjective expected utility theory in a Bayesian decision task. *Organizational Behavior and Human Performance, 3,* 239–252.

Walster, E., Berscheid, E., & Walster, G. W. (1973). New directions in equity research. *Journal of Personality and Social Psychology, 25,* 151–176.

Wason, P. C. (1960). On the failure to eliminate hypotheses in a conceptual task. *Quarterly Journal of Experimental Psychology, 12,* 129–140.

Wason, P. C. (1968). Reasoning about a rule. *Quarterly Journal of Experimental Psychology, 20,* 273–281.

Wason, P. C., & Johnson-Laird, P. N. (1972). *The psychology of reasoning: Structure and content.* London: Batsford.

Watson, W. E., Michaelsen, L. K., & Sharp, W. (1991). Member competence, group interaction, and group decision making: A longitudinal study. *Journal of Applied Psychology, 76,* 803–809.

Yates, J. F. (1990). *Judgment and decision making.* Englewood Cliffs, NJ: Prentice Hall.

Zaccaro, S. J., Gualtieri, J., & Minionis, D. (1995). Task cohesion as a facilitator of team decision making under temporal urgency. *Military Psychology, 7,* 77–93.

Zeckhauser, R. J., & Viscusi, W. K. (1990). Risk within reason. *Science, 248,* 559–564.

Zeelenberg, M., Beattie, J., van der Pligt, J., & de Vries, N. K. (1996). Consequences of regret aversion: Effects of expected feedback on risky decision making. *Organizational Behavior and Human Decision Processes, 65,* 148–158.

CHAPTER 20

Career Dynamics

JEFFREY H. GREENHAUS

Careers evolve over time (Greenhaus, Callanan, & Godshalk, 2000). Indeed, time is what distinguishes the career from other work-related concepts. Careers are also a product of the times—influenced by the economic, political, cultural, and interpersonal environments in which they are embedded. Recent changes in the global economy have had dramatic effects on the way work organizations are structured and on the manner in which they operate (Arthur, Inkson, & Pringle, 1999). Moreover, these changes in work organizations—in conjunction with shifts in the composition and values of the workforce—have had a substantial effect on the meaning of a career, the evolution of a career over time, the meaning of career success, and the relationship between work and family.

Therefore, it is an opportune time to examine the current concepts and research in career dynamics. The aims of this chapter are to review the recent research on careers, to connect this research to the emerging changes in the landscape of work, and to suggest areas in which additional research would be particularly fruitful. To accomplish these aims, I first discuss recent changes in the world of work—focusing on the movement toward boundaryless organizations (Arthur et al., 1999), the revision of the traditional psychological contract

between employers and employees (Rousseau, 1995), and the implications of these changes for the conceptualization of a career. I then examine theory and research in three areas that are critical to understanding career dynamics: career success, stages of career development, and career decision making. I conclude with suggestions regarding the direction of future research on careers.

The review of the literature is necessarily selective. For example, my focus on the success, development, and decision making associated with individuals' careers precludes extensive discussion of the links between business strategies and career systems at the organizational level (Gunz & Jalland, 1996). Moreover, because other chapters in this volume focus extensively on diversity (Alderfer & Sims) and international issues (Erez), this chapter does not devote substantial attention to these topics. However, gender issues are examined in some depth because of the strong connections among gender, family life, and careers.

THE CH\ANGING LANDSCAPE OF WORK AND CAREERS

Contemporary careers are increasingly pursued in economic and organizational settings that are considerably different from those in the recent past. Characteristics of the so-called new economy and the boundaryless organizations that

---

The author thanks Romila Singh for her helpful comments on an earlier version of the chapter.

comprise it (Arthur et al., 1999) are discussed next to set the stage for exploring the meaning of *career* in the twenty-first century.

Perhaps the most visible sign of the turbulence of the late twentieth century was the heightened loss of jobs. It has been estimated that 43 million jobs were lost in the United States between 1979 and 1995. Moreover, the pace of job loss accelerated in the 1990s, with 3.2 million jobs lost per year on average—an increase of nearly 40% over the 1980s (Uchitelle & Kleinfeld, 1996). This extensive job loss has been attributed to technological advances that render many jobs obsolete, the pursuit of increased efficiency in an intensely competitive global economy, the shedding of bloated staffing levels that had arisen in the 1960s and 1970s, and the rising rate of mergers and acquisitions (Callanan & Greenhaus, 1999).

The loss of established jobs and the creation of new jobs (often in different segments of the economy) reflect the turbulence and uncertainty of the new economy. This turbulence has produced a diminished sense of job security—especially among managers and professionals, who had been shielded from prior layoffs (Cappelli, 1999)—although it is not clear whether job insecurity has resulted in deteriorated work attitudes (Kinnunen, Mauno, Nätti, & Happonen, 2000; Pearce, 1998).

In addition, many organizations have changed their structure and their human resources (HR) practices in significant ways. It has been suggested (Allred, Snow, & Miles, 1996; Byrne, 1993; Nicholson, 1996) that an increasing number of employers will be characterized by a small, permanent core workforce supplemented by a larger number of contingent, part-time, and contract workers; a flatter hierarchy with self-managed, cross-functional teams responsible for most decisions; extensive alliances with internal and external partners; a continual utilization of advanced technology into work processes; and ongoing efforts to eliminate unprofitable ventures and to seek more promising enterprises.

These emerging characteristics of the new economy are believed to be motivated by the need for substantial speed and flexibility to respond to intensely competitive market forces produced by a technology-driven global economy (Arthur et al., 1999). In support of his belief that career jobs are dead, Cappelli (1999) argues that employers have increasingly incorporated a market-driven orientation through outsourcing, benchmarking, and decentralized responsibility for performance. Cappelli contends that these outside market forces determine how organizations select, reward, and develop their workforce.

This emergent form of organization is considered *boundaryless* (Weick, 1996) because a variety of boundaries have become more permeable. Members of organizations regularly move across functional, hierarchical, and national boundaries, and boundaries between the organization itself and its external suppliers and partners are loosening. In addition, boundaryless organizations represent weak situations that offer few explicit guides for action (Weick, 1996). It is argued that boundaryless organizations have spurred boundaryless careers (Arthur et al., 1999).

Before discussing the nature of contemporary careers, it is important to consider the shift in the psychological contract between employer and employee. The psychological contract contains perceptions regarding the reciprocal obligations that exist between employees and employers—that is, employees' beliefs regarding their obligations to the employer and the employer's obligations to employees (Shore & Tetrick, 1994). Psychological contracts provide employees with greater certainty and direct their behavior without the need for external monitoring (Shore & Tetrick, 1994). Most researchers believe that the psychological contract is best viewed through the eyes of the employee (Morrison & Robinson, 1997; Rousseau, 1995), although there is some disagreement on that issue (Guest, 1998).

The concept of the psychological contract is not new (Argyris, 1960). However, there has been a recent resurgence of interest in psychological contracts, accompanied by a large stream of empirical research. Scholars have developed theories regarding the formation of psychological contracts (Shore & Tetrick, 1994) and have examined the determinants (Robinson & Wolfe Morrison, 2000) and the consequences (Robinson, Kraatz, & Rousseau, 1994; Robinson & Morrison, 1995; Robinson & Rousseau, 1994; Turnley & Feldman, 2000) of contract violations.

This renewed interest often focuses on the distinction between relational and transactional terms of psychological contracts (Rousseau, 1995) and the corresponding belief that psychological contracts have changed with the emergence of the new economy from relational to transactional (Hall & Mirvis, 1995). Rousseau (1995) believes that relational and transactional terms are two ends of a contractual continuum. Relational contracts involve a high degree of emotional investment on the part of employer and employee and tend to be long-term in nature. Employees' beliefs that effort and loyalty on their part will be rewarded with long-term job security and opportunities for career advancement exemplify the relational contract.

Transactional contracts, involving short-term and monetizable items (Rousseau, 1995), are predicated on performance-based pay, involve lower levels of commitment, and permit easy exit from the agreement (Callanan & Greenhaus, 1999). Instead of exchanging effort and loyalty for job security and career advancement, transactional contracts exchange employee flexibility and willingness to develop new skills for employability derived from opportunities for continued professional development (Waterman, Waterman, & Collard, 1994). A recent factor analysis of psychological contract items has provided some support for the distinction between relational and transactional contract terms (Millward & Hopkins, 1998).

It is not difficult to imagine why organizations operating in the new economy would favor transactional psychological contracts. The need to remain flexible and responsive to an increasingly competitive environment may be better served by just-in-time staffing, contingent employment, and a general unwillingness to make long-term career commitments to employees. Although empirical evidence regarding the evolution of psychological contracts is scarce, Rousseau (1995) makes a strong case that psychological contracts within what have been called postbureaucratic adhocracies are unlikely to be purely relational and may be more varied in their inclusion of relational and transactional terms. It may be premature to proclaim the death of the relational contract, but it seems reasonable to conclude that fewer employees can expect long-term security and continued hierarchical advancement within a single employer (Arthur et al., 1999). The movement away from purely relational psychological contracts requires that the meaning of a career needs to be sufficiently broad to incorporate shorter-term relationships with multiple employers and occupations over the life span.

THE MEANING OF A CAREER

The *Random House Dictionary* (Stein et al., 1969, p. 223) provides a number of definitions that accurately reflect the meaning of a career in the mid-twentieth century: "an occupation or profession, especially one requiring special training," "success in a profession," "to run or move rapidly along; go at full speed." The everyday meaning of *career* in the era of bureaucratic organizations has had a number of themes (Greenhaus et al., 2000; Hall, 1976). One dominant theme reflected in these definitions—advancement or success—suggests that only individuals who are moving along (so to speak), advancing, and succeeding have a career. The phrase *a stalled career* clearly implies that a normal career involves movement, progress, and advancement. A second theme implicit in the meaning of a career is the requirement of a professional occupation. Doctors and lawyers—not sanitation workers or welders—have a career. Finally, stability in an occupation has often been seen as a precondition for a career. An individual who has worked as a high school teacher, a guidance counselor, a principal, and finally a superintendent of a school system has a career as an educator. On the other

hand, an individual who has shifted from teaching to public relations to real estate sales is thought to have merely pursued a series of jobs or perhaps three different careers.

These themes limited our understanding of careers because they confined the concept to a small segment of society—professionals advancing in a clearly recognizable path—and restricted the kinds of research questions that could be posed. A pioneering break from these constraints was provided by Hall (1976), who defined a career as "the individually-perceived sequence of attitudes and behaviors associated with work-related experiences and activities over the span of a person's life" (p. 4). Similarly broad definitions quickly followed in the literature (Feldman, 1988; Greenhaus, 1987; London & Stumpf, 1982).

Taken together, these newer definitions suggest that everyone has a work career—not only professionals on the fast track. They also legitimized the study of individuals' perceptions and attitudes regarding their careers and recognized that it is the entirety of an individual's work-related experiences—not just the pursuit of one occupation in a single organization—that constitutes a career.

An additional shift in the meaning of career has recently appeared that is designed to be more consistent with the contemporary economic environment. A number of researchers—most prominently Arthur and colleagues (Arthur, 1994; Arthur et al., 1999; Arthur & Rousseau, 1996)—have concluded that an increasing number of careers are no longer bounded to single organizations. In other words, the organizational career has been replaced by the boundaryless career.

Sullivan (1999) has provided an excellent distinction between the characteristics of boundaryless careers and traditional, organizational careers. This distinction goes beyond the setting of a career in multiple organizations (vs. one or two organizations) to include the nature of the psychological contract (transactional), the type of skills that are required (portable), and the vehicle for acquiring the skills (on-the-job learning). Moreover, the conceptualization of boundaryless careers expands the meaning of career success (psychological success), suggests different criteria for the concept of milestones or development (learning- rather than age-related), and places the responsibility for career management squarely on the shoulders of the individual.

There has also been a reemergence of the concept of a protean career originally introduced by Hall (1976) and remarkably consistent with the notion of a boundaryless career. Named for Proteus, the Greek god who could change shape at will, a protean career is under the control of the individual—not the organization—and its aim is the pursuit of psychological success through continuous learning and identity change (Hall, 1976, 1996; Mirvis & Hall, 1994).

The recent focus on boundaryless and protean careers has been useful because it provides an explicit alignment between the nature of career patterns and types of economic and organizational environments in which careers are pursued. What is particularly interesting is that it took radical and visible shifts toward a new economy to recognize the value of Hall's (1976) early insights. This recent emphasis does not necessarily mean that the boundaryless career is the only or the dominant model, but rather that an increasing segment of the population is likely to pursue a career with boundaryless characteristics. Individual careers may follow a variety of patterns, a position recognized in the literature for quite some time (Brousseau, Driver, Eneroth, & Larsson, 1996; Sullivan, Carden, & Martin, 1998).

Changes in the economic environment, organizational structure, and psychological contract may require revisions in the meaning of career success, adjustments in theories of career development, and scrutiny of effective career decision making. The next three sections of the chapter examine these concepts.

CAREER SUCCESS

The Meaning of Career Success

Consistent with the view that careers can be viewed from an external or an internal perspective, career success has been measured in terms of external or objective criteria as well as internal or subjective criteria. Objective criteria include compensation or salary, organizational level, and advancement or promotion rate. Subjective indicators include career satisfaction, perceived career success, job satisfaction, and life satisfaction.

Although objective indicators of career success are certainly relevant, the pursuit of boundaryless or protean careers places an emphasis on understanding career success from a subjective perspective. In one recent study, Friedman and Greenhaus (2000) had business professionals rate the importance of 15 different elements to their belief that their career is successful. A factor analysis of the items revealed five dimensions of the meaning of career success: status, time for self, challenge, security, and social considerations. With the exception of status, the dimensions of the meaning of career success reveal a considerable emphasis on success criteria that go beyond the external trappings of prestige, power, money, and advancement.

There is additional evidence that the meaning of career success has expanded in recent years. A recent survey of master's of business administration (MBA) students from around the world asked respondents what career goals they hoped to attain after they received their MBA (Universum

Intituted, 1998). The most popular response, selected by 44% of the sample, was to balance career and personal life. Similar preferences have also been revealed by high school students (Sanders, Lengnick-Hall, Lengnick-Hall, & Steele-Clapp, 1998) and by job seekers (Shellenbarger, 1991).

The Determinants of Career Success

Empirical research has predicted a variety of career success indicators—both objective and subjective. Whereas some studies include only one measure of career success, others contain multiple or composite indicators of success. The majority of the studies use cross-sectional designs, either single-gender or undifferentiated samples, and managerial or professional samples. Most of the studies also examine direct effects of blocks of variables on success, although an increasing number of studies have introduced process models that are capable of detecting direct and indirect effects. Despite somewhat different terminology or classification schemes among researchers, most of the predictors of career success can be grouped into seven categories of variables: human capital investments, motivational factors, interpersonal relationships, career choices or strategies, personality characteristics, organizational characteristics, and family status.

There is substantial support for the impact of *human capital investments* on career success. For example, age and years of work experience have consistently been associated with objective indicators of career success (Judge & Bretz, 1994; Melamed, 1995; Seibert, Crant, & Kraimer, 1999; Seibert & Kraimer, 2001; Tharenou, Latimer, & Conroy, 1994). Nevertheless, the impact of employment gaps—which serve to limit one's work experience—on career advancement has been inconsistent (Tharenou, 1997). In some studies (Dreher & Ash, 1990; Judiesch & Lyness, 1999; Seibert et al., 1999), employment gaps have been shown to restrict career advancement, whereas in other studies (Bretz & Judge, 1994; Judge & Bretz, 1994; Schneer & Reitman, 1995) they have not.

Activities designed to enhance skills have also been associated with career success. For example, the level, type, and quality of one's educational background (Boudreau, Boswell, & Judge, 2001; Judge, Cable, Boudreau, & Bretz, 1995; Seibert & Kraimer, 2001; Seibert et al., 1999; Tharenou et al., 1994) have been related to career success. Participation in training and development programs (Scandura, 1992; Tharenou et al., 1994), job competence (Aryee, Chay, & Tan, 1994), and opportunities for on-the-job learning (McCauley, Ruderman, Ohlott, & Morrow, 1994) have also been associated with high levels of success. Presumably, such human capital investments enhance job performance, which promote career advancement opportunities (Tharenou, 1997). The evidence linking human capital variables to subjective career success is more limited, with age, education, competence, and job performance enhancing satisfaction (Aryee et al., 1994; Judge et al., 1995) and employment gaps restricting satisfaction (Judge & Bretz, 1994).

Motivational variables also play a prominent role in the pursuit of career success. Behavioral work involvement (i.e., the number of hours worked) and psychological involvement in work (salience, identity, ego involvement) show positive relationships to career advancement (Judge & Bretz, 1994; Judge et al., 1995; Lobel & St. Clair, 1992; Schneer & Reitman, 1995; Seibert et al., 1999). The motivation to advance and career ambition have also been consistently associated with high levels of career advancement (Judge et al., 1995; Seibert et al., 1999; Tharenou, 1997). Despite their positive effect on career advancement, ambition, work role salience, and the motivation to advance have also been associated with low levels of subjective success (Aryee et al., 1994; Judge et al., 1995; Seibert et al., 1999).

Many *personality variables* have been studied as antecedents to career advancement, although few of them have been examined extensively across many studies. Achievement motivation, self-monitoring, leadership motivation, masculinity, self-confidence, extraversion, optimism, and proactivity have been associated with career advancement (Seibert et al., 1999; Tharenou, 1997; Tharenou et al., 1994; Turban & Dougherty, 1994), and proactivity has been related to subjective career success (Seibert et al., 1999). Two recent studies demonstrated the relationship between Big Five personality characteristics and career success. They further showed that the impact of personality on career success may depend on the countries in which employees work (Boudreau et al., 2001) and the types of occupations they pursue (Seibert & Kraimer, 2001).

Certain elements of the *interpersonal environment* have been associated with objective and subjective indicators of career success. Strong social ties inside and outside the organization (Tharenou, 1997), congruence in values between the individual and the organization (Aryee et al., 1994), career support and encouragement (Friedman & Greenhaus, 2000; Tharenou et al., 1994), and a relationship with a mentor (Judge & Bretz, 1994; Wayne, Liden, Kraimer, & Graf, 1998) can all promote advancement and satisfaction in one's career. Mentoring is such a powerful factor in career success that it is treated in more detail in a subsequent section of this chapter.

Career choices and strategies have also been frequently examined as precursors to career success. Some strategies, such as relocation and extensive involvement in work, have been consistently associated with high levels of career success

(Tharenou, 1977). Other strategies, such as frequent changes in jobs and employers have produced inconsistent results (Tharenou, 1997), and still others—such as supervisor ingratiation and self-nomination (Judge & Bretz, 1994)—have not been examined extensively in recent years.

Organizational characteristics can serve to enhance or restrict career success. At the organizational level, Malos and Campion (2000) demonstrated how a firm's HR staffing and development strategies affect its overall promotion rate. Moreover, the particular industry and region in which an organization operates have been associated with individuals' advancement and subjective success (Judge et al., 1995; Seibert et al., 1999; Spell & Blum, 2000), as has the presence of an internal labor market (Aryee et al., 1994). Nevertheless, the impact of many characteristics of an organization (size, length of the promotional ladder, success or growth) and the individual's location within an organization (functional area, line versus staff, type of job) has been inconsistent (Tharenou, 1997).

The recognition of the interdependence of work and family roles over the past 20 years led many researchers to examine the effect of employees' *family characteristics* on career success. Marital status, parenthood, time devoted to home and family, psychological involvement in family life, and spouse attitudes and behavior have been tested for their effects on a range of career-related outcomes, often with contradictory results (Singh, Greenhaus, & Parasuraman, 2002). Because of the persistent differences between men and women regarding participation in—and involvement with—work and family activities (Friedman & Greenhaus, 2000), the effect of family life on career success is discussed shortly when considering the relationship between gender and career success.

In sum, many different variables have been shown to be associated with career success—some of them rather consistently. However, the factors that influence income or advancement do not necessarily affect satisfaction or perceived career success (Aryee et al., 1994; Judge & Bretz, 1994; Judge et al., 1995; Kirchmeyer, 1998; Seibert et al., 1999; Wayne et al., 1999). The mentoring process, which has the capacity to affect a range of career outcomes, both objective and subjective, is discussed next.

Mentoring and Career Success

Having the support of a mentor has long been regarded as a crucial determinant of career success (Roche, 1979). A mentor is generally defined as an individual with advanced experience and knowledge who is committed to providing upward mobility and support to the protégé's career (Ragins, 1997). A mentor is believed to provide career functions to enhance the protégé's career advancement and psychosocial functions to enhance the protégé's competence, sense of identity, and effectiveness (Kram, 1983). Career functions include sponsorship, exposure and visibility, coaching, protection, and challenging assignments. Psychosocial functions include role modeling, acceptance and confirmation, counseling, and friendship. Mentors may be inside or outside of the protégé's organization, and mentoring relationships may be formal or informal and homogenous or diversified (Ragins, 1997).

There is substantial evidence that mentoring can enhance a protégé's career. Having experienced a mentoring relationship has been associated with compensation (Chao, 1997; Chao, Walz, & Gardner, 1992; Dreher & Ash, 1990; Whitely, Dougherty, & Dreher, 1991), advancement (Dreher & Ash, 1990; Scandura, 1992), and career satisfaction (Fagenson, 1989). Other protégé outcomes attributed to mentoring include job satisfaction, job involvement, increased power, effective socialization, and organizational commitment (Chao, 1997; Chao et al., 1992; Fagenson, 1988; Koberg, Boss, & Goodman, 1998; Ostroff & Kozlowski, 1993).

Most of this research has examined the effects of informal or spontaneous mentoring relationships on protégés' careers. Research has recently begun to examine formal or facilitated mentoring relationships; it has also explored the impact of mentoring not only on the protégé but also on the mentor.

For example, Ragins and Cotton (1999) found that informal mentoring relationships were superior to formal mentoring relationships in a variety of ways. Informal mentors provided more sponsorship, coaching, protection, challenging assignments, exposure, friendship, social support, role modeling, and acceptance than did formal mentors. Moreover, protégés with a history of informal mentors attained greater compensation (but not more promotions) and were more satisfied with their mentors than were those with a history of formal mentors. They also found that individuals with a history of informal mentoring earned more money than did nonmentored employees, whereas employees with a history of formal mentoring earned no more money than did those who reported no mentoring experiences. Moreover, Seibert (1999) compared employees who had participated in a facilitated mentoring program with those who had not had a mentor. He found that although mentored individuals were more satisfied with their jobs than were nonmentored individuals, there were no differences in organizational commitment, work stress, or self-esteem at work. These findings are generally consistent with prior research on formal and informal mentoring (Green & Bauer, 1995; Noe, 1988). However, a recent study by Ragins, Cotton, and Miller (2000) revealed

that the level of satisfaction with a mentoring relationship explained more variance in work attitudes than did the relationship's level of formality. In fact, individuals in highly satisfying formal relationships generally reported more positive work attitudes than did those in dissatisfying informal relationships.

Research has also started to examine the mentoring relationship from the mentor's perspective. Levinson, Darrow, Klein, Levinson, and McKee (1978) pointed out that mentors benefit from the relationship by satisfying their generativity needs through assisting younger employees to achieve career success. Consistent with this view, Allen, Poteet, and Burroughs (1997) found that many mentors cited the desire to pass on information to others, the desire to help others, and gratification derived from seeing others succeed as important reasons why they decided to become a mentor. In addition, the research of Mullen and Noe (1999) suggests that mentors see protégés as a source of information that can help the mentors in their work.

These findings raise the broader question of why individuals choose to mentor. Those individuals who express a willingness to mentor others tend to have prior experience in a mentoring relationship, either as mentor or as a protégé (Allen, Poteet, Russell, & Dobbins, 1997; Ragins & Scandura, 1999) and work in organizations that have a supportive culture (Aryee, Lo, & Kang, 1999). Personality characteristics—such as locus of control, positive affectivity, and altruism—have also predicted the desire to serve as a mentor (Allen et al., 1997; Aryee et al., 1999).

Ragins and Scandura (1999) developed a scale to assess the expected benefits and costs of being a mentor. A factor analysis revealed five dimensions of benefits (rewarding experience, improved job performance, loyal base of support, recognition by others, and generativity) and five dimensions of costs (more trouble than it's worth, fear of a dysfunctional relationship, concern about claims of nepotism, concerns about a negative effect on the mentor's reputation, and fears about energy drain). The resulting factors were consistent in many respects with the qualitative findings reported by Allen et al. (1997). Moreover, Ragins and Cotton (1999) found individuals with a strong intention to serve as a mentor perceived low costs and high benefits and had been a mentor or protégé in the past. In addition, the impact of costs and benefits on mentoring intentions was especially strong for individuals who had prior experience as a mentor, a protégé, or both.

Individuals also develop preferences for the type of protégé they wish to mentor. Mentors have been found to prefer those who are high performers, strongly motivated, open to learning and accepting feedback, willing to express a need for help, and similar to the mentors themselves in important respects (Allen, Poteet, & Russell, 2000; Burke, McKeen, & McKenna, 1993).

The majority of the research in this area has focused on the potential benefits of mentoring. Scandura (1998) provides a different perspective by exploring the dysfunctional characteristics of mentoring relationships. She developed a typology of dysfunctional career and psychosocial behaviors that could either reflect intentions to help others or to harm others. By focusing on such potentially dysfunctional behaviors as bullying, revenge, and betrayal, Scandura (1998) has applied the psychological literature on abusive relationships to the mentoring process and has broadened the scope of future research on the mentoring process.

Gender and Career Success

The glass ceiling that represents a barrier to the careers of women (Martin, 1991) serves to remind us that women's careers can be dramatically different from men's careers. In fact, there seem to be two ways in which the meaning of career success is different for women and men. First, men have historically placed substantial importance on money and advancement as yardsticks to assess their success in the world of work. It has been suggested that many men equate masculinity with success in the workplace (Kimmel, 1993) and judge their career and their life against these standards. Men have been found to value such outcomes as money, advancement, or power more than women have (Konrad, Ritchie, Lieb, & Corrigall, 2000; Universum Instituted, 1998). Women, on the other hand, define their career accomplishment differently and in ways that are perhaps broader than those of men. Women tend to value feelings of accomplishment, growth and development, and challenge in their work, and they place substantial importance on interpersonal relationships and on opportunities to help others at work (Konrad, Corrigall, Lieb, & Ritchie, 2000; Konrad, Ritchie, et al., 2000; Universum Instituted, 1998).

Moreover, whereas men define career success in terms of accomplishments residing within the work domain, women view career success in terms of achieving balance between career and family (Gerson, 1993; Gordon & Whelan, 1998). Gallos (1989) has suggested that women's pursuit of career success is often tempered by an enduring concern for significant relationships with others. According to Gallos, many women pursue a split dream that provides balance between career and relationships.

It seems, then, that what constitutes a successful career is different and perhaps more complex for women than for men. However, the literature on career success, as discussed

previously, has tended to focus on money and advancement (and to a lesser extent, career satisfaction) as career success outcomes. Nevertheless, psychologists must rely on that literature to explore whether women have achieved a different level of career success than have men and whether the path to career success varies for men and women.

The most glaring evidence that women's managerial careers lag behind men's has been the persistent glass ceiling that limits women's hierarchical advancement. Although women have entered the managerial ranks in increasing numbers—women represented 44% of managerial positions in 1998—they continue to occupy senior management positions at dramatically lower rates than do men. Depending on the definition of senior manager that is adopted, estimates of women's representation at the highest organizational levels in 1998 range from 11.2% to less than 1% (Powell, 1999). Women's compensation also continues to lag substantially behind men's, and their recent earning gains may have reached a plateau (Roos & Gatta, 1999). Studies of managers and professionals continue to report a significant gender gap in earnings, advancement, or both (Kirchmeyer, 1998; Stroh, Brett, & Reilly, 1992; Tharenou et al., 1994)—especially at higher organizational levels (Lyness & Judiesch, 1999).

Explanations for these differences through the use of control or mediating variables has produced mixed results. Kirchmeyer (1998) found that the gender difference in income favoring men disappeared when controlling for organizational tenure, total years of work experience, mentorship experiences, and having a nonemployed spouse. Stroh et al. (1992), on the other hand, found that even when women had all the right stuff, so to speak (i.e., when they were similar in education and work experience to men), they still lagged behind men in salary progression and geographical mobility but not in rates of promotion. To complicate the matter further, Tharenou et al. (1994) found both direct and indirect effects of gender on advancement. Men's more substantial work experience, participation in training and development activities, and career encouragement only partially explained why they achieved greater advancement than did women.

The literature reveals a wide range of career experiences that favor men, including access to training, job challenge, relocation opportunities, and career support (Stroh & Reilly, 1999; Tharenou, 1997). Even at senior management levels, men report greater authority, more geographical and international mobility, less frequent career interruptions, and greater satisfaction with career opportunities (Lyness & Thompson, 1997). Although these findings suggest an array of factors that may limit the career progress of female managers, women have not always experienced restricted advancement relative to men (Powell & Butterfield, 1994). Thus, an organization's commitment to diversity, culture, and HR practices may play a significant role in determining the presence of a glass ceiling.

In addition to examining gender differences in the level of career success, research has recently explored whether the determinants of career success are similar or different for men and women. The findings have not provided overwhelming support for the notion that different factors predict the career success of men and women. For example, Kirchmeyer (1998) found that gender moderated 8 of the 36 relationships between predictors and criteria, and Melamed (1995) found that gender moderated 9 of the 46 predictor-criterion relationships she examined. Thus, there may be more similarities than differences in the determinants of career success for men and women.

That conclusion does not mean, however, that the antecedents of career success are identical for men and women. The investment of time at work—total work experience, number of hours worked, employment gaps, and organizational tenure—is more predictive of career success for men than it is for women (Kirchmeyer, 1998; Konrad & Cannings, 1997), as are human capital investments in training and development (Tharenou et al., 1994). Yet the level and type of education—also forms of human capital—seem to be more predictive of the career success of women than of men (Kirchmeyer, 1998; Tharenou et al., 1994). And whereas masculinity had a stronger effect on perceived career success for women than for men (Kirchmeyer, 1998), independence—typically thought to be a masculine trait—had a stronger effect on salary for men than for women (Melamed, 1995).

It appears that the use of the external labor market is a more effective career strategy for men than it is for women. Specifically, interorganizational mobility has a stronger impact on advancement (Lyness & Judiesch, 1999) and salary (Brett & Stroh, 1997) for men than it does for women. These findings are consistent with Lyness and Judiesch's (1999) observation that women managers are less likely to attain new management positions by external hiring than by internal promotions. Moreover, Dreher and Cox (2000) established that the use of the external labor market was effective only for white males—not for women or people of color.

Whereas many studies examined the impact of gender on relationships between predictors and career success, Tharenou et al. (1994) developed and tested process models of career advancement separately for men and women. Through structural equation modeling, they observed a number of paths to career success that varied by gender. One such path revealed that home and family commitments limited women's careers and boosted men's careers. Therefore, understanding the link between family and work may potentially explain at least a portion of the gender differences in career success.

Gender, Family, and Career Success

Because of the growing representation of dual-earner partners and single parents in the workforce over the past 25 years, scholars have increasingly recognized the interdependence of work and family roles. Indeed, family responsibilities have often been invoked as an explanation for the limited progression of women in managerial careers (Powell, 1999). In a broad sense, we can think of family life as interfering with the pursuit of a career (a family-work conflict perspective) or family life as enhancing career opportunities and career success (a family-work enhancement perspective), although conflict and enhancement are not mutually exclusive (Singh et al., 2002).

Some evidence does suggest that family responsibilities and demands can interfere with career success, especially—but not exclusively—for women. For example, married women are more likely than are unmarried women to hold part-time or low-status jobs (Drobnic, Blossfeld, & Rohwer, 1999)—in some cases because they tend to be the trailing spouse in relocations for their husband's career (Brett, Stroh, & Reilly, 1992). A man's marital status generally does not influence his selection of career roles.

Research regarding the effect of marriage on the traditional indicators of career success has produced mixed results. Studies have indicated that married employees earn greater incomes than do those who are unmarried (Bretz & Judge, 1994; Judge et al., 1995; Landau & Arthur, 1992). However, the relationship between marital status and income has often been found to be either nonsignificant for women (Landau & Arthur, 1992; Friedman & Greenhaus, 2000) or even negative (Jacobs, 1992). Moreover, most of the research has found no relationship between marital status and career advancement (Aryee et al., 1994; Dreher & Ash, 1990; Judge et al., 1995; Whitely et al., 1991), especially for women (Friedman & Greenhaus, 2000; Schneer & Reitman, 1993).

There is also inconsistent evidence that marriage affects career satisfaction. Friedman and Greenhaus (2000) found that married men were more satisfied with their careers than were unmarried men but that marriage neither helped nor hindered the career satisfaction of women. A majority of the studies observed no effect of marital status on such subjective dimensions of career success as career satisfaction, job satisfaction, and perceived career success (Aryee et al., 1994; Brett et al., 1992; Bretz & Judge, 1994; Judge et al., 1995; Kirchmeyer, 1998; Seibert et al., 1999).

In sum, the research suggests that the positive effects of marriage on income and career advancement may be more pronounced for men than for women, and the inhibiting effects of marriage on the selection of a career role and on financial rewards seem more prevalent among women than among men. Nevertheless, these differential relationships have not been consistently observed.

Responsibility for dependents appears to have a more pronounced effect than does marriage on career achievements, although again the results have not been overwhelmingly consistent. For example, Glass and Camarigg (1992) did not support their expectation that mothers would select less strenuous and more flexible jobs that are compatible with family responsibilities. Yet researchers have found that parents work fewer hours per week than do nonparents (Brett et al., 1992) especially in the case of women (Friedman & Greenhaus, 2000; Greenberger & O'Neil, 1993; Singh, Greenhaus, Collins, & Parasuraman, 1998).

Turning to the prediction of career success, much of the research found that income was *not* affected by parental responsibilities (Bretz & Judge, 1994; Jacobs, 1992; Lobel & St. Clair, 1992). Some research has revealed that the impact of children on income was positive only for men—especially single-earner fathers (Brett et al., 1992; Friedman & Greenhaus, 2000; Landau & Arthur, 1992; Schneer & Reitman, 1993). The impact of children on women's income is inconsistent. Although several studies found that mothers earned less money than did women without children (Friedman & Greenhaus, 2000; Jacobs, 1992), other studies found that dual-earner mothers earned as much as did other married women and more than did unmarried women (Brett et al., 1992; Landau & Arthur, 1992; Schneer & Reitman, 1993, 1995).

The effects of children on career advancement and career satisfaction are also uncertain. Most of the research has shown no relationship between parental responsibilities and advancement (Aryee et al., 1994; Friedman & Greenhaus, 2000; Kirchmeyer, 1998; Konrad & Cannings, 1997) or satisfaction (Aryee et al., 1994; Bretz & Judge, 1994; Judge et al., 1995; Kirchmeyer, 1998). One exception was the study by Friedman and Greenhaus (2000), who found that fathers were more satisfied with their careers than were men without children, whereas mothers were less satisfied with their careers than were women without children.

In short, employees with extensive parental responsibilities may limit their time involvement in work and may experience restricted opportunities for career growth. Although these effects can occur for both men and women, there is some evidence that women's careers are more likely than are men's careers to be affected by their dependent care responsibilities (Friedman & Greenhaus, 2000).

Family-career interference may be explained by the process of accommodation (Lambert, 1990), in which involvement in one role is lessened to accommodate the demands of a more salient role. In other words, a parent's limited investment in work may reflect his or her intention to accommodate the career for the needs of the family. If in fact women's careers are more likely to be constrained by family responsibilities than are men's careers, it could be speculated that women are either more willing—or more strongly coerced—than are men to make career accommodations for their families.

The prior section has focused on the potential constraints that family life can place on careers. However, resources derived from the family domain can promote career success, and the quality of the family role may spill over into work. The most prominent type of family resource is the social support provided by members of the family. Both tangible and emotional support from one's family can enable the individual to cope more effectively with work-related problems and reduce the extent to which family interferes with work. There is some evidence that support from a partner or spouse—tangible and emotional—is associated with high levels of income and career satisfaction (Friedman & Greenhaus, 2000). In part, this effect can be explained by the fact that individuals who receive substantial support from a spouse or partner tend to spend more time at work (Parasuraman, Singh, & Greenhaus, 1997) and therefore may demonstrate high levels of job performance (Friedman & Greenhaus, 2000).

However, the benefits of social support go beyond the instrumental assistance that frees up time for work. Business professionals who receive extensive emotional support from their partners have been found to experience greater opportunities for career development through such mechanisms as coaching and visible job assignments (Friedman & Greenhaus, 2000). Presumably, the understanding, acceptance, and encouragement of a family member provide an individual with the information, self-confidence, or motivation to seek out career-building experiences.

Resources derived from family experiences also include the skills, knowledge, and perspectives that can be effectively applied to work. For example, it is plausible that skills in parenting (nurturance, empathy, active listening) can be particularly important in team-based, collaborative organizations. Although this form of enrichment has been discussed extensively in the literature (Greenhaus & Parasuraman, 1999), relatively little empirical research has examined the dynamics that underlie this process. However, Kirchmeyer (1992) has shown that Canadian business school graduates believe that the skills, knowledge, and perspectives they derive from their parenting experiences are helpful at work.

Another important dimension of family life is the quality of the family role. Marital and family satisfaction, quality of family life, family tensions, and distress are frequent indicators of family role quality. Although several studies found that marital quality did not contribute to attendance or satisfaction at work (Aryee et al., 1994; Erickson, Nichols, & Ritter, 2000), other research indicates that stress within the family role is associated with negative emotions at work (Frone, Yardley, & Markel, 1997).

Gender, Mentoring, and Career Success

It is reasonable to wonder whether women's careers are restricted because they experience difficulties establishing or benefiting from a relationship with a mentor. However, the literature does not find a ready answer to this question. For example, although women may experience more barriers to developing a relationship with a mentor than do men (Ragins & Cotton, 1991), most of the research indicates that women are as likely as men are to have had a mentor (Ragins, 1999). It is also generally believed that women in mentoring relationships derive benefits (compensation, advancement, and satisfaction) similar to those derived by men (Dreher & Ash, 1990; Fagenson, 1989; Ragins, 1999). Moreover, much—although not all—of the research indicates that men and women receive the same level of career and psychosocial support from mentoring (Koberg et al., 1998; Ragins & McFarlin, 1990; Turban & Dougherty, 1994; Whitely et al., 1991).

However, because of the limited number of women in high managerial positions, women protégés are more likely than are men to experience a cross-gender mentoring relationship (Ragins & Cotton, 1991). It has been observed that cross-gender mentor relationships can be delicate to manage because of the potential for sexual tension and rumors of sexual intimacy (Ragins & Cotton, 1991), but it is not clear whether cross-gender relationships are less effective than same-gender relationships. Protégés in same-gender relationships have been found to receive more psychosocial support from their mentors than do protégés in cross-gender relationships (Koberg et al., 1998; Thomas, 1990), although this has not always been observed (Ragins & Cotton, 1999).

A recent comprehensive study of formal and informal mentoring has revealed the complex consequences of diversified mentoring relationships. Ragins and Cotton (1999) found that male protégés with male mentors earned higher salaries than did any other gender combination, which could be explained by the power of the male mentor and the similarity introduced into the relationship by virtue of both parties' being of the same sex. The least amount of money was earned by female protégés with female mentors—suggesting that gender similarity does not compensate for a mentor without much power in the organization. Moreover, female protégés with male mentors had a higher promotion rate (but earned less money) than did male protégés with male mentors. Despite these differences, there appeared to be many more similarities than differences in the career development and psychosocial functions provided by mentors in the different mentor-protégé categories.

It is clear that more research needs to be conducted on homogeneous and diversified mentoring to understand the subtle relationships between gender and career success. Ragins (1997) has identified processes that are thought to characterize diversified relationships (e.g., stereotyping, interpersonal comfort, work group support) and has developed sophisticated process models linking the composition of mentoring relationships to outcomes for both protégés and mentors.

STAGES OF CAREER DEVELOPMENT

It is not the mere passage of time that characterizes a career; rather, it is the pattern of experiences that an individual encounters. If there were no underlying regularities in work experiences over time, then the career concept would be unnecessary. However, beliefs regarding patterns of career development have changed dramatically in recent years.

Historically, the most influential models of career development have proposed a series of stages that were closely linked to age. For example, Super (1957, 1980) identified five stages—growth, exploration, establishment, maintenance, and decline—that were thought to capture individuals' work-related experiences from the years of childhood to retirement. Miller and Form (1951) and Hall and Nougaim (1968) also identified five career stages, and Schein (1978) proposed a sequence of nine stages of career development.

All of these models identified age ranges in which individuals typically encountered the tasks associated with each stage of career development. Moreover, the models appear to have assumed that individuals pursue a continuous linear career within one occupation, in perhaps one or two organizations, and without major disruptions or redirections. Why else would individuals go through an exploration or establishment stage only once in their lifetimes?

These approaches to career development—along with Levinson et al.'s (1978) model of adult life development—were enormously influential because they sought to identify patterns of experiences that evolved over the course of an individual's life. Moreover, these theories were compatible with the pursuit of an organizational career that was prominent during the era in which the theories were proposed. Nevertheless, consistent support for these theories has proved elusive—in part because of the subtlety of many of the changes that the theories propose and because of the difficulties in conceptualizing and measuring career stages (Greenhaus & Parasuraman, 1986; Sullivan, 1999).

There is an emerging belief that career stages or cycles currently are shorter in duration and reoccur periodically over the course of a person's career. It is thought that career cycles are now compressed because of the frequent and dramatic changes or transitions associated with pursuing a boundaryless career (Arthur et al., 1999; Hall & Mirvis, 1995). These multiple transitions produce cycles of change, each of which requires "preparation, encounter, adjustment, stabilization, and renewed preparation" (Arthur & Rousseau, 1996, p. 33). Mirvis and Hall (1994) view these cycles as opportunities for gaining new skills and prefer to view development through a career cycle in terms of an individual's career age rather than chronological age.

Arthur et al. (1999) have recently identified three career cycles or modes—fresh energy, informed direction, and seasoned engagement—that are generally consistent with exploration, establishment, and maintenance, respectively. Although fresh energy is typically displayed in the early career, informed direction in midcareer, and seasoned engagement in late career, Arthur et al. (1999) demonstrate how individuals periodically recycle back to earlier modes as they change projects, jobs, employers, or occupations. Smart and Peterson (1997) have provided additional support for recycling in the midst of a career transition.

Arthur et al. (1999) believe that individuals' willingness to explore and experiment enables them to experience continual growth and development in their careers. Moreover, career growth is thought to depend on the development of three types of career competencies: knowing why, knowing how, and knowing whom (Arthur et al., 1999). These career competencies are compatible with the two metaskills that Mirvis and Hall (1994) believe are crucial to experience psychological success: personal identity development and adaptability.

In basic agreement with the notion of compressed and recurrent career cycles, Parasuraman, Greenhaus, and Linnehan (2000) believe that chronological age may still play a significant role in understanding the unfolding of a career over a lifetime. They proposed a model of lifelong career transitions to detect patterns that cut across multiple career cycles as an individual becomes older. Specifically, they developed three different scenarios in which individuals experience an increase in person-career fit, a stability in fit, or a decline in fit as they move from one career cycle to another.

In sum, the concept of development within a career seems to have changed to become more compatible with careers in the new economy. Research on career stages has declined because interest in traditional career stage models has waned, and the recent focus on recycling through shorter career cycles is still too new to have guided a great deal of empirical research. Nevertheless, research continues on topics that are often associated with a particular career stage. Research on the socialization process (often linked to the early career) is burgeoning, and the examination of employee reactions to a variety of different career transitions is also growing. In addition, the traditional stages of career development have increasingly come under attack as severely limited in their capacity to understand the careers of women.

Organizational Socialization

Organizational socialization refers to the "process by which an individual comes to appreciate the values, abilities, expected behaviors, and social knowledge essential for assuming an organizational role, and for participating as an organizational member" (Louis, 1980, pp. 229–230). Indicators of successful socialization include effective job performance, the establishment of satisfactory work relationships with other people, the understanding of the political structure within the organization, and an appreciation of the organization's goals, values, history, and language (Chao, O'Leary-Kelly, Wolf, Klein, & Gardner, 1994). Research has examined the antecedents and consequences of successful socialization as well as the stages that comprise the socialization process.

Although socialization or establishment is a stage within most theories of career development, research on socialization has generally been conducted independent of a particular theory of career development. Understanding the socialization process should shed light on boundaryless or protean careers because individuals pursuing these careers need to confront the socialization tasks periodically as they move across functional, organizational, and occupational boundaries with increasing frequency (Wanberg & Kammeyer-Mueller, 2000).

Bauer, Morrison, and Callister's (1998) excellent review of the research on organizational socialization identified a number of trends in the literature, three of which have particular relevance to this chapter: the range of transitions that require socialization, proactivity during socialization, and the impact of mentoring during socialization.

The short-duration career cycles that characterize boundaryless careers require repeated resocialization to new job responsibilities and new work settings. A number of studies have examined the ease or effectiveness of socialization following transitions that represent different degrees of contrast from the prior work setting. Socialization and adjustment tend to go more smoothly when the new setting is not dramatically different from the old setting (Chao et al., 1994), although some research has found either no relationship or a negative relationship between the similarity of work settings and socialization (Adkins, 1995; Anakwe & Greenhaus, 2000). These inconsistent findings reveal the complexity of the process by which prior work experiences translate into effective socialization.

Bauer et al. (1998) also observed an emerging focus on the individual as an active agent of socialization. Scholars have proposed different types of information needs during socialization and techniques used to acquire this information (Morrison, 1993; Ostroff & Kozlowski, 1992). Given this focus on the individual's role during socialization, it is not surprising that proactivity has been increasingly examined in socialization research. In fact, Saks and Ashforth (1997) include proactive strategies and behavior in their multilevel process model of organizational socialization. Ashford and Black (1996) assessed seven types of proactive socialization tactics relevant to organizational newcomers: information seeking, feedback seeking, general socializing, relationship building with one's boss, networking, negotiation of job changes, and positive framing. They found employees' desire for control was related to five of the seven proactive socialization tactics, four of the proactive tactics were related to job satisfaction, and two of the tactics were associated with job performance.

Wanberg and Kammeyer-Mueller (2000) examined the antecedents and consequences of a variety of proactive socialization behaviors. They found that two Big Five personality characteristics (extraversion and openness) were related to participation in proactive social behaviors and that several of the proactive behaviors were associated with such work outcomes as social integration, role clarity, job satisfaction, and withdrawal tendencies. Saks and Ashforth (2000) also supported the notion that dispositional factors (negative affectivity and self-efficacy expectations) can influence the adjustment of organizational newcomers. The changing view of the new employee from a passive to an active socialization agent (Bauer et al., 1998; Saks & Ashforth, 1997) is consistent with the recent emphasis on the individual as a proactive manager of his or her career (Arthur et al., 1999; Greenhaus et al., 2000; Hall, 1996).

Bauer et al. (1998) also cited evidence that mentoring can assist in the socialization process. More recent research has illustrated the positive impact of peer mentors on the socialization of newcomers (Allen, McManus, & Russell, 1999) and the importance of personal and situational factors in facilitating the receipt of mentoring for employees in their early careers (Aryee et al., 1999).

Career Transitions

Although the socialization research has examined adjustment to a new work setting, other streams of research have studied different types of career transitions. Stephens (1994) provided a comprehensive review of the literature on subjective career transitions and proposed a model to predict the success of career transitions from a wide range of individual and situational variables.

Much of the research on career transitions has focused on reactions to job loss. Hanisch (1999) reviewed the literature on job loss and unemployment—addressing such as issues as the unemployment experience, outcomes of unemployment, coping with job loss, and the impact of unemployment on family members. Latack, Kinicki, and Prussia (1995) developed a model of coping with job loss based extensively on a control theory perspective. The model proposes that the appraisal of job loss as a potential harm or threat, in conjunction with coping efficacy, influence coping goals that—along with coping resources—determine the type of coping strategies enacted.

Empirical research on the coping process following job loss has been extensive. For example, Leana, Feldman, and Tan (1998) examined coping behavior following a layoff. They identified a range of personal and situational factors that predicted problem-focused and symptom-focused coping, and they found that an initial positive appraisal of the job loss was associated with extensive problem- and symptom-focused coping. In another longitudinal study of job loss, Kinicki, Prussia, and McKee-Ryan (2000) demonstrated that coping does not end with reemployment and that coping subsequent to reemployment depends on the quality of reemployment, income loss, and the availability of coping resources.

However, the use of specific coping techniques has not always produced similar results. For example, Gowen, Riordan, and Gatewood (1999) found that psychological distancing as a coping behavior reduced stress and enhanced the likelihood of successful reemployment, whereas proactive job search activities did not promote reemployment. Wanberg (1997), on the other hand, found that proactive search facilitated reemployment and distancing did not.

Just as unemployment can have substantial negative effects on an individual's well-being (Hanisch, 1999), so too can underemployment, which may be increasing in today's turbulent economy. Feldman and Turnley (1995) examined underemployment among recent business college graduates. They identified four attributes of underemployment (e.g., underutilization of skills) and found that the attributes had negative effects on such outcomes as job satisfaction, work commitment, and internal work motivation. In a subsequent manuscript, Feldman, Leana, and Turnley (1997) applied a relative deprivation perspective to understand the underemployment experience.

Underemployment brings to mind another career transition—the career plateau—that may be increasingly prevalent in the new economy. There has not been a great deal of recent research on career plateauing, despite the fact that organizational restructuring and downsizing can result in individuals' spending more time in one job with limited opportunities for hierarchical advancement (Allen, Russell, Poteet, & Dobbins, 1999).

There are two promising developments in the study of the career plateau. One is the distinction between structural or hierarchical plateauing—in which future promotions are unlikely—and job content plateauing, in which increases in responsibility on the current job are unlikely (Bardwick, 1986). This distinction was supported in a recent factor analysis of career plateau perceptions conducted by Allen, Russell, et al. (1999). They further demonstrated that although there were some common predictors of the two types of career plateauing, there were several unique predictors as well. Moreover, Allen, Poteet, and Russell (1998) observed that employees who reached a structural plateau were more satisfied with their jobs and expressed a lower intention to quit than did employees who reached a plateau in their job content. This is consistent with the finding that being passed over for a promotion does not inevitably lead to decline in work attitudes (Lam & Schaubroeck, 2000). Not surprisingly, Allen et al. (1998) also found that employees who were content *and* who were at structural plateaus experienced the lowest levels of job involvement and organizational commitment.

A second innovative approach to the study of the career plateau has been the examination of the attributions that employees invoke to explain why they are at a plateau. Godshalk (1997) identified three types of career plateau attributions (organizational constraints, a negative assessment of the individual by his or her organization, and personal choice) and found that career plateau attributions were associated with employees' reactions to their plateau status.

Gender and Career Development

The relevance of traditional theories of career development to women's careers has been a topic of considerable discussion and some research. Those studies designed to test the applicability of career stage models—in particular, those of Super and Levinson—to women's careers have not met with

success (Sullivan, 1999). There are good reasons to question whether career development models developed largely on male samples can adequately reflect the development of women's careers. As noted earlier, the theories are generally based on an organizational career model that is pursued continuously and often in the same organization and occupation. Therefore, the sequential stages of exploration, establishment, achievement, maintenance, and decline—each associated with approximate age ranges—made some sense. So did Levinson et al.'s (1978) demarcation of life development into early, middle, and late adulthood, with specific issues arising within each era of adulthood.

Because of extensive family responsibilities, women are more likely than are men to experience career interruptions or employment gaps (Lyness & Thompson, 1997) that sever the close connection between age and career stage. Moreover, women have generally displayed a greater variety of career patterns than do men (e.g., employment-then-motherhood, employment-motherhood-employment), thereby rendering their sequence of activities and challenges more unpredictable than those of men (Sekaran & Hall, 1989).

In addition, traditional theories of career development assume that work is the primary focus in life—especially in the early career stages of exploration, establishment, and achievement, in which the tasks of finding, establishing, and succeeding in a career are paramount. The formulation and pursuit of the "Dream," which usually contains extensive reference to occupational success, has been seen as a primary task of early adulthood (Levinson et al., 1978).

However, women may hold a more complex view of how their careers fit into their lives than do men, emphasizing both career and relationships. Gallos' (1989) notion of women's split dream was supported by a recent study demonstrating that achieving an appropriate balance between work and family responsibilities was a significant need for women professionals early in their careers as well as in midlife (Gordon & Whelan, 1998).

Powell and Mainiero (1992) identified two themes that emerged from their review of the literature on women's career development. They observed that issues of balance, connectedness, and interdependence were salient to women throughout the life course. Perhaps as a result of this dual perspective, they saw women's careers and lives as involving complex choices and constraints and characterize women's simultaneous concerns about careers and relationships as "cross-currents in the river of time" (p. 215).

The implication of women's dual focus on work and relationships—on career and family—is that the tasks, challenges, and needs that they experience may not follow the same pattern or sequence traditionally associated with different stages of career development. The work-relationship duality and the variety of career patterns women follow may explain why they have adopted more subjective and somewhat different meanings of career success than men typically have. However, the tendency of younger men and women to place substantial importance on achieving work-family balance (Shellenbarger, 1991) and the emergence of the boundaryless career may serve to weaken the links between age and career stage for many employees, regardless of their sex.

CAREER DECISION MAKING

A career decision refers to the selection of a course of action that has implications for an individual's work-related experiences over time (Singh, 2000). Many career-related behaviors explicitly or implicitly involve a career decision: to pursue a particular job, to increase or decrease involvement in work, or to change occupational fields. Although each situation is different, they all involve action in the face of alternatives. It is reasonable to expect that the emergence of shorter and more frequent career cycles will require individuals to make a greater number of significant career decisions over the course of their lives. However, we know relatively little about how employees make—or should make—career decisions.

At the most basic level, career decision making requires an individual to be able and willing to make a decision when confronted with the necessity of choosing between alternatives. The literature has distinguished between career-decided and career-undecided individuals. The concept of career decidedness (or its converse, career indecision) has been examined extensively among student populations, in which the career decision that has been made (or has not been made) is either the selection of a college major or of an occupational field. However, virtually no research has studied the career indecision experienced by employees. In a study designed to address that gap, Callanan and Greenhaus (1990) identified seven different reasons why managers and professionals experienced career indecision: a lack of information (about themselves, their current organization, or the external environment), a lack of self-confidence, decision-making fear and anxiety, nonwork demands, and situational constraints.

A widespread assumption is that indecision about one's future career is dysfunctional. However, the literature on student populations has distinguished between being developmentally undecided (because of a temporary lack of information) from being chronically undecided or indecisive—characterized by an enduring tendency to avoid making career decisions. A cluster analysis conducted by Callanan and Greenhaus

(1992) confirmed this distinction between developmentally and chronically undecided managers and professionals. They also found two types of career-decided employees—those who made a career decision based on information about themselves and the world of work (the vigilant group) and those who made a decision in order to relieve excessive fear and anxiety (the hypervigilant group). Their findings suggest that individuals need to know when to make a career decision and when to postpone a decision until sufficient information and insight are attained.

The research on career indecision also raises the broader question regarding how employees go about the task of making a career decision. A great deal of research has been conducted on the career decision-making styles used by students in making educational and occupational decisions. Harren (1979) developed an extensively researched typology that consisted of rational, intuitive, and dependent career decision-making styles. A rational style involves a logical and systematic approach to a career decision with an extensive search for career-related information. An intuitive style focuses on present feelings rather than information about potential outcomes, and a dependent style relies heavily on the opinions and recommendations of other people in making a career decision.

The empirical research conducted on students has not supported the widespread expectation that a rational approach to making a career decision is necessarily superior to an intuitive style, although a dependent style is generally ineffective (Phillips & Strohmer, 1982). However, there has been little research on the career decision-making styles used by employees, prompting Singh (2000) to develop a model that specifies the conditions under which different styles are most likely to lead to effective career decisions among managers and professionals.

Arthur et al.'s (1999) in-depth qualitative study of the careers of 75 New Zealanders also addressed the issue of decision strategies and styles. Consistent with Weick's (1996) perspective on the enactment of a career, Arthur et al. concluded that careers are more likely to be characterized by spontaneous responses to changing situations than by the pursuit of predetermined plans and goals. They argue that the advantages of career planning have been exaggerated and that "the career is less about a planned destination than it is about a series of lived experiences along the way" (Arthur et al., 1999, p. 47). They praise the virtue of exploration because it provides opportunities for ongoing learning.

It is difficult to disagree with the virtues of exploration, openness to continuous learning, and flexibility. Moreover, it is likely that rational goal setting is susceptible to tunnel vision and inflexibility (McCaskey, 1977). Nevertheless, the advantages and disadvantages of different career decision-making styles are still not well understood.

CONCLUSIONS AND DIRECTIONS FOR FUTURE RESEARCH

Much of the current theory and research on career dynamics is aligned with the significant issues facing individuals and organizations in today's work environment. The specific topics that have dominated the literature—psychological contracts, socialization, coping with transitions, and diversified mentoring, to mention a few—are clearly relevant to the contemporary work scene. Moreover, the research in certain areas such as socialization, psychological contracts, and transitional coping are increasingly rigorous, using longitudinal designs to test sophisticated process models.

However, much of the research has not caught up with the more inclusive definition of a career that has emerged over the past 20 years. Despite the belief that careers are not limited to incumbents of high-status occupations, the vast majority of the research has used managerial or professional samples (Arthur & Rousseau, 1996). The most occupationally heterogeneous samples seem to have been studied in the research on coping with job loss.

Although it is certainly legitimate to study managerial and professional careers, a near-exclusive focus on this group prevents us from understanding the similarities and differences in the patterns of work experiences of individuals from different walks of life. In a sense, the narrow focus on managers and professionals impedes our ability to test the usefulness of a career perspective across a broad population. It may also detract from understanding and ameliorating the career problems faced by under-studied groups such as the working poor (Kossek, Huber-Yoder, Castellino, & Lerner, 1997). Arthur et al.'s (1999) comprehensive study is noteworthy in its deliberate attempt to sample participants from a variety of occupational backgrounds.

Most of the research reviewed in this chapter was organized into three broad areas—career success, career development, and career decision-making. In this concluding section of the chapter, I offer suggestions for future research in each area, explicitly attempting to link the suggested research to the contemporary work scene whenever possible.

Career Success

Studies of career success should more extensively incorporate subjective indicators of success to make them more relevant to the pursuit of boundaryless or protean careers. Although the examination of career satisfaction and perceived career success represents a step in the right direction, it does not go far enough. The use of these composite measures can mask relationships that might otherwise emerge with more fine-grained assessments of subjectively defined career success.

It would be particularly useful to develop scales that assess a variety of dimensions of the meaning of career success. As noted earlier, Friedman and Greenhaus (2000) observed five dimensions along which career success is gauged. Scale development efforts should attempt to develop and validate a measure that captures most individuals' conception of what it means for them to be successful in their careers. Studies could then predict accomplishments or perceived success in each of these areas. Different models of career success—not merely objective success and subjective success—could result from these studies that represent alternative paths to fulfillment in a career.

The models are likely to include somewhat different predictors because the factors that determine advancement, for example, may not be the same as those that determine work-family balance. It is trite to recommend that the predictors of success should be based on a theoretical framework, but the current studies are not particularly strong in that regard. Although most of the studies include reasonable sets of variables (e.g., human capital, motivational), the theoretical rationale for the specific variables within these sets has not always been persuasive.

The inclusion of a more varied set of career success indicators could also provide information regarding the tendency of individuals to experience career success along more than one dimension. For example, is it likely to experience success simultaneously with regard to advancement strivings and needs to establish strong interpersonal relationships? What are the individual and situational factors that distinguish patterns of career success (e.g., high in advancement and low in work-family balance vs. high in both)? In short, an expanded conceptualization of career success should produce research that is relevant to individuals pursuing a wide array of career motives.

Career Development

Despite many of the outmoded assumptions of age-related theories of development, it is important not to disregard the effects of age. Individuals change in important ways as they get older. The specific age ranges associated with early, middle, and later adulthood (Levinson et al., 1978) may have to be revised in light of longer life spans and more varied lifestyles, but aging is inevitable. One can cycle back to the previously encountered tasks of socialization and establishment when one changes projects, jobs, employers, or occupations. But one cannot cycle back from late adulthood to middle adulthood to early adulthood. We accumulate experiences and psychological baggage that are not easily displaced. Levinson et al.'s (1978) conception of life development as a series of alternating stable and transitional phases as individuals move through adulthood is as compelling in boundaryless careers as in organizational careers, even though the theory has not received extensive support.

Therefore, a major challenge of career development theory is to connect the career learning cycles that have been proposed (exploration, establishment, maintenance, decline) with the developmental challenges of adulthood to understand the interplay between career age and chronological age. For example, an accountant who becomes a public school teacher at age 55 needs to face the tasks of socialization and establishment; however, that individual must do so from the vantage point of middle age. Research on psychological contract formation, socialization, and mentoring could benefit by examining the experiences of older employees who are entering a new career cycle.

It is therefore important to determine whether the tasks associated with entering and managing a career cycle are handled more effectively or differently as one gets older. Parasuraman et al. (2000) proposed three different patterns of changes in person-career fit as individuals move from one career cycle to another. The pattern of increasing fit is predicated on greater self-esteem and competence in career decision making over time, but there are likely to be wide individual differences in these qualities as a person gets older and accumulates life experiences.

Arthur et al.'s (1999) three career competencies (knowing why, how, and whom) and Mirvis and Hall's (1994) metaskills of personal identity and adaptability could be fruitfully applied to individuals with different degrees of work experience and at differences stages of life development. Hall and Mirvis' (1995) prescriptions for older workers in the new economy require considerable self-insight and adaptability. Understanding whether and how these two qualities are enhanced through routine busting, as the authors suggest, will require substantial research on the learning process at different stages of life. Such research should also provide insight into the factors that encourage individuals to exit one career cycle for the uncertainty of another cycle. In a similar vein, research could examine the factors that promote growth in Arthur et al.'s (1999) career competencies over the life span.

Research should also examine the development of contingent employees, who make up a growing segment of the workforce. Scholars have begun to explore the psychological experiences of contingent employees (Beard & Edwards, 1995) and have linked contingent employment to the socialization process (Bauer et al., 1998), the psychological contract (McLean Parks, Kidder, & Gallagher, 1998), and job design (Pearce, 1998). Additional research in this area could shed considerable light on the nature of career cycles and career development in the new economy.

Career Decision Making

Because so little research has been conducted on the career decision-making strategies used by employees, it is less a matter of suggesting ways to make the research more relevant to the contemporary work scene than it is of encouraging researchers to enter this arena in the first place. In fact, any insight into the effectiveness of career decision making should be timely because of the frequency and magnitude of decisions that are likely to be required in boundaryless careers.

Although Harren's (1979) typology is not the only classification of decision-making strategies, it is a useful starting point because it contains both rational and intuitive styles. Given the failure of the prior research on students to confirm the superiority of a rational style, and the contention that a spontaneous style is more typical and perhaps more effective (Arthur et al., 1999), this area seems ripe for additional study.

Research should examine the possibility that the effectiveness of a rational decision-making style is contingent upon the situation. Singh (2000) has proposed two situational factors that moderate the impact of career decision style on the effectiveness of a career decision—the time constraint imposed to make the decision and the magnitude of the difference between the prior work setting and the new work setting. It would also be useful to examine interactions between different career decision-making styles. For example, research may find that a combination of rational and intuitive behavior, of facts and feelings, of attending to the mind and to the heart that produces the most effective career decisions.

Gender Issues in Careers

Research should examine multiple indicators of career success for men and women at different stages of their lives. In that way, an understanding of gender differences in the paths to career success would incorporate different meanings of success. It is possible that women are less successful than are men in some respects and are more successful in other respects. Such analyses could also reveal the obstacles faced by women and men in achieving different forms of career success.

The impact of family dynamics on the careers of women and men also warrants additional study. In particular, research should examine not only the mechanisms by which family experiences constrain careers but also the ways in which they can promote career success. Research should examine the extent to which women's more substantial accommodation of work for the well-being of their family is due to their values, the lack of support from their family, or the inflexibility and bias of their employers (Singh et al., 2002).

Research is also needed to determine the various ways by which family experiences can enrich life at work. Family-derived resources include financial assets; assistance with children, elders, and housework; emotional support; and the development of skills that can be applied to the work domain (Friedman & Greenhaus, 2000). Although Kirchmeyer (1992) has provided some support for the presence of positive spillover between family and work, additional research is needed to specify the family resources and experiences that are associated with different types of enrichment.

Finally, research should acknowledge that despite substantial gender differences in career dynamics, there are likely to be considerable within-gender variations as well (Parasuraman & Greenhaus, in press). It is just as inappropriate to assume that all women are the same as it is to assume that women and men experience the same opportunities and obstacles in their careers. Therefore, even those studies that focus on gender differences in careers should examine additional variables (e.g., work and family orientation, family structure, organizational practices) that may interact with gender or even supercede gender as an explanation for a phenomenon.

In conclusion, research on career-related topics is sophisticated conceptually and methodologically. The topics are wide ranging because the concept of a career is necessarily inclusive. It is unlikely that a single theory will be capable of explaining such diverse phenomena as career success, career development, and career decision making—not to mention the various processes within each of these three areas. However, researchers should continue to develop and test midrange theories that explain facets of career dynamics, combine them when possible to explain the intersection of two or more phenomena, and keep them current with the issues that individuals face at any given point in history.

REFERENCES

Adkins, C. L. (1995). Previous work experience and organizational socialization: A longitudinal examination. *Academy of Management Journal, 38,* 839–862.

Allen, T. D., McManus, S. E., & Russell, J. E. A. (1999). Newcomer socialization and stress: Formal peer relationships as a source of support. *Journal of Vocational Behavior, 54,* 453–470.

Allen, T. D., Poteet, M. L., & Burroughs, S. M. (1997). The mentor's perspective: A qualitative inquiry and future research agenda. *Journal of Vocational Behavior, 51,* 70–89.

Allen, T. D., Poteet, M. L., & Russell, J. E. A. (1998). Attitudes of managers who are more or less career plateaued. *Career Development Quarterly, 47,* 159–172.

Allen, T. D., Poteet, M. L., & Russell, J. E. A. (2000). Protégé selection by mentors: What makes the difference? *Journal of Organizational Behavior, 21,* 271–282.

Allen, T. D., Poteet, M. L., Russell, J. E. A., & Dobbins, G. H. (1997). A field study of factors related to willingness to mentor others. *Journal of Vocational Behavior, 50,* 1–22.

Allen, T. D., Russell, J. E. A., Poteet, M. L., & Dobbins, G. H. (1999). Learning and development factors related to perceptions of job content and hierarchical plateauing. *Journal of Organizational Behavior, 20,* 1113–1137.

Allred, B. B., Snow, C. C., & Miles, R. E. (1996). Characteristics of managerial careers in the 21st century. *Academy of Management Executive, 10*(4), 17–27.

Anakwe, U. P., & Greenhaus, J. H. (2000). Prior work experience and socialization experiences of college graduates. *International Journal of Manpower, 21*(2), 95–111.

Argyris, C. (1960). *Understanding organizational behavior.* Homewood, IL: Dorsey.

Arthur, M. B. (1994). The boundaryless career: A new perspective for organizational inquiry. *Journal of Organizational Behavior, 15,* 295–306.

Arthur, M. B., Inkson, K., & Pringle, J. K. (1999). *The new careers: Individual action and economic change.* London: Sage.

Arthur, M. B., & Rousseau, D. M. (1996). A career lexicon for the 21st century. *Academy of Management Executive, 10*(4), 28–39.

Aryee, S., Chay, Y. W., & Tan, H. H. (1994). An examination of the antecedents of subjective career success among a managerial sample in Singapore. *Human Relations, 47,* 487–509.

Aryee, S., Lo, S., & Kang, I. (1999). Antecedents of early career stage mentoring among Chinese employees. *Journal of Organizational Behavior, 20,* 563–576.

Ashford, S. J., & Black, J. S. (1996). Proactivity during organizational entry: The role of desire for control. *Journal of Applied Psychology, 81,* 199–214.

Bardwick, J. M. (1986). *The plateauing trap.* Toronto, Canada: Bantam Books.

Bauer, T. N., Morrison, E. W., & Callister, R. R. (1998). Organizational socialization: A review and directions for future research. *Research in Personnel and Human Resources Management, 16,* 149–214.

Beard, K. M., & Edwards, J. R. (1995). Employees at risk: Contingent work and the psychological experience of contingent workers. In C. L. Cooper & D. M. Rousseau (Eds.), *Trends in organizational behavior* (Vol. 2, pp. 109–126). West Sussex, UK: Wiley.

Boudreau, J. W., Boswell, W. R., & Judge, T. A. (2001). Effects of personality on executive career success in the United States and Europe. *Journal of Vocational Behavior, 58,* 53–81.

Brett, J. M., & Stroh, L. K. (1997). Jumping ship: Who benefits from an external labor market career strategy? *Journal of Applied Psychology, 82,* 331–341.

Brett, J. M., Stroh, L. K., & Reilly, A. H. (1992). What is it like being a dual-career manager in the 1990s? In S. Zedeck (Ed.), *Work and family* (pp. 138–167). San Francisco: Jossey-Bass.

Bretz, R. D., & Judge, T. A. (1994). Person-organization fit and theory of work adjustment. *Journal of Vocational Behavior, 44,* 32–54.

Brousseau, K. R., Driver, M. J., Eneroth, K., & Larsson, R. (1996). Career pandemonium: Realigning organizations and individuals. *Academy of Management Executive, 10*(4), 52–66.

Burke, R. J., McKeen, C. A., & McKenna, C. (1993). Correlates of mentoring in organizations: The mentor's perspective. *Psychological Reports, 72,* 883–896.

Byrne, J. A. (1993, December 20). The horizontal corporation. *Business Week,* 76–81.

Callanan, G. A., & Greenhaus, J. H. (1990). The career indecision of managers and professionals: Development of a scale and test of a model. *Journal of Vocational Behavior, 37,* 79–103.

Callanan, G. A., & Greenhaus, J. H. (1992). The career indecision of managers and professionals: An examination of multiple subtypes. *Journal of Vocational Behavior, 41,* 212–231.

Callanan, G. A., & Greenhaus, J. H. (1999). Personal and career development: The best and worst of times. In A. I. Kraut & A. K. Korman (Eds.), *Evolving practices in human resource management: Responses to a changing world of work* (pp. 146–171). San Francisco: Jossey-Bass.

Cappelli, P. (1999). Career jobs are dead. *California Management Review, 42*(1), 146–167.

Chao, G. T. (1997). Mentoring phases and outcomes. *Journal of Vocational Behavior, 51,* 15–28.

Chao, G. T., O'Leary-Kelly, A. M., Wolf, S., Klein, H. J., & Gardner, P. (1994). Organizational socialization: Its content and consequences. *Journal of Applied Psychology, 79,* 730–743.

Chao, G. T., Walz, P. M., & Gardner, P. D. (1992). Formal and informal mentorships: A comparison on mentoring functions and contrast with nonmentored counterparts. *Personnel Psychology, 45,* 619–636.

Dreher, G. F., & Ash, R. A. (1990). A comparative study of mentoring among men and women in managerial, professional, and technical positions. *Journal of Applied Psychology, 75,* 539–546.

Dreher, G. F., & Cox, T. H. (2000). Labor market mobility and cash compensation: The moderating effects of race and gender. *Academy of Management Journal, 43,* 890–900.

Drobnic, S., Blossfeld, H. P., & Rohwer, G. (1999). Dynamics of women's employment patterns over the family life course: A comparison of the United States and Germany. *Journal of Marriage and the Family, 61,* 133–146.

Erickson, R. J., Nichols, L., & Ritter, C. (2000). Family influences on absenteeism: Testing an expanded process model. *Journal of Vocational Behavior, 57,* 246–272.

Fagenson, E. A. (1988). The power of a mentor: Protégés and non-protégés' perceptions of their own power in organizations. *Group and Organization Studies, 13,* 182–192.

Fagenson, E. A. (1989). The mentor advantage: Perceived career/job experiences of protégés versus nonprotégés'. *Journal of Organizational Behavior, 10,* 309–320.

Feldman, D. C. (1988). *Managing careers in organizations.* Glenview IL: Scott Foresman.

Feldman, D. C., Leana, C. R., & Turnley, W. H. (1997). A relative deprivation approach to understanding underemployment. In C. L. Cooper & D. M. Rousseau (Eds.), *Trends in organizational behavior* (Vol. 4, pp. 43–60). West Sussex, UK: Wiley.

Feldman, D. C., & Turnley, W. H. (1995). Underemployment among recent business college graduates. *Journal of Organizational Behavior, 16,* 691–706.

Friedman, S. D., & Greenhaus, J. H. (2000). *Allies or enemies? How choices about work and family affect the quality of men's and women's lives.* New York: Oxford University Press.

Frone, M. R., Yardley, J. K., & Markel, K. S. (1997). Developing and testing an integrative model of work-family interface. *Journal of Vocational Behavior, 50,* 145–167.

Gallos, J. V. (1989). Exploring women's development: Implications for career theory, practice, and research. In M. B. Arthur, D. T. Hall, & B. S. Lawrence (Eds.), *Handbook of career theory* (pp. 110–132). Cambridge, UK: Cambridge University Press.

Gerson, K. (1993). *No man's land: Men's changing commitments to family and work.* New York: Basic Books.

Glass, J., & Camarigg, V. (1992). Gender, parenthood and job-family compatibility. *American Journal of Sociology, 98,* 131–151.

Godshalk, V. M. (1997). *The effects of career plateauing on work and nonwork outcomes.* Unpublished doctoral dissertation, Drexel University, Philadelphia, PA.

Gordon, J. R., & Whelan, K. S. (1998). Successful professional women in midlife: How organizations can more effectively understand and respond to the challenges. *Academy of Management Executive, 12*(1), 8–24.

Gowen, M. A., Riordan, C. M., & Gatewood, R. D. (1999). Test of a model of coping with involuntary job loss following a company closing. *Journal of Applied Psychology, 84,* 75–86.

Green, S. G., & Bauer, T. N. (1995). Supervisory mentoring by advisers: Relationships with doctoral student potential, productivity, and commitment. *Personnel Psychology, 48,* 537–561.

Greenberger, E., & O'Neil, R. (1993). Spouse, parent, worker: Role commitments and role-related experiences in the construction of adults' well-being. *Developmental Psychology, 29,* 181–197.

Greenhaus, J. H. (1987). *Career management.* Hinsdale, IL: Dryden Press.

Greenhaus, J. H., Callanan, G. A., & Godshalk, V. M. (2000). *Career management* (3rd ed.). Fort Worth, TX: Dryden Press.

Greenhaus, J. H., & Parasuraman, S. (1986). Vocational and organizational behavior, 1985: A review. *Journal of Vocational Behavior, 29,* 115–176.

Greenhaus, J. H., & Parasuraman, S. (1999). Research on work, family, and gender: Current status and future directions. In G. N. Powell (Ed.), *Handbook of gender and work* (pp. 391–412). Newbury Park, CA: Sage.

Guest, D. E. (1998). Is the psychological contract worth taking seriously? *Journal of Organizational Behavior, 19,* 649–664.

Gunz, H. P., & Jalland, R. M. (1996). Managerial careers and business strategies. *Academy of Management Review, 21,* 718–756.

Hall, D. T. (1976). *Careers in organizations.* Glenview, IL: Scott Foresman.

Hall, D. T. (1996). Protean *careers* of the 21st Century. *Academy of Management Executive, 10*(4), 8–16.

Hall, D. T., & Mirvis, P. H. (1995). The new career contract: Developing the whole person at midlife and beyond. *Journal of Vocational Behavior, 47,* 269–289.

Hall, D. T., & Nougaim, K. (1968). An examination of Maslow's need hierarchy in an organizational setting. *Organizational Behavior and Human Performance, 3,* 12–35.

Hanisch, K. A. (1999). Job loss and unemployment research from 1994 to 1998: A review and recommendations for research and intervention. *Journal of Vocational Behavior, 55,* 188–220.

Harren, V. A. (1979). A model of career decision making for college students. *Journal of Vocational Behavior, 14,* 119–133.

Jacobs, J. A. (1992). Women's entry into management. *Administrative Science Quarterly, 37,* 282–301.

Judge, T. A., & Bretz, R. D. (1994). Political influence processes and career success. *Journal of Management, 20,* 43–65.

Judge, T. A., Cable, D. M., Boudreau, J. W., & Bretz, R. D. (1995). An empirical investigation of the predictors of executive career success. *Personnel Psychology, 48,* 485–519.

Judiesch, M. K., & Lyness, K. S. (1999). Left behind? The impact of leaves of absence on managers' career success. *Academy of Management Journal, 42,* 641–651.

Kimmel, M. S. (1993). What do men want? *Harvard Business Review, 71*(6), 50–63.

Kinicki, A. J., Prussia, G. E., & McKee-Ryan, F. M. (2000). A panel study of coping with involuntary job loss. *Academy of Management Journal, 43,* 90–100.

Kinnunen, U., Mauno, S., Nätti, J., & Happonen, M. (2000). Organizational antecedents and outcomes of job insecurity: A longitudinal study in three organizations in Finland. *Journal of Organizational Behavior, 21,* 443–459.

Kirchmeyer, C. (1992). Nonwork participation and work attitudes: A test of scarcity vs. expansion models of personal resources. *Human Relations, 45,* 775–795.

Kirchmeyer, C. (1998). Determinants of managerial career success: Evidence and explanation of male/female differences. *Journal of Management, 24,* 673–692.

Koberg, C. S., Boss, R. W., & Goodman, E. (1998). Factors and outcomes associated with mentoring among health-care professionals. *Journal of Vocational Behavior, 53,* 58–72.

Konrad, A. M., & Cannings, K. (1997). The effects of gender role congruence and statistical discrimination on managerial advancement. *Human Relations, 50,* 1305–1328.

Konrad, A. M., Corrigall, E., Lieb, P., & Ritchie, J. E. (2000). Sex differences in job attribute preferences among managers and business students. *Group and Organization Management, 25,* 108–131.

Konrad, A. M., Ritchie, J. E., Lieb, P., & Corrigall, E. (2000). Sex differences and similarities in job attribute preferences: A meta-analysis. *Psychological Bulletin, 126,* 593–641.

Kossek, E. E., Huber-Yoder, M., Castellino, D., & Lerner, J. (1997). The working poor: Locked out of careers and the organizational mainstream? *Academy of Management Executive, 11*(1), 76–92.

Kram, K. E. (1983). Phases of the mentor relationship. *Academy of Management Review, 26,* 608–625.

Lam, S. S. K., & Schaubroeck, J. (2000). The role of locus of control in reactions to being promoted and being passed over: A quasi experiment. *Academy of Management Journal, 43,* 66–78.

Lambert, S. J. (1990). Processes linking work and family: A critical review and research agenda. *Human Relations, 43,* 239–257.

Landau, J., & Arthur, M. B. (1992). The relationship of marital status, spouse's career status, and gender to salary level. *Sex Roles, 27,* 665–681.

Latack, J. C., Kinicki, A. J., & Prussia, G. E. (1995). An integrated process model of coping with job loss. *Academy of Management Review, 20,* 311–342.

Leana, C. R., Feldman, D. C., & Tan, G. Y. (1998). Predictors of coping behavior after a layoff. *Journal of Organizational Behavior, 19,* 85–97.

Levinson, D. J., Darrow, C. N., Klein, E. B., Levinson, M. H., & McKee, B. (1978). *Seasons of a man's life.* New York: Knopf.

Lobel, S. A., & St. Clair, L. (1992). Effects of family responsibilities, gender, and career identity salience on performance outcomes. *Academy of Management Journal, 35,* 1057–1069.

London, M., & Stumpf, S. A. (1982). *Managing careers.* Reading, MA: Addison-Wesley.

Louis, M. E. (1980). Career transitions: Varieties and commonalities. *Academy of Management Review, 5,* 329–340.

Lyness, K. S., & Judiesch, M. K. (1999). Are women more likely to be hired or promoted into management positions? *Journal of Vocational Behavior, 54,* 158–173.

Lyness, K. S., & Thompson, D. E. (1997). Above the glass ceiling? A comparison of matched samples of female and male executives. *Journal of Applied Psychology, 82,* 359–375.

Malos, S. B., & Campion, M. A. (2000). Human resource strategy and career mobility in professional service firms: A test of an options-based model. *Academy of Management Journal, 43,* 749–760.

Martin, L. (1991). *A report on the glass ceiling.* Washington, DC: U.S. Department of Labor.

McCaskey, M. B. (1977). Goals and direction in personal planning. *Academy of Management Review, 2,* 454–462.

McCauley, C. D., Ruderman, M. N., Ohlott, P. J., & Morrow, J. E. (1994). Assessing the developmental components of managerial jobs. *Journal of Applied Psychology, 79,* 544–560.

McLean Parks, J., Kidder, D. L., & Gallagher, D. G. (1998). Fitting square pegs into round holes: Mapping the domain of contingent work arrangements onto the psychological contract. *Journal of Organizational Behavior, 19,* 697–730.

Melamed, T. (1995). Career success: The moderating effect of gender. *Journal of Vocational Behavior, 47,* 35–60.

Miller, D. C., & Form, W. H. (1951). *Industrial sociology.* New York: Harper and Row.

Millward, L. J., & Hopkins, L. J. (1998). Psychological contracts, organizational and job commitment. *Journal of Applied Social Psychology, 28,* 1530–1556.

Mirvis, P. H., & Hall, D. T. (1994). Psychological success and the boundaryless career. *Journal of Organizational Behavior, 15,* 365–380.

Morrison, E. W. (1993). Longitudinal study of the effects of information seeking on newcomer socialization. *Journal of Applied Psychology, 78,* 173–183.

Morrison, E. W., & Robinson, S. L. (1997). When employees feel betrayed: A model of how psychological contract violation develops. *Academy of Management Review, 22,* 226–256.

Mullen, E. J., & Noe, R. A. (1999). The mentoring information exchange: When do mentors seek information from their protégés? *Journal of Organizational Behavior, 20,* 233–242.

Nicholson, N. (1996). Career systems in crisis: Change and opportunity in the information age. *Academy of Management Executive, 10,* 40–51.

Noe, R. A. (1988). An investigation of the determinants of successful assigned mentoring relationships. *Personnel Psychology, 41,* 457–479.

Ostroff, C., & Kozlowski, S. W. J. (1992). Organizational socialization as a learning process: The role of information acquisition. *Personnel Psychology, 45,* 849–874.

Ostroff, C., & Kozlowski, S. W. J. (1993). The role of mentoring in the information gathering processes of newcomers during early organizational socialization. *Journal of Vocational Behavior, 42,* 170–183.

Parasuraman, S., & Greenhaus, J. H. (in press). Toward reducing some critical gaps in work-family research. *Human Resource Management Review.*

Parasuraman, S., Greenhaus, J. H., & Linnehan, F. (2000). Time, person-career fit, and the boundaryless career. In C. L. Cooper & D. M. Rousseau (Eds.), *Trends in organizational behavior* (Vol. 7, pp. 63–78). West Sussex, UK: Wiley.

Parasuraman, S., Singh, R., & Greenhaus, J. H. (1997). The influence of self and partner family variables on career development opportunities of professional women and men. In P. Tharenou (Ed.), *Best paper and abstract proceedings of the Australian industrial and organizational psychology conference* (pp. 125–129). Melbourne, Australia: The Australian Psychological Society.

Pearce, J. L. (1998). Job insecurity is important, but not for the reasons you might think: The example of contingent workers. In C. L. Cooper & D. M. Rousseau (Eds.), *Trends in organizational behavior* (Vol. 5, pp. 31–46). West Sussex, UK: Wiley.

Phillips, S. D., & Strohmer, D. C. (1982). Decision-making style and vocational maturity. *Journal of Vocational Behavior, 20,* 215–222.

Powell, G. N. (1999). Reflections on the glass ceiling: Recent trends and future prospects. In G. N. Powell (Ed.), *Handbook of gender and work* (pp. 325–345). Newbury Park, CA: Sage.

Powell, G. N., & Butterfield, D. A. (1994). Investigating the "glass ceiling" phenomenon: An empirical study of actual promotions to top management. *Academy of Management Journal, 37,* 68–86.

Powell, G. N., & Mainiero, L. A. (1992). Cross-currents in the river of time: Conceptualizing the complexities of women's careers. *Journal of Management, 18,* 215–237.

Ragins, B. R. (1997). Diversified mentoring relationships in organizations: A power perspective. *Academy of Management Review, 22,* 482–521.

Ragins, B. R. (1999). Gender and mentoring relationships: A review and research agenda for the next decade. In G. N. Powell (Ed.), *Handbook of gender and work* (pp. 347–370). Newbury Park, CA: Sage.

Ragins, B. R., & Cotton, J. L. (1991). Easier said than done: Gender differences in perceived barriers to gaining a mentor. *Academy of Management Journal, 34,* 939–951.

Ragins, B. R., & Cotton, J. L. (1999). Mentor functions and outcomes: A comparison of men and women in formal and informal mentoring relationships. *Journal of Applied Psychology, 84,* 529–550.

Ragins, B. R., Cotton, J. L., & Miller, J. S. (2000). Marginal mentoring: The effects of type of mentor, quality of relationship, and program design on work and career attitudes. *Academy of Management Journal, 43,* 1177–1194.

Ragins, B. R., & McFarlin, D. (1990). Perceptions of mentor roles in cross-gender mentoring relationships. *Journal of Vocational Behavior, 37,* 321–339.

Ragins, B. R., & Scandura, T. A. (1999). Burden or blessing? Expected costs and benefits of being a mentor. *Journal of Organizational Behavior, 20,* 493–509.

Robinson, S. L., Kraatz, M. S., & Rousseau, D. M. (1994). Changing obligations and the psychological contract: A longitudinal study. *Academy of Management Journal, 37,* 137–152.

Robinson, S. L., & Morrison, E. W. (1995). Psychological contracts and OCB: The effect of unfulfilled obligations on civic virtue behavior. *Journal of Organizational Behavior, 16,* 289–298.

Robinson, S. L., & Rousseau, D. M. (1994). Violating the psychological contract: Not the exception but the norm. *Journal of Organizational Behavior, 15,* 245–259.

Robinson, S. L., & Morrison, E. W. (2000). The development of psychological contract breach and violation: A longitudinal study. *Journal of Organizational Behavior, 21,* 525–546.

Roche, G. R. (1979). Much ado about mentors. *Harvard Business Review, 57*(1), 14–28.

Roos, P. A., & Gatta, M. L. (1999). The gender gap in earnings: Trends, explanations, and prospects. In G. N. Powell (Ed.), *Handbook of gender and work* (pp. 95–123). Newbury Park, CA: Sage.

Rousseau, D. M. (1995). *Psychological contracts in organizations: Understanding written and unwritten agreements.* Newbury Park, CA: Sage.

Saks, A. M., & Ashforth, B. E. (1997). Organizational socialization: Making sense of the past and present as a prologue for the future. *Journal of Vocational Behavior, 51,* 234–279.

Saks, A. M., & Ashforth, B. E. (2000). The role of dispositions, early stressors, and behavioral plasticity theory in predicting newcomers' adjustment to work. *Journal of Organizational Behavior, 21,* 43–62.

Sanders, M. M., Lengnick-Hall, M. L., Lengnick-Hall, C. A., & Steele-Clapp, L. (1998). Love and work: Career-family attitudes of new entrants into the labor force. *Journal of Organizational Behavior, 19,* 603–619.

Scandura, T. A. (1992). Mentorship and career mobility: An empirical investigation. *Journal of Organizational Behavior, 13,* 169–174.

Scandura, T. A. (1998). Dysfunctional mentoring relationships and outcomes. *Journal of Management, 24,* 449–467.

Schein, E. H. (1978). *Career dynamics: Matching individual and organizational needs.* Reading, MA: Addison-Wesley.

Schneer, J., & Reitman, F. (1993). The effects of alternate family structures on managerial career paths. *Academy of Management Journal, 36,* 830–843.

Schneer, J., & Reitman, F. (1995). The impact of gender as managerial careers unfold. *Journal of Vocational Behavior, 47,* 290–315.

Seibert, S. (1999). The effectiveness of facilitated mentoring: A longitudinal quasi-experiment. *Journal of Vocational Behavior, 54,* 483–502.

Seibert, S. E., Crant, J. M., & Kraimer, M. L. (1999). Proactive personality and career success. *Journal of Applied Psychology, 84,* 416–427.

Seibert, S. E., & Kraimer, M. L. (2001). The five-factor model of personality and career success. *Journal of Vocational Behavior, 58,* 1–21.

Sekaran, U., & Hall, D. T. (1989). Asynchronism in dual-career couples. In M. B. Arthur, D. T. Hall, & B. S. Lawrence (Eds.), *Handbook of career theory* (pp. 159–180). Cambridge, UK: Cambridge University Press.

Shellenbarger, S. (1991, November 15). More job seekers put family needs first. *The Wall Street Journal,* pp. B1, B12.

Shore, L. M., & Tetrick, L. E. (1994). The psychological contract as an explanatory framework in the employment relationship. In C. L. Cooper & D. M. Rousseau (Eds.), *Trends in organizational behavior* (Vol. 1, pp. 91–109). West Sussex, UK: Wiley.

Sieber, S. D. (1974). Toward a theory of role accumulation. *American Sociological Review, 39,* 567–578.

Singh, R. (2000). *The effectiveness of alternative career decision making styles: Development and test of a model.* Unpublished manuscript, Drexel University, Philadelphia, PA.

Singh, R., Greenhaus, J. H., Collins, K. M., & Parasuraman, S. (1998). The influence of family responsibilities, gender and social support on the career involvement of professionals. *Proceedings of the 35th Annual Meeting of the Eastern Academy of Management, 35,* 267–270.

Singh, R., Greenhaus, J. H., & Parasuraman, S. (2002). The impact of family life on career decisions and outcomes. In C. L. Cooper & R. J. Burke (Eds.), *The new world of work*: *Challenges and opportunities* (pp. 95–112). Oxford, UK: Blackwell.

Smart, R., & Peterson, C. (1997). Super's career stages and the decision to change careers. *Journal of Vocational Behavior, 51,* 358–374.

Spell, C. S. & Blum, T. C. (2000). Getting ahead: Organizational practices that set boundaries around mobility patterns. *Journal of Organizational Behavior, 21,* 299–314.

Stein, J., et al. (Eds.). (1969). *The Random House dictionary of the English language.* New York: Random House.

Stephens, G. K. (1994). Crossing internal career boundaries: The state of research on subjective career transitions. *Journal of Management, 20,* 479–501.

Stroh, L. K., Brett, J. M., & Reilly, A. H. (1992). All the right stuff: A comparison of female and male managers' career progression. *Journal of Applied Psychology, 77,* 251–260.

Stroh, L. K., & Reilly, A. H. (1999). Gender and careers: Present experiences and emerging trends. In G. N. Powell (Ed.), *Handbook of gender and work* (pp. 307–324). Newbury Park, CA: Sage.

Sullivan, S. E. (1999). The changing nature of careers: A review and research agenda. *Journal of Management, 25,* 457–484.

Sullivan, S. E., Carden, W. A., & Martin, D. F. (1998). Careers in the next millennium: Directions for future research. *Human Resource Management Review, 8,* 165–185.

Super, D. E. (1957). *The psychology of careers.* New York: Harper and Row.

Super, D. E. (1980). A life-span, life-space approach to career development. *Journal of Vocational Behavior, 16,* 282–298.

Tharenou, P. (1997). Managerial career advancement. In C. L. Cooper & I. T. Robertson (Eds.), *International review of industrial and organizational psychology* (Vol. 12, pp. 39–94). Chichester, UK: Wiley.

Tharenou, P., Latimer, S., & Conroy, D. (1994). How do you make it to the top? An examination of influences on women's and men's managerial advancement. *Academy of Management Journal, 37,* 899–931.

Thomas, D. A. (1990). The impact of race on managers' experiences of developmental relationships (mentoring and sponsorship): An intra-organizational study. *Journal of Organizational Behavior, 11,* 479–491.

Turban, D. B., & Dougherty, T. W. (1994). Role of protégé personality in receipt of mentoring and career success. *Academy of Management Journal, 37,* 688–702.

Turnley, W. H., & Feldman, D. C. (2000). Re-examining the effects of psychological contract violations: Unmet expectations and job dissatisfaction as mediators. *Journal of Organizational Behavior, 21,* 25–42.

Uchitelle, L., & Kleinfield, N. R. (1996, March 3). On the battlefields of business, millions of casualties. *The New York Times,* p. 1.

Universum Intituted. (1998). *American graduate survey 1988.* Stockholm, Sweden: Author.

Wanberg, C. R. (1997). Antecedents and outcomes of coping behaviors among unemployed and reemployed individuals. *Journal of Applied Psychology, 82,* 731–744.

Wanberg, C. R., & Kammeyer-Mueller, J. D. (2000). Predictors and outcomes of proactivity in the socialization process. *Journal of Applied Psychology, 85,* 373–385.

Waterman, R. H., Waterman, J. A., & Collard, B. A. (1994). Toward a career resilient workforce. *Harvard Business Review, 72*(4), 87–95.

Wayne, S. J., Liden, R. C., Kraimer, M. L., & Graf, I. K. (1999). The role of human capital, motivation and supervisor sponsorship in predicting career success. *Journal of Organizational Behavior, 20,* 577–595.

Weick, K. E. (1996). Enactment and the boundaryless career: Organizing as we work. In M. B. Arthur & D. M. Rousseau (Eds.), *The boundaryless career* (pp. 40–57). New York: Oxford University Press.

Whitely, W., Dougherty, T. W., & Dreher, G. F. (1991). Relationship of career mentoring and socioeconomic origin to managers' and professionals' early career progress. *Academy of Management Journal, 34,* 331–351.

CHAPTER 21

Human Factors and Ergonomics

WILLIAM C. HOWELL

NATURE AND CONTEXT OF THE FIELD

The customary introduction to a field of endeavor begins with a succinct defining statement. Unfortunately, the field of *human factors and ergonomics* (HF/E) does not lend itself to simple definition because, among those who identify with it, universal agreement on how it should be characterized is lacking. One report cites some 130 definitions (Licht, Polzella, & Boff, 1991), and many of the differences, although subtle, are significant. In fact, as we shall see momentarily, there is not even a consensus on what the field should be called.

Because these unresolved issues are rooted in history and shaped by philosophical disagreements that will undoubtedly have an impact on the field's future course, glossing over them in the interest of expository convenience would do gross injustice to the field. HF/E is, in truth, a work in progress, and any representation to the contrary would be misleading. Therefore, in lieu of the conventional introduction, I shall begin by examining those facets of the field on which there is and is not a consensus. HF/E will consistently be referred to as a *field* rather than a *discipline,* a *specialty,* a *science,* or a *profession,* because the latter terms are closely linked to the issues on which consensus is lacking.

Commonalities and Distinctions

The one unifying concept the entire field subscribes to is the notion that humans and the artifacts they create for coping with their world should be viewed together rather than separately in the design process—a perspective typically referred to as the *human-machine system model.*

As illustrated in Figure 21.1, human capabilities, limitations, and tendencies should be identified and accommodated at the critical interfaces where human and machine meet. A good fit promotes efficient, safe accomplishment of whatever the system is designed to do; a poor one virtually ensures ineffective performance, costly errors, and accidents.

This seemingly obvious concept, which has found its way into the popular vernacular as the term *user-friendliness,* is neither as simple nor as commonplace as one might expect. Widely publicized cases of systems designed without regard for the demands placed on human operators abound: Disasters such as the Three Mile Island nuclear accident (Rubinstein & Mason, 1979), the accidental destruction of a passenger airliner by the USS Vincennes (U.S. Navy, 1988), and a number of fatal medical accidents (Institute of Medicine, 1999) all involved tasks that were unnecessarily difficult for even highly trained personnel to carry out. More mundane examples, such as difficult-to-program VCRs, confusing road signs, and poorly formatted election ballots, can be found everywhere.

The principal reason is that design professionals such as engineers, computer scientists, and architects have tended to focus on *artifacts,* seeking to maximize the reliability, efficiency, and aesthetics of the *machine* component alone rather

Work Environment

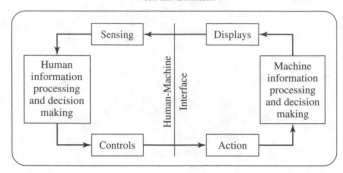

Figure 21.1 Schematic representation of the person-machine system. *Source:* Howell (1991).

than the performance of the entire system. What consideration they have given to usability has typically been from a naive personal perspective rather than the substantial body of scientific data that exist on human performance. For example, evolution of the personal computer was delayed considerably because the early software was designed from the perspective of computer experts rather than the ultimate—unsophisticated—user.

Another, more fundamental reason for the neglect of the human in systems design is cultural. In our society, it is generally assumed that poor or unsafe performance is the fault of the user (i.e., to err is human) rather than the machine. This bias has, among other things, hampered the development of safer systems in such high-profile domains as transportation, defense, and medicine by focusing accident investigations on the assignment of culpability rather than on true diagnosis (Woods, 2000). As Reason (1990) notes, accidents "are rarely if ever caused by any one factor, either mechanical or human" (p. 197).

The field of HF/E, then, is about user-oriented design within the conceptual framework of the human-machine system model, and on that point there is little disagreement. Where opinions begin to diverge is over the question of how this philosophy can best be represented within the institutions of the scientific and professional world. The core issue is whether it justifies—and can support—a distinct new discipline, replete with all the institutional trappings of a recognized science or profession, or whether it should instead be integrated into existing disciplines for which human-oriented design is most relevant. Those favoring the independent-discipline view consider establishing the identity and status of HF/E a top priority, whereas those favoring the shared-philosophy view believe that trying to carve out and defend professional territory is counterproductive (Howell, 1994). The most recent survey data suggest that the field is fairly evenly split on this issue (Hendrick, 1996).

Irrespective of status, there is no question that the field's scope has expanded dramatically. Originally limited chiefly to psychology and engineering (in fact, the field was once known as *human engineering*), it now lays claim to material from computer science, biomechanics, cognitive science, architecture, sociology, organizational behavior, anthropometry, neuroscience, and even medicine and forensics. At the same time, however, new specialties have been evolving that seem more inclined toward establishing their own unique identity than supporting HF/E's professional aspirations. Notable examples include *human-computer interaction (HCI)* and *cognitive engineering (CE),* multidisciplinary specialties that are currently among the most vigorous promoters of the human-oriented design philosophy.

HF/E Institutions

Designation Issues

Not only has definition been a problem for HF/E, but settling on a name has proven equally challenging. A number of labels have been adopted over the years, and there is still no universal consensus. Whereas the U.S. contingent settled on *human factors* several decades ago, and most of its institutions (e.g., professional organizations, training programs, publications) adopted that name, Europe and the rest of the world preferred *ergonomics* and labeled their institutions accordingly (Howell & Goldstein, 1971). As Helander (1997) notes, the European preference for the term *ergonomics* stemmed from its origin in industrial engineering, whereas the American preference for *human factors* reflected its psychological heritage.

However, with the internationalization of industry and the expanding content of the field, this discrepancy became increasingly problematic, prompting the U.S. contingent (the world's largest) to adopt *human factors and ergonomics* as its official designation—hence the consistent use of HF/E throughout this chapter. This somewhat awkward compromise has never been fully accepted, however, and the term *ergonomics*—which is becoming increasingly common in the popular vernacular—remains ambiguous. For some, it carries strong physical-work connotations; for others, it includes mental or cognitive facets as well.

Organizations, Publications, and Training

A necessary, if not sufficient, condition for identification as a field, discipline, or specialty is the evolution of formal institutions for exchanging and disseminating knowledge, advancing professional objectives, and training future professionals (scientists and practitioners). Despite its relative youth (just over a half-century), the field of HF/E has established a solid institutional presence in all three of these areas. Foremost among its professional organizations are the U.S.-based Human Factors and Ergonomics Society (HFES), its counterpart societies in other countries and regions of the world, and the International Ergonomics Association (IEA)—a consortium of some 35 of these societies. The total number of professionals identified with HF/E worldwide has been estimated at more than 25,000, about one-fifth of whom are members of HFES (by far the largest of the individual societies), although precise numbers are difficult to pin down since not all those engaged in the field are affiliated with its organizations (Helander, 1997).

Training varies widely, as would be expected considering the field's geographical, conceptual, and disciplinary diversity (VanCott & Huey, 1992). In the United States, the majority of programs reside in either engineering schools or psychology departments. Nearly half (44%) of the current members of HFES hold degrees in psychology, with the vast majority of those being at the doctoral level; only about 12% hold engineering degrees, and the majority of those are at the bachelor's or master's level. Overall, there are about as many master's-level as doctoral-level professionals in the field (nearly 40% each), with another 15% at the bachelor's level (HFES, 2000).

Pressures resulting from the push for professional recognition have led to various efforts to control the quality of HF/E services and those who render them (Hopkins, 1995; Wilson, 1998). The HFES does this through accreditation of graduate programs, thereby hoping to ensure at least minimal competence in those graduated, and through the promulgation of various design standards, thereby hoping to influence design directly. Many self-appointed groups have set up certification programs that award credentials to individual practitioners purporting to verify their competence. The fact that these programs vary so widely in rigor—some requiring little more than payment of a fee—throws considerable doubt on the validity of this credential. Many in the field, the author included, question the merit of all these quality-control mechanisms given the field's breadth and the lack of consensus over precisely what collection of knowledge and skills the well-trained practitioner should have. Moreover, in a field driven to some extent by technology and fast-moving research, the useful half-life of any set of evidence-based standards or requirements is likely to be very short (see 10-year comparison in Rhodenizer, Bowers, Pharmer, & Gerber, 1999a, 1999b).

The final set of institutions involves communication, and HF/E offers a large and growing array of books, journals, professional meetings, and Web sites (e.g., http://hfes.org) for those interested in the field and its products. The leading

comprehensive journals are *Human Factors* and *Ergonomics,* which are managed by the HFES and the IEA, respectively, and feature original research. HFES also publishes a magazine, *Ergonomics in Design,* that reports work of a more applied nature in a less technical style. The *Handbook of Human Factors and Ergonomics* (Salvendy, 1997), the second edition of what a decade earlier was entitled the *Handbook of Human Factors* (Salvendy, 1987), also provides comprehensive exposure to the field. The title change and expanded scope of content represented in these two volumes serves as a dramatic illustration of the field's growing diversity and definition problems. The most widely used textbooks are those by Sanders and McCormick (1993) and Wickens (1992).

Related Disciplines and Institutions

The principal fields HF/E intersects with are the design disciplines (e.g., engineering, information systems, architecture) on the applications side, and the human-oriented sciences (e.g., biological, behavioral, cognitive, social) on the knowledge-generation side. Among these, the relationship between engineering specialties (notably the industrial and systems ones) and psychology (notably the experimental and cognitive branches) has the longest history and remains the strongest. Nevertheless, HF/E exists on the fringes of each, and is virtually absent from some disciplinary specialties where logic would suggest the interaction should be the most vigorous. The industrial and organizational (I/O) branch of psychology is the most salient example for present purposes, but equally neglected are the disciplines concerned with the larger social, political, and cultural environment (Hendrick, 1997; Moray, 2000; Rasmussen, 2000). Moray makes this point using Figure 21.2 as an illustration, noting with concern that HF/E has traditionally limited its attention to the innermost layers of the diagram.

The I/O-HF/E Disconnect

Both I/O psychology and HF/E claim commitment to a systems philosophy in which outputs are viewed as a function of human and nonhuman components interacting within an environmental context (Harris, 1994). Both subscribe to the goal of improving system outputs by improving the fit among these major components. However, they have traditionally differed in the scope of their systems focus, and in the dominant strategies for improving the fit. Whereas the HF/E systems model (Figure 21.1) tends to focus on the microlevel represented by the two inner layers in Figure 21.2, I/O psychology subscribes to the more macrolevel, *open-systems* version that encompasses the entire diagram (Katz & Kahn,

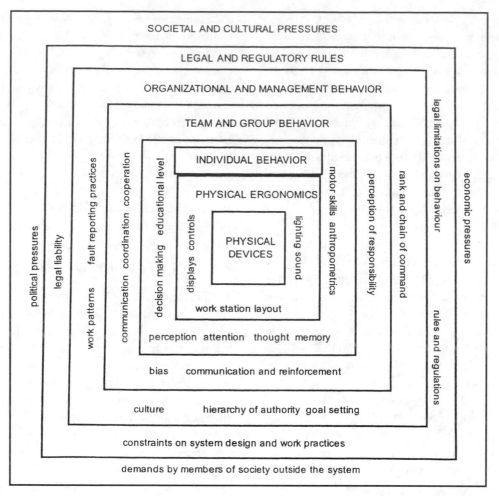

Figure 21.2   Illustration of disciplinary interest domains within the sociotechnical systems model.   *Source:* Moray (2000).

1978). For HF/E, the work organization has traditionally been considered part of the environment—basically, a given; for I/O psychology, it has been a primary focus of attention, with the givens being the outermost (societal) and innermost (technological) layers of the system.

Thus, whereas HF/E's strategies for improving the system have typically stopped at the individual-technology interface (i.e., design), those of I/O psychology have spanned the individual (e.g., selection, placement), team (e.g., team-building, leadership), and organizational (e.g., compensation systems, organizational development) levels. However, I/O psychology has shown little interest in interventions at the technology level (design). The one intervention strategy shared by both fields has been that of training, but even there, the emphasis has been somewhat different: HF/E's interest has been primarily in training *technologies,* especially for skill acquisition and maintenance; that of I/O psychology has been primarily in training *programs* for everything from manual skills to executive management.

As we shall see in a moment, the disconnect between HF/E and I/O psychology has a strong historical and cultural basis but

shows some signs of weakening. The HF/E community has begun to recognize the serious implications of neglecting social and other organizational considerations when designing interfaces, and the I/O psychology community has begun to appreciate how much of an impact technology can have on seemingly unrelated facets of organizational functioning (Harris, 1994; Howard, 1995; B. Schneider & Klein, 1994). Within HF/E, one indication of the growing interest in organizational factors is the emergence of a new specialty that calls itself *macroergonomics* (Hendrick, 1997). A recent survey of those identified with the specialty suggests that its principal focus is on precisely the same topics that have occupied the attention of organizational psychologists and organizational theorists for the last half-century (Kleiner, 2000). Yet the term *macroergonomics* is virtually unknown within either of the latter disciplines, and evidence of cross-fertilization is sparse (Ilgen & Howell, 1999). In the author's view, this is still another illustration of the down side of trying to establish HF/E as a unique discipline rather than strengthening interdisciplinary linkages.

Identification of macroergonomics as a specialty has, however, served to raise the consciousness of the HF/E community to organizational variables and thereby improves the prospects for productive interactions in the future. By contrast, no comparable movement is evident within the institutions of I/O psychology. While technology issues appear frequently in its current literature, there is little indication that I/O psychology has increased its appreciation for HF/E's role—past or future—in addressing them. The present volume, of course, serves as a noteworthy exception, and other encouraging examples may be found in Coovert (1995) and Harris (1994), and in the convergence of HF/E and I/O psychology—along with other fields—on the topics of team training and cooperative work that we will encounter later on.

A Bit of History

Having observed the institutional chasm that separates HF/E and I/O psychology today, it is instructive to note that their heritage includes both shared and very distinct traditions. Space does not allow a full historical account of either field, so we shall focus on illustrative developments that bear directly on their relationship.

Scientific Management and Classical Bureaucracy

Early studies aimed at improving the design of work were carried out by an industrial engineer (Frederick Taylor) and an industrial psychologist and her husband (Lillian and Frank Gilbreth) in the early twentieth century. Both relied heavily on detailed measurements of workers performing manual tasks (so-called *time and motion studies*) and a philosophy known as *scientific management* (Taylor, 1911). The basic idea was to simplify and standardize jobs to improve efficiency, reduce accidents and errors, and minimize the skills required of workers (thereby capitalizing on the large, cheap, unskilled labor force of the day).

This approach complemented nicely the prevailing management philosophy (classical organization theory) in which both workers and machines were regarded as instruments of production whose roles—along with everything else in the organization—were prescribed and controlled by a rational bureaucracy preoccupied with maximizing efficiency. Division of labor, a rigid hierarchy of command, formal rules and procedures, and centralized (top-down) decision making were the key features of this model (Pugh, 1966).

The legacy of *Taylorism* is apparent in both the *job analysis* techniques used by I/O psychologists and the *task analysis* techniques used by HF/E professionals. The irony is that the two analytic threads evolved independently and resulted in very different products. Only now, with the intellectual demands of work taking center stage, are the threads converging: *cognitive task analysis (CTA),* discussed in a later section, constitutes the principal common ground.

Human Relations and Technology Theories

By midcentury, organization and management theorists were beginning to take seriously the importance of human and technological considerations in the design and management of work. Research demonstrated that neglecting the complex array of human needs, motives, and attitudes could undermine the most perfectly conceived organizational design, and ignoring the influence of technology and its associated uncertainties could result in chronically outmoded structures and methods. The resulting *human relations movement* (Pugh, 1966) and *technology theory* (Woodward, 1958) perspectives were instrumental in transforming industrial psychology into industrial/organizational psychology. Its domain was expanded to include motivational, attitudinal, and social considerations along with the traditional personnel ones—for example, job analysis, selection, and training (Katzell & Austin, 1992). The new organizational component developed in close concordance with another emerging field, *organizational behavior.* By contrast, these new organizational perspectives had no apparent impact on the infant field of HF/E, which, although developing around the same time, was preoccupied with efficient and safe design at the production level.

Experimental and Individual-Differences Traditions

The most important historical basis for the institutional chasm that developed between the HF/E (engineering) and I/O specialties within psychology can be traced to competing methodological traditions within psychology itself (Cronbach, 1957). One—the *experimental* tradition—used controlled (usually laboratory) experimentation and hypothesis testing to establish psychological principles representative of the typical individual; the other—the *individual-differences* or *psychometric* tradition—sought to measure (usually with multivariate techniques) how individuals differ on psychologically relevant characteristics in order to predict future behavior patterns. The former was favored by basic researchers; the latter by those with more applied interests, such as industrial selection, educational and career counseling, and clinical assessment. Industrial psychology developed within the individual-differences tradition; engineering psychology, within the experimental tradition.

World War Influences

Applications of psychology to industry preceded WWI but received a substantial boost as a result of its contributions to selection and placement of personnel during that conflict. Comparable applications to system design originated chiefly under the exigencies of WWII. Leading experimental psychologists were teamed with engineers in an effort to identify and correct the causes of aviation accidents and other mishaps that were ultimately traced to poorly *human-engineered* designs (e.g., Fitts & Jones, 1961). This relationship (and philosophy) gravitated to postwar civilian industry, particularly in aviation and other military contractors, and returned with its participants to the halls of academe where HF/E-type programs began appearing in both psychology and engineering departments. Most of the formal HF/E institutions came into being during the late 1950s.

The Present

Several of the noteworthy developments in HF/E since mid-century, including the institutional barriers that have inhibited its fruitful interaction with I/O psychology, have already been discussed. The field has grown, diversified, and become increasingly focused on establishing itself as a unique professional discipline. It has in place most of the formal institutions through which such identification is typically achieved, yet HF/E remains underutilized at a time when the need for what it has to offer could hardly be greater (Nickerson, 1992; Rouse, Kober, & Mavor, 1997). There is no question that technology is driving many facets of society and is doing so at a frightening pace, yet neglect of human implications is as prevalent as ever—a paradox that merits one final comment.

Despite a rather impressive track record, neither the field of HF/E nor its contributions are widely appreciated by the general public, its elected officials, organizational decision-makers, or even the field's own parent disciplines of psychology and engineering. Few are aware that valuable innovations such as the high-mounted rear taillight on automobiles (Malone, 1986) and ergonomically designed computer workstations (Grandjean, Hunting, & Pidermann, 1983) owe their existence directly to HF/E research. The bulk of the contributions in areas such as computer technology, virtual reality, simulation, and complex systems have come about as a result of collaborations among designers, HF/E experts, and professionals from other disciplines.

The net result of this lack of recognition is that HF/E is often called upon as a last resort to diagnose and address human-oriented design flaws after the system is in operation and the damage has already been done (Rouse & Boff, 1997). This was the prevailing atmosphere when the field was born, and despite some progress, it remains the atmosphere today. Moreover, because some of the human-factors solutions appear so intuitive once implemented, the field is often portrayed by its detractors as little more than glorified common sense. What the detractors fail to explain is why society is saddled with so many poorly designed artifacts that obviously conformed to somebody's common sense, and why, when subjected to scientific evaluation, some common-sense solutions turn out to be demonstrably superior to others. The common-sense fallacy has been, and continues to be, responsible for countless preventable inefficiencies, accidents, injuries, and even deaths.

HF/E ROLES, STRATEGIES, AND METHODS

The philosophy and content of HF/E have influenced systems through a number of direct and indirect routes. In this section we will examine a few of the more prominent ones, organized according to four major roles through which these strategies and methods are typically executed: actual design, consulting, public policy (including forensics), and research. Space does not permit the detailed account of specific methodologies; instead, the description is limited to a rather gross characterization of generic approaches, some of which will be revisited in later sections. The interested reader is referred to Salvendy (1997) for a more comprehensive and detailed discussion of methods.

System Design Role

Contrary to the popular notion of design as a highly structured process that proceeds from conceptualization through a series of stages to actual production, the reality is that it is implemented in a wide variety of ways depending on such factors as the nature of the product, the context in which it is used, and tradition. In the relatively young, fast-moving, highly competitive software industry, for instance, the pressure to minimize the lag between innovation and production is intense, so design, test, and evaluation progress more or less together (an approach frequently referred to as *concurrent engineering*), whereas in the more traditional manufacturing industries, the process tends to be more serial. Meister (1987) described the process as a series of overlapping planning, design, testing and evaluation, and production phases, but more recently has characterized it as essentially one of problem solving that incorporates all the elements and idiosyncrasies usually associated with that activity (Meister & Enderwick, 2001).

In the younger industries, HF/E professionals are often included in the design teams that work collaboratively throughout the concurrent-engineering process. Thus the opportunity exists to incorporate human considerations into the design from the outset. By contrast, their role in the more traditional industries is typically limited to the test and evaluation phase, their main contribution being to identify features of already-articulated designs that are likely to pose a problem for the human user. Among the techniques most commonly used for this purpose are *task analyses* of various kinds (Luczak,

1997), and *usability tests* (Nielsen, 1997) aimed at determining how well the proposed system (or the human subsystem) actually performs. In systems involving highly complex tasks such as piloting spacecraft or supervising automated process-control operations, the analyses often include estimates of cognitive requirements such as *mental workload* demands and *human information-processing* requirements. Usability tests typically employ system prototypes or high-fidelity simulations with human operators *in the loop* to determine not only how well the system performs, but also how acceptable it is likely to be to prospective users.

Prototyping and testing, however, are very costly, so system developers have come to rely heavily on modeling techniques in both the design and test phases (Elkind, Card, Hochberg, & Huey, 1989; Laughery & Corker, 1997; Pew & Mavor, 1998). Computer-assisted design (CAD), for example, is now standard practice in architectural, industrial, and systems-development applications, with powerful graphics (and virtual reality—VR—technologies) enabling designers to examine directly and quickly the implications of alternative design features, including total system performance (Harris, 1994). Of course, the accuracy of these projections rests heavily on the adequacy of the component models, and in those systems where an operator is involved, the weakest link is inevitably the *human* model. A number of such models have been developed to simulate human performance in both mechanical (Kroemer, Snook, Meadows, & Deutsch, 1988; Marras, 1997) and cognitive (Eberts, 1997) task domains, but few have been adequately validated. Addressing this deficiency represents an obvious means by which HF/E can exert a positive influence on the initial design as well as the test phase, and work toward that end is beginning to appear (Pew & Mavor, 1998).

Another mechanism through which HF/E considerations are occasionally incorporated in the early phases of design is that of mandates from customers. Procurement of military systems, for example, is guided by military standards documents, some of which specify human-oriented design criteria (e.g., MIL-STD-1472C; Department of Defense, 1981). In addition, each branch of the armed services has developed approaches to design that stress human-machine integration (e.g., the Army's Manpower and Personnel Integration [MANPRINT] program; see Booher, 1988, 1990). When such guidance is followed in preparing procurement documents, it shows up in the form of explicit specifications derived from HF/E research. Unfortunately, it is all too often ignored in preference to hardware, cost, reliability, tradition, and other more conventional considerations.

Influencing design, of course, calls for more than just techniques; it requires a relevant, valid body of knowledge—in the case of HF/E, knowledge of human-performance characteristics derived from a variety of research efforts (see the "Research Role" section, later). There does, in fact, exist a large and growing knowledge base in HF/E, but opinions differ on how useful it is in the forms in which it is usually found—journal articles, handbooks, textbooks, and the like. Some argue that general human-performance principles are difficult to translate into specific design applications because their validity rests heavily on particular systems characteristics (Meister & Enderwick, 2001). According to this view, the emphasis in design applications should shift from reliance on general principles to gathering data in situ using appropriate observational, analytic, and test methods (Rasmussen, 2000; Vicente, 1999; Woods, 1999a). Others believe the problem lies more in translation, and that the emphasis should be directed toward casting the basic knowledge of human performance into a form that designers understand and can more easily use. Boff and Lincoln (1988), for example, pursued this strategy in compiling their massive *Engineering Data Compendium* in the area of human perception.

Consultant Role

Many HF/E professionals, including full-time employees of firms that engage in design, serve as consultants to (rather than direct participants in) the design process. That is, they are called upon to provide HF/E expertise whenever and wherever it is needed rather than as full-fledged members of design teams. The distinction is subtle but important—another illustration of the design community's reluctance to accept HF/E knowledge as integral to design. The majority of today's HF/E professionals are practitioners, according to a recent survey, and 23% of those responding are employed exclusively as consultants—whether self-employed or as employees of consulting firms (Hendrick, 1996). Typically, their services are rendered through contracts with industrial or government customers that are limited in function and scope, but run the gamut from research projects to the test and evaluation phase of system design.

Some HF/E consultants influence design indirectly as safety experts, working in domains such as hazard analysis, accident investigation, personal injury litigation, and the promulgation of design standards and regulations. For convenience these related functions are combined here under the heading of *policy*.

Policy Role

The traditional way HF/E professionals seek to influence design involves convincing industry that human-oriented design has practical merit (Rouse & Boff, 1997; Rouse et al., 1997). However, frustration over industry's general reluctance to embrace this philosophy—and when it has, to do so without drawing upon the available body of HF/E knowledge—has led the field to pursue other strategies (Woods, 1999b).

Litigation

One such strategy that has been growing rapidly over the past several decades and has clearly had an impact on both system design and public awareness of the field involves the justice system—in particular, bringing HF/E content and methods to bear on the adjudication of product liability, workplace injury, and other civil (and occasionally, even criminal) actions. Trial lawyers have discovered that HF/E professionals and the body of knowledge they represent can be extremely useful in both building and defending cases against manufacturers, distributors, retailers, and employers for damages (including injury and death) sustained by plaintiffs in the use of consumer products or in places of work and commerce. As most people know, such litigation has reached astounding proportions in the United States. Thus HF/E has found its way into the legal process through the testimony of expert witnesses. In 1980, it was estimated that there were some 600 HF/E professionals engaged in this type of work (Sanders & McCormick, 1993), but their number and frequency of appearance in litigation has undoubtedly increased substantially since then.

As a result, manufacturers and other potential defendants have been forced to recognize the human implications of design, and to make greater use of HF/E principles. They have been obliged to answer for failure to conduct systematic hazard analyses of work sites, for example, and for failure to guard or warn adequately against foreseeable misuse of their products by consumers. Since a considerable amount of information on both now exists in the HF/E literature (Laughery & Wogalter, 1997; Rogers, Lamson, & Rousseau, 2000), industries that ignore it do so at great risk; and over the years, a substantial amount of case law has accumulated, making that risk even higher.

While unquestionably influential, HF/E's involvement in the litigation arena is not without its drawbacks. All too frequently opinions rendered by self-proclaimed HF/E experts are based more on the hiring attorney's theory than on solid scientific evidence, and in many instances, involve issues that may not legitimately call for HF/E expertise at all. When HF/E experts are hired by both sides in a dispute and render directly conflicting testimony, the impression is conveyed that the factual basis on which the field rests is suspect. Furthermore, some industries have come to view the HF/E discipline as an enemy rather than a partner in pursuit of the mutually beneficial goal of safer products and work environments. Finally, design changes forced by litigation are not always consistent with the goal of improving safety. The 20-plus warning messages that appear in an inconspicuous place on all metal ladders sold today, for instance, have far more to do with avoiding litigation than with protecting users. In sum, one can only hope that the positive impact of litigation based on HF/E considerations will outweigh the negative over the long run, for the good of both the field and society.

Statutes, Regulations, and Professional Standards

Whereas influencing design-related policy through the courts is indirect and idiosyncratic, other means to this end are more direct and explicit. Legislative bodies can mandate design requirements directly through statutes or, more often, by authorizing agencies such as the Occupational Safety and Health Administration (OSHA), the Nuclear Regulatory Commission (NRC), the Federal Aviation Administration (FAA), and the Food and Drug Administration (FDA) to promulgate regulations that have the force of law. Following investigation of the highly publicized accident at the Three Mile Island nuclear power plant, for example, HF/E considerations were incorporated into the design regulations adopted by the NRC (U.S. Nuclear Regulatory Commission, 1983).

More recently, OSHA promulgated a set of ergonomic standards to address the costly problem of work-related musculoskeletal injuries. It has been estimated that lower back injuries alone cost society between $25–95 billion annually, and this type of trauma represents only about 22% of the total for which workers' compensation claims are filed (Marras, 1997). The intent of the standards was to reduce the incidence and severity of these injuries through incorporation of ergonomic principles in the design of physical tasks. Over strong resistance by the trucking industry and other affected employers, the standards were adopted in the waning days of the Clinton administration, only to be rescinded through a parliamentary maneuver spearheaded by the incoming Bush administration.

The point of this illustration is that scientific evidence alone, no matter how strong, is rarely sufficient to bring about positive design changes when financial and political interests are at stake—as they were, at the extreme, in this case. Not only did the initiative fail, it generated a strong backlash against the whole HF/E field. Despite positive reviews by the nation's most trusted institutions for evaluating research (the National Research Council and Institute of Medicine, 2001), policymakers and the media were quick to dismiss HF/E evidence as *pseudoscience* or *voodoo science*. Maintaining an apolitical position while effectively *informing* policy, therefore, is becoming an almost impossible feat, leading some in the field to advocate a more proactive stance—instead of merely presenting the facts, *promoting* them vigorously in the public policy arena (Fischhoff, 1996; Woods, 1999b).

Enlightened industries, along with those hoping merely to forestall government regulation, often develop evidence-based standards of their own, and HF/E has been an active participant in the self-regulation process for some years. The American National Standards Institute (ANSI) and the International Standards Organization (ISO) are the foremost organizations through which this process is executed. ANSI and ISO standards now provide HF/E guidance in a number of design areas, including computer workstations (ANSI, 1988) and hazard warnings (ANSI, 1998). In those areas where industry standards exist, they have a profound impact on design, since the process is heavily supported—both technically and financially—by the industries themselves, and the standards carry considerable weight in litigation.

In sum, HF/E can have a significant impact on systems by ensuring that its knowledge base is included in the rules—statutes, regulations, standards—that govern the design process in specific industries. Although it has made progress in this regard, its contribution to date is limited to a relatively small segment of the industrial population. Part of the reason is its fairly recent entry into the policy arena, part is due to the problem of overcoming popular misconceptions, and part involves limitations in the HF/E database itself—a situation that can be addressed only through sustained research. Hence we turn our attention to the last HF/E role.

Research Role

The proportion of HF/E professionals engaged primarily in teaching and research is approximately the same as that for I/O psychologists and psychologists in general: about one-third (Hendrick, 1996). Such figures, however, are somewhat misleading in that they depend on how one defines *research* and whom one considers an HF/E professional. If activities such as usability testing, accident or task analysis, and case studies are included, the proportion undoubtedly includes a majority of the field; if scientists whose work on basic human-performance functions (such as sensory, perceptual, and cognitive processes) are included, the proportion is even larger. For present purposes, we will limit discussion of the research role to activities performed by those explicitly trained as HF/E professionals.

Most graduate-level HF/E programs include training in the conventional methods used in psychological research (e.g., experimental, quasi-experimental, and multivariate designs), along with at least the rudiments of psychophysical and psychometric measurement. Most also include techniques (e.g., modeling, simulation) drawn from the engineering and design

fields and various analytic methods (e.g., workload, reliability, hazard, and accident/error/failure). Thus it is fair to say that HF/E, like I/O psychology, equips its professionals with a rather wide array of research tools even though most do not become active scientists in the sense of contributing to the archival literature. However, a survey of HF/E specialists indicates that many of them rely on one or another of these techniques in the course of performing their design or test and evaluation functions (Rhodenizer et al., 1999b; VanCott & Huey, 1992).

As noted earlier, the expanding scope of HF/E applications and diversity of participating disciplines has led to growing debate over which research techniques and what sorts of data should have priority in the field. There is little doubt that the preponderance of original research appearing in the leading journals still employs experimental or quasi-experimental methods and is carried out in laboratory settings. Thus, it maximizes scientific rigor at the expense of demonstrated *external validity,* and leads to broad (often theory-based) generalizations rather than data that can be directly applied. The traditional view is that only through principles based on research of this kind can the field progress, although as previously noted, some means of translation is required.

Equally obvious is the fact that the amount of research being conducted in the field to address specific design issues—often at the expense of reliability and generalizability of findings to similar issues in other contexts—is growing dramatically. Such work employs methods as varied as focus groups, surveys, knowledge-elicitation techniques, controlled observation, and model comparison, along with adaptations of traditional experimental designs (see, e.g., Suri, 2000—a case study that used observation, task analysis, brainstorming, simulation, and test in the design of a portable defibrillator). It tends to be atheoretical, descriptive, and ad hoc. When findings are reported at all, it is usually through technical reports, conferences, or trade magazines rather than archival journals, but frequently the data are considered proprietary and are not disseminated. When statistical tests are performed, practical rather than conventional significance criteria are commonly used. Those engaged in such research argue that it offers the most effective way to get human considerations into the design process. They believe traditional research has its place, but is incapable of keeping pace with today's rapidly moving design requirements.

One final consideration in this debate is the fact that as the complexity of systems and the human role in them have increased, the gap between what can meaningfully be addressed in the laboratory and what exists in the field has widened. Context becomes critical, and even the most sophisticated laboratory simulations and complex experimental designs fail to capture all the relevant variables and interactions that characterize the actual system. This dilemma has led a growing number of HF/E researchers to seek alternatives to the dichotomy between laboratory experimentation and idiosyncratic field studies. One such alternative, the so-called *ecological approach,* will be revisited in a later section. While taking various forms, its distinguishing features include (a) gathering data in the field using structured observations and trained observers, (b) extracting nonobservable task and performance information from subject matter experts (SMEs), (c) developing models or design alternatives and meaningful criterion measures, (d) evaluating the alternatives in context using these criteria, and (e) expressing findings in ways that permit accumulation of knowledge and evolving generalization. In short, the ecological approach regards field settings as *natural laboratories* (Hoffman & Woods, 2000b).

HF/E SETTINGS AND CONTENT DOMAINS

The last comprehensive survey of HF/E utilization was published a decade ago (VanCott & Huey, 1992), although a limited follow-up conducted in 1998 revealed some interesting trends in the types of work HF/E professionals are performing and the topic areas they find most relevant (Rhodenizer et al., 1999a, 1999b). As noted earlier, the breadth of topics appearing in the HF/E literature has expanded, and some of the newer topics—such as computer-supported cooperative work (CSCW), situation awareness (SA), naturalistic decision making (NDM), and cognitive task analysis (CTA)—have replaced more traditional ones such as mental workload measurement, vigilance and signal detection, stimulus (S)-response (R) compatibility, and perceptual-motor skills in popularity. This section begins with an overview of both the settings where HF/E is practiced and the topics of major interest, followed by selected illustrations from the matrix of settings and topics. No attempt is made to represent the entire domain; rather, the selection is biased in favor of topics on which current activity is on the increase and relevance for I/O psychology is clear.

Application Settings

According to the 1992 NRC survey (VanCott & Huey, 1992), 60% of the HF/E professionals work in one of three major settings: computers, aerospace, or industrial processes. Another 25% are almost equally distributed among health and safety, communications, and other transportation settings, while only about 5% are found in the energy, consumer products, and office products industries. Despite the field's historic link

TABLE 21.1   Comparative Frequencies of Tasks Performed by HF/E Professionals, 1989–1999

Task	1989 (%)	1998 (%)
Designing software-user interfaces	48.0	64.7
Performing safety analyses	31.0	44.0
Assessing performance risks	27.0	45.7
Performing human-reliability analyses	22.0	37.6
Preparing product warnings	18.0	27.5
Supporting product liability	11.0	22.0
Collecting and analyzing accident and error data	39.0	50.3
Conducting training	37.0	58.7
Developing training content	35.0	66.7
Designing simulation systems	24.0	55.9

Source: Rhodenizer, Bowers, Pharmer, & Gerber (1999).

with the military, the vast majority (74%) are now employed in the private sector, with only 15% working for any branch of the government. Of course, some private-sector employers are heavily involved in military contract work (e.g., most of those working in aerospace spend more than half their time on military applications, compared to only about 10% of those working in computers and communications, and far fewer in the each of the other identified settings).

The 1998 follow-up survey shows little change in this general employment pattern, although it reveals some marked shifts in the kinds of activities performed. As shown in Table 21.1, dramatic increases have occurred in software interface design; training-related activities; safety, reliability, and risk analyses; and activities bearing on consumer protection and litigation—warnings, product liability, and the like (Rhodenizer et al., 1999a).

The profile of activities and roles performed by HF/E professionals also varies considerably with the work setting. For example, those working in the industrial processes setting are much more likely to be engaged in tasks such as measuring physical workload and performing safety analyses than are those working in areospace, where assessing mental workload, conducting research, and interpreting test and evaluation results are more common. Some functions, such as analyzing tasks and applying human-factors principles, are fairly common across settings. The complete picture of these activity profiles is far too complex to present here, but can be found in VanCott and Huey (1992). Keeping in mind this general overview of where and how HF/E knowledge is applied, we move now to an examination of the knowledge itself: the content of the field.

Content Domains

It is very difficult to do justice in a simple taxonomy to the content of any field, particularly one as diverse as HF/E. The fairly broad categories shown in Table 21.2 have been used for several years by the journal *Human Factors* to classify its

TABLE 21.2   Classification Currently Used by the Journal *Human Factors* to Cluster HF/E Topics

Classification	Associated Topics
Accidents, safety, human error	Pilot, crew behavior.
	Systems design features.
Aging	
Attentional processes	Automatic and controlled processsing.
	Dual-task performance.
	Mental workload.
	Multiple recources.
	Situation awareness.
	Vigilance, monitoring.
Automation, expert systems	Expert-novice differences.
	Function allocation.
	Knowledge elicitation.
	Mode awareness.
Biomechanics, anthropometry, work physiology	Interventions.
	Models and measures.
	Physical work, loading.
Cognitive processes	Decision making, naturalistic decision making.
	Knowledge representation.
	Language.
	Learning, memory.
	Mental models.
	Problem solving, reasoning.
Communication systems	Macrodesign features (networks, Web, conferencing, etc.).
	Microdesign features (coding, media, etc.).
Computer systems	Graphics.
	Groupware.
	Human-computer interaction.
	Interface evaluation, usability.
	Menus.
Consumer products, tools	
Displays and controls	Auditory displays.
	Display-control compatibility.
	Haptic and other displays.
	Keyboards.
	Speech production and recognition.
	Trackballs, mice, joysticks, other output devices.
	Visual, pictorial, object displays.
Health and medical systems	
Individual differences	
Macroergonomics and the environment	Ambient conditions.
	Organizational behavior and design.
Manufacturing, process-control systems	Operations research.
	Reliability issues.
	Robotics.
	Scheduling.
Psychological states	Boredom, monotony.
	Effort and motivation.
	Fatigue.
	Induced states (e.g., alcohol, drugs, sleep deprivation).
	Stress.
Psychomotor processes	Eye movement, tracking.
	Reaction time.
	Skills (development, maintenance).
Sensory and perceptual processes	Audition.
	Detection.
	Haptics and other senses.
	Recognition.
	Search.
	Vision.
Simulation and virtual reality	
Surface transportation systems	Driver behavior.
	Highway and vehicle design.
	Maritime issues.
Training, education, instructional systems	Embedded, cross-, and team training.
	Training technologies.
Miscellaneous	

content and, although they are by no means standard, constitute a useful framework for present purposes. One common distinction they fail to make is between material that focuses primarily on the *human* (e.g., sensory/perceptual, cognitive, biomechanical, and social processes) and that which is oriented more toward the *system* (e.g., component and overall systems analyses, design principles, modeling, HCI). Another is between *principles* (or the body of knowledge per se) and *methods* for acquiring and applying that knowledge. The topics selected for further examination cut across all four of these content categories.

SELECTED ILLUSTRATIONS

Attentional Processes: Concepts and Techniques

It is common knowledge that most tasks humans perform require some level of attention, and when it is insufficient or misdirected, the chances of errors and accidents increase. What is far less obvious is exactly how the mental processes governing attention operate, how they relate to the characteristics of the tasks to which attention must be applied, and most importantly, how an understanding of these functions can be used to advantage in systems design. Few psychological constructs have stimulated more sustained interest among HF/E researchers and practitioners than those involving attention, so the remainder of this section will touch upon all six of the attentional-process topics listed in Table 21.2.

Before proceeding, however, it is important to recognize that the dominant theoretical paradigm that has guided research in this and related areas for a half-century is the conceptualization of the human as an *information-processing system*. As illustrated in simplified form in Figure 21.3, this model identifies the structures (e.g., memory stores) and processes (e.g., perception, decision) believed to underlie human cognition and action, along with the functional relationships among them. Attention influences all the cognitive processes. Both the general framework depicted here and the more detailed textbook versions are supported by a vast literature in cognitive psychology and cognitive science that is derived largely from controlled laboratory experimentation. Some generalizations from this work have been validated externally, both through field research and useful applications, but many have not—a situation that has led to growing dissatisfaction within the HF/E research community over the field's heavy reliance on this model and on the cognitivist approach to studying systems that it features. As we saw earlier and will encounter again, the call for a totally different (ecological) approach is a fairly recent development that seems to be gaining momentum.

Vigilance and Monitoring

HF/E's interest in attentional issues is as old as the field itself. *Human engineers* became engaged in this topic during WWII when they discovered that operators of the crude radar systems of that era tended to miss rare (but critical) signals, and to do so more frequently as their watch progressed—and, presumably, their attention waned. This phenomenon, which became known as the *vigilance decrement,* was brought into the laboratory for study in the hope of finding ways to mitigate it (Mackworth, 1948), and in fact a number of strategies were conceived—most derived from prevailing theories of attention (Parasuraman, Warm, & Dember, 1987).

However, the vigilance decrement was but one of a host of practical problems involving the extraction of information from displays with which early HF/E professionals were

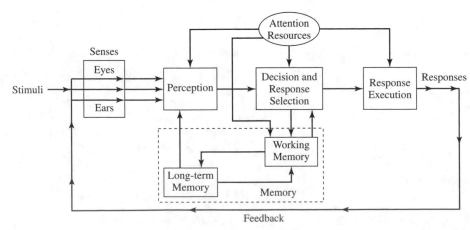

Figure 21.3   A greatly simplified model of human information-processing structures and processes. *Source:* Wickens & Carswell (1997).

concerned. Others included the problem of distinguishing auditory signals from noise (or other concurrent signals), and that of requiring operators to perform more than one task at once (as was increasingly the case in advanced systems). Attention seemed to play a role in all these problems, but so too did other psychological processes. Hence the collective research on such issues led to a number of important generalizations and theories of human information processing from which current conceptualizations of the attentional process evolved.

Signal Detection

One of these, the *theory of signal dectability (TSD),* dealt with the generic problem of extracting relevant signals from irrelevant ones (i.e., the noise problem), and has become a standard technique for analyzing human performance on such tasks (Wickens, 1992). In the TSD model, signal detection is composed of two distinct components: one purely sensory, the other, cognitive (an implicit decision criterion that an observer sets in classifying an observation as *signal* or *noise*). Since the TSD model provides a means of estimating both parameters for any detection task, it has enabled investigators to establish empirically which variables affect which human processes and to design interventions accordingly. Vigilance performance, for example, which does not always decline over time, appears to involve both sensitivity and decision functions, but in different proportions depending on other task characteristics (Balakrishman, 1998; Parasuraman et al., 1987). Therefore, the tendency to miss signals might be addressed in one case through training and incentives (which would affect the observer's *decision* criterion), and in another by highlighting or color-coding relevant signals (which would affect the *sensitivity* function).

Attention is not explicitly featured in TSD, but the distinction between the decision and sensitivity functions implies a fundamental principle: the fact that attention is controlled by both *external* factors (e.g., stimulus characteristics, such as highlighting, that attract attention) and *internal* factors (e.g., expectancies and motives that affect attention-allocation decisions). This distinction between stimulus-driven (or *bottom-up*) and observer-driven (or *top-down*) control of attention is one of several core concepts that underlie current theories of attention. Others include the distinction between *focused* and *selective* modes of attention (the former being more stimulus driven than the latter); representation of attention as a *searchlight* that illuminates focal stimuli more completely than peripheral stimuli or as a finite *mental resource* that the observer allocates in processing stimulus information; and the conceptualization of attention as a skill or an ability (Wickens, 1992).

Resource Theories and Divided Attention

Space does not permit examination of all the current variations on these themes or their implications, but one—the *mental resource* notion—does merit further elaboration by virtue of the research and applications it has generated. The basic idea is that humans have a limited supply of processing capacity that can be allocated differentially to available tasks (whether through top-down or bottom-up modes); hence investing more capacity in one mental activity leaves less for others. Focusing attention on a map or a cell-phone conversation while one is driving, for example, would deplete the amount available for recognizing an impending accident.

Some versions of this theory suggest a single resource pool whereas others posit multiple pools, each with its own properties and capacity limits (Kahneman, 1973; Navon & Gopher, 1979). Tasks will interfere with each other to the extent that they draw on a common pool. Thus if the cell-phone conversation does not require the same resources as watching the road—or if there is plenty of capacity to accommodate both tasks—the two could be performed concurrently with no decrement in either. If the two tasks share resources, however, one or the other is likely to suffer (e.g., Dingus, Antin, Hulse, & Wierwille, 1989).

Although by no means universally accepted, the multiple-resource model has received considerable support in the literature, and has led to some important practical developments. One is a methodology for predicting the extent to which alternative display or task designs are likely to pose attentional (and hence performance) problems, thereby enabling designers to make sound decisions early in the planning process. Another is a technique known as the *dual-task paradigm,* which has proven useful in measuring the mental workload associated with various tasks (Damos, 1991). We will return to the topic of workload measurement in a moment, but before leaving the discussion of resource theory one final construct should be mentioned: *automaticity* (W. Schneider & Shiffrin, 1977).

Automatic and controlled processing. Many tasks can be trained to a high enough skill level that they can be performed without any apparent mental effort or even sustained awareness of the activity—and when developed to that level, have little apparent impact on other tasks performed concurrently. The routine aspects of driving an automobile constitute a familiar example. Such overlearned skills are seen to involve a kind of processing (*automatic* processing) that draws minimally on attentional resources, in contrast with another kind—*controlled* processing—that is resource intensive. While thus consistent in some respects with resource theory, automaticity theory is unique in its practical implications and emphasis. Basically, it seeks to identify those task characteristics that are most amenable to automaticity training, and those training procedures that are most effective in producing automaticity, rather than focusing on the inherent attentional demands of tasks. The more routine functions that can be *automated* through such training, the more capacity remains for performing nonroutine (often crucial) system functions such as fault detection, planning, and decision making. Many of today's advanced systems place a heavy cognitive burden on the human operator, so any potential means of freeing-up processing capacity would likely enhance system performance. However, in order to address such problems through design, training, selection, or other means—or to evaluate specific interventions—it is necessary to measure the core attentional constructs. The constructs of *mental workload* and *situation awareness* have proven particularly fruitful in this regard, so we will consider each in turn.

Mental workload. Interest in the mental workload construct—derived mainly from resource theory—grew out of the realization that technologically advanced systems that supposedly were making the operator's task easier (and hence were making system performance less subject to *human error*) were having just the opposite effect. While off-loading much of the routine work to sophisticated software, such designs often increased the scope and responsibility of the human's role, thereby making the task more demanding while increasing the potential seriousness of errors (Moray, 1982). Hence the demand for ways to measure this unobservable cognitive burden grew, and the resulting research has produced both a variety of useful measurement techniques and a clearer picture of the mental workload construct.

Four principal approaches have emerged—subjective, psychophysiological, performance-based, and analytic—each offering a variety of measurement techniques (Tsang & Wilson, 1997; Wickens, 1992). The two leading subjective instruments, the Subjective Workload Assessment Technique (SWAT) and the National Aeronautics and Space Administration Task Loading Index (NASA TLX), both consist of dimensional rating scales that operators complete immediately after performing a task or a task component. Others involve comparative judgments, retrospective judgments, and unidimensional ratings. All these instruments have been evaluated in the laboratory and the field, and have demonstrated reasonable psychometric propertics as well as sensitivity to various task-demand manipulations. They are far and away the most frequently used techniques for measuring workload demands of existing systems and for estimating those associated with designs under development—in part, because they are easy to use and preferred by the ultimate users.

The principal psychophysiological measures include heart rate, brain activity (especially certain electroencephalograph components and evoked potentials), and blink-rate recordings, all of which have also proven sensitive to task manipulations. Although having the advantage of tracking the operator's workload in real time, these techniques present a number of implementation problems that to date have limited their use primarily to the laboratory. However, technological improvements in instrumentation are rapidly overcoming these limitations (especially that of cumbersome recording devices), and such measures promise to see much wider application in the future.

Neither the performance-based nor the analytic approach has had much direct impact on systems design to this point. Performance-based methods derive from resource theory and the dual-task paradigm introduced earlier: Workload demand for the task of interest is estimated from the measured interference that results when the operator is required to perform a second (reference) task concurrently. This general approach has proven useful for laboratory exploration of theoretical issues such as the interference patterns predicted from multiple-resource theory, and theoretical knowledge of this sort has obvious long-range implications for design. However, the fact that it requires rigorous experimentation limits its usefulness in direct application. The analytic approach, on the other hand, has considerable application potential—especially in early design phases—but is still in its infancy (Tsang & Wilson, 1997). Basically, it relies on task analyses and modeling techniques that are beyond the scope of this chapter.

Research on mental workload measurement has slowed in recent years, in large part because it has generated useful tools that have already made the transition from the laboratory to the field (Howell, 1993; Tsang & Wilson, 1997). Estimates of workload demands are now commonplace among the requirements specified in the development of complex systems—especially military systems. By contrast, these tools have been largely ignored by I/O psychologists who express concern over the changing nature of work (Howard, 1995), and the fact that they are in wide use in some contexts does not imply that the book on mental workload is closed. Much remains to be learned about their theoretical underpinnings and the implications of this knowledge for improved measurement. For one thing, the empirical evidence reveals that the various approaches do not correlate highly, indicating that mental workload is either a multidimensional construct or multiple constructs—either way, no single measure captures the total loading picture (B. H. Kantowitz, 1992). For another thing, the practical potential of techniques capable of predicting the more complex interactive effects among concurrent tasks or their underlying constructs has yet to be fully exploited. Development of such techniques awaits a deeper understanding of the underlying cognitive mechanisms.

Situation awareness. Closely related to, but conceptually and operationally distinguishable from, mental workload is the topic of *situation awareness* (or *SA*), essentially the extent to which an operator is able to keep track of, interpret, and deal with large amounts of information on an ongoing basis. A conceptual model illustrating the nature and role of this construct in complex task performance is shown in Figure 21.4. A combat pilot, for example, must maintain a sense of his position relative to the enemy and the outside world; the status of his own aircraft, imminent threats, and his offensive and defensive capabilities for dealing with them; and various tactical options while flying the aircraft—all under rapidly changing conditions. Clearly, mission success in this or any other complex, dynamic task environment requires appropriate and timely decisions which, in turn, require maintaining a grasp of the total situation. Mental workload is one of many factors that would affect SA.

The consensus of those who function in such complex environments is that the condition of maintaining or losing that mental grasp is a unique subjective reality; hence the term *situation awareness* was in common use long before the late 1980s, when it began attracting serious interest among HF/E

scientists (in part, because *loss of SA* was listed as the official cause of the vast majority of military aviation mishaps). If, it was reasoned, this construct could be uniquely identified and measured, all the traditional human-resource strategies—selection, training, and systems design—might be used to enhance it. So during the decade of the 1990s, SA replaced mental workload as the dominant focus of applied research on attention, with studies conducted in a wide variety of operational settings (Gilson, 1995).

While not without controversy—some believe that SA demonstrates no unique properties that cannot be accommodated by other well-established constructs (Flach, 1995), and others simply feel that SA needs more rigorous definition (Sarter & Woods, 1991)—this work has shed considerable light on the phenomenon (Endsley, 1995a). It has also produced measurement techniques that, like their mental-workload counterparts, have proven useful for evaluating systems design and, to a lesser extent, for training and selection applications (Endsley, 1995b; Howell, 1993; Pew & Mavor, 1998). The most widely used measurement approach, the Situation Awareness Global Assessment Technique (SAGAT), requires operators to respond to carefully designed memory probes inserted throughout the course of a complex task. By this means, it is possible to track over time the individual's understanding of

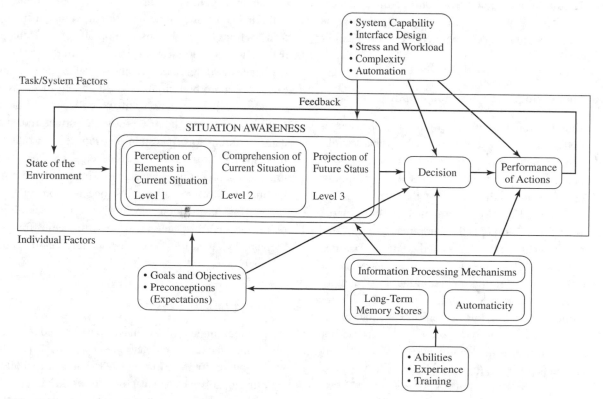

Figure 21.4 A model of situation awareness represented within the framework of the traditional (cognitivist) human information-processing model. *Source:* Endsley (1995a).

what he or she has observed and what it means. Although SAGAT suffers from limitations such as the cueing potential of the memory probes and the disruptive effect of interrupting the task to obtain them, alternative approaches—surrogate behavioral measures and subjective measures—have limitations of their own, and from a face-validity and acceptance standpoint, SAGAT has proven superior.

In concluding this sampling from the attentional-process content, it should be pointed out that more space is accorded these topics than the remaining ones because the former play a role in most of the latter, they are deeply rooted in psychology, they illustrate mature techniques that are being applied in a variety of settings, and for the most part, they represent the cognitivist tradition.

They are also relevant to the work demands posed by systems of the future. As noted before, technology drives systems development, including the macrosystems that comprise the workplace, with human implications an afterthought. Much of the capability that technology provides in terms of physical and computational power, bandwidth, mobility, intelligence, and so forth winds up imposing new, often greater, net demands on human mental performance. Therefore, understanding constructs such as mental capacity, workload, and SA, and developing practical and valid ways to measure them, can only become more critical as advances continue—indeed, HF/E professionals rated *workload* among the most salient of the 52 topics listed in a recent survey, well above its standing in a comparable survey conducted a decade earlier (Rhodenizer et al., 1999b).

Cognitive Engineering: Processes and Applications

As noted earlier, CE (also known as cognitive systems engineering, or CSE) has become a highly visible, interdisciplinary content area that either overlaps with, or is encompassed by, HF/E depending on one's point of view. Good illustrations could be drawn from any of the topics listed under "Cognitive processes" in Table 21.2, along with most of those under "Automation, expert systems" and "Computer systems," and some that appear under the "Displays and controls" heading. Although Vicente (1999) defines CE in a way that would be difficult to differentiate from organization theory—"a multidisciplinary area of research that is concerned with the analysis, design, and evaluation of complex sociotechnical systems" (p. 5)—most of the work seems to be focused on melding human and machine intelligence to maximum advantage in systems that are highly complex and heavily automated. Flach's (1998) definition of CE describes it as "application and design integration of information technology to facilitate work" (p. 3). Thus there is heavy emphasis on

topics such as techniques for capturing and modeling domain expertise (e.g., knowledge elicitation, mental models); describing and understanding the mental operations that underlie individual performance in complex systems, including problem-solving and decision-making functions (e.g., CTA); and articulating the additional facets of these intellectual operations that come into play when teams of operators function collaboratively (e.g., team SA, shared mental models, team decision making). Superimposed on these topic areas are those involving computer applications (e.g., function allocation, decision aiding, CSCW). For present purposes, our sampling will be limited to illustrations drawn primarily from the CTA, knowledge-elicitation, NDM, and CSCW areas, although it should be noted that virtually all topics in CE are interrelated.

Task Analysis

Since the days of Taylorism, *task analysis* has played a central role in human-oriented design efforts. Basically, it involves a detailed decomposition of functions or roles (e.g., laying bricks, controlling air traffic, making command decisions) into component tasks and subtasks, specification of the demands associated with each, and representation of the logical and temporal relationships among them in some sort of graphic, tabular, or diagrammatic form (Luczak, 1997). Techniques for gathering and compiling this information take many different forms—from the crude, observation-and-stopwatch approach that Taylor used, to methods derived from theories of human performance (e.g., biomechanical and cognitive models). Some use more bottom-up or unstructured methods, hoping to induce generalizations from the collection of descriptive material; others are more top-down or structured, gathering data according to a preestablished conceptualization of the fundamental operations involved (e.g., theories of human information processing, decision making, or problem solving). Ultimately, however, all rely on one or more of four basic sources of information: documentation, observation, self-report, and performance measures—the same four sources, incidentally, that I/O psychologists rely on in conducting job analyses.

Cognitive Task Analysis (CTA)

As the predominant work demands have shifted from the physical to the mental, the emphasis in task analysis has shifted to the cognitive domain (Flach, 1998; This shift should not be overstated, however, since physical work has certainly not vanished, and the demands imposed by tasks such as materials handling and repetitive motion have serious consequences.

Advances in analytic techniques and biomechanical models have kept pace with those in the cognitive domain; Marras, 1997). Because mental operations are not as accessible to direct observation and measurement as physical ones, it has become necessary to adapt analysis to this new challenge, and the result has been a spate of variations on traditional themes, referred to collectively as CTA methods. Most rely heavily on subject matter experts (SMEs) in either the data-gathering or interpretation phases of the analysis, and also on the self-report of operators performing the task. Consider the following hypothetical example.

An operator is required to think aloud, so to speak, while functioning as a combat information officer aboard a cruiser engaged in an air defense exercise, describing in real time the thought processes leading to each threat assessment, decision, and action. These verbal protocols are recorded along with objective data describing the unfolding scenario, and both sets of records are subsequently reviewed in detail by an SME (or perhaps two, if a reliability estimate is desired). The SME analyzes the records on the basis of either a checklist of predetermined cognitive elements (task-specific or generic) or his or her personal knowledge (e.g., identification of critical events), and the resulting data are organized in a manner consistent with the purposes of the analysis (e.g., design of automated decision aids or improved displays; identification of flaws or biases in the operator's assessment of information for consideration in the design of training curricula).

Verbal protocol analysis and performance records, of course, are not the only techniques used to infer the cognitive elements involved in complex tasks of this sort. Survey instruments, questionnaires, and guided debriefing exercises are also in common use. One verbal protocol approach involves a structured dialogue between two SMEs that is focused on carefully selected problem-solving tasks. Although extremely labor intensive, this technique has proven useful in analyzing ill-defined, poorly structured problems (Hall, Gott, & Pokorny, 1995).

Cognitivist Versus Ecological Perspectives

This fundamental methodological distinction, touched upon in earlier sections, becomes particularly relevant in the context of CTA. As Vicente (1999) explains, the *normative cognitivist approach* is oriented chiefly toward identifying the human information-processing constraints (e.g., limited mental resources; decision biases; reaction times; storage limits, etc.) that must be dealt with in order for the system to achieve its goals. The mainly descriptive *ecological approach,* on the other hand, focuses on understanding the environmental constraints or context—the physical and social realities—facing

the system that must be taken into account in seeking to optimize the system's performance and the human's role in it.

Traditional CTA techniques like the attentional ones presented earlier derive from cognitivist thinking: They use information-processing models from cognitive psychology as a top-down framework for analysis. For example, the *goals-operators-methods-selection rules* (or *GOMS*) *model* (see Figure 21.5, panel A), which is used widely in the design of human-computer interfaces and describes cognitive tasks in terms of production rules, grew out of the influential work by Newell and Simon (1972) on human problem solving (Eberts, 1997).

By contrast, the ecological approach is more bottom-up, observing the situation systematically in the field with whatever means are most conducive to accurate description—often verbal protocols—and constructing a representation of the work domain. Figure 21.5, panel B illustrates one such representation (for electronics problem-solving) that was derived from verbal reports organized within a generic (*abstraction-decomposition*) framework developed by Rasmussen (1986). In the ecological view the distinctions among research, systems analysis, and design become quite blurred: The common goal of understanding cognitive processes in context encompasses all three. A number of excellent examples of the ecological approach are provided in Rasmussen, Pejtersen, and Goodstein (1994), Vicente (1999), and a special section of *Human Factors* (Hoffman & Woods, 2000a). One direct outgrowth of this work is the concept of an *ecological interface,* which has been attracting considerable attention among those concerned with the design of displays for supervisory control tasks (Burns, 2000; Czaja, 1997). Basically, it involves organizing and presenting information to operators in a manner consistent with their normal mode of interpreting such information (i.e., their cognitive representation of how the system functions).

The ecological philosophy, then, is a thread that connects a number of topic areas in which CTA is implicated, including our final three illustrations: knowledge elicitation, NDM, and CSCW (Hoffman & Woods, 2000b).

Knowledge Elicitation

As we have just seen, ecological analysis and description of intellectually demanding tasks requires extracting key information (declarative and procedural knowledge) from recognized SMEs, including experienced operators. The end product, a representation of the SMEs' conceptualizations of the task, is typically referred to as a *mental model.* Sometimes such information is also gathered from novices, and the expert-novice comparison serves as a basis for identifying qualitative differences for use in articulating the properties of

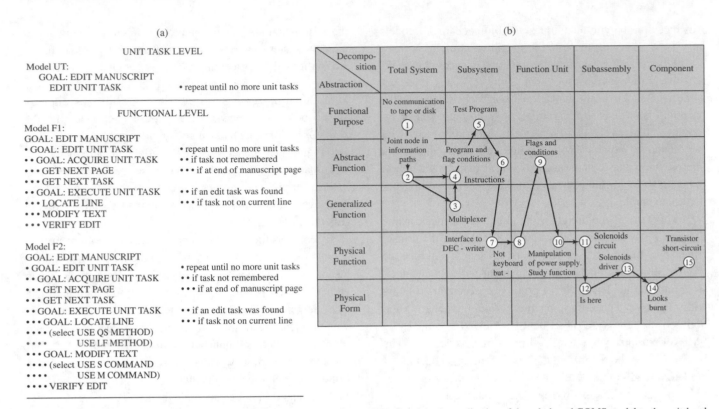

(a)

UNIT TASK LEVEL

Model UT:
    GOAL: EDIT MANUSCRIPT
        EDIT UNIT TASK   • repeat until no more unit tasks

FUNCTIONAL LEVEL

Model F1:
GOAL: EDIT MANUSCRIPT
• GOAL: EDIT UNIT TASK   • repeat until no more unit tasks
• • GOAL: ACQUIRE UNIT TASK   • • if task not remembered
• • • GET NEXT PAGE   • • • if at end of manuscript page
• • • GET NEXT TASK
• • GOAL: EXECUTE UNIT TASK   • • if an edit task was found
• • • LOCATE LINE   • • • if task not on current line
• • • MODIFY TEXT
• • • VERIFY EDIT

Model F2:
GOAL: EDIT MANUSCRIPT
• GOAL: EDIT UNIT TASK   • repeat until no more unit tasks
• • GOAL: ACQUIRE UNIT TASK   • • if task not remembered
• • • GET NEXT PAGE   • • • if at end of manuscript page
• • • GET NEXT TASK
• • GOAL: EXECUTE UNIT TASK   • • if an edit task was found
• • • GOAL: LOCATE LINE   • • • if task not on current line
• • • • (select USE QS METHOD)
• • • •   USE LF METHOD)
• • • GOAL: MODIFY TEXT
• • • • (select USE S COMMAND
• • • •   USE M COMMAND)
• • • • VERIFY EDIT

Figure 21.5 Examples comparing the ecological and cognitivist approaches to CTA: Panel A, the application of the rule-based GOMS model to the unit-level task of editing a manuscript (*Source:* Eberts, 1997); Panel B, the troubleshooting behavior of an electronics technician in an abstraction-decomposition space (*Source:* Vicente, 1999).

expertise and for developing artificial intelligence software, training programs, machine aids, evaluation criteria, and other purposes. A number of methods have been used to elicit this information, including the self-report and verbal-protocol techniques alluded to earlier (Cooke, 1999). One unique approach, *Pathfinder,* uses multidimensional scaling to map the cognitive structure underlying relatedness judgments obtained from the SME; thus it represents elements of both performance-based and subjective methods (Gillan & Schvaneveldt, 1999).

Naturalistic Decision Making (NDM)

This topic represents the ecological perspective as it appears in research and applications involving judgment and decision-making processes in complex systems. Again, it is based on the premise that traditional models, notably the normative (primarily economic) theories of rational decision behavior and the descriptive (primarily psychological) ones that emphasize human biases and heuristics, are not representative of actual expert decision-makers in real-world systems. Consequently, in applying the same knowledge-elicitation techniques discussed earlier in a variety of field settings, advocates of this perspective have accumulated a considerable

and rapidly growing body of evidence in support of alternative models of the decision process (Klein, Orasanu, Calderwood, & Zsambok, 1993; Zsambok & Klein, 1997). For instance, experienced decision makers faced with a large, complex, dynamic array of diagnostic information tend to reduce their task to manageable proportions by converting it mentally into a pattern-recognition problem—a strategy called *recognition-primed decision making,* or *RPD* (Klein, 1989). Basically they compare the situation they are observing with stored representations of similar patterns and interpret it in terms of the closest fit. Traditional cognitivist decision theories, most of which posit more computational kinds of mental strategies, cannot easily accommodate such evidence, and RPD is but one strategy that the NDM research has uncovered. Applications from this research have begun appearing in display design, decision-aiding, and training contexts (Cannon-Bowers & Salas, 1998; Zsambok & Klein, 1997).

Computer Supported Cooperative Work (CSCW)

Our final strand in the ecological CTA thread, CSCW, is still in its infancy but promises to grow rapidly as the capability for, and incidence of, distributed work (e.g., telecommuting, teleconferencing, distributed mission rehearsal, telerobotics, etc.)

becomes more commonplace, and increasing reliance is vested in coordinated teams (distributed and otherwise). Clearly, evolving computer technologies enable a variety of collaboration modes, but our understanding of the processes involved and how best to exploit these new capabilities is still fairly primitive. This is largely because the earliest research tended to be driven by disciplinary interests while understanding requires a convergence of disciplinary perspectives. Thus CSCW emerged in the mid-1980s as an interdisciplinary effort aimed at understanding "how people accomplish their activities cooperatively in the workplace" (Bannon, 2001).

Work published to date bearing on CSCW runs the gamut from laboratory research carried out within the cognitivist tradition (Kiesler & Sproull, 1992), to studies of team decision-making and problem-solving in simulated military settings (Cannon-Bowers & Salas, 1998), to use of CTA techniques to describe *team mental models* and *team SA* (Cooke, Salas, Cannon-Bowers, & Stout, 2000; Cooke, Stout, & Salas, 2001). There presently exists a considerable literature on topics related to CSCW, but its parts lie in different corners of the disciplinary universe and do not represent a coherent whole (Barua, Chellappa, & Whinston, 1997). Hence a primary objective of the CSCW movement is to integrate this fragmented knowledge and extend it through targeted research and emergent theory. Space does not permit a more explicit account of this work here, but an excellent overview of the concepts, methods, and applications is available in McNeese, Salas, and Endsley (2001).

Certainly the topics discussed in this section offer a variety of points at which I/O psychology and HF/E should, and hopefully will, converge in the future. Some, such as mental workload measurement and mental resource theory (which are largely foreign to the I/O community) are clearly related to concepts of current interest to I/O practitioners, such as stress and downsizing. The same could be said for vigilance and boredom, for task- and job-analysis techniques, and for a number of other such pairings. It would appear that the greatest liklihood for convergence, however, lies in the newer areas of research and application that have evolved from CTA in general and the ecological approach in particular. Understanding cognitive functions in complex systems based on systematic observations gathered in the field represents a departure from the laboratory-based principles and microsystems tradition of HF/E—one that would appear far more compatible with the traditions of organizational researchers. Techniques and knowledge developed in areas such as SA, knowledge elicitation, naturalistic decision making, and CSCW have important implication for organizational design, management training, job restructuring, and other standard

I/O applications. In its inherently eclectic composition, CSCW is currently drawing upon social-psychological and organizational knowledge, and thus perhaps represents a model for future collaboration between I/O psychology and HF/E.

Other Illustrations

The selection of content illustrations presented here has necessarily omitted a number of highly active areas of HF/E research and application (see Table 21.2), so we will close by commenting briefly on a few of those with above-average implications for I/O psychology: individual differences, function allocation (and automation), and training (including simulation and virtual reality). By contrast, topics such as HCI, display and control design, consumer product applications, and driver behavior, while maintaining a high profile in the field, focus on the more traditional (micro-) aspects of human-machine system affairs as discussed in the section on HF/E roles. Those topics dealing with physical work, such as biomechanical models and interventions, are only tangentially related to psychology.

Individual Differences and Aging

The rapidly shifting demography of America's population and workforce has numerous implications for systems design on both micro and macro levels—particularly issues associated with the accommodation of older workers, those from different cultures, those with disabilities, and women who seek to combine career and family goals. As demonstrated earlier, HF/E's heritage does not include a strong interest in individual differences, either in its research orientation and methodology or its applications. Hence its generalizations have been based primarily on population norms; the validity of its design principles for atypical human operators has been largely unknown. However, the last decade has seen a dramatic growth in the literature on age-related changes (Czaja, 1990; Fisk & Rogers, 1999), and—stimulated by the antidiscrimination and accommodation mandates of the Americans With Disabilities Act—a similar trend is beginning to appear with respect to the functionally impaired (Gardner-Bonneau, 1990; Vanderheiden, 1997). Population characteristics such as sex, ethnicity, and culture, to which the I/O psychology community has devoted considerable attention since the 1960s, are still neglected by HF/E researchers.

Not only has the topic of group differences become more visible within HF/E, so too has the use of aptitude, personality, and other trait variables for modeling and predicting human performance. For example, while hypothesized global traits such as *accident proneness* have not proven useful, significant relationships have been demonstrated between certain personality measures and accident or error rates in specific systems contexts (Arthur, Barrett, & Alexander, 1991; Deery & Fildes, 1999; Hale & Glendon, 1987; Lawton & Parker, 1998).

Function Allocation

Determining which function should be performed by humans and which by machines in systems design was once guided chiefly by lists of comparative strengths and weaknesses. However, technological advances—especially in artificial intelligence—have seriously eroded the assumptions underlying these comparisons, with automation becoming a viable option in many areas previously reserved for humans. So the emphasis has shifted from attribute lists to modeling and evaluating design options with the help of flowcharts, CTA data, contextual constraints lists, and occasionally even empirical tests (H. H. Kantowitz & Sorkin, 1987; Sharit, 1997).

Unfortunately, however, designer bias is generally toward machine allocation, automating everything that feasibly can be and leaving the operator with significant responsibility (e.g., supervisory control) but serious handicaps in exercising it—notably due to breakdowns in the interaction between the automated and human components. For example, faced with a malfunction or emergency, pilots of highly automated aircraft often have difficulty interpreting what the system is doing and diagnosing the problem (Wiener & Curry, 1980). Moreover, the system sometimes presents them with difficult-to-interpret (conflicting, unreliable) information—termed *automation surprises*—that can result in inappropriate action or inaction and accidents (Sarter, Woods, & Billings, 1997). Sometimes, when faced with incongruous information, they will put too much trust in the automation; sometimes, not enough. All of this, of course, has implications for SA and mental workload. The transition from supervisory (normal) to manual (abnormal, emergency) control seriously exacerbates the accompanying increase in mental workload (Huey & Wickens, 1993).

These automation problems have been well documented after the fact, and a substantial literature is accumulating on their cognitive correlates and possible design interventions (Parasuraman, 2000; Sharit, 1997). One concept that is receiving considerable attention currently is that of *dynamic function allocation*—building into the system the capability for adapting to circumstances, relying either more or less on automation depending, for example, on whether the human is overloaded or has lost faith in the automated aid's performance. This concept, of course, raises a host of other issues such as the validity of human judgment in taking over control

and the rules under which the machine would decide that the human was overloaded.

Training

Training research and application is undoubtedly the area in which HF/E and I/O psychology have shown the most convergence, probably because most training innovations were developed under military sponsorship through organizations responsible for *human systems,* broadly defined (i.e., encompassing personnel, manpower, training, and human engineering functions). Because this topic is dealt with in depth in another chapter, we will examine only the difference in emphasis that training has received from the two fields.

Basically, the emphasis in HF/E has been on developing and evaluating training technology, particularly that involved in learning and maintaining skills. Thus it has been heavily involved in simulation technology, including that which exploits the potential of VR, computer networking, and embedded-training software (i.e., that which enables personnel to practice simulated exercises at their operational workstations). Working closely with educational technologists, HF/E professionals have also played a role in the development of intelligent tutoring programs and other computer-based training systems (Brock, 1997).

CONCLUDING COMMENT

The field of HF/E is in a state of expansion and evolution, but exactly how this will play out is not altogether clear. Whether it will succeed in establishing itself as a widely recognized discipline, or settle for influencing design through more established disciplines and emerging specialties, is difficult to predict. Either way, its content and methods are driven to a large extent by advances in technology (especially information technology) and cultural forces (as reflected in public policy, litigation, and social issues; Howell, 1993). So, too, are its linkages with other disciplines.

Its traditional linkages were with experimental psychology and engineering; its principal model, the human-machine system; its conceptualization of the human component, the human information-processing model. Today, although it has not abandoned this heritage, HF/E's *cognitivist* approach is being challenged by an *ecological* one that has profound implications for the direction of both research and application. Among other things, this alternative approach emphasizes systematic field observation aimed at understanding systems *in the wild (so to speak),* blurs the distinction between research and application, and is highly eclectic—recognizing the need for many disciplinary perspectives if complex systems are to be truly understood (Hutchins, 1995; Moray, 2000; Rasmussen, 2000). In this regard, the ecological perspective supports the growing awareness within HF/E that limiting attention to just the human-machine (micro-) system level hampers the field's ability to contribute to human-oriented design—the view advocated by the fledgling macroergonomics specialty (which, interestingly enough, does not overlap as much with the ecological wing of the CE community as one might expect).

Most importantly for present purposes, however, both the macroergonomics and ecological perspectives within HF/E would seem conducive to the establishment of linkages with I/O psychology. Although movement to date has been minimal, the climate for convergence of the two fields on technology-driven issues connected with work has never been more favorable. The workplace, the nature of work, and the workforce are changing in ways that neither field is equipped to deal with alone, but each has an important—and complementary— contribution to make (Harris, 1994; Howard, 1995). By presenting today's HF/E in both historical and future perspectives, the present chapter seeks to highlight those areas in which the prospects for convergence with I/O psychology appear brightest.

REFERENCES

ANSI. (1988). *American national standard for human factors engineering of visual display terminal workstations* [ANSI/HFS Standard No. 100-1988]. Santa Monica, CA: Human Factors Society.

ANSI. (1998). *ANSI Z 5e5.1-Z535.5-1998*. Rosslyn, VA: National Electrical Manufacturers Association.

Arthur, W., Barrett, G. V., & Alexander, R. A. (1991). Prediction of vehicular accident involvement: A meta-analysis. *Human Performance, 4,* pp. 89–105.

Balakrishman, J. D. (1998). Measures and interpretation of vigilance performance: Evidence against the detection criterion. *Human Factors, 40,* 601–623.

Bannon, L. J. (2001). Towards a social and societal ergonomics: A perspective on CSCW. In M. McNeese, E. Salas, & M. Endsley (Eds.), *New trends in cooperative activities: Understanding system dynamics in complex environments* (pp. 9–21). Santa Monica, CA: Human Factors and Ergonomics Society.

Barua, A., Chellappa, R., & Whinston, A. B. (1997). Social computing: Computer supported cooperative work and groupware. In G. Salvendy (Ed.), *Handbook of human factors and ergonomics* (pp. 1760–1782). New York: Wiley.

Boff, C. R., & Lincoln, J. E. (Eds.). (1988). *Engineering data compendium*. Wright-Patterson Air Force Base, OH: Harry G. Armstrong Aerospace Medical Research Laboratory.

Booher, H. R. (1988). Progress of MANPRINT—The Army's human factors program. *Human Factors Society Bulletin, 31,* 1–3.

Booher, H. R. (Ed.). (1990). *MANPRINT: An approach to systems integration*. New York: van Nostrand Reinhold.

Brock, J. F. (1997). Computer-based instruction. In G. Salvendy (Ed.), *Handbook of human factors and ergonomics* (pp. 578–593). New York: Wiley.

Burns, C. M. (2000). Putting it all together: Improving display integration in ecological displays. *Human Factors, 42,* 226–241.

Cannon-Bowers, J. A., & Salas, E. (Eds.). (1998). *Making decisions under stress*. Washington, DC: American Psychological Association.

Cooke, N. J., (1999). Knowledge elicitation. In F. T. Durso, R. S. Nickerson, R. W. Schvaneveldt, S. T. Dumais, D. S. Lindsay, & M. T. H. Chi (Eds.), *The handbook of applied cognition* (pp. 479– 509). Chichester, UK: Wiley.

Cooke, N. J., Salas, E., Cannon-Bowers, J. A., & Stout, R. J. (2000). Measuring team knowledge. *Human Factors, 42,* 151–177.

Cooke, N. J., Stout, R., & Salas, E. (2001). A knowledge elicitation approach to the measurement of team situation awareness. In M. McNeese, E. Salas, & M. Endsley (Eds.), *New trends in cooperative activities: Understanding system dynamics in complex environments* (pp. 114–139). Santa Monica, CA: Human Factors and Ergonomics Society.

Coovert, M. D. (1995). Technological changes in office jobs: What we know and what we can expect. In A. Howard (Ed.), *The changing nature of work* (pp. 175–208). San Francisco: Jossey-Bass.

Cronbach, L. J. (1957). The two disciplines of scientific psychology. *American Psychologist, 12,* 671–684.

Czaja, S. J. (Ed.). (1990). Aging [Special issue]. *Human Factors, 32,* 509–619.

Czaja, S. J. (1997). Systems design and evaluation. In G. Salvendy (Ed.), *Handbook of human factors and ergonomics* (pp. 17–40). New York: Wiley.

Damos, D. L. (Ed.). (1991). *Multiple-task performance*. London: Taylor and Francis.

Deery, H. A., & Fildes, B. N. (1999). Young novice driver subtypes: Relationship to high-risk behavior, traffic accident record, and simulation driving performance. *Human Factors, 41,* 628–643.

Department of Defense. (1981, May 2). *Human engineering requirements for military systems, equipment, and facilities (MIL-STD 1472C)*. Washington, DC: Author.

Dingus, T. A., Antin, J. A., Hulse, M. C., & Wierwille, W. W. (1989). Attentional demand requirements of an automobile moving-map navigation system. *Transportation Research, 23A,* 301–315.

Eberts, R. (1997). Cognitive modeling. In G. Salvendy (Ed.), *Handbook of human factors and ergonomics* (pp. 1328–1374). New York: Wiley.

Elkind, J. I., Card, S. K., Hochberg, J., & Huey, B. M. (Eds.). (1989). *Human performance models for computer-aided engineering*. Washington, DC: National Academy Press.

Endsley, M. R. (1995a). Toward a theory of situation awareness in dynamic systems. *Human Factors, 37,* 32–64.

Endsley, M. R. (1995b). Measurement of situation awareness in dynamic systems. *Human Factors, 37,* 65–84.

Fischhoff, B. (1996). Psychology and public policy. In R. P. Lorian, I. Iscoe, P. H. DeLeon, & G. R. VandenBos (Eds.), *Psychology and public policy* (pp. 249–262). Washington, DC: American Psychological Association.

Fisk, A. D., & Rogers, W. A. (Eds.). (1999). *Handbook of human factors and the older adult*. New York: Academic Press.

Fitts, P. M., & Jones, R. E. (1961). Psychological aspects of instrument display. In H. W. Sinaiko (Ed.), *Selected papers on human factors in the design and use of control systems* (pp. 359–396). New York: Dover.

Flach, J. (1995). Situation awareness: proceed with caution. *Human Factors, 37,* 149–157.

Flach, J. (1998). *Victory by design: War, information, and cognitive systems engineering* (Tech. Rep. No. AFRL 1998-0074). Wright-Patterson Air Force Base, OH: Human Effectiveness Directorate.

Gardner-Bonneau, D. J. (1990). People with functional impairments [Special issue]. *Human Factors, 32,* 379–501.

Gillan, D. J., & Schvaneveldt, R. W. (1999). Applying cognitive psychology: Bridging the gulf between basic research and cognitive artifacts. In F. T. Durso, R. S Nickerson, R. W. Schvaneveldt, S. T. Dumais, D. S. Lindsay, & M. T. H. Chi (Eds.), *Handbook of applied cognition* (pp. 3–31). New York: Wiley.

Gilson, R. D. (Ed.). (1995). Situation awareness [Special section]. *Human Factors, 37,* 3–157.

Grandjean, E., Hunting, W., & Pidermann, M. (1983). VDT workstation design: Preferred settings and their effects. *Human Factors, 25,* 161–175.

Hale, A. R., & Glendon, A. I. (1987). *Individual behavior in the control of danger*. Amsterdam: Elsevier.

Hall, E. P., Gott, S. P., & Pokorny, R. A. (1995). *A procedural guide to cognitive task analysis: The PARI methodology* (Tech. Rep. No. AL/Hr-TR-1995-0108). Brooks Air Force Base, TX: AFMC.

Harris, D. H. (Ed.). (1994). *Organizational linkages: Understanding the productivity paradox*. Washington, DC: National Academy Press.

Helander, M. G. (1997). The human factors profession. In G. Salvendy (Ed.), *Handbook of human factors and ergonomics* (pp. 3–16). New York: Wiley.

Hendrick, H. W. (1996). All-member survey: Preliminary results. *Human Factors and Ergonomics Society Bulletin, 39,* 1–4.

Hendrick, H. W. (1997). Organizational design and macroergonomics. In G. Salvendy (Ed.), *Handbook of human factors and ergonomics* (pp. 594–636). New York: Wiley.

Hoffman, R. R., & Woods, D. D. (Eds.). (2000a). Cognitive task analysis [Special section]. *Human Factors, 42,* 1–101.

Hoffman, R. R., & Woods, D. D. (2000b). Studying cognitive systems in context. *Human Factors, 42,* 1–7.

Hopkins, C. O. (1995). Accreditation: The international perspective. *Human Factors and Ergonomics Society Bulletin, 38,* 1–5.

Howard, A. (1995). *The changing nature of work*. San Francisco: Jossey-Bass.

Howell, W. C. (1991). Human factors in the workplace. In M. Dunnette & L. Hough (Eds.), *Handbook of industrial & organizational psychology* (pp. 209–269). Palo Alto, CA: Consulting Psychologists Press.

Howell, W. C. (1993). Engineering psychology in a changing world. *Annual Review of Psychology, 44,* 231–263.

Howell, W. C. (1994). Human factors and the challenges of the future. *Psychological Science, 5,* 1–7.

Howell, W. C., & Goldstein, I. L. (Eds.). (1971). *Engineering psychology: Current perspectives in research*. New York: Appleton-Century-Crofts.

Huey, B. M., & Wickens, C. D. (Eds.). (1993). *Workload transition*. Washington, DC: National Academy Press.

Human Factors and Ergonomics Society. (2000). *Directory and yearbook*. Santa Monica, CA: Author.

Hutchins, E. (1995). *Cognition in the wild*. Cambridge, MA: MIT Press.

Ilgen, D. R., & Howell, W. C. (1999). The National Research Council's Committee on Human Factors (or "Human factors: It's more than you think"). *The Industrial-Organizational Psychologist, 37,* 39–41.

Institute of Medicine. (1999). *To err is human: Building a safer health system*. Washington, DC: National Academy Press.

Kahneman, D. (1973). *Attention and effort*. Englewood Cliffs, NJ: Prentice Hall.

Kantowitz, B. H. (1992). Selecting measures for human factors research. *Human Factors, 34,* 387–398.

Kantowitz, H. H., & Sorkin, R. D. (1987). Allocation of functions. In G. Salvendy (Ed.), *Handbook of human factors* (pp. 355–369). New York: Wiley.

Katz, D., & Kahn, R. L. (1978). *The social psychology of organizations* (2nd ed.). New York: Wiley.

Katzell, R. A., & Austin, J. T. (1992). From then to now: The development of industrial-organizational psychology in the United States. *Journal of Applied Psychology, 77,* 803–835.

Kiesler, S., & Sproull, L. (1992). Group decision making and communication technology. *Organizational Behavior and Human Decision Processes, 52,* 96–123.

Klein, G. A. (1989). Recognition-primed decisions. In W. B. Rouse (Ed.), *Advances in man-machine systems research* (Vol. 5, pp. 47–92). Greenwich, CT: JAI Press.

Klein, G. A., Orasanu, J., Calderwood, R., & Zsambok, C. E. (Eds.). (1993). *Decision making in action: Models and methods*. Norwood, NJ: Ablex.

Kleiner, B. (June, 2000). Report on taxonomy. *Macroergonomics Technical Group Newsletter,* 8–13.

Kroemer, K. H. E., Snook, S. H., Meadows, S. K., & Deutsch (Eds.). (1988). *Ergonomic models of anthropometry, human biomechanics, and operator-equipment interfaces.* Washington, DC: National Academy Press.

Laughery, K. R., Jr., & Corker, K. (1997). Computer modeling and simulation. In G. Salvendy (Ed.), *Handbook of human factors and ergonomics* (pp. 1375–1408). New York: Wiley.

Laughery, K. R., Sr., & Wogalter, M. S. (1997). Warnings and risk perception. In G. Salvendy (Ed.), *Handbook of human factors and ergonomics* (pp. 1174–1197). New York: Wiley.

Lawton, R., & Parker, D. (1998). Individual differences in accident liability: A review and integrative approach. *Human Factors, 40,* 655–671.

Licht, D. M., Polzella, D. J., & Boff, K. R. (1991). *Human factors, ergonomics and human factors engineering: An analysis of definitions* (Rep. No. 89-01). Wright-Patterson Air Force Base, OH: CSERIAC.

Luczak, H. (1997). Task analysis. In G. Salvendy (Ed.), *Handbook of human factors and ergonomics* (pp. 340–416). New York: Wiley.

Mackworth, N. H. (1948). The breakdown of vigilance during prolonged visual search. *Quarterly Journal of Experimental Psychology, 1,* 6–21.

Malone, T. B. (1986). The centered high-mounted brake light: A human factors success story. *Human Factors Society Bulletin, 29,* 1–4.

Marras, W. S. (1997). Biomechanics of the human body. In G. Salvendy (Ed.), *Handbook of human factors and ergonomics* (pp. 233–267). New York: Wiley.

McNeese, M., Salas, E., & Endsley, M. (Eds.). (2001). *New trends in collaborative activities: Understanding system dynamics in complex environments.* Santa Monica, CA: Human Factors and Ergonomics Society.

Meister, D. (1987). Systems design, development, and testing. In G. Salvendy (Ed.), *Handbook of human factors* (pp. 17–42). New York: Wiley.

Meister, D., & Enderwick, T. P. (2001). *Human factors in system design, development, and testing.* Mawah, NJ: Erlbaum.

Moray, N. (1982). Subjective mental work load. *Human Factors, 23,* 25–40.

Moray, N. (2000). Culture, politics, and ergonomics. *Ergonomics, 43,* 858–868.

National Research Council & Institute of Medicine. (2001). *Musculoskeletal disorders and the workplace.* Washington, DC: National Academy Press.

Navon, D., & Gopher, D. (1979). On the economy of human processing systems. *Psychological Review, 86,* 254–255.

Newell, A., & Simon, H. (1972). *Human problem solving.* Englewood Cliffs, NJ: Prentice Hall.

Nickerson, R. S. (1992). *Looking ahead: Human factors challenges in a changing world.* Hillsdale, NJ: Erlbaum.

Nielsen, J. (1997). Usability testing. In G. Salvendy (Ed.), *Handbook of human factors and ergonomics* (pp. 1543–1568). New York: Wiley.

Parasuraman, R. (2000). Designing automation for human use: Empirical studies and quantitative models. *Ergonomics, 43,* 931– 951.

Parasuraman, R., Warm, J. S., & Dember, W. N. (1987). Vigilance: Taxonomy and utility. In L. S. Mark, J. S. Warm, & R. L. Huston (Eds.), *Ergonomics and human factors* (pp. 11–32). New York: Springer-Verlag.

Pew, R. W., & Mavor, A. S. (Eds.). (1998). *Human modeling and organizational behavior.* Washington, DC: National Academy Press.

Pugh, D. S. (1966). Modern organization theory. *Psychological Bulletin, 66,* 235–251.

Rasmussen, J. (1986). *Information processing and human-machine interaction: An approach to cognitive engineering.* New York: North-Holland.

Rasmussen, J. (2000). Human factors in a dynamic information society: Where are we heading? *Ergonomics, 43,* 869–879.

Rasmussen, J., Pejtersen, A. M., & Goodstein, L. P. (1994). *Cognitive system engineering.* New York: Wiley.

Reason, J. (1990). *Human error.* Cambridge, UK: Cambridge University Press.

Rhodenizer, L. G., Bowers, C. A., Pharmer, J. A., & Gerber, T. N. (1999a). HF Competencies: Who are we, and what do we do? *Human Factors and Ergonomics Society Bulletin, 42, 5,* 1–4.

Rhodenizer, L. G., Bowers, C. A., Pharmer, J. A., & Gerber, T. N. (1999b). Human factors competencies, part II. *Human Factors and Ergonomics Society Bulletin, 42*(10), 1–5.

Rogers, W. A., Lamson, N., & Rousseau, G. K. (2000). Warning research: An integrative perspective. *Human Factors, 42,* 102–139.

Rouse, W. B., & Boff, K. R. (1997). In G. Salvendy (Ed.), *Handbook of human factors and ergonomics* (pp. 1617–1643). New York: Wiley.

Rouse, W. B., Kober, N., & Mavor, A. (Eds.). (1997). *The case for human factors in industry and government.* Washington, DC: National Academy Press.

Rubinstein, T., & Mason, A. F. (1979, November). The accident that shouldn't have happened: An analysis of Three Mile Island. *IEEE Spectrum,* 33–57.

Salvendy, G. (Ed.). (1987). *Handbook of human factors.* New York: Wiley.

Salvendy, G. (Ed.). (1997). *Handbook of human factors and ergonomics.* New York: Wiley.

Sanders, M. S., & McCormick, E. J. (1993). *Human factors in engineering and design* (7th ed.). New York: McGraw-Hill.

Sarter, N. B., & Woods, D. D. (1991). Situation awareness: A critical but ill-defined phenomenon. *International Journal of Aviation Psychology, 1,* 45–57.

Sarter, N. B., Woods, D. D., & Billings, C. E. (1997). Automation surprises. In G. Salvendy (Ed.), *Handbook of human factors and ergonomics* (pp. 1926–1943). New York: Wiley.

Schneider, B., & Klein, K. J. (1994). What is enough? A systems perspective on individual-organizational performance linkages. In D. H. Harris (Ed.), *Organizational linkages* (pp. 81–104). Washington, DC: National Academy Press.

Schneider, W., & Shiffrin, R. (1977). Controlled and automatic human information processing: Detection, search, and attention. *Psychological Review, 84,* 1–66.

Sharit, J. (1997). Allocation of functions. In G. Salvendy (Ed.), *Handbook of human factors and ergonomics* (pp. 301–339). New York: Wiley.

Suri, J. F. (2000). Saving lives through design. *Ergonomics in Design, 8,* 1–12.

Taylor, F. W. (1911). *The principles of scientific management.* New York: Harper and Row.

Tsang, P., & Wilson, G. F. (1997). Mental workload. In G. Salvendy (Ed.), *Handbook of human factors and ergonomics* (pp. 417–449). New York: Wiley.

U.S. Navy. (1988). *Investigating report: Formal investigation into the circumstances surrounding the downing of Iran Air flight 655 on 3 July 1988.* Washington, DC: Department of Defense Investigation Report.

U.S. Nuclear Regulatory Commission. (1983). *U.S. Nuclear Regulatory Commission human factors program plan (NUREG-0985).* Springfield VA: National Technical Information Service.

VanCott, H. P., & Huey, B. M. (Eds.). (1992). *Human factors specialists' education and utilization: Results of a survey.* Washington, DC: National Academy Press.

Vanderheiden, G. C. (1997). Designing for people with functional limitations resulting from disability, aging, or circumstance. In G. Salvendy (Ed.), *Handbook of human factors and ergonomics* (pp. 2010–2052). New York: Wiley.

Vicente, K. J. (1999). *Cognitive work analysis.* Mahwah, NJ: Erlbaum.

Wickens, C. D. (1992). *Engineering psychology and human performance.* New York: HarperCollins.

Wickens, C. D., & Carswell, C. M. (1997). Information processing. In G. Salvendy (Ed.), *Handbook of human factors and ergonomics* (pp. 89–129). New York: Wiley.

Wiener, E. L., & Curry, R. E. (1980). Flight deck automation: Promises and problems. *Ergonomics, 23,* 995–1011.

Wilson, J. R. (1998). Education and recognition of ergonomists. *Human Factors and Ergonomics Society Bulletin, 41,* 1–4.

Woods, D. D. (1999a). The age of ergonomics problems. *Human Factors and Ergonomics Society Bulletin, 42*(1), 1–6.

Woods, D. D. (1999b). Human factors, politics, and stakeholders. *Human Factors and Ergonomics Society Bulletin, 42*(9), 1–8.

Woods, D. D. (2000). Patient safety and human factors opportunities. *Human Factors and Ergonomics Society Bulletin, 43*(5), 1–4.

Woodward, J. (1958). *Management and technology, problems of progress in industry.* London: Her Majesty's Stationery Office.

Zsambok, C., & Klein, G. (Eds.). (1997). *Naturalistic decision making.* Hillsdale NJ: Erlbaum.

CHAPTER 22

Organizational Culture and Climate

CHERI OSTROFF, ANGELO J. KINICKI, AND MELINDA M. TAMKINS

Organizational culture and climate focus on how organizational participants *experience* and make sense of organizations (Schneider, 2000) and are fundamental building blocks for describing and analyzing organizational phenomena (Schein, 2000). Although culture and climate have been approached from different scholarly traditions and have their roots in different disciplines, they are both about understanding psychological phenomena in organizations. Both concepts rest upon the assumption of shared meanings—a shared understanding of some aspect of the organizational context.

Historically, the construct of climate preceded the construct of culture. Climate was introduced in the 1960s, primarily based on the theoretical concepts proposed by Kurt Lewin (1951; Lewin, Lippitt & White, 1939) and followed by the empirical research conducted in both educational settings (e.g., Stern, 1970) and organizational settings (e.g., Litwin & Stringer, 1968). Organizations were examined from a cultural perspective as early as the 1930s (Trice & Beyer, 1993); however, organizational culture did not become a popular issue for study in the management literature until the 1980s, largely following the publication of several best-selling trade books.

Since that time, research and thinking about culture have tended to overshadow that about climate (Schneider, 2000).

In recent years, a great deal of attention has been devoted to the question of whether the constructs of culture and climate are different, the same, or interrelated (cf. Dennison, 1996; Payne, 2000; Schein, 2000). In this chapter, we view culture and climate as two complementary constructs that reveal overlapping yet distinguishable nuances in the psychological lives of organizations (Schneider, 2000). Each is deserving of attention as a separate construct as well as attention to the relationship between the two constructs. Furthermore, the continued study of culture and climate is important to the field of industrial and organizational (I/O) psychology around the world because these constructs provide a context for studying organizational behavior. That is, the social and symbolic processes associated with the emergence of organizational culture and climate influence both individual and group behaviors, including turnover, job satisfaction, job performance, safety, customer satisfaction, service quality, and financial performance. We structure this chapter by providing separate reviews and discussion of the culture and climate literature before turning to the relationships between the two constructs and the processes underlying their emergence, strength, and change.

INTEGRATED MODEL OF CULTURE AND CLIMATE

Before providing an overview of our integrated model shown in Figure 22.1, it is important to define the constructs of culture and climate. *Climate* is an experientially based description of what people see and report happening to them in an organizational situation (L. R. James & Jones, 1974; L. R. James, Joyce, & Slocum, 1988; Schneider, 2000). Climate involves employees' perceptions of what the organization is like in terms of practices, policies, procedures, routines, and rewards (e.g., A. P. Jones & James, 1979; Rentsch, 1990; Schneider, 1990). Hence, climate's focus is on the situation and its link to the perceptions, feelings, and behavior of employees. It can be viewed as temporal, subjective, and possibly subject to manipulation by authority figures (Dennison, 1996).

Whereas climate is about experiential descriptions or perceptions of what happens, *culture* helps define why these things happen (Schein, 2000; Schneider, 2000). It pertains to employees' fundamental ideologies (Trice & Beyer, 1993) and assumptions (Schein, 1992) and is influenced by symbolic interpretations of organizational events and artifacts (Hatch, 1993). Culture represents an evolved context embedded in systems (Dennison, 1996; Schein, 2000), is more stable than climate, has strong roots in history (Rowlinson & Procter, 1999), is collectively held, and is resistant to manipulation (Dennison, 1996).

Thus, climate is more immediate than culture. Individuals can sense the climate upon entering an organization through things such as the physical appearance of the place, the emotionality and attitudes exhibited by employees, and the experiences and treatment of visitors and new employee members. In contrast, culture is a deeper phenomenon based on symbolic meanings (Hatch, 1993) that reflect core values and underlying ideologies and assumptions (Schein, 1992; Trice & Beyer, 1993). This interpretative process explains the *why* of organizational behavior. Climate develops from the deeper core of culture. Climate, or the *what* of the culture, can result from espoused values and shared tacit assumptions and reflects the surface organizational experience based on policies, practices, and procedures (Guion, 1973; Schein, 2000).

Figure 22.1 represents a heuristic model for locating culture and climate in a conceptual framework across aggregate and individual levels of analysis and is used to help structure our review. Figure 22.1 shows that organizational culture is a function of industry and environmental characteristics, national culture, and an organization's vision, goals, and strategy (Aycan, Kanungo, & Sinha, 1999). The relationship between societal or national culture and organizational culture, however, may be more complex than depicted in our multilevel model. National culture and organizational culture are likely to influence organizational practices interactively (Kopelman, Brief, & Guzzo, 1990), but research is needed to examine the veracity of this notion.

Returning to Figure 22.1, organizational culture is expected to effect structure, practices, policies, and routines in the organization that in turn provide the context for climate

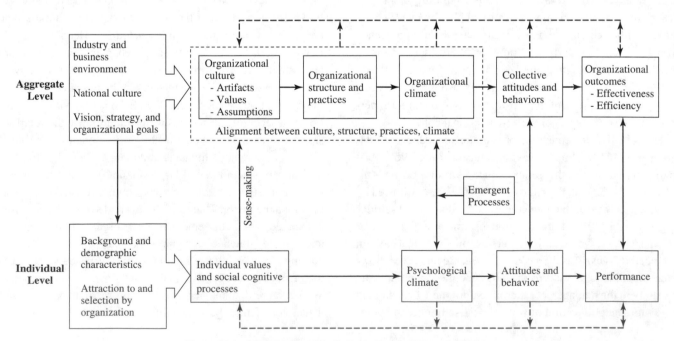

Figure 22.1   Multi-level model of organizational culture and climate.

perceptions. These organizational practices are the means through which employee perceptions, and subsequent attitudes, responses, and behaviors, are shaped. At the organizational level, cultural values and assumptions lead managers to the explicit or implicit adoption of structural features and practices that influence the climate that develops. Collective attitudes and behaviors of employees are shaped by climate and in turn effect organizational outcomes (e.g., financial performance, customer service, efficiency, productivity). Culture, as a shared meaning across employees, develops through individuals' sense-making process.

Figure 22.1 shows that individuals' background characteristics and process of joining the organization are related to individuals' values and social cognitive processes, which in turn influence psychological climate. When these climate perceptions are shared across an organization's employees, organizational climate is said to emerge. We also propose that these shared perceptions will develop only when strong emergent processes are enacted in the organization (practices delivered in such a way as to create a strong situation, homogeneity of attributes among employees, social interaction processes, and leadership). When the emergent process is weak, idiosyncratic perceptions within an organization develop, which produces wide variability in perceptions of climate and can result in wide variability in individual attitudes and behaviors, diminishing the relationship to organizational performance. We also note that there are reciprocal relationships between the variables across the aggregate and individual level. Individual-level constructs are influenced in part by the existing organizational-level constructs (e.g., individual climate perceptions are influenced by the existing organizational climate; individual attitudes and behaviors are influenced in part by the collective attitudes and behaviors). At the same time, individual constructs have a role in creating the contextual variables. Finally, we include feedback loops at both the organizational and individual levels. It is important to note that the model is not comprehensive and we did not include all possible linkages and variables in Figure 22.1. Rather, our purpose was to highlight those relationships that are most critical for integrating culture and climate across levels of analysis; boxes in boldface represent the constructs and linkages that are our primary focus.

ORGANIZATIONAL CULTURE

This section begins by providing a brief historical review of the construct of organizational culture. We then consider the levels of organizational culture, the content or types of organizational cultures, and the antecedents and outcomes of organizational culture.

Historical Foundation and Definition of Organizational Culture

Research on organizational culture has its roots in anthropology. This research relies heavily on qualitative methods that use participant observation, interviews, and examination of historical information to understand how culture provides a context for understanding individual, group, and societal behavior. The first systematic attempt to investigate work organizations in cultural terms began in the 1930s during the final phase of the Hawthorne studies at the Western Electric Company (Trice & Beyer, 1993). This study began as an empirical investigation of the relationship between light intensity and productivity, but qualitative methods (i.e., employee interviews) were used to explain counterintuitive results showing that productivity increased for a select group of employees regardless of the physical surroundings. Although this study's results have been questioned, it still represents one of the first qualitative studies of individual and group behavior. Furthermore, Gardner published the first textbook that examined organizations from a cultural perspective in 1945. Interest in an anthropological approach to studying work organizations nonetheless waned from the 1940s through early 1960s. Although there was a resurgence in anthropologically based studies in the 1960s (e.g., Trice, Belasco, & Alutto, 1969) and 1970s (e.g., Mintzberg, 1973), the topic of organizational culture did not become prominent until the 1980s.

This interest in organizational culture was stirred by anecdotal evidence contained in three best-selling books: Ouchi's (1981) *Theory Z: How American Business Can Meet the Japanese Challenge;* Deal and Kennedy's (1982) *Corporate Cultures: The Rites and Rituals of Corporate Life;* and Peters and Waterman's (1982) *In Search of Excellence*. Each suggested that strong organizational cultures were associated with organizational effectiveness. The number of applied and scholarly publications on the topic of organizational culture has mushroomed since 1982 (Barley, Meyer, & Gash, 1988) and is likely to continue in light of findings suggesting that organizational culture is one of the biggest barriers to creating and leveraging knowledge assets (De Long & Fahey, 2000), to effectively implementing total quality management programs (Tata & Prasad, 1998) and to successfully implementing technological innovations (DeLisi, 1990).

The concept of organizational culture has a variety of meanings and connotations. For example, Verbeke, Volgering, and Hessels (1998) identified 54 different definitions in the literature between 1960 and 1993. Part of this inconsistency is due to the fact that culture researchers represent an eclectic group that come from a variety of disciplines such as sociology, anthropology, and psychology and use different epistemologies and methods to investigate organizational culture. That said, Hofstede, Neuijen, Ohayv, and Sanders (1990) conclude that there are some common characteristics across the different definitions of organizational culture. These commonalities include the notion that organizational culture includes multiple layers (Schein, 1992) and aspects (i.e., cognitive and symbolic) of an organizational context (Mohan, 1993), that organizational culture is a socially constructed phenomenon influenced by historical and spatial boundaries (Rowlinson & Procter, 1999; Schein, 2000), and the concept of "shared" meaning that is central to understanding an organization's culture.

Although a variety of definitions of culture that integrate these commonalities have been offered, the most comprehensive one was offered by Schein (1992), who concludes that the culture of a group—the term *group* refers here to social units of all sizes—is defined as

> a pattern of shared basic assumptions that the group learned as it solved its problems of external adaptation and internal integration, that has worked well enough to be considered valid and, therefore, to be taught to new members as the correct way to perceive, think, and feel in relation to those problems. (p.12)

Schein suggests that organizational culture is learned by group members who pass it on to new group members through a variety of socialization and communication processes. This definition also implies that overt behavior, although not directly part of organizational culture, is clearly influenced by the basic assumptions or ideologies (Trice & Beyer, 1993) people hold. Finally, Schein does not specify the size of the social unit to which a culture can be applied. This implies that organizations can have subcultures and that it is inappropriate to talk about a so-called *universal culture,* a notion that is still being debated in the literature (Harris & Ogbonna, 1999)

Layers of Organizational Culture

Numerous scholars have proposed that organizational culture possesses several layers or levels that vary along a continuum of accessibility and subjectivity (Hofstede et al., 1990; Mohan, 1993; Rousseau, 1990; Schein, 1992). Schein (1985, 1992) concludes that there are three fundamental layers at which culture manifests itself: observable artifacts, espoused values, and basic underlying assumptions.

Observable Artifacts

Artifacts are surface-level realizations of underlying values that represent manifestations of deeper assumptions (Schein, 1992) or ideologies (Trice & Beyer, 1993). Artifacts include the

> visible products of the group such as the architecture of its physical environment, its language, its technology and products, its artistic creations, and its style as embodied in clothing, manners of address, emotional displays, myths and stories told about the organization, published lists of values, observable rituals and ceremonies, and so on. For purposes of cultural analysis this level also includes the visible behavior of the group and the organizational processes into which such behavior is made routine. (Schein, p. 17)

Trice and Beyer conclude that there are four major categories of cultural artifacts: *symbols* (e.g., natural and manufactured objects, physical settings, and performers and functionaries), *organizational language* (e.g., jargon and slang, gestures, signals, signs, songs, humor, jokes, gossip, rumor, metaphors, proverbs, and slogans), *narratives* (e.g., stories, legends, sagas, and myths), and *practices* (e.g., rituals, taboos, rites, and ceremonies). They recommend using ethnographic studies of these artifacts to decipher an organization's culture. It is important to note, however, that artifacts can be misleading in terms of interpreting organizational culture because they are easy to observe but difficult to interpret accurately (Schein).

Espoused Values

Schwartz (1992) notes that *values* possess five key components: "Values (1) are concepts or beliefs, (2) pertain to desirable end-states or behaviors, (3) transcend situations, (4) guide selection or evaluation of behavior and events, and (5) are ordered by relative importance" (p. 4). *Espoused values* are those that are specifically endorsed by management or the organization at large. In contrast, *enacted values* are those that are exhibited or converted into employee behavior. The difference between espoused and enacted values is important because the gap is related to employee attitudes and behavior (Clarke, 1999). Clarke's results revealed that employees were more cynical about a corporate safety program when there was a gap between management's espoused and enacted values about safety.

The role of values in understanding organizational culture was recently questioned by Stackman, Pinder, and Connor (2000). These authors note that the construct of values is an individual-level variable and that it is a logical error to attribute, other than metaphorically, human properties such as values to aggregations of individuals such as groups or organizations. Organizations do not possess values. Rather, key individual leaders possess values and these individuals can influence organizational goals, processes, and systems in directions that are consistent with their values. These authors conclude that it is meaningless to speak of an organization's singular culture or its values and suggest that future research should consider new modes of thinking about values and their role in organizations. Future research is clearly needed to address the concerns raised by Stackman and colleagues and to determine the veracity of using aggregated measures of individual values as proxies for organizational values.

Basic Assumptions

Basic assumptions are unobservable and reside at the core of organizational culture, according to Schein (1990, 1992). Deeply held assumptions frequently start out as values that over time become so ingrained or are taken so much for granted that they take on the character of assumptions. When a basic assumption is strongly held by a group (e.g., Herb Kelleher, chief executive officer of Southwest Airlines, tells personnel that they, the employees, are a more important constituent than customers), employees will find organizational behavior that violates this assumption as inconceivable (e.g., Southwest Airlines' putting customer satisfaction ahead of employees' welfare). Schein concludes that basic assumptions are rarely confronted or debated and are extremely difficult to change. Challenging basic assumptions produces anxiety and defensiveness because they provide security through their ability to define what employees should pay attention to, how they should react emotionally, and what actions they should take in various kinds of situations (Schein, 1992). To date, research has not attempted to identify the antecedents or outcomes associated with an organization's basic assumptions.

Moreover, Trice and Beyer (1993) and Hatch (1993) criticize Schein's proposal that basic assumptions represent the core of culture because assumptions ignore the symbolic nature of culture. Trice and Beyer suggest that ideologies represent the core content or substance of a culture. *Ideologies* are "shared, relatively coherently interrelated sets of emotionally charged beliefs, values, and norms that bind some people together and help them to make sense of their world" (Trice & Beyer, p. 33). Hatch also believes that Schein's model is deficient because it fails to consider interactive processes among artifacts, values, and assumptions. We concur with Hatch's evaluation and recommend that future work investigate the dynamic relationships among the levels of culture.

The Content of Organizational Culture

Interpreting the different layers of organizational culture helps define the content or substance of culture. Most researchers either conduct a qualitative analysis to assess the deeper layers of organizational culture (e.g., Brannen & Salk, 2000; Casey, 1999; Schein, 1992) or use surveys to assess espoused values and beliefs quantitatively (e.g., Buenger,

Daft, Conlon, & Austin, 1996; Cooke & Szumal, 2000; O'Reilly, Chatman, & Caldwell, 1991) or a set of work practices thought to underlie organizational culture (e.g., Christensen & Gordon, 1999; Hofstede, 1998; Hofstede et al., 1990). Ashkanasy, Broadfoot, and Falkus (2000) reviewed questionnaire measures of organizational culture and concluded that many are used for consultative purposes, lack a sound theoretical basis, are infrequently used, and lack validity. Furthermore, other researchers (e.g., Schein, 1992, 2000; Trice & Beyer, 1993) do not accept the premise that surveys are a valid measure of organizational culture and conclude that they should not be used as the principal method for assessing organizational culture.

That said, we uncovered four frequently used surveys that are theoretically based and have been subjected to preliminary validation. Each is based on a different conceptual framework and results in a different taxonomy of organizational culture. These taxonomies are the basis of the Organizational Culture Inventory (OCI; Cooke & Lafferty, 1987), the Competing Values Framework (CVF; Quinn & Rohrbaugh, 1983), the Organizational Culture Profile (OCP; O'Reilly et al., 1991), and the work practices survey (Hofstede et al., 1990).

The Organizational Culture Inventory (OCI)

The OCI is a 120-item survey that assesses 12 sets of normative beliefs. These norms are categorized into three types of organizational cultures. A *constructive culture,* the first cultural type, endorses normative beliefs associated with achievement, self-actualizing, humanistic-encouraging, and affiliative. The second type, a *passive-defensive culture,* reinforces values related to seeking approval, being conventional or dependent, and avoiding accountability. Finally, an *aggressive-defensive culture* endorses beliefs characterized as oppositional, power oriented, competitive, and perfectionist. See Cooke and Szumal (2000) for a complete description of the theoretical foundation of the OCI.

A series of studies reported in Cooke and Szumal (2000) reveal that the three types of culture are significantly correlated with antecedent variables reflecting organizational structure, management practices, technology, leadership, and a variety of individual (motivation, social loafing, performance, job satisfaction, stress), group (teamwork, quality of work relations, unit-level quality), and organizational (quality of customer service) outcomes. Cooke and Szumal conclude that strong norms for constructive behaviors are more likely to lead to desirable outcomes. Evidence supporting the reliability and validity of the OCI is provided by Cooke and Rousseau (1988) and Cooke and Szumal (1993, 2000).

Competing Values Framework (CVF)

The CVF was developed by Quinn and his associates (Quinn & McGrath, 1985; Quinn & Rohrbaugh, 1983) to explain differences in the values or ideologies underlying models of organizational effectiveness. The CVF can be used to "explore the deep structures of organizational culture, the basic assumptions that are made about such things as the means to compliance, motives, leadership, decision making, effectiveness, values and organizational forms" (Quinn & Kimberly, 1984, p. 298), which results in classifying culture into four types. A *group culture,* the first cultural type, is based on values associated with affiliation, emphasizing the development of human resources and employee participation in decision making. The second type, the *developmental culture,* is driven by a positive orientation toward change, with values focusing on flexibility and the accomplishment of organizational goals. A *hierarchical culture,* the third type, endorses values and norms associated with a bureaucracy. Here, culture tends to be inwardly focused and management information systems are used to create stability and control. The fourth type, the *rational culture,* reflects values and norms associated with achievement, planning, productivity, and efficiency.

Researchers using the CVF tend to use case studies (Zammuto, Gifford, & Goodman, 2000; Zammuto & Krakower, 1991), Likert-type scales (e.g., Buenger et al., 1996; Chang & Weibe, 1996; McDermott & Stock, 1999), or short ipsative scales (Shortell et al., 1995; Smart & St. John, 1996). Although a few studies have supported the structure and integrity of the CVF (e.g., Howard, 1998; McDermott & Stock, 1999; Zammuto & Krakower, 1991), there has not been a comprehensive assessment of the construct validity of measures used to operationalize this model, and conclusions based on studies using the CVF should be interpreted with some caution.

The Organizational Culture Profile (OCP)

The OCP was originally developed to measure person-organization fit (O'Reilly et al., 1991). It contains 54 value statements that were derived from an extensive review of academic and practitioner writings on organizational culture. Respondents use the Q-sort methodology to sort the values into categories ranging from the least characteristic to most characteristic of their respective organizations or their personal preferences. Research using the OCP has shown that it possesses interrater reliability, test-retest reliability, within- and between-group differences, and predictive validity. However, factor analyses of the 54 items have identified different factor structures across samples (cf. O'Reilly et al., 1991; Vandenberghe, 1999). In an attempt to overcome

measurement problems associated with the original OCP, Ashkanasy, Broadfoot, et al. (2000) developed a 50-item survey to measure 10 dimensions of organizational culture. Unfortunately, validation studies of this instrument uncovered a two-factor solution, thereby failing to support the a priori dimensionality of this newly proposed instrument. When the original OCP was used as a measure of person-organization fit, fit was positively associated with individuals' organizational commitment, job satisfaction, intention to quit (O'Reilly et al.), and turnover (Vandenberghe, 1999).

Work Practices Surveys

Hofstede et al. (1990) developed a 61-item measure of perceived work practices based on a series of in-depth interviews with nine informants from 20 work units spanning ten different organizations in Denmark and the Netherlands. Hofstede et al. proposed that work practices are the visible part of organizational culture. Factor analysis of these perceptual items resulted in six underlying dimensions of organizational culture: *process oriented versus results oriented, employee oriented versus job oriented, parochial versus professional, open system versus closed system, loose versus tight control,* and *normative versus pragmatic.* Work practices were used to identify organizational subcultures (Hofstede, 1998) and were associated with measures of organizational values, work structure, top management demographics, organizational demographics (Hofstede et al., 1990) and revenue growth (Christensen & Gordon, 1999).

Examination of the work practice measures indicates that they assess employees' perceptions of general and specific work-environment characteristics. Consistent with our definitions of culture and climate, we believe that these measures are actually tapping climate, not culture, and recommend that they not be used as indicators of organizational culture.

Summary

Controversy still exists about the appropriateness of various methods for assessing culture. Some researchers reject the validity of quantitative studies because these studies are based on the assumption that culture represents something that an organization *has,* rather than something an organization *is* (Smircich, 1983). In contrast, others reject the subjective and idiosyncratic interpretations associated with qualitative case studies. We concur with Schultz and Hatch (1996) that it is impossible and illusionary to resolve this paradigmatic argument and thus echo Ashkanasy, Broadfoot, et al. (2000) and Rousseau (1990) in suggesting that researchers should use multiple methods to assess multiple levels of organizational culture.

Antecedents of Organizational Culture

To date, there has not been a comprehensive examination of the antecedents of organizational culture. What has been written in this regard is predominantly theoretical. For example, Aycan et al. (1999) propose that the enterprise environment, which includes market characteristics, nature of the industry, ownership or control, resource availability, and sociocultural dimensions, is a direct antecedent of organizational culture. Tesluk, Farr, and Klein (1997) similarly hypothesize that industry and business environments are the key antecedents of organizational culture. Other models of organizational effectiveness or productivity, however, treat organizational culture as an exogenous variable (e.g., Kopelman et al., 1990) and do not attempt to identify antecedents of culture. In partial support of these propositions, the extent of strategic planning (Oswald, Stanwick, & LaTour, 1997) and manufacturing strategy strength (Bates, Amundson, Schroeder, & Morris, 1995) were significantly associated with organizational culture.

A somewhat different hypothesis was proposed by G. George, Sleeth, and Siders (1999) and by Schein (1983). They predicted that senior leaders' vision and behaviors were the key antecedents of an organization's artifacts and values and that an organization's culture is originally formed by the founder's values. Future research is clearly needed to examine the antecedents of organizational culture and to investigate the techniques leaders use to embed culture.

Outcomes of Culture

Culture has been viewed as a key driver of organizational effectiveness and performance (e.g., Deal & Kennedy, 1982; Peters & Waterman, 1982) and a source of sustained competitive advantage (Barney, 1986). We identified three summary reviews of literature pertaining to the relationship between culture and performance (Lim, 1995; Siehl & Martin, 1990; Wilderom, Glunk, & Maslowski, 2000), and all three resulted in similar conclusions.

Siehl and Martin (1990, p. 242) concluded "that it is unwise and misleading to justify studying culture in terms of its links to financial performance, since such a link has not been—and may well never be—empirically demonstrated." They noted that there were measurement problems plaguing past research as well as a lack of theory to explain why such a relationship should be expected in the first place. Lim (1995) summarized both idiographic and nomothetic studies and concluded that "the present examination does not seem to indicate a relationship between culture and the short-term performance of organizations, much less to show a causal relationship between culture and performance" (p. 20). Based

on a review of 10 quantitative studies, Wilderom et al. (2000) concluded that most studies were cross-sectional, used unvalidated and ad hoc measures of culture, relied on measures of performance that were convenient and accessible rather than theoretically based, and could not clearly establish the direction of the relationship between culture and climate.

Our search of the literature was consistent with these reviews. There is a lack of theoretical development around the relationship between culture and performance, there are problems with the measurement of both culture and financial performance, empirical evidence does not support the idea that organizational culture predicts organizational performance, and longitudinal research is lacking. We also note that researchers have not examined a more inclusive list of outcomes other than financially based measures (Sheridan, 1992, is an exception, showing that a culture emphasizing interpersonal relationship values had lower turnover rates than a culture focusing on accomplishment of work values). Furthermore, inconsistent relationships between organizational culture and performance may be due to the failure to examine potential moderators (e.g., industry) and mediators (e.g., organizational climate), as suggested in Figure 22.1.

CLIMATE

This section provides a brief review of the climate construct. We begin by discussing the historical roots and theoretical underpinnings of the construct, elucidating issues pertaining to the objective versus perceptual aspect of climate, and aggregation. We then examine the content of climate and summarize research findings on antecedent and outcome relationships.

Historical Roots and Theoretical Foundations

Climate is widely defined as the perception of formal and informal organizational policies, practices, and procedures (Reichers & Schneider, 1990). However, the definition of climate and the focus of climate research have evolved over the years since Lewin's early studies of experimentally created social climates (1951; Lewin et al., 1939). Lewin and his colleagues were interested in examining the climate or atmosphere created by different leadership styles and the consequences these different climates had on the behaviors and attitudes of group members—in this case, young boys.

From a theoretical perspective, the relationship between people and their social environment was framed in the formulation: *Behavior* is a function of person and the environment (Lewin, 1951). Hence, the environment is created by or studied as a construct that is separate from the people who operate within it (Dennison, 1996; Roberts, Hulin, & Rousseau, 1978). *Climate* is an abstraction of the environment—a gestalt that is based on the patterns of experiences and behaviors that people perceive in the situation (Schnieder, Bowen, Ehrhart, & Holcombe, 2000). The agents (e.g., leaders, management) or factors that create the climate (e.g., structure, strategy, practices) are either assumed or not directly studied (Dennison, 1996). Rather, the focus is on a climate that is perceived by employees yet can be measured and studied separately from individuals, and on the impact this climate has on the people within it. This perspective has continued to dominate much of climate research.

Following the work of Lewin, research in the late 1950s through the early 1970s emphasized the human context of organizations, with particular emphasis on organizational effectiveness outcomes as well as the impact on attitudinal outcomes (Schneider et al., 2000). For example, a number of theorists (e.g., Argyris, 1964; Likert, 1967; McGregor, 1960) suggested that the social context, climate, or atmosphere created in the workplace have important consequences. Researchers proposed that organizational productivity was achieved through employee satisfaction and attention to workers' physical and emotional needs; the conditions created in the workplace influenced the extent to which an employee was satisfied, gave his or her services wholeheartedly to the organization, and performed up to potential in patterns of activity that were directed toward achieving the organization's objectives. Similarly, a number of researchers documented consistency between climates and the needs or personalities of individuals within them (e.g., J. R. George & Bishop, 1971; Pervin, 1967) and showed the impact that climates have on the performance and attitudes of individuals that work within them (e.g., Litwin & Stringer, 1968; Pritchard & Karasick, 1973; Schneider & Bartlett, 1968, 1970). Litwin and Stringer further articulated a framework in which climate was a mediator between the effects of organizational system factors and individual motivation and subsequent behavior, while others tested the notion the climate was a moderator of relationships between individual differences and individual performance (e.g., Schneider & Bartlett, 1968).

Controversies and Resolutions

Despite climate's strong historical foundation, the concept was still somewhat ill defined and as work continued throughout the 1970s and 1980s, the construct became plagued by controversies, ambiguities, and methodological difficulties (Kozlowski & Doherty, 1989). These issues centered around the objective versus perceptual nature of climate, the appropriate level of analysis for addressing climate, and the aggregation of climate perceptions.

Objective versus Perceptual Climate and Levels of Analysis

In contrast to the approach based on Litwin's work (that climate was driven largely by leadership and practices), Payne and Pugh (1976) suggested that climate was produced by the objective context and structure of the organization—for example, the organization's size, hierarchy, span of control, resources, and rate of turnover. These authors concluded, based on a review of research, that relationships between structure and climate were modest at best. Yet, controversy continued over whether climate was an objective organizational property or a subjective and perceptual one (Taguiri & Litwin, 1968). A related controversy centered on whether climate was an individual or organizational attribute (e.g., Guion, 1973).

To resolve this issue, a distinction between *psychological climate*, in which climate is conceptualized and measured at the individual level, and *organizational climate*, in which climate is conceptualized and studied as an organizational variable, was proposed (Hellriegel & Slocum, 1974; L. R. James & Jones, 1974). This proposition extended the original Lewinian basis for climate to include interactionist and cognitive theoretical perspectives. That is, climate was conceptualized as sets of perceptually based descriptions of organizational features, events, and processes. At the individual level, these perceptions represent cognitive interpretations of the context and arise from individuals' interactions with context and with each other (e.g., L. R. James, Hater, Gent, & Bruni, 1978; L. R. James & Jones, 1974; A. P. Jones & James, 1979). Thus, while early researchers tended to define *climate* as enduring organizational or situational characteristics that were perceived by organizational members (e.g., Schneider & Bartlett, 1968), more attention was now given to individuals' perceptions than to organizational characteristics, and psychological meaningfulness became an explicit part of the definition (Rentsch, 1990).

A related concern was raised about individual-level climate perceptions, questioning whether climate is a measure of affective responses similar to job satisfaction (e.g., Guion, 1973; Payne & Pugh, 1976). This issue was resolved through a series of papers showing that climate and satisfaction are conceptually distinct and the constructs are not necessarily correlated (e.g., LaFollette & Sims, 1975; Payne, Fineman, & Wall, 1976; Schneider & Snyder, 1975).

Nevertheless, debate continued into the 1980s over whether organizational climate should be measured through objective features of organizations (Glick, 1985, 1988) or through assessments of how individuals perceive the organization (L. R. James et al., 1988). L. R. James and his colleagues (e.g., L. R. James et al., 1988; L. A. James & James, 1989) argued that because organizational climate arises out of the cognitive appraisals, social constructions, and sense-making of individuals, measures of organizational climate should rely on the individual as the basic unit of theory and thus it is appropriate and productive to describe organizations in psychological terms. That is, since organizational climate is fundamentally an individual-level construct, the unit of measurement must begin at the individual level. When consensus among individuals in their perceptions of climate can be demonstrated, the perceptions can be meaningfully aggregated to represent subunit or organizational climate (L. R. James, 1982). The distinction between psychological climate as an individual perception and organizational climate as a shared perception, and the appropriateness of using aggregated individual perceptions to represent a higher level (e.g., organizational) climate, are widely accepted today (Schneider et al., 2000).

The formation of climate has been traditionally regarded as primarily an individual-level process based on sense-making and cognitive representations of meaning inherent in organizational features and processes (Schneider, 1983). This process, however, also was viewed as interactive and reciprocal (Ashforth, 1985; Kozlowski & Doherty, 1989; Schneider, 1983). Because similar types of individuals are attracted to the same sort of organizational settings, are selected by similar types of organizational settings, are socialized in similar ways, are exposed to similar features within the setting, and share their interpretations of the setting with others, consensus among climate perceptions of individuals in the same setting develops.

Aggregation

Although the definition of organizational climate as a summary perception became widely accepted, concerns were raised about the reliability of aggregated data and how to demonstrate consensus, or shared perceptions. For many years, attitudinal-like scales have been used to capture an organization's climate and individual data aggregated to represent the climate (Ashkanasy, Wilderom, & Peterson, 2000). A great deal of attention has been devoted to the aggregation problem in climate, and the fundamental controversies have been largely resolved (cf. Bliese, 2000; Klein et al., 2000).

The Content of Climate

Climate research has been content dominated through attempts to determine the dimensions of the climates. Early

work often focused on global or molar concepts of climate, with the assumption that individuals develop global or summary perceptions of their organization (e.g., L. R. James & Jones, 1974; Schneider & Bartlett, 1968). Furthermore, early attention was devoted to the study of multiple climates within an organization. Research and rhetoric surrounded attempts to delineate different dimensions or define a set of dimensions thought to best represent the most important aspects of organizational climate (e.g., Campbell, Dunnette, Lawler, & Weick, 1970; Likert, 1967; Litwin & Stringer, 1968).

By the end of the 1970s, the number of dimensions identified as relevant for climate had grown quite large and included facets such as structure, reward, risk, warmth, support, standards, conflict, identity, democraticness, autocraticness, supportiveness, innovativeness, peer relations, cooperation, cohesion, pressure, and many more. New dimensions were being added to the conceptualization of climate each time a researcher thought climate might be useful for understanding some interesting phenomenon (Schneider, 2000). At the same time, many researchers were more concerned with organizational effectiveness than with climate per se, with climate being used as a way to understand why some organizations were more effective than others (Reichers & Schneider, 1990), even though critical reviews at the time concluded that there were only weak relationships between organizational climate and organizational effectiveness (e.g., Campbell et al., 1970; Payne & Pugh, 1976).

Schneider (1975) concluded that the molar concept of climate was too amorphous, inclusive, and multifaceted to be useful; that is, attempting to describe organizational situations simultaneously along 10 or so generic facets has no focus, and thus relationships to some specific outcome will be modest at best (Schneider et al., 2000). He proposed that climate be conceptualized and studied as a specific construct that has a particular referent or strategic focus, indicative of the organization's goals (Reichers & Schneider, 1990; Schneider). That is, climate research should shift from a molar, abstract perspective that includes everything that happens in an organization to linking climate to a specific, even strategic, criterion or outcome—a climate *for* something, such as a climate for service (Schneider, 1975, 1990). The underlying premise is similar to that in attitude research (Ajzen & Fishbein, 1975) in that the predictor and criterion variables not only should be conceptually linked, but also should be operationalized at the same level of specificity (Schneider & Reichers, 1983). The notion of a strategic criterion or a climate-for approach appears to be gaining wide acceptance, addressing issues such as climates for safety (Zohar, 2000), service (Schneider, 1990), sexual harassment

(Fitzgerald, Drasgow, Hulin, Gelfand, & Magley, 1997), innovation (Klein & Sorra, 1996), justice (Naumann & Bennett, 2000), citizenship behavior (Schneider, Gunnarson, & Niles-Jolly, 1994), and ethics (Victor & Cullen, 1988), to name a few.

Antecedents of Climate

A comprehensive treatment of the factors that create climate is largely lacking in the literature. Much more attention has been directed toward studying the outcomes of climate, rather than how climate develops or the features that create climate (Dennison, 1996). The organizational context and organizational practices are two potentially important antecedent variables can be gleaned from the literature.

Based on an extensive review of research, Payne and Pugh (1976) proposed a model indicating how organizational climate was produced from organizational context (e.g., purpose, size, resources, technology) and structure (hierarchy, authority system, structuring of role activities). However, research evidence has only modestly supported this model (e.g., A. P. Jones & James, 1979; Payne & Pugh, 1976). Nevertheless, given more recent developments in the conceptualization of climate around a specific strategic focus, it is likely that structural aspects may yet be important antecedents of climate. For example, technical, structural, and reward systems have been related to a climate for technical updating (Kozlowski & Hults, 1987). Vertical differentiation has been proposed as an important factor influencing organizational silence (Morrison & Milliken, 2000), and contextual variables such as size, differentiation, and centralization may be related to the number of subclimates that might be found in organizations.

Little research has examined the relationship between actual practices, policies, and procedures and measures of climate. This is surprising because (a) definitions of climate clearly indicate that climate is based on these practices, policies, procedures, and routines; (b) organizational practices are believed to at least partially influence organizational productivity and effectiveness (Kopelman et al., 1990); and (c) climate, as a cumulative construct, suggests that an organization's practices and policies for a particular type of climate may be more predictive of organizational outcomes than focusing on the determinants of climates themselves (Klein & Sorra, 1996). It is widely believed that practices, policies, and procedures—particularly human resource management practices—create the foundation for particular types of climate to develop (e.g., Klein & Sorra, 1996; Schneider, 1990), yet little research has tested this notion and climate is rarely studied as an outcome variable (Kopelman et al., 1990).

Furthermore, the beliefs, values, and role of top management have been proposed as important direct or indirect factors influencing organizational climate (e.g., Ostroff & Bowen, 2000). Additional issues pertaining to the formation of climate are addressed later in the climate emergence section.

Outcomes of Climate

A wide variety of global climate dimensions (e.g., participation, cooperation) and climates-for (e.g., for service) have been related to various attitudinal and performance-based outcomes. By far, the most studied group of climate outcomes includes those experienced by individuals in the workplace, although some work has examined relationships between group or organizational climate and group or organizational outcomes.

Individual-Level Outcomes

Two types of studies have typically been conducted to examine the impact of climate on individual outcomes: (a) individual-level studies examining relations between psychological climate perceptions and individual outcomes and (b) cross-level studies whereby aggregated unit or organizational climate scores are assigned to individuals and relationships to individual outcomes are examined. Empirical research has demonstrated relationships between overall climate (or global dimensions of psychological climate) and satisfaction (e.g., Johnson & McIntye, 1998), performance (e.g., Pritchard & Karasick, 1973), stress (e.g., Day & Bedeian, 1995; Feldt, Kinnunen, & Mauno, 2000; Hemingway & Smith, 1999), involvement (Shadur, Kienzle, & Rodwell, 1999), role-ambiguity stressors (Hemingway & Smith, 1999), and leader-member exchange relationships (e.g., Cogliser & Schriesheim, 2000). Individual perceptions of climates-for have also been related to affective and behavioral outcomes. For example, climate for technical updating has been related to commitment, satisfaction, and performance (Kozlowski & Hults, 1987), climate for justice to commitment and to helping behaviors (Naumann & Bennett, 2000), and climate for tolerance of sexual harassment to reports of harassment incidents (Hulin, Fitzgerald, & Drasgow, 1996). Cross-level studies have shown that unit or organizational climate is related to performance (Litwin & Stringer, 1968), helping behavior (Naumann & Bennett, 2000), accidents (e.g., Zohar, 2000), satisfaction, commitment, turnover intentions, absenteeism, and involvement (e.g., Jackofsky & Slocum, 1988; Joyce & Slocum, 1984; Ostroff, 1993b). Furthermore, the extent of agreement on overall climate has been related both to individual outcomes and to similarity in outcomes among organizational members (Lindell & Brandt, 2000).

Subunit- and Organizational-Level Outcomes

Climate for service has been the most consistently examined climate-for at the unit and organizational levels, with studies showing relationships to customer satisfaction ratings (e.g., Johnson, 1996); customer perceptions of service quality (e.g., Schneider & Bowen, 1985; Schneider, Parkington, & Buxton, 1980; Schneider, White, & Paul, 1998); and employee perceptions of service performance, which in turn are related to financial performance (e.g., Borucki & Burke, 1999). In addition, group-level climate for safety, as indexed through perceptions of supervisory actions of safety practices, has been related to objectively measured injuries (Zohar, 2000). Global climate dimensions have been related to organizational effectiveness (e.g., Lindell & Brandt, 2000; Ostroff & Schmitt, 1993), total quality management outcomes (Lin, Madu, & Kuei, 1999), and unit-level effectiveness and satisfaction (e.g., Pritchard & Karasick, 1973).

Summary

Despite the now–widely accepted definition of *climate* as a summary perception or summated meaning that people attach to particular features of the work setting, and the shift in climate from a largely generic, molar concept to one centered around a specific target or outcome, much work is needed in this area. While early research focused on links between climate and key organizational variables, for many years, investigations of climate have been largely based on solving methodological and definitional issues. Only recently have substantive climate investigations been gaining momentum. We believe the emerging research on "strategic climates" is a step in the right direction, but only a few climates-for have been empirically studied, and relatively little work has been conducted at the organizational level with only a narrow range of organizational outcomes studied.

More work is needed in specifying and testing theories that relate strategic climates to specific, commensurate outcomes. Similarly, it is generally acknowledged that multiple types of climate exist within an organization (e.g., Schneider & Snyder, 1975) and that organizations operate in multiple performance domains (e.g., Cameron, 1978). Yet, the work on climates-for has almost exclusively examined one climate for something at a time. It may be fruitful to simultaneously examine multiple climates-for such as a climate for employee justice, a climate for efficiency, and a climate for customer service. Different configurations of climates are likely to be related to effectiveness outcomes in different performance domains, and different configurations of climates may be related to more global indicators of effectiveness, such as market-based performance. Furthermore, work is also needed

to determine the relative importance of global versus strategic climate dimensions for different sets of outcomes. For example, it may be that global dimensions are more relevant for individual-level attitudes and outcomes whereas strategic dimensions are important for both individual behaviors and indices of organizational effectiveness.

RELATIONSHIP BETWEEN CULTURE AND CLIMATE

There are several key issues to consider when discussing the relationship between culture and climate and elucidating the relationships presented in Figure 22.1. We begin by exploring the theoretical and empirical overlap among the constructs and propose that organizational practices are the linking mechanism that mediates the relationship between culture and climate. We then explore the role of levels of analysis in the culture and climate literatures and the techniques for using aggregated data to represent these constructs at higher levels of analysis.

Overlap and Confusion Between Culture and Climate

Although researchers traditionally made theoretical distinctions between culture and climate, a number of recent articles have been devoted to what, if any, is the difference between these two concepts (cf. Dennison, 1996; Payne, 2000; Reichers & Schnieder, 1990; Trice & Beyer, 1993). Schein (2000) notes that in much of the popular management press, the term *culture* is often used when an examination of what is being said indicates that *climate* is the more appropriate term. We believe the root cause for the blurring of *culture* and *climate* stems not so much from theoretical treatments as from empirical attempts to assess the constructs.

Traditionally, culture was studied with qualitative methodologies using case studies, whereas climate research has been largely quantitative and survey based, asking employees about their perceptions of the organizational context. However, although early work in culture and climate retained a clear distinction between the two constructs both theoretically and methodologically, in more recent years, many empirical culture studies have become virtually indistinguishable from traditional climate research (Dennison, 1996; Hofstede, 1998).

Two types of studies have contributed to the overlap between climate and culture. First, during the 1990s, a number of quantitative culture studies began appearing, using a survey-based methodology much like that used in climate studies (e.g., Chatman, 1991; Cooke & Szumal, 1993) and often focusing on the same dimensions originally investigated in climate research (e.g., support, achievement, innovation). Many of the items in such so-called culture surveys are often very similar to items in climate surveys (Hofstede, 1998; Payne, 2000). In the culture literature, these dimensions (e.g., support, innovation, achievement) are often referred to as *values,* while in the climate literature they are often referred to as *climate dimensions* or the *organizational context*. We argue that, in these studies, the *why* of culture and the *what* of climate are not clearly distinguished.

The second research stream that has contributed to the blurring of these constructs involves culture studies that focus on quantitative assessments of perceptions of organizational practices (e.g., Christensen & Gordon, 1999; Hofstede, 1998; Hofstede et al., 1990). Here, it appears that researchers are using practices and procedures as a proxy of sorts for cultural assumptions, in that, based on practices, one can infer the culture. However, the items and dimensions assessed in these studies are often very similar to traditional climate research and more closely resemble climate as the perceptions of practices, policies, and procedures.

These types of studies tend to focus on what Schein (1992) terms *artifacts* and represent an overlap between research in climate and in culture. Although Schein (2000) explicitly defines *climate* as a cultural artifact resulting from espoused values and shared tacit assumptions, we argue, similar to others (e.g., Moran & Volkwein, 1992), that artifacts are the overlapping area between climate, as perceptions of practices, and culture, as deep-rooted assumptions and values. The focus on broad dimensions (e.g., risk-taking, supportiveness) or organizational practices represents the more artifact or surface aspects of culture but does not always clearly reflect underlying meaning or summary perceptions based on policies, practices, and procedures.

Organizational Practices: The Linking Mechanism Between Culture and Climate

Practices, policies, procedures, and routines play a role in both culture and climate. They are viewed as artifacts in culture (Schein, 1992), whereas in the climate literature (e.g., L. R. James, 1982; Schneider & Reichers, 1983) they are viewed as the basis for the formation of climate perceptions. We propose that the set of actual practices, policies, and procedures is the linking mechanism between culture and climate (see Figure 22.1), *not* a measure of either culture or climate.

Several researchers and theorists (e.g., Burke & Litwin, 1992; Kopelman et al., 1990) assert that the organizational practices, management practices, policies, and procedures

(hereafter referred to generically as *practices*) adopted in an organization reflect cultural influences. Similarly, other work has examined the degree of (in)congruence between culture and actual organizational practices and has taken this to be a measure of culture strength or consistency or alignment (e.g., Dennison, 1990; Smart & St. John, 1996). That is, alignment between culture and practices is a separate variable or construct. This implies that (a) culture is not practices and (b) culture should lead to a set of practices, policies, procedures, and routines that are consistent with the underlying cultural values (e.g., Kopelman et al., 1990). To the degree that alignment is achieved, organizational functioning and effectiveness should be enhanced.

However, alignment between culture and practices is not sufficient for organizational effectiveness. Organizational members must perceive the practices in a manner consistent with the underlying values and intended strategic goals. It is well accepted that practices are key ingredients in the determination of an organization's climate (e.g., Burke & Litwin, 1992; L. R. James & Jones, 1974; Reichers & Schnieder, 1990). Yet it is not the objective practices themselves that are climate, but rather, organizational members' interpretations and perceptions of these properties in psychologically meaningfully terms (Rentsch, 1990) that define climate.

Therefore, culture can lead to a set of relevant practices that are then perceived by organizational members. Based on cultural assumptions, certain sets of practices and procedures should be adopted, in concordance with strategic goals. For example, a set of reward practices about how to treat customers, selection standards, and so forth may be adopted to be consistent with a culture that values the customer. To the extent that organizational members perceive these practices to be consistent with a service focus and agree among themselves on their perceptions, a service-based organizational climate is said to exist in the firm (Schneider, 1990). This suggests the importance of *practices* as a mediating mechanism for linking culture and climate (Kopelman et al., 1990). Furthermore, it suggests that inconsistencies between culture and climate are likely to have occurred through some misalignment or poor implementation of the set of practices. If the adopted practices do not reflect the culture, or if practices are poorly implemented, climate perceptions may develop that are counter to the underlying cultural values and assumptions. In addition, these climate perceptions provide employees with direction and orientation about where they should focus their skills, attitudes, and behaviors in pursuit of organizational goals (Schneider et al., 1994). As implied in Figure 22.1, alignment between culture, practices, and climate is necessary for employees to respond and behave in ways that will lead to organizational effectiveness (e.g., Ostroff & Bowen, 2000).

It also is important to point out that organizations operate in multiple domains (Cameron, 1978) and that different configurations of organizational attributes will be relevant to different performance and effectiveness criteria (Ostroff & Schmitt, 1993). Hence we propose in Figure 22.1 that contextual features and strategic goals should enhance the formation of different cultures, which in turn are expected to result in the adoption of different sets of practices and perceptions of organizational climate.

Moving Across Levels of Analysis

In the culture literature, the term *levels* has been used to discuss the different layers of culture (artifacts, values, assumptions, ideologies) identified by Schein (1985, 1992) and others (Trice & Beyer, 1993). In the climate literature, the term *levels* has been used in a manner consistent with the literature on levels of analysis (i.e., on distinguishing among hierarchical levels in the organization; e.g., Klein, Dansereau, & Hall, 1994; Ostroff, 1993a). Here, we use the term *levels* to refer to the organizational levels-of-analysis literature, and we distinguish among the individual, subunit (e.g., group, division, plant, function), and organizational levels. We use the term *organizational* or *unit-level* generically to refer to higher level constructs.

Levels-of-analysis issues are implicit in the culture literature. Culture has been treated almost exclusively as a construct that resides at the organizational level. Yet, the conceptualization of culture rests upon shared meaning. Individuals are believed to construct shared meanings based on their social construction of organizational realities. Thus, by definition, a multilevel process takes place in culture, moving from individual constructions of the situation and sensemaking to the creation of shared meanings across people (see Figure 22.1).

In the climate area, levels issues are explicit. A levels-based distinction has been made between psychological and organizational climates (L. R. James & Jones, 1974) with the relationship between them viewed as *compositional*. That is, there is isomorphism in the manifestations of the construct at different levels of analysis whereby the constructs share the same content, meaning, and construct validity across levels of analysis (Chan, 1998; L. R. James, 1982; Kozlowski & Klein, 2000). Because researchers have acknowledged that climate is based on the psychological meaning of the situation to individuals (e.g., Rentsch, 1990), the unit of measurement begins with the individual. Only when these perceptions are shared across people does organizational climate become a meaningful construct (e.g., L. R. James, 1982; Payne, 1990). These levels-based constructs of composition are implicitly assumed

in culture. Theory is based on shared meanings of culture but little research has examined whether shared meaning exists, and whether isomorphism and composition models are necessary or appropriate in culture.

Furthermore, there is the assumption that different cultures and climates can exist at different organizational levels of analysis. Culture researchers, for example, have documented the existence of subcultures (e.g., Hofstede, 1998; Martin & Siehl, 1983), and climate researchers propose that functions, departments, or groups within an organization may develop different climates (e.g., Schneider & Bowen, 1985). We acknowledge that the *content* of the culture and climate can vary across groups within the organization and return to the implications of this after exploring the notion that climate and culture are emergent properties of organizations.

Shared Meaning and Perceptions

Shared meanings and perceptions are the foundation of organizational-level or unit-level culture and climate. We now discuss a variety of issues associated with the methods used to establish the extent of shared meaning or convergence of perceptions.

Demonstrating Agreement

In the culture area, meaning has most often been assessed through qualitative studies. Culture researchers elicit interpretations of what the organizational context means to employees (e.g., Langan-Fox & Tan, 1997) and from these assessments summarize meaning into some aggregated qualitative description of the culture. Thus, although studies of culture have assessed interpretations of events, the qualitative method does not well allow for objective comparisons across units or for direct assessment of the extent of agreement.

In contrast to the culture literature, climate researchers have devoted considerable attention to measuring and documenting the degree to which organizational members share perceptions of the organizational climate (Schneider, 2000). The most common procedure is to use a mean or aggregated score across individuals within the same unit to represent a higher level climate. However, procedures and criteria for determining whether the mean scores can be interpreted as an indicator of the higher level climate have been a source of debate (Patterson, Payne, & West, 1996). One criterion rests on the demonstration of between-group differences between units on their mean scores (cf. Glick, 1988; L. R. James, 1982). A second criterion rests on the demonstration of within-unit agreement or consensus to show that climate, conceptualized and operationalized at the individual level, is functionally isomorphic to another form of the construct (e.g., organizational climate) at the higher level (cf. Danserau, Alluto, & Yammarino, 1984; L. R. James, 1982; L. R. James, Demaree, & Wolfe, 1984). While debate continues about the most appropriate indices, researchers have generally agreed that some form of within-unit agreement or consensus in responses and sufficient between-unit variability be demonstrated in order to justify using the mean score to represent a higher level climate (Klein et al., 2000).

A related issue pertains to the referent or focal point for assessing climate. Many assessments of climate have had the focal point of measurement as the individual (e.g., *I perceive . . .*). However, some researchers (e.g., Chan, 1998; Klein, Cohn, Smith, & Sorra, 2001) have argued that rather than measure an individual's own climate perceptions, we should assess how an individual believes most people in the organization perceive the climate and whether there is within-unit consensus in such beliefs. Thus, conceptualization of the climate construct is still at the level of individual perception, but the referent of the content is changed to the unit level (from self to others). Finally, consensus or agreement can be imposed by having individuals discuss and come to agreement on the climate as a group. The resulting score is then used as the indicator of the climate, making statistical indices of agreement unnecessary. More research is needed to determine the implications of this shift in focal point and the use of group-based agreement techniques for the construct meaning of climate across levels of analysis.

(Dis)agreement

The absence of shared perceptions has been addressed in both the culture and climate literatures. For example, the *deviance model* (Martin, 1992) or the *dissensus model* (Trice & Beyer, 1993) of culture highlights disagreement or lack of consensus. However, there is debate as to whether deviance or dissensus in an organization indicates that a culture exists, a fragmented culture exists, or no culture exists. In the climate literature, large variability in perceptions among members indicates that aggregated perceptions do not adequately represent a construct of climate at the higher level (e.g., L. R. James, 1982; Klein et al., 2001).

Empirical studies of climate have often found that although agreement on climate may be adequate from a methodological standpoint for the study as a whole, there is still considerable variability in perceptions, and some groups or organizations in the sample have less than adequate agreement on climate perceptions. Thus, additional models for addressing the link between individual perceptions and aggregate constructs have been suggested. For example, in a *dispersion model* (e.g.,

Chan, 1998; Kozlowski & Klein, 2000), the degree of variability of responses (e.g., an r_{wg} score) can be an important variable in its own right (not only a justification for an aggregate score), independent of the level of the content of climate (e.g., mean climate on some climate dimension). To the extent that greater homogeneity in perceptions of climate is present, collective perceptions and responses should be more uniform and organizational-level relationships can emerge and be meaningfully examined (Ostroff & Bowen, 2000).

Collectivities

Recently, cluster analysis has been used to form *subcultures* (e.g., Hofstede, 1998) and *collective climates,* which represent clusters of employees who perceive the organization similarly (e.g., Jackofsky & Slocum, 1984; Patterson et al., 1996; González-Romá, Peiró, Lloret, & Zornoza, 1999). Because subcultures and collective climates are formed by grouping people based on the similarity of their perceptions, the agreement problem is essentially solved (Payne, 1990). Nevertheless, collective climates may not be representative of a meaningful organizational construct, but rather may be statistical artifacts, particularly if they do not correspond to any defined, formally or informally structured collectivity such as workgroups, divisions, or hierarchical levels (Patterson et al., 1996; Payne, 1990). The foundation of this argument is relevant to the unresolved and underresearched question about how individuals come to share similar perceptions of the work environment (Schneider & Reichers, 1983; Young & Parker, 1999).

EMERGENCE OF SHARED MEANING AND PERCEPTIONS

Culture and climate are viewed, at least partly, as emergent properties of organizations. As defined by Kozlowski and Klein (2000, p. 55), "a phenomenon is emergent when it originates in the cognition, affect, behaviors or other characteristics of individuals, is amplified by their interaction, and manifests as a higher level, collective phenomenon" Two distinct dimensions of emergent processes are delineated: elemental content and interaction. *Elemental content* is the raw material of emergence and refers to the cognitions, affect, perceptions, or mental representations. *Interaction* denotes the process of emergence (e.g., how elemental content becomes shared) through communication and information exchange, sharing of ideas, exchanging work products, and other forms of interactions among employees. In combination, the elemental content and form of the interaction process comprise the *emergent phenomenon.* While much has been written about the process of social information processing, in which individuals use schema and scripts contained in cognitive categories to interpret stimuli (cf. Corner, Kinicki, & Keats, 1994; Fiske & Taylor, 1984; Weick, 1995), group members can share the same schema for important work-related events, enabling them to act more effectively and efficiently with one another and within the context of the situation (Schneider, 1975). These shared interpretations form the basis for a shared sense of culture and for the emergence of a unit-level climate. Thus, it is important to understand *how* similar cognitive maps (Weick, 1995) can be created across people, thereby allowing an analysis of the situation as a whole as opposed to analysis of individual differences in the perception of situations (Magnusson & Endler, 1977).

Emergence of Organizational Culture

Hatch (1993), Peterson and Smith (2000), and Trice and Beyer (1993) discuss the sense-making process underlying organizational culture. According to Trice and Beyer, "Sense making is a cognitive process in that it involves knowing and perceiving, it is a behavioral process in that it involves doing things, and it is a social process in that it involves people doing things together" (p. 81). They note that sense-making occurs at both nonconscious and conscious levels and is both retrospective and prospective in nature. Sense-making about culture, however, occurs between and among people because culture involves shared interpretations about an organization. Social processes and interactions are thus at the core of emergent processes regarding culture (Kilduff & Corley, 2000; Peterson & Smith; Trice & Beyer).

Strain-Theory Perspective

Trice and Beyer (1993) use *strain theory* to explain how culture emerges. Given that people are averse to strain and its associated negative consequences, Trice and Beyer propose that *ideologies,* which represent the core content of an organization's culture, are used to make social situations comprehensible, more structured, and less stressful. They propose that an organization's culture ultimately is shaped by the conflict and strain that exits among competing ideologies. Although Trice and Beyer note that shared experiences, socialization, communication, social interactions, and the related processes of influence, power, and leadership affect the sense-making process, they do not specifically detail how conflict among ideologies manifests in the emergence of organizational culture.

Symbolic-Process Perspective

Hatch's (1993) model includes a role for symbolic processes and specifies linkages with Schein's (1985, 1992) three layers of culture. The dynamic, emergent nature of Hatch's model is captured by a conceptualization of the links among artifacts, values, assumptions, and symbols as being influenced by four processes: manifestation, realization, symbolization, and interpretation. These four processes create both *forward* (proactive/prospective) and *backward* (retrospective/retroactive) temporal modes of operation.

The embedding process begins through the manifestation and realization of specific assumptions, values, or behavioral norms. Cultural artifacts are the product of manifestation and realization processes. According to Hatch (2000, p. 250), "artifacts realize underlying values and assumptions in the sense that they are made real (tangible, explicit, material) via actions that are culturally shaped and directed." Once an artifact is realized, the symbolization and interpretation processes take over and lead to the emergence of organizational culture. An artifact becomes a *cultural symbol* when people use the symbol to make sense of an event or artifact. For example, a company pin becomes an artifact whenever someone wears it. *Symbolization* represents the process of linking artifacts with meanings through the recognition of personal or social significance. Symbolization is largely influenced by the social context associated with the artifact. Finally, *interpretation* specifies the meaning attached to a symbol. Returning to the example of wearing a corporate pin, this artifact could be symbolic of company pride or of an ingratiating person, depending on the social context operating at the time the pin is worn. It thus appears that culture becomes emergent when large segments of the unit or organization share the symbolic interpretations of assumptions, values, and behavioral norms. Although Hatch's model helps explain the dynamic nature of how organizational culture emerges, researchers have not yet begun to empirically examine the model's key propositions.

Role-Theory Perspective

Peterson and Smith (2000) explain the emergent process using *role theory.* Their fundamental proposition is that sense-making is derived by linking events to interpretative structures. The interpretative structures contain a taxonomy of sources of meaning that are intraorganizational (rules, superiors, colleagues, subordinates, and self) and extraorganizational (international, national, and local societal rules; primary groups; professional rules; professional peers; other rules and parties; and societal self). Organizational members are viewed as using these sources to make sense of specific events. Furthermore,

Peterson and Smith believe that people occupying various roles (e.g., a chief executive officer, or CEO) can deliberately attempt to influence sense-making. For example, a CEO may try to create the impression that downsizing is a good event because it helps the organization reduce costs and improve customer service. Similar to Hatch (2000), Peterson and Smith note that research is needed to investigate how influence- or power-based approaches affect the social construction process and the emergence of culture. Unfortunately, they do not specifically explain how a shared view of an organization's culture is formed by the interactions of various role holders and sources of meaning.

Summary

The writings by Corner et al. (1994), Peterson and Smith (2000), Trice and Beyer (1993), and Weick (1995) help frame the social cognitive processes that influence organizational sense-making, but only Hatch (1993) provides a detailed explanation of how emergence actually occurs. We suspect that the inherent complexity of the phenomenon precludes a precise explanation for the emergence of organizational culture. Clearly, conceptual work is needed to further understand how individual interpretations of organizational events are transformed into shared meanings.

Emergence of Organizational Climate

Schneider and Reichers (1983) delineated three perspectives on the formation of climate: *structuralist, attraction-selection-attrition (ASA)* or *homogeneity,* and *social interaction.* Although it is sometimes considered part of the structuralist perspective, we also discuss separately the importance of leadership as well as the impact of an individuals' immediate workgroup.

Structure and Practices

In the *structuralist* perspective, climate purportedly arises out of structural characteristics of an organization. With its roots in Lewin's (1951) field theory, this approach assumes that organizational characteristics such as size and structure establish a common reality that provides the basis for shared perception. The person is analytically separate from the social context (Roberts et al., 1978). Support for this perspective has rested on research showing that climate perceptions are related to structural variables such as size, centralization, structure, and hierarchical level (e.g., Payne & Pugh, 1976).

More consistent with current definitions of climate, the set of policies, practices, and procedures of the organization are

the features that provide the basis for shared perceptions to emerge. However, merely introducing and implementing a set of practices around some strategic focus is not sufficient. Unless the practices are designed and implemented in such a way as to create a strong situation (Mischel, 1973), idiosyncratic psychological climate perceptions are likely to emerge (Ostroff & Bowen, 2000). Organizational practices, such as *human resource management (HRM)* practices, are often viewed as communications from the employer to employee (Rousseau, 1995; Tsui, Pearce, Porter, & Tripoli, 1997). Yet two employees can interpret the same practice differently because there is considerable variance among employees in the sense-making strategies they use in interpreting these messages (Guzzo & Noonan, 1994). Differences in category systems or cognitive maps can exist across people (Kelly, 1955). To the extent that the situational stimulus is ambiguous or unclear, multiple categorization is likely (Feldman, 1981) and different people are likely to use different cognitive categories to attend to different aspects of the situation, making subsequent attributions different. This can result in divergent views about appropriate behaviors (Rousseau & Wade-Benzoni, 1994).

On the other hand, collective sense-making can occur when practices are designed to induce a strong situation, regardless of the type of practice implemented. For example, when practices represent a coherent and internally consistent whole; are made very visible; are communicated widely and clearly; are administered consistently throughout the organization; and are fair, legitimate, and valid, a collective perception of climate based on these practices is more likely to emerge (Ostroff & Bowen, 2000). These metacharacteristics of the practices help reduce ambiguity and enhance clarity of interpretation in the setting, thereby allowing for similar cognitive maps to develop across people so that the context and appropriate ways of behaving are understood. A strong process of delivering practices creates the elemental content and this content is shared because interpretations are consistent across people. One implication is that in today's world of virtual organizations or virtual teams, in which interaction and communication are often limited, climate could be perceived similarly if the practices are unambiguous and delivered in a strong manner (although climate in general may be less useful as an explanatory variable with such distributed work arrangements).

Homogeneity

This approach is based on the ASA process (Schneider & Reichers, 1983) in which individuals are attracted to and want to join organizations that have similar attributes to their own views and attributes. Selection procedures attempt to ensure that the applicants hired fit the organizational context, and people tend to leave organizations when the work context does not fit their personal characteristics. As a result, an organization is likely to consist of very similar people (Schneider, 1987). These effects may be furthered by the socialization processes that can change new organizational members' personal attributes, goals, and values in the direction of those of the organization (Fisher, 1986; Ostroff & Rothausen, 1997). Due to this homogeneity process, individuals should perceive the organization similarly and sense-making should not yield idiosyncratic interpretations, but should yield agreement (Schneider, 1983).

Little empirical work has explicitly tested the relationship between homogeneity and the development of shared climate perceptions. Early work, largely in educational settings, showed that personality was related to organizational climate perceptions (e.g., J. R. George & Bishop, 1971; Stern, 1970). Recently, group cohesiveness has been positively related to agreement on climate perceptions (Naumann & Bennett, 2000) and needs have been related to collective climate membership (Young & Parker, 1999).

Social Interaction and Communication

The third approach to the emergence and formation of organizational climate is based on social interaction, with roots in symbolic interactionism. Shared perception and meaning evolve from communications and interaction patterns among members of the same group. Work contexts are created by the individuals within them—that is, "the people make the place" (Schneider, 1987); and at the same time, the context and individuals' interpretations of it have a large influence and impact on behavior and responses (e.g., Ashforth, 1985; Morgeson & Hofmann, 1999; Schneider & Reichers, 1983).

Overlapping schemas or cause maps across people can be facilitated through social exchange and transactions among employees. In such a way they can agree on the appropriate aspects of the environment to attend to, and on how to interpret these aspects and respond to them appropriately (Weick, 1995; Wicker, 1992). As explained by Morgeson and Hofmann (1999), within any collective, individuals are likely to meet one another and interact. Each interaction results in a discrete event, and subsequent interactions are termed *event cycles*. The structure of any collective group can be viewed as a series of ongoing events, activities, and events cycles among the individuals. These interdependencies and interactions among individuals over time can result in jointly produced responses, and it is this structure that forms the basis for the eventual emergence of collective constructs. Group

members construct the meaning of organizational events from repeated social interactions and it is these interactions that are likely to result in conformity (Ashforth, 1985).

Some recent empirical studies have shown that collective climates (defined through clusters of people with similar perceptions) are related to formal workgroup membership (e.g., Jackofsky & Slocum, 1988; Young & Parker, 1999). However, other research has found little or no relationship between collective climates and workgroup membership, regional membership, job type, or hierarchical level (e.g., Patterson et al., 1996; González-Romá et al., 1999). One explanation for these contradictory findings is based on informal interaction groups, which may have more influence on the development of shared climate perceptions than structurally imposed interaction groups. Indeed, research has shown that informal interaction groups attached similar meanings to the organizational context (Rentsch, 1990) and that individuals' climate perceptions were more similar to those of others with whom stronger communication ties were maintained (Fink & Chen, 1995). Clearly, more research is needed in this area. For example, researchers should investigate the extent to which interactions and interdependencies actually occur in structurally imposed groups, and whether it is these interactions that form shared perceptions. Likewise, given that exposure to and participation in various work practices can result in more positive perceptions about the practices and the organization (Katz & Kahn, 1978), much more research is needed in determining how individuals shape the climate and affect climate perceptions.

Leadership

Finally, shared perceptions may result through leadership processes. Original conceptualizations of climate focused largely on the role of the leader in creating climates (e.g., Lewin et al., 1939; McGregor, 1960) and experimental studies showed that climates became increasingly differentiated over time in a manner consistent with a leader's style (Litwin & Stringer, 1968). Leaders or supervisors serve as interpretive filters of relevant organizational processes, practices, and features for all group members, contributing to the development of common climate perceptions (Kozlowski & Doherty, 1989). By exposing employees to the same policies, practices, and procedures, leaders act as "climate engineers" (Naumann & Bennett, 2000) or "meaning managers" (Smircich & Morgan, 1982).

For example, in a study of service climates, the importance of service to managers was related to employee perceptions of the service climate (Borucki & Burke, 1999). This is likely due to the fact that managers and leaders are largely responsible for communicating meaning (Schein, 1992). Leaders explicitly and directly communicate their own interpretations and, in conjunction with interacting with most members, will be able to introduce a common interpretation among unit members (Rentsch, 1990). Indeed, in a recent study, agreement among workgroup members on climate was stronger when the supervisor was seen as visible in implementing organizational procedures and enforcing policies (Naumann & Bennett, 2000). Moreover, several studies have indicated that high-quality-exchange relationships with a leader are related to climate perceptions and that subordinates in high-quality-exchange leader-member relationships had greater within-unit consensus on climate perceptions (e.g., Kozlowski & Doherty, 1989; Scott & Bruce, 1994). The causal direction of the relationship between climate and leader-member relationships, however, is not yet known (Cogliser & Schriesheim, 2000).

Furthermore, the literature on social influence and authority indicates that individuals are willing to adjust their behavior in response to the inductions of some influencing agent (Kelman & Hamilton, 1989). The influencing agent, or in this case leader or supervisor, can exert influence and induce uniform behavior through informing the person about the nature of the situation and what is at stake for him or her in this situation, explaining practices, policies, and procedures and the consequences for adhering or failing to adhere to them, and enacting the organizational practices. Not only can a leader create shared perceptions by serving as a filter of and model for organizational practices, policies, and procedures, but through influence can induce uniform responses in accordance with these practices, which are then interpreted by members in forming perceptions of climate. The role of the leader in forming climate perceptions is an area ripe for research.

Workgroup Influences

As noted earlier, the aggregate level of analysis refers to any higher level (e.g., division, function, unit). The most immediate and proximal level is likely to have the greatest influence (Katz & Kahn, 1978; Rousseau, 1985); hence, processes within an individual's immediate workgroup or team should help in the formation of shared cognitions.

Recent work in the area of teams has highlighted the concept of shared mental models as an underlying mechanism for team effectiveness, enabling team members to respond appropriately and effectively in their work environments (Kozlowski, Gully, Salas, & Cannon-Bowers, 1996; Marks, Zaccaro, & Mathieu, 2000). For example, using a technique called *concept mapping*, Marks et al. showed that leader communication in the form of transmitting, exchanging, reporting, and passing on information about the task and the work

environment as well as training focused on team interaction were related to the development of shared mental models about how the work system and environment operate. Similarly, Hofmann and Stetzer (1996) showed that the group process (e.g., sharing information, coordinating efforts, interdependence) was related to shared perceptions of a climate for safety, and that both group process and climate were related to individual-level and group-level safety outcomes.

While we acknowledge that the factors discussed previously (structure, ASA, communication, leader roles) are likely to have effects on the emergence of shared perceptions within a work unit similar to the effects they have for any level of analysis, the proximal nature of the immediate workgroup makes it worthy of separate mention. There are also other workgroup processes, such as task characteristics and workgroup structure, and common workgroup experiences such as successes and failures (Marks et al., 2000), that are likely to influence the development of shared perceptions among workgroup or team members. In this regard, researchers might find the perspective offered by *structuration theory* (Poole, 1999) useful. *Structuration* is a general theory that can be applied to any emergent or developmental phenomenon in groups and that acknowledges the role of action, group interaction, and their products. Essentially, this theory focuses on understanding the structuring process, or the explicit and implicit rules and resources that members use to generate and sustain the group system and that serve as guides for action.

Implications and Research Directions

Emergent Process

Elemental content differs between culture and climate. For example, the cognitions, interpretations, and schemas are based around the policies, practices, procedures, and routines in climate (Schneider & Reichers, 1983), whereas in culture they are based on assumptions, ideologies, values, and artifacts (Schein, 1992; Trice & Beyer, 1993). However, the interaction process of emergence shares common features across culture and climate. Both can be based on homogeneity, communication, social interactions, and leadership.

A fruitful avenue for culture and climate research would be combining the research traditions of each (cf. Rentsch, 1990; Sparrow & Gaston, 1996). For example, if a researcher is interested in studying the service-oriented climate, from a quantitative perspective, the description and shared nature of the climate can be delineated. From a qualitative culture-oriented perspective, the deeper meanings and values behind this descriptively based, shared climate can be discerned. Both qualitative and quantitative studies can examine the features that led to the shared interpretation of a service-oriented climate.

Furthermore, in climate it has been argued that perceptions must be similar to justify moving from individual-level perceptions to higher level climate. However, the notion of *compilation* (Kozlowski & Klein, 2000) is based on the assumption that organizational practices, policies, procedures, the socialization process, the ASA process, and related processes are not so strong as to eliminate all meaningful differences in individual members' elemental characteristics such as their cognitions, perceptions, and behaviors. For example, some organizations may desire to build an organization that has some heterogeneity of employees in order to create flexibility or promote change (Schneider & Reichers, 1983) and may intentionally select individuals for their varying idiosyncratic strengths (Kozlowski & Klein). Likewise, interactions among organizational members might result in some dissimilarity or polarization of employees (Kozlowski & Klein). Although too much variability in fundamental elements would indicate either a fragmented climate or culture or no climate or culture at all, variability in fundamental elements may not necessarily lead to lack of emergence of shared properties. Different mental models can be compatible, fit together in a complementary way (Kozlowski & Klein), and create a complementarity whereby the whole is more than the sum of the parts (Milgrom & Roberts, 1995). This implies that a configural approach (Doty & Glick, 1994) might be appropriate in that it is the *pattern* of individual elements or cognitions in conjunction with interaction patterns that results in the emergence of shared meanings and perceptions. Emergence can be equifinal in that collective phenomena may emerge in different ways and with different profiles and patterns. Thus, heterogeneity in individual elements does not preclude the emergence of a collective property (Kozlowski & Klein, 2000).

Strength

The emergent property of organizational culture or climate can be strong or weak. The general notion of strong versus weak situations is largely derived from Mischel's (1973) such that situations are strong to the degree that "they lead all persons to construe the particular events the same way, induce uniform expectancies regarding the most appropriate response pattern, provide adequate incentives for the performance of that response pattern, and instill the skills necessary for its satisfactory construction and execution" (p. 276). Weak situations are ambiguously coded or not uniformly interpreted across individuals, do not generate uniform expectancies concerning the desired behavior, do not offer sufficient incentives for its performance, or fail to provide the learning needed for behaving appropriately.

The terms *strong culture* and *strong climate* have emerged in the literature, but have not been defined in consistent ways. We delineate three aspects of strength that encompass strong situations: (a) *agreement-based strength,* dealing with the extent to which employees interpret and encode the organizational situation in the same way, that is, the extent of agreement on culture or climate; (b) *system-based strength,* pertaining to the notion that culture or climate is pervasive and all-encompassing throughout the entire domain of organizational life, imposes strong expectations on employees, and attempts to induce uniform behaviors (e.g., strong socialization programs, training, sanctions for behaving outside norms); and (c) *alignment-based strength,* referring to the congruence between culture and actual organizational practices (e.g., Dennison, 1990; Smart & St. John, 1996) and between organizational practices and climate.

In the emergence of organizational climate, it is likely that the perspectives delineated previously (structure, homogeneity, social interaction, and leadership) will influence the strength of the climate. Agreement-based strength is fostered when (a) practices are administered in a way that allows individuals to interpret them similarly, (b) members are homogenous and thus predisposed to view the organization similarly, (c) shared interpretations are developed through social interactions, or (d) leaders serve as filters and communicators of practices, policies, and procedures to influence members to interpret situations the same way. Indeed, without agreement-based strength or a shared sense of the climate, linkages between organizational climate and subsequent outcomes at the aggregate level are unlikely to be realized (see Figure 22.1).

Yet, the emergence of climate and the fostering of agreement-based strength do not necessarily lead to alignment-based strength. The climate that is perceived should be one that was intended through the set of practices. The practices, policies, and procedures, when administered in a strong (e.g., salient, consistent, fair, valid) way, provide the elemental content in the form of a cognitive representation of the climate. To the extent that the homogeneity process is strong *and* the process of administering practices is strong, similar cognitive elements should form and shared perceptions of climate should emerge that are consistent with the intent of the practices (thereby creating alignment-based strength). However, to the extent that the homogeneity process is weak or that practices are not administered in a way to create a strong situation, social interaction and leadership processes can lead to the formation of shared perceptions of climates that may or may not be consistent with what was ultimately intended.

Finally, system-based strength is fostered when a set of practices is developed that is internally consistent and intensive. *Internal consistency* is achieved when the members of the set of practices reinforce and support one another around a specific focus. For example, if innovation is the strategic focus and value, all the practices should help build an interpretation of innovation and reinforce behaviors aligned with that focus. *Intensity* is achieved when the organization implements a wide range of practices that pervade all aspects of organizational life. For example, some organizations adopt low-intensity HRM systems, utilizing a minimum of practices. In contrast, high-performance HRM systems (e.g., Becker & Huselid, 1998; Lawler, 1992) are based on the premise that employee involvement and participation are cornerstones of a productive workforce. These systems encompass practices such as teams, expanding job duties, employee ownership, performance-sensitive pay, and rewards based on group or organizational performance. Such a system of practices would be considered intense because it involves a wide range of practices requiring a great deal of participation on the part of employees and encompass the range of organizational activities (Ostroff, 1995). Intense systems affect a large number of employees and are designed to induce a uniform set of behaviors among employees (Ostroff & Bowen, 2000).

When agreement-based strength is fostered in conjunction with alignment-based strength between the climate and practices and in conjunction with system-based strength, an organizational climate emerges that is consistent with what was intended by the practices. This does not necessarily mean, however, that the resulting climate is consistent with the strategic goals and culture. Alignment-based strength between culture and practices and a strong system-based culture with intense practices that induce and reward uniform values and behavior are also needed. When strength and alignment are achieved across culture *and* climate, expected relationships between climate and organizational outcomes are more likely to be realized.

Subcultures and Subclimates

Subcultures and subclimates can emerge throughout the organization. Within-unit social interactions, communication, interdependencies, and different leadership processes can lead to the formation of emergence of a culture or climate within a group that may differ between groups in the same organization (Hofstede, 1998).

Although some have argued that subcultures and climates can meaningfully exist when core values or perceptions are consistent with the organizational culture and climate, much work is needed in examining the implications of subunit cultures and climates. For example, this raises the question of whether in today's large, diversified, geographically dispersed organizations, there can be such a thing as organizational culture and climate. Can shared meanings and perceptions develop across such an organization?

Furthermore, studies have documented different team- or group-level climates within an organization. However, few studies have examined the degree of climate consistency among groups within an organization, although Griffin and Mathieu (1997) showed that aggregated climate perceptions across hierarchical levels within an organization were related. Studies are needed that include multiple groups from multiple organizations to determine whether groups within an organization are more similar to one another than groups across organizations.

Although the concept of countercultures implies a negative connotation, we argue that the effects of subcultures and subclimates depend on the extent to which they are contradictory or in opposition to each other or the extent to which they complement one another and potentially form a complementarity. Clearly, if two subcultures or climates produce negativity, conflict, politics, and negative competition between groups, the subcultures are not complementary or compatible and may be detrimental both to individual responses and to organizational outcomes. However, subclimates can exist simultaneously without creating conflict (O. Jones, 2000). For example, an innovation-based climate in one division may complement a quality-based climate in another division. If the organization's strategy is to provide high-quality service or products, but at the same time it also wants to explore entry into new markets, these two different climates may exist simultaneously in different divisions and yet produce a complementarity at the organizational level. Again, this suggests that patterns across multiple strategic climates should be investigated and that different patterns of climates may be equifinal for organizational effectiveness.

CULTURE AND CLIMATE CHANGE

The change process is relevant to both culture and climate. More attention has been devoted to the process of culture change than that of climate change in the literature. Yet, culture should be more resistant to change than climate (Schein, 2000).

Culture Change

There is much controversy about whether organizational culture can and should be consciously changed by management (e.g., Harris & Ogbonna, 1999; Martin, 1985; Sathe & Davidson, 2000; Smircich, 1983). Opinions range from management can and should change culture (Sathe & Davidson) to the manipulation of culture can only occur naturally and is not the consequence of management's direct intervention (Ogbonna, 1993). The value and appropriateness of discussing cultural change depend on one's philosophical orientation.

Sathe and Davidson (2000) reviewed the cultural change literature and made observations about two key unresolved issues. The first pertains to whether a culture's fundamental assumptions or ideologies can be changed, and they concluded that, in fact, some values and beliefs can. This conclusion was supported by idiographic studies showing that cultural change programs resulted in changes in employee behaviors that were consistent with the desired culture (e.g., Langan-Fox & Tan, 1997; Ogbonna & Harris, 1998) and that cultural change programs resulted in corresponding changes in organizational systems, structure, and strategy (Ogbonna & Harris). These positive results, however, must be tempered by findings from case studies showing that employees' reactions to cultural change are not always what they seem. Ogbonna and Harris's case study revealed that some of the employees' behavioral change actually represented resigned compliance rather than authentic change. Their results also indicated that value changes were not uniformly positive and ranged from rejection to reorientation.

Moreover, Gilmore, Shea, and Useem (1997) identified four key side effects or unintended consequences of culture-change initiatives based on their personal observations of culture change across numerous organizations over the course of six years. These side effects include *ambivalent authority* (i.e., who is responsible for leading change and who decides what must change), *polarized images* (i.e., contrasting images of and comfort with the new and old ways of doing things can polarize employees), *disappointment and blame* (i.e., initial success can give rise to resistance and disappointment, which is frequently followed by finger-pointing toward perceived malcontents and scapegoats), and *behavioral inversion* (i.e., new values, beliefs, and behaviors are absorbed into old ones, making the old seem new and thus preserving the status quo without appearing to do so). All told, cultural change can change fundamental values, but management must be aware of negative side effects that are likely to occur. Planning for these side effects should be included in planning a cultural-change initiative.

Sathe and Davidson's (2000) second unresolved issue is associated with the decision of how best to refreeze (Lewin, 1951) or reinforce culture change. That is, should management use extrinsic and intrinsic forms of reinforcement, and

when should they be used? Sathe and Davidson conclude that both forms of reinforcement are needed at different points in the change process. This recommendation is consistent with Stajkovic and Luthans (1997) meta-analysis of organizational behavior modification (OB Mod) research, which revealed that behavioral changes aimed at increasing productivity resulted in a 17% increase in performance when desired behaviors where specifically tied to contingent consequences. Furthermore, Sathe and Davidson also endorsed Luthans and Kreitner's (1985, p. 128) conclusion that

natural rewards are potentially the most powerful and universally applicable reinforcers. In contrast to contrived rewards, they do not generally lead to satiation (people seldom get tired of compliments, attention, or recognition) and can be administered on a very contingent basis.

Climate Change

Little research has explicitly tested whether climates change in reaction to changes in practices (Schuster et al., 1997, is an exception), and no research that we are aware of has explicitly examined the process of *how* climate perceptions change over time. Nevertheless, testable theoretical explanations have been offered about the change process in climate.

Climate is formed from the practices, policies, and procedures of the organization. Thus, a change in practices should result in a change in the content of climate (Kopelman et al., 1990) and force a reevaluation of the situation (Guzzo & Noonan, 1994). The employee is deemed to be a receiver of the communicative content of practices and procedures (Guzzo & Noonan, 1994; Rousseau, 1995). In making interpretations of these practices, either automatic or systematic processing of communications (Eagley & Chaiken, 1993; Feldman, 1981) will be evoked (Guzzo & Noonan, 1994). *Automatic processing* entails a superficial perception and assessment of signals. In contrast, *systematic processing* involves careful attention to stimuli, extensive evaluation of and comparison with present knowledge and belief, and the making of inferences about how all this might affect one's attitudes and behaviors. Changes in practices and communications are likely to trigger systematic processing as employees derive conscious explanations of the information (i.e., as they engage in sense-making; Guzzo & Noonan, 1994). Changes in particular practices (e.g., a change from a merit-based system to profit sharing, or adding a new practice such as teams) will evoke a process of reinterpreting what the organization expects.

Furthermore, constructs may shift levels over time (Dansereau, Yammarino, & Kohles, 1999). Changes in the set of practices may initially cause discord and disagreement among individuals in an organization. Hence a previously homogenous group with shared perceptions that lead to an organizational climate may lose their agreement with a change in practices, thereby enabling a focus on psychological climates only. Thus, a change in practice may not produce the desired change in climate content unless the process of the changed practices is delivered in an effective manner (e.g., they evoke salience, understandability, visibility, and so forth; Ostroff & Bowen, 2000). In addition, climate change is likely to fail if we do not take into consideration the underlying cultural assumptions (Schein, 2000). As noted by Reichers and Schnieder (1990), a climate survey may not yield sufficient data about the inner workings of an organization and is unlikely to be a good source of information for promoting change toward a new focus or strategic objective. In promoting climate change, it may be necessary to examine underlying cultural assumptions through other methodologies (e.g., qualitative study, attributional analysis) to determine whether the desired climate change is consistent with underlying cultural assumptions and to derive more information about the organization's functioning.

CONCLUSIONS AND DIRECTIONS FOR FUTURE RESEARCH

We believe that the definitional distinction between *what* and *why* highlighted initially is a useful one because it indicates the interrelationship between the two constructs of culture and climate as well as their differences. Researchers, theorists, and practitioners are urged to attend more carefully to whether they are referring to climate or culture and to whether they are referring to psychological or organizational climate (as defined previously) in an effort to help to reduce the emerging confusion between the two constructs. Although culture and climate are similar and interrelated in that they both focus on the creation and impact of social contexts, maintaining a distinction between them is important if we are to understand different aspects of the social context and shared meaning and perceptions that develop in organizational life. At the same time, we argue that there is much to be learned by examining the two streams of research simultaneously rather than approaching each as a separate body of literature.

Much theory and research has addressed the layers of culture, how employees and new members learn about the culture, and how culture can be changed. Yet culture research, although theoretically strong in the notion of shared meaning, has done little in the way of empirically measuring or determining the extent to which shared meaning exists, nor does it

have a strong tradition in defining the dimensions of culture or of developing categories of culture (Schein, 2000). In contrast, in climate research, much attention has been devoted to content or delineating different types of climates and the types of organizational practices, policies, and goals that lead to these types of climate, but very little attention in climate has been devoted to process or *how* shared interpretations of climate emerge. Some of the difference in emphasis in culture and climate work is likely due to measurement techniques that have dominated these research areas. Climate's tradition of survey research is deductive and requires that content of climate be specified a priori, whereas culture's tradition of observational techniques, qualitative studies, and case studies is more inductive and allows for the emergence of cultural properties but not for robust comparisons with other organizations (Ashkanasy, Wilderom, et al., 2000). Our understanding of climate could be advanced if we used the qualitative and quantitative techniques from culture research to examine the deeper values and assumptions that help lead to climate (Schein, 2000; Schneider, 2000). Similarly, climate researchers could learn from culture researchers about studying the change process, while culture researchers could borrow from the strong measurement tradition, particularly about aggregation and agreement, inherent in climate research (Dennison, 1996; Schneider, 2000) to examine shared meaning.

Research is also needed to test many of the linkages specified in Figure 22.1, both within and between levels. Theorists and researchers are urged to take a multilevel perspective in examining culture and climate. In particular, a much-neglected area of research is the emergence from the individual level to higher levels in the formation of culture and climate. Research is needed to explore *how* these constructs emerge in organizations.

We also specified that the structural context and set of organizational practices, policies, and procedures are the mediating mechanism between culture and climate. Future research is needed to test this notion. For example, research could assess cultural values and assumptions; actual practices as reported by managers, HR directors, and written documents; and employee perceptions of these practices to test the linkages specified in Figure 22.1. Related research should test alignment among culture, practices, and climate. For example, climates inconsistent with culture may result when practices are not consistent with culture or are not delivered in a way that creates a strong situation that allows for the formation of shared perceptions. Additional research is needed to determine both how alignment-based strength is fostered and its relationship to agreement-based and system-based strength in the emergence and impact of culture and climate.

The lack of relationship between culture and performance may be due to the failure to take into account the mediating mechanisms specified in Figure 22.1. Although a few studies have demonstrated relationships between climate and organizational performance, much more work is needed in this area. For example, there is emerging work on the link between HRM practices and organizational performance (e.g., Becker & Huselid, 1998) with assumed mediators of climate and collective attributes of employees, but little work has explicitly tested these relationships. Indeed, some of the contradictory findings of organizational practice-outcome relationships may be due to fact that organizational climate did not emerge (e.g., due to poor agreement-based or alignment-based strength) and hence expected relationship between practices and outcomes were not realized. Thus, multilevel research is needed to determine the emergence and strength of climate from practices and its relationship to collective attributes and performance.

Finally, there is a lack of longitudinal research that tests reciprocal relationships among constructs and across levels. For example, organizational outcomes can have a reciprocal relationship with climate (Schneider et al., 1998). Research is needed to determine how the other feedback loops contained in Figure 22.1 operate to more fully understand relationships among culture, climate, and the effective functioning of organizations.

REFERENCES

Ajzen, I., & Fishbein, M. (1975). Attitudinal and normative variables as predictors of specific behaviors. *Journal of Personality and Social Psychology, 27,* 41–57.

Argyris, C. (1964). *Integrating the individual and the organization.* New York: Wiley.

Ashforth, B. E. (1985). Climate formation: Issues and extensions. *Academy of Management Review, 10,* 837–847.

Ashkanasy, N. M., Broadfoot, L. E., & Falkus, S. (2000). Questionnaire measures of organizational culture. In N. M Ashkanasy, C. P. M. Wilderom, & M. F. Peterson (Eds.), *Handbook of organizational culture & climate* (pp. 131–146). Thousand Oaks, CA: Sage.

Ashkanasy, N. M., Wilderom, C. P. M., & Peterson, M. F. (2000). Introduction. In N. M Ashkanasy, C. P. M. Wilderom, & M. F. Peterson (Eds.), *Handbook of organizational culture & climate* (pp. 1–18). Thousand Oaks, CA: Sage.

Aycan, Z., Kanungo, R. N., & Sinha, J. B. P. (1999). Organizational culture and human resource management practices: The model of culture fit. *Journal of Cross-Cultural Psychology, 30,* 501–526.

Barley, S. R., Meyer, G. W., & Gash, D. C. (1988). Cultures of culture: Academics, practitioners and the pragmatics of normative control. *Administrative Science Quarterly, 33,* 24–60.

Barney, J. B. (1986). Organizational culture: Can it be a source of sustained competitive advantage? *Academy of Management Review, 11,* 656–665.

Bates, K. A., Amundson, S. D., Schroeder, R. G., & Morris, W. T. (1995). The crucial interrelationship between manufacturing strategy and organizational culture. *Management Science, 41,* 1565–1580.

Becker, B. E., & Huselid, M. A. (1998). High performance work systems and firm performance: A synthesis of research and managerial implications. *Research in Personnel and Human Resource Management, 16,* 43–101.

Bliese, P. D. (2000). Within-group agreement, non-independence, and reliability: Implications for data aggregation and analysis. In K. J. Klein & S. W. J. Kozlowski (Eds.), *Multilevel theory, research and methods in organizations* (pp. 512–556). San Francisco: Jossey-Bass.

Borucki, C. C., & Burke, M. J. (1999). An examination of service-related antecedents to retail store performance. *Journal of Organizational Behavior, 20,* 943–962.

Brannen, M. Y., & Salk, J. E. (2000). Partnering across borders: Negotiating organizational culture in a German-Japanese joint venture. *Human Relations, 53,* 451–487.

Buenger, V., Daft, R. L., Conlon, E. J., & Austin, J. (1996). Competing values in organizations: Contextual influences and structural consequences. *Organization Science, 7,* 557–576.

Burke, W. W., & Litwin, G. H. (1992). A causal model of organizational performance and change. *Journal of Management, 18,* 523–545.

Cameron, K. (1978). Measuring organizational effectiveness in institutes of higher education. *Administrative Science Quarterly, 23,* 604–632.

Campbell, J. P., Dunnette, M. D., Lawler, E. E., III, & Weick, K. E. (1970). *Managerial behavior, performance, and effectiveness.* New York: McGraw-Hill.

Casey, C. (1999). "Come, join our family": Discipline and integration in corporate organizational culture. *Human Relations, 52,* 155–178.

Chan, D. (1998). Functional relations among constructs in the same content domain at different levels of analysis: A typology of composition models. *Journal of Applied Psychology, 83,* 234–246.

Chang, F. S., & Weibe, H. A. (1996). The ideal culture profile for total quality management: A competing values perspective. *Engineering Management Journal, 8,* 19–26.

Chatman, J. A. (1991). Matching people and organizations: Selection and socialization in public accounting firms. *Administrative Science Quarterly, 36,* 459–484.

Christensen, E. W., & Gordon, G. G. (1999). An exploration of industry, culture, and revenue growth. *Organization Studies, 20,* 397–422.

Clarke, S. (1999). Perceptions of organizational safety: Implications for the development of safety culture. *Journal of Organizational Behavior, 20,* 185–198.

Cogliser, C. C., & Schriesheim, C. A. (2000). Exploring work unit context and leader-member exchange: A multi-level perspective. *Journal of Organizational Behavior, 21,* 487–511.

Cooke, R. A., & Lafferty, J. C. (1987). *Organizational Culture Inventory.* Plymouth, MI: Human Synergistics.

Cooke, R. A., & Szumal, J. L. (1993). Measuring normative beliefs and shared behavioral expectations in organizations: The reliability and validity of the organizational culture inventory. *Psychology Reports, 72,* 1299–1330.

Cooke, R. A., & Szumal, J. L. (2000). Using the organizational culture inventory to understand the operating cultures of organizations. In N. M Ashkanasy, C. P. M. Wilderom, & M. F. Peterson (Eds.), *Handbook of organizational culture & climate* (pp. 147–162). Thousand Oaks, CA: Sage.

Corner, P. D., Kinicki, A. J., & Keats, B. W. (1994). Integrating organizational and individual information processing perspectives on choice. *Organization Science, 5,* 294–308.

Dansereau, F., Alluto, J. A., & Yammarino, F. J. (1984). *Theory testing in organizational behavior: The varient approach.* Englewood Cliffs, NJ: Prentice Hall.

Dansereau, F., Yammarino, F. J., & Kohles, J. C. (1999). Multiple levels of analysis from a longitudinal perspective: Some implications for theory building. *Academy of Management Journal, 24,* 346–357.

Day, D., & Bedeian, A. G. (1995). Personality similarity and work-related outcomes among African-American nursing personnel: A test of the supplementary model of person-environment congruence. *Journal of Vocational Behavior, 46,* 55–70.

Deal, T. E., & Kennedy, A. A. (1982). *Corporate cultures: The rites and rituals of corporate life.* Reading, MA: Addison-Wesley.

DeLisi, P. S. (1990). Lessons from the stell axe: Culture, technology, and organizational change. *Sloan Management Review, 32,* 83–93.

De Long, D. W., & Fahey, L. (2000). Diagnosing cultural barriers to knowledge management. *Academy of Management Executive, 14,* 113–126.

Dennison, D. R. (1990). *Corporate culture and organizational effectiveness.* New York: Wiley.

Dennison, D. R. (1996). What is the difference between organizational culture and organizational climate? A native's point of view on a decade of paradigm wars. *Academy of Management Review, 21,* 619–654.

Doty, D. H., & Glick, W. H. (1994). Typologies as a unique form of theory building: Toward improved understanding and modeling. *Academy of Management Review, 19,* 230–251.

Eagley, A. H., & Chaiken, S. (1993). *The psychology of attitudes.* Fort Worth, TX: Harcourt, Brace, Jovanovich.

Feldman, J. M. (1981). Perception, cognition, and the organization. *Journal of Applied Psychology, 66,* 128–138.

Feldt, T., Kinnunen, U., & Mauno, S. (2000). A mediational model of sense of coherence in the work context: A one-year follow-up study. *Journal of Organizational Behavior, 21,* 461–476.

Fink, E. L., & Chen, S. S. (1995). A galileo analysis of organizational climate. *Human Communication Research, 21,* 494–521.

Fisher, C. D. (1986). Organizational socialization: An integrative review. In K. M. Rowland & G. R. Ferris (Eds.), *Research in personnel and human resources* (pp. 101–145). Greenwich, CT: JAI Press.

Fiske, S. T., & Taylor, S. E. (1984). *Social cognition.* New York: Random House.

Fitzgerald, L. F., Drasgow, F., Hulin, C. L., Gelfand, M. J., & Magley, V. J. (1997). Antecedents and consequences of sexual harassment in organizations: A test of an integrated model. *Journal of Applied Psychology, 82,* 578–589.

Gardner, B. B. (1945). *Human relations in industry.* Chicago: Richard D. Irwin.

George, G., Sleeth, R. G., & Siders, M. A. (1999). Organizing culture: Leader roles, behaviors, and reinforcement mechanisms. *Journal of Business and Psychology, 13,* 545–560.

George, J. R., & Bishop, L. K. (1971). Relationship of organizational structure and teacher personality characteristics to organizational climate. *Administrative Science Quarterly, 16,* 467–475.

Gilmore, T. N., Shea, G. P., & Useem, M. (1997). Side effects of corporate cultural transformations. *Journal of Applied Behavioral Science, 33,* 174–189.

Glick, W. H. (1985). Conceptualizing and measuring organizational and psychological climate: Pitfalls in multi-level research. *Academy of Management Review, 10,* 601–616.

Glick, W. H. (1988). Organizations are not central tendencies: Shadowboxing in the dark, round 2 [Response]. *Academy of Management Review, 13,* 133–137.

González-Romá, V., Peiró, J. M., Lloret, S., & Zornoza, A. (1999). The validity of collective climates. *Journal of Occupational and Organizational Psychology, 72,* 25–40.

Griffin, M. A., & Mathieu, J. E. (1997). Modeling organizational processes across hierarchical levels: Climate, leadership, and group process in work groups. *Journal of Organizational Behavior, 18,* 731–744.

Guion, R. M. (1973). A note on organizational climate. *Organizational Behavior and Human Performance, 9,* 120–125.

Guzzo, R. A., & Noonan, K. A. (1994). Human resource practices as communications and the psychological contract. *Human Resource Management, 33,* 447–462.

Harris, L. C., & Ogbonna, E. (1999). Developing a market oriented culture: A critical evaluation. *Journal of Management Studies, 36,* 177–196.

Hatch, M. J. (1993). The dynamics of organizational culture. *Academy of Management Review, 18,* 657–693.

Hatch, M. J. (2000). The cultural dynamics of organizing and change. In N. M. Ashkanasy, C. P. M. Wilderom, & M. F. Peterson (Eds.), *Handbook of organizational culture & climate* (pp. 245–260). Thousand Oaks, CA: Sage.

Hellriegel, D., & Slocum, J. W. (1974). Organizational climate: Measures, research and contingencies. *Academy of Management Review, 17,* 255–280.

Hemingway, M. A., & Smith, C. S. (1999). Organizational climate and occupational stressors as predictors of withdrawal behaviours and injuries in nurses. *Journal of Occupational and Organizational Psychology, 72,* 285–299.

Hofstede, G. (1998). Attitudes, values and organizational culture: Disentangling the concepts. *Organization Studies, 19,* 477–492.

Hofstede, G., Neuijen, B., Ohayv, D. D., & Sanders, G. (1990). Measuring organizational cultures: A qualitative and quantitative study across twenty cases. *Administrative Science Quarterly, 35,* 286–316.

Hofmann, D. A., & Stetzer, A. (1996). A cross-level investigation of factors influencing unsafe behaviors and accidents. *Personnel Psychology, 49,* 307–340.

Howard, L. W. (1998). Validating the competing values model as a representation of organizational cultures. *International Journal of Organizational Analysis, 6,* 231–250.

Hulin, C. L., Fitzgerald, L. F., & Drasgow, F. (1996). Organizational influences on sexual harassment. In M. S. Stockdale (Ed.), *Sexual harassment in the workplace* (pp. 127–150). Thousand Oaks, CA: Sage.

Jackofsky, E. F., & Slocum, J. W., Jr. (1988). A longitudinal study of climates. *Journal of Organizational Behavior, 8,* 319–334.

James, L. A., & James, L. R. (1989). Integrating work environment perceptions: Explorations in the measurement of meaning. *Journal of Applied Psychology, 74,* 739–751.

James, L. R. (1982). Aggregation bias in estimates of perceptual agreement. *Journal of Applied Psychology, 67,* 219–229.

James, L. R., Demaree, R. G., & Wolf, G. (1984). Estimating within-group interrater reliability with and without response bias. *Journal of Applied Psychology, 69,* 85–98.

James, L. R., Hater, J. J., Gent, M. J., & Bruni, J. R. (1978). Psychological climate: Implications from cognitive social learning theory and interactional psychology. *Personnel Psychology, 31,* 783–813.

James, L. R., & Jones, A. P. (1974). Organizational climate: A review of theory and research. *Psychological Bulletin, 81,* 1096–1112.

James, L. R., Joyce, W. F., & Slocum, J. W., Jr. (1988). Comment: Organizations do not cognize. *Academy of Management Review, 13,* 129–132.

Johnson, J. W. (1996). Linking employee perceptions of service climate to customer satisfaction. *Personnel Psychology, 49,* 831–852.

Johnson, J. J., & McIntye, C. L. (1998). Organizational culture and climate correlates of job satisfaction. *Psychological Reports, 82,* 843–850.

Jones, A. P., & James, L. R. (1979). Psychological climate: Dimensions and relationships of individual and aggregated work environment perceptions. *Organizational Behavior and Human Performance, 23,* 201–250.

Jones, O. (2000). Scientific management, culture and control: A first-hand account of Taylorism in practice. *Human Relations, 53,* 631–653.

Joyce, W. F., & Slocum, J. W., Jr. (1984). Collective climate: Agreement as a basis for defining aggregate climates in organization. *Academy of Management Journal, 27,* 721–742.

Katz, D., & Kahn, R. L. (1978). *The social psychology of organizations.* New York: Wiley.

Kelly, G. A. (1955). *The psychology of personal constructs.* New York: W. W. Norton.

Kelman, H. C., & Hamilton, V. C. (1989). *Crimes of obedience: Toward a social psychology of authority and responsibility.* New Haven, CT: Yale University Press.

Kilduff, M., & Corley, K. G. (2000). Organizational culture from a network perspective. In N. M. Ashkanasy, C. P. M. Wilderom, & M. F. Peterson (Eds.), *Handbook of organizational culture & climate* (pp. 211–221). Thousand Oaks, CA: Sage.

Klein, K. J., Bliese, P. D., Kozlowski, S. W. J., Dansereau, F., Gavin, M. B., Griffin, M. A., Hofmann, D. A., James, L. R., Yammarino, F. J., & Bligh, M. C. (2000). Multilevel analytical techniques: Commonalities, differences and continuing questions. In K. J. Klein & S. W. J. Kozlowski (Eds.), *Multilevel theory, research and methods in organizations* (pp. 512–556). San Francisco: Jossey-Bass.

Klein, K. J., Dansereau, F., & Hall, R. J. (1994). Levels issues in theory development, data collection, and analysis. *Academy of Management Review, 19,* 195–229.

Klein, K. J., Cohn, A. B., Smith, D. B., & Sorra, J. S. (2001). Is everyone in agreement? An exploration of within-group agreement in employee perceptions of the work environment. *Journal of Applied Psychology, 86,* 3–16.

Klein, K. J., & Sorra, J. S. (1996). The challenge of innovation and implementation. *Academy of Management Review, 21,* 1055–1088.

Kopelman, R. E., Brief, A. P., & Guzzo, R. A. (1990). The role of climate and culture in productivity. In B. Schneider (Ed.), *Organizational climate and culture* (pp. 282–318). San Francisco: Jossey-Bass.

Kozlowski, S. W. J., & Doherty, M. L. (1989). Integration of climate and leadership: Examination of a neglected issue. *Journal of Applied Psychology, 74,* 721–742.

Kozlowski, S. W. J., Gully, S. M., Salas, E., & Cannon-Bowers, J. A. (1996). Team leadership and development: Theory, principles, and guidelines for training leaders and teams. In M. Beyerlein, D. Johnson, & S. Beyerlein (Eds.), *Advances in interdisciplinary studies of work teams: Team leadership* (pp. 351–389). Greenwich, CT: JAI Press.

Kozlowksi, S. W. J., & Hults, B. M. (1987). An exploration of climates for technical updating and performance. *Personnel Psychology, 40,* 539–563.

Kozlowski, S. W. J., & Klein, K. J. (2000). A multilevel approach to theory and research in organizations: Contextual, temporal, and emergent processes. In K. J. Klein & S. W. J. Kozlowski (Eds.), *Multilevel theory, research and methods in organizations* (pp. 3–90). San Francisco: Jossey-Bass.

LaFollette, W. R., & Sims, H. P., Jr. (1975). Is satisfaction redundant with climate? *Organizational Behavior and Human Performance, 13,* 257–278.

Langan-Fox, J., & Tan, P. (1997). Images of culture in transition: Personal constructs of organizational stability and change. *Journal of Occupational and Organizational Psychology, 70,* 273–293.

Lawler, E. E., III. (1992). *The ultimate advantage: Creating the high-involvement organization.* San Francisco: Jossey-Bass.

Lewin, K. (1951). *Field theory in social science.* New York: Harper and Row.

Lewin, K., Lippitt, R., & White, R. K. (1939). Patterns of aggressive behavior in experimentally created "social climates." *Journal of Social Psychology, 10,* 271–299.

Likert, R. L. (1967). *The human organization.* New York: McGraw-Hill.

Lim, B. (1995). Examining the organizational culture and organizational performance link. *Leadership and Organization Development Journal, 16,* 16–21.

Lin, C., Madu, C. N., & Kuei, C. H. (1999). The association between organizational climate and quality management practices: An empirical study on small- and medium-sized manufacturing companies in Taiwan. *Total Quality Management, 10,* 863–868.

Lindell, M. K., & Brandt, C. J. (2000). Climate quality and climate consensus as mediators of the relationship between organizational antecedents and outcomes. *Journal of Applied Psychology, 85,* 331–348.

Litwin, G. H., & Stringer, R. A. (1968). *Motivation and organizational climate.* Boston: Harvard University Press.

Luthans, F., & Kreitner, R. (1985). *Organizational behavior modification and beyond.* Glenview, IL: Scott, Foresman.

Magnusson, D., & Endler, N. S. (1977). *Personality at the crossroads: Current issues in interactional psychology.* Hillsdale, NJ: Erlbaum.

Marks, M. A., Zaccaro, S. J., & Mathieu, J. E. (2000). Performance implications of leader briefings and team-interaction training for team adaptation to novel environments. *Journal of Applied Psychology, 85,* 971–986.

Martin, J. (1985). Can organizational culture be managed? In P. J. Frost, L. F. Moore, M. R. Louis, C. C. Lundburg, & J. Martin (Eds.), *Organizational culture* (pp. 95–98). London: Sage.

Martin, J. (1992). *Cultures in organizations: Three perspectives.* New York: Oxford University Press.

Martin, J., & Siehl, C. J. (1983). Organizational culture and counterculture: An uneasy symbiosis. *Organizational Dynamics, 12,* 52–64.

McDermott, C. M., & Stock, G. N. (1999). Organizational culture and advanced manufacturing technology implementation. *Journal of Operations Management, 17,* 521–533.

McGregor, D. M. (1960). *The human side of enterprise.* New York: McGraw-Hill.

Mischel, W. (1973). Toward a cognitive social learning conceptualization of personality. *Psychological Review, 80,* 252–283.

Milgrom, P., & Roberts, J. (1995). Complementarities and fit: Strategy, structure, and organizational change in manufacturing. *Journal of Accounting and Economics, 19,* 179–208.

Mintzberg, H. (1973). *The nature of managerial work.* New York: Harper and Row.

Mohan, M. L. (1993). *Organizational communication and cultural vision: Approaches for analysis.* Albany, NY: State University of New York Press.

Moran, E. T., & Volkwein, J. F. (1992). The cultural approach to the formation of climate. *Human Relations, 45,* 19–47.

Morgeson, F. P., & Hofmann, D. A. (1999). The structure and function of collective constructs: Implications for multilevel research and theory development. *Academy of Management Review, 24,* 249–285.

Morrison, E. W., & Milliken, F. J. (2000). Organizational silence: A barrier to change and development in a pluralistic world. *Academy of Management Review, 25,* 706–725.

Naumann, S. E., & Bennett, N. (2000). A case for procedural justice climate: Development and test of a multi-level model. *Academy of Management Journal, 43,* 881–889.

Ogbonna, E. (1993). Managing organizational culture: Fantasy or reality? *Human Resource Management Journal, 3,* 42–54.

Ogbonna, E., & Harris, L. C. (1998). Managing organizational culture: Compliance or genuine change? *British Journal of Management, 9,* 273–288.

O'Reilly, C. A., III, Chatman, J. A., & Caldwell, D. F. (1991). People and organizational culture: A profile comparison approach to assessing person-organization fit. *Academy of Management Journal, 34,* 487–516.

Ostroff, C. (1993a). Comparing Correlations based on individual-level and aggregated data. *Journal of Applied Psychology, 77,* 693–974.

Ostroff, C. (1993b). The effects of climate and personal influences on individual behavior and attitudes in organizations. *Organizational Behavior and Human Decision Processes, 56,* 56–90.

Ostroff, C. (1995). SHRM/CCH survey. *Human Resources Management: Ideas and Trends in Personnel* (356), 1–12.

Ostroff, C., & Bowen, D. E. (2000). Moving HR to a higher level: HR practices and organizational effectiveness. In K. J. Klein & S. W. J. Kozlowski (Eds.), *Multilevel theory, research and methods in organizations* (pp. 211–266). San Francisco: Jossey-Bass.

Ostroff, C., & Rothausen, T. R. (1997). The moderating effect of tenure in person-environment fit: A field study in educational organizations. *Journal of Occupational and Organizational Psychology, 70,* 173–188.

Ostroff, C., & Schmitt, N. (1993). Configurations of organizational effectiveness and efficiency. *Academy of Management Journal, 36,* 1345–1361.

Oswald, S., Stanwick, P., & LaTour, M. (1997). The effect of vision, strategic planning, and cultural relationships on organizational performance: A structural approach. *International Journal of Management, 14,* 521–529.

Ouchi, W. G. (1981). *Theory Z: How American business can meet the Japanese challenge.* Reading, MA: Addison-Wesley.

Patterson, M., Payne, R., & West, M. (1996). Collective climates: A test of their sociopsychological significance. *Academy of Management Journal, 39,* 1675–1691.

Payne, R. L. (1990). Madness in our method. A comment on Jackofsky and Slocum's paper, "A longitudinal study of climates." *Journal of Organizational Behavior, 11,* 77–80.

Payne, R. L. (2000). Climate and culture: How close can they get? In N. M. Ashkanasy, C. P. M. Wilderom, & M. F. Peterson (Eds.), *Handbook of organizational culture & climate* (pp. 163–176). Thousand Oaks, CA: Sage.

Payne, R. L., Fineman, S., & Wall, T. D. (1976). Organizational climate and job satisfaction: A conceptual synthesis. *Organizational Behavior and Human Performance, 16,* 45–62.

Payne, R. L., & Pugh, D. S. (1976). Organizational structure and climate. In M. D. Dunnette (Ed.), *Handbook of industrial and organizational psychology* (pp. 1125–1173). Chicago: Rand-McNally.

Pervin, L. R. (1967). A twenty-college study of student x college interaction using TAPE (Transactional analysis of personality and environment): Rationale, reliability and validity. *Journal of Educational Psychology, 58,* 290–302.

Peters, T. J., & Waterman, R. (1982). *In search of excellence.* New York: Harper and Row.

Peterson, M. F., & Smith, P. B. (2000). Sources of meaning, organizations, and culture: Making sense of organizational events. In N. M. Ashkanasy, C. P. M. Wilderom, & M. F. Peterson (Eds.), *Handbook of organizational culture & climate* (pp. 101–116). Thousand Oaks, CA: Sage.

Poole, M. S. (1999). Group communication theory. In L. R. Frey, D. S. Gouran, & M. S. Poole (Eds.), *The handbook of group communication theory and research* (pp. 37–70). Thousand Oaks, CA: Sage.

Pritchard, R. D., & Karasick, B. W. (1973). The effects of organizational climate on managerial job performance and job satisfaction. *Organizational Behavior and Human Performance, 9,* 126–146.

Quinn, R. E., & Kimberly, J. R. (1984). Paradox, planning, and perseverance: Guidelines for managerial practice. In J. R. Kimberly & R. E. Quinn (Eds.), *Managing organizational translations* (pp. 295–313). Homewood, IL: Dow Jones-Irwin.

Quinn, R., E., & McGrath, M. R. (1985). The transformation of organizational cultures: A competing values perspective. In P. J. Frost, L. F. Moore, M. R. Louis, C. C. Lundberg, & J. Martin (Eds.), *Organizational culture* (pp. 315–334). Beverly Hills, CA: Sage.

Quinn, R. E., & Rohrbaugh, J. (1983). A spatial model of effectiveness criteria: Toward a competing values approach to organizational analysis. *Management Science, 29,* 363–377.

Reichers, A. E., & Schneider, B. (1990). Climate and culture: An evolution of constructs. In B. Schneider (Ed.), *Organizational climate and culture* (pp. 5–39). San Francisco: Jossey-Bass.

Rentsch, J. R. (1990). Climate and culture: Interaction and qualitative differences in organizational meanings. *Journal of Applied Psychology, 75,* 668–681.

Roberts, K. H., Hulin, C. L., & Rousseau, D. M. (1978). *Developing an interdisciplinary science of organizations.* San Francisco: Jossey-Bass.

Rousseau, D. M. (1985). Issues of level in organizational research: Multi-level and cross-level perspectives. In B. M. Staw & L. L. Cummings (Eds.), *Research in organizational behavior* (pp. 1–37). Greenwich, CT: JAI Press.

Rousseau, D. M. (1990). Assessing organizational culture: The case for multiple methods. In B. Schneider (Ed.), *Organizational climate and culture* (pp 153–192). San Francisco: Jossey Bass.

Rousseau, D. M. (1995). *Psychological contracts in organizations.* Thousand Oaks, CA: Sage.

Rousseau, D. M., & Wade-Benzoni, K. A. (1994). Linking strategy and human resource practices: How employee and customer contracts are created. *Human Resource Management, 33,* 463–490.

Rowlinson, M., & Procter, S. (1999). Organizational culture and business history. *Organization Studies, 20,* 369–396.

Sathe, V., & Davidson, E. J. (2000). Toward a new conceptualization of culture change. In N. M. Ashkanasy, C. P. M. Wilderom, & M. F. Peterson (Eds.), *Handbook of organizational culture & climate* (pp. 279–296). Thousand Oaks, CA: Sage.

Schein, E. H. (1983). The role of the founder in creating organizational culture. *Organizational Dynamics, 12,* 13–28.

Schein, E. H. (1985). *Organizational culture and leadership.* San Francisco: Jossey-Bass.

Schein, E. H. (1990). Organizational culture. *American Psychologist, 45,* 109–119.

Schein, E. H. (1992). *Organizational culture and leadership: A dynamic view.* San Francisco: Jossey-Bass.

Schein, E. H. (2000). Sense and nonsense about culture and climate. In N. M. Ashkanasy, C. P. M. Wilderom, & M. F. Peterson (Eds.), *Handbook of organizational culture & climate* (pp. xxiii–xxx). Thousand Oaks, CA: Sage.

Schneider, B. (1975). Organizational climates: An essay. *Personnel Psychology, 28,* 447–479.

Schneider, B. (1983). Work climates: An interactionist perspective. In N. W. Feimer & E. S. Geller (Eds.), *Environmental psychology* (pp. 106–128). New York: Praiger.

Schneider, B. (1987). The people make the place. *Personnel Psychology, 40,* 437–453.

Schneider, B. (1990). The climate for service: An application of the climate construct. In B. Schneider (Ed.), *Organizational climate and culture* (pp. 383–412). San Francisco: Jossey-Bass.

Schneider, B. (2000). The psychological life of organizations. In N. M. Ashkanasy, C. P. M. Wilderom, & M. F. Peterson (Eds.),

Handbook of organizational culture & climate (pp. xvii–xxi). Thousand Oaks, CA: Sage.

Schneider, B., & Bartlett, J. (1968). Individual differences and organizational climate: I. The research plan and questionnaire development. *Personnel Psychology, 21,* 323–333.

Schneider, B., & Bartlett, J. (1970). Individual differences and organizational climate: II. Measurement of organizational climate by the multitrait-multirater matrix. *Personnel Psychology, 23,* 493–512.

Schneider, B., & Bowen, D. E. (1985). Employee and customer perceptions of service in banks: Replication and extension. *Journal of Applied Psychology, 70,* 423–433.

Schneider, B., Bowen, D. E., Ehrhart, M. G., & Holcombe, K. M. (2000). The climate for service: Evolution of a construct. In N. M. Ashkanasy, C. P. M. Wilderom, & M. F. Peterson (Eds), *Handbook of organizational culture & climate* (pp. 21–36). Thousand Oaks, CA: Sage.

Schneider, B., Brief, A. P., & Guzzo, R. A. (1996). Creating a climate and culture for sustainable organizational change. *Organizational Dynamics, 24,* 6–19.

Schneider, B., Gunnarson, S. K., & Niles-Jolly, K. (1994). Creating the climate and culture of success. *Organizational Dynamics, 23,* 17–29.

Schneider, B., Parkington, J. J., & Buxton, V. M. (1980). Employee and customer perceptions of service in banks. *Administrative Science Quarterly, 25,* 252–267.

Schneider, B., & Reichers, A. A. (1983). On the etiology of climates. *Personnel Psychology, 36,* 19–39.

Schneider, B., & Snyder, M. (1975). Some relationships between job satisfaction and organizational climate. *Journal of Applied Psychology, 60,* 318–328.

Schneider, B., White, S. S., & Paul, M. C. (1998). Linking service climate and customer perceptions of service quality: Test of a causal model. *Journal of Applied Psychology, 83,* 150–163.

Schultz, M., & Hatch, M. J. (1996). Living with multiple paradigms: The case of paradigm interplay in organizational culture studies. *Academy of Management Review, 21,* 529–557.

Schuster, F. E., Morden, D. L., Baker, T. E., McKay, I. S., Dunning, K. E., & Hagan, C. M. (1997). Management practice, organization climate, and performance. *Journal of Applied Behavioral Science, 33,* 209–226.

Schwartz, S. H. (1992). Universals in the content and structure of values: Theoretical advances and empirical tests in 20 countries. In M. P. Zanna (Ed.), *Advances in experimental social psychology* (Vol. 25, pp. 1–65). San Diego, CA: Academic Press.

Scott, S. G., & Bruce, R. A. (1994). Determinants of innovative behavior in the workplace. *Academy of Management Journal, 37,* 580–607.

Shadur, M. A., Kienzle, R., & Rodwell, J. J. (1999). The relationship between organizational climate and employee perceptions of involvement. *Group & Organization Management, 24,* 479–503.

Sheridan, J. E. (1992). Organizational culture and employee retention. *Academy of Management Journal, 35,* 1036–1056.

Shortell, S. M., O'Brien, J. L., Carman, J. M., Foster, R., Hughes, E. F. X., Boerstler, H., & O'Connor, E. J. (1995). Assessing the impact of continuous quality improvement/total quality management: Concept versus implementation. *Health Services Research, 30,* 377–401.

Siehl, C., & Martin, J. (1990). Organizational culture: A key to financial performance? In B. Schneider (Ed.), *Organizational climate and culture* (pp. 241–281). San Francisco: Jossey-Bass.

Smart, J. C., & St. John, E. P. (1996). Organizational culture and effectiveness in higher education: A test of the "culture type" and "strong culture" hypotheses. *Educational Evaluation and Policy Analysis, 18,* 219–241.

Smircich, L. (1983). Concepts of culture and organizational analysis. *Administrative Science Quarterly, 28,* 339–358.

Smircich, L., & Morgan, G. (1982). Leadership: The management of meaning. *Journal of Applied Behavioral Science, 18,* 257–273.

Sparrow, P. R., & Gaston, K. (1996). Generic climate maps: A strategic application of climate survey data? *Journal of Organizational Behavior, 17,* 679–698.

Stackman, R. W., Pinder, C. C., & Connor, P. E. (2000). Values lost: Redirecting research on values in the workplace. In N. M. Ashkanasy, C. P. M. Wilderom, & M. F. Peterson (Eds.), *Handbook of organizational culture & climate* (pp. 37–54). Thousand Oaks, CA: Sage.

Stajkovic, A. D., & Luthans, F. (1997). A meta-analysis of the effects of organizational behavior modification on task performance, 1975–95. *Academy of Management Journal, 40,* 1122–1149.

Stern, G. G. (1970). *People in context: Measuring person-environment congruence in education and industry.* New York: Wiley.

Taguiri, R., & Litwin, G. (Eds.). (1968). *Organizational climate: Explorations of a concept.* Boston: Harvard Business School, Division of Research.

Tata, J., & Prasad, S. (1998). Cultural and structural constraints on total quality management implementation. *Total Quality Management, 9,* 703–710.

Tesluk, P. E., Farr, J. L., & Klein, S. R. (1997). Influences of organizational culture and climate on individual creativity. *Journal of Creative Behavior, 31,* 27–41.

Trice, H. M., & Beyer, J. M. (1993). *The cultures of work organizations.* Englewood Cliffs, NJ: Prentice Hall.

Trice, H. M., Belasco, J., & Alutto, J. A. (1969). The role of ceremonials in organizational behavior. *Industrial and Labor Relations Review, 23,* 40–51.

Tsui, A. S., Pearce, J. L., Porter, L. W., & Tripoli, A. M. (1997). Alternative approaches to employee-organization relationship: Does investment in employees pay off? *Academy of Management Journal, 40,* 1089–1121.

Vandenberghe, C. (1999). Organizational culture, person-culture fit, and turnover: A replication in the health care industry. *Journal of Organizational Behavior, 20,* 175–184.

Verbeke, W., Volgering, M., & Hessels, M. (1998). Exploring the conceptual expansion within the field of organizational behaviour: Organizational climate and organizational culture. *Journal of Management Studies, 35,* 303–329.

Victor, B., & Cullen, J. B. (1988). The organizational bases of ethical work climates. *Administrative Science Quarterly, 33,* 101–125.

Weick, K. E. (1995). *Sensemaking in organizations.* Thousand Oaks, CA: Sage.

Wicker, A. W. (1992). Making sense of environments. In W. B. Walsh, K. H. Craik, & R. H. Price (Eds.), *Person-environment psychology* (pp. 157–192). Hillsdale, NJ: Erlbaum.

Wilderom, C. P. M., Glunk, U., & Maslowski, R. (2000). Organizational culture as a predictor of organizational performance. In N. M. Ashkanasy, C. P. M. Wilderom, & M. F. Peterson (Eds.), *Handbook of organizational culture & climate* (pp. 193–210). Thousand Oaks, CA: Sage.

Young, S. A., & Parker, C. P. (1999). Predicting collective climates: Assessing the role of shared work values, needs, employee interaction and work group membership. *Journal of Organizational Behavior, 20,* 1199–1218.

Zammuto, R. F., Gifford, B., & Goodman, E. A. (2000). Managerial ideologies, organization culture, and the outcomes of innovation: A competing values perspective. In N. M. Ashkanasy, C. P. M. Wilderom, & M. F. Peterson (Eds.), *Handbook of organizational culture & climate* (pp. 261–278). Thousand Oaks, CA: Sage.

Zammuto, R. F., & Krakower, J. Y. (1991). Quantitative and qualitative studies of organizational culture. In R. W. Woodman & W. A. Pasmore (Eds.). *Research in organizational change and development* (Vol. 5, pp. 83–114). Greenwich, CT: JAI Press.

Zohar, D. (2000). A group-level model of safety climate: Testing the effect of group climate on microaccidents in manufacturing jobs. *Journal of Applied Psychology, 85,* 587–596.

CHAPTER 23

Diversity in Organizations

CLAYTON P. ALDERFER AND ADRIENNE D. SIMS

Stimulated by the Hudson Institute Report from Johnston and Packer (1987) predicting an increase in the diversity of U.S. workers, the fields of social and industrial psychology have given more attention than they previously had to understanding the effects of a workforce that is less and less dominated by *native white males* (the language used in the original document). As one might have anticipated, these efforts have reflected the culture and norms of the subdiscipline. The field's primary modes of conducting research traditionally have emphasized the inductive accumulation of empirical findings (as contrasted with theory development) with a focus on individual and interpersonal relations (as contrasted to group and intergroup dynamics). As time has passed, however, this orientation alone has proved to be less and less satisfactory, and efforts have been directed toward having theory play a larger role in research and addressing more complex entities in addition to individuals.

As research gives theory a larger role, investigators face more explicit questions about the way theory affects the conduct of research and how choices among alternative (sometimes competing, sometimes complementary) theories can be made (Alderfer & Thomas, 1988). In a general sense, these questions have long been the focus of historians and philosophers of science (Kaplan, 1964; Kuhn, 1996). Until recently, however, they have not been a central concern for industrial

and organizational (I/O) psychology, given the subdiscipline's historical preference for inductively driven research. In this chapter, we shall examine how social and I/O psychology deal with diversity in organizations by comparing the key theoretical orientations that have been brought to bear on the topic.

Meanings of Diversity

The word *diversity* is a term with both straightforward and highly complex meanings. Milliken and Martins (1996) note the dictionary meaning (variety, or a point or respect in which things differ) and recognize that in the context of organizations, other, more emotional interpretations (e.g., affirmative action or hiring quotas) arise. These two meanings differ in the reactivity they evoke. In the first instance, the meaning is neutral, and in the second, reactions tend to be both favorable and unfavorable. The positive focus stems from a desire to increase the inclusion of groups historically kept out of particular jobs within organizations and for the resources available for this task. The negative meaning arises when efforts to increase diversity are made in ways that are (or are perceived to be) unfair to other groups not previously facing unfair treatment (Harrington & Miller, 1992). Neither meaning, however, is directly tied to specific theories that address group and intergroup relations. Following the perspective developed by Kuhn (1996), we believe that as knowledge advances, definitions of phenomena become part of theory and change when theories change. Without one or more strong theories, definitions tend to lack widely shared meanings.

This chapter compares theories that deal with group and intergroup relations in organizations as a means to better understand diversity. From this perspective, then, *diversity* is about group and intergroup relations. Meanings of the term that pertain exclusively to individual-level attributes, such as skills or personality traits, fall outside this set of conceptual systems. This orientation takes account of individuals from an intragroup perspective as group members and from an intergroup perspective as group representatives (Alderfer, 1987; Rice, 1969).

AN INITIALLY INDUCTIVE DIVERSITY STUDY

We begin with a relatively detailed account of one study by Stewart and Shapiro (2000) entitled, "Selection Based on Merit Versus Demography: Implications Across Race and Gender Lines." The aim is to illustrate problems that can arise when key theoretical issues are ambiguous. Initially, the authors carried out a factorial experiment with two levels of four independent variables: (a) race, (b) gender, (c) selection criterion, and (d) feedback about task performance. Dependent variables consisted of self-assessments of leadership ability, performance evaluation, responsibility for performance, and desire to remain a leader. Due to unexpected results, the authors conducted a second experiment, which employed two independent variables, (a) race of the experimenter and (b) race of respondents, and two dependent variables, (a) change in self-assessed performance of respondents and (b) change in self-esteem.

Stewart and Shapiro's (2000) original experiment was designed to determine whether a set of empirical findings pertaining to the effect of merit versus gender preference on undergraduate respondents' self-assessments showed the same effects for race preference. When the empirical results did not generalize as expected, a second study, which drew on relational demography theory to predict the impact of race, was carried out. When the results of the second study only partially met expectations, additional concepts from other theories were brought to bear.

Particularly significant in diversity research is the manner by which investigators address African American and white racial dynamics as they exist today in the United States. Some treat race as if it were roughly the equivalent of other diversity variables. This assumption seems to have guided

Stewart and Shapiro as they designed their first experiment to determine whether effects observed for gender in earlier research would also be found for race in their research. The authors' exact words were, "If the [other authors'] explanation, which rests on group membership (gender), is valid, then the same pattern observed in the women . . . should appear in studies whose samples consist of African Americans" (Stewart & Shapiro, 2000, p. 220).

There is substantial research on African American and white race relations in the United States' organizations (e.g., Alderfer, 2000; Alderfer & Thomas, 1988; Alderfer, Tucker, Morgan, & Drasgow, 1983; Cox, 1990; Jaynes & Williams, 1989; Myrdal, Sterner, & Rose, 1944; Star, Williams, & Stouffer, 1949; Thomas & Gabarro, 1999). Perhaps beginning with Myrdal et al. (pp. 1035–1064) these analyses have drawn attention to effects of tacit theories and values on the interpretation of research on race relations. We provide a similar examination of the Stewart and Shapiro (2000) article as a means to identify hazards that can arise during research and practice pertaining to race relations and other aspects of diversity. In doing so, we do not wish our analysis to be taken as personal criticism of the authors or journal editors. Analysis of the research as one example of diversity research shows why comparing theories that address questions of diversity in organizations can be critically important.

Merit Versus Demography

A crucial aspect of both studies was comparing two experimental conditions in which respondents were told either that they were selected to be a leader because they scored better on an exam (the merit condition), or because there just were not enough members of their gender and race in the group, regardless of test scores (the demography condition). The two conditions relied on an interpretation of affirmative action by the U.S. Equal Employment Opportunity Commission (EEOC; Stewart & Shapiro, 2000, p. 219). The authors were asking whether potential beneficiaries of affirmative action (females of both racial groups, and black men) might be hurt if criteria other than merit were employed for selection.

It is significant that there were only two selection conditions, merit and demography. The formulation suggests that the two conditions occupy different locations on a single continuum. Thus, merit implies either more or less demography and vice versa. Merit and demography, however, can be distinctly different variables. To investigate the effects of merit and demography on the dependent variables, the investigators might have established four experimental conditions: (a) neither demography nor merit; (b) demography but not merit; (c) merit but not demography; and (d) demography and merit. On the other hand, the study might be viewed as comparing two policy alternatives that are used to implement selection practices to meet affirmative action guidelines. An implicit assumption of the study is that affirmative action requires choosing demography over merit at least often enough to collect data relevant to the comparison. Others differ from that point of view (Harrington & Miller, 1992).

An important yet little known study by Nordlie (1979) showed that in the U.S. Army at the time of his research, white enlisted personnel were promoted more rapidly if they had higher mental ability test scores, while African American enlisted personnel were promoted more rapidly if they had lower mental ability test scores. More than a decade later, Alderfer (1992), during research on a 14-year organizational intervention to reduce barriers against the promotion of African American managers, found that some white male managers intentionally selected underqualified African Americans to promote as a means to undermine corporate affirmative action policies. These managers framed their alternatives as if they were forced to choose between qualified candidates and African American candidates. The implication was that they could not find employees who were both qualified for promotion and African American. Believing that they were being forced to promote African American people, who in their minds were inevitably underqualified, they then actively sought especially underqualified African Americans to promote. In subsequent conversations, they would criticize affirmative action for forcing them to promote unqualified (African American) managers. The informal managerial practices designed to resist affirmative action in the intervention study and the promotion practices reported in the military reflect a particularly problematic form of selection based on merit versus demography. Did Stewart and Shapiro (2000) intend to reinforce the kinds of practices found by the military in the 1970s or in corporations in the 1970s and 1980s? We imagine they did not. At the same time, they showed limited awareness of the hazards for policy and practice from the way they framed their study.

Race Relations and the Temporary Laboratory Organization

The effect of theory in research potentially pertains not only to how independent variables are conceptualized, but also to how experiments themselves are conducted. Laboratory investigators do construct temporary organizations in order to study the phenomena of their interest (Alderfer, 1985, p. 55). Typically, these systems have three levels of hierarchy (i.e., principal investigator, experimenter, respondent). Moreover, the laboratory-as-temporary-organization is embedded in the larger social system. Filling organizational positions within the laboratory involves choices about the race and gender of the people chosen for each level. Consequently, conducting experiments involves negotiations between the laboratory organization and its environment. Experimenters seldom explicitly take account of such group and organizational variables, even though studies have shown that laboratories are rarely the closed systems that most experimental methods sections imply (cf. Vidmar & Hackman, 1971; Wuebben, 1974). Stewart and Shapiro (2000), however, came to believe that the way they managed the group and organizational dynamics of their two experiments provided plausible explanations for their findings.

Respondents in the first experiment carried out their activities in the presence of an experimenter and a confederate, both of whom were white men. Thus, racially speaking, African American respondents faced dramatically different conditions than white respondents. Compared to whites, African Americans were both outnumbered and outranked by members of the other racial group. African American women faced a situation in which they differed by gender as well. White respondents, on the other hand, did not differ in race from their confederate peers or from their supervisors in the study. Both white men and white women, however, faced peer confederates who differed by gender. The writers explained that they employed these procedures in order to maintain consistency with other investigators, who had studied merit versus demography for gender using only white respondents. Until they obtained anomalous results from the initial experiment, the investigators apparently had no reason to consider that the racial group dynamics of the study might be different for African American and white participants. The investigators seemed to be race blind in anticipating the experimental effects on their dependent variables, even as they were race conscious in establishing their independent variables.

What they found, contrary to expectation, was that African American respondents who received experimentally manipulated negative performance evaluations expressed higher evaluations of their own leadership ability than whites did in the similar condition. In contrast, whites, as expected, showed lower self-assessments after the failure treatment than after success treatment. Moreover, African Americans who were told their selection was based on demography rather than merit demonstrated this apparently defensive effect of failure, but African Americans who were told their selection was based on merit did not. In an attempt to understand these unanticipated findings, Stewart and Shapiro (2000) carried out a second experiment, which varied only the race of experimenter and the race of respondent, and all respondents received negative feedback. They based the new experimental design on *relational demography theory,* which suggests that race-alike boss-subordinate pairs should show similar effects independent of which race was involved (Williams & O'Reilly, 1998). Beyond systematically varying the race of the experimenter for all respondents, the second study also provided same-race peer-confederates for all respondents. The experimental conditions were therefore two-person, race-alike African American groups with African American or white experimenters in charge and two-person, race-alike white groups with African American or white experimenters in charge. The study focused on change in self-esteem of respondents. Consistent with their expectations, the authors found that the self-esteem of African American respondents increased more than that of white respondents after they received the negative feedback. Inconsistent with their expectations, however, they did not find a significant difference between African American respondents who received feedback from African American rather than white experimenters.

Relational demography theory focuses explicitly only upon the demographic similarity or difference between individuals. According to this view, a race-alike white group with a African American experimenter was equivalent to a race-alike African American group with a white experimenter. The results, however, did not support this view. Reflecting on the second round of unanticipated findings, the authors observed that in both experiments, respondents were students in a predominantly white university. If one were to take the perspective of *embedded intergroup relations theory,* one would say that the two types of groups with experimenters racially different from members were not equivalent but rather were embedded differently in the laboratory organization (Alderfer & Smith, 1982). To obtain a more equivalent setting for both kinds of cross-race authority patterns, the study should have been carried out in a setting such as a historically African American university as well as in a predominantly white setting. If that were done, then the two-person groups would have had roughly equivalent external as well internal conditions. Larkey (1996), drawing on an extensive literature review, makes a nearly equivalent proposal, referring to situational effects in workgroup contexts. The implication from embedded intergroup relations theory and Larkey's analysis is that the external conditions of groups, whether in the laboratory or more permanent settings, affect the experiences of group members.

As designed, however, the experimental groups—while matched in their internal conditions (i.e., peer and immediate authority relations)—were not matched in their external conditions. After their second experiment failed to produce all of the expected results, the authors were stimulated to think further about how their study was embedded. What they took from their self-observation, however, was not what we have suggested here. Rather, they noted that in real organizations (their words) it is not uncommon for women and minorities (again their words) to have a white male authority and to be the only persons of their demography (again, their words) to be members of their workgroups. The authors thus argue from what we believe to be a conceptual limitation of relational demography theory (i.e., the failure to adequately take account of the external dynamics of groups) and end by defending the status quo. Gerard and Miller (1975, pp. 64–65) made a similar argument as part of their research on public school desegregation. Tacit reasoning of this kind reflects a perspective similar to the racially conservative biases in U.S. social science that Myrdal et al. (1944) described more than half a century ago.

Alternative ways of thinking do exist. We use the remainder of this chapter to examine the most widely used theories of group and intergroup relations for addressing questions of diversity in organizations. The perspective from which we make these analyses is that of embedded intergroup relations theory (Alderfer, 1987; Alderfer & Smith, 1982).

INDIVIDUALISM-COLLECTIVISM THEORY

When Dunnette and Hough published the second edition of the *Handbook of Industrial and Organizational Psychology* in the early 1990s, they called upon Triandis, Kurowski, and Gelfand (1994) to formulate the topic of diversity in organizations. These authors addressed a broad range of issues concerned with workplace diversity and drew heavily upon the theory of *individualism and collectivism* developed by Triandis and his colleagues. We first examine the theory and then address how the authors used the theory to address questions about diversity.

Concepts and Propositions

Perhaps the key formulation in the theory is the notion of a continuum of cultures that places *individualism* at one end and *collectivism* at the other. These key terms refer to properties of social entities, not of persons taken one at a time. Individualistic cultures give individual goals (particularly those pertaining to material ends) higher priority than collective goals. Collectivistic cultures give collective goals higher priority than individual goals. In addition, analogous terms exist for properties of individuals. *Idiocentric* persons, independent of the culture in which they live, place their own personal objectives ahead of those of the collective. *Allocentric* people, independent of the culture in which they live, place collective goals ahead of individual goals. This fundamental distinction has been subject to extensive conceptual analysis and empirical testing (cf. Triandis, 1989, 1990).

Speaking empirically, one observes that the theory of individualism and collectivism is about the self in relation to groups and cultures. The crucial measurement tools employed by Triandis and his colleagues were questionnaires administered to individuals. These instruments asked about both individuals and cultures, and they thereby allow the researchers to make empirically based statements about cultures, such as how to arrange them along the individualism-collectivism continuum. The Triandis methodological procedure, however, does not examine properties of cultures in ways other than through the eyes of individuals, who often were students when responding to the fixed alternative questionnaire items. The researchers neither systematically observed the cultures, nor did they attempt to bring about change based on the understanding they developed. Consequently, what they are able to understand from their studies pertained to individuals thinking about properties of groups and cultures, but not to groups or cultures as they occur concretely in nature. As we shall explain later, this distinction turns out to be quite important when one chooses theories for purposes of intervention, as one inevitably must, if he or she is to deal effectively with the dynamics (i.e., with change processes) associated with increasing (or decreasing) diversity. By comparing individual responses across cultures, Triandis, Vassiliou, Vassiliou, Tanaka, and Shanmugam's (1972) data suggest how powerful collective entities can be for individual members. Yet individualism-collectivism theory, if it is not to go beyond what the data show, should focus only upon individuals, because the findings produced by the research pertain only to what exists in the minds of individuals. In fact, this is what Triandis, Brislin, and Hui (1988) do when they propose a series of recommendations for cross-cultural training.

Assessing the dynamics of a group or a more complex collective entity (especially for purposes of explaining, predicting, or shaping change) calls for more than conventional linear measurement. That is, it is not like measuring a table with a tape measure, such that the measurements become increasingly precise as one takes more readings on the same dimensions; rather, it is like fitting together the pieces of a jigsaw puzzle—each observation adds a complementary perspective, such that averaging is not automatically the most effective way to combine data points. Various members perceive and interpret group events differently based upon their subgroup memberships and roles (Alderfer, 1977a). Consider, for example, a foreperson and her or his workgroup of hourly employees. The foreperson will notice, remember,

speak, and act differently in the workgroup than will an informal leader of the workers who reports to the foreperson (cf. Lieberman, 1950; Roethlisberger & Dickson, 1939). Averaging perspectives across subgroups and roles can obfuscate rather than clarify subgroup and role differences within group and cultural dynamics.

Individualism-collectivism theory distinguishes among three orders of the self in relation to cultures: (a) the private self; (b) the public self; and (c) the collective self. These orders refer to the person as known to herself or himself intrapsychically, the person as known to members of her or his own in-groups, and the person as known in situations in which he or she represents his or her own group during intergroup relations, respectively. According to the theory, as groups and cultures vary along the individualism-collectivism dimension, they evoke and involve the several senses of self in different degrees. Thus, on the one hand, individualistic cultures provide more opportunity for people to acknowledge and develop their private selves; on the other hand, collective cultures call forth greater expression of public and collective selves. These elements of individualism-collectivism theory fit well with other perspectives that promote understanding of diversity in organizations (cf. Alderfer & Thomas, 1988; Thompson & Carter, 1997). Taken on their own terms, the concepts are not dependent upon examining groups and cultures only from within the minds of their individual members. Instead, they point investigators' attention to what occurs both among members inside groups and among groups in intergroup relations.

Certain additional questions, however, can be raised about the single-continuum proposition from individualism-collectivism theory. Are groups and cultures that encourage self-development and self-differentiation inevitably at odds with collective entities that are notable for the cohesion and commitment of their members? As a general rule (as compared to certain circumstances), are individual goals in conflict with group goals, as the central proposition of the theory asserts? Our view and a key proposition in embedded intergroup relations theory is that individuals and groups (or the cultures contained by groups) are, conceptually speaking, independent (Alderfer, 1987; Alderfer & Thomas, 1988). There are conditions when individuals and groups are in conflict, as, for example, when groups demand conformity from their members as a price for continued acceptance. However, there are also instances in which cohesive and committed groups can serve the development of well-differentiated autonomous individuals, as, for example, when effectively functioning families nourish and support the development of their members (Bowen, 1978). Indeed, we suggest that persistent strains between individuals and their groups may be signs of dysfunction, which may be normative in a statistical sense (i.e., few groups and organizations are *not* dysfunctional). Strains of this kind, however, are neither inevitable descriptively, nor desirable pragmatically. An alternative perspective states that when people who differ from conventional norms belong to groups, the collective entities may or may not exist in a state that induces strain between the members' unique and the group's common qualities. A theory such as individualism-collectivism that sees as inevitable any conflict between uniquely individual properties and strong collectives will have comparatively little to say about how one might proceed to alter potentially dysfunctional conflicts. In contrast, a theory that sees conflict between individual and collective properties as one condition among many that may exist between individuals and groups will have more to offer to the problems of diversity in organizations (Smith & Berg, 1985).

Implications for Diversity and Organizations

The chapter provides an important form of legitimacy for researchers, educators, and consultants within the tradition of I/O psychology to address questions about identity groups in organizations. Groups named and explicitly discussed are those based on race, ethnicity, gender, sexual orientation, and physical ability. Recognizing the groups and presenting crucial aspects of their perspectives on questions concerning the workplace reduces the potential for denial often associated with investigators who think exclusively in terms of individual differences. Although identity-group memberships do reflect ways that individuals differ, these differences are not only about individuals. They are also about groups and how group representatives relate to one another—that is, they are about intergroup relations. Identity groups and their intergroup relations have long histories and face contemporary problems shaped by historical events. From an intergroup perspective, we are all members of these groups and participate in the contemporary events in ways partially shaped by history. Not to acknowledge the role of historical events in shaping policies on the intergroup dynamics of such matters as affirmative action and sexual harassment is to be less prepared than is desirable.

In regard to group-level thinking, Triandis et al. (1994) make an important distinction between stereotypes and sociotypes. *Stereotypes* are the inaccurate and prejudicial views held about one group by members of another group. Especially within social psychology, the concept of stereotypes (coupled with the desire to be seen as personally not having them) has a long history. *Sociotypes* are the relatively accurate

understanding of group differences based on mutual respect and achieved through direct contact and inquiry. One potentially constructive effect of placing the stereotype-sociotype distinction into I/O psychology's professional vocabulary is to reduce the guilt about potential political incorrectness that often prevents psychologists from explicitly addressing group differences. Instead, the new term may encourage those who wish to understand to proceed—undoubtedly with some anxiety—to learn about their own groups and others.

We do, however, have an additional perspective on how professionals orient themselves and others to learning about groups other than their own. The practice of writing about other groups without identifying one's own groups, reflecting upon one's own relationship to one's own groups, or examining the relationship between one's own groups and other groups can be problematic. The practice may fail to take account of the universal tendency toward *unconscious projection,* which consists of attributing both favorable and unfavorable characteristics to other groups while denying their appropriateness to one's own groups. Our belief is that we psychologists are no less subject to these forces than are other human beings (Alderfer, 1985). In their handbook chapter, Triandis et al. (1994) briefly describe workplace perspectives of Asian Americans, African Americans, Hispanics, women, Gay Males and Lesbians, and people with disabilities. Presenting this material in the manner that they do implies comparisons with other groups, such as white, northern European, men, heterosexual, and able-bodied people. Including the perspectives of these groups as well and acknowledging their own memberships in and relationships to them is a means by which authors can reduce tendencies toward unconscious projection among themselves and their readers.

According to embedded intergroup relations theory, a precursor to learning about other groups as a means to improve one's capacity to work respectfully and effectively with these groups is to study more deeply about one's own groups (cf. Alderfer, 1982, 1994, as this point pertains to the first author). Learning about one's own groups is a counterforce to unconscious projection. To the degree that one accepts the sources of pride and shame associated with one's own groups, one is less likely to project those qualities unwittingly onto other groups. This element pertains to the intrapsychic component of intergroup relations. There are also the intragroup and intergroup components. To the degree that one understands one's own groups, one is more able to serve diversity from within. To the degree that one understands intergroup relationships that include one's own groups, one is better equipped to serve diversity from without. Speaking metaphorically, we note that many may be familiar with the aphorism stating that one should not judge others until one has walked in their shoes. This principle is often used as a basis for having people role-play members of groups other than their own. We suggest a complementary principle: One is more prepared to attempt to walk in the footsteps of others after one has examined one's own groups and has attempted to accept both their flaws and accomplishments.

In Triandis et al.'s (1994) chapter, the writers address what they term *intergroup difficulties* and identify another distinction, which they refer to as *intergroup versus interpersonal*. They explain the latter distinction as follows: "When a person relates to another person by paying attention primarily to the other's group memberships, the relationship is intergroup. When a person attends only to the other's personal attributes, the relationship is interpersonal" (p. 790). Their definition implies that whether a relationship has intergroup components depends wholly upon what is in the mind of the individual people who enact the relationship. This orientation follows directly from individualism-collectivism theory—a connection the authors make when they define the continuum. An alternative perspective—consistent with other terms in individualism-collectivism theory—is that all relationships have intrapersonal, intragroup, and intergroup components (Alderfer, 1987; Rice, 1969).

Not taking account of all three dimensions can unintentionally lead to unnecessarily difficult exchanges. Imagine a white, male, quantitative methods instructor saying to a dark-skinned African American male student, "I never noticed you were Black, because you have done so well in my [extremely challenging] course." The statement is framed from an interpersonal perspective. Knowing the instructor involved, one would attribute to him the conscious desires both to be color-blind and to convey an authentically felt compliment to the student. On the other hand, the episode does have a significant racial component. Whether African American or white, anyone knowing African American-white race relations in the United States probably would sense the unfortunate impact of the statement. The limitation is rooted in the white male instructor's failure to understand the interracial component contained in his interpersonal relationship with male African American student.

The 1994 Triandis et al. chapter gives two messages about whether all relationships have intergroup components. On the one hand, the authors have a section on what they term the *culture of [intergroup] relationships* (p. 795). On the other hand, reasoning from individualism-collectivism theory, they present a framework emphasizing *perceived similarity*, defined as perceiving another person as a member of one's in-group rather than of an out-group (p. 779). The aim of their

model was to accumulate empirical findings from research about perceived similarity in a manner that can be used to predict positive intergroup attitudes. In the concrete example given previously, the instructor spoke consciously to include the student as a member of the instructor's in-group (i.e., individuals who performed well in quantitative methods). Yet his words failed to appreciate their impact in the history of African American and white race relations in the United States. In this instance, instructor and student both would have been better served if the instructor had simply given the student a deserved compliment for his achievements in quantitative methods. In this instance, *not* speaking about the racial differences between the two people while giving an unqualified compliment involves recognizing the negative impact that some historically white views of African American intellectual abilities have had and without reproducing those negative effects.

SOCIAL IDENTITY THEORY

Social identity theory was initially developed in Europe in the years following World War II by Henri Tajfel (see Tajfel, 1981) and subsequently brought to the United States by Marilyn Brewer (1995) and her associates. Formulation of the theory was aided by the development of the *minimal group technique* for use in social psychology laboratories. Following this procedure, investigators brought respondents to the laboratory and randomly assigned each to an essentially meaningless social category or group membership. Based on this treatment alone, respondents were found to discriminate in favor of in-group and against out-group members. Over the years, numerous studies attempted to show that alternative artifactual explanations lay at the root of category-based discrimination. The social category explanation, however, has withstood robust challenges and today is widely accepted as a causal explanation for what is termed *in-group/out-group discrimination* (Turner, 1981, p. 100).

Within the history of social psychology, social identity theory was developed as an alternative formulation to the functional theory of intergroup conflict and cooperation originally proposed by Sherif and Sherif (1969). The older theory argued that groups competed or cooperated because they either had conflicting goals (e.g., both could not win a tug-of-war contest) or shared a superordinate goal (e.g., both had to work together in order to repair broken equipment needed by all). *Social identity theory* proposed that perceived group membership alone—even of the most trivial form, as demonstrated in the laboratory experiments—was more potent than functional conflict or interdependence in shaping intragroup and intergroup behavior and attitudes. Over the years, crucial laboratory experiments comparing functional with social category formulations consistently produced findings that favored social identity theory over functional theory (Turner, 1981, pp. 93–96). Noting these results, however, one should be aware that the kinds of experimental settings employed by social identity theorists were rooted in the laboratory and attended to the cognitions and behavior of individuals. The intergroup phenomena observed by Sherif and Sherif (1969) were based on field experiments that utilized intact groups of young boys, who had substantial histories with one another.

In social identity research, investigators combine the use of a particular mode of investigation (the minimal group technique) with the drawing of conclusions that make comparisons with another theory that was developed using a different method of investigation (field experimentation with intact groups). Minimal group technique was employed to investigate responses in the minds of individuals. The Sherif and Sherif (1969) studies created, observed, intervened in, and measured the responses of both individuals and groups. Although it seems reasonable to view social identity theory as being superior to functional theory for explaining what happens in the minds of individuals treated as group representatives, the minimal group procedures really do not address full-blown group and intergroup dynamics. In other words, experimental procedures were confounded with theory preference in this and other bodies of research. One therefore has reason to be cautious in drawing inferences about groups and intergroup relations (and about the effects of groups on individuals) based on studies exclusively focused on individuals—perhaps especially when the experiments use treatments purposely designed to be weak (i.e., minimal group technique). The caution is especially appropriate when investigators wish to make inferences from data obtained in one kind of organizational setting (i.e., the social psychological laboratory) to another (i.e., diversity dynamics in day-to-day organizations), where group forces affecting individuals tend to be very potent (Brewer, 1995).

The Personal Experience of Henri Tajfel

As noted in the preceding sections, an important element in the formulation of any theory of human behavior is how people who use the theory understand themselves in relation to the conceptual formulation. In particular, do they show an awareness of how their concepts derive from and relate to experiences from their own lives? If they do not, there is a danger that the theory serves more of a defensive than an explanatory function for the writers. On the other hand, if theorists do demonstrate this sort of self-understanding, then there is more reason to believe the theory is relatively unhampered by unconscious projection, and the author does not believe he or she can free him- or herself from the laws of human behavior when conducting research (cf. Berg & Smith, 1985).

Tajfel (1981, p. 1) provided enough of his personal history for readers to understand how his fundamental insight arose and to sense how connected his laboratory work was to his own personal history. In a brief autobiographical account, he explained that his education for research in social psychology occurred after World War II. He viewed himself as belonging to a generation of European Jews who were born in the first part of the twentieth century and survived the "raging storm" and "came in from very cold and very far" to express and reflect upon what happened to them and to others. Tajfel was a Holocaust survivor who, after developing some distance from the trauma, went into social research in part to try to understand what the Nazis had done to the Jews and how. Viewed in the most basic terms, minimal group experiments were at the core of how Hitler and his associates condemned Jews to the most horrific forms of suffering and death. At the height of Nazi terror, Hitler's agents identified Jews and required them to wear a yellow Star of David to make them readily identifiable for mistreatment, abuse, and death (Shoenberner, 1969). The minimal group experimental treatment had a historical precursor that could hardly have been less minimal.

Concepts and Propositions

Social identity theory has at its core several key propositions. The first of these pertains to the formation of social categories in the minds of individuals based on persons' memberships in cognitively defined groups (Turner, 1981, p. 78). From this cognitive process there follows a boundary division that separates one's in-group from the out-group. The use of these terms in social identity theory seems to be basically in accord with the same terminology employed in individualism-collectivism theory. According to social identity theory, an effect of the social categorization process is intergroup discrimination. Once social categorization has taken place, individuals perceive in-group members as being like themselves and show favorable attitudes and behavior toward them. Conversely, they perceive out-group members as being unlike themselves and demonstrate unfavorable attitudes and behavior toward them.

Even though, according to the theory, social categorization occurs in the minds of individuals, researchers who use the theory draw implications for defining and explaining group-level phenomena. Turner (1981, pp. 86–87) showed how the definition of a group differs between those who employ social identity theory and those who employ functional theory. For social identity theorists, a social group consists of two or more individuals who perceive themselves as members of the same social category or share a common social identification. This definition of a group depends wholly on the contents of the minds of individuals. The functional model, in contrast, includes (along with social categorization) patterns of interaction, role and status relationships among members, and shared norms and values. Thus, for functional theorists, the concept of a group has an externally observable, concrete reality along with categories that exist in the minds of individuals. In these contrasting definitions, we may be seeing researchers formulating conceptual definitions of a phenomenon (in this case, a group) to fit their preferred style of research (i.e., laboratory or field studies), rather than asking what the essential properties of groups as entities are and then developing research methods to address them. Either definition of a group (and other definitions as well) has implications for understanding diversity in organizations and for designing diversity interventions.

The second core proposition of social identity theory pertains to how individuals relate to groups and to social comparison processes. Depending on which social identity theorist one examines (e.g., compare Brown, 1995, with Brewer, 1995), one finds relatively greater attention focusing either on the impact of (in-)group membership on the individual or on the individual's relation to the self as partly mediated by (in-)group memberships. These distinctions follow closely the difference between intrapsychic relations of self to group (i.e., *How do I think of myself in relation to a group?*) and intragroup relations of group to self (i.e., *How is my sense of self shaped by membership in this group?*) Each of the several theories (individualism-collectivism, social identity, and embedded intergroup relations) addresses these questions—albeit with differing emphases.

Social identity theory, however, has its particular formulation of self-motivations, which from a certain normative perspective can be problematic. The key theoretical questions pertain to how a concept of self is formulated and what implications that formulation has for group and intergroup relations. The view proposed by social identity theory is oriented to preserving and enhancing a positive picture of the self. As Brown (1995) puts it,

> [self-identity theorists] assume that people generally have a preference for seeing themselves positively rather than negatively. Since part of our self-image is defined in terms of our group memberships, this implies that there will also be a preference

to see our groups in a positive light in relation to those groups to which we do not belong. It is this general tendency to make biased intergroup comparisons which serves as the motivation core of . . . [the] theory. (p. 170)

A number of empirical studies conducted by social identity theorists using the minimal group procedure support this proposition. One example is the study is by Sachdev and Bourhis (1987), who show monotonically increasing satisfaction with the in-group as low-status, equal-status, and high-status groups are compared. We do not doubt the reliability of this empirical finding or of others equivalent to it. Rather, we raise conceptual questions about the implications of viewing self-motivations primarily as a pursuit of a positive self-image.

An alternative formulation is to view the maturing self—in its intrapsychic, intragroup, and intergroup senses—in terms of a quest for greater wholeness and complexity, as well as for becoming more favorable. A strong foundation for this alternative view can be found in the writings of personality theorists, who have developed their conceptual perspectives by attending to unconscious processes in clients and themselves during long-term psychotherapy and psychoanalysis (cf. Jung & Jaffe, 1961; Klein, 1960; Miller, 1984; von Franz, 1968). In citing these views, we acknowledge that for some purposes—different than those of this chapter—there are important theoretical differences among the several theories of the personal and archetypal unconscious; but these variations tend not to be about the direction toward greater wholeness as personality matures, nor about the diminishing inclination toward unconscious projection as wholeness increases. *Greater wholeness* means a person is increasingly able to hold, accept, and own (rather than to avoid, deny, or project onto other individuals and out-groups) those aspects of the self that are disturbing and troublesome. In the context of diversity and intergroup relations, this perspective implies a greater capacity to accept one's personal biases and blind spots along with the problematic aspects of one's in-groups, and less tendency toward unconscious projecting of the troublesome parts of oneself and one's groups onto other individuals and groups. Thus, if one were a member of a high-status group (or aspired to such membership) and held this perspective, he or she would relate to that membership not only as a basis for positive self-feelings but also with openness about the limitations and biases associated with the higher status group. More generally, the social-identity proposition about the quest for an increasingly positive self-image through group and intergroup relations might be viewed as an important property of conscious-rational thinking, which could usefully be complemented by attention to the kinds of characteristically mixed feelings observed in unconscious processes.

Social identity theorists also speak about a *continuum* from interpersonal to intergroup relations (Brown, 1988, pp. 5–9). By this they mean that relations between individuals can be understood as being relatively more interpersonal and relatively less intergroup, or vice versa. They illustrate this conceptual point with two examples. For the extreme case of interpersonal (and nonintergroup) relations, they choose an intimate conversation between two lovers, and to identify an equivalent situation in the other direction, they propose a conflict between strikers and police. Each example contains the seeds of important conceptual limitations. If the lovers are of different genders, a significant portion of their intimacy will be based on the fact that each one represents a different gender group. If the lovers are of the same gender, the two will share a common fate in relation to a heterosexual community that is often extremely biased against them (Shilts, 1987). Viewed in this manner, even the most intimate interpersonal relationship will have intergroup components. Conversely, there will be interpersonal components present even in the most severe intergroup conflict. It is not difficult to imagine, even if one has not had the actual experience, that police officers and demonstrators do speak to each other as individuals in the midst of heated conflict and agree on such matters as how to conduct a demonstration in a manner that minimizes violence. During the Civil War, in what is perhaps the worst conflict the United States has ever experienced, soldiers from the North and South found ways between battles to meet and talk with each other in a mode of mutual respect (Reynolds, 1991).

The alternative to employing a continuum from interpersonal to intergroup relations is to view human relations in a manner that gives conceptually independent places to intrapsychic, interpersonal (or intragroup), and intergroup relations, an orientation shared by a variety of researchers (Alderfer, 1987; Rice, 1969; Triandis, 1989). The result is that one does not necessarily have less of any of the three components as one has more of another. One implication is that one can retain individuality in relation to one's own and other groups even in the midst of severe conflict. In addition, using three independent dimensions instead of a single continuum implies that persons can find unique ways of being members of their groups and relating to other groups without denying either their group memberships or intergroup differences. People can speak about their own racial, ethnic, and gender identities in these terms (cf. Thompson & Carter, 1997). For example, one might ask of the present authors, "In what manner does the first author understand his being a senior white man?" "In what manner does the second author understand her being a junior African American woman?" and "What implications does this combination of authority-racial-gender identities have for how this chapter was

written?" There are most certainly intrapsychic and interpersonal components in the answers to these questions, *and* they in no measure diminish the several intergroup relationships that also are operative. The authors have worked cooperatively for several years, discussed explicitly their authority, racial, generational, and gender-group memberships, and expressed both agreement and disagreement on these matters directly to one another. On occasion, these discussions have included strong, disturbing emotions.

The benefits of taking account of multiple group memberships and of the positive and negative feelings people may have about their own and other groups were also underlined in Larkey's (1996) formulation of propositions concerning communication in culturally diverse workgroups. In her view, seeing another person or a subgroup of people as belonging to one or more groups different than one's own (i.e., fitting into different categories) need not automatically produce negative reactions. More balanced and predominantly favorable responses can occur that need not involve viewing others only as unique individuals, but also as persons with memberships in groups different than one's own.

Implications for Diversity and Organizations

Social identity theory has contributed a major theoretical insight in recognizing and demonstrating the impact of even relatively minimal group memberships on intergroup discrimination. Having seen the effects of minimal group treatments in the laboratory, researchers and practitioners should be far less likely to overlook or deny the impact of group memberships in other, more long-lasting group and organizational relationships. As it turns out, however, the fundamental insight can be a two-edged sword in terms of how it affects behavior in organizations. On the problematic side, it may tempt investigators to believe they can effect significant changes by invoking or promoting larger, suprasystem social identities when attempting to bring greater cohesion to diverse work groups composed of members who represent potentially conflicting subgroups. Williams and O'Reilly (1998, p. 119), for example, propose just such an intervention to enhance group process and performance. Brewer (1995, p. 63), on the other hand, recognizes the hazards of acting as if minimal group inventions developed for the laboratory can be taken into more permanent organizational settings without taking account of the powerful forces set into motion by intact groups with substantial histories. The use of superordinate social categories that work in the laboratory as temporary organization may not work equally well in more permanent organizations, and they are likely to have other less-than-desirable side effects.

From the perspective of embedded intergroup relations theory, the resolution of these apparent differences of opinion among social identity theorists turns on how one conceives of a group and addresses the question of *group boundary permeability* (cf. Alderfer, 1987). With exception of some discussion about individual mobility between groups and about individuals dealing with multiple group memberships simultaneously, social identity theorists tend to see (cognitive) boundaries or social categories as either present or absent. Thus, once invoked, a social category defines an in-group/out-group difference, and a given person either belongs to or is excluded from a defined group. Another alternative is to think of group boundaries as varying in their degree of permeability and as influencing the flow of information, matter, and energy inward and outward from the focal system. Thinking in this manner means that groups consist of more than social categories; that both beneficial and harmful exchanges can occur between groups of different kinds; and that groups (as well as other entities) can become dysfunctional from both too much *and* too little boundary permeability. From this point of view, defining a group by a social category is only the cognitive part of the story. Moreover, the fact that given people or groups are nonmembers does not preclude them from visiting the defined group and participating in exchanges with that group. Boundary management tasks for the group include making adjustments for both too much and too little boundary permeability (Alderfer, 1987).

Social identity theory has tended to address the problem of what is termed here as too little boundary permeability of a subgroup by proposing to substitute a superordinate identity. Thus, identification with the smaller, less inclusive unit is to be replaced by a new identification with a larger, more comprehensive entity. This solution contains problematic elements, however, if carried to its logical conclusion. First, each subsequently more inclusive entity forms another in-group/out-group differentiation, about which one can predict from social identity theory that there will be intergroup discrimination. Thus, if a supervisor says only, "Please give your first loyalty to the department over and above your profession [or some other meaningful group, such as gender]," the effect will be to exacerbate interdepartmental (or intergender) conflict. Next, to reducing interdepartmental (or intergender) conflict will require a higher level manager to make a similar statement about the next most inclusive organizational entity, for example, a division. This process cannot continue indefinitely in a meaningful fashion. Furthermore, the more the process does continue within realistic limits, the more it will cause the smaller entities to have too much boundary permeability and thereby risk losing their ability to function effectively.

An alternative, according to embedded intergroup relations theory, is to conceptualize leadership and consultation tasks as adjusting boundary permeability—toward either increases or decreases, depending on what is appropriate for the circumstances. A group with too little boundary permeability would thus be led toward greater acceptance of valid criticisms of itself, and a group with too much boundary permeability would be encouraged to recognize more of its positive qualities. These sorts of exchanges do not involve altering social categories, but they do consist of participating in new kinds of within-group and between-group dialogues (cf. Alderfer, Alderfer, Bell, & Jones, 1992). They are consistent with Larkey's (1996) recognition that perceiving groups as different than one's own can, under the right circumstances, be associated with favorable responses to those individuals and groups.

RELATIONAL DEMOGRAPHY

Relational or organizational demography is the name of a third body of concepts and propositions that organizational researchers have brought to bear on understanding diversity in organizations (Milliken & Martins, 1996; Pfeffer, 1985; Williams & O'Reilly, 1998). Pfeffer (p. 303) refers to *demography* as "the composition, in terms of basic attributes such as age, sex, educational level, length of service or residence, race, and so forth of the social entity under study." Used in this way, organizational demography is not a theory for explaining diversity in the same sense as other theories considered in this chapter. Rather, *organizational demography* identifies a class of variables, which can assist in understanding diversity when used in conjunction with other theories presented here (Williams & O'Reilly, 1998). In presenting the empirical and conceptual cases for attending to organizational demography, Pfeffer emphasized that central tendency (in the statistical sense of mean, median, or mode) was not all that is significant about an organization's stable and changing demography. Of equal or greater importance are demographic distributions. Thus, if one examines the distribution of age, one then observes the numbers of people in each of several age ranges. Beyond a simple distribution of age, one would additionally inquire about joint distributions. How, for instance, does age vary with functional assignments, location in the hierarchy, and other demographic variables? Pfeffer's fundamental insight is that organizations vary across time and among one another in their demographic composition. Moreover, the multidimensional demographic composition of an organization can serve both as dependent variables, based on how organizations relate to their environments, and as independent variables, shaping outcomes to organizations and their members.

Tenure as the Prototypic Demographic Variable

After having provided a list of potential demographic variables, Pfeffer (1985) then proceeded to develop in detail an analysis of how tenure as a demographic variable could be employed productively to explain and predict various aspects of organizational behavior. He began by recognizing that turnover is often related to age and tenure; yet the three variables are conceptually and operationally different and may have different relationships with each other. Hypothetical conditions that might affect the distribution of tenure (and other demographic variables) included growth, technology, personnel policies and practices, and unionization (pp. 310–320).

As he examined the relationship between tenure distribution and organizational performance, Pfeffer (1985, p. 320) identified advantages and disadvantages of turnover. *Turnover,* in this sense, can be viewed as the rate of change of tenure. Depending on the circumstances, too little turnover can be associated limited ability to adapt and innovate. Too high a rate of turnover, on the other hand, will be associated with chaos and disorganization. With this formulation, we have a statement that comes close to becoming an empirical generalization for many organizational demography researchers. With considerable care and analysis, the proposition has been extended to other demographic variables (cf. Milliken & Martins, 1996; Williams & O'Reilly, 1998). Before turning to a careful examination of empirical findings and theoretical analysis of this potential generalization about diversity, however, we examine one more important—although subtly conveyed—element in Pfeffer's argument.

After discussing the role of tenure distribution in organizational control and the distribution of power, Pfeffer (1985, p. 335) turned to a discussion of what he termed *cohort identity and intercohort conflict*. With the introduction of these terms, Pfeffer, without explicitly acknowledging what he was doing, introduced a version of intergroup theory into his analysis of organizational demography. He noted that length of service could define cohorts in part because members of cohorts experience the same events within the same interval. Organizational members, in turn, identify with others in their same cohorts and may engage in conflict with members of other cohorts. This language moves his analysis of tenure demography to a discussion of what some have called *generational intergroup relations* (Alderfer, 1971, 1987; Feuer, 1969). Moreover, as we imagine Pfeffer would agree, generational groups may form based on events outside as well as inside organizations. *Cohorts,* as Pfeffer used the term, are

generational groups formed within organizations based on members' entering at similar points in history and participating in common experiences.

The picture of cohort group dynamics conveyed by Pfeffer (1985) suggests that he was reasoning in a manner largely consistent with social identity theory (even if not explicitly stated). Thus, he saw people from the same cohort as behaving like an in-group who knew one another, cooperated on behalf of organizational objectives, and even accepted subordinate roles in relation to each other. In terms of relations between cohorts, Pfeffer commented only about patterns of conflict. From the perspective of embedded intergroup relations theory, however, the picture he painted was accurate as far as it went but was also notably incomplete. Alderfer (1971), studying a group of high-potential bank managers, found not only that they cooperated with one another in relation to other groups (e.g., non-high-potential managers) but also competed internally as well—that is, the high-potential in-group did have significant internal conflict. In addition, both the group and individual members had relationships of mutual support as well as conflict with senior officers of the bank. Indeed, mentor-protégé relationships by definition cut across generational groups and, in doing so, provided benefits to members of both generations (Kram, 1985; Levinson, Darrow, Levinson, & McKee, 1978; Sims, 2002; Thomas, 1993). Consequently, one can observe that the conceptual picture of cohort identity and intercohort relations painted by Pfeffer was, in important ways, limited. Utilizing the perspective of embedded intergroup relations theory, we would propose a connection between the acceptance of conflict within the younger high-potential group and the capacity for both cooperation and conflict by this group with older senior managers (cf. Alderfer, 1977b, 1987; Smith & Zane, 1999). The ability of the high-potential group to tolerate disturbing emotions within their group made possible some degree of cooperation between cohort groups. The capacity of group members to deal with troublesome emotions among themselves meant they were less inclined to project those feelings onto the senior group and consequently less likely to exacerbate irrational forms of conflict between the groups.

Diversity Dynamics and Performance

In the years following Pfeffer's (1985) original paper, organizational researchers were stimulated to undertake numerous empirical studies designed to understand the impact of various demographic variables on dependent measures of group and organizational performance. Milliken and Martins (1996) provided a review covering six years. More recently, Williams and O'Reilly (1998) provided a review covering 40 years and examining 27 laboratory and 62 field studies. This latter review addressed five kinds of demographic differences as independent variables: (a) tenure, (b) background, (c) age, (d) sex, and (e) race and ethnicity. In conceptualizing group performance, Williams and O'Reilly were primarily influenced by Hackman's (1987) focus on three different aspects of group functioning: (a) productive output, (b) social processes involved in carrying out the work, and (c) need satisfaction of individual group members. From the outset, the authors framed their review as being aimed at addressing the tension between those who argue for the value in diversity and those who suggest that increasing diversity makes group functioning more difficult (p. 77); the earlier review by Milliken and Martins showed a similar orientation. In addition, Williams and O'Reilly suggested that a portion of the apparent disagreement may turn on whether studies seeming to answer the question one way or the other were conducted in the laboratory or in the field. Their suggestion was that laboratory studies were more likely to show positive effects for diversity, whereas field studies were more likely to underline various group-process problems associated with inadequate cohesion, poor communication, and unproductive conflict (p. 79).

In accord with Pfeffer's (1985) original formulation, the empirical literature review proposes that both too little and too much diversity are likely to have negative effects on group performance. The authors' exact words are, "Taken together, the overall effect of increasing diversity is likely to have a[n inverted] U-shaped form with some increments of diversity having large positive effects in group problem-solving. . . . Large amounts of diversity in groups may offer little in the way of added value from unique information and make group cohesion and functioning difficult" (Williams & O'Reilly, 1998, p. 90). The authors then proceed to assess the empirical literature in each of the five demographic areas and, on balance, interpret the empirical findings as being in accord with their primary conceptual-empirical proposition—but with notable caution. "Under ideal conditions increased diversity may have the positive effects predicted by information and decision theories. However, . . . the preponderance of empirical evidence suggests that, by itself, diversity is more likely to have to have negative than positive effects on group performance" (p. 120).

Given this overall conclusion, questions also arise uniquely for specific demographic variables. The formulation of these questions and the implications of their answers pertain both to specific demographic dimensions and to the general topic of diversity. Two of the diversity dimensions—namely, tenure and (professional) background—tend to be more readily linked to task activities. The three other diversity dimensions—namely age, sex, and race-ethnicity—

in addition to their relevance for tasks (e.g., product design, marketing, sales, service delivery) also relate to personal identity and powerful social, political, and historical forces (cf. Cox, 1995; Nkomo, 1995). Investigators associated with schools of management sometimes find it easier to envision the potential benefits of increasing diversity on the first two dimensions, whereas they tend to be more uncertain, if not outright anxious, about highly emotional (and therefore, according to some conceptual systems, unproductive) conflict. In the case of sex diversity, for example, Williams and O'Reilly (1998, p. 108) note that men in the minority position are likely to show more negative psychological reactions than are women in the minority position. In the case of racial diversity, they suggest that aversive racism may be an appropriate response. They explain *aversive racism* in the following: "Faced with strong normative pressures to override invidious social categorizations, group members may enhance their ability to perform by consciously overriding the propensity to differentiate in-groups and out-groups. This may improve team-work [*sic*] because of the awareness of social stigma attached to socially inappropriate social categorization" (p. 119). They give no concrete examples of this practice. The present writers, however, find themselves thinking of words (spoken or unspoken) that would have the effect of denying the gender, racial, or ethnic identity of people. Would a statement such as "I never thought of you as . . . [with the relevant gender, racial, or ethnic group membership included]" be an example? From the perspective of embedded intergroup relations theory, either explicit or tacit denial removes the psychological aspect of identity-group boundaries—even when motivated by the best of intentions. Whether acknowledged or not, identity-group dynamics do occur. The challenge of diversity is to work with group differences in ways that serve the individuals involved, their groups, and their organizations—not to deny the impact of these forces.

Avoiding, Managing, Addressing, and Working With Identity-Group Conflict

The four terms describing this subsection show an ordered sequence employed by various authors when they propose responses to the emotional conflict associated with identity-group dynamics (Ely, 1995; Kossek, Zonia, & Young, 1996; Northcroft, Polzer, Neale, & Kramer, 1995; Tsui, Xin, & Egan, 1995). *Avoiding conflict* means preventing highly charged issues from arising. *Managing conflict* emphasizes controlling events so that the overt emotion present at any time is minimal. *Addressing conflict* involves allowing the disturbing issues to emerge in largely uncensored form *once* with the expectation that, having been addressed, they will not reappear. *Working with conflict* means accepting the notion that many forms of group conflict have complex histories and require repeated, sustained, and sometimes emotional conversations to be dealt with productively in the long run. In defining the continuum, we do not wish to imply that one form of dealing with intergroup conflict is always more appropriate than the others. The terms, however, do describe degrees of engagement with conflict.

To the extent that one's objectives pertain to long-term development for human beings in complex organizations, we do believe that actions involving more engagement—provided they are undertaken in ways that are theoretically and behaviorally sound—offer more promise for constructively utilizing diverse demographic differences. We close this subsection with a concrete example to illustrate the alternative modes. Propositions from embedded intergroup relations theory help to explain the alternative actions.

A human resources staff group of six professionals charged with corporate management development, of whom five were I/O psychologists, met to discuss the progress their company had made during the preceding year in meeting established goals to increase the diversity of their executive-level workforce. Three members of the group were white men; two were white women; and the sixth was an African American woman. The team's data indicated that the percentage of white women had increased by approximately 2.5% during the year; the proportion of Hispanics and Asians had remained constant; and the fraction of African Americans had decreased. The group's conversation included reference to the fact that in general, involuntary terminations had increased and voluntary terminations had decreased. White members of the team interpreted the turnover data to indicate that the company was doing a better job of terminating poorly performing and retaining highly performing executives. As the conversation unfolded, the African American member asked whether the team was going to consider why the corporation seemed unable to increase the racial and ethnic diversity of its executive ranks. The senior white male in charge of the group indicated that such questions belonged with the corporate director of diversity, not to management development. One white male and one white female spoke to support this view. The African American female, in turn, suggested forming a partnership between management development and diversity to address the question. At this point, the group dropped the topic from further discussion.

Had the management development team—alone or in collaboration with the diversity team—been able to engage more fully the question of the corporation's inability to increase racial and ethnic diversity at the executive level, certain questions might have asked. In what ways, if any, were the

corporation's selection tools for executive positions impeding the selection of highly competent men and women of color? Given that organizational fit was important for this corporation, how was that concept defined, especially when people from diverse racial and ethnic backgrounds were assessed for executive positions? In what ways, if any, were individuals who influenced assessment and evaluation decisions asked to become conscious of bias as they collected and analyzed data about potential candidates for executive positions? In what ways could selection teams be formed to in order to bring compensating biases to bear when evaluating candidates? How might the behavior of effectively or ineffectively functioning diverse selection teams affect the behavior of candidates during selection processes and ultimately their perceived value as executives? Because the group changed the subject (thereby avoiding overt conflict), these and other questions of a similar kind were not addressed. Soon after, the African American female left the management development unit and the corporation.

EMBEDDED INTERGROUP RELATIONS THEORY

The first author and a number of collaborators developed embedded intergroup relations theory over several decades (Alderfer, 1977a, 1987; Alderfer & Simon, 2002; Alderfer & Smith, 1982; Alderfer & Thomas, 1988). The theory has been influenced by data obtained through surveys using organic questionnaires, long-term organizational intervention programs, case studies, and field experiments (Alderfer, 1971, 1977b; Alderfer & Brown, 1975; Alderfer & Tucker, 1996; Alderfer et al., 1983). In later years, the theory was also employed in a deductive fashion to design, implement, and assess educational and organizational interventions (e.g., Alderfer, 1990, 1992; Alderfer et al., 1992). We mention these features because, as is apparent from both the Williams and O'Reilly (1998) review and our own observations, often an association exists between the method investigators use and the concepts and conclusions they formulate. Embedded intergroup relations theory is based upon a broad array of field methods but has not employed laboratory experimentation. Moreover, from the perspective of embedded intergroup relations theory, methodology includes not only methodological procedures (i.e., survey, case, experiment) but also the identity and organizational group memberships of the research team and the relationships among team members (Alderfer, 1985). As noted above, two people who differed by race, gender, and seniority and who explicitly discuss their different perspectives prepared this chapter. Diverse teams whose composition was relevant to the subject matter of the studies carried out many of the embedded intergroup relations studies on which the theory was based. In the material that follows, we present those portions of the theory that bear directly on the work of this chapter.

Proposition 1. Whether acknowledged or not, individuals in interaction with others represent multiple identity and organizational groups; the groups that become salient in a transaction depend on which people representing which other groups are present and on the historical and contemporary relationship among those individuals and groups.

Proposition 2. Intergroup relations occur simultaneously at three interdependent levels—the intrapsychic (or personal), the intragroup (or interpersonal), and the intergroup (or group representational).

These first two propositions are in general consistent with Rice's (1969) formulation that organizational-group relationships always have intergroup components, and with those aspects of individualism-collectivism theory that address these specific three levels of analysis. They are also in accord with Wells's (1980) formulation about groups-as-wholes employed for experiential education and organizational consultation. Embedded intergroup relations theory does not employ ingroup/out-group logic as stated explicitly by individual-collectivism and social identity theories and (tacitly) by relational demography theory. Rather, the present theory treats groups as concrete entities on their own terms (conceptually independent of individuals, even as they are made up of individuals).

The intrapsychic component recognizes that individuals have within themselves conscious and unconscious feelings and thoughts concerning how they relate to their groups. Which messages from their various groups do they inwardly accept, and which do they reject? When do they feel pride and when shame about their multiple group memberships? The intragroup component reflects that each individual has observable concrete relationships with each of her or his multiple groups. How does each individual behave in response to the internal group dynamics of her or his own groups? In response to which group messages do they express agreement and which disagreement? The intergroup component reflects the fact that each group member makes choices (some conscious and some unconscious) about how to behave in relation to members of other groups, and that in turn, his or her thoughts and feelings about those groups influenced are by what occurs during intergroup transactions.

A crucial feature of embedded intergroup relations theory assumes that individuals in professional roles are influenced by the same forces as those they study and serve. Thus, each statement derived from propositions contained in the theory has implications for those who do research and consultation as well as for their respondents and clients. Writers from the perspectives of individualism-collectivism, social identity, and relational demography do not address the question of how professionals, as they do their work, relate to the phenomena they study. The omission suggests they might believe professionals are immune to these forces as a consequence of their professional roles. Empirical research on these matters suggests otherwise (cf. Alderfer & Thomas, 1988).

Proposition 3. Group boundaries (which are both subjective and material) have two functions: (a) they distinguish an entity from its environment, and (b) they regulate the flow of matter, energy, and information between an entity and its environment.

Proposition 4. The capacity of a group to survive in a malevolent environment or to thrive in a benevolent environment (y) follows an inverse square function of its boundary permeability (x), that is, $y = (x - h)^2/4p$, where h refers to the relative benevolence of the environment and p expresses the relative sensitivity of system vitality to changes in boundary permeability.

Proposition 5a. The boundary permeability of any focal identity or organizational group depends upon the relative boundary permeability of the subgroups within that group: (a) If all subgroup boundaries are optimally or excessively permeable, the focal group boundaries will be excessively or optimally permeable; (b) if one or more subgroups' boundaries are excessively impermeable, then the focal group boundaries will be excessively permeable.

Proposition 5b. The boundary permeability of subgroups within any focal identity or organizational group depends on the boundary permeability of the focal group: (a) If the focal group boundaries are excessively impermeable, the subgroup boundaries will be excessively permeable; (b) if the focal group boundaries are excessively permeable, the subgroup boundaries will reflect their larger group's condition independent of the focal group.

These propositions place forming, tightening, loosening, and removing boundaries at the center of group and intergroup relations. In-group to out-group discrimination is reframed as a condition of excessive boundary impermeability. In contrast with other theories, which do not discuss boundary permeability (i.e., relational demography) or view boundaries as either absent or present (i.e., social identity theory), embedded intergroup relations theory makes boundary permeability central. Thus, recognizing subgroups within a focal group (whether those subgroups are based on identity or organization) is not an automatic threat to the boundaries of the focal group—as is suggested by an empirical law relating too little and too much diversity to group effectiveness.

Instead, the central diagnostic question becomes understanding the relative boundary permeability of subgroups and the focal group. Providing more support for subgroup boundaries from outside (i.e., the exact opposite of reducing diversity) will enable those boundaries to become more permeable (i.e., as the group becomes less in need of defending itself) and thus enable the focal group boundaries to become less permeable. An intervention based on this principle is especially appropriate for identity and organization groups with less power who exist under greater threat. Conversely, enabling groups who have more power and face less threat from the environment to engage in self-reflection (i.e., by becoming more open to internal criticism) will enable their boundaries to become more permeable and thereby enable the focal group boundaries to become less impermeable. Yet a third condition exists when the focal group boundaries are excessively impermeable. In this case, tightening the boundaries of the subgroups will increase the boundary permeability of the focal group and allow it to become more permeable in exchanges with other comparable groups in the organization.

In these several ways, the analysis derived from embedded intergroup relations theory does not imply a necessary tension between individual and group levels of analysis (i.e., both are important) or between too little or too much diversity. Indeed, Proposition 3 provides a basis for conceptually reframing the phenomena of too much and too little diversity as an alternative way to understand the inverted U-shaped function proposed by several investigators. The focus of attention shifts from too little or too much diversity to adjusting subgroup and focal group boundaries. Accepting and respecting subgroups (rather than rejecting or denying their presence) thus becomes a vehicle for moving toward optimal boundary permeability for the focal group. This orientation calls for explicit understanding of group-level phenomena in terms of emotions, cognitions, and behavior. Needed concepts include more than the cognitions that exist in the minds of individuals and require interventions addressed toward groups as entities (cf. Alderfer et al., 1992; Alderfer & Tucker, 1996).

To make these concepts concrete, we return to the example from the corporate management development team described in the preceding section. How might these propositions been employed to adjust the group and subgroup boundaries of that team and improve upon its stated goal of increasing the diversity in the company's executive ranks? Inwardly, the team would have recognized and discussed the various meanings of its own race and gender composition (i.e., a white male leader, two white men, two white women, and a lone African American woman). They would have acknowledged the difficulties associated with the white members' listening and the African American members' speaking about executives of color. This kind of conversation would have the effect of increasing the boundary permeability of the white subgroup, reducing the boundary permeability of the African American subgroup (i.e., both the one person in the room and other peo-

ple of color throughout the corporation) and thereby would have increased the boundary permeability of the focal group. One effect of increased boundary permeability of the management development team would be to increase the likelihood of that group's working cooperatively with the diversity director on what could become their joint goals. Had these sorts of changes in the boundaries of the management development team occurred, the likelihood of the African American female's leaving the group and the organization would have been reduced.

> *Proposition 6.* Deriving from intrapsychic conditions and the dynamics of identity and organizational groups, individuals and groups participate in unconscious parallel processes by projecting their own emotions onto others and by absorbing the projections of others onto themselves.
>
> *Proposition 7.* Two crucial tasks of any group's leadership (alone or in cooperation with consultants) are (a) to assess and alter as appropriate the focal group's and subgroups' boundary permeabilities and (b) to assist individual members and the group as a whole in raising unconscious parallel processes into awareness.

Of the propositions contained within embedded intergroup relations theory, the portion most different from the other theories examined in this chapter pertains to propositions 6 and 7. The other theories do not explicitly address unconscious phenomena at either the individual or group levels. Their attention goes only to the conscious-rational level of human affairs. We suggest that their preferences to avoid conflict noted previously (which varies by theory and investigator) reflects a largely out-of-awareness understanding of the power of these phenomena. There is, in addition, an empirical and conceptual literature from both psychoanalytic psychotherapy and organizational intervention describing, analyzing, explaining, and utilizing the phenomena of parallel processes (e.g., Alderfer, 1977b, 1987; Alderfer & Simon, 2002; Frawley-O'Dea & Sarnat, 2001; Krantz & Gilmore, 1991; Smith & Zane, 1999).

From the management development team episode, we find two indications of the likelihood of unconscious parallel processes operating in the relationship among whites and between whites and people of color. The first instance arises from the unexamined, yet tacitly reported, association between the increase in retention of high-performing managers and the decrease in proportion of managers of color. The group did not examine how they understood these seemingly (but perhaps not) related phenomena. Did they consciously mean to suggest that managers of color on average were less likely to be high performers? Perhaps less of a positive association between the two variables was intended. Maybe the corporation included forces that pushed out high-performing managers of color; if so, then examining those forces (and changing them as appropriate) would increase both the proportion of high performers *and* the proportion of managers of color available to become executives.

The second likely manifestation of unconscious parallel processes was in the group's disinclination to examine its internal subgroup dynamics. To what degree, if any, were the white leader and white members encouraging their African American female member to offer her perspective on the matter before them? To what degree, if any, were members of the group, beginning with the white male leader, prepared to question how their own biases about ethnicity, race, and gender might be affecting deliberations? Why did the group flee so readily from the topic they had met to examine? Framed as they are for this chapter, these questions might seem reasonable and straightforward, but in the case described, they were not. Asking them, which the team did not do, would have been a means to inquire about whether and how unconscious parallel processes might have been shaping the group's relations among its own members and with other groups in the corporation.

A recent field study about the career paths of minority executives (their terms) by Thomas and Gabarro (1999) provided a strong basis for believing that organizations need not choose between too much and too little diversity or between "merit and demography." Employing both case studies and sophisticated quantitative techniques, they found that career paths of white and minority executives to the executive suite were decidedly different. Minority managers with backgrounds largely comparable to those of white managers took longer to reach the executive level than their white counterparts. Longer career paths were particularly notable in the early years; minority executives required more time in the early phases of their careers to convince senior management of their competence than did their white peers. This meant that when they actually reached senior executive positions, they had more experience and had endured more frustrations than white counterparts. The study was undertaken in three companies that over three decades had maintained visible public commitments (which differed in important concrete ways) to diversity. Their findings implied that a sophisticated commitment to both performance and diversity could produce more on these dimensions than either one alone—even as organizations address questions of discrimination and fairness for all people.

CONCLUSION

As I/O psychology gives increasing attention to questions of diversity, benefits will accrue, we believe, if more work is devoted to clarifying and comparing theories. Theories are not neutral in how they shape data collection, inform procedures, interpret findings, or lead to actions. Attempting to avoid the biases of any given theory by being primarily inductive does not escape the problem. Tacit assumptions and unspoken values will still be present. Being more explicit about theoretical issues and observing how theories become connected to methods involves balancing a set of complex tensions.

Even the process of comparing theories is not a neutral process. Critical empirical studies can be conducted, and their results may be interpreted as favoring one point of view over another. As Kuhn (1996) has observed in the physical sciences, however, anomalous results will continue to exist, and theories will differ in how they interpret that data—or even whether they consider the findings relevant. We have shown how the perspective of embedded intergroup relations theory can be employed to examine both inductively derived empirical findings and various theories used to explain diversity effects in organizations. In doing so, we have attempted to make our conceptual and value biases clear. Other researchers, taking alternative theories as stepping-off points, may disagree.

While differing in how they proceeded, the several theories underlined that important diversity dynamics occur at the individual, group, and intergroup levels. We propose that these forces operate as separate dimensions and affect investigators and consultants in a manner similar to the way they influence respondents and clients. The empirical evidence and the concrete examples show that the phenomena are complex and call for conceptual formulations capable of addressing subtlety and nuance. Both identity and organizational-group dynamics carry powerful historical elements. To be dealt with fruitfully, they call for sophisticated competencies to discuss the issues and maintain long-term commitments to learn and change.

REFERENCES

Alderfer, C. P. (1971). The effects of individual, group and intergroup relations on attitudes toward a management development program. *Journal of Applied Psychology, 55,* 302–311.

Alderfer, C. P. (1977a). Group and intergroup relations. In J. R. Hackman & J. L. Suttle (Eds.), *Improving life at work: Behavioral science approaches to organizational change* (pp. 227–296). Santa Monica, CA: Goodyear.

Alderfer, C. P. (1977b). Improving organizational communication through long-term intergroup intervention. *Journal of Applied Behavioral Science, 13,* 193–210.

Alderfer, C. P. (1982). Problems of changing white males' behavior and beliefs concerning race relations. In P. S. Goodman (Ed.), *Change in organizations* (pp. 122–165). San Francisco: Jossey-Bass.

Alderfer, C. P. (1985). Taking our selves seriously as researchers. In D. N. Berg & K. K. Smith (Eds.), *The self in social inquiry* (pp. 35–70). Beverly Hills, CA: Sage.

Alderfer, C. P. (1987). An intergroup perspective on group dynamics. In J. Lorsch (Ed.), *Handbook of organizational behavior* (pp. 190–222). Englewood Cliffs, NJ: Prentice-Hall.

Alderfer, C. P. (1990). Staff authority and leadership in experiential groups. In J. Gillette & M. McCollom (Eds.), *Groups in context: A new perspective on group dynamics* (pp. 252–275). Reading, MA: Addison-Wesley.

Alderfer, C. P. (1992). Changing race relations embedded in organizations: Report on a long-term project with the XYZ corporation. In S. Jackson (Ed.), *Diversity in the workplace* (pp. 138–166). New York: Guilford.

Alderfer, C. P. (1994). A white man's perspective on the unconscious processes within black-white relations in the United States. In E. J. Trickett, R. J. Watts, & Dina Birman (Eds.), *Human diversity: Perspectives on people in context* (pp. 201–229). San Francisco: Jossey-Bass.

Alderfer, C. P. (2000). National culture and the new corporate language for race relations. In R. T. Carter (Ed.), *Addressing cultural issues in organizations: Beyond the corporate context* (pp. 19–33). Thousand Oaks, CA: Sage.

Alderfer, C. P., Alderfer, C. J., Bell, E. L., & Jones, J. (1992). The race relations competence workshop: Theory and results. *Human Relations, 45,* 1259–1291.

Alderfer, C. P., & Brown, L. D. (1975). *Learning from changing: Organizational diagnosis and development.* Newbury Park, CA: Sage.

Alderfer, C. P., & Simon, A. F. (2002). Non-response rates to organic questionnaire items as evidence of parallel processes during organizational diagnosis. *Journal of Applied Behavioral Science,* in press.

Alderfer, C. P., & Smith, K. K. (1982). Studying intergroup relations embedded in organizations. *Administrative Science Quarterly, 27,* 35–65.

Alderfer, C. P., & Thomas, D. A. (1988). The significance of race and ethnicity for organizational behavior. In C. L. Cooper & I. Robertson (Eds.), *International review of industrial and organizational psychology* (pp. 1–41). New York: Wiley.

Alderfer, C. P., & Tucker, R. C. (1996). A field experiment for studying race relations embedded in organizations. *Journal of Organizational Behavior, 17,* 43–57.

Alderfer, C. P., Tucker, R. C., Morgan, D., & Drasgow, F. (1983). Black and white cognitions of changing race relations. *Journal of Occupational Behavior, 4,* 105–136.

Berg, D. N., & Smith, K. K. (1985). *The self in social inquiry: Researching methods.* Newbury Park, CA: Sage.

Bowen, M. (1978). *Family therapy and clinical practice.* New York: Aronson.

Brewer, M. B. (1995). Managing diversity: The role of social identities. In S. E. Jackson & M. N. Ruderman (Eds.), *Diversity in work teams: Research paradigms for a changing workplace* (pp. 47–68). Washington, DC: American Psychological Association.

Brown, R. (1988). *Group processes: Dynamics within and between groups.* Cambridge, MA: Blackwell.

Brown, R. (1995). *Prejudice: Its social psychology.* Oxford, UK: Blackwell.

Cox, T. (1990). Problems with research by organizational scholars on issues of race and ethnicity. *Journal of Applied Behavioral Science, 26,* 5–23.

Cox, T. (1995). The complexity of diversity: Challenges and directions for future research. In S. E. Jackson & M. N. Ruderman (Eds.), *Diversity in work teams: Research paradigms for a changing workplace* (pp. 235–246). Washington, DC: American Psychological Association.

Ely, R. J. (1995). The role of dominant identity and experience in organizational work on diversity. In S. E. Jackson & M. N. Ruderman (Eds.), *Diversity in work teams: Research paradigms for a changing workplace* (pp. 161–186). Washington, DC: American Psychological Association.

Feuer, L. S. (1969). *The conflict of generations: The character and significance of student movements.* New York: Basic Books.

Frawley-O'Dea, M. G., & Sarnat, J. E. (2001). *The supervisory relationship: A contemporary psychodynamic approach.* New York: Guilford Press.

Gerard, H. B., & Miller, N. (1975). *School desegregation: A long-term study.* New York: Plenum.

Hackman, J. R. (1987). The design of work teams. In J. Lorsch (Ed.), *Handbook of organizational behavior* (pp. 315–342). Englewood Cliffs, NJ: Prentice-Hall.

Harrington, H. J., & Miller, N. (1992). Overcoming resistance of affirmative action in industry: A social psychological perspective. In P. Sudfeld & P. Tetlock (Eds.), *Psychology and social policy* (pp. 137–147). New York: Hemisphere.

Jaynes, G. D., & Williams, R. M. (1989). *Blacks and American society: A common destiny.* Washington, DC: National Academy Press.

Johnston, W. B., & Packer, A. H. (1987). *Workforce 2000: Work and workers for the twenty-first century.* Indianapolis, IN: Hudson Institute.

Jung, C. G., & Jaffe, A. (1961). *Memories, dreams and reflections.* New York: Random House.

Kaplan, A. (1964). *The conduct of inquiry: Methodology for behavioral science.* San Francisco: Chandler.

Klein, M. (1960). On mental health. In M. Klein (Ed.), *Envy and gratitude and other works 1946–1963* (pp. 268–274). London, UK: Hogarth Press.

Kossek, E. E., Zonia, S. C., & Young, W. (1996). The limitations of organizational demography: Can diversity climate be enhanced in the absence of teamwork? In M. N. Ruderman, M. W. Hughes-James, & S. E. Jackson (Eds.), *Selected research on work team diversity* (pp. 121–154). Washington, DC: American Psychological Association.

Kram, K. E. (1985). *Mentoring at work: Developmental relationships in organizational life*. Glenville, IL: Scott, Foresman.

Krantz, J., & Gilmore, T. N. (1991). Understanding the dynamics between consulting teams and client systems. In M. F. R. Kets de Vries (Ed.), *Clinical perspectives on organizational behavior and change* (pp. 307–330). San Francisco: Jossey-Bass.

Kuhn, T. S. (1996). *The structure of scientific revolutions* (3rd ed.). Chicago, IL: University of Chicago Press.

Larkey, L. K. (1996). Toward a theory of communicative interactions in culturally diverse workgroups. *Academy of Management Review, 21,* 463–491.

Levinson, D. J., Darrow, C. N., Levinson, M. H., & McKee, B. (1978). *Seasons of a man's life*. New York: Knopf.

Lieberman, S. (1950). The effects of changes in the roles on the attitudes of role occupants. *Human Relations, 9,* 385–403.

Miller, A. (1984). Adolf Hitler's childhood: From hidden to manifest horror. In A. Miller (Ed.), *For your own good: Hidden cruelty in child-rearing and the roots of violence* (pp. 142–197). Toronto, Ontario, Canada: McGraw-Hill Ryerson.

Milliken, F. J., & Martins, L. L. (1996). Searching for common threats: Understanding the multiple effects of diversity in organization groups. *Academy of Management Review, 21,* 402–433.

Myrdal, G., Sterner, R., & Rose, A. (1944). *An American dilemma: The Negro problem and modern democracy* (Vol. 2). New York: Random House.

Nkomo, S. M. (1995). Identities and the complexity of diversity. In S. E. Jackson & M. N. Ruderman (Eds.), *Diversity in work teams: Research paradigms for a changing workplace* (pp. 247–256). Washington, DC: American Psychological Association.

Nordlie, P. G. (1979). Proportion of black and white army officers in command positions. In R. Alvarez & K. G. Lutterman (Eds.), *Discrimination in organizations* (pp. 158–171). San Francisco: Jossey-Bass.

Northcraft, G. B., Polzer, J. T., Neale, M. A., & Kramer, R. M. (1995). Diversity, social identity, and performance: Emergent social dynamics in cross-functional teams. In S. E. Jackson & M. N. Ruderman (Eds.), *Diversity in work teams: Research for a changing workplace* (pp. 69–96). Washington, DC: American Psychological Association.

Pfeffer, J. (1985). Organizational demography. *Research in Organizational Behavior, 5,* 299–357.

Reynolds, C. G. (1991). *The civil war*. New York: Mallard Press.

Rice, A. K. (1969). Individual, group, and intergroup processes. *Human Relations, 22,* 565–584.

Roethlisberger, F. J., & Dickson, W. J. (1939). *Management and the worker* (pp. 379–510). New York: Wiley.

Sachdev, I., & Bourhis, R. (1987). Status development and intergroup behavior. *European Journal of Social Psychology, 17,* 277–293.

Schoenberner, G. (1969). *The yellow star*. New York: Bantam.

Sherif, M., & Sherif, C. W. (1969). *Social psychology*. New York: Harper & Row.

Shilts, R. (1987). *And the band played on: Politics, people, and the AIDS epidemic*. New York: Penguin.

Sims, A. (2002). *An intergroup examination of African-American executives' mentoring relationships: Traversing the invisible hurdles of corporate America*. Unpublished doctoral dissertation, Rutgers, The State University of New Jersey.

Smith, K. K., & Berg, D. N. (1985). *Paradoxes of group life*. San Francisco: Jossey-Bass.

Smith, K. K., & Zane, N. (1999). Organizational reflections: Parallel processes at work in a dual consultation. *Journal of Applied Behavior Science, 35,* 145–162.

Star, S. A., Williams, R. M., & Stouffer, S. A. (1949). Negro soldiers. In S. A. Stouffer, E. A. Suchman, L. C. Devinney, S. A. Star, & R. M. Williams (Eds.), *The American soldier: Adjustment during army life* (Vol. 1, pp. 486–599). New York: Wiley.

Stewart, M. M., & Shapiro, D. L. (2000). Selections based on merit versus demography: Implications across race and gender lines. *Journal of Applied Psychology, 85,* 219–231.

Tajfel, H. (1981). *Human groups and social categories: Studies in social psychology*. London: Cambridge University Press.

Thomas, D. A. (1993). Racial dynamics in cross-race developmental relationships. *Administrative Science Quarterly, 38,* 169–194.

Thomas, D. A., & Gabarro, J. J. (1999). *Breaking through: The making of minority executives in corporate America*. Boston: Harvard Business School.

Thompson, C. E., & Carter, R. T. (1997). *Racial identity theory: Applications to individual, group, and organizational interventions*. Mahwah, NJ: Erlbaum.

Triandis, H. C. (1989). The self and social behavior in differing cultural contexts. *Psychological Review, 96,* 506–520.

Triandis, H. C. (1990). Cross-cultural studies of individualism and collectivism. In J. Berman (Ed.), *Nebraska Symposium on Motivation, 1989* (pp. 44–133). Lincoln: University of Nebraska Press.

Triandis, H. C., Brislin, R., & Hui, H. C. (1988). Cross-cultural training across the individualism-collectivism divide. *International Journal of Intercultural Relations, 12,* 269–289.

Triandis, H. C., Kurowski, L. L., & Gelfand, M. J. (1994). Workplace diversity. In H. C. Triandis, M. D. Dunnette, & L. M. Hough (Eds.), *Handbook of industrial and organizational psychology* (2nd ed., Vol. 4, pp. 769–827). Palo Alto, CA: Consulting Psychologists Press.

Triandis, H. C., Vassiliou, V., Vassiliou, G., Tanaka, Y., & Shanmugam, A. W. (1972). *The analysis of subjective culture*. New York: Wiley.

Tsui, A. S., Xin, K. R., & Egan, T. D. (1995). Relational demography: The missing link in vertical dyad linkage. In S. E.

Jackson & M. N. Ruderman (Eds.), *Diversity in work teams: Research paradigms for a changing workplace* (pp. 97–130). Washington, DC: American Psychological Association.

Turner, J. C. (1981). The experimental social psychology of intergroup behavior. In J. C. Turner & H. Giles (Eds.), *Intergroup behavior* (pp. 66–101). Chicago, IL: University of Chicago Press.

Vidmar, N., & Hackman, J. R. (1971). Interlaboratory generalizability of small group research: An experimental study. *Journal of Social Psychology, 83,* 129–139.

von Franz, M. L. (1968). The process of individuation. In C. G. Jung (Ed.), *Man and his symbols* (pp. 157–254). New York: Dell.

Wells, L., Jr. (1980). The group-as-a-whole: A systemic socio-analytic perspective on interpersonal and group relations. In C. P. Alderfer & C. L. Cooper (Eds.), *Advances in experiential social processes* (Vol. 2, pp. 165–200). Chichester, England: Wiley.

Williams, K. Y., & O'Reilly, C. A. (1998). Demography and diversity in organizations: A review of 40 years of research. In L. L. Cummings & B. M. Staw (Eds.), *Research in organizational behavior* (Vol. 20, pp. 77–140). Thousand Oaks, CA: Sage.

Wuebben, P. L. (1974). Dissemination of experimental information by debriefed subjects: What is told to whom, when. In P. L. Wuebben, B. C. Straits, & G. I. Schulman (Eds.), *The experiment as a social occasion* (pp. 173–186). Berkeley, CA: Glendessary Press.

Author Index

Subject Index